E-BUSINESS & E-COMMERCE MANAGEMENT

STRATEGY, IMPLEMENTATION AND PRACTICE

Visit the *E-Business and E-Commerce Management*, fifth edition Companion Website at **www.pearsoned.co.uk/chaffey** to find valuable **student** learning material including:

- Self-assessment questions to check your understanding
- Links to relevant sites on the Web
- Additional case studies
- An online glossary to explain key terms
- Flashcards to test your understanding of key terms
- A smarter online searching guide
- Link to Dave Chaffey's blog with a collection of articles and links
- Link to Dave Chaffey's Twitter feed
- Latest updates from Dave Chaffey

We work with leading authors to develop the
strongest educational materials in business and
management, bringing cutting-edge thinking and
best learning practice to a global market.

Under a range of well-known imprints, including
Financial Times Prentice Hall, we craft high quality
print and electronic publications which help readers
to understand and apply their content, whether
studying or at work.

To find out more about the complete range of our
publishing, please visit us on the World Wide Web at:
www.pearsoned.co.uk

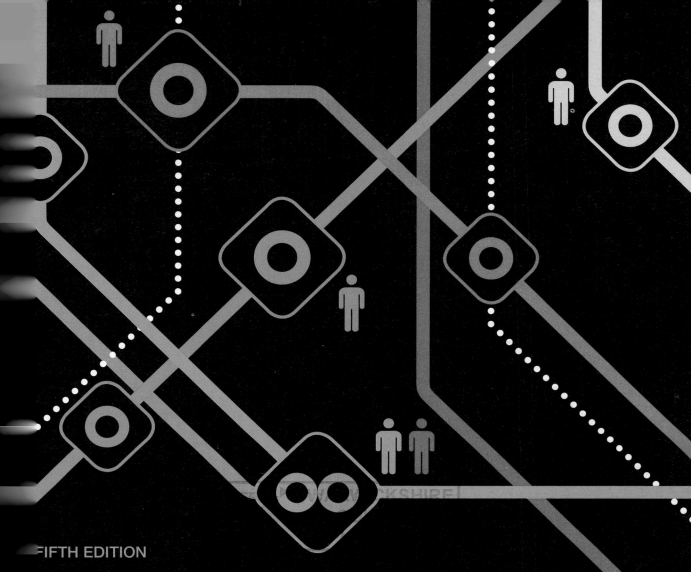

FIFTH EDITION

E-BUSINESS &
E-COMMERCE
MANAGEMENT

STRATEGY, IMPLEMENTATION
AND PRACTICE

DAVE CHAFFEY

**Financial Times
Prentice Hall
is an imprint of**

PEARSON

Harlow, England • London • New York • Boston • San Francisco • Toronto
Sydney • Tokyo • Singapore • Hong Kong • Seoul • Taipei • New Delhi
Cape Town • Madrid • Mexico City • Amsterdam • Munich • Paris • Milan

Pearson Education Limited
Edinburgh Gate
Harlow
Essex CM20 2JE
England

and Associated Companies throughout the world

Visit us on the World Wide Web at:
www.pearsoned.co.uk

First published 2002
Second edition published 2004
Third edition published 2007
Fourth edition published 2009
Fifth edition published 2011

ISBN: 978-0-273-75201-1

British Library Cataloguing-in-Publication Data
A catalogue record for this book is available from the British Library

Library of Congress Cataloging-in-Publication Data
Chaffey, Dave, 1963-
   E-business and e-commerce management : strategy, implementation and practice /
Dave Chaffey. -- 5th ed.
       p. cm.
   ISBN 978-0-273-75201-1 (pbk.)
  1. Electronic commerce. 2.   Business enterprises--Computer networks. I. Title.
   HF5548.32.C472 2011
   658.8'72--dc22

                                                                2011007808

10 9 8 7 6 5 4 3 2
14 13 12

Typeset in 10/12pt Minion by 30
Printed and bound by Rotolito Lombarda, Italy

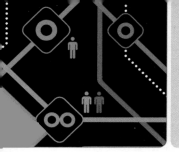

Brief contents

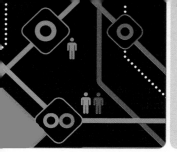

Contents

Part 2

Strategy and applications | 235

Supporting resources

Visit **www.pearsoned.co.uk/chaffey** to find valuable online resources:

Companion Website for students

- Self-assessment questions to check your understanding
- Links to relevant sites on the Web
- Additional case studies
- An online glossary to explain key terms
- Flashcards to test your understanding of key terms
- A smarter online searching guide
- Link to Dave Chaffey's blog with a collection of articles and links
- Link to Dave Chaffey's Twitter feed
- Latest updates from Dave Chaffey

For instructors

- Complete, downloadable Instructor's Manual
- PowerPoint slides that can be downloaded and used for presentations
- Testbank of question material

Also: The Companion Website provides the following features:

- Search tool to help locate specific items of content
- E-mail results and profile tools to send results of quizzes to instructors
- Online help and support to assist with website usage and troubleshooting

For more information please contact your local Pearson Education sales representative or visit **www.pearsoned.co.uk/chaffey**

Preface

In 1849 a group of settlers travelling west towards the Promised Land, California, entered a then unnamed valley. The valley presented a harsh environment with a barrier of mountains to the west making the way forward unclear. Some of the settlers lost their lives as they sought to find a route west before eventually reaching California and what was to become one of the most prosperous places on Earth. As the group left the valley, one of the women in the group turned and said, 'Goodbye, Death Valley', and hence the valley got its name. The route to e-business success is also not straightforward and similarly fraught with difficulties of selecting the correct strategic direction and surviving in an increasingly harsh competitive environment. Not all who follow the route survive. However, the competitive drivers to follow this route, such as demand from customers and adoption by competitors, make this journey essential. The rewards are evident from those adopters who identified the opportunity early and steered their companies in the right direction, adopting innovative ways to engage with their customers, suppliers and other partners.

But the journey to e-business can never be completed, because of the relentless evolution in technology and new commercial approaches which exploit it. Smart e-businesses have an agile approach which enables them to review and select the appropriate technologies at the right time. For example, businesses which have adopted social media marketing techniques have been able to enhance awareness and interaction with their brands while their competitors seem more remote from their customers.

Flagship e-businesses with headquarters in California, such as eBay, Facebook and Google, are now leading global brands with turnovers of billions of dollars, yet this has happened less than 300 years after the first modern settlers arrived.

This book is intended to equip current and future managers with some of the knowledge and practical skills to help them navigate their organization towards e-business. It is your guide to how all types of companies can prosper through e-business.

A primary aim of this book is to identify and review the key management decisions required by organizations moving to e-business and consider the process by which these decisions can be taken. Key questions are the following: What approach to e-business strategy do we follow? How much do we need to invest in e-business? Which processes should be our e-business priorities? Should we adopt new business and revenue models? What are the main changes that need to be made to the organization to facilitate e-business?

Given the broad scope of e-business, this book takes an integrative approach drawing on new and existing approaches and models from many disciplines including information systems, strategy, marketing, supply chain management, operations and human resources management.

What is e-business management?

Electronic business (e-business)
All electronically mediated information exchanges, both within an organization and with external stakeholders, supporting the range of business processes.

As we will see in Chapter 1, **electronic business (e-business)** is aimed at enhancing the competitiveness of an organization by deploying innovative information and communications technology throughout an organization and beyond, through links to partners and customers. It does not simply involve using technology to automate existing processes, but should also achieve process transformation by applying technology to help change these processes. To be successful in managing e-business, a breadth of knowledge is needed of different business processes and activities from across the value chain such as marketing and sales, through new

Supply chain management (SCM)

The coordination of all supply activities of an organization from its suppliers and partners to its customers.

product development, manufacturing and inbound and outbound logistics. Organizations also need to manage the change required by new processes and technology through what have traditionally been support activities such as human resources management.

From this definition, it is apparent that e-business involves looking at how electronic communications can be used to enhance all aspects of an organization's **supply chain management**. It also involves optimizing an organization's **value chain**, a related concept that describes the different value-adding activities that connect a company's supply side with its demand side. The e-business era also involves management of a network of interrelated value chains or **value networks**.

Value chain

A model for analysis of how supply chain activities can add value to products and services delivered to the customer.

What is e-commerce management?

Value networks

The links between an organization and its strategic and non-strategic partners that form its external value chain.

To this point we have exclusively used the term 'e-business', but what of 'e-commerce'? Both these terms are applied in a variety of ways; to some they mean the same, to others they are quite different. As explained in Chapter 1, what is most important is that they are applied consistently within organizations so that employees and external stakeholders are clear about how the organization can exploit electronic communications. The distinction made in this book is to use **'electronic commerce' (e-commerce)** to refer to all types of electronic transactions between organizations and stakeholders, whether they are financial transactions or exchanges of information or other services. These e-commerce transactions are either **buy-side e-commerce** or **sell-side e-commerce** and the management issues involved with each aspect are considered separately in Part 2 of the book. 'E-business' is applied as a broader term encompassing e-commerce but also including all electronic transactions within an organization.

Electronic commerce (e-commerce)

All electronically mediated information exchanges between an organization and its external stakeholders.

Management of e-commerce involves prioritizing buy-side and sell-side activities and putting in place the plans and resources to deliver the identified benefits. These plans need to focus on management of the many risks to success, some of which you may have experienced when using e-commerce sites, from technical problems such as transactions that fail, sites that are difficult to use or are too slow, through to problems with customer service or fulfilment, which also indicate failure of management. Today, the **social media** or peer-to-peer interactions that occur between customers on company websites, blogs, communities and social networks have changed the dynamics of online commerce. Likewise, adoption of mobile phones and **mobile apps** offer new platforms to interact with stakeholders which must be evaluated and prioritized. Deciding which technologies not to adopt is a challenge for all organizations.

Buy-side e-commerce

E-commerce transactions between an organization and its suppliers and other partners.

Sell-side e-commerce

E-commerce transactions between an organization and its customers.

How is this book structured?

Social media

A category of media focusing on participation and peer-to-peer communication between individuals with sites providing the capability to develop user-generated content (UGC) and to exchange messages and comments between different users.

The overall structure of the book, shown in Figure P.1, follows a logical sequence: introducing e-business terms, concepts and history of development in Part 1; reviewing alternative strategic approaches and applications of e-business in Part 2; and how strategy can be implemented in Part 3. Within this overall structure, differences in how electronic communications are used to support different business processes are considered separately. This is achieved by distinguishing between how electronic communications are used, from buy-side e-commerce aspects of supply chain management in Chapters 6 and 7, to the marketing perspective of sell-side e-commerce in Chapters 8 and 9. Figure P.1 shows the emphasis of perspective for the particular chapters.

Mobile apps
A software application that is designed for use on a mobile phone, typically downloaded from an App store. iPhone Apps are best known, but all Smart Phones support the use of apps which can provide users with information, entertainment or location-based services such as mapping.

Part 1: Introduction (Chapters 1–4)

Part 1 introduces e-business and e-commerce. It seeks to clarify basic terms and concepts by looking at different interpretations of terms and applications through case studies.

- **Chapter 1: Introduction to e-business and e-commerce**. Definition of the meaning and scope of e-business and e-commerce. Social media, social commerce and mobile apps are also introduced. Introduction to business use of the Internet – what are the benefits and barriers to adoption and how widely used is it?
- **Chapter 2: Marketplace analysis for e-commerce**. Introduction to new business models and marketplace structures enabled by electronic communications.
- **Chapter 3: E-business infrastructure**. Background on the hardware, software and tele-communications that need to be managed to achieve e-business.
- **Chapter 4: E-environment**. Describes the macro-environment of an organization that presents opportunities and constraints on strategy and implementation.

Part 2: Strategy and applications (Chapters 5–9)

In Part 2 of the book approaches to developing e-business strategy and applications are reviewed for the organization as a whole (Chapter 5) and with an emphasis on buy-side e-commerce (Chapters 6 and 7) and sell-side e-commerce (Chapters 8 and 9).

- **Chapter 5: E-business strategy**. Approaches to developing e-business strategy. Differences from traditional strategic approaches. Relation to IS strategy.

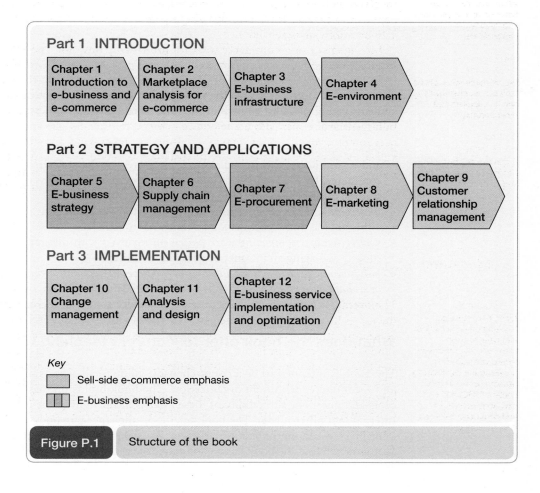

| **Figure P.1** | Structure of the book |

- **Chapter 6: Supply chain management**. A supply chain perspective on strategy with examples of how technology can be applied to increase supply chain and value chain efficiency.
- **Chapter 7: E-procurement**. Evaluation of the benefits and practical issues of adopting e-procurement.
- **Chapter 8: E-marketing**. A sell-side e-commerce perspective to e-business, reviewing differences in marketing required through digital media. Structured around developing an e-marketing plan.
- **Chapter 9: Customer relationship management**. Reviews marketing techniques that apply e-commerce for acquiring and retaining customers.

Part 3: Implementation (Chapters 10–12)

Management of e-business implementation is described in Part 3 of the book in which we examine practical management issues involved with creating and maintaining e-business solutions.

- **Chapter 10: Change management**. How to manage the organizational, human and technology changes required in the move to e-business.
- **Chapter 11: Analysis and design**. We discuss the main issues of analysis and design raised by e-commerce systems that need to be discussed by managers and solutions providers.
- **Chapter 12: E-business implementation and optimization**. How should e-commerce systems be managed and monitored once they are live?

Who should use this book?

Students

This book has been created as the main student text for undergraduate and postgraduate students taking specialist courses or modules which cover e-business, e-commerce information systems or e-marketing. The book is relevant to students who are:

- *undergraduates on business programmes* which include modules on the use of the Internet and e-commerce; this includes specialist degrees such as electronic business, electronic commerce, Internet marketing and marketing or general business degrees such as business studies, business administration and business management;
- *undergraduate project students* who select this topic for final-year projects or dissertations – this book is an excellent resource for these students;
- *undergraduates completing work placement* involved with different aspects of e-business such as managing an intranet or company website;
- *postgraduate students on specialist masters degrees in electronic commerce, electronic business or e-marketing and generic MBA, Certificate in Management, or Diploma in Management Studies* which involve modules or electives for electronic commerce and digital marketing.

What does the book offer to lecturers teaching these courses?

The book is intended to be a comprehensive guide to all aspects of deploying e-business and e-commerce within an organization. The book builds on existing theories and concepts and questions the validity of these models in the light of the differences between the Internet and other media. The book references the emerging body of literature specific to e-business, e-commerce and e-marketing. As such, it can be used across several modules. Lecturers will find the book has a good range of case studies, activities and exercises to support their teaching. These activities assist in using the book for student-centred learning as part of directed study. Web links given in the text and at the end of each chapter highlight key information sources for particular topics.

Practitioners

There is also much of relevance in this book for the industry professional, including:

- *Senior managers and directors* seeking to apply the right e-business and e-commerce approaches to benefit their organization.
- *Information systems managers* who are developing and implementing e-business and e-commerce strategies.
- *Marketing managers* responsible for defining an e-marketing strategy and implementing and maintaining the company website.
- *Supply chain, logistics and procurement managers* wanting to see examples of best practice in using e-commerce for supply chain management.
- *Technical project managers or webmasters* who may understand the technical details of building a site, but have a limited knowledge of business or marketing fundamentals.

Student learning features

A range of features have been incorporated into this book to help the reader get the most out of it. They have been designed to assist understanding, reinforce learning and help readers find information easily. The features are described in the order you will encounter them.

At the start of each chapter

- *Chapter at a glance*: a list of main topics, 'focus on' topics and case studies.
- *Learning outcomes*: a list describing what readers can learn through reading the chapter and completing the activities.
- *Management issues*: a summary of main issues or decisions faced by managers related to the chapter topic area.
- *Web support*: additional material on the Companion Website.
- *Links to other chapters*: a summary of related topics in other chapters.
- *Introductions*: succinct summaries of the relevance of the topic to marketing students and practitioners together with content and structure.

In each chapter

- *Activities*: short activities in the main text that develop concepts and understanding, often by relating to student experience or through reference to websites. Model answers are provided to activities at the end of the chapter where applicable.
- *Case studies*: real-world examples of issues facing companies that implement e-business. Questions at the end of the case study highlight the main learning points from that case study.
- *Real-world e-business experiences*: interviews with e-commerce managers at a range of UK, European and US-based organizations concerning the strategies they have adopted and their approaches to strategy implementation.
- *Box features*: these explore a concept in more detail or give an example of a principle discussed in the text.

- '*Focus on*' *sections*: more detailed coverage of specific topics of interest.
- *Questions for debate*: suggestions for discussion of significant issues for managers involved with the transformation required for e-business.
- *Definitions*: when significant terms are first introduced the main text contains succinct definitions in the margin for easy reference.
- *Web links*: where appropriate, web addresses are given for further information, particularly those to update information.
- *Chapter summaries*: intended as revision aids and to summarize the main learning points from the chapter.

At the end of each chapter

- *Self-assessment exercises*: short questions which will test understanding of terms and concepts described in the chapter.
- *Discussion questions*: require longer essay-style answers discussing themes from the chapter, and can be used for essays or as debate questions in seminars.
- *Essay questions*: conventional essay questions.
- *Examination questions*: typical short-answer questions found in exams and can also be used for revision.
- *References*: these are references to books, articles or papers referred to within the chapter.
- *Further reading*: supplementary texts or papers on the main themes of the chapter. Where appropriate a brief commentary is provided on recommended supplementary reading on the main themes of the chapters.
- *Web links*: these are significant sites that provide further information on the concepts and topics of the chapter. All website references within the chapter, for example company sites, are not repeated here. The website address prefix 'http://' is omitted from www links for clarity.

At the end of the book

- *Glossary*: a list of all definitions of key terms and phrases used within the main text.
- *Index*: all key words and abbreviations referred to in the main text.

Learning techniques

The book is intended to support a range of learning styles. It can be used for an active or student-centred learning approach whereby students attempt the activities through reflecting on questions posed, answering questions and then comparing to a suggested answer at the end of the chapter. Alternatively, students can proceed straight to suggested answers in a more traditional learning approach, which still encourages reflection about the topic.

Module guide

Table B presents one mapping of how the book could be used in different weekly lectures and seminars through the core eleven weeks of a module where the focus is on management issues of e-business and e-commerce.

A full set of PowerPoint slides and accompanying notes to assist lecturers in preparing lectures is available on the lecturer's side of the Companion Website.

Enhancements for the fifth edition

The effective chapter structure of previous editions has been retained, but many other changes have been incorporated based on lecturer and student feedback.

The most significant additions to the content reflect the growth in importance of social commerce, social media marketing and mobile commerce. We have also integrated more video content to assist teaching and learning.

Each chapter has been rationalized to focus on the key concepts and processes recommended to evaluate capability and develop e-business strategies. The main updates for the fifth edition on a chapter-by-chapter basis are:

- *Chapter 1.* Starts with a look at the amazing innovation in business model that the web has facilitated. The introduction to different e-commerce concepts now covers mobile, Web 2.0 and social commerce concepts in more detail. The six main options for reaching and interacting with online audiences are introduced.
- *Chapter 2.* Renamed 'Marketplace analysis for e-commerce', is updated with the latest tools for online marketplace analysis for e-business which can be used by students working on case studies or practitioners in business and is described with new diagrams and links to information sources. A new case study about i-to-i, an organization offering adventure travel in different markets, is included.
- *Chapter 3.* The chapter has been updated to review the business applications of augmented reality, APIs, mobile apps and microformats. Coverage of software as a service and the issues in managing these services have been added to. Chapter 3 includes a case study on Google technology and innovation and mini case studies on Amazon Web Services and Twitter.
- *Chapter 4.* The chapter has been simplified and privacy implications of behavioural targeting and remarketing are presented.
- *Chapter 5.* Chapter simplified, still using established strategy process frameworks.
- *Chapter 6.* New research on Operations Planning (S&OP) Systems and a mini case study on how Argos uses e-supply chain management to improve customer convenience.
- *Chapter 7.* New research on business benefits of e-procurement through case studies of three companies is presented.
- *Chapter 8.* Some new concepts incorporated include content strategy and crowd sourcing.
- *Chapter 9.* Increased depth on social media and introduction to social CRM.
- *Chapter 10.* A new mini case study on conversion optimization by Def-Shop and a case study of a failed e-project.
- *Chapter 11.* A new section on using the star schema in data warehouses and business intelligence systems. Coverage of web user feedback tools.
- *Chapter 12.* Content management and content strategy discussion updated.

Table A	In-depth case studies in *E-Business and E-Commerce Management*, 5th edition

Chapter		Case study	
1	Introduction to e-business and e-commerce	1.1	A short history of Facebook
		1.2	North West Supplies extends its reach online
		1.3	eBay – the world's largest e-business
2	Marketplace analysis for e-commerce	2.1	i-to-i – a global marketplace for a start-up company
		2.2	Zopa launches a new lending model
3	E-business infrastructure	3.1	Innovation at Google
		3.2	New architecture or just new hype?
4	E-environment	4.1	The implications of globalization for consumer attitudes
5	E-business strategy	5.1	Capital One creates value through e-business
		5.2	Setting the Internet revenue contribution at Sandvik Steel
		5.3	Boo hoo – learning from the largest European dot-com failure
6	Supply chain management	6.1	Shell Chemicals redefines its customers' supply chains
		6.2	Argos uses e-supply chain management to improve customer convenience
		6.3	RFID: keeping track starts its move to a faster track
7	E-procurement	7.1	Cambridge Consultants reduce costs through e-procurement
		7.2	Covisint – a typical history of a B2B marketplace?
8	E-marketing	8.1	The e-volution of easyJet's online revenue contribution
		8.2	Dell gets closer to its customers online
		8.3	The new Napster changes the music marketing mix
9	Customer relationship management	9.1	Tesco.com increases product range and uses triggered communications to support CRM
10	Change management	10.1	Process management: making complex business simpler
		10.2	Using Enterprise 2.0 tools to support knowledge management at Janssen-Cilag Australia
11	Analysis and design	11.1	Dabs.com refines its web store
		11.2	Building an e-business fortress
12	E-business service implementation and optimization	12.1	Learning from Amazon's culture of metrics

Table B	Module guide

Week	Lecture topic	Seminar or tutorial topics		Notes
1	LI Introduction to e-business and e-commerce	Activity 1.1 Case study 1.2 Case study 1.3 Debate 1.1	Introduction NW Supplies eBay E-business vs IS	Chapter 1 and Chapter 3 (technical introduction)
2	L2 E-commerce micro-environment	Activity 2.1 Case study 2.1 Case study 2.2 Debate 2.1	Introduction i-to-i Zopa.com Online intermediaries	Chapter 2
3	L3 E-commerce macro-environment	Activity 4.1 Case study 4.1 Debate 4.2	Introduction Globalization E-government	Chapters 3 and 4
4	L4 E-business strategy: (a) Situation analysis and objective setting	Activity 5.2 Case study 5.1 Debate 5.1	B2C/B2B analysis Capital One E-business responsibility	Chapter 5
5	L5 E-business strategy: (b) Strategy and tactics	Activity 5.4 Case study 5.3 Debate 5.2	B2C/B2B strategies Boo.com Board-level representation	Chapter 5
6	L6 E-business applications: (a) Supply chain management	Activity 6.1 Case study 6.1 Case study 6.2 Debate 6.1	Introduction Shell Chemicals Argos Value chain	Chapter 6
7	L7 E-business applications: (b) E-procurement	Activity 7.1 Case study 7.1 Case study 7.2 Debate 7.2	Introduction Cambridge Consultants Covisint B2B exchanges	Chapter 7
8	L8 E-business applications: (c) E-marketing	Activity 8.2 Case study 8.1 Case study 8.3 Debate 8.1	Competitor benchmarking easyJet The new Napster E-marketing planning	Chapter 8
9	L9 E-business applications: (d) E-CRM	Activity 9.1 Case study 9.1 Debate 9.1	Introduction Tesco.com Permission marketing	Chapter 9

| Table B | Continued |

Week	Lecture topic	Seminar or tutorial topics		Notes
10	L10 Change management	Activity 10.1	Introduction	Chapter 10
		Case study 10.1	Process management: making complex business simpler	
		Case study 10.2	Janssen-Cilag	
		Debate 10.1	E-business function	
11	L11 Evaluation and maintenance	Activity 12.1	Introduction	Chapters 11 and 12
		Case study 11.1	Dabs.com	
		Case study 12.1	Amazon	
		Debate 12.1	Standards control	

Table C	The author's timeline

		1960
1963	Born	Black and white television
		1970
1976		Colour television
		1980
1982		First used computer-programmed mainframe using punched cards
1985	BSc, Imperial College, London	
1988	PhD, University of Leeds	Wrote PhD on mainframe
1989	Project Manager in software house developing GIS for marketing planning	First used PC
		1990
1991	Software Engineering Manager for company producing packaged and bespoke engineering software	Sent first e-mail
1994	Project Manager for customer-facing financial services systems	Started using World Wide Web
1995	Senior Lecturer, Business Information Systems, Derbyshire Business School, University of Derby	First ordered book online
1997	Delivering CIM Internet Marketing seminars	Built first website
1998	*Groupware, Workflow and Intranets* published	Mobile phone
1999	*Business Information Systems* published	
		2000
2000	*Internet Marketing* published	Interactive digital TV
2000	MSc E-commerce course launched at Derby	WAP phone
2003	Nominated by CIM as one of 50 'gurus' to have 'shaped the future of marketing' along with Philip Kotler and Michael Porter!	
2004	Recognized by the Department of Trade and Industry, NOP World and E-consultancy as one of the 'Top 100 people commended by the industry as key influencers and drivers, who have driven the development and growth of e-commerce in the UK over the last ten years'	
2005	Second edition of *E-marketing Excellence* published	Blogging and RSS on www.davechaffey.com
2006	Third edition of *E-Business and E-Commerce Management* published	Participating in social networks such as Facebook and Linked-In
2008	E-consultancy Managing Digital Channels research report published	Using Twitter to stay up to date with technology innovation

This timeline supports Activity 3.2. This considers the diffusion of technological innovation at home and in the workplace. The author first started using a computer regularly when he was 18, yet his 4-year-old daughter is already an Internet user. Readers can compare their own adoption of computer technology at home and at work. How do you think the use of the Internet and its successors for e-commerce and e-entertainment will change as successive generations become increasingly computer literate?

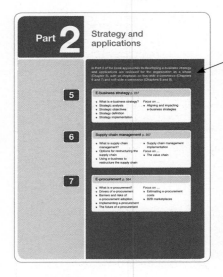

Part introduction Each part of the book is summarized with a brief list of chapter contents and 'focus on' issues.

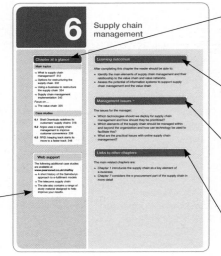

Chapter at a glance This feature summarizes the main topics of the chapter and the case studies.

Learning outcomes These are set out clearly at the start of each chapter.

Management issues These list the strategic and practical implications of each topic and case study.

Links to other chapters To highlight the connections between chapters.

Web support To highlight additional support material on the Companion Website.

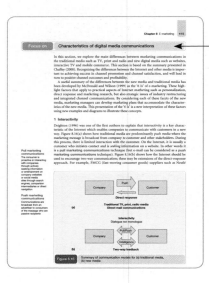

Focus on 'Focus on' sections contain more detailed coverage of key areas.

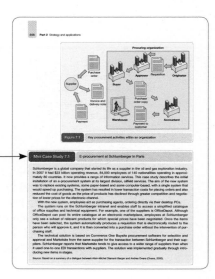

Mini Case Study Extra smaller case studies have been added to give students more examples of e-commerce within business.

Activity To test students' understanding of key topics.

Essay, Discussion and Examination questions These provide engaging activities for students and lecturers in and out of the classroom.

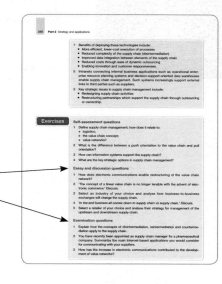

Real-world E-Business experiences Interviews with industry leaders in the e-commerce world to give personal insight to students.

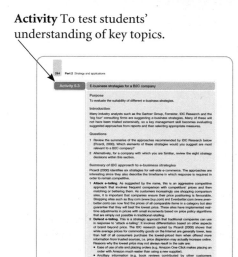

Student Companion Website Contains a variety of materials to aid learning and studying.

Case Study Integrated throughout the text with many taken from the *Financial Times*, illustrating current examples of e-commerce and its applications.

Dave Chaffey BSc, PhD, FCIM, HIDM

Dave manages his own E-business, Smart Insights (www.smartinsights.com), an online publisher and analytics company providing advice and alerts on best practice and industry developments for digital marketers and Ecommerce managers. The advice is also created to help readers of Dave's books. The most relevant information is highlighted at www.smartin-sights.com/book-support.

Dave also works as an independent Internet marketing trainer and consultant for Marketing Insights Limited. He has consulted on digital marketing and Ecommerce strategy for companies of a range of sizes from larger organizations like 3M, Barclaycard, HSBC, Mercedes-Benz and Nokia to smaller organizations like Arco, Confused.com, Euroffice, Hornbill and i-to-i.

Dave's passion is educating students and marketers about latest and best practices in digital marketing, so empowering businesses to improve their online performance through getting the most value from their web analytics and market insight. In other words making the most of online opportunities and avoiding waste.

He is proud to have been recognized by the Department of Trade and Industry as one of the leading individuals who have provided input and influence on the development and growth of e-commerce and the Internet in the UK over the last 10 years. Dave has also been recognized by the Chartered Institute of Marketing as one of 50 marketing 'gurus' world-wide who have helped shape the future of marketing. He is also proud to be an Honorary Fellow of the IDM.

Dave is a visiting lecturer on e-commerce courses at different universities, including Birmingham, Cranfield, Derby, Manchester Metropolitan and Warwick universities. He is a tutor on the IDM Diploma in Digital Marketing, for which he is also senior examiner.

In total, Dave is author of five best-selling business books including *Internet Marketing: Strategy, Implementation and Practice*, *eMarketing eXcellence* (with PR Smith) and *Total E-mail Marketing*. Many of these books have been published in new editions since 2000 and translations include Chinese, Dutch, German, Italian and Serbian.

When offline he enjoys fell-running, indie guitar music and travelling with his family.

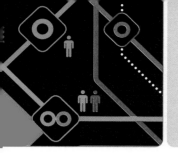

Acknowledgements

The author would like to thank the team at Pearson Education in Harlow, in particular Gabrelle James, Emma Violet, Kelly Miller, Philippa Fiszzon, Cats Pellegrino, Stephen Pepper and Annette Abel for their help in the creation of this book. I would particularly like to thank the reviewers who undetook detailed reviews for the second, third and fourth editions – these reviews have been important in shaping the book: Magdy Abdel-Kader, University of Essex; Poul Andersen, Aarhus Business School, Denmark; Michelle Bergadaa, University of Geneva, Switzerland; Bruce Bowhill, University of Portsmouth; Yaw Busia, University of Middl sex; Hatem El-Gohary, Bradford University; Janet French, Barking College; Andy Gravell, Univesity of Southampton; Ulf Hoglind, Örebro University, Sweden; Judith Jeffcoate, University of Buckingham; Britt-Marie Johansson, University of Jönköping, Sweden; Matthias Klaes, Keele University; Mette P. Knudsen, University of Southern Denmark; Tuula Mittila, University of Tampere, Finland; Barry Quinn, University of Ulster; Gerry Rogers, EdExcel-Qualifications Leader; Chandres Tejura, University of North London; Ian Watson, University of Northumbria; Steve Wood, Liverpool John Moores University.

Thanks also to these reviewers who were involved at earlier stages with this book: Fintan Clear, Brunel University; Neil Doherty, Loughborough University; Jean-Noel Ezingeard, Henley Management College; Dr Felicia Fai, University of Bath; Lisa Harris, Brunel University; Sue Hartland, Gloucestershire Business School at Cheltenham and Gloucester College of Higher Education; Mike Healy, University of Westminster; Eric van Heck, Rotterdam School of Management, The Netherlands; Dipak Khakhar, Lund University, Sweden; Robert Proops, University of Westminster; Professor Michael Quayle, University of Glamorgan; Richard Riley, University of Central England; Gurmak Singh, University of Wolverhampton; John Twomey, Brunel University; Gerry Urwin, Coventry University.

Publisher's acknowledgements

We are grateful to the following for permission to reproduce copyright material:

Figures

Figure 1.2, 1.3, 1.4, 2.1, 3.7, 3.14, 4.12, 4.15, 5.12, 5.18, 6.8a, 7.4, 8.8, 8.20 and 9.2 from *Internet Marketing : Strategy, Implementation and Practice*, 2nd ed., Financial Times Prentice Hall (Chaffey, D., Meyer, R., Johnston, K. and Ellis-Chadwick, F. 2003) Copyright © 2003 Pearson Education Ltd; Figure 1.9 after Nova Spivack blog posting. How the WebOS evolves? 2009, http://novaspivack.typepad.com/nova_spivacks_weblog/2007/02/steps_towards_a.html, www.novaspivack.com, reprinted with permission; Figure 1.11 from Eurostat, Data in focus Industry, trade and services, figure 2: illustrating Enterprises' websites by facilities provided, EU-27, January 2009 (% of enterprises having a website). isoc_ci_cd_en2, © European Union 1995-2011; Figure 1.13 from Business in the Information Age, *International Benchmarking Study 2002* (DTI 2002), Crown Copyright material is reproduced with permission under the terms of the Click-Use Licence; Figure 1.15 from Individuals Accessing the Internet, *Report from the UK National Statistics Omnibus Survey, published online at www.statistics.gov. uk* (UK Statistics 2006), Crown Copyright material is reproduced with permission under the terms of the Click-Use Licence; Figure 3.5 adapted from http://news.netcraft.com/archives/category/web-server-survey, Courtesy of Netcraft and www.netcraft.com; Figure 3.17 adapted from Information system integration, *Communications of the ACM*, 43 (6), pp.33-38 (Hasselbring, W. 2000), ACM Press

Books and Journals, Copyright © 2000 ACM, Inc., reprinted by permission, and reproduced by kind permission of the author; Figure 3.21 from The State of Mobile Apps, June 1, 2010, Nielsen Wire, 2010, The Nielsen Company, http://blog.nielsen.com/nielsenwire/online_mobile/the-state-of-mobile-apps/, reprinted with permission; Figure 4.2 adapted from Based on Table 1d(2), OECD Broadband Portal, http://www.oecd.org/sti/ict/broadband (last updated: 6 December 2010), reprinted with permission; Figure 4.5 from European Interactive Advertising Association (www.eiaa.net), Mediascope Europe 2008, reprinted with permission; Figure 4.6 from Eurostat community survey on ICT usage and eCommerce by enterprises, Europe's Digital Competitiveness Report 2010, figure 6.7 illustrating Problems with and barriers to electronic sales, 2009. http://ec.europa.eu/information_society/digital-agenda/documents/edcr.pdf, © European Union 2010-2011; Figure 4.9 from Nielsen Buzzmetrics, www.blogpulse.com, reprinted by permission of Nielsen Buzzmetrics; Figure 4.11 from International E-Economy: Benchmarking the World's Most Effective Policy for the E-Economy, report published 19 November, London, www.e-envoy.gov.uk/oee/nsf/sections/summit_benchmarking/$file/indexpage.htm (Booz Allen Hamilton 2002), Crown Copyright material is reproduced with permission under the terms of the Click-Use Licence; Figure 4.13 from at http://www.gartner.com/it/page.jsp?id=1447613.; Figure 5.9 from Towards a manager's model of e-business strategy decisions, *Journal of General Management*, 30 (4) (Perrott, B. Summer 2005), The Braybrooke Press; Figure 5.12 from *'Hard choices for Senior Managers'. In Mastering Information Management,* Financial Times Prentice Hall, Harlow (Marchand, D. in Marchand, D. et al. eds. 1999) pp. 187-192, Copyright © Pearson Education; Figure 5.17 from E-consultancy, 2008. Managing digital channels research report by Dave Chaffey, reprinted with permission; Figures 6.8b, 6.9 adapted from *Executive's Guide to E-Business : From Tactics to Strategy* (Deise, M. et al. 2000) Copyright © 2000 John Wiley & Sons, Inc. Reproduced with permission of John Wiley & Sons, Inc.; Figure 6.12 from European Commission, 2008, i2010 Annual Information Society Report 2008, mid-term report, published at http://ec.europa.eu/information_society/eeurope/i2010/mid_term_review_2008/index_en.htm © European Communities, 1995-2008; Figure 7.2 from An E-valuation framework for developing net enabled business metrics through functionality interaction, *Journal of Organizational Computing and Electronic Commerce*, 17 (2), pp. 175-203 (Riggins, F. and Mitra, S. 2007), Reprinted by permission of the publisher (Taylor & Francis Group, http://www.informaworld.com); Figures 8.1, 8.5 from Managing digital teams. Integrating digital marketing into your organisation. Author: Dave Chaffey. Available at http://econsultancy.com, reprinted with permission; Figure 8.9 from Bowen Craggs & Co., www.bowencraggs.com, reprinted with permission; Figures 8.25, 8.26, 9.6 from *BrandNewWorld* (Anne Mollen/AOL UK, Cranfield School of Management/ Henley Centre 2004); Figure 9.16 adapted from Putting the service-profit chain to work, *Harvard Business Review*, March-April, p. 167 (Heskett, J. et al. 1994), Copyright © 1994 by the Harvard Business School Publishing Corporation, all rights reserved; Figures 10.2, 10.10 from Managing an E-commerce team. Integrating digital marketing into your organisation. Author: Dave Chaffey., Available from www.e-consultancy.com, reprinted with permission; Figures 10.3, 10.8 from Managing an E-commerce team. Integrating digital marketing into your organisation. Author: Dave Chaffey. Available from www.e-consultancy.com, reprinted with permission; Figures 10.4, 10.5 from E-Consultancy, 2007, Web project management. The practices behind successful web projects. Research report by Sonia Kay available from http://econsultancy.com, reprinted with permission; Figure 10.9 adapted from Organizing for digital marketing, *McKinsey Quarterly*, No. 4, pp. 183-192 (Parsons, A., Zeisser, M. and Waitman, R. 1996), www.mckinsey-quarterly.com, McKinsey & Co., Inc.; Figure 11.1 adapted from *Groupware, workflow and intranets--Re-engineering the enterprise with collaborative software*, 1 ed., Digital Press, Woburn, MA (Chaffey, D. 1998) Elsevier, reprinted by permission of Elsevier Science; Figure 11.19 from Department of Business, Enterprise and Regulatory Reform (BERR) Information Security Breaches Survey 2008, published at http://www.pwc.co.uk/eng/publications/berr_information_security_breaches_survey_2008.html, Crown Copyright material is reproduced with permission under the terms of the Click-Use Licence; Figure 11.20 from Code Red (CRv2) Spread Animation, CAIDA/UC San Diego, www.cse.ucsd.edu/~savage/papers/IEEESP03.pdf, Copyright © 2001 The Regents of the University of California, reprinted by permission of the Regents of the University of California; Figure 11.21 from Department of Business, Enterprise and Regulatory Reform (BERR) Information Security Breaches Survey 2008, published at http://www.pwc.co.uk/eng/publications/berr_information_security_breaches_survey_2008.html; Figure 11.22 from Marshal Ltd., www.marshal.com, reprinted by permission of Marshal Ltd.; Figure 11.23 from *Department of Trade and Industry Information Security Breaches Survey* (DTI 2006), Crown Copyright material is reproduced with permission under the terms of the Click-Use Licence; Figure 12.1 adapted from *Image from "The Art of Agile Development"*, O'Reilly (Shore, J. and Warden, S. 2008) Copyright © 2007 James Shore and Shane Warden, Used with permission from O'Reilly Media, Inc. All rights reserved;

Figure 12.2 from Port80 software, www.port80software.com/surveys/top1000appservers; Figure 12.8 from *The Multichannel Challenge*, Butterworth-Heinemann (Wilson, H. 2008) Copyright Elsevier 2008; Figure 12.13 from Maxymiser Ltd, Multivariate testing results reproduced by the kind permission of Maxymiser, www.maxymiser.com.

Screenshots

Screenshot 1.1 from Wayback Machine Archive, http://web.archive.org/web/19981111183552/google. stanford.edu; Screenshot 1.5 from Yammer, https://www.yammer.com/, reprinted with permission; Screenshot 1.7 from www.qype.com, reprinted with permission; Screenshot 2.4 from http://trends. google.com/websites, reprinted by permission of Google, Inc. Google™ is a trademark of Google, Inc.; Screenshot 2.10 from Google Adwords, https://adwords.google.com/select/KeywordToolExternal, reprinted by permission of Google, Inc. Google Adwords™ is a trademark of Google, Inc.; Screenshot 2.13 from http://econsultancy.com, reprinted with permission; Screenshot 2.14 from www.firebox. com, reprinted with permission; Screenshot 2.15 from www.zopa.com, reprinted with permission; Screenshot 3.16 from Twitter; Screenshot 3.20 from http://www.salesforce.com, reprinted with permission; Screenshot 3.22 from www.giagia.co.uk/?cat=63, created by www.giagia.co.uk/?page_id=2 blog, Image courtesy of Twentieth Century Fox Home Entertainment; Screenshot 3.23 from www. hypertag.com, reproduced by kind permission of Hypertag Ltd.; Screenshot 3.24 from http://mtld. mobi/emulator.php, reprinted with permission from the Site owner; Screenshot 4.7 from feedjit. com/stats/davechaffey.com/map; Screenshot 4.10 from www.hsbc.co.uk, reprinted with permission; Screenshot 4.14 from www.innocentive.com, reprinted with permission; Screenshot 5.3 from www. britishairways.com, reprinted with permission; Screenshot 5.13 from www.arenaflowers.com, reprinted with permission; Screenshot 6.4 from www.bluescopesteelconnect.com, reprinted with permission; Screenshot 6.11 from http://www.e2open.com/, reprinted with permission; Screenshot 7.7 from www.supply2.gov.uk, reprinted with permission; Screenshot 8.14 from http://www. firebox.com, reprinted with permission; Screenshot 8.27 from http://www.napster.co.uk/, reprinted with permission; Screenshot 9.9 from google.com, reprinted by permission of Google, Inc. Google Analytics™ search engine is a trademark of Google, Inc.; Screenshot 9.15 from http://www.toptable. com, reprinted with permission; Screenshot 11.9 from www.dulux.co.uk, Dulux is a trademark of ICI © ICI; Screenshot 11.13 from www.rswww.com, Screenshot of RS Components homepage supplied courtesy of RS Components (http://rswww.com); Screenshot 11.18 from www.hsbc.com, with permission from HSBC Holdings plc; Screenshot 12.11 from www.google.com/analytics/reporting/ visitors?id, reprinted by permission of Google, Inc. Google Analytics™ is a trademark of Google, Inc.; Screenshot 12.12 from National Express website, reprinted with permission.

Tables

Table 1.2 from comScore, comScore MobiLens 2010 reprinted with permission; Table 2.1 from Hitwise Press Release : UK Internet visits to flower websites at highest ever peak in February, London, 6 March 2008 , reprinted with permission; Table 2.3 adapted from *New Marketing : Transforming the Corporate Future*, Butterworth-Heinemann (McDonald, M and Wilson, H. 2002) Copyright 2002, with permission from Elsevier; Table 2.4 adapted from The All-In-One-Market, *Harvard Business Review*, p. 2-3 (Nunes, P., Kambil, A. and Wilson, D. 2000) © 2000 by the Harvard Business School Publishing Corporation, all rights reserved; Table 2.6 from Comscore, comScore media metrix ranks top-growing properties and site categories for April 2010. Press Release, May 10th, http:// www.comscore.com/Press_Events/Press_Releasees/2010/5/comScore_Media_Metrix_Ranks_Top-Growing_Properties_and_Site_Categories_for_April_2010, reprinted with permission; Table 3.2 adapted from Road map to the e-revolution *Information Systems Management (previously Journal of Information Systems Management)*, 17 (2), pp. .1–15 (Kampas, P. 2000), Reprinted by permission of the publisher (Taylor&Francis Group, http://www.informaworld.com); Table 4.4 from European Interactive Advertising Association (www.eiaa.net) EIAA, Mediascope Europe 2008, reprinted with permission; Table 4.5 from CIFAS, 2008, CIFAS (Credit Industry Fraud Association) Press Release: Figures emphasise the change in UK's fraud landscape., http://www.cifas.org.uk/default.asp?edit_ id=839-57, Published by permission of CIFAS--the UK's Fraud Prevention Service; Table 5.2 from E-Consultancy, 2008. Managing Digital Channels Research Report by Dave Chaffey. Available from http://econsultancy.com, reprinted with permission; Table 5.11 adapted from E-Consultancy, 2008, managing digital channels research report. Author Dave Chaffey. Available from http://econsultancy.com, reprinted with permission; Table 7.3 adapted from Reducing the costs of goods sold: role of complexity, design relationships *McKinsey Quarterly*, Vol. 2, pp. 212–215 (Kluge, J. 1997), www.mckinsey-quarterly.com, McKinsey & Co., Inc.; Table 7.7 adapted from E-hubs: the new B2B marketplaces *Harvard Business Review*, May–June, p. 99 (Kaplan, S. and Sawhney, M. 2000) © 2000 by the Harvard Business School Publishing Corporation, all rights reserved; Table 8.6 adapted from *eShock 2000. The Electronic Shopping Revolution: Strategies for retailers and manufacturers*, 2 ed., Palgrave Macmillan (de Kare-Silver, M. 1999) reproduced with permission of Palgrave Macmillan; Table 9.1 from Efficient Frontier, www.efficientfrontier.com, reprinted with permission; Table 9.2 from Data from Interactive Advertising Bureau www.iab.net/xmos., XMOS is a registered trademark of the IAB; Table 9.4 adapted from Your secret weapon on the web, *Harvard Business Review*, July–August, pp. 105-113 (Reichheld, F. and Schefter, P. 2000) © 2000 by the Harvard Business School Publishing Corporation, all rights reserved; Table 10.6 adapted from How risky is your company?, *Harvard Business Review*, May–June, p. 87 (Simon, R. 1999) © 1999 by the Harvard Business School Publishing Corporation, all rights reserved; Table 11.6 adapted from *Internet Marketing* (Hofacker, C.F. 2001) Copyright © 2001 John Wiley & Sons, Inc. Reproduced with permission of John Wiley & Sons, Inc.; Table 11.8 from Department of Business, Enterprise and Regulatory Reform Information Security Breaches Survey 2008, published at http://www.pwc.co.uk/eng/publications/berr_information_security_breaches_survey_2008.html, Crown Copyright material is reproduced with permission under the terms of the Click-Use Licence; Table 12.3 adapted from *Software testing : a craftsman's approach* (JORGENSEN, PAUL C.) Copyright 1995 in the format Textbook via Copyright Clearance Center.; Table 12.5 from ABC Electronic www.abce.org.uk, ABC ELECTRONIC, reprinted with permission; Table 12.7 from Coremetrics monthly metrics benchmark produced for UK retailers, July 2008, http://www.coremetrics.co.uk/solutions/benchmarking.php, reprinted with permission.

Text

Interview on pages 8-10 from E-consultancy, http://econsultancy.com/news-blog/newsletter/3200/interview-ted-speroni-director-emea-hp-com.html, reprinted with permission; Case Study 1.2 from North-West Supplies Extends its Reach Online, written by Peter Davies, Ecommerce adviser, Mentermon, www.mentermon.com, with permission from Peter Davies; Interview on pages 50-54 from E-consultancy, www.Econsultancy.com/news-blog/366073/q-a-more-than-s-roberto-hortal-munoz-on-comparison-sites.html, reprinted with permission; Case Study 2.3 adapted from various sources , With thanks to www.firebox.com; Interview on pages 96-98 from E-consultancy, Posted 15 September 2009 09:53am by Graham Charlton, http://econsultancy.com/blog/4612-q-al-lastminute-com-s-marko-balabanovic-on-innovation, reprinted with permission; Box 3.1 adapted from 12 ways to use your intranet to cut your costs. Member briefing paper August 2008. Published by the Intranet Benchmarking Forum www.ibforum.com, with permission from IBF; Box 3.3 from blog by Matt Cutts, www.mattcutts.com/blog/seo-glossary-url-definitions/, with permission from Matt Cutts; Box 3.4 from Office of Communications report: The International Communications Market 2007. Report published December 2007 at http://www.ofcom.org.uk/research/cm/icmr07/overview/landscape/. © Ofcom Copyright 2007; Extract on page 206 from Privacy and Electronic Communications Regulations (PECR) Act 2003, Crown Copyright material is reproduced with permission under the terms of the Click-Use Licence; Interview on pages 183-185 from E-consultancy, http://econsultancy.com/uk/blog/4275-q-a-lingo24-founder-christian-arno, reprinted with permission; Extract on pages 199-202 from Data Protection Act 1984, 1998 (DPA), Crown Copyright material is reproduced with permission under the terms of the Click-Use Licence; Case Study 4.1 from The Futures Company, http://www.hchlv.com/, reprinted with permission from The Futures Company; Box 4.5 adapted from Eric Goldman Technology and Marketing Law Blog. Rhino Sports, Inc. v. Sport Court, Inc., 8 May 2007 blog.ericgoldman.org/archives/2007/05/broad_matching.htm, with permission from Eric Goldman; Box 4.6 adapted from various sources, with permission from HSBC Bank; Interview on pages 238-241 from E-consultancy, http://econsultancy.com/news-blog/newsletter/3504/interview-with-standard-life-s-sharon-shaw.html, reprinted with permission; Case Study 5.1 adapted from Campaign of the month, *Revolution* (Rigby, E. 2005), Reproduced from Revolution magazine with the permission of the copyright owner, Haymarket Business Publications Limited; Case Study 5.1 adapted from Company annual reports and an article in The Banker 2003, reprinted by permission of Capital One Bank (Europe) plc; Case Study 5.2 from E-Consultancy e-Business briefing, Arena Flowers' Sam Barton on web design and development, e-newsletter interview 12/03/2008, reprinted with permission;

Case Study 6.2 from Econsultancy, 2010, Multichannel accounts for 43% of Argos sales. By Graham Charlton, 4 May 2010, http://econsultancy.com/blog/5850-multichannel-accounts-for-43-of-argos-sales, reprinted with permission; Case Study 7.1 from RS Components White Paper, www.rswww.com, Courtesy of R.S. Components Ltd. © R. S. Components Ltd; Case Study 7.2 adapted from various sources; Interview on pages 385-386 from E-consultancy, www.econsultancy.com/news-blog/newsletter/3415/steve-nicholas-assistant-director-of-e-commerce-at-guess.html, reprinted with permission; Case Study 8.3 adapted from various sources, reprinted by permission of Napster LLC; Interview on pages 453-455 from E-consultancy, http://econsultancy.com/blog/5523-q-a-peter-cobb-of-ebags, Reproduced with permission; Case Study 9.1 from Facebook bidding by Nicola Smith, 7 October 2010, http://www.nma.co.uk/features/facebook-bidding/3019000.article, with permission from NMA; Case Study 9.2 from Blog posting, 9 September 2008, http://www.arenaflowers.com/blog/2008/09/09/wiser-about-web-from-a-flowers-website-to-academic-text/#comment-4361, with permission from Arena Flowers; Case Study 9.4 from Product placement, *New Media Age*, *www.nma.co.uk* (Hargrave, S.), with permission from NMA; Interview on pages 532-534 from E-consultancy, http://econsultancy.com/uk/blog/6624-q-a-confused-com-s-tom-beverley-on-multichannel-marketin, reprinted with permission; Case Study 10.2 from e-gineer.com blog by Nathan Wallace, www.e-gineer.com/v2/blog/2007/08/our-intranet-wiki-case-study-of-wiki.htm, with permission from Nathan Wallace; Interview on pages 579-581 from www.econsultancy.com/news-blog/newsletter/3722/arena-flowers-8217-sam-barton-on-web-design-and-development,html, Reproduced with permission; Case Study 11.1 from case study developed by Agency.com available through the IAB (www.iabuk.net) and presented at Engage 2007, reprinted with permission; Box 11.2 from E-Consultancy, 2007, e-business briefing interview. Bruce Tognazzini on Human-Computer interaction. Interview published November. http://econsultany.com/blog/1862-q-a-bruce-tognazzini-on-human-computer-interaction, reprinted with permission; Interview on pages 651-653 from E-consultancy, http://econsultancy.com/blog/4647-q-a-dane-atkinson-ceo-of-squarespace, reprinted with permission; Box 12.2 from Search engine ranking factors v2, 2 April 2007, www.seomoz.org/article/search-ranking-factors, reprinted with permission.

The Financial Times

Screenshot 2.2 from www.ft.com, reprinted with permission; Case Study 3.2 from New architecture or just new hype?, *The Financial Times*, 08/03/2006 (Waters, Richard), The Financial Times, reprinted with permission; Newspaper Headline on page 293 from Boo.com collapses as investors refuse funds. Online sports retailer becomes Europe's first big internet casualty, *The Financial Times*, 18/05/2000 (Barker, T. and Daniel, C.); Case Study 6.1 from Did IT work? Service was paramount when enhancing supply chain, *The Financial Times*, 30/01/2008 (Pritchard, S.), reprinted with permission; Case Study 6.3 from Keeping track starts its move to a faster track *The Financial Times*, 20/04/2005 (Nairn,G.), reprinted with permission; Screenshot 7.6 from FT.com, reprinted with permission; Case Study 10.1 from Process Management: Making complex business a lot simpler?, *The Financial Times*, 14/05/2008 (Cane, A.), reprinted with permission; Case Study 11.2 from A different approach to protection, *The Financial Times*, 09/11/2005 (Thomas, D.).

In some instances we have been unable to trace the owners of copyright material, and we would appreciate any information that would enable us to do so.

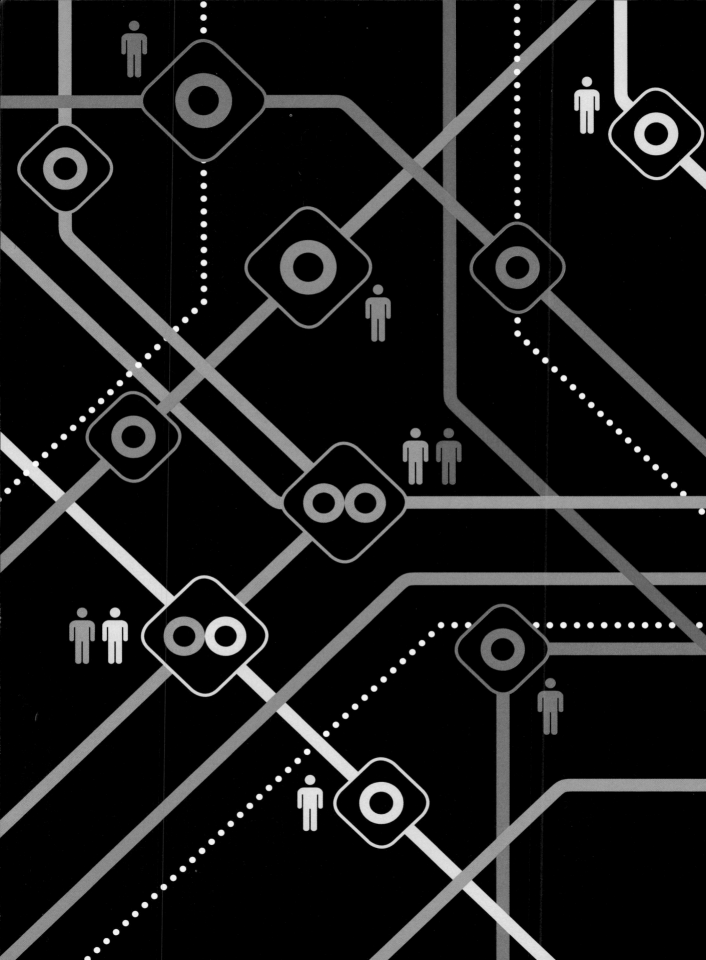

Part 1

Introduction

Part 1 introduces e-business and e-commerce and their relevance to businesses and consumers. It clarifies e-business terms and concepts such as online business, revenue and technology models by reviewing alternative applications through activities and case studies.

1

Introduction to e-business and e-commerce p. 3

- The impact of electronic communications on traditional businesses
- What is the difference between e-commerce and e-business?
- E-business opportunities

- Business adoption of digital technologies for e-commerce and e-business
- E-business risks and barriers to business adoption
- Management responses to e-commerce and e-business

2

Marketplace analysis for e-commerce p. 48

- The e-commerce environment
- Location of trading in the marketplace
- Business models for e-commerce

Focus on …
- Auction business models
- Internet start-up companies – the 'dot-coms'

3

E-business infrastructure p. 92

- Internet technology
- Web technology
- Internet-access software applications
- How does it work? Internet standards
- Managing e-business infrastructure

Focus on …
- Internet governance
- Web services, SaaS and service-oriented architecture (SOA)
- Mobile commerce

4

E-environment p. 179

- Social and legal factors
- Environmental and green issues related to Internet usage
- Taxation
- Economic and competitive factors
- Political factors
- E-government
- Technological innovation and technology assessment

Focus on ...

- E-commerce and globalization

1

Introduction to e-business and e-commerce

Web support

The following additional case studies are available at
www.pearsoned.co.uk/chaffey

→ SME adoption of sell-side e-commerce

→ Death of the dot-com dream

→ Encouraging SME adoption of sell-side e-commerce

The site also contains a range of study material designed to help improve your results.

Learning outcomes

After completing this chapter the reader should be able to:

● Define the meaning and scope of e-business and e-commerce and their different elements

● Summarize the main reasons for adoption of e-commerce and e-business and barriers that may restrict adoption

● Outline the ongoing business challenges of managing e-business and e-commerce in an organization

Management issues

The issues for managers raised in this chapter include:

● How do we explain the scope and implications of e-business and e-commerce to staff?

● What is the full range of benefits of introducing e-business and what are the risks?

● How do we evaluate our current e-business capabilities?

Links to other chapters

The main related chapters are:

● *Chapter 2* examines the principal e-commerce business and marketplace models in more detail

● *Chapter 3* introduces the technical infrastructure of software and hardware that companies must incorporate to achieve e-commerce

● *Chapter 5* describes approaches to e-business strategy introduced in *Chapter 1*

Introduction

The Internet

'The Internet' refers to the physical network that links computers across the globe. It consists of the infrastructure of network servers and communication links between them that are used to hold and transport information between the client PCs and web servers.

World Wide Web (WWW)

The most common technique for publishing information on the Internet. It is accessed through web browsers which display web pages of embedded graphics and HTML/XML-encoded text.

Wireless communications

Electronic transactions and communications conducted using mobile devices such as laptops and mobile phones (and fixed access platforms) with different forms of wireless connection.

Organizations have now been applying technologies based on **the Internet, World Wide Web** and **wireless communications** to transform their businesses for over 20 years since the creation of the first website (http://info.cern.ch) by Sir Tim Berners-Lee in 1991. Deploying these technologies has offered many opportunities for innovative e-businesses to be created based on new approaches to business. Table 1.1 highlights some of the best-known examples and in Activity 1.1 you can explore some of the reasons for success of these e-businesses.

For the author, e-business and e-commerce is an exciting area to be involved with, since many new opportunities and challenges arise yearly, monthly and even daily. Innovation is a given, with the continuous introduction of new technologies, new business models and new communications approaches. For example, Google innovates relentlessly. Its service has developed a long way since 1998 (Figure 1.1) with billions of pages now indexed and other services such as web mail, pay-per-click adverts, analytics and social networks all part of its offering. Complete Activity 1.1 or view Table 1.1 to see other examples of the rate at which new innovations occur.

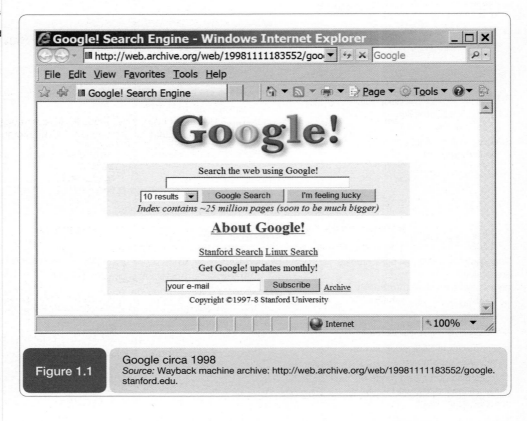

| Figure 1.1 | Google circa 1998
Source: Wayback machine archive: http://web.archive.org/web/19981111183552/google.stanford.edu. |

Table 1.1	Timeline of websites indicating innovation in business model or marketing communications approach	

Year founded	Company / site	Category of innovation and business model
1994	Amazon	Retailer
1995 (March)	Yahoo! (yahoo.com)	Directory and portal
1995 (Sept)	eBay	Online auction
1995 (Dec)	AltaVista (altavista.com)	Search engine
1996	Hotmail (hotmail.com)	Web-based e-mail Viral marketing (using e-mail signatures to promote service) Purchased by Microsoft in 1997
1998	GoTo.com (goto.com) Overture (2001)	Pay-per-click search marketing Purchased by Yahoo! in 2003
1998	Google (google.com)	Search engine
1999	Blogger (blogger.com)	Blog publishing platform Purchased by Google in 2003
1999	Alibaba (alibaba.com)	B2B marketplace with $1.7 billion IPO on Hong Kong stock exchange in 2007. See case in Chapter 2
1999	MySpace (myspace.com) Formerly eUniverse	Social network Purchased by News Corp in 2005
2001	Wikipedia (wikipedia.com)	Open encyclopedia
2002	Last.fm	A UK-based Internet radio and music community website, founded in 2002. On 30 May 2007, CBS Interactive acquired Last.fm for £140m (US$280m)
2003	Skype (skype.com)	Peer-to-peer Internet telephony VoIP – Voice over Internet Protocol Purchased by eBay in 2005
2003	Second Life (secondlife.com)	Immersive virtual world
2004	Facebook (facebook.com)	Social network applications and groups
2005	YouTube (youtube.com)	Video sharing and rating
2007	Hulu (hulu.com)	Quality video broadcast service IPTV – Internet Protocol TV
2009	Foursquare (foursquare.com)	A location-based social media website designed for mobile access. Video explanation: http://bit.ly/EBEC-Foursquare
??	The future	??

Activity 1.1	Innovative e-businesses

Purpose

To illustrate innovation in online business models and communications approaches.

Questions

1 Think about the innovation that you have witnessed during the time you have used the Internet and World Wide Web. What would you say are the main sites used in your country that have been created which have changed the way we spend our time or buy online?

> 2 We talk about these businesses being 'successful', but what is success for a new e-business?
>
> 3 What do these sites have in common that you think has made them successful?
>
> *Answers to activities can be found at* www.pearsoned.co.uk/chaffey

The impact of electronic communications on traditional businesses

Social media

A category of media focusing on participation and peer-to-peer communication between individuals with sites providing the capability to develop user-generated content (UGC) and to exchange messages and comments between different users.

Social network

A site that facilitates peer-to-peer communication within a group or between individuals through providing facilities to develop user-generated content (UGC) and to exchange messages and comments between different users.

During the same period managers at established businesses have had to determine how to apply new electronic communications technologies to transform their organizations. As we will see later in this chapter, existing businesses have evolved their approaches to e-business through a series of stages. Innovation in e-business is relentless, with the continuous introduction of new technologies, new business models and new communications approaches. So all organizations have to review new electronic and Internet-based communications approaches for their potential to make their business more competitive and also manage ongoing risks such as security and performance. For example, many businesses are reviewing the benefits, costs and risks of implementing:

- The growth in popularity of **social media** and in particular **social networks** such as Facebook, Twitter and for business-to-business users Linked In, **virtual worlds** such as Habbo Hotel and Second Life, and **blogs** created by many individuals and businesses.
- **Rich media** such as online video and interactive applications into their websites.
- A selection of **mobile commerce** services which exploit the usage of mobile phones and other portable wireless devices such as laptops around the world. The potential of mobile commerce is evident from research by ITU (2010) which estimated that by the end of 2010 there would be 5 billion mobile subscriptions of whom 1 billion would have mobile broadband access. The growth in popularity of **mobile apps** (Chapter 3), from the iPhone store, Google Android store and other handset vendors, is another significant development in mobile communications.
- Location-based tracking of goods and inventory as they are manufactured and transported.

| Activity 1.2 | The most popular apps today |

Virtual worlds

An electronic environment which simulates interactions between online characters known as avatars. Also known as Massively Multiplayer Online Roleplaying Games (MMORPG).

Blog

Personal online diary, journal or news source compiled by one person, an internal team or external guest authors. Postings are usually in different categories. Typically comments can be added to each blog posting to help create interactivity and feedback.

This can be completed individually or as a group activity comparing popular apps for different mobile handsets. Review the most popular apps today, either using the App Store for your mobile phone or a compilation from an information provider such as Nielsen.

Questions

1 Identify the most popular categories of apps from the top 10 or 20 most popular apps.

2 Discuss the opportunities for companies to promote their brands or services using apps.

At the time of writing the most popular categories of apps catalogued by Nielsen (2010) in order of popularity on Smart Phones were:

1 Games

2 Music

3 Social networking

Rich media
Digital assets such as ads are not static images, but provide animation, audio or interactivity as a game or form to be completed.

Mobile commerce (m-commerce)
Electronic transactions and communications conducted using mobile devices such as laptops, PDAs and mobile phones, and typically with a wireless connection.

Mobile apps
A software application that is designed for use on a mobile phone, typically downloaded from an app store. iPhone Apps are best known, but all Smart Phones support the use of apps which can provide users with information, entertainment or location-based services such as mapping.

4   News/weather

5   Maps/navigation

6   Video/movies

7   Entertainment/food

8   Sports

9   Communication

10 Banking/finance

You can see that an organization's capability to manage technology-enabled change is the essence of successfully managing e-business. The pace of change and the opportunities for new communications approaches make e-business and e-commerce an exciting area of business to be involved in.

In *E-Business and E-Commerce Management* we will explore approaches managers can use to assess the relevance of different e-business opportunities and then devise and implement strategies to exploit these opportunities. We will also study how to manage more practical risks such as delivering a satisfactory service quality, maintaining customer privacy and managing security. We introduce some of the opportunities and risks later in this chapter.

In this chapter we start by introducing the scope of e-business and e-commerce. Then we review the main opportunities and risks of e-business together with the drivers and barriers to adoption of e-business services.

Managing social media

Managing social media is one of the most pressing challenges for many businesses seeking to engage with their prospects and customers online. Some would suggest that managing social media is not possible. But with web users spending an increasing proportion of their time online using social media sites, an approach to determine how to engage users of social networks and communities with brands and monitor and respond to their comments is a priority for many companies today. If you visit the latest list of popular sites worldwide compiled by Google-owned company Doubleclick (www.google.com/adplanner/static/top1000) you will see that Facebook is the most popular site and, of course, within different countries and for different interests each has its own area of interest. Given the importance of social media opportunities, this is a common theme throughout this book.

Real-world E-Business experiences   **The Econsultancy interview**

Ted Speroni, Director, EMEA (Europe, Middle East and Asia), HP.com

Overview and main concepts covered

Ted Speroni heads the European operations of HP.com, as well as the tech giant's regional preferred online partner programme. This practitioner interview highlights some of the challenges and opportunities for a traditional organization in managing e-commerce. It also introduces some of the important online marketing communications techniques such as search engine marketing, affiliate marketing, social media and widget marketing which are described in Chapter 9.

The interview

Q. Can you briefly summarise your role at HP.com?

Ted Speroni, HP.com: I look after HP.com for the EMEA region. We have around 40 country websites throughout the region in something like 28 languages, so that's my responsibility. I'm also responsible for all of our electronic content management across Europe, which is where we intersect with the online retail community.

At HP, we have a clear strategy of making our products available wherever our customers want to buy them – through high street shops, proximity resellers, online retailers, e-resellers and direct through HP.

We only sell direct through HP.com in five countries in Europe – the UK, France, Germany, Switzerland and Spain. So in most countries, we connect in with the leading etailers. We get daily feeds from all of them on their product availability and pricing, and we display them on HP.com. We then deep link into the shopping basket on each etailer, so we're generating leads for them.

It's just like an affiliate programme [a commission-based sales arrangement covered in Chapter 9], but we don't get a commission because it's for our own products. We track the number and quality of leads we are sending each retailer and their conversion rates. We have all the data on which products sell and which cross-sell.

It's a pretty big programme – we have about 150 partners in Europe that are part of it and we generate quite a considerable amount of leads and traffic for them. You have to qualify to be part of it – there are certain criteria you have to meet.

Q. What are you doing at the moment to drive more traffic to these etailers?

Ted Speroni, HP.com: The first thing is the integrated marketing approach we have. Search engine marketing (SEM) and search engine optimisation (SEO) are probably the two biggest areas we are working on.

The fundamental principle is that we want to drive all that traffic to pages where we give the customer choice. All the marketing traffic drives people to landing pages that give people a choice about where to purchase the product.

Our investment in SEM is probably in line with the growth we see overall in the industry. We're also making quite heavy investments internally in SEO, because a much higher percentage of our traffic comes from natural search and the conversion rate is not that dissimilar to SEM.

Natural search is a big area of focus for us at the moment. With SEM, we always get people to the right page, to specific landing pages. With natural search, we're not as convinced we're always getting people to the correct page.

For that, we're analysing where the traffic is going from natural search results so that we can give the customer choice on those pages, and also looking at how to make sure people go to the pages they want to go to.

Q. How difficult is it to maintain communication with partners across multiple channels?

Ted Speroni, HP.com: We're pretty happy with the multi-channel approach we have taken. Encompassing all the different ways customers want to buy products is the most important thing.

We've struggled with that for a long time and we're just trying to make each channel as efficient as possible. We still have a way to go – I'm still working on a number of projects to optimise the different channels.

One thing is the question of high street retailers and the question of integration of inventory. When a customer wants to buy a specific camera they want to know whether it is in stock today, and I don't want the site to send them to the wrong place.

Q. How are you managing the syndication of your product content to your partners in the programme? How challenging is that?

Ted Speroni, HP.com: My team syndicates out [electronically distributes] all the content to our resellers. What this is all about is we want to control the HP brand in relation to our products. We produce electronic content feeds in 28 languages of all the product information – pictures, marketing messaging, specifications, everything.

Whenever a customer anywhere in Europe is seeing information about an HP product, there's a very high probability that that will be content we have created. The picture is the picture we want people to see. We feel it's been very successful for us – not only in terms of controlling our brand, but also in terms of cutting costs for our partners. They don't need to do content acquisition.

We'll either syndicate the content via XML feeds, or sometimes the resellers are buying the content through content aggregators. And this extends beyond simple product information – we also syndicate out our recommended cross-sell products. If you buy an HP printer, we have a list of recommended accessories.

This is a key thing – similar to what Dell have talked about in terms of increasing the average shopping basket. Our top priority partners are partners that sell complete HP solutions, so this tool helps them sell complete HP solutions. Resellers can't say they don't know which products sell well with others, because we are telling them.

I should also mention another component – we're not just syndicating content, we also syndicate a configurator for configuring PCs.

We feed all the data into the configurator about the different configurations you can build. You as a customer configure the PC and the information goes into the shopping basket of the retailer, as well as coming through to the HP factory so we can build the configuration. We then match up the order when the retailer passes the order through to us, and we ship it.

It goes beyond syndicating content – you're syndicating widgets, real web apps that can be integrated into websites.

Q. How else are you looking to use widgets?

Ted Speroni, HP.com: Another area is product advisors. We have product advisors on HP.com and we would like to syndicate them out. The principle behind this is that we don't want to provide a link on retailers' websites to HP.com, we want to keep the customers on their sites. As we move HP.com to a more modular, Web 2.0-type approach, we'll see which components we can syndicate out. We also have flash demos so there's an opportunity for resellers to have them on their website, although the resellers do have to have some merchandising people that know about the products. Their sites also have to be Web 2.0-enabled.

Q. What are you doing in terms of social media and social shopping?

Ted Speroni, HP.com: We're starting to pilot some social tagging concepts on our product pages, so that people can easily embed our product pages into different sites, like Myspace profiles for example.

It's at a very early stage but it's about the whole concept of exporting our stuff onto the social networking sites, as opposed to trying to get people onto our sites. We haven't implemented it in Europe, but in the US we have started some pilots.

For a while now, we have also had RSS links on promotions from our site – we've had some uptake of that, but it's not a killer app I would say. We're basically looking at how we can help people who want to create content around our products, and facilitate that.

There's a lot of HP content on YouTube – lots of people make videos about how to make the new HP printer, for example. So our approach is 'if people want to do this, let's help them and let's benefit from it'. If we can get user generated linkage to our products, it's incredibly powerful.

Q. Have you looked at user generated reviews?

Ted Speroni, HP.com: We're doing a pilot in the US with user generated reviews. We haven't started that yet in Europe – I'm trying to work out a scaleable model with all the language issues.

We have to have some quality control on the user reviews – we can't depend completely on community policing. We need some proactive moderation – since it's on our website, we can't take risks with legal issues and so on.

You can say our products aren't good but you have to use appropriate language. Also, we don't want you to be able to comment on our competitors' products. You can say what you want about our products but you can't push competitors' products.

We've been runnning this for about six months in the US and there's been good uptake, and we haven't had big issues with appropriateness. In Europe, I am looking to deploy something and looking into the multi-language issues.

Source: www.econsultancy.com/news-blog/newsletter/3200/interview-ted-speroni-director-emea-hp-com. html. Econsultancy.com provides information, training and events on best practice in online marketing and e-commerce management.

What is the difference between e-commerce and e-business?

The rapid advancement of technology and its application to business has been accompanied by a range of new terminology and jargon. The use of the term 'electronic commerce' has been supplemented by additional terms such as e-business and digital marketing, and more specialist terms such as e-CRM, e-tail and e-procurement. Do we need to be concerned about the terminology? The short answer is no; Mougayer (1998) noted that it is understanding the services that can be offered to customers and the business benefits that are obtainable through e-business that are important. However, labels are convenient in defining the *scope* of the changes we are looking to make within an organization through using electronic communications. Managers need to communicate the extent of changes they are proposing through introducing digital technologies to employees, customers and partners. **Social commerce** is an increasingly important part of e-commerce for site owners since incorporating reviews and ratings into a site and linking to social networking sites can help understand customers' needs and increase conversion to sale. It can also involve group buying, using a coupon service like Groupon.

E-commerce defined

Electronic commerce (e-commerce) is often thought simply to refer to buying and selling using the Internet; people immediately think of consumer retail purchases from companies such as Amazon. But e-commerce involves much more than electronically mediated *financial* transactions between organizations and customers. E-commerce should be considered as *all* electronically mediated transactions between an organization and any third party it deals with. By this definition, non-financial transactions such as customer requests for further information would also be considered to be part of e-commerce. Kalakota and Whinston (1997) refer to a range of different perspectives for e-commerce:

Social commerce
A subset of e-commerce which encourages participation and interaction of customers in rating, selecting and buying products through group buying. This participation can occur on an e-commerce site or on third-party sites.

Electronic commerce (e-commerce)
All electronically mediated information exchanges between an organization and its external stakeholders.

1 A *communications perspective* – the delivery of information, products or services or payment by electronic means.
2 A *business process perspective* – the application of technology towards the automation of business transactions and workflows.
3 A *service perspective* – enabling cost cutting at the same time as increasing the speed and quality of service delivery.
4 An *online perspective* – the buying and selling of products and information online.

The UK government also used a broad definition when explaining the scope of e-commerce to industry:

> *E-commerce is the exchange of information across electronic networks, at any stage in the supply chain, whether within an organization, between businesses, between businesses and consumers, or between the public and private sector, whether paid or unpaid.* (Cabinet Office, 1999)

These definitions show that electronic commerce is not solely restricted to the actual buying and selling of products, but also includes pre-sale and post-sale activities across the supply chain.

When evaluating the strategic impact of e-commerce on an organization, it is useful to identify opportunities for buy-side and sell-side e-commerce transactions as depicted in Figure 1.2, since systems with different functionalities will need to be created in an

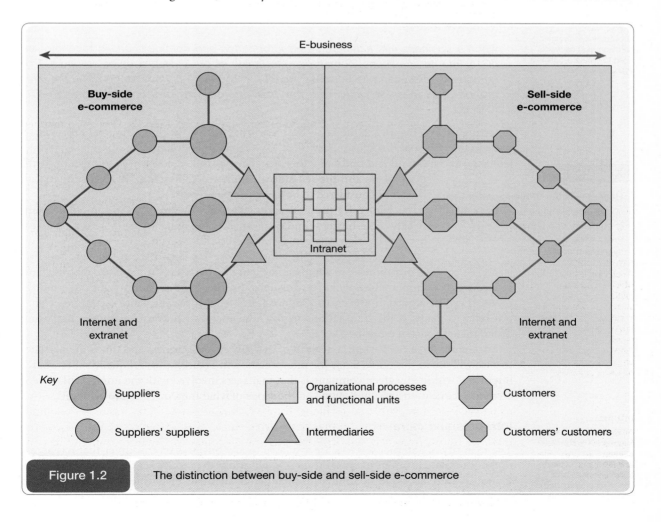

| Figure 1.2 | The distinction between buy-side and sell-side e-commerce |

Buy-side e-commerce

E-commerce transactions between a purchasing organization and its suppliers.

Sell-side e-commerce

E-commerce transactions between a supplier organization and its customers.

organization to accommodate transactions with buyers and with suppliers. **Buy-side e-commerce** refers to transactions to procure resources needed by an organization from its suppliers. In Chapter 6, Case Study 6.1 reviews how Shell has developed an e-business capability that enables buy-side e-commerce for its customers. **Sell-side e-commerce** refers to transactions involved with selling products to an organization's customers. So e-commerce transactions between organizations can be considered from two perspectives: sell-side from the perspective of the selling organization and buy-side from the perspective of the buying organization.

E-business defined

Electronic business (e-business)

All electronically mediated information exchanges, both within an organization and with external stakeholders supporting the range of business processes.

Information and communication technology (ICT or IT)

The software applications, computer hardware and networks used to create e-business systems.

Given that Figure 1.2 depicts different types of e-commerce, what then is **e-business**? Let's start from the definition by IBM (www.ibm.com/e-business), which was one of the first suppliers to use the term in 1997 to promote its services:

> *e-business (e'biz'nis) – the transformation of key business processes through the use of Internet technologies.*

In an international benchmarking study analysing the adoption of e-business in SMEs the Department of Trade and Industry emphasizes the application of technology (**information and communications technologies (ICTs)**) in the full range of business processes, but also emphasizes how it involves innovation. DTI (2000) described the initial applications of e-business as follows:

> *when a business has fully integrated information and communications technologies (ICTs) into its operations, potentially redesigning its business processes around ICT or completely reinventing its business model... e-business, is understood to be the integration of all these activities with the internal processes of a business through ICT.* (DTI, 2000)

Referring back to Figure 1.2, the key e-business processes are the organizational processes or units in the centre of the figure. They include research and development, marketing, manufacturing and inbound and outbound logistics. The buy-side e-commerce transactions with suppliers and the sell-side e-commerce transactions with customers can also be considered to be key business processes.

Debate 1.1

How new is the e-business concept?

'E-business is just a new label – there is no distinction between the role of e-business and traditional information systems management.'

Figure 1.3 presents some alternative viewpoints of the relationship between e-business and e-commerce. In Figure 1.3(a) there is a relatively small overlap between e-commerce and e-business. From Figure 1.2 we can reject Figure 1.3(a) since the overlap between buy-side and sell-side e-commerce is significant. Figure 1.3(b) seems to be more realistic, and indeed many commentators seem to consider e-business and e-commerce to be synonymous. It can be argued, however, that Figure 1.3(c) is most realistic since e-commerce does not refer to many of the transactions *within* a business, such as processing a purchasing order, that are part of e-business.

So, e-commerce can best be conceived of as a subset of e-business and this is the perspective we will use in this book. Since the interpretation in Figure 1.3(b) is equally valid, what is important within any given company is that managers involved with the implementation of e-commerce or e-business are agreed on the scope of what they are trying to achieve!

Intranets and extranets

Intranet

A private network within a single company using Internet standards to enable employees to access and share information using web publishing technology.

The majority of Internet services are available to any business or consumer that has access to the Internet. However, many e-business applications that access sensitive company information require access to be limited to qualified individuals or partners. If information is restricted to employees inside an organization, this is an **intranet,** as is shown in Figure 1.4.

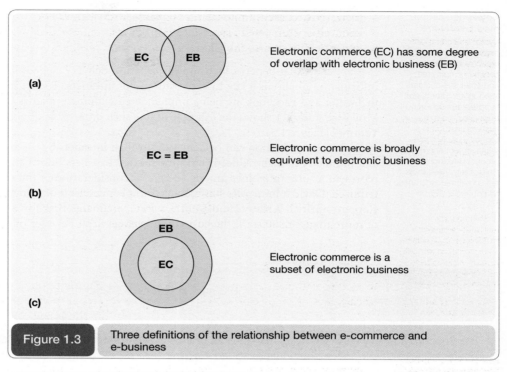

Figure 1.3   Three definitions of the relationship between e-commerce and e-business

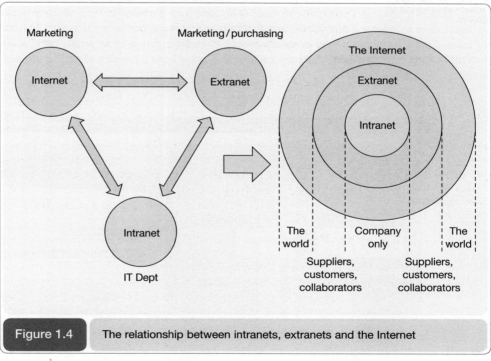

Figure 1.4   The relationship between intranets, extranets and the Internet

In a survey of 275 managers responsible for an intranet featured in *CIO* (2002), the main benefits mentioned by managers were:

1. Improved information sharing (customer service), 97%
2. Enhanced communications and information sharing (communications), 95%
3. Increased consistency of information (customer service), 94%

4 Increased accuracy of information (customer service), 93%

5 Reduced or eliminated processing, 93%

6 Easier organizational publishing, 92%

It is apparent that benefits focus on information delivery, suggesting that management of information quality is a key to successful use of intranets. Today, software services similar to Twitter and Facebook are being implemented within companies to achieve similar goals. Mini case study 1.1 shows the example of one such **enterprise social media software** tool, Yammer (Figure 1.5).

Direct cost reduction can be achieved through intranets by the reduced cost of printing and indirectly though reduced staff time needed to access information. However, intranets represent a substantial investment, so careful consideration of the return on investment is required. David Viney, who has managed implementation of intranets at Pricewaterhouse Coopers, British Airways and Centrica PLC, estimates that for a large implementation of more than 10,000 staff, the cost could average £250 per user or seat (Viney, 2003). He

---

Mini Case Study 1.1	Suncorp implement an internal social network

The Suncorp financial services group manages 25 brands in Australia and New Zealand spanning banking, insurance, investment and superannuation. Suncorp has over 219,000 shareholders, over 16,000 employees and around 7 million customers.

Suncorp has used enterprise social networking tool Yammer to help geographically dispersed people and teams to connect, share, discuss and innovate. It has also helped Suncorp create a culture where collaboration is more natural by enabling people to interact online in an open, informal and transparent way. Within a matter of months, Yammer membership grew from a handful of early adopters to over 1,700 users and continues to grow.

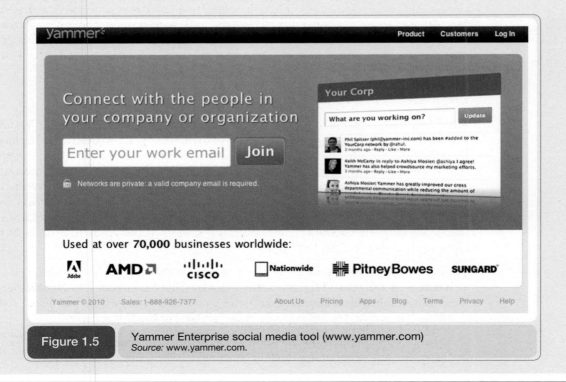

Figure 1.5	Yammer Enterprise social media tool (www.yammer.com) *Source:* www.yammer.com.

Jeff Smith, Suncorp, the Chief Information Office of Yammer explains the benefits as follows:

Yammer has enabled us to harness the wisdom of our people who are spread across multiple teams, geographies and brands to help achieve our purpose of delivering business solutions for competitive advantage.

Brian Robbins, Chief Marketing Office (CMO) added:

We recently signed up for Yammer and are seeing it spread virally among our employees. It is helping us accelerate collaboration and internal communications across our 20,000 employees in 300 offices in 30 countries. We're seeing all kinds of serendipitous connections across projects, cultures and time zones.

The benefits of applying a tool like Yammer to Suncorp can be summarized as:

- Increased informal knowledge flow across the organization through microblogging.
- Overcome barriers to collaboration, providing instant connection for people, teams, informal networks, communities of practice and other shared interest groups.
- Improved alignment between executives and employees by use of broadcast message to communicate messages and quickly crowdsource to get ideas, suggestions and answers to questions.
- Helped stimulate greater sharing and discussion among common role groups e.g. developers, architects and testers.

Source: Adapted from Yammer (2010).

suggests this cost breaks down into four categories: software (content management systems), hardware (servers to store content and applications), integration of information sources and applications, and process change (staff costs and opportunity costs associated within implementation). He also suggests that if the portal project involves integration with ERP systems, this could add £150 per seat.

If access to an organization's web services is extended to some others, but not everyone beyond the organization, this is an **extranet**. Whenever you log on to an Internet service such as that for an e-retailer or online news site, this is effectively an extranet arrangement, although the term is most often used to mean a business-to-business application such as the Shell SIMON capability described in Case Study 6.1 where certain customers or suppliers are given shared access. We look at examples of intranets and extranets in Chapter 3 including the Dell Premier extranet.

Extranet

A service provided through Internet and web technology delivered by extending an intranet beyond a company to customers, suppliers and collaborators.

Different types of sell-side e-commerce

Sell-side e-commerce doesn't only involve selling products such as books and DVDs online, but also involves using Internet technologies to market services using a range of techniques we will explore in Chapters 8 and 9. Not every product is suitable for sale online, so the way in which a website is used to market products will vary. It is useful to consider the five main types of online presence for sell-side e-commerce, which each have different objectives and are appropriate for different markets. These are not clear-cut categories of websites since any company may combine these types, but with a change in emphasis according to the market they serve. As you review websites, note how organizations have different parts of the site focusing on these five functions:

1 **Transactional e-commerce sites**. These enable purchase of products online. The main business contribution of the site is through sale of these products. The sites also support the business by providing information for consumers that prefer to purchase products offline. These include retail sites, travel sites and online banking services.
2 **Services-oriented relationship-building websites**. Provide information to stimulate purchase and build relationships. Products are not typically available for purchase online. Information is provided through the website and e-newsletters to inform purchase

decisions. The main business contribution is through encouraging offline sales and generating enquiries or leads from potential customers. Such sites also add value to existing customers by providing them with information to help support them.

3 **Brand-building sites.** Provide an experience to support the brand. Products are not typically available for online purchase. Their main focus is to support the brand by developing an online experience of the brand. They are typical for low-value, high-volume fast-moving consumer goods (FMCG brands) for consumers.

4 **Portal, publisher or media sites.** Provide information, news or entertainment about a range of topics. 'Portal' refers to a gateway of information. This is information both on the site and through links to other sites. Portals have a diversity of options for generating revenue, including advertising, commission-based sales and sale of customer data (lists).

5 **Social networks.** Social networks could be considered to be in the previous category since they are often advertising-supported, but the influence of social networks such as Facebook, Linked In and Twitter on company and customer communications suggests they form a separate category.

Complete Activity 1.3 to consider examples of these different types of site.

Activity 1.3	Understanding different types of online presence

Purpose

To help you assess how different types of online presence are used for marketing.

Activity

Review the popularity of the different site types in your country or globally. The recommended information sources are:

- The Doubleclick AdPlanner compilation of the 1,000 most-visited sites on the web (www.google.com/adplanner/static/top1000/).
- The Hitwise Data Centers (e.g. www.hitwise.com/us/resources/data-center) available for Australia, Canada, France, Hong Kong, Singapore, New Zealand, UK, and US.

Visit each of the sites below and then indicate which of the five categories of online presence are their primary and secondary focus:

1 Transactional e-commerce site.
2 Services-oriented relationship-building website.
3 Brand-building site.
4 Portal or media site.
5 Social network.

Example sites

- Business site: Silicon (www.silicon.com)
- Bank, e.g. HSBC (www.hsbc.com)
- Lingerie manufacturer, e.g. Gossard (www.gossard.com)
- Management consultants such as PricewaterhouseCoopers (www.pwcglobal.com) and Accenture (www.accenture.com)
- Beverage manufacturers, e.g. Tango (www.tango.com), Guinness (www.guinness.com)
- Travel company, e.g. Thomas Cook (www.thomascook.com)
- An end-product manufacturer such as Vauxhall (www.vauxhall.co.uk)
- Consumer site, e.g. Yahoo! (www.yahoo.com)
- Online retailer such as Amazon (www.amazon.com)

Answers to activities can be found at www.pearsoned.co.uk/chaffey

Digital marketing

Digital marketing, e-marketing or Internet marketing is yet another field that is closely related to e-commerce. 'Digital marketing' is a term increasingly used by specialist e-marketing agencies, in recruitment of specialist staff, and the new media trade publications such as *New Media Age* (www.nma.co.uk) and *Revolution* (www.revolutionmagazine.com) to refer to sell-side e-commerce. We cover digital marketing in more detail in Chapters 8 and 9.

To help explain the scope and approaches used for digital marketing the IDM (www.theidm.com) has developed a more detailed explanation of digital marketing:

Digital marketing involves:

Applying these technologies which form online channels to market:

– Web, e-mail, databases, plus mobile/wireless and digital TV.

To achieve these objectives:

– Support marketing activities aimed at achieving profitable acquisition and retention of customers ... within a multi-channel buying process and customer lifecycle.

Through using these marketing tactics:

– Recognising the strategic importance of digital technologies and developing a planned approach to reach and migrate customers to online services through e-communications and traditional communications. Retention is achieved through improving our customer knowledge (of their profiles, behaviour, value and loyalty drivers), then delivering integrated, targeted communications and online services that match their individual needs.

Let's now look at each part of this description in more detail. The first part of the description illustrates the range of access platforms and communications tools that form the online channels which e-marketers use to build and develop relationships with customers including PCs, PDAs, mobile phones, interactive digital TV and radio.

Different access platforms deliver content and enable interaction through a range of different online communication tools or media channels. Some are well-established techniques which will be familiar to you, like websites, search engines, e-mail and text messaging. One of the most exciting things about working in digital media is the introduction of new tools and techniques which have to be assessed for their relevance to a particular marketing campaign.

Recent innovations which we discuss further in Chapters 8 and 9 include blogs, **feeds, podcasts** and **social networks.** The growth of social networks has been documented by Boyd and Ellison (2007) who describe social networking sites (SNS) as:

Web-based services that allow individuals to (1) construct a public or semi-public profile within a bounded system, (2) articulate a list of other users with whom they share a connection, and (3) view and traverse their list of connections and those made by others within the system.

The interactive capabilities to post comments or other content and rate content are surprisingly missing from this definition.

The six key types of digital media channels

There are many online communications techniques which marketers must review as part of their e-business communications strategy or as part of planning an online marketing campaign. To assist with planning, Chaffey and Smith (2008) recommend reviewing these six main types of **digital media channels** for reaching audiences shown in Figure 1.6. Note that offline communications should also be reviewed for their role in driving visitors to a company website or social network presence.

In Chapters 8 and 9, we review these tools in detail, but here is a summary of each digital media channel.

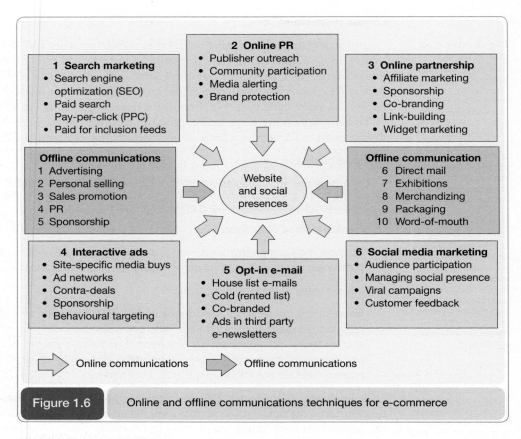

Figure 1.6 Online and offline communications techniques for e-commerce

1 Search engine marketing

Placing messages on a search engine to encourage clickthrough to a website when the user types a specific keyword phrase. Two key search marketing techniques are: paid placements or sponsored links using **pay-per-click**, and placements in the natural or organic listings using **search engine optimization (SEO)**.

2 Online PR

Maximizing favourable mentions and interactions with a company's brands, products or websites using third-party sites such as social networks or blogs that are likely to be visited by your target audience. It also includes responding to negative mentions and conducting public relations via a site through a press centre or blog. It is closely related to social media marketing.

3 Online partnerships

Creating and managing long-term arrangements to promote your online services on third-party websites or through e-mail communications. Different forms of partnership include link building, affiliate marketing, aggregators such as price comparison sites like Money supermarket (www.moneysupermarket.com), online sponsorship and co-branding.

4 Interactive advertising

Use of online ads such as banners and rich media ads to achieve brand awareness and encourage clickthrough to a target site.

5 Opt-in e-mail marketing

Renting e-mail lists or placing ads in third-party e-newsletters or the use of an in-house list for customer activation and retention.

6 Social media marketing

Social media marketing
Monitoring and facilitating customer–customer interaction and participation throughout the web to encourage positive engagement with a company and its brands. Interactions may occur on a company site, social networks and other third-party sites.

Social media marketing is an important category of digital marketing which invovles encouraging customer communications on a company's own site, or a social presence such as Facebook or Twitter, or in specialist publisher sites, blogs and forums. It can be applied as a traditional broadcast medium, for example companies can use Facebook or Twitter to send messages to customers or partners who have opted in. However, to take advantage of the benefits of social media it is important to participate in customer conversations. These can be related to products, promotions or customer service and are aimed at learning more about customers and providing support, so improving the way a company is perceived. In Chapter 9 we identify six main applications of social media.

Facebook is an example of an e-business that is now vital to companies seeking to reach and engage their audience online. Read the case study to understand the drivers behind the growth of the company and the challenges of managing an e-business.

Case Study 1.1	A short history of Facebook

Context

This case is about the social network Facebook. According to its owners,

> Facebook is a social utility that helps people communicate more efficiently with their friends, family and coworkers. The company develops technologies that facilitate the sharing of information through the social graph, the digital mapping of people's real-world social connections. Anyone can sign up for Facebook and interact with the people they know in a trusted environment.

In many countries Facebook is one of the most popular sites and in February 2010 exceeded 400 million active worldwide users for the first time. The case illustrates some of the challenges for an owner of a social network managing growth in usage, providing new features, advertising and managing user privacy. It also highlights the challenges for partners and advertisers considering working with a social network.

The case is presented through key events during the development of Facebook.

Facebook launched and extended – 4 February 2004

Facebook was founded while Mark Zuckerberg was a student at Harvard University. Initially membership was limited to Harvard students. The initial viral effect of the software was indicated since more than half of the undergraduate population at Harvard registered on the service within the first month!

Zuckerberg used open-source software PHP and the MySQL database to create the original 'TheFacebook. com' site and these technologies are still in use today.

When Facebook first launched in February 2004, there were just three things that users could do on the site which are still core to the functionality of the site. Users could create a profile with their picture and information, view other people's profiles, and add people as friends.

Since 2004, Facebook has introduced other functionality to create the Facebook experience. Some of the most significant of these include:

- A wall for posting messages
- News feeds
- Messages
- Posting of multiple photos and videos
- Groups
- Applications
- Facebook or engagement ads
- Access by mobile phones

Intellectual property dispute – September 2004 and ongoing

There has been an ongoing dispute on ownership of Facebook since another Harvard-originated social networking site 'HarvardConnection', which later changed its name to ConnectU, alleged in September 2004 that Zuckerberg had used their source code to develop Facebook when they originally contracted him to help in building their site.

It is also alleged that another system predated Facebook. Aaron J. Greenspan, a Harvard student, in 2003 created a simple web service that he called house-SYSTEM. It was used by several thousand Harvard students for a variety of online college-related tasks – six months before Facebook started and eight months before ConnectU went online. Mark Zuckerberg was briefly an early participant. No suit has been filed by Greenspan, but he has published a book about his experience.

Brand identify established – 23 August 2005

In August, Facebook bought the domain name facebook.com from the Aboutface Corporation for $200,000 and dropped 'the' from its name.

International expansion – 11 December 2005

Throughout 2005, Facebook extended its reach into different types of colleges and by the end of 2005 included most small universities and junior colleges in the United States, Canada and Mexico. It was also made available in many universities in the UK and Ireland and by December, Australia and New Zealand were added to the Facebook network, bringing its size to more than 2,000 colleges and over 25,000 high schools.

Initial concerns about privacy of member data – 14 December 2005

Two MIT students downloaded over 70,000 Facebook profiles from four schools (MIT, NYU, the University of Oklahoma, and Harvard) using an automated script, as part of a research project on Facebook privacy.

Facebook receives $25 million in funding – April 2006; Microsoft invests October 2007

In May 2005 Facebook received a $13 million cash infusion from venture firm Accel Partners, followed in April 2006 by a further $25 million from a range of partners including Greylock Partners, Meritech Capital Partners, and investor Peter Thiel, the co-founder of PayPal.

Facebook spokesman Chris R. Hughes explained the rationale for the investment when he said:

> This investment supports our goal to build an industry-leading company that will continue to grow and evolve with our users. We're committed to building the best utility to enable people to share information with each other in a secure and trusted environment.

Paul S. Madera, Meritech's managing director, said his firm was impressed by Facebook's rapid growth and its potential for further expansion in the coveted college-age market. 'They've been designated by their community as the chosen community portal,' Madera said. 'This is a company that the entire venture community would love to be a part of.'

In October 2007 Microsoft took a $240 million equity stake in Facebook based on a $15 billion valuation of Facebook. Under the terms of this strategic alliance, Microsoft would be the exclusive third-party advertising platform partner for Facebook, and begin to sell advertising for Facebook internationally in addition to the United States.

New feed functionality launched – September 2006

New information feeds were launched in mid-2006 which show the challenges of balancing the benefit of new functionality against disrupting existing user habits.

Writing in the Facebook blog in September 2006 Mark Zuckerberg said:

> We've been getting a lot of feedback about Mini-Feed and News Feed. We think they are great products, but we know that many of you are not immediate fans, and have found them overwhelming and cluttered.
>
> Other people are concerned that non-friends can see too much about them. We are listening to all your suggestions about how to improve the product; it's brand new and still evolving.

Later, in an open letter on the blog dated 8 September 2006, Zuckerberg said:

> We really messed this one up. When we launched News Feed and Mini-Feed we were trying to provide you with a stream of information about your social world. Instead, we did a bad job of explaining what the new features were and an even worse job of giving you control of them. I'd like to try to correct those errors now.

Categorizing friends into different types (Friends Lists – December 2007) is one approach that has helped to manage this.

Facebook Platform for applications launched – 24 May 2007

The Facebook Platform provides an API (Application Programming Interface) which enables software developers to create applications that interact with core Facebook features. This was a significant move since the openness enabled applications to grow in popularity and other sites to embed Facebook Fan page and follower information.

By January 2008, over 18,000 applications had been built on Facebook Platform with 140 new applications added per day. More than 95% of Facebook members have used at least one application built on Facebook Platform.

Facebook Platform for mobile applications was launched in October 2007, although many Facebook users already interacted with their friends through mobile phones.

Facebook passes 30 million active users – July 2007

Facebook active users passed 30 million according to the Facebook blog in July 2007. Mashable (http://

mashable.com/2007/07/10/facebook-users-2) reported that this represented a doubling in the first half of 2007.

Data produced by querying the Facebook ad targeting tool (www.facebook.com/ads) completed in November 2007 by blogger P.K. Francis suggests that the majority of Facebook users in many countries are female: http://midnightexcess.wordpress.com/2007/11/ 23/facebook-member-stats-an-update.

In terms of user engagement metrics, Facebook (www.facebook.com/press/info.php?statistics) shows there are:

- 68 million active users
- An average of 250,000 new registrations per day since January 2007
- Sixth most trafficked site in the United States (comScore)
- More than 65 billion page views per month
- More than half of active users return daily
- People spend an average of 20 minutes on the site daily (comScore)

Advertisers assess reputational damage – Summer 2007

In August 2007, the BBC announced that six major mainly financial services firms (First Direct, Vodafone, Virgin Media, the AA, Halifax and the Prudential) had withdrawn advertisements from Facebook, after they appeared on a British National Party page.

At a similar time, bank HSBC was forced to respond to groups set up on Facebook criticizing them for introduction of new student banking charges (although not until the case had been featured in the national media).

Facebook Ads launched – 7 November 2007

Some of the features of Facebook Ads (www.facebook.com/ads) include:

- Targeting by age, gender, location, interests, and more.
- Alternative payment models: cost per click (CPC) or impression-based (CPM).
- 'Trusted Referrals' or 'Social Ads' – ads can also be shown to users whose friends have recently engaged with a company's Facebook page or engaged with the company website through Facebook Beacon.

At the time of the launch the Facebook blog made these comments, which indicates the delicate balance between advertising revenue and user experience. They said, first of all, what's not changing:

- *'Facebook will always stay clutter-free and clean.*
- *Facebook will never sell any of your information.*

- *You will always have control over your information and your Facebook experience.*
- *You will not see any more ads than you did before this.'*

And what is changing:

- *'You now have a way to connect with products, businesses, bands, celebrities and more on Facebook.*
- *Ads should be getting more relevant and more meaningful to you.*
- *You now have the option to share actions you take on other sites with your friends on Facebook.'*

Commercial companies or more commonly not-for-profit organizations (e.g. www.facebook.com/joinred) can also create their own Facebook pages (currently free). Facebook users can then express their support by adding themselves as a fan, writing on the company Wall, uploading photos, and joining other fans in discussion groups. When users become fans, they can optionally agree to be kept up to date about developments which then appear in their news feeds.

Privacy concerns sparked by 'Beacon technology' – November 2007

Facebook received a lot of negative publicity on its new advertising format related to the 'Beacon' tracking system. Mark Zuckerberg was forced to respond to on the Facebook blog (5 December 2007). He said:

About a month ago, we released a new feature called Beacon to try to help people share information with their friends about things they do on the web. We've made a lot of mistakes building this feature, but we've made even more with how we've handled them. We simply did a bad job with this release, and I apologize for it. While I am disappointed with our mistakes, we appreciate all the feedback we have received from our users. I'd like to discuss what we have learned and how we have improved Beacon.

When we first thought of Beacon, our goal was to build a simple product to let people share information across sites with their friends. It had to be lightweight so it wouldn't get in people's way as they browsed the web, but also clear enough so people would be able to easily control what they shared. We were excited about Beacon because we believe a lot of information people want to share isn't on Facebook, and if we found the right balance, Beacon would give people an easy and controlled way to share more of that information with their friends.

But we missed the right balance. At first we tried to make it very lightweight so people wouldn't have to touch it for it to work. The problem with our initial approach of making it an opt-out system instead of opt-in was that if someone forgot to decline to share something, Beacon still went ahead and shared it with their friends. It took us too long after people started contacting us to change the product so that users had to explicitly approve what they wanted to share. Instead of acting quickly, we took too long to decide on the right solution. I'm not proud of the way we've handled this situation and I know we can do better.

New friends list functionality launched – December 2007

A criticism levelled at Facebook has been the difficulty in separating out personal friends and business acquaintances.

In December 2007, Facebook launched a significant new functionality called Friend Lists to enhance the user experience. Friend Lists enables users to create named groups of friends in particular categories, e.g. business or personal and these private lists can be used to message people, send group or event invitations, and to filter updates from certain groups of friends.

December 2007/January 2008 – first drop in numbers using Facebook and new data centres to manage growth in users

Application spam has been considered one of the possible causes to the drop in visitors to Facebook at the beginning of 2008. The fall in visitors between December 2007 and January 2008 was its first drop since the website first launched.

To put this in context, the Facebook blog reported at the end of 2007 that nearly 2 million new users from around the world sign up for Facebook each week.

Facebook expands internationally – February 2008

Despite the hype generated amongst English speakers, Facebook only announced the launch of a Spanish site in February 2008 with local language versions planned for Germany and France. It seems that Facebook will inevitably follow the path taken by other social networks such as MySpace in launching many local language versions.

Privacy setting concerns – Autumn to 2009 to Spring 2010

In December 2009, Facebook implemented new privacy settings. This meant some information, including 'lists of friends', was 'publicly available', when it was previously possible to restrict access to this information. Photos and some personal information were also public unless users were sufficiently knowledgeable and active to limit access. Privacy campaigners including the Electronic Frontier Foundation and American Civil Liberties Union criticized the changes. In May 2010 further changes were made to give users greater control and simplify the settings.

Source: Facebook (www.facebook.com), Facebook press room (www.facebook.com/press.php), Facebook Statistics (www.facebook.com/press/info.php?statistics, Facebook blog (http://blog.facebook.com), Wikipedia (2010) Wikipedia Pages for Facebook (http://en.wikipedia.org/wiki/Facebook), Criticism of Facebook (http://en.wikipedia.org/wiki/Criticism_of_Facebook) and Mark Zuckerberg (http://en.wikipedia.org/wiki/Mark_Zuckerberg)

Questions

1 As an investor in a social network such as Facebook, which financial and customer-related metrics would you use to assess and benchmark the current business success and future growth potential of the company?
2 Complete a situation analysis for Facebook focusing on an assessment of the main business risks which could damage the future growth potential of the social network.
3 For the main business risks to Facebook identified in Question 2, suggest approaches the company could use to minimize these risks.

Video explanation: http://bit.ly/EBEC-Facebook-Video.

Mobile services adoption is increasing rapidly as users purchase the latest models. Table 1.2 shows how more advanced 'Smartphone' devices with improved functionality and download speed encourage adoption of services.

An example of the popularity of location-based mobile services is Qype (www.qype.com). Founded in 2006, Qype is Europe's largest site for user-generated reviews and recommendations of places, events and experiences. Qype allows users to search for and read reviews about a restaurant, shop, service or experience and, with the Qype App, users can read and add reviews on their phone and use the application as a personal satnav to find

Table 1.2	Internet usage habits among mobile phone subscribers, EU-5 3-month average ending March 2010, age 13+

	Reach (%) of Mobile Subscribers					
	EU5	**UK**	**France**	**Germany**	**Italy**	**Spain**
Sent text message to another phone	82.2%	90.1%	80.4%	80.9%	77.5%	82.0%
Used application (including games)	35.0%	39.2%	25.9%	33.8%	39.4%	37.4%
Used browser	25.0%	33.6%	24.0%	20.3%	23.6%	22.9%
Listened to music on mobile phone	23.8%	22.6%	21.1%	25.8%	21.1%	30.0%
Accessed Social Networking Site or Blog	13.7%	20.7%	12.6%	8.8%	14.2%	12.1%
Accessed news	11.1%	15.5%	10.3%	9.2%	12.0%	7.9%
Smartphone	24.5%	25.0%	17.1%	18.6%	33.3%	30.5%
3G Subscribers	44.0%	43.3%	38.6%	40.4%	45.6%	55.0%

Source: MobiLens (2010).

places nearby. Available in seven different languages, Qype is a pan-European local review site with 2.2 million reviews covering more than 166,000 cities worldwide. (See Figure 1.7)

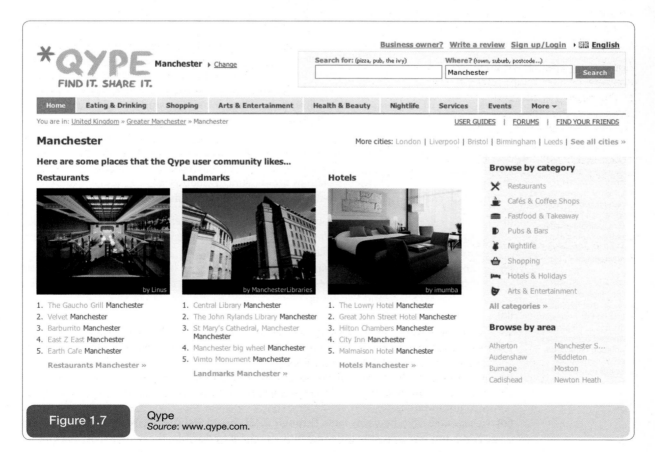

Figure 1.7	Qype *Source*: www.qype.com.

Multi-channel marketing
Customer communications and product distribution are supported by a combination of digital and traditional channels at different points in the buying cycle

Multi-channel marketing strategy
Defines how different marketing channels should integrate and support each other in terms of their proposition development and communications based on their relative merits for the customer and the company.

Customer journey
A description of modern multi-channel buyer behaviour as consumers use different media to select suppliers, make purchases and gain customer support.

Customer-centric marketing
An approach to marketing based on detailed knowledge of customer behaviour within the target audience which seeks to fulfil the individual needs and wants of customers.

Customer insight
Knowledge about customers' needs, characteristics, preferences and behaviours based on analysis of qualitative and quantitative data. Specific insights can be used to inform marketing tactics directed at groups of customers with shared characteristics.

Web 2.0 concept
A collection of web services that facilitate interaction of web users with sites to create user-generated content and encourage behaviours such as community or social network participation, **mashups**, content rating, use of **widgets** and tagging.

The second part of the definition of digital marketing shows that it should not be the technology that drives digital marketing, but the business returns from gaining new customers and maintaining relationships with existing customers. It also emphasizes how digital marketing does not occur in isolation, but is most effective when it is integrated with other communications channels such as phone, direct mail or face-to-face. The role of the Internet in supporting **multi-channel marketing** and **multi-channel marketing strategy** is another recurring theme in this book and Chapters 2 and 5 in particular explain its role in supporting different customer communications channels and distribution channels. Online channels should also be used to support the whole buying process or **customer journey** from pre-sale to sale to post-sale and further development of customer relationships. This clarifies how different marketing channels should integrate and support each other in terms of their proposition development and communications based on their relative merits for the customer and the company.

The final part of the description summarizes approaches to **customer-centric marketing.** It shows how success online requires a planned approach to migrate existing customers to online channels and acquire new customers by selecting the appropriate mix of e-communications and traditional communications. Gaining and keeping online customers needs to be based on developing **customer insight** by researching their characteristics and behaviour, what they value and what keeps them loyal, and then delivering tailored, relevant web and e-mail communications.

Web 2.0

Since 2004, the **Web 2.0 concept** has increased in prominence among website owners and developers. The main technologies and principles of Web 2.0 have been explained in an influential article by Tim O'Reilly (O'Reilly, 2005). Behind the label 'Web 2.0' lies a bewildering range of interactive tools and social communications techniques such as blogs, podcasts and social networks. These are aimed at increasing user participation and interaction on the web. With the widespread adoption of high-speed broadband in many countries, rich media experiences are increasingly used to engage customers with the hope they will have a viral effect, i.e. they will be discussed online or offline and more people will become aware of or interact with the brand campaign. Mini case study 1.2 gives an example of a viral campaign which helped sell products.

Web 2.0 also references methods of exchanging data between sites in standardized formats, such as the feeds merchants use to supply shopping comparison sites with data about products offered and their prices. We include examples of Web 2.0 e-business applications throughout the book and discuss them in more detail in Chapter 3.

The main characteristics of Web 2.0 are that it typically involves:

(i) Web services or interactive applications hosted on the web such as Flickr (www.flickr.com), Google Maps™ (http://maps.google.com) or blogging services such as Blogger.com or Typepad (www.typepad.com).

(ii) Supporting participation – many of the applications are based on altruistic principles of community participation best represented by the most popular social networks such as Bebo, MySpace and Facebook.

(iii) Encouraging creation of user-generated content – blogs are the best example of this. Another example is the collaborative encyclopedia Wikipedia (www.wikipedia.com).

(iv) Enabling rating of content and online services – services such as Delicious (www.delicious.com) and traceback comments on blogs support this.

(v) Ad funding of neutral sites – web services such as Google Mail/GMail™ and many blogs are based on contextual advertising such as Google Adsense™ or Overture/Yahoo! Content Match.

(vi) Data exchange between sites through XML-based data standards. RSS is based on XML, but has relatively little semantic mark-up to describe the content. An attempt by Google to facilitate exchange and searching is Google Base™ (http://base.google.com).

Mini Case Study 1.2	BlendTec uses rich media and viral marketing to grow awareness and sales

This example shows how an engaging idea can be discussed initially online and then in traditional media to help increase the awareness of a brand. On the WillItBlend campaign micro-site (www.willitblend.com, Figure 1.8) a blender designed for making smoothies has blended an iPhone, an iPod, golf balls, glow sticks, a video camera and more. It's only meant to make smoothies and milk shakes! As well as the micro-site for the viral campaign, there is also a brand channel on YouTube (www.youtube.com/user/blendtec) where different ads received several million views. There is also a blog (http://blog.blendtec.com) for new announcements and providing information for journalists. The blender has also been extensively featured on traditional media such as TV, newspapers, magazines and radio, showing that traditional media are important in increasing awareness further after the initial impact.

The viral idea was developed by Blendtec employee George Wright who came up with the viral idea and announced that in 2007 sales increased tremendously: '*because we're a smaller company, we were able to put out something edgy and fun. In terms of the product you see on YouTube, our sales have gone up by 500 per cent.*'

Figure 1.8	Blendtec viral campaign micro-site *Source*: www.willitblend.com.

Micro-formats

A simple set of formats based on XHTML for describing and exchanging information about objects including product and travel reviews, recipes and event information.

Mashups

Websites, pages or widgets that combine the content or functionality of one website or data source with another to create something offering a different type of value to web users from the separate types of content or functionallity.

This allows users to upload data about particular services in a standardized format based on XML. Data can also be exchanged through standard **micro-formats** such as hCalendar and hReview which are used to incorporate data from other sites into the Google listings (see www.microformats.org for details). New classes of content can also be defined and **mashups** created.

(vii) Use of rich media or creation of rich Internet applications (RIA) which provide for a more immersive, interactive experience. These may be integrated into web browsers or may be separate applications like that downloaded for Second Life (www.secondlife.com).

(viii) Rapid application development using interactive technology approaches known as 'Ajax' (Asynchronous JavaScript and XML). The best-known Ajax implementation is Google Maps which is responsive since it does not require refreshes to display maps.

Figure 1.9 summarizes the evolution of digital and web-related technologies. Box 1.1 discusses the emerging concept of Web 3.0.

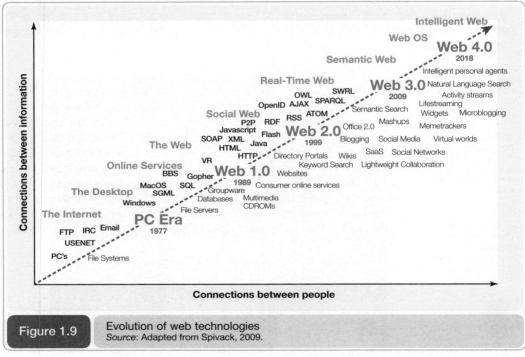

Figure 1.9	Evolution of web technologies
	Source: Adapted from Spivack, 2009.

Box 1.1	**Whither Web 3.0?**

Web 3.0 concept

Next-generation web incorporating high-speed connectivity, complex cross-community interactions, full range of digital media (text, voice, video) and an intelligent or semantic web where automated applications can access data from different online services to assist searchers to perform complex tasks of supplier selection.

Since the Web 2.0 concept has been widely applied, it is natural that commentators would try to evolve the concept to **Web 3.0**, although the term hasn't been widely applied to date. We can suggest that as web functionality evolves, these approaches will become more important:

• *Web applications*. Usage of web-based applications and services (like Google word processor and spreadsheets). This is sometimes termed '*cloud computing*' where all that is really needed for many activities is a computer with a web browser, with local software applications used less widely.

• *Syndication*. Increased incorporation of syndicated content and services from other sites or a network into a site (using tools such as Yahoo! Pipes and XML exchange between **widgets**). We refer to this concept as 'atomization' in Chapter 9.

Widget

A badge or button incorporated into a site or social network space by its owner, with content or services typically served from another site making widgets effectively a mini-software application or web service. Content can be updated in real time since the widget interacts with the server each time it loads.

- *Streamed video or IPTV.* Increased use of streamed video from existing TV providers and user-generated content (as suggested by use of YouTube and IPTV services such as Hulu).
- *Virtual worlds.* Increased use of immersive virtual environments such as Second Life.
- *Personal data integration.* Increased exchange of data between social networks fulfilling different needs (as indicated by the recent Google development of OpenSocial).
- *The semantic web.* Increased use of semantic mark-up leading to the semantic web envisioned by Tim Berners-Lee over 10 years ago. Semantic mark-up will be needed to develop artificial intelligence applications which recommend content and services to web users without their actively having to seek them and apply their own judgement as to the best products and brands.

Video explanation: Kate Ray interviews semantic web commentator Nova Spivack: http://bit.ly/EBEC-Semantic-Web-Video.

Supply chain management (SCM)

The coordination of all supply activities of an organization from its suppliers and partners to its customers.

Value chain

A model for analysis of how supply chain activities can add value to products and services delivered to the customer.

Value network

The links between an organization and its strategic and non-strategic partners that form its external value chain.

Business-to-consumer (B2C)

Commercial transactions between an organization and consumers.

Business-to-business (B2B)

Commercial transactions between an organization and other organizations (interorganizational marketing).

Consumer-to-consumer (C2C)

Informational or financial transactions between consumers, but usually mediated through a business site.

Consumer-to-business (C2B)

Consumers approach the business with an offer.

Supply chain management

When distinguishing between buy-side and sell-side e-commerce we are looking at different aspects of managing an organization's supply chain. **Supply chain management (SCM)** is the coordination of all supply activities of an organization from its suppliers and delivery of products to its customers. The opportunities for using e-commerce to streamline and restructure the supply chain are described in more detail in Chapter 6. The **value chain** is a related concept that describes the different value-adding activities that connect a company's supply side with its demand side. We can identify an *internal* value chain within the boundaries of an organization and an *external* value chain where these activities are performed by partners. Note that in the era of e-business a company will manage many interrelated value chains, so in Chapter 6 we also consider the concept of a **value network**.

Business or consumer models of e-commerce transactions

It is now commonplace to describe e-commerce transactions between an organization and its stakeholders according to whether they are primarily with consumers (**business-to-consumer – B2C**) or other businesses (**business-to-business – B2B**).

Figure 1.10 gives examples of different companies operating in the business-to-consumer (B2C) and business-to-business (B2B) spheres. Often companies such as BP or Dell Computer will have products that appeal to both consumers and businesses, so will have different parts of their site to appeal to these audiences.

Referring to the well-known online companies in Table 1.1 initially suggests these companies are mainly focused on B2C markets. However, B2B communications are still important for many of these companies since business transactions can drive revenue, as for example eBay Business (http://business.ebay.com/), or the B2C service may need to be sustained through advertising provided through B2B transactions; for example, Google's revenue is largely based on its B2B AdWords (http://adwords.google.com/) and advertising service and advertising-based revenue is also important to sites such as YouTube, MySpace and Facebook.

Figure 1.10 also presents two additional types of transaction, those where consumers transact directly with other consumers (**C2C**) and where they initiate trading with companies (**C2B**). These monikers are less widely used (e.g. *Economist*, 2000), but they do highlight significant differences between Internet-based commerce and earlier forms of commerce. Consumer-to-consumer interactions (also known as peer-to-peer or person-to-

From: Supplier of content/service

	Consumer or citizen	Business (organization)	Government
Consumer or citizen	**Consumer-to-Consumer (C2C)** • eBay • Peer-to-Peer (Skype) • Blogs and communities • Product recommendations • Social networks: MySpace, Bebo	**Business-to-Consumer (B2C)** • Transactional: Amazon • Relationship-building: BP • Brand-building: Unilever • Media owner – News Corp • Comparison intermediary: Kelkoo, Pricerunner	**Government-to-Consumer (G2C)** • National government transactional: Tax – inland revenue • National government information • Local government services
Business (organization)	**Consumer-to-Business (C2B)** • Priceline • Consumer-feedback, communities or campaigns	**Business-to-Business (B2B)** • Transactional: Euroffice • Relationship-building: BP • Media Owned: Emap business publications • B2B marketplaces: EC21	**Government-to-Business (G2B)** • Government services and transactions: tax • Legal regulations
Government	**Consumer-to-Government (C2G)** • Feedback to government through pressure group or individual sites	**Business-to-Government (B2G)** • Feedback to government businesses and non-governmental organizations	**Government-to-Government (G2G)** • Inter-government services • Exchange of information

To: Consumer of content/service

Figure 1.10   Summary and examples of transaction alternatives between businesses, consumers and governmental organizations

person, P2P) were relatively rare, but are now very common in the form of social networks. Hoffman and Novak (1996) suggested that C2C interactions are a key characteristic of the Internet that is important for companies to take into account, but it is only in recent years with the growth of always-on broadband connections and mobile access to the web that these have become so popular. P2P transactions are also the main basis for some online business models for e-businesses such as Betfair (see Mini case study 1.3) and eBay (www. ebay.com, see Case study 1.2) which are still run on a business basis, and some blogs which are not run by companies but by individuals.

Finally, the diagram also includes government and public services organizations which deliver online or e-government services. As well as the models shown in Figure 1.10, it has also been suggested that employees should be considered as a separate type of consumer through the use of intranets which are referred to as employee-to-employee or E2E.

Mini Case Study 1.3   Betfair profits with C2C online gambling service

Betfair provides a great example of the creation of an ebusiness with an innovative business model. It holds licences to operate in the UK, USA, Australia, Austria, Germany, Italy and Malta with over 50% of all new registrations coming from outside the UK and Ireland. It has grown rapidly over the last five years with revenue rising from £107m in 2005 to £303m for 2009, while adjusted EBITDA has more than doubled from £30m in 2005 to £72m for 2009.

Betfair is the world's biggest online sports betting company and pioneered the first successful betting exchange in 2000. Driven by cutting-edge technology, Betfair enables customers to choose their own odds and bet even after the event has started. The company now processes over 6 million transactions a day from its 3 million registered customers around the world (the 3 million mark was passed in 2010).

Betfair introduced a novel form of betting which replaces the typical role of the bookmaker such as Ladbrokes or William Hill who provided fixed odds and take their own risk on the outcome. With Betfair, all bets placed are with other Betfair customers rather than with Betfair which has no risks on the outcome. As with all forms of gambling, there is a risk of corruption 'throwing the bet'; to reduce this risk Betfair has a transparent approach where evidence of corruption may be shared with the governing body of a sport.

Through providing an online service, there are additional aspects of its proposition:

- You can either place bets conventionally or request your own odds.
- You can choose the odds you want to play at.
- You can bet whilst the game is in play.

Betfair's revenue model

Betfair charges a commission (typically 5%) on each player's net winnings on a market. If a player loses, there is no commission. There is a discount on commission; when you place more bets this rewards regular punters.

Betfair's growth

This outline history of Betfair shows how it has extended its product range and partnerships to support its growth:

1 2000 – The Sporting Exchange Ltd launches Betfair.com from Russell Square, London. At launch funds were limited, so the company used 'guerrilla marketing' to promote it, such as a procession through the City of London with coffins with banners 'death of the bookmaker' and fake demonstrations with 'Betfair – unfair' banners.
2 2001 – Betfair matches £1 million in seven days for the first time.
3 2002 – Betfair announces a merger with competitor Flutter and sponsorship of Fulham Football Club.
4 2003 – Betfair launches sites in German, Danish, Greek, Italian, Swedish, Norwegian, Finnish and Chinese.
5 2004 – Betfair launches Betfair poker, which today has 60,000 registered players. Betfair signs joint venture with Australia's Publishing and Broadcasting Limited.
6 2005 – Betfair sponsors the Channel 4 Ashes Cricket coverage and records the highest-ever single market turnover, matching £36 million on the Fifth Ashes Test Match alone! Betfair signs exclusive deal with Yahoo! UK and Ireland to launch a simplified betting exchange as well as a co-branded betting exchange.
7 Betfair's key performance indicators are suggested by an annual report for year ending 30 April 2007 when it had an annual turnover in excess of £180 million with operating profit of £35 million based on 18 million 'active player days' which is a key performance measure derived from the 433,000 active customers and an average 9 player-days per month per active customer. International revenues grew most rapidly and contributed 23 per cent of exchange revenues compared with 18 per cent in the previous year.
8 By 2010 Betfair employed over 1,700 people globally. Its headquarters are in Hammersmith in West London, while its international business is based in Malta. It also has large operational bases in the UK in Stevenage, Australia in Tasmania and Melbourne, a software development hub in Romania, as well as offices in Los Angeles and San Francisco.
9 Technology challenges are indicated by the 6 million transactions a day processed, equating to 360 bets a second. Using Oracle database technology, Betfair processes 99.9 per cent of bets in less than one second.
10 In April 2010 an iTunes App was released with Betfair noting that their registered mobile users increased 40% in 2009 with a a 50% increase in year on year mobile revenues.

Source: Corporate site (www.betfaircorporate.com).

E-government defined

E-government
The application of
e-commerce technologies
to government and public
services for citizens and
businesses.

E-government refers to the application of e-commerce technologies to government and public services. In the same way that e-business can be understood as transactions with customers (citizens), suppliers and internal communications, e-government covers a similar range of applications:

- *Citizens* – facilities for dissemination of information and use of online services at local and national levels. For example, at a local level you can find out when refuse is collected and at national level it is possible to fill in tax returns.
- *Suppliers* – government departments have a vast network of suppliers. The potential benefits (and pitfalls) of electronic supply chain management and e-procurement described in Chapters 6 and 7 are equally valid for government.
- *Internal communications* – this includes information collection and dissemination and e-mail and workflow systems for improving efficiency within government departments.

E-government is now viewed as important within government in many countries. The European Union set up 'i2010' (*European Information Society in 2010*) whose aims included

> *providing an integrated approach to information society and audio-visual policies in the EU, covering regulation, research, and deployment and promoting cultural diversity.* (eEurope, 2005)

E-business opportunities

E-business has introduced new opportunities for small and large organizations to compete in the global marketplace. Many commentators have noted that one of the biggest changes introduced by electronic communications is how approaches to transmitting and transforming information can be used for competitive advantage. A significant commentary on the disruptive, transformational nature of electronic communications is provided in Box 1.2.

Box 1.2	Evans and Wurster on the impact of disruptive Internet technologies

Evans and Wurster of Harvard argue in their classic 1997 paper 'Strategy and the new economics of information' that there are three characteristics of information which, when combined with **disruptive Internet technologies,** can have a major impact on a marketplace. These characteristics of information are reach, richness and affiliation:

Disruptive Internet technologies
New Internet-based
communications
approaches which
change the way in
which information about
products is exchanged,
which impact the basis
for competition in a
marketplace.

1 *Reach.* Conventionally, 'reach' refers to the potential number of customers a business can interact with. The Internet enables reach to be increased nationally and internationally at low cost through making content available via search engines. 'Reach' also refers to the number of different categories and products a consumer interface (e.g. store, catalogue or website) can cover: witness the large range of products available through e-businesses such as Amazon, eBay and Kelkoo.com and existing companies such as easyJet.com and Tesco.com which have used the web to extend their product range.

2 *Richness.* This is a characteristic of the information itself. The Internet enables more detailed information about products, prices and availability to be made available. It also enables more interactivity and customization to engage customers and to provide more up-to-date information. But, Evans and Wurster also note that richness is limited by bandwidth (the volume of information that can be

> transmitted using a communications link in a given time), the accuracy or reliability of information and its security.
>
> 3 *Affiliation*. This refers to the effectiveness of links with partners. In an online context, an organization which has the most and richest links with other compatible organizations will be able to gain a larger reach and influence. Consider how e-businesses such as eBay, Google and Yahoo! have successfully formed partnerships or acquired other companies to provide new diverse information services such as social networking, mapping, voice communications and online photography, to name just a few.
>
> In markets such as car sales which have been transformed by the Internet, understanding how to improve reach, richness and affiliation is crucial. This is not because a large proportion of people buy cars online, but rather the majority research online their preferred make, model and supplier.

The Internet also provides significant opportunities for many businesses to build closer relationships with their existing customers and suppliers online to help achieve customer retention. Encouraging use of online, e-business services by customers and suppliers can significantly reduce costs while providing a new, convenient channel for purchase and customer service. Through providing high-quality online services, organizations can build lasting relationships with their stakeholders. While it is sometimes said that '*online, your customers are only a mouse click away from your competitors*', this is a simplification, and encouraging use of online services can help achieve '**soft lock-in**'. This means that a customer or supplier continues to use a service since they find the service valuable, they have invested time in learning the service or integrating it with their systems and there are some costs in switching. Think of online services you use for different purposes. How often do you switch between them? Of course, the ideal is that the service meets the needs of its users so well and delivers value such that they are satisfied and do not consider switching.

Soft lock-in
Customers or suppliers continue to use online services because of the switching costs.

Business adoption of digital technologies for e-commerce and e-business

As managers, we need to assess the impact of e-commerce and e-business on our marketplace and organizations. What are the drivers of changed consumer and business behaviour? How should we respond? How much do we need to invest? What are our priorities and how quickly do we need to act? Answering these questions is an essential part of formulating an e-business and e-marketing strategy and is considered in more detail in Part 2. To answer these questions marketing research will need to be conducted as described in Chapters 2 to 4 to determine the current levels of adoption of the Internet for different activities among customers and competitors in our market sector and in other sectors.

Drivers of business Internet adoption

Business adoption of e-commerce and e-business is driven by benefits to different parts of the organization. First and foremost, businesses are concerned about how the benefits of e-business will impact on profitability or generating value to an organization. The two main ways in which this can be achieved are:

- Potential for increased revenue arising from increased reach to a larger customer base and encouraging loyalty and repeat purchases among existing customers.
- Cost reduction achieved through delivering services electronically. Reductions include staff costs, transport costs and costs of materials such as paper.

At a relatively early point in e-business adoption, a government report (DTI, 2000) identified two main categories of drivers which remain relevant today:

Cost/efficiency drivers

1 Increasing speed with which supplies can be obtained
2 Increasing speed with which goods can be despatched
3 Reduced sales and purchasing costs
4 Reduced operating costs

Competitiveness drivers

5 Customer demand
6 Improving the range and quality of services offered
7 Avoiding losing market share to businesses already using e-commerce

More recently, in interviews with Australian businesses, Perrott (2005) identifies four key areas driving performance which are cost–benefit, competitive pressures, market advantage and value adding, i.e. improving customer satisfaction while building strong relationships.

When reviewing potential benefits, it is useful to identify both tangible benefits (for which monetary savings or revenues can be identified) and intangible benefits (for which it is more difficult to calculate cost savings). The types of potential benefits are summarized in Table 1.3.

In Chapter 5 (Figure 5.12), an alternative information-based model of value creation is discussed in relation to financial services organization Capital One. This reviews new opportunities for adding value, reducing costs, managing risks and creating a new reality (transformation).

Brochureware
Brochureware describes a web site in which a company has migrated its existing paper-based promotional literature on to the Internet without recognizing the differences required by this medium.

Doherty *et al.* (2003) researched the drivers and barriers to retailers' adoption of Internet technologies to determine the most important factors. Table 1.4 summarizes the ranking in importance for different degrees of Internet adoption from static **brochureware (A)**, through an active website containing product information (B) to a transactional site where items can be purchased (C). You can see that the two most important factors which correlate with adoption are 'Internet target segment', i.e. customers in their market are typically

Table 1.3	Tangible and intangible benefits from e-commerce and e-business

Tangible benefits	**Intangible benefits**
• Increased sales from new sales leads giving rise to increased revenue from: – new customers, new markets – existing customers (cross-selling) • Marketing cost reductions from: – reduced time in customer service – online sales – reduced printing and distribution costs of marketing communications • Supply-chain cost reductions from: – reduced levels of inventory – shorter cycle time in ordering • Administrative cost reductions from more efficient routine business processes such as recruitment, invoice payment and holiday authorization.	• Corporate image communication • Enhancement of brand • More rapid, more responsive marketing communications including PR • Faster product development lifecycle enabling faster response to market needs • Improved customer service • Learning for the future • Meeting customer expectations to have a website • Identifying new partners, supporting existing partners better • Better management of marketing information and customer information • Feedback from customers on products

Table 1.4	Summary of factors most important in encouraging Internet adoption amongst e-retailers		

Factor influencing adoption		A	B	C
1	Internet target segment	3	2	1
2	Internet strategy	1	1	6
3	Internet marketplace	4	5	2
4	Infrastructure and development capability	2	3	5
5	Internet communications	5	6	4
6	Cost of Internet trading	8	9	10
7	Internet cost opportunity	6	8	7
8	Market development opportunity	7	4	3
9	Concerns	9	10	9
10	Consumer preferences	10	7	8

A = Internet adoption (static website), B = active website, C = online sales (transactional site)
Based on a compilation from separate tables in Doherty *et al.* (2003).

adopters of the Internet, and 'Internet strategy', i.e. a defined Internet strategy is in place. This suggests, as would be expected, that companies that do not have a coherent Internet or e-business strategy are less likely to use higher levels of Internet services. Many larger organizations that have responded to the challenge of e-business have created a separate e-commerce plan and separate resources to implement it. This book covers what needs to go into such a plan and the issues to consider when implementing it.

More recently, in Europe, research completed for the i2010 initiative monitored usage of the Internet by business (European Commission, 2010) and found that around 95% of businesses in the majority of countries surveyed have Internet access, although this figure masks lower levels of access for SMEs (small and medium-sized enterprises) and particularly micro-businesses (Figure 1.11).

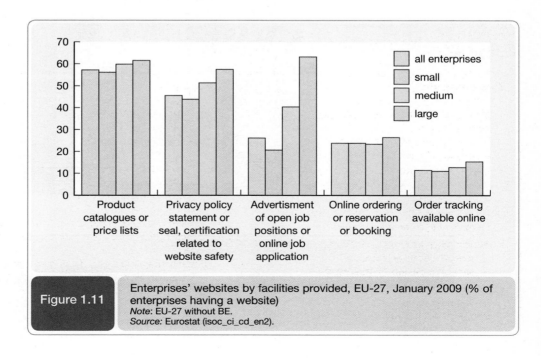

| Figure 1.11 | Enterprises' websites by facilities provided, EU-27, January 2009 (% of enterprises having a website)
Note: EU-27 without BE.
Source: Eurostat (isoc_ci_cd_en2). |
|---|---|

Case Study 1.2 illustrates the benefits of setting up an online operation for a small or medium enterprise (SME). It also highlights some of the challenges of managing an online business and highlights the need for continued investment to refine online services and the marketing needed to attract visitors to the website.

Case Study 1.2	North West Supplies extends its reach online

North West Supplies (Figure 1.12) was launched as a business in March 1999 when Andrew Camwell, a member of the RAF Volunteer Reserve at the time, spotted a gap in the UK market for mail order supplies of military garments to people active in the Volunteer Reserve and the Air Cadet Force. Andrew, his wife Carys, and her sister Elaine Hughes started running a mail order business out of shop premises in the village of Cemaes Bay.

The web store at www.northwestsupplies.co.uk has been online since November 2002. As it can take several months for a website to be indexed by search engines, NWS used pay-per-click advertising (PPC – see Chapter 9) as a method of very quickly increasing the website's presence in the major search engines. This marketing method proved successful. The directors were pleasantly surprised as they had previously been somewhat dubious about the prospect of the Internet generating sales in their sector. Within six months of running the website, the company had increased turnover by £20,000, but further advances would incur a high advertising cost. Following an eCommerce Review by Opportunity Wales, the company decided to tackle the issues by implementing search engine optimization (SEO – see Chapter 9) and a site redesign which included:

Figure 1.12	North West Supplies Ltd *Source*: www.northwestsupplies.co.uk; Opportunity Wales.

- *Improved graphic design* – this was to be changed to a more professional and up-to-date look.
- *Best, featured and latest products* – the introduction of a dynamic front page to entice customers to revisit the site on a regular basis. The contents of this page would feature the best sellers, and latest or featured products.
- *Reviews and ratings* – to provide confidence to consumers and allow some kind of interaction with them, this would allow users to review products they have purchased and give them a star rating.
- *Cross-selling* – when customers view a product other products or categories that may be of interest or complementary would be displayed.
- *Segmentation* – the site would be split into two sections emphasizing the segmentation of product lines into military wear and outdoor wear sectors, thus being less confusing, and easier to use.
- *Navigation by sub-categories* – as the product range had expanded, the additional pages created in each category made it harder for customers to find specific items. The introduction of sub-categories would provide a clear link to the areas of interest and contain fewer pages to browse, thus helping the customer to make a choice more easily and more quickly. A new search tool and order tracking were also seen as important parts of the online customer experience (Chapter 8).

Benefits

The owners describe the benefits of the improvements to the site as follows:

- *Increased direct sales* – 'The new launch increased sales and appealed to a broader audience – young and old.' The annual turnover of the business has increased from £250,000 to £350,000 and this is mainly attributable to the new website. The high-profile launch aimed at existing customers, the greater visibility in search engines, and the greater usability of the site have all contributed to this.
- *Improved promotion of the whole range of stock* – 'We started selling stuff that we hadn't sold before.' The changes in navigation, particularly division into two market segments (military and outdoors) and greater use of sub-categories, meant that products were easier to find and hence easier to buy, leading to increased sales of products that had previously been slow sellers.
- *New customers* – 'We now send more items abroad.' The better performance of the site in search engines has led to an increase in orders from new customers and from abroad. The company now has regular sales to Canada, Australia, New Zealand and various European states. Sixty per cent of orders are from new customers – not bad for a business that was initially set up on the premise of a niche market for UK-based cadet forces.
- *Adding value to the brand* – 'New corporate clients could look at our website and see we weren't fly-by-night and that we meant business.' Improvements to the design have raised confidence levels in visitors and this has led to increased sales. But perhaps more significantly, the professional image of the site was a good boost to confidence for potential business partners in the emerging business-to-business division that started to trade as North Star Contracts.

Question

Discuss the new opportunities and risks that need to be managed by North West Supplies with the increased importance of its online channel to market.

E-business risks and barriers to business adoption

Opportunities have to be balanced against the risks of introducing e-business services which include strategic and practical risks. One of the main strategic risks is making the wrong decision about e-business investments. In every business sector, some companies have taken advantage of e-business and gained a competitive advantage. But others have invested in e-business without achieving the hoped-for returns, either because the execution of the plan was flawed, or simply because the approaches were inappropriate. The impact of the Internet and technology varies by industry. Andy Grove, Chairman of Intel, one of the early adopters of e-business, noted that every organization needs to ask whether, for them:

The Internet is a typhoon force, a ten times force, or is it a bit of wind? Or is it a force that fundamentally alters our business? (Grove, 1996)

This statement still seems to encapsulate how managers must respond to different digital technologies; the impact will vary through time from minor for some companies to significant for others, and an appropriate response is required.

There are also many practical risks to manage which, if ignored, can lead to bad customer experiences and bad news stories which damage the reputation of the company. In the section on e-business opportunities, we reviewed the concept of soft lock-in; however, if the customer experience of a service is very bad, they will stop using it, and switch to other online options. Examples of poor online customer experience include:

- Websites that fail because of a spike in visitor traffic after a peak-hour TV advertising campaign.
- Hackers penetrating the security of the system and stealing credit card details.
- A company e-mails customers without receiving their permission, so annoying customers and potentially breaking privacy and data protection laws.
- Problems with fulfilment of goods ordered online, meaning customer orders go missing or are delayed.
- E-mail customer-service enquiries from the website don't reach the right person and are ignored.

Debate 1.2

Limited SME adoption of e-business

'Adoption of e-business by established SMEs is generally less than that in larger businesses. This is principally a consequence of the negative attitude of managing directors and CEOs to the business benefits of information and communication technology.'

The perception of these risks may result in limited adoption of e-business in many organizations, which is suggested by the data in Figure 1.11. This is particularly the case for small and medium enterprises (SMEs). We study adoption levels and drivers in this type of business further in Chapter 4.

A DTI (2002) study evaluated some of the barriers to B2B e-commerce (Figure 1.13) which remain valid today. You can see that reasons of cost were the most important factors. This suggests the importance of managers

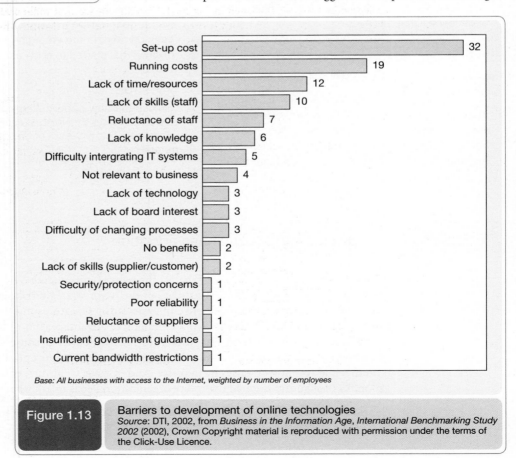

Base: All businesses with access to the Internet, weighted by number of employees

Figure 1.13 Barriers to development of online technologies
Source: DTI, 2002, from *Business in the Information Age, International Benchmarking Study 2002* (2002), Crown Copyright material is reproduced with permission under the terms of the Click-Use Licence.

assessing e-business to develop a cost–benefit analysis that considers both the initial investment costs and the ongoing costs that form the **total cost of ownership (TCO)** against the value created from the tangible and intangible benefits. The difficulties in implementation which we will review later in this book, such as the lack of the right resources or difficulty in integrating systems, are also indicated.

Another approach to reviewing the strategy issues involved with implementing e-business is the classic McKinsey 7S strategy instrument (Waterman *et al.*, 1980) which is summarized in Table 10.1.

Evaluating an organization's e-business capabilities

Assessment of an organization's existing e-business capabilities is a starting point for the future development of their e-business strategy. We will see in Chapter 5 how different forms of **stage models** can be used to assess e-business capability. An example of a basic stage model reviewing capabilities for sell-side and buy-side e-commerce is shown in Figure 1.14. This shows how companies will introduce more complex technologies and extend the range of processes which are e-business-enabled. Stage 5 includes social commerce.

Drivers of consumer Internet adoption

To determine investment in sell-side e-commerce, managers need to assess how to adopt new services such as web, mobile and interactive TV and specific services such as blogs, social networks and feeds. In Chapter 4, we see how such demand analysis is conducted in a structured way. One example of demand analysis is popularity or adoption rates for different online services. The range of different ways in which consumers use the Internet to research or transact is shown in Figure 1.15. You can see that male and female usage of the Internet for different activities is now very similar, but with downloading of digital content generally more popular among males.

Total cost of ownership (TCO)
TCO refers to the total cost for a company operating a computer system or other investment. This includes not only the purchase or leasing cost, but also the cost of all the services needed to maintain the system and support the end-user.

Stage models
Used to review how advanced a company is in its use of information and communications technology (ICT) to support different processes.

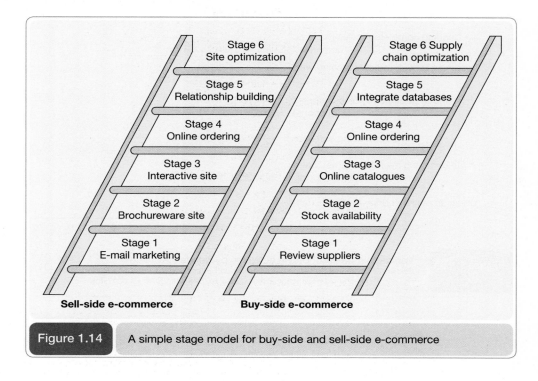

Figure 1.14   A simple stage model for buy-side and sell-side e-commerce

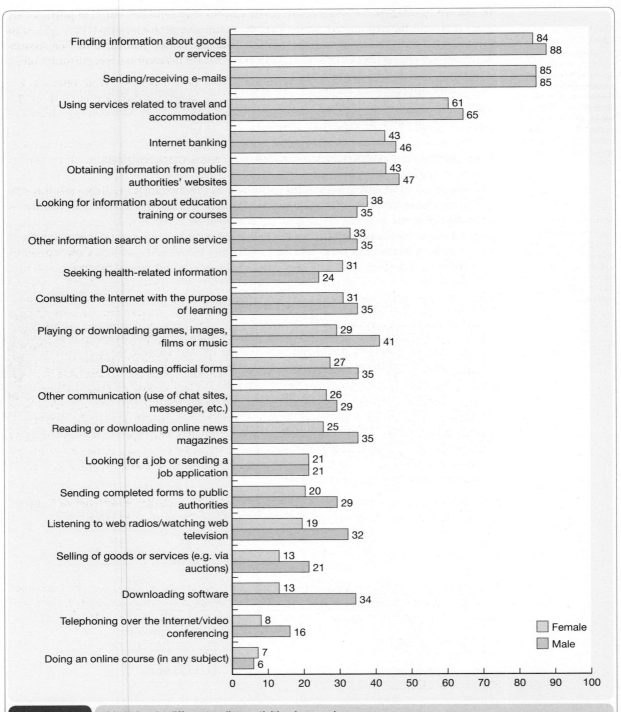

| Figure 1.15 | Variation in different online activities by gender
Source: UK National Statistics (2009) *Individuals accessing the Internet – Report from the UK National Statistics Omnibus Survey.* Published online at www.ststistics.gov.uk/StatBase/Product.asp?vlnk=5672. |

We will see in Chapter 4 on strategy development for e-business how it is important that companies offering e-commerce services create a clear **online value proposition (OVP)** to encourage customers to use their specific online services. Typical benefits of online services are summarized by the 'Six Cs', a simple mnemonic to show different types of customer value:

Online value proposition (OVP)
A statement of the benefits of online services reinforces the core proposition and differentiates from an organization's offline offering and those of competitors.

1 *Content* – In the mid-1990s it was often said that 'content is king'. Well, relevant rich content is still king. This means more detailed, in-depth information to support the buying process for transactional or relationship-building sites or branded experiences to encourage product usage for FMCG brands.

2 *Customization* – In this case mass customization of content, whether received as website pages such as '*Amazon recommends*' or e-mail alerts, and commonly known as 'personalization'.

3 *Community* – The Internet liberates consumers to discuss anything they wish through forums, chat-rooms and blog comments. We will explore these techniques more in Chapters 2 and 3.

4 *Convenience* – This is the ability to select, purchase and in some cases use products from your desktop at any time: the classic $24 \times 7 \times 365$ availability of a service. Online usage of products is, of course, restricted to digital products such as music or other data services. Amazon has advertised offline using creative ads showing a Christmas shopper battling against a gale-swept street clutching several bags to reinforce the convenience message.

5 *Choice* – The web gives a wider choice of products and suppliers than via conventional distribution channels. The success of online intermediaries such as Kelkoo (www.kelkoo.com) and Screentrade (www.screentrade.com) is evidence of this. Similarly, Tesco.com provides Tesco with a platform to give consumers a wider choice of products (financial, travel, white goods) with more detailed information than are physically available in-store.

6 *Cost reduction* – The Internet is widely perceived as a relatively low-cost place of purchase. Often customers expect to get a good deal online as they realize that online traders have a lower cost-base as they have lower staff and distribution costs than a retailer that runs a network of high-street stores. A simple price differential is a key approach to encouraging usage of online services. In the late 1990s, low-cost airline easyJet encouraged the limited change behaviour required from phone booking to online booking by offering a £2.50 discount on online flight bookings.

Note that the 7Cs of Rayport and Jaworski (2003) provide a similar framework of Context, Content, Community, Customization, Communication, Connection and Commerce.

Barriers to consumer Internet adoption

An indication of some of the barriers to using the Internet, in particular for consumer purchases, is clear from a survey (Booz Allen Hamilton, 2002) of perceptions in different countries. It noted that consumer barriers to adoption of the Internet included:

- No perceived benefit
- Lack of trust
- Security problems
- Lack of skills
- Cost

This lack of demand for Internet services from this group needs to be taken into account when forecasting future demand.

To complete this chapter, read Case study 1.3 for the background on the success factors which have helped build one of the world's biggest e-businesses.

| Case Study 1.3 | eBay – the world's largest e-business |

This case summarizes the strategic approach used by eBay to take advantage of increased consumer adoption of the Internet. It summarizes its objectives, strategy and proposition and some of the risks that need management.

Context

It's hard to believe that one of the most celebrated dot-coms has now been established over 15 years. Pierre Omidyar, a 28-year-old French-born software engineer living in California coded the site while working for another company, eventually launching the site for business on Monday, 4 September 1995 with the more direct name 'Auction Web'. Legend reports that the site attracted no visitors in its first 24 hours. The site became eBay in 1997. In 2009, eBay had 90 million active users globally, with the total worth of goods sold on eBay $60 billion, which is equivalent to $2,000 every second. Total revenue was $8.7 billion.

Mission

eBay describes its purpose as to 'pioneer new communities around the world built on commerce, sustained by trust, and inspired by opportunity'.

At the time of writing eBay comprises two major businesses:

1 *The eBay marketplaces (approximately 66% of net revenues in Quarter 4 2009).* These include other sites like comparison site Shopping.com and StubHub.The mission for the core eBay business is to 'create the world's online marketplace'. The marketplace platforms include an average of 100 million products for sale on each day! In 2007, eBay's SEC filing notes some of the success factors for this business for which eBay seeks to manage the functionality, safety, ease-of-use and reliability of the trading platform. In 2010 the strategic priorities had changed to trust, value, selection and convenience.
2 *PayPal (approximately 34% of net revenues in 2009).* The mission is to 'create the new global standard for online payments'. This company was acquired in 2003 and is now a significant contributor to eBay revenue with the service incorporated in many other e-commerce sites.

A third part of the business, *Skype Internet telephony,* was acquired in 2005 by eBay and sold to an investor group in November 2009 with a 30% share retained by eBay.

Advertising and other net revenues represented 4% of total net revenues during 2007. This case focuses on the best-known eBay business, the eBay marketplace.

Revenue model

The vast majority of eBay's revenue is for the listing and commission on completed sales. For PayPal purchases an additional commission fee is charged. Margin on each transaction is phenomenal since once the infrastructure is built, incremental costs on each transaction are tiny – all eBay is doing is transmitting bits and bytes between buyers and sellers.

Advertising and other non-transaction net revenues represent a relatively small proportion of total net revenues and the strategy is that this should remain the case. Advertising and other net revenues totalled $94.3 million in 2004 (just 3% of net revenue).

Proposition

The eBay marketplace is well known for its core service which enables sellers to list items for sale on an auction or fixed-price basis giving buyers the opportunity to bid for and purchase items of interest. At the end of 2007, there were over 532,000 online storefronts established by users in locations around the world.

Software tools are provided, particularly for frequent traders, including Turbo Lister, Seller's Assistant, Selling Manager and Selling Manager Pro, which help automate the selling process, plus the Shipping Calculator, Reporting tools, etc. Today over 60% of listings are facilitated by software, showing the value of automating posting for frequent trading.

Fraud is a significant risk factor for eBay. BBC (2005) reported that around 1 in 10,000 transactions within the UK were fraudulent; 0.0001% is a small percentage, but scaling this up across the number of transactions, this is a significant volume.

eBay has developed 'Trust and Safety Programs' which are particularly important to reassure customers since online services are prone to fraud. For example, the eBay feedback forum can help establish credentials of sellers and buyers. Every registered user has a feedback profile that may contain compliments, criticisms and/or other comments by users who have conducted business with that user. The Feedback Forum requires feedback to be related to specific transactions and Top Seller status was introduced in 2010 to increase trust in the service. There is also a Safe Harbor data protection method and a standard purchase protection system.

According to the SEC filing, eBay summarizes the core messages to define its proposition as follows:

For buyers:

- Trust
- Value
- Selection
- Convenience

In 2007, eBay introduced Neighbourhoods (http://neighborhoods.ebay.com) where groups can discuss brands and products they have a high involvement with.

For sellers:

- Access to broad global markets
- Efficient marketing and distribution
- Opportunity to increase sales

In January 2008, eBay announced significant changes to its marketplaces business in three major areas: fee structure, seller incentives and standards, and feedback. These changes have been controversial with some sellers, but are aimed at improving the quality of experience. Detailed Seller Ratings (DSRs) enable sellers to be reviewed in four areas: (1) item as described, (2) communication, (3) delivery time and (4) postage and packaging charges. This is part of a move to help increase conversion rate by increasing positive shopping experiences, for example by including more accurate descriptions with better pictures and avoiding excessive shipping charges. Power sellers with positive DSRs will be featured more favourably in the search results pages and will gain additional discounts.

eBay obtained increased use of mobile e-commerce in 2009 and into 2010. The eBay mobile app for iPhone was downloaded 7 million times by January 2010. Consumers are shopping more and more via their mobile phones with more than $600 million worth of sales transacted through mobile applications in 2009.

Competition

Although there are now few direct competitors of online auction services in many countries, there are many indirect competitors. SEC (2008) describes competing channels as including online and offline retailers, distributors, liquidators, import and export companies, auctioneers, catalogue and mail order companies, classifieds, directories, search engines, products of search engines, virtually all online and offline commerce participants and online and offline shopping channels and networks.

BBC (2005) reports that eBay is not complacent about competition. It has pulled out of Japan due to competition from Yahoo! and within Asia and China is also facing tough competition by Yahoo! which has a

portal with a broader range of services more likely to attract subscribers.

Before the advent of online auctions, competitors in the collectables space included antique shops, car boot sales and charity shops. Anecdotal evidence suggests that all of these are now suffering. Some have taken the attitude of 'if you can't beat 'em, join 'em'. Many smaller traders who have previously run antique or car boot sales are now eBayers. Even charities such as Oxfam now have an eBay service where they sell high-value items contributed by donors. Other retailers such as Vodafone have used eBay as a means to distribute certain products within their range.

Objectives and strategy

The overall eBay aims are to increase the gross merchandise volume and net revenues from the eBay marketplace. More detailed objectives are defined to achieve these aims, with strategies focusing on:

1 *Acquisition* – increasing the number of newly registered users on the eBay marketplace.
2 *Activation* – increasing the number of registered users that become active bidders, buyers or sellers on the eBay marketplace.
3 *Activity* – increasing the volume and value of transactions that are conducted by each active user on the eBay marketplace. eBay had approximately 83 million active users at the end of 2007, compared to approximately 82 million at the end of 2006. An active user is defined as any user who bid on, bought, or listed an item during the most recent 12-month period.

The focus on each of these three areas will vary according to strategic priorities in particular local markets.

eBay marketplace growth is also driven by defining approaches to improve performance in these areas. First, category growth is achieved by increasing the number and size of categories within the marketplace, for example Antiques, Art, Books, and Business and Industrial. Second, formats for interaction. The traditional format is auction listings, but it has been refined now to include the 'Buy-It-Now' fixed-price format. This fixed-price listing now accounts for 53% of all transactions, suggesting adaptability into the eBay offering. Another format is the 'Dutch Auction' format, where a seller can sell multiple identical items to the highest bidders. eBay Stores was developed to enable sellers with a wider range of products to showcase their products in a more traditional retail format. eBay says it is constantly exploring new formats, often through acquisition of other comapnies, for example through the acquisition in 2004 of mobile.de in Germany and

Marktplaats.nl in the Netherlands, as well as investment in craigslist, the US-based classified ad format. Another acquisition is Rent.com, which enables expansion into the online housing and apartment rental category. In 2007, eBay acquired StubHub, an online ticket marketplace, and it also owns comparison marketplace Shopping.com. Finally, marketplace growth is achieved through delivering specific sites localized for different geographies as follows. You can see there is still potential for greater localization, for example in parts of Scandinavia, Eastern Europe and Asia.

Localized eBay marketplaces:

- Australia
- Austria
- Belgium
- Canada
- China
- Singapore
- South Korea
- Spain
- France
- Germany
- Hong Kong
- India
- Ireland
- Sweden
- Switzerland
- Taiwan
- Italy
- Malaysia
- Netherlands
- New Zealand
- Philippines
- United Kingdom
- United States

eBay's growth strategy

In its SEC filing, success factors eBay believes are important to enable it to compete in its market include:

- ability to attract buyers and sellers;
- volume of transactions and price and selection of goods;
- customer service; and
- brand recognition.

According to its 2010 SEC filing:

Our growth strategy is focused on reinvesting in our customers by improving the buyer experience and seller economics by enhancing our products and services, improving trust and safety and customer support, extending our product offerings into new formats, categories and geographies, and implementing innovative pricing and buyer retention strategies.

Over the course of 2009, we continued to make significant changes that were designed to improve the user experience on all of our sites, including changes to pricing and shipping policies. In 2009, we also made significant steps to create a faster and more streamlined search experience with a greater focus on relevance when sorting search results. Pricing changes reduced the upfront cost of listing fixed price items on eBay so that fees are now based more on the successful sale of items, for both smaller and larger sellers. We encourage sellers to offer free or inexpensive shipping to our buyers by promoting their listings through our 'Best Match' search algorithm.

It also notes that in the context of its competitors, other factors it believes are important are:

- community cohesion, interaction and size;
- system reliability;
- reliability of delivery and payment;
- website convenience and accessibility;
- level of service fees; and
- quality of search tools.

This implies that eBay believes it has optimized these factors, but its competitors still have opportunities for improving performance in these areas which will make the market more competitive.

Risk management

The SEC filing lists the risks and challenges of conducting business internationally as follows:

- regulatory requirements, including regulation of auctioneering, professional selling, distance selling, banking, and money transmitting;
- legal uncertainty regarding liability for the listings and other content provided by users, including uncertainty as a result of less Internet-friendly legal systems, unique local laws, and lack of clear precedent or applicable law;
- difficulties in integrating with local payment providers, including banks, credit and debit card associations, and electronic fund transfer systems;
- differing levels of retail distribution, shipping, and communications infrastructures;
- different employee–employer relationships and the existence of workers' councils and labour unions;
- difficulties in staffing and managing foreign operations;
- longer payment cycles, different accounting practices, and greater problems in collecting accounts receivable;
- potentially adverse tax consequences, including local taxation of fees or of transactions on websites;
- higher telecommunications and Internet service provider costs;
- strong local competitors;
- different and more stringent consumer protection, data protection and other laws;
- cultural ambivalence towards, or non-acceptance of, online trading;
- seasonal reductions in business activity;
- expenses associated with localizing products, including offering customers the ability to transact business in the local currency;
- laws and business practices that favour local competitors or prohibit foreign ownership of certain businesses;

- profit repatriation restrictions, foreign currency exchange restrictions, and exchange rate fluctuations;
- volatility in a specific country's or region's political or economic conditions; and
- differing intellectual property laws and taxation laws.

Results

Financial results are presented in the table below. The growth and profitability figures show that eBay is no longer growting at its original rates. It is useful to identify active users who contribute revenue to the business as a buyer or seller. eBay had 56 million active users at the end of 2004 who are defined as any user who has bid, bought or listed an item during a prior 12-month period. This had increased to 90 million by 2009.

Video explanations: http://bit.ly/EBEC-Ebay-Video;
eBay interactive timeline: http://www.ebayinc.com/list/milestones.

Question

Assess how the characteristics of the digital media and the Internet together with strategic decisions taken by its management team have supported eBay's continued growth.

	Year ended December 31 2007	Year ended December 31 2008	Year ended December 31 2009	Percent change from 2007 to 2008	Percent change from 2008 to 2009
	(In thousands, except percentage changes)				
Net Revenues by Type:					
Net transaction revenues					
Marketplaces	$ 4,680,835	$ 4,711,057	$ 4,461,845	1%	(5)%
Payments	1,838,539	2,320,495	2,641,194	26%	14%
Communications	364,564	525,803	575,096	44%	9%
Total net transaction revenues	6,883,938	7,557,355	7,678,135	10%	2%
Marketing services and other revenues					
Marketplaces	683,056	875,694	849,169	28%	(3)%
Payments	88,077	83,174	154,751	(6)%	86%
Communications	17,258	25,038	45,307	45%	81%
Total marketing services and other revenues	788,391	983,906	1,049,227	25%	7%
Total net revenues	$ 7,672,329	$ 8,541,261	$ 8,727,362	11%	2%

Source: SEC (2010), BBC (2005).

Summary

1   Electronic commerce traditionally refers to electronically mediated buying and selling.

2   Sell-side e-commerce or digital marketing involves all electronic business transactions between an organization and its customers, while buy-side e-commerce involves transactions between an organization and its suppliers. Social commerce encourages customers to interact to support sales goals.

3   'Electronic business' is a broader term, referring to how technology can benefit all internal business processes and interactions with third parties. This includes buy-side and sell-side e-commerce and the internal value chain.

4   Digital marketing involves the application of 6 key digital marketing media channels of search engine marketing, online PR and social media, partnerships, display advertising, email marketing and viral marketing.

5   Web 2.0 is used to referred to web services that facilitate interaction of web users with sites to create user-generated content and encourage behaviours such as community or social network participation, mashups, content rating, use of widgets and tagging.

5   The main business drivers for introducing e-commerce and e-business are opportunities for increased revenues and reducing costs, but many other benefits can be identified that improve customer service and corporate image.

6   Consumer adoption of the Internet is limited by lack of imperative, cost of access and security fears. Business adoption tends to be restricted by perceptions of cost, making return on investment difficult to quantify.

7   Introducing new technology is not all that is required for success in introducing e-commerce and business. Clearly defined objectives, creating the right culture for change, mix of skills, partnerships and organizational structure are arguably more important.

Exercises

Answers to these exercises are available online at www.pearsoned.co.uk/chaffey

Self-assessment questions

1   Distinguish between e-commerce and e-business.

2   Explain what is meant by buy-side and sell-side e-commerce.

3   Explain the scope and benefits of social media and social commerce to an organization of your choice.

4   Summarize the consumer and business adoption levels in your country. What seem to be the main barriers to adoption?

5   Outline the reasons why a business may wish to adopt e-commerce.

6   What are the main differences between business-to-business and business-to-consumer e-commerce?

7   Summarize the impact of the introduction of e-business on different aspects of an organization.

8   What is the relevance of intermediary sites such as Kelkoo (www.kelkoo.com) to the B2C company?

Essay and discussion questions

1   Suggest how an organization can evaluate the impact of digital technology on its business. Is it a passing fad or does it have a significant impact?

2   Explain the concepts of social media and social commerce and how they can assist organizations in reaching their objectives.

3   Similar benefits and barriers exist for the adoption of sell-side e-commerce for both B2B and B2C organizations. Discuss.

4   Evaluate how social media marketing techniques can be applied within an organization and with its stakeholders.

5   The web presence of a company has similar aims regardless of the sector in which the company operates.

Examination questions

1 Explain the relationship between the concepts of e-commerce and e-business.
2 Distinguish between buy-side and sell-side e-commerce and give an example of the application of each.
3 Summarize three reasons why a company may wish to introduce e-commerce.
4 Describe three of the main barriers to adoption of e-commerce by consumers and suggest how a company could counter these.
5 Outline the internal changes a company may need to make when introducing e-business.
6 Summarize the benefits of applying social media marketing approaches to an organization.
7 Name three risks to a company that introduces buy-side e-commerce.
8 Name three risks to a company that introduces sell-side e-commerce.

References

BBC (2005) eBay's 10-year rise to world fame. By Robert Plummer. Story from BBC News, 2 September **http://news.bbc.co.uk/go/pr/fr/-/l/hi/business/42075/10.stm**.

Booz Allen Hamilton (2002) International E-Economy: Benchmarking the World's Most Effective Policies for the E-Economy. Report published 19 November 2002, London.

Boyd, D. and Ellison, N. (2007) Social network sites: definition, history, and scholarship, *Journal of Computer-Mediated Communication*, 13 (1), 210–30.

Cabinet Office (1999) E-commerce@its.best.uk. A Performance and Innovation Unit report – September. UK Cabinet Office. Available online at: **www.cabinet-office.gov.uk/inno-vation/1999/ecommerce/ec.body.pdf**.

CIO (2002) Measuring the ROIs of Intranets – Mission Possible? By Toby Ward. *CIO Magazine*, October. Available online at: **www.cio.com/research/intranet/study_2002.html**.

comScore (2010) comScore Media Metrix Ranks Top-Growing Properties and Site Categories for April 2010. Press release, 10 May: **http://www.comscore.com/Press_Events/Press_Releases/2010/5/comScore_Media_Metrix_Ranks_Top-Growing_Properties_and_Site_Categories_for_April_2010**.

Doherty, N., Ellis-Chadwick, F. and Hart, C. (2003) An analysis of the factors affecting the adoption of the Internet in the UK retail sectors. *Journal of Business Research*, 56, 887–97.

DTI (2000) *Business in the Information Age – International Benchmarking Study 2000*. UK Department of Trade and Industry.

DTI (2002) *Business in the Information Age – International Benchmarking Study 2002*. UK Department of Trade and Industry.

Economist (2000) E-commerce survey. Define and sell. *Supplement*, 26 February, 6–12.

eEurope (2005) Information Society Benchmarking Report. From eEurope (2005) initiative. Published at: **http://europa.eu.int/information_society/eeurope/i2010/docs/bench-marking/ 051222%20Final%20Benchmarking%20Report.pdf**.

eSuperbrands (2005) *eSuperbrands 2006: Your Guide to Some of the Best Brands on the Web*. Superbrands Ltd, London.

European Commission (2010) i2010 Annual Information Society Report ICT usage in enterprises, 2009. Issue number 1/2010. Published at: **http://epp.eurostat.ec.europa.eu/portal/page/portal/product_details/publication?p_product_code=KS-QA-10-001**.

Evans, P. and Wurster, T.S. (1997) Strategy and the new economics of information. *Harvard Business Review*, September–October, 70–82.

Grove, A. (1996) *Only the Paranoid Survive*. Doubleday, New York.

Hoffman, D.L. and Novak, T.P. (1996) Marketing in hypermedia computer-mediated environments: conceptual foundations, *Journal of Marketing*, 60 (July), 50–68.

ITU (2010) ITU sees 5 billion mobile subscriptions globally in 2010. News release, 15 February 2010: **http://www.itu.int/net/pressoffice/press_releases/2010/06.aspx**.

Kalakota, R. and Whinston, A. (1997) *Electronic Commerce: A Manager's Guide*. Addison-Wesley, Reading, MA.

Mougayer, M. (1998) E-commerce? E-business? Who e-cares? *Computer World* website (**www.computerworld.com**), 2 November.

Nielsen (2010) The State of Mobile Apps, June 2010: **http://blog.nielsen.com/nielsenwire/online_mobile/the-state-of-mobile-apps/**.

ONS (2005) *Social Trends* 35, 2005 edition: **www.statistics.gov.uk/pdfdir/inta0807.pdf**.

O'Reilly, T. (2005) What Is Web 2? Design Patterns and Business Models for the Next Generation of Software. Web article, 30 September. O'Reilly Publishing, Sebastopol, CA.

Perrott, B. (2005) Towards a manager's model of e-business strategy decisions. *Journal of General Management*, 30 (4), Summer.

Rayport, J. and Jaworski, B. (2003) *Introduction to E-Commerce*, 2nd edn. McGraw-Hill, New York.

SEC (2010) United States Securities and Exchange Commission submission Form 10-K. eBay submission for the fiscal year ended 31 December 2009: **http://yahoo.brand.edgar-online.com/displayfilinginfo.aspx?FilingID=7062869-11669-66791&type=sect&dcn=0001193125-10-033324**.

Spivack (2009) Nova Spivack blog posting. How the WebOS Evolves? 9 February: **http://novaspivack.typepad.com/nova_spivacks_weblog/2007/02/steps_towards_a.html**.

Viney, D. (2003) Intranet portal guide (online article: **www.viney.com/DFV**).

Waterman, R.H., Peters, T.J. and Phillips, J.R. (1980) Structure is not organization. *McKinsey Quarterly* in-house journal. McKinsey & Co., New York.

Welch, J. (2001) CEO of GE speech to Annual Shareowners Meeting, Atlanta, GA, 25 April.

Yammer (2010) Suncorp case study accessed May 2010, Yammer website: **https://www.yammer.com/about/case_studies**.

Further reading

Chaffey, D., Ellis-Chadwick, F., Mayer, R. and Johnston, K. (2009) *Internet Marketing: Strategy, Implementation and Practice*, 4th edn. Financial Times Prentice Hall, Harlow. Chapters 10 and 11 highlight the differences between B2C and B2B e-commerce.

Web links

Sites giving general information on market characteristics of e-business:

ClickZ Experts (**www.clickz.com/experts/**) An excellent collection of articles on online marketing communications. US-focused.

ClickZ Stats (**www.clickz.com/stats/**) The definitive source of news on Internet developments, and reports on company and consumer adoption of the Internet and characteristics in Europe and worldwide. A searchable digest of most analyst reports.

European Commission Information Society Statistics (http://ec.europa.eu/information_society/digital-agenda/index_en.htm) Reports evaluating e-business activity and consumer adoption across the European Union.

Econsultancy.com (www.econsultancy.com) Research, best practice reports and supplier directory for online marketing.

Ofcom (http://stakeholders.ofcom.org.uk/) The Office of Communication has an annual Communications Market report on the adoption of digital media including telecommunications and the Internet (including broadband adoption), digital television and wireless services.

University-sponsored research projects on e-business and e-commerce:

Centre for Digital Business @ MIT (http://ebusiness.mit.edu) Created by MIT Sloan School of Management, contains summaries of over 50 research projects.

Intranet Life (http://www.intranetlife.com) A blog summarizing the work of the intranet benchmarking forum.

NetAcademy on Electronic Markets (www.electronicmarkets.org) Research compiled in *Electronic Markets – The International Journal of Electronic Commerce and Business Media.*

Sloan Center for Internet Retailing (http://ecommerce.vanderbilt.edu) Originally founded in 1994 as Project 2000 by Tom Novak and Donna Hoffman at School of Management, Vanderbilt University, to study marketing implications of the Internet. Useful links/papers.

Smart Insights (www.smartinsights.com) Guidance on digital marketing best practice from Dave Chaffey to help businesses succeed online. It includes alerts on the latest developments in applying digital technology and templates to create marketing plans and budgets.

Trade magazines

E-commerce Times (www.ecommercetimes.com) Has 'daily news e-business news and analysis'.

New Media Age (www.newmediazero.com) A weekly New Media magazine, with partial content online.

International country government sites encouraging e-business adoption

Australian Government Information Management Office (www.agimo.gov.au) Formerly the Australian National Office for the Information Economy.

Business.gov.sg (www.business.gov.sg) Singapore government portal for encouragement of e-business.

New Zealand Government E-Commerce (www.ecommerce.govt.nz) Information on e-commerce policy and initiatives.

UK CIO Council (www.cio.gov.uk) The UK government now has a Chief Information Office tasked with managing e-government for 'ensuring that IT supports the business transformation of government itself so that we can provide better, more efficient, public services'.

US Office of Electronic Government and Technology (www.estrategy.gov) US agency facilitating e-government in the USA.

UK Office of Government Commerce (www.ogc.gov.uk) Information on e-government and e-procurement.

2

Marketplace analysis for e-commerce

Web support

The following additional case studies are available at
www.pearsoned.co.uk/chaffey

→ Dynamic pricing at GlaxoSmithKline
→ Ahold explores new ways to reach customers
→ The implications of broadband access
→ Learning from the dot-coms

The site also contains a range of study material designed to help improve your results.

Learning outcomes

After completing this chapter the reader should be able to:

- Complete an online marketplace analysis to assess competitor, customer, and intermediary use of the Internet as part of strategy development
- Identify the main business and marketplace models for electronic communications and trading
- Evaluate the effectiveness of business and revenue models for online businesses

Management issues

The fundamentals of e-commerce imply these questions for managers:

- What are the implications of changes in marketplace structures for how we trade with customers and other partners?
- Which business models and revenue models should we consider in order to exploit the Internet?
- What will be the importance of online intermediaries and marketplace hubs to our business and what actions should we take to partner these intermediaries?

Links to other chapters

The main related chapters are:

- *Chapter 3* explains the hardware and software infrastructure enabling these new business models
- *Chapters 4* and *5* consider appropriate strategic responses to these new models and paradigms
- *Chapter 6* explores new models of the value chain in more detail
- *Chapter 7* explores the effect of new intermediaries and marketplaces on procurement
- *Chapter 9* discusses models of online customer behaviour which is another aspect of environment analysis

Introduction

Disruptive technologies

New technologies that prompt businesses to reappraise their strategic approaches.

Destination site

Typically a retailer or manufacturer site with sales and service information. Intermediaries such as media sites may be destination sites for some.

Online intermediaries

Websites which help connect web users with content they are seeking on destination sites. Include new online intermediaries such as search engines and shopping comparison sites and traditional brokers, directories and newspaper and magazine publishers that now have an online presence.

Online marketplace

Exchanges of information and commercial transactions between consumers, businesses and governments completed through different forms of online presence such as search engines, social networks, comparison sites and destination sites.

Situation analysis

Collection and review of information about an organization's external environment and internal processes and resources in order to inform its strategies.

Environmental scanning and analysis

The process of continuously monitoring the environment and events and responding accordingly.

Electronic communications are **disruptive technologies** that have caused major changes in industry structure, marketplace structure and business models. Consider a B2B organization. Traditionally it has sold its products through a network of distributors. With the advent of e-commerce it now has the opportunity to bypass distributors and trade directly with customers via a destination website, and it also has the opportunity to reach customers through new B2B marketplaces. Similarly, for B2C organizations such as an e-retail **destination site** there is the opportunity to market its products through **online intermediaries** such as search engines, price comparison sites, social networks, blogs and other publisher sites.

Another key feature of electronic communications and digital technology is that they increase dynanism within the marketplace. The **online marketplace** itself doesn't remain static as new digital technologies and ways of using them develop. For example, in 2010 when writing the 5th edition, these changes are noteworthy:

- Social networks rather than search engines have become the most popular sites (Hitwise, 2010).
- The iPad was launched which many commentators described as 'gamechanger' since it encourages 'family sofa browsing and collaboration' and increased use of apps and e-books on devices using the iOS operating system for iPad, iPod and iPhone.
- YouTube passed 2 billion video views daily according to Mashable (2010), showing the increased importance of streamed video for communications.
- Groupon became market leader for an emerging type on online commerce called collective buying. Groupon and its competitors partner with businesses to offer members a product or service at a major discount (40% off or more). For example, a spa service that might normally cost $100 would be available to Groupon members for $40, as long as 1,000 people agreed to buy the service for that price. Previous collective buying approaches such as Letsbuyit.com were launched during the dot-com boom, but were perhaps too early for their time.

Organizations that monitor, understand and respond appropriately to changes in their online marketplace have the greatest opportunities to use digital technologies to compete effectively. Understanding the online elements of an organization's environment, as illustrated in Figure 2.1, is a key part of **situation analysis** for e-business strategy development. There is also the need for a process to continually monitor the environment which is often referred to as **environmental scanning**.

Knowledge of the opportunities and threats presented by these marketplace changes is essential to those involved in defining business, marketing and information systems strategy. In this chapter we introduce a number of frameworks for analysing the immediate marketplace of the micro-environment. In Chapter 4 we examine the issues of the broader *e-commerce environment* in more detail using the SLEPT framework to examine Social, Legal, Economic, Political and Technological issues.

The chapter starts by considering the different participants and constraints in the e-commerce environment. We will show you how different information sources can be used to assess customer usage of different types of intermediaries. We then look at how electronic communications have facilitated restructuring of the relationships between members of the electronic marketplace – a key feature of e-commerce. Electronic communications have also given rise to many exciting new business and revenue models and we investigate how the potential of these can be assessed. Throughout this chapter we mainly consider the sell-side elements of e-commerce rather than the e-business as a whole. A review of the entire supply chain is completed in Chapter 6. To conclude the chapter, we evaluate the success factors for Internet-only businesses known as 'pureplays'.

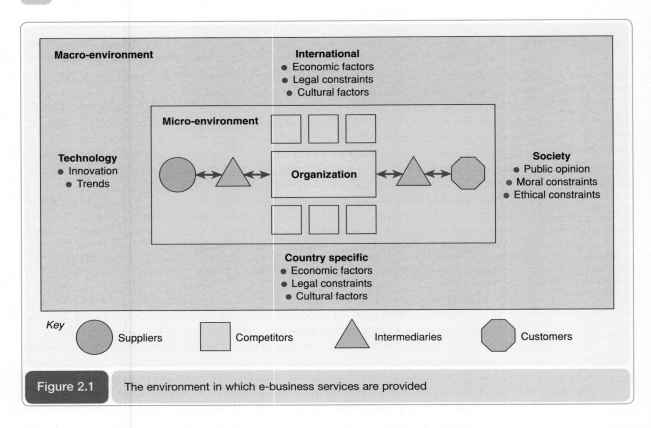

Macro-environment

International
- Economic factors
- Legal constraints
- Cultural factors

Micro-environment

Technology
- Innovation
- Trends

Organization

Society
- Public opinion
- Moral constraints
- Ethical constraints

Country specific
- Economic factors
- Legal constraints
- Cultural factors

Key ⬤ Suppliers   ▢ Competitors   ▲ Intermediaries   ⬣ Customers

| Figure 2.1 | The environment in which e-business services are provided |

The Real-world e-business experiences case studies show the importance of new online intermediaries for an existing company within the financial services sector.

Real-world E-Business experiences   **The Econsultancy interview**

MORE TH>N's Roberto Hortal Munoz on comparison sites

Overview and main concepts covered

Roberto Hortal Munoz is the head of e-business at insurance company MORE TH>N. The importance of online intermediaries and social networks in the marketplace of an organization are reviewed in this interview. In the interview he explains his brand's use of comparison sites amid growing concerns in the sector over their value to brands. We also dig into the challenge of sales attribution across different channels and the company's various efforts around online communities.

Q. Is the intense competition between comparison sites delivering value to insurance providers?

Roberto Hortal, MORE TH>N: Certainly, some insurance providers are getting value from the explosive adoption of price comparison sites. Price comparison sites change the rules of the market quite significantly, bringing scalability into the equation.

Previously an insurer's reach was more or less proportional to their marketing budget. Now, we can all reach the same amount of people just by taking part in the aggregator market. Those insurance providers that adapt quickest to the implications that a scalable market brings will certainly extract a lot of value from this new ecosystem.

I think financial services brands could do worse than looking back to what has happened in travel in the past few years: a wave of disintermediation [explained later in this chapter] spawned a myriad of direct brands across the value chain, in turn creating an ideally fragmented marketplace for aggregators to thrive in.

Some direct brands have been very successful in that environment – doing a bit of aggregating themselves to fend off the intermediaries – while others have become utilities and drastically dialled down their direct distribution to cut costs and focus on their core competencies.

The question is: What are the options that open up to insurance providers, and who will have the courage, skills and flexibility to seize on them first?

Q. What effect are comparison sites having on your Return on Investment from paid search on Google, as well as other advertising costs?

Roberto Hortal, MORE TH>N: Seen purely from a customer acquisition perspective and ignoring the deeper implications for the insurance market, I believe price comparison sites actually help reduce overall acquisition costs.

Their revenue model remains a fairly basic CPA-based one [cost per action – explained in Chapter 9], typically charging flat or near-flat fees on conversion only so costs remain predictable. After Google changed the rules about brand protection, I haven't actually seen many aggregators buying branded keywords, at least not the brands of those insurers in their panel, so they are not having such an impact there either.

Where they do massively impact costs is in generic keywords. Words like 'car insurance' have become prohibitive for all but the deepest-pocketed direct insurers. These words tend to be typically low converting so the impact on actual sales or direct ROI is not big.

The missed opportunity from not being able to effectively use those keywords as part of your brand activity is more difficult to ascertain and easy to underestimate.

Aggregators have made the drive to find a better value attribution model to replace today's 'last click takes all' more urgent. Until such time, and purely from the perspective of generating sales, comparison sites don't seem to be significantly increasing our marketing costs.

Q. Could you see more insurance providers taking the Direct Line approach to comparison sites?

Roberto Hortal, MORE TH>N: I can certainly see some scenarios where direct insurers may decide to pursue similar policies. I can even think of some where this may be a very successful move for a strong direct financial services brand.

However, I would caution anyone thinking about going down that route to stop to think for a minute about the reasons behind aggregators' wild success, and the lessons that need to be learned from it.

Customers have loudly voted with their clicks for a channel that brings convenience to them and helps them make a choice on the basis of what the vast majority of them consider to be the key decision points: choice and price. Anyone looking to buck the trend and go against consumers' clearly stated expectations would do so at their own peril.

Q. Is the rise of price comparison sites impacting premiums or levels of insurance coverage?

Roberto Hortal, MORE TH>N: Financial services is a very strongly regulated marketplace. Consumers can be sure that, whatever the market pressures, regulation ensures cover levels and premiums are reasonable and appropriate.

I have seen some companies launching basic cover products to more effectively compete on the aggregators. I haven't seen reliable adoption figures for those products so I wouldn't be able to tell whether these are really being adopted by consumers or are they just adding noise to an already deafening marketplace. This is not something MORE TH>N is doing.

In terms of premiums, price comparison is making providers' pricing a lot more transparent, and may be driving some to lower their premiums to better compete in the marketplace. Again, I can't say this is something particularly impacting on MORE TH>N premiums, as we are fully aware of the need to grow a sustainable business over the long term.

Q. How do cashback sites compare to comparison sites in terms of effectiveness?

Roberto Hortal, MORE TH>N: Cashback sites share just two characteristics with price comparison sites: they are consumers' favourites and they offer us a predictable marketing cost model based on CPA which makes it easy to work with them. That's really where the similarities end, as far as I'm concerned.

For consumers, cashbacks provide none of the convenience that aggregators do. For merchants, cashbacks firmly root the market back to nonscalable territory. They provide no real extra reach – at least nothing compared with aggregators' ability to display an insurer's prices to all its visitors.

From that point of view, cashbacks are just glorified online directories, so basic in fact that they need to incentivize people to visit them and give away listings' impressions to merchants in order to generate business. Cashbacks are important because they have found the single proposition that consumers value over convenience: hard cash.

I see cashbacks as competing with, rather than complementing, comparison sites. Savvy consumers are already making comparisons on the aggregators, then heading off to Quidco to make the purchase. This behaviour threatens the long-term sustainability of the price comparison sites in their current incarnation, as well as opening the door to interesting opportunities for cooperation and cross-pollination among them.

What is most interesting to me is the social media potential of cashback sites. Cashback sites work with their customers purely on trust. This trust is generated via tools (such as merchant ratings, discussion forums, blogs, etc.) that allow users to weed out the bad merchants and promote the good ones. An active community of users potentially recommending your brand to their mates for immediate purchase? Who wouldn't want a piece of that?

Q. How are retention rates working out for customers referred from comparison sites, affiliates, search, cashback sites etc?

Roberto Hortal, MORE TH>N: It's been widely reported that retention rates for customers from channels which prime price over value are lower than average. It's not just the channels themselves; the barrage of insurance advertising people are constantly under is helping educate people about the potential savings to be had by churning.

From my point of view, lower retention rates are largely a long-term trend of our own making. Car insurance, much like mobile phones, is largely a saturated market and companies grow their books primarily by taking others' customers.

Aggregators and cashbacks have certainly accelerated this trend and are making it even more urgent for the industry to find a way to reinvent itself so that either this long-term trend is reversed (by aggressively rewarding loyalty, perhaps) or the industry adapts to provide the shorter-term products people seem to prefer these days.

Q. What proportion of your sales is being generated through the web, and can you break that down by channel (e.g. affiliates, comparison sites etc)?

Roberto Hortal, MORE TH>N: I am not able to give a precise figure. However, I will say that eBusiness (that's what we call the aggregate of Direct Web and Aggregators at MORE TH>N) is our main sales channel.

People have clearly adopted the internet as their preferred option when it comes not just to research, but also to purchase of general insurance, and we're clearly seeing this ourselves.

Q. How does online acquisition compare to offline in terms of cost?

Roberto Hortal, MORE TH>N: While individual channels' Cost Per Sale vary, and it could be claimed that online channels tend to carry a lower 'last click' CPS, the truth is that offline spend contributes massively to creating awareness and driving searches, direct visits, affiliate clicks, etc.

I am not convinced that talk about 'online costs' and 'offline costs' contributes much. I prefer to spend my energy trying to find a good model to split each sale's attributed value proportionally to every single activity that, over time, contributed to this individual customer finally making a decision to purchase our product.

Q. Are there still a lot of consumers out there that research online but convert offline?

Roberto Hortal, MORE TH>N: I'm not seeing a lot of those cases any more. People did display that behaviour years ago but most are now familiar and comfortable with the Internet as a distribution channel. People are also aware of the many ways in which merchants, payment providers and regulators protect their online transactions. Indeed, it seems to me I'm better protected when shopping online – from disreputable merchants – than offline.

We do see consumers doing research on price comparison sites, then visiting direct and getting a quote before they eventually buy. That figure is made up of early adopters and is rapidly decreasing as well, on the back of familiarity, trust and changes by the price comparison sites which mean that prices displayed are more accurate and less likely to change now.

Q. Are you doing anything to move away from the last click wins [attribution of sale to the last referrer to a site discussed in Chapter 9] model?

Roberto Hortal, MORE TH>N: As I've already mentioned a couple of times, this is a priority for me. I believe finding such a model could be a huge competitive advantage for a marketer. We're working hard internally and with our agencies to develop and test various approaches to a much more complex way to attribute sales to the 'marketing value chain', with some success so far although we're still well into the journey.

Q. Are you looking at other forms of online marketing like viral?

Roberto Hortal, MORE TH>N: I'm always looking at opportunities to do things differently. We did an interesting thing with viral last Christmas where we bridged online and the real world. Our Personal Customer Managers emailed customers to let them know of our Christmas opening hours and included, as a little present, a papercraft model of our MORE TH>N wood people, the ones featured in our ad campaign.

The models could be printed, folded and glued into Christmas decorations. We had quite a few downloads and I'm sure we made a few people smile. Some may have even decided to stay with us.

Q. Can you talk a bit about Living, your green social network; the reasons for its launch and the challenges of execution?

Roberto Hortal, MORE TH>N: Living is our main social networking activity. We're not new to social networking by any means – we've been successfully running PetHealthcare.co.uk, a community and forum for pet owners, for a number of years.

In the spirit of MORE TH>N, We Do More, last year we started looking for more opportunities for MORE TH>N to enable conversations around other topics of interest to our potential customers.

We commissioned iCrossing, our SEO [search engine optimization, explained in Chapter 9] partner, to use its Network Sense methodology to map the networks of topics and conversations where our product, brand or site featured as part of the discussion. This work identified a gap that we could step in to fill – we couldn't find a neutral, authoritative, trusted and consumer-friendly space to discuss practical issues around how to live greener daily lives.

If it was to succeed, the site had to be genuine: countless companies have tried and failed to infiltrate the social space (remember Zuzzid?) when the only workable approach is to contribute and share freely. To be genuine useful. To really participate.

So we set it up using the tools that most bloggers use (Wordpress and plugins), gave it an independent voice (the writers, all professionals, are completely independent from MORE TH>N and have complete editorial control), freed the content by using a non-restrictive Creative Commons licence throughout the site and allowed it to become part of the fabric of social networking by providing countless ways to share, bookmark, recommend, rate and comment.

We also made sure the site was easy to use, accessible and effective at interacting with search engines. And of course we give it daily in-depth, engaging, original content so our audience will always find a new topic to add to their online conversations.

The site is clearly delivering its stated goals of being eminently useful and creating long-term engagement with the brand. It's constantly developing as a result of user feedback, broadening the topics covered and providing the types of content and services its increasingly numerous audience find useful. It is really taking on a life of its own.

And all the while, it is delivering a branded experience to the thousands of people who decide to spend the time of the day in conversation with MORE TH>N.

Source: Econsultancy (2008) Q&A: MORE TH>N's Roberto Hortal Munoz on comparison sites, 8 August: www.Econsultancy.com/news-blog/366073/q-a-more-th-n-s-roberto-hortal-munoz-on-comparison-sites.html.

The e-commerce environment

All organizations operate within an environment that influences the way in which they conduct business. Strategy development should be strongly influenced by considering the environment the business operates in, as illustrated in Figure 2.1. To inform e-commerce strategy, the most significant influences are those of the immediate marketplace of the micro-environment that is shaped by the needs of customers and how services are provided to them through competitors and intermediaries and via upstream suppliers. Wider influences are provided by local and international economic conditions and legislation together with whatever business practices are acceptable to society. Finally, technological innovations are vital in providing opportunities to provide superior services to competitors or through changing the shape of the marketplace.

Strategic agility
The capability to innovate and so gain competitive advantage within a marketplace by monitoring changes within an organization's marketplace and then to efficiently evaluate alternative strategies and select, review and implement appropriate candidate strategies.

Strategic agility

The capacity to respond to these environmental opportunities and threats is commonly referred to as **strategic agility**. Strategic agility is a concept strongly associated with knowledge management theory and is based on developing a sound process for reviewing marketplace opportunities and threats and then selecting the appropriate strategy options. See Mini case study 2.1 for an excellent video introduction to the principles of strategic agility.

Mini Case Study 2.1	The Marine Corps demonstrates strategic agility

Professor Donald N. Sull is an Associate Professor of Management Practice in the Strategy and International Management faculty at the London Business School.

In the first video tutorial, 'Fog of the Future' on strategic agility (visit www.ft.com/multimedia and search for 'London Business School'), he asserts that traditional management models of creating a long-term vision are flawed since our knowledge of the future is always imperfect and marketplace conditions are changing continuously. Rather than being the captain of a ship surveying the far horizon, analogous with the top-down model of strategy, the reality for managers is that their situation is more akin to that of a racing car driver on a foggy day, constantly looking to take the right decisions based on the mass of information about their surroundings coming through the fog. He believes that having a clear long-term vision, particularly where it isn't based on environment analysis, isn't practical in most industries. Instead he says that companies should '*keep vision fuzzy but current priorities clear*'.

In a second video tutorial, 'Strategic Agility', Sull explains the basis for strategic agility. He explains that all knowledge of the future is based on uncertainty, but that managers must act now so they need to put in

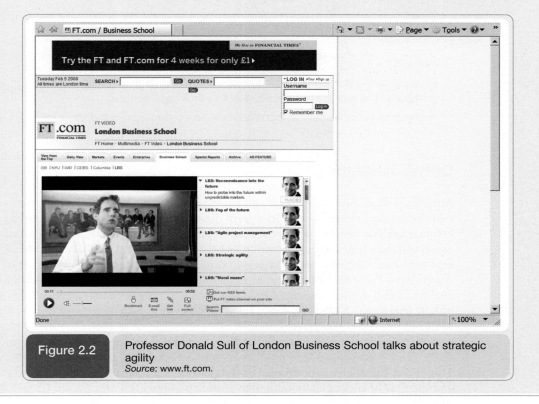

Figure 2.2	Professor Donald Sull of London Business School talks about strategic agility *Source*: www.ft.com.

place US Marine Corps-style reconnaissance missions as an army would in order to make their battle plans. He gives the example of Dell, explaining how they spend relatively little on research and development, but are instead constantly probing the marketplace, trialling new ideas with multiple probes into the approach. He stresses the importance of finding anomalies in the marketplace where it doesn't appear as expected and these may represent learnings or opportunities. Detailed customer insights and business performance are necessary to identify these anomalies. Finally, he makes the point of the need to act rapidly to have scalability to 'swarm the gap in the defences of the enemy' where there is a strong opportunity.

In an e-business context, we can see that strategic agility requires these characteristics and requirements for an organization to be successful in its strategy development:

1 Efficient collection, dissemination and evaluation of different information sources from the micro- and macro-environment.
2 Effective process for generating and reviewing the relevance of new strategies based on creating new value for customers.
3 Efficient research into potential customer value against the business value generated.
4 Efficient implementation of prototypes of new functionality to deliver customer value.
5 Efficient measurement and review of results from prototypes to revise further to improve proposition or to end trial.

Now complete Activity 2.1 to review the importance of these environmental influences.

Activity 2.1	Why are environmental influences important?

Purpose

To emphasize the importance of monitoring and acting on a range of environmental influences.

Activity

For each of the environmental influences shown in Figure 2.1, give examples of why it is important to monitor and respond in an e-business context.

Answers to activities can be found at www.pearsoned.co.uk/chaffey

Online marketplace analysis

Analysis of the online marketplace or 'marketspace' is a key part of developing a long-term e-business plan or creating a shorter-term digital marketing campaign. Completing a marketplace analysis helps to define the main types of online presence that are part of a 'click ecosystem' which describes the consumer behaviour (Chapter 9) or flow of online visitors between search engines, media sites and other intermediaries to an organization and its competitors. Prospects and customers in an online marketplace will naturally turn to search engines to find products, services, brands and entertainment. Search engines act as a distribution system which connects searchers to different intermediary sites for different phrases, so the flow of visits between sites must be understood by the marketer in their sector.

To help understand and summarize the online linkages between online businesses and traffic flows it is worthwhile to produce an online marketplace map, as shown in Figure 2.3. This shows the relative importance of different online intermediaries in the marketplace and the flow of clicks between different customer segments, company site(s) and different competitors via the intermediaries.

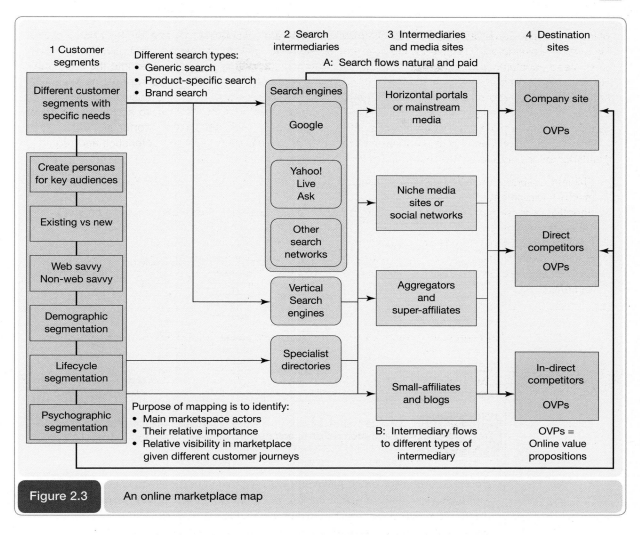

| Figure 2.3 | An online marketplace map |

The main elements of the online marketplace map presented in Figure 2.3 are:

1 **Customer segments**

   The marketplace analysis should identify and summarize different target segments for an online business in order to then understand their online media consumption, buyer behaviour and the type of content and experiences they will be looking for from intermediaries and your website.

2 **Search intermediaries**

   These are the main search engines in each country. Typically they are Google, Yahoo!, Microsoft Live Search and Ask, but others are important in some markets such as China (Baidu), Russia (Yandex) and South Korea (Naver). You can use audience panel data from different providers indicated in Box 2.1 to find out their relative importance in different countries. The Google Trends tool (Figure 2.4) is a free tool for assessing site popularity and the searches used to find sites and how they vary seasonally, which is useful for student assignments.

   Companies need to know which sites are effective in harnessing search traffic and either partner with them or try to obtain a share of the search traffic using the search engine marketing and affiliate marketing techniques explained in Chapter 9. Well-known, trusted brands which have developed customer loyalty are in a good position to succeed online

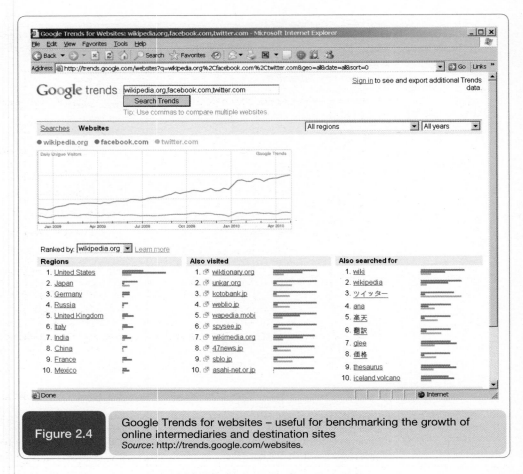

Figure 2.4	Google Trends for websites – useful for benchmarking the growth of online intermediaries and destination sites *Source*: http://trends.google.com/websites.

Share of search
The audience share of Internet searches achieved by a particular audience in a particular market.

Aggregators
An alternative term for *price comparison sites*. Aggregators include product, price and service information, comparing competitors within a sector such as financial services, retail or travel. Their revenue models commonly include affiliate revenues (CPA), pay-per-click advertising (CPC) and display advertising (CPM).

Affiliate
A company promoting a merchant typically through a commission-based arrangement either direct or through an affiliate network.

since a common consumer behaviour is to go straight to the site through entering a URL, a bookmark, e-mail or searching for the brand or URL. Hitwise provides this type of insight, as shown in Table 2.1. Through evaluating the type and volume of phrases used to search for products in a given market it is possible to calculate the total potential opportunity and the current share of search terms for a company. '**Share of search**' can be determined from web analytics reports from the company site which indicate the precise key phrases used by visitors to actually reach a site.

3 Intermediaries and media sites

Media sites and other intermediaries such as aggregators and affiliates are often successful in attracting visitors via search or direct since they are mainstream brands. Companies need to assess potential online media and distribution partners in the categories shown in Figure 2.3 such as:

(a) **Mainstream news media sites or portals**. Include traditional, e.g. FT.com or Times, or Pureplay, e.g. Google news, an aggregator.

(b) **Niche or vertical media sites,** e.g. Econsultancy, ClickZ.com in B2B.

(c) **Price comparison sites** (also known as **aggregators**), e.g. Moneysupermarket, Kelkoo, Shopping.com, uSwitch.

(d) **Superaffiliates**. **Affiliates** gain revenue from a merchant they refer traffic to using a commission-based arrangement based on the proportion of sale or a fixed amount. They are important in e-retail markets, accounting for tens of percent of sales.

(e) **Niche affiliates or bloggers**. These are often individuals, but they may be important; for example, in the UK, Martin Lewis of Moneysavingexpert.com receives millions of visits every month. Smaller affiliates and bloggers can be important collectively.

Table 2.1	Top 10 generic and branded search terms sending traffic to a Hitwise custom category of the top 25 flower websites in the UK over the four weeks ending 1 March 2007

	Branded term popularity	Generic term popularity
1	interflora	flowers
2	flying flowers	mothers day flowers
3	tesco	flower delivery
4	interflora uk	mothers day
5	tesco flowers	flowers delivered
6	next flowers	mothers day gifts
7	flowers by post	florists
8	next	flowers for mothers day
9	asda	valentines flowers
10	asda flowers	send flowers

Source: Hitwise press release: UK Internet visits to flower web sites at highest-ever peak in February, London, 6 March 2008.

Again, the relative importance of these site types can be assessed using the services summarized in Box 2.1.

4 **Destination sites**

These are the sites that the marketer is trying to generate visitors to, whether these are transactional sites, like retailers, financial services or travel companies or manufacturers or brands. Figure 2.3 refers to OVP or **online value proposition** which is a summary of the unique features of the site (see Chapters 4 and 8). The OVP is a key aspect to consider within marketplace analysis – marketers should evaluate their OVPs against competitors' as part of competitor analysis and think about how they can refine them to develop a unique online experience. Competitor analysis is also covered in Chapter 8.

Online value proposition (OVP)
A statement of the benefits of e-commerce service that ideally should not be available in competitor offerings or offline offerings.

Box 2.1	Resources for analysing the online marketplace

There is a wealth of research about current Internet usage and future trends which strategists can use to understand their marketplace. In Table 2.2, we summarize a selection of free and paid for services which can be used for online marketplace analysis to assess the number of people searching for information and the popularity of different types of sites measured by the number of **unique visitors**.

E-consultancy (www.e-consultancy.com) provides a summary of many of the latest research from these sources together with its own reports such as the Internet Statistics compendium.

Unique visitors
Individual visitors to a site measured through cookies or IP addresses on an individual computer.

Table 2.2	Research tools for assessing your e-marketplace

Service	Usage
1 Alexa (www.alexa.com). Free tool, but not based on a representative sample, see also www.compete.com. The Google Trends for Websites (http://trends.google.com/websites, Figure 2.4) gives this information using a larger sample size.	Free service owned by Amazon which provides traffic ranking of individual sites compared to all sites. Works best for sites in top 100,000. Sample dependent on users of the Alexa toolbar.
2 Hitwise (www.hitwise.com). Paid tool, but free research available at http://weblogs.hitwise.com and Data centres.	Paid service available in some countries to compare audience size and search and site usage. Works through monitoring IP traffic to different sites through ISPs.
3 Netratings (www.netratings.com). Paid tool. Free data on search engines and intermediaries available from press release section.	Panel service based on at-home and at-work users who have agreed to have their web usage tracked by software. Top rankings on site gives examples of most popular sites in several countries.
4 Comscore (www.comscore.com). Paid tool. Free data on search engines and intermediaries available from press release section.	A similar panel service to Netratings, but focusing on the US and UK. A favoured tool for media planners.
5 ABCE Database (www.abce.org.uk). Free tool. (Choose ABCE Database.)	The Audit Bureau of Circulation (Electronic) gives free access to its database of portals (not destination sites) that have agreed to have their sites audited to prove traffic volumes to advertisers.
6 Search keyphrase analysis tools. Compilation available from www.davechaffey.com/seo-keyword-tools. See also the Google Agency Toolkit (www.google.com/agencytoolkit).	Tools such as the Google Keyword tool and Google Traffic Estimator can be used to assess the popularity of brands and their products reflected by the volume of search terms typed into Google and other search engines. The Yahoo! Site Explorer can be used to assess links between sites.
7 Forrester (www.forrester.com). Paid research service. Some free commentary and analysis within blogs (http://blogs.forrester.com).	Offers reports on Internet usage and best practice in different vertical sectors such as financial services, retail and travel. Free research summaries available in press release section and on its Marketing blog (http://blogs.forrester.com).
8 Gartner (www.gartner.com).	Another research service, in this case focusing on technology adoption. See also Jupiter Research (www.jupiterresearch.com) which often has good reports on e-mail marketing best practice.
9 Internet or Interactive Advertising Bureau (IAB) US: www.iab.net, UK: iab.uk.net, Europe: www.iabeurope.eu (see also www.eiaa.net)	Research focusing on investment in different digital media channels, in particular display ads and search marketing.
10 Internet Media in Retail Group (IMRG) (www.imrg.org).	The IMRG has compilations on online e-commerce expenditure and most popular retailers in the UK.

Location of trading in the marketplace

Electronic marketplace

A virtual marketplace such as the Internet in which no direct contact occurs between buyers and sellers.

While traditional marketplaces have a physical location, an Internet-based market has no physical presence – it is a virtual marketplace. Rayport and Sviokla (1996) used this distinction to coin a new term: **electronic marketplace**. This has implications for the way in which the relationships between the different actors in the marketplace occur.

The new electronic marketspace has many alternative virtual locations where an organization needs to position itself to communicate and sell to its customers. Managers need to understand the relative importance of different types of sites and consumer and business interactions and information flows. In this section we will review how marketplace channel structures, the location of trading and multichannel marketing models can be assessed to inform e-business strategy. Finally, we will review commercial arrangements for transactions.

Review of marketplace channel structures

Marketplace channel structures describe the way a manufacturer or selling organization delivers products and services to its customers. Typical channel structures between business and consumer organizations are shown in Figure 2.5.

A distribution channel will consist of one or more intermediaries such as wholesalers and retailers. For example, a music company is unlikely to distribute its CDs directly to retailers, but will use wholesalers who have a large warehouse of titles which are then distributed to individual branches according to demand. Of course, today they can distribute digital tracks straight to online retailers such as iTunes and Napster, a major change to their channel strategy. Bands can even bypass retailers and sell direct; for example, in 2008 Radiohead released their *In Rainbows* album direct from their site, allowing purchasers to name their own price!

The relationship between a company and its channel partners shown in Figure 2.5 can be dramatically altered by the opportunities afforded by the Internet. This occurs because the

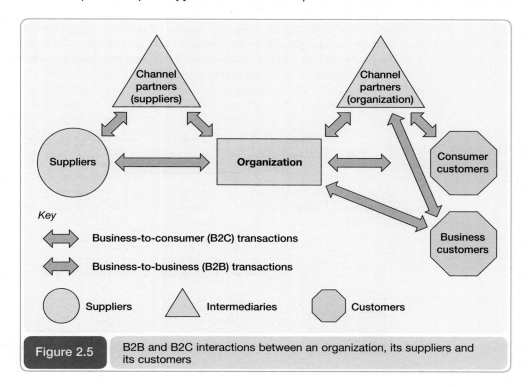

| Figure 2.5 | B2B and B2C interactions between an organization, its suppliers and its customers |

Disintermediation

The removal of intermediaries such as distributors or brokers that formerly linked a company to its customers.

Internet offers a means of bypassing some of the channel partners. This process is known as **disintermediation** or 'cutting out the middleman'.

Figure 2.6 illustrates disintermediation in a graphical form for a simplified retail channel. Further intermediaries such as additional distributors may occur in a business-to-business market. Figure 2.6(a) shows the former position where a company marketed and sold its products by 'pushing' them through a sales channel. Figures 2.6(b) and (c) show two different types of disintermediation in which the wholesaler (b) or the wholesaler and retailer (c) are bypassed, allowing the producer to sell and promote direct to the consumer. The benefits of disintermediation to the producer are clear – it is able to remove the sales and infrastructure cost of selling through the channel. Benjamin and Weigand (1995) calculated that, using the sale of quality shirts as an example, it is possible to make cost savings of 28 per cent in the case of (b) and 62 per cent for case (c). Some of these cost savings can be passed on to the customer in the form of cost reductions.

Vauxhall (www.vauxhall.co.uk), the UK part of General Motors, provides a good example of the response to the opportunities provided by new electronic channels. The initial aims for this website were not limited to online sales generation but included raising the profile and branding awareness of Vauxhall and lead generation for dealerships (such as brochure and test drive requests). Online approaches included differential pricing ('Vauxhall Internet Price'), an online sales support tool ('Vauxhall Advisor') and an e-mail newsletter. CIO (Chief Information Officer) (2002) reported that in November 2001, eGM – a group created in 1999 to manage e-business projects and processes throughout General Motors – was dismantled and rolled back into GM's traditional business units. While sceptics may point to this as evidence of disappointing results from e-business, the article reports that GM executives, including CEO Rick Wagoner and CIO's Ralph Szygenda, say the changes at eGM are not indicative of a wholesale retreat from e-business:

> *The intent from the beginning was to create a separate function for two to three years to drive [e-business capabilities] across GM. The dismantling of the eGM group is seen as a sign of success, with e-business now an integral part of the company's fabric.*

GM managers also point to the role of the Internet in generating leads for dealer sales. In September 2001, the GM BuyPower US website delivered an average of more than 2,000 leads to dealers per day with 20% of dealer leads generated through BuyPower converting into sales. This pattern of the incorporation of e-business back into traditional structures is commonplace amongst the advanced adopters of e-business who have successfully integrated e-business into their organizations.

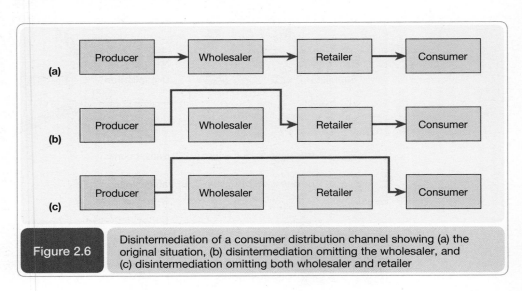

| Figure 2.6 | Disintermediation of a consumer distribution channel showing (a) the original situation, (b) disintermediation omitting the wholesaler, and (c) disintermediation omitting both wholesaler and retailer |

Reintermediation
The creation of new intermediaries between customers and suppliers providing services such as supplier search and product evaluation.

Although disintermediation has occurred, **reintermediation** is perhaps a more significant phenomenon resulting from Internet-based communications. Figure 2.7 illustrates this concept. Figure 2.7(a) shows the traditional situation in which many sales were through brokers such as the Automobile Association (www.theaa.co.uk). With disintermediation (Figure 2.7(b)) there was the opportunity to sell direct, initially via call centres as with Direct Line (www.directline.co.uk) and then more recently by their transactional website. Purchasers of products still needed assistance in the selection of products and this led to the creation of new intermediaries, the process referred to as reintermediation (Figure 2.7(c)).

In the UK Screentrade (www.screentrade.com) and Confused (www.confused.com) are examples of a new entrant broker providing a service for people to find online insurance at a competitive price. Esurance.com and Insurance.com are US examples. Reintermediation removes this inefficiency by placing an intermediary between purchaser and seller. This intermediary performs the price evaluation stage since its database has links updated from prices contained within the databases of different suppliers. Screentrade was purchased by Lloyds TSB, a traditional financial services provider, but is still positioned as independent from its parent.

Debate 2.1

Countermediation

'The advent of e-commerce means that marketers cannot rely on the online presence of existing intermediaries – instead they must create their own online intermediaries.'

What are the implications of reintermediation for the e-commerce manager? First, it is necessary to make sure that your company, as a supplier, is represented on the sites of the new intermediaries operating within your chosen market sector. This implies the need to integrate databases containing price information with those of different intermediaries. Forming partnerships or setting up sponsorship with some intermediaries can give better online visibility compared to competitors. Second, it is important to monitor the prices of other suppliers within this sector (possibly by using the intermediary website). Third, it may be appropriate to create your own intermediary, for example DIY chain B&Q set up its own intermediary to help budding DIYers, but it is positioned separately from its owners. Such tactics to counter or take advantage of reintermediation are sometimes known as **countermediation**. Screentrade is another example of countermediation, except that here the strategy of Lloyds TSB was to use the lower-risk approach of purchasing an existing online intermediary rather than creating its own intermediary. A further example is Opodo (www.opodo.com) which was set up by nine European airlines including Air France, BA, KLM and Lufthansa. Such collaboration would have been inconceivable just a short time ago.

Countermediation
Creation of a new intermediary by an established company.

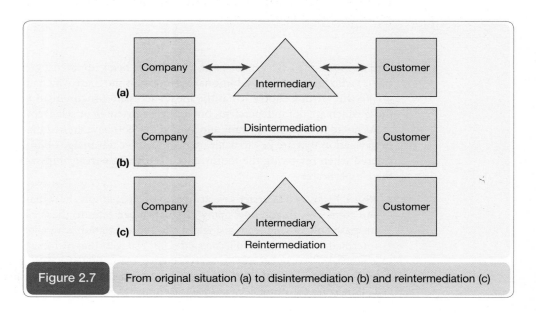

| Figure 2.7 | From original situation (a) to disintermediation (b) and reintermediation (c) |

Location of trading in the marketplace

Another perspective on the configuration of the marketplace relates to the position of trading and relative strength between different players within the marketplace.

Berryman *et al.* (1998) created a useful framework for this, identifying three different types of location. Seller-controlled sites are the main home page of the company and are e-commerce-enabled. Buyer-controlled sites are intermediaries that have been set up so that the buyer initiates the market-making. In procurement posting, a purchaser specifies what they wish to purchase, and a message is sent by e-mail to suppliers registered on the system and then offers are awaited. Aggregators involve a group of purchasers combining to purchase a multiple order, thus reducing the purchase cost. Neutral sites are independent evaluator intermediaries that enable price and product comparison.

Table 2.3	Different places for online representation	

Place of purchase	Examples of sites
A Seller-controlled	• Vendor sites, i.e. home site of organization selling products, e.g. www.dell.com
B Seller-oriented	• Intermediaries controlled by third parties to the seller such as distributors and agents, e.g. Opodo (www.opodo.com) represents the main air carriers
C Neutral	• Intermediaries not controlled by buyer's industry, e.g. EC21 (www.ec21.com) • Product-specific search engines, e.g. CNET (www.computer.com) • Comparison sites, e.g. MoneySupermarket (www.moneysupermarket.com) • Auction space, e.g. eBay (www.ebay.com)
D Buyer-oriented	• Intermediaries controlled by buyers, e.g. Covisint used to represent the major motor manufacturers (www.covisint.com) although they now don't use a single marketplace, but each manufacturer uses the technology to access its suppliers direct • Purchasing agents and aggregators
E Buyer-controlled	• Website procurement posting on company's own site, e.g. Deutsche Telekom Corporate Procurement portal (www.einkauf.telekom.de) which controls part of the company's €23 billion purchasing budget

Source: Adapted from McDonald and Wilson (2002).

The framework of Berryman *et al.* (1998) has been updated by McDonald and Wilson (2002) who introduce two additional locations for purchase which are useful (Table 2.3).

We will see in Chapter 7 that the most successful procurement intermediaries are often those which are not independent, but are seller-oriented or seller-controlled.

As noted in Chapter 1, Evans and Wurster (1999) have argued that there are three aspects of navigation that are key to achieving competitive advantage online. These should be considered when reviewing the importance of forming partnerships with intermediaries. The three aspects are:

● *Reach.* Evans and Wurster say: 'It [reach] means, simply, how many customers a business can connect with and how many products it can offer to those customers.' Reach can be increased by moving from a single site to representation with a large number of different intermediaries. Allen and Fjermestad (2001) suggest that niche suppliers can readily reach a much wider market due to search-engine marketing (Chapter 8). Evans and Wurster also suggest reach refers to the range of products and services that can be offered since this will increase the number of people the company can appeal to.

- *Richness.* This is the depth or detail of information which is both collected about the customer and provided to the customer. The latter is related to the richness of product information and how well it can be personalized to be relevant to the individual needs.
- *Affiliation.* This refers to whose interest the selling organization represents – consumers or suppliers – and stresses the importance of forming the right partnerships. This particularly applies to retailers . The authors suggest that successful online retailers will provide customers who provide them with the richest information on comparing competitive products.

The importance of multi-channel marketplace models

Customer journey
A description of modern multi-channel buyer behaviour as consumers use different media to select suppliers, make purchases and gain customer support.

Multi-channel marketing strategy
Defines how different marketing channels should integrate and support each other in terms of their proposition development and communications based on their relative merits for the customer and the company.

Online purchasers typically use a combination of channels as they follow their **customer journeys.** As they select products and interact with brands, they do not use the Internet in isolation – they consume other media such as print, TV, direct mail and outdoor ads. It follows that an effective approach to using the Internet is as part of a **multi-channel marketing strategy.** This defines how different marketing channels should integrate and support each other in terms of their proposition development and communications based on their relative merits for the customer and the company.

Developing 'channel chains' to help us understand multi-channel behaviour is a powerful technique recommended by McDonald and Wilson (2002) for analysing the changes in a marketplace introduced by the Internet. A channel chain shows alternative customer journeys for customers with different channel preferences. It can be used to assess the current and future performance of these different customer journeys. An example of a channel chain is shown in Figure 2.8. A market map can show the flow of revenue between a manufacturer or service provider and its customers through intermediaries and new types of intermediaries. Thomas and Sullivan (2005) give the example of a US multi-channel retailer that used cross-channel tracking of purchases through assigning each customer a unique identifier to calculate channel preferences, as follows: 63% bricks-and-mortar store only, 12.4% Internet-only customers, 11.9% catalogue-only customers, 11.9% dual-channel customers and 1% three-channel customers.

Commercial arrangement for transactions

Markets can also be considered from another perspective – that of the type of commercial arrangement that is used to agree a sale and price between the buyer and supplier. The main types of commercial arrangement are shown in Table 2.4.

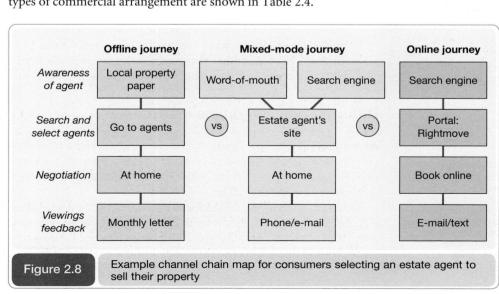

	Offline journey	Mixed-mode journey	Online journey
Awareness of agent	Local property paper	Word-of-mouth Search engine	Search engine
Search and select agents	Go to agents vs	Estate agent's site vs	Portal: Rightmove
Negotiation	At home	At home	Book online
Viewings feedback	Monthly letter	Phone/e-mail	E-mail/text

Figure 2.8   Example channel chain map for consumers selecting an estate agent to sell their property

Table 2.4	Commercial mechanisms and online transactions

Commercial (trading) mechanism	Online transaction mechanism of Nunes *et al.* (2000)
1 **Negotiated deal** *Example:* can use similar mechanism to auction, as on Commerce One (www.commerceone.net)	Negotiation – bargaining between single seller and buyer. Continuous replenishment – ongoing fulfilment of orders under pre-set terms
2 **Brokered deal** *Example:* intermediaries such as Screentrade (www.screentrade.co.uk)	Achieved through online intermediaries offering auction and pure markets online
3 **Auction** *Examples:* C2C: eBay (www.ebay.com); B2B: Industry to Industry (http://business.ebay.co.uk/)	Seller auction – buyers' bids determine final price of sellers' offerings. Buyer auction – buyers request prices from multiple sellers. Reverse – buyers post desired price for seller acceptance
4 **Fixed-price sale** *Examples:* all e-tailers	Static call – online catalogue with fixed prices. Dynamic call – online catalogue with continuously updated prices and features
5 **Pure markets** *Example:* electronic share dealing	Spot – buyers' and sellers' bids clear instantly
6 **Barter** *Examples:* www.intagio.com and www.bartercard.co.uk	Barter – buyers and sellers exchange goods. According to the International Reciprocal Trade Association (www.irta.com), barter trade was over $9 billion in 2002

Source: Adapted from The All-In-One-Market, *Harvard Business Review*, pp. 2–3 (Nunes, P., Kambil, A. and Wilson, D. 2000) © 2000 by the Harvard Business School Publishing Corporation, all rights reserved.

Each of these commercial arrangements is similar to traditional arrangements. Although the mechanism cannot be considered to have changed, the relative importance of these different options has changed with the Internet. Owing to the ability to rapidly publish new offers and prices, auction has become an important means of selling on the Internet. A turnover of several billion dollars has been achieved by eBay from consumers offering items such as cars and antiques.

An example of a completely new commercial mechanism that has been made possible through the web is provided by priceline.com (www.priceline.com). This travel site is characterized by its unique and proprietary 'Name Your Own Price™' buying service. Here, users enter the price they wish to pay for airline tickets, hotel rooms or car hire together with their credit card details. If priceline.com can match the user's price and other terms with inventory available from its participating suppliers, the deal will go ahead. The brand has also been licensed in the UK and Asia.

Debate 2.2

Innovative business models

The new business models associated with the dot-com era were, in fact, existing models in an online context. Business models and revenue models have not changed.'

Different types of online intermediary

As we showed through Figure 2.3, identifying different types of online intermediary as potential partners to promote an e-business is a key part of marketplace analysis. In this section, we take a more in-depth look at the different types of intermediaries and the business and revenue models they adopt.

Sarkar *et al.* (1996) identified many different types of new intermediaries (mainly from a B2C perspective) which they refer to using the dated term 'cybermediaries'. Hagel and Rayport (1997) use '**infomediary**' specifically to refer to sale of customer information. See Box 2.2 for further information on this concept and the related concept of the metamediary.

Infomediary

A business whose main source of revenue derives from capturing consumer information and developing detailed profiles of individual customers for use by third parties.

Some of the main new intermediaries identified by Sarkar *et al.* (1996) were:

| Box 2.2 | Infomediaries and metamediaries |

Infomediaries that have developed in response to the online marketplace include:

- *Online audience panel* or research providers selling information on online audience behaviour and media consumption such as Comscore, Hitwise and Nielsen Netratings listed in Table 2.2.
- *E-mail list brokers* who obtain permission to e-mail consumers or businesses, for example TMN Group plc (www.tmnplc.com) holds over 8 million e-mail addresses of UK consumers and businesses.
- *Advertising networks* such as DoubleClick (www.doubleclick.com) which is now owned by Google, or Google AdWords (http://adwords.google.com) which through relationships with publishers offers advertising services which are based partly on audience behaviour in responding to ads.

Metamediaries
Intermediaries providing information to assist with selection and discussion about different products and services.

'**Metamediary**'. This is an important class of intermediary that bring buyers and sellers together, providing independent information. The prefix 'meta' is from the Greek term meaning 'adjacent or with' and can be thought of as information an intermediary can provide about a product or service to assist with product selection. Metacritic (www.metacritic.com, Figure 2.9) provides reviews of music and movies from traditional publications and community reviewers and adds value by ranking them in order – an essential site! It is an ad-funded Internet start-up which was purchased by CNET Networks, also known for their comparison sites about electronic products and their shareware service (www.download.com).

Price comparison sites can be considered to be a type of metamediary although how truly independent they are will depend on their advertising and editorial policies!

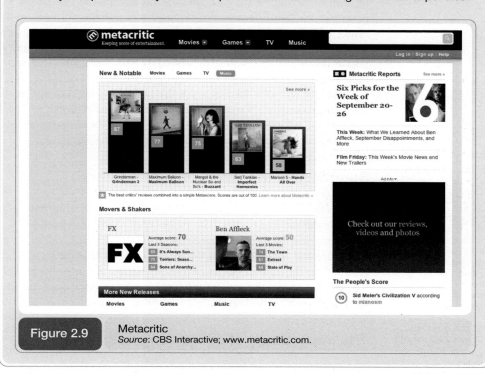

| Figure 2.9 | Metacritic
Source: CBS Interactive; www.metacritic.com. |

- Directories (such as Yahoo!, Excite).
- Search engines (AltaVista, Infoseek).
- Malls (BarclaySquare, Buckingham Gate).
- Virtual resellers (own-inventory and sell-direct, e.g. Amazon, CDNow).
- Financial intermediaries (offering digital cash and cheque payment services, such as Digicash).
- Forums, fan clubs and user groups (referred to collectively as 'virtual communities').
- Evaluators (sites which perform review or comparison of services).

Timmers (1999) identified another categorization of site types which we will review in the section on business models later in this chapter. It is useful to review how the role of online intermediaries has changed since this time to evaluate the importance of different types of intermediaries today in reaching and influencing an audience. General directories are now less important and have mainly merged with search engines since search is now the preferred form of access through the search engines that have risen to the top of the pile, namely Google, Yahoo! and Microsoft Bing. However, traditional directory owners such as the Yellow Pages (www.yell.com) and many small-scale directories of sites still exist in vertical sectors which give opportunities for visibility to be reviewed by companies.

Online shopping malls, which were online equivalents of the offline phenomenon, did not prove effective since there was no consumer benefit in visiting a shopping mall retailer when you could go direct to the retailer's website. Instead, sites in the evaluator category such as the price comparison search engines we considered earlier in this chapter such as Kelkoo and Pricerunner have become important destinations since they enable a choice of many suppliers across many categories based on price. E-retailers such as Amazon have remained important, but many such as CDNow have failed since they could not balance the expenditure on customer acquisition with the need to retain customers. Many of the forms of digital currency such as Digicash and E-cash did not prove popular. Instead, PayPal (www.paypal.com) became popular and was purchased by eBay (www.ebay.com, see Case Study 1.3). Paying for apps or books through Apple iTunes has also proved popular and micropayments via mobile phone service providers are increasing in popularity. The C2C virtual communities category described by Sarkar *et al.* has proved to be where many online users spend the most time via the social network.

A further type of intermediary is the *virtual marketplace* or virtual trading community of the B2B marketplace. From the supplier's or manufacturer's perspective they provide a new channel for selling their products. The form of these marketplaces is considered in more detail in '*Focus on* Electronic B2B marketplaces' in Chapter 7.

Summary of the types of intermediary

Portal

A website that acts as a gateway to information and services available on the Internet by providing search engines, directories and other services such as personalized news or free e-mail.

Search engines, spiders and robots

Automatic tools known as 'spiders' or 'robots' index registered sites. Users search this by typing keywords and are presented with a list of pages.

Intermediaries vary in scope and the services they offer, so naturally terms have evolved to describe the different types. The main types of intermediary you will identify as part of an online marketplace analysis are shown in Table 2.5. It is useful, in particular for marketers, to understand these terms since they act as a checklist for how their companies can be represented on the different types of intermediaries, online publishers and **portals**.

Table 2.6 shows the scale of the Internet can provide opportunities for providing content to niche or vertical audiences.

The importance of search engines

Search engines are a key type of intermediary for organizations marketing their services online, since today they are the primary method of finding information about a company and its products. Research compiled by Searchenginewatch (www.searchenginewatch. com) shows that over 90% of web users state that they use search engines to find informa-

Table 2.5	Different types of online intermediary

Type of intermediary	Characteristics	Example
Access portal	Associated with ISP or mobile service provider	• Orange (www.orange.co.uk) • Sky (www.bskyb.com)
Blog	Content updated through time, typically text-based, but can include video or audio delivered by RSS feeds (see Chapter 3 for details)	• Blogger (www.blogger.com) hosts many blogs • Many company blogs are created using Wordpress (www.wordpress.com) or Movable Type (www.movabletype.com)
Directory	Listings of sites and businesses details in categories	• Business.com (www.business.com) Yell (www.yell.com)
Geographical (region, country, local)	May be: • horizontal • vertical	• Google country versions • Yahoo! country and city versions • Craigslist (www.craigslist.com)
Horizontal or functional portal	Range of services: search engines, directories, news, recruitment, personal information management, shopping, etc.	• Yahoo! (www.yahoo.com) • Microsoft MSN (www.msn.com) • Google (www.google.com) which for a long period just focused on search
Marketplace or auction site	May be: • horizontal • vertical • geographical	• EC21(www.ec21.com) • eBay (www.ebay.com)
Price comparison site or aggregator	Compares products or services on different criteria including price	• Kelkoo in Europe and Asia (www.kelkoo.com) • Epinions in US (www.epinions.com)
Publisher site	Main focus is on consumer or business news or entertainment	• BBC (www.bbc.co.uk) • Guardian (www.guardian.co.uk) • ITWeek (www.itweek.co.uk)
Search engine	Main focus is on search	• Google (www.google.com) • Ask (www.ask.com) • Baidu in China (www.baidu.com) • Naver in S. Korea (www.naver.com)
Media type	May be: • voice (audio podcasts) • video (video webcasts) Delivered by streaming media or downloads of files	• Audio podcasts, for example Odeo (www.odeo.com) • Video, for example YouTube (www.youtube.com) • Multimedia publisher, e.g. BBC (www.bbc.co.uk)
Vertical intermediary	Covers a particular market or niche audience such as construction with news and other services	• Construction Plus (www.constructionplus.co.uk) • Chem Industry (www.chemindustry.com) • Barbour Index for B2B resources (www.barbour-index.com) • E-consultancy (www.econsultancy.com) • Focuses on e-business resources

tion online. Their importance can also be seen from their audience sizes by applying the tools in Table 2.2. We will show how search engines can be used for marketing in more detail in Chapter 9. As part of marketplace analysis it is useful for companies to assess demand for products and brand preferences in different countries using tools such as the Google Keyword

Table 2.6	Top 10 gaining properties by percentage change in unique visitors (US) April 2010 vs March 2010: Total US – home, work and university locations			
	Total unique visitors (000)			
	Mar-10	**Apr-10**	**% Change**	**Rank by unique visitors**
Total Internet : Total Audience	*212,593*	*213,019*	*0*	*N/A*
MLB.COM	8,126	13,588	67	102
NHL Network	4,527	6,092	35	232
Buzzle.com	4,804	5,697	19	244
ChaCha.com	5,779	6,686	16	207
The Mozilla Organization	29,798	34,244	15	28
The Home Depot, Inc.	11,200	12,597	12	111
Vevo	38,894	43,255	11	20
Ford Motor Company	5,011	5,571	11	247
Examiner.com Sites	12,563	13,936	11	97
Conduit.com	10,015	11,105	11	125

Source: comScore (2010).

Tool (Figure 2.10) which shows the volume of searches by consumers related to clothes in the UK in a one-month period. CPC is the cost per click charged to advertisers. Google uses this tool to encourage advertisers to use its Adwords advertising service.

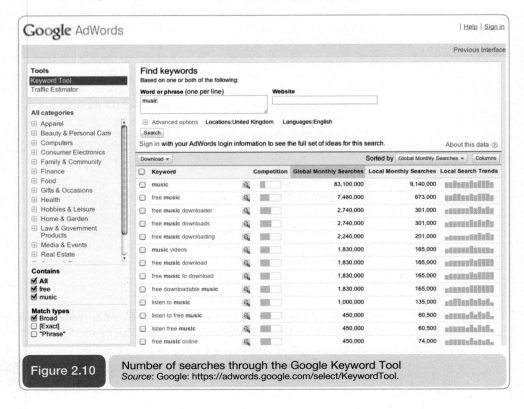

Figure 2.10	Number of searches through the Google Keyword Tool
	Source: Google: https://adwords.google.com/select/KeywordTool.

Business models for e-commerce

Online business model

A summary of how a company will generate a profit identifying its core product or service value proposition, target customers in different markets, position in the competitive online marketplace or value chain and its projections for revenue and costs.

A review of the different **online business models** made available through e-commerce is of relevance to existing companies, but in particular, start-up companies and online intermediaries. Venkatram (2000) pointed out that existing businesses needed to use the Internet to build on current business models, while at the same time experimenting with new business models. New business models may be important to gain a competitive advantage over existing competitors, while at the same time heading off similar business models created by new entrants. More commonly, they may simply offer a different revenue stream through advertising or charging for services in a new way. For Internet start-ups the viability of a business model and in particular their sources of revenue will be crucial to funding from venture capitalists. But what is a business model? Timmers (1999) defines a 'business model' as:

> *An architecture for product, service and information flows, including a description of the various business actors and their roles; and a description of the potential benefits for the various business actors; and a description of the sources of revenue.*

Investors will require eight key elements of the business model to be defined which will summarize the organization's e-business strategy:

1 **Value proposition.** Which products and or services will the company offer? This is supplemented by the added value defined using the online value proposition described in Chapter 5.
2 **Market or audience.** Which audience will the company serve and target with its communications? For example, business-to-business, business-to-consumer or not-for-profit? Within these categories are there particular audience segments that will be targeted? The scope of geographical markets such as countries, regions or towns needs to be defined. A communications plan as described in Chapters 8 and 9 will detail how the audience will be reached and influenced using online communications and offline communications such as advertising and public relations.
3 **Revenue models and cost base.** What are the specific revenue models that will generate different income streams? What are the main costs of the business forming its budget? How are these forecast to change through time?
4 **Competitive environment.** Who are the direct and indirect competitors for the service and which range of business models do they possess?
5 **Value chain and marketplace positioning.** How is the company and its services positioned in the value chain between customers and suppliers and in comparison with direct and indirect competitors?
6 **Representation in the physical and virtual world.** What is its relative representation in the physical and virtual world, e.g. high-street presence, online only, intermediary, mixture? How will the company influence its audience through a multi-channel buying process?
7 **Organizational structure.** How will the organization be internally structured to create, deliver and promote its service? (See Chapter 10.) How will it partner with other companies to provide services, for example through outsourcing?
8 **Management.** What experience in similar markets and companies do the managers have? Will they attract publicity?

Timmers (1999) identifies no less than eleven different types of business model that can be facilitated by the web. These are described mainly in terms of their revenue models and value chain or marketplace positioning. You will notice that many of these are in common with the intermediary types identified by Sarkar which we reviewed earlier in the chapter:

1 *E-shop* – marketing of a company or shop via the web.
2 *E-procurement* – electronic tendering and procurement of goods and services.

3 *E-malls* – a collection of e-shops such as Indigo Square (www.indigosquare.com).

4 *E-auctions* – eBay (www.ebay.com) is the best-known example and offers both B2B and B2C offerings.

5 *Virtual communities* – these can be B2C communities such as the major social networks or B2B communities such as those built around trade publishers; these are important for their potential in e-marketing and are described in the section on virtual communities in Chapter 9.

6 *Collaboration platforms* – these enable collaboration between businesses or individuals, e.g. E-groups, now part of Yahoo! (www.yahoo.com) services.

7 *Third-party marketplaces* – marketplaces are described in '*Focus on* Electronic B2B marketplaces' in Chapter 7.

8 *Value-chain integrators* – offer a range of services across the value chain.

9 *Value-chain service providers* – specialize in providing functions for a specific part of the value chain, such as the logistics company UPS (www.ups.com).

10 *Information brokerage* – provide information for consumers and businesses, often to assist in making the buying decision or for business operations or leisure.

11 *Trust and other services* – examples of trust services include Internet Shopping is Safe (ISIS) (www.imrg.org/isis) or TRUSTe (www.truste.org) which authenticate the quality of service provided by companies trading on the web.

Publishers are a major type of business model that is not clearly represented in the Timmers categories. We examine the revenue models for these in the next section. Riggins and Mitra (2007) have a more recent evaluation of alternative online marketplace players which we review in Chapter 7. Regardless of the descriptors used, the important point is that as part of strategy development, organizations should identify relevant partners and develop tactics for working with them appropriately.

Finally, Michael Rappa, a professor at North Carolina State University, has a useful compilation of examples of online business models in these and other categories in the link shown at the end of the chapter. At a lower level, Rappa identifies utilities providers that provide online services such as the Internet service providers and hosting companies we discuss in Chapter 3. Now complete Activity 2.2 to assess whether it is possible to simplify these business models and read Case study 2.2 to see examples of new revenue models that can be used by a forward-looking retailer.

Figure 2.11 suggests a different perspective for reviewing alternative business models. There are three different perspectives from which a business model can be viewed. Any individual organization can operate in different categories, as the examples below show, but most will focus on a single category for each perspective. Such a categorization of business models can be used as a tool for *formulating e-business strategy*. The three perspectives, with examples, are:

Activity 2.2	Exploring business models

Purpose

To explore the different types of business model available on the web and suggest a structure for evaluating business models.

Question

Identify overlap between the different business models identified by Timmers (1999). Can you group the different business models into different types of services? Do you think these business models operate in isolation?

Answers to activities can be found at www.pearsoned.co.uk/chaffey

1   *Marketplace position perspective.* The book publisher here is the manufacturer, Amazon is a retailer and Yahoo! is both a retailer and a marketplace intermediary.
2   *Revenue model perspective.* The book publisher can use the web to sell direct while Yahoo! and Amazon can take commission-based sales. Yahoo! also has advertising as a revenue model.
3   *Commercial arrangement perspective.* All three companies offer fixed-price sales, but, in its place as a marketplace intermediary, Yahoo! also offers alternatives.

Revenue models

Revenue models
Describe methods of generating income for an organization.

Revenue models specifically describe different techniques for generation of income. For existing companies, revenue models have mainly been based upon the income from sales of products or services. This may be either for selling direct from the manufacturer or supplier of the service or through an intermediary that will take a cut of the selling price. Both of these revenue models are, of course, still crucial in online trading. There may, however, be options for other methods of generating revenue; a manufacturer may be able to sell advertising space or sell digital services that were not previously possible.

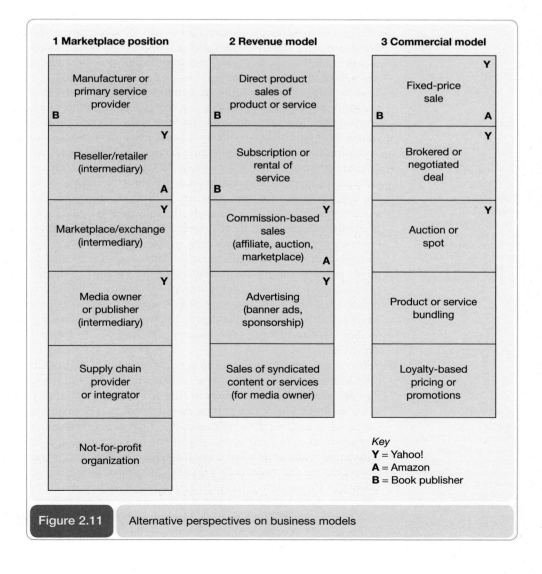

1 Marketplace position	**2 Revenue model**	**3 Commercial model**
Manufacturer or primary service provider **B**	Direct product sales of product or service **B**	**Y** Fixed-price sale **B** **A**
Y Reseller/retailer (intermediary) **A**	Subscription or rental of service **B**	**Y** Brokered or negotiated deal
Y Marketplace/exchange (intermediary)	**Y** Commission-based sales (affiliate, auction, marketplace) **A**	**Y** Auction or spot
Y Media owner or publisher (intermediary)	**Y** Advertising (banner ads, sponsorship)	Product or service bundling
Supply chain provider or integrator	Sales of syndicated content or services (for media owner)	Loyalty-based pricing or promotions
Not-for-profit organization		*Key* **Y** = Yahoo! **A** = Amazon **B** = Book publisher

Figure 2.11   Alternative perspectives on business models

Online publisher and intermediary revenue models

For a publisher, there are many options for generating revenue online based around advertising and fees for usage of the online service. These options, particularly the first four in the list below, can also be reviewed by other types of business such as price comparison sites, aggregators, social networks and destination sites which can also carry advertising to supplement revenue. The main types of online revenue model are:

CPM (cost per thousand)

The cost to the advertiser (or the revenue received by the publisher) when an ad is served 1,000 times.

CPC (cost per click)

The cost to the advertiser (or the revenue received by the publisher) of each click of a link to a third-party site.

1 **CPM display advertising on site. CPM** stands for 'cost per thousand' where M denotes 'mille'. This is the traditional method by which site owners charge a fee for advertising. The site owner charges advertisers a rate card price (for example £50 CPM) according to the number of times ad are served to site visitors. Ads may be served by the site owner's own ad server or more commonly through a third-party ad network service such as DoubleClick (which is owned by Google).

2 **CPC advertising on site (pay-per-click text ads)** CPC stands for 'cost per click'. Advertisers are charged not simply for the number of times their ads are displayed, but according to the number of times they are clicked upon. These are typically text ads served by a search engine such as Google (www.google.com) on what is known as its content network. Google has its Adsense (http://adsense.google.com) programme for publishers which enables them to offer text- or image-based ads typically on a CPC basis, but optionally on a CPM basis. Typical costs per click can be surprisingly high, i.e. they are in the range £0.10 to £4, but sometimes up to £20 for some categories such as 'life insurance'. The revenue for search engines and publishers from these sources can also be significant: Google's annual reports (http://investor.google.com) show that this is between a quarter and a third of Google's revenue.

3 **Sponsorship of site sections or content types (typically fixed fee for a period).** A company can pay to advertise a site channel or section. For example, the bank HSBC sponsors the Money section on the Orange broadband provider portal (www.orange.co.uk). This type of deal is often struck for a fixed amount per year. It may also be part of a reciprocal arrangement, sometimes known as a 'contra-deal' where neither party pays.

CPA (cost per acquisition)

The cost to the advertiser (or the revenue received by the publisher) for each outcome such as a lead or sale generated after a click to a third-party site.

4 **Affiliate revenue (CPA, but could be CPC).** Affiliate revenue is commission-based, for example I display Amazon books on my site SmartInsights.com and receive around 5% of the cover price as a fee from Amazon. Such an arrangement is sometimes known as **cost per acquisition (CPA)**. Increasingly, this approach is replacing CPM or CPC approaches where the advertiser has more negotiating power. For example, manufacturing company Unilever negotiates CPA deals with online publishers where it is paid for every e-mail address captured by a campaign rather than a traditional CPM deal. However, it depends on the power of the publisher, who will often receive more revenue overall for CPM deals. After all, the publisher cannot influence the quality of the ad creative or the incentivization to click which will affect the clickthrough rate and so earnings from the ad.

5 **Transaction fee revenue.** A company receives a fee for facilitating a transaction. Examples include eBay and Paypal who charge a percentage of the transaction cost between buyer and seller.

6 **Subscription access to content or services.** A range of documents can be accessed from a publisher for a fixed period. These are often referred to as premium services on websites.

7 **Pay-per-view access to documents.** Here payment occurs for single access to a document, video or music clip which can be downloaded. It may or may not be protected with a password or **digital rights management**. I pay to access detailed best-practice guides on Internet marketing from Marketing Sherpa (www.marketingsherpa.com).

Digital rights management (DRM)

The use of different technologies to protect the distribution of digital services or content such as software, music, movies or other digital data.

8 **Subscriber data access for e-mail marketing.** The data a site owner has about its customers are also potentially valuable since it can send different forms of e-mail to its customers if they have given their permission that they are happy to receive e-mail from either the publisher or third parties. The site owner can charge for adverts placed in its newsletter or can deliver a separate message on behalf of the advertiser (sometimes known as 'list rental'). A related approach is to conduct market research with the site customers.

Calculating revenue for an online business

Site owners can develop models (Figure 2.11) of potential revenue depending on the mix of revenue-generating techniques from the four main revenue options they use on the site given in the options above.

Consider the capacity of a site owner to maximize revenue or 'monetize' their site – which factors will be important? The model will be based on assumptions about the level of traffic and number of pages viewed plus the interaction with different types of ad unit. Their ability to maximize revenue will be based on these factors which can be modelled in the spreadsheet shown in Figure 2.12:

- *Number and size of ad units.* This is a delicate balance between the number of ad units in each site section or page – too many obtrusive ad units may present a bad experience for site users, too few will reduce revenue. Figure 2.12 has a parameter for the number of ad units or containers in each ad revenue category. There is a tension with advertisers who know that the awareness and response they generate from their ads is maximized when they are as large as practical and in prominent placements. A more accurate revenue model would develop revenue for different page types such as the home page and different page categories, e.g. the money or travel sections.
- *Capacity to sell advertising.* Figure 2.12 also has a parameter for the percentage of ad inventory sold in each category – for example, for the CPM ad display revenue only 40% of inventory may be sold. This is why you may see publisher sites with their own 'house ads' – it is a sign they have been unable to sell all their ad space. A benefit of using the Google AdSense publisher programme is that inventory is commonly all used.
- *Fee levels negotiated for different advertising models.* These will depend on the market competition or demand for advertising space. For 'pay-per-performance' advertising options such as the CPC and CPA models, it also depends on the response. In the first case, the site owner only receives revenue when the ad is clicked upon and in the second case, the site owner only receives revenue when the ad is clicked upon and a product is purchased on the destination merchant site.
- *Traffic volumes.* More visitors equate to more opportunities to generate revenue through serving more pages (which helps with CPM-based advertising) or more clicks to third-party sites (which helps generate revenue from CPC and CPA deals).
- *Visitor engagement.* The longer visitors stay on a site (its 'stickiness'), the more page views that will accumulate, which again gives more opportunities for ad revenue. For a destination site a typical number of page views per visit would be in the range 5 to 10, but for a social network, media site or community the figure could be greater than 30.

Considering all of these approaches to revenue generation together, the site owner will seek to use the best combination of these techniques to maximize the revenue. An illustration of this approach is shown in Figure 2.12.

To assess how effective different pages or sites in their portfolio are at generating revenue using these techniques, site owners will use two approaches. The first is eCPM, or effective cost per thousand. This looks at the total the advertiser can charge (or cost to advertisers) for each page or site. Through increasing the number of ad units on each page this value will increase. The other alternative to assess page or site revenue-generating effectiveness is revenue per click (RPC), also known as 'earnings per click' (EPC). Alternatively, revenue can be calculated as ad revenue per 1,000 site visitors. This is particularly important for affiliate marketers who make money through commission when their visitors click through to third-party retail sites, and then purchase there.

Activity 2.3 explores some of the revenue models that are possible.

Ad revenue option	Measure	Site
	Pages served	**100,000**
Display advertising (CPM)	CPM (Cost Per Thousand)	£2
	% Inventory served	40%
	Avg. Clickthrough (CTR %)	0.10%
	Ad units served per page	2
	Clicks – CPM ads	80
	Revenue – display ads	**£160**
	Earnings per 100 clicks (EPC)	**£200.0**
	eCPM – display ads	**£1.60**
Fixed run-of-site sponsorship	% Inventory served	100%
	Avg. Clickthrough (CTR %)	0.30%
	Ad units served 1	1
	Clicks – fixed	300
	Revenue – fixed sponsorship	**£3,000**
	Earnings per 100 clicks (EPC)	**£1,000.0**
	eCPM – fixed	**£30.00**
Text ad advertising (CPC)	% Inventory served	100%
	Avg. Clickthrough (CTR %)	1.00%
	Avg. Cost Per Click	£0.30
	Ad units served per page	1
	Clicks – CPC ads	1,000
	Revenue – CPC ads	**£300**
	Earnings per 100 clicks (EPC)	**£30.0**
	eCPM – CPC ads	**£3**
Affiliate commission	% Inventory served	100%
	Avg. Clickthrough (CTR %)	0.50%
	Ad units served per page	1
	Clicks – Affiliates	500
	Desination conversion rate (%)	3%
	Average order value	£100
	Commission %	10%
	Revenue – affiliates	**£150**
	Earnings per 100 clicks (EPC)	**£30.0**
	eCPM – affiliates	**£1.50**
Overall metrics for site	**Clicks – total**	**1,880**
	Revenue – total	**£3,610**
	Earnings per 100 clicks (EPC) – total	**£192.02**
	eCPM – total	**£36.10**

Blue cells = input variables – vary these for 'what-if' analysis

Orange cells = Output variables (calculated – **do not overtype**)

Figure 2.12 Example spreadsheet for calculating a site revenue model
Note: Available for download at www.smartinsights.com/conversion-model-spreadsheets/.

Activity 2.3	Revenue models at e-business portals

Purpose

To illustrate the range of revenue-generating opportunities for an online publisher. This site looks at three alternative approaches for publishing, referencing three different types of portal.

Question

Visit each of the sites in this category:

1 Summarize the revenue models which are used for each site by looking at the information for advertisers and affiliates.

2 What are the advantages and disadvantages of the different revenue models for the site audience and the site owner?

3 Given an equivalent audience, which of these sites do you think would generate the most revenue? You could develop a simple spreadsheet model based on the following figures:
- *Monthly site visitors*: 100,000, 0.5% of these visitors click through to affiliate sites where 2% go on to buy business reports or services at an average order value of €100.
- *Monthly page views*: 1,000,000, average of three ads displayed for different advertisers at €20 CPM (we are assuming all ad inventory is sold, which is rarely true in reality).
- *Subscribers to weekly newsletter*: 50,000. Each newsletter broadcast four times per month has four advertisers each paying at a rate of €10 CPM.

Note: These are not actual figures for any of these sites.

The sites are:
- Econsultancy (www.econsultancy.com), Figure 2.13.
- Marketing Sherpa (www.marketingsherpa.com).

Answers to activities can be found at www.pearsoned.co.uk/chaffey

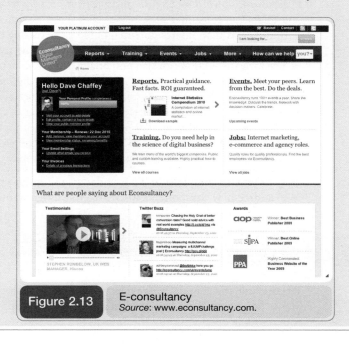

Figure 2.13	E-consultancy *Source*: www.econsultancy.com.

Auction business models

With the success of eBay (www.ebay.com, Case study 1.3), auctions have been highlighted as one of the new business models for the Internet. But how do auctions work, what infrastructure is required and what is the potential for B2B auctions? In this section we will address some of these issues.

Auctions involve determination of the basis for product or service exchange between a buyer and seller according to particular trading rules that help select the best match between the buyer and seller from a number of participants.

Klein (1997) identifies different roles for auction:

1 *Price discovery* – an example of price discovery is in the traditional consumer auction involving bidding for antiques. Antiques do not have standardized prices, but the auction can help establish a realistic market price through a gathering of buyers.
2 *Efficient allocation mechanism* – the sale of items that are difficult to distribute through traditional channels falls into this category. Examples include 'damaged inventory' that has a limited shelf life or is only available at a particular time such as aircraft flight or theatre tickets. Lastminute.com (www.lastminute.com) has specialized in disposal of this type of inventory in Europe, not always by means of auctions.
3 *Distribution mechanism* – as a means of attracting particular audiences.
4 *Coordination mechanism* – here the auction is used to coordinate the sale of a product to a number of interested parties; an example is the broadband spectrum licences for 3G telecoms in the UK (www.spectrumauctions.gov.uk).

Offer

A commitment by a trader to sell under certain conditions.

Bid

A commitment by a trader to purchase under certain conditions.

To understand auctions it is important to distinguish between offers and bids. An **offer** is a commitment for a trader to sell under certain conditions such as a minimum price. A **bid** is made by a trader to buy under certain conditions such as a commitment to purchase at a particular price.

There are many potential combinations of the sequence of bids and offers and these have been described by Reck (1997). Despite the combinations, two main types of auction can be identified:

1 *Forward, upward or English auction (initiated by seller)*. These are the types of auctions available on consumer sites such as eBay. For these auctions, the seller sets the rules and the timing, and then invites potential bidders. Increasing bids are placed within a certain time limit and the highest bid will succeed provided the reserve (minimum) price is exceeded. The forward auction can also potentially be used to perform price discovery in a market.
2 *Reverse, downward or Dutch auction (initiated by buyer)*. These are more common on business-to-business marketplaces. For these auctions, the buyer sets the rules and the timing. Here, the buyer places a request for tender or quotation (RFQ) and many suppliers compete, decreasing the price, with the supplier whom the buyer selects getting the contract. This will not necessarily be the lowest price since other factors such as quality and capability to deliver will be taken into account. Companies may use reverse auctions to:

- rationalize suppliers in a particular spending category;
- source new components in an area they are unfamiliar with.

Internet start-up companies

Dot-coms

Businesses whose main trading presence is on the Internet.

To conclude the chapter, we review how to evaluate the potential of new Internet start-ups. Many 'dot-coms' were launched in response to the opportunities of new business and revenue models opened up by the Internet in the mid-to-late 1990s. We also consider what lessons can be learnt from the dot-com failures. But Table 1.1 showed that innovation and the growth of Internet pureplays did not end in 2000, but rather many successful online companies such as digital publishers and social networks have developed since then.

From 'bricks and mortar' to 'clicks and mortar'

Bricks and mortar
A traditional organization with limited online presence.

Clicks and mortar
A business combining an online and offline presence.

Clicks only or Internet pureplay
An organization with principally an online presence.

These expressions were introduced in 1999/2000 to refer to traditional '**bricks and mortar**' enterprises with a physical presence, but limited Internet presence. In the UK, an example of a 'bricks and mortar' store would be the bookseller Waterstones (www.waterstones.co.uk), which when it ventured online would become '**clicks and mortar**'. Significantly, in 2001 Waterstones decided it was most cost-effective to manage the Internet channel through a partnership with Amazon (www.amazon.co.uk). In 2006 it reversed this decision and set up its own independent site once more. As mentioned above, some virtual merchants such as Amazon that need to operate warehouses and shops to sustain growth have also become 'clicks and mortar' companies. An **Internet 'pureplay'** which only has an online representation is referred to as '**clicks only**'. A pureplay typically has no retail distribution network. They may have phone-based customer service, as is the case with office supplier Euroffice (www.euroffice.co.uk), or not, as is the case with financial services provider Zopa (www.zopa.com), or may offer phone service for more valuable customers, as is the case with hardware provider dabs.com (www.dabs.com).

Assessing e-businesses

Internet pureplay companies are often perceived as dynamic and successful owing to the rapid increase in visitors to sites, or sales, or due to initial valuations on stock markets. In reality, it is difficult to assess the success of these companies since despite positive indications in terms of sales or audience, the companies have often not been profitable. Consider the three major socal networks: Bebo, Facebook or MySpace – none of these was profitable at the time of writing the fourth edition.

Boo.com is an interesting case of the potential and pitfalls of an e-commerce start-up and criteria for success, or one could say of 'how not to do it'. The boo.com site was launched in November 1999 following two significant delays in launching and in January 2000 it was reported that 100 of its 400 employees had been made redundant due to disappointing initial revenues of about £60,000 in the Christmas period. Boo faced a high '**burn rate**' because of the imbalance between promotion and site development costs and revenues. As a consequence, it appeared to change its strategy by offering discounts of up to 40 per cent on fashions from the previous season. Closure followed in mid-2000 and the boo.com brand was purchased by an American entrepreneur who still continues to use the brand, as you can see on www.boo.com. Boo.com features as a case study in Chapter 5. Investors provided a reported £74 million in capital. This enthusiasm is partly based on the experience of two of the founders in creating bokus.com, a relatively successful online bookseller.

Burn rate
The speed at which dot-coms spent investors' money.

As with all new companies, it is difficult for investors to assess the long-term sustainability of start-ups. There are a number of approaches that can be used to assess the success and sustainability of these companies. There have been many examples where it has been suggested that dot-com companies have been overvalued by investors who are keen to make a fast return from their investments. There were some clear anomalies if traditional companies are compared to dot-coms.

Valuing Internet start-ups

Desmet *et al.* (2000) apply traditional discounted cash flow techniques to assess the potential value of Internet start-ups or dot-coms. They point out that traditional techniques do not work well when profitability is negative, but revenues are growing rapidly. They suggest that for new companies the critical factors to model when considering the future success of a company are:

1 The cost of acquiring a customer through marketing.
2 The contribution margin per customer (before acquisition cost).
3 The average annual revenues per year from customers and other revenues such as banner advertising and affiliate revenues.
4 The total number of customers.
5 The customer **churn rate**.

Churn rate

The proportion of customers (typically subscribers) that no longer purchase a company's products in a time period.

As would be expected intuitively, modelling using these variables indicates that for companies with a similar revenue per customer, contribution margin and advertising costs, it is the churn rate that will govern their long-term success. To look at this another way, given the high costs of customer acquisition for a new company, it is the ability to retain customers for repeat purchases which governs the long-term success of companies. This then forces dot-com retailers to compete on low prices with low margins to retain customers.

A structured evaluation of the success and sustainability of UK Internet start-ups has been undertaken by management consultancy Bain and Company in conjunction with *Management Today* magazine and was described in Gwyther (1999). Six criteria were used to assess the companies as follows.

1 Concept

This describes the strength of the business model. It includes:

- potential to generate revenue including the size of the market targeted;
- superior 'customer value', in other words how well the value proposition of the service is differentiated from that of competitors;
- first-mover advantage (less easy to achieve today).

2 Innovation

This criterion looks at another aspect of the business concept, which is the extent to which the business model merely imitates existing real-world or online models. Note that imitation is not necessarily a problem if it is applied to a different market or audience or if the experience is superior and positive word-of-mouth is generated.

3 Execution

A good business model does not, of course, guarantee success. If there are problems with aspects of the implementation of the idea, then the start-up will fail. Aspects of execution that can be seen to have failed for some companies are:

- Promotion – online or offline techniques are insufficient to attract sufficient visitors to the site.
- Performance, availability and security – some sites have been victims of their own success and have not been able to deliver fast access to the sites or technical problems have meant that the service is unavailable or insecure. Some sites have been unavailable despite large-scale advertising campaigns due to delays in creating the website and its supporting infrastructure.
- Fulfilment – the site itself may be effective, but customer service and consequently brand image will be adversely affected if products are not despatched correctly or promptly.

4 Traffic

This criterion is measured in terms of the number of visitors, the number of pages they visit and the number of transactions they make which control the online ad revenues. Page impressions or visits are not necessarily an indication of success but are dependent on the business model. After the viability of the business model, how it will be promoted is arguably the most important aspect for a start-up. For most companies a critical volume of loyal, returning and revenue-generating users of a service is required to repay the investment in these companies. Promotion from zero base is difficult and costly if there is a need to reach a wide audience. An important decision is the investment in promotion and how it is split between online and offline techniques. Perhaps surprisingly, to reach the mass market, traditional advertising was required to get the message about the service across clearly to the numbers required. For example, Boo had major TV and newspaper campaigns which generated awareness and visits, but didn't translate to sufficient initial or repeat transactions. Some of the other start-up companies such as lastminute.com and Zopa.com have been able to grow without the initial investment in advertising. These have grown more organically, helped by favourable word of mouth and mentions in newspaper features supported by some traditional advertising. Promotion for all these companies seems to indicate that the Internet medium is simply adding an additional dimension to the communications mix and that traditional advertising is still required.

5 Financing

This describes the ability of the company to attract venture capital or other funding to help execute the idea. It is particularly important given the cost of promoting these new concepts.

6 Profile

This is the ability of the company to generate favourable publicity and to create awareness within its target market.

These six criteria can be compared with the other elements of business and revenue models which we discussed earlier in this chapter.

Case Study 2.1	i-to-i – a global marketplace for a start-up company

This case is about a specialist travel and education company, focusing on its online TEFL (Teaching English as a Foreign Language) courses. The case illustrates the importance of marketplace analysis.

i-to-i background

i-to-i (www.i-to-i.com) is an international organization with offices in the UK, USA, Ireland and Australia. Twenty thousand people have selected i-to-i as they travel on ventures to support 500 worthwhile projects in five continents and it has also trained a further 80,000 people as TEFL (Teaching English as a Foreign Language) teachers. This service is offered through the main site and also through a specialist online TEFL site (www.onlinetefl.com) on which this case focuses.

The history of i-to-i

The founder of i-to-i, Deirdre Bounds, was inspired to create the company following a career break which

took her to teach English in Japan, China and Greece and drive a backpackers' bus in Sydney. The company initially started through creating TEFL courses eventually leading to organizing volunteer projects.

Since 2003 the company has supported the i-to-i Foundation, a registered charity committed to providing funds to the most needy community and ecological projects in the i-to-i family.

In 2007, i-to-i became part of the TUI travel group.

Proposition

The main features of the i-to-i TEFL proposition are:

- *International accreditation*: i-to-i is externally accredited by the ODLQC in order to ensure that its courses are rigorously monitored and always meet the highest industry standards.
- *World-class reputation*: i-to-i has four offices worldwide and it has over 12 years' experience teaching TEFL.

- *Partnership*: i-to-i is preferred TEFL course provider for STA Travel, Opodo and Lonely Planet.
- *Complete student support*: Students receive advice on how to get work abroad, how best to prepare for their time away and up to the minute advice on current job opportunities.
- *Highly experienced tutors*: All i-to-i tutors have at least three years' overseas teaching experience.

This proposition is backed up by 'the i-to-i TEFL Promise'.

1 We will beat any equivalent and cheaper course by 150%.
2 If you're not entirely satisfied after the first seven days, we'll give you a full refund.
3 Our experience, our high academic standards and the quality of our courses mean that i-to-i TEFL certificates are recognized by thousands of language schools worldwide.

Additionally i-to-i can offer to help students find TEFL jobs abroad.

Audience segmentation

The main segmentation used by i-to-i is geographic:

- UK
- North America
- Europe
- Australia and New Zealand
- Rest-of-world (same as UK)

Different brochures are also available for each geographical area.

Information is also collected on an optional basis about prospects' age and status, although these are not used for targeting e-mails. Status categories are:

- Student
- Employed
- Self-employed
- Career break
- Unemployed
- Retired

Since optional information is restricted to certain lead tools it is not used to target e-mails. For weekend TEFL courses, postcode / city is used to target courses to prospects.

Competitors

Some of the main competitors for online TEFL courses based in the UK and Australia include:

- www.cactustefl.com
- www.teflonline.com
- www.eslbase.com

In the US, competitors who also operate in the UK and other countries include:

- www.teflcorp.com/
- ITTP (International Tefl-Tesol-Online) www.tefl-tesol-online.com

Media mix

i-to-i use a combination of these digital media channels to drive visits, leads and sales:

- Pay per click (PPC) (mainly Google AdWords)
- Social media marketing using Facebook, Twitter and i-to-i's own traveller community
- Natural search
- Affiliate marketing
- Display advertising
- E-mail marketing

Conversion process

Detailed content to help visitors decide on purchasing a course is available on the site. This includes module outlines and FAQs. Specific landing pages have not been used to convert visitors from paid search or affiliates, for example. Instead, the destination page for visitors from referring sites is the main category page for the product preference indicated by the search performed (for example, online TEFL).

A number of engagement devices are used to generate leads, including brochures, 'TEFL tasters', an e-mail guide and campaign promotions such as winning a course.

Such leads are followed up through a series of welcome e-mails. Results are monitored, but e-mails are not proactively followed up on. There is no phone follow-up of leads due to the relative low value of the products, but site visitors are encouraged to ring or set up a call-back which often leads to higher conversion rates.

Marketplace challenges

The main marketplace challenges faced by i-to-i are:

1 Increasing their presence and conversion effectiveness in a competitive market in different geographies:

(a) i-to-i have good exposure in the UK, its primary market, but operate in a cluttered marketplace with price being the main differentiator (products are similar and some competitors are just as established etc.).

(b) Research suggests that there is good opportunity within the US, but exposure is more limited because of the cost of pay per click advertising and because presence in natural search favours the US.

(c) Rest-of-world sales (outside of UK, USA, Canada, Ireland/Europe, Australia, New Zealand) are increasing and this is believed to be a growing market. i-to-i seek to penetrate these markets, but in a cost-effective way that will not distract attention from main markets.

2 Increasing demand through reaching and educating those considering travel who are not aware of TEFL courses and the opportunities they unlock. For example, many will look for casual work in other countries, e.g. in bars or in agriculture, but will be unaware of TEFL.

Source: Smart Insights (2010) i-to-i case study. Written by Dave Chaffey and Dan Bosomworth with agreement from the company.

Questions

1 Select one country that i-to-i operate in and summarize the main types of sites and businesses involved using a marketplace map (Figure 2.3).

2 Review the different factors that i-to-i will need to review to gauge the commercial effectiveness of their online presence in different geographic markets.

Why dot-coms failed

At the end of Chapter 5 we review the reasons for failed e-business strategies and, in Case study 5.3, we examine the reasons for one of the most spectacular dot-com failures – Boo. com. We will see that in many cases it was a case of an unsound business strategy, or ideas before their time. Many of the dot-coms were founded on innovative ideas which required a large shift in consumer behaviour. A rigorous demand analysis would have shown that, at the time, there were relatively few Internet users, with the majority on dial-up connections, so there wasn't the demand for these services. We see in the Boo.com example that there were also failings in implementation, with technology infrastructure resulting in services that were simply too slow and the consequent poor experience leading to sales conversion rates and returning customer rates that were too low for a sustainable business.

Remember, though, that many companies that identified a niche and carefully controlled their growth did survive, of which 'boys' toys site' Firebox (Mini case study 2.2) is a great example.

Mini Case Study 2.2	Firebox.com survives the dot-com boom and bust

Firebox.com (Figure 2.14) opened its virtual doors in 1998 as hotbox.co.uk, an Internet retailer which was founded by university flatmates Michael Smith and Tom Boardman. Initially operating out of Cardiff, the company saw rapid initial growth due to the success of the founders' invention, the Shot Glass Chess Set. In the summer of 1999 the company moved to London and relaunched as Firebox.com.

eSuperbrands (2005) described Firebox products as 'unique, unusual and quirky products from around the world'. Examples include glowing alarm clocks, light sabres, duct tape wallets and, of course, lava lamps. With many traditional retailers and other niche players operating in this sector now, Firebox positions itself as being one of the first outlets for innovative products. Firebox makes use of the collaborative nature of the web with C2C interactions where Firebox.com customers describe their experiences with products and even send in photos and videos of them in action!

Initially a 'pureplay' Internet-only business, Firebox is now a multi-channel retailer, providing a mail-order service via its catalogue and corporate products (including sales promotion and staff incentives for Yahoo!, Oracle, Five, Siemens and Santander plus wholesale and trade suppliers). The trade suppliers then distribute products to other online and offline e-retailers.

Firebox received £500,000 of investment from New Media Spark, with further funding from private investors. Sales have grown 156% a year from £262,000 in 2000 to £4.4m in 2003 and £8 million in 2004 from 175,000 orders. In the same year, it received 4.5 million page impressions and 680,000 monthly unique visitors, according to the Nielsen//Netratings panel (eSuperbrands, 2005). Firebox.com became profitable in 2001.

One of the reasons for the success of Firebox is the way it has embraced traditional channels to market. Silicon.com (2004) reports that head of PR Charlie Morgan explained:

In a market place that was fast becoming cluttered there was a strong need to both expand the customer base and ensure that Firebox itself grew as a brand. By building in a programme of catalogue drops, Firebox aimed to recruit many new customers who had not thought of the internet as a purchasing medium, increase turnover and of course grow the brand.

In 2009, the company reported that the Firebox.com website attracted nearly 10m visits in 2009 and served 48m page impressions according to Google Analytics. The e-mail newsletter is sent fortnightly to over 550,000 recipients while 7 million copies of the catalogue are circulated annually. In 2008, revenue of the business was £11 million.

Source: Company website, About Us, eSuperbrands (2005) and Silicon.com (2004). With thanks to www.firebox.com.

Figure 2.14   Firebox
Source: www.firebox.com.

As a conclusion to this chapter, consider Case study 2.2 which highlights the issues faced by a new e-business launched in 2005.

Case Study 2.2	Zopa launches a new lending model

This case shows how it is still possible to develop radical new online business models. It shows how an online business can be launched without large-scale expenditure on advertising and how it needs to be well targeted at its intended audience.

Context

It might be thought that innovation in business models was left behind in the dot-com era, but still fledgling businesses are launching new online services. Zopa is an interesting example of a pureplay social or peer-to-peer lending service launched in March 2005, with US and Italian sites launching in 2007, and the Japanese site in 2008. By 2010 Zopa lenders had lent Zopa borrowers more than £100m since launch.

Zopa is an online service which enables borrowers and lenders to bypass the big high-street banks. Since launch in March 2005, £20 million in unsecured personal loans have been arranged at Zopa in the UK. There are over 150,000 UK members and 200,000 worldwide. Zopa is an example of a consumer-to-consumer (peer-to-peer) exchange intermediary. It illustrates the challenges and opportunities of launching a new business online, especially one with a new business model.

Zopa stands for 'zone of possible agreement' which is a term from business theory. It refers to the overlap between one person's bottom line (the lowest they're prepared to receive for something they are offering) and another person's top line (the most they're prepared to pay for something). In practice, this approach underpins negotiations about the majority of types of products and services.

The business model

The exchange provides a matching facility between people who want to borrow with people who want to lend. Significantly, each lender's money is parcelled out between at least 50 borrowers. Zopa revenue is based on charging borrowers 1 per cent of their loan as a fee, and from commission on any repayment protection insurance that the borrower selects. At the time of launch, Zopa estimated it needed to gain just a 0.2 per cent share of the UK loan market to break even, which it could achieve within 18 months of launch.

In 2007, listings were launched (http://uk.zopa.com/ZopaWeb/Listings/) where loans can be requested by individuals in a similar way to eBay listings.

The main benefit for borrowers is that they can borrow relatively cheaply over shorter periods for small amounts.

This is the reverse of banks, where if you borrow more and for longer it gets cheaper. The service will also appeal to borrowers who have difficulty gaining credit ratings from traditional financial services providers.

For lenders, higher returns are possible than through traditional savings accounts if there are no bad debts. These are in the range of 20 to 30% higher than putting money in a deposit account, but of course, there is the risk of bad debt. Lenders choose the minimum interest rate that they are prepared to accept after bad debt has been taken into account for different markets within Zopa. Borrowers are placed in different risk categories with different interest rates according to their credit histories (using the same Equifax-based credit ratings as used by the banks) and lenders can decide which balance of risk against return they require.

Borrowers who fail to pay are pursued through the same mechanism as banks use and also get a black mark against their credit histories. But, for the lender, their investment is not protected by any compensation scheme, unless they have been defrauded.

The *Financial Times* reported that banks don't currently see Zopa as a threat to their high-street business. One financial analyst said Zopa was 'one of these things that could catch on but probably won't'.

Zopa does not have a contact centre. According to its website, enquiries to Zopa are restricted to e-mail in order to keep its costs down. However, there is a service promise of answering e-mails within 3 hours during working hours.

Although the service was launched initially in the UK in 2005, *Financial Times* (2005) reported that Zopa has 20 countries where people want to set up franchises. Other countries include China, New Zealand, India and some South American countries.

The peer-to-peer lending marketplace now has several providers. For example, the social lending site Kiva allows lenders to give to a specific entrepreneur in a poor or developing world country. In the US, Prosper (www.prosper.com) has over 600,000 members and uses a loan listing model.

About the founders

The three founders of Zopa are chief executive Richard Duvall, chief financial officer James Alexander and David Nicholson, inventor of the concept and business architect. All were involved with Egg, with Richard Duvall creating the online bank for Prudential in 1998. Mr Alexander had been strategy director at Egg after

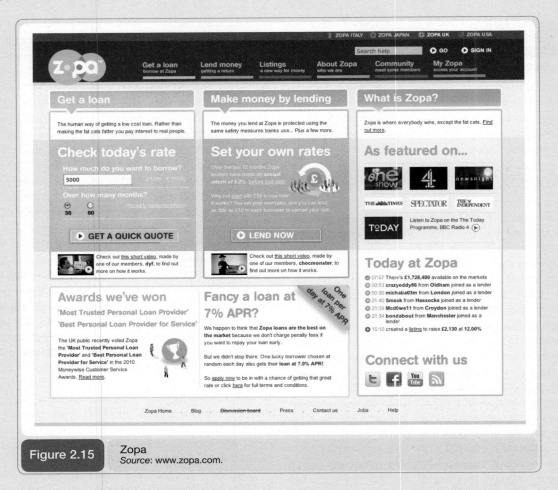

Figure 2.15	Zopa

Source: www.zopa.com.

joining in 2000, and previously had written the business plan for Smile, another online bank owned by the Co-operative Bank. The founders were also joined by Sarah Matthews from Egg who was Egg's brand development director.

Target market

The idea for the business was developed from market research that showed there was a potential market of 'freeformers' to be tapped.

Freeformers are typically not in standard employment, rather they are self-employed or complete work that is project-based or freelance. Examples include consultants and entrepreneurs. Consequently, their incomes and lifestyles may be irregular, although they may still be assessed as creditworthy. According to James Alexander, 'they're people who are not understood by banks, which value stability in people's lives and income over everything else'. The Institute of Directors (IOD) (2005) reported that the research showed that freeformers had 'much less of a spending model of money and much more of an asset model'.

Surprisingly, the research indicated a large number of freeformers. *New Media Age* reported Duvall as estimating that in the UK there may be around 6 million freeformers (of a population of around 60 million). Duvall is quoted as saying: 'it's a group that's growing really quickly. I think in 10 or 15 years time most people will work this way. It's happening right across the developed world. We've been doing some research in the US and we think there are some 30 or 40 million people there with these attitudes and behaviours.'

Some of the directors see themselves as freeformers: they have multiple interests and do not only work for Zopa; James Alexander works for one day a week in a charity and Sarah Matthews works just 3 days a week for Zopa. You can see example personas of typical borrowers and lenders on the website: www.zopa.com/ ZopaWeb/public/how/zopamembers.shtml.

From reviewing the customer base, lenders and borrowers are often united by a desire to distance themselves from conventional institutions. James Alexander says: 'I spend a lot of time talking to members and have found enormous goodwill towards the idea, which is really like lending to family members or within a community.'

But he also says that some of the lenders are simply entrepreneurs who have the funds, understand portfolio diversification and risk and are lending on Zopa alongside other investments.

Business status

The *Financial Times* (2005) reported that Zopa had just 300 members at launch, but within 4 months it had 26,000 members. According to James Alexander, around 35 per cent are lenders, who between them have £3m of capital waiting to be distributed. The company has not, to date, revealed how much has been lent, but average loans have been between £2,000 and £5,000. Moneyfacts.co.uk isn't showing any current accounts with more than 5 per cent interest, but Zopa is a riskier product, so you'd expect better rates. Unlike a deposit account, it's not covered by any compensation schemes.

Marketing communications

The launch of Zopa has been quite different from Egg and other dot-coms at the turn of the millennium. Many companies at that time invested large amounts in offline media such as TV and print to rapidly grow awareness and to explain their proposition to customers.

Instead, Zopa has followed a different communications strategy which has relied on word of mouth and PR with some online marketing activities where the cost of customer acquisition can be controlled. The launch of such a model and the history of its founders make it relatively easy to have major pieces about the item in relevant newspapers and magazines such as *The Guardian, The Financial Times, The Economist* and the Institute of Directors house magazine, which its target audience may read. Around launch, IOD (2005) reports that Duvall's PR agency, Sputnik, achieved 200 million

opportunities for the new company to be read about. Of course, not all coverage is favourable: many of the articles explored the risk of lending and the viability of the start-up. However, others have pointed out that the rates for the best-rated 'A category' borrowers are better than any commercial loan offered by a bank and for lenders, rates are better than any savings account. The main online marketing activities that Zopa uses are search engine marketing and affiliate marketing. In 2007 Zopa created its own Facebook application 'People Like You', which lets Facebookers compare their personality with other people's. Zopa communicates with its audience in an informal way through its blogs (http://blog.zopa.com).

Funding

Zopa initially received funding from two private equity groups, Munich-based Wellington Partners and Benchmark Capital of the US. Although the model was unique within financial services, its appeal was increased by the well-publicized success of other peer-to-peer Internet services such as Betfair, the gambling website, and eBay, the auction site.

Sources: Financial Times (2005), New Media Age (2005), Institute of Directors (2005), Zopa website (www.zopa.com) and blog http://blog.zopa.com.

Question

Imagine you are a member of the team at the investors reviewing the viability of the Zopa business. On which criteria would you assess the future potential of the business and the returns on your investment based on Zopa's position in the marketplace and its internal capabilities?

Summary

1 The constantly changing e-business environment should be monitored by all organizations in order to be able to respond to changes in social, legal, economic, political and technological factors together with changes in the immediate marketplace that occur through changes in customer requirements and competitors' and intermediaries' offerings.

2 The e-business marketplace involves transactions between organizations and consumers (B2C) and other businesses (B2B). Consumer-to-consumer (C2C) and consumer-to-business categories (C2B) can also be identified.

3 The Internet can cause *disintermediation* within the marketplace as an organization's channel partners such as wholesalers or retailers are bypassed. Alternatively, the Internet can cause *reintermediation* as new intermediaries with a different purpose are formed to help bring buyers and sellers together in a *virtual*

marketplace or marketspace. Evaluation of the implications of these changes and implementation of alternative *countermediation* strategies is important to strategy.

4 Trading in the marketplace can be sell-side (seller-controlled), buy-side (buyer-controlled) or at a neutral marketplace.

5 A business model is a summary of how a company will generate revenue identifying its product offering, value-added services, revenue sources and target customers. Exploiting the range of business models made available through the Internet is important to both existing companies and start-ups.

6 The Internet may also offer opportunities for new revenue models such as commission on affiliate referrals to other sites or banner advertising.

7 The opportunities for new commercial arrangements for transactions include negotiated deals, brokered deals, auctions, fixed-price sales and pure spot markets, and barters should also be considered.

8 The success of dot-com or Internet start-up companies is critically dependent on their business and revenue models and traditional management practice.

Exercises

Answers to these exercises are available online at www.pearsoned.co.uk/chaffey

Self-assessment questions

1 Outline the main options for trading between businesses and consumers.

2 Explain the concepts of disintermediation and reintermediation with reference to a particular industry; what are the implications for a company operating in this industry?

3 Describe the three main alternative locations for trading within the electronic marketplace.

4 What are the main types of commercial transactions that can occur through the Internet or in traditional commerce?

5 E-business involves re-evaluating value chain activities. What types of changes can be introduced to the value chain through e-business?

6 List the different business models identified by Timmers (1999).

7 Describe some alternative revenue models for a website from a magazine publisher.

8 Draw a diagram summarizing the different types of online marketplace.

Essay and discussion questions

1 'Disintermediation and reintermediation occur simultaneously within any given market.' Discuss.

2 For an organization you are familiar with, examine the alternative business and revenue models afforded by the Internet and assess the options for the type and location of e-commerce transitions.

3 For a manufacturer or retailer of your choice, analyse the balance between partnering with portals and providing equivalent services from your website.

4 Contrast the market potential for B2B and B2C auctions.

5 Select an intermediary site and assess how well it makes use of the range of business models and revenue models available to it through the Internet.

Examination questions

1　Explain disintermediation and reintermediation using examples.

2　Describe three different revenue models for a portal such as Yahoo!

3　What is meant by buy-side, sell-side and marketplace-based e-commerce?

4　What are the different mechanisms for online auctions?

5　Describe two alternative approaches for using e-business to change a company's value chain.

6　Explain what a business model is and relate it to an Internet pureplay of your choice.

7　Outline the elements of the e-business environment for an organization and explain its relevance to the organization.

8　Give three different transaction types that an industry marketplace could offer to facilitate trade between buyers and suppliers.

References

Allen, E. and Fjermestad, J. (2001) E-commerce marketing strategies: a framework and case analysis. *Logistics Information Management*, 14(1/2), 14–23.

Benjamin, R. and Weigand, R. (1995) Electronic markets and virtual value-chains on the information superhighway. *Sloan Management Review*, Winter, 62–72.

Berryman, K., Harrington, L., Layton-Rodin, D. and Rerolle, V. (1998) Electronic commerce: three emerging strategies. *McKinsey Quarterly*, no. 1, 152–9.

CIO (2002) GM Shifts Gears. Article by Derek Slater, 1 April. Available online at: **www.cio. com/archive/040102/matters_content.html**.

comScore (2010) comScore Media Metrix Ranks Top-Growing Properties and Site Categories for April 2010. Press release, 10 May: **http://www.comscore.com/ Press_Events/Press_Releases/2010/5/comScore_Media_Metrix_Ranks_Top-Growing_Properties_and_Site_Categories_for_April_2010**.

Covisint (2002) E-business at DaimlerChrysler is paying off: savings exceed present investment. Press release on **www.covisint.com**, 4 February.

Desmet, D., Francis, T., Hu, A., Koller, M. and Riedel, G. (2000) Valuing dot coms. *McKinsey Quarterly*, no. 1. Available online at **www.mckinseyquarterly.com**.

Emiliani, V. (2001) Business-to-business online auctions: key issues for purchasing process improvement. *Supply Chain Management: An International Journal*, 5(4), 176–86.

eSuperbrands (2005) eSuperbrands 2006. *Your Guide to Some of the Best Brands on the Web.* Superbrands Ltd, London.

Evans, P. and Wurster, T.S. (1999) Getting real about virtual commerce. *Harvard Business Review*, November, 84–94.

Financial Times (2005) Lending exchange bypasses high street banks. Paul J. Davies, 22 August. *Financial Times*.

Gwyther, M. (1999) Jewels in the web. *Management Today*, November, 63–9.

Hagel, J. and Rayport, J. (1997) The new infomediaries. *McKinsey Quarterly*, no. 4, 54–70.

Institute of Directors (2005) Profile – Richard Duvall. IOD House magazine, *Director*, pp. 51–5.

Hitwise (2010) Robin Goad Analyst Weblog: Social networks now more popular than search engines in the UK, 8 June 2010. **http://weblogs.hitwise.com/robin-goad/2010/06/ social_networks_overtake_search_engines.html**.

Klein, S. (1997) Introduction to electronic auctions. *International Journal of Electronic Markets*, 4(7), 3–6.

Mashable (2010) YouTube Surpasses Two Billion Video Views Daily, Blog posting, **http://mashable.com/2010/05/17/youtube-2-billion-views/**.

McDonald, M. and Wilson, H. (2002) *New Marketing: Transforming the Corporate Future*. Butterworth-Heinemann, Oxford.

New Media Age (2005) Personal lender, Dominic Dudley, *New Media Age*, 18 August.

Nunes, P., Kambil, A. and Wilson, D. (2000). The all-in-one market. *Harvard Business Review*, May–June, 2–3.

Pant, S. and Ravichandran, T. (2001) A framework for information systems planning for e-business. *Logistics Information Management*, 14(1), 85–98.

Rayport, J. and Sviokla, J. (1996) Exploiting the virtual value-chain. *McKinsey Quarterly*, no. 1, 20–37.

Reck, M. (1997) Trading characteristics of electronic auctions. *International Journal of Electronic Markets*, 4(7), 17–23.

Riggins, F. and Mitra, S. (2007) An e-valuation framework for developing net-enabled business metrics through functionality interaction. *Journal of Organizational Computing and Electronics Commerce*, 17(2), 175–203.

Sarkar, M., Butler, B. and Steinfield, C. (1996) Intermediaries and cybermediaries. A continuing role for mediating players in the electronic marketplace. *Journal of Computer Mediated Communication*, 1(3). Online-only journal, no page numbers.

Silicon.com (2004) Ecommerce sites: 'Long live ... the catalogue?' 23 November. Author, Will Sturgeon (**www.silicon.com**).

Simons, M. (2000) Setting the banks alight. *Computer Weekly*, 20 July, 6.

Thomas, J. and Sullivan, U. (2005) Managing marketing communications with multi-channel customers. *Journal of Marketing*, 69 (October), 239–51.

Timmers, P. (1999) *Electronic Commerce Strategies and Models for Business-to-Business Trading*. Series on Information Systems, Wiley, Chichester.

Venkatram, N. (2000) Five steps to a dot-com strategy: how to find your footing on the web. *Sloan Management Review*, Spring, 15–28.

Further reading

Deise, M., Nowikow, C., King, P. and Wright, A. (2000) *Executive's Guide to E-Business. From Tactics to Strategy*. Wiley, New York. Introductory chapters consider buy- and sell-side options and later chapters look at value-chain transformation.

Fingar, P., Kumar, H. and Sharma, T. (2000) *Enterprise E-Commerce*. Meghan-Kiffler Press, Tampa, FL. These authors present a model of the different actors in the e-marketplace that is the theme throughout this book.

Novak, T.P. and Hoffman, D.L. (2002) Profitabilty on the web: business models and revenue streams. Vanderbilt position paper. Available online at **http://elab.vanderbilt.edu/research/manuscripts/index.htm**.

Timmers, P. (1999) *Electronic Commerce Strategies and Models for Business-to-Business Trading*. Series on Information Systems, Wiley, Chichester. Provides coverage of value-chain analysis and business model architectures in Chapter 3.

Turban, E., Lee, J., King, D. and Chung, H. (2000) *Electronic Commerce: A Managerial Perspective*. Prentice-Hall, Upper Saddle River, NJ. Chapter 1 introduces industry structures and models for e-commerce.

Variani, V. and Vaturi, D. (2000) Marketing lessons from e-failures. *McKinsey Quarterly*, no. 4, 86–97. Available online at **www.mckinseyquarterly.com**.

Web links

Adoption of Internet and online services

These sources are listed at the end of Chapter 4 and examples given in that chapter.

Business model development

Business 2 (**http://money.cnn.com/magazines/business2**) Also covers the development of business models with a US focus.

FastCompany (**www.fastcompany.com**) Also covers the development of business models with a US focus.

Ghost sites (**www.disobey.com/ghostsites**) Steve Baldwin's compilation of failed e-businesses, including the Museum of E-failure!

Paid Content (**www.paidcontent.org**) Covers the development of revenue models for publishers.

Paid Content UK (**www.paidcontent.co.uk**) Covers developments in start-up companies within the UK.

Commentators on online business models

Mohansawhney.com (**www.mohansawhney.com**) Papers from e-business specialist, Mohanbir Sawhney of Kellogg School of Management, Northwestern University, Evanston, IL, USA.

Michael Rappa's Business Models page (**http://digitalenterprise.org/models/models.html**) Michael Rappa is a professor at North Carolina State University.

Dave Chaffey's Smart Insights (**www.smartinsights.com**) Discussion on business models and spreadsheets for modelling publishing and e-commerce revenue.

3

E-business infrastructure

Web support

The following additional case studies are available at
www.pearsoned.co.uk/chaffey

→ Selecting a supplier for hosting website services
→ Achieving integration between different systems through EAI
→ The site also contains a range of study material designed to help improve your results.

Learning outcomes

After completing this chapter the reader should be able to:

● Outline the hardware and software technologies used to build an e-business infrastructure within an organization and with its partners
● Outline the hardware and software requirements necessary to enable employee access to the Internet and hosting of e-commerce services

Management issues

The issues for managers raised in this chapter include:

● What are the practical risks to the organization of failure to manage the e-commerce infrastructure adequately?
● How should staff access to the Internet be managed?
● How should we evaluate the relevance of web services and open source software?

Links to other chapters

This chapter is an introduction to Internet hardware and software technologies. It gives the technical background to Chapters 1 and 2 and to Parts 2 and 3. Its focus is on understanding the technology used but it also gives an introduction to how it needs to be managed. The main chapters that cover management of the e-business infrastructure are:

● *Chapter 10*, Change management
● *Chapter 11*, Analysis and design (including architecture design)
● *Chapter 12*, Implementation and maintenance – this focuses on the issues in selecting the software used for publishing content such as content management systems and blogs

Introduction

Defining an adequate technology infrastructure is vital to all companies adopting e-business. The infrastructure directly affects the quality of service experienced by users of the systems in terms of speed and responsiveness. The e-business services provided through a standardized infrastructure also determine the capability of an organization to compete through differentiating itself in the marketplace. Mcafee and Brynjolfsson (2008) suggest that to use digital technology to support competition the mantra for the CEO should be:

> *'Deploy, innovate, and propagate': First, deploy a consistent technology platform. Then separate yourself from the pack by coming up with better ways of working. Finally, use the platform to propagate these business innovations widely and reliably. In this regard, deploying IT serves two distinct roles – as a catalyst for innovative ideas and as an engine for delivering them.*

Our 'Real-world e-business' experience interview in this chapter highlights the role of managing innovation and the need for a flexible approach to selecting and deploying relevant e-business technology.

E-business infrastructure refers to the combination of hardware such as servers and client PCs in an organization, the network used to link this hardware and the software applications used to deliver services to workers within the e-business and also to its partners and customers. Infrastructure also includes the architecture of the networks, hardware and software and where it is located. Finally, infrastructure can also be considered to include the methods for publishing data and documents accessed through e-business applications. A key decision with managing this infrastructure is which elements are located within the company and which are managed externally.

It is also important that the e-business infrastructure and the process of reviewing new technology investments be flexible enough to support changes required by the business to compete effectively. One example of organizations who haven't had the flexibility or commitment to investment in infrastructure is provided by a speech to the American Society of Newspaper Editors by Rupert Murdoch of News Corporation:

> *Scarcely a day goes by without some claim that new technologies are fast writing newsprint's obituary. Yet, as an industry, many of us have been remarkably, unaccountably complacent. Certainly, I didn't do as much as I should have after all the excitement of the late 1990s. I suspect many of you in this room did the same, quietly hoping that this thing called the digital revolution would just limp along.*
>
> *Well it hasn't … it won't …. And it's a fast developing reality we should grasp as a huge opportunity to improve our journalism and expand our reach.* (News Corporation, 2005)

In 2010 Murdoch introduced 'paywalls' to some of his UK-based titles with full-content only available to paid subscribers indicating a commitment to a change in infrastructure.

We refer above to an *adequate* e-business infrastructure, but what does this mean? For the manager in the e-business, this is a key question. While it is important to be able to understand some of the technical jargon and concepts when talking to suppliers, what is of crucial importance is to be aware of some of the limitations (and also the business potential) of the infrastructure. Through being aware of these problems, managers of an organization can work with their partners to ensure a good level of service is delivered to everyone, internal and external, who is using the e-business infrastructure. To highlight some of the problems that may occur if the infrastructure is not managed correctly, complete Activity 3.1.

E-business infrastructure
The architecture of hardware, software, content and data used to deliver e-business services to employees, customers and partners.

Infrastructure risk assessment

Purpose

To indicate potential problems to customers, partners and staff of the e-business if technical infrastructure is not managed adequately.

Activity

Make a list of the potential technology problems faced by customers of an online retailer. Consider problems faced by users of e-business applications which are either internal or external to the organization. Base your answer on problems you have experienced on a website that can be related to network, hardware and software failures or problems with data quality.

Answers to activities can be found at www.pearsoned.co.uk/chaffey

E-business infrastructure components

Figure 3.1 summarizes how the different components of e-business architecture relate to each other. The different components can be conceived of as layers with defined interfaces between each layer. The different layers can best be understood in relation to a typical task performed by a user of an e-business system. For example, an employee who needs to book a holiday will access a specific human resources application or program that has been created to enable the holiday to be booked (Level I in Figure 3.1). This application will enable a holiday request to be entered and will forward the application to their manager and human resources department for approval. To access the application, the employee will

	Examples
I **E-business services –** **applications layer**	CRM, supply chain management, data mining, content management systems
II **Systems software layer**	Web browser and server software and standards, networking software and database management systems
III **Transport or** **network layer**	Physical network and transport standards (TCP/IP)
IV **Storage/physical** **layer**	Permanent magnetic storage on web servers or optical backup or temporary storage in memory (RAM)
V **Content and** **data layer**	Web content for intranet, extranet and Internet sites, customers' data, transaction data, clickstream data

Figure 3.1 A five-layer model of e-business infrastructure

use a web browser such as Microsoft Internet Explorer, Mozilla Firefox or Google Chrome using an operating system such as Microsoft Windows or Apple OS X (Level II). This systems software will then request transfer of the information about the holiday request across a network or transport layer (Level III). The information will then be stored in computer memory (RAM) or in long-term magnetic storage on a web server (Level IV). The information itself which makes up the web pages or content viewed by the employee and the data about their holiday request are shown as a separate layer (Level V in Figure 3.1), although it could be argued that this is the first or second level in an e-business architecture.

Kampas (2000) describes an alternative five-level infrastructure model of what he refers to as 'the information system function chain':

1 *Storage/physical.* Memory and disk hardware components (equivalent to Level IV in Figure 3.1).
2 *Processing.* Computation and logic provided by the processor (processing occurs at Levels I and II).
3 *Infrastructure.* This refers to the human and external interfaces and also the network, referred to as 'extrastructure'. (This is Level III , although the human or external interfaces are not shown there.)
4 *Application/content.* This is the data processed by the application into information. (This is Level V.)
5 *Intelligence.* Additional computer-based logic that transforms information to knowledge (Level I).

Each of these elements of infrastructure presents separate management issues which we will consider separately. In this chapter, infrastructure management issues are introduced, while more detailed discussion of management solutions is presented in Chapters 10, 11 and 12.

We start our coverage of e-business infrastructure by considering the technical infrastructure for the Internet, extranets, intranets and the World Wide Web, which are Levels II and III.

We then look at how these facilities work by reviewing the standards that are used to enable electronic communications, including communications standards such as TCP/IP and EDI and publishing standards such as HTML and XML.

In the second part of the chapter, some management issues of hosting e-business services are then reviewed, specifically management of Level I applications and services by external parties and how to manage staff access to the Internet. Finally, we focus on how new access platforms such as mobile phones and interactive digital TV will change the way the Internet is used in the future (Level II).

We return to some issues of e-business infrastructure management later in this book. Table 3.1 provides a summary of the main issues facing businesses and where they are covered in this chapter and later in the book.

Table 3.1	Key management issues of e-business infrastructure	
Main issue	**Detail**	**Where covered?**
Which type of e-business applications do we prioritize for development?	For example, supply chain management, e-procurement, secure online ordering, customer relationship management	Chapter 5 sections on e-business services and stage models, Chapters 7, 8 and 9 on specific e-business applications
Which technologies do we use?	For example, e-mail, web-based ordering vs EDI, web services	This chapter introduces different technologies at different levels of Figure 3.1, Chapter 4 discusses adoption of new technologies
How do we achieve quality of service in applications?	Requirements are: business fit, security, speed, availability and errors	Section on ISPs in this chapter, Chapter 11 on design, Chapter 12 on implementation
Where do we host applications?	Internal or external sourcing and hosting via web services?	'*Focus on* ASPs' section in this chapter, Managing partnerships section in Chapter 7 on SCM
Application integration	Integration of e-business solutions with: – legacy systems – partner systems – B2B exchanges and intermediaries	Section on integrating information systems into supply chain management in Chapter 6
Which access platforms do we support? Which development technologies and standards do we use?	Mobile access, interactive digital TV, e.g. CGI, Perl, .Net, .PHP	'*Focus on* Access devices' in this section in Chapter 12
How do we publish and manage content and data quality?	How are content and data updated so that they are up to date, accurate, easy to find and easy to interpret?	Web content management, blogs and feeds are introduced in this chapter and in more detail in Chapters 11 and 12
How do we manage employee access to the Internet?	Staff can potentially waste time using the Internet or can act illegally	Covered in Chapter 11 in '*Focus on* Security design for e-business'
How do we secure data?	Content and data can be deleted in error or maliciously	Safeguards are described in Chapter 11

Real-world E-Business experiences   The E-consultancy interview

Marko Balabanovic of lastminute.com on the opportunities for deploying digital technology

Context

Management of the opportunities presented by innovation in digital technology is a significant challenge for the people responsible for e-business or e-commerce within an organization. Since the previous edition, I have noticed more roles in larger organizations specifically for managing innovation, i.e. reviewing and selecting the most relevant new digital technologies for an organization. This example provides a snapshot of some of the issues involved with technology innovation. Marko is head of innovation at lastminute.com; here he talks about how the team looks to innovate, and some of the products it has created...

Q. Can you tell me about the innovation team at lastminute.com?

Marko Balabanovic, lastminute.com: Within the European side of the business, we have a small group called lastminute.com labs, which is responsible for the more 'risky' projects. This means we can develop and build new projects and launch them in beta to see if it works out or not, and get feedback from customers.

Q. Where does it sit within the organization? Do you have much autonomy?

Marko Balabanovic, lastminute.com: It is designed to be reasonably independent, and operates a little like a start-up within lastminute.com. Unlike the average start-up though, we are launching a lot of different products, four last year, and three so far in 2009.

We operate reasonably separately from the rest of the company, and we have licence to try things out. If something doesn't work, we can quickly withdraw a new product or service and kill it.

However, if it turns out to be successful, then we can transfer the product to another area of the company.

Q. What kind of innovations have you introduced recently?

Marko Balabanovic, lastminute.com: This year, we are concentrating exclusively on mobile products, but last year we worked on different ways to do search on the site.

With most travel sites, people have to enter destinations, leaving dates, airports, return dates: lots of fields to fill in before they can search, which is sometimes not very inspiring.

To get around this, we created Pronto which is a single box where you can type in a specific query. For example, 'I want to go to Paris', 'I want a hotel in Venice' and so on. Pronto makes sense of these sentences and produces results that match.

Q. When did it come about?

Marko Balabanovic, lastminute.com: The lab team has been going for two years in its current form, but there was previously a smaller team looking at the development of new products. There are seven of us in the team, including me.

One element is trying to encourage innovation across the company as a whole, so we have events like a bi-annual hack day, where we have 24 hours to build and create something new.

We're not the only part of the company that is innovative, but this was set up because it is easier to look at new technical ideas in this way.

Q. Which of your concepts have been adopted for the main website?

Marko Balabanovic, lastminute.com: The Pronto search feature has gone from an experimental activity to being something that customers can use. It isn't heavily pro-moted on the UK site, but it's a tool we offer our affiliate networks, and it's a search option on the French version of the website. We're in the process of proving its worth.

Q. How has it worked so far?

Marko Balabanovic, lastminute.com: It has been quite popular so far, and it has the added benefit that, because you have given people a search box that enables them to type what they want, you can learn more about the kinds of searches that people want to do.

This is information you wouldn't normally find out through the standard search fields, and helps us to see trends and adapt the main site to suit this.

Q. Can you tell me about the NRU iPhone / Android app?

Marko Balabanovic, lastminute.com: We've been trying to see how, with the new classes of mobile handsets that have been released over the last 9–12 months, with features like compasses and accelerometers, we can create apps to make the most of these phones. It provides the opportunity to build a much more interactive experience for customers.

NRU visualizes the things that are available around you, cafés, restaurants, by moving the phone around. We launched it for Android phones at the beginning of the year, and more recently for the new iPhone 3GS.

Q. Where does the content for the app come from?

Marko Balabanovic, lastminute.com: In Europe, we use a mixture of restaurants from our FoneFood app, and also pull in content and reviews from Qype. In the US we partner with ZAGAT for content and reviews.

Q. What else are you doing with mobile this year?

Marko Balabanovic, lastminute.com: We're trying to move beyond our current apps, and to be cleverer about recommending based on the current context; location for instance. We have three new products launching soon, but I'm unable to give any detail on those at the moment.

We are trying to take a step back from the current model that a person is at a desk typing search terms into Google and accessing the site's home page.

As things progress, there will be more contexts in which people are accessing the site and services, there will be more movement between different devices; laptops, iPhones, netbooks etc.

If you develop just for the desktop web, you don't have to worry about contexts, but there are a lot of ideas that could work in different situations and on different devices.

Q. Do you see customers booking and making transactions on lastminute.com via mobile?

Marko Balabanovic, lastminute.com: Completely. Even now, there is nothing to stop this happening, other than the fact that many companies are not adapting their sites to allow this to happen, creating smaller versions of booking forms and checkouts.

Source: Q&A: lastminute.com's Marko Balabanovic on innovation. Posted 15 September 2009 09:53am by Graham Charlton: http://econsultancy.com/blog/4612-q-al-lastminute-com-s-marko-balabanovic-on-innovation.

Internet
The physical network that links computers across the globe. It consists of the infrastructure of network servers and communication links between them that are used to hold and transport information between the client computers and web servers.

Client–server
The client/server architecture consists of *client* computers, such as PCs, sharing resources such as a database stored on a more powerful *server* computer.

Internet technology

Internet service provider (ISP)
A provider providing home or business users with a connection to access the Internet. They can also host web-based applications.

Backbones
High-speed communications links used to enable Internet communications across a country and internationally.

As you will know, the **Internet** enables communication between millions of connected computers worldwide, but how does the seamless transfer of data happen? Requests for information are transmitted from client computers and mobile devices whose users request services to server computers that hold information and host business applications that deliver the services in response to requests. Thus, the Internet is a large-scale **client–server** system.

Figure 3.2 shows how the client computers within homes and businesses are connected to the Internet via local **Internet service providers (ISPs)** which, in turn, are linked to larger ISPs with connection to the major national and international infrastructure or **backbones** which are managed by commercial organizations. These high-speed links can be thought of as the motorways on the 'information superhighway', while the links provided from ISPs to consumers are equivalent to slow country roads.

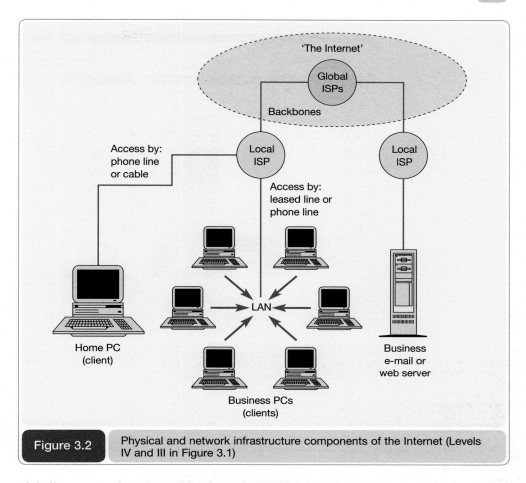

| Figure 3.2 | Physical and network infrastructure components of the Internet (Levels IV and III in Figure 3.1) |

Globally, many submarine cables form the backbone between countries, which are susceptible to damage. For example, in January 2008 a ship's anchor severed a cable in the Mediterranean resulting in a dramatic slowdown in Internet access for people in India, Sri Lanka, Pakistan and the Middle East!

Hosting of websites and e-business services

Hosting provider
A service provider that manages the server used to host an organization website and its connection to the Internet backbones.

While it is possible for companies to manage their own services by setting up web servers within their own company offices, or to use their ISP, it is common practice to use a specialist **hosting provider** to manage this service. For example, Rackspace (Figure 3.3) describes itself as 'Europe's fastest growing hosting company'. Since 2001 Rackspace has been hosting and supporting mission critical websites, Internet applications, e-mail servers, security and storage services for over 4,000 customers. Rackspace also has US offices.

We will return to the issues of selecting and managing a hosting provider later in this chapter.

The Internet timeline

The Internet is only the latest development in the way that the human race has used technology to disseminate information (see Figure 3.4). Kampas (2000) identifies ten stages that are part of five 'megawaves' of change. It is evident that many of the major advances in the use of information have happened within the last hundred years (see Table 3.2). This indicates that the difficulty of managing technological change is likely to continue. Kampas goes on to speculate on the impact of access to lower-cost, higher-bandwidth technologies.

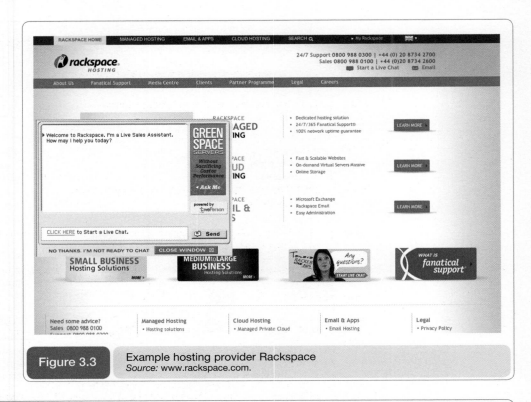

Figure 3.3   Example hosting provider Rackspace
Source: www.rackspace.com.

Table 3.2   Six stages of advances in the dissemination of information

Stage		Enabling technology	Killer applications* and impact
1	Documentation: 3500 BC to ad 1452	Written language and the development of clay tablets in Mesopotamia	Taxes, laws and accounting giving rise to the development of civilization and commerce
2	Mass publication: 1452 to 1946	The Gutenburg press of movable metal type	Demand for religious and scientific texts resulting in scientific advances and ideological conflicts
3	Automation: 1946 to 1978	Electric power and switching technologies (vacuum tubes and transistors)	Code breaking and scientific calculations. Start of information age
4	Mass interaction: 1978 to 1985	Microprocessor and personal computer	Spreadsheets and word processing
5	Infrastructuralization: 1985 to 1993	Local- and wide-area networks, graphical user interfaces	E-mail and enterprise resource planning
6	Mass communication: 1993 to c. 2010	Internet, World Wide Web, Java	Mass information access for communications and purchasing

*Very useful applications which will encourage adoption of a technology.
Source: Adapted and republished with permission of CRC Press LLC from table on pp. 8–22 from 'Road map to the e-revolution', by Kampas, P., in *Information Systems Management Journal,* Spring 2000, Auerbach Publications, Copyright © 2000 by CRC Press LLC; permission conveyed through Copyright Clearance Center, Inc.

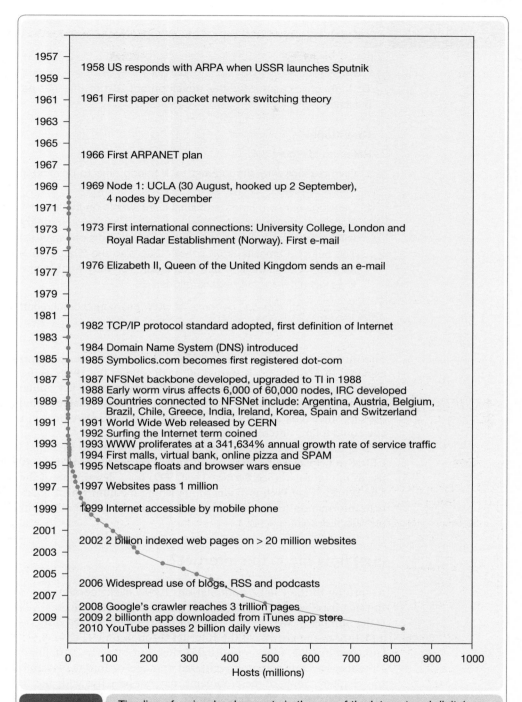

1957

1958 US responds with ARPA when USSR launches Sputnik

1959

1961 First paper on packet network switching theory

1961

1963

1965

1966 First ARPANET plan

1967

1969 Node 1: UCLA (30 August, hooked up 2 September),
4 nodes by December

1971

1973 First international connections: University College, London and
Royal Radar Establishment (Norway). First e-mail

1975

1976 Elizabeth II, Queen of the United Kingdom sends an e-mail

1977

1979

1981

1982 TCP/IP protocol standard adopted, first definition of Internet

1983

1984 Domain Name System (DNS) introduced

1985 Symbolics.com becomes first registered dot-com

1987 NFSNet backbone developed, upgraded to TI in 1988

1988 Early worm virus affects 6,000 of 60,000 nodes, IRC developed

1989 Countries connected to NFSNet include: Argentina, Austria, Belgium,
Brazil, Chile, Greece, India, Ireland, Korea, Spain and Switzerland

1991 World Wide Web released by CERN

1992 Surfing the Internet term coined

1993 WWW proliferates at a 341,634% annual growth rate of service traffic

1994 First malls, virtual bank, online pizza and SPAM

1995 Netscape floats and browser wars ensue

1997 Websites pass 1 million

1999 Internet accessible by mobile phone

2002 2 billion indexed web pages on > 20 million websites

2006 Widespread use of blogs, RSS and podcasts

2008 Google's crawler reaches 3 trillion pages

2009 2 billionth app downloaded from iTunes app store

2010 YouTube passes 2 billion daily views

Hosts (millions)

Figure 3.4 Timeline of major developments in the use of the Internet and digital technologies

<table>
<tr><td>Activity 3.2</td><td>The development of the Internet and digital technologies</td></tr>
</table>

Purpose

To highlight reasons for the development of the Internet as a vital enabler for business.

Questions

Referring to Figure 3.4:

1 Give reasons why the Internet took a long time to develop into today's essential business tool.

2 Develop your own timeline of significant events on the Internet. A key source is the Hobbes Internet timeline (www.zakon.org/robert/internet/timeline/) or a relevant wikipedia page, for example: http://en.wikipedia.org/wiki/History_of_the_Internet. The author's timeline is on p. xxiii. See also the 'Focus on New access devices' section towards the end of this chapter. You may want to speculate on how time-lines will differ for future generations.

Answers to activities can be found at www.pearsoned.co.uk/chaffey

The Internet has taken a relatively long time to become an essential part of business, as explored in Activity 3.2. It started life at the end of the 1960s as the ARPAnet research and defence network in the USA which linked servers used by key military and academic collaborators. It was established as a network that would be reliable even if some of the links were broken, since data and messages sent between users were broken up into smaller packets and could follow different routes.

It is the advent of the World Wide Web, which was invented by Tim Berners-Lee of CERN to help share research easily, that is responsible for the massive growth in business use of the Internet. (See Berners-Lee (1999) for a description of the invention of the web.) The World Wide Web provides a publishing medium which makes it easy to publish and read information using a web browser and also to link to related information. (See section on Web technology p. 112.)

Just how big is the Internet?

According to the ClickZ compilations (www.clickz.com/stats/), there are over 1 billion Internet users worldwide; but how big is the infrastructure they are accessing? One measure is the number of web servers. Netcraft has regularly surveyed the servers since 1995 to give a picture of the growth of the Internet through time (Figure 3.5). The first survey it ran, launched in 1995, found only 18,957 sites, but by early 2010, there were over 200 million! Note that Netcraft measures registered domains or Internet IP addresses (explained later in this chapter). Some of these domains may not be active with and there has been a decrease in rate of growth, as the chart shows.

Another way at looking at the scale of the Internet is to look at the number of pages indexed by search engines. A good indication of the size of the web is the number of pages indexed by Google. The first index by Google in 1998 found 26 million pages (Figure 1.1).

Google doesn't index every page since many pages are duplicates or 'web spam' used to mislead the search engine and its users to help companies gain a place in Google's coveted listings. However, the number of pages visited by its main crawler or robot GoogleBot reached over 1 trillion in 2008 according to Google (2008). That's 1,000,000,000,000 pages!

Google indexes 1 trillion URLs, equivalent to 50,000 times larger than the US road network.

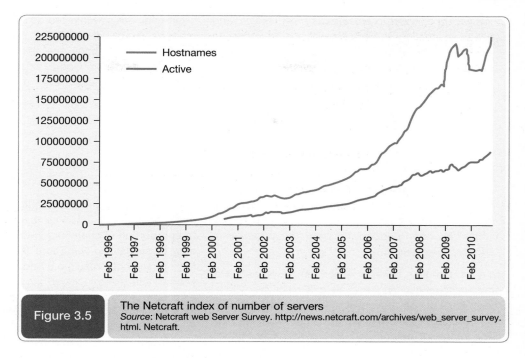

Figure 3.5	The Netcraft index of number of servers
	Source: Netcraft web Server Survey. http://news.netcraft.com/archives/web_server_survey. html. Netcraft.

In their blog posting Google engineers explain:

Google downloads the web continuously, collecting updated page information and re-processing the entire web-link graph several times per day. This graph of one trillion URLs is similar to a map made up of one trillion intersections. So multiple times every day, we do the computational equivalent of fully exploring every intersection of every road in the United States. Except it'd be a map about 50,000 times as big as the US, with 50,000 times as many roads and intersections.

Google no longer publishes the number of pages indexed on its home page, perhaps due to accusations that it is 'evil big brother'; however, it is generally reckoned to exceed 10 billion.

Case Study 3.1   Innovation at Google

Context

In addition to being the largest search engine on Earth, mediating the searches of tens of billions of searches daily, Google is an innovator. All involved in e-business should follow Google to see the latest approaches it is trialling.

Google's mission

Google's mission is encapsulated in the statement '*to organize the world's information ... and make it universally accessible and useful*.' Google explains that it believes that the most effective, and ultimately the most profitable, way to accomplish its mission is to put the needs of its users first. Offering a high-quality user experience has led to strong word-of-mouth promotion and strong traffic growth.

Notable tenets of the Google philosophy are:

- Focus on the user and all else will follow.
- It's best to do one thing really, really well.
- You can make money without doing evil.

Further details on the culture and ethics of Google is available at www.google.com/intl/en/corporate/tenthings. html.

Putting users first is reflected in three key commitments in the Google SEC filing:

1 *We will do our best to provide the most relevant and useful search results possible, independent of financial incentives. Our search results will be objective and we will not accept payment for inclusion or ranking in them.*

2 *We will do our best to provide the most relevant and useful advertising. Advertisements should not be an annoying interruption. If any element on a search result page is influenced by payment to us, we will make it clear to our users.*

3 *We will never stop working to improve our user experience, our search technology and other important areas of information organization.*

In the SEC filing, the company explains 'How we provide value to our users':

We serve our users by developing products that quickly and easily find, create, organize, and share information. We place a premium on products that matter to many people and have the potential to improve their lives.

Some of the key benefits which are explained are: Comprehensiveness and relevance; Objectivity; Global access; Ease of use; Pertinent, useful commercial information; Multiple access platforms and Improving the web.

The range of established Google services is well known and is listed at http://www.google.com/options/.

Google's commitment to innovation is indicated by these more recent services:

- Google TV (announced 2010) as part of a partnership agreement with Sony
- Nexus One Phone using the Google Android mobile operating system launched in January 2010 (www.google.com/phone)
- Google Mobile advertising (although Google has offered text ads for some time, the 2009 acquisition of AdMob enables improvements in sophistication of this approach)
- Google Chrome OS (a lightweight operating sysytem announced in 2009 and targeted initially at Netbooks)
- Google Chrome (a browser announced as a beta in 2008 and a full product for Windows in 2009)

For 2009, Google spent around 12% of its revenue in research and development, an increase from less than 10% in 2005, a larger amount than sales and marketing (8.4%).

Google revenue models

Google generated approximately 99% of its revenues in 2007 and 97% in 2008 and 2009 from its advertisers with the remainder from its enterprise search products where companies can install search technology through products such as the Google Appliance and Google Mini.

Google AdWords, the auction-based advertising programme that enables advertisers, is the main source of revenue. Advertisers pay on a 'pay-per-click' cost basis within the search engines and within other services such as Gmail, but with cost-per-thousand payment options available on Google Networks members' websites. Google has introduced classified-style ad programmes for other media, including:

- Google Audio Ads (ads are placed in radio programmes)
- Google Print Ads
- Google TV Ads
- Google Promoted Video Ads within YouTube, user-initiated click-to-play video ads.

So, Google's revenues are critically dependent on how many searches it achieves in different countries and the proportion of searchers who interact with Google's ads. Research by comScore (2008) suggests around 25% of searches result in an ad click where sponsored search results are included (around 50% of searches). Of course Google is also looking to increase the number of advertisers and invests heavily in this through trade communications to marketers. Increased competition to advertise against a search term will result in increased bid amounts and so increased revenue for Google.

International revenues accounted for approximately 53% of total revenues in Q4 2009, and more than half of user traffic came from outside the US. In Q4 2009, 12% of ad revenue was from the UK alone.

Thirty-one per cent of Google's revenue is from the Network of content partners who subscribe to the Google Adsense programme.

Risk factors

Some of the main risk factors that Google declares include:

1 **New technologies could block Google ads**. Ad-blocking technology could, in the future, adversely affect Google's results, although there has not been widespread adoption of these approaches.

2 **Litigation and confidence loss through click fraud**. Click fraud can be a problem when competitors click on a link, but this is typically small-scale. A larger problem for is structured click fraud where site owners on the Google content network seeks to make additional advertising feeds.

3 **Index spammers could harm the integrity of Google's web search results**. This could damage Google's reputation and cause its users to be dissatisfied with products and services.

Google says:

There is an ongoing and increasing effort by 'index spammers' to develop ways to manipulate our web search results. For example, because our web search technology ranks a web page's relevance based in part on the importance of the web sites that link to it, people have attempted to link a group of web sites together to manipulate web search results.

At 31 December 2009, Google had 19,835 employees. All of Google's employees are also equity-holders, with significant collective employee ownership. As a result, many employees are highly motivated to make the company more successful. Google's engineers are encouraged to spend up to 10% of their time identifying new approaches.

Further reading: Bala and Davenport (2008)

You can find updates on this case study by searching at SmartInsights. com for 'Google marketing updates'.

Web video explanation: http://www.google.com/howgoogleworks/. Further information on how Google works is available in Chapter 9 in the section on search engine marketing.

In the further reading for this chapter, we reference Arnold (2010) who describes how Google is incorporating semantic web approaches.

> ### Question
> Explain how Google generates revenue and exploits innovation in digital technology to identify future revenue growth. You should also consider the risk factors for future revenue generation.

Intranets and extranets

In Chapter 1, illustrated by Figure 1.4, we introduced the concept of intranets and extranets.

Intranet applications

Intranets are used extensively for supporting sell-side e-commerce from within the marketing function. They are also used to support core supply-chain management activities as described in the next section on extranets. Today, they are typically deployed as web-based services supplemented by messages and alerts delivered by e-mail or when users login to a company network. A marketing intranet has the following advantages:

- Reduced product life cycles – as information on product development and marketing campaigns is rationalized we can get products to market faster.
- Reduced costs through higher productivity, and savings on hard copy.
- Better customer service – responsive and personalized support with staff accessing customers over the web.
- Distribution of information through remote offices nationally or globally.

Intranets are also used for internal marketing communications since they can include:

- Staff phone directories.
- Staff procedures or quality manuals.
- Information for agents such as product specifications, current list and discounted prices, competitor information, factory schedules, and stocking levels, all of which normally have to be updated frequently and can be costly.
- Staff bulletin or newsletter.
- Training courses.

Total cost of ownership (TCO)
The sum of all cost elements of managing information systems for end-users, including purchase, support *and* maintenance.

Intranets can be used for much more than publishing information, as shown in Box 3.1. Web browsers also provide an access platform for business applications which were traditionally accessed using separate software programs. This can help reduce the **total cost of ownership (TCO)** of delivering and managing information systems. Applications delivered through a web-based intranet or extranet can be cheaper to maintain since no installation is required on the end-user's PC, upgrades are easier and there are fewer problems with users reconfiguring software. Applications include tools for workgroups to collaborate on projects, self-service human resources (e.g. to book a holiday or arrange a job review), financial modelling tools and a vehicle-build tracking system. Traditional information such as competitive intelligence, company news and manufacturing quality statistics can also be shared.

Box 3.1	12 ways to use your intranet to cut your costs

This guidance is from the Intranet Benchmarking Forum (IBF), the world's leading intranet and portal benchmarking group.

1 *Build bridges with internal customers.* Intranet initiatives are driven from the business units that will benefit. They say: '*Where intranets are achieving cost-savings, the impetus often comes from business units or functions, not the central intranet team. From HR and finance to manufacturing units and customer service operations, it is these business areas that are best placed to identify inefficient processes and practices in their area, and then approach the intranet team for help.*'

2 *Research users' needs.* This is, of course, a prerequisite of any successful information systems project. The IBF advise: '*The leaders in the field carry out research with the aim of building a picture, for each of their main employee groups, of their working patterns, the processes they follow and where the frustrations, blockages and inefficiencies lie, as well as finding out in detail about how they currently use the intranet and where they think it could help them work more efficiently.*'

3 *Implement or expand self-service.* Re-engineering process to enable self-service is '*The most significant way intranets cut costs for organisations is by enabling administrative processes to be reengineered – particularly in the HR area – and migrated online via the intranet. This can make processes far more cost-efficient (and effective) for the organisation and individual users*'. They give the example of how the British Airways intranet has achieved some impressive results following its re-launch as a self-service intranet:
    - 100 per cent of internal recruitment is now carried out on the intranet
    - 100 per cent of staff travel is booked on the intranet
    - 33 per cent of staff training is delivered through the intranet
    - 80 per cent of employees update their contact details on the intranet
    - The most popular self-service application has been the relatively simple e-Pay tool where employees access their payslip. This alone delivered BA savings of £90,000 per year.

4 *Target further design, print and distribution savings.* Reduction in physical and distribution costs through moving towards a 'paperless office'.

5 *Improve usability.* Making it quicker to find information through improving information architecture and 'findability', i.e. better browsing and searching functionality.

6 *Revamp HR content.* As indicated by the examples given above, improvements to HR functionality often give the biggest benefits to the employees and the business.

7 *Create content for customer-facing staff.* The example is given of the UK-based insurance group Prudential which has used its intranet to provide content and tools that help contact centre staff respond rapidly to telephone, e-mail and postal enquiries from customers.

8 *Create internal helpdesk content.* Costs of internal helpdesks, for example for IT, HR or Finance, can be delivered more efficiently via the intranet. The IBF suggests it costs about £8 to £10 to respond to each request for help by telephone, and about £5 to do so by e-mail.

9 *Enhance the employee directory.* The IBF say: '*A good people search can be a killer app: many intranet experts agree that, more than anything else, staff want to use the intranet to get in touch with one another.*'

10 *Put senior leaders online.* Intranets make it easier and more cost-effective for senior leaders to communicate their ideas and 'walk the virtual floor' – for example through blogs that allow staff to comment on posts, or through a regular online webcast or chat Q&A sessions.

11 *Leverage online meetings*. This is web conferencing which, although not directly enabled by the intranet, should facilitate collaboration.

12 *Measure savings*. The IBF state that: '*Few organisations have made progress in measuring the cost savings they can attribute to the intranet, or even to parts of it.*' This is partly because it is difficult to measure cause and effect. But the study does give some examples:

- Ford estimates that online training delivered via its portal will drive down training costs to an average of $0.21 per class, down from $300–$2,500 per class.
- Cisco cut the cost of processing employee expense reports from $50.69 with the previous forms-based system to $1.90 three years later. Total corporate savings by that third year were $7m. The average elapsed time for processing each expense report dropped from 21 to 4 days.
- BT's implementation of e-procurement encompassed 95 per cent of all its goods – including desktop computing, stationery, clothing, travel and agency staff – so reduced the average purchasing transaction cost from £56 to £40 inside a year. Another example is the introduction of an online room booking service some years ago. For a total development cost of £150,000, the service initially reduced direct costs by about £450,000 p.a. The cost savings were achieved through the near elimination of a call centre that previously handled the bookings.

Source: Adapted from IBF (2008).

In addition to these 'classical' uses of intranets, intranet developer Odyssey (www.odyssey-i.com) identifies some less common intranet applications :

1 *Employee incentive scheme.* Companies reward the best employees according to anonymous voting by their peers. At the end of each quarter, prizes such as DVD players and televisions are awarded.

2 *Text messaging.* A distribution company keeps in touch with its sales staff and drivers through enabling staff to contact colleagues who are 'on the road' using **SMS** text messaging.

3 *Holiday booking.* A workflow system forwards holiday requests to the relevant manager and informs the applicant automatically. Team managers can also check on the intranet when people within their group have booked holidays.

4 *Resource booking.* Viewing and making bookings of meeting rooms is another simple application that can save time.

5 *News screen.* Displaying the company's latest news and most recent achievements on a dedicated screen can give a focal point to a waiting room or foyer area.

6 *Integrated external resources.* Route planning, mapping or traffic news sites can be integrated into the intranet to save time for staff. One example of this is a housing authority that stores its list of properties on the intranet. Each house has a link to a mapping site (e.g. Multimap www.multimap.com), which will display the location of the property based on its postcode.

SMS (short message services)
The formal name for text messaging.

Intranets need to include a suitable technology to enable staff to create and manage their own content. **Content management system (CMS)** features are built into intranet and extranet systems to achieve this (see Chapter 12). For example, Microsoft Sharepoint Server is commonly used for intranet management (http://sharepoint.microsoft.com).

The management challenges of implementing and maintaining an intranet (see *Intranet Journal*, 2009) are similar to those of an extranet. In the next section, we examine five key management issues of extranets.

Content management system (CMS)
Software used to manage creation, editing and review of web-based content.

Extranet applications

Although an extranet may sound complex, from a user point of view it is straightforward. If you have bought a book or CD online and have been issued with a username and password to access your account, then you have used an extranet. This is a consumer extranet. Extranets are also used to provide online services which are restricted to business customers. If you visit the Ifazone (www.ifazone.com) extranet of financial services company Standard Life, which is designed for the independent financial advisers who sell its products, you will see that the website only has three initial options – log-in, register and demonstrations. The Ifazone extranet is vital to Standard Life since 90 per cent of business is now introduced through this source. This usage of the term 'extranet', referring to electronic business-to-business communications, is most typical (see, for example, Vlosky *et al.*, 2000). Hannon (1998) concurs, and also notes the relationship of extranets with intranets, describing an extranet as

> *any network connected to another network for the purpose of sharing information and data. An extranet is created when two businesses connect their respective intranets for business communication and transactions.*

Dell Premier is an example of a business customer extranet for a large corporation. You can read how Dell positions the benefits in Mini case study 3.1. The system helps Dell encourage customer loyalty since once integration occurs customers are less likely to change suppliers due to switching costs. It is an example of 'soft lock-in' which we introduced in Chapter 1. Dell also encourages consumers to make suggestions about new products through its IdeaStorm (www.ideastorm.com) service for which customers have to be registered to add comments, so could be considered as a form of extranet although Dell Premier is a better example since it shows how a service can be provided continuously.

Mini Case Study 3.1   Dell Premier customer extranet provides e-business services

Dell provides Premier Dell.com (formerly Premier Pages) for its business customers. This is how Dell describes the service to customers:

Premier.Dell.com is a secure, customizable procurement and support site designed to save your organization time and money through all phases of I/T product ownership.

- *Easy Ordering – A custom online store ensures access to your products at your price.*
- *Easy Tracking – View real-time order status, online invoices and purchase history details.*
- *Easy Control – Custom access groups define what users can see and do within Premier.*

It explains how Dell Premier can be used for e-procurement as follows:

Dell integrates a customized Premier catalog with your Enterprise Resource Planning (ERP) system to give you more control over your purchasing process and to help ensure accurate and efficient transactions.

Aligning with your Procurement System *– Dell can integrate with a variety of ERP applications, including: Ariba, Commerce One, Lawson, Oracle Purchasing, SAP, SciQuest and more.*

Dramatic Savings *– E-Procurement integration can reduce purchasing overhead and order processing time. Consolidating purchase records into one system streamlines administration, while electronic invoicing and payment save employee processing time.*

The Solution for You *– Return your shopping contents to your ERP system electronically as Dell's integrated platform is designed to help improve efficiencies and order accuracy, while reducing product delivery times.*

Source: http://premier.dell.com.

Vlosky *et al.* (2000) refer to these business benefits of an extranet:

1 *Information sharing in secure environment.* Information needed to support business through a range of business partners can be shared using an extranet. Vlosky *et al.* (2000) give the example of advertising agency Saatchi using an extranet to allow their advertisers to access draft advertising material during a project. Information for suppliers is often shared by providing a log-in to a database which shows demand for products.

2 *Cost reduction.* Operating processes can be made more efficient through an extranet. The example given by these authors is Merisel, a $3.5 billion computer hardware reseller reducing its order processing costs by 70%. Such cost reductions are achieved by reducing the number of people involved in placing orders and the need to rekey information from paper documents.

3 *Order processing and distribution.* The authors refer to an 'electronic integration effect'. For example, an extranet can connect a retailer's point of sales terminals to a supplier's delivery system, ensuring prompt replenishment of goods sold. This potentially means less lost sales because of out-of-stock items and a lower inventory holding is needed.

4 *Customer service.* Improving levels of service is one of the main benefits of the Premier Dell.com extranet described above, although it also has the other benefits listed above. Distributors or agents of companies can also find information such as customized pricing or advertising materials. For example, 3M provides open web access to individual customers to find information about its office products such as Post-it notes and transparent films (www.3m.com/uk/office), but it also offers an extranet for distributors such as Spicers (www.spicers.net) and Euroffice (www.euroffice.co.uk).

Many of the management issues involved with managing extranets are similar to those for intranets. These are five key questions that need to be asked when reviewing an existing extranet or when creating a new extranet:

1 *Are the levels of usage sufficient?* Extranets require a substantial investment, so efforts need to be made to encourage usage since we are asking the users of the service to change their behaviour. It is in the organization's interest to encourage usage, to achieve a return on their investment and achieve the cost efficiencies intended.

2 *Is it effective and efficient?* Controls must be put in place to assess how well it is working and improve its performance. Return on investment should be assessed. For example, visitor levels can be measured for different types of audiences and the level of usage for accessing different types of information can be assessed. The direct and indirect cost savings achieved through each extranet transaction can be calculated to help assess effectiveness. For example, 3M, manufacturer of many products including office products such as Post-it notes, has an extranet to connect to the office supply retailers (see www.3m.com/uk/easy). Retailers download the latest price lists and promotional information such as product pictures. Each digital download represents a significant saving in comparison to shipping physical items to the retailer.

3 *Who has ownership of the extranet?* Functions with an interest in an extranet include IT (technical infrastructure), Finance (setting payments and exchanging purchase orders and invoices), Marketing (providing marketing materials and sales data to distributors or providing services to customers) and Operations Management (exchanging information about inventory). Clearly the needs of these different parties must be resolved and management controls established.

4 *What are the levels of service quality?* Since an extranet will become a vital part of an organization's operating process, a problem with the speed or availability of the extranet could cause loss of a lot of money; it is arguably more important than the public-facing Internet site.

5 *Is the quality of the information adequate?* The most important attributes of information quality is that it is up to date and accurate. Vlosky *et al.* (2000) point out the importance of liability if information is inaccurate or the extranet crashes.

It will be seen in Chapter 6 that extranets are used extensively to support supply chain management as resources are ordered from suppliers and transformed into products and services delivered to customers. At Marshall Industries, for example, when a new customer order is received across the extranet it automatically triggers a scheduling order for the warehouse (transferred by intranet), an order acknowledgement for the customer and a shipping status when the order is shipped (Mougayer, 1998). To enable different applications on the intranet to communicate, **middleware** is used by systems integrators to create links between organizational applications or between different members of a supply chain. For example, within a supply chain management system, middleware will translate requests from external systems such as a sales order so they are understood by internal systems (relevant fields are updated in the database) and then it will trigger follow-up events to fulfil the order.

Middleware is now also referred to as **enterprise application integration (EAI)** (*Internet World*, 1999). Such applications include a sales-order processing system and a warehousing system. It now also includes software programs from different organizations.

A final example of the use of an extranet on a global basis is that of Mecalux (www.mecalux.com). Mecalux, based in Barcelona, is involved in the design, manufacture and assembly of storage systems. Since it was formed in 1996, the company has expanded and has offices in Argentina, Germany, the UK, France, Portugal, Singapore and Mexico. One of the challenges of this expansion was to improve communications between its representatives around the world and to supply them with the information needed to improve customer service. The management team wanted to create a paperless company where information flows freely in all locations around the world. This makes it easier for the engineers to have the information necessary to respond to any customer's requirements. The extranet created to solve this problem has, for example, enabled representatives in Singapore to tap into data held on the server in Spain to check the availability of the product and get it to a local customer in the shortest possible timeframe. The solution also permits technicians and engineers to collaborate on ideas and work together on future designs from anywhere in the world.

Firewalls

Firewalls ensure that outside access to confidential information does not occur. Firewalls are usually created as software mounted on a separate server at the point where the company is connected to the Internet. Firewall software can then be configured to accept links only from trusted domains representing other offices in the company. A firewall has implications for e-marketing since staff accessing a website from work may not be able to access some content such as graphics plug-ins.

The use of firewalls within the infrastructure of a company is illustrated in Figure 3.6. It is evident that multiple firewalls are used to protect information on the company. The information made available to third parties over the Internet and extranet is partitioned by another firewall using what is referred to as the 'demilitarized zone' (DMZ). Corporate data on the intranet are then mounted on other servers inside the company.

The design of security measures for e-business is reviewed in '*Focus on* Security design for e-business' (Chapter 11, p. 624).

Encouraging use of intranets and extranets

Intranets and extranets often represent a change to existing methods of working for business people so encouraging usage is often a challenge. They may be launched to a great fanfare, but, if their content is neglected, their usage will dwindle. Common warning signs identified in the KM Column (2002) are:

Middleware

Software used to facilitate communications between business applications including data transfer and control.

Enterprise application integration (EAI)

Software used to facilitate communications between business applications including data transfer and control.

Firewall

A specialized software application mounted on a server at the point where the company is connected to the Internet. Its purpose is to prevent unauthorized access into the company from outsiders.

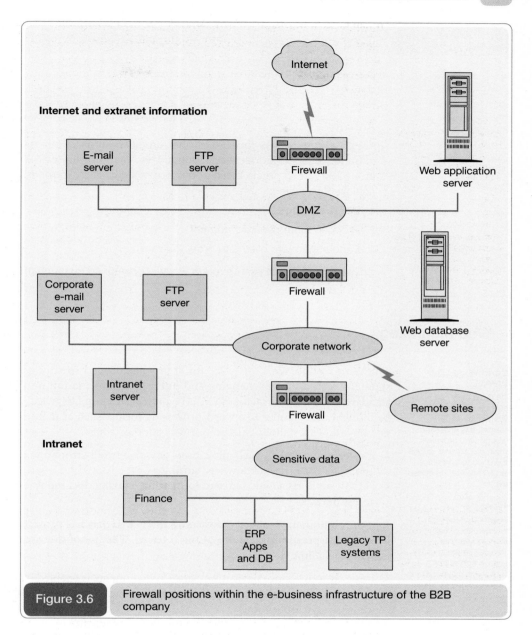

| Figure 3.6 | Firewall positions within the e-business infrastructure of the B2B company |

- Staff usage of the intranet is low, and not growing.
- The majority of content is out of date, incomplete or inaccurate.
- The intranet is very inconsistent in appearance, particularly across sections managed by different groups.
- Almost all information on the intranet is reference material, not news or recent updates.
- Most sections of the intranet are used solely to publicize the existence of the business groups within the organization.

To explore solutions to limited usage of intranets and extranets, complete Activity 3.3.

Activity 3.3	Overcoming limited use of intranets and extranets in a B2B company

Purpose

To illustrate solutions to limited usage of intranets and extranets.

Activity

A B2B company has found that after an initial surge of interest in its intranet and extranet, usage has declined dramatically. Many of the warning signs mentioned in the KM (2002) article listed above are evident. The e-business manager wants to achieve these aims:

1 Increase usage.

2 Produce more dynamic content.

3 Encourage more clients to order (extranet).

Answers to activities can be found at www.pearsoned.co.uk/chaffey

Web technology

World Wide Web (WWW)

The most common technique for publishing information on the Internet. It is accessed through web browsers which display web pages of embedded graphics and HTML/XML-encoded text.

Hyperlink

A method of moving between one website page and another, indicated to the user by an image or text highlighted by underlining and/or a different colour.

The **World Wide Web**, or 'web' for short, has proved so successful since it provides a standard method for exchanging and publishing information on the Internet. The main standard document format is HTML (Hypertext Markup Language, Chapter 12), which can be thought of as similar to a word-processing format such as that used for Microsoft Word documents. This standard has been widely adopted since:

- it offers **hyperlinks** which allow users to move readily from one document or website to another – the process known as 'surfing';
- HTML supports a wide range of formatting, making documents easy to read on different access devices.

It is the combination of web browsers and HTML that has proved so successful in establishing widespread business use of the Internet. The use of these tools provides a range of benefits including:

- It is easy to use since navigation between documents is enabled by clicking on hyperlinks or images. This soon becomes a very intuitive way of navigation which is similar across all websites and applications.
- Interactivity is supported by web forms which enable discussions through social networks and purchase on e-commerce sites.
- It can provide a graphical environment supporting multimedia which is popular with users and gives a visual medium for advertising.
- The standardization of tools and growth in demand means information can be exchanged with many businesses and consumers.
- Flexibility in the style of designs and tailoring them for using on different access devices from desktop computers to wireless devices.
- Browser capabilities are extensible through the use of browser **plug-ins**, **extensions** and toolbars which enable users to access standard services.

Browser plug-in

An add-on program to a web browser, providing extra functionality such as animation.

Browser extensions

The capability of a browser to add new services through new add-ons or plug-ins or customizing through different visual themes, particularly used in Mozilla Firefox browser.

Browser extensions and toolbars can be useful for site owners to add value through new functionality and encourage continued usage of their services. Think of examples such as the Google Toolbar (http://toolbar.google.com) and the Facebook toolbar for Firefox. Gadgets within Windows provide similar opportunities.

Web browsers and servers

Web browsers
Browsers such as Mozilla Firefox or Microsoft Internet Explorer provide an easy method of accessing and viewing information stored as web documents on different servers.

Web servers
Store and present the web pages accessed by web browsers.

Cascading style sheets (CSS)
Enable web designers to define standard styles (e.g. fonts, spacing and colours) to hypertext markup language documents. By separating the presentation style of documents from the content of documents, CSS simplifies web authoring and site maintenance since style can be defined across a whole site (or sections of sites).

Static web page
A page on the web server that is invariant.

Dynamically created web page
A page that is created in real time, often with reference to a database query, in response to a user request.

Web application frameworks
A standard programming framework based on reusable library functions for creating dynamic websites through a programming language.

Web application server
A collection of software processes which is accessed by a standard programming interface (API) of a web application framework to serve dynamic website functionality in response to requests received from browsers.

Transaction log files
A web-server file that records all page requests.

Web analytics system
Information on visitor volumes, sources and pages visited are analysed through web analytics systems.

Web browsers are software which we use to access the information on the WWW that is stored on **web servers**.

Web servers are used to store, manage and supply the information on the WWW. The main web browsers are Microsoft Internet Explorer and Mozilla Firefox with the Apple Safari browser and Google Chrome having relatively small market share. Browsers display the text and graphics accessed from websites and provide the interactions. As described in Chapter 11, **cascading style sheets** (CSS) are now used by most websites to enable standard styling and interaction features.

Figure 3.7 indicates the process by which web browsers communicate with web servers. A request from the client PC is executed when the user types in a web address, clicks on a hyperlink or fills in an online form such as a search. This request is then sent to the ISP and routed across the Internet to the destination server using the mechanism described in the section on *protocols* in networking standards, below. The server returns either a **static (fixed) web page**, or, if it requires reference to a database, such as a request for product information, it will pass the query on to a database server and will then return this to the customer as a **dynamically created web page**.

Dynamic websites with e-commerce facilities are not created simply using static HTML; instead they are implemented through additional functions defined in a **web application framework** which use standard programming conventions or application programming interfaces (APIs) in combination with data storage to achieve different tasks such as simply adding a user to a system or rendering the different page elements of a site. They provide standard functions in libraries to make it quicker to develop functionality than starting from lower-level coding. Functions in the web application framework are executed by a **web application server** which comprises software processes running on the server which accepts and actions requests via the principal web server software (e.g. Apache or Microsoft Information Server).

Information on each page request is stored in a **transaction log file** or **web analytics system** which records the page requested, potential errors and the time it was made and

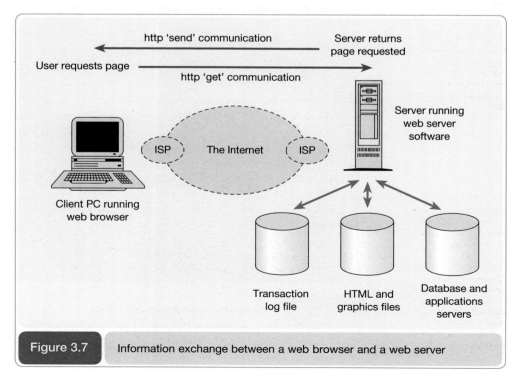

| Figure 3.7 | Information exchange between a web browser and a web server |

the source of the referral or originating site. This enables analysis of the performance of e-business systems. This information can be analysed to assess the success of the website, as explained in Chapter 12 (p. 680). Box 3.2 gives some background information on transaction log files.

Box 3.2 | Inside transaction log files – why hits stands for 'how idiots track success'

Figure 3.8 shows the detail recorded within a transaction log file. This shows the level of work that web servers have to do. This server extract is from DaveChaffey.com which uses the open-source Apache server to serve content. This example shows 10 requests received over a period of 5 seconds. Each line represents a GET request from a web browser for a file on the server. For each page, there are multiple lines or hits since each image or an embedded reference to a script or stylesheet in the page is downloaded separately. In Chapter 12 we show how hits should not be used as a measure for success.

Looking at individual lines shows the information collected available from each transaction:

```
92.236.80.105 - - [08/Sep/2008:17:48:15 -0500] "GET /
Internet-Marketing/C8-Communications/E-tools/Online-PR/what-is-
atomisation-web-2-0/ HTTP/1.1" 200 76137
"http://www.google.co.uk/search?hl=en&client=firefox-a&rls=org.
mozilla%3Aen-GB%3Aofficial&hs=hBc&q=atomised+marketing&btnG=
Search&meta=" "Mozilla/5.0 (Windows; U; Windows NT 5.1; en-GB;
rv:1.8.1.14) Gecko/20080404 Firefox/2.0.0.14"
```

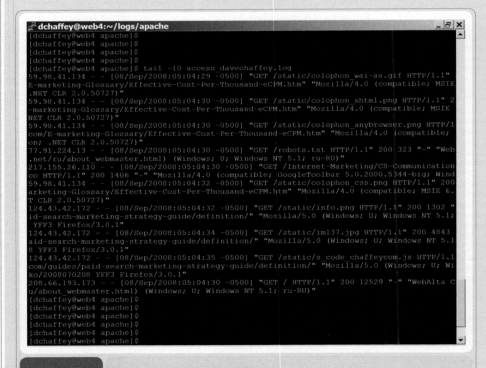

Figure 3.8 Transaction log file example

Here are the elements of the HTTP request step-by-step:

1 *IP address requesting the page*. 92.236.80.105. This can be used to determine the location of the computer or IP assigned address accessing the page.

2 *Date/time stamp for transaction*. [08/Sep/2008:17:48:15 –0500]. This enables site owners to see visitors returning to the site (usually in combination with cookies).

3 *Page request*. "GET /Internet–Marketing/C8–Communications/E-tools/ Online–PR/what–is–atomization–web–2–0/". This is the particular file requested from the server. Subsequently other page components will be downloaded.

4 *Response status code on server*. 200. Important status codes include:

- *200 OK*, the standard response for successful HTTP requests.
- *301 Moved Permanently*, used to tell the browser or user agent that the page has moved forever and future requests should be to the new address – for example when an old site structure is migrated to a new site structure.
- *302 Found (Moved temporarily)*, used for temporary redirection.
- *304 Not Modified*, indicating the page or file hasn't been modified since last requested by the browser. This saves bandwidth and reprocessing on both the server and client.
- *404 Not Found*, this is a significant code since it shows where the requested resource could not be found. These should be monitored so that errors such as links pointing to an invalid address are corrected. Special pages should also be constructed to explain to users what has happened.
- *500 Internal Server Error*, this and other server errors show the server cannot respond due to an error, for example with the content management system.

5 *Referring site*.

```
"http://www.google.co.uk/search?hl=en&client=firefox-a&rls=org.
mozilla%3Aen–GB%3Aofficial&hs=hBc&q=atomized+marketing&btnG=
Search&meta="
```

In this example, this shows us the visit has been referred from Google UK and the search term 'atomized marketing' that the searcher was seeking. You can see this is very useful information for marketers trying to determine why visitors are accessing their site.

6 *User agent*.

```
"Mozilla/5.0 (Windows; U; Windows NT 5.1; en-GB; rv:1.8. 1.14)
Gecko/20080404 Firefox/2.0.0.14".
```

This is a software or browsing device that is used to make the request which is useful for site designers, in this case version 2.0.0.14 of the Mozilla browser. Other significant user agents include search robots such as Googlebot/2.1 (+http://www.google.com/bot.html) and feed readers, for example Feedfetcher-Google (+http://www.google.com/feedfetcher.html).

Browser compatibility
Cross-browser compatibility is the capability of a site to render and deliver interactivity correctly in different versions of web browsers, in particular the most popular browsers: Microsoft Internet Explorer, Mozilla Firefox, Apple Safari and Google Chrome.

Transaction logs also contain information on errors which should be assessed to determine problems with a service.

The main management implication for changes in browser usage is ensuring sites have appropriate **browser compatibility**. An example of a tool for designers to test compatibility is shown in Figure 3.9. We discuss this issue further in Chapter 11 in the context of web design.

| Figure 3.9 | Browsershots – a service for testing cross-browser compatibility
Source: www.browsershots.org. |

Internet-access software applications

Many software tools have been developed to help find, send and receive information across the Internet. These tools are summarized in Table 3.3. In this section we will briefly discuss how to assess the relevance and challenges of managing the most significant of these tools in today's organization. The other tools have either been superseded or are of less relevance from a business perspective.

Really Simple Syndication (RSS) Feeds

Blog, news or other content is published by an XML standard and syndicated for other sites or read by users in RSS reader software services. Now usually shortened to 'feed', e.g. news feed or sports feed.

Web 2.0

In recent years, many tools have been developed which exploit the interactivity and extensibility capabilities of the web. These Web 2.0 services were introduced in Chapter 1 and described in the influential article by Tim O'Reilly (O'Reilly, 2005). We will discuss some of the technologies behind Web 2.0 later in this section.

Table 3.3	Applications of different Internet tools

Internet tool	Summary
Augmented reality	Blends real-world digital data capture to create a browser-based digital representation or experience mimicking that of the real world.
Blogs	Web-based publishing of regularly updated information in an online diary-type format using tools such as Blogger.com, Typepad or WordPress.
Electronic mail or e-mail	Sending messages or documents, such as news about a new product or sales promotion, between individuals is a key Internet capability. In a 2007 report on global e-mail volume, IDC predicted that a staggering 97 billion e-mails would be sent daily in 2007, over 40 billion of which were spam (which we discuss in Chapter 4).
Feeds	**Really Simple Syndication (RSS)** is a well-known XML-based content distribution format commonly used for syndicating and accessing blog information. Standard XML feed AOIformats are also used by merchants updating price comparison sites.
APIs	**Application Programming Interfaces (API)** provide another method, similar to feeds, of transferring information between different web services.
FTP file transfer	The File Transfer Protocol is used as a standard for moving files across the Internet. Commonly used to upload HTML and other files to web servers. FTP is still used for e-business applications such as downloading files such as product price lists or specifications.
Gophers, Archie and WAIS	These tools were important before the advent of the web for storing and searching documents on the Internet. They have largely been superseded by the web and search engines.
Instant Messaging (IM) and Internet Relay Chat (IRC)	These are synchronous communications tools for text-based 'chat' between different users who are logged on at the same time. IM, from providers such as Yahoo and MSN and Twitter (described in Mini case study 3.4), has largely replaced IRC and provides opportunities for advertising to users.
IPTV	Digital TV channels are made available via broadband Internet either as streamed live broadcasts or as archived broadcasts of TV programmes. This is discussed towards the end of this chapter.
Usenet newsgroups	Forums to discuss a particular topic such as a sport, hobby or business area. Traditionally accessed by special newsreader software, but now typically accessed via a web browser from http://groups.google.com.
Secure Shell (SSH) and Telnet	These allow remote command-line access to computer systems. SSH is a more secure replacement for Telnet. For example, a retailer could check to see whether an item was in stock in a warehouse using SSH.
Peer-to-peer file sharing	Peer-to-peer file-sharing technology used to enable sharing of large audio and video files in BitTorrent or approaches such as Kontiki.
Podcasting	A method of downloading and playing audio or video clips (webcasts), targeting portable devices such as the iPod or MP3 players or fixed devices.
Voice over Internet Protocol (VOIP)	Technology for digitally transmitting voice over a LAN or Internet.
Widget	A badge or button incorporated into a site or social network space by its owner, with content or services typically served from another site, making widgets effectively a mini-software application or web service. Content can be updated in real time since the widget interacts with the server each time it loads.
World Wide Web	Widely used for publishing information and running business applications over the Internet accessed through web browsers.

Augmented reality

Augmented reality (AR)
Blends real-world digital data capture typically with a digital camera in a webcam or mobile phone to create a browser-based digital representation or experience mimicking that of the real world.

Augmented reality (AR) is an exciting concept which can help companies improve their customer experience. It is best explained through examples:

1 Glasses Direct created its 'Video Mirror' app (Figure 3.10) which enabled site visitors to model pairs of glasses using their webcam.
2 BMW used AR within a campaign launching their Z4 model on a 'virtual' test drive around the desk!
3 Layar demonstrated an estate agent application using the camera on a mobile phone while overlaying property information in a similar form to Google Street View.

Blogs and blogging

Blog
An online diary or news source prepared by an individual or a group of people. From 'web log'.

'**Blogs**'(web logs) give an easy method of regularly publishing web pages. Many blogs provide commentary or news on a particular subject; others function as more personal online diaries. A typical blog combines text, images, and links to other blogs, web pages, and other media related to its topic. The capability for readers to leave comments in an interactive format is an important part of many blogs. Feedback (traceback) comments from other sites are also sometimes incorporated. Frequency can be hourly, daily, weekly or less frequently.

An example of a useful blog which can keep marketing professionals up to date about e-business developments is Smart Insightsblog (Figure 3.11). Business blogs are created by people within an organization. They can be useful in showing the expertise of those within the organization, but need to be carefully controlled to avoid releasing damaging information. Technology company Sun Microsystems has several hundred bloggers and has a policy to control them to make positive comments.

Figure 3.10	Video Mirror from Glasses Direct
	Source: www.glassesdirect.co.uk.

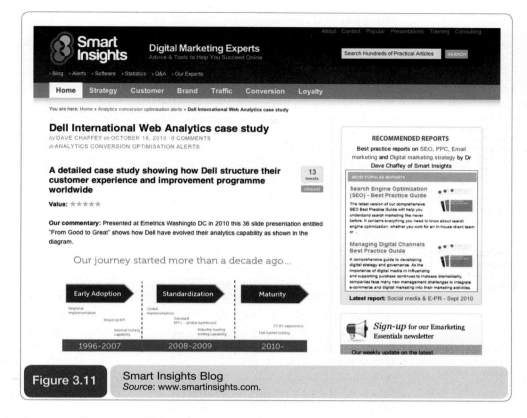

Figure 3.11   Smart Insights Blog
Source: www.smartinsights.com.

Services to enable blogging

There are many free services which enable anyone to blog (for example www.blogger.com which was purchased by Google in 2003). Blogs were traditionally accessed through online tools (e.g. Google Reader) or software readers (www.rssreader.com) but were incorporated into mainstream software in 2005–6.

The main tools, to create blogs for individuals or companies, in approximate order of popularity, are:

1 *Movable Type* (www.movabletype.org) from Six Apart is a download for management on your servers. Paid service.
2 *Typepad* (www.typepad.com), also from Six Apart, offers this as an online service like most of those below, which is easier for smaller businesses. Paid service.
3 *Blogger* (www.blogger.com), purchased by Google some time ago – the best free option?
4 *Wordpress* (www.wordpress.com) – open-source alternative. Highly configurable. Used by many personal bloggers.
5 *Other open-source CMSs more often used for corporate sites, e.g. Plone, Drupal and Mambo* or corporate content management systems such as Microsoft Office SharePoint server (see Chapter 12 for discussion of the management issues).

The blogging format enables the content on a website to be delivered in different ways. For example, the Smart Insights blog (Figure 3.11) has a lot of rich content related to Internet marketing which can be delivered in different ways:

- *By topic* (in categories or topics to browse) – example, online PR category.
- *By tag* (more detailed topics – each article will be tagged with several tags to help them appear in searches) – example, 'blogs and blogging' tag.
- *By author* (features from different columnists who can be internal or external).
- *By time* (all posts broken down by the different methods above are in reverse date order).

Tagging and folksonomies

A defining characteristic of Web 2.0 closely related to blogs is '**tagging**' whereby users add their own meta-data to content they produce, consume and share. On Flickr (www.flickr. com) and Delicious (www.delicious.com), for example, any user can attach tags to digital media items (files, bookmarks, images). The aggregation of tags creates an organic, free-form, 'bottom-up' taxonomy. The information architect Thomas van der Wal coined the term 'folksonomy' derived from the idea of a 'folk-taxonomy' (Fitzgerald, 2006). **Folksonomies** are flat (that is, they have no hierarchy, and show no parent–child relationships) and, critically, are completely uncontrolled. A key implication of their lack of structure is that they do not support functions such as drill-down searching and cross-referencing. There is much discussion of the potential for folksonomies to coexist with and complement the 'official' taxonomies (Johnston, 2008).

Electronic mail or e-mail

E-mail is now an essential business communication tool and is also widely used for personal use For the individual, managing these communications in their e-mail inbox is rapidly becoming impossible! For the information services manager and indeed any business manager, there are four main controls that need to be considered to reduce the amount of time staff spend reading **inbound e-mail**:

1 Spam (unsolicited e-mail).
2 Internal business e-mail.
3 External business e-mail.
4 Personal e-mail (friends and family).

At the same time the policy will seek to improve productivity and the quality of response to customers and partners. The controls that can be introduced in each area are described in Chapter 11.

 Outbound e-mail marketing is an important tool for communicating with customers, as explained in Chapter 9.

Feeds

Feeds are an important method of exchanging different types of information using standard formats typically based on XML.

 The best-known type of feed is **Really Simple Syndication (RSS)**, also sometimes known as 'Rich Site Summary', which is an Internet standard for publishing and exchanging content using XML. From a practical viewpoint it enables two things. First, content that originates on one site can be syndicated or published on another site. Second, and of much greater interest to promoting a website, it is a relatively new method of distributing alerts to customers. Initially, the RSS messages were received by specialist software such as RSS Reader (www.rssreader.com) or sites which receive feeds such as Netvibes (www.netvibes. com), iGoogle (www.google.com/ig) and Bloglines (www.bloglines.com). These RSS readers, or aggregators, poll for RSS at a defined interval.

 RSS has been embraced by major publishers such as the BBC. It enables you to subscribe to very specific content that interests you and then provides you with an alert when a new story is published. For example, I subscribe to the e-commerce news channel and that for Arsenal, my football team. In this arrangement subscription does not require opt-in, it just requires a request of the feed. So RSS is potentially a threat to the permission marketing model since there is no data exchange and it is easy for subscribers to switch them on and off.

 More technical information on RSS is available at: www.rss-specifications.com/rss-submission.htm.

RSS feeds are now more widely adopted since it is available beyond specialist readers in the still ubiquitous Microsoft Internet Explorer and Outlook products. According to Avenue A – Razorfish (2008) 55% of web users in the US consume feeds, although this figure will be significantly lower in other geographical areas. However, the benefits of feeds for consumers are clear:

1 More granular control of communications (e.g. choose content updates from any channel on the BBC site such as channels about a sport, team or any news topic.
2 Can switch on and off without registration (reduces control of marketers). Someone could subscribe to holiday offers from a travel website within a 2-week period, for instance.
3 Little or no spam since messages are pulled to the reader from the server (currently – although ads may be placed within a feed).

RSS is a threat to e-mail marketers since typically users profile and qualify themselves before opt-in to e-mail. With RSS this permission marketing isn't necessary since it is a pull service where the user retrieves information from the website hosting the RSS feed.

Application programming interfaces (APIs)

Traditionally, organizations have sought to keep proprietary information within their firewalls for security reasons and to protect their intellectual property. But in the Internet era, this strategy may limit opportunities to add value to their services or share information via other online companies and their web services to increase their potential reach. Here are some examples from retail, publishing and software companies where APIs, sometimes known as the the 'Programmable Web', have been used to help gain competitive advantage.

- *Amazon Web Services* (http://aws.amazon.com). One example of AWS allows affiliates, developers and website publishers to use Amazon Product Discovery which enables other sites to incorporate data about Amazon products and pricing.
- *Facebook* and *Twitter* use their APIs to help other sites embed social content into their sites.
- *The Guardian Newspaper Open Platform* (www.guardian.co.uk/open-platform) enables sharing of content and statistics from *The Guardian*. In one application developed initially as a student project, WhatCouldICook.com uses recipes from *The Guardian* as part of an arrangement to share ad revenue.
- *Google APIs* exist for a number of its services, most notably Google Maps which, according to this directory (http://www.programmableweb.com/apis/directory), is one of the most popular mashups created through an API. The Google Analytics API has enabled many businesses and third-party application developers to visualize web performance data in a more tailored way.
- *Kayak* is an aggregator which allows third-party sites to integrate kayak.com searches and results into their website, desktop application, or mobile phone application.
- *Tesco* launched a public API for its grocery products in 2008 which was closed in 2010. The API powered some internal services such as iPhone apps and continues as a private API.

IPTV (Internet TV)

IPTV (Internet Protocol television)
Digital television service is delivered using Internet Protocol, typically by a broadband connection. IPTV can be streamed for real-time viewing or downloaded before playback.

The growth in popularity of **IPTV** or 'Internet TV', where TV and video are streamed via broadband across the Internet, is one of the most exciting developments in recent years. In 2007 services offering streamed viewing of hundreds of channels from providers such as the Europe-based Joost (Figure 3.12, www.joost.com) and the US service Hulu (www.hulu.com) launched, and there are many competitors such as Babelgum, Vuze and Veoh. IPTV is sometimes referred to as non-linear TV or on-demand broadcasting.

IPTV is also used to deliver standard channels available on satellite. Then there is also the IPTV option of digital TV downloaded before playback, as is possible with many traditional broadcasters such as the BBC, Sky or ITV using peer-to-peer distribution, where many users download and share small chunks of the programme. Who pays for the large bandwidth required by IPTV is an ongoing debate, covered in the next section on net neutrality.

Figure 3.12 Joost service

It will be essential for marketers and ad agencies to learn how to exploit IPTV in order to reach online audiences

Providers of IPTV services are experimenting with new ad formats. Research by Moorey-Denholm and Green (2007) has shown that effective video ads are substantially shorter, with brief pre-rolls and interstitial ads between shots being the order of the day. A further challenge is that advertisers will only want their ads associated with certain types of content for targeting purposes and to avoid damage to their brand by association. IPTV also offers opportunities for programme makers to involve more interaction with their audiences through chat and channel forums. Brands can provide their own channels such as the brand channels available on YouTube (www.youtube.com/advertise).

Brand advertisers can develop their own brief IPTV viral clips to spread their message – witness the 2007 video viral clips from Cadbury and a follow-up spoof from Wonderbra which gained millions of views on YouTube. Because of limits on the amount of video that can be uploaded and control of the environment there are some subscription payment video-hosting services such as MyDeo (www.mydeo.com) emerging.

Voice over IP (VoIP)

Voice over IP (VOIP)
Voice data is transferred across the Internet – it enables phone calls to be made over the Internet.

Voice over IP (VoIP) can be used for transmitting voice over a LAN or on a wider scale. You will remember that IP stands for Internet Protocol and so VoIP enables phone calls to be made over the Internet. IP enables a single network to handle all types of communications needs of an organization, i.e. data, voice and multimedia. VoIP (pronounced 'voyp') is proving increasingly popular for reducing the cost of making phone calls within an office and between offices, particularly internationally. IOD (2005) estimates that after initial investment, the cost of managing a converged VoIP communications system could be 50 per cent lower than managing separate voice and data systems. In the longer term major telecommunications companies such as AT&T and BT will replace their existing voice networks with IP networks.

Other benefits include:

- Click-to-call – users click the number they want from an on-screen directory.
- Call forwarding and conferencing to people at other locations.
- Unified messaging. E-mails, voicemails and faxes are all integrated into a single inbox.
- Hot-desking – calls are routed to staff wherever they log-in – on-site or off-site.
- Cost control – review and allocation of costs between different businesses is more transparent.

Several options are available:

1 Peer-to-peer. The best-known peer-to-peer solution is Skype which offers free calls or video-conferencing between Internet-connected PCs that are enabled with a head-set (sometimes called 'softphones'). A service called SkypeOut enables calls to landlines or mobile phones at a reduced cost compared to traditional billing. This service is only really suited to smaller businesses, but could be used in larger businesses for some staff who call abroad frequently to bypass the central system.

2 Hosted service. A company makes use of a large centralized IP-based system shared between many companies. This potentially reduces costs, but some companies might be concerned about outsourcing their entire phone directory.

3 Complete replacement of all telephone systems. This is potentially costly and disruptive in the short term, but new companies or relocating companies may find this the most cost-effective solution.

4 Upgrading existing telephone systems to use VoIP. Typically, the best compromise for existing companies.

Widgets

Widgets
A badge or button incorporated into a site or social network space by its owner, with content or services typically served from another site, making widgets effectively a mini-software application or web service. Content can be updated in real time since the widget interacts with the server each time it loads.

Widgets are tools made available on a website or on a user's desktop. They either provide some functionality, like a calculator, or they provide real-time information, for example on news or weather.

Site owners can encourage partners to place them on their sites and this will help educate people about your brand, possibly generate backlinks for SEO purposes (Chapter 9) and also engage with a brand when they're not on the brand owner's site. Widgets offer partner sites the opportunity to add value to their visitors through the gadget functionality or content, or to add to their brand through association with you (co-branding).

The main types of widget are:

1 *Web widgets.* Web widgets have been used for a long time as part of affiliate marketing, but they are getting more sophisticated, enabling searches on a site, real-time price updates or even streaming video.

2 *Google gadgets.* Different content can be incorporated onto a personalized Google 'iGoogle' home page.

3 *Desktop and operating system gadgets.* Microsoft Windows makes it easier to create and enable subscription to these widgets and place them into sidebars.

4 *Social media widgets.* These encourage site visitors to subscribe to RSS or to bookmark the page on their favourite social media site like Delicious, Digg or Technorati.

5 *Facebook applications.* Facebook has opened up its API (application programming interface) to enable developers to create small interactive programs that users can add to their space to personalize it.

Atomization

Atomization
In a Web 2.0 context, refers to a concept where the content on a site is broken down into smaller fundamental units which can then be distributed via the web through links to other sites. Examples of atomization include the stories and pages in individual feeds being syndicated to third-party sites and widgets.

Atomization is a concept which incorporates some of the marketing techniques we have reviewed such as posts on social networks, feeds and widgets.

Atomization traditionally refers to fine particles of powder or liquid, but in a Web 2.0 context it describes how the content on a website can be broken down into smaller components and then can be released on to the web where they can be aggregated together with other content to provide content and services valuable for other site owners and visitors. These are typically implemented through standard APIs that can be embedded in a page through JavaScript.

For site owners, options to consider for the application of atomization include:

1 Providing content feeds in different categories through their content management system. The BBC effectively provides tens of thousands of newsletters at the level of detail or granularity to support the interests of their readers, i.e. separate feeds at different levels of aggregation, e.g. sport, football, Premier League football or a fan's individual team.

2 Separate out content which should be provided as a data feed of news stories or statistics into widgets on other sites. Example – the 2007-launched UK retail statistics widget dashboard for iGoogle.

3 Develop web services which update widgets with data from their databases. A classic example is the justgiving widget (www.justgiving.com) where money raised by a charity donor is regularly updated.

4 Create badges which can be incorporated within blogs or social networks by their fans or advocates.

5 Review whether widgets or feeds from other companies can be included within their content to provide value for their users. For example, the Facebook plug-ins (http://developers.facebook.com/plugins) have helped companies integrate Facebook within their site.

How does it work? Internet standards

In this section we look briefly at Internet standards which have been adopted to enable information transfer. Knowledge of these terms is useful for anyone involved in the management of e-commerce since discussion with suppliers may involve them.

Networking standards

Internet standards are important in that they are at the heart of definitions of the Internet. According to Leiner *et al.* (2000), on 24 October 1995 the Federal Networking Council unanimously passed a resolution defining the term 'Internet':

> *'Internet' refers to the global information system that – (i) is logically linked together by a globally unique address space based on the Internet Protocol (IP) or its subsequent extensions/follow-ons; (ii) is able to support communications using the Transmission Control Protocol/Internet Protocol (TCP/IP) suite or its subsequent extensions/follow-ons, and/or other IP-compatible protocols; and (iii) provides, uses or makes accessible, either publicly or privately, high level services layered on the communications and related infrastructure described herein.*

TCP/IP

TCP/IP

The Transmission Control Protocol is a transport-layer protocol that moves data between applications. The Internet Protocol is a network-layer protocol that moves data between host computers.

TCP/IP development was led by Robert Kahn and Vince Cerf in the late 1960s and early 1970s and, according to Leiner *et al.* (2000), four rules controlled Kahn's early work on this protocol:

1 Distinct networks would be able to communicate seamlessly with other networks.

2 Communications would be on a best-effort basis, that is, if a data packet did not reach the final destination, it would be retransmitted from the source until successful receipt.

3 Black boxes would be used to connect the networks; these are now known as 'gateways' and 'routers'.

4 There would be no global control of transmissions – these would be governed by the requester and sender of information.

It can be seen that simplicity, speed and independence from control were at the heart of the development of the TCP/IP standards.

The data transmissions standards such as TCP/IP are part of a larger set of standards known as the Open Systems Interconnection (OSI) model. This defines a layered model that enables servers to communicate with other servers and clients. When implemented in software, the combined layers are referred to as a 'protocol stack'. The seven layers of the OSI model are:

- *Application.* The program such as a web browser that creates and receives messages.
- *Presentation.* These protocols are usually part of the operating system.
- *Session.* This includes data-transfer protocols such as SMTP, HTTP and FTP.
- *Transport.* This ensures the integrity of data transmitted. Examples include TCP and Novell SPX.
- *Network.* Defines protocols for opening and maintaining links between servers. The best known are the Internet protocol IP and Novell IPX.
- *Data link.* Defines the rules for sending and receiving information.
- *Physical.* Low-level description of physical transmission methods.

The postal service is a good analogy for the transmission of data around the Internet using the TCP/IP protocol. Before we send mail, we always need to add a destination address. Likewise, the IP acts as an addressed envelope that is used to address a message to the appropriate IP address of the receiver (Figure 3.13).

The Internet is a packet-switched network that uses TCP/IP as its protocol. This means that, as messages or packets of data are sent, there is no part of the network that is dedicated to them. This is like the fact that when your letters and parcels are sent by post they are mixed with letters and parcels from other people The transmission media of the Internet such as telephone lines, satellite links and optical cables are the equivalent of the vans, trains and planes that are used to carry post. Transmission media include analogue media such as phone lines and faster, digital media such as Integrated Service Digital Network technology (ISDN) and more recently the Asynchronous Digital Subscriber Line (ADSL).

Addressing information goes at the beginning of messages; this information gives the network enough information to deliver the packet of data. The **IP address** of a receiving server is usually in the form 207.68.156.58 (as shown in Figure 3.8) which is a numerical representation of a better-known form such as www.microsoft.com. Each IP address is unique to a given organization, server or client, in a similar way to postal codes referring to a small number of houses. The first number refers to the top-level domain in the network, in this case .com. The remaining numbers are used to refer to a particular organization.

For efficiency, information sent across IP networks is broken up into separate parts called **packets**. The information within a packet is usually between 1 and 1,500 characters long. This helps to route information most efficiently and fairly, with different packets sent by

IP address

The unique numerical address of a computer.

Packet

Each Internet message such as an e-mail or http request is broken down into smaller parts for ease of transmission.

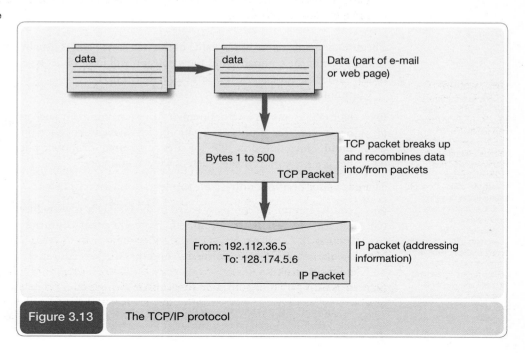

| Figure 3.13 | The TCP/IP protocol |

different people gaining equal priority. TCP performs the task of splitting up the original message into packets on dispatch and reassembling it on receipt. Combining TCP and IP, you can think of an addressed IP envelope containing a TCP envelope which contains part of the original message that has been split into a packet (Figure 3.13).

The HTTP protocol

HTTP, the **Hypertext Transfer Protocol**, is the standard used to allow web browsers and servers to transfer requests for delivery of web pages and their embedded graphics. When you click on a link while viewing a website, your web browser will request information from the server computer hosting the website using HTTP. Since this protocol is important for delivering the web pages, the letters http:// are used to prefix almost all web addresses. HTTP messages are divided into HTTP 'get' messages for requesting web pages and HTTP 'send' messages as shown in Figure 3.13. The web pages and graphics transferred in this way are transferred as packets.

The inventor of HTTP, Tim Berners-Lee, describes its purpose as follows (Berners-Lee, 1999):

> *HTTP rules define things like which computer speaks first, and how they speak in turn. When two computers agree they can talk, they have to find a common way to represent their data so they can share it.*

Uniform resource locators (URLs)

Web addresses refer to particular pages on a web. The technical name for web address is **uniform (or universal) resource locator (URL)**. URLs can be thought of as a standard method of addressing, similar to postcodes or ZIP codes, that make it straightforward to find the name of a site.

Web addresses are structured in a standard way as follows:

http://www.domain-name.extension/filename.html

Domain names

The domain name refers to the name of the web server and is usually selected to be the same as the name of the company, and the extension will indicate its type. The extension is commonly known as the generic top-level domain (gTLD).

Common gTLDs are:

(i) **.com** represents an international or American company such as www.travelocity.com.

(ii) **.org** are not-for-profit organizations (e.g. www.greenpeace.org).

(iii) **.mobi** – introduced in 2006 for sites configured for mobile phones.

(iv) **.net** is a network provider such as www.demon.net.

There are also specific country-code top-level domains (ccTLDs):

(v) **.co.uk** represents a company based in the UK such as www.thomascook.co.uk.

(vi) **.au, .ca, .de, .es, .fi, .fr, .it, .nl,** etc. represent other countries (the co.uk syntax is an anomaly!).

(vii) **.ac.uk** is a UK-based university or other higher education institution (e.g. www.cranfield.ac.uk).

(viii) **.org.uk** is for an organization focusing on a single country (e.g. www.mencap.org.uk).

The 'filename.html' part of the web address refers to an individual web page, for example 'products.html' for a web page summarizing a company's products.

It is important that companies define a **URL strategy** which will help customers or partners find relevant parts of the site containing references to specific products or campaigns when printed in offline communications such as adverts or brochures.

There is further terminology associated with a URL which will often be required when discussing site implementation or digital marketing campaigns, as shown in the box 'What's in a URL?'.

Box 3.3 | **What's in a URL?**

A great example of different URL components is provided by Google engineer Matt Cutts (Cutts, 2007). He gives this example:

http://video.google.co.uk:80/videoplay?docid=-7246927612831078230&hl=en#00h02m30s

Here are some of the components of the url:

- The *protocol* is http. Other protocols include https, ftp, etc.
- The *host* or *hostname* is video.google.co.uk.
- The *subdomain* is video.
- The *domain name* is google.co.uk.
- The *top-level domain* or *TLD* is uk (also known as gTLD). The uk domain is also referred to as a country-code top-level domain or ccTLD. For google.com, the TLD would be com.
- The *second-level domain* (SLD) is co.uk.
- The *port* is 80, which is the default port for web servers (not usually used in URLs when it is the default, although all web servers broadcast on ports).
- The *path* is /videoplay. Path typically refers to a file or location on the web server, e.g. /directory/file.html.
- The URL parameter is docid and the value of that parameter is -7246927612831078230. These are often called the 'name, value' pair. URLs often have lots of parameters. Parameters start with a question mark (?) and are separated with an ampersand (&).
- The *anchor* or fragment is '#00h02m30s'.

Domain name registration

The process of reserving a unique web address that can be used to refer to the company website.

Domain name registration

Most companies own several domains, for different product lines or countries or for specific marketing campaigns. Domain name disputes can arise when an individual or company has registered a domain name which another company claims they have the right to. This is sometimes referred to as 'cybersquatting'.

Managers or agencies responsible for websites need to check that domain names are automatically renewed by the hosting company (as most are today). For example, the .co.uk domain must be renewed every two years. Companies that don't manage this process potentially risk losing their domain name since another company could potentially register it if the domain name lapsed.

The mini case study shows one example of the value of domains and the need to protect them, which we examine in more detail in Chapter 4.

Mini Case Study 3.2	How much is a domain worth?

One of the highest values attached to a domain in Europe was paid in 2008 when the website cruise.co.uk paid the German travel company Nees Reisen £560,000 for the rival name cruises.co.uk. *Guardian* (2008a) reported the new owner of cruises.co.uk as saying that he hopes to use the new domain differently – by turning the site into an online intermediary or community for cruising enthusiasts while its existing cruise. co.uk will concentrate on offering the best deals for voyages. Explaining the valuation cruise.co.uk's managing director, Seamus Conlon, said:

> *'Cruises' is consistently ranked first on Google, with 'cruise' just behind. We wanted the top positions so that when internet users are searching for cruise deals, reviews or news we are the first port of call.*

In the US, the record domain values are higher than when they were exchanged in the late 1990s, including

- Sex.com for $12m
- Business.com for $7.5m
- Beer.com for $7m in 1999.

Web presentation and data exchange standards

Content

The design, text and graphical information that forms a web page. Good content is the key to attracting customers to a website and retaining their interest or achieving repeat visits.

The information, graphics and interactive elements that make up the web pages of a site are collectively referred to as **content**. Different standards exist for text, graphics and multimedia. The saying 'content is king' is often applied to the World Wide Web, since the content will determine the experience of the customer and whether he or she will return.

HTML (Hypertext Markup Language) – display of unstructured text content

HTML (Hypertext Markup Language)

A standard web-page presentation format used to define the text and layout of web pages. HTML files usually have the extension .HTML or .HTM.

Web-page text has many formatting options including applying fonts, emphasis (bold, italic, underline) and placing information in tables. The web browser applies these formats according to instructions that are contained in the file that makes up the web page. This is usually written in **HTML** or **Hypertext Markup Language**. HTML is an international standard established by the World Wide Web Consortium (and published at www.w3.org) intended to ensure that any web page authored according to the definitions in the standard will appear the same in any web browser.

Content management systems (CMS, Chapter 12) are used to shield business content editors from the complexity of HTML.

A brief example of HTML is given for a simplified home page for an example B2B company in Figure 3.14. The HTML code used to construct pages has codes or instruction tags such as <TITLE> to indicate to the browser what is displayed. The <TITLE> tag indicates what appears at the top of the web browser window. Each starting tag has a corresponding end tag usually marked by a '/', for example, <B>plastics</B> to embolden 'plastics'.

XML (eXtensible Markup Language) – display and exchange of structured text and data

Meta-data

A definition of the structure and content of a collection of data or documents. 'Data about data'.

While HTML has proved powerful in providing a standard method of displaying information that was easy to learn, it is largely presentational. HTML only had a limited capability for describing the data on web pages. A capability for summarizing the content of pages is an example of **meta-data**. 'Meta' is part of the ancient Greek language, and in an information management context can be summarized as providing a description or definition about a topic or item.

HTML meta-tags

Standard HTML codes used to specify the content and characteristics of the document.

HTML also has a limited capability for describing documents through **HTML meta-tags**. These are presented at the start of the document in the header area. As the example

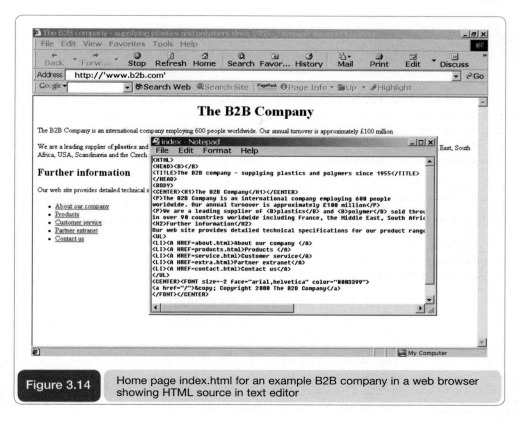

Figure 3.14 Home page index.html for an example B2B company in a web browser showing HTML source in text editor

below shows, they can be used to specify a document's author, last update and type of content. This uses only some examples of meta-tags; the full definition and an introduction to HTML are available from the World Wide Web Consortium at www.w3.org/MarkUp.

```
<HEAD>
   <TITLE>An intranet document example</TITLE>
   <META name="author" content="Dave Chaffey">
   <META name="keywords" content="phone directory, address
   book">
   <META name="description" content="An online phone book">
   <META name="date" content="2005-11-06T08:49:37+00:00">
</HEAD>
```

One application of meta-tags and an illustration of meta-data is that they are used by search engines to identify the content of documents. Early search engines such as AltaVista ranked higher in their listings documents which had meta-keywords that corresponded to the words typed into the search engine by its user. This led to abuse by companies that might include the name of their competitor or repeat keywords several times in the meta-tags, a process known as 'search engine spamming'. As a result, most search engines now attach limited importance to the keyword meta-tags – in fact Google does not use them at all for ranking purposes, but may use them to identify unique documents. However, most search engines including Google do attach relevance to the <TITLE> tag, so it is important that this does not just contain a company name. For example, easyJet.com used the following title tag which incorporates the main phrases potential visitors may type into a search engine.

```
<title>easyJet.com - easyjet low cost airline, easy jet, flight,
air fares, cheap flights</title>
```

XML or eXtensible Markup Language
Standard for transferring structured data, unlike HTML which is purely presentational.

The limited capability within HTML for meta-data and data exchange has been acknowledged and, in an effort coordinated by the World Wide Web Consortium, the first **XML or eXtensible Markup Language** was produced in February 1998. This is not strictly a replacement for HTML since HTML and XML can coexist – they are both markup languages. To help developers use HTML and XML together a new standard, confusingly known as XHTML, was adopted. XHTML and XML are based on Standardized General Markup Language (SGML). The key word describing XML is 'extensible'. This means that new markup tags can be created that facilitate the searching and exchange of information. For example, product information on a web page could use the XML tags <NAME>, <DESCRIPTION>, <COLOUR> and <PRICE>. Examples of tags relevant to a product catalogue are shown below.

Example XML for online marketplace catalogue

This example is a standard for publishing catalogue data. It can be seen that specific tags are used to identify:

- Product ID
- Manufacturer
- Long and short description
- Attributes of product and associated picture.

There is no pricing information in this example.

```
<CatalogData>
<Product>
<Action Value5"Delete"/>
<ProductID>118003-008</ProductID>
</Product>
<Product Type5"Good" SchemaCategoryRef5"C43171801">
<ProductID>140141-002</ProductID>
<UOM><UOMCoded>EA</UOMCoded></UOM>
<Manufacturer>Compaq</Manufacturer>
<LeadTime>2</LeadTime>
<CountryOfOrigin>
<Country><CountryCoded>US</CountryCoded></Country>
</CountryOfOrigin>
<ShortDescription xml:lang5"en">Armada M700 PIII 500
12GB</ShortDescription>
<LongDescription xml:lang5"en">
This light, thin powerhouse delivers no-compromise performance
in a sub-five pound form factor. Size and Weight(HxWxD): 12.4 X
9.8 X 1.1 in 4.3-4.9 lbs (depending on configuration) Processor:
500-MHZ Intel Pentium III Processor with 256K integrated cache
Memory: 128MB of RAM, expandable to 576MB Hard Drive: 12.0GB
Removable SMART Hard Drive Display Graphics: 14.1-inch color
TFT with 1024 x 768 resolution (up to 16M colors internal)
Communication: Mini-PCI V.90 Modem/Nic Combo Operating System:
Dual Installation of Microsoft Windows 95 &amp; Microsoft
Windows 98
```

```
</LongDescription>
<ProductAttachment>
<AttachmentURL>file:\5931.jpg</AttachmentURL>
<AttachmentPurpose>PicName</AttachmentPurpose>
<AttachmentMIMEType>jpg</AttachmentMIMEType>
</ProductAttachment>
<ObjectAttribute>
<AttributeID> Processor Speed</AttributeID>
<AttributeValue>500MHZ</AttributeValue>
</ObjectAttribute>
<ObjectAttribute>
<AttributeID>Battery Life</AttributeID>
<AttributeValue>6 hours</AttributeValue>
</ObjectAttribute>
</Product>
```

An XML implementation typically consists of three parts: the XML document, a document type definition (DTD) and a stylesheet (XSL), which are usually stored as separate files. We need a simple example to understand how these relate. Let's take the example of a bookstore cataloguing different books. You will see from this example that it is equivalent to using a database such as Microsoft Access to define database fields about the books and then storing and displaying their details.

The XML document contains the data items, in this case the books, and it references the DTD and XSL files:

Data Items: The Xml Document <books.xml>

```
<?xml version="1.0"?>
<!DOCTYPE Bookstore SYSTEM "books.dtd">
<?xml-stylesheet type="text/html" href="books.xsl"?>

<Bookstore>
<Book ID="101">
     <Author>Dave Chaffey</Author>
     <Title>E-business and E-commerce Management</Title>
     <Date>30 November 2003</Date>
     <ISBN>0273683780</ISBN>
     <Publisher>Pearson Education</Publisher>

</Book>
<Book ID="102">
     <Author>Dave Chaffey</Author>
     <Title>Total E-mail Marketing</Title>
     <Date>20 February 2003</Date>
     <ISBN>0750657545</ISBN>
     <Publisher>Butterworth Heinemann</Publisher>

</Book>
</Bookstore>
```

Note: The tags such as Bookstore, Book and Author are defined for this particular application. They are defined in a separate Data Type Definition document which is shown below.

The DTD referenced at the start of the XML document defines the data items associated with the root element, which in this case is the bookstore:

Data Definition: Document Type Definition <books.dtd>

```
<!ELEMENT BookStore (Book)*>
<!ELEMENT Book (Title, Author+, Date, ISBN, Publisher)>

<!ATTLIST Book ID #REQUIRED>
<!ELEMENT Title (#PCDATA)>
<!ELEMENT Author (#PCDATA)>
<!ELEMENT Date (#PCDATA)>
<!ELEMENT ISBN (#PCDATA)>
<!ELEMENT Publisher (#PCDATA)>
```

Notes:
*The Bookstore can contain many books.
Bookstore is known as the 'Root element'.
+ Allows for one or more author.
PCDATA stands for parsed character data, i.e. a text string; further validation of fields could be used.
REQUIRED shows that this field is essential.

The XSL document uses HTML tags to instruct the browser how the data within the XML file should be displayed. Separation of data from their presentation method makes this a more powerful approach than combining the two since different presentation schemes such as with and without graphics can readily be switched between according to user preference.

This stylesheet would display the data as follows:

Presentation: Document Style Sheet File <books.xsl>

```
<?xml version="1.0"?>
<xsl:stylesheet xmlns:xsl="http://www.w3.org/TR/WD-xsl">
<xsl:template match="/">
    <html> <body>
        <table cellpadding="2" cellspacing="0" border="1"
        bgcolor="#FFFFD5"> <tr>
        <th>Title</th>
            <th>Author</th>
            <th>Publisher</th>
            <th>Date</th>
            <th>ISBN</th>
        </tr> <xsl:for-each select="Bookstore/Book">
        <tr><td><xsl:value-of select="Title"/></td>
            <td><xsl:value-of select="Author"/></td>
            <td><xsl:value-of select="Publisher"/></td>
            <td><xsl:value-of select="Date"/></td>
            <td><xsl:value-of select="ISBN"/></td>
            </tr> </xsl:for-each>
        </table>
    </body> </html>
</xsl:template>
</xsl:stylesheet>
```

Note: The style sheet uses standard HTML tags to display the data.

Display of data through browser

Title	Author	Publisher	Date	ISBN
E-business and E-commerce Management	Dave Chaffey	Pearson Education	30 November 2003	0273683780
Total E-mail Marketing	Dave Chaffey	Butterworth Heinemann	20 February 2003	0750657545

Examples of XML applications

One widely adopted XML application is the Dublin Core meta-data initiative (DCMI) (www.dublincore.org), so called since the steering group first met in Dublin, Ohio, in 1995, which has been active in defining different forms of meta-data to support information access across the Internet. An important part of this initiative is in defining a standard method of referencing web documents and other media resources. If widely adopted this would make it much more efficient to search for a document produced by a particular author in a particular language in a particular date range. Up to now, it has mainly been applied within content management systems to assist in knowledge management for data on intranets and extranets rather than on the public Internet.

The significance of XML is indicated by its use for facilitating supply chain management. For example, Microsoft's BizTalk server (www.microsoft.com/biztalk) for B2B application integration is based on XML. Since this is a proprietary standard, an open standard 'RosettaNet' (www.rosettanet.org) was created by a consortium of many of the world's leading information technology, electronic components and semiconductor manufacturing companies such as Intel, Sony and Nokia. BizTalk server enables different enterprise applications such as SAP and JDEdwards to exchange information as part of improved supply chain management. Microsoft summarize the benefits of BizTalk as:

1. Reduced 'time to value', i.e. development time and cost of application integration.
2. Easy integration with virtually any application or technology.
3. Scalability to any size of application.
4. Support for industry standards such as EDI, XML and Simple Object Access Protocol (SOAP).
5. Reliable document delivery including 'once-only' delivery of documents, comprehensive document tracking, and logging and support for failover (automatic recovery of documents from a backup system).
6. Secure document exchange – this is not an integral feature of XML but has been built into this application.
7. Automation for complex business processes.
8. Management and monitoring of business processes.
9. Automated trading partner management.
10. Reduced complexity in development.

Another widely adopted application of XML is ebXML (www.ebxml.org). This standard has been coordinated by Oasis (www.oasis-open.org) which is an international not-for-profit consortium for promoting Internet standards. The original project was intended to define business exchange using five standards:

- business processes
- core data components

- collaboration protocol agreements
- messaging
- registries and repositories.

Oasis defines three types of transaction that form business processes:

1 *Business transaction.* A single business transaction between two partners, such as placing an order or shipping an order.
2 *Binary collaboration.* A sequence of these business transactions, performed between two partners, each performing one role.
3 *Multi-party collaboration.* A series of binary collaborations composed of a collection of business partners.

One application developed using ebXML enables different accounting packages to communicate with online order processing systems. This new standard has been recognized by 85% of the accounting industry, the World Wide Web Consortium and the United Nations. Over 120 national and international accounting software vendors have confirmed that they are developing interfaces. Exchequer Software Ltd (www.exchequer.com) is the first company to embed this new technology in its products, which means it receives orders via e-mail directly into its own accounting system. This has resulted in a reduction of 30% in processing costs and a sales increase of 40%. The e-business module of the accounting software can be used to provide a remotely hosted e-commerce shopping cart system with regular updates of stock details, pricing matrices, account information and transactional data, such as outstanding orders and invoices.

Governments are also using XML to standardize data transfer between departments.

Semantic web standards

Semantic web
Interrelated content including data with defined meaning, enabling better exchange of information between computers and between people and computers.

The **semantic web** is a concept promoted by Tim Berners-Lee and the World Wide Web Consortium (www.w3.org) to improve upon the capabilities of the current World Wide Web. Semantics is the study of the meaning of words and linguistic expressions. For example, the word 'father' has the semantic elements male, human and parent and 'girl' has the elements female, human and young. The semantic web is about how to define meaning for the content of the web to make it easier to locate relevant information and services rapidly. As mentioned above, finding information on a particular topic through searching the web is inexact since there isn't a standard way of describing the content of web pages. The semantic web describes the use of meta-data through standards such as the XML, RDF and the Dublin Core to help users find web resources more readily. Another benefit of the semantic web is that it will enable data exchange between software **agents** running on different server or client computers.

Agents
Software programs that can assist humans by automatically gathering information from the Internet or exchanging data with other agents based on parameters supplied by the user.

Agents are software programs created to assist humans in performing tasks. In this context they automatically gather information from the Internet or exchange data with other agents based on parameters supplied by the user.

The applications of the semantic web are best illustrated through examples. Berners-Lee *et al.* (2001) give the example of a patient seeking medical treatment for a particular condition. They envisage a patient having a personal software agent (effectively a search engine) which is used to find the best source of treatment. The patient's agent will interact with the doctor's agent which will describe the symptoms and search pages from different healthcare providers which detail their services. The patient's agent will then give them the different treatment options in terms of cost, effectiveness, waiting time and location. Similarly, a personal agent could be used to find the best flight or a business agent could be used to participate in a reverse auction.

Wiki
A collaborative interactive web service which enables users to modify content contributed by others.

Although the concept of the semantic web has been established for over 10 years, there have been relatively few commercial applications, suggesting the difficulty of implementation together with the lack of demand since the search engines perform well in returning relevant information. The World Wide Web Consortium (www.w3c.org) has compiled some examples which it updates at www.w3.org/2001/sw/sweo/public/UseCases/. The mini case study shows how the concept of the semantic web has been applied at EDF to help knowledge management within their intranet.

Mini Case Study 3.3	Enhancement and integration of corporate social software using the semantic web at Electricité de France

Electricité de France, the largest electricity company in France, recently introduced the use of social software within its R&D department, embracing the Enterprise 2.0 movement. The use of blogs, **wikis**, free-tagging, and the integration of external RSS feeds offers new possibilities for knowledge management and collaboration between engineers and researchers. Yet, these tools raise various issues, such as:

- Querying data across applications is not straightforward as different applications use different formats (database structure or output format) to model their data.
- Knowledge created using wikis cannot be easily understood by computers. For instance, a user cannot run a query such as 'List all companies working on solar energy and based in the US'. The user would need instead to browse various pages to find the answer.
- Free-tagging leads to heterogeneity and ambiguity which complicates the search for relevant content. For instance, a query about 'solar' will not retrieve documents tagged with 'solar energy' or 'solar_energy'.
- RSS feeds tend to produce a lot of incoming data, which, for example, makes it difficult to follow all information about a given company.

The solution

To solve these problems and offer new and value-added services to end-users, we developed a solution that uses semantic web technologies and relies on various components that act together and provide a mediation system between those services and the users. This mediation system provides a common model for meta-data and for document content. It achieves this using ontologies, plug-ins for existing tools to create data according to these ontologies, a central storage system for this data, and services to enrich information retrieval and data exchange between components.

Since our first requirement was to provide a common and machine-readable model of meta-data for content from any service, we decided that the model should be implemented in RDF. We then took part in the development of the SIOC (Semantically-Interlinked Online Communities) ontology which provides a model for describing activities of online communities in RDF. For example, SIOC can be used to describe what is a blog post, what properties a blog has, and how a blog post relates to a user and user comments. SIOC takes advantage of commonly used vocabularies such as FOAF (Friend Of A Friend) and Dublin Core. SIOC exporters and translators were added to our services so that wherever the data comes from (blogs, wikis, RSS feeds), it is automatically modelled in a common way, offering a first layer of unified semantics over existing tools in our mediation architecture.

As much valuable knowledge is contained within our wikis, we extended the wiki server with semantic functionalities in order to model some of its content in a machine-readable way. To do this we created ontologies which model the concepts within the knowledge fields of our wikis. For example, we designed an ontology to model information about companies, their industry, and location. In order to benefit from existing models and data, our ontologies extend or reuse existing ones such as Geonames and SKOS (Simple Knowledge Organization System). Moreover, to allow users to easily publish and maintain ontology instances from wiki pages, our add-on provides the ability for wiki administrators to define form templates for wiki pages and to map them to the classes and properties of the ontologies. Thus, users create and maintain instances by editing wiki pages, which is as simple as what they were doing prior to implementing semantic web technologies. For instance, instead of writing that '*EDF is an organization located in France*', a user fills in the template so that the following RDF triples will be immediately created when saving the page, thus providing a second layer of semantics for the mediator:

```
athena:EDF rdf:type foaf:Organization;
      geonames:locatedIn <http://sws.geonames.org/3017382/>.
```

In order to provide a bridge between the advantages and openness of tagging, and the powerful but complex use of ontologies and semantic annotation, we developed a framework called MOAT (Meaning

Of A Tag). MOAT allows users to collaboratively provide links between tags and their meanings. The resources (classes or instances) of the ontologies in our system define the meaning. Thus, users can keep using free-keywords when tagging content, since this layer helps to solve ambiguity and heterogeneity problems, as different tags can be related to the same resource (e.g. '*solar*' and '*solar_energy*' linked to athena:SolarEnergy). Moreover, users can browse a human-readable version (using labels instead of URLs) of the ontology in case they want to add a new link or if the tag leads to ambiguity and they must choose the relevant resource when tagging content. Furthermore, when saving tagged content, the links between content and resources are exported in a RDF export using SIOC and MOAT.

Each time a service produces a new document, the storage system is notified by the plug-ins of our mediation architecture, saves its RDF data instantaneously and merges it with other data using the architecture shown in Figure 3.15. This allows us to benefit from a unique view of the many integrated data sources (e.g. blogs, wikis, RSS) and to have access to up-to-date information. Then, using the SPARQL query language and protocol, we can query across the many data sources, and services can be plugged in on top of the central storage system.

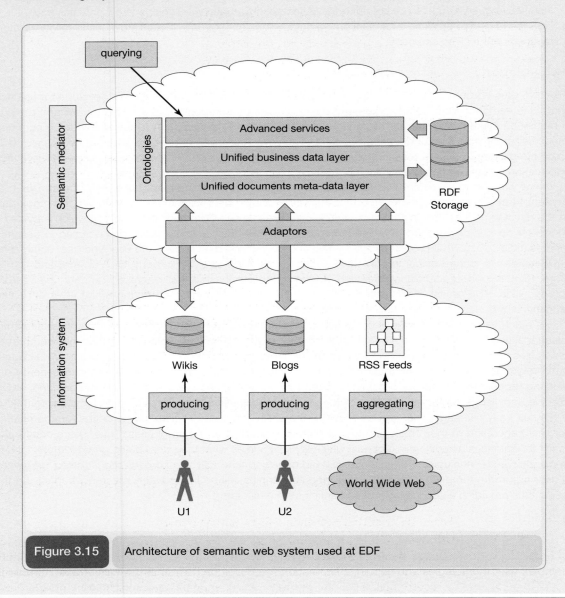

Figure 3.15 Architecture of semantic web system used at EDF

The most beneficial service we developed is a dedicated semantic search engine, which allows users to find information by concept, from a given keyword, using all available sources of information. When a user searches for '*France*', the system will suggest all instances containing that word whether it is used in the label or the tag. For example, the user will retrieve '*Association des Maires de France*', '*France*' and '*Electricité de France*'. This approach allows the user to define precisely what they are looking for and to then display related information from wikis, blogs, and RSS feeds. In addition, our system can also reuse resources labels to provide a first step of semi-automatic indexing of incoming RSS feeds. The system also proposes to extend search regarding relationships between concepts that exist in our ontologies, for example, suggesting '*Solar energy*' when searching for '*Renewable energies*'.

Another interesting component we can now provide due to the technology is wiki content geolocation. Since we primarily use the Geonames ontology to model location, we can reuse the freely-available data from the Geonames project to build geolocation services at zero cost to the company.

Key benefits of using semantic web technologies

- unifying Web 2.0 and the semantic web with lightweight ontologies;
- common semantics to model meta-data of existing Web 2.0 services with SIOC;
- advanced and collaborative knowledge modeling using wikis;
- interlinking tags, ontology instances and tagged content with MOAT;
- reusing ontologies and RDF data available on the web;
- ability to merge and query data from various services using a central storage system;
- ontology based querying;
- suggesting related content thanks to relationships in the ontology;
- evolution of query services thanks to the SPARQL language and protocol.

Finally, one of the most important points of our system is that most of the semantics are hidden from end-users who do not need to struggle with complex semantic web modelling principles to benefit from the services.

Source: EDF (2008).

Microformats

A simple set of formats based on XHTML for describing and exchanging information about objects including product and travel reviews, recipes and event information.

GIF (Graphics Interchange Format)

A graphics format and compression algorithm best used for simple graphics.

JPEG (Joint Photographics Experts Group)

A graphics format and compression algorithm best used for photographs.

PNG (Portable Network Graphics)

A graphics format defined to supersede the GIF format. Its features include compression, transparency and progressive loading.

Microformats

Microformats are a practical example of the way the semantic web will develop. Data can be exchanged through standard microformats such as hCalendar and hReview which are used to incorporate data from other sites into the Google listings (see www.microformats. org for details). You can see examples of microformats which Google has incorporated as star ratings from sites it has indexed if you perform a search on movies, hotels or popular products. In the further reading for this chapter, we reference Arnold (2010) who describes how Google is incorporating semantic web approaches.

Graphical images (GIF, JPEG and PNG files)

Graphics can be readily incorporated into web pages as images. **GIF (Graphics Interchange Format)**, **JPEG (Joint Photographics Experts Group)** and **Portable Network Graphics (PNG)** refer to the standard file formats most commonly used to present images on web pages. GIF files are limited to 256 colours and are best used for small simple graphics such as banner adverts, while JPEG is best used for larger images where quality is important, such as photographs. Both formats use image compression technology to minimize the size of downloaded files.

Animated graphical information (GIFs and plug-ins)

GIF files can also be used for interactive banner adverts. **Plug-ins** are additional programs, sometimes referred to as 'helper applications', that work in association with the web browser to provide features not present in the basic web browser. Adobe Acrobat is used to display documents in .pdf format (www.adobe.com) and the Macromedia Flash and

Plug-in
A program that must be downloaded to view particular content such as an animation.

Shockwave products for producing interactive graphics (www.macromedia.com). Silverlight (www.silverlight.net) is a similar service introduced by Microsoft in 2007 for delivery of applications and streamed media.

Audio and video standards

Streaming media
Sound and video that can be experienced within a web browser before the whole clip is downloaded.

Traditionally sound and video, or 'rich media', have been stored as the Microsoft standards .wav and .avi. A newer sound format for music is mp3. **Streaming media** are now used for many multimedia sites since they enable video or audio to start playing within a few seconds – it is not necessary for the whole file to be downloaded before it can be played. Formats for streaming media have been established by Real Networks (www.realnetworks.com). Rich media such as Flash applications, audio or video content can also be stored on a web server, or a specialist streaming media server.

Focus on	Internet governance

In Chapter 4 we will look briefly at how governments promote and control, through laws, the use of the Internet in their jurisdiction. In this section, we look at the growth of the Internet as a global phenomenon and how the standards described in the previous section were devised. The Internet is quite different from all previous communication media since it is much less easy for governments to control and shape its development. Think of print, TV, phone and radio and you can see that governments can exercise a fair degree of control on what they find acceptable.

Internet governance
Control of the operation and use of the Internet.

Esther Dyson (1998) has been influential in advising on the impact of the Internet on society; she describes **Internet governance** as the control put in place to manage the growth of the Internet and its usage. The global nature of the Internet makes it less practical for a government to control cyberspace. Dyson says:

Now, with the advent of the Net, we are privatizing government in a new way – not only in the traditional sense of selling things off to the private sector, but by allowing organizations independent of traditional governments to take on certain 'government' regulatory roles. These new international regulatory agencies will perform former government functions in counterpoint to increasingly global large companies and also to individuals and smaller private organizations who can operate globally over the Net.

Dyson (1998) describes different layers of jurisdiction. These are:

1 Physical space comprising individual countries in which their own laws such as those governing taxation, privacy, and trading and advertising standards hold.
2 ISPs – the connection between the physical and virtual worlds.

There are number of established non-profit-making organizations that control different aspects of the Internet. These are sometimes called 'supra-governmental' organizations since their control is above government level.

The net neutrality principle

Network neutrality
'Net neutrality' is the principle of provision of equal access to different Internet services by telecommunications service providers.

Net or network neutrality is based on the organic way in which the Internet grew during the 1980s and 1990s. The principle enshrines equal access to the Internet and the web which is threatened by two different forces. First and the most common context for net neutrality is the desire by some telecommunications companies and ISPs to offer tiered access to particular Internet services. The wish of the ISPs is to potentially offer different quality of service, i.e. speed, to consumers based on the fee paid by the upstream content provider.

So potentially ISPs could charge companies such as TV channels more because they stream content such as video content which has high bandwidth requirements.

Concerns over tiered access to services appear strongest in the United States where two proposed Bills to help achieve neutrality, the 2006 Internet Freedom and Nondiscrimination Act and 2006 Communications Opportunity, Promotion and Enhancement Act, did not become law. The ISPs were strong lobbyists against these Bills and subsequently it has been alleged that provider Comcast has discriminated against users accessing peer-to-peer traffic from BitTorrent (Ars Technica, 2007). In European countries such as the UK, ISPs offer different levels of access at different bandwidths.

The second and less widely applied, but equally concerning, concept of net neutrality is the wish by some governments or other bodies to block access to certain services or content. For example, the government in China limits access to certain types of content in what has been glibly called '*The Great Firewall of China*' (*Wired*, 2007), which describes the development of the Golden Shield which is intended to monitor, filter and block sensitive online content. More recently Google has been criticized for censoring its search results in China for certain terms such as 'Tiananmen Square'. In 2009/2010 Google considered withdrawing its business from China.

Box 3.4	Ofcom on net neutrality in Europe and the United States

Ofcom is the regulator of the Internet in the UK. Its position on net neutrality has a clear description of the potential need for governance on this issue.

The concept of net neutrality

The issue of net neutrality concerns whether and where there should be a principle of non-discrimination regarding different forms of internet traffic carried across networks.

The communications sector is entering a period where there is rapidly increasing traffic on the internet, such as video and peer-to-peer applications (for example, games and VoIP services). This rapid increase in traffic is generating substantial congestion in some parts of the internet. Moreover many of these applications are time-sensitive and are far less tolerant of delay than, say, email or web browsing.

To respond to these new applications and their associated demands, service providers are developing a range of business models that facilitate the prioritisation of different types of traffic. This is enabled by improvements in network technology that are allowing greater identification of internet packets associated with different applications, which can then be prioritised, accordingly.

Ofcom goes on to explain the arguments for and against net neutrality and the current position in Europe.

Arguments for and against net neutrality

Proponents of net neutrality argue that it is fundamental to the protection of consumer choice and innovation on the internet, and advocates in the US have cited the First Amendment to the constitution, arguing that net neutrality is necessary to ensure freedom of speech. Some large internet application and content companies tend to be advocates of net neutrality, alongside some consumer rights groups.

Opponents to net neutrality argue that they should be able to offer different qualities of service, both in order to recover their infrastructure investment costs and to enable quality of service guarantees to improve the consumer experience for services such as VoIP or video streaming. In the United States, cable and incumbent telecom operators have also claimed that the First Amendment supports opposition to net neutrality, arguing that they cannot be compelled to promote speech with which they disagree.

Differences between the European Union and United States

A contrasting set of circumstances exists in the European Union, compared to the United States. Specifically, the net neutrality debate was triggered in the United States by the deregulation of wholesale access services including access to the internet. In the EU there are obligations to offer unbundled local loops and bitstream access and these continue to be seen as key tools in addressing competition problems.

As part of its proposals to amend the existing EU regulatory framework, the European Commission has proposed a range of measures to ensure that consumers have access to lawful content including proposals to ensure that consumers are made aware of changes to the terms of service offered by their communications provider and the ability to switch contracts with penalty. In addition, the Commission proposed to empower national regulators with the ability to impose minimum quality of service obligations on communications providers subject to a set of standards agreed at European level.

Source: Ofcom (2007).

The Internet Corporation for Assigned Names and Numbers (ICANN, www.icann.org)

The Internet Corporation for Assigned Names and Numbers (ICANN) is the non-profit body formed for domain name and IP address allocation and management. These were previously controlled through US government contract by IANA (Internet Assigned Numbers Authority) and other entities.

According to the ICANN Fact Sheet (www.icann.org/general/fact-sheet.htm):

In the past, many of the essential technical coordination functions of the Internet were handled on an ad hoc basis by US government contractors and grantees, and a wide network of volunteers. This informal structure represented the spirit and culture of the research community in which the Internet was developed. However, the growing international and commercial importance of the Internet has necessitated the creation of a technical management and policy development body that is more formalized in structure, more transparent, more accountable, and more fully reflective of the diversity of the world's Internet communities.

The independence of such bodies raises several questions, such as who funds them and who they answer to – are they regulated? Incredibly, in 2002 ICANN had just 14 staff and a 19-member volunteer board of directors chaired by Dr Vinton Cerf, who many consider as 'father of the Internet'. Funding is through the fees charged for domain registration by commercial companies. The policy statements on the sites suggest that ICANN policy is influenced by various stakeholders, but the main control is an independent review body of ten.

The Internet Society (www.isoc.org)

The Internet Society (ISOC) is a professional membership society formed in 1992. It summarizes its aims as

To provide leadership in addressing issues that confront the future of the Internet, and is the organization home for the groups responsible for Internet infrastructure standards, including the Internet Engineering Task Force (IETF) and the Internet Architecture Board (IAB).

A key aspect of the society's mission statement (www.isoc.org/isoc/mission) is:

To assure the open development, evolution and use of the Internet for the benefit of people throughout the world.

Although it focuses on technical issues of standards and protocols, it is also conscious of how these will affect global society.

The Internet Engineering Task Force (IETF, www.ietf.org)

This is one of the main technical bodies. It is an international community of network designers, operators, vendors and researchers concerned with the development of the Internet's architecture and its transport protocols such as IP. Significant subgroups are the Internet Architecture Board, a technical advisory group of ISOC with a wide range of responsibilities, and the Internet Engineering Steering Group, which is responsible for overseeing the activities of the IETF and the Internet standards process.

The World Wide Web Consortium (www.w3.org)

This organization is responsible for web standards. Its director is Tim Berners-Lee. Today, it focuses on improving publishing standards such as HTML and XML. The consortium also aims to promote accessibility to the web for those with disabilities – for instance.

Telecommunications Information Networking Architecture Consortium TINA-C (www.tina.com)

This consortium takes a higher-level view of how applications communicate over communications networks. It does not define detailed standards. Its principles are based on an object-oriented approach to enable easier integration of systems. In its terms:

> The purpose of these principles is to insure interoperability, portability and reusability of software components and independence from specific technologies, and to share the burden of creating and managing a complex system among different business stakeholders, such as consumers, service providers, and connectivity providers.

Although it has been established since the 1990s, it has had limited success in establishing solutions which are branded as 'TINA-compliant'.

How can companies influence or take control of Internet standards?

It can be argued that companies seek control of the Internet to gain competitive advantage. For example, Microsoft used what have been judged as anti-competitive tactics to gain a large market share for its browser, Internet Explorer. In a five-year period, it achieved over 75% market share, which has given it advantages in other areas of e-commerce such as advertising revenue through its portal MSN (www.msn.com) and retail through its sites such as travel site Expedia (www.expedia.com). Microsoft has also sought to control standards such as HTML and has introduced rival standards or variants of other standards.

The existence of global Internet standards bodies arguably means that it is less likely that one company can develop proprietary standards, although Microsoft has been successfully using this approach for many years. Today, companies such as Microsoft have to lobby independent organizations to have their input into standards such as XML. Businesses can protect their interests in the Internet by lobbying these organizations or governments, or subscribing as members and having employees involved with development of standards

Many remain worried about the future control of the Internet by companies; the 'World of Ends' campaign (www.worldofends.com) illustrates some of the problems where control can limit consumer choice and stifle innovation. But the future of the Internet is assured because the three core principles espoused in the World of Ends document remain true:

- No one owns it.
- Everyone can use it.
- Anyone can improve it.

Open-source software

Open-source software
Is developed collaboratively, independent of a vendor, by a community of software developers and users.

The selection of **open-source software** to support e-business applications is a significant decision for anyone managing technology infrastructure for a company. Open-source software is now significant in many categories relevant to e-business including operating systems, browsers, web servers, office applications and content management systems (including blogs).

The Open Source Organization (www.opensource.org) explains its benefits as follows:

> *The basic idea behind open source is very simple: When programmers can read, redistribute, and modify the source code for a piece of software, the software evolves. People improve it, people adapt it, people fix bugs. And this can happen at a speed that, if one is used to the slow pace of conventional software development, seems astonishing.*
>
> *We in the open source community have learned that this rapid evolutionary process produces better software than the traditional closed model, in which only a very few programmers can see the source and everybody else must blindly use an opaque block of bits.*

Table 3.4 summarizes some of the main advantages and disadvantages of open-source software. To gain an appreciation of the issues faced by a technical manager pondering the open-source dilemma, complete Activity 3.4.

Table 3.4	Three advantages and three disadvantages of open-source software
Advantages of open-source software	**Counter-argument**
1 Effectively free to purchase	Cost of migration from existing systems may be high and will include costs of disruption and staff training
2 Lower cost of maintenance since upgrades are free	There is not a specific counter-argument for this, but see the disadvantages below
3 Increased flexibility	Organizations with the resources can tailor the code. Frequent patches occur through collaborative development
Disadvantages of open-source software	**Counter-argument**
1 Has less functionality than commercial software	Simplicity leads to ease of use and fewer errors. Many functions not used by the majority of users
2 More likely to contain bugs compared to commercial software since not tested commercially	Evidence does not seem to suggest this is the case. The modular design needed by collaborative development enables problems to be isolated and resolved
3 Poor quality of support	Organizations with the resource can fix problems themselves since they have access to the code. Companies such as IBM, SuSe and RedHat do offer support for Linux for a fee. Finding skilled staff for emerging open-source technologies can be difficult

Activity 3.4	Selecting open-source software

visit the www

Purpose

This activity looks at a common issue facing technical managers: should they adopt standard software promoted by the largest companies or open-source software or cheaper software from other vendors?

Questions

1 For the different alternatives facing a technical manager below, assess:
   (a) Which is most popular (research figures).
   (b) The benefits and disadvantages of the Microsoft solution against the alternatives.

2 Make recommendations, with justifications, of which you would choose for a small–medium or large organization.
   A Operating system: Microsoft /Windows XP/Server or Linux (open-source) for server and desktop clients.
   B Browser: Internet Explorer browser or rivals such as Mozilla Firefox or Google Chrome which is part based on open source.
   C Programming language for dynamic e-commerce applications: Microsoft.Net or independent languages/solutions such as the LAMP combination (Linux operating system, Apache server software plus the MySQL open-source database and scripting languages such as PHP, Perl or Python).

Answers to activities can be found at www.pearsoned.co.uk/chaffey

Managing e-business infrastructure

e-business infrastructure

The architecture of hardware, software, content and data used to deliver e-business services to employees, customers and partners.

As explained at the start of the chapter, **e-business infrastructure** comprises the hardware, software, content and data used to deliver e-business services to employees, customers and partners. In this part of the chapter we look at the management of e-business infrastructure by reviewing different perspectives on the infrastructure. These are:

1 *Hardware and systems software infrastructure.* This refers mainly to the hardware and network infrastructure discussed in the previous sections. It includes the provision of clients, servers, network services and also systems software such as operating systems and browsers (Layers II, III and IV in Figure 3.1).

2 *Applications infrastructure.* This refers to the applications software used to deliver services to employees, customers and other partners (Layer I in Figure 3.1).

A further perspective is the management of data and content (Layer V in Figure 3.1) which is reviewed in more detail in the third part of this book.

Microblogging

Publishing of short posts through services such as Twitter.com and Tumblr.com.

To illustrate the importance and challenges of maintaining an adequate infrastructure, read the mini case study about the **microblogging** service Twitter. Twitter is a fascinating case of the challenges of monetizing an online service and delivering adequate service levels with a limited budget and a small team. This case study shows some of the successes and challenges for the start-up e-business.

Mini Case Study 3.4 The popularity of twittering gives infrastructure challenges

The microblogging service Twitter (Figure 3.16) enables users to post short messages or 'tweets' of up to 140 characters by different web services, Instant Messenging (IM) or mobile to keep in touch with 'followers' around the world. While Twitter might appear to have similar functionality to IM, each subscriber follows others and in turn is followed by other users. Its open architecture has also enabled many publishing applications, from the BBC using it to cover breaking news or sports, through US presidential election candidates, to companies such as Cisco and Woot.com using it to provide product and service information via RSS feeds.

In April 2010 Twitter revealed these details about its scale at its user conference:

- Twitter has 105,779,710 registered users.
- New users are signing up at the rate of 300,000 per day.
- 180 million unique visitors come to the site every month.
- 75% of Twitter traffic comes from outside Twitter.com (i.e. via third-party applications).
- Twitter gets a total of 3 billion requests a day via its API.
- Twitter users are, in total, tweeting an average of 55 million tweets a day.
- Twitter's search engine receives around 600 million search queries per day.
- Of Twitter's active users, 37% use their phone to tweet.

Figure 3.16 Twitter
Source: www.twitter.com/davechaffey.

For many years, Twitter didn't have a stated revenue model. In an interview (*Guardian*, 2008b) co-founder Evan Williams explained that there is sufficient venture capital investment to pay for what Williams called '*the usual startup stuff: salaries, servers, rent*' adding '*there will need to be an income eventually*'. He explains that unlike many services, placing ads is not their preferred revenue method, instead explaining that '*we are striving for (and believe we can achieve) a built-in revenue model that is compatible with the open nature of Twitter and its ecosystem, rather than something tacked-on*'.

In 2009 Twitter agreed to share real-time search data with Microsoft and Google in separate agreements which it was estimated provided millions in development. In 2010 Twitter trialled 'Promoted Tweets' which are text ads occurring within a user's message stream. But at the time of writing, the long-awaited method of charging business or personal users for enhanced presence wasn't available.

Twitter was founded in 2006 and by 2008 had developed to a small company of 24 full-time employees and contractors who manage the service in five teams. The make-up of the teams shows the main challenges of managing an online service:

- *Product team* who define, design and support the Twitter service.
- *User Experience* who create the user experience and create applications, craft the user experiences of the products, and develop tools that safeguard those experiences.
- *API (application programming interface)* team who develop the software interfaces accessed by other services such as Twhirl, a desktop application enabling users to review and post messages, and Twitterfeed, which enables blog postings to be added to Twitter.
- *Services* who develop the main applications and service which form the Twitter functionality.
- *Operations* who architect, deploy, operate, measure and monitor the infrastructure, products and services.

The Twitter team has grappled with sustaining service with the growth. This is catalogued in the Twitter status blog (http://status.twitter.com) which shows that in May 2008 uptime fell to a low of 97.14% or 21 hours across the month. While Twitter has a stated goal to make Twitter 'a reliable global communication utility', system outages indicated by an animated 'Fail Whale' became familiar during early 2008.

Twitter was originally developed on the Ruby on Rails open-source web application development framework which while sometimes used for development of content management systems didn't scale to the capacity required by a messaging system such as Twitter. The open-source MySQL database was initially used for storing and retrieving updates and this also caused problems since at one stage there was a single physical database used for storing updates. However, a new lead architect and the acquisition of Summize, a company specializing in searching archived Tweets, had stablized uptime and response times at the time of writing.

Source: Twitter Blog (http://blog.twitter.com) and *Guardian* (2008b).

Updates at: www.davechaffey.com/E-commerce-Internet-marketing-case-studies/twitter-case-study/

Managing hardware and systems software infrastructure

Management of the technology infrastructure requires decisions on Layers II, III and IV in Figure 3.1.

Layer II – Systems software

The key management decision is standardization throughout the organization. Standardization leads to reduced numbers of contacts for support and maintenance and can reduce purchase prices through multi-user licences. Systems software choices occur for the client, server and network. On the client computers, the decision will be which browser software to standardize on. Standardized plug-ins should also be installed across the organization. The systems software for the client will also be decided on; this will probably be a variant of Microsoft Windows, but open-source alternatives such as Linux may also be considered. When considering systems software for the server, it should be remembered that there may be many servers in the global organization, both for the Internet and intranets. Using standardized web-server software such as Apache will help maintenance. Networking software will also be decided on.

Layer III – Transport or network

Decisions on the network will be based on the internal company network, which for the e-business will be an intranet, and for the external network either an extranet or VPN (p. 161) or links to the public Internet. The main management decision is whether internal or external network management will be performed by the company or outsourced to a third party. Outsourcing of network management is common. Standardized hardware is also needed to connect clients to the Internet, for example a modem card or external modem in home PCs or a network interface card (NIC) to connect to the company (local-area) network for business computers.

Layer IV – Storage

The decision on storage is similar to that for the transport layer. Storage can be managed internally or externally. This is not an either–or choice. For example, intranet and extranet are commonly managed internally while Internet storage such as the corporate website is commonly managed externally or at an application service provider (p. 153). However, intranets and extranets can also be managed externally.

We will now consider decisions involving third-party service providers of the hardware and systems software infrastructure.

Managing Internet service and hosting providers

Service providers who provide access to the Internet are usually referred to as 'ISPs' or 'Internet service providers'. ISPs may also host the websites which publish a company's website content. But many organizations will turn to a separate hosting provider to manage the company's website and other e-business services accessed by customers and partners such as extranets, so it is important to select an appropriate hosting provider.

ISP connection methods

Figure 3.2 shows the way in which companies or home users connect to the Internet. The diagram is greatly simplified in that there are several tiers of ISPs. A user may connect to one ISP which will then transfer the request to another ISP which is connected to the main Internet backbone.

Dial-up connection
Access to the Internet via phone lines using analogue modems.

High-speed broadband is now the dominant home access method rather than the previously popular **dial-up connection**.

However, companies should remember that there are significant numbers of Internet users who have the slower dial-up access. Ofcom (2010) reported that the proportion of individuals with access to broadband services in the UK is 71% (fixed broadband 65% and mobile broadband 15%).

Broadband connection
Access to the Internet via phone lines using a digital data transfer mechanisim.

Broadband uses a technology known as ADSL or asymmetric digital subscriber line, which means that the traditional phone line can be used for digital data transfer. It is asymmetric since download speeds are typically higher than upload speeds. Small and medium businesses can also benefit from faster continuous access than was previously possible.

The higher speeds available through broadband together with a continuous 'always on' connection have already transformed use of the Internet. Information access is more rapid and it becomes more practical to access richer content such as digital video.

Issues in management of ISP and hosting relationships

The primary issue for businesses in managing ISPs and hosting providers is to ensure a satisfactory service quality at a reasonable price. As the customers and partners of organizations become more dependent on their web services, it is important that downtime be minimized. But severe problems of downtime can occur, as shown in Box 3.5, and the consequences of these need to be avoided or managed.

Box 3.5	Downtime is inevitable

The Register (www.register.co.uk) catalogues challenges of managing IT. Here is a recent selection of downtime article headlines which indicate the type of problem:

- Thieves take out Cable & Wireless centre (10 July 2008)
- Fasthosts' dedicated servers go titsup (15 April 2008)
- Fasthosts customers still frozen out of websites (5 December 2007)
- Fasthosts customers blindsided by emergency password reset (30 November 2007)
- Banking data fears over Fasthosts intruder (19 October 2007)
- Fasthosts customer? Change your password now (18 October 2007)
- Fasthosts admits email destruction fiasco (17 October 2007)
- Fasthosts hit by severe floods (23 July 2007)
- Fasthosts 'electrical issue' halts service for four hours (17 July 2007)
- Level 3 floored by robbery (1 November 2006)
- Level 3 has a little lie-down in the sun (25 July 2006)
- Pipex hosting service floored by electrical fault (20 January 2006)

In the United States, a fire at hosting provider The Planet's H1 data centre in Houston caused downtime for many company websites delivered around the world including the author's website DaveChaffey.com, which, as for many businesses, is hosted by another hosting provider that uses The Planet's data centre for their services. The company blamed a faulty transformer for a fire which meant that the local fire department asked the hosting provider to switch off all generators and evacuate the building. No servers or networking equipment were damaged, but the data centre remained without power after The Planet shut down all generators 'as instructed by the fire department'. Around 10,000 servers were affected and some sites were down for as much as 3 days.

Speed of access

A site or e-business service fails if it fails to deliver an acceptable download speed for users. In the broadband world this is still important as e-business applications become more complex and sites integrate rich media. But what is acceptable?

Research supported by Akamai (2006) suggested that content needs to load within 4 seconds, otherwise site experience suffers. The research also showed, however, that high product price and shipping costs and problems with shipping were considered more important than speed. However, for sites perceived to have poor performance, many shoppers said they would not be likely to visit the site again (64%) or buy from the e-retailer (62%).

In 2010 Google introduced speed as a signal into its ranking algorithm, effectively penalizing slower sites by positioning them lower in its listings. The announcement suggested this would only affect 1% of sites (Google, 2010). The announcement also summarized more recent research from Akamai which suggested that less than 2 seconds was now an acceptable download speed for e-commerce site users. With Google taking page download speed into account when ranking some particularly slow sites it's worth comparing your 'page weight' or bloat compared to other sites. The average page size is 320Kb according to this compilation: http://code.google.com/speed/articles/web-metrics.html.

Speed of access to services is determined by both the speed of the server and the speed of the network connection to the server. The speed of the site governs how fast the response is to a request for information from the end-user. This will be dependent on the speed of the server machine on which the website is hosted and how quickly the server processes the information. If there are only a small number of users accessing information on the server, then there will not be a noticeable delay on requests for pages. If, however, there are thousands of users

| Box 3.6 | How long before you become impatient? |

Usability specialist Jacob Nielsen noted (Nielsen, 1994) that the basic advice for response times for human–computer interaction has been about the same for 30 years. He describes these requirements for response:

- 0.1 second is about the limit for having the user feel that the system is reacting instantaneously, meaning that no special feedback is necessary except to display the result.
- 1.0 second is about the limit for the user's flow of thought to stay uninterrupted, even though the user will notice the delay. Normally, no special feedback is necessary during delays of more than 0.1 but less than 1.0 second, but the user does lose the feeling of operating directly on the data.
- 10 seconds is about the limit for keeping the user's attention focused on the dialogue. For longer delays, users will want to perform other tasks while waiting for the computer to finish, so they should be given feedback indicating when the computer expects to be done. Feedback during the delay is especially important if the response time is likely to be highly variable, since users will then not know what to expect.

requesting information at the same time then there may be a delay and it is important that the combination of web server software and hardware can cope. Web server software will not greatly affect the speed at which requests are answered. The speed of the server is mainly controlled by the amount of primary storage (for example, 1024 Mb RAM is faster than 512 Mb RAM) and the speed of the magnetic storage (hard disk). Many of the search-engine websites now store all their index data in RAM since this is faster than reading data from the hard disk. Companies will pay ISPs according to the capabilities of the server.

Dedicated server
Server only contains content and applications for a single company.

An important aspect of hosting selection is whether the server is **dedicated** or shared (co-located). Clearly, if content on a server is shared with other sites hosted on the same server then performance and downtime will be affected by demand loads on these other sites. But a dedicated server package can cost 5 to 10 times the amount of a shared plan, so many small and medium businesses are better advised to adopt a shared plan, but take steps to minimize the risks with other sites going down.

For high-traffic sites, servers may be located across several computers with many processors to spread the demand load. New distributed methods of hosting content, summarized by Spinrad (1999), have been introduced to improve the speed of serving web pages for very large corporate sites by distributing content on servers around the globe, and the most widely used service is Akamai (www.akamai.com). These are used by companies such as Yahoo! Apple and other 'hot-spot' sites likely to receive many hits.

Bandwidth
Indicates the speed at which data are transferred using a particular network medium. It is measured in bits per second (bps).

The speed is also governed by the speed of the network connection, commonly referred to as the network '**bandwidth**'. The bandwidth of a website's connection to the Internet and the bandwidth of the customer's connection to the Internet will affect the speed with which web pages and associated graphics load. The term is so called because of the width of range of electromagnetic frequencies an analogue or digital signal occupies for a given transmission medium.

As described in Box 3.7, bandwidth gives an indication of the speed at which data can be transferred from a web server along a particular medium such as a network cable or phone line. In simple terms bandwidth can be thought of as the size of a pipe along which information flows. The higher the bandwidth, the greater the diameter of the pipe, and the faster information is delivered to the user. Many ISPs have bandwidth caps, even on 'unlimited' Internet access plans, for users who consume high volumes of bandwidth.

Box 3.7   Bandwidth measures

Bandwidth measures are in bits per second where one character or digit, such as the number '1', would be equivalent to 8 bits. So a modem operating at 57,600 bits per second (57.6 kbps) will transfer information at 7,200 characters per second (57,600/8). When selecting an ISP or hosting provider it is important to consider the bandwidth of the connection between the ISP and the Internet. Choices may be:

- ISDN – 56 kbps up to 128 kbps
- Frame relay – 56 kbps up to a T1 communications channel (1.55 Mbps)
- Dedicated point-to-point – 56 kbps up to T3 (45 Mbps): connected to the Internet backbone.

    kbps is one kilobit per second or 1,000 bps (a modem operates at up to 56.6 kbps)
    Mbps is one megabit per second or 1,000,000 bps (company networks operate at 10 or more Mbps)
    Gbps is one gigabit per second or 1,000,000,000 bps (fibre-optic or satellite links operate at Gbps).

A major factor for a company to consider when choosing an ISP is whether the server is *dedicated* to one company or whether content from several companies is located on the same server. A dedicated server is best, but it will attract a premium price.

Availability

The availability of a website is an indication of how easy it is for a user to connect to it. In theory this figure should be 100 per cent, but sometimes, for technical reasons such as failures in the server hardware or upgrades to software, the figure can drop substantially below this. Box 3.8 illustrates some of the potential problems and how companies can evaluate and address them.

Box 3.8   Preventing wobbly shopping carts

The extent of the problem of e-commerce service levels was indicated by *The Register* (2004) in an article titled 'Wobbly shopping carts blight UK e-commerce'. The research showed that failure of transactions once customers have decided to buy is often a problem. As the article said, '*UK E-commerce sites are slapping customers in the face, rather than shaking them by the hand. Turning consumers away once they have made a decision to buy is commercial suicide.*' The research showed this level of problems:

(ix) 20% of shopping carts did not function for 12 hours a month or more.
(x) 75% failed the standard service level availability of 99.9% uptime.
(xi) 80% performed inconsistently with widely varying response times, time-outs and errors – leaving customers at best wondering what to do next and at worst unable to complete their purchases.

Similarly, SciVisum, a web-testing specialist, found that three-quarters of Internet marketing campaigns are impacted by website failures, with 14% of failures so severe that they prevented the campaign meeting its objectives. The company surveyed marketing professionals from 100 UK-based organizations across the retail, financial, travel and online gaming sectors. More than a third of failures were rated as 'serious to severe', with many customers complaining or unable to complete web transactions. These are often seen by marketers as technology issues which are owned by others in the business, but marketers need to ask the right questions. The SciVisum (2005) research showed that nearly two-thirds of marketing professionals did not know how many users making transactions their websites could support, despite an average transaction value of £50 to £100, so they were not able to factor this into campaign plans. Thirty-seven per cent could not put a monetary value on losses caused by customers abandoning web transactions. A quarter of organizations experienced website overloads and crashes as a direct result of a lack of communication between the two departments.

SciVisum recommends that companies do the following:

1   Define the peak visitor throughput requirements for each customer journey on the site. For example, the site should be able to support at the same time: approximately ten checkout journeys per second, thirty add-to-basket journeys per second, five registration journeys per second, two check-my-order-status journeys per second.

2   Service-level agreement. More detailed technical requirements need to be agreed for each of the transaction stages. Home-page delivery time and server uptime are insufficiently detailed.

3   Set up a monitoring programme that measures and reports on the agreed journeys 24/7.

Service-level agreements

Service-level agreement (SLA)
A contractual specification of service standards a contractor must meet.

To ensure the best speed and availability a company should check the **service-level agreements (SLAs)** carefully when outsourcing website hosting services. The SLA will define confirmed standards of availability and performance measured in terms of the *latency* or network delay when information is passed from one point to the next. The SLA also includes notification to the customer detailing when the web service becomes unavailable with reasons why and estimates of when the service will be restored.

Security

Security is another important issue in service quality. How to control security was referred to in the earlier section on firewalls and is considered in detail in '*Focus on* Security design for e-business' (Chapter 11, p. 624).

Managing employee access to the Internet and e-mail

This is covered in Chapter 11 in the '*Focus on* Security design for e-business' section.

Managing e-business applications infrastructure

E-business applications infrastructure
Applications that provide access to services and information inside and beyond an organization.

Management of the **e-business applications infrastructure** concerns delivering the right applications to all users of e-business services. The issue involved is one that has long been a concern of IS managers, namely to deliver access to integrated applications and data that are available across the whole company. Traditionally businesses have developed applications silos or islands of information, as depicted in Figure 3.17(a). These silos may develop at three different levels: (1) there may be different technology architectures used in different functional areas, (2) there will also be different applications and separate databases in different areas, and (3) processes or activities followed in the different functional areas may also be different.

Applications silos are often a result of decentralization or poorly controlled investment in information systems, with different departmental managers selecting different systems from different vendors. This is inefficient in that it will often cost more to purchase applications from separate vendors, and also it will be more costly to support and upgrade. Such a fragmented approach stifles decision making and leads to isolation between functional units. For example, if a customer phones a B2B company for the status of a bespoke item they have ordered, the person in customer support may have access to their personal details but not the status of their job, which is stored on a separate information system in the manufacturing unit. Problems can also occur at tactical and strategic levels. For example, if a company is trying to analyse the financial contribution of customers, perhaps to calculate lifetime values, some information about customers' purchases may be stored in a marketing information system, while the payments data will be stored in a separate system within the finance department. It may prove difficult or impossible to reconcile these different data sets.

To avoid the problems of a fragmented applications infrastructure, companies attempted throughout the 1990s to achieve the more integrated position shown in Figure 3.17(b).

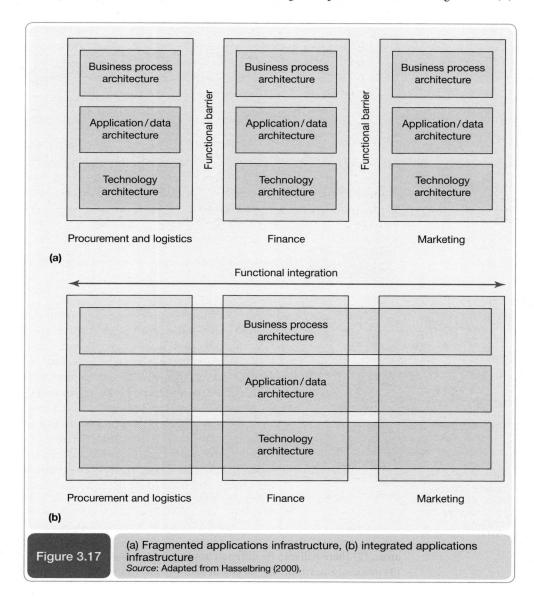

Figure 3.17 (a) Fragmented applications infrastructure, (b) integrated applications infrastructure
Source: Adapted from Hasselbring (2000).

Enterprise resource planning (ERP) applications
Software providing integrated functions for major business functions such as production, distribution, sales, finance and human resources management.

Many companies turned to **enterprise resource planning (ERP)** vendors such as SAP, Baan, PeopleSoft and Oracle.

The approach of integrating different applications through ERP is entirely consistent with the principle of e-business, since e-business applications must facilitate the integration of the whole *supply chain* and *value chain*. It is noteworthy that many of the ERP vendors such as SAP have repositioned themselves as suppliers of e-business solutions! The difficulty for those managing e-business infrastructure is that there is not, and probably never can be, a single solution of components from a single supplier. For example, to gain competitive edge, companies may need to turn to solutions from innovators who, for example, support new channels such as WAP, or provide knowledge management solutions or sales management solutions. If these are not available from their favoured current supplier, do they wait until these components become available or do they attempt to integrate new software into the application? Thus managers are faced with a precarious balancing act between standardization or core product and integrating innovative systems where applicable. Figure 3.18 illustrates this dilemma. It shows how different types of applications tend to have strengths in different areas.

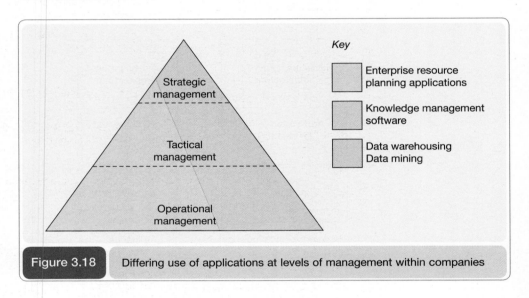

| Figure 3.18 | Differing use of applications at levels of management within companies |

Debate 3.2

Best of breed vs single-source systems

Selecting 'best-of-breed' applications from multiple system vendors for different e-business applications such as enterprise resource planning, customer relationship management, transactional e-commerce and supply chain management is a better approach for an effective e-business infrastructure than using a single-vendor solution.

ERP systems were originally focused on achieving integration at the operational level of an organization. Solutions for other applications such as business intelligence in the form of data warehousing and data mining tended to focus on tactical decision making based on accessing the operational data from within ERP systems. Knowledge management software (Chapter 10) also tends to cut across different levels of management. Figure 3.18 only shows some types of applications, but it shows the trial of strength between the monolithic ERP applications and more specialist applications looking to provide the same functionality.

The issues of managing e-business infrastructure are examined in more detail later in the book. Figure 3.19 summarizes some of these management issues and is based on the layered architecture introduced at the start of this section.

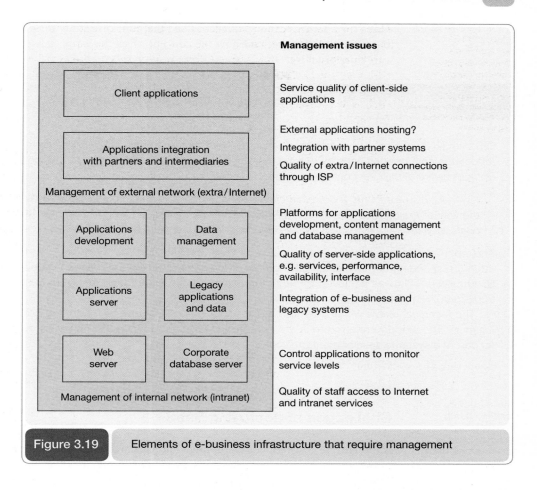

Figure 3.19   Elements of e-business infrastructure that require management

Web services, SaaS and service-oriented architecture (SOA)

Web services

Business applications and software services are provided through Internet and web protocols with the application managed on a separate server from where it is accessed through a web browser on an end-user's computer.

'**Web services**' or 'software as a service (SaaS)' refers to a highly significant model for managing software and data within the e-business age. The web services model involves managing and performing all types of business processes and activities through accessing web-based services rather than running a traditional executable application on the processor of your local computer.

Benefits of web services or SaaS

SaaS are usually paid for on a subscription basis, so can potentially be switched on and off or payments paid according to usage, hence they are also known as 'on demand'. The main business benefit of these systems is that installation and maintenance costs are effectively outsourced. Cost savings are made on both the server and client sides, since the server software and databases are hosted externally and client applications software is usually delivered through a web browser or a simple application that is downloaded via the web.

In research conducted in the US and Canada by Computer Economics (2006), 91% of companies showed a first-year return on investment (ROI) from SaaS. Of these, 57% of the total had economic benefits which exceeded the SaaS costs and 37% broke even in year one. The same survey showed that in 80% of cases, the total cost of ownership (TCO) came in either on budget or lower. There would be few cases of traditional applications where these figures can be equalled. Read the mini case study for details on the benefits of a SaaS implementation and how the concept of service usage can also be applied to hardware infrastructure.

Mini Case Study 3.5	How Intel benefits from SaaS, IaaS and PaaS!

CIO.com (2010) describes how Intel built an intranet for its research and development group. Its aims were to reduce the cost of operations by making more use of existing infrastructure and making users of computing services aware of their cost of their utilization. Das Kamhout, the project lead, explained the benefits as follows:

'Overall, this represents a dramatic change in mindset. On-demand self-service allows IT to get out of the way of the business so we can up-level IT and be a strategic business partner. And with transparent costs, departments across Intel now know what they're costing and what they're consuming.

This approach to server utilization is known as **IaaS (Infrastruture as a Service)**. Through reduced infrastructure spending and avoiding building new data centre facilities, the company expected to save nearly $200 million. This was achieved through improving its server utilization rate from 59% in the first half of 2006 to 80% in 2010.

The technical teams within Intel also applied the **PaaS (Platform as a Service)** concept as part of the initiative. The platform referred to is the specific type of SaaS for developing new software and hardware as part of a systems development project.

Source: Adapted from CIO (2010).

Infrastructure as a Service (IaaS)
Hardware used to provide support for end-user applications is outsourced and paid for according to level of usage. The hardware infrastructure used includes servers and networks.

PaaS (Platform as a Service)
Provision of software services for application design, development, data storage, testing and hosting together with messaging tools for collaboration on the development project.

Challenges of deploying SaaS

Although the cost reduction arguments of SaaS are persuasive, what are the disadvantages of this approach? The pros and cons are similar to the 'make or buy' decision discussed in Chapter 12. SaaS will obviously have less capability for tailoring to exact business needs than a bespoke system.

The most obvious disadvantage of using SaaS is dependence on a third party to deliver services over the web, which has these potential problems:

● Downtime or poor availability if the network connection or server hosting the application or server fails.
● Lower performance than a local database. You know from using Gmail or Hotmail that although responsive, they cannot be as responsive as using a local e-mail package like Outlook.
● Reduce data security since traditionally data would be backed up locally by in-house IT staff (ideally also off-site). Since failures in the system are inevitable, companies using SaaS need to be clear how back-up and restores are managed and the support that is available for handling problems which is defined within the SLA.
● Data protection – since customer data may be stored in a different location it is essential that it is sufficiently secure and consistent with the data protection and privacy laws discussed in Chapter 4.

Multi-tenancy SaaS
A single instance of a web service is used by different customers (tenants) run on a single server or load-balanced across multiple servers. Customers are effectively sharing processor, disk usage and bandwidth with other customers.

These potential problems need to be evaluated on a case-by-case basis when selecting SaaS providers. Disaster recovery procedures are particularly important since many SaaS applications such as customer relationship management and supply chain management are mission-critical. Managers need to question service levels since often services are delivered to multiple customers from a single server in a **multi-tenancy** arrangement rather than a **single-tenancy** arrangement. This is similar to the situation with the shared server or dedicated server we discussed earlier for web hosting. An example of this in practice is shown in Box 3.9.

| Box 3.9 | Is my SaaS single-tenancy or multi-tenancy? |

Single-tenancy SaaS
A single instance of an application (and/or database) is maintained for all customers (tenants) who have dedicated resources of processor, disk usage and bandwidth. The single instance may be load-balanced over multiple servers for improved performance.

Smoothspan (2007) has estimated the level of multi-tenancy for different web services, which is also dependent on the number of seats or users per server. He estimates that in 2006 Salesforce was running 40 Dell PowerEdge servers with 6,700 customers (tenants) and 134,000 seats. This is equivalent to 168 tenants per server, and 3,350 seats per server! Although this figure suggests the disadvantage of multi-tenancy, he also estimates there is a 16:1 cost advantage of multi-tenant over single tenant.

An example of a consumer SaaS, word processing, would involve visiting a website which hosts the application rather than running a word processor such as Microsoft Word on your local computer through starting 'Word.exe'. The best-known consumer service for online word processing and spreadsheet use is Google Docs (http://docs.google.com) which was launched following the purchase in 2006 by Google of start-up Writely (www.writely.com). Google Docs also enables users to view and edit documents offline, through Google Gears, an open-source browser extension. 'Microsoft Office Live' is a similar initiative from Microsoft.

Google Apps enables organizations to manage many of their activities. The basic service is free, with the Premier Edition, which includes more storage space and security, being $50 per user account per year.

Utility computing
IT resources and in particular software and hardware are utilized on a pay-per-use basis and are managed externally as 'managed services'.

A related concept to web services is **utility computing**. Utility computing involves treating all aspects of IT as a commodity service such as water, gas or electricity where payment is according to usage. A subscription is usually charged per month according to the number of features, number of users, volume of data storage or bandwidth consumed. Discounts will be given for longer-term contracts. This includes not only software which may be used on a pay-per-use basis, but also using hardware, for example for hosting. An earlier term is '**applications service providers**' (ASP).

Application service provider
An application server provides a business application on a server remote from the user.

Figure 3.20 shows one of the largest SaaS or utility providers Salesforce.com where customers pay from £5 to £50 per user per month according to the facilities used. The service is delivered from the Salesforce.com servers to over 50,000 customers in 15 local languages.

Cloud computing
The use of distributed storage and processing on servers connected by the Internet, typically provided as software or data storage as a subscription service provided by other companies.

In descriptions of web services you will often hear, confusingly, that they access 'the cloud' or the term '**cloud computing**'. The cloud referred to is the combination of networking and data storage hardware and software hosted externally to a company, typically shared between many separate or 'distributed' servers accessed via the Internet. So, for example, Google Docs will be stored somewhere 'in the cloud' without any knowledge of where it is or how it is managed since Google stores data on many servers. Of course you can access the document from any location. But there are issues to consider about data stored and served from the cloud: 'Is it secure, is it backed up, is it always available?' The size of Google's cloud is indicated by Pandia (2007), which estimated that Google had over 1 million servers running the open-source Linux software.

Examples of cloud computing web services

Think of examples of web services that you or businesses use, and you will soon see how important they are for both personal and business applications. Examples include:

- Web mail readers.
- E-commerce account and purchasing management facilities such as Amazon.com.
- Many services from Google such as Google Maps, GMail, Picasa and Google Analytics.
- Customer relationship management applications from Salesforce.com and Siebel/Oracle.
- Supply chain management solutions from SAP, Oracle and Covisint.
- E-mail and web security management from companies like MessageLabs (part of Symantec).

| Figure 3.20 | Salesforce.com
Source: www.salesforce.com. |

From the point of view of managing IT infrastructure these changes are dramatic since traditionally companies have employed their own information systems support staff to manage different types of business applications such as e-mail. Costs associated with upgrading and configuring new software on users' client computers and servers are dramatically decreased.

As seen in the mini case study below, many smaller businesses and start-ups use cloud computing services to provide web-based services at a relatively low cost with the flexibility to meet short-term (high demand spikes) or longer growth in demand for their services.

Mini Case Study 3.6   Amazon Web Services supports start-ups through their growth

View the examples at Amazon Web Services (AWS) (**http://aws.amazon.com/solutions/case-studie**s) to gain an idea of the services used by start-up businesses. Here are some examples:

- **Application hosting**: 99designs' massive design marketplace has received over 3.1 million unique design submissions from over 53,000 designers around the world and runs entirely on AWS.
- **Back-up and storage**: ElephantDrive turns to Amazon S3 to store client data, expanding their total amount of storage by nearly 20% each week while avoiding increased capital expenses.
- **Content delivery:** HyperStratus teams with the Silicon Valley Education Foundation to support AWS cloud-based content management serving 13,000 teachers in the Silicon Valley area.

- **E-commerce:** The Talk Market uses Amazon Flexible Payments Service to power their credit card processing pipeline.
- **High-performance computing:** Harvard's Laboratory for Personalized Medicine (LPM) uses customized Oracle AMIs on Amazon EC2 to run genetic testing models and simulations.
- **Media hosting:** Fotopedia hosts 500,000 photos using Amazon EC2, Elastic IPs, and Elastic Load Balancing for hosting and Amazon S3 and CloudFront for media hosting and for internal log and data storage.
- **On-demand workforce:** Using Amazon Mechanical Turk, Channel Intelligence was able to leverage human intelligence around the globe and decrease task-specific costs by 85%.
- **Search engines:** Alexa delivers high-volume search and information services, storing over 12 million objects in Amazon SimpleDB and performing over 5 million queries daily.
- **Web hosting:** Online mobile commerce provider Gumiyo runs a complete production environment with Amazon Web Services, including web servers, database servers and load balancers.

Activity 3.5	Opportunities for using web services by a B2B company

Purpose

To highlight the advantages and disadvantages of the web services approach.

Question

Develop a balanced case for the managing director explaining the web services approach and summarizing its advantages and disadvantages.

Answers to activities can be found at www.pearsoned.co.uk/chaffey

Virtualization

Virtualization
The indirect provision of technology services through another resource (abstraction). Essentially one computer is using its processing and storage capacity to do the work of another.

Virtualization is another approach to managing IT resource more effectively. However, it is mainly deployed within an organization. VMware was one of the forerunners, offering virtualization services which it explains as follows (VMware, 2008):

The VMware approach to virtualization inserts a thin layer of software directly on the computer hardware or on a host operating system. This software layer creates virtual machines and contains a virtual machine monitor or 'hypervisor' that allocates hardware resources dynamically and transparently so that multiple operating systems can run concurrently on a single physical computer without even knowing it.

However, virtualizing a single physical computer is just the beginning. VMware offers a robust virtualization platform that can scale across hundreds of interconnected physical computers and storage devices to form an entire virtual infrastructure.

They go on to explain that virtualization essentially lets one computer do the job of multiple computers, by sharing the resources of a single computer across multiple environments. Virtual servers and virtual desktops let you host multiple operating systems and multiple applications. So virtualization has these benefits:

- Lower hardware costs through consolidation of servers (see mini case study below).
- Lower maintenance and support costs.
- Lower energy costs.
- Scalability to add more resource more easily.
- Standardized, peronalized desktops can be accessed from any location, so users are not tied to an individual physical computer.
- Improved business continuity.

The mini case study gives an example of these benefits.

| **Mini Case Study 3.7** | Virtualization cuts costs and improves service |

The Association of Teachers and Lecturers (ATL) is using virtualization not only to cut hardware costs, but also to recover quickly from systems failures and maintain business continuity. The Association of Teachers and Lecturers is an independent, registered trade union and professional association representing approximately 160,000 teachers, lecturers and support staff in maintained and independent nurseries, schools, sixth forms, and tertiary and further education colleges in the UK.

Ann Raimondo, head of information technology at ATL, is responsible for managing the IT infrastructure for the ever-expanding organization, including deploying equipment, IT support and training for its 150 employees. In addition to offices in London, Belfast and Cardiff, the ATL has a large volunteer base of remote workers throughout the UK who require IT systems and support. In her role, Raimondo was faced with the following challenges:

- Fifty per cent of the available server storage space was not utilized.
- Seventy-two per cent of the storage space purchased was not being used.
- Storage space could not be reallocated to other systems in need of additional storage.
- Data were physically bound to a server, so if corruption occurred to the operating system or applications, the data on physical drives could not be reattached easily to another server and would need to be restored from back-up.

The implementation resulted in the following benefits:

- **Server consolidation**. ATL consolidated from 22 servers to 11, reducing hardware requirements and costs by 50 per cent.
- **Flexibility and responsiveness**. Prior to bringing in ESX Server, deploying a new server would require approximately three weeks for sourcing, ordering and implementing hardware. With VMware virtual infrastructure, this same process takes less than one hour.
- **Lowered the cost of disaster recovery**. The hardware independence of VMware virtual infrastructure helps mitigate failures caused by hardware and enables recovery from a disaster in a matter of minutes, matching and improving on user downtime expectations.

Source: VMware (2007).

Service-oriented architecture (SOA)

Service-oriented architecture
A service-oriented architecture is a collection of services that communicate with each other as part of a distributed systems architecture comprising different services.

The technical architecture used to build web services is formally known as a '**service-oriented architecture**'. This is an arrangement of software processes or agents which communicate with each other to deliver the business requirements.

The main role of a service within SOA is to provide functionality. This is provided by three characteristics:

1 An interface with the service which is platform-independent (not dependent on a particular type of software or hardware). The interface is accessible through applications development approaches such as Microsoft .Net or Java and accessed through protocols such as SOAP (Simple Object Access Protocol) which is used for XML-formatted messages.
2 The service can be dynamically located and invoked. One service can query for the existence of another service through a service directory – for example an e-commerce service could query for the existence of a credit card authorization service.
3 The service is self-contained. That is, the service cannot be influenced by other services; rather it will return a required result to a request from another service, but will not change state. Within web services, messages and data are typically exchanged between services using XML.

The examples of web services all imply a user interacting with the web service. But with the correct business rules and models to follow, there is no need for human intervention and different applications and databases can communicate with each other in real time. A web service such as Kelkoo.com exchanges information with all participating merchants through XML using an SOA. The concept of the semantic web mentioned above and business applications of web services such as CRM, SCM and ebXML are also based on an SOA approach..

Read Case study 3.2 to explore the significance and challenges of SOA further.

| Case Study 3.2 | New architecture or just new hype? | FT |

Depending on whom you listen to, it could be the most important shift in corporate computing since the advent of the Internet – or it could be just the latest excuse for technology companies to hype their products in a dismal market.

'We believe it's the Next Big Thing,' says Henning Kagermann, chairman of SAP, Europe's biggest software company.

'It's the new fashion statement,' counters Mark Barrenechea, chief technology officer of Computer Associates. 'I'm sceptical.'

The 'it' in question goes by the ungainly name of 'service-oriented architecture', or SOA for short. According to the big software companies, its impact on computing will be as big as the client–server revolution of the early 1990s, or the arrival of web-based applications with the internet.

'Every five or 10 years, we see this in the industry,' says John Wookey, the executive in charge of Oracle's Project Fusion, the giant effort to re-engineer all of the software applications inherited as a result of that company's various acquisitions.

For those with ambitions to dominate the next phase of corporate software – SAP, Oracle, IBM and Microsoft – it represents an important turning-point. 'When these transitions occur you have your best opportunity to change the competitive landscape,' adds Mr Wookey.

Yet for customers, the benefits and costs of this next transformation in the underlying computing architecture are still hard to ascertain.

Bruce Richardson, chief research officer at AMR Research, draws attention to the unexpected costs that came with the rise of client–server computing: the soaring hardware and software expenses, the difficulty of supporting such a wide array of machines, and the cost of dealing with security flaws.

'That ended up being a huge bill,' he notes.

It is hardly surprising that enterprise software companies – those that create the heavy-duty software that big corporations and governments use to run their operations – are so eager to latch on to the next big thing.

An industry still in its infancy is facing potential disruptive upheaval. New licensing models and ways of delivering software, along with open-source approaches to development and distribution, are turning the young software industry on its head.

At the same time, the maturity of existing applications and the technology platform on which they run has left the best-established enterprise software companies stuck in a period of slow growth.

That is fertile soil for extravagant marketing claims to take root in.

Even if SOA risks are being over-hyped, however, it still seems likely to represent an important step forward for today's often monolithic corporate IT systems.

By harnessing industry-wide technology standards that have been in development since the late 1990s, it promises at least a partial answer to one of the biggest drawbacks of the current computing base: a lack of flexibility that has driven up the cost of software development and forced companies to design their business processes around the needs of their IT systems, rather than the other way around.

Software executives say that the inability to redesign IT systems rapidly to support new business processes, and to link those systems to customers and suppliers, was one of the main reasons for the failure of one of the great early promises of the internet – seamless 'B2B', or business-to-business, commerce.

'It's what killed the original [B2B] marketplaces,' says Shai Agassi, who heads SAP's product and technology development.

SAP is certainly further ahead than others in the race to build a more flexible computing platform. While Oracle and Microsoft are busy trying to create coherent packages of software applications from the corporate acquisitions they have made, SAP is halfway through a revamp of its technology that could give it a lead of two years or more.

'If they're right, it will be a huge thing for them,' says Charles Di Bona, software analyst at Sanford C. Bernstein.

Underlying the arrival of SOA has been the spread of so-called web services standards – such as the mark-up language XML and communications protocol SOAP – that make it easier for machines to exchange data automatically.

This holds the promise of automating business processes that run across different IT systems, whether inside a single company or spanning several business partners: a customer placing an order in one system could automatically trigger production requests in another and an invoice in a third.

Breaking down the different steps in a business process in this way, and making them available to be recombined quickly to suit particular business needs, is the ultimate goal of SOA. Each step in the process becomes a service, a single reusable component that is 'exposed' through a standard interface.

The smaller each of these software components, the more flexibility users will have to build IT systems that fit their particular needs.

SAP has created 300 services so far; that number will rise to 3,000 by the end of this year, says Mr Agassi. Through NetWeaver, the set of 'middleware' tools that provide the glue, it has also finalised much of the platform to deliver this new set of services. The full 'business process platform' will be complete by the end of next year, SAP says.

'The factory is running – we have all the tools ready now,' says Peter Graf, head of solution marketing at SAP. To get customers to start experimenting with the new technology, he adds, 'we need to come up with killer apps.'

The first full-scale demonstration will come from a project known as Mendecino, under which SAP and Microsoft have been working to integrate their 'back-end' and 'front-end' systems and which is due to be released in the middle of this year.

By linking them to the widely used components of Microsoft's Office desktop software, SAP's corporate applications will become easier to use, says Mr Graf: for instance, when a worker enters a holiday in his or her Outlook calendar, it could automatically trigger an approval request to a manager and cross-check with a system that records holiday entitlements.

While such demonstrations may start to show the potential of SOA, however, the real power of this architectural shift is likely to depend on a much broader ecosystem of software developers and corporate users.

'People want to extend their business processes to get closer to customers,' says Mr Richardson at AMR. To do that through the 'loosely coupled' IT systems promised by SOA will require wider adoption of the new technology architecture.

A number of potential drawbacks stand in the way.

Along with uncertainty about the ultimate cost, points out Mr Richardson, is concern about security: what safeguards will companies need before they are willing to let valuable corporate data travel outside their own IT systems, or before they open up their own networks to code developed elsewhere?

A further question is whether SOA can fulfil one of its most important promises: that the technology platforms being created by SAP and others will stimulate a wave of innovation in the software industry, as developers rush to create new and better applications, many of them suited to the specific needs of particular industries or small groups of companies.

That depends partly on whether companies such as SAP can create true technology 'ecosystems' around their platforms, much as Microsoft's success in desktop software depended on its ability to draw developers to its desktop software platform.

'We were told three years ago that we didn't know how to partner,' says Mr Agassi at SAP, before dismissing such criticism as 'quite funny', given what he says was the success of its earlier software applications in attracting developers. 'We are more open than we have ever been, we are more standards-based than we have ever been,' he adds – a claim that is contested by Oracle, which has tried to make capital from the fact that its German rival's underlying technology still depends on a proprietary computing language, ABAP.

However, even if the future SOA-enabled platforms succeed in stimulating a new generation of more flexible corporate software, one other overriding issue remains: rivals such as SAP and Oracle will see little to gain from linking their rival platforms to each other. Full inter-operability will remain just a dream.

'To make SOA real, you have to have a process start in one system and end in another, with no testing or certification needed,' says Mr Barrenechea at Computer Associates – even if those systems are rival ones from SAP and Oracle.

The software giants, he says, 'have to be motivated to make it work'.

According to Mr Agassi, companies will eventually 'have to choose' which of the platforms they want to use as the backbone for their businesses.

The web services standards may create a level of inter-operability between these different backbones, but each will still use its own 'semantics', or way of defining business information, to make it comprehensible to other, connected systems.

Like a common telephone network, the standards should make it easier to create connections, but they can do nothing if the people on either end of the line are talking a different language.

If different companies in the same industry, or different business partners, adopt different software platforms, there will still be a need for the expensive manual work to link the systems together.

'You will have to spend the same amount of money on systems integrators that you spend today,' says Mr Graf.

Despite that, the new service-oriented technology should still represent a leap forward from today's monolithic IT systems. Even the sceptics concede that the gains could be substantial. It should lead to 'better [software] components and better interfaces – which equals better inter-operability,' says Mr Barrenechea.

As with any sales pitch from the technology industry, however, it is as well to be wary of the hype.

Source: Richard Waters, New architecture or just new hype? *The Financial Times*, 8 March 2006. Reprinted with permission.

> **Question**
>
> Discuss the extent to which SOA will reduce reliance on a single provider of enterprise software and increase flexibility in deploying new applications and functionality.

EDI

Electronic data interchange (EDI)

The exchange, using digital media, of structured business information, particularly for sales transactions such as purchase orders and invoices between buyers and sellers.

Financial EDI

Aspect of electronic payment mechanism involving transfer of funds from the bank of a buyer to the bank of a seller.

Electronic funds transfer (EFT)

Automated digital transmission of money between organizations and banks.

Internet EDI

Use of EDI data standards delivered across non-proprietary IP networks.

Value-added network (VAN)

A secure wide-area network that uses proprietary rather than Internet technology.

Virtual private networks (VPN)

A secure, encrypted (tunnelled) connection between two points using the Internet, typically created by ISPs for organizations wanting to conduct secure Internet trading.

Transactional e-commerce predates the World Wide Web and service-oriented architecture by some margin. In the 1960s, **electronic data interchange (EDI)**, **financial EDI** and **electronic funds transfer (EFT)** over secure private networks became established modes of intra- and inter-company transaction. The idea of standardized document exchange can be traced back to the 1948 Berlin Airlift, where a standard form was required for efficient management of items flown to Berlin from many locations. This was followed by electronic transmission in the 1960s in the US transport industries. The EDIFACT (Electronic Data Interchange for Administration, Commerce and Transport) standard was later produced by a joint United Nations/European committee to enable international trading. There is also a similar X12 EDI standard developed by the ANSI Accredited Standards Committee.

Clarke (1998) considers that EDI is best understood as the replacement of paper-based purchase orders with electronic equivalents, but its applications are wider than this. The types of documents exchanged by EDI include business transactions such as orders, invoices, delivery advice and payment instructions as part of EFT. There may also be pure information transactions such as a product specification, for example engineering drawings or price lists. Clarke (1998) defines EDI as:

> *the exchange of documents in standardised electronic form, between organisations, in an automated manner, directly from a computer application in one organisation to an application in another.*

EDI is one form, or a subset, of electronic commerce. A key point is that direct communication occurs between applications (rather than between computers). This requires information systems to achieve the data processing and data management associated with EDI and integration with associated information systems such as sales order processing and inventory control systems.

EDI is developing through new standards and integration with Internet technologies to achieve **Internet EDI**.

Internet EDI enables EDI to be implemented at lower costs since, rather than using proprietary so-called **value-added networks (VANs)**, it uses the same EDI standard documents, but using lower-cost transmission techniques through **virtual private networks (VPNs)** or the public Internet. Reported cost savings are up to 90% (*EDI Insider*, 1996). *EDI Insider* estimated that this cost differential would cause an increase from the 80,000 companies in the United States using EDI in 1996 to hundreds of thousands. Internet EDI also includes EDI-structured documents being exchanged by e-mail or in a more automated form using FTP.

There is now a wide choice of technologies for managing electronic transactions between businesses. The Yankee Group (2002) refers to these as 'transaction management (TXM)' technologies which are used to automate machine-to-machine information exchange between organizations. These include:

document and data translation, transformation, routing, process management, electronic data interchange (EDI), eXtensible Mark-up Language (XML), Web services ... Value-added networks, electronic trading networks, and other hosted solutions are also tracked in the TXM market segment.

Focus on   Mobile commerce

Mobile commerce or m-commerce
Electronic transactions and communications conducted using mobile devices such as laptops, PDAs and mobile phones, and typically with a wireless connection.

In Chapter 1 we explained that e-commerce refers to both informational and financial transactions through digital media. Similarly, **mobile commerce (m-commerce)** refers to the use of wireless devices such as mobile phones for both informational and monetary transactions.

While fixed access to the Internet has dominated to date in many developed countries, in future this situation will change due to the ubiquity of the mobile phone and the adoption of higher-speed services and more sophisticated handsets. In some countries, such as Japan and China, the majority of web access is via mobile phone and we can expect to see increased mobile use in all countries. In China there are more mobile subscribers (over half a billion) than the whole US population (Belic, 2007) and according to the regularly updated Comscore panel data (www.comscore.com), use of the web by mobile devices in Japan is equal to that of traditional computer access.

Box 3.10   Adoption and potential for mobile commerce around the world

The potential of mobile commerce is evident from research by Wireless Intelligence (2008) which found that at the end of 2007, globally there were 3 billion subscriber connections and, if there was one active subscription per person, that would represent half the planet's population. But they explain that because of multiple SIM ownership there is always a lag between connections and subscribers, so there is still some way to go before half the world's population is connected. They also note that penetration is relatively low in developing countries such as India (21%) and China (41%), showing the potential for future growth. Some of the other figures are staggering:

- More than 1 billion mobile phones were sold in 2007.
- It took 12 years to get to 1 billion GSM connections and just 30 months to get to 2 billion.
- There are 1.2 million new GSM connections every day.
- Nearly 7 billion text messages are sent every day.

Table 4.3 gives figures for different content and applications of mobile phones in China, the US and several European countries.

Wireless Internet access standards

The capabilities of mobile phones have evolved tremendously since the first-generation brick-like phones were introduced in the 1980s. There is a bewildering range of data transfer standards which are summarized in Table 3.5. Many subscribers are still using the second-generation GSM technology which does not permit Internet access, but many have the option for 2.5G web access via WAP. The 3G and 3.5G phones support video calls and broadband speed access.

Table 3.5	Comparison of mobile phone technologies		
Generation of mobile technology	**Main standards**	**Maximum data transfer rate (downlink)**	**Approximate adoption levels 2008**
1G Analogue cellphones of 1980s	Frequency Division Multiple Access (FDMA)	9600 bits/sec	N/A
2G Circuit-switched, digital cellphones introduced in 1991	GSM (Global System for Mobile communications) Code division multiple access(CDMA) TDMA ('time division multiple access')	13 kbit/s	c80% globally
2.5G Introduced in 2001	GPRS (General Packet Radio Service) EDGE (Enhanced Data rates for Global Evolution)	114 kbit/s	N/A
3G Packet-switched introduced in 2004	UMTS (Universal Mobile Telecommunications System) W-CDMA (Wideband Code Division Multiple Access) HSDPA (High-Speed Downlink Packet Access)	14.4 Mbit/s	c28% in Europe and US according to Comscore
3.5G 2008	Evolved HSPA / HPSA+	42 Mbit/s	N/A
4G 2012–15	Fourth generation No agreed standards	2012–15 time scale	N/A

Wireless Application Protocol (WAP)
WAP is a technical standard for transferring information to wireless devices, such as mobile phones.

'Wireless Application Protocol', or WAP, offers the facility to access information on websites that has been specially tailored using Wireless Markup Language (WML) for display on the small screens of mobile phones. When first introduced around 2000, levels of product purchase by mobile phone and content access proved very low in comparison with the Internet, even for standardized products such as books and CDs. Many m-commerce providers such as Sweden's M-box went into receivership.

i-Mode
A mobile access platform that enables display of colour graphics and content subscription services.

One other form of mobile access popularity is the Japanese i-Mode standard which uses a derivative of HTML for content display. It has not been successful elsewhere. Mobile phone ringtones and other music downloads are the most popular i-Mode purchases, followed by other paid-for information services such as dating.

Wireless access devices

Site owners and marketers need to consider support for the following:

- Mobile phones using short-code response to campaigns or interactive sites based on WAP or use of rich-media streaming supported by broadband 3G technology.
- Personal digital assistants or smartphones such as the BlackBerry and Windows mobile 'Pocket PC' phones.
- Traditional PCs such as laptops accessing the web over Wi-Fi.
- Gaming platforms with a lower screen resolution accessing the web via Wi-Fi such as the Nintendo DS Lite or Sony PlayStation Plus (PSP).

Popularity of applications of mobile communications

Mobile technologies have been touted for many years as the future for Internet access. They are widely used, but still primarily for text messaging within Europe and the US. Mobile phones are important in terms of paid content services.

The benefits that mobile or wireless connections offer to their users are ubiquity (can be accessed from anywhere), reachability (their users can be reached when not in their normal location) and convenience (it is not necessary to have access to a power supply or fixed-line connection). They also provide security – each user can be authenticated since each wireless device has a unique identification code; their location can be used to tailor content; and they provide a degree of privacy compared with a desktop PC. An additional advantage is that of instant access or being 'always-on'; here there is no need to dial up a wireless connection. Table 3.6 provides a summary of the mobile or wireless Internet access proposition. There are considerable advantages in comparison to PC-based Internet access, but it is still limited by the display limitations.

Table 3.6	Summary of mobile or wireless Internet access consumer proposition
Element of proposition	**Evaluation**
No fixed location	The user is freed from the need to access via the desktop, making access possible when commuting, for example
Location-based services	Mobiles can be used to give geographically based services, e.g. an offer in a particular shopping centre. Future mobiles will have global positioning services integrated
Instant access/convenience	The latest General Packet Radio Service (GPRS) and 3G services are always on, avoiding the need for lengthy connection
Privacy	Mobiles are more private than desktop access, making them more suitable for social use or for certain activities such as an alert service for looking for a new job
Personalization	As with PC access, personal information and services can be requested by the user, although these often need to be set up via PC access
Security	In the future mobiles may become a form of wallet, but thefts of mobiles make this a source of concern

Mobile apps

Mobile apps
A software application that is designed for use on a mobile phone, typically downloaded from an AppStore. iPhone apps are best known, but all Smartphones support the use of apps which can provide users with information, entertainment or location-based services such as mapping.

Mobile apps are a highly significant development in mobile communications, indeed all digital communications, since they highlight a change in the method of delivering interactive services and content via mobile phones. Until the advent of apps, popularized by Apple iPhone, the web browser had been seen as the main model by most for delivering content via mobile phones.

For this author, the growth in popularity of apps for the iPhone has been incredible, with Apple announcing in January 2010 that 3 billion apps had been downloaded in the 18 months following the launch of the AppStore. iPhoneDev (2010) compiled a summary of the growth based on official figures from the Apple AppStore and showed these characteristics of apps from the AppStore in June 2010:

- Number of apps downloaded per month = 500 million
- The number iOS users = 100 million
- Average number of apps downloaded by an iOS user = 5 per month
- Of which paid apps are 25% i.e. 1.25 apps
- Average spend by an iOS user = 1.25 × \$1.25 = \$1.5 per month
- Total paid apps sales amount = \$1.5 × 100M = \$150M

These figures show the potential benefits of apps to marketers in reaching audiences and potentially in selling apps, although the latter will generally be limited to publishers or specialist software developers. It's also worth remembering that other handsets use other operating systems which in total are nearly as popular as the iPhone in terms of apps downloaded. The most significant of these include Android OS from Google, Symbian OS from Nokia and BlackBerry. So app producers also have to decide whether to support these. For example, Tesco launched a Nokia grocery app (www.tesco.com/apps/) in advance of its iPhone app to reach the substantial audience of non-iPhone app users.

Through reviewing the types of apps which have proved popular, businesses can assess the potential for them to develop applications for their audiences (Figure 3.21).

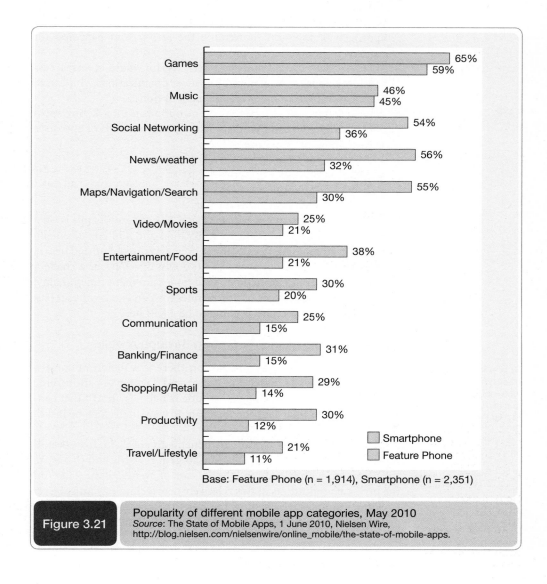

Base: Feature Phone (n = 1,914), Smartphone (n = 2,351)

| **Figure 3.21** | **Popularity of different mobile app categories, May 2010**
Source: The State of Mobile Apps, 1 June 2010, Nielsen Wire,
http://blog.nielsen.com/nielsenwire/online_mobile/the-state-of-mobile-apps. |

The key questions to ask are:

1 *Are apps a strategic priority for us?* The goal of apps for most organizations will be to increase awareness and sales or, for publishers, revenue from advertising or subscriptions. For many companies, this won't be a priority because they will have to put budget into higher priority areas such as improving the experience on-site or in their social network presence. Owing to volume of users reached through these other platforms incremental improvements here are likely to give better returns. But the figures presented above show the potential benefits of apps to marketers in reaching audiences and potentially in selling apps, although the latter will be generally limited to publishers or specialist software developers. For these types of organization, apps are likely to be a priority.

2 *Do we build our own app and/or leverage existing apps?* Creating an app is only one of the marketing options – advertising and sponsorship options may be a more cost-effective method to build reach and awareness of a brand. A good example of sponsorship fit is the Canon sponsorship of the excellent Guardian Eyewitness phototgraphy app. There are also options of new iAds from Apple and Google Adsense mobile display networks.

3 *Free or paid apps?* Retailers will generally offer free apps offering choice and convenience in return for loyalty. Brands offering entertainment will likely also go the free route to increase customer engagement. But for publishers or software houses, a freemium approach of free app showcasing the serivce and paid app for improved features or content is the standard approach.

4 *Which category of application to target?* As you would expect, accessing social networks and music via apps is popular, but for most organizations, you can see from Figure 3.21 that games and entertainment are the main options.

5 *How to best promote mobile apps?* The options for marketing apps were also researched by Nielsen, which found that the most popular methods of app discovery are:
   - Searching the AppStore
   - Recommendations from friends and family
   - Mention on device or network carrier page
   - E-mail promotion
   - Offline mention in TV and print

6 *How to refine apps in line with feedback.* The success of apps is very dependent on feedback in the AppStores and the need to fix bugs and add enhancements to compete shows the need for an ongoing development cycle with frequent updates. A whole new area of app analytics and new solutions will no doubt develop but a challenge with apps, similar to that of Flash apps before them, is that measurement functionality needs to be specified in advance. Careful review of hurdle rates for percentage of user base who are using the app or its different functions is going to be a KPI here.

Social location-based marketing through mobile

Social location-based marketing
Where social media tools give users the option of sharing their location, and hence give businesses the opportunity to use proximity or location-based marketing to deliver targeted offers and messages to consumers and collect data about their preferences and behaviour.

In **social location-based marketing** there is a fusion of social and mobile marketing. Foursquare, Gowalla, Facebook Places and Twitter Locations are all options available to consumers. There's also Google Latitude which has an API that can be used to ask users for access to update their latitude location or view their current location if they have enabled their location history in Google.

Businesses can offer consumers benefits to check-in, for example, to gain points, be the most regular visitor to that location, to gain rewards and prizes from advertisers, to share their location with friends and, in the case of events, to meet like-minded people. Of course the privacy implications of this relatively new technology must be carefully reviewed.

Some examples which show the potential power of future mobile applications are suggested through an initiative by Google, explained in Box 3.11.

Mini Case Study 3.8	Location-based marketing

If you're thinking that location-based marketing is just for corporates with large budgets, the likes of Starbucks and McDonald's, then think again. ClickZ (2010) has reported how AJ Bombers, a specialty burger bar in Milwaukee, attributed a sale increase of 110% to Foursquare. It has 1,400 people on its Foursquare page who have checked in 6,000 times. The mayor gets a free burger, and currently that's 'Amy,' who has had to check in 40 times in the last 60 days at the one-location establishment in order to achieve the distinction.

Engagement is also increased through people who add a tip to the restaurant's Foursquare page, getting rewarded with a free cookie when they show it to a waiter or cashier.

The sales increase figure is based on a single campaign which saw 161 check-ins on 28 February, a 110% sales increase when compared to a normal Sunday. Joe Sorge, owner of the restaurant, promoted an AJ Bombers-branded 'Swarm Badge' event to his Foursquare-using regulars. Such a custom badge is awarded to users who check in at a location where at least 50 other users are simultaneously checked in.

The restaurant owner advised that success involves implementing Foursquare as a regular part of operations:

Our staff encourages the use and engagement of Foursquare by virtue of our Foursquare specials being very prominent throughout our business. It encourages our customers to ask questions of our staff. Education of that staff is the key.

Box 3.11	Google Android Developer Challenge highlights future of mobile

Android is a new initiative by Google to develop an operating system for mobile phones. The first phones were launched in 2008. To help build awareness and adoption of the service, it initiated the Android Developer Challenge (http://code. google. com/android/adc_gallery/). Out of 50 teams of finalists, 10 teams received a $275,000 award each and 10 teams received a $100,000 award each. The most interesting applications, many of which are location-based, include:

- **GoCart Price Comparison** – scan a product's barcode with your phone's camera and view all the best prices online and at nearby local stores.
- **Ecorio** – automatically tracks your mobile carbon footprint, suggests transit and car pooling alternatives and lets you stay carbon-neutral by off-setting your trips easily.
- **TuneWiki Social Media Player** – featuring synchronized lyrics for audio or video, translation, music maps and a social network.
- **Wertago** – the mobile application nightlifers have been waiting for. Find the hottest parties in town and connect with friends and others all night long.

SMS applications

The importance of SMS messaging by businesses should not be underestimated. Texting has proved useful for business in some niche applications. For example, banks now notify customers when they approach an overdraft and provide weekly statements using SMS. Text has also been used by consumer brands to market their products, particularly to a younger audience as the case studies at text agency Flytxt (www.flytxt.com) and Text.It, the organization promoting text messaging (www.text.it), show. Texting can also be used in supply chain management applications for notifying managers of problems or deliveries.

For companies marketing themselves electronically, SMS is potentially a great way to get closer to customers, particularly those in the youth market who are difficult to reach with other media. However, it is important that companies that follow this path respect the opt-in and privacy legislation which is described in Chapter 4.

These are some of the SMS applications showcased on Text.it (www.text.it):

1 *Database building/direct response to ads/direct mail or on-pack.* This is one of the most significant applications. For example, Ford engaged its audience when promoting the Ford Ka by offering consumers a unique code printed on their postcard to text in for entry into a prize draw.

2 *Location-based services.* Text for the nearest pub, club, shop or taxi. In London you can now text for the nearest available taxi and pay the congestion charge.

3 *Sampling/trial.* Nestlé used an opt-in SMS database to offer samples of a new chocolate bar to consumers in its target group.

4 *Sales promotions.* Timed e-coupons can be sent out to encourage footfall in real and virtual stores. Drinks brand WKD offered its consumers 'Peel Off and Win' labels on its bottles. The competition offered prizes of 3,000 football club shirts, mini footballs, 10,000 referee cards, and 1 million exclusive ringtones and logos. Half a million people played the game, a campaign response rate of 3%. A 3,000-strong opt-in database of the company's 18–24-year-old customer base was created.

5 *Rewarding with offers for brand engagement.* Valuable content on mobiles can be offered via SMS, for example free ringtones, wallpaper, Java games or credits can be offered to consumers via text.

6 *Short codes.* **Short codes** are easy to remember: 5-digit numbers combined with text that can be used by advertisers or broadcasters to encourage consumers to register their interest. **Quick Response (QR)** code is a kind of bar code published in newspapers or

Short code

5-digit numbers combined with text that can be used by advertisers or broadcasters to encourage consumers to register their interest. They are typically followed up by an automated text message from the advertiser with the option to opt-in to further information by e-mail or to link through to a WAP site.

Quick Response (QR) code

A QR code is a two-dimensional matrix bar code. QR codes were invented in Japan where they are a popular type of two-dimensional code used for direct response.

Figure 3.22	Use of QR code for promotion of film *28 Days Later*
	Source: www.giagia.co.uk/?cat=63, created by www.giagia.co.uk/?page_id=2 blog.

billboards which can be scanned by a mobile phone camera and then linked directly through to a website. It does require specific software. Figure 3.22 shows an example.

7 *Offering paid-for WAP services and content.* Any service such as a ringtone delivered by WAP can be invoked from a text message. For example, Parker's Car Guides now prints ad text 'go parkers' to 89080 (a short code) for quick access to the Parker's WAP site which provides car prices on the go, at £1 for 10 minutes.

SMS messaging has recently been augmented by picture messaging or multimedia messaging services (MMS). While volumes have been relatively low initially, the overlap between text messaging and e-mail marketing will decrease as there are more handsets with larger screens. The integration of SMS alerts with social networks has proved popular, as the box shows.

Box 3.12	Social networking sites turn to mobile

Much social networking is already completed via mobiles, despite the relative immaturity of social networks.

Mark Donovan, senior analyst at M:Metrics, says:

Nearly every online social networking site has added the ability to connect to these communities with a mobile phone, allowing people to access profiles and share content while they're on the go. With the mobile phone playing a central role in people's social lives, it's only natural that social networking sites are working to bridge the gap between the online and mobile worlds.

MySpace and Facebook are the top two social networking sites accessed via mobile in both the US and the UK (see Table 3.7). MySpace attracts 3.7 million US and 440,000 UK mobile users. In America, Facebook's mobile audience is about 2 million, and in Britain, about 307,000. Number three is YouTube in the US, with 901,000 mobile visitors and Bebo in the UK, with 288,000.

New Media Age (2008) reports how important the owner of MySpace considers mobile access to social networks to be; he says: 'over half of the site's traffic will be from mobile within five years. We're pushing aggressively to enable us to capitalize on that. We don't see ourselves as a website: we're a set of tools and a service for people to connect with other people.'

Table 3.7	Social network access via mobile in Europe and the US

	France	Germany	Italy	Spain	UK	US
Almost every day	0.8%	0.5%	1.5%	0.7%	0.3%	0.7%
At least once each week	0.2%	0.4%	0.4%	0.6%	0.7%	1.1%
Once to three times throughout the month	0.7%	1.0%	0.9%	1.0%	1.4%	1.8%
Ever in month	1.7%	1.9%	2.8%	2.3%	2.5%	3.5%

Source: M: Metrics (2007).

Wi-Fi ('wireless-fidelity') mobile access

Wi-Fi ('wireless fidelity')
A high-speed wireless local-area network enabling wireless access to the Internet for mobile, office and home users.

'Wi-Fi' is the shorthand often used to describe a high-speed wireless local-area network. Most Wi-Fi networks use a standard protocol known as *802.11 a,b, g or n*, which offers data rates of up to 300 Mbps, which is relatively fast compared to ADSL, although this depends on signal strength. Wi-Fi can be deployed in an office or home environment, but it has attracted most attention for its potential for offering wireless access in cities and towns without the need for a fixed connection.

Airports, cafés and hotels started offering Wi-Fi 'hotspots' which allowed customers access to the Internet from their laptops or other mobile devices. For wireless local-area networks (WLANs) additional hardware is needed.

Bluetooth

Bluetooth
A wireless standard for transmission of data between devices over short ranges (less than 100 m).

Bluetooth is used for short-range data transmission between devices. Applications of Bluetooth include wireless keyboards and beaming data between a PDA and a desktop or a laptop and a printer. Transmission distances between Bluetooth-enabled devices were initially limited to 10 m, but can now be up to 100 m, so there is now the option for using the technology for networking like Wi-Fi. However, Bluetooth is significantly slower than the main Wi-Fi standard at 723 kbps.

Bluetooth wireless applications

Proximity marketing
Marketing messages are delivered in real time according to customers' presence based on the technology they are carrying, wearing or have embedded. *Bluecasting* is the best-known example.

Bluetooth technology has potential for different forms of local marketing campaigns known as **proximity marketing**: (1) viral communication, (2) community activities (dating or gaming events), (3) location-based services – electronic coupons as you pass a store. It is currently in its infancy, but some trials of **bluecasting** such as that shown in Figure 3.23 where sample music tracks are downloaded and in Mini case study 3.9 have been successful.

Bluecasting
Bluecasting involves messages being automatically pushed to a consumer's Bluetooth-enabled phone or they can pull or request audio, video or text content to be downloaded from a live advert. In the future ads will be able to respond to those who view them.

Figure 3.23   Using proximity marketing to download music tracks

Mini Case Study 3.9	Bluecasting encourages trial of new album

One of the early commercial uses of Bluecasting was to support the launch of the Coldplay X&Y album where a London-based campaign involved 13,000 fans downloading free pre-release video clips, never-before-seen interviews, audio samples and exclusive images on to their mobile, via Bluetooth, from screens at mainline train stations. In this campaign, 87,000 unique handsets were 'discovered' and 13,000 people opted in to receive the material, a response rate of 15%. The busiest day was Saturday 4 June – two days before the official album launch date – when over 8,000 handsets were discovered and over 1,100 users opted in to receive a video file. The Bluecast systems can deliver time-sensitive contextual content, so, for example, in the morning the user would get an audio clip of the track 'Fix You' and be prompted to tune in to Radio One, but in the afternoon the clip would be the same but the user would be prompted to watch Jonathan Ross on BBC1.

Bluejacking

Sending a message from a mobile phone or transmitter to another mobile phone which is in close range via Bluetooth technology.

Bluecasting has also caused concern over permission where the user does not proactively agree to receive communications as with the examples above, but instead the message is sent to any local mobile where Bluetooth is set up to detect connections. **Bluejacking** involves sending a message from a mobile phone (or other transmitter) to another mobile phone which is in close range and set up to connect with other Bluetooth devices such as from a store to customers.

Bank HSBC used this approach in a 2007 trial to offer one of its investment products to passers-by at its Canary Wharf branch. The risks of this approach can be seen from the write-up in Finextra which was headlined '*HSBC spams passersby in mobile marketing ploy*'. Although the UK Information Commissioner has acknowledged that the technique isn't covered adequately by privacy rules, obviously care needs to be taken since this technique could be seen as intrusive.

Debate 3.3

Predicting the future of the mobile Internet

'Future-generation mobile access devices using such technologies as 3G will supersede PCs as the main consumer access device for the Internet within 5 years.'

The advent of new mobile technologies for customers to access content poses a dilemma for organizations that have adopted e-commerce since, to be competitive, the decision to adopt must be made before the extent of its impact is apparent. These issues apply, in particular, to business-to-consumer companies since the content made available for new access devices has mainly been targeted at consumers. Imagine you are the e-commerce manager or brand manager at a consumer company: what would be the benefits and drawbacks of updating your e-commerce systems to m-commerce? The benefits of deciding to invest could include:

- Early-mover advantage
- Learning about the technology
- Customer acquisition
- Customer retention
- Improving corporate or brand image

However, it will be difficult to estimate the number of new customers who may be acquired and the profitability of the project may be sacrificed to achieve the other benefits above. As new technologies become available, companies need to assess the technology, understand the services that may be relevant to their customers and work out a strategy and implementation plan. It also becomes necessary to support development across multiple platforms, for example retailers such as WH Smith Online use a database to generate book catalogue content for display on web, mobile or interactive digital TV platforms.

Technology convergence

A trend in which different hardware devices such as TVs, computers and phones merge and have similar functions.

Although it may appear there is a divergence in access devices from PC to phone to TV, in the long term most commentators expect **technology convergence** to occur.

Mougayer (1998) identifies different types of convergence:

- *Infrastructure convergence* – this is the increase in the number of delivery media channels for the Internet such as phone lines, microwave (mobile phones), cable and satellite.
- *Information appliance (technology) convergence* – the use of different hardware devices to access and deliver the content of the Internet.
- *Supplier convergence* – the overlap between suppliers such as Internet service providers, online access providers and more traditional media suppliers such as the telecommunications and cable companies.

Strategies for mobile commerce

Different types of strategy can be identified for two main types of players. For portal and media owners the options are to migrate their own portal to a text version (the option followed by the BBC for example (www.bbc.co.uk/mobile/). The BBC offers a standard (WAP) version which can be used on all mobile devices, and is the fastest and cheapest option, and an Enhanced (XHTML) version which includes both video and audio downloads has been designed for use on 3G phones. There is also a PDA version and the standard desktop version so that is four different versions that have to be supported.

Mobile sites can also be made available through a .mobi domain where a WAP site is available for download of content. The example in Figure 3.24 shows a feed of news items repurposed for mobile.

Figure 3.24	Example mobile site at an emulator on Mobi.com
	Source: Site owner.

Repurposing
Developing content for a new access platform which was previously used for a different platform such as the web.

Alternatively, an organization may decide the cost of **repurposing** is too high and they may wait for users to access the web with 3G devices which will require less repurposing since the screen resolution is higher. A stylesheet can be defined to simplify the design for visitors to the website who are accessing the web through a mobile device.

Revenue models for mobile access for site owners are similar to those described for publishers in Chapter 2. They may include advertising, sponsorship or subscription for individual content items or be on a subscription basis.

For destination sites such as retailers, banks and travel companies, mobile marketing options include:

- marketing communications (to support purchase) using banner advertising;
- e-commerce (sale of products on-site);
- brand building – improving brand image by being one of the first suppliers to offer an innovative service.

Summary

1 The Internet is a global communications network that is used to transmit the information published on the World Wide Web (WWW) in a standard format based on Hypertext Markup Language (HTML) using different standard protocols such as HTTP and TCP/IP.

2 Companies deliver e-business services to employees and partners through web servers which are often hosted at third-party companies known as 'Internet service providers' (ISPs). Web servers will be linked to applications servers, database servers and legacy applications to deliver these services.

3 Consumers and business users access these e-business services using web browser software, with connections to the Internet also managed by an ISP through which they can access web servers.

4 Intranets are private networks used inside companies to share information. Internet-based tools such as e-mail, FTP and the World Wide Web are all used as methods of sharing this information. Not all Internet users can access intranets since access is restricted by firewalls and password controls. Extranets are similar to intranets, but they are extended beyond the company to third parties such as suppliers, distributors or selected customers.

5 Standards to enable delivery of information include:
   - Communications standards such as TCP/IP and HTTP.
   - Text information standards such as HTML, XML and WML.
   - Graphical information standards such as GIF and JPEG.
   - Multimedia standards such as Shockwave, Flash and streaming audio and video.

6 Managing staff access to the Internet involves taking decisions about the number of staff with access and how much time can be permitted and the nature of monitoring used for e-mails and web pages.

7 Managers need to decide on internal or external management of the technology and applications infrastructure of an organization. The benefits and risks of cloud computing should be assessed.

8 Electronic data interchange (EDI) involves the structured transfer of information, particularly for online B2B purchasing transactions. It can now occur over the Internet as Internet EDI.

9 Applications service providers are increasingly important as businesses look to reduce infrastructure costs and improve e-business service delivery through external hosting of applications and data outside an organization.

10 Managers of e-commerce services need to monitor the adoption of new access devices for the Internet including mobile phones. An e-commerce infrastructure should be designed to readily enable new access media to be supported as they develop.

Exercises

Self-assessment questions

1 What is the difference between the Internet and the World Wide Web?

2 Describe the two main functions of an Internet service provider (ISP). How do they differ from applications service providers?

3 Distinguish between intranets, extranets and the Internet.

4 Describe the standards involved when a web page is served from a web server to a user's web browser.

5 What are the management issues involved with enabling staff access to a website?

6 Explain the following terms: HTML, HTTP, XML, FTP.

7 What is the difference between static web content written in HTML and dynamic content developed using a scripting language such as JavaScript?

8 What software and hardware are required to access the Internet from home?

Essay and discussion questions

1 'Without the development of the World Wide Web by Tim Berners-Lee, the Internet is unlikely to have become a commercial medium.' Discuss.

2 'In the future the distinction between intranets, extranets and the Internet for marketing purposes is likely to disappear.' Discuss.

3 Discuss the merits and disadvantages of locating company e-business services inside a company, in comparison with outsourcing to an ISP or ASP.

4 You are consultant to a small retailer interested in setting up a transactional e-commerce site. Create a summary guide for the company about the stages that are necessary in the creation of a website and the management issues involved.

Examination questions

1 You have been tasked with arranging Internet access for other employees in your company. Summarize the hardware and software needed.

2 How would you explain to a friend what they need to purchase to access the World Wide Web using the Internet? Explain the hardware and software needed.

3 Explain the term 'electronic data interchange'. Is it still relevant to companies?

4 Describe how the following tools would be used by a company hosting a website: HTML, FTP, RSS.

5 The existence of standards such as HTML and HTTP has been vital to the success and increased use of the World Wide Web. Explain why.

6 What benefits to a business-to-business company does the XML standard offer beyond those of HTML?

7 Explain why the e-business coordinator of a company might investigate the use of applications service providers.

8 Explain the differences between intranet, extranet and the Internet from an e-business perspective.

References

Ahonen, T. and Moore, A. (2007) *Communities Dominate Brands.* Future Text, London. Supported by blog: **http://communities-dominate.blogs.com/**.

Akamai (2006) Akamai and JupiterResearch Identify '4 Seconds' as the New Threshold of Acceptability for Retail Web Page Response Times. Press release, 6 November, **www.akamai.com/html/about/press/releases/2006/press_110606.html**.

Ars Technica (2007) Evidence mounts that Comcast is targeting BitTorrent traffic. *Ars Technica,* The Art of Technology, by Jacqui Cheng, 19 October. **http://arstechnica.com/news.ars/post/20071019-evidence-mounts-that-comcast-is-targeting-bittorrent-traffic.html**.

Avenue A – Razorfish (2008) Avenue A | Razorfish 2008 Digital Outlook Report available online at **www.avenuea-razorfish.com**.

Belic, D. (2007) China mobile subscribers surpass total population of the United States. *IntoMobile,* 7 April.

Berners-Lee, T. (1999) *Weaving the Web: The Past, Present and Future of the World Wide Web by its Inventor.* Orion Publishing, London.

Berners-Lee, T., Hendler, J. and Lassila, O. (2001) The Semantic Web. *Scientific American,* May. Published online at: **www.sciam.com**.

ClickZ (2010) Foursquare Marketing Hits and Misses: 5 Case Studies. Christopher Heine, 28 September. **www.clickz.com/clickz/news/1735591/foursquare-marketing-hits-misses-case-studies**.

CIO (2010) IaaS: Why Intel Dumped the Grid. Article on CIO.com online magazine. By Rick Swanborg, 9 June 2010. **www.cio.com/article/596387/IaaS_Why_Intel_Dumped_the_Grid?taxonomyId=3017**.

Clarke, R. (1998) *Electronic Data Interchange* (EDI): An Introduction. **www.anu.edu.au/people/Roger.Clarke/EC/EDIIntro.html**.

Computer Economics (2006) Software as a Service Shows Attractive Payback. Research Report, June.

comScore (2008) Why Google's surprising paid click data are less surprising. By Magid Abraham, 28 February. Published at: **www.comscore.com/blog/2008/02/whygoogles-surprisingpaidclickdataarelesssuprising.html**.

Cutts, M. (2007) *Talk like a Googler: parts of a url.* Blog posting, 14 August. **www.mattcutts.com/blog/seo-glossary-url-definitions/**.

DTI (2000) Business in the Information Age – International Benchmarking Study 2000. UK Department of Trade and Industry.

Dyson, E. (1998) *Release 2.1: A Design for Living in the Digital Age.* Penguin, London.

EDF (2008) Alexandre Passant, Electricité de France R&D and LaLIC, Université Paris-Sorbonne, France, June. Semantic Web case study published at: **http://www.w3.org/2001/ sw/sweo/public/UseCases/EDF/**.

EDI Insider (1996) Internet EDI: separating hope from hype. *EDI Insider,* 1(1), Washington Publishing Company, Washington, DC. **www.wpc-edi.com/Insider/Articles/V1/I-1B.html**.

Fitzgerald, M. (2006) The name game: tagging tools let users describe the world in their own terms as taxonomies become folksonomies. *CIO Magazine,* 1 April.

Gillies, J. and Cailliau, R. (2000) *How the Web Was Born.* Oxford University Press, New York.

Google (2008) We knew the web was big... Blog posting, Official Google Blog, 25 July. **http://googleblog.blogspot.com/2008/07/we-knew-web-was-big.html**.

Google (2010) **http://googlewebmastercentral.blogspot.com/2010/05/you-and-site-performance-sitting-in.html**.

Guardian (2008a) Porn? Sex? Britons value cruises much more. *The Guardian,* Richard Wray, Wednesday 6 February.

Guardian (2008b) Twitter searches for the next step. Giles Turnbull, The Guardian, Thursday 24 July. **www.guardian.co.uk/technology/2008/jul/24/blogging. socialnetworking.**

Hannon, N. (1998) *The Business of the Internet.* Course Technology, New York.

Hasselbring, W. (2000) Information system integration. *Communications of the ACM,* 43(6), 33–8.

Huffington Post (2010) Twitter User Statistics Revealed, First posted: 04-14-10 (no author given). **www.huffingtonpost.com/2010/04/14/twitter-user-statistics-r_n_537992.html.**

IBF (2008) *12 ways to use your intranet to cut your costs.* Member Briefing Paper, August. Published by the Intranet Benchmarking Forum (**www.ibforum.com**).

IDC (1999) *Reinventing EDI: Electronic Data Interchange Services Market Review and Forecast, 1998–2003.* International Data Corporation, Framingham, MA.

IDC (2007) Worldwide Email Usage 2007–2011 Forecast: Resurgence of Spam Takes Its Toll. Report summarized in press release 'IDC Reveals the Future of Email As It Navigates Through A Resurgence of Spam and Real-Time Market Substitutes', 9 April.

Internet World (1999) Enterprise application integration – middleware apps scale firewalls. *Internet World,* 17 May.

IOD (2005) Voice Over IP. Institute of Directors (**www.iod.com**), February, London.

Intranet Journal (2009) Creating your SharePoint Governance Plan. Robert Bogue, 4 June 2009, Intranet Journal (online magazine). **www.intranetjournal.com/articles/200906/ ij_06_04_09a.html.**

iPhoneDev(2010) App Store average earning per month per paid app is $700. **http://iphone-dev.tumblr.com/post/754296222/appstore-average-earning.** Blog post, 30 June 2010.

Johnston, K. (2008) Folksonomies, collaborative filtering and e-business: Is Enterprise 2.0 one step forward and two steps back? *European Journal of Knowledge Management,* 5(4), 411–18.

Kampas, P. (2000) Road map to the e-revolution. *Information Systems Management Journal,* Spring, 8–22.

KM Column (2002) September 2002 issue: Sixteen steps to a renewed corporate intranet. Published by Step Two Designs at: **www.steptwo.com.au/papers/kmc_renewintranet/ index.html.**

Leiner, B., Cerf, V., Clark, D., Kahn, R., Kleinrock, L., Lynch, D., Postel, J., Roberts, J. and Wolff, S. (2000) *A Brief History of the Internet.* The Internet Society, **www.isoc.org/ internet-history/brief.html**, continuously updated document.

Mcafee, A. and Brynjolfsson, E. (2008) Investing in the IT that makes a competitive difference. *Harvard Business Review.* July–August, 99: 107.

MMetrics (2007) M:Metrics Press Release, Mobile Social Networking Has 12.3 Million Friends in the US and Western Europe, 15 August.

Moorey-Denholm, S. and Green, A. (2007) The effectiveness of online video advertising. *AdMap,* March, 45–7.

Mougayar, W. (1998) *Opening Digital Markets – Battle Plans and Strategies for Internet Commerce,* 2nd edn. CommerceNet Press, McGraw-Hill, New York.

New Media Age (2008) Profile – Travis Katz, Author: Luan Goldie. *New Media Age* magazine, published 31 January.

News Corporation (2005). Press release. Speech by Rupert Murdoch to the American Society of Newspaper Editors, 13 April: **www.newscorp.com/news/news_247.html.**

Nielsen, J. (1994) Response Times: The Three Important Limits. Online white paper, published 1994: **www.useit.com/papers/responsetime.html.**

Ofcom (2007) The International Communications Market 2007. Report published December 2007. Extract from section 1.3, the regulatory landscape. **www.ofcom.org.uk/ research/cm/icmr07/overview/landscape/.**

Ofcom (2010) The UK Communications Market Report 2010 (August). **http://stakeholders. ofcom.org.uk/market-data-research/.**

O'Reilly, T. (2005) What is Web 2? Design patterns and business models for the next generation of software. Web article, 30 September. O'Reilly Publishing, Sebastopol, CA.

Pandia (2007) Google: one million servers and counting. Pandia Search Engine News: **www.pandia.com/sew/481-gartner.html.**

SciVisum (2005) Internet Campaign Effectiveness Study. Press Release, July. **www.scivisum.co.uk.**

Smoothspan (2007) How Many Tenants For a Multitenant SaaS Architecture? Blog posting, 30 October. **http://smoothspan.wordpress.com/2007/10/30/how-many-tenants-for-a-multitenant-saas-architecture/.**

Spinrad, P. (1999). The new cool. Akamai overcomes the Internet's hotspot problem. *Wired*, 7 August, 152–4.

The Register (2004) Wobbly shopping carts blight UK e-commerce: *The Register.Co.uk*, 4 June.

Vlosky, R., Fontenot, R. and Blalock, L. (2000) Extranets: impacts on business practices and relationships. *Journal of Business and Industrial Marketing*, 15(6), 438–57.

VMware (2007) Association of Teachers and Lecturers, customer success story. **www.vmware.com/a/customers.**

VMware (2008) Virtualization Basics. **www.vmware.com/virtualization.**

Wired (2007) The Great Firewall: China's Misguided – and Futile – Attempt to Control What Happens Online. *Wired* 15.11, by Oliver August, 10.23.07.

Wireless Intelligence (2008) Global mobile market Q4 2007. Published by GSM World: **www.gsmworld.com/documents/20_year_factsheet.pdf.**

Yankee Group (2002). E-business evolution: transaction management costs, benefits, and market development. *Yankee Group Research Report 2002*. Available online at: **www.sterlingcommerce.com/go/yankeegroup/yankeeWP_07-02.pdf.**

Further reading

Arnold, S. (2010) *Could Google Become the Semantic Web?* Blog post by Stephen E. Arnold, 21 February 2010. **www.semanticuniverse.com/articles-could-google-become-semantic-web.html**

Bala, I. and Davenport, T. (2008) Reverse engineering Google's innovation machine. *Harvard Business Review*, 86(4), 58–68.

Berners-Lee, T. (1999) *Weaving the Web. The Past, Present and Future of the World Wide Web by its Inventor.* Orion Publishing, London. A fascinating, readable description of how the concept of the web was developed by the author, with his thoughts on its future development.

Gillies, J. and Cailliau, R. (2000) *How the Web Was Born.* Oxford University Press, New York. Another readable book, this time, despite the title, on the whole history of the Internet.

Web links

A brief history of the Internet (**www.zakon.org/robert/internet/timeline**) An Internet timeline.

CIO Magazine (**www.cio.com/research/intranet**) Intranet and extranet research centre.

Digital Future Reports (**www.digitalcenter.org**) USC Annenberg School Center for the Digital Future.

Free Online Dictionary of Computing (www.foldoc.org) Comprehensive non-commercial site with succinct definitions supported by Imperial College London. Particularly good for Internet standards.

Forrester Marketing Blog (http://blogs.forrester.com/marketing/) Forrester analysts write about developments in technology.

Google (www7.scu.edu.au/programme/fullpapers/1921/com1921.htm) Interesting, but technical, article on Google, 'The anatomy of a large-scale hypertextual web search engine'.

Howstuffworks (www.howstuffworks.com) Good explanations with diagrams of many Internet technologies.

Intranet Benchmarking Forum (www.ibforum.com). Membership service disseminating intranet best practice from corporate organizations. Their blog (www.intranetlife.com) has discussion of topical intranet management issues and extracts of research.

Intranet Focus (www.intranetfocus.com) Best-practice guidelines and links on intranets, portals and content management systems.

Intranet Journal (**www.intranetjournal.com**) Articles on intranet management.

IT Toolbox (www.ittoolbox.com) Guidelines, articles on e-business, ERP, CRM and data warehousing.

Mobile Commerce World (**www.mobilecommerceworld.com**) Industry news.

ReadWriteWeb (www.readwriteweb.com) Site focusing on digital technology trends and developments in content management, web applications and social media.

RosettaNet (www.rosettanet.org) Organization promoting exchange of B2B data.

SmoothSpan (http://smoothspan.wordpress.com) Blog by Bob Warfield covering developments in SaaS, Web 2.0 and cloud computing.

Whatis.com (www.whatis.com) Succinct explanations of technical terms.

XMLEDI (www.xmledi.com/.net) Organization promoting use of XML to support EDI.

XML.com (www.xml.com) XML resources.

Mobile marketing resources

- Direct Marketing Association Mobile Marketing Council, Mobile Marketing Help Notes (http://mobile.dma.org.uk/content/Inf-Case.asp) aimed at guiding businesses through the commercial options available to them.
- IAB has a portal on mobile advertising (www.iabuk.net/en/1/mobileadvertising.html).
- The worldwide Mobile Marketing Association (www.mmaglobal.com) has case studies and statistics of adoption.
- Mobile Data Association's text.it (www.text.it) focuses on marketing for SMS and picture messaging.
- Mobile Marketing Magazine (www.mobilemarketingmagazine.co.uk) An online magazine focusing on emerging approaches and case studies.

4

E-environment

Web support

The following additional case studies are available at
www.pearsoned.co.uk/chaffey

→ Singapore government creates 'intelligent island'
→ Variations in take-up of online services for Orient Overseas Container Line (OOCL)
→ Is there a future for print?
→ The wired GP

The site also contains a range of study material designed to help improve your results.

Learning outcomes

After completing this chapter the reader should be able to:

- Identify the different elements of an organization macro-environment that impact on an organization's e-business and e-marketing strategy
- Assess the impact of legal, privacy and ethical constraints or opportunities on a company
- Assess the role of macro-economic factors such as economics, governmental e-business policies, taxation and legal constraints

Management issues

The issues for managers raised in this chapter include:

- What are the constraints such as legal issues placed by the e-environment on developing and implementing an e-business strategy?
- How can trust and privacy be assured for the customer while seeking to achieve marketing objectives of customer acquisition and retention?
- Assessment of the business relevance of technological innovation

Links to other chapters

The main related chapters are:

- *Chapter 2* Marketplace analysis for e-commerce – introduces the different elements of the e-environment
- The strategic approaches outlined in *Part 2 (Chapters 5, 6 and 8)* require consideration of the constraints placed on strategy by the e-environment

Introduction

Table 4.1 presents the main marketplace or macro-environmental factors and the micro-environmental factors that directly affect an organization.

Table 4.1	Factors in the macro- and micro-environment of an organization

Macro-environment	Micro-environment (e-marketplace)
Social	The organization
Legal, ethical and taxation	Its customers
Economic	Its suppliers
Political	Its competitors
Technological	Intermediaries
Competitive	The public at large

In Chapter 2 we introduced the importance of monitoring changes in the online marketplace or micro-environment and how they impact on an organization. In this chapter we concentrate on the role of the macro-environmental forces using the widely used SLEPT framework. Often, these factors are known as the PEST factors, but we use SLEPT since it is useful to stress the importance of the law in influencing Internet marketing practices. The SLEPT factors are:

- *Social factors* – these include the influence of consumer perceptions in determining usage of the Internet for different activities.
- *Legal and ethical factors* – determine the method by which products can be promoted and sold online. Governments, on behalf of society, seek to safeguard individuals' rights to privacy.
- *Economic factors* – variations in economic performance in different countries and regions affect spending patterns and international trade.
- *Political* – national governments and transnational organizations have an important role in determining the future adoption and control of the Internet and the rules by which it is governed.
- *Technological factors* – changes in technology offer new opportunities to the way products can be marketed.

For each factor we look at new issues raised for managers responsible for e-commerce trading. For those actively involved in the implementation of e-business, and in particular sell-side e-commerce, factors associated with buyer behaviour are also important when implementing e-commerce. These are covered separately in Chapter 9, p. 463.

Now complete Activity 4.1 to reflect on the most important macro-environmental factors that have to be considered by the e-business manager. When completing a review it's important to not give all of them equal weighting, but instead focus on the ones that matter most in the current environment such as legislation and technology innovation.

The issues identified in Activity 4.1 and others such as economic and competitive pressures tend to change rapidly, particularly dynamic factors associated with advances in technology.

List all the social, legal and ethical issues that the manager of a sell-side e-commerce website needs to consider to avoid damaging relationships with users of his or her site or which may leave the company facing prosecution. You can base your answer on current issues which may concern you, your friends or your family when accessing a website.

Answers to activities can be found at www.pearsoned.co.uk/chaffey

An indication of the challenge of assessing the macro-environment factors is presented in Figure 4.1. This figure of the 'waves of change' shows how fluctuations in the characteristics of different aspects of the environment vary at different rates through time. The manager has to constantly scan the environment and assess which changes are relevant to their sphere of influence. Changes in social culture and particularly pop culture tend to be very rapid. Introduction of new technologies and changes in their popularity tend to be frequent too. Governmental and legal changes tend to happen over longer timescales but new laws can be introduced relatively fast. The trick for managers is to identify those factors which are critical to competitiveness and service delivery and monitor these. The technological and legal factors are most important to managing e-commerce, so we focus on these.

Since the law is one of the most important issues for the e-commerce manager to address, the six most important legal issues for managers are introduced in Table 4.2. Each of these is covered in more detail later in the chapter.

Organizations that either do not monitor these environmental factors or do not respond to them adequately will not remain competitive and may fail. The process of monitoring the environment is usually referred to as **environmental scanning**. This often occurs as an *ad*

Environmental scanning
The process of continuously monitoring the environment and events and responding accordingly.

Behavioural ad targeting
Advertisers target ads at a visitor as they move within or between sites dependent on their viewing particular sites or types of content that indicate their preferences.

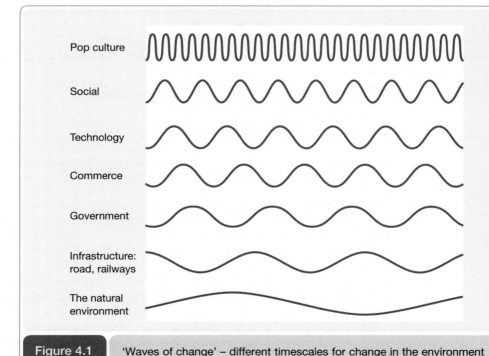

| Figure 4.1 | 'Waves of change' – different timescales for change in the environment |

Table 4.2	Significant laws which control digital marketing

Legal issue	Digital marketing activities affected
1 Data protection and privacy law	☑ Collection, storage, usage and deletion of personal information directly through data capture on forms and indirectly through tracking behaviour through web analytics ☑ E-mail marketing and SMS mobile marketing ☑ Use of viral marketing to encourage transmission of marketing messages between consumers ☑ Use of cookies and other techniques for personalizing content and tracking on-site ☑ Use of cookies for tracking between sites, for example for advertising networks and company site using '**behavioural ad targeting**' ☑ Use of customer information from social networks ☑ Use of digital assets installed on a user's PC for marketing purposes, e.g. toolbars or other downloadable utilities sometimes referred to as 'malware'
2 Disability and discrimination law	☑ Accessibility of content such as images for the visually impaired within different digital environments: 　☑ Website 　☑ E-mail marketing 　☑ Mobile marketing 　☑ IPTV ☑ Accessibility affecting other forms of disability including hearing difficulties and motor impairment
3 Brand and trademark protection	☑ Use of trademarks and brand names within: 　☑ Domain names 　☑ Content on site (for search engine optimization) 　☑ Paid search advertising campaigns (e.g. Google AdWords) ☑ Representation of a brand on third-party sites including partners, publishers and social networks ☑ Defamation of employees
4 Intellectual property rights	☑ Protection of digital assets such as text content, images, audio and sounds through digital rights management (DRM)
5 Contract law	☑ Validity of electronic contracts relevant to: 　☑ Cancellations 　☑ Returns 　☑ Errors in pricing ☑ Distance-selling law ☑ International taxation issues where the e-commerce service provider is under a different tax regime from the purchaser
6 Online advertising law	☑ Similar issues to traditional media: 　☑ Representation of offer 　☑ Causing offence (e.g. viral marketing)

hoc process, but if there is not a reporting mechanism then some major changes may not be apparent to managers. Environmental analysis is required to evaluate information and respond accordingly.

The real-world e-business experiences case below shows how a translation service has reviewed and exploited changes within their marketplace.

The E-consultancy interview

Interview with Christian Arno of Lingo24 around the challenges of localizing web content for different countries.

Overview and main concepts covered

Lingo24 is a company which offers online translation services to a range of clients, including Orange, BP, Bloomberg, RBS and T Mobile. It was founded In Aberdeen by Christian Arno in 2001 and now employs staff all around the world.

Q. Can you explain what Lingo24 does?

Christian Arno, Lingo24: We are a web-focused translation company. Most traditional translation firms did not grasp the potential of the web at the time of the dot-com boom, and also tended to have an academic slant. I saw the opportunity to move this service online.

There is a lot of content on the Internet, and websites are not necessarily achieving their full potential because they are limited to an English-speaking market. People will generally search and look for content in their own languages, so companies have an opportunity if they cater for these users.

With the majority of online content in the English language, it is more difficult for companies to gain prominence, but there are plenty of opportunities in foreign language markets. Take German for instance, there is a potential market there of 100 million German speakers for companies to target.

Q. What kind of clients do you have?

Christian Arno, Lingo24: One of our biggest clients is a hotel marketing group, and we translate its content into several different languages.

Orange is another client, it is very specific about its brand and the language it uses, so we work very closely with them on the tone of voice they use to foreign customers.

Q. What are the challenges in translating sales and marketing messages and keeping them relevant?

Christian Arno, Lingo24: It's not just a question of direct translation from one language to another, it becomes much more complicated than that. A lot of marketing plays on culture and common experience that is specific to individual countries or languages, so it can be difficult to adapt to foreign markets.

Even with the same countries, marketing can vary a lot. I live in Edinburgh, and the advertising messages I see are often very different to those meant for a London audience.

When you are looking to target different languages and cultures, there is a lot to think about; even colours can have different associations, for instance.

We offer clients different levels of service, from straight translation of documents etc. to a higher level where we work closely with clients to consider the target audience, and completely take apart the marketing message and reconstruct it.

It also helps that our linguists are all based in the country for which marketing messages are intended, so they have that local knowledge of what type of language will work best. Also, we employ people who have experience in the specific sectors clients come from, so they will understand industry terminology.

Q. How many people do you employ now?

Christian Arno, Lingo24: We crept over the 100 employee mark recently. We only employ three full-time translators, but we have a network of 4,000 around the world that we monitor regularly to maintain quality.

Our Head Office is in Edinburgh, where we employ 10 staff, though the majority of our team (70 people) is based in Romania, which is the hub of our European operations. Romania was a good choice because it is a very multi-lingual country.

We also have four staff in New Zealand and two in China, as well as an office in Panama.

Q. It must be a challenge leading a team that is spread so widely...

Christian Arno, Lingo24: It is a real challenge in terms of keeping a community feel amongst the workforce. The main tool we use to keep everyone in touch is a daily newsletter, which lets people know about any key information, policy changes etc.

Q. How did you get the site started in the beginning?

Christian Arno, Lingo24: I studied languages at university, and had a year abroad in Italy as part of the course, and saw an opportunity to provide a service online and undercut established translation businesses.

I started a very basic website, and managed to get some business this way. One of my first clients was Fuzzybrush, the Liverpool Tourist Board another. This proved that there was a demand out there for this kind of service.

It was perhaps only one project per month, but enough to persuade my friends and me that there was an opportunity here, so we decided to make the website and service more professional, and charge prices to match this.

Q. How did you fund the business at first?

Christian Arno, Lingo24: I worked from my parents' house in Aberdeen to keep costs down, but I also got lucky with share dealings while in Italy. I invested £500 of my student loan and managed to turn it into £15,000, which gave me a cushion while I got the business up and running.

I also kept costs low by giving people I worked with a share of the business.

Q. Have you taken any funding at any point?

Christian Arno, Lingo24: No, I've managed to grow the business gradually, as more clients came on board, and have expanded as and when we have needed to.

Q. You have experienced growth of 30% during the recession – how have you achieved this?

Christian Arno, Lingo24: It's partly a reflection of our continued investment in sales and marketing, and a lot of the growth has come from international markets; the UK now accounts for less than 50% of our business.

We also have a very diversified selection of services, something which has helped us to survive and grow during the recession.

Q. What trends have you been seeing recently?

Christian Arno, Lingo24: Whereas five years ago companies expected people to speak English to be able to view their websites, I think that there is an increasing recognition of the need to cater to international audiences.

In other European countries, companies would naturally have a website in English as well as their own language, but this was not always the case for the UK.

People should look at translation as a way to open up another sales channel; it allows a business to reach a new market, and it can be much easier to get good search rankings in another language.

Q. What advice would you offer to other online start-ups?

Christian Arno, Lingo24: Think internationally from the start; in terms of buying domain names and marketing websites, this will save a lot of headaches and problems later on.

Source: www.econsultancy.com/uk/blog/4275-q-a-lingo24-founder-christian-arno.

Social and legal factors

The social and cultural impacts of the Internet are important from an e-commerce perspective since they govern demand for Internet services and propensity to purchase online and use different types of e-commerce services. For example, in Figures 1.11 and 1.15 respectively we saw how businesses and consumers have adopted different online services.

Complete Activity 4.2 to start to review some of the social issues associated with the Internet.

Factors governing e-commerce service adoption

It is useful for e-business managers to understand the different factors that affect how many people actively use the Internet, so that action can be taken to overcome some of these barriers. For example, marketing communications can be used to reduce fears about the value proposition, ease of use and security. Chaffey *et al.* (2009) suggest that the following factors are important in governing adoption of any e-commerce service:

Activity 4.2	Understanding enablers and barriers to consumer adoption

Purpose

To identify reasons why businesses or consumers may be encouraged online or may resist.

visit the www

Activity

Access a recent survey in your country of attitudes to the Internet. In particular, you should concentrate on reasons why customers have used the Internet or have not used the Internet at all. A compilation of research about the Internet and technology adoption is available at www.clickz.com/stats. Examples of data are provided in Figures 1.10 and 1.14.

1 Summarize and explain the reasons for the levels of usage of the medium for different activities.
2 What are the main enablers and barriers to higher levels of adoption of these different activities and which actions should organizations take to increase adoption?

Alternatively, devise an *ad hoc* survey to investigate attitudes to and use of the Internet using friends, family or classmates as respondents. Example questions might include the following: What have you bought online? If nothing, why not? How many hours do you spend online each month? How many e-mails do you receive or send? What stops you using the Internet more? What aspects of the Internet are you concerned about?

Answers to activities can be found at www.pearsoned.co.uk/chaffey

1 *Cost of access.* This is certainly a barrier for those who do not already own a home computer. The other main costs are the cost of using an ISP to connect to the Internet and the cost of using the media to connect. Free access would certainly increase adoption and usage.
2 *Value proposition.* Customers need to perceive a need to be online – what can the Internet offer that other media cannot? Examples of value propositions include access to more supplier information and possibly lower prices.
3 *Ease of use.* This includes the ease of first connecting to the Internet using the ISP and the ease of using the web once connected.
4 *Security.* While this is only, in reality, a problem for those who shop online, the perception may be that if you are connected to the Internet then your personal details may not be secure. It will probably take many years for this fear to diminish.
5 *Fear of the unknown.* Many will simply have a general fear of the technology and the new media, which is not surprising since much of the news about the Internet will concern pornography, fraud and privacy infringements.

An attempt has been made to quantify the magnitude of barriers to access in a UK government-sponsored survey (Booz Allen Hamilton, 2002) of different countries. Barriers for individuals included:

- No perceived benefit
- Lack of trust
- Security problems
- Lack of skills
- Cost

The authors of the report note that:

> significant (national) variation exists in what citizens perceive to be the most important barriers to further use, and in governments' chosen role in tackling those barriers. Using the internet and ICTs in education seems to be a significant driver of citizens' confidence in their own skills. Several governments, notably Italy and France, have attempted to tackle the skill issue later in life through a range of courses in computer skills.

These barriers to access and usage of the web still remain and governments are concerned about 'social exclusion' where some sectors of society have lower levels of access and opportunity. As expected, there is a strong correlation between Internet use and PC penetration. Countries such as Sweden have encouraged home use most actively through government initiatives. This appears to exert more influence than reduction in costs of access.

Understanding users' access requirements

To fully understand online customer propensity to use online service we also need to consider the user's access location, access device and 'webographics'. 'Webographics' is a term coined by Grossnickle and Raskin (2001), which includes:

- Usage location (from home or work)
- Access device (browser and computer platform including mobile devices)
- Connection speed – broadband versus dial-up connections
- ISP
- Experience level
- Usage type
- Usage level

Competition in the marketplace amongst broadband providers has caused a great increase in the Internet access options available for consumers and small businesses. But these vary significantly by country, as shown by Figure 4.2, so web services should be tested for lower-speed Internet access.

Variations in usage of mobile services are shown in Table 4.3. You can see that this type of data is vital for managers considering investment in mobile e-commerce services. Again there are large variations in usage of services in different countries, but with overall use of mobile applications relatively low.

Consumers influenced by using the online channel

To help develop effective online services, we need to understand customers' **online buyer behaviour** and motivation (this topic is considered in more depth in Chapter 9, p. 463). As we saw in Figure 4.1, finding information about goods and services is a popular online activity, but each organization needs to capture data about online influence in the buying

Online buyer behaviour

An assessment of how consumers and business people use the Internet in combination with other communications channels when selecting and buying products and services.

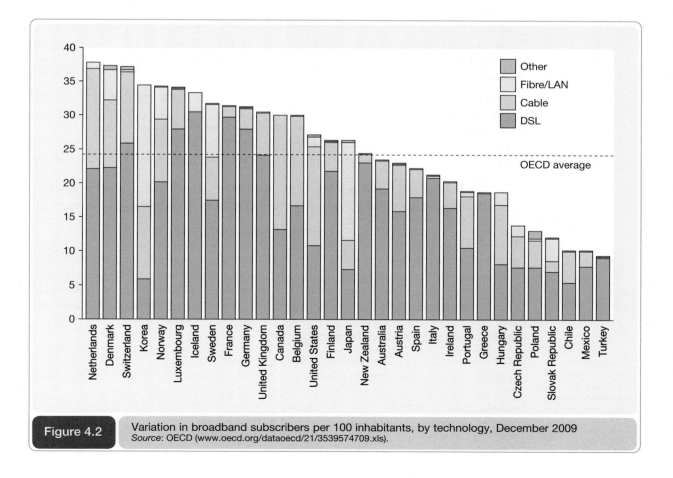

| Figure 4.2 | Variation in broadband subscribers per 100 inhabitants, by technology, December 2009
Source: OECD (www.oecd.org/dataoecd/21/3539574709.xls). |

Table 4.3	Percentage of mobile subscriber monthly consumption of content and applications

	USA	France	Germany	Italy	Spain	UK	China
Watched video	4.2%	5.0%	2.5%	6.0%	7.7%	5.1%	0.9%
Listened to music	5.7%	12.9%	15.0%	13.3%	20.0%	18.9%	34.8%
Accessed news/info via browser	12.6%	9.2%	5.2%	7.6%	7.5%	15.5%	6.1%
Played downloaded game	9.1%	4.0%	7.6%	8.7%	13.0%	11.0%	10.0%
Accessed downloaded application	4.2%	1.3%	2.2%	4.0%	2.5%	3.3%	2.4%
Sent/received photos or videos	20.5%	24.3%	21.7%	31.3%	31.7%	29.7%	15.2%
Purchased ringtones	9.7%	4.3%	4.2%	4.6%	4.6%	3.7%	4.4%
Used e-mail	11.6%	6.7%	6.9%	10.2%	9.0%	9.1%	2.5%
Accessed social networking sites	3.6%	1.7%	1.4%	1.9%	2.4%	3.6%	2.2%

Source: comScore M:Metrics (2008) M:Metrics, Inc., Copyright © 2008. Survey of mobile subscribers. Data based on three-month moving average for period ending 30 November 2007, mobile subscribers in France, n = 12,867 Germany, n = 15,700; Italy, n = 13,107; Spain, n = 12,877; United Kingdom, n = 15,588; United States, n = 33,237, and the cities of Beijing, Shanghai, Guangzhou, Shenyang, Chengdu, Wuhan and Xi'an for the three-month average ending 31 December 2007, n = 5,163.

process for their own market. Managers also need to understand how the types of sites shown in Figure 2.3 influence consumers, for example are blogs, social networks or traditional media sites more trusted? We can understand significant features of online buyer behaviour from research summarized in the AOL-sponsored BrandNewWorld (2004) study which showed that:

1 The Internet is a vital part of the research process with 73% of Internet users agreeing that they now spend longer researching products.
2 The Internet is used at every stage of the research process from the initial scan to the more detailed comparison and final check before purchase.
3 Consumers are more informed from a multiplicity of sources; price is not exclusively the primary driver.
4 Online information and experience (and modified opinions about a brand or product) also translates into offline purchase. This is an important but sometimes underestimated role of e-commerce (Figure 4.3).

There is also a wide variation in influence according to type of product, so it is important to assess the role of the web in supporting buying decisions for a particular market. Understanding the potential reach of a website and its role in influencing purchase is clearly important in setting e-marketing budgets. A different perspective on this is indicated by Figure 4.3 which shows the proportion of people who purchase offline after online research.

Motivation for use of online services

Psychographic segmentation
A breakdown of customers according to different characteristics.

Marketers can also develop **psychographic segmentations** which help explain motivation. Specialized psychodemographic profiles have been developed for web users. See Box 4.1 for an example of this type of segmentation applied to responsiveness to online advertising. Which profile do you fit?

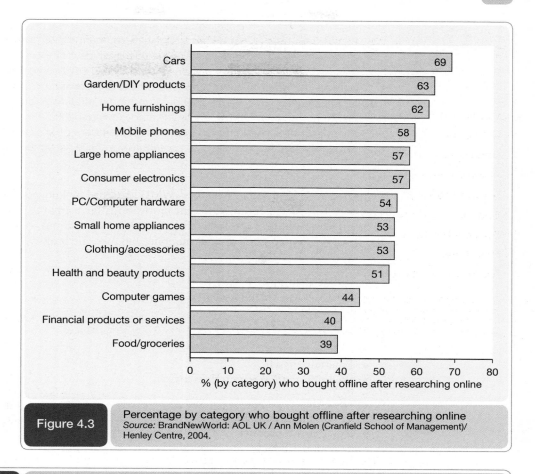

Figure 4.3	**Percentage by category who bought offline after researching online** *Source:* BrandNewWorld: AOL UK / Ann Molen (Cranfield School of Management)/ Henley Centre, 2004.

Box 4.1	**Psychographic segmentation for transactional e-commerce**

Digital marketing agency Digitas (2007) developed this segmentation to represent different attitudes to online advertising (OLA) and usage of different online services.

1 Casual user (20%) – To the casual user, the Internet is a fun and entertaining way to spend time. Generally, the casual user visits the same small set of sites on a regular basis and does not engage other users online. The oldest of the segments with an average age of 55, this is the segment most likely to subscribe to a daily newspaper, to find value in weekly newspaper circulars, and believe that companies should never send them e-mail.

2 Task-based user (24%) – The task-based user believes that technology is moving too fast and sees Internet usage specifically as a chore. Non-responsive to OLA, this segment is also most likely to feel the need for assistance when using the Internet. Their online behaviours focus on completing a specific task such as online banking or making travel arrangements.

3 Researcher (16%) – The research segment enjoys being online and conducts online research prior to making offline purchases. They consider themselves to be trendsetters. However, they do not transact online. OLA is a trusted source of information and enables them to learn about new products and services.

4 Emerging user (19%) – This segment is the traditional 'sweet spot' for online advertisers. The segment is the most responsive to OLA, and they conduct research online as well as transact online.

> **5** Established user (17%) – The established segment consists of e-commerce veterans who nurture and develop online relationships. They consider themselves to be trendsetters but do not pay attention to online advertising. Rather, they rely on peer reviews to gain information on products and services.
>
> **6** Next Gen user (5%) – The youngest and most affluent of all the segments, the Next Gen segment grew up online and consider their mobile phone a natural extension of their Internet experience. Members of this segment enjoy being online and are the most likely to contribute via social networking tools.

The revised Web Motivation Inventory (WMI) identified by Rodgers *et al.* (2007) is a useful framework for understanding different motivations for using the web. The four motives which cut across cultures are: research (information acquisition), communication (socialization), surfing (entertainment) and shopping and these are broken down further below.

1 *Community*
   - Get to know other people
   - Participate in an online chat
   - Join a group.

2 *Entertainment*
   - Amuse myself
   - Entertain myself
   - Find information to entertain myself.

3 *Product trial*
   - Try on the latest fashions
   - Experience a product
   - Try out a product.

4 *Information*
   - Do research
   - Get information I need
   - Search for information I need.

5 *Transaction*
   - Make a purchase
   - Buy things
   - Purchase a product I've heard about.

6 *Game*
   - Play online games
   - Entertain myself with Internet games
   - Play online games with individuals from other countries.

7 *Survey*
   - Take a survey on a topic I care about
   - Fill out an online survey
   - Give my opinion on a survey.

8 *Downloads*
   - Download music
   - Listen to music
   - Watch online videos.

9 *Interaction*
  - Connect with my friends
  - Communicate with others
  - Instant message others I know.

10 *Search*
  - Get answers to specific questions
  - Find information I can trust.

11 *Exploration*
  - Find interesting web pages
  - Explore new sites
  - Surf for fun.

12 *News*
  - Read about current events and news
  - Read entertainment news.

Web advertisers and site owners can use this framework to review the suitability of facilities to meet these needs.

Purchased online

Increasing numbers of consumers are now purchasing online. Figure 4.4 shows that initially Internet users may restrict themselves to searching for information or using e-mail. As their confidence grows their use of the Internet for purchase is likely to increase. This is often coupled with the use of broadband. For this reason, there is still good potential for e-retail sales, even if the percentage of the population with access to the Internet plateaus.

You can see from Figure 4.4 that Internet users take longer to become confident to purchase more expensive and more complex products. Figure 4.5 shows that the result is a dramatic difference in online consumer behaviour for products according to their price and

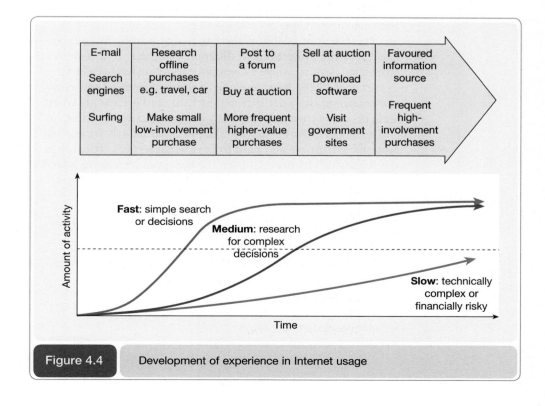

Figure 4.4   Development of experience in Internet usage

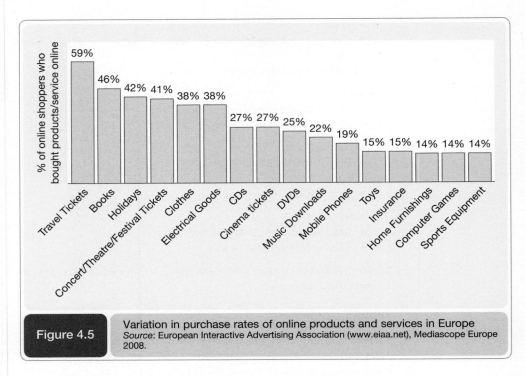

| Figure 4.5 | Variation in purchase rates of online products and services in Europe
Source: European Interactive Advertising Association (www.eiaa.net), Mediascope Europe 2008. |

complexity. For some products such as travel and cinema and theatre tickets, the majority buy online, while fewer people purchase clothes and insurance online. However, there is now less difference between the products than there was two or three years ago. Figure 4.5 suggests that the way companies should use digital technologies for marketing their products will vary markedly according to product type. In some, such as cars and complex financial products such as mortgages, the main role of online marketing will be to support research, while for standardized products there will be a dual role in supporting research and enabling purchase.

The extent of adoption also varies significantly by country – see Table 4.4. This will affect revenue projections in different countries. It also shows the potential for further growth in countries where e-commerce adoption has been lower.

Bart *et al.* (2005) have developed a widely referenced conceptual model that links website and consumer characteristics, online trust, and behaviour. We have summarized the eight main drivers of trust from the study in Figure 9.5 in the section on buyer behaviour.

The model of Bart *et al.* (2005) and similar models are centred on a single site, but perceptions of trust are also built from external sources. The role of social media and friends was highlighted by research from the European Interactive Advertising Association (2008), which rated key sources for research among European consumers:

- Search engines (66%)
- Personal recommendations (64%)
- Price comparison websites (50%)
- Websites of well-known brands (49%)
- Newspapers/magazines (49%)
- Customer website reviews (46%)
- Expert website reviews (45%)
- Retailer websites (45%)
- Sales people in shops (46%)
- Content provided by ISPs (30%)

Table 4.4	Variation in amount spent and number of purchases in Europe (2008)

Country	% of Internet users who shop online	Average amount spent online per online shopper
Sweden	99%	€731
Denmark	98%	€910
Norway	98%	€1077
UK	93%	€1100
Netherlands	89%	€746
Germany	87%	€561
Europe average	84%	€701
France	81%	€523
Spain	79%	€537
Belgium	76%	€708
Italy	62%	€431

Source: European Interactive Advertising Association (www.eiaa.net), Mediascope Europe 2008.

Business demand for e-commerce services

The B2B market is more complex than B2C in that variation in demand will occur according to different types of organization and people within the buying unit in the organization. This analysis is also important as part of the *segmentation* of different groups within a B2B target market. We need to profile business demand according to:

1 *Variation in organization characteristics*
   - Size of company (employees or turnover)
   - Industry sector and products
   - Organization type (private, public, government, not-for-profit)
   - Division
   - Country and region.

2 *Individual role*
   - Role and responsibility from job title, function or number of staff managed
   - Role in buying decision (purchasing influence)
   - Department
   - Product interest
   - Demographics: age, sex and possibly social group.

B2B profiles

We can profile business users of the Internet in a similar way to consumers by assessing:

1 *The percentage of companies with access.* In the business-to-business market, Internet access levels are higher than for business-to-consumer. The European Commission (2010) study showed that over 99% of businesses in the majority of countries surveyed have Internet access (Figure 1.11). Understanding access for different members of the organizational buying unit amongst their customers is also important for marketers. Although the Internet seems to be used by many companies, it doesn't necessarily reach the right people in the buying unit.

2 *Influenced online.* In B2B marketing, the high level of access is consistent with a high level of using the Internet to identify suppliers. As for consumer e-commerce, the Internet is important in identifying online suppliers rather than completing the transaction online. This is particularly the case in the larger companies.

3 *Purchase online.* The European Commission (2010) survey revealed that there is a large variation in the proportion of businesses in different countries who order online, with the figure substantially higher in countries such as Sweden and Germany in comparison to Italy and France for example. This shows the importance of understanding differences in the environment for e-commerce in different countries.

In summary, to estimate online revenue contribution to determine the amount of investment in e-business we need to research the number of connected customers, the percentage whose offline purchase is influenced online and the number who buy online.

Adoption of e-business by businesses

The European Commission (2010) reviewed adoption of the Internet across Europe.

In 2009, 81% of medium and 90% of large enterprises had a website, the average being 65% for all enterprises (up from 61% in 2005). They noted that 'Over time, there has been significant fragmentation in website availability for small enterprises across countries. Small enterprises in Austria, Bulgaria, Germany, Estonia, Spain, Finland, Hungary, Lithuania, Luxenbourg, Latvia, Netherlands, Poland, Portugal, Slovenia and Slovakia have seen increases of around 10% up to 20%, while no relevant progress has been registered in other countries.'

The e-business options offered through websites were as follows:

- 45% of enterprises with a website display a privacy policy statement/seal/certification
- 57% of enterprises with a website offer a product catalogue or price list
- 23–25% of enterprises with a website have an ordering, reservation or booking facility
- 11.3% of enterprises with a website have an order-tracking facility

It can be seen that many companies have not yet seen sufficient reasons to invest in e-commerce and/or the barriers are too great. Figure 4.6 gives a summary of these barriers. You can see that the lack of relevance or need for e-commerce is the largest barrier, but organizational governance issues are also important.

Daniel *et al.* (2002) researched e-business adoption in UK SMEs and noted four clusters: (1) developers, which were actively developing services, but were limited at the time of research; (2) communicators, which use e-mail to communicate internally and with customers and suppliers; (3) web presence; (4) transactors.

The luxury of sufficient resources to focus on planning and implementing an Internet strategy isn't open to many small businesses and is likely to explain why they have not been such enthusiastic adopters of e-business.

Privacy and trust in e-commerce

Ethical standards
Practice or behaviour which is morally acceptable to society.

Ethical standards are personal or business practices or behaviour which are generally considered acceptable by society.

Ethical issues and the associated laws constitute an important consideration of the Internet business environment for marketers. Privacy of consumers is a key ethical issue that affects all types of organization regardless of whether they have a transactional e-commerce service. For example, we saw in Case study 1.1 that Facebook has encountered resistance from its users for its approach to managing their information.

A further ethical issue for which laws have been enacted in many countries is providing an accessible level of Internet services for disabled users. Other laws have been developed for managing commerce and distance-selling online. In many cases, the laws governing e-commerce are in their infancy and lag behind the applications of technology.

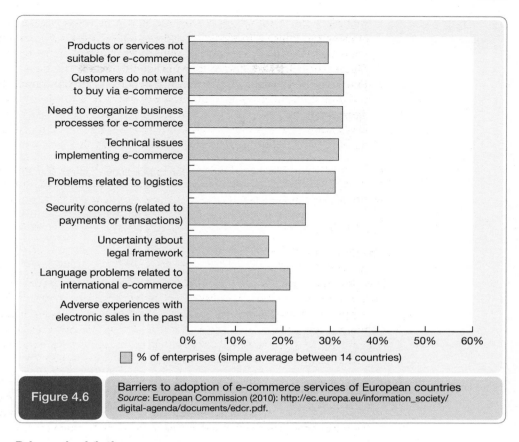

Figure 4.6 — Barriers to adoption of e-commerce services of European countries
Source: European Commission (2010): http://ec.europa.eu/information_society/
digital-agenda/documents/edcr.pdf.

Privacy legislation

Privacy

A moral right of individuals to avoid intrusion into their personal affairs.

Identity theft

The misappropriation of the identity of another person without their knowledge or consent.

Privacy refers to a moral right of individuals to avoid intrusion into their personal affairs by third parties. Privacy of personal data such as our identities, likes and dislikes is a major concern to consumers, particularly with the dramatic increase in **identity theft**. This is clearly a major concern for many consumers when using e-commerce services since they believe their privacy and identity may be compromised. This is not unfounded, as Box 4.2 shows.

While identity theft is traumatic, in the majority of cases the victim will *eventually* be able to regain any lost funds through their financial services providers.

Why personal data are valuable for e-businesses

While there is much natural concern amongst consumers about their online privacy, information about these consumers is very useful to marketers. Through understanding their customers' needs, characteristics and behaviours it is possible to create more personalized, targeted communications, which help increase sales. How should marketers respond to this dilemma? An obvious step is to ensure that marketing activities are consistent with the latest data protection and privacy laws. However, different interpretations of the law are possible and since these are new laws they have not been tested in court. As a result, companies have to take their own business decision based on the business benefits of applying particular marketing practices, against the financial and reputational risks of less strict compliance.

What are the main information types used by the Internet marketer which are governed by ethics and legislation? The information needs are:

1 *Contact information.* This is the name, postal address, e-mail address and, for B2B companies, website address.

Box 4.2	Types of identity fraud

Table 4.5 illustrates different types of identity fraud. The data show that it's still a growing problem with a 20% increase in impersonation between 2009 and 2010.

Table 4.5	Identity fraud categories in the UK		

	Jan to Mar 2009	Jan to Mar 2010	% change
Identity fraud – granted	13,350	19,322	44.73%
Identity fraud – not granted	11,469	10,427	-9.09%
Identity fraud – total	24,819	29,749	19.86%
Application fraud – granted	3,206	1,784	-44.35%
Application fraud – not granted	13,384	9,985	-25.40%
Application fraud – total	16,590	11,769	-29.06%
False insurance claim	138	161	16.67%
Facility takeover fraud	5,856	5,617	-4.08%
Asset conversion	87	119	36.78%
Misuse of facility	12,991	12,235	-5.82%
Victims of impersonation	20,730	26,874	22.86%
Victims of takeover	6,211	5,717	-8.64%

Notes:
- Identity fraud cases include cases of false identity and identity theft.
- Application fraud/false insurance claim relates to applications or claims with material falsehood (lies) or false supporting documentation where the name has not been identified as false.
- Facility takeover fraud occurs where a person (the 'facility hijacker') unlawfully obtains access to details of the 'victim of takeover', namely an existing account holder or policy holder (or of an account or policy of a genuine customer or policy holder) and fraudulently operates the account or policy for their own (or someone else's) benefit.
- Asset conversion relates to the sale of assets subject to a credit agreement where the lender retained ownership of the asset (for example a car or a lorry).
- Misuse of facility is where an account, policy or other facility is used fraudulently.

Source: CIFAS (2010).

2 *Profile information.* This is information about a customer's characteristics that can be used for segmentation. They include age, sex and social group for consumers, and company characteristics and individual role for business customers. The specific types of information and how they are used is referenced in Chapters 2 and 6. Research by Ward *et al.* (2005) found that consumers in Australia were willing to give non-financial data if there is an appropriate incentive.

3 *Platform usage information.* Through web analytics systems it is possible to collect information on type of computer, browser and screen resolution used by site users (see Chapter 7). For example, Figure 4.7 shows detail collected by a widget installed on DaveChaffey. com. As well as the platform used, the search term referred from Google is shown. Visits are tracked in this way on virtually all sites, but it is not possible to identify an individual unless they have agreed to give information through a web form.

4 *Behavioural information (on a single site).* This is purchase history, but also includes the whole buying process. Web analytics (Chapter 12) can be used to assess the web and e-mail content accessed by individuals.

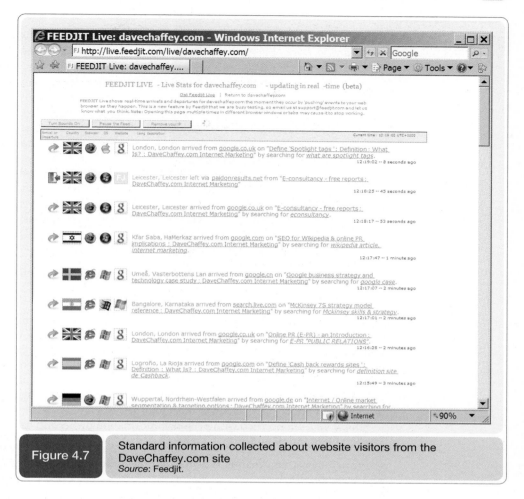

Figure 4.7 Standard information collected about website visitors from the DaveChaffey.com site
Source: Feedjit.

5 *Behavioural information (across multiple sites).* This can show how a user accesses multiple sites and responds to ads across sites. Typically these data are collected and used using an anonymous profile based on cookie or IP addresses which is not related to an individual. Complete Activity 4.3 to find out more about behavioural targeting and form an opinion of whether it should be regulated more.

Activity 4.3   **Attitudes to behavioural ad targeting**

Imagine you are a web user who has just found out about behavioural targeting.
Use the information sources provided by the industry to form an opinion. Discuss with others studying your course whether you believe behavioural ad targeting should be banned (as has been proposed in some countries) or whether its is acceptable.
Suggested information sources:

- Internet Advertising Bureau guide to behavioural advertising and privacy (www. youronlinechoices.co.uk).
- Web Analytics Association (www.webanalyticsassociation.org/?page=privacy). A trade association of online tracking vendors.
- Google 'Interest-based advertising': How it works (www.google.com/ads/preferences/html/about.html), which explains the process and benefits as follows:

Many websites, such as news sites and blogs, use Google's AdSense program ('a network of publishers using advertising through Google') to show ads on their sites. It's our goal to make these ads as relevant as possible for you. While we often show you ads based on the content of the page you are viewing, we also developed new technology that shows some ads based on interest categories that you might find useful. The following example explains this new technology step by step:

Mary's favorite hobby is gardening. With Google's interest-based advertising technology, Mary will see more relevant gardening ads because she visits many gardening websites. Here's how that works: When Mary visits websites that display ads provided by Google's AdSense program, Google stores a number in her browser (using a 'cookie') to remember her visits. That number could look like this: 114411. Because many of the websites that Mary visits are related to gardening, Google puts her number (114411) in the 'gardening enthusiast' interest category.

As a result, Google will show more gardening ads to Mary (based on her browser) as she browses websites that use AdSense.

Answers to activities can be found at www.pearsoned.co.uk/chaffey

Table 4.6 summarizes how these different types of customer information are collected and used. The main issue to be considered by the marketer is disclosure of the types of information collection and tracking data used. The first two types of information in the table are usually readily explained through a privacy statement at the point of data collection, which is usually a legal requirement. However, with the other types of information, users would only know they were being tracked if they have cookie monitoring software installed or if they seek out the privacy statement of a publisher which offers advertising.

Ethical issues concerned with personal information ownership have been summarized by Mason (1986) into four areas:

- *Privacy* – what information is held about the individual?
- *Accuracy* – is it correct?
- *Property* – who owns it and how can ownership be transferred?
- *Accessibility* – who is allowed to access this information, and under which conditions?

Fletcher (2001) provides an alternative perspective, raising these issues of concern for both the individual and the marketer:

- *Transparency* – who is collecting what information and how do they disclose the collection of data and how it will be used?
- *Security* – how is information protected once it has been collected by a company?
- *Liability* – who is responsible if data are abused?

All of these issues arise in the next section, which reviews actions marketers should take to achieve privacy and trust.

Data protection legislation is enacted to protect the individual, to protect their privacy and to prevent misuse of their personal data. Indeed, the first article of the European Union directive 95/46/EC (see http://ec.europa.eu/justice_home/fsj/privacy/) specifically refers to personal data. It says:

Member states shall protect the fundamental rights and freedoms of natural persons [i.e. a named individual at home or at work], and in particular their right to privacy with respect to the processing of personal data.

In the UK, the enactment of the European legislation is the Data Protection Act 1984, 1998 (DPA). It is managed by the 'Information Commissioner' and summarized at www.ico.gov. uk. This law is typical of what has evolved in many countries to help protect personal information. Any company that holds personal data on computers or on file about customers or

Malware

Malicious software or toolbars, typically downloaded via the Internet, which acts as a 'trojan horse' by executing unwanted activities such as keylogging of user passwords or viruses which may collect e-mail addresses

Table 4.6	Types of information collected online and related technologies

Type of information	Approach and technology used to capture and use information
1 Contact information	• *Online forms* – online forms linked to customer database • *Cookies* – are used to remember a specific person on subsequent visits
2 Profile information including personal information	• *Online forms* • Cookies can be used to assign a person to a particular segment by linking the cookie to a customer database record and then offering content consistent with their segment
3 Access platform usage	• Web analytics system – identification of computer type, operating system and screen characteristics based on http attributes of visitors
4 Behavioural information on a single site	• Purchase histories are stored in the sales order database. Web analytics store details of IP addresses against clickstreams of the sequence of web pages visited • Web beacons in e-mail marketing – a single-pixel GIF is used to assess whether a reader had opened an e-mail • First-party cookies are also used for monitoring visitor behaviour during a site visit and on subsequent visits • **Malware** can collect additional information such as passwords
5 Behavioural information across multiple sites	• Third-party cookies used for assessing visits from different sources such as online advertising networks or affiliate networks (Chapter 9) • Search engines such as Google use cookies to track advertising through its AdWords pay-per-click programme • Services such as Hitwise (www.hitwise.com) monitor IP traffic to assess site usage of customer groups within a product category

Notification

The process whereby companies register with the data protection registrar to inform about their data holdings.

Personal data

Any information about an individual stored by companies concerning their customers or employees.

Data controller

Each company must have a defined person responsible for data protection.

Data subject

The legal term to refer to the individual whose data are held.

employees must be registered with the data protection registrar (although there are some exceptions which may exclude small businesses). This process is known as **notification**.

The guidelines on the eight data protection principles are produced by legal requirements of the 1998 UK Data Protection Act. These principles state that **personal data** should be:

1 Fairly and lawfully processed.

In full: '*Personal data shall be processed fairly and lawfully and, in particular, shall not be processed unless – at least one of the conditions in Schedule 2 is met; and in the case of sensitive personal data, at least one of the conditions in Schedule 3 is also met.*'

The Information Commissioner has produced a 'fair processing code' which suggests how an organization needs to achieve 'fair and lawful processing'. This requires:

• Appointment of a **data controller** who has defined responsibility for data protection within a company.
• Clear details in communications such as on a website or direct mail of how a '**data subject**' can contact the data controller or a representative.
• Before data processing 'the data subject has given his consent' or the processing must be necessary either for a 'contract to which the data subject is a party' (for example as part of a sale of a product) or because it is required by other laws.

- Sensitive personal data require particular care, these include:
  - the racial or ethnic origin of the data subject;
  - political opinions;
  - religious beliefs or other beliefs of a similar nature;
  - membership of a trade union;
  - physical or mental health or condition;
  - sexual life;
  - the commission or alleged commission or proceedings of any offence.
- No other laws must be broken in processing the data.

2 **Processed for limited purposes.**
In full: '*Personal data shall be obtained only for one or more specified and lawful purposes, and shall not be further processed in any manner incompatible with that purpose or those purposes.*'

This implies that the organization must make it clear why and how the data will be processed at the point of collection. Figure 4.8 suggests some of the issues that should be considered when a data subject is informed of how the data will be used. Important issues are:

- Whether future communications will be sent to the individual (explicit consent is required for this in online channels).
- Whether the data will be passed on to third parties (again explicit consent is required).
- How long the data will be kept.

3 **Adequate, relevant and not excessive.**
In full: '*Personal data shall be adequate, relevant and not excessive in relation to the purpose or purposes for which they are processed.*'

This specifies that the minimum necessary amount of data is requested for processing. There is difficulty in reconciling this provision between the needs of the individual and the needs of the company. The more details that an organization has about a customer,

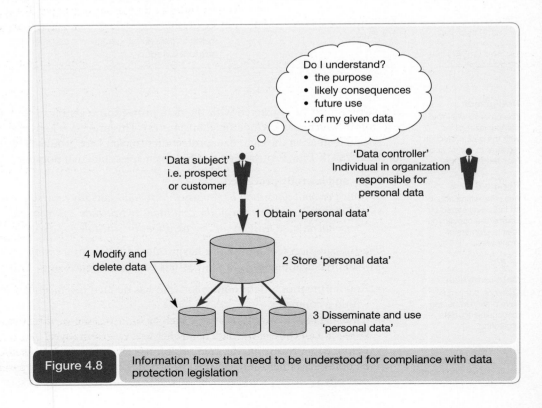

Figure 4.8   Information flows that need to be understood for compliance with data protection legislation

the better they can understand that customer and so develop products and marketing communications specific to that customer.

4 **Accurate**.

In full: '*Personal data shall be accurate and, where necessary, kept up to date.*'

It is clearly also in the interest of an organization in an ongoing relationship with a partner that the data is kept accurate and up to date. Inaccurate data is defined in the guidelines as: 'incorrect or misleading as to any matter of fact'.

The guidelines go on to discuss the importance of keeping information up to date. This is only necessary where there is an ongoing relationship and the rights of the individual may be affected if they are not up to date.

5 **Not kept longer than necessary**.

In full: '*Personal data processed for any purpose or purposes shall not be kept for longer than is necessary for that purpose or those purposes.*'

The guidelines state: '*To comply with this Principle, data controllers will need to review their personal data regularly and to delete the information which is no longer required for their purposes.*'

It might be in a company's interests to 'clean data' so that records that are not relevant are archived or deleted. However, there is the possibility that the customer may still buy again, in which case the information would be useful. For example, a car manufacturer could justifiably hold data for several years.

If a relationship between the organization and the data subject ends, then data should be deleted. This will be clear in some instances, for example when an employee leaves a company their personal data should be deleted.

6 **Processed in accordance with the data subject's rights**.

In full: '*Personal data shall be processed in accordance with the rights of data subjects under this Act.*'

One aspect of the data subject's rights is the option to request a copy of their personal data from an organization for payment of a small fee such as £10 or £30; this is known as a '**subject access request**'. This includes all information on paper files and on computer.

Other aspects of a data subject's rights are designed to prevent or control processing which:

Subject access request
A request by a data subject to view personal data from an organization.

- causes damage or distress (for example repeatedly sending mailshots to someone who has died);
- is used for direct marketing (for example, in the UK consumers can subscribe to the mail, e-mail or telephone preference service to avoid unsolicited mailings, e-mails or phone calls). This invaluable service is provided by the Direct Marketing Association (www.dmaconsumers.org). Organizations must check against these 'exclusion lists' before contacting you.
- is used for automatic decision taking – automated credit checks, for example, may result in unjust decisions on taking a loan.

7 **Secure**.

In full: '*Appropriate technical and organizational measures shall be taken against unauthorised or unlawful processing of personal data and against accidental loss or destruction of, or damage to, personal data.*'

Techniques for managing data security are discussed in Chapter 11.

Of course, the cost of security measures will vary according to the level of security required. The Act allows for this through this provision:

(i) *Taking into account the state of technological development at any time and the cost of implementing any measures, the measures must ensure a level of security appropriate to: (a) the harm that might result from a breach of security; and (b) the nature of the data to be protected. (ii) The data controller must take reasonable steps to ensure the reliability of staff having access to the personal data.*

8 **Not transferred to countries without adequate protection**.

In full: '*Personal data shall not be transferred to a country or territory outside the European Economic Area, unless that country or territory ensures an adequate level of protection of the rights and freedoms of data subjects in relation to the processing of personal data.*'

Transfer of data beyond Europe is likely for multinational companies. This principle prevents export of data to countries that do not have sound data processing laws. If the transfer is required in concluding a sale or contract or if the data subject agrees to it, then transfer is legal. Data transfer with the US is possible through companies registered through the Safe Harbor scheme (www.export.gov/safeharbor).

Anti-spam legislation

Laws have been enacted in different countries to protect individual privacy and with the intention of reducing **spam** or unsolicited commercial e-mail (UCE). Spammers rely on sending out millions of e-mails in the hope that even if there is only a 0.01% response they may make some money, if not get rich.

Anti-spam laws do not mean that e-mail cannot be used as a marketing tool. As explained below, permission-based e-mail marketing based on consent or opt-in by customers and the option to unsubscribe or opt out is the key to successful e-mail marketing.

Before starting an e-mail dialogue with customers, according to law in Europe, America and many countries in the Asia–Pacific region, companies must ask customers to provide their e-mail address and then give them the option of 'opting into' further communications.

Legal opt-in e-mail addresses and customer profile information are available for purchase or rental from a database traditionally known by marketers as a '**cold list**'. Your name will also potentially be stored on an opt-in **house list** where you have given your consent to be contacted by a company you have purchased from or its partners.

Regulations on privacy and electronic communications

While the Data Protection Directive 95/46 and Data Protection Act afford a reasonable level of protection for consumers, they were quickly superseded by advances in technology and the rapid growth in spam. As a result, in 2002 the European Union passed the '2002/58/EC Directive on Privacy and Electronic Communications' to complement previous data protection law (see Box 4.3). This Act applies specifically to electronic communications such as e-mail and the monitoring of websites using technologies such as cookies.

Worldwide regulations on privacy and electronic communications

In the USA, there is a privacy initiative aimed at education of consumers and business (www.ftc.gov/privacy), but legislation is limited other than for e-mail marketing. In January 2004, a new federal law known as the CAN-SPAM Act (www.ftc.gov/spam) was introduced to assist in the control of unsolicited e-mail. CAN-SPAM stands for 'Controlling the Assault of Non-Solicited Pornography and Marketing' (an ironic juxtaposition between pornography and marketing). The Act requires unsolicited commercial e-mail messages to be labelled (though not by a standard method) and to include opt-out instructions and the sender's physical address. It prohibits the use of deceptive subject lines and false headers in such messages.

Anti-spam legislation in other countries can be accessed:

- Australia enacted a spam Act in 2003 (www.privacy.gov.au)
- Canada has a privacy Act (www.privcom.gc.ca)
- New Zealand Privacy Commissioner (www.privacy.org.nz)
- Summary of all countries (www.privacyinternational.org and www.spamlaws.com).

While such laws are clearly in consumers' interests, some companies see the practice as restrictive. In 2002, ten companies including IBM, Oracle and VeriSign, who referred to

---

Spam

Unsolicited e-mail (usually bulk-mailed and untargeted).

Cold list

Data about individuals that are rented or sold by a third party.

House list

Data about existing customers used to market products to encourage future purchase.

themselves as the 'Global Privacy Alliance (GPA)', lobbied the EU saying that it put too much emphasis on the protection of individuals' privacy, and not enough on ensuring the free flow of information between companies! More positively, the Online Privacy Alliance (www.privacyalliance.org) is a 'group of more than 30 global corporations and associations who have come together to introduce and promote business-wide actions that create an environment of trust and foster the protection of individuals' privacy online'.

| **Box 4.3** | UK and European e-mail marketing law |

As an example of European privacy law which covers use of e-mail, SMS and cookies for marketing, we review the implications for managers of the UK enactment of 2002/58/EC Directive on Privacy and Electronic Communications. We will contrast this with the law in other European countries.

This came into force in the UK on 11 December 2003 as the **Privacy and Electronic Communications Regulations (PECR) Act**. The law is published at http://www.legislation.gov.uk/uksi/2003/2426/contents/made. Consumer marketers in the UK also need to heed the Code of Advertising Practice from the Advertising Standards Agency (ASA CAP code, www.asa.org.uk/the_codes). This has broadly similar aims and places similar restrictions on marketers to the PECR law.

The PECR law is a surprisingly accessible and common-sense document – many marketers will be practising similar principles already. Clauses 22 to 24 are the main clauses relevant to e-mail communications. The PECR law:

1 **Applies to consumer marketing using e-mail or SMS text messages**. 22(1) applies to '*individual subscribers*', which currently means consumers, although the Information Commissioner has stated that this may be reviewed in future to include business subscribers as is the case in countries such as Italy and Germany.

    Although this sounds like great news for business-to-business (B2B) marketers, it could be dangerous. The Advertising Standards Agency found against a B2B organization which had unwittingly e-mailed consumers from what they believed was a list of B2B customers.

2 **Is an 'opt-in' regime**. The law applies to '*unsolicited communications*' (22(1)) and was introduced with a view to reducing spam, although its impact will be limited on spammers beyond Europe. The recipient must have '*previously notified the sender that he consents*' (22(2)) or has proactively agreed to receive commercial e-mail. This is opt-in. Opt-in can be achieved online or offline through asking people whether they want to receive e-mail. Online this is often done through a tick box. In fact, the PECR law does not mandate a tick box option (except for receiving communications from third parties) provided consent is clearly indicated, such as by pressing a button.

Privacy and Electronic Communications Regulations Act
A law intended to control the distribution of e-mail and other online communications including cookies.

Opt-in
A customer proactively agrees or consents to receive further communications.

Permission marketing
Customers agree (opt in) to be involved in an organization's marketing activities, usually as a result of an incentive.

Debate 4.1

How far should opt-in go?

'*Companies should always use an opt-in privacy policy for*
(a) *e-mailing prospects and customers*
(b) *monitoring website visitors using site analysis software*
(c) *identifying repeat visitors using cookies.*'

The approach required by the law has been used by many organizations for some time, as sending unsolicited e-mails was thought to be unethical and also not in the best interests of the company because of the risk of annoying customers. In fact, the law conforms to an established approach known as '**permission marketing**', a term coined by US commentator Seth Godin (1999) (see *Chapter 9*, p. 458).

Opt-out
A customer declines the offer to receive further information.

3 **Requires an opt-out option in all communications**. An opt-out or method of 'unsubscribing' is required so that the recipient does not receive future communications. In a database this means that a 'do not e-mail' field must be created. A 'simple means of refusing' future communications is required both when the details were first collected and in each subsequent communication.

4 **Does not apply to existing customers when marketing similar products**. This common-sense clause (22(3)(a)) states that previous opt-in is not required if the contact details were obtained during the course of the sale or negotiations for the sale of a product or service. This is sometimes known as the 'soft or implied opt-in exception'. This clause is interpreted differently in different European countries with seven countries, Italy, Denmark, Germany, Austria, Greece, Finland and Spain, not including it. Marketers managing campaigns across Europe need to take the differences into account.

Clause 22(3)(b) adds that when marketing to existing customers the marketer may market 'similar products and services only'. Case law will help in clarifying this.

5 **Contact details must be provided**. It is not sufficient to send an e-mail with a simple sign-off from 'The marketing team' or 'Web team'. The law requires a name, address or phone number to whom a recipient can complain.

6 **The 'from' identification of the sender must be clear**. Spammers aim to disguise the e-mail originator. The law says that the identity of the person who sends the communication must not be 'disguised or concealed' and that a valid address to 'send a request that such communications cease' should be provided.

7 **Applies to direct marketing communications**. The communications that the legislation refers to are for 'direct marketing'. This suggests that other communications involved with customer service such as an e-mail about a monthly phone statement are not covered, so the opt-out choice may not be required here.

8 **Restricts the use of cookies**. Some privacy campaigners consider that the user's privacy is invaded by planting cookies or electronic tags on the end-user's computer. The concept of the cookie and its associated law is not straightforward, so it warrants separate discussion (see Box 4.4).

Cookies
Small text files stored on an end-user's computer to enable websites to identify them.

| Box 4.4 | Understanding cookies |

A 'cookie' is a data file placed on your computer that identifies the individual computer.

Types of cookies
The main cookie types are:

- **Persistent cookies** – these stay on a user's computer between multiple sessions and are most valuable for marketers to identify repeat visits to sites.
- **Temporary or session cookies** – single session – useful for tracking within pages of a session such as on an e-commerce site.
- **First-party cookies** – served by the site you are currently using – typical for e-commerce sites. These can be persistent or session cookies.
- **Third-party cookies** – served by another site to the one you are viewing – typical for portals where an ad network will track remotely or where the web analytics software places a cookie. These are typically persistent cookies.

Cookies are stored as individual text files in a directory on a personal computer. There is usually one file per website. For example: dave_chaffey@british-airways.txt contains encoded information as follows:

```
FLT_VIS  |K:bapzRnGdxBYUU|D:Jul-25-1999| british-airways.com/
         0 425259904 293574 26 1170747936 29284034 *
```

Persistent cookies
Cookies that remain on the computer after a visitor session has ended. Used to recognize returning visitors.

Session cookies
Cookies used to manage a single visitor session.

First-party cookies
Served by the site you are currently using – typical for e-commerce sites.

Third-party cookies
Served by another site to the one you are viewing – typical for portals where an ad network will track remotely or where the web analytics software places a cookie.

The information is essentially just an identification number and a date of the last visit, although other information can be stored.

Cookies are specific to a particular browser and computer, so if a user connects from a different computer or starts using a different browser, the website will not identify him or her as a similar user.

Browser suppliers are keen to protect users' online privacy as part of their value proposition. 2008 saw the launch of Internet Explorer 8 and its InPrivate feature and Google Chrome with its Incognito mode. These are intended for temporary use for a session where someone is browsing sites they don't want others in the family or office to know about. They won't delete previous cookies, but new permanent cookies won't be created in these situations.

What are cookies used for?

Common marketing applications of cookies include:

A *Personalizing a site for an individual.* Cookies are used to identify individual users and retrieve their preferences from a database.

For example, I subscribe to the E-consultancy service www.e-consultancy.com; each time I return I do not have to log in because it remembers my previous visit. Many sites feature a 'Remember Me' option which implies using a cookie to remember a returning visitor. Retailers such as Amazon can use cookies to recognize returning visitors and recommend related items. This approach generally has benefits for both the individual (it is a hassle to sign in again and relevant content can be delivered) and the company (tailored marketing messages can be delivered).

B *Online ordering systems.* This enables a site such as Tesco.com to track what is in your basket as you order different products.

C *Tracking within a site.* Web analytics software such as Webtrends (www.webtrends.com) relies on persistent cookies to find the proportion of repeat visitors to a website. Webtrends and other tools increasingly use first-party cookies since they are more accurate and less likely to be blocked.

D *Tracking across sites.* Advertising networks use cookies to track the number of times a particular computer user has been shown a particular banner advertisement; they can also track adverts served on sites across an ad network.

Affiliate networks and pay-per-click ad networks such as Google Adwords and Yahoo! Search services (Overture) may also use cookies to track through from a click on a third-party site to a sale or lead being generated on a destination or merchant site. These approaches tend to use third-party cookies. For example, if conversion tracking is enabled in Google Adwords, Google sets a cookie when a user clicks through on an ad. If this user buys the product, then the purchase confirmation page will include script code supplied by Google to make a check for a cookie placed by Google. If there is a match, the sale is attributed to Adwords. An alternative approach is that different online campaigns have different tracking parameters or codes within the links through to the destination site and when the user arrives on a site from a particular source this is identified and a cookie is set. When purchase confirmation occurs, this can then be attributed back to the original source and the particular referrer.

Owing to the large investments now made in pay-per-click and affiliate marketing, this is the area of most concern for marketers since the tracking can become inaccurate. However, sale should still occur even if the cookies are blocked or deleted, so the main consequence is that the ROI of online advertising or pay-per-click marketing may look lower than expected. In affiliate marketing, this phenomemon may benefit the marketer in that payment may not need to be made to the third party if a cookie has been deleted (or blocked) between the time of original clickthrough and sale.

Privacy issues with cookie use

The problem for Internet marketers is that, despite these important applications, blocking by browsers or security software and deletion by users has increased dramatically. In 2005 Jupiter Research claimed that 39% of online users may be deleting cookies from their primary computer monthly, although this is debated.

Many distrust cookies since they indicate that 'big brother' is monitoring your actions. Others fear that their personal details or credit card details may be accessed by other websites. This is very unlikely since all that cookies contain is a short identifier or number that is used to link you to your record in a database. In most cases, the worst that someone can do who gets access to your cookies is to find out which sites you have been visiting.

It is possible to block cookies, but this is not straightforward and many customers either do not know or do not mind that their privacy may be infringed. In 2003 an interesting survey on the perception and behaviour with regards to cookies was conducted on cookie use in the UK (RedEye, 2003). Of the 1,000 respondents:

- 50% had used more than one computer in the last three months;
- 70% said that their computer was used by more than one person;
- 94% said they either accepted cookies or did not know what they were, although 20% said they only accepted session cookies;
- 71% were aware of cookies and accepted them. Of these, only 18% did not know how to delete cookies, and 55% of them were deleting them on a monthly basis;
- 89% knew what cookies were and how to delete them and said that they had deleted them once in the last three months.

Legal constraints on cookies

The PECR law limits the use of cookies. It states: *'a person shall not use an electronic communications network to store information, or to gain access to information stored, in the terminal equipment of a subscriber or user unless the following requirements are met'*.

The requirements are:

(a) the user is provided with clear and comprehensive information about the purposes of the storage of, or access to, that information; and

(b) the user is given the opportunity to refuse the storage of or access to that information.

(a) suggests that it is important that there is a clear **privacy statement** and (b) suggests that opt-in to cookies is required. In other words, on the first visit to the site, a box would have to be ticked to agree to the use of cookies. This was thought by many commentators to be a curious provision since this facility is already available in the web browser. A further provision clarifies this. The law states: 'where such storage or access is strictly necessary for the provision of an information society service requested by the subscriber or user'. This indicates that for an e-commerce service session cookies are legitimate without the need for opt-in. It is arguable whether the identification of return visitors is 'strictly necessary' and this is why some sites have a 'remember me' tick box next to the log-in. Through doing this they are compliant with the law.

Privacy statement
Information on a website explaining how and why an individual's data are collected, processed and stored.

Viral marketing
In an online context, 'Forward to a friend' e-mail used to transmit a promotional message from one person to another. 'Online word of mouth.'

Viral e-mail marketing

One widespread business practice that is not covered explicitly in the PECR law is '**viral marketing**', as discussed in Chapter 3 and reviewed in Chapter 9, p. 498.

Several initiatives are being taken by industry groups to reassure web users about threats to their personal information. The first of these is TRUSTe (www.truste.org), sponsored by IBM and with sites validated by PricewaterhouseCoopers and KPMG. The validators will audit the site to check each site's privacy statement to see whether it is valid. For example, a privacy statement will describe:

- how a site collects information;
- how the information is used;
- who the information is shared with;
- how users can access and correct information;
- how users can decide to deactivate themselves from the site or withhold information from third parties.

A UK accreditation initiative aimed at *reassurance* coordinated by the Internet Media in Retail Group is ISIS, a trade group for e-retailers (Internet Shopping Is Safe) (www.imrg.org/ISIS). Another initiative, aimed at *education*, is GetSafeOnline (www.getsafeonline.org) which is a site created by government and business to educate consumers to help them understand and manage their online privacy and security.

Government initiatives will also define best practice in this area and may introduce laws to ensure guidelines are followed.

We conclude this section on privacy legislation with a checklist summary of the practical steps that are required to audit a company's compliance with data protection and privacy legislation. Companies should:

1 Follow privacy and consumer protection guidelines and laws in all local markets. Use local privacy and security certification where available.
2 Inform the user, before asking for information:
   - who the company is;
   - what personal data are collected, processed and stored;
   - what is the purpose of collection.
3 Ask for consent for collecting sensitive personal data, and it is good practice to ask before collecting any type of data.
4 Reassure customers by providing clear and effective privacy statements and explaining the purpose of data collection.
5 Let individuals know when 'cookies' or other covert software are used to collect information about them.
6 Never collect or retain personal data unless it is strictly necessary for the organization's purposes. If extra information is required for marketing purposes this should be made clear and the provision of such information should be optional.
7 Amend incorrect data when informed and tell others. Enable correction on-site.
8 Only use data for marketing (by the company, or third parties) when a user has been informed this is the case and has agreed to this. (This is opt-in.)
9 Provide the option for customers to stop receiving information. (This is opt-out.)
10 Use appropriate security technology to protect the customer information on your site.

Other e-commerce legislation

Sparrow (2000) identified eight areas of law which need to concern online marketers. Although laws have been refined since that time, this is still a useful framework.

1 Marketing your e-commerce business

Domain name

The domain name refers to the name of the web server and it is usually selected to be the same as the name of the company.

Sparrow used this category to refer to purchasing a **domain name** for a website, but other legal constraints now also fall under this category.

A Domain name registration

Most companies are likely to own several domains, perhaps for different product lines, countries or for specific marketing campaigns. Domain name disputes can arise when an individual or company has registered a domain name which another company claims they have the right to (see Chapter 3).

A related issue is brand and trademark protection. Online brand reputation management and alerting software tools offer real-time alerts when comments or mentions about a brand are posted online. Some basic tools are available including:

- Googlealert (www.googlealert.com) and Google Alerts (www.google.com/alerts) which will alert companies when any new pages appear that contain a search phrase such as your company or brand names.
- Blog Pulse (www.blogpulse.com) gives trends and listings of any phrase (see example in Figure 4.9) and individual postings can be viewed.
- Paid tools (see listing at www.davechaffey.com/online-reputation-management-tools).

B Using competitor names and trademarks in meta-tags (for search engine optimization)

Meta-tags are used to market websites by enabling them to appear more prominently in search engines as part of search engine optimization (SEO) (see Chapter 9). Some companies have tried putting a competitor company name within the meta-tags. Case law has found against companies that have used this approach. Privacy law for e-mail marketing was considered in the previous section.

C Using competitor names and trademarks in pay-per-click advertising

Pay-per-click (PPC) search marketing
A company pays for text adverts to be displayed on the search engine results pages when a specific key phrase is entered. The marketer pays for each time the link in the ad is clicked on.

A similar approach can potentially be used in **pay-per-click marketing** (see Chapter 9) to advertise on competitors' names and trademarks. For example, if a search user types 'Dell laptop' can an advertiser bid to place an ad offering an 'HP laptop'? There is less case law in this area and differing findings have occurred in the US and France. One example of the types of issue that can arise is highlighted in Box 4.5.

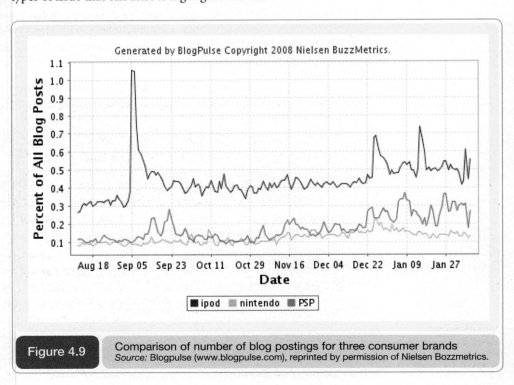

Figure 4.9	Comparison of number of blog postings for three consumer brands
	Source: Blogpulse (www.blogpulse.com), reprinted by permission of Nielsen Bozzmetrics.

Box 4.5	Who owns the term 'sport court'

This case involved two competitors who manufacture synthetic sports flooring. In 2002, Sport Court sued Rhino Sports for trademark infringement, and the parties settled with a permanent injunction restricting Rhino Sports from 'directly or indirectly using in commerce the mark SPORT COURT'. This injunction listed the digital assets or advertising where this might occur: *'on or in connection with the Internet, such as in an Internet domain name, as a sponsored link, in connection with an Internet web page, or as HTML code for an Internet website in any manner, such as the title or keyword portions of a metatag, or otherwise'.*

However, because of the broad matching facility in Google AdWords this didn't cover another activity which arose in 2006. Sport Court discovered that a Rhino Sports ad appeared as a sponsored link in response to the search term 'sport court' (without quotations) and went to court claiming that Rhino Sport was in contempt of the original injunction. However, the ad copy didn't contain the phrase 'sport court', and Rhino Sports said it bought the broad-matched keyword terms 'court' and 'basketball court', which triggered the ad. As a result, the complaint was rejected. Goldman explains:

First, the literal terms of the injunction only restrict using the term 'Sport Court ... as a sponsored link'. Arguably, invisible keyword triggering using 'Sport Court' wouldn't violate this provision. Second, Rhino Sports didn't buy the keyword 'Sport Court,' and the injunction doesn't restrict Rhino Sports' purchase of generic terms like 'court' or 'basketball court'.

This court's reasoning is solid, but I'm interested by the fact that the court didn't discuss Rhino Sports' ability to negative keyword match the phrase 'sport court'. This would be easy for Rhino Sports to do and it would appear to solve Sport Court's problem. Given that the court didn't bail the plaintiff out here, plaintiffs drafting injunctions may need to update their boilerplate injunction language to contemplate the different technologies offered by the ad networks, both now and in the future.

Source: Goldman (2007).

D Accessibility law

Accessibility legislation
Legislation intended to protect users of websites with disabilities including visual disability.

Laws relating to discriminating against disabled users who may find it more difficult to use websites because of audio, visual or motor impairment are known as **accessibility legislation**. This is often contained within disability and discrimination Acts. In the UK, the relevant Act is the Disability and Discrimination Act 1995.

Web accessibility refers to enabling all users of a website to interact with it regardless of disabilities they may have or the web browser or platform they are using. The visually impaired or blind are the main audience that designing an accessible website can help. Coverage of the requirements that accessibility places on web design are covered in Chapter 7.

Internet standards organizations such as the World Wide Web Consortium have been active in promoting guidelines for web accessibility (www.w3.org/WAI). This site describes such common accessibility problems as:

images without alternative text; lack of alternative text for imagemap hot-spots; misleading use of structural elements on pages; uncaptioned audio or undescribed video; lack of alternative information for users who cannot access frames or scripts; tables that are difficult to decipher when linearized; or sites with poor color contrast.

A tool provided to assess the WWW standards is BOBBY (http://bobby.cast.org).

In 2000, Bruce Maguire, a blind Internet user who uses a refreshable Braille display, brought a case against the Sydney Organizing Committee for the Olympic Games. Maguire successfully demonstrated deficiencies in the site which prevented him using it adequately, which were not successfully remedied. He was protected under the 1992 Australian Disability Discrimination Act and the defendant was ordered to pay AU\$20,000. This was the first case brought in the world, and it showed organizations in all countries that they could be guilty of discrimination if they did not audit their sites against accessibility guidelines. Discrimination Acts are now being amended in many countries to specifically refer to online discrimination.

2 Forming an electronic contract (contract law and distance-selling law)

We will look at two aspects of forming an electronic contract: the country of origin principle and distance-selling laws.

Country of origin principle

The contract formed between a buyer and a seller on a website will be subject to the laws of a particular country. In Europe, many such laws are specified at the regional (European Union) level, but are interpreted differently in different countries. This raises the issue of the jurisdiction in which law applies – is it that for the buyer or the seller (merchant)? In 2002 attempts were made by the EU to adopt the '*country of origin principle*', where the law for the contract will be that where the merchant is located. The Out-Law site produced by lawyers Pinsent Mason gives more information on jurisdiction (**www.out-law.com/page-479**).

Distance-selling law

Sparrow (2000) advises different forms of disclaimers to protect the retailer. For example, if a retailer made an error with the price or the product details were in error, then the retailer is not bound to honour a contract, since it was only displaying the products as 'an invitation to treat', not a fixed offer.

One e-retailer offered televisions for £2.99 due to an error in pricing a £299 product. Numerous purchases were made, but the e-retailer claimed that a contract had not been established simply by accepting the online order, although the customers did not see it that way! Unfortunately, no legal precedent was established since the case did not come to trial.

Disclaimers can also be used to limit liability if the website service causes a problem for the user, such as a financial loss resulting from an action based on erroneous content. Furthermore, Sparrow suggests that terms and conditions should be developed to refer to issues such as timing of delivery and damage or loss of goods.

The distance-selling directive also has a bearing on e-commerce contracts in the European Union. It was originally developed to protect people using mail-order (by post or phone). The main requirements are that e-commerce sites must contain easily accessible content which clearly states:

(i)   The company's identity including address.
(ii)   The main features of the goods or services.
(iii)   Price information, including tax and, if appropriate, delivery costs.
(iv)   The period for which the offer or price remains valid.
(v)   Payment, delivery and fulfilment performance arrangements.
(vi)   Right of the consumer to withdraw, i.e. cancellation terms.
(vii)   The minimum duration of the contract and whether the contract for the supply of products or services is to be permanent or recurrent, if appropriate.
(viii) Whether an equivalent product or service might be substituted, and confirmation as to whether the seller pays the return costs in this event.

After the contract has been entered into, the supplier is required to provide written confirmation of the information provided. An e-mail confirmation is now legally binding provided both parties have agreed that e-mail is an acceptable form for the contract. It is always advisable to obtain an electronic signature to confirm that both parties have agreed the contract, and this is especially valuable in the event of a dispute. The default position for services is that there is no cancellation right once services begin.

The Out-Law site also gives information on distance selling (**www.out-law.com/page-430**).

3 Making and accepting payment

For transactional e-commerce sites, the relevant laws are those referring to liability between a credit card issuer, the merchant and the buyer. Merchants need to be aware of their liability for different situations such as the customer making a fraudulent transaction.

4 Authenticating contracts concluded over the Internet

'Authentication' refers to establishing the identity of the purchaser. For example, to help prove a credit card owner is the valid owner, many sites now ask for a 3-digit authentication code. This helps reduce the risk of someone buying fraudulently who has, for instance, found a credit card number. Using digital signatures is another method of helping to prove the identity of purchasers (and merchants).

5 E-mail risks

One of the main risks with e-mail is infringing an individual's privacy. Specific laws have been developed in many countries to reduce the volume of spam, as explained in the previous section on privacy.

A further issue with e-mail is defamation, where someone makes a statement that is potentially damaging to an individual or a company. In 2000, a statement was made on the Norwich Union Healthcare internal e-mail system in England which falsely alleged that rival company WPA was under investigation and that regulators had forced them to stop accepting new business. The posting was published on the internal e-mail system, but it was not contained and became more widespread. WPA sued for libel and the case was settled out of court when Norwich Union paid £415,000 to WPA. Such cases are relatively rare.

6 Protecting intellectual property (IP)

Intellectual property rights (IPR)

Protect the intangible property created by corporations or individuals that is protected under copyright, trade secret and patent laws.

Intellectual property rights (IPR) protect designs, ideas and inventions and include content and services developed for e-commerce sites. Copyright law is designed to protect authors, producers, broadcasters and performers through ensuring they see some returns from their works every time they are experienced. The European Directive of Copyright (2001/29/EC) came into force in many countries in 2003; it covers new technologies and approaches such as streaming a broadcast via the Internet.

IP can be misappropriated in two senses online.

First, an organization's IP may be misappropriated: it is relatively easy to copy web content and republish on another site. Reputation management services can be used to assess how an organization's content, logos and **trademarks** are being used on other websites. Tools such as Copyscape (www.copyscape.com) can be used to identify infringement of content where it is 'scraped' off other sites using 'screenscrapers'.

Trademark

A trademark is a unique word or phrase that distinguishes your company. The mark can be registered as plain or designed text, artwork or a combination.

Secondly, an organization may misappropriate content inadvertently. Some employees may infringe copyright if they are not aware of the law. Additionally, some methods of designing transactional websites have been patented. For example, Amazon has patented its 'One-click' purchasing option.

7 Advertising on the Internet

Advertising standards that are enforced by independent agencies such as the UK's Advertising Standards Authority Code also apply in the Internet environment. They are traditionally less strongly policed, leading to more 'edgy' creative executions online which are intended to have a viral effect.

The Out-Law site gives more information (www.out-law.com/page-5604).

8 Data protection

Data protection has been referred to in depth in the previous section.

Environmental and green issues related to Internet usage

The future state of our planet is a widely held social concern. Technology is generally seen as detrimental to the environment, but there are some arguments that e-commerce and digital communications can have environmental benefits. Companies can sometimes also make cost savings while positioning themselves as environmentally concerned – see Box 4.6.

Potentially, online shopping can also have environment benefits. Imagine a situation where we no longer travelled to the shops, and 100% of items were efficiently delivered to us at home or at work. This would reduce traffic considerably! Although this situation is inconceivable, online shopping is growing considerably and it may be having an impact. Research by the Internet Media in Retail Group (www.imrg.org) shows the growing importance of e-commerce in the UK where over 10% of retail sales are now online. In 2007 IMRG launched a Go Green, Go Online campaign where it identified six reasons why it believes e-commerce is green. They are:

| Box 4.6 | HSBC customers plant virtual forest |

HSBC has committed to improving the environment since it became a climate-neutral company globally in November 2005. Through the use of green technologies and emission-offset trading, HSBC counteracts all CO_2 emissions generated by its building operations and corporate travel. In 2006, 35% of operations in North America were offset by investments in Renewable Energy Certificates from wind power alone.

Another aspect of HSBC green policy is its online banking service, where it encourages paperless billing. For example, in the UK in 2007, over 400,000 customers switched from paper statements to online delivery, creating a virtual tree each time (Figure 4.10), and for every 20 virtual trees, HSBC promised to plant a real one.

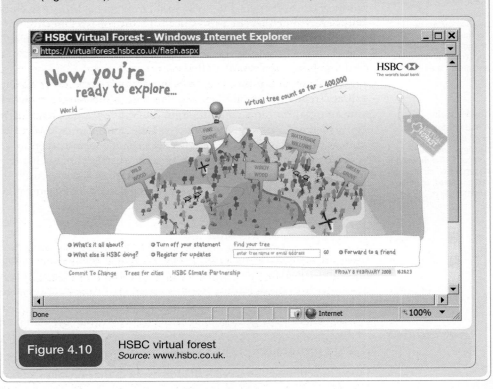

| Figure 4.10 | HSBC virtual forest |

Source: www.hsbc.co.uk.

1 *Less vehicle-miles.* Shopping is the most frequent reason for car travel in the UK, accounting for 20% of all trips, and for 12% of mileage. A study by the Swiss online grocer LeShop.ch calculated that each time a customer decides to buy online rather than go shopping by car, 3.5 kg of CO_2 emissions are saved.

2 *Lower inventory requirements.* The trend towards pre-selling online – i.e. taking orders for products before they are built, as implemented by Dell – avoids the production of obsolete goods that have to be disposed of if they don't sell, with associated wastage in energy and natural resources.

3 *Fewer printed materials.* Online e-newsletters and brochures replace their physical equivalent so saving paper and distribution costs. Data from the Direct Mail Information Service (www.dmis.co.uk) show that direct mail volumes have fallen. This must be partly due to marketing e-mails which the DMA e-mail benchmarks (www.dma.org.uk) show number in their billions in the UK alone.

4 *Less packaging.* Although theoretically there is less need for fancy packaging if an item is sold online this argument is less convincing, since most items like software or electronic items still come in packaging. At least those billions of music tracks downloaded don't require any packaging or plastic.

5 *Less waste.* Across the whole supply chain of procurement, manufacturing and distribution the Internet can help reduce product and distribution cycles. Some even claim that auction services like eBay and Amazon Marketplace can promote recycling and reuse.

6 *Dematerialization.* Better known as 'digitization', this is the availability of products like software, music and video in digital form.

If companies trading online can explain these benefits to their customers effectively, as HSBC has done, then this can benefit these online channels.

But how much could e-shopping reduce greenhouse gas emissions? A study by Finnish researchers Siikavirta *et al.* (2003), limited to e-grocery shopping, has suggested that it is theoretically possible to reduce the greenhouse gas emissions generated by grocery shopping by 18% to 87% compared with the situation in which household members go to the store. The researchers estimated that this would lead to a reduction of all Finland's greenhouse gas emissions of as much as 1%, but in reality the figure is much lower since only 10% of grocery shopping trips are online.

Cairns (2005) has completed a study for the UK which shows the importance of grocery shopping – she estimates that car travel for food and other household items represents about 40% of all UK shopping trips by car, and about 5% of all car use. She considers that a direct substitution of car trips by van trips could reduce vehicle-km by 70% or more. A broader study by Ahmed and Sharma (2006) used value chain analysis to assess the role of the Internet in changing the amount of energy and materials consumed by businesses for each part of the supply chain. However, no estimates of savings are made.

Taxation

How to change tax laws to reflect globalization through the Internet is a problem that many governments have grappled with. The fear is that the Internet may cause significant reductions in tax revenues to national or local governments if existing laws do not cover changes in purchasing patterns. Basu (2007) notes that around a third of government taxation revenue is from domestic consumption tax with revenue from import taxation around 17%. Governments are clearly keen that this revenue is protected.

Government revenue is normally protected since, taking the UK as an example, when goods are imported from a non-EU territory, an excise duty is charged at the same rate as VAT. While this can be levied for physical goods imported by air and sea it is less easy to administer for services. Here agreements have to be reached with individual suppliers.

In Europe, the use of online betting in lower-tax areas such as Gibraltar has resulted in lower revenues to governments in the countries where consumers would have formerly paid gaming tax to the government via a betting shop. Large UK bookmakers such as William Hill and Victor Chandler are offering Internet-based betting from 'offshore' locations. Retailers have set up retail operations on Jersey to sell items such as DVDs and CDs which cost less than an £18 Low Value Consignment Relief threshold, so no VAT or excise duty needs to be paid.

This trend has been dubbed LOCI or 'location-optimized commerce on the Internet' by Mougayer (1998).

Since the Internet supports the global marketplace it could be argued that it makes little sense to introduce tariffs on goods and services delivered over the Internet. Such instruments would, in any case, be impossible to apply to products delivered electronically. This position is currently that of the USA. In the document 'A Framework for Global Electronic Commerce', President Clinton stated that:

> *The United States will advocate in the World Trade Organization (WTO) and other appropriate international fora that the Internet be declared a tariff-free zone.*

Tax jurisdiction

Tax jurisdiction determines which country gets tax income from a transaction. Under the pre-electronic commerce system of international tax treaties, the right to tax was divided between the country where the enterprise that receives the income is resident ('residence country') and that from which the enterprise derives that income ('source country'). In 2002, the EU enacted two laws (Council Directive 2002/38/EC and Council Regulation (EC) 792/2002) on how value added tax (VAT) was to be charged and collected for electronic services. These were in accordance with the principles agreed within the framework of the Organization for Economic Co-operation and Development (OECD) at a 1998 conference in Ottawa. These principles establish that the rules for consumption taxes (such as VAT) should result in taxation in the jurisdiction where consumption takes place (the country of origin principle referred to above). These laws helped to make European countries more competitive in e-commerce.

The OECD also agreed that a simplified online registration scheme, as now adopted by the European Council, is the only viable option today for applying taxes to e-commerce sales by non-resident traders. The tax principles are as follows in the UK interpretation of this law implemented in 2003 for these electronic services:

- supply of websites or web-hosting services
- downloaded software (including updates of software)
- downloaded images, text or information, including making databases available
- digitized books or other electronic publications
- downloaded music, films or games
- electronic auctions or
- Internet service packages.

The UK VAT rules are as follows:

- if the supplier (residence) and the customer (source) are both in the UK, VAT will be chargeable;
- exports to private customers in the EU will attract either UK VAT or local VAT;
- exports outside the EU will be zero-rated (but tax may be levied on imports);
- imports into the UK from the EU or beyond will attract local VAT, or UK import tax when received through customs (for which overseas suppliers need to register);
- services attract VAT according to where the supplier is located. This is different from products and causes anomalies if online services are created. This law has since been reviewed.

Freedom-restrictive legislation

Although governments enact legislation in order to protect consumer privacy on the Internet, some individuals and organizations believe that legislation may also be too restrictive. In the UK, a new Telecommunications Act and Regulation of Investigatory Powers Act (RIP) took several years to enact since it involved giving security forces the ability to monitor all communications passing through ISPs. This was fiercely contested due to cost burdens placed on infrastructure providers and in particular ISPs, and of course many citizens and employees were not happy about being monitored either!

Freedom House (www.freedomhouse.org) is a human rights organization created to reduce censorship. It notes in a report (Freedom House, 2000) that governments in many countries, both developed and developing, are increasingly censoring online content. Only 69 of the countries studied have completely free media, while 51 have partly free media and 66 countries suffer heavy government censorship. Censorship methods include implementing licensing and regulation laws, applying existing print and broadcast restrictions to the Internet, filtering content and direct censoring after dissemination. In Asia and the Middle East, governments frequently cite protection of morality and local values as reasons for censorship. Even the US government tried to control access to certain Internet sites with the Communications Decency Act in 1996, but this was unsuccessful. Refer to Activity 4.4 to discuss these issues.

Activity 4.4	Government and company monitoring of electronic communications

Purpose

To examine the degree to which governments and organizations should monitor electronic communications.

Activity

Write down the arguments for and against each of these statements, debate individually or as a group to come to a consensus:

1 *'This house believes that organizations have no right to monitor employees' use of e-mail or the web.'* Use Moreover (www.moreover.com) to research recent cases where employees have been dismissed for accessing or sending e-mails or web content that is deemed unsuitable. Is this just used as an excuse for dismissing staff?

2 *'This house believes that governments have no right to monitor all Internet-based communications passing through ISPs.'* Use Moreover (www.moreover.com) to research action taken by the government of your country to monitor and control Internet communications.

What action do you think managers should take with regard to monitoring employee access? Should laws be set at a national level or should action be taken by individual companies?

Answers to activities can be found at www.pearsoned.co.uk/chaffey

Economic and competitive factors

E-economy
The dynamic system of interactions between a nation's citizens, the businesses and government that capitalize upon online technology to achieve a social or economic good.

The economic health and competitive environment in different countries will determine their e-commerce potential. Managers developing e-commerce strategies in multinational companies will initially target the countries that are most developed in the use of the technology. A comprehensive framework for assessing an '**e-economy**' has been developed by Booz Allen Hamilton (2002). The report authors define the e-economy as:

> *the dynamic system of interactions between a nation's citizens, the businesses and government that capitalize upon online technology to achieve a social or economic good.*

The framework is based upon four layers of environment, readiness, uptake and use, and impact, and three major stakeholder groups: citizens, businesses and government, as shown in Figure 4.11.

A review of how different governments have tried to improve the health of their e-economies is presented later in this chapter.

Knowledge of different economic conditions is also part of budgeting for revenue from different countries. In China there is regulation of foreign ownership of Internet portals and ISPs which could hamper development.

The trend towards globalization can arguably insulate a company to some extent from fluctuations in regional markets, but is, of course, no protection from a global recession. Managers can also study e-commerce in leading countries to help predict future e-commerce trends in their own country.

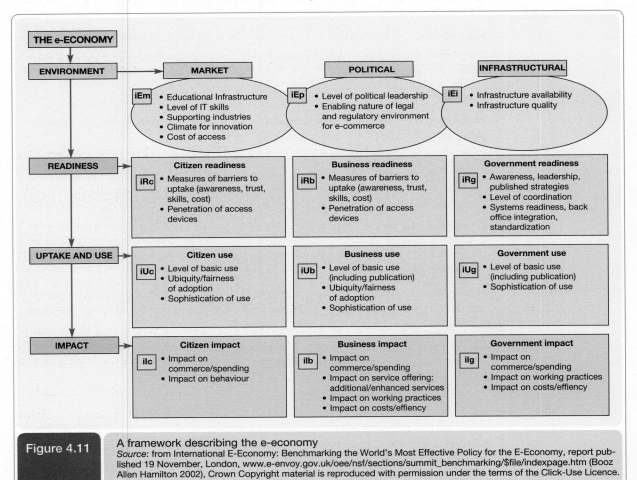

Figure 4.11

A framework describing the e-economy
Source: from International E-Economy: Benchmarking the World's Most Effective Policy for the E-Economy, report published 19 November, London, www.e-envoy.gov.uk/oee/nsf/sections/summit_benchmarking/$file/indexpage.htm (Booz Allen Hamilton 2002), Crown Copyright material is reproduced with permission under the terms of the Click-Use Licence.

Globalization
The increase of international trading and shared social and cultural values.

Globalization refers to the move towards international trading in a single global market-place and also to blurring of social and cultural differences between countries. We saw in Chapter 1 that for both SMEs and larger organizations, electronic communications gives the opportunity for increasing the reach of the company to achieve sales around the world.

Quelch and Klein (1996) point out some of the obvious consequences for organizations that wish to compete in the global marketplace; they say a company must have:

- *a 24-hour order-taking and customer service response capability;*
- *regulatory and customs-handling experience to ship internationally;*
- *in-depth understanding of foreign marketing environments to assess the advantages of its own products and services.*

Language and cultural understanding may also present a problem and an SME is unlikely to possess the resources to develop a multi-language version of its site or employ staff with sufficient language skills. Similarly, Quelch and Klein (1996) note that the growth of the use of the Internet for business will accelerate the trend of English becoming the lingua franca of commerce. Tailoring e-commerce services for individual countries or regions is referred to as **localization**. A website may need to support customers from a range of countries with:

Localization
Tailoring of website information for individual countries or regions.

- different product needs;
- language differences;
- cultural differences.

The importance of localization is highlighted by a report by Common Sense Advisory (2002). According to them, for many US Fortune 500 firms, non-US revenue – or what they refer to as 'xenorevenue' – accounts for 20 to more than 50% of their global income. A similar situation is likely to exist for non-US multinational organizations.

It may be necessary to vary:

- The language that content is provided in.
- Tone and style of copy.
- Site design – certain colours or images may be unsuitable or less effective in some countries.
- Range of product offerings.
- Product pricing.
- Promotional offers used to encourage acquisition of customer e-mail address (see Chapter 9). This may be affected by local data protection, taxation and trading laws.
- Local contact points.

Localization will address all these issues. In order to be effective, a website often needs more than translation, since different promotion concepts may be needed for different countries. For example, Durex (www.durex.com) localizes content for many countries since language and the way in which sexual issues can be discussed vary greatly. 3M (www.3m.com), however, only localizes content in local language for some countries such as France, Germany and Spain. For large multinational companies, localization is a significant strategic issue for e-commerce. The decision on the level of localization will need to be taken on a regional or country basis to prioritize different countries according to the size of the market and the importance of having localization.

Singh and Pereira (2005) provide an evaluation framework for the level of localization:

1 **Standardized websites (not localized).** A single site serves all customer segments (domestic and international).
2 **Semi-localized websites.** A single site serves all customers; however, there will be contact information about foreign subsidiaries available for international customers.

3 **Localized websites**. Country-specific websites with language translation for international customers, wherever relevant.

4 **Highly localized websites**. Country-specific websites with language translation; they also include other localization efforts in terms of time, date, postcode, currency formats, etc.

5 **Culturally customized websites**. Websites reflecting complete 'immersion' in the culture of target customer segments.

Deciding on the degree of localization is a difficult challenge for managers since while it has been established that local preferences are significant, it is often difficult to balance costs against the likely increase or conversion rate. In a survey published in *Multilingual* (2008), 88% of managers at multinational companies stated that localization is a key issue, with 76% of them saying that it is important specifically for international customer satisfaction. Yet, over half of these respondents also admitted that they allocate only between 1% and 5% of their overall budget for localization.

An indication of the importance of localization in different cultures has been completed by Nitish *et al.* (2006) for the German, Indian and Chinese cultures, assessing localized websites in terms not only of content, but cultural values such as collectivism, individualism, uncertainty avoidance and masculinity. The survey suggests that without cultural adaptation, confidence or flow falls, so resulting in lower purchase intent.

A further aspect of localization to be considered is search engine optimization (SEO, see Chapter 9) since sites which have local language versions will be listed more prominently by local versions of the search engines. Many specialist companies have been created to help manage these content localization issues for companies, for example agency Web Certain maintains a forum advising on localization (www.multilingual-seo.com).

One example of the effect of localization on conversion rates is provided by MySpace CEO Mike Katz, who stated in NMA (2008) that: 'All the 27 sites are localised, we don't believe that one size fits all. We know that from the first day we localise in any language, we triple our sign-ups on original users.' In 2008, 45 million of the 130 million MySpace users were outside the US; new sites were planned for Russia, India, Poland and Korea, each requiring a local version.

To explore the implications of globalization for consumer-oriented companies, refer to Case study 4.1.

Case Study 4.1 — The implications of globalization for consumer attitudes

The article starts by discussing anti-globalization. It then explores the implications of variations in the characteristics of different cultures on businesses providing services to them. At the end of the article, research about attitudes to globalization is summarized, along with its implications for businesses trading internationally.

Globalisation, or maybe more specifically, anti-globalisation issues, are never far from the headlines, whether it's coverage of the latest anti-WTO demonstration or news that McDonald's has replaced Ronald McDonald in France with Asterix – in a move to 'appease anti-globalisation protesters'.

But what does globalisation actually mean? Stemming from the application of free market principles it has manifested the belief that the world is small and that consumers are becoming more and more alike,

thus allowing companies to use the same advertising and marketing across regions and countries. Such a doctrine has enabled companies to act global and think global, much to the distaste of the anti-globalisation lobbies. Indeed, in 1985 it was Friends of the Earth that coined the slogan 'think global, act local' in its desire to counter such global forces – particularly with regards to environmental issues.

However, such 'glocalisation' [global localisation] makes a lot of sense for multinational companies operating today and planning new market entry, for a number of reasons. Firstly, the term globalisation for many Europeans is virtually synonymous with that of 'Americanisation'. For some this has negative connotations of materialism, loss of native culture and the encroachment of the English language. At its extreme, it drives many of the anti-globalisation activists. Thus there is real risk that companies will damage their brand and reputation if they don't recognise the importance of localisation when considering market entry.

Secondly, consumers are as different as they are similar – local and regional cultures have a profound effect in shaping consumer demand. These differences are potentially more interesting than the similarities, in that they can allow product and service differentiation as well as new approaches to segmentation and marketing communications. To take advantage of such opportunities, businesses have to have a clear insight into how and why consumers in one market may differ from ones in another.

Feelings of anti-Americanisation are a strong undercurrent in Europe. Businesses have to plan how to counter such a groundswell of feeling if planning on entering new markets – given that some 50% of Europeans believe that 'our society is too Americanised' and such an attitude has increased over the past 10 years. While the degree of agreement varies within Europe (e.g. 67% of Spaniards agreeing with the statement, as compared with 44% of Brits) it is a significant influence of customer behaviour. To compound matters, multinational companies are the least trusted of 27 entities when European consumers have been asked to state which they trust to be honest and fair.

As a result, not only have we seen an increase in consumer activism (such as anti-WTO protests, growth of the slow food movement in Europe etc.), but also we have seen global brands coming under threat from emergent local brands which are gaining in currency. We would expect this to continue. This is not to say that there is no room for global brands! Many global brands have successfully tapped into local culture and tastes and recognised the need to either modify the product/ service completely or change different elements of the offer and how it is ultimately marketed. Thus companies expanding into new geographic markets have to ensure that their strategies are based on a real understanding of regional and local markets.

Globalisation is not making the world a smaller, homogeneous place. While this presents many opportunities for businesses, it also implies a need for a clear understanding of what shapes consumer needs and desires in the different nations. Not surprising perhaps that many businesses found the notion of a 'globalised' world compelling given the significant implications for researching a multitude of different markets in terms of time and money budgets. Similarly, it is easy to understand the temptation of taking well-established national stereotypes and assuming that they are representative of the truth.

Recent attitudinal studies in Europe and the US undertaken by the Henley Centre show the complexity of attempting to categorise consumers on a broad scale. Let's take an example. At one level, results show that all consumers take pride in their family, so a global advertising campaign using the 'family' as a theme may feel like safe territory. To some extent it is. Dig down a bit deeper, however, and you find that different people define 'family' in very different ways, so what people take pride in will be subtly different. At a country level, many more differences expose themselves.

Businesses wanting to broaden their geographic reach have to consider at a strategic level what level of understanding of consumer needs they require. Generalisations are important and are a good place to start, but it is critical to then delve further – national stereotypes are too simplistic. Differences, rather than similarities, have to be considered, and interrogated in terms of how these will impact customer needs.

Source: The Henley Centre (www.henleycentre.com).

Question

Based on this article and your experiences, debate the statement: 'Site localization is essential for each country for an e-commerce offering to be successful in that country.'

The implications of e-commerce for international B2B trading

Hamill and Gregory (1997) highlight the strategic implications of e-commerce for international business-to-business trading. They note that there will be increasing standardization of prices across borders as businesses become more aware of price differentials. Secondly, they predict that the importance of traditional intermediaries such as agents and distributors will be reduced by Internet-enabled direct marketing and sales.

Larger organizations typically already compete in the global marketplace, or have the financial resources to achieve this. But what about the smaller organization? Most governments are encouraging SMEs to use electronic commerce to tap into the international market. Hamill and Gregory (1997) identify the barriers to SME internationalization shown in Table 4.7. Complete Activity 4.5 to look at the actions that can be taken to overcome these barriers.

More recent research suggests SMEs have been relatively slow to adopt the Internet. Research by Arnott and Bridgewater (2002) tests the level of sophistication by which SMEs are using the Internet (see stage models in Chapter 5). They find that the majority of firms are using the Internet for information provision rather than interactive, relationship-building or transactional facilities. Smaller firms are using significantly fewer Internet tools than their larger counterparts. Quayle (2002) has assessed issues considered by SMEs to be strategically important. In the UK 298 SMEs were surveyed. Issues of marketing, leadership and waste reduction were given highest priority and supplier development, financial management, time to market and supply chain management were medium priority. Perhaps unsurprisingly, the lowest priority was given to technology, research and development, e-commerce, customer management and purchasing – all closely related to e-business. In further research, Meckel *et al.* (2004) analysed e-business adoption by several hundred SMEs in the NW of England and found that fewer than 15% had formal, documented e-business strategies.

Activity 4.5	Overcoming SME resistance to international e-commerce

Purpose

To highlight barriers to exporting amongst SMEs and suggest measures by which they may be overcome by governments.

Activity

For each of the four barriers to internationalization given in Table 4.7 suggest the management reasons why the barriers may exist and actions that governments can take to overcome these barriers. Evaluate how well the government in your country communicates the benefits of e-commerce through education and training.

Table 4.7	Issues in SME resistance to exporting

Barrier	Management issues	How can barrier be overcome?
1 Psychological		
2 Operational		
3 Organizational		
4 Product/market		

Source: Barriers from Hamill and Gregory (1997) and Poon and Jevons (1997).

Answers to activities can be found at www.pearsoned.co.uk/chaffey

Political factors

The political environment is shaped by the interplay of government agencies, public opinion, consumer pressure groups such as CAUCE (the Coalition Against Unsolicited E-mail – www.cauce.org), and industry-backed organizations such as TRUSTe (www.truste.org) that promote best practice amongst companies.

Political action enacted through government agencies to control the adoption of the Internet can include:

- promoting the benefits of adopting the Internet for consumers and business to improve a country's economic prosperity;
- enacting legislation to protect privacy or control taxation, as described in previous sections;
- providing organizations with guidelines and assistance for compliance with legislation;
- setting up international bodies to coordinate the Internet (see Chapter 3).

Political involvement in many of these activities is intended to improve the economic competitiveness of countries or groups of countries. Quayle (2002) summarizes six strands of the UK government strategy for e-commerce which are intended to increase industry competitiveness:

1 Establish a brand in e-commerce both domestically and internationally.
2 Transform existing businesses.
3 Foster e-commerce creation and growth.
4 Expand the e-commerce talent pool (skills).
5 Provide leadership in international e-commerce policy development.
6 Government online should be a priority.

These goals are typical for many countries and specific targets are set for the proportion of people and businesses that have access, including public access points for those who cannot currently afford the technology. Managers who are aware of these initiatives can tap into sources of funding for development or free training to support their online initiatives. Alternatively, there may be incentives such as tax breaks.

The European Commission (EC) provides some other examples of the role of government organizations in promoting and regulating e-commerce:

Information society
A society with widespread access to and transfer of digital information within business and the community.

- The EC Information Society initiative was launched in 1998 with the aims of increasing public awareness of the impact of the **information society** and stimulating people's motivation and ability to participate (reducing social exclusion); increasing socio-economic benefits and enhancing the role of Europe in influencing the global information society. Information society was defined by the UK INSINC working party on social inclusion in the information society in 1997 as:

    A society characterized by a high level of information intensity in the everyday life of most citizens, in most organizations and workplaces; by the use of common or compatible technology for a wide range of personal, social, educational and business activities; and by the ability to transmit and receive digital data rapidly between places irrespective of distance.

    UNESCO has also been active in advancing the information society in less developed countries (http://portal.unesco.org/ci).

- The European Community has set up 'i2010' (*European Information Society in 2010*) whose aims include:

    providing an integrated approach to information society and audio-visual policies in the EU, covering regulation, research, and deployment and promoting cultural diversity.
    (eEurope, 2005)

- In 1998 new data protection guidelines were enacted to help protect consumers and increase the adoption of e-commerce by reducing security fears. Since 2000, cross-Europe laws have been enacted to control online consumer privacy, electronic selling and taxation.

Booz Allen Hamilton (2002) review approaches used by governments to encourage use of the Internet. They identify five broad themes in policy:

1 *Increasing the penetration of 'access devices'.* Approaches include either home access through Sweden's PC Tax Reform, or in public places, as in France's programme to develop 7,000 access points by a specific year/target date. France also offers a tax incentive scheme, where firms can make tax-free gifts of PCs to staff for personal use.
2 *Increasing skills and confidence of target groups.* These may target potentially excluded groups, as with France's €150 million campaign to train the unemployed. Japan's IT training programmes use existing mentors.
3 *Establishing 'driving licences' or 'passport' qualifications.* France, Italy and the UK have schemes which grant simple IT qualifications, particularly aimed at low-skilled groups.
4 *Building trust, or allaying fears.* The US 1998 Child Online Protection Act used schemes to provide 'kitemark'-type verification, or certification of safe services.
5 *Direct marketing campaigns.* According to the report, only the UK, with its UK Online campaign, is marketing directly to citizens on a large scale.

Internet governance

Internet governance
Control of the operation and use of the Internet.

Internet governance describes the control put in place to manage the growth of the Internet and its usage – as discussed in Chapter 3.

Dyson (1998) describes the different layers of jurisdiction. These are:

1 Physical space comprising each individual country where its own laws hold.
2 ISPs – the connection between the physical and virtual worlds.
3 Domain name control (www.icann.net) and communities.
4 Agencies such as TRUSTe (www.truste.org).

The organizations that manage the infrastructure also have a significant role in governance.

E-government

E-government
The application of e-commerce technologies to government and public services.

E-government is distinct from Internet governance. In Chapter 1, we noted that e-government is a major strategic priority for many countries. To achieve the potential cost savings, some governments have set targets for both buy- and sell-side e-government. In the UK, the government's main target was:

That by 2005, 100% of dealings with Government should be capable of being delivered electronically, where there is a demand.

Although this target is to be applauded, one can view this as the UK government's dot-com investment. Although many services have been created, adoption rates tend to be low and the government is having to invest in marketing usage of these services.

In Australia, the National Office for the Information Economy, NOIE (www.noie.gov.au), has created a strategic framework which has the following themes. This summarizes the types of actions that many governments are taking to encourage e-business within their countries.

Debate 4.2

Getting value from e-government

'Efforts by national governments to deliver e-government services for citizens represent a massive waste of public money, given the limited demand for these services.'

1 *Access, participation and skills* – Encouraging all sectors of the community to actively participate in the information economy.

2 *Adoption of e-business* – The government is working to provide more efficient communication between businesses to help improve the productivity of the Australian economy.

3 *Confidence, trust and security* – The government is working to build public trust and confidence in going online, and addressing barriers to consumer confidence in e-commerce and other areas of online content and activity.

4 *E-government strategies and implementation* – The use of new technologies for government information provision, service delivery and administration has the potential to transform government, which will improve the lives of Australians.

5 *Environment for information economy firms* – Provide research on the environmental variables that drive innovation and growth in the information economy and underpin its future development.

6 *International dimensions* – NOIE, in cooperation with other government bodies, represents Australia in world forums where decisions are made that may affect national interests in the information economy.

Mini Case Study 4.1   SourceUK

SourceUK (www.sourceuk.org.uk) is a successful e-government initiative that has been responsible for the delivery and the management of the busiest electronic communication and e-procurement channels to UK government and wider public-sector departments in line with the Modernising Government Agenda legislation. Approximately 250,000 senior managers, budget holders and decision makers have direct access to the channels for their on-the-minute must-have news and information needs and for the sourcing of their goods and services.

SourceUK is proven to be one of the most accredited, respected, well known and busiest portals of its sort available to this marketplace. The portal is currently receiving on average 500,000 visits each month.

Source: SourceUK e-mail alert, 2008.

Technological innovation and technology assessment

One of the great challenges of managing e-commerce is the need to be able to assess which new technological innovations can be applied to give competitive advantage – what is 'the next big thing'? The truth is no one can predict the future, and many companies have misunderstood the market for products:

> *This 'telephone' has too many shortcomings to be seriously considered as a means of communication. The device is inherently of no value to us.*
>
> Western Union internal memo, 1876

> *Who the hell wants to hear actors talk?*
>
> H. M. Warner, Warner Brothers, 1927

> *I think there is a world market for maybe five computers.*
>
> Thomas Watson, chairman of IBM, 1943

> *There is no reason for any individual to have a computer in their home.*
>
> Ken Olson (President of Digital Equipment Corporation) at the Convention of the World Future Society in Boston in 1977

I personally believe the best that organizations can do is to analyse the current situation and respond rapidly where appropriate. As the Canadian science-fiction writer William Gibson said:

The future is here. It's just not widely distributed yet.

A slightly different, and more forward-looking, perspective came from Bruce Toganizzi, who founded the Human Interface Team at Apple and developed the company's first interface guidelines (E-consultancy, 2007):

Successful technology-predicting is based on detecting discontinuities and predicting the trends that will flow from them.

He gives the example of the introduction of the Apple iPhone and the other devices based on gestural interfaces that will follow.

In addition to technologies deployed on the website, the suitability of new approaches for attracting visitors to the site must be evaluated – for example, should registration at a paid-for search engine, or new forms of banner adverts or e-mail marketing be used (Chapter 9)? Decisions on strategy are covered in Chapter 5.

When a new technique is introduced, a manager faces a difficult decision as to whether to:

- Ignore the use of the technique, perhaps because it is felt to be too expensive or untried, or the manager simply doesn't believe the benefits will outweigh the costs – a cautious, 'wait-and-see' approach.
- Enthusiastically adopt the technique without a detailed evaluation since the hype alone convinces the manager that the technique should be adopted – a risk-taking, early-adopter approach.
- Evaluate the technique and then take a decision whether to adopt it according to the evaluation – an intermediate approach.

Early adopters
Companies or departments that invest in new technologies and techniques.

This diffusion–adoption process (represented by the bell curve in Figure 4.12) was identified by Rogers (1983), who classified those trialling new products as innovators, **early adopters**, early majority, late majority, or laggards.

Figure 4.12 can be used in two main ways as an analytical tool. First, it can be used to understand the stage customers have reached in adoption of a technology, or any product. For example, the Internet is now a well-established tool and in many developed countries we are into the late majority phase of adoption, which suggests it is essential to use this

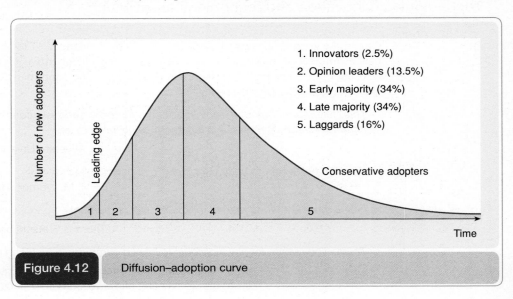

1. Innovators (2.5%)
2. Opinion leaders (13.5%)
3. Early majority (34%)
4. Late majority (34%)
5. Laggards (16%)

Conservative adopters

Number of new adopters

Leading edge

Time

Figure 4.12 Diffusion–adoption curve

medium for marketing purposes. Second, managers can look at adoption of a new technique by other businesses – from an organizational perspective. For example, an online supermarket could look at how many other e-tailers have adopted personalization to evaluate whether it is worthwhile adopting the technique.

An alternative graphic representation of diffusion of innovation has been developed by technology analyst Gartner for assessing the maturity, adoption and business application of specific technologies (Figure 4.13). Gartner (2010) recognizes the following stages within a **hype cycle**, an example of which is given in Figure 4.13 for trends current in 2010:

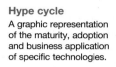

Hype cycle

A graphic representation of the maturity, adoption and business application of specific technologies.

1 **Technology trigger** – The first phase of a hype cycle is the 'technology trigger' or breakthrough, product launch or other event that generates significant press and interest.
2 **Peak of inflated expectations** – In the next phase, a frenzy of publicity typically generates over-enthusiasm and unrealistic expectations. There may be some successful applications of a technology, but there are typically more failures.
3 **Trough of disillusionment** – Technologies enter the 'trough of disillusionment' because they fail to meet expectations and quickly become unfashionable. Consequently, the press usually abandons the topic and the technology.
4 **Slope of enlightenment** – Although the press may have stopped covering the technology, some businesses continue through the 'slope of enlightenment' and experiment to understand the benefits and practical application of the technology.
5 **Plateau of productivity** – A technology reaches the 'plateau of productivity' as the benefits of it become widely demonstrated and accepted. The technology becomes increasingly

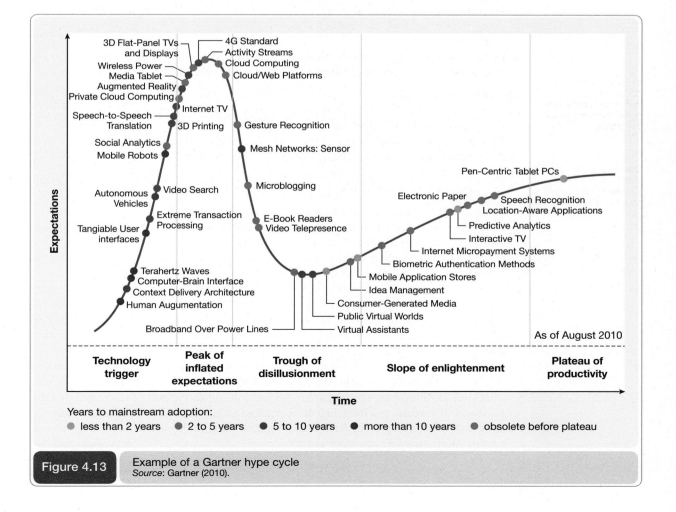

| Figure 4.13 | Example of a Gartner hype cycle
Source: Gartner (2010). |

stable and evolves in second and third generations. The final height of the plateau varies according to whether the technology is broadly applicable or benefits only a niche market.

Trott (1998) identifies different requirements that are necessary within an organization to be able to respond effectively to technological change or innovation:

- *Growth orientation* – a long-term rather than short-term vision.
- *Vigilance* – the capability of environment scanning.
- *Commitment to technology* – willingness to invest in technology.
- *Acceptance of risk* – willingness to take managed risks.
- *Cross-functional cooperation* – capability for collaboration across functional areas.
- *Receptivity* – the ability to respond to externally developed technology.
- *Slack* – allowing time to investigate new technological opportunities.
- *Adaptability* – a readiness to accept change.
- *Diverse range of skills* – technical and business skills and experience.

The problem with being an early adopter (as an organization) is that the leading edge is often also referred to as the 'bleeding edge' due to the risk of failure. New technologies will have bugs, may integrate poorly with the existing systems, or the marketing benefits may simply not live up to their promise. Of course, the reason for risk taking is that the rewards are high – if you are using a technique that your competitors are not, then you will gain an edge on your rivals.

Approaches to identifying emerging technology

PMP (2008) describes four contrasting approaches to identifying new technologies, which may give a company a competitive edge:

Technology scouting
A structured approach to reviewing technology innovations akin to football scouting.

1 *Technology networking.* Individuals monitor trends through their personal network and **technology scouting** and then share them through an infrastructure and process that supports information sharing. PMP (2008) explains that Novartis facilitates sharing between inside and outside experts on specific technologies through an extranet and face-to-face events.

Crowdsourcing
Utilizing a network of customers or other partners to gain insights for new product or process innovations.

2 *Crowdsourcing.* **Crowdsourcing** facilitates access to a marketplace of ideas from customers, partners or inventors for organizations looking to solve specific problems. Lego is well known for involving customers in discussion of new product developments. InnoCentive (Figure 4.14) is one of the largest commercial examples of crowdsourcing. It is an online marketplace which connects and manages the relationship between 'seekers' and 'solvers'. Seekers are the companies conducting research and development that are looking for new solutions to their business challenges and opportunities. Solvers are the 170,000 registered members of InnoCentive who can win cash prizes ranging from $5,000 to $1,000,000 for solving problems in a variety of domains including business and technology.

3 *Technology hunting.* This is a structured review of new technology through reviewing the capabilities of start-up companies. For example, British Telecom undertakes a structured review of up to 1,000 start-ups to assess relevance for improving their own capabilities which may ultimately be reduced to five companies that BT will enter into a formal arrangement with each year.

4 *Technology mining.* A traditional literature review of technologies described in published documents. Deutsche Telekom AG use technology to automate the process through software such as Autonomy which searches for patterns indicating potential technology solutions within patents, articles, journals, technological reports and trend studies. A simpler approach is setting up a keyword search for technologies through a free service such as Google Alerts (www.google.com/alerts).

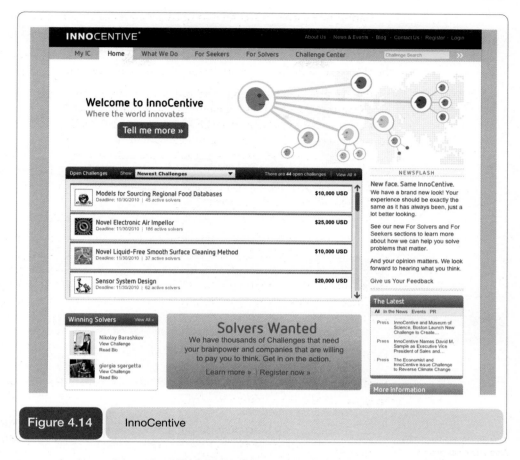

Figure 4.14	InnoCentive

It may also be useful to identify how rapidly a new concept is being adopted. When a product or service is adopted quickly this is known as 'rapid diffusion'. Access to the Internet is an example of this – in developed countries the use of the Internet has become widespread more rapidly than the use of TV, for example. Internet-enabled mobile phones are relatively slow-diffusion products.

So, what action should e-commerce managers take when confronted by new techniques and technologies? There is no straightforward rule of thumb, other than that a balanced approach must be taken. It would be easy to dismiss many new techniques as fads, or classify them as 'not relevant to my market'. However, competitors will probably be reviewing new techniques and incorporating some, so a careful review of new techniques is required. This indicates that benchmarking of 'best of breed' sites within sectors and in different sectors is essential as part of environmental scanning. However, by waiting for others to innovate and reviewing the results on their website, a company may have already lost 6 to 12 months.

Figure 4.15 summarizes the choices. The stepped curve I shows the variations in technology through time. Some may be small incremental changes such as a new operating system, others such as the introduction of personalization technology are more significant in delivering value to customers and so improving business performance. Line A is a company that is using innovative business techniques, that adopts technology early, or is even in advance of what the technology can currently deliver. Line C shows the conservative adopter whose use of technology lags behind the available potential. Line B, the middle ground, is probably the ideal situation where a company monitors new ideas as early adopters trial them and then adopts those that will have a positive impact on the business.

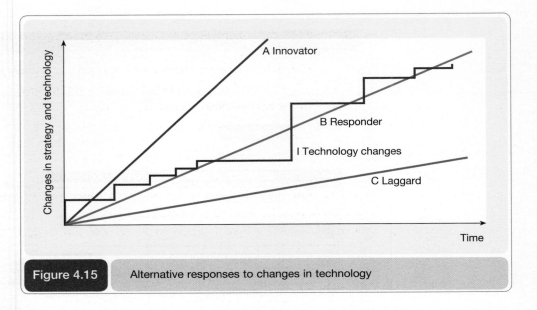

| Figure 4.15 | Alternative responses to changes in technology |

Summary

1   Environmental scanning and analysis are necessary in order that a company can respond to environmental changes and act on legal and ethical constraints on its activities.

2   Environmental constraints are related to the micro-environment variables reviewed in Chapter 5 and the macro-environment variables in this chapter using the SLEPT mnemonic.

3   Social factors that must be understood as part of the move to the Information Society include buyer behaviour characteristics such as access to the Internet and perceptions about it as a communications tool.

4   Ethical issues include the need to safeguard consumer privacy and security of personal information. Privacy issues include collection and dissemination of customer information, cookies and the use of direct e-mail.

5   Legal factors to be considered by e-commerce managers include: accessibility, domain name registration, copyright and data protection legislation.

6   Economic factors considered in the chapter are the regional differences in the use of the Internet for trade. Different economic conditions in different markets are considered in developing e-commerce budgets.

7   Political factors involve the role of governments in promoting e-commerce, but also trying to control it.

8   Rapid variation in technology requires constant monitoring of adoption of the technology by customers and competitors and appropriate responses.

Exercises

Self-assessment questions

1   Why is environmental scanning necessary?

2   Give an example how each of the macro-environment factors may directly drive the content and services provided by a website.

3   Summarize the social factors that govern consumer access to the Internet. How can companies overcome these influences once people venture online?

4   What actions can e-commerce managers take to safeguard consumer privacy and security?

5   What are the general legal constraints that a company acts under in any country?

6   How do governments attempt to control the use of the Internet?

7   Summarize adoption patterns across the continents.

8   How should innovation be managed?

Essay and discussion questions

1   You recently started a job as e-commerce manager for a bank. Produce a checklist of all the different legal and ethical issues that you need to check for compliance on the existing website of the bank.

2   How should the e-commerce manager monitor and respond to technological innovation?

3   Benchmark different approaches to achieving and reassuring customers about their privacy and security using three or four examples for a retail sector such as travel, books, toys or clothing.

4   'Internet access levels will never exceed 50% in most countries.' Discuss.

5   Select a new Internet access technology that has been introduced in the last two years and assess whether it will become a significant method of access.

6   Assess how the eight principles of the UK Data Protection Act (www.dataprotection. gov.uk) relate to actions an e-commerce manager needs to take to ensure legal compliance of their site.

Examination questions

1   Explain the different layers of governance of the Internet.

2   Summarize the macro-environment variables a company needs to monitor.

3   Explain the purpose of environmental scanning.

4   Give three examples of how web sites can use techniques to protect the user's privacy.

5   What are the three key factors which affect consumer adoption of the Internet?

6   Explain the significance of the diffusion–adoption concept to the adoption of new technologies to:

   (a) Consumers purchasing technological innovations.

   (b) Businesses deploying technological innovations.

7   What action should an e-commerce manager take to ensure compliance with ethical and legal standards of their site?

References

Ahmed, N.U. and Sharma, S.K. (2006) Porter's value chain model for assessing the impact of the internet for environmental gains. *International Journal of Management and Enterprise Development*, 3(3), 278–95.

Arnott, D. and Bridgewater, S. (2002) Internet, interaction and implications for marketing. *Marketing Intelligence and Planning*, 20(2), 86–95.

Bart, Y., Shankar, V., Sultan, F., and Urban, G. (2005) Are the drivers and role of online trust the same for all web sites and consumers? A large-scale exploratory empirical study. *Journal of Marketing*, October, 133–52.

Basu, D. (2007) *Global Perspectives on E-commerce Taxation Law*. Ashgate, Aldershot.

Booz Allen Hamilton (2002) *International E-Economy Benchmarking. The World's Most Effective Policies for the E-Economy*. Report published 19 November, London. **www.e-envoy. gov.uk/oee/oee.nsf/sections/esummit-benchmarking/$file/indexpage.htm.**

BrandNewWorld (2004) AOL Research published at **www.brandnewworld.co.uk.**

Cairns, S. (2005) Delivering supermarket shopping: more or less traffic? *Transport Reviews*, 25(1), 51–84.

Chaffey, D., Mayer, R., Johnston, K. and Ellis-Chadwick, F. (2009) *Internet Marketing: Strategy, Implementation and Practice*, 4th edn. Financial Times Prentice Hall, Harlow.

CIFAS (2010) CIFAS (Credit Industry Fraud Association) Press release: Fraud continues to pose problems in 2010. Press release: **www.cifas.org.uk/default.asp?edit_id=1014-57.**

Common Sense Advisory (2002) Beggars at the globalization banquet. White Paper available at: **www.commonsenseadvisory.com.** Editor: Don Da Palma. No locale given.

Computer Weekly (2004) Assessing the real risk of being online. *Computer Weekly*. Article by Stewart King. Thursday 9 December; **www.computerweekly.com.**

comScore M:Metrics (2008) M:metrics now measuring China, the world's largest mobile market, Seattle, WA, 9 February: **www.mmetrics.com/press/PressRelease.aspx?article=20080211-china-market.**

Daniel, L., Wilson, H. and Myers, A. (2002) Adoption of e-commerce by SMEs in the UK. Towards a stage model. *International Small Business Journal*, 20(3), 253–70.

Digitas (2007) Segmenting Internet Users: Implications for online advertising. White Paper published at: **http://digitalhive.blogs.com/digiblog/files/WebDotDigitas.pdf.**

Dyson, E. (1998) *Release 2.1. A Design for Living in the Digital Age*. Penguin, London.

E-consultancy (2007) E-business briefing interview. Bruce Tognazzini on human–computer interaction. Interview published November: **www.econsultancy.com/news-blog/ news-letter/link_track.asp?id=3515&link_id=#1.**

eEurope (2005) Information Society Benchmarking Report. From eEurope (2005) initiative.

European Commission (2010) i2010 Annual Information Society Report: ICT usage in enterprises – 2009. Issue number 1/2010.

European Interactive Advertising Association (2008) EIAA Online Shoppers 2008 Report: **www.eiaa.net/Ftp/casestudiesppt/ EIAA_Online_Shoppers_Report.pdf.**

Fletcher, K. (2001) Privacy: the Achilles heel of the new marketing. *Interactive Marketing*, 3(2), 128–40.

Freedom House (2000) *Censoring dot-gov report*. 17 April: **www.freedomhouse.org/news/pr041700.html**, New York.

Gartner (2010) Gartner's Hype Cycle: Special Report for 2010. Report summary available at **http://www.gartner.com/it/page.jsp?id=1447613.**

Godin, S. (1999) *Permission Marketing*. Simon and Schuster, New York.

Goldman, E. (2007) Eric Goldman Technology and Marketing Law blog. Rhino Sports, Inc. v. Sport Court, Inc., 8 May 2007: **http://blog.ericgoldman.org/archives/2007/05/ broad_matching.htm.**

Grossnickle, J. and Raskin, O. (2001) *The Handbook of Online Marketing Research: Knowing Your Customer Using the Net*. McGraw-Hill, New York.

Hamill, J. and Gregory, K. (1997) Internet marketing in the internationalisation of UK SMEs. *Journal of Marketing Management*, 13, 9–28.

HMRC (2003) Electronically supplied services and broadcasting services: New EU rules. HMRC Reference: VAT Info Sheet 01/03. HM Revenue and Customs.

Mason, R. (1986) Four ethical issues of the information age. *MIS Quarterly*, March.

Meckel, M., Walters, D. Greenwood, A. and Baugh, P. (2004) A taxonomy of e-business adoption and strategies in small and medium sized enterprises. *Strategic Change* 13, 259–69.

Mougayer, W. (1998) *Opening Digital Markets – Battle Plans and Strategies for Internet Commerce*, 2nd edn. CommerceNet Press, McGraw-Hill, New York.

Multilingual (2008) Localizing a localizer's website: the challenge. Jan/Feb, 30–33.

Nitish, S., Fassott, G., Zhao, H. and Boughton, P. (2006) A cross-cultural analysis of German, Chinese and Indian consumers' perception of web site adaptation. *Journal of Consumer Behaviour*, 5, 56–68.

NMA (2008) Profile – Travis Katz. Author: Luan Goldie. *New Media Age magazine*, published 31 January.

PMP (2008) Supply Chain & Manufacturing Systems Report. PMP Research Report published at **www.conspectus.com**. March.

Poon, S. and Jevons, C. (1997) Internet-enabled international marketing: a small business network perspective. *Journal of Marketing Management*, 13, 29–41.

Quayle, M. (2002) E-commerce: the challenge for UK SMEs in the twenty-first century. *International Journal of Operation and Production Management*, 22(10), 1148–61.

Quelch, J. and Klein, L. (1996) The Internet and international marketing. *Sloan Management Review*, Spring, 61–75.

RedEye (2003) A study into the accuracy of IP and cookie-based online management information. The RedEye Report. Available at **www.redeye.com.**

Rodgers, S., Chen, Q., Wang, Y. Rettie, R. and Alpert, F. (2007) The Web Motivation Inventory. *International Journal of Advertising*, 26(4), 447–76.

Rogers, E. (1983) *Diffusion of Innovations*, 3rd edn. Free Press, New York.

Siikavirta, H., Punakivi, M., Karkkainen, M. and Linnanen, L. (2003) Effects of e-commerce on greenhouse gas emissions: a case study of grocery home delivery in Finland. *Journal of Industrial Ecology*, 6(2), 83–97.

Singh, N. and Pereira, A. (2005) *The Culturally Customized Web Site, Customizing Web Sites for the Global Marketplace*. Butterworth-Heinemann, Oxford.

Sparrow, A. (2000) *E-Commerce and the Law. The Legal Implications of Doing Business Online*. Financial Times Executive Briefings, London.

Trott, P. (1998) *Innovation Management and New Product Development*. Financial Times Prentice Hall, Harlow.

Ward, S., Bridges, K. and Chitty, B. (2005) Do incentives matter? An examination of on-line privacy concerns and willingness to provide personal and financial information. *Journal of Marketing Communications*, 11(1), 21–40.

Further reading

Booz Allen Hamilton (2002) *International E-Economy Benchmarking. The World's Most Effective Policies for the E-Economy*. Report published 19 November, London. A detailed study (177-page report) reviewing government attempts to influence use of the Internet by citizens and businesses.

Dibb, S., Simkin, L., Pride, W. and Ferrell, O. (2000) *Marketing. Concepts and Strategies*, 4th edn. Houghton Mifflin, Boston. In Chapter 2, the authors introduce the different elements of the marketplace from a marketing perspective.

Dyson, E. (1998) *Release 2.1. A Design for Living in the Digital Age*. Penguin, London. Chapters 5 (Governance), 8 (Privacy), 9 (Anonymity) and 10 (Security) are of particular relevance.

Garfinkel, S. (2000) *Database Nation*. O'Reilly, San Francisco. This book is subtitled 'The death of privacy in the 21st century' and this is the issue on which it focuses (includes Internet- and non-Internet-related privacy).

Slevin, J. (2000) *The Internet and Society*. Polity Press, Oxford. A book about the Internet that combines social theory, communications analysis and case studies from both academic and applied perspectives.

Web links

Dave Chaffey's link directory (**www.davechaffey.com**) A directory of e-business-related Internet adoption and usage links is maintained by Dave Chaffey to support this book.

Guide to Smarter Internet Searching (**www.pearsoned.co.uk/chaffey**) A detailed explanation from the author of this book on how to use the Internet more effectively to search for business and academic sources. Includes a description of an advanced searching approach using Google.

The Oxford Internet Institute (OII) (**www.oii.ox.ac.uk**) Research institute focused on the study of the impact of the Internet on society.

Government sources on Internet usage and adoption

- European government (**http://europa.eu.int/comm/eurostat**)
- OECD (**www.oecd.org**). OECD broadband research (**www.oecd.org/sti/ict/broadband**)
- UK government (**www.statistics.gov.uk**)
- Ofcom (**www.ofcom.org.uk**) Ofcom is the independent regulator and competition authority for the UK communications industries, with responsibilities across television, radio, telecommunications and wireless communications services and has in-depth reports on communications markets
- US government (**www.stat-usa.gov**)

Online audience panel media consumption and usage data

These are fee-based data, but contain useful free data within press release sections.

- comScore (**www.comscore.com**)
- Hitwise (**www.hitwise.com**). Hitwise blog (**http://weblogs.hitwise.com**). Sample reports from Hitwise on consumer search behaviour and importance of different online intermediaries
- Netratings (**www.netratings.com**)

Other major online research providers

- The European Interactive Advertising Association (**www.eiaa.net**). The EIAA is a pan-European trade organization with surveys of media consumption and usage across Europe
- International Telecommunications Union (**www.itu.int/ITU-D/icteye**). Adoption of Internet and mobile phone statistics by company
- The Pew Internet & American Life Project (**www.pewinternet.org**). Produces reports that explore the impact of the Internet on families, communities, work and home, daily life, education, healthcare, and civic and political life

Privacy

- **Australian Privacy Commissioner** (**www.privacy.gov.au**). Information on privacy laws in Australia such as the Privacy Act and the Telecommunications Act
- **European Data Protection resources** (**http://europa.eu.int/comm/justice_home/fsj/privacy/index_en.htm**). These laws are coordinated centrally, but interpreted differently in different countries
- **Federal Trade commission** (**www.ftc.gov/privacy**). US privacy initiatives

- **GetSafeOnline** (**www.getsafeonline.org**). Site created by government and business to educate consumers to help them understand and manage their online privacy and security
- **Home Office Identify theft web site** (**www.identitytheft.org**). An awareness site created by the government
- **iCompli** (**www.icompli.co.uk**). Portal and e-newsletter about privacy and data protection compliance
- **Information Commissioner** (**www.informationcommisioner.gov.uk**). Site explaining law for UK consumers and businesses
- **Marketing Law** (**www.marketinglaw.co.uk**). Useful e-mail update on the latest privacy law developments
- **Outlaw** (**www.out-law.com**). Compilation of the latest technology-related law
- **Office of Electronic Government and Technology** (**www.estrategy.gov**). US agency facilitating e-government in the USA
- **Privacy International** (**www.privacyinternational.org**). A human rights group formed in 1990 as a watchdog on surveillance and privacy invasions by governments and corporations

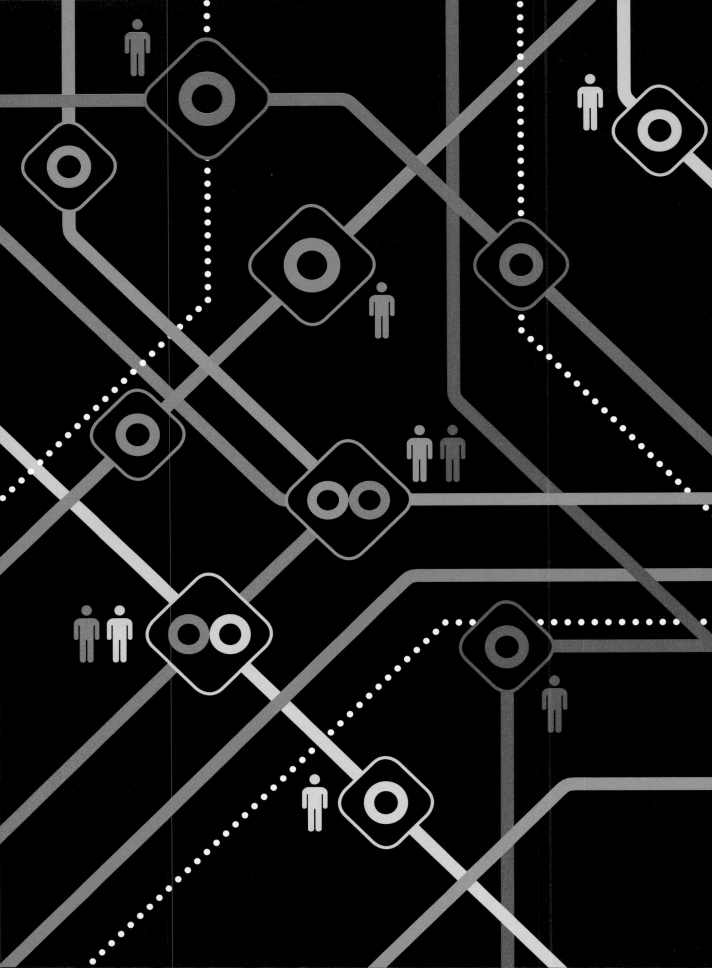

Part 2

Strategy and applications

In Part 2 of the book approaches to developing e-business strategy and applications are reviewed for the organization as a whole (Chapter 5), with an emphasis on buy-side e-commerce (Chapters 6 and 7) and sell-side e-commerce (Chapters 8 and 9).

E-business strategy p. 237

- What is e-business strategy?
- Strategic analysis
- Strategic objectives
- Strategy definition
- Strategy implementation

Focus on …
- Aligning and impacting e-business strategies

6

Supply chain management p. 307

- What is supply chain management?
- Options for restructuring the supply chain
- Using e-business to restructure the supply chain
- Supply chain management implementation

Focus on …
- The value chain

7

E-procurement p. 354

- What is e-procurement?
- Drivers of e-procurement
- Barriers and risks of e-procurement adoption
- Implementing e-procurement
- The future of e-procurement

Focus on …
- Estimating e-procurement costs
- B2B marketplaces

8

E-marketing p. 382

- What is e-marketing?
- E-marketing planning
- Situation analysis
- Objective setting
- Strategy
- Tactics
- Actions
- Control

Focus on ...
- Characteristics of digital media communications
- Online branding

9

Customer relationship management p. 450

- What is e-CRM?
- Conversion marketing
- The online buying process
- Customer acquisition management
- Customer retention management
- Customer extension
- Technology solutions for CRM

Focus on ...
- Marketing communications for customer acquisition
- Social media and social CRM strategy
- Excelling in e-commerce service quality

5

E-business strategy

Web support

The following additional case study is available at
www.pearsoned.co.uk/chaffey

→ Evolving business models in the Internet car sales market
→ The site also contains a range of study material designed to help improve your results.

Learning outcomes

After completing this chapter the reader should be able to:

- Follow an appropriate strategy process model for e-business
- Apply tools to generate and select e-business strategies
- Outline alternative strategic approaches to achieve e-business

Management issues

Consideration of e-business strategy raises these issues for management:

- How does e-business strategy differ from traditional business strategy?
- How should we integrate e-business strategy with existing business and information systems strategy?
- How should we evaluate our investment priorities and returns from e-business?

Links to other chapters

The main related chapters are:

- *Chapters 6 and 7* review the specific enactment of e-business strategy to supply chain and procurement management processes
- *Chapters 8 and 9* explain how e-marketing and customer relationship management relate to the concept of e-business, and e-commerce and e-marketing planning are approached
- *Chapters 10, 11 and 12* look at practical aspects of the implementation of e-business strategy

Introduction

Developing an e-business strategy requires a fusion of existing approaches to business, marketing, supply chain management and information systems strategy development. In addition to traditional strategy approaches, commentators have exhorted companies to apply innovative techniques to achieve competitive advantage. Around 2000, many articles, fuelled by the dot-com hype of the time, urged CEOs to 'innovate or die'. For many existing companies this was neither desirable nor necessary and they have made a more gradual approach to e-business practice. Those companies that have successfully managed the transformation to e-business have done so by applying traditional strategy approaches. At the same time there have been many start-ups featured as cases in previous chapters, such as eBay, Lastminute.com and Zopa.com, that have succeeded through innovative business models. But these companies also have succeeded through applying established principles of business strategy, planning and risk management.

In this chapter we seek to show how an e-business strategy can be created through following these established principles, but also through careful consideration of how to best identify and exploit the differences introduced by new electronic channels. In a nutshell, e-business isn't just about defining '*how to do business online*'; it defines '*how to do business differently online*'. The e-business strategy defines how.

We start the chapter by introducing e-business strategy and then discuss appropriate strategy process models to follow as a framework for developing e-business strategy. The chapter is structured around this four-stage strategy process model:

1 Strategic evaluation.
2 Strategic objectives.
3 Strategy definition.
4 Strategy implementation.

For each of these components of strategy, we cover management actions to review and refine e-business strategy. A recurring theme through this chapter is the need to align e-business strategy with business strategy while also identifying opportunities for e-business strategy to impact business strategy. '*Focus on* Aligning and impacting e-business strategies' at the end of this chapter covers these in more depth.

Real-world E-Business experiences   The E-consultancy interview

Standard Life's Sharon Shaw on strategy and planning

Overview and main concepts covered

Developing a new e-commerce strategy can be a daunting experience. We spoke to Sharon Shaw, e-commerce manager at Standard Life about her experiences of strategy creation, including budgets, KPIs, incentives and structures.

Q. When developing a new digital strategy, how do you start? What models are out there for you to base it on? We have developed a wheel framework for acquisition, conversion and retention, but what approach did you use?

Sharon Shaw, Standard Life: Standard Life and Avenue A/Razorfish have used an Attract, Convert, Support, Extend model, which is very similar to the E-consultancy framework, though its meaning is evolving as the role of digital changes within the organisation. Measurement and optimisation are fundamentals in both.

Building the model, we combine existing business and brand strategies with primary and secondary customer research, competitor audits and innovation trends.

The customer research covers online attitudes and behaviours and cross-channel preferences and needs. The competitor audit includes a SWOT analysis of our own site and an evaluation against business objectives and user expectations.

Q. Someone said the evolution to digital is 'a bit like global warming' – we all know it's happening but fixed goalposts or yardsticks are hard to find. What references and benchmarks can you use for targets and comparisons?

Sharon Shaw, Standard Life: The boon with digital is that it is so measurable. As such, setting financial targets and comparisons is easier than in traditional media. ROI stands out as the most obvious measure for individual projects, varying for brand campaigns and e-commerce builds (but always positive!).

Overall, we like to look at the percentage contribution digital makes to total sales volumes and we can set a benchmark target of around 15% for a mature multi-channel retail business.

Strategically, the aim is to reference the customer experience online and across channels to make sure it is consistent and mutually constructive. This can be measured through online and offline surveys, and increasingly through 'buzz' metrics on the social web.

Standard Life is considering using services like eBenchmarkers to compare site performance with competitors. It provides metrics for our site in comparison to aggregated scores across all their registered sites.

Q. What are the key success metrics and what reliable data is out there to compare 'like with like'?

Sharon Shaw, Standard Life: Ultimately, success in e-commerce is measured through improved profits across sales and marketing activity.

Conversion rates and basket value are therefore the most important numbers for the site, followed by (and related to) campaign ROI and/or CPA. Natural and paid search performance are key traffic generation metrics.

Other measures include dwell time to evaluate customer engagement with rich media, and a recency–frequency model to score customer loyalty. For reliable data, we refer to the IMRG, Hitwise, comScore, Mintel, eMarketer and TGI.

Q. What are the challenges and opportunities of moving towards multi-channel measurement and integration?

Sharon Shaw, Standard Life: Both the biggest opportunities and biggest challenges lie in the integration of online and offline systems and databases.

We know that allowing each channel the same view of the customer and their transactional history can drive KPIs up, through delivering a consistent and personalised customer experience at every touchpoint.

But it is rare that such integration can happen easily as most organisations have developed their online and offline architectures in isolation.

Which leads us nicely on to the other key challenge – getting the budget, staff and (most importantly) board level buy-in to undertake the large-scale business change needed to deliver an effective multi-channel proposition.

Q. Where should e-commerce fit into the overall budget – should it have its own P&L, or is it a cost centre for other business units?

Sharon Shaw, Standard Life: It really depends on the organisation, its objectives and how far it has already gone with e-commerce.

A dedicated P&L is great for new e-commerce ventures that don't rely too much on other channels. The autonomy and flexibility of financial control allow the channel to change and grow at pace.

A more mature online channel that has significant crossover with offline will at the very least need to share elements of their P&L with other business units.

For instance, if an initial enquiry is made online and a sale is converted from the lead by telephone, who gets the credit?

A sensible approach would be to give the telephone centre 75% and the website 25%. If the telephone centre has a code to give customers when they go online, the reverse can be true. The point being, the P&L should be used to encourage a symbiotic relationship between channels.

If e-commerce is solely a cost-centre for other units, decision making will be slow, political manoeuvring common and the team fragmented.

Q. Where should e-commerce sit in the organisation and who should be the senior person responsible for it?

Sharon Shaw, Standard Life: We strongly recommend a dedicated team run e-commerce. The channel requires people with appropriate skills and experience to drive it forward and a mandate to give it their complete attention. The integration with the rest of the business should happen through collaboration on the ground and only through reporting lines at the most senior levels.

The organisation at the senior level is a point of some debate. It is fairly common in retail for a Commercial Director to take responsibility for e-commerce sales but the marketing team has a significant input and interest.

The online marketing budget to advertise and attract customers is growing all the time and there is a powerful need to integrate communications and the customer experience across channels.

One approach is to create a multi-channel role responsible for all online activity and how it is integrated with the rest of the business. This role could report into the Sales & Marketing Director or directly to the MD.

In terms of incentive structures and targets, if each channel has its own target, how do you avoid channels competing with each other to the detriment of the overall organisation's goals?

The challenge here is to motivate and reward the team that is tasked with growing a new channel without upsetting other channels that may be experiencing slower growth. The P&L attribution is a key factor but incentives can also help.

Most companies reward on total business performance to target first, followed by an individual's performance.

One way to motivate a channel team might be to introduce a middle-tier related to the channel performance to target, a factor that will give them a boost if they see strong growth in their area.

Q. Do you have any tips on staff recruitment and retention – finding and retaining the right skills for a reasonable price?

Sharon Shaw, Standard Life: The main issues for digital workers seem to be the environment in which they work, the variety of their work and their opportunities for personal development.

With a dedicated online team there is a great opportunity to create a fun and fast-paced workplace that feels dynamic and creative (even for the techies!). There is a risk of giving people repetitive work when administering a site so it is also important to make sure staff have a chance to try their hand at different tasks and project work. Back this up with the security of good HR and corporate benefits.

Finally, don't forget that the digital world doesn't stand still. Give all the team plenty of exposure to the latest research, emerging trends and breakthrough technologies.

Q. When a large business is going through a major reorganisation, what are the main ways this can impact upon the e-commerce/digital marketing team? What types of demands are placed on the team by different business units?

Sharon Shaw, Standard Life: The biggest problem tends to be a freeze on investment and/or significant change. Digital teams are expected to carry on delivering business as usual but won't be given the opportunities to make often long-awaited improvements until the reorganisation is complete.

Projects get put on hold and the team feel stuck in limbo. Strong leadership is needed to keep everyone on track.

Source: www.econsultancy.com/news-blog/newsletter/3504/interview-with-standard-life-s-sharon-shaw. html. Econsultancy.com provides information, training and events on best practice in online marketing and e-commerce management.

What is e-business strategy?

Strategy
Definition of the future direction and actions of a company defined as approaches to achieve specific objectives.

Strategy defines the future direction and actions of an organization or part of an organization. Johnson and Scholes (2006) define corporate strategy as:

the direction and scope of an organization over the long-term: which achieves advantage for the organization through its configuration of resources within a changing environment to meet the needs of markets and to fulfil stakeholder expectations.

Lynch (2000) describes strategy as an organization's sense of purpose. However, he notes that purpose alone is not strategy; plans or actions are also needed.

E-business strategies share much in common with corporate, business and marketing strategies. These quotes summarizing the essence of strategy could equally apply to each strategy:

- 'Is based on current performance in the marketplace.'
- 'Defines how we will meet our objectives.'
- 'Sets allocation of resources to meet goals.'
- 'Selects preferred strategic options to compete within a market.'
- 'Provides a long-term plan for the development of the organization.'
- 'Identifies competitive advantage through developing an appropriate positioning defining a value proposition delivered to customer segments.'

Johnson and Scholes (2006) note that organizations have different levels of strategy, particularly for larger or global organizations. These are summarized within Figure 5.1. They identify *corporate strategy* which is concerned with the overall purpose and scope of the organization, *business unit strategy* which defines how to compete successfully in a particular market and *operational strategies* which are concerned with achieving corporate and business unit strategies. Additionally, *functional strategies* describe how the corporate and business unit strategies will be operationalized in different functional areas or business processes. Functional or process strategies refer to marketing, supply chain management, human resources, finance and information systems strategies.

E-business strategy
Definition of the approach by which applications of internal and external electronic communications can support and influence corporate strategy.

Where does **e-business strategy** fit? Figure 5.1 does not show at which level e-business strategy should be defined, since for different organizations this must be discussed and agreed. We can observe that there is a tendency for e-business strategy to be incorporated

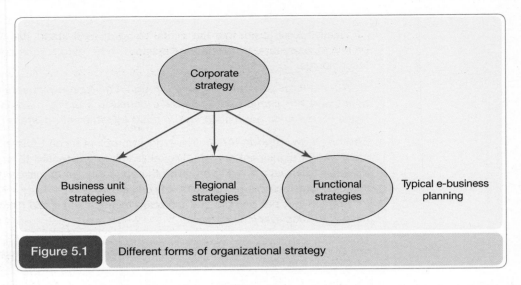

| **Figure 5.1** | Different forms of organizational strategy |

within the functional strategies, for example within a marketing plan or logistics plan, or as part of information systems (IS) strategy. A danger with this approach is that e-business strategy may not be recognized at a higher level within organizational planning. A distinguishing feature of organizations that are leaders in e-business, such as Cisco, Dell, HSBC, easyJet and General Electric, is that e-business is an element of corporate strategy development.

There is limited research on how businesses have integrated e-business strategy into existing strategy, although authors such as Doherty and McAulay (2002) have suggested it is important that e-commerce investments be driven by corporate strategies. We return to approaches of alignment later in the chapter. Box 5.1 illustrates some of the challenges in integrating e-business into existing planning processes.

Box 5.1   Perspectives on senior management buy-in to e-commerce

Research of retail banks by Hughes (2001) suggested that, in the early phases of e-business development, there is no clarity in e-commerce strategy at a senior level. In one of the responding companies, interviewees comment that:

> *My perception would be that they are not leading e-commerce as actively as they are other parts of change within the organisation.*
>
> (Organisation development manager, case 1)

Another comments:

> *There is a lack of understanding of the new technology and its implications by the executive team: Whereas if it's a life and pensions decision they can take that because it's in their blood. If it's a technology decision, it's much more difficult.*
>
> (Marketing manager, case 1)

However, problems in defining strategy can occur, even though clear control is evident. In company 3 the importance of senior involvement is stressed:

> *The ability to drive forward a project without a very high level sponsor is doomed to failure really. [In our organization] The allocation of budgets is decided at the highest level.*

In organization 3, three senior managers are responsible for driving e-commerce: the chief executive, the head of the electronic channel and the technology director.

However, the marketing manager feels that the marketing function has not been sufficiently central in e-commerce development:

What marketing is trying to do is say there should be a strong consumer voice within there who can think about it purely from the marketing side. We're trying to make sure that we've got strong representation.

Although these quotes date back to an early phase in e-business strategy development in organizations, they are still instructive in indicating the importance of senior management sponsorship and ownership of e-business strategy. E-consultancy (2005, 2008a) research into managing digital channels again showed the challenges and importance of senior sponsorship. The main challenges identified by e-commerce managers from over a hundred participating companies from Europe and the United States showed that gaining buy-in into e-commerce involved significant challenges for many. These are the ratings for the main challenges:

- Gaining senior management buy-in or resource (68% agreed that this was a challenge, 68% in 2005)
- Gaining buy-in / resource from traditional marketing functions / brands (68% agreed that this was a challenge, 66% in 2005)
- Gaining IT resource / technical support (68% agreed that this was a challenge, 69% in 2005)
- Finding suitable staff appeared to have got more challenging (75% agreeing that this was a challenge compared to 60% in 2005).

However, enormous strides have still been made with almost three-quarters of respondents agreeing with the statement: *'Digital channels are fully recognised and integrated into our annual planning and budgeting process'*.

The imperative for e-business strategy

Think about the implications if e-business strategy is not clearly defined. The following may result:

- Missed opportunities from lack of evaluation of opportunities or insufficient resourcing of e-business initiatives. These will result in more savvy competitors gaining a competitive advantage.
- Inappropriate direction of e-business strategy (poorly defined objectives, for example, with the wrong emphasis on buy-side, sell-side or internal process support).
- Limited integration of e-business at a technical level resulting in silos of information in different systems.
- Resource wastage through duplication of e-business development in different functions and limited sharing of best practice.

To help avoid these problems, organizations will want e-business strategy to be based on corporate objectives. As Rowley (2002) has pointed out, it is logical that e-business strategy should support corporate strategy objectives and it should also support functional marketing and supply chain management strategies.

However, these corporate objectives should be based on new opportunities and threats related to electronic network adoption, which are identified from environment analysis and objectives defined in an e-business strategy. So it can be said that e-business strategy should not only support corporate strategy, but should also influence it. Figure 5.2 explains how e-business strategy should relate to corporate and functional strategies. It also shows where these topics are covered in this book.

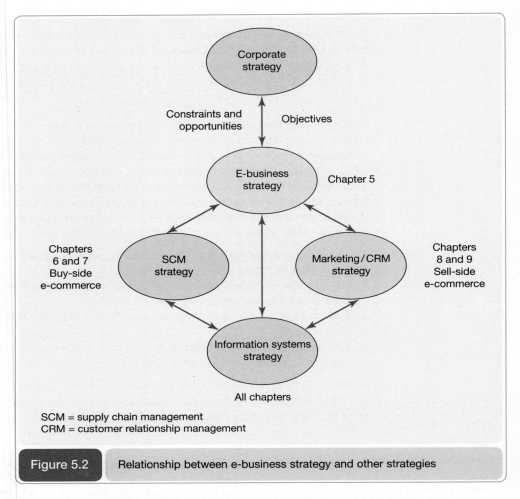

SCM = supply chain management
CRM = customer relationship management

| Figure 5.2 | Relationship between e-business strategy and other strategies |

E-channel strategies

E-channel strategies
Define how a company should set specific objectives and develop specific differential strategies for communicating with its customers and partners through electronic media.

An important aspect of e-business strategies is that they create new 'e-channel strategies' for organizations.

E-channel strategies define specific goals and approaches for using electronic channels. This is to prevent simply replicating existing processes through e-channels, which will create efficiencies but will not exploit the full potential for making an organization more effective through e-business. E-channel strategies also need to define how electronic channels are used in conjunction with other channels as part of a **multi-channel e-business strategy**. This defines how different marketing and supply chain channels should integrate and support each other in terms of their proposition development and communications based on their relative merits for the customer and the company. Finally, we also need to remember that e-business strategy also defines how an organization gains value internally from using electronic networks, such as sharing employee knowledge and improving process efficiencies through intranets. Myers *et al.* (2004) provide a useful summary of the decisions required about multi-channel marketing.

Multi-channel e-business strategy
Defines how different marketing and supply chain channels should integrate and support each other to drive business efficiency and effectiveness.

The characteristics of a multi-channel e-business strategy are:

- E-business strategy is a channel strategy.
- Specific e-business objectives need to be set to benchmark adoption of e-channels.
- E-business strategy defines how we should:
  1 *Communicate the benefits of using e-channels*
  2 *Prioritize audiences or partners targeted for e-channel adoption*

3 *Prioritize products sold or purchased through e-channels*
4 *Achieve our e-channel targets.*

- E-channel strategies thrive on creating *differential value* for all parties to a transaction.
- *But* e-channels do not exist in isolation, so we still need to manage *channel integration* and acknowledge that the adoption of e-channels will not be appropriate for all products or services or generate sufficient value for all partners. This selective adoption of e-channels is sometimes referred to as 'right-channelling' in a sell-side e-commerce context. Right-channelling can be summarized as:
  - *Reaching the right customer*
  - *Using the right channel*
  - *With the right message or offering*
  - *At the right time.*
- E-business strategy also defines how an organization *gains value internally* from using electronic networks, such as through sharing employee knowledge and improving process efficiencies through intranets.

As an example of how an e-channel strategy is implemented and communicated to an audience, see Mini case study 5.1: BA asks 'Have you clicked yet?' This shows how BA communicates its new e-channel strategy to its customers in order to show them the differential benefits of their using the channel, and so change their behaviour. BA would use 'right-channelling' by targeting a younger, more professional audience for adoption of e-channels, while using traditional channels of phone and post to communicate with less web-savvy customers who prefer to use these media.

Mini Case Study 5.1	BA asks 'Have you clicked yet?'

In 2004, British Airways launched online services which allowed customers to take control of the booking process, so combining new services with reduced costs. BA decided to develop a specific online ad campaign to create awareness and encourage usage of its Online Value Proposition (OVP). BA's UK marketing manager said about the objective:

> *British Airways is leading the way in innovating technology to simplify our customers' journey through the airport. The role of this campaign was to give a strong message about what is now available online, over and above booking tickets.*

The aim of the campaign was to educate and change the way in which BA's customers behave before, while and after they travel. The campaign focused on the key benefits of the new online services – speed, ease and convenience – and promoted the ability to check in online and print out a boarding pass. The two main target audiences were quite different, early adopters and those who use the web occasionally, but don't rely on it. Early adopters were targeted on sites such as T3.co.uk, Newscientist.com and DigitalHomeMag.com. Occasional users were reached through ads on sites such as JazzFM.com, Vogue.com and Menshealth.com.

Traditional media used to deliver the 'Have you clicked yet?' message included print, TV and outdoor media. The print ad copy, which details the OVP, was:

> *Your computer is now the airport. Check in online, print your own boarding pass, choose your seat, change your booking card and even find hire cars and hotels. Simple.*

A range of digital media were used, including ATMs, outdoor LCD transvision screens such as those in London rail stations which included Bluecasting where commuters could receive a video on their Bluetooth-enabled mobile phone, and digital escalator panels. More than 650,000 consumers interacted with the ATM screen creative. Online ads included overlays and skyscrapers which showed a consumer at this computer, printing out a ticket and walking across the screen to the airport. Such rich-media campaigns generated 17% clickthrough and 15% interaction. The website used in the campaign is shown in Figure 5.3.

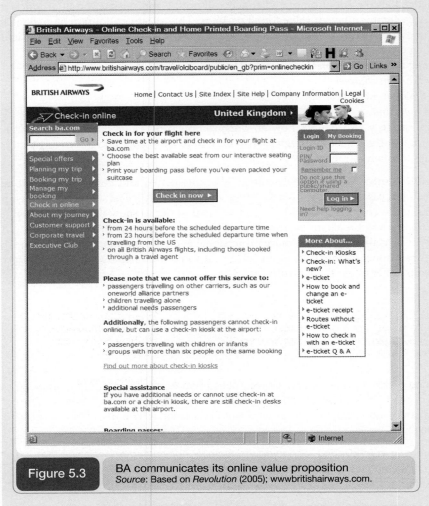

| Figure 5.3 | **BA communicates its online value proposition**
Source: Based on *Revolution* (2005); wwwbritishairways.com. |

Source: Adapted from Campaign of the month, *Revolution* (Rigby, E. 2005). Reproduced from *Revolution* magazine with the permission of the copyright owner, Haymarket Business Publications Limited.

Strategy process model

A framework for approaching strategy development.

Strategy process models for e-business

Before developing any type of strategy, a management team needs to agree the process they will follow for generating and then implementing the strategy. A **strategy process model** provides a framework that gives a logical sequence to follow to ensure inclusion of all key activities of e-business strategy development. It also ensures that e-business strategy can be evolved as part of a process of continuous improvement.

Before the advent of e-business, many strategy process models had been developed for the business strategies described above. To what extent can management teams apply these models to e-business strategy development? Although strategy process models differ in emphasis and terminology, they all have common elements. Complete Activity 5.1 to discuss what these common elements are.

Debate 5.1

E-business responsibility

'A single person with specific e-business responsibility is required for every medium-to-large business. It is not sufficient for this to be the responsibility of a non-specialist manager.'

Activity 5.1	Selecting an e-business strategy process model

Purpose

To identify the applicability of existing strategy process models to e-business.

Activity

Review three or four strategy process models that you have encountered. These could be models such as those shown in Table 5.1. Note that columns in this table are independent – the rows do not correspond across models.

Questions

1 What are the strengths and weaknesses of each model?
2 What common features do the models share? List the key elements of an appropriate strategy process model.

Answers to activities can be found at www.pearsoned.co.uk/chaffey

Table 5.1	Alternative strategy process models

Jelassi and Enders (2008) E-business strategy framework	Johnson and Scholes (2006) Parallel corporate strategy model	McDonald (1999) Sequential marketing strategy model	Smith (1999) SOSTAC™ Sequential marketing strategy model (see Chapter 8)
SWOT summarizing external analysis (e.g. marketplace, customers, competitors); internal analysis (e.g. human, financial and operational)	Strategic analysis (environment, resources, expectations, objectives and culture)	Situation review (marketing audit, SWOT analysis, assumptions)	Situation analysis
Mission and objectives	Strategic choice (generation of options, evaluation of options, selection of strategy)	Goal setting (mission, corporate objectives)	Objective setting
Strategy formulation to create and capture value through sustaining competitive advantage and exploring new market spaces	Strategic implementation (resource planning, people and systems, organization structure)	Strategy formulation (marketing objectives and strategy, estimate expected results, identify alternative plans and mixes)	Strategy
Strategy implementation including internal organization, interaction with suppliers and users or customers		Resource allocation and monitoring (budget, first-year implementation plan)	Tactics Actions Control

Common elements include:

1 Internal and external environment scanning or analysis is needed. Scanning occurs both during strategy development and as a continuous process in order to respond to competitors.
2 A clear statement of vision and objectives is required. Clarity is required to communicate the strategic intention to both employees and the marketplace. Objectives are also vital to act as a check as to whether the strategy is successful!
3 Strategy development can be broken down into strategy option generation, evaluation and selection.
4 After strategy development, enactment of the strategy occurs as strategy implementation.
5 Control is required to monitor operational and strategy effectiveness problems and adjust the operations or strategy accordingly.

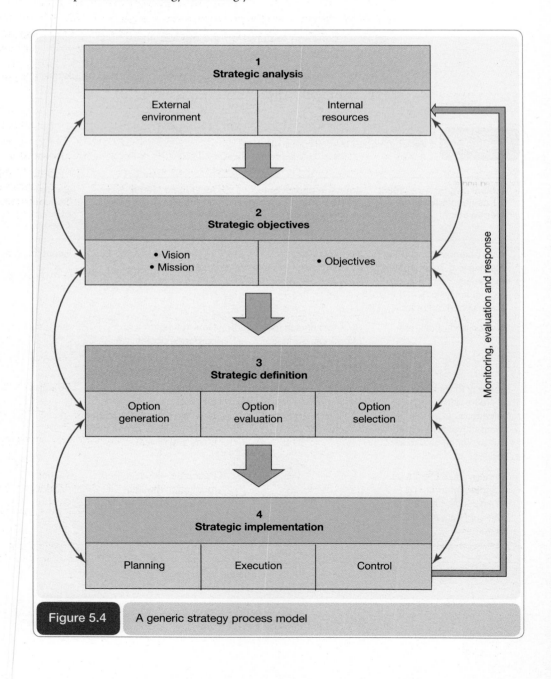

| Figure 5.4 | A generic strategy process model |

Additionally, the models suggest that these elements, although generally sequential, are also iterative and require reference back to previous stages. In reality there is overlap between these stages.

To what extent, then, can this traditional strategy approach be applied to e-business?

Jelassi and Enders (2008) suggest that there are three key dimensions for defining e-business strategy:

1 *Where will the organization compete?* (That is, within the external micro-environment.)
2 *What type of value will it create?* (Strategy options to generate value through increased revenue or reduced costs.)
3 *How should the organization be designed to deliver value?* (Includes internal structure and resources and interfaces with external companies.)

The arrows in Figure 5.4 highlight an important distinction in the way in which strategy process models are applied. Referring to the work of Mintzberg and Quinn (1991), Lynch (2000) distinguishes between prescriptive and emergent strategy approaches. In the **prescriptive strategy** approach strategic analysis is used to develop a strategy, and it is then implemented. In other words, the strategy is prescribed in advance. Alternatively, in the **emergent strategy** approach, strategic analysis, strategic development and strategy implementation are interrelated.

In reality, most organizational strategy development and planning processes have elements of prescriptive and emergent strategy. The prescriptive elements are the structured annual or six-monthly budgeting process or a longer-term three-year rolling marketing planning process. But, on a shorter timescale, organizations also need an emergent process to enable strategic agility (introduced in Chapter 2) and the ability to rapidly respond to marketplace dynamics. E-consultancy (2008a) has researched approaches used to encourage emergent strategies or strategic agility based on interviews with e-commerce practitioners – see Table 5.2.

Prescriptive strategy
Strategic analysis, strategic development and strategy implementation are linked together sequentially.

Emergent strategy
Strategic analysis, strategic development and strategy implementation are interrelated and are developed together.

Table 5.2	Summary of approaches used to support emergent strategy

Aspect of emergent strategy	Approaches used to support emergent digital strategy
Strategic analysis	• Staff in different parts of organization encouraged to monitor introduction of new approaches by competitors in-sector or out of sector • Third-party benchmarking service reporting monthly or quarterly on new functionality introduced by competitors • *Ad hoc* customer panel used to suggest or review new ideas for site features • Quarterly longitudinal testing of usability to complete key tasks • Subscription to audience panel data (comScore, Netratings, Hitwise) reviews changes in popularity of online services
Strategy formulation and selection	• Budget flexible to reassign priorities • Dedicated or 'ring-fenced' IT budget up to agreed limits to reduce protracted review cycles • Digital channel strategy group meets monthly, empowered to take decisions about which new web functionality to implement
Strategy implementation	• Use of agile development methodologies to enable rapid development • Area of site used to showcase new tools currently under trial (for example Google Labs (http://labs.google.com)).

Source: E-consultancy, 2008a.

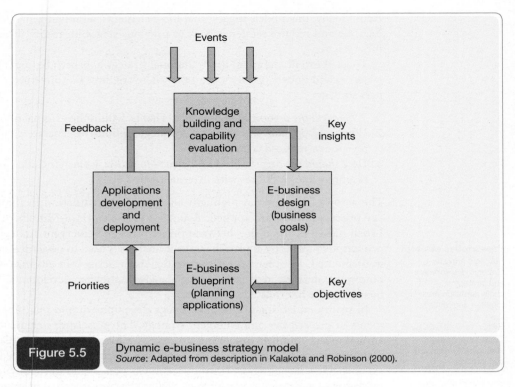

Figure 5.5	Dynamic e-business strategy model
	Source: Adapted from description in Kalakota and Robinson (2000).

Kalakota and Robinson (2000) recommend a dynamic emergent strategy process specific to e-business – see Figure 5.5. It essentially shares similar features to Figure 5.4, but with an emphasis on responsiveness with continuous review and prioritization of investment in new applications.

Strategic analysis

Strategic analysis
Collection and review of information about an organization's internal processes and resources and external marketplace factors in order to inform strategy definition.

Strategic analysis or situation analysis involves review of:

- The internal resources and processes of the company to assess its e-business capabilities and results to date in the context of a review of its activity in the marketplace.
- The immediate competitive environment (micro-environment), including customer demand and behaviour, competitor activity, marketplace structure and relationships with suppliers, partners and intermediaries, as described in Chapter 2.
- The wider environment (macro-environment) in which a company operates; this includes the social, legal, economic and political factors reviewed in Chapter 4.

These are summarized in Figure 5.6. For the effective, responsive e-business, as explained earlier, it is essential that situation analysis or environmental scanning be a continuous process with clearly identified responsibilities for performing the scanning and acting on the knowledge acquired.

Resource and process analysis

Resource analysis
Review of the technological, financial and human resources of an organization and how they are utilized in business processes.

Resource analysis for e-business is primarily concerned with its e-business capabilities, i.e. the degree to which a company has in place the appropriate *technological and applications infrastructure* and financial and human resources to support it. These resources must be harnessed together to give efficient *business processes*.

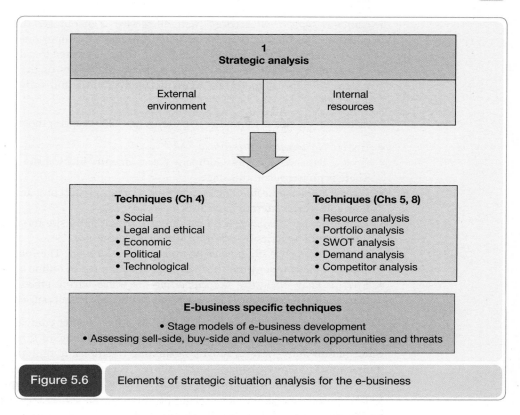

1
Strategic analysis

External environment	Internal resources

Techniques (Ch 4)
- Social
- Legal and ethical
- Economic
- Political
- Technological

Techniques (Chs 5, 8)
- Resource analysis
- Portfolio analysis
- SWOT analysis
- Demand analysis
- Competitor analysis

E-business specific techniques
- Stage models of e-business development
- Assessing sell-side, buy-side and value-network opportunities and threats

Figure 5.6	Elements of strategic situation analysis for the e-business

Jelassi and Enders (2008) distinguish between analysis of resources and capabilities:

- Resources are the tangible and intangible assets which can be used in value creation. Tangible resources include the IT infrastructure, bricks and mortar, and financial capital. Intangible resources include a company's brand and credibility, employee knowledge, licences and patents.
- Capabilities represent the ability of a firm to use resources effectively to support value creation. They are dependent on the structure and processes used to manage e-business.

Stage models of e-business development

Stage models are helpful in reviewing how advanced a company is in its use of information and communications technology (ICT) resources to support its processes. Stage models have traditionally been popular in the analysis of the current application of business information systems (BIS) within an organization. For example, the six-stage model of Nolan (1979) refers to the development of use of information systems within an organization from initiation with simple data processing through to a mature adoption of BIS with controlled, integrated systems. A simple example of a stage model was introduced in Figure 1.14.

When assessing the current use of ICT within a company or across a market it is instructive to analyse the extent to which an organization has implemented the technological infrastructure and support structure to achieve e-business. Quelch and Klein (1996) developed a five-stage model referring to the development of sell-side e-commerce. The stages remain relevant today. Research referenced in Chapter 1 and Chapter 4 shows that many companies still have limited e-business capabilities and are at an early stage in the model. For existing companies the stages are:

1 *Image and product information* – a basic 'brochureware' website or presence in online directories.
2 *Information collection* – enquiries are facilitated through online forms.

3 *Customer support and service* – 'web self-service' is encouraged through frequently asked questions and the ability to ask questions through a forum or online.
4 *Internal support and service* – a marketing intranet is created to help with support process.
5 *Transactions* – financial transactions such as online sales or the creation of an e-CRM system where customers can access detailed product and order information through an extranet.

Considering sell-side e-commerce, Chaffey *et al.* (2009) suggest there are six options:

- *Level 0: No website or presence on web.*
- *Level 1: Basic web presence.* Company places an entry in a website listing company names. There is no website at this stage.
- *Level 2: Simple static informational website.* Contains basic company and product information, sometimes referred to as 'brochureware'.
- *Level 3: Simple interactive site.* Users are able to search the site and make queries to retrieve information. Queries by e-mail may also be supported.
- *Level 4: Interactive site supporting transactions with users.* The functions offered will vary according to company but they will usually be limited to online buying.
- *Level 5. Fully interactive site supporting the whole buying process.* Provides relationship marketing with individual customers and facilitating the full range of marketing exchanges.

Research by Arnott and Bridgewater (2002) assessed whether companies of different sectors and sizes and located in different countries had reached one of three stages: informational (information only – level 2 above), facilitating (relationship building – level 3 above) and transactional (online exchange – level 4 above). They found that a majority of firms were still using the Internet for information provision. This is also supported by research published in 2007 (Figure 1.11 and Figure 4.7). Sophistication was greater in larger companies and where the Internet was being used to support international sales. Stage models have also been applied to SME businesses where Levy and Powell (2003) reviewed different adoption ladders which broadly speaking have four stages of (1) publish, (2) interact, (3) transact and (4) integrate.

Considering buy-side e-commerce, the corresponding levels of product sourcing applications can be identified:

- *Level I.* No use of the web for product sourcing and no electronic integration with suppliers.
- *Level II.* Review and selection from competing suppliers using intermediary websites, B2B exchanges and supplier websites. Orders placed by conventional means.
- *Level III.* Orders placed electronically through EDI, via intermediary sites, exchanges or supplier sites. No integration between organization's systems and supplier's systems. Rekeying of orders into procurement or accounting systems necessary.
- *Level IV.* Orders placed electronically with integration of company's procurement systems.
- *Level V.* Orders placed electronically with full integration of company's procurement, manufacturing requirements planning and stock control systems.

In Chapter 6, the case of BHP Steel (p. 314) is an illustration of such a stage model.

We should remember that typical stage models of website development such as those described above are most appropriate to companies whose products can be sold online through transactional e-commerce. In fact, stage models could be developed for a range of different types of online presence and business models each with different objectives. In Chapter 1, we identified the four major different types of online presence for marketing: (1) transactional e-commerce site, (2) services-oriented relationship-building website, (3) brand-building site and (4) portal or media site. A stage model for increasing sophistication in each of these areas can be defined. As a summary to this section Table 5.3 presents a synthesis of stage models for e-business development. Organizations can assess their position on the continuum between stages 1 and 4 for the different aspects of e-business development shown in the column on the left.

Table 5.3	A stage model for e-business development

	1 Web presence	**2 E-commerce**	**3 Integrated e-commerce**	**4 E-business**
Services available	Brochureware or interaction with product catalogues and customer service	Transactional e-commerce on buy-side or sell-side	Buy- and sell-side integrated with enterprise resource planning (ERP) or legacy systems. Personalization of services	Full integration between all internal organizational processes and elements of the value network
Organizational scope	Isolated departments, e.g. marketing department	Cross-organizational	Cross-organizational	Across the enterprise and beyond ('extraprise')
Transformation	Technological infrastructure	Technology and new responsibilities identified for e-commerce	Internal business processes and company structure	Change to e-business culture, linking of business processes with partners
Strategy	Limited	Sell-side e-commerce strategy, not well integrated with business strategy	E-commerce strategy integrated with business strategy using a value-chain approach	E-business strategy incorporated as part of business strategy

When companies devise the strategies and tactics to achieve their objectives they may return to the stage models to specify which level of innovation they are looking to achieve in the future.

Application portfolio analysis

Analysis of the current portfolio of business applications within a business is used to assess current information systems capability and also to inform future strategies. A widely applied framework within information systems study is that of McFarlan and McKenney (1993) with the modifications of Ward and Griffiths (1996). Figure 5.7 illustrates the results of a portfolio analysis for a B2B company applied within an e-business context. It can be seen that current applications such as human resources, financial management and production-line management systems will continue to support the operations of the business and will not be a priority for future investment. In contrast, to achieve competitive advantage, applications for maintaining a dynamic customer catalogue online, online sales and collecting marketing intelligence about customer buying behaviour will become more important. Applications such as procurement and logistics will continue to be of importance in an e-business context. Of course, the analysis will differ greatly according to the type of company; for a professional services company or a software company, its staff will be an important resource, hence systems that facilitate the acquisition and retention of quality staff will be strategic applications.

Portfolio analysis is also often used to select the most appropriate future Internet projects. A weakness of the portfolio analysis approach is that today applications are delivered by a single e-business software or *enterprise resource planning* application. Given this, it is perhaps more appropriate to define the services that will be delivered to external and internal customers through deploying information systems.

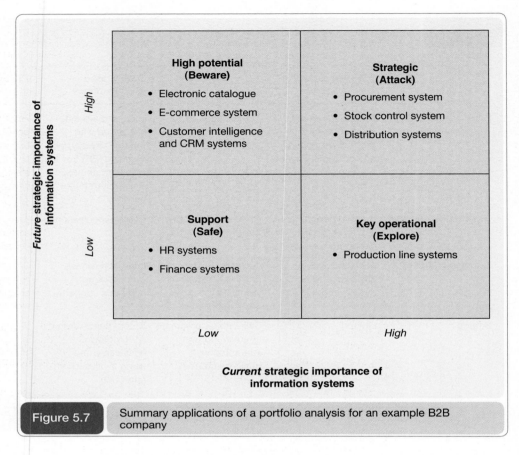

Figure 5.7 Summary applications of a portfolio analysis for an example B2B company

E-consultancy (2008a) uses a form of portfolio analysis as the basis for benchmarking current e-commerce capabilities and identifying strategic priorities. The six areas for benchmarking are:

1 *Digital channel strategy*. The development of a clear strategy including situation analysis, goal setting, identification of key target markets and audience and identification of priorities for development of online services.
2 *Online customer acquisition*. Strategies for gaining new customers online using alternative digital media channels shown in Figure 1.6, including search engine marketing, partner marketing and display advertising.
3 *Online customer conversion and experience*. Approaches to improve online service levels and increase conversion to sales or other online outcomes.
4 *Customer development and growth*. Strategies to encourage visitors and customers to continue using online services using tactics such as e-mail marketing and personalization.
5 *Cross-channel integration and brand development*. Integrating online sales and service with customer communications and service interactions in physical channels.
6 *Digital channel governance*. Issues in managing e-commerce services such as structure and resourcing including human resources and the *technology infrastructure* such as hardware and networking facilities to deliver these applications.

Organizational and IS SWOT analysis

SWOT analysis
Strengths, weaknesses, opportunities and threats.

SWOT analysis is a relatively simple yet powerful tool that can help organizations analyse their internal resources in terms of strengths and weaknesses and match them against the external environment in terms of opportunities and threats. SWOT analysis is of greatest value when it is used not only to analyse the current situation, but also as a tool to

The organization	Stengths – S 1 Existing brand 2 Existing customer base 3 Existing distribution	Weaknesses – W 1 Brand perception 2 Intermediary use 3 Technology/skills 4 Cross-channel support
Opportunities – O 1 Cross-selling 2 New markets 3 New services 4 Alliances/co-branding	SO strategies Leverage strengths to maximize opportunities = **Attacking strategy**	WO strategies Counter weaknesses through exploiting opportunities = **Build strengths for attacking strategy**
Threats – T 1 Customer choice 2 New entrants 3 New competitive products 4 Channel conflicts	ST strategies Leverage strengths to minimize threats = **Defensive strategy**	WT strategies Counter weaknesses and threats = **Build strengths for defensive strategy**

Figure 5.8   SWOT analysis

formulate strategies. To achieve this it is useful once the strengths, weaknesses, opportunities and threats have been listed to combine them, as shown in Figure 5.8. This can be used to develop strategies to counter the threats and take advantage of the opportunities and can then be built into the e-business strategy.

Figure 8.7 gives an example of an e-marketing SWOT using the approach shown in Figure 5.8.

Human and financial resources

Resource analysis will also consider these two factors:

1 *Human resources.* To take advantage of the opportunities identified in strategic analysis the right resources must be available to deliver e-business solutions.
2 *Financial resources.* Assessing financial resources for information systems is usually conducted as part of investment appraisal and budgeting for enhancements to new systems which we consider later in the chapter.

Evaluation of internal resources should be balanced against external resources. Perrott (2005) provides a simple framework for this analysis (Figure 5.9). He suggests that adoption of e-business will be determined by the balance between internal capability and incentives and external forces and capabilities. Figure 5.9 defines a matrix where there are four quadrants which businesses within a market may occupy:

- *Market driving strategy* (high internal capabilities/incentives and low external forces/incentives). This is often the situation for the early adopters.
- *Capability building* (low internal capabilities/incentives and high external forces/incentives). A later adopter.
- *Market driven strategy.* Internal capabilities/incentives and external forces/incentives are both high.
- *Status quo.* There isn't an imperative to change since both internal capabilities/incentives and external forces/incentives are low.

An organization's position in the matrix will be governed by benchmarking of external factors suggested by Perrott (2005) which include the proportion of competitors' products or services delivered electronically, proportion of competitors' communications to customers done electronically, and proportion of different customer segments (and suppliers or

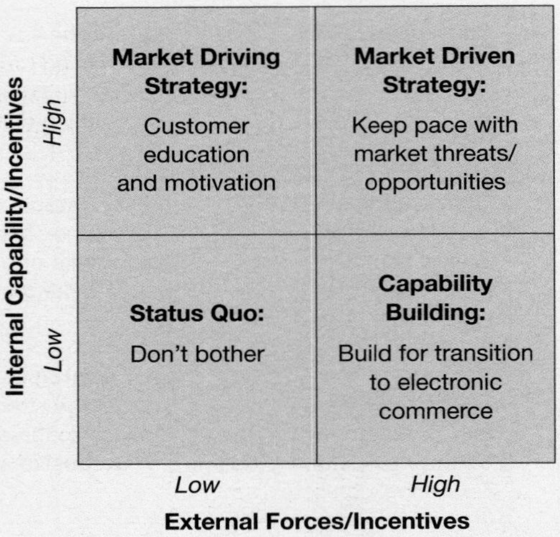

Figure 5.9 Matrix for evaluation of external capability against internal capability
Source: Perrott (2005).

partners on the supply side) attracted to electronic activity. Internal factors to be evaluated include technical capabilities to deliver through internal or external IT providers, desire or ability to move from legacy systems and the staff capability (knowledge, skills and attitudes necessary to conduct electronic business). The cost differential of savings made against implementation costs is also included here.

Stage models can also be used to assess internal capabilities and structures. For example, Atos Consulting (2008, Table 5.4) have defined a capability maturity framework. This is based on the well-known capability maturity models devised by Carnegie Mellon Software Engineering Institute (www.sei.cmu.edu/cmmi/) to help organizations improve their software development practices. In Chapter 10 there is more detail on how to achieve management of change between these stages.

Table 5.4 Capability maturity model of the adoption of e-business

Carnegie Mellon Software development maturity process	Atos consulting e-business capability framework
Level 1 Initial	*E-business unplanned*. E-business initiatives are *ad hoc*, unplanned and even chaotic. The organization lacks the capability to meet commitments consistently
Level 2 Repeatable	*E-business aware*. Basic e-business processes established necessary to repeat earlier successes but not yet part of planning process. The focus is on developing the capabilities of the organization
Level 3 Defined	*E-business enabled*. Central e-business strategy and planning process towards a centralized model (IT and competencies)
Level 4 Managed	*E-business integrated*. E-business part of departmental and business unit planning. Detailed performance measures of e-business process and applications collected and used for control
Level 5 Optimized	*Extended enterprise*. E-business core part of corporate strategy with continuous evaluation of e-business improvements enabled by quantitative feedback, piloting innovative ideas and technologies

Competitive environment analysis

External factors are also assessed as part of strategic analysis. We have already considered how marketplace analysis can be undertaken to identify external opportunities and threats for a business in Chapter 2, but here we consider demand analysis and look at competitive threats in more detail.

Demand analysis

Demand analysis

Assessment of the demand for e-commerce services amongst existing and potential customer segments.

A key factor driving e-business strategy objectives is the current level and future projections of customer, partner and internal access and usage of different types of e-commerce services, **demand analysis**. This is one of the main external factors referenced by Perrott (2005). In particular, demand analysis is a key activity in producing an e-marketing plan which will feed into the e-business strategy. It is described in more detail in Chapter 8.

Further information on demand for services will be indicated by data on the volume of searches, as shown in Figure 2.10, for example.

For buy-side e-commerce a company also needs to consider the e-commerce services its suppliers offer: how many offer services for e-commerce and where they are located (Chapter 7, p. 371).

Assessing competitive threats

Michael Porter's classic 1980 model of the five main competitive forces that affect a company still provides a valid framework for reviewing threats arising in the e-business era. Table 5.5 summarizes the analysis by Michael Porter of the impact of the Internet on business using the five forces framework (Porter, 2001).

Placed in an e-business context, Figure 5.10 shows the main threats updated to place emphasis on the competitive threats applied to e-business. Threats have been grouped into buy-side (upstream supply chain), sell-side (downstream supply chain) and competitive threats. The main difference from the five forces model of Porter (1980) is the distinction between competitive threats from intermediaries (or partners) on the buy-side and sell-side.

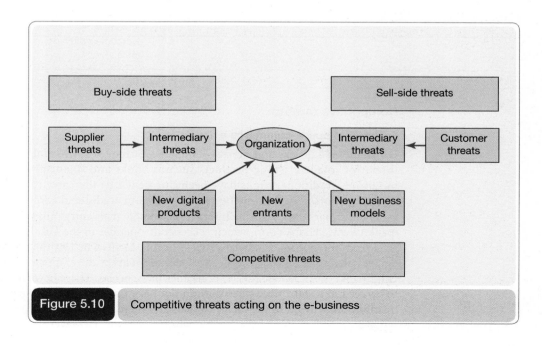

| Figure 5.10 | Competitive threats acting on the e-business |

Table 5.5	Impact of the Internet on the five competitive forces

Bargaining power of buyers	Bargaining power of suppliers	Threat of substitute products and services	Barriers to entry	Rivalry amongst existing competitors
• The power of online buyers is increased since they have a wider choice and prices are likely to be forced down through increased customer knowledge and price transparency, i.e. switching behaviour is encouraged. • For a B2B organization, forming electronic links with customers may deepen a relationship and it may increase switching costs, leading to 'soft lock-in'.	• When an organization purchases, the bargaining power of its suppliers is reduced since there is wider choice and increased commoditization due to e-procurement and e-marketplaces. • The reverse arguments also apply as for bargaining power of buyers. • Commoditization reduces differentiation of suppliers. • E-procurement can reduce switching costs although use of preferred systems can achieve lock-in.	• Substitution is a significant threat since new digital products or extended products can be more readily introduced. • The introduction of new substitute products and services should be carefully monitored to avoid erosion of market share. • Internet technology enables faster introduction of products and services. • This threat is related to new business models which are covered in a later section in this chapter.	• Barriers to entry are reduced through lower fixed costs, enabling new competitors, particularly for retailers or service organizations that have traditionally required a high-street presence or a mobile sales force. • New entrants must be carefully monitored to avoid erosion of market share. • Internet services are easier to imitate than traditional services, making it easy for 'fast followers'. The cost of establishing a recognized, trusted brand is a major barrier or cost of entry and new entrants have to encourage customers to overcome switching costs.	• The Internet encourages commoditization which makes it less easy to differentiate products. • Rivalry becomes more intense as product life cycles shorten and lead times for new product development decrease. • The Internet facilitates the move to the global market with potentially lower cost-base also potentially increasing the number of competitors.

Competitive threats

1 Threat of new e-commerce entrants

For traditional 'bricks and mortar' companies (Chapter 2, p. 79) this has been a common threat for retailers selling products such as books and financial services. For example, in Europe, traditional banks have been threatened by the entry of completely new start-up competitors such as Zopa (www.zopa.com) or traditional companies from a different geographic market that use the Internet to facilitate their entry into an overseas market. Citibank (www.citibank.com), which successfully operates in the UK, has used this approach. ING, another existing financial services group, formed in 1991 and based in the Netherlands, has also used the Internet to facilitate market development. The Icelandic bank Landsbanki (www.landsbanki.is) is another new entrant. These new entrants have been able to succeed in a short time since they do not have the cost of developing and maintaining a distribution network to sell their products and these products do not require a manufacturing base. In other words, the *barriers to entry* are low. However, to succeed, new entrants need to be market leaders in executing marketing and customer service. The costs of achieving these will be high. These could perhaps be described as *barriers to success* rather than barriers to entry. This competitive threat is less common in vertical business-to-business markets involving manufacture and process industries such as the chemical or oil industry since the investment barriers to entry are much higher.

2 Threat of new digital products

This threat can occur from established or new companies. The Internet is particularly good as a means of providing information-based services at a lower cost. The greatest threats are likely to occur where digital product fulfilment can occur over the Internet, as is the case with delivering share prices, digital media content or software. This may not affect many business sectors, but is vital in some, such as newspaper, magazine and book publishing, and music and software distribution. In photography, Kodak has responded to a major threat of reduced demand for traditional film by increasing its range of digital cameras to enhance this revenue stream and by providing online services for customers to print and share digital photographs. The extent of this threat can be gauged by a review of product in the context of Figure 5.10.

3 Threat of new business models

This threat can also occur from established or new companies. It is related to the competitive threat in that it concerns new methods of service delivery. The threats from existing competitors will continue, with the Internet perhaps increasing rivalry since price comparison is more readily possible and the rival e-businesses can innovate and undertake new product development and introduce alternative business and revenue models with shorter cycle times than previously. This again emphasizes the need for continual environment scanning. See the section on business and revenue models in Chapter 2 for examples of strategies that can be adopted in response to this threat. Case study 2.2 about Zopa shows how a new peer-to-peer lending model has changed the loans market.

Sell-side threats

1 Customer power and knowledge

This is perhaps the single biggest threat posed by electronic trading. The bargaining power of customers is greatly increased when they are using the Internet to evaluate products and compare prices. This is particularly true for standardized products which can be compared through price comparison engines. For commodities, auctions on business-to-business exchanges can also have a similar effect of driving down price. Purchase of some products that have not traditionally been thought of as commodities may become more price-sensitive. This

Commoditization
The process whereby product selection becomes more dependent on price than differentiating features, benefits and value-added services.

process is known as 'commoditization'. Examples of goods that are becoming commoditized are electrical goods and cars. The issue of online pricing is discussed in Chapter 8.

In the business-to-business arena, a further issue is that the ease of use of the Internet channel makes it potentially easier for customers to swap between suppliers – switching costs are lower. With a specific EDI (electronic data interchange) link that has to be set up between one company and another, there may be reluctance to change this arrangement (**soft lock-in** due to switching costs). Commentators often glibly say 'online, your competitor is only a mouse click away', but it should be remembered that soft lock-in still exists on the web – there are still barriers and costs to switching between suppliers since, once a customer has invested time in understanding how to use a website to select and purchase a particular type of product, they may not want to learn another service.

Soft lock-in
Electronic linkages between supplier and customer increase switching costs.

2 Power of intermediaries

A significant downstream channel threat is the potential loss of partners or distributors if there is a channel conflict resulting from *disintermediation* (Chapter 2, p. 62). The tensions between intermediaries, and in particular aggregators and strategies to resolve them, are shown by the public discussion between direct insurer Direct Line (www.directline.com) and aggregator MoneySupermarket (www.moneysupermarket.com) in Box 5.2.

| Box 5.2 | The balance of power between brands and aggregator sites |

Guardian (2007) reported on an ongoing spat which saw Direct Line disparaging comparison engines like MoneySupermarket, Confused.com and Go Compare in a multi-million-pound TV campaign. It reported Roger Ramsden, strategy director for Royal Bank of Scotland Insurance, which owns Direct Line, as saying:

> *Direct Line has never been available through a middleman of any sort and never will be, and that's what these [comparison] sites are. They are commercial operations rather than a public service, and the [advertising] campaign is responding to our customers who tell us they are unaware of this and find the sites confusing.*

His assertion is partially true in that although MoneySupermarket covers approximately 80% of the motor insurance market, it does not list quotes from some large insurers such as Norwich Union or other insurers owned by the Royal Bank of Scotland including Direct Line, Churchill, Privilege and Tesco Personal Finance.

In a counter-argument, Richard Mason, director of MoneySupermarket.com, said that Direct Line's campaign:

> *smacks of complete desperation. We are the new kids on the block and Direct Line don't like it. They have lost their market share since we came on the scene – they were in a position where consumers thought they were competitive and kept renewing their policies. They spent hundreds of millions of pounds on advertising. But now consumers can find cheaper alternatives and are doing so in their droves.*

Data from Hitwise (2006) supports MoneySupermarket's position. It suggests this site achieves around a third of its visits from price-sensitive searchers looking to compare by typing generic phrases such as 'car insurance', 'cheap car insurance' and 'compare car insurance'. It has also invested in traditional advertising through TV, print and outdoor media to increase brand awareness.

An additional downstream threat is the growth in number of intermediaries (another form of partners) to link buyers and sellers. These include consumer portals such as Bizrate (www.bizrate.com) and business-to-business exchanges such as EC21 (www.ec21.com). If a company's competitors are represented on a portal while the company is absent or, worse still, they are in an exclusive arrangement with a competitor, then this can potentially exclude a substantial proportion of the market.

Buy-side threats

1 Power of suppliers

This can be considered as an opportunity rather than a threat. Companies can insist, for reasons of reducing cost and increasing supply chain efficiency, that their suppliers use electronic links such as EDI or Internet EDI to process orders. Additionally, the Internet tends to reduce the power of suppliers since barriers to migrating to a different supplier are reduced, particularly with the advent of *business-to-business exchanges*. However, if suppliers insist on proprietary technology to link companies, then this creates 'soft lock-in' due to the cost or complexity of changing supppliers.

2 Power of intermediaries

Threats from buy-side intermediaries such as business-to-business exchanges are arguably less than those from sell-side intermediaries, but risks arising from using these services should be considered. These include the cost of integration with such intermediaries, particularly if different standards of integration are required for each. They may pose a threat from increasing commission once they are established.

From the review above, it should be apparent that the extent of the threats will be dependent on the particular market a company operates in. Generally the threats seem to be greatest for companies that currently sell through retail distributors and have products that can be readily delivered to customers across the Internet or by parcel. Case study 5.1 highlights how one company has analysed its competitive threats and developed an appropriate strategy.

Co-opetition

Co-opetition
Interactions between competitors and marketplace intermediaries which can mutually improve the attractiveness of a marketplace.

Jelassi and Enders (2008) note that while the five forces framework focuses on the negative effects that market participants can have on industry attractiveness, the positive interactions between competitors within an industry can have a positive effect on profitability. Examples of interactions encouraged through **co-opetition** include:

- *Joint standards setting* for technology and other industry standards. For example, competitors within mobile commerce can encourage development of standard approaches such as 3G which potential customers can be educated about and to make it easier to enable customer switching.
- *Joint developments* for improving product quality, increasing demand or smoothing e-procurement. For example, competing car manufacturers DaimlerChrysler, Ford and General Motors set up Covisint, a common purchasing platform (Chapter 7).
- *Joint lobbying* for favourable legislation, perhaps through involvement in trade associations.

Competitor analysis

Competitor analysis for e-business
Review of e-business services offered by existing and new competitors and adoption by their customers.

Competitor analysis is also a key aspect of e-business situation analysis. It is also a key activity in producing an e-marketing plan which will feed into the e-business strategy, which is described in more detail in Chapter 8.

Resource-advantage mapping

Core competencies
Resources, including skills or technologies, that provide a particular benefit to customers.

Customer value
Value dependent on product quality, service quality, price and fulfilment time.

It is useful to map the internal resource strengths against external opportunities, to identify, for example, where competitors are weak and can be attacked. To identify internal strengths, definition of **core competencies** is one approach. Lynch (2000) explains that core competencies are the resources, including knowledge, skills or technologies, that provide a particular benefit to customers, or increase **customer value** relative to competitors. Customer value is defined by Deise *et al.* (2000) as dependent on product quality, service quality, price and fulfilment time. So, to understand core competencies we need to understand how the organization is differentiated from competitors in these areas. Benchmarking e-commerce services of competitors, as described in Chapter 8, is important here. The cost-base of a company relative to its competitors' is also important since lower production costs will lead to lower prices. Lynch (2000) argues that core competencies should be emphasized in objective setting and strategy definition.

Strategic objectives

Strategic objectives
Statement and
communication of an
organization's mission,
vision and objectives.

Defining and communicating an organization's **strategic objectives** is a key element of any strategy process model since (1) the strategy definition and implementation elements of strategy must be directed at how best to achieve the objectives, (2) the overall success will be assessed by comparing actual results against objectives and taking action to improve strategy, and (3) clear, realistic objectives help communicate the goals and significance of an e-business initiative to employees and partners. Note that objective setting typically takes place in parallel with strategic analysis, defining a vision and strategy for e-business as part of an iterative process.

Figure 5.11 highlights some of the key aspects of strategic objective setting that will be covered in this section.

Defining vision and mission

Corporate vision is defined in Lynch (2000) as 'a mental image of the possible and desirable future state of the organization'. Defining a specific company vision for e-business is helpful since it contextualizes e-business in relation to a company's strategic initiatives (business alignment) and its marketplace. It also helps give a long-term emphasis on e-business transformation initiatives.

**Vision or mission
statement**
A summary of the scope
and broad aims of an
organization.

Vision or mission statements for e-businesses are a concise summary defining the scope and broad aims of digital channels in the future, explaining how they will contribute to the organization and support customers and interactions with partners. Jelassi and Enders (2008) explain that developing a mission statement should provide definition of:

- *Business scope (where?).* Markets including products, customer segments and geographies where the company wants to compete online.

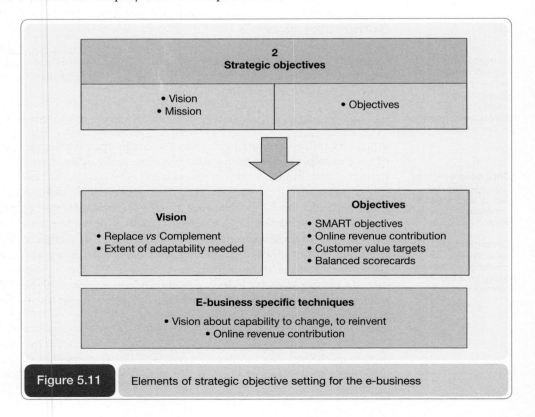

| **Figure 5.11** | Elements of strategic objective setting for the e-business |

- *Unique competencies (how?).* A high-level view of how the company will position and differentiate itself in terms of e-business products or services.
- *Values (why?).* Less commonly included, this is an emotional element which can indicate what inspires the organization or its e-business initiative.

Many organizations have a top-level mission statement which is used to scope the ambition of the company and to highlight the success factors for the business. Some examples are shown in Box 5.3.

Box 5.3   **Example vision or mission statements from e-businesses**

Here are some examples from well-known e-businesses featured in the case studies in this book. Assess how well they meet the criteria we have discussed for an effective vision statement.

Amazon.com Our vision is to be earth's most customer-centric company, to build a place where people can come to find and discover anything they might want to buy online.

Dell Dell listens to customers and delivers innovative technology and services they trust and value.

eBay eBay pioneers communities built on commerce, sustained by trust, and inspired by opportunity. eBay brings together millions of people every day on a local, national and international basis through an array of websites that focus on commerce, payments and communications.

Facebook Facebook is a social utility that helps people communicate more efficiently with their friends, family and co-workers. The company develops technologies that facilitate the sharing of information through the social graph, the digital mapping of people's real-world social connections. Anyone can sign up for Facebook and interact with the people they know in a trusted environment.

Google Google's mission is to organize the world's information and make it universally accessible and useful.

Vision statements can also be used to define a longer-term picture of how the channel will support the organization through defining strategic priorities. The disadvantage with brief vision statements such as those shown in Box 5.3 is that they can be generic, so it is best to make them as specific as possible by:

- Referencing key business strategy and industry issues and goals.
- Referencing aspects of online customer acquisition, conversion or experience and retention.
- Making memorable through acronyms or mnemonics.
- Linking through to objectives and strategies to achieve them through high-level goals.

Dell expands on the simple vision outline in the box to explain:

Our core business strategy is built around our direct customer model, relevant technologies and solutions, and highly efficient manufacturing and logistics; and we are expanding that core strategy by adding new distribution channels to reach even more commercial customers and individual consumers around the world. Using this strategy, we strive to provide the best possible customer experience by offering superior value; high-quality, relevant technology; customized systems and services; superior service and support; and differentiated products and services that are easy to buy and use.

A more detailed vision statement for a multi-channel retailer might read:

> Our <u>digital channels</u> will make it easy for shoppers to <u>find, compare and select</u> products using a structured approach to <u>merchandising and improving conversion</u> to produce an <u>experience rated as excellent</u> by the majority of our customers.

Different aspects of the vision statement (underlined) can then be expanded upon when discussing with colleagues, for example:

- *Digital channels* = the website supported by e-mail and mobile messaging.
- *Find* = improvements to site search functionality.
- *Compare and select* = using detailed product descriptions, rich media and ratings.
- *Merchandising and improving conversion* = through delivery of automated merchandising facilities to present relevant offers to maximize conversion and average order value. Additionally, use of structured testing techniques such as AB testing (see Chapter 12) and multivariate testing will be used.
- *Experience rated as excellent* = we will regularly review customer satisfaction and advocacy against direct competitors and out-of-sector to drive improvements with the website.

Scenario-based analysis

Models of the future environment are developed from different starting points.

Scenario-based analysis is a useful approach to discussing alternative visions of the future prior to objective setting. Lynch (2000) explains that scenario-based analysis is concerned with possible models of the future of an organization's environment. He says:

> The aim is not to predict, but to explore a set of possibilities; scenarios take different situations with different starting points.

Lynch distinguishes qualitative scenario-based planning from quantitative prediction based on demand analysis, for example. In an e-business perspective, scenarios that could be explored include:

1 One player in our industry becomes dominant through use of the Internet.
2 Major customers do not adopt e-commerce due to organizational barriers.
3 Major disintermediation (Chapter 2) occurs in our industry.
4 B2B marketplaces do or do not become dominant in our industry.
5 New entrants or substitute products change our industry.

Through performing this type of analysis, better understanding of the drivers for different views of the future will result, new strategies can be generated and strategic risks can be assessed.

Simons (2000a) illustrates the change in thinking required for e-business vision. He reports that to execute Barclays Bank's vision, 'a high tolerance of uncertainty' must be introduced. The group CEO of Barclays (Matt Barrett) said:

> our objective is to use technology to develop entirely new business models ... while transforming our internal structure to make us more efficient and effective. Any strategy that does not achieve both is fundamentally flawed.

Speaking at E-metrics 2008, Julian Brewer, Head of Online Sales and Content, Barclays UK Retail Banking explained how Barclays Bank was using digital technology today to make their e-commerce more efficient and effective, including:

- using predictive web analytics (see Chapter 12) which connects online data to effective action by drawing reliable conclusions about current conditions and future events;
- advanced tracking of different online media across customer touchpoints, in particular paid search such as Google AdWords which accounts for 60% of Barclays' spend on digital media.

Benefits in 2006 were a 5% improvement in paid search costs worth £400k in saved costs (showing that around £8 million annually was spent on paid search and the importance of developing a search engine marketing strategy). An additional 6% of site traffic was generated by applying analytics to improve search practice equating to £1.3 million income (Brewer, 2008).

From a sell-side e-commerce perspective, a key aspect of vision is whether the Internet will *complement* or *replace* the company's other channels. It is important to communicate this to staff and other stakeholders.

Clearly, if it is believed that e-commerce will primarily replace other channels, then it is important to invest in the technical, human and organizational resources to achieve this. Kumar (1999) suggests that replacement is most likely to happen when:

1 customer access to the Internet is high;
2 the Internet can offer a better value proposition than other media (i.e. propensity to purchase online is high);
3 the product can be delivered over the Internet (it can be argued that this is not essential for replacement);
4 the product can be standardized (user does not usually need to view to purchase).

If at least two of Kumar's conditions are met there may be a replacement effect. For example, purchase of travel services online fulfils criteria 1, 2 and 4. As a consequence, physical outlets for these products may no longer be viable. The extent to which these conditions are met will vary through time, for example as access to the Internet and propensity to purchase online increase. A similar test is de Kare-Silver's (2000) *Electronic Shopping Test* (Chapter 8, p. 406).

A similar vision of the future can be developed for buy-side activities such as procurement. A company can have a vision for how e-procurement and e-enabled supply chain management (SCM) will complement or replace paper-based procurement and SCM.

How can e-business create business value?

As Chaffey and White (2010) have emphasized, much of the organizational value created by e-business is due to more effective use of information. The strategic importance of business information management in an organization can be reviewed and communicated as part of the vision using Figure 5.12. This analytic tool, devised by Professor Don Marchand, shows different ways in which information can create value for organizations. The main methods are:

1 *Adding value.* Value is added through providing better-quality products and services to an organization's customers. Information can be used to better understand customer characteristics and needs and their level of satisfaction with services. Information is also used to sense and respond to markets. Information about trends in demands, competitor products and activities must be monitored so organizations can develop strategies to compete in the marketplace. For example, all organizations will use databases to store personal characteristics of customers and details of their transaction history which shows when they have purchased different products, responded to marketing campaigns or used different online services. Analysis of these databases using data mining can then be used to understand customer preferences and market products that better meet their needs. Companies can use **sense and respond communications**. The classic example of this is the personal recommendations provided by Amazon.

2 *Reduce costs.* Cost reduction through information is achieved through making the business processes shown in Figure 10.2 more efficient. Efficiency is achieved through using information to source, create, market and deliver services using fewer resources than previously. Technology is applied to reduce paperwork, reduce the human resources needed to operate the processes through automation and improve internal and external communications. Capital One (Case study 5.1) has used Internet technology so that customers can apply for and service their credit cards online.

3 *Manage risks.* Risk management is a well-established use of information within organizations. Marchand (1999) notes how risk management has created functions and professions

Sense and respond communications
Organizations monitor consumers' preferences indicated by their responses to websites or e-mail communications in order to target them with relevant, peronalized and targeted communications.

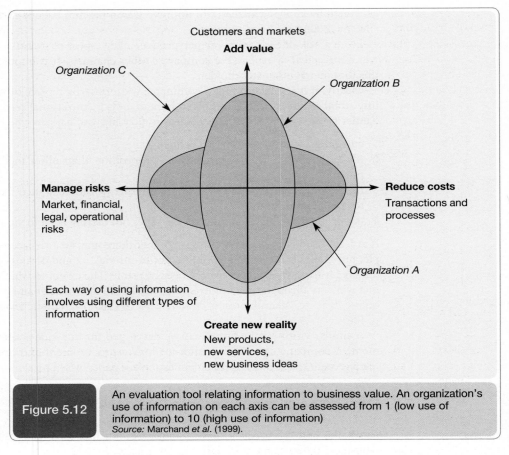

Customers and markets
Add value

Organization C

Organization B

Manage risks ← → **Reduce costs**

Market, financial,
legal, operational
risks

Transactions and
processes

Organization A

Each way of using information
involves using different types of
information

Create new reality

New products,
new services,
new business ideas

Figure 5.12	An evaluation tool relating information to business value. An organization's use of information on each axis can be assessed from 1 (low use of information) to 10 (high use of information) *Source: Marchand et al.* (1999).

such as finance, accounting, auditing and corporate performance management. For example, Capital One uses information to manage its financial risks and promotions through extensive modelling and analysis of customer behaviour.

4   *Create new reality.* Marchand uses the expression 'create new reality' to refer to how information and new technologies can be used to innovate, to create new ways in which products or services can be developed. This is particularly apt for e-business. Capital One has used technology to facilitate the launch of flexible new credit products which are micro-targeted to particular audiences.

Case Study 5.1	Capital One creates value through e-business

Capital One was established in 1995. It offers credit cards, savings, loans and insurance products in the UK, Canada and the US. It is a financially successful company, achieving high returns of 20% earnings per share growth and 20% return on equity growth. It has been profitable every quarter in its existence and in less than ten years it achieved net income of over $1 billion.

Capital One uses what it calls an Information-Based Strategy (IBS), which brings marketing, credit, risk, operations and IT together to enable flexible decision making. It describes IBS as 'a rigorously scientific test-

and-learn methodology that has enabled us to excel at product innovation, marketing and risk management – the essentials of success in consumer financial services'. For customers it aims to offer financial solutions tailored to individual customers' needs. It does this through mass-customization: offering different rates and fees structures to different customers depending on their risk status. Its mission can be summarized as to deliver the right product, at the right price, to the right customer, at the right time through continual testing, learning and innovation.

The scale of use of information is indicated by different operations in the business. In corresponding with customers, *The Banker* reported that Capital One sends out 1 billion items of mail per year and handles 90 million inbound calls, 300 million outbound calls, 230 million Internet impressions and 40 million transactions per day. Together with its subsidiaries, the company had 45.8 million managed accounts and $60.7bn in managed loans outstanding as of June 2003.

The IBS is managed by the Chief Information Officer, Gregor Bailar. He is in charge of operations related to computer systems, analysis of customer data, data protection, setting data standards, business continuity and information security.

According to *The Banker*, Gregor says:

CIOs today need to be technology alchemists. They need to be strong in professional technical method-ologies so that their conversation is a disciplined one but, at the same time, they need to understand the business, be it banking, credit cards or loans.

Their job is not to know the future of technology, nor the latest and greatest of delivery networks, but to be focused on balancing the set of business needs, and choosing or creating the best possible solutions that can be provided from a technical perspective.

On the one hand, the CIO has to be an advocate for the business into the technology world, and on the other hand, the voice of technology in the best respect of how it can respond to the business. This is a relatively new role and the challenge is to interpret and prioritise correctly the business needs and make the technology systems really responsive.

The CIO is expected to be involved not only in strategy development, but also in business and product inno-vation. Now, more than ever, CIOs are being held accountable for driving the business value, not just for keeping the lights blinking on the computers.

In their 2007 Annual Report, Capital One (2008) stressed their commitment to technology to support a strategy based on a superior customer experience.

Our brand is not defined by our television commer-cials. It is defined by the quality of our products and our customer experience. At Capital One, our brand is premised on empowering our customers with informed choice, great value, and excellent service. We are building on our heritage of bringing our customers great value without the hassle by investing in our customer experience to drive ongoing customer loyalty. We also are investing in world-class customer infrastructure, such as an integrated view of customer relationships and enhanced online servicing capabilities.

These investments will enable us to provide all of our national and local customers with better products at lower cost.

Source: Based on company annual reports and an article in *The Banker* (2003). Reproduced by permission of Capital One Bank (Europe) plc. 2007 annual report available from http://library.corporate-ir.net/library/70/706/70667/items/283356/2007AnnualRpt.pdf.

Question

Explain with reference to Figure 5.12 how Capital One has achieved competitive advantage through creating value through e-business.

Objective setting

Effective strategies link objectives, strategies and performance. One method of achiev-ing this is through tabulation, as shown for a fictitious company in Table 5.6. Each of the performance indicators should also have a timeframe in which to achieve these objec-tives. Despite the dynamism of e-business, some of the goals that require processes to be re-engineered cannot be achieved immediately. Prioritization of objectives can help in com-municating the e-business vision to staff and also when allocating resources to achieve the strategy. As with other forms of strategic objectives, e-business objectives should be *SMART* (Box 5.4) and include both efficiency and effectiveness measures.

Efficiency

Minimizing resources or time needed to complete a process: 'doing the thing right'.

Effectiveness

Meeting process objectives, delivering the required outputs and outcomes: 'doing the right thing'.

Put simply, **efficiency** is 'doing the thing right' – it defines whether processes are com-pleted using the least resources and in the shortest time possible. **Effectiveness** is 'doing the right thing' – conducting the right activities, producing the required outputs and out-comes, and applying the best strategies for competitive advantage. When organizations set goals for e-business and e-commerce, there is a tendency to focus on the efficiency metrics but such measures often do not capture the overall value that can be derived. Effectiveness measures will assess how many customers or partners are using the e-business services and

Box 5.4	Setting SMART objectives

SMART is used to assess the suitability of objectives set to drive different strategies or the improvement of the full range of business processes.

(i)   *Specific.* Is the objective sufficiently detailed to measure real-world problems and opportunities?

(ii) *Measurable.* Can a quantitative or qualitative attribute be applied to create a metric?

(iii) *Actionable.* Can the information be used to improve performance?

(iv) *Relevant.* Can the information be applied to the specific problem faced by the manager?

(v)   *Time-related.* Does the measure or goal relate to a defined timeframe?

The key performance indicators column in Table 5.6 gives examples of SMART e-business objectives.

the incremental benefits that contribute to profitability. For example, an airline such as BA.com could use its e-channel services to reduce costs (increased efficiency), but could be facing a declining share of online bookers (decreased effectiveness). Effectiveness may also refer to the relative importance of objectives for revenue generation through online sales and improving internal process or supply chain efficiency. It may be more effective to focus on the latter.

Some examples of sell-side e-commerce SMART performance indicators of an online flower business are shown in Mini case study 5.2.

Table 5.6	Objectives, strategies and performance indicators for an example B2B company (in order of priority)

Objectives	Strategies to achieve goals	Key performance indicators (critical success factors)
1 Develop revenue from new geographical markets 2 Increase revenue from smaller-scale purchases from retailers 3 Ensure retention of key account customers 4 Improve efficiency of sourcing raw materials 5 Reduce time to market and costs for new product development 6 Protect and increase efficiency of distributor and partner network	1 Create e-commerce facility for standard products and assign agents to these markets 2 Create e-commerce facility for standard products 3 Attain soft lock-in by developing extranet facilities and continued support from sales reps 4 Develop e-procurement system 5 Use collaboration and project management tools 6 Create partner extranet and aim for paperless support	1 Achieve combined revenue of £1m by year-end. Online revenue contribution of 70% 2 Increase sales through retailers from 15% to 25% of total by year 2. Online revenue contribution of 30% 3 Retain five key account customers. Online revenue contribution of 100% from these five 4 Reduce cost of procurement by 5% by year-end, 10% by year 2. Achieve 80% of purchasing online 5 Reduce cost and time to market by average of 10% by year 3 6 Reduce cost of sales in each of five main geographical markets by 30%

Mini Case Study 5.2	Arena Flowers controls its growth through key performance indicators

Arena Flowers (Figure 5.13) is an online florist based in London. The business was incorporated in July 2006 and went live with a transactional website in September 2006. The company delivered £2 million net sales in year one and broke even within the first 12 months of trading. At the time of the interview they are forecasting sales of £4 million in year two and to make a healthy profit. The head of design and development Sam Barton sees opportunities to keep growing both sales and profitability at a similar rate going forward through various initiatives. For example, the company has developed a Facebook application that provides 15% of the site traffic – an opportunity that has been missed by many of its more established rivals.

Average order values (AOVs) have developed from an initial £30 and have grown month on month. The current level is £42. Ways of increasing AOV have included options to add a vase, make a deluxe bouquet and buy Prestat's chocolates alongside the flowers.

The essence of the Arena Flowers proposition is to cut out all middlemen and buy direct from growers. There are no 'relay' fees and, because of their high stock turnover, they get fresh flowers in daily and they go straight to the customer, rather than sitting in a hot shop window. Arena Flowers offer free delivery on all their products and were the first online florist in the UK to offer FFP-accredited, ethically sourced flowers. That has been a good 'unique selling point' and enables Arena to offer something different from other suppliers such as supermarkets.

Source: E-consultancy (2008b) E-business Briefing. Arena Flowers' Sam Barton on web design and development, E-newsletter interview 12 March 2008. The full interview is presented at the start of Chapter 11.

Figure 5.13	Arena Flowers *Source*: www.arenaflowers.com.

Performance management systems are needed to monitor, analyse and refine the performance of an organization. The use of systems such as web analytics in achieving this is covered in Chapter 12.

The online revenue contribution

Online or Internet revenue contribution (ORC)
An assessment of the direct or indirect contribution of the Internet to sales, usually expressed as a percentage of overall sales revenue.

By considering the demand analysis, competitor analysis and factors such as those defined by Kumar (1999) an **Internet or online revenue contribution (ORC)** objective can be set. This states the percentage of company revenue *directly* generated through online transactions. An *indirect* online contribution can be stated where the sale is influenced by the online presence but purchase occurs using conventional channels. Online revenue contribution objectives can be specified for different types of products, customer segments and geographic markets. They can also be set for different digital channels such as web or mobile commerce.

Conversion modelling for sell-side e-commerce

Conversion marketing
Using marketing communications to maximize conversion of potential customers to actual customers.

Experienced e-commerce managers build conversion or waterfall models of the efficiency of their web marketing to assist with forecasting future sales. Using this approach, the total online demand for a service in a particular market can be estimated and then the success of the company in achieving a share of this market determined. **Conversion marketing** tactics can then be created to convert as many potential site visitors as possible into actual visitors and then convert these into leads, customers and repeat customers. Box 5.5 gives further details.

So, to assess the potential impact of digital channels it is useful to put in place tracking or research which assesses the cross-channel conversions at different stages in the buying process. For example, phone numbers which are unique to the website can be used as an indication of the volume of callers to a contact centre influenced by the website. This insight can then be built into budget models of sales levels such as that shown in Figure 5.14. This shows that of the 100,000 unique visitors in a period we can determine that 5,000 (5%) may actually become offline leads.

E-channel service contribution
The proportion of service-type processes that are completed using electronic channels.

The **e-channel service contribution** gives an indication of the proportion of service-type processes that are completed using electronic channels. Examples include e-service (proportion of customers who use web self-service), e-procurement (proportion of different types of purchases bought online) and administrative process facilities used via an intranet or extranet.

Box 5.5	Conversion modelling

A widely quoted conceptual measurement framework based on the industrial marketing concepts of purchasing decision processes and hierarchy of effects models, which can be applied for conversion marketing, was proposed by Berthon *et al*. (1998). The model assesses efficiency of offline and online communications in drawing the prospect through different stages of the buying decision. The main measures defined in the model are the following ratios:

1 *Awareness efficiency*: target web-users/all web-users.
2 *Locatability or attractability efficiency*: number of individual visits/number of seekers.
3 *Contact efficiency*: number of active visitors/number of visits.
4 *Conversion efficiency*: number of purchases/number of active visits.
5 *Retention efficiency*: number of repurchases/number of purchases.

This model is instructive for improving Internet marketing within an organization since these different types of conversion efficiency are key to understanding how effective online and offline marketing communications are in achieving marketing outcomes.

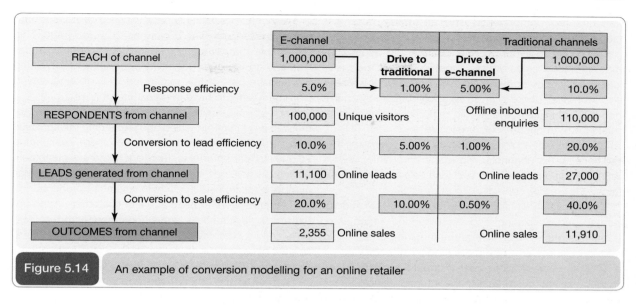

	E-channel				Traditional channels
REACH of channel	1,000,000	**Drive to traditional**	**Drive to e-channel**		1,000,000
Response efficiency	5.0%	1.00%	5.00%		10.0%
RESPONDENTS from channel	100,000	Unique visitors	Offline inbound enquiries		110,000
Conversion to lead efficiency	10.0%	5.00%	1.00%		20.0%
LEADS generated from channel	11,100	Online leads	Online leads		27,000
Conversion to sale efficiency	20.0%	10.00%	0.50%		40.0%
OUTCOMES from channel	2,355	Online sales	Online sales		11,910

Figure 5.14   An example of conversion modelling for an online retailer

An example of objective setting within a particular company, then at a relatively early stage of adoption, is provided by Case study 5.2 and for different industries in Activity 5.2.

Case Study 5.2   Setting the Internet revenue contribution at Sandvik Steel

Sandvik Steel, a company selling into many international markets, provides a good illustration of how Internet revenue contribution can be used to set objectives for different geographical markets.

When dotcom mania was at its height, so-called old economy companies, such as Sweden's Sandvik, tended to be overshadowed as the brash new online stars took the limelight.

But now that the collapse of Internet and other technology stocks has injected a harsh dose of reality into the stock market and business scene, many established names are back in favour again.

As the experience of Sandvik, founded in 1862, shows, skilful use of the Internet can lead to huge improvements in links with customers and suppliers, bringing considerable cost savings.

Based north of Stockholm in Sandviken, the company's activities seem remote from the virtual world of the Internet. It makes cutting tools, specialty steels and mining and construction equipment.

However, the group is a long-time advocate of IT. Its annual IT budget is some SKr1bn.

'We first formulated our IT strategy in 1969,' says Clas Ake Hedstrom, the chief executive. 'We didn't foresee the Internet.' Only recently, he adds, has IT moved from serving the company to benefiting customers.

Transferring its 30-year-old IT experience to the age of the web requires more than a deep understanding of technology, says Arnfinn Fredriksson, director of internet business development at the group's Coromant tooling business.

'The major challenges are not IT and systems, but "soft" things such as attitudes, insights and getting people to understand and accept that this is part of their daily work.' This means focusing hard on business needs and cutting through the Internet hype.

Sandvik Steel, the specialty steel operation, also goes beyond transactions to find solutions for its customers. Its extranet enables users to obtain worldwide stock information, catalogues and training aids, as well as take part in online discussions.

At both Coromant and Sandvik Steel, e-business activities are mainly directed towards enhancing links with customers. 'Customer value comes when our product is used, not when it is purchased,' Mr Fredriksson says.

Thus, Coromant allows customers not only to buy tools over the web but also to design their own products – within parameters set by Coromant – and receive advice on how best to use them.

Choosing the right cutting tools and using them effectively can save around 10% of the total cost of manufactured components. The e-business strategy had to take account of this.

It also had to avoid channel conflict, the bypassing of its traditional sales outlets. Most Coromant tools are sold directly to customers, but 40% goes through resellers. Moreover, there are big regional variations; more than 80% of sales in the Nordic region are direct, while most North American sales are indirect.

The company's approach was to work with the traditional sales channels. 'So many companies try to bypass traditional channels and lose sales and relationships,' Mr Fredriksson says.

It is the relationship with the customer – including greater personalization and an extended reach into global markets – which will be the most important pillar of its e-business strategy in the long term, he says.

This is what provides real competitive advantage. Shifting existing customers to the Internet, winning new ones and saving costs are also important. But other companies will be doing the same.

At present, only a small part of Coromant's orders are transacted over the web. Nordic countries are leading the way. Around 20% of all orders from Denmark are online and 31% of those from Sweden.

The proportion in the US, however, is only 3%, since most business goes through distributors and is conducted by EDI (electronic data interchange), the pre-Internet means of e-commerce.

Over the next six months, the company hopes to raise the US figure to 40%. Mr Fredriksson hopes that in two years, between 40 and 50% of total orders will come via the web.

To enhance its online service to customers, Coromant plans to offer each one a personalized web page. This will enable the company to offer new products, materials and advice on productivity improvements. Training will also be part of this expanded web offering, which Coromant aims to have in place later this year.

For both Coromant and Sandvik Steel, the value of the web lies in strengthening and expanding relationships with customers. In the case of Coromant, with some 25,000 standard products, there are numerous customers buying low volumes. With Sandvik Steel, however, a small number of customers buy a high volume of products.

'Our aims were to have 200 key customers using the extranet by a fixed time; and a confirmation from at least 80% of key customers that they consider the extranet to be a major reason to deal with Sandvik,' says Annika Roos, marketing manager at Sandvik Steel.

By putting the Internet at the heart of its business, the Sandvik group intends to penetrate deeply into the minds and ambitions of its customers. 'The challenge is not just doing e-business, it is becoming an e-business,' she adds.

Source: Andrew Fisher, Sandvik Steel, 4 June 2001.

Questions

1 Summarize Sandvik Steel's e-business strategy as described in the article.
2 Suggest why the proportion of online purchases varies in the different countries in which Sandvik trades.

Activity 5.2	Assessing the significance of digital channels

Purpose

To illustrate the issues involved with assessing the suitability of the Internet for e-commerce.

Activity

For each of the following products and services assess the suitability of the Internet for delivery of the product or service and position it on the grid in Figure 5.15 with justification and make estimates in Table 5.7 for the direct and indirect online revenue contribution in two, five and ten years' time for different products in your country. Choose specific products within each category.

No suggested answer supplied.

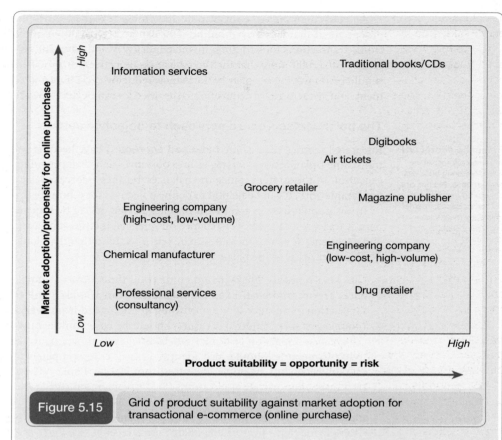

Figure 5.15 — Grid of product suitability against market adoption for transactional e-commerce (online purchase)

Table 5.7 — Vision of online revenue contribution for a B2B company

Products/services	Now	2 years	5 years	10 years
Example: Cars, US	5%	10%	25%	50%
Direct online sales	50%	70%	90%	95%
Indirect online sales				
Financial services				
Direct online sales				
Indirect online sales				
Clothing				
Direct online sales				
Indirect online sales				
Business office supplies				
Direct online sales				
Indirect online sales				

An equivalent buy-side measure to the online revenue contribution is the proportion of procurement that is achieved online. This can be broken down into the proportions of electronic transactions for ordering, invoicing, delivery and payment, as described in Chapter 7. Deise *et al.* (2000) note that the three business objectives for procuring materials and services should be improving supplier performance, reducing cycle time and cost for indirect procurement, and reducing total acquisition costs. Metrics can be developed for each of these.

The balanced scorecard approach to objective setting

Balanced scorecard
A framework for setting and monitoring business performance. Metrics are structured according to customer issues, internal efficiency measures, financial measures and innovation.

Integrated metrics such as the **balanced scorecard** have become widely used as a means of translating organizational strategies into objectives and then providing metrics to monitor the execution of the strategy. Since the balanced business scorecard is a well-known and widely used framework, it can be helpful to define objectives for e-business in the categories below.

It was popularized in a *Harvard Business Review* article by Kaplan and Norton (1993). In part, it was a response to over-reliance on financial metrics such as turnover and profitability and a tendency for these measures to be retrospective rather than looking at future potential.

The main areas of the balanced scorecard are:

1. *Customer concerns.* These include time (lead time, time to quote, etc.), quality, performance, service and cost. Example measures from Halifax Bank from Olve *et al.* (1999): satisfaction of mystery shoppers visiting branches and from branch customer surveys.
2. *Internal measures.* Internal measures should be based on the business processes that have the greatest impact on customer satisfaction: cycle time, quality, employee skills, productivity. Companies should also identify critical core competencies and try to guarantee market leadership. Example measures from Halifax Bank: ATM availability (%), conversion rates on mortgage applications (%), arrears on mortgage (%).
3. *Financial measures.* Traditional measures such as turnover, costs, profitability and return on capital employed. For publicly quoted companies this measure is key to shareholder value. Example measures from Halifax Bank: gross receipts (£), mortgage offers (£), loans (£).
4. *Learning and growth: innovation and staff development.* Innovation can be measured by change in value through time (employee value, shareholder value, percentage and value of sales from new products).

For each of these four areas management teams will define objectives, specific measures, targets and initiatives to achieve these targets. For some companies, such as Skandia Life, the

Table 5.8	An example of an e-business balanced scorecard for a B2B company
Scorecard component	**Objective metric**
Customer perspective	Customer acquisition rate (leads generated online) Customer retention rate (% using online services) Customer satisfaction index
Process	Average time for new product development (months) Procurement lead times Sales cycle lead time
Financial	Revenue contribution from online channel Margin from online channel Cost savings from partners using different e-services
Innovation and employee development	Number of new product releases per year Training hours attended per employee: target 30 hours/year

balanced scorecard provides a framework for the entire business strategy process. Olve *et al.* (1999) make the point that a further benefit of the scorecard is that it does not solely focus on outcomes, but also considers performance drivers that should positively affect the outcomes. For example, investment in technology and in employee training are performance drivers.

More recently, it has been suggested that it provides a useful tool for aligning business and IS strategy; see, for example, der Zee and de Jong (1999).

Table 5.8 outlines how the balanced scorecard could be deployed in a B2B organization to support its e-business strategy. A more detailed example is given in Chapter 8.

Strategy definition

Strategy definition
Formulation, review and selection of strategies to achieve strategic objectives.

The **definition of strategy** is driven by the objectives and vision referred to in the previous sections. As strategy is formulated based on vision and objectives, so it is necessary to frequently revisit and revise them.

In this section the key strategic decisions faced by a management team developing e-business strategy are reviewed. For each of the areas of strategy definition that we cover, managers will want to generate different options, review them and select them as shown in Figure 5.16. We start by considering the sell-side-related aspects of e-business and then review the buy-side-related aspects.

Selection of e-business strategy options

When reviewing e-business strategy options, there will be a range of possible strategies and e-business service alternatives to be evaluated. Limited resources will dictate that only some applications are practical. Typical options for an organization which has a brochureware site might be to implement:

- transactional e-commerce facility;
- online catalogue facility;

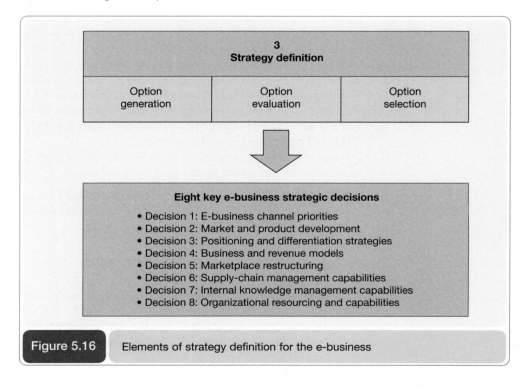

Figure 5.16   Elements of strategy definition for the e-business

- e-CRM system – lead generation system;
- e-CRM system – customer service management;
- e-CRM system – personalization of content for users;
- e-procurement system for office supplies;
- partner relationship management extranet for distributors and agents;
- social network or customer forum.

Portfolio analysis can be used to select the most suitable e-business projects. Daniel *et al.* (2001) suggest that potential e-commerce opportunities should be assessed for the value of the opportunity to the company against its ability to deliver. Similarly, McDonald and Wilson (2002) suggest evaluations should be based on a matrix of attractiveness to customer against attractiveness to company.

Tjan (2001) also suggested a matrix approach of viability (return on investment) against fit (with the organization's capabilities) for Internet applications. He presents the following metrics for assessing viability of each application. For 'fit' these are:

- Alignment with core capabilities.
- Alignment with other company initiatives.
- Fit with organizational structure.
- Fit with company's culture and value.
- Ease of technical implementation.

For 'viability' the metrics are:

- Market value potential (return on investment).
- Time to positive cash flow.
- Personnel requirement.
- Funding requirement.

E-consultancy (2008a) also recommends a form of portfolio analysis (Figure 5.17) as the basis for benchmarking current e-commerce capabilities and identifying strategic priorities. The five criteria used for organizational value and fit (together with a score or rating for their relative effectiveness) are:

- *Business value generated (0–50).* These should be based on *incremental* financial benefits of the project. These can be based on conversion models showing estimated changes in number of visitors attracted (new and repeat customers), conversion rates and results produced. Consideration of lifetime value should occur here.
- *Customer value generated (0–20).* This is a 'softer' measure which assesses the impact of the delivered project on customer sentiment, for example would they be more or less likely to recommend a site, would it increase their likelihood to visit or buy again?
- *Alignment with business strategy (0–10).* Projects which directly support current business goals should be given additional weighting.
- *Alignment with digital strategy (0–10).* Likewise for digital strategy.
- *Alignment with brand values (0–10).* And for brand values.

The cost elements for potential e-business projects are based on requirements for internal people resource (cost/time), agency resource (cost/time), set-up costs and technical feasibility, ongoing costs and business and implementation risks.

Decision 1: E-business channel priorities

The e-business strategy must be directed according to the priority of different strategic objectives such as those in Table 5.6. If the priorities are for the *sell-side downstream channel*, as are objectives 1 to 3 in Table 5.6, then the strategy must be to direct resources at these objectives. For a B2B company that is well known in its marketplace worldwide and cannot

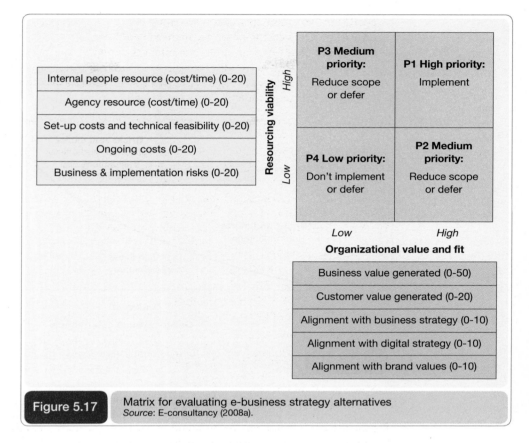

Figure 5.17   Matrix for evaluating e-business strategy alternatives
Source: E-consultancy (2008a).

offer products to new markets, an initial investment on *buy-side upstream channel* e-commerce and value chain management may be more appropriate.

E-business channel strategy priorities can be summarized in the words of Gulati and Garino (2000): '*Getting the right mix of bricks and clicks*'. This expression usually refers to sell-side e-commerce. The general options for the mix of 'bricks and clicks' are shown in Figure 5.18. This summarizes an organization's commitment to e-commerce and its implication for traditional channels. The other strategy elements that follow define the strategies for how the target online revenue contribution will be achieved.

A similar figure was produced by de Kare-Silver (2000) who suggests that strategic e-commerce alternatives for companies should be selected according to the percentage of the target market who can be persuaded to migrate to use the e-channel and the benefits to the company of encouraging migration in terms of anticipated sales volume and costs for initial customer acquisition and retention.

Although being Internet-only is impractical for many businesses, companies are moving along the curve in this direction. In the UK, the Automobile Association and British Airways have closed the majority of their retail outlets since orders are predominately placed via the Internet or by phone. But both of these companies still make extensive use of the phone channel since its interactivity is needed for many situations. Essentially they have followed a 'bricks and clicks' approach; indeed, most businesses require some human element of service.

The transition to a service that is clicks-only is unlikely for the majority of companies. Where a retailer is selling a product such as a mobile phone or electronic equipment many consumers naturally want to compare the physical attributes of products or gain advice from the sales person. Even dot-coms such as lastminute.com have set up a call centre and experimented with a physical presence in airports or train stations since this helps them

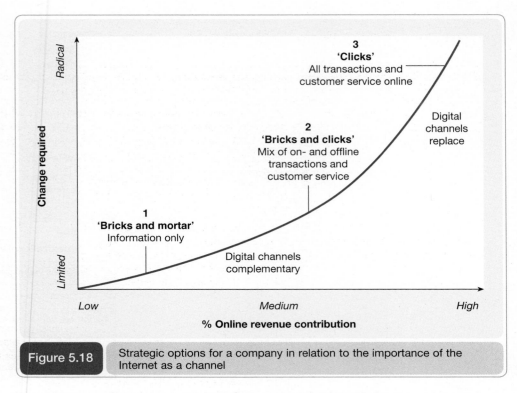

| Figure 5.18 | Strategic options for a company in relation to the importance of the Internet as a channel |

to reach a key audience and has benefits in promoting the brand. Another example of the importance of a physical presence related by Tse (2007) is this quote from the CEO of Charles Tyrwhitt, a London-based shirtmaker that makes heavy use of the online channel:

> *The picture of its Jermyn Street flagship store on our website is worth as much as having the store (in the shoppers' native countries). Jermyn Street meant something to the customers, especially those in the US.*

Right-channelling

Prioritization of different communications channels to achieve different e-business objectives is an important aspect of e-business strategy, which is often referred to as '**right-channelling**'. It can be summarised as:

> – *The Right Person*
>   – *At the Right Time*
>   – *Using the Right Communications Channel*
>   – *With a Relevant Offer, Product or Message*

Some examples of right-channelling are given in Table 5.9.

Decision 2: Market and product development strategies

Deciding on which markets to target through digital channels to generate value is a key strategic consideration. Managers of e-business strategy have to decide whether to use new technologies to change the scope of their business to address new markets and new products. As for Decision 1, it is a balance between fear of the do-nothing option and fear of poor return on investment for strategies that fail. The model of Ansoff (1957) is still useful as a means for marketing managers to discuss market and product development using electronic technologies. This decision is considered from an e-marketing perspective in Chapter 8. The

Right-channelling
This is selective adoption of e-channels by business for some products or markets in order to best generate value for the organization according to stakeholder preferences.

Table 5.9	Examples of 'right-channelling' applications

Right-channelling strategy example	Application and tactics to achieve channel adoption	Typical sector and company examples
1 Sell to and serve SMEs through online channels.	Using the Internet for sales and service through an extranet to lower-sales-volume SME customers who cannot be serviced direct through account managers. Customer channel adoption encouraged by convenience and lack of other options.	B2B. Hardware: Dell, software services such as MessageLabs Antivirus; anti-spam and e-mail management services. Commercial banks such as HSBC.
2 Account-managed relationships with larger companies offline, either direct or through partner companies.	The converse of strategy 1. Using face-to-face and phone meetings with large, high-sales-volume clients through account managers. Customer channel adoption encouraged by personal service and capability to negotiate service levels and buying options.	B2B. Account managers at Dell for larger clients. Bank 'relationship managers' who discuss financial management with 'higher-wealth' individuals.
3 Encourage consumers to buy through online channels.	Customers buying online have lower cost of sale. However, there is a risk of customers evaluating competitor offerings and lower conversion rates during the sales process. Customer channel adoption encouraged by reduced 'Internet prices' compared to offline channels and explaining proposition of more choice, more convenience.	Insurance companies such as DirectLine.com and morethan.com. Retailers such as Tesco and Comet.
4 Provide offline conversion to sale options during sales process.	Offer a phone callback or live chat facility from within web sales process since strategy 3 may involve lower conversion rates than an in-store or call-centre customer interaction. Customer channel adoption encouraged by providing clear contact numbers on site (but not on home page, when part-way through customer journey).	Insurance companies such as DirectLine.com and morethan.com.
5 Migrate customers to web self-service.	Customers are encouraged to use the web to manage their accounts which results in a lower cost-to-serve for the company. E-mail notification and e-billing. Customer channel adoption encouraged by marketing campaigns which encourage e-channel adoption, possibly including savings on service.	B2C. Service providers such as mobile phone companies, utility companies, banks and government (tax returns).
6 Selective service levels for different customer types.	With integrated CRM systems (Chapter 9), companies can determine, in real time, the value of customers and then assess where they are placed in queue or which call-centre they are directed to.	Most companies would not publicly admit to this, but the practice is common amongst financial services companies, mobile phone network providers and some pureplays.

market and product development matrix (Figure 5.19) can help identify strategies to grow sales volume through varying what is sold (the product dimension on the x-axis) and who it is sold to (the market dimension on the y-axis). Specific objectives need to be set for sales generated via these strategies, so this decision relates closely to that of objective setting.

1 *Market penetration.* This strategy involves using digital channels to sell more existing products into existing markets. The Internet has great potential for achieving sales growth or maintaining sales by the market penetration strategy. Figure 5.19 indicates some of the main ways in which the Internet can be used for market penetration:
   - *Market share growth* – companies can compete more effectively online if they have websites that are efficient at converting visitors to sale and mastery of online marketing communications techniques.
   - *Customer loyalty improvement* – companies can increase their value to customers and so increase loyalty by migrating existing customers online by adding value to existing products, services and brand by developing their online value proposition (see Decision 6).
   - *Customer value improvement* – the value delivered by customers to the company can be increased by increasing customer profitability by decreasing cost to serve (and so price to customers) and at the same time increasing purchase or usage frequency and quantity.

2 *Market development.* Here online channels are used to sell into new markets, taking advantage of the low cost of advertising internationally without the necessity for a supporting sales infrastructure in the customer's country.

   Existing products can also be sold to new market segments or different types of customers. This may happen simply as a by-product of having a website. The Internet may offer further opportunities for selling to market sub-segments that have not been previously targeted. Many companies have found that the audience and customers of their website are quite different from their traditional audience, so this analysis should inform strategy.

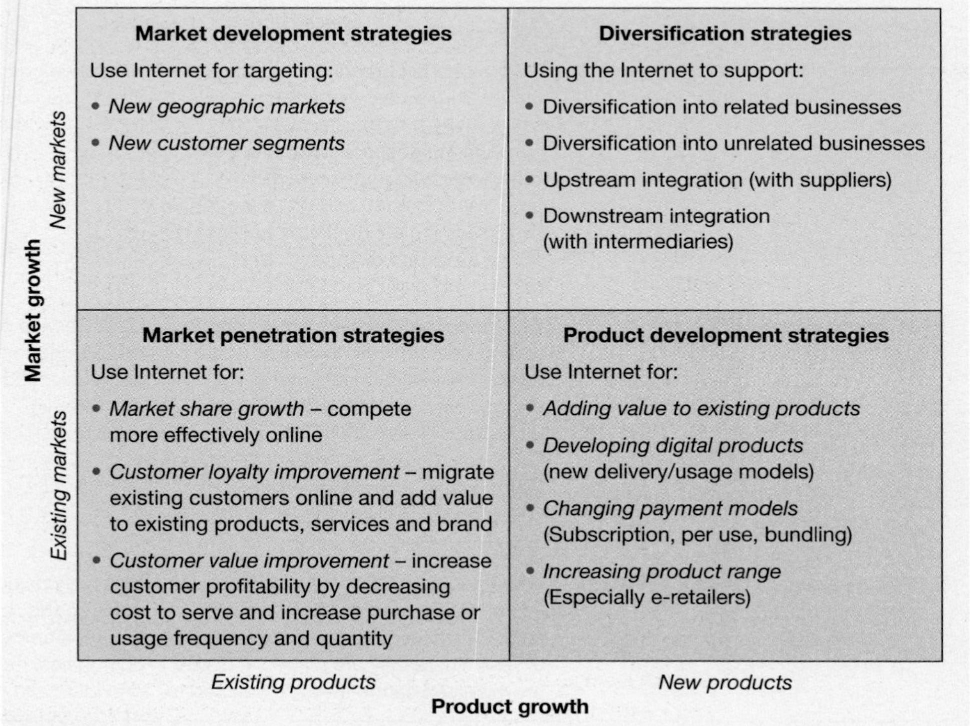

Figure 5.19 Using the Internet to support different growth strategies

3 *Product development.* The web can be used to add value to or extend existing products for many companies. For example, a car manufacture can potentially provide car performance and service information via a website. But truly new products or services that can be delivered by the Internet only apply for some types of products. These are typically digital media or information products. Retailers can extend their product range and provide new bundling options online also.

4 *Diversification.* In this sector, new products are developed which are sold into new markets. The Internet alone cannot facilitate these high-risk business strategies, but it can facilitate them at lower costs than have previously been possible. The options include:

- *Diversification into related businesses* (for example, a low-cost airline can use the website and customer e-mails to promote travel-related services).
- *Diversification into unrelated businesses* – again the website can be used to promote less-related products to customers.
- *Upstream integration* – with suppliers – achieved through data exchange between a manufacturer or retailer with its suppliers to enable a company to take more control of the supply chain.
- *Downstream integration* – with intermediaries – again achieved through data exchange with distributors such as online intermediaries.

The danger of diversification into new product areas is illustrated by the fortunes of Amazon, which was infamous for limited profitability despite multi-billion-dollar sales. Phillips (2000) reported that for books and records, Amazon sustained profitability through 2000, but it is following a strategy of product diversification into toys, tools, electronics and kitchenware. This strategy gives a problem through the cost of promotion and logistics to deliver the new product offerings. Amazon is balancing this against its vision of becoming a 'one-stop shop' for online shoppers.

Target marketing strategy
Evaluation and selection of appropriate segments and the development of appropriate offers.

A closely related issue is the review of how a company should change its **target marketing strategy**. This starts with segmentation, or identification of groups of customers sharing similar characteristics. Targeting then involves selectively communicating with different segments. This topic is explored further in Chapter 8. Some examples of customer segments that are commonly targeted online include:

- *The most profitable customers* – using the Internet to provide tailored offers to the top 20% of customers by profit may result in more repeat business and cross-sales.
- *Larger companies (B2B)* – an extranet could be produced to service these customers, and increase their loyalty.
- *Smaller companies (B2B)* – large companies are traditionally serviced through sales representatives and account managers, but smaller companies may not warrant the expense of account managers. However, the Internet can be used to reach smaller companies more cost-effectively.
- *Particular members of the buying unit (B2B)* – the site should provide detailed information for different interests which supports the buying decision, for example technical documentation for users of products, information on savings from e-procurement for IS or purchasing managers and information to establish the credibility of the company for decision makers.
- *Customers who are difficult to reach using other media* – an insurance company looking to target younger drivers could use the web as a vehicle for this.
- *Customers who are brand-loyal* – services to appeal to brand loyalists can be provided to support them in their role as advocates of a brand as suggested by Aaker and Joachimsthaler (2000).
- *Customers who are not brand-loyal* – conversely, incentives, promotion and a good level of service quality could be provided by the website to try to retain such customers.

Decision 3: Positioning and differentiation strategies

Once segments to target have been identified, organizations need to define how to best position their online services relative to competitors according to four main variables: product quality, service quality, price and fulfilment time. As mentioned earlier, Deise *et al.* (2000) suggest it is useful to review these through an equation of how they combine to influence customer perceptions of value or brand:

$$Customer\ Value\ (Brand\ perception) = \frac{Product\ quality \times Service\ quality}{Price \times Fulfilment\ time}$$

Strategies should review the extent to which increases in product and service quality can be matched by decreases in price and time. As we look at some other opinions of positioning strategies for e-businesses, refer back to the customer value equation to note similarities and differences.

Chaston (2000) argues that there are four options for strategic focus to position a company in the online marketplace. He says that these should build on existing strengths, but can use the online facilities to enhance the positioning as follows:

- *Product performance excellence.* Enhance by providing online product customization.
- *Price performance excellence.* Use the facilities of the Internet to offer favourable pricing to loyal customers or to reduce prices where demand is low (for example, British Midland Airlines uses auctions to sell underused capacity on flights).
- *Transactional excellence.* A site such as software and hardware e-tailer Dabs.com (www. dabs.com) offers transactional excellence through combining pricing information with dynamic availability information on products.
- *Relationship excellence.* This is related to the creation of an exceptional brand-experience which is described by Figure 11.8. It comprises emotional, design-influenced factors and rational factors based on ease of use, content quality and performance. For example, personalization features enable customers to review sales order history and place repeat orders as on the RS Components site (www.rswww.com). The complexity of the interplay between these factors means that it is important to use the user research and feedback techniques covered in Chapters 11 and 12 to understand the quality of the experience as perceived by customers.

These positioning options remain relevant since they share much in common with Porter's competitive strategies of cost leadership, product differentiation and innovation (Porter, 1980). Porter has been criticized since many commentators believe that to remain competitive it is necessary to combine excellence in all of these areas. It can be suggested that the same is true for sell-side e-commerce and that the experience of the brand is particularly important. These are not mutually exclusive strategic options, rather they are prerequisites for success. This is the view of Kim *et al.* (2004) who concluded that for online businesses, '*integrated strategies that combine elements of cost leadership and differentiation will outperform cost leadership or differentiation strategies*'.

The type of criteria on which customers judge performance can be used to benchmark the proposition. Table 5.10 summarizes criteria typically used for benchmarking. It can be seen that the criteria are consistent with the strategic positioning options of Chaston (2000). Significantly, the retailers with the best overall score at the time of writing, such as Tesco (grocery retail), smile (online banking) and Amazon (books), are also perceived as the market leaders and are strong in each of the scorecard categories. These ratings have resulted from strategies that enable the investment and restructuring to deliver customer performance.

Plant (2000) also identifies four different positional e-strategic directions which he refers to as technology leadership, service leadership, market leadership and brand leadership. The author acknowledges that these are not exclusive. It is interesting that this author does not

Online value proposition (OVP)
A statement of the benefits of online services reinforces the core proposition and differentiates from an organization's offline offering and those of competitors.

see price differentiation as important, rather he sees brand and service as important to success online.

In Chapter 8 we look further at how segmentation, positioning and creating differential advantage should be integral to Internet marketing strategy. We also see how the differential advantage and positioning of an e-commerce service can be clarified and communicated by developing an **online value proposition (OVP)**.

To conclude this section on e-business strategies, complete Activity 5.3 for a different perspective on e-business strategies.

Table 5.10	Example scorecard criteria for rating e-tailers

Scorecard category	Scorecard criteria
1 Ease of use	• Demonstrations of functionality • Simplicity of account opening and transaction process • Consistency of design and navigation • Adherence to proper user interaction principles • Integration of data providing efficient access to information commonly accessed by consumers
2 Customer confidence	• Availability, depth and breadth of customer service options, including phone, e-mail and branch locations • Ability to resolve accurately and readily a battery of telephone calls and e-mails sent to customer service, covering simple technical and industry-specific questions • Privacy policies, service guarantees, fees and explanations of fees • Each ranked website is monitored every 5 minutes, 7 days a week, 24 hours a day for speed and reliability of both public and secure (if available) areas • Financial strength, technological capabilities and independence, years in business, years online and membership of trade organizations
3 On-site resources	• Availability of specific products • Ability to transact in each product online • Ability to seek service requests online
4 Relationship services	• Online help, tutorials, glossary and frequently asked questions • Advice • Personalization of data • Ability to customize a site • Reuse of customer data to facilitate future transactions • Support of business and personal needs such as tax reporting or repeated buying • Frequent-buyer incentives
5 Overall cost	• A basket of typical services and purchases • Added fees due to shipping and handling • Minimum balances • Interest rates

Business model
A summary of how a company will generate revenue, identifying its product offering, value-added services, revenue sources and target customers.

Revenue models
Describe methods of generating income for an organization.

Decision 4: Business, service and revenue models

A further aspect of Internet strategy formulation closely related to product development options is the review of opportunities from new **business** and **revenue models** (first introduced in Chapter 2). Constantly reviewing innovation in services to improve the quality of experience offered is also important for e-businesses. For example, innovations, as holiday company Thomson (www.thomson.co.uk) have included: travel guides to destinations, video tours of destinations and hotels, 'build your own' holidays and the use of e-mail alerts

Activity 5.3	E-business strategies for a B2C company

Purpose

To evaluate the suitability of different e-business strategies.

Introduction

Many industry analysts such as the Gartner Group, Forrester, IDC Research and the 'big four' consulting firms are suggesting e-business strategies. Many of these will not have been trialled extensively, so a key management skill becomes evaluating suggested approaches from reports and then selecting appropriate measures.

Questions

1 Review the summaries of the approaches recommended by IDC Research below (Picardi, 2000). Which elements of these strategies would you suggest are most relevant to a B2C company?

2 Alternatively, for a company with which you are familiar, review the eight strategy decisions within this section.

Summary of IDC approach to e-business strategies

Picardi (2000) identifies six strategies for sell-side e-commerce. The approaches are interesting since they also describe the timeframe in which response is required in order to remain competitive.

1 **Attack e-tailing**. As suggested by the name, this is an aggressive competitive approach that involves frequent comparison with competitors' prices and then matching or bettering them. As customers increasingly use shopping comparison sites, it is important that companies ensure their price positioning is favourable. Shopping sites such as Buy.com (www.buy.com) and Evenbetter.com (www.even-better.com) can now find the prices of all comparable items in a category but also guarantee that they will beat the lowest price. These sites have implemented real-time adjustments in prices with small increments based on price policy algorithms that are simply not possible in traditional retailing.

2 **Defend e-tailing**. This is a strategic approach that traditional companies can use in response to 'attack e-tailing'. It involves differentiation based on other aspects of brand beyond price. The IDC research quoted by Picardi (2000) shows that while average prices for commodity goods on the Internet are generally lower, less than half of all consumers purchase the lowest-priced item when offered more information from trusted sources, i.e. price dispersion may actually increase online. Reasons why the lowest price may not always result in the sale are:

- Ease of use of site and placing orders (e.g. Amazon One-Click makes placing an order with Amazon much easier than using a new supplier).
- Ancillary information (e.g. book reviews contributed by other customers enhances Amazon service).
- After-sales service (prompt, consistent fulfilment and notification of dispatch from Amazon increases trust in the site).
- Trust with regard to security and customer privacy.

These factors enable Amazon to charge more than competitors and still achieve the greatest sales volume of online booksellers. In summary, trust becomes the means of differentiation and loyalty. As a result, price comparison sites are being superseded by sites that independently rate the overall service, such as Gomez (www.gomez.com), or use customers' opinions to rate the service, such as Bizrate (www.bizrate.com) and Epinions (www.epinions.com).

3 **E2E (end-to-end) integration**. This is an efficiency strategy that uses the Internet to decrease costs and increase product quality and shorten delivery times. This strategy is achieved by moving towards an automated supply chain (Chapter 8) and internal value chain.

4 **Market creation**. Picardi (2000) defines market creation as '*the business of supplying market clearing and ancillary services in cyberspace, resulting in the creation of an integrated ecosystem of suppliers*'. In tangible terms, this strategy involves integrating and continuously revising supply chains with market-maker sites such as business-to-business exchanges (Chapter 8).

5 **Customer as designer**. This strategy uses the technology to enable customers to personalize products, again as a means of differentiation. This approach is particularly suited to information products, but manufactured products such as cars can now be specified to a fine degree of detail by the customer.

6 **Open-source value creation**. The best-known example of this is the creation and commercial success of the operating system Linux by over 300,000 collaborators worldwide. Picardi (2000) suggests that organizations will make more use of external resources to solve their problems.

Answers to activities can be found at www.pearsoned.co.uk/chaffey

and RSS (Really Simple Syndication, Chapter 3) feeds with holiday offers. Such innovations can help differentiate from competitors and increase loyalty to a brand online.

Evaluating new models and approaches is important since if companies do not review opportunities to innovate then competitors and new entrants certainly will. Andy Grove of Intel famously said: '*Only the paranoid will survive*', alluding to the need to review new revenue opportunities and competitor innovations. A willingness to test and experiment with new business models is also required. Dell is another example of a tech company that regularly reviews and modifies its business model, as shown in Mini case study 5.3. Companies at the bleeding edge of technology such as Google and Yahoo! constantly innovate through acquiring other companies.

Early (first) mover
An early entrant into the marketplace.

These companies also invest in internal research and development and continuously develop and trial new services.

Mini Case Study 5.3	Innovation in the Dell business model

One example of how companies can review and revise their business model is provided by Dell Computer. Dell gained **early-mover** advantage in the mid-1990s when it became one of the first companies to offer PCs for sale online. Its sales of PCs and peripherals grew from the mid-1990s with online sales of $1 million per day to 2000 sales of $50 million per day. Based on this success it has looked at new business models it can use in combination with its powerful brand to provide new services to its existing customer base and also to generate revenue through new customers. In September 2000, Dell announced plans to become a supplier of IT consulting services through linking with enterprise resource planning specialists such as software suppliers, systems integrators and business consulting firms. This venture enabled Dell's Premier B2B customer extranet to be integrated into the procurement component of ERP systems such as SAP and Baan, thus avoiding the need for rekeying and reducing costs. Dell Business Solutions is now an important contributor to its business.

In a separate initiative, Dell launched a B2B marketplace (formerly www.dellmarketplace.com) in mid-2000 aimed at discounted office goods and services procurements including PCs, peripherals, software, stationery and travel. This strategic option did not prove sustainable, but it was able to test a model and then move on – it closed the marketplace after just 4 months! This was Dell's dot.com disaster. However, it does offer Dell Outlet, a relatively low-cost purchase method for returned, refurbished PCs.

More recently, in 2007, Dell launched Ideastorm (www.ideastorm.com), a site encouraging user participation where anyone can suggest new products and features which can be voted on. Importantly, Dell 'close the loop' through a separate 'Ideas in Action' section where they update consumers on actions taken by the company. As well as improvements to customer service, they have explained how they have introduced systems with a non-Windows Linux operating system in response to suggestions on Ideastorm. In 2008 Dell also has a raft of online options to engage with customers and other partners including:

- A corporate blog, Direct2Dell (www.direct2dell.com), which is 'a blog about Dell products, services and customers'.
- Studio Dell (www.studiodell.com) 'designed to help you get the most from your Dell experience'.
- A brand channel on YouTube (www.youtube.com/DellVlog).
- Dell Community / Dell Conversations (www.dell.com/conversations) 'interactive ways for you to share and learn with others and with us'.

To sound a note of caution, flexibility in the business model should not be to the company's detriment through losing focus on the core business. A 2000 survey of CEOs of leading UK Internet companies such as Autonomy, Freeserve, NetBenefit and QXL (Durlacher, 2000) indicates that although flexibility is useful, this may not apply to business models. The report states:

> A widely held belief in the new economy in the past, has been that change and flexibility is good, but these interviews suggest that it is actually those companies who have stuck to a single business model that have been to date more successful. CEOs were not moving far from their starting vision, but that it was in the marketing, scope and partnerships where new economy companies had to be flexible.

So, with all strategy options, managers should also consider the 'do-nothing option'. Here a company will not risk a new business model, but will adopt a 'wait-and-see' or 'fast-follower' approach to see how competitors perform and respond rapidly if the new business model proves sustainable.

Less radical changes to revenue models that are less far-reaching may nevertheless be worthwhile. For example:

- Transactional e-commerce sites (for example Tesco.com and lastminute.com) can sell advertising space or run co-branded promotions on site or through their e-mail newsletters or lists to sell access to their audience to third parties.
- Retailers or media owners can sell-on white-labelled services through their online presence such as ISP, e-mail services or photo-sharing services.
- Companies can gain commission through selling products which are complementary (but not competitive to their own). For example, a publisher can sell its books through an affiliate arrangement with an e-retailer.

Decision 5: Marketplace restructuring

We saw in Chapter 2 that electronic communications offer opportunities for new market structures to be created through *disintermediation, reintermediation and countermediation* within a marketplace. The options for these should be reviewed.

In Mini case study 5.4 we review the example of 3M (www.3m.com), manufacturer of tens of thousands of products such as Post-it notes and reflective Scotchlite film. These options can be reviewed from both a buy-side and a sell-side perspective.

| Mini Case Study 5.4 | 3M innovates in the e-marketplace |

3M was founded in 1902 at the Lake Superior town of Two Harbors, Minnesota, when five businessmen set out to mine a mineral deposit for grinding-wheel abrasives. But the deposits proved to be of little value, and the new Minnesota Mining and Manufacturing Co. was formed to focus on sandpaper products.

Today 3M is a diversified technology company known for product innovation with a worldwide presence in consumer and office; display and graphics; electro and communications; healthcare; industrial and transportation; and safety, security and protection services. In 2005 it had a turnover of $21 billion and 69,000 employees. With 3M products sold in nearly 200 countries and over 60% of its turnover occurring outside its US base, 3M has risen to the challenge of using e-channels to distribute its products and services worldwide.

The following are some of the strategies it has pursued to use online channels to change its relationship with its marketplace.

Sell-side

- *Disintermediation (sell-direct) strategy.* 3M has traditionally sold through retail partners, but now offers some products direct through an e-store (www.3mselect.co.uk).
- *Create a new online intermediary (countermediation) strategy.* This is a strategy 3M has not followed due to its diversity of products. Instead it has focused on its destination site, www.3m.com, which has a tool to help potential customers to research and select products. Localized content is available for many countries with 'Where to Buy' links to relevant suppliers in these countries. As an example of a countermediation strategy, in the banking sector, banks such as Barclays have created new portals, such as ClearlyBusiness (www.clearlybusiness.com), in this case to reach small, start-up businesses online.
- *Partner with new online or existing intermediary or retailer strategy.* 3M has integrated its product catalogue with online office retailers such as Euroffice (www.euroffice.co.uk). If a customer is on the 3M site and reviewing a product, when they select the 'Where to Buy' option they are linked directly to the relevant page on Euroffice which enables them to buy. Data is exchanged between 3M and Euroffice using XML data feeds.
- *Do nothing!* This is not a realistic strategy for any company, but 3M has gradually made the transition to e-business over a ten-year period. The strength of existing distribution has meant that 3M had to decide when customer usage of the web became such that it needed to offer new online services. This point, of course, varies in different markets.

Buy-side

In keeping with its innovative market position, 3M was one of the first organizations to adopt e-procurement on a large scale. Starting in the mid-1990s, 3M used different e-procurement products to help manage the enormous task of integrating the buying of a wide range of products from suppliers in many countries. This gave the typical benefits of e-procurement we will see in Chapter 7. 3M used Ariba's Enterprise Spend Management (ESM) solutions for sourcing and procurement across the entire business.

- *Disintermediation (buy direct, bypassing distributors).* 3M has used its sourcing system to buy more services direct from suppliers. In keeping with exploring new business models and services enabled through e-business, 3M has developed its own HighJump's RFID-enabled product suite (www.highjumpsoftware.com) to help its clients with complex, global supply chains to source, manufacture, develop and distribute products more readily.
- *Buy through new intermediaries such as B2B exchanges.* 3M was involved in the pilot of the Dell B2B marketplace launched in 2000 as a supplier, but it did not prove successful. As we will see in Chapter 7, the use of these marketplaces has not become widespread since using direct e-procurement with suppliers has proved more sustainable.
- Do nothing!

Decision 6: Supply-chain management capabilities

Supply chain management and e-procurement are discussed further in Chapters 6 and 7. The main e-business strategy decisions that need to be reviewed are:

- How should we integrate more closely with our suppliers, for example through creating an extranet to reduce costs and decrease time to market?
- Which types of materials and interactions with suppliers should we support through e-procurement?
- Can we participate in online marketplaces to reduce costs?

Decision 7: Internal knowledge management capabilities

Organizations should review their internal e-business capabilities and in particular how knowledge is shared and processes are developed. Questions to ask are:

- How can our intranet be extended to support different business processes such as new product development, customer and supply chain management?
- How can we disseminate and promote sharing of knowledge between employees to improve our competitiveness?

We reviewed intranet management issues in Chapter 3 and we explore knowledge management issues in more detail in Chapter 10 in the 'Focus on' section.

Decision 8: Organizational resourcing and capabilities

Once the e-business strategy decisions we have described have been reviewed and selected, decisions are then needed on how the organization needs to change in order to achieve the priorities set for e-business.

Gulati and Garino (2000) identify a continuum of approaches from integration to separation. The choices are:

1 *In-house division (integration).*
2 *Joint venture (mixed).*
3 *Strategic partnership (mixed).*
4 *Spin-off (separation).*

Gulati and Garino (2000) give the advantages of the integration approach as being able to use existing brands, being able to share information and achieving economies of scale. They say the spin-off approach gives better focus, more flexibility for innovation and the possibility of funding through flotation. For example, financial services company Egg was able to create a brand distinct from Prudential when first launched and has developed new revenue models such as retail sales commission. Gulati and Garino say that separation is preferable in situations where:

- a different customer segment or product mix will be offered online;
- differential pricing is required between online and offline;
- there is a major channel conflict;
- the Internet threatens the current business model;
- additional funding or specialist staff need to be attracted.

The other aspects of organizational capability that should be reviewed and changed to improve their ability to deliver e-business strategies are shown in Table 5.11. These include:

- *Strategy process and performance improvement.* The process for selecting, implementing and reviewing e-business initiatives.
- *Structure.* Location of e-commerce and the technological capabilities through the software, hardware infrastructure used and staff skills.
- *Senior management buy-in.* E-business strategies are transformational, so require senior management sponsorship.
- *Marketing integration.* We have stressed the importance of integrated customer and partner communications through right-channelling. Staff members responsible for technology and marketing need to work together more closely to achieve this.
- *Online marketing focus.* Strategic initiatives will focus on the three core activities of customer acquisition (attracting site visitors), conversion (generating leads and sales) and retention (encouraging continued use of digital channels).

Within a business there are many issues for changing internal capabilities; these options are considered in more depth in Chapter 10, 'Change management'.

| Table 5.11 | Capability maturity model of e-commerce adoption based on E-consultancy (2008a) research |

Level	Strategy process and performance improvement	Structure: Location of e-commerce	Senior management buy-in	Marketing integration	Online marketing focus
1 Unplanned	*Limited* Online channels not part of business planning process. Web analytics data collected, but unlikely to be reviewed or actioned	*Experimentation* No clear centralized e-commerce resources in business. Main responsibility typically within IT	*Limited* No direct involvement in planning and little necessity seen for involvement	*Poor integration* Some interested marketers may experiment with e-communications tools	*Content focus* Creation of online brochures and catalogues. Adoption of first style guidelines
2 Diffuse management	*Low-level* Online referenced in planning, but with limited channel-specific objectives. Some campaign analysis by interested staff	*Diffuse* Small central e-commerce group or single manager, possibly with steering group controlled by marketing. Many separate web sites, separate online initiatives, e.g. tools adopted and agencies for search marketing, e-mail marketing. E-communications funding from brands or businesses may be limited	*Aware* Management becomes aware of expenditure and potential of online channels	*Separate* Increased adoption of e-communications tools and growth of separate sites and microsites continues. Media spend still dominantly offline	*Traffic focus* Increased emphasis on driving visitors to site through pay-per-click search marketing and affiliate marketing

Table 5.11	Continued

Level	Strategy process and performance improvement	Structure: Location of e-commerce	Senior management buy-in	Marketing integration	Online marketing focus
3 Centralized management	*Specific*	*Centralized*	*Involved*	*Arm's-length*	*Conversion and customer experience focus*
	Specific channel objectives set. Web analytics capability not integrated to give unified reporting of campaign effectiveness	Common platform for content management and web analytics. Preferred-supplier list of digital agencies. Centralized, independent e-commerce function, but with some digital-specific responsibilities by country, product or brand	Directly involved in annual review and ensures review structure involving senior managers from Marketing, IT, operations and finance	Marketing and e-commerce mainly work together during planning process. Limited review within campaigns. Senior e-commerce team-members responsible for encouraging adoption of digital marketing throughout organization	Initiatives for usability, accessibility and revision of content management system (including search engine optimization) are common at this stage
4 Decentralized operations	*Refined* Close cooperation between e-commerce and marketing. Targets and performance reviewed monthly. Towards unified reporting. Project debriefs	*Decentralized* Digital marketing skills more developed in business with integration of e-commerce into planning and execution at business or country level. E-retailers commonly adopt direct-channel organization of which e-commerce is one channel. Online channel profit and loss accountability sometimes controlled by businesses or brands, but with central budget for continuous e-communications spend (search, affiliates, e-communications)	*Driving* Performance Involved in review at least monthly	*Partnership* Marketing and e-commerce work closely together through year. Digital media spend starts to reflect importance of online channels to business and consumers	*Retention focus* Initiatives on analysis of customer purchase and response behaviour and implementation of well-defined touch strategies with emphasis on e-mail marketing. Loyalty drivers well known and managed

Table 5.11	Continued

Level	Strategy process and performance improvement	Structure: Location of e-commerce	Senior management buy-in	Marketing integration	Online marketing focus
5 Integrated and optimized	*Multi-channel process* The interactions and financial contribution of different channels are well understood and resourced and improved accordingly	*Integrated* Majority of digital skills within business and e-commerce team commonly positioned within marketing or direct sales operation. 'Front-end' systems development skills typically retained in e-commerce team	*Integral* Less frequent in-depth involvement required. Annual planning and six-monthly or quarterly review	*Complete* Marketing has full complement of digital marketing skills, but calls on specialist resource from agencies or central e-commerce resource as required. Online potential not constrained by traditional budgeting processes	*Optimization focus* Initiatives to improve acquisition, conversion and retention according to developments in access platform and customer experience technologies. May use temporary multi-disciplinary team to drive performance

Strategy implementation

Strategy implementation
Planning, actions and controls needed to achieve strategic goals.

Strategy implementation includes all tactics used to achieve strategic objectives. The main tactics and actions required are summarized in Figure 5.20. These actions are described in more detail in the remainder of Part 2 and in Part 3, as indicated in the figure.

Chapter 10 focuses on approaches to managing the change associated with e-business implementation. Figure 10.2 summarizes different implementation marketing activities that need to be completed by an online retailer structured according to customer acquisition, conversion and retention activities.

Failed e-business strategies

Unsurprisingly, there are few companies that want to have their mistakes detailed in public, but the names of failures are well known: Boo (clothing retail – see Case study 5.3), eToys (retail), CDNow (retail), Peapod (online grocer), VerticalNet (online B2B marketplaces) and Mondus (B2B marketplaces). Many other Internet companies have failed or merged, and many existing companies invested in e-commerce without achieving a satisfactory return on investment.

What then can be learned from these? There are usually more fundamental problems resulting in failure of Internet companies. Miller (2003) has reviewed these misjudgements from an analysis of many Internet failures. He believes that the biggest mistake companies made was to '*massively overestimate the speed at which the marketplace would adopt dot com innovations*'. Furthermore, it was assumed that new innovations would rapidly displace existing product offerings, for example online grocery shopping would rapidly replace conventional grocery shopping. Even Tesco.com, one of the most successful online retailers, achieves a single-digit percentage of its retail sales from the Internet – and this has taken several years to achieve. Other reasons mentioned by Miller include:

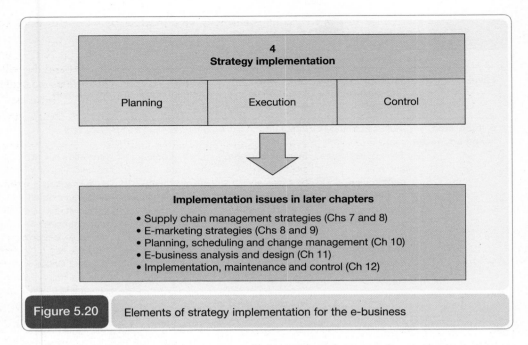

4 **Strategy implementation**		
Planning	Execution	Control

Implementation issues in later chapters
- Supply chain management strategies (Chs 7 and 8)
- E-marketing strategies (Chs 8 and 9)
- Planning, scheduling and change management (Ch 10)
- E-business analysis and design (Ch 11)
- Implementation, maintenance and control (Ch 12)

Figure 5.20 Elements of strategy implementation for the e-business

- *Timing errors*: for example, services for download of digital entertainment that were offered before high-speed broadband Internet access was widely available. The learning is that insufficient research had been conducted about demand for online products.
- *Lack of creativity*: many services copied existing business models, or other online retail services. The learning is that insufficient research had been conducted about competitor differentiators and capabilities and whether these would be sufficient to encourage consumers to switch providers.
- *Offering free services*: many services were offered free to gain site visitors and registration, and it then became difficult to encourage payment for marginally better services. This is a difficult balance to get right.
- *Over-ambition*. To achieve investor funding amongst many competing companies, some entrepreneurs exaggerated the demand for their products and the growth.

Beyond these reasons, we can also point to classic mistakes that start-up and existing businesses have always made. These include:

- *Situation analysis* – insufficient rigour in researching demand for new products and competitive forces.
- *Objective setting* – setting unrealistic objectives or, worse still, not setting clear objectives.
- *Strategy definition* – poor decisions about business and revenue models, target markets, product differentiation, pricing, distribution, etc.
- *Implementation* – problems with customer service quality, infrastructure and change management, as described in Chapter 10.

E-business strategy implementation success factors for SMEs

An assessment of success factors for e-business strategy implementation in SMEs has been produced by Jeffcoate *et al.* (2002). They suggest these 11 critical success factors, which can also be usefully applied to larger organizations:

1 *Content.* The effective presentation of products or services.
2 *Convenience.* The usability of the website.
3 *Control.* The extent to which organizations have defined processes that they can manage.
4 *Interaction.* The means of relationship building with individual customers.
5 *Community.* The means of relationship building with groups of like-minded individuals or organizations.

6 *Price sensitivity*. The sensitivity of a product or service to price competition on the Internet.

7 *Brand image*. The ability to build up a credible brand name for e-commerce.

8 *Commitment*. A strong motivation for using the Internet and the will to innovate.

9 *Partnership*. The extent to which an e-commerce venture uses partnerships (value chain relationships) to leverage Internet presence and expand its business.

10 *Process improvement*. The extent to which companies can change and automate business processes.

11 *Integration*. The provision of links between underlying IT systems in support of partnership and process improvement.

As a counterpoint to Case study 5.3, consider Mini case study 2.2 which shows how SME Firebox.com has survived and prospered.

Case Study 5.3   Boo hoo – learning from the largest European dot-com failure

Context

'*Unless we raise $20 million by midnight, boo.com is dead*.' So said boo.com CEO Ernst Malmsten on 18 May 2000. Half the investment was raised, but this was too little, too late, and at midnight, less than a year after its launch, Boo.com closed. The headlines in the *Financial Times* the next day read: '*Boo.com collapses as investors refuse funds. Online sports retailer becomes Europe's first big Internet casualty*.'

The Boo.com case remains a valuable case study for all types of business, since it doesn't only illustrate the challenges of managing e-commerce for a clothes retailer, but rather highlights failings in e-commerce strategy and management that can be made in any type of organization.

Company background

Boo.com was founded in 1998 by three Swedish entrepreneurs, Ernst Malmsten, Kajsa Leander and Patrik Hedelin. Malmsten and Leander had previous business experience in publishing where they created a specialist publisher and had also created an online bookstore, bokus.com, which in 1997 became the world's third largest book e-retailer behind Amazon and Barnes & Noble. They became millionaires when they sold the company in 1998. At Boo.com, they were joined by Patrik Hedelin who was also the financial director at bokus, and at the time they were perceived as experienced European Internet entrepreneurs by the investors who backed them in their new venture.

Company vision

The vision for Boo.com was for it to become the world's first online global sports retail site. It would be a European brand, but with a global appeal. Think of it as a sports and fashion retail version of Amazon. At launch it would open its virtual doors in both Europe and America with a view to 'amazoning the sector'. Note, though, that Amazon did not launch simultaneously in all markets. Rather it became established in the US before providing local European distribution.

The boo.com brand name

According to Malmsten *et al.* (2001), the boo brand name originated from film star Bo Derek, best known for her role in the movie *10*. The domain name 'bo.com' was unavailable, but adding an 'o', they managed to procure the domain 'boo.com' for $2,500 from a domain name dealer. According to Rob Talbot, director of marketing for Boo.com, Boo were '*looking for a name that was easy to spell across all the different countries and easy to remember ... something that didn't have a particular meaning*'.

Target market

The audience targeted by Boo.com can be characterized as 'young, well-off and fashion-conscious' 18-to-24-year-olds. The concept was that globally the target market would be interested in sports and fashion brands stocked by Boo.com.

The market for clothing in this area was viewed as very large, so the thought was that capture of only a small part of this market was required for Boo.com to be successful. The view at this time on the scale of this market and the basis for success is indicated by *New Media Age* (1999):

The $60b USD industry is dominated by Gen X'ers who are online and according to market research in need of knowing what is in, what is not and a way *to receive such goods quickly. If boo.com becomes known as the place to keep up with fashion and can supply the latest trends then there is no doubt that there is a market, a highly profitable one at that, for profits to grow from.*

The growth in market was also supported by retail analysts, with Verdict predicting online shopping in the United Kingdom to grow from £600 million in 1999 to £12.5 billion in 2005.

However, New Media Age (2005) does note some reservations about this market, saying:

Clothes and trainers have a high rate of return in the mail order/home shopping world. Twenty year olds may be online and may have disposable income but they are not the main market associated with mail order. To date there is no one else doing anything similar to boo.com.

The Boo.com proposition

In their proposal to investors, the company stated that 'their business idea is to become the world-leading Internet-based retailer of prestigious brand leisure and sportswear names'. They listed brands such as Polo, Ralph Lauren, Tommy Hilfiger, Nike, Fila, Lacoste and Adidas. The proposition involved sports and fashion goods alongside each other. The thinking was that sports clothing has more standardized sizes with less need for a precise fit than designer clothing.

The owners of Boo.com wanted to develop an easy-to-use experience which re-created the offline shopping experience as far as possible. As part of the branding strategy, an idea was developed of a virtual salesperson, initially named Jenny and later Miss Boo. She would guide users through the site and give helpful tips. When selecting products, users could drag them on to models, zoom in and rotate them in 3D to visualize them from different angles. The technology to achieve this was built from scratch along with the stock control and distribution software. A large investment was required in technology with several suppliers being replaced before launch which was 6 months later than promised to investors, largely due to problems with implementing the technology.

Clothing the mannequin and populating the catalogue was also an expensive challenge. For 2000, about $6 million was spent on content about spring/summer fashion wear. It cost $200 to photograph each product, representing a monthly cost of more than $500,000.

Although the user experience of Boo.com is often criticized for its speed, it does seem to have had that wow factor that influenced investors. Analyst Nik Margolis, writing in *New Media Age* (1999), illustrates this by saying:

What I saw at boo.com is simply the most clever web experience I have seen in quite a while. The presentation of products and content are both imaginative and offer an experience. Sure everything loads up fast in an office but I was assured by those at boo.com that they will keep to a limit of 8 seconds for a page to download. Eight seconds is not great but the question is will it be worth waiting for?

Of course, today, the majority of European users have broadband, but in the late 1990s the majority were on dial-up and had to download the software to view products.

Communicating the Boo.com proposition

Early plans referred to extensive 'high-impact' marketing campaigns on TV and newspapers. Public relations were important in leveraging the novelty of the concept and human side of the business – Leander was previously a professional model and had formerly been Malmsten's partner. This PR was initially focused within the fashion and sportswear trade and then rolled out to publications likely to be read by the target audience. The success of this PR initiative can be judged by the 350,000 e-mail pre-registrations who wanted to be notified of launch. For the launch Malmsten *et al.* (2001) explains that '*with a marketing and PR spend of only $22.4 million we had managed to create a worldwide brand*'.

To help create the values of the Boo.com brand, Boom, a lavish online fashion magazine, was created, which required substantial staff for different language versions. The magazine wasn't a catalogue which directly supported sales, rather it was a publishing venture competing with established fashion titles. For existing customers the Look Book, a 44-page print catalogue was produced which showcased different products each month.

The challenges of building a global brand in months

The challenges of creating a global brand in months are illustrated well by Malmsten *et al.* (2001). After an initial round of funding, including investment from JP Morgan, LMVH Investment and the Benetton family, which generated around $9 million, the founders planned towards launch by identifying thousands of individual tasks, many of which needed to be completed by staff yet to be recruited. These tasks were divided into twenty-seven areas of responsibility familiar to many organizations including office infrastructure, logistics, product information, pricing, front-end applications, call centres, packaging, suppliers, designing logos, advertising//PR, legal issues, and recruitment. At its zenith, Boo.com had 350 staff, with over one hundred in London and new offices in Munich, New York, Paris and Stockholm. Initially boo.com was available in UK English, US English, German, Swedish, Danish and Finnish with localized versions for France, Spain and Italy added after launch. The website was tailored for individual countries using the local language and currency and also local prices. Orders were fulfilled and shipped out of one of two warehouses: one in Louisville, Kentucky and the other in Cologne, Germany. This side of the business was relatively successful with on-time delivery rates approaching 100% achieved.

Boo possessed classic channel conflicts. Initially, it was difficult getting fashion and sports brands to offer their products through Boo.com. Manufacturers already had a well-established distribution network through large high-street sports and fashion retailers and many smaller retailers. If clothing brands permitted Boo.com to sell their clothes online at discounted prices, then this would conflict with retailers' interests and would also portray the brands in a negative light if their goods were in an online 'bargain bucket'. A further pricing issue is where local or *zone pricing* in different markets exists, for example lower prices often exist in the US than Europe and there are variations in different European countries.

Making the business case to investors

Today it seems incredible that investors were confident enough to invest $130 million in the company and, at the high point, the company was valued at $390 million. Yet much of this investment was based on the vision of the founders to be a global brand and achieve 'first-mover advantage'. Although there were naturally revenue projections, these were not always based on an accurate detailed analysis of market potential. Immediately before launch, Malmsten *et al.* (2001) explain a meeting with would-be investor Pequot Capital, represented by Larry Lenihan who had made successful investments in AOL and Yahoo! The Boo.com management team were able to provide revenue forecasts, but unable to answer fundamental questions for modelling the potential of the business, such as *'How many visitors are you aiming for? What kind of conversion rate are you aiming for? How much does each customer have to spend? What's your customer acquisition cost? And what's your payback time on customer acquisition cost?'* When these figures were obtained, the analyst found them to be 'far-fetched' and reputedly ended the meeting with the words. *'I'm not interested. Sorry for my bluntness, but I think you're going to be out of business by Christmas.'*

When the site launched on 3 November 1999, around 50,000 unique visitors were achieved on the first day,

but only 4 in 1,000 placed orders (a 0.25% conversion rate). This shows the importance of modelling conversion rates accurately. This low conversion rate was also symptomatic of problems with technology. It also gave rise to negative PR. One reviewer explained how he waited: *'Eighty-one minutes to pay too much money for a pair of shoes that I still have to wait a week to get?'* These rates did improve as problems were ironed out – by the end of the week 228,848 visits had resulted in 609 orders with a value of $64,000. In the 6 weeks from launch, sales of $353,000 were made and conversion rates had more than doubled to 0.98% before Christmas. However, a relaunch was required within 6 months to cut download times and to introduce a 'low-bandwidth version' for users using dial-up connections. This led to conversion rates of nearly 3% on sales promotion. Sales results were disappointing in some regions, with US sales accounting for 20% compared to the planned 40%.

The management team felt that further substantial investment was required to grow the business from a presence in 18 countries and 22 brands in November to 31 countries and 40 brands the following spring. Turnover was forecast to rise from $100 million in 2000/01 to $1,350 million by 2003/04 which would be driven by $102.3 million in marketing in 2003/04. Profit was forecast to be $51.9 million by 2003/4.

The end of Boo.com

The end of Boo.com came on 18 May 2000, when investor funds could not be raised to meet the spiralling marketing, technology and wage bills.

Source: Prepared by Dave Chaffey from original sources including Malmsten *et al.* (2001) and *New Media Age* (1999).

Questions

1 Which strategic marketing assumptions and decisions arguably made Boo.com's failure inevitable? Contrast these with other dot-com-era survivors that are still in business, for example lastminute.com, Egg.com and Firebox.com.

2 Using the framework of the marketing mix, appraise the marketing tactics of Boo.com in the areas of Product, Pricing, Place, Promotion, Process, People and Physical evidence.

3 In many ways, the visions of Boo's founders were 'ideas before their time'. Give examples of e-retail techniques used to create an engaging online customer experience which Boo adopted that are now becoming commonplace.

| Focus on | Aligning and impacting e-business strategies |

An essential part of any e-business strategy is consideration of how information systems strategy supports change. The importance to e-business success of utilizing information systems to manage information is highlighted by Willcocks and Plant (2000) who found in a study of 58 major corporations in the USA, Europe and Australasia that the leading companies were astute at *distinguishing the contributions of information and technology, and considering them separately*. They make the point that competitive advantage *comes not from technology, but from how information is collected stored, analysed and applied*.

An established aspect of information systems strategy development is the focus of IS strategy on business impact or alignment. In the **business-alignment** approach, a top-down approach is used to review how information systems can be used to directly support a defined business strategy. Referring to e-business strategy, Pant and Ravichandran (2001) say:

> Alignment models focus on aligning the information system's plans and priorities with organizational strategy and business goals.

Business-alignment IS strategy
The IS strategy is generated from the business strategy through techniques such as CSF analysis.

The importance of alignment is stressed in the digital channel strategic initiative business-case prioritization investment matrix (Figure 5.7). Linking information systems to objectives and critical success factors (CSF) (Table 5.6) is one approach for using the alignment approach. Another is the use of business systems planning methodology which focuses on deriving data and applications needs by analysis of existing business processes.

In the **business-impacting** approach, a bottom-up approach is used to determine whether there are new opportunities from deploying information systems that may impact positively on a business strategy. New hardware and software technologies are monitored by the IS manager and other managers to evaluate whether they can achieve competitive advantage. Pant and Ravichandran (2001) say:

Business-impacting IS strategy
IS strategy analyses opportunities for new technologies and processes to favourably impact the business strategy.

> impact models focus on the potential impact of information technology on organizational tasks and processes and use this as a basis to identify opportunities for deploying information systems.

The impacting approach may also involve redesigning business processes to integrate with partners. Sultan and Rohm (2004), based on a study of three organizations, identify different forms of aligning Internet strategies with business goals, with their framework identifying these strategic objectives:

- *Cost reduction and value chain efficiencies.* For example, B2B supplier AB Dick used the Internet to sell printer supplies via the Internet to reduce service calls.
- *Revenue generation.* Reebok uses the Internet for direct licensed sales of products such as treadmills which do not have strong distribution deals.
- *Channel partnership.* Partnering with distributors using extranets.
- *Communications and branding.* Car company Saturn developed the MySaturn site to foster close relationships with customers.

Value chain analysis (Chapter 6, p. 328) can be used for the impact approach. For example, this might identify the need for e-procurement which can be used as part of an effort to reduce costs and increase efficiency as part of business strategy. This technique has merit in that it not only considers internal use of information systems, but also how they can be used to integrate with external organizations such as suppliers, perhaps through innovative methods such as marketplace exchanges.

The impact and alignment techniques need not be mutually exclusive. During initial development of an e-business strategy, a business-alignment approach can be applied to ensure that IS strategy supports e-business strategy. A business-impacting approach is also useful to see which new opportunities IS produce. For instance, managers could consider how a relatively new technology such as workflow management software (Chapter 11, p. 585) can be used to improve efficiency and customer service.

Perhaps the ultimate expression of using IS to impact business performance is through business process re-engineering, which is considered in Chapter 10.

The application of an impacting or aligning strategy with respect to IS and business strategy is dependent on the importance attached to IS within an organization.

Elements of IS strategy

Ward and Griffiths (1996) suggest an IS strategy plan contains three elements:

1 *Business information strategy.* How information will support the business. This will include applications to manage particular types of business.
2 *IS functionality strategy.* Which services are provided?
3 *IS/IT strategy.* Providing a suitable *technological, applications and process infrastructure* (see Chapter 3).

The advent of e-business clearly increases the strategic importance of information systems resources of an organization. However, developing an IS strategy to achieve e-business goals is complex because it can be viewed from many different perspectives (Table 5.12). This table is essentially a checklist of different aspects of IS strategy that have to be implemented by an IS manager in the e-business. Many of these aspects are solutions to business and technical problems that are described in Parts 2 and 3 of this book as summarized in the table.

We will now consider one of the most important issues facing IS managers in more detail.

Investment appraisal

In the e-business context, investment appraisal can refer to:

1 Overall levels of spending on information systems to support e-business.
2 Decisions about which business applications to invest in (portfolio analysis).
3 Assessment of the cost/benefit for individual applications.

Decisions about which business applications to invest in

A portfolio analysis such as that illustrated for a B2B company in Figure 5.7 can also be used to decide priorities for application by selecting those that fall within the strategic and turnaround categories for further investment. Relative priorities and the amount of investment in different applications can also be assisted if priorities for e-business objectives have been assigned, as is the case with Table 5.4.

Traditionally investments in information systems have been categorized according to their importance and contribution to the organization. For example, Robson (1997) describes four types of BIS investment:

1 *Operational value investment.* These investments are in systems that are key to the day-to-day running of the organization. Such systems are often valuable in increasing efficiency or reducing costs, but they do not contribute directly to the performance of the business.
2 *Strategic value investment.* Strategic investments will enhance the performance of a business and should help in developing revenue. A customer relationship management system would increase customer loyalty, resulting in additional sales from existing customers.

Table 5.12	Different elements of IS strategy

IS strategy element	What needs to be specified	Approaches to aid selected tactics (applications)	Specification
1 Business contribution perspective (Chapter 5)	How applications achieve e-business objectives	Impact and alignment Portfolio analysis Investment types	Implementation of key systems
2 Information management strategy (Chapter 10)	Strategy for integrated information and knowledge management	Audit information management and knowledge management requirements by internal and external resources Security audit	Committee to standardize company information Enterprise resource planning, knowledge management, data warehousing, intranet and extranet projects
3 Applications perspective (Chapters 3 and 11)	Priorities for applications acquisition	Portfolio analysis Investment appraisal	As above
4 Process perspective (supply chain perspective to e-business) (Chapters 6 and 11)	How do applications and infrastructure support processes and value chain activities? Are new processes required?	Process mapping and analysis Value chain analysis	Enterprise resource planning integrated with transactional e-commerce
5 Departmental (functional) perspective (Chapters 3 and 10)	Which applications support different departments?	Portfolio analysis	Standardization of applications
6 Infrastructure perspective (Chapters 3 and 11)	Network capacity and service levels	Cost/benefit feasibility study of applications	Managing total cost of ownership Outsourcing
7 Communications perspective (Chapter 9)	Using technology to improve process efficiency and customer service quality	Audit communications volume and complexity Prioritize	E-mail, groupware and workflow systems Knowledge management
8 User services perspective (Chapter 9)	Helpdesk services for internal and external system users	Audit service levels, impact on business and then prioritize	Outsourcing Enquiry management systems
9 Customer and partner relationship management perspective (Chapters 6 and 9)	Investment in systems for managing customer and partner relationships	Customer relationship management and partner relationship management systems Use of standards for integration: EDI and XML	CRM facilities on website Integration
10 Resourcing perspective (Chapter 10)	How are relevant IS skills acquired and developed?	Skills audit and industry comparison End-user computing	Technology partners Outsourcing Recruitment tactics E-learning and skills transfer
11 Change management perspective (Chapter 10)	How organizational culture and structure change to achieve e-business are managed	Apply existing change management approaches	Risk management Project management
12 Internal integration perspective (Chapters 3 and 11)	Overall applications architecture across the value chain	Analyse information access constraints, rekeying	Enterprise resource planning
13 External integration perspective (Chapters 3 and 11)	How are links between internal applications and partners managed?	Analyse ease of setting up links, prioritize	Outsourcing to systems integrator Standardization through ERP Integration of IS systems with buy- and sell-side intermediaries
14 Legal constraints approach (Chapter 4)	How do we ensure company stays within international legal and ethical constraints?	Seek specialist advice	Specialist lawyers and privacy statements

3 *Threshold investment.* These are investments in BIS that a company must make to operate within a business. They may have a negative return on investment but are needed for competitive survival.

4 *Infrastructure investment.* These can be substantial investments which result in gain in the medium-to-long term. Typically this includes investment in internal networks, electronic links and new hardware.

Companies can prioritize potential information systems investments in the above categories according to their impact on the business. A similar approach is to specify the applications portfolio described in the section on situation analysis. It is evident that priority should be given to applications that fall into the strategic and high-potential categories in Figure 5.7. Now complete Activity 5.4.

Activity 5.4	E-business investment types

Purpose

To gain an appreciation of how to prioritize IS investments.

Questions

1 Referring to the four investment categories of Robson (1997), discuss in groups which category the following investments would fit into:

(a) E-procurement system.

(b) Transactional e-commerce website.

(c) Contract with ISP to host web server and provide Internet connectivity for staff.

(d) Workflow system to manage complex customer orders (e.g. processing orders).

(e) Upgrading a company network.

2 Assume you only had sufficient funds to invest in two of these options. Which two would you choose?

Answers to activities can be found at www.pearsoned.co.uk/chaffey

---

The productivity paradox

Productivity paradox
Research results indicating a poor correlation between organizational investment in information systems and organizational performance measured by return on equity.

All discussion of investment appraisals in information systems should acknowledge the existence of the **productivity paradox**. Studies in the late 1980s and 1990s summarized by Brynjolfsson (1993) and Strassman (1997) suggested that there is little or no correlation between a company's investment in information systems and its business performance measured in terms of profitability or stock returns. Strassman's work, based on a study of 468 major North American and European firms, showed a random relationship between IT spending per employee and return on equity.

To the present day, there has been much dispute about the reality of the productivity paradox. Carr (2003) suggested that information technology has become commoditized to such an extent that it no longer delivers a competitive advantage. Carr says:

> *What makes a resource truly strategic – what gives it the capacity to be the basis for a sustained competitive advantage is not ubiquity, but scarcity. You only gain an edge over rivals by having something that they can't have or can't do. By now the core functions of IT – data storage, data processing and data transport have become available and affordable to all... They are becoming costs of doing business that must be paid by all but provide distinction to none.*

Carr's argument is consistent with the productivity paradox concept, since although IT investments may help in increasing productivity, this does not necessarily yield a competitive advantage if all competitors are active in making similar IT investments.

Today, most authors, such as Brynjolfsson and Hitt (1998) and Mcafee and Brynjolfsson (2008), refute the productivity paradox and conclude that it results from mismeasurement, the lag occurring between initial investment and payback and the mismanagement of information systems projects. Mcafee and Brynjolfsson (2008) suggest that to use digital technology to support competition the mantra should be:

> *'Deploy, innovate, and propagate': First, deploy a consistent technology platform. Then separate yourself from the pack by coming up with better ways of working. Finally, use the platform to propagate these business innovations widely and reliably. In this regard, deploying IT serves two distinct roles – as a catalyst for innovative ideas and as an engine for delivering them.*

More recent detailed studies such as that by Sircar *et al.* (2000) confirm the findings of Brynjolfsson and Hitt (1998). They state that:

> *Both IT and corporate investments have a strong positive relationship with sales, assets, and equity, but not with net income. Spending on IS staff and staff training is positively correlated with firm performance, even more so than computer capital.*

In conclusion they state:

> *The value of IS staff and staff training was also quite apparent and exceeded that of computer capital. This confirms the positions of several authors, that the effective use of IT is far more important than merely spending on IT.*

The disproportionate allocation of spend to implementation was highlighted by the *Financial Times* (2003), which said:

> *Prof Brynjolfsson and colleagues found that of the $20m total cost of an enterprise resource planning (ERP) system, only about $3m goes to the software supplier and perhaps $1m towards the acquisition of new computers. The $16m balance is spent on business process redesign, external consultants, training and managerial time. The ratio between IT investment and this 'supporting' expenditure varies across projects and companies. But, over a range of IT projects, Prof Brynjolfsson believes that a 10:1 ratio is about right. Returns on these investments commonly take 5 years to materialise.*

The 10:1 ratio between total investment in new information management practices and IT also shows that applying technology is only a relatively small part in achieving returns – developing the right approaches to process innovation, business models and change management are more important, and arguably more difficult and less easy to replicate. Some leading companies have managed to align investment in e-business with their business strategies to achieve these unique gains.

For example, Dell has used a range of IT-enabled techniques mentioned earlier in the chapter such as online ordering, the Dell Premier extranet for large purchasers, vendor-managed inventory, adaptive supply chains, and build-to-order to gain competitive advantage.

Research into the productivity paradox highlights the importance of considering the information, people and technology resources together when planning for e-business strategy and implementation. It also suggests that e-business contributes to productivity gains only when combined with investments in process redesign, organizational change management and innovation.

Summary

1 E-business strategy process models tend to share the following characteristics:
   - Continuous internal and external environment scanning or analysis is required.
   - Clear statement of vision and objectives is required.
   - Strategy development can be broken down into formulation and selection, a key emphasis being assessing the differential benefits provided by e-channels for company and stakeholders and then selecting the most appropriate channels for different business activities and partners ('right-channelling').
   - After strategy development, enactment of the strategy occurs as strategy implementation.
   - Control is required to detect problems and adjust the strategy accordingly.
   - They must be responsive to changes in the marketplace.

2 In this chapter a four-stage model is used as a framework for e-business strategy development. Key e-business issues within this framework are outlined below.

3 *Strategic analysis*. Continuous scanning of the micro- and macro-environment of an organization is required, with particular emphasis on the changing needs of customers, actions and business models of competitors, and opportunities afforded by new technologies.

4 *Strategic objectives*. Organizations must have a clear vision on whether digital media will complement or replace other media, and their capacity for change. Clear objectives must be defined and in particular goals for the online revenue contribution should be set.

5 *Strategy definition*. Six key elements of e-business strategy that were reviewed are:
   - E-business priorities – significance to organization (replace or complement) and emphasis on buy-side or sell-side.
   - Form of restructuring required.
   - Business and revenue models.
   - Marketplace restructuring.
   - Market and product development strategies.
   - Positioning and differentiation strategies.

6 Strategy implementation. Detailed in the remainder of Part 2 and in Part 3.

7 Information systems strategy should use a combination of impact and alignment techniques to govern e-business strategy. IS strategy can take a number of perspectives, of which those that focus on information or knowledge management and technological and applications infrastructure are most important.

Exercises

Self-assessment questions

1 What are the key characteristics of an e-business strategy model?

2 Select a retailer or manufacturer of your choice and describe what the main elements of its situation analysis should comprise.

3 For the same retailer or manufacturer suggest different methods and metrics for defining e-business objectives.

4 For the same retailer or manufacturer assess different strategic options to adopt for e-business.

Essay and discussion questions

1 Evaluate the range of restructuring options for an existing 'bricks-and-mortar' organization to move to 'bricks-and-clicks' or 'clicks-only' contributing a higher online revenue.

2 Explain the main strategy definition options or decisions available to an organization intending to become an e-business.

3 Between 1994 and 1999 Amazon lost more than $500m, but at the end of this period its valuation was still more than $20bn. At the start of 2000 Amazon.com underwent its first round of job cuts, sacking 150 staff or 2% of its worldwide workforce. Later in 2000 its valuation dropped to less than half.

   Write an essay on the strategy of Amazon.com exploring its history, different criteria for success and its future. See the *Wired Magazine* archive for profiles of Amazon (www.wired.com).

4 Analyse the reasons for the failure of the original boo.com. Research and assess the sustainability of the new boo.com business model.

5 What can existing businesses learn from the business approaches of the dot-com organizations?

6 What are the similarities and differences between the concepts of business process re-engineering (BPR) and e-business? Will the e-business concept face the same fate as BPR?

7 Discuss this statement by David Weymouth, Barclays Bank chief information officer (Simons, 2000b):

   There is no merit in becoming a dot-com business. Within five years successful businesses will have embraced and deployed at real-scale across the whole enterprise, the processes and technologies that we now know as dot-com.

8 Compare and contrast different approaches to developing e-business strategy.

Examination questions

1 Define the main elements of an e-business strategy.

2 You are the incumbent e-business manager for a domestic airline. What process would you use to create objectives for the organization? Suggest three typical objectives and how you would measure them.

3 Explain the productivity paradox and its implications for managers.

4 What choices do executives have for the scope and timeframe of implementing e-business?

References

Aaker, D. and Joachimsthaler, E. (2000) *Brand Leadership*. Free Press, New York.

Ansoff, H. (1957) Strategies for diversification. *Harvard Business Review*, September–October, 113–24.

Arnott, D. and Bridgewater, S. (2002) Internet, interaction and implications for marketing. *Marketing Intelligence and Planning*, 20(2), 86–95.

Atos Consulting (2008) Ebusiness maturity framework. Published 4 November at **www.maxx-online.nl/?p=273**.

Banker (2003) Why does the CIO have so many hats? *The Banker*, 2 December. **www.thebanker.com/news/fullstory.php/aid/921/Why_ does the CIO have so manyhats_.html?PHPSESSID=6127f5720bc3f4cb3bd386bf1f31087a.**

Berthon, P., Lane, N., Pitt, L. and Watson, R. (1998) The World Wide Web as an industrial marketing communications tool: models for the identification and assessment of opportunities. *Journal of Marketing Management*, 14, 691–704.

Brewer, J. (2008) Analytics Meets Targeting Meets CRM. Presentation to eMetrics Marketing Optimization Summit. London, 20–21 May.

Brynjolfsson, E. (1993) The productivity paradox of information technology. *Communications of the ACM*, 36(12), 67–77.

Brynjolfsson, E. and Hitt, L. (1998) Beyond the productivity paradox. *Communications of the ACM*, 41(8), 49–55.

Carr, N. (2003) IT doesn't matter. *Harvard Business Review*, May, 5–12.

Chaffey, D. and White, G. (2010) *Business Information Management: Improving Performance Using Information Systems*. 2nd edn. Financial Times Prentice Hall, Harlow.

Chaffey, D., Mayer, R., Johnston, K. and Ellis-Chadwick, F. (2009) *Internet Marketing: Strategy, Implementation and Practice*, 4th edn. Financial Times Prentice Hall, Harlow.

Chaston, I. (2000) *E-Marketing Strategy*. McGraw-Hill, Maidenhead.

Damanpour, F. (2001) E-business, e-commerce, evolution: perspective and strategy. *Managerial Finance*, 27(7), 16–33.

Daniel, E., Wilson, H., McDonald, M. and Ward, J. (2001) *Marketing Strategy in the Digital Age*. Financial Times Prentice Hall, Harlow.

Deise, M., Nowikow, C., King, P. and Wright, A. (2000) *Executive's Guide to E-Business. From Tactics to Strategy*. Wiley, New York.

de Kare-Silver, M. (2000) *EShock 2000. The Electronic Shopping Revolution: Strategies for Retailers and Manufacturers*. Macmillan, London.

der Zee, J. and de Jong, B. (1999) Alignment is not enough: integrating business and information technology management with the balanced business scorecard. *Journal of Management Information Systems*, 16(2), 137–57.

Doherty, N. and McAulay, L. (2002) Towards the formulation of a comprehensive framework for the evaluation of investments in sell-side e-commerce. *Evaluation and Program Planning*, 25, 159–65.

Durlacher (2000) Trends in the UK new economy. *Durlacher Quarterly Internet Report*, November, 1–12.

E-consultancy (2005) Managing an e-commerce team. Integrating digital marketing into your organisation. 60-page report by Dave Chaffey. Available from **www.econsultancy.com.**

E-consultancy (2008a) Managing Digital Channels Research Report. Author: Dave Chaffey. Available from **www.econsultancy.com.**

E-consultancy (2008b) E-business Briefing. Arena Flowers' Sam Barton on web design and development, E-newsletter interview, 12 March.

Financial Times (2003) Buried treasure. Article by Simon London. *Financial Times*, 10 December.

Guardian (2007) Beware when you compare Harriet Meyer, Friday 22 June, *Guardian* **http://money.guardian.co.uk/insurance _/story/0,,21 08482,00.html.**

Gulati, R. and Garino, J. (2000) Getting the right mix of bricks and clicks for your company. *Harvard Business Review*, May–June, 107–14.

Hackbarth, G. and Kettinger, W. (2000) Building an e-business strategy. *Information Systems Management*, Summer, 78–93.

Hitwise (2006). Paid and Organic Search: Profile of MoneySupermarket. Hitwise blogposting: **http://weblogs.hitwise.com/heather-hopkins/2006/09/paid and organic search profil.html.**

Hughes, S. (2001) Market orientation and the response of UK financial services companies to changes in market conditions as a result of e-commerce. *International Journal of Bank Marketing*, 19(6), 222–31.

Jeffcoate, J., Chappell, C. and Feindt, S. (2002) Best practice in SME adoption of e-commerce. *Benchmarking: An International Journal*, 9, 122–32.

Jelassi, T. and Enders, A. (2008) *Strategies for e-Business: Creating Value through Electronic and Mobile Commerce*, 2nd edn. Financial Times Prentice Hall, Harlow.

Johnson, G. and Scholes, K. (2006) *Exploring Corporate Strategy: Text and Cases*, 7th edn. Financial Times Prentice Hall, Harlow.

Kalakota, R. and Robinson, M. (2000) *E-Business. Roadmap for Success*. Addison-Wesley, Reading, MA.

Kaplan, R.S. and Norton, D.P. (1993) Putting the balanced scorecard to work. *Harvard Business Review*, September–October, 134–42.

Kim, E., Nam, D. and Stimpert, D. (2004) The applicability of Porter's generic strategies in the digital age: assumptions, conjectures and suggestions. *Journal of Management*, 30, 569–89.

Kumar, N. (1999) Internet distribution strategies: dilemmas for the incumbent. *Financial Times*, Special Issue on Mastering Information Management, no. 7, Electronic Commerce.

Levy, M. and Powell, P. (2003) Exploring SME Internet adoption: towards a contingent model. *Electronic Markets*, 13(2), 173–81, **www.electronicmarkets.org**.

Lynch, R. (2000) *Corporate Strategy*. Financial Times Prentice Hall, Harlow.

Mcafee, A. and Brynjolfsson, E. (2008) Investing in the IT that makes a competitive difference. *Harvard Business Review*, 7/8, 98–107.

McDonald, M. (1999) Strategic marketing planning: theory and practice. In *The CIM Marketing Book*, 4th edn, M. Baker (ed.). Butterworth-Heinemann, Oxford, pp. 50–77.

McDonald, M. and Wilson, H. (2002) *New Marketing: Transforming the Corporate Future*. Butterworth-Heinemann, Oxford.

McFarlan, F. and McKenney, J. (1993) *Corporate Information Systems Management*. Prentice Hall, London.

Malmsten, E., Portanger, E. and Drazin, C. (2001) *Boo Hoo. A Dot.com Story from Concept to Catastrophe*. Random House, London.

Marchand, D. (1999) Hard choices for senior managers. In *Mastering Information Management*, D. Marchand, T. Davenport and T. Dickson (eds). Financial Times Prentice Hall, Harlow, pp. 187–92.

Marchand, D., Kettinger, W. and Rollins, J. (2002) *Information Orientation: The Link to Business Performance*. Oxford University Press, Oxford, UK.

Miller, T. (2003) Top ten lessons from the Internet shakeout. Article on Webmergers.com. Available online at: **www.webmergers.com/data/article.php?id=48**.

Mintzberg, H. and Quinn, J. (1991) *The Strategy Process*, 2nd edn. Prentice-Hall, Upper Saddle River, NJ.

Myers, J., Pickersgill, A, and Van Metre, E. (2004) Steering customers to the right channels. *McKinsey Quarterly*, no. 4.

New Media Age (1999) Will boo.com scare off the competition? By Budd Margolis. *New Media Age*, 22 July. Online only, **www.nma.co.uk**.

New Media Age (2005) Delivering the goods. By Nic Howell. *New Media Age*, 5 May.

Nolan, R. (1979) Managing the crisis in data processing. *Harvard Business Review*, March–April, 115–26.

Olve, N., Roy, J. and Wetter, M. (1999) *Performance Drivers. A Practical Guide to Using the Balanced Scorecard*. Wiley, Chichester.

Pant, S. and Ravichandran, T. (2001) A framework for information systems planning for e-business. *Logistics Information Management*, 14(1), 85–98.

Perrott, B. (2005) Towards a manager's model of e-business strategy decisions. *Journal of General Management*, 30(4), 73–89.

Phillips, S. (2000) Retailer's crown jewel is a unique customer database. *Financial Times*, 4 December.

Picardi, R. (2000) *EBusiness Speed: Six Strategies for eCommerce Intelligence*. IDC Research Report. IDC, Framingham, MA.

Plant, R. (2000) *ECommerce: Formulation of Strategy*. Prentice-Hall, Upper Saddle River, NJ.

Porter, M. (1980) *Competitive Strategy*. Free Press, New York.

Porter, M. (2001) Strategy and the Internet. *Harvard Business Review*, March, 62–78.

Quelch, J. and Klein, L. (1996) The Internet and international marketing. *Sloan Management Review*, Spring, 60–75.

Revolution (2005) Campaign of the Month, by Emma Rigby. *Revolution*, October, 69.

Robson, W. (1997) *Strategic Management and Information Systems: An Integrated Approach*. Pitman, London.

Rowley, J. (2002) Synergy and strategy in e-commerce. *Marketing Intelligence and Planning*, 20(4), 215–20.

Simons, M. (2000a) Barclays gambles on web big bang. *Computer Weekly*, 13 July, p. 1.

Simons, M. (2000b) Setting the banks alight. *Computer Weekly*, 20 July, p. 6.

Sircar, S., Turnbow, J. and Bordoloi, B. (2000) A framework for assessing the relationship between information technology investments and firm performance. *Journal of Management Information Systems*, Spring, 16(4), 69–98.

Smith, P. (1999) *Marketing Communications: An Integrated Approach*, 2nd edn. Kogan Page, London.

Strassman, P. (1997) *The Squandered Computer*. Information Economics Press, New Canaan, CT.

Sultan, F. and Rohm, A. (2004) The evolving role of the Internet in marketing strategy. *Journal of Interactive marketing*, 19(2), 6–19.

Tjan, A. (2001) Finally, a way to put your Internet portfolio in order. *Harvard Business Review*, February, 78–85.

Tse, T. (2007) Reconsidering the source of value of e-business strategies. *Strategic Change*, 16, 117–26.

Ward, J. and Griffiths, P. (1996) *Strategic Planning for Information Systems*. Wiley, Chichester.

Willcocks, L. and Plant, R. (2000) Business Internet strategy – moving to the net. In *Moving to E-Business*, L. Willcocks and C. Sauer (eds). Random House, London, pp. 19–46.

Further reading

Hackbarth, G. and Kettinger, W. (2000) Building an e-business strategy. *Information Systems Management*, Summer, 78–93. An information systems perspective to e-business strategy.

Jelassi, T. and Enders, A. (2008) *Strategies for e-Business. Creating Value through Electronic and Mobile Commerce*, 2nd edn. Financial Times Prentice Hall, Harlow. Provides a roadmap for developing e-business strategy focusing on sell-side e-commerce, but excluding communications strategy.

Johnson, G. and Scholes, K. (2006) *Exploring Corporate Strategy. Text and Cases*, 7th edn. Financial Times Prentice Hall, Harlow. The classic text on business strategy development.

Porter, M. (2001) Strategy and the Internet. *Harvard Business Review*, March, 63–78. Michael Porter defends his existing models in the new economy context.

Web links

CIO Magazine e-commerce resource centre (**www.cio.com/forums/ec**) One of the best online magazines from a business and technical perspective – see other research centres also, e.g. intranets, knowledge management.

DaveChaffey.com (**www.davechaffey.com/E-business**) Updates by the author about all aspects of e-business, including strategy.

E-commerce Times (**www.ecommercetimes.com**) An online newspaper specific to e-commerce developments.

Knowledge@Wharton (**http://knowledge.wharton.upenn.edu/www**) Knowl-edge@ Wharton is an online resource that offers the latest business insights, information, and research from a variety of sources.

Financial Times Digital Business (**http://news.ft.com/reports/digitalbusiness**) Monthly articles based on case studies.

McKinseyQuarterly (**www.mckinseyquarterly.com**) Articles regularly cover digital marketing strategy.

E-consultancy (**www.econsultancy.com**) E-business portal with links to news and White Papers on other sites.

MIT Center for Digital Business (**http://digital.mit.edu**) in the MIT Sloan School of Management. Resources and papers from leading researchers into digital business including Professor Erik Brynjolfsson (**http://digital.mit.edu/erik**).

Mohansawney.com (**www.mohansawney.com**) Case studies and White Papers from one of the leading US authorities on e-commerce.

6

Supply chain management

Web support

The following additional case studies are available at
www.pearsoned.co.uk/chaffey

→ A short history of the Sainsburys approach to e-fulfilment models
→ The telecoms supply chain
→ The site also contains a range of study material designed to help improve your results.

Learning outcomes

After completing this chapter the reader should be able to:

- Identify the main elements of supply chain management and their relationship to the value chain and value networks
- Assess the potential of information systems to support supply chain management and the value chain

Management issues

The issues for the manager:

- Which technologies should we deploy for supply chain management and how should they be prioritized?
- Which elements of the supply chain should be managed within and beyond the organization and how can technology be used to facilitate this?
- What are the practical issues with online supply chain management?

Links to other chapters

The main related chapters are:

- *Chapter 1* introduces the supply chain as a key element of e-business
- *Chapter 7* considers the e-procurement part of the supply chain in more detail

Introduction

In the end business all comes down to supply chain vs supply chain.

(Robert Rodin, then CEO of Marshall Industries, one of the largest global distributors of electronic components, 1999)

Supply chain management is essentially the optimization of material flows and associated information flows involved with an organization's operations. To manage these flows e-business applications are today essential to bring the benefits illustrated in Box 6.1. Supply chain management is presented as the premier application of e-business in Part 2 of this book since it is a unifying concept that incorporates both e-procurement (Chapter 7) and sell-side e-commerce (Chapters 8 and 9). By applying information systems, companies can enhance or radically improve many aspects of the supply chain. In the context of Figure 1.1, which was used to introduce the concept of e-business, supply chain management can be enhanced through buy-side e-commerce, internal communications, relationships with partners and sell-side e-commerce. E-business technologies enable information flows to be redefined to facilitate the sharing of information between partners, often at lower costs than were previously possible.

Supply chain management capabilities are best known for their importance in delivering profitability. For example, AMR (2008) reported that Nike, a company best known for its marketing, used improvements to its supply chain to increase operating margins of between 10 and 15% in each of the preceding four years. But for Nike and other companies which constantly innovate to renew products, selecting the right technology is important to '*orchestrate the constant collaboration between supply, demand, and product management groups that brings profitable new products to market*'. Managing distribution and returns from e-commerce sites is a further challenge. *Internet Retailing* (2010) reported that while the average rates of return to a high street retailer can be as high as 10%, the average for UK e-commerce sites is 22%.

The importance of supply chain management capabilities to customer satisfaction and so repeat business for an e-business is highlighted by Mini case study 6.1.

Mini Case Study 6.1	Premier Farnell uses its global supply chain system to improve customer satisfaction

Constant investment in technology is vital for electronics component distributor *Premier Farnell*, a growing business with a mission to deliver industry-leading customer service.

The FTSE-250 company, which supplies electronic components in North America, Europe and Asia has a demanding group of valuable customers who need to know swiftly and accurately when their order will be shipped.

Most of them are design engineers building prototypes of high-tech goods, working for manufacturers of a wide range of equipment.

'For our customers, service is paramount,' explains Laurence Bain, chief operating officer. 'They are looking for a product and they are looking for it now.

'So we had to address the completeness of our product range, our stock levels, and ensure next-day delivery.' As a result, an efficient supply chain operation is essential.

Premier Farnell sets a tough target: 99.9 per cent of shipments must arrive the next day. Shipments also need to be complete.

Add to this a move into China – Premier Farnell now offers next-day delivery to 90 cities for items in its Chinese distribution centre – and the company would seem a prime candidate for investing in a new supply chain management or ERP system.

This option was considered carefully, says Mr Bain. The company, however, decided to keep its existing technology. This allowed it to focus its resources on improving connections between the supply chain systems in North America, Europe and Asia, and critically, improving business processes.

This freed resources for investment in e-commerce and front-office systems, including a three-year project to install a Siebel-based customer relationship management system.

Forty per cent of European orders are now online and Mr Bain expects this to rise to 50%. In the US, all orders, save those placed by new customers, are handled without manual intervention.

'We did a review of our order processes, looking at the level of interconnectivity between our systems and our ability to transfer data,' says Mr Bain.

'We looked at the processes end to end. We used quality techniques to identify the gaps that created the greatest opportunity for error. It was not just about the cycle time [the time from taking an order to shipment] but the quality of the orders.'

As a result, Premier Farnell decided to maintain its existing supply chain management system, but improve the links between its parts, as well as its capacity.

'We looked at our supply chains holistically and identified the areas where we needed the systems to interface and talk to each other,' explains Mr Bain. 'Our supply chain group specified the enhancements needed to interface the systems and ensure data completeness.'

The task of updating the system fell to Premier Farnell's 200-strong in-house IT team. The project had to be managed in a way that ensured the supply chain targets were met, but without drawing too many resources away from the company's Siebel deployment or its expanding e-commerce operations.

'We have a fairly strong governance designed to ensure business strategy translates into IT priorities,' Mr Bain points out. 'We have an IT leadership group that meets quarterly to assess the evolution of that strategy and a global IT leadership group that signs off IT projects.'

This way, Premier Farnell has ensured customers can see orders placed across all channels, including the web, phone or, in the US, a branch, when they log in to their online accounts.

'We have to be able to capture all transactions,' says Mr Bain. 'You have to take the customer with you. For us, all roads lead to IT: we are a high-volume, high-service distributor dealing in massive numbers of transactions on a daily basis.

'The traffic on our website is growing strongly and we rely on IT to manage these transactions effectively and on a real-time basis.'

Premier Farnell also likes to differentiate itself by its speed in bringing new products to market.

The company recently added 55,000 products to its catalogue. These need to appear simultaneously in its web ordering and back office systems, as well as in the supply chain system so orders reach suppliers on time.

Other material, such as specifications and product data sheets, also have to be loaded before a new product is sold.

As well as the flexibility to handle new products, Premier Farnell relies on its supply chain management system to monitor key aspects of performance. 'In terms of the supply chain, the key metric is our distribution performance,' says Mr Bain.

'We compare it, and have targets, for each facility. We look at the cost of processing an order, the efficiency of goods in and out, and service measures.' Head office collates the data monthly, but operations managers in each distribution facility monitor the figures daily.

The result has been a tough set of targets for engineers tasked with updating a supply chain management system that many less prudent – or less confident – companies might have replaced.

But for Premier Farnell, the combination of clear objectives, a capable in-house team of developers and the lower risks of updating rather than replacing made it the most effective choice.

'Our overall services were good but not as good as they are now. We were confident we could enhance our systems and improve our processes,' says Mr Bain.

'We were comfortable we had the capacity. We had to invest, but it cost a lot less than replacing the back office system, and that allowed us to prioritise our investments in CRM and our web channels.'

Source: Did IT work? Service was paramount when enhancing supply chain. Stephen Pritchard, *The Financial Times*, 30 January 2008. Reprinted with permission.

Box 6.1	The benefits of supply chain management

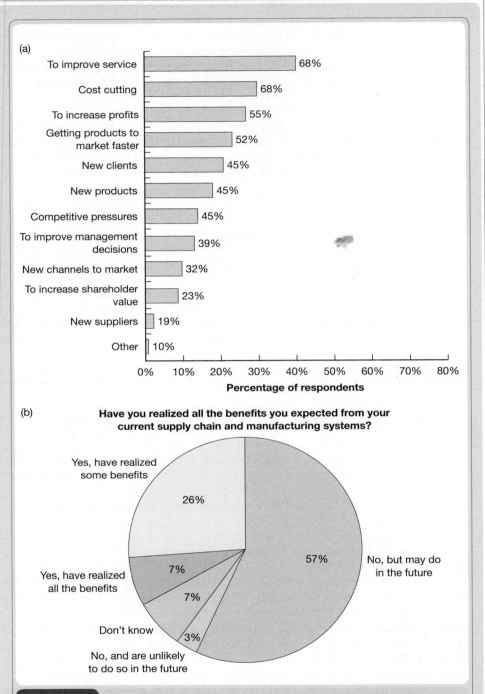

(a) Benefits of supply chain management, (b) Realization of benefits
Note: Respondents could select all benefits that apply.
Source: PMP (2008).

Figure 6.1

The benefits of supply chain management according to a PMP (2008) survey are shown in Figure 6.1. You can see that although benefits of reducing costs and increasing profitability are mentioned frequently, many respondents mentioned that supply chain management also assists with delivering better service to customers.

The figure also shows the challenges of implementing supply chain management technology since a large proportion had not fully realised the intended benefits, although the majority believed they would in the long term.

Much of the excitement generated by the e-business concept concerns the benefits that companies can achieve through increasing the efficiency of the whole supply chain. Companies such as Argos (Case Study 6.2), which have enthusiastically embraced technology to manage the supply chain, have been reaping the benefits for many years.

Problems of supply chain management

Using e-business technology to support SCM can help to avoid some problems that can occur in a supply chain (Table 6.1). This introduces many of the key concepts of technology enabled supply chain management.

Table 6.1 A summary of the problems of supply chain management and how e-business technology can assist

Problems of supply chain management	How e-business technology can reduce problems in SCM
Pressure to reduce costs of manufacturing and distributing products in order to remain competitive	Reduction in paperwork through electronic transmission of orders invoices and delivery notes. Reduced inventory holdings needed through better understanding of demand. Reduced time for information and component supply across the supply chain. Lower SCM system purchase and management costs through use of online services (SaaS)
Demand forecasting	Sharing of demand by customers with suppliers as part of efficient consumer response (ECR)
Failure to deliver products on time consistently or lack of items on shelf in retailer	Supplier becomes responsible for item availability through vendor-managed inventory
Failure to deliver or ship correct product	Human error reduced. 'Checks and balances can be built into system'
High inventory costs	Inventory reduced throughout the supply chain through better demand forecasting and more rapid replenishment of inventory
Time for new product development	Improved availability of information about potential suppliers and components, for example through online marketplaces

What is supply chain management?

Supply chain management (SCM)
The coordination of all supply activities of an organization from its suppliers and partners to its customers.

Upstream supply chain
Transactions between an organization and its suppliers and intermediaries, equivalent to buy-side e-commerce.

Downstream supply chain
Transactions between an organization and its customers and intermediaries, equivalent to sell-side e-commerce.

Supply chain network
The links between an organization and all partners involved in multiple supply chains.

Efficient consumer response (ECR)
Creating and satisfying customer demand by optimizing product assortment strategies, promotions, and new product introductions.

Supply chain management (SCM) involves the coordination of all supply activities of an organization from its suppliers and delivery of products to its customers. Figure 6.2 introduces the main players in the supply chain. In Figure 6.2(a) the main members of the supply chain are the organizations that manufacture a product and/or deliver a service.

For most commercial and not-for-profit organizations we can distinguish between **upstream supply chain** activities which are equivalent to buy-side e-commerce and **downstream supply chain** activities which correspond to sell-side e-commerce. In this chapter and the next we focus mainly on improving the efficiency of upstream supply chain activities, while in Chapters 8 and 9 the emphasis is on the marketing aspects of improving downstream supply chain activities.

Remember also from Figure 1.1 that supply chain management includes not only supplier and buyer, but also the intermediaries such as the supplier's suppliers and the customer's customers (Figure 6.2(b)). Indeed, some companies may have first-tier suppliers, second-tier and even third-tier suppliers or first-, second- and higher-tier customers. Because each company effectively has many individual supply chains for different products, the use of the term 'chain' is limiting and **supply chain network** is a more accurate reflection of the links between an organization and its partners.

Technology is vital to supply chain management since managing relationships with customers, suppliers and intermediaries is based on the flow of information and the transactions between these parties. The main strategic thrust of enhancing the supply chain is to provide a superior value proposition to the customer, of which **efficient consumer response (ECR**, see Box 6.2) is important within the retail and packaged consumer goods market. As explained in Chapter 5, improving customer value involves improving product quality, customer service quality and/or reducing price and fulfilment times. Increasing efficiency in obtaining resources from a supplier organization or distributing products to customers reduces operational costs and so increases profitability.

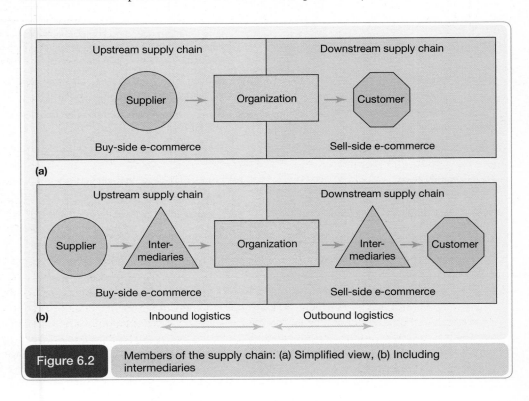

| Figure 6.2 | Members of the supply chain: (a) Simplified view, (b) Including intermediaries |

Box 6.2	Efficient consumer response (ECR)

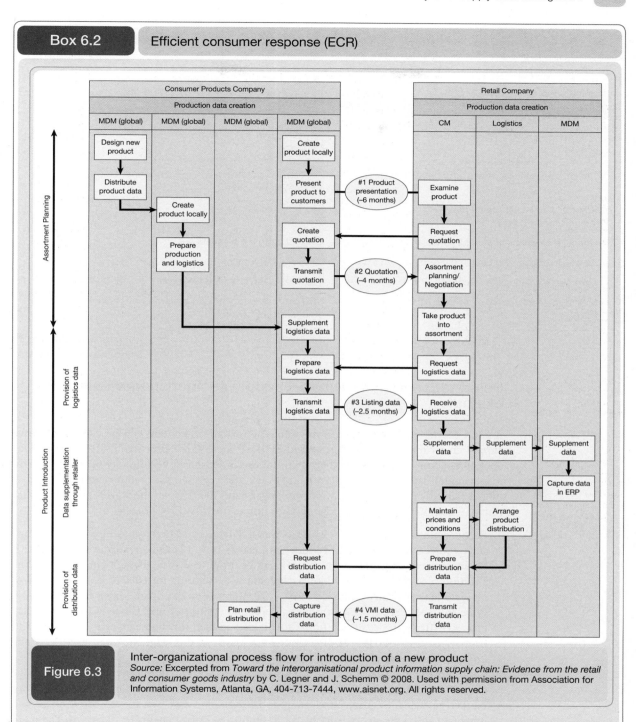

Figure 6.3 Inter-organizational process flow for introduction of a new product
Source: Excerpted from Toward the interorganisational product information supply chain: Evidence from the retail and consumer goods industry by C. Legner and J. Schemm © 2008. Used with permission from Association for Information Systems, Atlanta, GA, 404-713-7444, www.aisnet.org. All rights reserved.

The ECR concept was developed for the food retailing business in the USA but since then it has been applied to other products and in other countries. It was originally developed by David Jenkins, then chairman of Shaw's supermarkets, to compete with other players such as Wal-Mart. Supply chain management had traditionally focused on efficient product replenishment whereas the focus of ECR is on demand management aimed at creating and satisfying customer demand by optimizing product assortment strategies, promotions and new product introductions (Legner and Schemm, 2008). Figure 6.3 shows the complexity and lead times of a process where a new consumer product is introduced and then stocked. ECR focuses on improving this process.

Table 6.2 shows that some of the aims and strategic approaches generated by ECR can also apply to business customers.

Table 6.2	Objectives and strategies for effective consumer response (ECR)
Objective	**Strategy**
Timely, accurate, paperless information flow	Revision of organization processes supported by information systems
Smooth, continual product flow matched to variations in consumption levels	See strategies below
Optimize productivity of retail space and inventory	Efficient store assortments
Optimize for time and cost in the ordering process	Efficient replacement
Maximize efficiency of promotions	Promotions are integrated into entire supply chain planning
Maximize effectiveness of new product development (NPD)	NPD process improved and better forward planning with other partners

Using technology to support supply chain management – an example

A good example of how the introduction of information systems can be used to improve supply chain management is provided by BHP Steel (now BlueScope Steel, www.bluescopesteel.com.au), an Australian firm. Its use of PC-based technology for supply chain management dates back to the 1980s and e-business represents a change of emphasis rather than a radically new approach. Chan and Swatman (2000) assess the stages in implementation of e-commerce for this company. The authors identify three phases:

1 *Early implementation: 1989–93.* This was a PC-based EDI purchasing system. At this stage, objectives were to (1) reduce data errors to 0, (2) reduce administration costs, (3) improve management control, (4) reduce order lead time. Benefits included rationalization of suppliers to 12 major partnerships (accounting for 60% of invoices); 80% of invoices placed electronically by 1990; 7,000 items were eliminated from the warehouse, to be sourced directly from suppliers, on demand. Shorter lead times in the day-to-day process – from 10 days to 26 hours for items supplied through a standard contract and from 42 days to 10 days for direct-purchase items. At this stage the main barriers to the implementation were technological.

2 *Electronic trading gateway: 1990–4.* This was again EDI-based, but involved a wider range of parties both externally (from suppliers through to customers) and internally (from marketing, sales, finance, purchasing and legal). The aim was to provide a combined upstream and downstream supply chain solution to bring benefits to all parties. The main learning from this process was the difficulty of getting customers involved – only four were involved after 4 years, although an industry-standard method for data exchange was used. This was surprising since suppliers had been enthusiastic adopters. From 1994, there was no further uptake of this system.

3 *The move towards Internet commerce: 1996 onwards.* The Internet was thought to provide a lower-cost alternative to traditional EDI for smaller suppliers and customers, through using a lower-cost value-added network. So, one objective of the project was to extend

the reach of electronic communications with supply chain partners. The second was to broaden the type of communications to include catalogue ordering, freight forwarding and customer ordering. The strategy divided transactions into three types: (1) strategic (high volume, high value, high risk) – a dedicated EDI line was considered most appropriate; (2) tactical (medium volume, value and risk) – EDI or Internet EDI was used; (3) consumer transactions (low volume, value and risk) – a range of lower-cost Internet-based technologies could be used. The main barriers to implementation at this stage have been business issues, i.e. convincing third parties of the benefits of integration and managing the integration process.

More recently, BlueScope Steel has introduced bluescopesteelconnect.com (Figure 6.4) which is a secure Internet-based steel procurement solution which allows customers to order and confirm the status of products. It also offers users the ability to check statements and download invoices in real time, simplifying reconciliations.

The implementation of SCM at BHP Steel reflects changing developments in the wider industry which are summarized in Box 6.3.

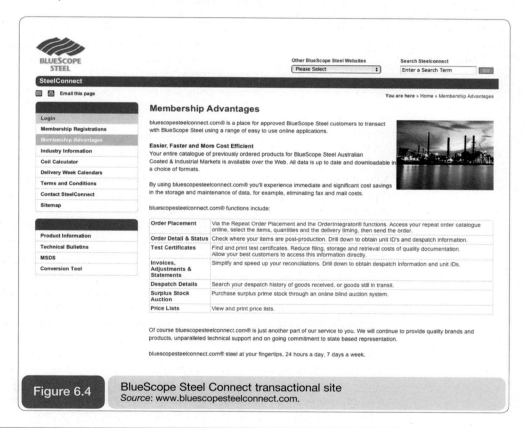

Figure 6.4   BlueScope Steel Connect transactional site
Source: www.bluescopesteelconnect.com.

Box 6.3   The past, present and future of SCM

Professor Alan Braithwaite of LCP Consulting, writing in PMP (2008), identifies these developments in SCM technology:

The 70s were characterised by monster batch-processing mainframes, manual data entry and primarily custom programming. These systems were driven by finance and generated huge piles of printout with little useful management information.

The 80s were the time when the minicomputer and the PC emerged, computing power became more accessible and the debate was between packaged software or customised solutions. Custom code was still the preferred route for many, but information rather than data was emerging.

The 90s saw a huge 'Windows-based' expansion of computing power – with packages overtaking custom software as their functionality matured – and the emergence of ERP. The debate was about best of breed versus all-in-one integrated software.

The end of the 90s was focused on the Y2K question as companies replaced their solutions wherever the risk of corruption in old legacy systems was too high – ERP was again a big winner from this.

In the first decade of the new century, the internet has come of age as a transaction medium, with exponential growth in computing power and storage encouraging the introduction of more and more sophisticated supply chain solutions and management information.

Braithwaite goes on to make these predictions about the future of SCM:

A fundamental principle of supply chain management is to secure end-to-end visibility and a single version of the truth – one number for forecasts, inventory, orders, billings and commitments; ERP in principle seeks to achieve that goal.

A second fundamental principle is that end-to-end visibility includes inventory and processes that extend beyond the focal firm and its ERP. The internet provides this capability in a way that was barely conceivable 10 years ago.

There are three key points from the growth of ERP and the internet that form the basis for my prediction of the future of supply chain systems …

The first is that managing the extended supply chain with a requirement to continually optimise means integrated ERP versus best of breed is an irrelevant argument. Systems in the future will be more open and include core and extended supply chain integration and optimisation. ERP is less good at the smart stuff and the data structures are not organised to deal with the extended chain.

The second point is that most systems are not delivering business benefits to their full potential because supply chain business processes are not good enough and the systems are not set up right to handle good practice.

The third factor is that a surprising number of companies are still stranded with legacy systems that are so customised it is difficult to migrate to new more open architectures based on 'bestpractice' processes. These companies have to determine how they will reengineer their businesses and migrate their systems. At present they will not be able to access the smart optimisation and extended chain capabilities easily.

The implication of these trends is that the long-term direction for companies will be extended open system architectures with an ERP core. Application and data interchange maturity exist, and the industry now talks widely about service oriented architecture (SOA). The real challenge now is process design and simplification and being able to represent that in supply chain systems.

So the future of supply chain systems will be about simply more of the same on the latest platforms, only this time better and more flexible. It will be up to management to provide better process clarity and execution, and work with the systems community to exploit the capabilities that exist. Anything new technically may be a bonus, but not if it distracts from the core concepts.

Source: PMP (2008).

A simple model of a supply chain

An organization's supply chain can be viewed from a systems perspective as the acquisition of resources (inputs) and their transformation (process) into products and services (outputs). Such a perspective indicates that as part of moving to e-business, organizations can review the transformation process and optimize it in order to deliver products to customers with greater efficiency and lower cost. Note that the position of the systems boundary for SCM extends beyond the organization – it involves improving not only internal processes, but also processes performed in conjunction with suppliers, distributors and customers. However, this process perspective misses the strategic importance of supply chain management – it also provides great opportunities to improve product performance and deliver superior value to the customer as suggested by Figure 6.1. As a result, supply chain management can dramatically have an impact on the profitability of a company.

Figure 6.5 shows the supply chain for a sample business-to-business company. Complete Activity 6.1 to consider the issues involved in modifying the supply chain in response to e-business. Note that although this example is based on a business-to-business scenario, supply chain management is also vital to the management of business-to-consumer and service companies. With service companies, the resources managed tend not to be physical but human, financial and information resources. However, the same principles can be applied.

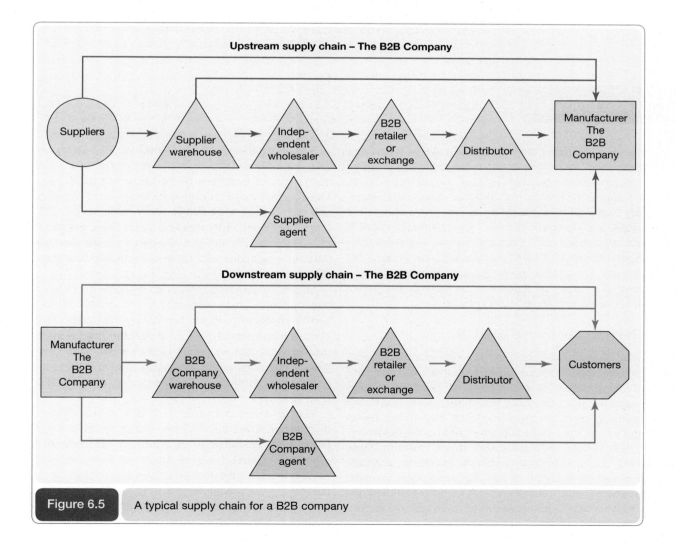

| Figure 6.5 | A typical supply chain for a B2B company |

Case study 6.1 shows how Shell Chemicals has developed a **vendor-managed inventory (VMI)** supply chain management system to enable delivery of supplies to be more responsive to customers' demands. VMI is a key concept in electronic supply chain and procurement management which shifts the day-to-day tasks of stock management, purchasing and order tracking from the customer to the supplier.

| **Activity 6.1** | **A supply chain for a typical B2B company** |

Vendor-managed inventory (VMI)
Supply chain partners manage the replenishment of parts or items for sale through sharing of information on variations in demand and stocking level for goods used for manufacture or sale.

Purpose

To examine the nature of a B2B supply chain and its potential for modification through restructuring and information systems as part of e-business development.

Questions

1 Referring to Chapter 2 and the section on disintermediation and reintermediation, discuss the opportunities for a B2B company to restructure its supply chain as part of the move to e-business, and the benefits this may bring.

2 How can information systems be used to accomplish the changes you have identified in question 1?

Answers to activities can be found at www.pearsoned.co.uk/chaffey

---

| **Case Study 6.1** | **Shell Chemicals redefines its customers' supply chains** |

This case illustrates the evolution of a typical e-business application for supply chain management within one company. Shell Chemicals originally introduced SIMON, a bespoke system to manage their customers' inventory based on data shared by its customers about their usage and forecast demand for chemicals. SIMON was then used for upstream supply chain management. Ultimately, Shell Chemicals switched to using the Elemica marketplace portal for supply chain management since this was thought to be more cost-effective than maintaining an in-house system.

The introduction of SIMON

Shell Chemicals (www.shell.com/chemicals) manufactures the chemicals used by other manufacturers of many industrial and consumer products. Shell's customers use detergents, solvents, plastics, and epoxy resins to produce everything from automotive paints and aircraft structures to diapers and plastic bottles.

Within such an organization, supply chain management has a dramatic impact on customer satisfaction and profitability. Shell Chemicals have invested in SIMON which stands for 'Shell Inventory Managed Order Network' for managing both upstream and downstream relationships.

SIMON was originally launched in 1995 using the IBM Lotus Notes Domino application server and is one of the earliest examples of an e-business application. This represented a change from the industry standard practice of using electronic data interchange (EDI) forms, telephone orders and paper invoices. EDI didn't give Shell the flexibility it needed to accommodate data on exceptions and up-to-date information about dynamic processes.

Initially, Shell used SIMON to manage their downstream supply chain processes which involve distribution of chemical products for use by their customers. The system enabled SHELL to assume the inventory management role on behalf of their customers. Once it was successful in this role it was then applied to the upstream processes of Shell acquiring raw materials from suppliers.

For customers, the benefits of the SIMON system are that responsibility for inventory management is transferred from customer to supplier. A Shell Chemicals customer doesn't need to place an order. Instead, SIMON manages the amount of inventory in stock at the customers' manufacturing locations.

Before the introduction of SIMON, there were a lot of manual, time-consuming transactions, often initiated by the customer, that required a lot of phone calls and faxes. There was also the danger that Shell's customers might run out of an essential chemical, so that plant time and then revenues would be lost. To avoid this, companies tend to maintain 'safety stock' levels. Re-ordering then occurs when inventory gets too close to these safety stock levels. The problem was that a typical re-supply order can take at least two weeks from the time the order is placed. This delay occurred since chemicals must be weighed at the plant, loaded on to railcars and then sent to the customer, who then weighs the materials at the other end before moving them into inventory. Miscalculations and errors can also occur.

For SIMON to enable a supplier to manage inventory, the customer needed to supply three types of information: the levels of current inventory; forecast demand for inventory; and the shipment details such as location, timing and quantities.

In addition to analysing inventory and consumption, SIMON also generates demand forecasts, calculates stock, tracks shipment status and generates a resupply plan.

SIMON 10 years on

In 2004, the Shell house magazine showed how the SIMON system is still in use nearly 10 years later and how it is used for supply chain management.

The Shell Chemicals Channel Captain programme provides customers with integrated inventory management. For Bayer in the US, the coordination and management of all phenol and acetone deliveries by one supplier offers both supply chain efficiencies and potential for competitive advantage.

As a supplier-managed inventory analyst for Shell Chemical LP, Denise Covin begins each day checking SIMON. This allows Covin to see the status of product shipments and reconcile product supply and demand so that her customer, Bayer Corporation, has a continuous supply of phenol and acetone for its BPA plant in Baytown, Texas.

What's unique about Covin's role is that she coordinates the entire supply chain inventory management process, working closely with the customer and even coordinating product delivery requests with another supplier, to manage Bayer's inventory.

While the Channel Captain service has been offered to numerous bulk supply customers around the world for several years, the relationship with Bayer is unique because it is the first to involve product deliveries by barge to the company's Business Process Automation (BPA) manufacturing facility.

In an industry often driven by spot market price advantage and future delivery schedules, the Channel Captain service is more than an inventory manage-

ment system. It's a working relationship between Shell Chemical LP and the customer to cut costs from within the total supply chain.

'It is costly to have extra inventory in your supply process,' says Phenol/Acetone sales manager Chuck Walker. 'The Channel Captain programme enables us to better understand inventory requirements and have only the product needed by the customer in the supply chain, thus helping us to better manage inventory and reduce carrying costs. The objective of the service is to realise increased value and savings to both parties in the supply management process.'

The key to the success of the Channel Captain service is close cooperation between the Shell Chemical people and their supply chain counterparts at the customer. In the case of Bayer, Shell Chemicals LP people worked closely with the customer to define the working relationship process and to identify key people involved and their responsibilities within the overall supply chain process.

'It's important to have people at all levels, within both companies, involved so everyone is aligned with the same vision,' says Matt Vandergrifft, Phenol/Acetone supply chain manager. 'This is not simply a process that takes a job from the customer's purchasing group and transfers it to Shell. Instead, we as supplier literally manage the inventory and billing process, so people on both sides get involved at different levels of the supply chain.'

Shell customer relationship coordinators, like Covin, use SIMON to get daily inventory readings, consumption forecasts, product receipts and current customer consumption in order to supply inventory on an as-needed basis. She also places product orders and coordinates delivery with another phenol and acetone supplier.

Barge delivery is a complicated process that can be impacted by weather, dock issues and ship channel traffic conditions.

'This is a customer who needs product on a just-in-time basis. Product flows very rapidly and there is not a lot of slack in the system,' she says.

It means, among other things, watching the weather. 'If there is a potential problem with fog, we may opt to load the barge ahead of time and reposition closer to the delivery location to get it to the customer on time. We must be able to keep the process moving regardless of any contingency.'

Covin works closely with production and shipping colleagues at the Deer Park phenol/acetone plant near Houston to make sure product is in the correct tanks for loading on to barges, and to coordinate movement of product at the docks.

If a barge is delayed due to weather conditions, dock congestion or any other reason, she's in contact with the barge company, logistics and supply people, as well as Bayer's purchasing and logistics people, to keep everyone informed.

Product transfers occur several times per week, so timing and close coordination for both loading and deliveries is critical. Deer Park production specialist Carl Pittman, who coordinates movement of product, says: 'We've developed a good team that works together to make sure both Bayer and Shell needs are met.'

The Shell Chemical LP customer service and production teams meet their customer counterparts on a quarterly basis for a general round table discussion, to foster good communications and to continually streamline the process.

'SIMON may appear on paper to be a computerised system that provides information, but the expertise really lies with the people who understand the value and know how to use the system effectively,' Walker adds.

Shell began the Channel Captain arrangements with Bayer in 2002. That same year, it was one of only twelve of Bayer's 4,000-plus suppliers to receive a Superior Supplier award for service quality and value provided. Only one other raw material supplier received the honour.

Duke Stiddard, procurement manager of raw materials for Bayer in Pittsburgh, Pennsylvania, says the Channel Captain service is more than just saving money. 'It's a concept that says Shell will share in your business and help you better manage your inventory processes. We don't view our relationship as ending at the point of barge delivery.'

'The service separates Shell from other suppliers,' Stiddard continues. 'A lot of people talk about doing this, but very few implement it. For Bayer, our low inventory is the biggest benefit. We don't have inventory in our system until we consume it.'

'Obviously, as a result, we save time and energy around scheduling and logistics. Plus, our people are free to work on other things,' he adds.

The relationship is a win–win for both supplier and customer. 'If we can streamline the supply management process and save the customer money at the same time, it goes a long way to help them have a competitive advantage in the marketplace,' says Walker.

Source: Shell Chemicals Magazine, Spring 2004: www.shellchemicals. com/magazine/1,1098,957-article_id=159,00.html.

Integration with the Elemica marketplace portal

By 2005, the Elemica chemical industry portal (www. elemica.com, Figure 6.6) had became an important part of the e-business strategy for Shell Chemical. It was reported in the *Shell Chemicals Magazine* that 30% of Shell Chemical business was online with an ambition to increase this to 50% by 2008.

Elemica was originally founded in 1999 by 22 leaders of the global chemical industry and by 2005 had a network of 1,800 industry trading partners, so it offered benefits of standardization:

With more than 1,500 active members and $50 billion in annual transactions, the value we extend to our customers continues to grow. As part of Elemica's industry-leading BPN, your enterprise can gain major competitive advantages through direct access to the latest supply chain technologies and intelligent business process capabilities.

Elemica describes the principles of its marketplace on its website as follows (http://www.elemica.com/About/Overview/page.aspx?):

'Elemica enables companies to achieve operational excellence by replacing complex approaches with automated systems and intelligent business processes. Utilizing leading-edge technology and in-depth process expertise, Elemica integrates disparate enterprise business systems and processes into one unified network across all customers, suppliers and third party service providers irrespective of company size or industry.

Elemica's innovative business process network (BPN) provides a fully connected operational framework that removes transactional and communication barriers and institutionalizes processes for integrating the information flow between global trading partners. With seamless access and visibility into the supply chain network, the enterprise can use fewer resources to do the same work more efficiently and release people, inventory, and assets that cover for these issues in the current process.

1 **Global reach and connectivity**
Our founding member companies are among the industry leaders and represent a significant proportion of the industry's buy and sell transactions, creating substantial initial liquidity. This foundation provides financial stability and global reach for Elemica, and the proven ability to scale quickly. This combination will continue to attract many additional buyers and sellers, resulting in an ever-growing reservoir of potential connections for new customers.

2 **Neutrality**
Elemica is an independent company with a dedicated management team. Our network is designed as an open network, embracing all industry buyers and sellers looking for a robust infrastructure, network and e-commerce solutions to improve core business processes. Elemica is not an

Figure 6.6	Elemica trading platform
	Source: www.elemica.com.

'aggregator' of material purchasing, nor a 'buyer', 'seller', or 'owner' of products – it is a facilitator of transactions.

3 **Security**

Elemica has incorporated state-of-the-art security measures to safeguard the flow and accessibility of information so that participants' individual transaction data is not shared with any other company. We have state-of-the-art security features and processes, including highly visible firewalls and strong data protection policies, a policy of confidentiality regarding handling of customer data, encryption technology to safeguard confidential data and secured information with access limited by individual user and regular independent auditing of these policies and procedures.

Integration with marketplace portals such as Elemica, which were not in existence earlier in the life cycle of SIMON, became important to Shell.

Elemica could offer similar benefits to SIMON, i.e. it could:

- Reduce transaction costs through reduction of human input to transactions

- Standardize business processes
- Reduce error sources
- Improve response time
- Improve cash flow through faster payment
- Increase customer satisfaction

The article describes this example of the practical benefits the new system could bring. A company in Europe shipped products directly from a Shell Chemical plant to their customers. Shell Chemical make the product; the company markets it and manages pick-up from the plant and delivery to the customer. Before the application of Elemica, these additional process stages or 'hand-offs' were required while each truck waited after loading:

- Paperwork was developed at the plant
- Then faxed to the partner company
- Then entered manually into their system
- Then faxed back to the Shell company – where the truck had been all along

A further complication was that the partner's offices closed earlier than the Shell traffic office. So, truck drivers could sit for hours waiting at the plant until the documents were faxed through! After switching to Elemica, paperwork was automatically processed 24 hours a day. Average truck-waiting times were cut from two hours to 15 minutes.

In addition to the process benefits which would create better customer service, Shell Chemical switched from using SIMON to Elemica for supply chain management since SIMON would require continued investment in ongoing development and maintenance costs. Elemica, as an outsourced solution, was more favourable in terms of ongoing costs and development. Since Elemica is not company-specific it also helped exchange of data since formats could be standardized across companies.

The data contained within SIMON was integrated to the Elemica chemical marketplace platform. In the *Shell Chemicals Magazine*, Spring 2005 (http://www.shellchemicals.com/magazine/1,1098,894-article_id=184,00.html), the benefits of integrating Elemica with SIMON VMI were described as:

> The supply chain service developed through Elemica captures and manages daily inventory readings, consumption forecasts, product receipts and current customer consumption. Its planning, forecasting and replenishment services are combined with the added advantages of ERP system integration through the Elemica hub. Improved product, technical and HSE (Health, Safety and the Environment) information has been brought together in the 'Customer Lounge'.

Global positioning systems also enable details on the railcar carrying the chemicals including current loca-

tion and estimated time of arrival. There are also links to road hauliers. For example, a link with Bertschi AG, one of the largest road transport logistics providers in Europe, enables thousands of transport instructions generated every month to be sent automatically, removing the need for manual faxing and reducing the potential for errors.

Bertschi transport planning manager, Stefan Bryner, explains the benefits as follows: '*It has reduced our paperwork and made the whole process more transparent. The potential for errors has been reduced and issues are easier to resolve.*'

Questions

1 The SIMON system supports both 'upstream and downstream' business relationships. Explain how this relates to Figure 1.1 and whether you would consider it an e-commerce system or an e-business system.

2 Draw a table summarizing the before and after implementation roles for Shell and their customers (downstream side).

3 This description of SIMON is explained from the Shell perspective. Using your answer to question 2, state whether you think the customer truly benefits, or is Shell transferring some of its workload to the customer?

4 Visit the Shell Chemicals website (www.shellchemicals.com). How are the benefits of these facilities explained?

What is logistics?

Logistics is a concept closely related to supply chain management. According to the Institute of Logistics and Transportation (www.iolt.org):

> Logistics is the time-related positioning of resource, or the strategic management of the total supply chain. The supply chain is a sequence of events intended to satisfy a customer. It can include procurement, manufacture, distribution, and waste disposal, together with associated transport, storage and information technology.

This definition of logistics is broad, reflecting its provenance. More typically, logistics is used to refer not to all supply chain activities, but specifically to the management of logistics or **inbound** and **outbound logistics** (Figure 6.2). Logistics is essential to the efficient management of the supply chain.

To understand why supply chain management plays an important role in modern management thinking, read Box 6.4.

Inbound logistics
The management of material resources entering an organization from its suppliers and other partners.

Outbound logistics
The management of resources supplied from an organization to its customers and intermediaries.

Box 6.4	Developments in supply chain management

In order to understand how e-commerce can be used to enhance supply chain and logistics management it is useful to consider the historical context of management approaches to supply chain management and how information systems have been used to support them. The following stages can be identified.

1960s/70s: Physical distribution management (PDM)

Physical distribution management (PDM) focused upon the physical movement of goods by treating stock management, warehousing, order processing and delivery as related rather than separate activities. Although information systems were developed to manage these processes they were often paper-based and not integrated across different functions. However, some leading companies started using EDI at this time. EDI was mainly used on a point-to-point basis for document automation with electronic purchaser orders sent to suppliers who responded with shipping notes and invoices. PDM was essentially about the management of finished goods but not about the management of materials and processes that impacted upon the distribution process. PDM was superseded by logistics management which viewed manufacturing storage and transport from raw material to final consumer as integral parts of a total distribution process.

1970s/80s: Logistics management (materials requirement planning (MRP) and just-in-time – JIT)

The just-in-time philosophy (JIT) aims to make the process of raw materials acquisition, production and distribution as efficient and flexible as possible in terms of material supply and customer service. Minimum order quantities and stock levels were sought by the customer and therefore manufacturers had to introduce flexible manufacturing processes and systems that interfaced directly with the customer who could call an order directly against a prearranged schedule with a guarantee that it would be delivered on time. Materials requirement planning systems were important in maintaining resources at an optimal level. The design for manufacture technique was used to simplify the number of components required for manufacture. An associated phenomenon is lean production and lean supply where supply chain efficiency is aimed at eliminating waste and minimizing inventory and work in progress.

1980s/90s: Supply chain management and efficient consumer response (ECR)

Effective management of the supply chain involved much closer integration between the supplier, customer and intermediaries and in some instances involved one organization in the channel taking over functions that were traditionally the domain of the intermediary. Bottlenecks or undersupply/oversupply can have a significant impact on an organization's profitability. The two primary goals of supply chain management are to maximize the efficiency and effectiveness of the total supply chain for the benefit of all the players, not just one section of the channel, and to maximize the opportunity for customer purchase by ensuring adequate stock levels at all stages of the process. These two goals impact upon the sourcing of raw materials and stockholding. A recent phenomenon has been the rapid growth in global sourcing of supplies from preferred suppliers, particularly amongst multinational or global organizations. The Internet will provide increased capability for smaller players to globally source raw materials and therefore improve their competitiveness. Quelch and Klein (1996) argue that the Internet will revolutionize the dynamics of international commerce and in particular lead to the more rapid internationalization of small and medium-sized enterprises. The web will reduce the competitive advantage of economies of scale in many industries, making it easier for smaller companies to compete on a worldwide basis.

New integrated information systems such as the SAP enterprise resource planning (ERP) system have helped manage the entire supply chain. ERP systems include modules which are deployed throughout the business and interface with suppliers through EDI or XML. These can potentially automate the requests for new orders. Technology has enabled the introduction of faster, more responsive and flexible ordering, manufacturing and distribution systems, which has diminished even further the need for warehouses to be located near to markets that they serve.

1990s/2000s: Technological interface management (TIM)
According to Hamill and Gregory (1997) the challenge facing suppliers, intermediaries and customers in the supply chain will shift from a focus on physically distributing goods to a process of collection, collation, interpretation and dissemination of vast amounts of information. Enterprise resource planning systems are continuously being updated to support direct data interfaces with suppliers and customers, for example to support EDI. A more recent development is interfacing of ERP systems with B2B intermediary sites or exchanges such as Elemica, referred to in Case study 6.1. See the 'Focus on B2B marketplaces' in Chapter 7 for further discussion of these. SAP has also created the mySAP facility to help customers manage and personalize their interactions with these exchanges. XML (Chapter 3) is increasingly used as the technical means by which technological interface management is achieved. (The critical resource possessed by these new intermediaries will be information rather than inventory. Hagel and Rayport (1997) take this a stage further by suggesting that customer information capture will serve customers rather than vendors in future. Currently customers leave a trail of information behind them as they visit sites and make transactions. This data can be captured and then used by suppliers and agents to improve targeting of offers. However, as customers become more aware of the value of information and as technology on the Internet enables them to protect private information relating to site visits and transactions, then the opportunity grows for intermediaries to act as customer agents and not supplier agents.)

Push and pull supply chain models

A change in supply chain thinking, and also in marketing communications thinking, is the move from push models of selling to pull models or to combined push–pull approaches. The **push model** is illustrated by a manufacturer who perhaps develops an innovative product, identifies a suitable target market and creates a distribution channel to push the product to the market – Figure 6.7(a). The typical motivation for a push approach is to optimize the production process for cost and efficiency.

The alternative approach consistent with ECR is the **pull model**, which is focused on the customer's needs and starts with analysis of their requirements through market research and close cooperation with customers and suppliers in new product development (Figure 6.7(b)). Here the supply chain is constructed to deliver value to the customer by reducing costs and increasing service quality. Figure 6.7(b) shows how there are much closer links between the elements of the supply chain through use of technology such as EDI to minimize document transfer and rekeying. The typical motivation for a pull approach is to optimize the production process for customer response, cost and efficiency. Such an approach is also consistent with management thinking about the similar concept of the value chain as illustrated in the 'Focus on The value chain' section.

Push supply chain
A supply chain that emphasizes distribution of a product to passive customers.

Pull supply chain
An emphasis on using the supply chain to deliver value to customers who are actively involved in product and service specification.

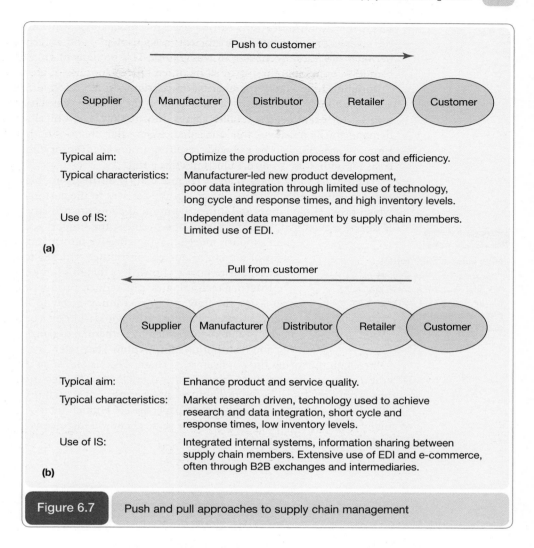

Push to customer

Supplier Manufacturer Distributor Retailer Customer

Typical aim:	Optimize the production process for cost and efficiency.
Typical characteristics:	Manufacturer-led new product development, poor data integration through limited use of technology, long cycle and response times, and high inventory levels.
Use of IS:	Independent data management by supply chain members. Limited use of EDI.

(a)

Pull from customer

Supplier Manufacturer Distributor Retailer Customer

Typical aim:	Enhance product and service quality.
Typical characteristics:	Market research driven, technology used to achieve research and data integration, short cycle and response times, low inventory levels.
Use of IS:	Integrated internal systems, information sharing between supply chain members. Extensive use of EDI and e-commerce, often through B2B exchanges and intermediaries.

(b)

Figure 6.7 Push and pull approaches to supply chain management

---

Focus on **The value chain**

Value chain
A model that considers how supply chain activities can add value to products and services delivered to the customer.

Michael Porter's **value chain (VC)** is a well-established concept for considering key activities that an organization can perform or manage with the intention of adding value for the customer as products and services move from conception to delivery to the customer (Porter, 1980). The value chain is a model that describes different value-adding activities that connect a company's supply side with its demand side. We can identify an *internal* value chain within the boundaries of an organization and an *external* value chain where activities are performed by partners. By analysing the different parts of the value chain managers can redesign internal and external processes to improve their efficiency and effectiveness. Benefits for the customer are created by reducing cost *and* adding value:

- *within each* element of the value chain such as procurement, manufacture, sales and distribution;
- *at the interface between* elements of the value chain such as between sales and distribution.

In equation form this is:

Value = (Benefit of each VC activity – Its cost) + (Benefit of each interface between VC activities – Its cost)

Electronic communications can be used to enhance the value chain by making activities such as procurement more efficient (see Chapter 7) and also enabling data integration between activities. According to IBF (2008), BT's implementation of e-procurement enabled 95% online purchasing of all its office-related supplies in the secondary value chain. This reduced the average purchasing transaction cost from £56 to £40, which is significant across hundreds of thousands of purchases. In the primary value chain, benefits can be even greater; for example, if a retailer shares information electronically with a supplier about demand for its products, this can enhance the value chain of both parties since the cycle time for ordering can be reduced, resulting in lower inventory holding and hence lower costs for both. Case study 6.1 illustrates this point.

Traditional value chain analysis (Figure 6.8(a)) distinguishes between *primary activities* that contribute directly to getting goods and services to the customer and *support activities* which provide the inputs and infrastructure that allow the primary activities to take place. It can be argued that, with the advent of e-business, the support activities offer much more than support; indeed, having effective information systems and management of human resources contributes critically to the primary activities. Michael Porter now acknowledges that this is the case.

Internet technologies can reduce production times and costs by increasing the flow of information as a way to *integrate* different value chain activities. Rayport and Sviokla (1996) contend that the Internet enables value to be created by gathering, organizing, selecting, synthesizing and distributing information. They refer to a separate parallel virtual value chain mirroring the physical value chain. The *virtual value chain* involves electronic commerce used to mediate traditional value chain activities such as market research, procurement, logistics, manufacture, marketing and distributing. The processing is machine-based or 'virtual' rather than paper-based. Human intervention is still required in many activities but the 'virtuality' of the value chain will increase as software agents increasingly perform these activities.

Debate 6.1

New value chain models

'The traditional value chain model of Michael Porter (Figure. 6.4(a)) is no longer useful as a framework for value chain management. Instead, Figure. 6.4(b) is more appropriate.'

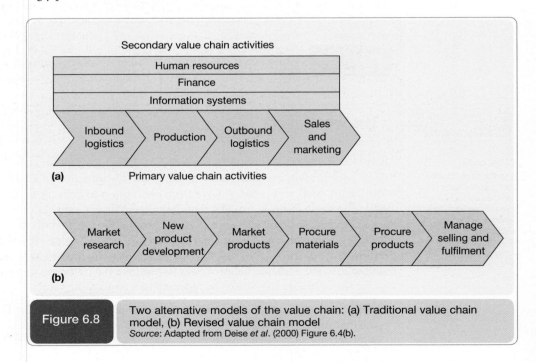

Figure 6.8 Two alternative models of the value chain: (a) Traditional value chain model, (b) Revised value chain model
Source: Adapted from Deise *et al.* (2000) Figure 6.4(b).

Restructuring the internal value chain

Traditional models of the value chain (such as Figure 6.8(a)) have been re-evaluated with the advent of global electronic communications. It can be suggested that there are some key weaknesses in the traditional value chain model:

- It is most applicable to manufacturing of physical products as opposed to providing services.
- It is a one-way chain involved with pushing products to the customer; it does not highlight the importance of understanding customer needs.
- The internal value chain does not emphasize the importance of value networks (although Porter (1980) did produce a diagram that indicated network relationships).

A revised form of the value chain has been suggested by Deise *et al.* (2000); an adaptation of this model is presented in Figure 6.8(b). This value chain starts with the market research process, emphasizing the importance of real-time environment scanning made possible through electronic communications links with distributors and customers. For example, leading e-tailers now monitor, on an hourly basis, how customers are responding to promotional offers on their website and review competitors' offers and then revise them accordingly. Similarly, manufacturers such as Cisco have feedback forms and forums on their site that enable them to collect information from customers and channel partners that can feed through to new product development. As new product development occurs the marketing strategy will be refined and at the same time steps can be taken to obtain the resources and production processes necessary to create, store and distribute the new product. Through analysis of the value chain and looking at how electronic communications can be used to speed up the process, manufacturers have been able to significantly reduce time to market from conception of a new product idea through to launch on the market. At the same time the use of technology increases value chain efficiency.

Electronic commerce also has implications for whether value chain activities are achieved internally or externally. These changes have been referred to as value chain *disaggregation* (Kalakota and Robinson, 2000) or *deconstruction* (Timmers, 1999) and value chain *reaggregation* (Kalakota and Robinson, 2000) or *reconstruction* (Timmers, 1999). Disaggregation can occur through deconstructing the primary activities of the value chain and approaching the elements in a new way. In reaggregation the value chain is streamlined to increase efficiency between each of the stages. Indeed, Timmers (1999) notes that the conventional wisdom of the value chain as a separate series of discrete steps may no longer be tenable as steps such as inbound logistics and operations become more tightly integrated through technology. We have only touched upon changes to the structure of the value chain here, since there is great similarity with the changes possible in the structure of the supply chain. This is evaluated in more depth in the sections on vertical integration and models for redefining the value chain.

The value stream

Value stream
The combination of actions required to deliver value to the customer as products and services.

The **value stream** is a concept closely related to the value chain. The difference is that it considers different types of tasks that are involved with adding value and looks at how the efficiency of these tasks can be improved. Womack and Jones (1998) define the value stream as:

the set of all the specific actions required to bring a specific product through the three critical management tasks of any business:

1 the problem-solving task *[the processes of new product development and production launch]*
2 the information management task *[the processes of order taking, scheduling to delivery]*
3 the physical transformation task *[the processes of transforming raw materials to finished product delivered to customers].*

Tasks 2 and 3 are traditional value chain activities (Figure 6.8(a)), but task 1 is not.

Returning to the definition of customer value from Deise *et al.* (2000) shown in the equation below, we can see that the lean thinking approach proposed by Womack and Jones is aimed at adding value by cutting out waste in each of these three management tasks. By reducing new product development and production times and costs, organizations can then either increase customer value by decreasing fulfilment time or price, and/or increasing product and service quality. Clearly e-commerce plays a key role in decreasing time to market and production times and costs.

$$\text{Customer value (brand perception)} = \frac{\text{Product quality} \times \text{Service quality}}{\text{Price} \times \text{Fulfilment time}}$$

Value chain analysis

This is an analytical framework for decomposing an organization into its individual activities and determining value added at each stage. In this way the organization can then assess how effectively resources are being used. It may be possible to use information systems to increase the efficiency of resource usage for each element in the value chain and even *between* activities.

How can an organization positively impact on its value chain by investing in new or upgraded information systems? Porter and Millar (1985) propose the following five-step process.

1 *Step 1* Assess the information intensity of the value chain (i.e. the level and usage of information *within* each value chain activity and *between* each level of activity). The higher the level of intensity and/or the higher the degree of reliance on good-quality information, the greater the potential impact of new information systems.
2 *Step 2* Determine the role of IS in the industry structure. It is also important here to understand the information linkages between buyers and suppliers within the industry and how they and competitors might be affected by and react to new information technology.
3 *Step 3* Identify and rank the ways in which IS might create competitive advantage. High-cost or critical activity areas present good targets.
4 *Step 4* Investigate how IS might spawn new businesses.
5 *Step 5* Develop a plan for taking advantage of IS, which is business-driven rather than technology-driven. The plan should assign priorities to the IS investments (which of course should be subjected to an appropriate cost–benefit analysis).

This process can also be applied to an organization's external value chain. Womack and Jones (1998) refer to *value stream analysis*, which considers how the whole production and delivery process can be made more efficient. They suggest that companies should map every activity that occurs in creating new products and delivering products or services to customers and then categorize them as:

1 Those that create value as perceived by the customer.
2 Those which create no value, but are required by product development or production systems and so cannot immediately be eliminated.
3 Those that don't add value, so can be immediately eliminated.

Having performed this analysis, plans can be made for removing the category 3 activities and then eliminating category 2 activities and enhancing category 1 activities. Womack and Jones give the example of the value stream for a cola can. Even a superficially simple product such as canned cola can have many activities involved in its production. Indeed there are several value streams: that in producing the can itself, those to produce the contents from beet field to sugar and corn field to caramel and those to produce the packaging. Taking the example of the can itself, value stream analysis can be performed to identify the stages in production as follows:

1 Mine bauxite.
2 Reduction mill.
3 Smelter.
4 Hot rolling mill.
5 Cold rolling mill.
6 Can maker.
7 Bottler.
8 Regional distribution centre (RDC).
9 Retail unit storage.
10 Home storage.

In value stream analysis, efficiency for each of the stages above will be calculated. For example, at stage 7, the bottler (adding the drink to the can), Womack and Jones (1998) give times of incoming storage four days, processing time one minute, finished storage five weeks. The need for such analysis is shown by the delays in the whole process which give incoming storage of five months, finished storage of six months, but processing time of only three hours. This gives a total cycle time of nearly a year from mine to home. Clearly, if information management can be used to reduce these storage times, it can create large savings in terms of reduced storage capacities. The benefits are evident for a retailer such as Tesco that has already undertaken value stream analysis and deployed e-commerce in the Tesco Information Exchange to reduce its storage in the RDC and in-store to only two and three days respectively. It has also been able to move to a system of continuous replenishment in 24 hours. Orders made by a Tesco store on a Monday night are delivered from suppliers via the RDCs to arrive before the store opens Wednesday morning!

At a practical level, improvements in the value chain are implemented through iterative improvements planning implemented through Sales and Operations Planning (S&OP) systems. Kjellsdotter and Jonsson (2010) have identified these benefits of e-business throughout the stages of an iterative planning cycle:

1 **Creating a consensus forecast**. Using statistical forecast methods, demand planning tools are able to integrate different departments and companies for improved decision support.
2 **Creating a preliminary delivery plan**. Reducing planning effort through applying the insights from the forecast.
3 **Creating a preliminary production plan**. Possibility to integrate several entities, coordination of different functions, possibility to use optimization models to find the most feasible solution.
4 **Adjusting delivery and production plan**. Visibility of information, scenario analysis, for example what-if analyses of the impact in resource availability and customer demands.
5 **Settle delivery and production plan**. Overall benefits of tangible cost savings and the intangible benefit of improved confidence in planning and scheduling.

Value networks

Reduced time to market and increased customer responsiveness are not simply the result of reviewing the efficiency of internal processes and how information systems are deployed, but also result through consideration of how partners can be involved to outsource some processes. Porter's original work considered not only the internal value chain, but also the **external value chain or value network**. As companies outsource more and more activities, management of the links between the company and its partners becomes more important. Deise *et al.* (2000) describe value network management as:

> *the process of effectively deciding what to outsource in a constraint-based, real-time environment based on fluctuation.*

External value chain or value network
The links between an organization and its strategic and non-strategic partners that form its external value chain.

Electronic communications have enabled the transfer of information necessary to create, manage and monitor outsourcing partnerships. These links are also mediated through intermediaries known as 'value chain integrators' or directly between partners. As a result the concept of managing a value network of partners has become commonplace.

Figure 6.9, which is adapted from the model of Deise *et al.* (2000), shows some of the partners of a value network that characterizes partners as:

1 Supply-side partners (upstream supply chain) such as suppliers, business-to-business exchanges, wholesalers and distributors.
2 Partners that fulfil primary or core value chain activities. In some companies the management of inbound logistics may be outsourced, in others different aspects of the manufacturing process. In the virtual organization all core activities may be outsourced.
3 Sell-side partners (downstream supply chain) such as business-to-business exchanges, wholesalers, distributors and customers (not shown, since conceived as distinct from other partners).
4 Value chain integrators or partners who supply services that mediate the internal and external value chain. These companies typically provide the electronic infrastructure for a company.

The similarity between elements of the value network of Figure 6.9 and the supply chain of a typical B2B company of Figure 6.5 will be apparent. But the value network offers a different perspective that is intended to emphasize:

- The electronic interconnections between partners and the organization and directly between partners that potentially enables real-time information exchange between partners.

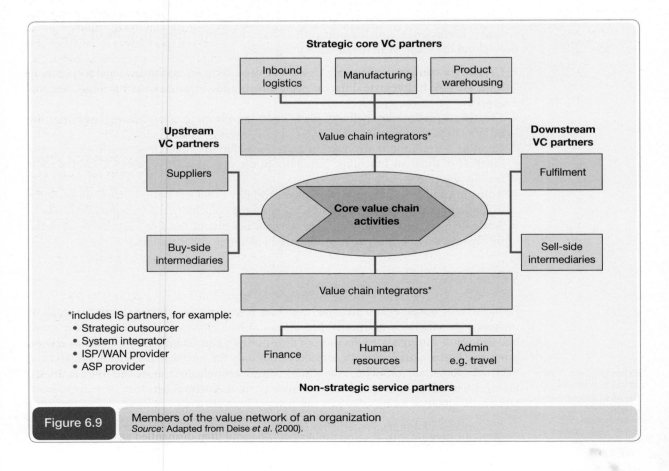

Figure 6.9   Members of the value network of an organization
Source: Adapted from Deise *et al.* (2000).

- The dynamic nature of the network. The network can be readily modified according to market conditions or in response to customer demands. New partners can readily be introduced into the network and others removed.
- Different types of links can be formed between different types of partners.

Wholesale outsourcing to third parties is not the only option. The different types of partnership that can be formed are described in more detail in the later section on 'Managing partnerships'. Remember also that outsourcing does imply cost reduction. Michael Dell relates that Dell do not see outsourcing as getting rid of a process that does not add value; rather they see it as a way of '*coordinating their activity to create the most value for customers*' (Magretta, 1998). Dell has improved customer service by changing the way it works with both its suppliers and distributors to build a computer to the customer's specific order within just six days.

Towards the virtual organization

Davidow and Malone (1992) describe a virtual corporation as follows:

> *To the outside observer, it will appear almost edgeless, with permeable and continuously changing interfaces between company, supplier and customer. From inside the firm, the view will be no less amorphous, with traditional offices, departments, and operating divisions constantly reforming according to need. Job responsibilities will regularly shift.*

Virtual organization
An organization which uses information and communications technology to allow it to operate without clearly defined physical boundaries between different functions.

An implication of increasing outsourcing of core activities is that companies will move towards the **virtual organization**. Benjamin and Wigand (1995) state that '*it is becoming increasingly difficult to delineate accurately the borders of today's organizations*'. Electronic networks make it easier to outsource aspects of the production and distribution of goods to third parties (Kraut *et al.*, 1998). This can lead to the boundaries between supplier and organization becoming blurred. Employees may work in any time zone and customers are able to purchase tailored products from any location. The absence of any rigid boundary or hierarchy within the organization should lead to a more responsive and flexible company with greater market orientation.

Virtual organizations can also be viewed as a way of transforming existing organizations. Malcolm Warner has defined a virtual organization, in this context, as follows:

> *Put simply, it is an organisational form that enables companies to reduce their physical assets (large headquarters, centralised plants and so on), relying instead on small decentralised units linked by a strong communications network. In other words, the old physical constraints of the plant and office building are broken down, and activities of co-ordination and control, which used to take place face-to-face, are now handled remotely 'over the wire'.* (Warner, 2001)

He suggests that companies are experimenting with different characteristics of virtual organizations, including:

- *Lack of physical structure*: virtual organizations have little or no physical existence.
- *Reliance on knowledge*: the lack of physical facilities and contacts means that knowledge is the key driving force of the virtual organization.
- *Use of communications technologies*: it follows that virtual organizations tend to rely on information technology.
- *Mobile work*: the reliance on communications technologies means that the traditional office or plant is no longer the only site where work is carried out.
- *Boundaryless and inclusive*: virtual companies tend to have fuzzy boundaries.
- *Flexible and responsive*: virtual organizations can be pulled together quickly from disparate elements, used to achieve a certain business goal and then dismantled again.

An alternative viewpoint on features of a virtual organization (Kraut *et al.*, 1998) is:

1 Processes transcend the boundaries of a single firm and are not controlled by a single organizational hierarchy.
2 Production processes are flexible with different parties involved at different times.
3 Parties involved in the production of a single product are often geographically dispersed.
4 Coordination is heavily dependent on telecommunications and data networks.

Virtualization
The process of a company developing more of the characteristics of the virtual organization.

Here, all companies tend to have some elements of the virtual organization. As these characteristics increase this is known as **virtualization**. Malone *et al.* (1987) argued that the presence of electronic networks tends to lead to virtualization since the governance and coordination of business transactions can be conducted effectively at lower costs.

Options for restructuring the supply chain

As part of strategy definition for e-business, managers will consider how the structure of the supply chain can be modified. These are mainly choices that have existed for many years but Internet technology provides a more efficient enabler and lower-cost communications.

Vertical integration
The extent to which supply chain activities are undertaken and controlled within the organization.

Supply chain management options can be viewed as a continuum between internal control ('**vertical integration**') and external control through outsourcing ('**virtual integration**'). The intermediate situation is sometimes referred to as 'vertical disintegration' or 'supply chain disaggregation'. This continuum is illustrated in Figure 6.10.

Virtual integration
The majority of supply chain activities are undertaken and controlled outside the organization by third parties.

There was a general trend during the second half of the twentieth century from vertical integration through vertical disintegration to virtual integration. In the car manufacturing industry traditionally car plants would be located near to a steelworks so that the input would be raw materials, with finished cars as the output. Other components of the car would also be manufactured by the company and other value chain activities such as marketing would largely be performed in-house. There has been a gradual move to sourcing more and more components such as lights, upholstery and trim and even engines to third parties. Marketing activities are now largely outsourced to marketing agencies. Another

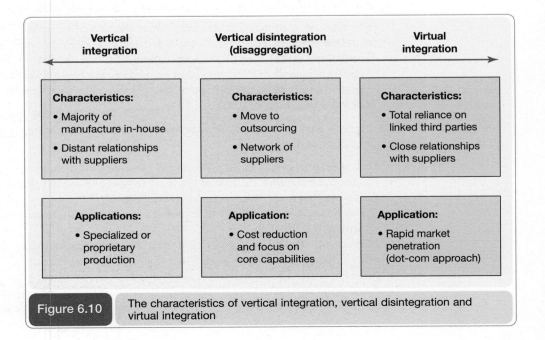

| Figure 6.10 | The characteristics of vertical integration, vertical disintegration and virtual integration |

Debate 6.2

Virtual integration and outsourcing of core processes

'The success of companies such as Dell in outsourcing core business processes and in virtual integration suggests that all companies need to adopt this model in order to be competitive.'

example is the purchase by pharmaceutical companies of pharmacy benefit managers (companies that manage drug distribution with private and company health schemes). By acquiring these companies which are part of a pharmaceutical company's downstream supply chain the aim is to 'get closer to the customer' while at the same time favourably controlling the distribution of the company's own drugs.

Hayes and Wheelwright (1994) provide a useful framework that summarizes choices for an organization's vertical integration strategy. The three main decisions are:

1 *The direction of any expansion.* Should the company aim to direct ownership at the upstream or downstream supply chain? The pharmaceuticals companies referred to above have decided to buy into the downstream part of the supply network (downstream vertical integration). This is sometimes referred to as an *offensive* strategic move since it enables the company to increase its power with respect to customers. Alternatively, if the pharmaceuticals company purchased other research labs this would be upstream-directed vertical integration which is strategically *defensive.*

2 *The extent of vertical integration.* How far should the company take downstream or upstream vertical integration? Originally car manufacturers had a high degree of vertical integration, but more recently they have moved from a *wide process span* to a *narrow process span.*

3 *The balance among the vertically integrated stages.* To what extent does each stage of the supply chain focus on supporting the immediate supply chain? For example, if a supplier to a motor manufacturer also produced components for other industries this would be an unbalanced situation.

Combining these concepts, we can refer to a typical B2B company (Figure 6.5). If it owned the majority of the upstream and downstream elements of the supply chain and each element was focused on supporting the activities of a B2B company, its strategy would be to follow upstream and downstream directions of vertical integration with a wide process span and a high degree of balance. Alternatively, if the strategy were changed to focus on core competencies it could be said to have a narrow process span.

How, then, can electronic communications support these strategies? Through increasing the flow of information between members of the supply chain, a strategy of narrower process span can be supported by e-commerce. However, this relies on all members of the supply chain being e-enabled. Companies undertaking offensive or defensive strategies will be in a better position to stipulate adoption of e-commerce, and so increase the overall efficiency of the supply chain. As we saw in Case study 6.1, a company such as Shell helps e-enable the supply chain by sharing information in its own databases with customers to increase the efficiency of the supply chain.

Our next example in the manufacture of personal computers also illustrates the concept of the two different supply chain products. Complete Activity 6.2 to review the benefits of each approach.

Activity 6.2   **Supply chain models in personal computer manufacture**

Activity

1 Review the approaches of the two companies illustrated below. Which tends to vertical integration and which tends to virtual integration?

2 Produce a table summarizing the benefits and disadvantages of each approach. Which do you think is the better approach?

3 How can information systems facilitate each approach?

Approach 1 IBM during the 1980s and early 1990s

Manufacture of many components by IBM plants in different locations including IBM processors, IBM hard disks, IBM cases and IBM monitors and even IBM mice. Distribution to companies by IBM logistics.

Approach 2 Dell during the 1990s and 2000s

Manufacture of all components by third parties in different locations including Intel processors, Seagate hard disks, Sony monitors and Microsoft mice. Assembly of some components in final product by third parties, e.g. adding appropriate monitor to system unit for each order.

Answers to activities can be found at www.pearsoned.co.uk/chaffey

---

Using e-business to restructure the supply chain

Information supply chain

An information-centric view of the supply chain which addresses the organizational and technological challenges of achieving technology-enabled supply chain management efficiency and effectiveness.

Using digital communications to improve supply chain efficiency is dependent on effective exchange and sharing of information. The challenges of achieving standardized data formats and data exchange have given rise to the study of optimization of the **information supply chain** (ISC) as suggested by Marinos (2005) and Sun and Yen (2005). March *et al.* (2007) describe the ISC as:

> *an information-centric view of physical and virtual supply chains where each entity adds value to the chain by providing the right information to the right entity at the right time in a secure manner. ISCs create value for the collaborating entities by gathering, organizing, selecting, synthesizing, and distributing information. The challenges to cultivating an ISC arise from both organizational and technological perspectives. Agility and flexibility in both internal and interorganizational business processes are required to benefit from technology investments in ISCs.*

This definition shows the scope and challenges of managing the ISC. Research by Legner and Schemm (2008) suggests two different types of information sharing and coordination problems in the retail and consumer goods industries: (1) the transactional information flow that allows for coordinating the physical demand and supply chain (demand signals, forecasts, orders, shipping, notifications, or invoices), and (2) the contextual information flow that ensures that retailers and manufacturers interpret data in the same way. They explain that a well-established problem is the 'bullwhip effect' or **information asymmetry** which results in amplification of the demand signal and fluctuation of inventory level

Information asymmetry

Imperfect information sharing between members of a supply chain which increases uncertainty about demand and pricing.

along a supply chain. The ECR concept introduced earlier in this chapter is an attempt to reduce information asymmetry. Although information asymmetry can be reduced through the use of technology, technical barriers such as the lack of standards, expertise or the cost of implementation will prevent it. Organizational issues such as the level of trust of supply chain partners and the competitive advantage that may result from keeping information are equally significant.

In this section we review efforts to optimize the ISC and describe the benefits of implementing ISC support technologies. We then consider how companies can use technologies to support the management of the upstream and downstream supply chain.

Technology options and standards for supply chain management

Some of the data transfer options and standards which enable e-SCM were introduced in Chapter 3. These include:

- EDI which is an established and relatively simple method of exchanging orders, delivery notes and invoices.
- XML- or XML-EDI-based data transfer enables more sophisticated one-to-many data transfers such as a request for orders being transmitted to potential suppliers.
- Middleware or software used to integrate or translate requests from external systems in real time so they are understood by internal systems and follow-up events will be triggered.
- Manual e-mail orders or online purchase through a traditional web-based e-commerce store for B2B.

These mechanisms enable data to be transferred to suppliers from clients using enterprise resource planning (ERP) systems which include material requirements planning modules which are used to model future demand for products, create a bill of materials of the relevant components needed to manufacture the products and then order them.

A rise in popularity of Software as a Service (SaaS, see Chapter 3) web applications has supported the growth of e-SCM systems as shown by Mini case study 6.2. In Chapter 3 we discuss some of the advantages and disadvantages of SaaS and in particular the single- or multi-tenancy decision.

Adoption rates of e-business applications

How popular are the e-business technologies for supply chain management? The European Commission Information Society report (European Commission, 2008) showed that the majority of businesses surveyed have Internet access; the proportion actively buying, selling or sharing information with partners online is much lower.

In 2006, the UK launched the Supplier Route to Government Portal (www.supply2.gov. uk) as part of its e-government initiative; this is an online marketplace for public-sector procurement valued at less than £100,000. Registered users can receive daily e-mail alerts about contracts appropriate to them, search for contracts online and post details of their offerings.

Mini Case Study 6.2	E2open prospers through e-SCM as SaaS

E2open (Figure 6.11) is a leading provider of multi-enterprise value chain solutions delivered on demand as a working business process in a pay-as-you-go model. Benefits of E2open according to the company include '*end-to-end visibility, collaboration and responsiveness over global value networks with faster time-to-value, lower total cost of ownership, a continuous value roadmap, and easier integration between internal enterprise applications and trading partners, including suppliers, customers, distributors and logistics providers.*' Over 45,000 companies worldwide currently use E2open which offers the choice of single tenancy or multi-tenancy.

Companies that use E2open to support supply chain management include the Boeing Company, Celestica, Cisco Systems, Flextronics, Hitachi, IBM, LG Electronics, LSI, Matsushita Electric Industrial (Panasonic), Motorola, Seagate Technology, Spansion, Vodafone, Wistron and YRC Worldwide.

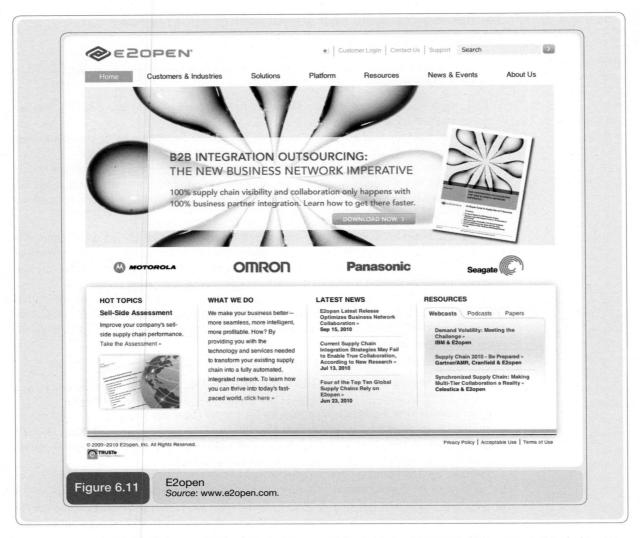

Figure 6.11 E2open
Source: www.e2open.com.

A European Union report (European Commission, 2008) also shows surprisingly low rates of adoption of different types of e-business applications. Figure 6.12 shows the popularity of different e-business applications. Despite the benefits of these applications, adoption is surprisingly low, particularly amongst smaller companies that use manual systems.

Benefits of e-supply chain management

Given the relative lack of adoption of e-SCM, particularly in SMEs, which opportunities are being missed that are available to adopters? Research by IDC (2004) into the challenges facing manufacturers in one sector (electronic component manufacture) showed that their main challenges (scored out of 5) were:

- Reduce order-to-delivery time (4.3)
- Reduce costs of manufacturing (4.1)
- Manage inventory more effectively (4.0)
- Improve demand forecasting (3.9)
- Reduce time to introduce new products (3.7)
- Improve after-market/post-sales operations (3.2)

Additional research on the benefits and challenges are presented in Figure 6.1.

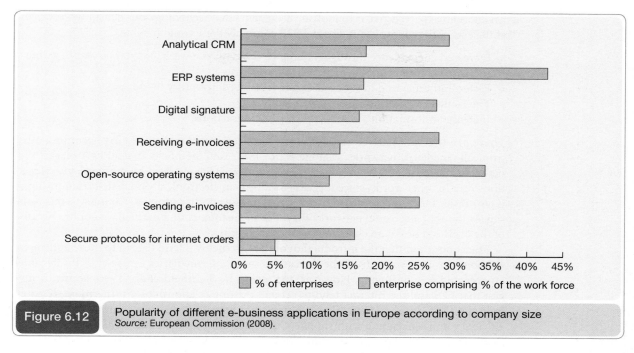

Figure 6.12	Popularity of different e-business applications in Europe according to company size

Source: European Commission (2008).

Typical benefits with respect to a B2B company include:

1 *Increased efficiency of individual processes.* If the B2B company adopts e-procurement this will result in a faster cycle time and lower cost per order, as described in Chapter 7.
Benefit: reduced cycle time and cost per order, as described in Chapter 7.
2 *Reduced complexity of the supply chain.* This is the process of disintermediation referred to in Chapter 2. Here the B2B company will offer the facility to sell direct from its e-commerce site rather than through distributors or retailers.
Benefit: reduced cost of channel distribution and sale.
3 *Improved data integration between elements of the supply chain.* The B2B company can share information with its suppliers on the demand for its products to optimize the supply process. Case study 6.2 on the Argos multichannel retail strategy shows the online sales growth that can be achieved through good integration of systems and data.
Benefit: reduced cost of paper processing.
4 *Reduced cost through outsourcing.* The company can outsource or use virtual integration to transfer assets and costs such as inventory holding costs to third-party companies.
Benefits: lower costs through price competition and reduced spend on manufacturing capacity and holding capacity.
5 *Innovation.* E-SCM should make it possible to be more flexible in delivering a more diverse range of products and to reduce time to market.
Benefit: better customer responsiveness.

Flexibility in adapting to new business requirements is a key capability of e-SCM systems. For example, in 2006, e-business system supplier and integrator SAP (www.sap.com) explained the three key capabilities of its SCM solution as:

- *Synchronize supply to demand* – Balance push and pull network planning processes. Replenish inventory and execute production based on actual demand.
- *Sense and respond with an adaptive supply chain network* – Drive distribution, transportation, and logistics processes that are integrated with real-time planning processes.
- *Provide networkwide visibility, collaboration, and analytics* – Monitor and analyse your extended supply chain.

Source: www.sap.com/solutions/business-suite/scm.

An alternative perspective is to look at the benefits that technology can deliver to customers at the end of the supply chain. For the B2B company these could include:

- Increased convenience through 24 hours a day, 7 days a week, 365 days a year ordering.
- Increased choice of supplier leading to lower costs.
- Faster lead times and lower costs through reduced inventory holding.
- The facility to tailor products more readily.
- Increased information about products and transactions.

There are two alternative, contradictory implications of supply chains becoming electronically mediated networks. Malone *et al.* (1987) and Steinfield *et al.* (1996) suggest that networks may foster electronic marketplaces that are characterized by more *ephemeral* relationships. In other words, since it is easier to form an electronically mediated relationship, it is also easier for the customer to break it and choose another supplier. Counter to this is the suggestion that electronic networks may *lock in* customers to a particular supplier because of the overhead or risk in changing to another supplier.

The conception that the introduction of the Internet will tend to lead to more ephemeral relationships may yet prove to be the case as more intermediaries evolve and this becomes an accepted way of buying. However, the review by Steinfield *et al.* (1996) seems to suggest that EDI and the Internet tend to cement existing relationships. Furthermore, research indicates that the use of networks for buying may actually reduce outcomes such as quality, efficiency and satisfaction with suppliers. If the findings of Steinfield *et al.* (1996) are confirmed in practice, then this calls into doubt the future of many B2B marketplaces (Chapter 7, p. 371). Personal relationships between the members of the buying unit and the supplier still seem to be important.

IS-supported upstream supply chain management

The key activities of upstream supply chain management are procurement and upstream logistics. The way in which information systems can be used to support procurement in the e-business is of such importance that a whole chapter is devoted to this (Chapter 7). However, in the current chapter we look at some examples of how technologies are used to improve upstream supply chain management.

Many grocery retailers have been at the forefront of using technology to manage their upstream supply chain. For example Tesco created the Tesco Information Exchange and other UK retailers have developed services such as 'Sainsbury Information Direct' and 'Safeway Supplier Information Service'. The Tesco Information Exchange (TIE) was developed in conjunction with GE Information Services (GEIS), and is an extranet solution that allows Tesco and its suppliers to collaboratively exchange trading information. TIE is linked to Tesco's key systems to give suppliers access to relevant and up-to-date information such as electronic point of sale (EPOS) data, to track sales and access the internal telephone/mail directory, so that suppliers can quickly find the right person to talk to.

RFID (radio-frequency identification microchip)

Radio-frequency identification (RFID)
Microchip-based electronic tags are used for monitoring anything they are attached to, whether inanimate products or animate (people).

RFID tags are a relatively recent innovation in e-SCM that are already widely used for logistics purposes. They can be attached to individual product items in a warehouse or in a retail location. With appropriate scanning technology they can then be used to assess stock levels.

RFID is still in a relatively early phase of its adoption with PMP (2008) reporting that only 3% of UK companies are using RFID extensively while 19% are deploying it in some areas. A further 3% only use it if mandated by their customers, while 16% are planning to use it in a few areas. The main disadvantage of RFID technology is still seen as its cost, cited by 42% of respondents to PMP (2008), while a lack of technology standards is mentioned by 32% and a lack of consumer understanding or distrust by 23%.

Case Study 6.2 Argos uses e-supply chain management to improve customer convenience

Retailer Argos is a leading proponent of using supply chain management to improve multichannel sales. The transactional Argos website was launched in 2000 when they were pioneers in implementing a reservation service. Sales have grown significantly since the launch over 10 years ago.

According to E-consultancy (2010), multichannel sales for Argos reached £1.9bn in 2009. Its 'Check and Reserve' feature, which enables visitors to check store availability and then order from a specific store for later pick-up, was responsible for 22% of the retailer's total sales in 2009, growing by 36%. Internet sales account for 32% of all sales. Some features of the system which rely on integration of the website with different logistics systems are superior to competitors'. For example, real-time stock availability information is shown and while some retailers make customers wait several days for in-store collection, items reserved on the Argos website can be collected straightaway.

David Tarbuck is head of multichannel retail at Argos. He explains the approach Argos has used for its fulfilment:

The way Argos is built is unique in the UK market, and this has made it easier for us to implement Check & Reserve. Since customers are in the front of the store, and the stock is held in the back, we have a clear picture of stock levels in our stores. This means we can be confident that, if we ask our systems about stock levels at any store, this information will be accurate.

Check & Reserve gained immediate adoption with customers, and this has accelerated over the last two or three years, with this channel growing by 36% for a second year in a row. People have caught on to it, and appreciate the convenience of being able to check before they leave the house and save themselves a wasted journey. While our model has been improved over the last ten years, other retailers have a more difficult and costly process for implementing this kind of service.

A further benefit for multichannel retailers like Argos is that they can broaden the available range of products available to shoppers by providing extended ranges on their websites, and Argos plans to add 10,000 online-only products in 2010. Argos also provides kiosk services in-store to help customers arrange home delivery.

Mobile commerce offers more order choice for Argos customers. In 2010, Argos launched its first iPhone app, in response to a 600% increase in traffic to Argos. co.uk from mobile devices. In December 2009, Argos had 750,000 visits from iPhones and iPods, suggesting demand for such a service.

The iPhone app initially asks you to set your home store to make subsequent reservations smoother. The app can also find the local store via GPS, or by entering the town name or postcode. Results of local stores are shown via Google Maps, and details are provided on opening hours, as well as driving directions, and the option to set this as your store. You can then use the search icon to search for stock held at that store. The stock checker works just like the machines in the Argos stores. Each product page comes with some detailed review information, which makes the app very useful for people to do some extra product research while in store. Once a product is selected, the reservation process is straightforward.

Argos is also well known for catalogues, which are also part of retail multichannel strategy since products featured can encourage purchase both in-store and on the web. Argos release two catalogues every year, each with a print run of 18 million. David Tarbuck explains how the catalogue fits into the multichannel strategy works:

We have large numbers of people who have our catalogue in their lounges, on their coffee tables, and this gives us a presence in people's homes.

Catalogues are often the starting point for customers shopping with Argos, they will flick through the catalogue, or browse the website at the same time.

We have over 11,000 products online that aren't in the catalogue, so people will come online to check this and for latest offers, so catalogues are used in conjunction with other channels. With catalogues or any other channel, it's all about talking to customers and working with them in whichever way they want to interact with us.

Tarbuck believes that the structure and focus of the team has also been important to success. He says:

We have a multichannel team, and I head up the development team and the operation of the website, overseeing online strategy.

We have e-commerce, marketing and commercial teams who respond to the trading side of the business, and make sure the various promotional campaigns are joined up, and there is consistency across channels. We've had a self-contained Internet-focused team in place for the last ten years, and this dedicated team has been very closely related to marketing and other areas of the business.

Fisher (1997) makes the distinction between two strategies that manufacturers can follow according to the type of product and the nature of its demand. For functional products, particularly those with easily predictable demand, the product does not need to be modified frequently in response to consumer demand. Here the implication is that the supply chain should be directed at cost reduction and efficiency. For more complex products, including those with less predictable demand, Fisher (1997) gives the example of two contrasting products, skiwear from Sport Obermayer and soup from Campbell. Each year, 95% of Sport Obermayer's products are new designs and demand forecasts may err by over 200%. In contrast, 95 per cent of Campbell's products are similar each year with predictable demand levels. The strategic response for these products is to develop a physically efficient supply chain in the former case and a market-responsive supply chain in the latter case.

In a company such as Campbell the biggest cost savings are possible by reviewing the structure of the supply chain as a whole. In 1991 the company operationalized what it referred to as a 'continuous replenishment programme'. It set up EDI links with major retailers and each morning retailers electronically inform Campbell of their demand for all products. Campbell then uses this information to determine which products require replenishment. Trucks leave Campbell's shipping plants and then arrive at the retailers' distribution centres each day. This approach reduced the inventory of participating retailers from about four weeks to two weeks with the associated cost reductions. This is the equivalent of a 1% increase in sales. This does not sound like a large improvement, but retailers' margins are thin, so this translates to a large increase in profitability on these product lines. The problem that Campbell encountered was that when it ran price promotions this could lead to up to five times the demand. This cannot be fulfilled on a short timescale so manufacture and retailer have to cooperate on advanced buying to meet these peaks in demand.

IS-supported downstream supply chain management

The key activities of downstream supply chain management are outbound logistics and fulfilment. In a B2B context the benefits for downstream customers are, of course, similar to the benefits that the organization receives through automating its upstream supply chain. These issues are considered from a marketing perspective in Chapters 8 and 9, but in this chapter we review the importance of fulfilment in achieving e-commerce success.

We also use the grocery retail market to illustrate the implications of e-commerce for management of the downstream supply chain. Tesco is one of the leaders in using e-commerce for downstream supply chain management. Tesco's downstream supply chain involves selling direct to customers, in other words it is operating a strategy of disintermediation (Chapter 2, p. 62) by reducing the role of its branches. Through being an early adopter, Tesco.com has developed as the world's largest online grocery site. You can read more on their latest developments at http://blogspot.technologyfortesco.com.

Outbound logistics management

The importance of outbound logistics relates to the expectations of offering direct sales through a website. In a nutshell, logistics is crucial to delivering the service promise established on the website.

A different angle on the importance of logistics and how it relates to the bottom line is illustrated by the fortunes of Amazon. Phillips (2000) reported that the fulfilment mechanism was adding to Amazon's costs because of split shipments, where multiple deliveries of items are necessary from a single order. This is a particular problem in the USA, which is the source of 86% of Amazon's revenue. Here the distance between population centres requires a network of seven distribution centres for shipments. Phillips (2000) explains that the need to fulfil a single order by shipping items from multiple locations increases costs for postage and the labour to assemble and dispatch goods. The alternative situation of stocking all distribution centres with every product is financially prohibitive. Some analysts suggest that Amazon should change its logistics strategy by separating out its distribution operation as a separate revenue source and outsourcing fulfilment to reduce costs.

The challenge for distribution companies is to deliver on time and provide services to enable customers to track shipment of products ordered online. The scale of the challenge can be gauged by looking at van Gend & Loos (vG&L, www.vgl.nl), a Dutch distribution company based within the Benelux countries. With over 4,000 employees, a fleet of 1,500 trucks, and annual revenues of approximately $500 million, vG&L wanted to offer its 40,000 customers the ability to track and trace their shipments over the Internet. While some distribution companies offer the facility for the sender to trace a package based on a consignment number, vG&L lets both the sender and the recipient track and trace packages based on date and destination searches. This key feature means that the sending parties can look at their information without the need for a special number, and they can look at all past shipments for the previous two months. At the same time, vG&L customers can also request pick-ups and shipments over the Internet.

IS infrastructure for supply chain management

Supply chain visibility
Access to up-to-date, accurate, relevant information about supply chain processes to different stakeholders.

Information systems need to deliver **supply chain visibility** to different parties who need to access the supply chain information of an organization, whether they be employees, suppliers, logistics service providers or customers. Users need to be able to personalize their view of the information according to their needs – customers want to see the status of their order, suppliers want to access the organization's database to know when their customer is next likely to place a major order. Security is also important – if a company has differential pricing, it will not want customers to see price differences.

These requirements for delivering supply chain information imply the need for an integrated supply chain database with different personalized views for different parties. A typical integrated information systems infrastructure for delivering supply chain management is illustrated in Figure 6.13. It can be seen that applications can be divided into those for planning the supply chain and those to execute the supply chain processes. Case studies 6.1 and 6.2 are both good examples of how new technologies are used to collect demand data and transfer data between different databases and applications. A key feature of a modern supply chain infrastructure is the use of a central operational database that enables information to be shared between supply chain processes and applications. This operational database is usually part of an enterprise resource planning system such as SAP, Baan or Prism and is usually purchased with the applications for supply chain planning and execution. Some of the planning applications such as network simulation and optimization are more likely to be supplied by separate software suppliers. The use of Internet technologies to deliver information over a TCP/IP protocol is becoming standard to reduce the costs of proprietary leased-line networks (Chapter 3). Information needed by managers to intervene

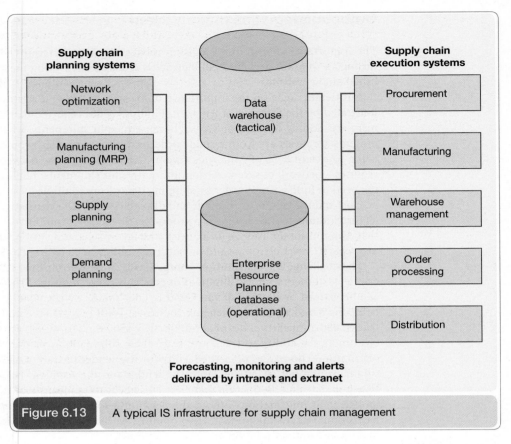

Figure 6.13 A typical IS infrastructure for supply chain management

in the supply chain process when problems occur is delivered as alerts or through continuous monitoring across secure private intranets or extranets used to link to partners.

Supply chain management implementation

The difficulties facing managers who are responsible for managing supply chains is indicated by these quotes from Conspectus (2000). When asked 'How difficult do you find it coordinating distribution and logistic plans at your sites?' a respondent from a UK mobile phone operator described his company's distribution and logistics process as 'an absolute nightmare'. Another commented:

Everything is moving so quickly within our industry at the moment that sourcing suppliers and changing our processes to fit with them is a constant battle. We are hoping our SCM software and the roll-out of our extranet will grow end-to-end ROI but it is easy to forget that we must constantly examine the business model to ensure we are doing things right.

By 2008, the PMP report showed that many companies have now invested in e-SCM (Figure 6.1). But there are great difficulties in delivering value from these systems.

Data standardization and exchange

The difficulties of exchanging information between incompatible systems has been a barrier limiting the adoption of SCM. Successful online marketplaces such as Elemica within the chemical industry have been based on collaboration between a limited number of partners within a vertical sector. But for markets with a more diverse range of products, standardization is more difficult. GDSN is a more recent development which should help accelerate adoption of e-SCM (see Box 6.5).

Some of the benefits of this approach for retailers identified by Schemm *et al.* (2007) include:

- Order and item administration improved by 50%
- Coupon rejection at the checkout reduced by 40%
- Data management efforts reduced by 30%
- Improvement of on-shelf availability, with out-of-stock items reduced from 8% to 3%

The supply chain management strategy process

A strategic approach for supply chain management can also be defined using the SOSTAC™ approach referred to in Chapters 5 and 8. Table 6.3 summarizes a SOSTAC™ approach to supply chain management strategy development based on the guidance of Hughes *et al.* (1998). Table 6.3 implies a linear approach to strategic thinking, but, as was pointed out in Chapters 4 and 5, an iterative approach is called for in which there is a joint development between the organization, the suppliers and other third parties.

Strategies for supply chain improvement have been categorized by Hughes *et al.* (1998) according to the scope of change and the speed of change. These dimensions of change are similar to those that are associated with business process re-engineering and business process improvement (Bocij *et al.*, 2005). Figure 6.14 illustrates four strategic options for the supply chain. The two strategies that are relatively limited in scope apply to individual processes such as procurement or outbound logistics and can be thought of as delivering

---

Box 6.5	Standardizing the world's data with GDSN

Every commercial organization has databases or catalogues containing information about the products they make, or sell, or buy. But, and it is a big but, the way in which they describe the information differs according to internal terminology, country, competing industry standards and when the database was last updated. This is one of the reasons for the development of barcodes and this principle has been developed further by supply chain trade organization Global Standards One (GS1) into the Electronic Product Code (EPC) and GDSN.

The Global Data Synchronisation Network (GDSN) was launched in 2005 to create standards for sharing information about retail products. By 2008 there were over 2 million items registered. G1, the organization that manages this standard, explains that there are five simple steps that allow trading partners to synchronize item, location and price data with each other:

1 *Load Data*. The seller registers product and company information in its data pool.
2 *Register Data*. A small subset of this data is sent to the GS1 Global Registry.
3 *Request Subscription*. The buyer, through its own data pool, subscribes to receive a seller's information.
4 *Publish Data*. The seller's data pool publishes the requested information to the buyer's data pool.
5 *Confirm & Inform*. The buyer sends a confirmation to the seller via each company's data pool, which informs the supplier of the action taken by the retailer using the information.

Table 6.3	A SOSTAC™ approach to supply chain management

Strategy element	SCM approach of Hughes *et al.* (1998)
Situation analysis	Gather the data: • Internal assessment of current approaches to the supply chain • External analysis of marketplace trends and customer opportunities
Objective setting	Set the objectives • Definition of required target returns and release of shareholder value
Strategy	Frame the strategies: • Development of supply chain strategies to achieve these goals (actions)
Tactics	Prioritization of operational improvement strategies and quick wins
Actions	Implement the change and challenge the thinking: • Formation of a supply chain strategy forum to assess the needs • Analysis of value-added, cost and cycle time of supply chain activities • Cascade of executive-led project groups to scrutinize key processes • Allocation of business development strategies to sponsor executives
Control	Measure the outcome: • Integration of supply chain measurement in corporation-wide reviews • Baselining to maintain pressure for performance delivery

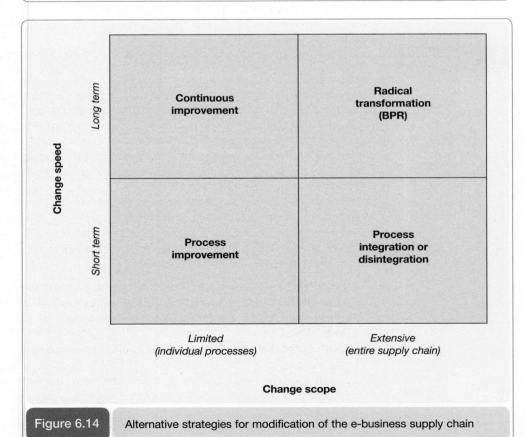

Figure 6.14	Alternative strategies for modification of the e-business supply chain

improvement at an operational level. These may give short-term benefits while minimizing the risk of more radical change. Conversely, where the scope of change is more extensive there is a greater risk, but also greater potential reward. These changes include complete re-engineering of processes or major changes to the supply chain.

Goal-setting and performance management for e-SCM

In an earlier section we discussed the benefits of e-supply chain management. To manage e-SCM effectively, the type of benefits such as time and cost savings and an improved service to customers should be developed into a performance management framework. Sambasivan *et al.* (2009) have consolidated performance measures described by other supply chain management researchers. In their measurement framework, they identified these categories of measures and gave examples of metrics within each:

1 **Cost in supply chain**: Total cost, distribution cost, manufacturing cost, inventory cost.
2 **Profitability**: ROI.
3 **Customer responsiveness**: Time required to produce, number of orders delivered on time, number of units produced, fill rate, stockout probability, number of back-orders, number of stockouts, customer response time, average lead time, shipping errors, customer complaints.
4 **Flexibility**: Volume flexibility, delivery flexibility, mix flexibility, new product flexibility, planned order procedures, order lead time, customer order path.
5 **Supply chain partnership**: Level and degree of information sharing, buyer–vendor cost-saving initiatives, extent of mutual cooperation leading to improved quality, extent of mutual assistance in problem-solving efforts, the entity and stage at which supplier is involved.
6 **Production level metric**: Range of products and services, effectiveness of scheduling techniques, capacity utilization.
7 **Delivery performance**: Delivery-to-request data, delivery-to-commit date, order fill lead time, number of faultless notes invoiced, flexibility of delivery systems to meet customer needs, total distribution cost, delivery lead time.
8 **Customer service and satisfaction**: Flexibility, customer query time, post-transaction measures of customer service, customer perception of service.
9 **Supply chain finance and logistics cost**: Cost associated with assets and ROI, total inventory cost, total cash flow time.
10 **Cost performance**: Material cost, labour cost, machinery energy cost, machinery material consumption, inventory and WIP level, total productivity, direct labour productivity, fixed capital productivity, indirect labour productivity, working capital productivity, value added productivity.
11 **Internal and external time performance**: Time to market, distribution lead time, delivery reliability, supplier lead time, supplier reliability, manufacturing lead time, standard run time, set-up time, wait time, move time, inventory turnover, order carrying-out time.
12 **Quality performance**: SPC measures, machine reliability, rework, quality system cost, inbound quality, vendor quality rating, customer satisfaction, technical assistance, returned goods.
13 **Customer relationship management**: Supplier relationship management and order fulfilment process: measures not discussed in paper.

To think about how e-SCM can assist in improving performance in this area, complete Activity 6.3.

| Activity 6.3 | An e-SCM performance management framework |

Purpose

To highlight the benefits of e-SCM and how improvements in performance and operational management of e-SCM can be achieved.

Questions

In a large group, each pair of students should take one of the categories of measures and then discuss:

1 How information systems can help improve performance.
2 The constraints that may limit performance improvements.

Managing partnerships

A key element of restructuring of the supply chain is examining the form of relationships with partners such as suppliers and distributors. This need to review the form of partnership has been accentuated with the globalization enabled by e-commerce. In this section we consider what forms these partnerships should take and how technology can be used to facilitate them.

Stuart and McCutcheon (2000) state that typically low cost is the main driver for partnership management in supply management (mainly upstream). According to these authors, the modification of supply chain partnerships usually follows what they describe as the 'received wisdom which many practitioners are rigidly following'. This approach requires companies to:

1 Focus on core competencies.
2 Reduce their number of suppliers.
3 Develop strong partnership relationships built on shared information and trust with the remaining suppliers.

Stuart and McCutcheon (2000) suggest that this approach may not suit all needs and the type of relationship required will be dependent on the ultimate objective. When reviewing partnerships, companies need to decide the options for the extent of their control of the supply chain process. Table 6.4 presents some strategic options for partnerships in order of increasing control and ownership over the process by the organization. Option 1 is total insourcing of a particular process while 2 to 9 give varying degrees of outsourcing. There is also a continuum between collaborative partnerships where risks are shared (options 1 to 5) and competitive sourcing where market competition is used to achieve the best combination of price and value. Note that although an organization may lose control of the *process* through outsourcing, a contractual arrangement will still enable them to exert a strong control over the *outputs* of the process.

From Table 6.4 it can be seen that as the depth of relationship between partners increases, the volume and complexity of information exchange requirements will increase. For a long-term arrangement information exchange can include:

- Short-term orders.
- Medium-to-long-term capacity commitments.
- Long-term financial or contractual agreement.
- Product design, including specifications.
- Performance monitoring, standard of product and service quality.
- Logistics.

Table 6.4	Strategic options for partnerships

Partnering arrangement	Technical infrastructure integration	Examples
1 Total ownership (more than 51% equity in company)	Technical issues in merging company systems	Purchase of Booker (distribution company) by Iceland (retailer). Since 1993 Cisco has made over 30 acquisitions (not all SCM-related)
2 Investment stake (less than 49% equity)	Technical issues in merging company systems	Cisco has also made over 40 investments in hardware and software suppliers
3 Strategic alliance	Collaboration tools and groupware for new product development	Cable and Wireless, Compaq and Microsoft new e-business solution called a-Services
4 Profit-sharing partnership	As above	Arrangement sometimes used for IS outsourcing
5 Long-term contract	See above. Tools for managing service level agreements important	ISPs have performance and availability SLAs with penalty clauses
6 Preferred suppliers	Permanent EDI or Internet EDI links set up with preferred partners	Tesco Information Exchange
7 Competitive tendering	Tenders issued at intermediary or buyer's website	Buyer-arranged auctions, (see Chapter 2)
8 Short-term contracts	As above	As above
9 Spot markets and auctions	Auctions at intermediary or buyer's website	Business-to-business marketplaces, e.g. www.freemarkets.com

For a short-term relationship simple information on transactions only, such as the EDI purchase order example in Chapter 3, is all that is required.

Stuart and McCutcheon (2000) present a more simplified set of partnership choices. They suggest that the partnering option chosen should be dependent on the core objective. If this is cost reduction, then a relationship with competitive tension is required (equivalent to options 6 to 9 in Table 6.4). Alternatively, if the core objective is value-added benefits such as improved delivery speed, additional design features or the need for customization, then the 'arm's-length' approach of options 6 to 9 may not be appropriate. In this case they suggest a strategic alliance or cooperative partnership is the best option. Stuart and McCutcheon point out that the competitive advantages achieved through cost reduction are likely to be short-lived so companies will increasingly need to turn to value-added benefits. Each supplier has to be considered for whichever type of partnership is most appropriate.

Managing global distribution

Arnold (2000) suggests action that manufacturers should follow as they enter new overseas markets enabled by the Internet. The seven actions are:

1 Select distributors. Do not let them select you.
2 Look for distributors capable of developing markets rather than those with new customer contacts.
3 Treat the local distributors as long-term partners, not temporary market entry vehicles.

4 Support market entry by committing money, managers and proven marketing ideas.
5 From the start, maintain control over marketing strategy.
6 Make sure distributors provide you with detailed market and financial performance data.
7 Build links among national distributors at the earliest opportunity.

Case Study 6.3   RFID: keeping track starts its move to a faster track

Over the years many techniques and technologies have been developed to make supply chains more efficient, but they often fail for the simple reason that it is notoriously difficult to get sufficient accurate information to be useful.

Radio frequency identification (RFID) technology tackles this problem using small radio tags to keep track of goods as they move through the supply chain.

Demand for these tags, which cost around 40 cents each, has soared because of mandates from US and European retailers – Wal-Mart is the best known – and the US Department of Defense which require large suppliers to put tags on pallets and cases as of 2005.

A clear sign that RFID is coming of age is that Nokia recently unveiled a kit to transform one of its phones into a mobile RFID reader. Despite the current hype, RFID is not a new technology. It was first used to identify aircraft in the Second World War and has been employed to tag cattle, collect road tolls and open doors for many years.

What is new is the application of RFID to supply chains.

The combination of RFID hardware with a unique number, called the electronic product code (EPC), enables businesses to associate a wealth of information with each tagged object. Not only is the information more detailed than a barcode, it can be read and updated using radio readers.

Early RFID technologies often delivered disappointing performance, but today's tags can be read reliably as packing cases are on a conveyor belt or even if the case is hidden behind others.

'RFID is a barcode on steroids,' says Lyle Ginsburg, RFID specialist at Accenture, the management consultancy. 'It promises tremendous productivity gains because you do not have the human intervention and line-of-sight issues that you get with barcodes.'

Many experts believe the combination of RFID and EPC has the potential to transform supply chains: no more inventory counts, no more lost or misdirected shipments, and no more guessing how much is in the supply chain or on the store shelves.

'Just by knowing what is in the store and what is still in the back room, you can get much greater visibility on

inventory,' says Peter Regen, vice president of global visible commerce at Unisys, the US IT company.

Visibility is sorely lacking from real-world supply chains, which is why companies hold buffer stocks and build warehouses. This lessens the chance of running out, but the annual cost of holding all this inventory – in warehousing, opportunity cost and obsolescence – adds up to $300bn, just in the US.

AMR Research estimates around $3 trillion of inventory is locked in US and European supply chains, which suffer order error rates of 20%. 'There is just too much waste in the supply chain,' says Michael Witty, an analyst with Manufacturing Insights, part of the IDC research group.

Even if RFID only manages to reduce inventory levels or error rates by a few percentage points, the benefits to the economy in terms of extra working capital are substantial. In the case of an emerging economy such as China, RFID's potential is even greater.

China's supply chains have not kept pace with the country's rapid rise as a manufacturing nation and bottlenecks now threaten its export-led growth. The Chinese government is keeping a close eye on RFID and officials recently attended a big RFID trade fair in the US.

'In China, there is a lot of interest in RFID, which has really surprised us,' says Amar Singh, VP of global RFID initiatives at SAP, the German software giant. In part, this interest is driven by Chinese manufacturers' need to fall into line with the RFID mandates of western customers, most notably Wal-Mart, which accounts for more than 10% of all US imports from China.

But the Chinese government also sees RFID as a strategic technology that will bring the country's supply chains up to the standards of developed nations. Several projects are under way to test the use of RFID in Chinese port and logistics operations.

In the past three years, ports have become more conscious about security. Shipping companies know they face delays and may be refused entry if they are carrying suspect containers. 'Before 9/11, there was not much concern about what was inside the container,' says Scott Brown, general manager for cargo security at GE, the US engineering giant.

GE has developed a 'smart box' that uses RFID to track the movements of maritime containers when they enter ports and sensors to detect if the containers have been opened. The smart box technology has been tested in GE's domestic appliance business, which imports most of its products from China.

'The impetus for doing this was security, but there are also potential supply chain benefits,' says Mr Brown. However, he admits that it is difficult to make a case for using RFID on these benefits alone.

This problem affects most RFID initiatives, according to Accenture's Mr Lyle. Unless forced to comply with an RFID mandate, many potential users prefer to wait. Standards are still evolving and the cost of the technology is still too high for many applications. Data security is another big issue.

Burt Kaliski, chief scientist at RSA Laboratories, a US security software firm, fears thieves could quickly discover how to destroy or change the information on RFID tags while hackers could launch 'denial-of-service' attacks with the potential to create chaos in RFID-equipped supply chains.

But the main reason not to jump in yet is that, mandates aside, there are too many hurdles that need to be overcome before RFID can show a clear return on investment.

'The business case for RFID is very challenging,' admits Mr Lyle.

Source: Geoffrey Nairn, Keeping track starts its move to a faster track, *The Financial Times*, 20 April 2005. Reprinted with permission.

Question

Select a manufacturing sector and then evaluate the benefits and risks of applying RFID in this sector.

Summary

1 Supply chain management involves the coordination of all supply activities of an organization from its suppliers and partners to its customers. Upstream supply chain activities (procurement and inbound logistics) are equivalent to buy-side e-commerce and downstream supply chain activities (sales, outbound logistics and fulfilment) correspond to sell-side e-commerce.

2 There has been a change in supply chain management thinking from a push-oriented supply chain that emphasizes distribution of a product to passive customers to a pull-oriented supply chain that utilizes the supply chain to deliver value to customers who are actively involved in product and service specification.

3 The value chain concept is closely allied to supply chain management. It considers how value can be added both between and within elements of the supply chain and at the interface between them.

4 Electronic communications enable value networks to be created that enable the external value chain to be dynamically updated in response to marketplace variables.

5 Supply chains and value chains can be revised by disaggregation or re-aggregation. Disaggregation may involve outsourcing core supply chain activities to external parties. As more activities are outsourced a company moves towards becoming a virtual organization.

6 Electronic communications have played a major role in facilitating new models of supply chain management. Technology applications that have facilitated supply chain management are:
- E-mail
- Web-based ordering
- EDI of invoices and payment
- Web-based order tracking.

7 Benefits of deploying these technologies include:
- More efficient, lower-cost execution of processes
- Reduced complexity of the supply chain (disintermediation)
- Improved data integration between elements of the supply chain
- Reduced costs through ease of dynamic outsourcing
- Enabling innovation and customer responsiveness.

8 Intranets connecting internal business applications such as operational enterprise resource planning systems and decision-support-oriented data warehouses enable supply chain management. Such systems increasingly support external links to third parties such as suppliers.

9 Key strategic issues in supply chain management include:
- Redesigning supply chain activities
- Restructuring partnerships which support the supply chain through outsourcing or ownership.

Exercises

Self-assessment questions

1 Define supply chain management; how does it relate to:
- logistics;
- the value chain concept;
- value networks?

2 What is the difference between a push orientation to the value chain and pull orientation?

3 How can information systems support the supply chain?

4 What are the key strategic options in supply chain management?

Essay and discussion questions

1 How does electronic communications enable restructuring of the value chain network?

2 'The concept of a linear value chain is no longer tenable with the advent of electronic commerce.' Discuss.

3 Select an industry of your choice and analyse how business-to-business exchanges will change the supply chain.

4 *In the end business all comes down to supply chain vs supply chain.*' Discuss.

5 Select a retailer of your choice and analyse their strategy for management of the upstream and downstream supply chain.

Examination questions

1 Explain how the concepts of disintermediation, reintermediation and countermediation apply to the supply chain.

2 You have recently been appointed as supply chain manager for a pharmaceutical company. Summarize the main Internet-based applications you would consider for communicating with your suppliers.

3 How has the increase in electronic communications contributed to the development of value networks?

4 What are the characteristics of a virtual organization? Using examples, explain how e-commerce can support the virtual organization.

5 Explain how information technologies can be employed for different elements of a purchaser–supplier relationship.

6 Using industry examples, summarize three benefits of using e-commerce to streamline the supply chain.

7 How can electronic commerce be used to support restructuring of the supply chain?

8 What are the differences and similarities of using information technology to support:

(a) the upstream supply chain;
(b) the downstream supply chain?

References

AMR (2008) The AMR Research Supply Chain Top 25 for 2008. Value Chain Report. Published at **www.amrresearch.com.**

Arnold, D. (2000) Seven rules of international distribution. *Harvard Business Review,* November–December, 131–7.

Benjamin, R. and Wigand, R. (1995) Electronic markets and virtual value-chains on the information superhighway. *Sloan Management Review,* Winter, 62–72.

Bocij, P., Chaffey, D., Greasley, A. and Hickie, S. (2005) *Business Information Systems. Technology, Development and Management,* 3rd edn. Financial Times Prentice Hall, Harlow.

Chan, C. and Swatman, P. (2000) From EDI to Internet commerce – the BHP Steel experience. *Internet Research Electronic Networks: Applications and Policy,* 10(1), 77–82.

Conspectus (2000) Supply chain management software issue. Prime Marketing Publications, June. PMP Research. **www.conspectus.com.**

Davidow, W.H. and Malone, M.S. (1992) *The Virtual Corporation: Structuring and Revitalizing the Corporation for the 21st Century.* HarperCollins, London.

Deise, M., Nowikow, C., King, P. and Wright, A. (2000) *Executive's Guide to E-Business. From Tactics to Strategy.* Wiley, New York.

Econsultancy (2010) Multichannel accounts for 43% of Argos sales. By Graham Charlton, 4th May 2010. **http://econsultancy.com/blog/5850-multichannel-accounts-for-43-of-argos-sales.**

European Commission (2008) i2010 Annual Information Society Report 2008, mid-term report published at: **http://ec.europa.eu/information_society/eeurope/i2010/mid_term_review_2008/index_en.htm.**

Field, C. (2000) Waterstone's: fully integrated into existing fulfilment systems. *Financial Times,* 3 May.

Fisher, M. (1997) What is the right supply chain for your product? *Harvard Business Review,* March–April, 105–16.

Hagel, J. III and Rayport, J. (1997) The new infomediaries. *McKinsey Quarterly,* no. 4, 54–70.

Hamill, J. and Gregory, K. (1997) Internet marketing in the internationalisation of UK SMEs. *Journal of Marketing Management,* 13, 1–3.

Hayes, R. and Wheelwright, S. (1994) *Restoring our Competitive Edge.* Wiley, New York.

Hughes, J., Ralf, M. and Michels, B. (1998) *Transform Your Supply Chain*. International Thomson Business Press, London.

IBF (2008) *12 ways to use your intranet to cut your costs*. Member Briefing Paper August 2008. Published by the Intranet Benchmarking Forum (**www.ibforum.com**).

IDC (2004) Increasing Supply Chain Responsiveness among Configured Electronic Systems Manufacturers, IDC White paper. Author: Meredith Whalen, January.

Internet Retailing (2010) Taking cost out of the reverse supply chain. *Internet Retailing*, 4 (6), September 2010.

Kalakota, R. and Robinson, M. (2000) *E-Business. Roadmap for Success*. Addison-Wesley, Reading, MA.

Kjellsdotter, L. and Jonsson, P. (2010) The potential benefits of advanced planning and scheduling systems in sales and operations planning, *Industrial Management & Data Systems*, 110(5), 659–81.

Kraut, R., Chan, A., Butler, B. and Hong, A. (1998) Coordination and virtualisation: the role of electronic networks and personal relationships. *Journal of Computer Mediated Communications*, 3(4).

Legner, C. and Schemm, J. (2008) Toward the inter-organizational product information supply chain – evidence from the retail and consumer goods industries. *Journal of the Association for Information Systems*, 9(3/4), 119–50, Special Issue.

Magretta, J. (1998) The power of virtual integration. An interview with Michael Dell. *Harvard Business Review*, March–April, 72–84.

Malone, T., Yates, J. and Benjamin, R. (1987) Electronic markets and electronic hierarchies: effects of information technology on market structure and corporate strategies. *Communications of the ACM*, 30(6), 484–97.

March, S., Raghu, T. and Vinze, A. (2007) Cultivating and securing the information supply chain. *Journal of the Association for Information Systems*, 9, pp. 95–7, Special Issue.

Marinos, G. (2005). The Information Supply Chain: Achieving Business Objectives by Enhancing Critical Business Processes. *DM Review*. **www.dmreview.com/article_sub. cfm?articleId=1023896.**

Phillips, S. (2000) Retailer's crown jewel is a unique customer database. *Financial Times*, 4 December.

PMP (2008) Supply Chain and Manufacturing Systems Report. PMP Research Report published at **www.conspectus.com,** March.

Porter, M. (1980) *Competitive Strategy*. Free Press, New York.

Porter, M. and Millar, V. (1985) How information gives you competitive advantage. *Harvard Business Review*, July–August, 149–60.

Quelch, J. and Klein, L. (1996) The Internet and international marketing. *Sloan Management Review*, Spring, 60–75.

Rayport, J. and Sviokla, J. (1996) Exploiting the virtual value-chain. *McKinsey Quarterly*, no. 1, 20–37.

Sambasivan, M., Tamizarasu, N. and Zainal, A. (2009) Consolidation of performance measures in supply chain environment. *Journal of Enterprise Information Management*, 22(6), 660–89.

Schemm, J. Legner, C. and Otto, B. (2007) Global Data Synchronization, Current Status and Future Trends. University of Gallen, Institute of Information Management, Research Report available at **www.gsl.org/productssolutions/gdsn/ds/retailers.html.**

Steinfield, C., Kraut, R. and Plummer, A. (1996) The impact of interorganizational networks on buyer–seller relationships. *Journal of Computer Mediated Communication*, 1(3).

Stuart, F. and McCutcheon, D. (2000) The manager's guide to supply chain management. *Business Horizons*, March–April, 35–44.

Sun, S. and Yen, J. (2005). Information supply chain: a unified framework for information-sharing, in *Intelligence and Security Informatics*, P. Kantor, G. Muresan, F. Roberts, D. Zeng, F.-Y. Wang, H. Chen and R. Merkle (eds). Springer, Berlin, pp. 422–9.

Timmers, P. (1999) *Electronic Commerce Strategies and Models for Business-to-Business Trading.* John Wiley Series in Information Systems. Wiley, Chichester.

Warner, M. (2001) Managing in virtual space. FT Mastering Management. Available online at: **www.ftmastering.com/mmo/mmo03_1.htm.**

Womack, J. and Jones, D. (1998) *Lean Thinking.* Touchstone, Simon and Schuster, London.

Further reading

Cagliano, R., Caniato, F. and Spina, G. (2005) E-business strategy: How companies are shaping their supply chain through the internet. *International Journal of Operations & Production Management*, 25(12), 1309–27. A classification of different levels of adoption of supply chain management including a literature review.

Johnson, E. and Whang, S. (2002), E-Business And Supply Chain Management: An Overview And Framework. *Production and Operations Management*, 11(4) Winter 2002, 413–23. An overview of different forms of E-SCM.

Murillo, L. (2001) Supply chain management and the international dissemination of e-commerce. *Industrial Management and Data Systems*, 101(7), 370–7. An introduction to changes in supply chain management introduced by e-commerce.

Smart, A. (2008) eBusiness and supply chain integration. *Journal of Enterprise Information Management*, 21(3), 227–46. Describes how four large organizations have approached the implementation of new E-SCM approaches including online order processing, e-procurement, reverse auctions, and a private exchange.

Web links

CIO Magazine E-commerce resource centre (**www.cio.com/forums/ec**) One of the best online magazines from a business/technical perspective – see other research centres also, e.g. intranets, knowledge management.

Conspectus (**www.conspectus.com**) Articles on different e-business applications including supply chain management.

CPFR (Collaborative Planning, Forecasting and Replenishment) (**www.cpfr.org**) CPFR is a concept that allows collaborative processes across the supply chain, using a set of process and technology models. The site includes generic models, White Papers and case studies.

Institute of Logistics and Transport (**www.iolt.org.uk**) Overview of logistics, plus links to related sites.

GS1 (**www.gs1.org**) Information on global standards for data exchange to support SCM.

ITtoolbox (**http://erp.ittoolbox.com**) Specialist portal containing news and articles about ERP (enterprise resource planning systems), one application of which is supply chain management.

Oracle SCM introduction (**www.oracle.com/applications/scm/**) Oracle is one of the biggest providers of SCM applications; here they introduce the benefits of their approach.

Technology for Tesco (**http://techfortesco.blogspot.com**) You can read more on the latest supply chain and marketing innovations applied by Tesco.

7

E-procurement

Web support

The following additional case studies
are available at
www.pearsoned.co.uk/chaffey

→ Worldwide oil exchange – the
   Shell perspective
→ E-procurement in the aerospace
   industry

The site also contains a range of
study materials designed to help
improve your results.

Learning outcomes

After reading this chapter the reader should be able to:

- Identify the benefits and risks of e-procurement
- Analyse procurement methods to evaluate cost savings
- Assess different options for integration of organizations'
  information systems with e-procurement suppliers

Management issues

Managers will be concerned with the following e-procurement
issues:

- What benefits and risks are associated with e-procurement?
- Which method(s) of e-procurement should we adopt?
- What organizational and technical issues are involved in
  introducing e-procurement?

Links to other chapters

The main related chapters are:

- *Chapter 2* – introduces business-to-business marketplaces,
  models of electronic trading and B2B auctions
- *Chapter 6* – covers the role of purchasing within supply chain
  management

Introduction

Procurement has not traditionally been a significant topic for management study in comparison with other areas such as marketing, operations or strategy. The concept of e-business has, however, highlighted its importance as a strategic issue since introducing electronic procurement or e-procurement can achieve significant savings and other benefits which directly impact upon the customer.

The potential importance of online procurement is highlighted by Christa Degnan, a senior analyst at the Aberdeen Group, who explains that purchased goods and services are often the largest expenditure at many companies:

> We estimate that for every dollar a company earns in revenue, 50 cents to 55 cents is spent on indirect goods and services – things like office supplies and computer equipment. That half dollar represents an opportunity: By driving costs out of the purchasing process, companies can increase profits without having to sell more goods. (Hildebrand, 2002)

In this chapter we consider the benefits and risks of e-procurement together with techniques that can be used to assess these benefits and risks. We also consider the selection and management of the different types of e-procurement including the hyped business-to-business marketplaces.

What is e-procurement?

The terms 'purchasing' and 'procurement' are sometimes used interchangeably, but as Kalakota and Robinson (2000) point out, 'procurement' generally has a broader meaning. 'Procurement' refers to all activities involved with obtaining items from a supplier; this includes purchasing, but also inbound logistics such as transportation, goods-in and warehousing before the item is used. The key procurement activities and associated information flows within an organization are shown in Figure 7.1. In this chapter we focus on these activities which include searching and specification of product by the end-user, purchasing by the buyer, payment by an account, and receipt and distribution of goods within a warehouse.

E-procurement should be directed at improving performance for each of the 'five rights of purchasing' (Baily *et al.*, 1994), which are sourcing items:

Electronic procurement (e-procurement)

The electronic integration and management of all procurement activities including purchase request, authorization, ordering, delivery and payment between a purchaser and a supplier.

1 at the right price
2 delivered at the right time
3 of the right quality
4 of the right quantity
5 from the right source.

Box 7.1 gives an additional perspective on e-purchasing.

Electronic procurement system (EPS)

An electronic system used to automate all or part of the procurement function.

E-procurement is not new; there have been many attempts to automate the process of procurement for the buyer using **electronic procurement systems (EPS)**, workflow systems and links with suppliers through EDI (Chapter 3). These involved online entry, authorization and placing of orders using a combination of data entry forms, scanned documents and e-mail-based workflow. It is convenient to refer to these as 'first-generation e-procurement'.

Read Mini case study 7.1 to understand how e-procurement occurs within an organization.

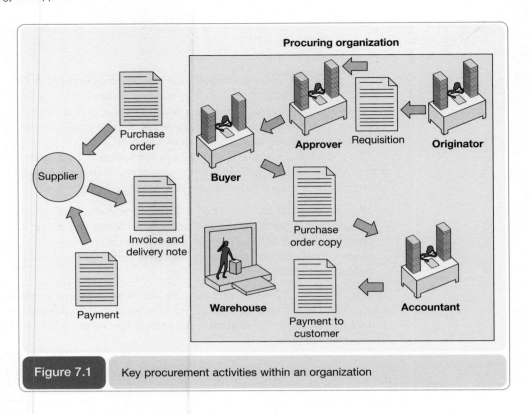

Figure 7.1 Key procurement activities within an organization

E-procurement at Schlumberger In Paris

Schlumberger is a global company that started its life as a supplier in the oil and gas exploration industry. In 2007 it had $23 billion operating revenue, 84,000 employees of 140 nationalities operating in approximately 80 countries. It now provides a range of information services. This case study describes the initial installation of an e-procurement system at its largest division, oilfield services. The aim of the new system was to replace existing systems, some paper-based and some computer-based, with a single system that would speed up purchasing. The system has resulted in lower transaction costs for placing orders and also reduced the cost of goods as the price of products has declined through greater competition and negotiation of lower prices for the electronic channel.

With the new system, employees act as purchasing agents, ordering directly via their desktop PCs.

The system runs on the Schlumberger intranet and enables staff to access a simplified catalogue of office supplies and technical equipment. For example, one of the suppliers is OfficeDepot. Although OfficeDepot can post its entire catalogue at an electronic marketplace, employees at Schlumberger only see a subset of relevant products for which special prices have been negotiated. Once the items have been selected, the system automatically produces a requisition that is electronically routed to the person who will approve it, and it is then converted into a purchase order without the intervention of purchasing staff.

The technical solution is based on Commerce One Buysite procurement software for selection and approval and Marketsite from the same supplier for the transaction between Schlumberger and their suppliers. Schlumberger reports that Marketsite tends to give access to a wider range of suppliers than when it used one-to-one EDI transactions with suppliers. The solution was implemented gradually through introducing new items in stages.

Source: Based on a summary of a dialogue between Alain-Michel Diamant-Berger and Andrea Ovans (Ovans, 2000).

| Box 7.1 | What is e-purchasing? |

This is how the Chartered Institute of Purchasing and Supply (CIPS, www.cips.org.uk) explains e-purchasing to its members:

The combined use of information and communications technology through electronic means to enhance external and internal purchasing and supply management processes. These tools and solutions deliver a range of options that will facilitate improved purchasing and supply management.

The range of potential options for improving purchasing processes are indicated by these benefits that are described by CIPS:

1. Evaluation of end-to-end trading cycles, e.g. evaluation and possible re-engineering of trading cycles leading to reduced cycle times; improved workflow of the internal procurement process enabling end-user self-service and decentralization with centralized control through company-specific catalogues; new functionality such as online bidding in e-auctions and e-requests for quotations (RFQs).

2. Use of more efficient and cheaper connectivity methods such as the Internet and XML. XML is not, however, a requirement for e-procurement.

3. Connectivity to external sources of information, e.g. portals, e-hubs, e-marketplaces.

4. Connectivity to external supply chains, e.g. extranets, EDI, e-hubs, e-marketplaces – allowing shared real-time information such as suppliers accessing real-time sales.

5. Sourcing, e.g. identifying new sources via the Internet, use of intelligent search engines.

6. Content management, e.g. private catalogues, public catalogues, internal inventory management, maintenance management.

7. Connectivity to internal systems and sources of information such as inventory management, maintenance management, materials resource planning (MRP) systems.

8. Payment systems, e.g. purchasing cards.

9. Multimedia (although e-procurement does not necessarily contain multimedia elements).

10. Improvements in localized supply chain mechanisms and consortia etc. leading to mutual benefit.

Source: CIPS (2008).

Understanding the procurement process

Before the advent of e-procurement, organizational purchasing processes had remained similar for decades. Table 7.1 highlights the paper-based process. It can be seen that it involves the end-user selecting an item by conducting a search and then filling in a paper requisition form that is sent to a buyer in the purchasing department (often after authorization by a manager, which introduces further delay). The buyer then fills in an order form that is dispatched to the supplier. After the item is delivered, the item and a delivery note are usually reconciled with the order form and an invoice and then payment occurs. Procurement also includes the transport, storage and distribution of goods received within the business – this is referred to as 'inbound logistics'. Activity 7.1 explains how the procurement process can be simplified through e-procurement.

Table 7.1	Process flow analysis for traditional procurement (typical cycle time, 5½ days)	

Task description	Chart symbols	Time
1 Search for goods	●⇨□D▽	1 hour
2 Fill in paper requisition	●⇨□D▽	10 min
3 Send to buyer	○➜□D▽	1 day
4 In buyer's in-tray	○⇨□▶▽	½ day
5 Buyer enters order number	●⇨□D▽	10 min
6 Buyer authorizes order	●⇨□D▽	10 min
7 Buyer prints order	●⇨□D▽	10 min
8 Order copies to supplier and goods-in	○➜□D▽	1 day
9 Delivery from supplier	○⇨□D▼	1 day
10 Order copy to accounts	○➜□D▽	1 day
11 Three-way invoice match	●⇨□D▽	1 day
12 Cheque payment	●⇨□D▽	10 min

Activity 7.1	Evaluating the benefits of the e-procurement process for a typical B2B company

Purpose

To highlight the tasks involved in organizational purchasing and to indicate the potential time savings from e-procurement.

Introduction

Table 7.1 illustrates a typical traditional procurement process using the flow-process chart symbols that are explained in more detail in Chapter 11. It is based on the actual procurement process for Cambridge Consultants described in Case study 7.1. Note that this process is for relatively low-value items that do not need authorization by senior managers. The timings are for a new item rather than a repeat buy for which searching would not be required. Table 7.2 summarizes the new procurement process.

Questions

1 Identify inefficiencies in the traditional procurement process (Table 7.1).

2 Identify process benefits to Table 7.1 that would be possible through the automation of a system through an e-mail-based workflow system.

3 Summarize why the e-procurement process in Table 7.2 is more efficient.

Answers to activities can be found at www.pearsoned.co.uk/chaffey

Table 7.2	Process flow analysis for new procurement (typical cycle time, $1\frac{1}{2}$ days)

	Chart symbols	Time
1 Search for goods	●⇨□D▽	20 min
2 Order on web	●⇨□D▽	10 min
3 Delivery from supplier	○⇨□D▼	1 day
4 Generate invoice	●⇨□D▽	10 min
5 Cheque payment	●⇨□D▽	10 min

Key to flow process chart symbols
○ Process
⇨ Transport
□ Inspection
D Delay
▽ Inbound goods

Types of procurement

To understand the benefits of e-procurement, and also to highlight some of the practical considerations with introducing e-procurement, we need to briefly consider the different types of items that are obtained by procurement (what is bought?) and types of ordering (how is it bought?).

Let us start us by reviewing what is bought by businesses. A B2B company might buy everything from steel for manufacturing products, through equipment to help machine products, to paper clips and pens for office use. There are two broad categories of procurement: those that relate to manufacturing of products (*production-related procurement*) and *operating* or *non-production-related procurement* that supports the operations of the whole business and includes office supplies, furniture, information systems, **MRO** goods and a range of services from catering, buying travel, and professional services such as consulting and training. Raw materials for the production of goods and MRO goods are particularly important since they are critical to the operation of a business. For the B2B company, they would include manufacturing equipment, network cables and computers to control the process.

Businesses tend to buy by one of two methods:

- *Systematic sourcing* – negotiated contracts with regular suppliers.
- *Spot sourcing* – fulfilment of an immediate need, typically of a commoditized item for which it is less important to know the credibility of the supplier.

Often items such as stationery are purchased repeatedly, either for identical items (straight rebuy) or with some changes (modified rebuy). E-procurement systems can make rebuys more straightforward.

Participants in different types of e-procurement

In Chapter 2 we showed how different types of online intermediaries such as price comparison sites changed the marketplace options for consumers. A similar understanding of new potential participants or actors in e-procurement is helpful. Riggins and Mitra (2007) identify eight types of intermediary that need to be reviewed to understand options for changes to procurement as part of developing an e-procurement strategy:

MRO
Maintenance, repairs and operations of manufacturing facilities.

- *Traditional manufacturers* which produce physical goods that are generally sold to other corporate customers.
- *Direct sales manufacturers,* similar to traditional manufacturers except that they bypass intermediaries and sell direct to end consumers via web or phone channels. These can include services companies. Direct sales manufacturer can be a cost-effective option for companies procuring business services such as flight bookings for staff.
- *Value-added procurement partners* act as intermediaries to sell products and services to other businesses; examples include travel agents and office solutions companies.
- *Online hubs* are industry-specific vertical portals such as Elemica (www.elemica.com) that generate revenues via B2B exchanges.
- *Knowledge experts* who produce information goods, for example E-consultancy.com and Hitwise.com have subscription services with innovation alerts, best practice and statistics of Internet usage.
- *Online information services* provide unique information to end users that is either original in its development or provides a unique editorial perspective. From an e-procurement perspective, as we saw in Chapter 6, SaaS services such as E2open (Figure 6.11) are available to manage the information supply chain.
- *Online retailers* include start-up e-businesses and more traditional multi-channel retailers. Euroffice (www.euroffice.co.uk) is an Internet pureplay providing office goods at lower prices than traditional providers. Traditional providers in this space with a network of stores include Staples (www.staples.com).
- *Portal communities* seek to aggregate different online information services into an integrated customer experience, for example personalized news stories, online bill presentment and payment, and community discussion features. These overlap with the online information services and knowledge experts.

Knudsen (2003) and Smart (2010) have reviewed a simple classification of different types or applications of e-procurement. These are the main types:

1 *E-sourcing.* Finding potential new suppliers using the Internet during the information gathering step of the procurement process.
2 *E-tendering.* The process of screening suppliers and sending suppliers requests for information (RFI) or requests for price (RFP).
3 *E-informing.* Qualification of suppliers for suitability. It doesn't involve transactions but instead handles information about the supplier's quality, financial status or delivery capabilities.
4 *E-reverse auctions.* Enable the purchasing company to buy goods and services that have the lowest price or combination of lowest price and other conditions via Internet technology.
5 *E-MRO and web-based ERP.* These involve the purchase and supply of products which are the core of most e-procurement applications. The software used manages the process of creating and approving purchasing requisitions, placing orders and receiving the goods or service ordered.

Drivers of e-procurement

Smart (2010) has completed a review of the business benefits of e-procurement through case studies of three companies. He identifies five key drivers or supplier selection criteria for e-procurement adoption related to improving:

- *Control* – improving compliance, achieving centralization, raising standards, optimizing sourcing strategy and improved auditing of data. Enhanced budgetary control is achieved through rules to limit spending and improved reporting facilities.

- *Cost* – improved buying leverage through increased supplier competition, monitoring savings targets and transactional cost reduction.
- *Process* – rationalization and standardization of e-procurement processes giving reduced cycle time, improved visibility of processes for management and efficient invoice settlement.
- *Individual performance* – knowledge sharing, value-added productivity and productivity improvements.
- *Supplier management* – reduced supplier numbers, supplier management and selection and integration.

Direct cost reductions are achieved through efficiencies in the process, as indicated by Tables 7.1 and 7.2. Process efficiencies result in less staff time spent in searching and ordering products and reconciling deliveries with invoices. Savings also occur due to automated validation of pre-approved spending budgets for individuals or departments, leading to fewer people processing each order, and in less time. It is also possible to reduce the cost of physical materials such as specially printed order forms and invoices.

There are also indirect benefits from e-procurement; Tables 7.1 and 7.2 show how the cycle time between order and use of supplies can be reduced. In addition e-procurement may enable greater flexibility in ordering goods from different suppliers according to best value. E-procurement also tends to change the role of buyers in the purchasing department. By removing administrative tasks such as placing orders and reconciling deliveries and invoices with purchase orders, buyers can spend more time on value-adding activities. Such activities may include more time spent with key suppliers to improve product delivery and costs or analysis and control of purchasing behaviour.

A useful framework for evaluating the benefits of e-procurement and e-SCM has been created by Riggins and Mitra (2007, Figure 7.2). This can also be used to review strategy since it highlights potential benefits in terms of process efficiency and effectiveness and strategic benefits to the company. Some of the main dimensions of value highlighted by the approach include:

- *Planning* – this shows the potential for an e-procurement system to increase the quality and dissemination of management information about e-procurement.
- *Development* – e-procurement systems can potentially be incorporated early in new product development to identify manufacturing costs; this can help accelerate development.
- *Inbound* – this is the main focus of e-procurement with efficiency gains from paperless transactions and more cost-effective sourcing possible through hubs or marketplaces. A strategic benefit is **vendor-managed inventory (VMI)** where supply chain partners will manage the replenishment of parts or items for sale as described in Case Study 6.1.
- *Production* – the integration of systems managing manufacture with the procurement systems used to ensure that manufacturing is not limited by poor availability of parts.
- *Outbound* – this is management of fulfilment of products to customers. It is not usually managed by the e-procurement system, but demand must be evaluated by linking through these systems to achieve **efficient consumer response (ECR)**.

Vendor-managed inventory (VMI)

Supply chain partners manage the replenishment of parts or items for sale through sharing of information on variations in demand and stocking level for goods used for manufacture or sale.

Efficient consumer response (ECR)

ECR is focused on demand management aimed at creating and satisfying customer demand by optimizing product assortment strategies, promotions and new product introductions. It creates operational efficiencies and cost savings in the supply chain through reducing inventories and deliveries.

Examples of the benefits of e-procurement

Case study 7.1 is a classic example illustrating many of the reasons why many companies are now introducing e-procurement. The primary driver is cost reduction, in this case from an average of £60 per order to £10 per order. In many cases the cost of ordering exceeds the value of the product purchased. In another example, BT's implementation of e-procurement enabled 95% of all its goods – including desktop computing, stationery, clothing, travel and agency staff – and so reduced the average purchasing transaction cost from £56 to £40 inside a year (IBF, 2008). Finally, Mini case study 7.2 gives a video example of the benefits of e-procurement according to the purchasing manager at a law firm.

Value Creation Dimension	Efficiency	Effectiveness	Strategic
Planning	Implement rich media for company-wide interaction	Provide online executive Information systems	Facilitate knowledge management between partners
Development	Standardize platform for cross-functional design	Share detailed requirements between partners	Enable concurrent design across virtual organization
Inbound	Support electronic transactions with supply partners	Generate supply flexibility through e-hub communities	Offload replenishment responsibility to supply partners
Production	Integrate internal systems	Exchange production data between partners	Optimize utilization of global capacity
Outbound	Support electronic transactions with customers	Furnish customized instantaneous order status	Institute direct fulfilment via logistics partners

Figure 7.2   E-business e-value grid
Source: Riggins and Mitra (2007).

Mini Case Study 7.2   IT procurement at a law firm

Mark Rowley, the head of purchasing at Herbert Smith, one of the ten largest law firms in the UK, explains how they use e-procurement systems to manage recurring orders and gain budget control. As a client-facing service, project managers at a law firm need to react straight away to a client's needs, and the system provides real-time visibility of their budget and spend at every stage so they maintain full control.

Video Explanation: www.proactis.co.uk/case-studies/video-case-studies/herbert-smith-video-case-study.aspx

---

Case Study 7.1   Cambridge Consultants reduce costs through e-procurement

Illustrates the potential benefits of e-procurement by reviewing the original and revised process and costs. The e-procurement system in this case is a direct link between the purchaser, Cambridge Consultants, and the web-based catalogue of one its major suppliers, RS Components.

Cambridge Consultants is a manufacturer offering technical product design and development services to commerce and industry. With hundreds of projects in hand at any one time, Cambridge needs a diverse range of components every day.

Purchasing is centralized across the company and controlled by its Purchasing Manager, Francis Pullen. Because of its varied and often unique requirements, Cambridge has a supplier base of nearly 4,000 companies, with 20 new ones added each month. Some of these companies are providing items so specialized that Cambridge purchases from them no more than twice a year. Of the total, only 400 are preferred suppliers. Of those, just 10% – 1% of the overall supplier base – have been graded key supplier by Cambridge. That number includes RS Components. Francis Pullen says, 'We charge our clients by the hour, so if a product is faulty or late we have engineers waiting for new parts to arrive. This doesn't align with our fast time to market business proposition. RS Components' guarantee of service and range of products fits in with our business ethos.'

The existing purchasing process

Pullen has seen many changes and improvements in the company's purchasing process as its suppliers have used new technology to introduce new services. The first was moving to CD-ROM from the paper-based catalogue. Next was an online purchasing card – an account card with detailed line item billing, passwords and controls. Using industry-standard guidelines from the Chartered Institute of Purchasing and Supply (CIPS), Francis Pullen analysed the internal cost of raising an order. This took into account every step, from the engineer raising a paper requisition, through processing by purchasing, the cost of handling the delivery once it arrived, invoice matching and clearance and even the physical cost of a four-part purchase order form. The whole process involved between eight and ten people and cost the company anywhere from £60 to £120, depending on the complexity of the order.

The main cost is in requisitioning, when engineers and consultants spend their revenue-producing time in identifying their needs and raising paperwork. (Centralized purchasing, by contrast, is very efficient, costing around £50 an order.)

Using the RS purchase card removes the need for engineers and consultants to raise a paper requisition. This makes low-value ordering much more cost-efficient. Invoice matching costs are also reduced, since the purchase-card statement lists all purchases made each month.

Although the purchase card is undoubtedly an advance, on its own it does not allow costs to be assigned to jobs in the system each day. The purchase-card statement takes a month to arrive, giving rise to an equivalent lag in showing the real costs on internal project accounts.

The e-procurement process

To enable the company to order online immediately, RS put Cambridge's pre-Internet trading records on the web server. Purchasing agreements and controls were thus automatically set up on the Internet order form, including correct pricing and special payment terms.

The benefit was instantly apparent. The use of the RS purchase card when ordering from the website meant that the complete order was automatically collated, with all controls in place. Accuracy was assured and the purchase process was speeded up, with the cost per transaction reduced significantly.

Pullen describes the change this has had on Cambridge's purchasing process:

'For the first time in our purchasing history, our financial controllers saw the benefit of distributed purchasing because of the cost savings, reassured by the central purchasing controls as back-up.

This has benefited us enormously. We have allowed three department heads to have their own purchasing cards, so that they can order independently from the website.

We have implemented a very efficient electronic workflow requisition system which is initiated by the purchase card holders and mailed to central purchasing. The orders are held in a mailbox and checked against physical delivery. This has cut out two layers of order activity.

In purchasing, we no longer spend our time passing on orders that they have raised, and there is no generation of paper during the order process. It doesn't just save time and money – it's also far more environmentally friendly. Passing on low-value orders each day adds very little value, so devolving this function back to our internal customers frees up our time in purchasing to work on higher-value tasks.

Benefits for staff

Francis Pullen continues: 'Our internal customers are also much happier. We leave at 6 p.m. but the engineers will often work late if they are on a deadline. Because they can order off the website from their desks (everyone at Cambridge has Internet access), they can add items to the order right up until RS's 8 p.m. deadline without our involvement. We maintain control because of the reporting functions on the site.'

Phase 2 of the rswww.com design has also made it possible for multiple orders to be opened during the day and then put against different cost centres internally.

Results

In the year to June 1999, Cambridge Consultants placed 1,200 orders with RS Components, totalling more than £62,000 in value. Of those transactions, 95% went via the Internet. Average order value over the Internet was £34 and accounted for £43,000 of the total business done. The remaining 60 orders were placed through traditional channels but had an average value of £317.

The cost to Cambridge of raising a paper-based order was identified as being £60. Using the combination of the RS purchasing card and rswww.com, this has been reduced to £10 an order. Over a year, this represents a saving of £57,000 to Cambridge. The net effect, therefore, is that its purchases from RS Components now cost it a mere £5,000 a year!

Francis Pullen again: 'RS has demonstrated its commitment to its customers in spending time and investing money in developing a world-class purchasing system that delivers tangible customer cost savings and benefits. We have welcomed their innovative approach to purchasing and believe they are way ahead of their competition in this sector.'

Source: RS Components White Paper (www.rswww.com), courtesy of RS Components Ltd © RS Components Ltd.

Questions

1 Given the scale of the purchasing operation at Cambridge Consultants, what benefits do you think e-procurement has brought?
2 Why are procurement costs currently as high as £60 to £100 per order?
3 How are procurement costs reduced through e-procurement?
4 What staff benefits accrue to Cambridge Consultants as a result of e-procurement?

Focus on   **Estimating e-procurement costs**

The general approach to estimating procurement costs is straightforward. First, we calculate the average procurement cost per item, then we multiply by the average number of requisitions. A Tranmit (1999) report provides some illustrations – typical medium-to-large companies issue between 1,000 and 5,000 requisitions a month and are spending between £600,000 and £3 million annually on the procurement process, based on the £50 median cost per item. In exceptional cases, the number of requisitions was between 30,000 and 40,000 per month. In these cases, the annual cost of procurement could be between £18 million and £43 million!

To calculate cost savings from e-procurement we perform the following calculation:

Savings = No. of requisitions × (Original cost – New cost)

For Cambridge Consultants (Case study 7.1) cost savings from orders placed with RS Components alone are as follows:

Savings = 1,300 × (£90 – £10) = £104,000

These are relative to a typical order value of £70, i.e. savings of £104,000 on purchase item costs of £91,000.

The impact of cost savings on profitability

A study by Kluge (1997) suggested that cost savings achieved through e-procurement may have a significant effect on profitability. Activity 7.2 illustrates how the savings will vary between companies according to their buying characteristics. The largest savings and impact on profitability will typically be for manufacturing companies in which procurement is a major cost element and there are many requisitions for relatively low-value items. Service industries have lower potential for savings. The consequence for this is that there will be a wide variation in potential savings according to industry, as illustrated in Table 7.3.

To conclude this *Focus on* topic, a note of caution should be struck. Many of the models used to calculate savings and return on investment are, of course, only as good as the assumptions they use.

Debate 7.1

E-procurement cost-savings

'The cost-saving benefits of e-procurement are theoretical rather than actual since only reduced headcount in procurement can result in savings.'

Table 7.3	Procurement as a percentage of cost of goods sold for different industry sectors (estimates from Kluge, 1997)

Industry	Procurement costs as a percentage of cost of goods sold
Consumer electronics	60–70%
Mini and personal computers	50–70%
Consumer goods	50–70%
Automotive	50–60%
Pharmaceuticals	25–50%
Service industry	10–40%

Activity 7.2 — Modelling cost savings and profitability arising from e-procurement

Purpose

To explore the different characteristics of purchasing in organizations that will govern the scale of savings made through e-procurement.

Activity

Imagine you are a procurement manager, IS manager or consultant who needs to demonstrate the cost savings of e-procurement to a senior management team in order to obtain approval for investment in an e-procurement system. Develop a spreadsheet model for each of two hypothetical companies to demonstrate the case as follows:

1 *Cost saving calculations*. Using the input parameters for the two companies in Table 7.4, develop a spreadsheet model to calculate traditional overall purchasing cost, new overall purchasing cost, percentage change in cost per order and percentage change in overall purchasing cost.

2 *Profitability calculations*. Using input parameters of turnover, traditional purchasing costs, other costs and a 5% reduction in purchasing costs, as shown in Table 7.5, develop a model that calculates the profitability before and after introduction of e-procurement and also shows the change in profitability as an absolute (£) and as a percentage.

Table 7.4	Input parameters for cost-saving calculations for two companies

Input parameters (Company A)		Input parameters (Company B)	
Number of orders	25,000	Number of orders	2,500
Traditional cost per order (average)	£50	Traditional cost per order (average)	£50
New cost per order (average)	£10	New cost per order (average)	£10
Average value of order	£150	Average value of order	£1,500

3 Analyse the sensitivity of the models to differences in volume of orders and values of purchases (Table 7.4) and the balance between traditional purchasing costs and other costs such as salaries and capital by using the parameters (Table 7.5). Explain to the managers the typical characteristics of a company that will make significant changes to profitability from introducing e-procurement.

Table 7.5	Input parameters for profitability calculations for two companies	
Parameter	**Company X**	**Company Y**
Turnover	£10,000,000	£10,000,000
Traditional purchasing costs	£5,000,000	£1,000,000
Other costs	£4,000,000	£8,000,000
Reduction in purchasing costs	20%	20%

Answers to activities can be found at www.pearsoned.co.uk/chaffey

Barriers and risks of e-procurement adoption

Of course, there are also barriers to adoption of e-procurement. CIPS (2008) identifies the following issues for suppliers:

- Competition issues, e.g. in exchanges using collaborative purchasing.
- Possible negative perception from suppliers, e.g. their margins reduced further from e-auctions.
- Negotiated procurement benefits may be shared with other exchange users who may be competitors.
- Creation of catalogues can be a long process and costly to suppliers.
- Culture profile within organizations, e.g. resistance to change.

These barriers are specific to e-procurement. There are also more general limitations to e-business adoption mentioned in Chapters 1 and 4, such as the cost of implementation and managing change.

If the cost savings referred to earlier in the chapter are to be achieved it may be necessary to redeploy staff, or in the worst case make them redundant. For a medium-sized company such as Cambridge Consultants the purchasing team of five people was reduced to four. The threat of redundancy or redeployment is likely to lead to resistance to the introduction of the system and this needs to be managed. The purchasing manager will have to carefully explain the reasons for introducing the new system, emphasizing the benefits to the company as a whole and how it should enable more variety to be introduced to the buying role.

Since the cost savings of e-procurement are achieved through empowerment of originators throughout the business to directly purchase their own items there is a risk that some originators may take advantage of this. 'Maverick or off-contract purchasing' occurs when items are ordered that are unnecessary or too expensive. Complete Activity 7.3 to review the mechanisms that can be used to reduce this risk.

Activity 7.3	Avoiding maverick purchasing

Purpose

To identify responses to problems of maverick purchasing.

Activity

To avoid maverick purchasing, businesses introducing e-procurement need to put safeguards into the e-procurement system. Think about the type of rules that could be written into an e-procurement system.

Answers to activities can be found at www.pearsoned.co.uk/chaffey

Implementing e-procurement

Implementing e-procurement has the challenges of change management associated with any information system which are discussed in Chapter 10. If the implementation can mirror existing practices, then it will be most straightforward, but many of the benefits will not be gained and the use of new technology often forces new processes to be considered. CIPS (2008) forcefully make the case that some re-engineering will be required:

> *Organisations should not simply automate existing procurement processes and systems but should consider improving ways of working and re-engineering business processes prior to the implementation of eSourcing / eProcurement. Purchasing and supply management professionals should challenge established procurement practices to test whether these have evolved around a paper-based system and as such can be replaced. CIPS strongly recommends that, wherever possible, processes should be re-engineered prior to implementing ePurchasing.*

These problems are also indicated by Carrie Ericson, consultant at e-procurement supplier AT Kearney (www.ebreviate.com), in an interview (logistics.about, 2003). She says that in her experience:

> *Challenges often come down to our classic change management dilemmas: getting folks to change the way they conduct business, disrupting long standing supplier agreements, issues around politics and control.*
>
> *In addition, the up front cost is often a challenge and the ROI [return on investment] can be perceived to be risky. I'm sure we've all heard a lot of stories about costly eprocurement implementations. Finally, the buyers are often nervous about perception. Will the new tools reflect that they have been doing a poor job in the past?*

To introduce e-procurement the IS manager and procurement team must work together to find a solution that links together the different people and tasks of procurement shown in Figure 7.1. Figure 7.3 shows how different types of information system cover different parts of the procurement cycle. The different type of systems are as follows.

- *Stock control system* – this relates mainly to production-related procurement; the system highlights that reordering is required when the number in stock falls below reorder thresholds.
- *CD or web-based catalogue* – paper catalogues have been replaced by electronic forms that make it quicker to find suppliers.
- *E-mail- or database-based workflow systems* integrate the entry of the order by the originator, approval by manager and placement by buyer. The order is routed from one person

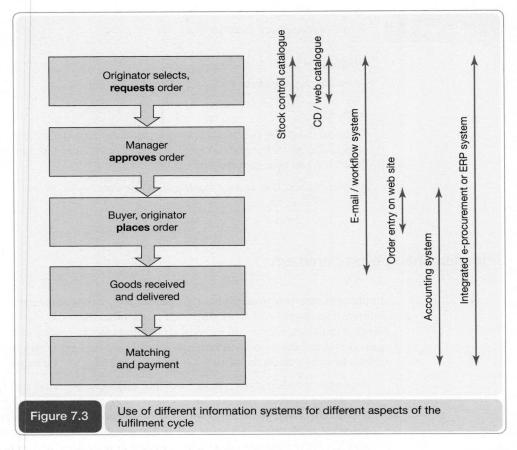

Figure 7.3   Use of different information systems for different aspects of the fulfilment cycle

to the next and will wait in their inbox for actioning. Such systems may be extended to accounting systems.

- *Order-entry on website* – the buyer often has the opportunity to order directly on the supplier's website, but this will involve rekeying and there is no integration with systems for requisitioning or accounting.
- *Accounting systems* – networked accounting systems enable staff in the buying department to enter an order which can then be used by accounting staff to make payment when the invoice arrives.
- *Integrated e-procurement or ERP systems* – these aim to integrate all the facilities above and will also include integration with suppliers' systems.

Companies face a difficult choice in achieving full-cycle e-procurement since they have the option of trying to link different systems or purchasing a single new system that integrates the facilities of the previous systems. Purchasing a new system may be the simplest technical option, but it may be more expensive than trying to integrate existing systems and it also requires retraining in the system.

Integrating company systems with supplier systems

We saw from the Shell case study in Chapter 6 the cost and cycle-time benefits that a company can achieve through linking its systems with those of its suppliers. If integrating systems within a company is difficult, then linking with other companies' systems is more so. This situation arises since suppliers will use different types of systems and different models for integration. As explained in Chapter 2, there are three fundamental models for location of

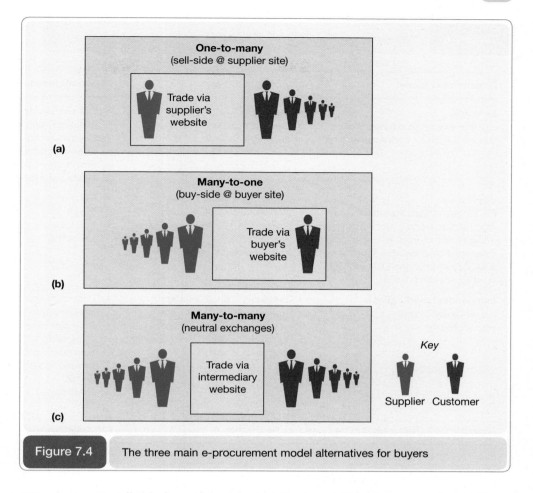

| Figure 7.4 | The three main e-procurement model alternatives for buyers |

B2B e-commerce: sell-side, buy-side and marketplace-based. These are summarized in Figure 7.4 and the advantages and disadvantages of each are summarized in Table 7.6.

Chapter 2 explained that companies supplying products and services had to decide which combination of these models would be used to distribute their products. From the buyer's point of view, they will be limited by the selling model their suppliers have adopted.

Figure 7.5 shows options for a buyer who is aiming to integrate an internal system such as an ERP system with external systems. Specialized e-procurement software may be necessary to interface with the ERP system. This could be a special e-procurement application or it could be middleware to interface with an e-procurement component of an ERP system. The e-procurement system can access price catalogues in two ways. Choice (a) is to house electronic catalogues from different suppliers inside the company and firewall. This traditional approach has the benefit that the data are housed inside the company and so can be readily accessed. However, electronic links beyond the firewall will be needed to update the catalogues, or this is sometimes achieved via delivery of a CD with the updated catalogue. Choice (b) is to use a **punchout catalogue** where access through the firewall is used to access catalogues either on a supplier site or at an intermediary site, ideally within a standard format. One of the benefits of linking to an intermediary site such as a B2B exchange is that this has done the work of collecting data from different suppliers and producing it in a consistent format.

Punchout catalogue
A purchasing company accesses a dynamic real-time catalogue hosted by a supplier or intermediary containing detailed product information, pricing and product images.

Table 7.6	Assessment of the procurement model alternatives for buyers	

Procurement model	Advantages to buyer	Disadvantages to buyer
Sell-side e.g. many catalogue-based B2B suppliers such as www.rswww.com	• Searching • Onus of maintaining data on supplier	• Different interface on each site (catalogue and ordering) • Restricted choice • Poor integration with ERP/ procurement systems • Limited purchase control
Buy-side Private exchanges hosted by manufacturers and major suppliers to these manufacturers, e.g. solutions developed by www.ebreviate.com, www.covisint.net and ERP suppliers such as SAP and Oracle	• Simplicity – single interface • Wider choice than sell-side • Integration with ERP/procurement systems • Good purchase control	• Onus of maintaining data is on buyer • Software licence costs • Retraining
Independent marketplace e.g. www.ec21.com, www.eutilia.net	• Simplicity – single interface • Potentially widest choice of suppliers, products and prices • Often unified terms and conditions and order forms	• Difficult to know which marketplace to choose (horizontal and vertical) • Poor purchase controls* • Uncertainty on service levels from unfamiliar suppliers • Interfacing with marketplace data format* • Relatively poor integration with ERP*

* Note that these disadvantages of the marketplace will disappear as marketplaces develop ERP integration.

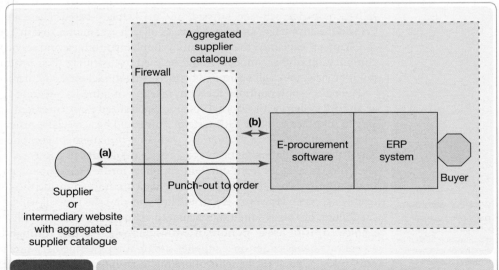

Figure 7.5	Integration between e-procurement systems and catalogue data

Focus on	B2B marketplaces

Before 2000, B2B marketplaces were heralded as transforming B2B purchases; however, many have had difficulty in achieving sustainable business models although we will see there are examples of successful marketplaces in vertical industries such as Elemica (www.elemica.com) within the chemicals industry which we referenced in Case study 6.1. Perhaps the prime example of a general e-marketplace is Alibaba.com, which is discussed in Mini case study 7.3.

Mini Case Study 7.3	Alibaba provides a global market for SMEs

Alibaba.com is one of the leading B2B e-commerce companies in China. It provides a marketplace connecting small and medium-sized buyers and suppliers from China and around the world. Its web presence includes an international marketplace (www.alibaba.com) focusing on global importers and exporters and a China marketplace (www.alibaba.com.cn) which focuses on suppliers and buyers trading domestically in China.

From a launch in 1999 the marketplaces have a community of more than 24 million registered users and over 255,000 paying members. In November 2007, Alibaba launched on the Hong Kong stock exchange and raised HK$13.1 billion (US$1.7 billion) in gross proceeds before offering expenses, making it the largest Internet IPO (initial public offering) in Asia and the second largest globally.

Jack Ma, the founder of Alibaba (Figure 7.6), first saw the Internet in 1995 when he went to Seattle as an interpreter for a trade delegation and a friend showed him the Internet. They searched for the word 'beer' on Yahoo and discovered that there was no data about China. They decided to launch a website and registered the name China Pages.

Mr Ma borrowed $2,000 to set up his first company and at the time knew nothing about personal computers or e-mails and had never touched a keyboard before. He described the experience as 'blind man riding on the back of a blind tiger'.

Initially, the business did not fare well, since it was a part of China Telecom and Jack Ma reflects that 'everything we suggested, they turned us down; it was like an elephant and an ant'.

He resigned, but in 1999, he gathered 18 people in his apartment and spoke to them for two hours about his vision. Everyone put their money on the table, and he got $60,000 to start Alibaba. He chose Alibaba as the name since it was easy to spell and associated with 'Open, Sesame', the command that Ali Baba used to open doors to hidden treasures in *The Thousand and One Nights*.

During the dot-com bubble, there were lay-offs, such that by 2002 there was only enough cash to survive for 18 months. They had a lot of free members using the site, and didn't know how they could make money. But they then developed a product for China exporters to meet US buyers online, which Ma said saved the company. By the end of 2002, Alibaba made $1 in profits! Each year since it has improved in profitability to the position where it was launched on the stock market.

Today, Jack Ma's vision is to build an e-commerce ecosystem that allows consumers and businesses to do all aspects of business online. They are partnering with Yahoo and have launched online auction and payment businesses. His vision is expansive, he says: 'I want to create one million jobs, change China's social and economic environment, and make it the largest Internet market in the world.'

You can view the video of CEO Jack Ma talking about the business on FT.com.

Source: Ali Baba Press releases Alibaba.com Limited Trading Debut, 7 November 2007: http://resources.alibaba.com/article/225276/Alibaba_com_Limited_Trading_Debut_.htm.

Riding the Blind Tiger: The Unlikely Rise of Alibaba CEO, Jack Ma, 8 January 2008: http://resources.alibaba.com/article/246718/Riding_the_Blind_Tiger_The_Unlikely_Rise_of_Alibaba_CEO_Jack_MA.htm.

Web Explanation: Interview with Jack Ma (search on Jack Ma) www.ft.com/cms/8a38c684-2a26-11dc-9208-000b5df10621.html.

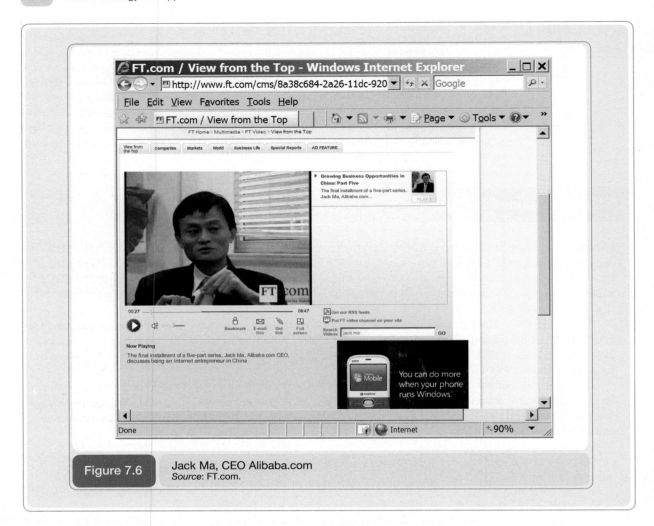

| Figure 7.6 | Jack Ma, CEO Alibaba.com
Source: FT.com. |

B2B electronic marketplaces, exchanges and hubs
Virtual locations with facilities to enable trading between buyers and sellers.

Electronic B2B marketplaces are variously known as 'marketplaces, exchanges or hubs'. Typically they are intermediaries that are part of the *reintermediation* (Chapter 2, p. 63) phenomenon and are independent of buyers and suppliers.

After a great deal of hype at the turn of the millennium, many B2B marketplaces have closed. Examples of independent B2B exchanges mentioned in the previous edition are Chemdex (www.chemdex.com), Vertical Net (www.vertical.net), CommerceOne Marketsite (www.commerceone.com) and Covisint (www.covisint.net), none of which now exists in its original form. As we saw in Chapter 5, in January 2001, Dell shut down one of its B2B online marketplaces, called Dell Marketplace, only four months after it opened, citing the lack of a mature e-commerce marketplace. *Computer World* (2001a) reported that of an estimated 900 business-to-business websites that were functioning worldwide in mid-2000, a little more than 400 were left by end-2000. Despite this, enthusiasm for the B2B marketplace concept still seems quite strong. Today, Googling 'B2B Exchanges' shows just a handful are still active.

The B2B exchange intermediaries that remain seem to be mainly for commodities or simple services (for example, EC21 (www.ec21.com), Elance (www.elance.com) and eBay Business (http://business.ebay.com)). One of the top categories on eBay Business is for tractors, with bids of between $10,000 and $20,000 common; another is photocopiers with over 3,000 listed, with a maximum price of $65,000.

Reasons for limited adoption of e-marketplaces

Johnson (2010) has investigated the reasons for limited adoption. Based on interviews with purchasing managers in a range of sectors, he believes the most significant are potentially misguided perceptions of the benefits, risks and trust in partners. However, these perceptions may be valid. He gives one example of a marketplace servicing the aerospace and defence industry where it couldn't recruit sufficient small suppliers because the e-market charged the same fee to all suppliers regardless of their size. The e-market charged suppliers $4,000 per year to use its catalogue software tool to create their own electronic catalogues, and a yearly subscription fee of $390. Although most small suppliers could afford the subscription, many could not afford to pay $4,000 per year in order to create electronic catalogues on the e-market.

From neutral to private B2B exchanges

So, these new online trading arrangements have not developed as open, neutral marketplaces as predicted by many analysts. This seems to be due to the complexity of business purchase decisions and negotiations and their destabilizing nature on markets. The *Computer World* (2001b) article gives these reasons why what it terms 'private exchanges' are proving successful:

> First, owners of private exchanges regulate supplier and customer access – and exclude competitors – making the sharing of sensitive information more likely.

> Second, owners can direct suppliers and customers to use the exchange through price incentives or by mandating changes in the way to conduct business.

> Third, private exchanges can be secured and tailored to serve specific projects and customers, unlike public exchanges, which must be generic so as to accommodate everyone.

The article gives the example of IBM which has well-established private marketplaces. IBM has saved about $1.7 billion since 1993 by being able to divulge sensitive price and inventory information over a private exchange built for 25,000 suppliers and customers. As host of the exchange, the company helped defray the cost of connecting suppliers. As a result, on-time delivery of systems to customers increased from around 50% to 90%.

Private B2B exchanges
A manufacturer or major supplier to different manufacturers creates a portal which is used for managing all aspects of procurement.

The approach that has evolved is that **private B2B exchanges** have developed. These are the buy-side exchanges referred to in Table 7.1. These are usually created by an individual manufacturer or supplier and include a 'walled garden of suppliers', i.e. everyone has to be approved as a member, although the forms to register as a supplier to bid in response to a particular Request for Quotation (RFQ) or to participate in a reverse auction are open to all, but with each vetted to avoid competitor involvement.

Case study 7.2 shows the history of the automotive marketplace Covisint. This pattern of a transition from a marketplace portal to a hosted e-procurement service has been followed by other B2B marketplaces from that time, including CommerceOne and Ariba.

Case Study 7.2 | Covisint – a typical history of a B2B marketplace?

This case studies a successful marketplace to prompt learning about what makes such a marketplace effective. It also illustrates the importance of online bidding in some industries.

The Covisint marketplace was originally created by Ford, GM and DaimlerChrysler (www.covisint.com).

Today, Covisint is not a marketplace, but is described by its owners Compuware as a 'connectivity solution'. Its service is still used by motor manufacturers (www.covisint.com) although they now don't use a single marketplace, rather each manufacturer uses technology to access its suppliers direct.

2002: Covisint used extensively for bidding

Covisint (2002) describes a high-level of activity on the exchange. Taking the example of DaimlerChrysler AG, 512 online bidding events were processed through Covisint over a twelve-month period from 2001 to 2002. In total, this amounted to €10 billion. In May 2001, DaimlerChrysler staged the largest online bidding event ever, with an order volume of €3.5 billion in just four days. In total, 43% of the total value of the parts for a future Chrysler model series was negotiated online with over 50 online bidding events in the third quarter of 2001 alone. As well as savings in material purchasing prices, DaimlerChrysler succeeded in reducing throughput times in purchasing by approximately 80%, thus saving on process costs. According to Dr Rüdiger Grube, Deputy Member of the Board of Management responsible for corporate development,

> the economic effects achieved with e-Procurement in the first year of implementation have already covered the costs of previous investment in e-Business and hold great potential for the future, too. Therefore, we will continue to pursue our e-Business activities to the fullest extent in 2002 as well.

With the online catalogue system 'eShop' which was part of the Covisint service at that time, DaimlerChrysler would be able to reduce process costs by 50% after the completion of the blanket rollout, which will give approximately 15,000 users the possibility of ordering several million articles. By the end of 2002 about 1,500 business partners would be connected to the electronic document exchange system 'eDocs', which would enable them to process approximately 500,000 document transmissions per year. Initial results using the 'FastCar' program for networking change management in automotive development at Chrysler show cuts in communication processes by 60–90%. In 2001, over 600 managers connected to the system developed over 300 product improvement suggestions online with the 'New Product Change Management' used in the development department of Mercedes-Benz.

'e-Business activities are already closely intertwined from development through procurement, logistics, sales and marketing. To a great extent, they are already a part of everyday business,' says Olaf Koch, Vice President of Corporate e-Business. Dr Grube: 'We're a good deal closer to our goal of making DaimlerChrysler the first automotive company to be networked throughout the entire value chain.'

2004: Covisint purchased by Compuware

Line56 (2004) summarizes the acquisition of Covisint by B2B software company Compuware. The article quotes Compuware CEO Pete Karmanos as predicting that the messaging and portal part of Covisint will contribute $20 million in 2005, and will eventually become a $100 million-plus business in the automotive industry alone. The primary e-procurement offering of Covisint is as a method of managing purchasing across the many different electronic business document formats including traditional EDI formats like ANSI X12 and EDIFACT along with XML purchasing formats such as OAGIS, STAR, RosettaNet and others. Different suppliers tend to have adopted different exchange formats, so a solution that integrates them is helpful. Covisint continues to offer a portal solution both for manufacturers and their suppliers, who in turn have tier 2 or 3 suppliers. A study for Covisint by AMR Research suggested that the Covisint Communicate service was found to help a company reduce the cost of developing and deploying a portal by up to 80% and reduce the annual cost of maintenance by 50%. You can see the portal solutions at: https://portal.covisint.com/wps/public/tradingPartners/_l/en/, one example being the Ford Supplier portal.

2008: Covisint used by more than 45,000 organizations in 96 countries

Today, Covisint describes itself as 'the leading provider of services that enable the integration of vital business information and processes between partners, customers and suppliers'. Many of its customers are still in the automotive industry, but now also in diverse industries including manufacturing, healthcare, aerospace, public-sector and financial services. The scale of operations is evident from these figures:

- Translation and secure transportation of over 40 million messages annually.
- Hosted infrastructure boasts 99.997% uptime.
- Provides critical portal, messaging and/or security services for users at over 45,000 organizations worldwide.

For each industry it has developed specific services particular to data exchange within these industries. Covisint Connect offers EDI and web EDI facilities for e-procurement. Covisint Communicate has over 300 applications available, some typical modules of which are used by DaimlerChrysler AG including:

- **Accounts payable** – enables suppliers to research past and future payment/information, resolve issues prior to payment due dates and download document information to the desktop for further analysis.
- **Cooperative raw material acquisition** – provides suppliers with access to a cooperative raw material supply program to leverage customers' purchasing power and maximize operational savings.

- **Product catalogue compilation tool** – collects and distributes information required to produce and update the company's catalogue of products.
- **Request for quote application** – enables customers to issue an online request for quotation process.
- **Supplier profile** – enables customers to maintain an accurate profile consisting of key information about the supplier.

Sources: Covisint website (www.covisint.com), Covisint (2002) and Line56 (2004).

> **Question**
>
> By reviewing the case study and examples of the different supplier portals available on Covisint (www.covisint.com) explain why Covisint has prospered as a supplier of e-procurement portals and business document data exchange rather than as a neutral marketplace.

Government marketplace exchanges

In the UK, the government has used reversed auctions on trial, but in 2006 launched two new initiatives which will highlight the value of recruitment. To give more options for small businesses to apply as suppliers to government, the UK government launched the Supplier Route to Government Portal (www.supply2.gov.uk, Figure 7.7) as part of its e-government initiative; this is an online marketplace for public-sector procurement valued at less than £100,000. Registered users can receive daily e-mail alerts about contracts appropriate to them, search for contracts online and post details of their offerings. The figure shows the

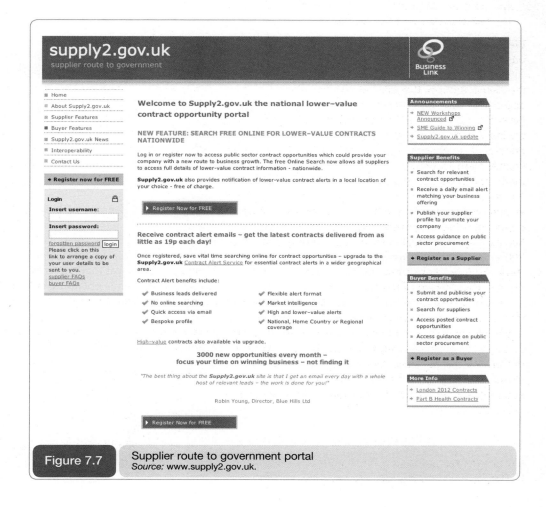

Figure 7.7 Supplier route to government portal
Source: www.supply2.gov.uk.

benefits of marketplaces for suppliers and buyers. The Office of Government Commerce (OGC) also unveiled an online marketplace for public sector procurement, called Zanzibar Managed Service (www.ogcbuyingsolutions.gov.uk/zanzibar/zanzibar.asp). The Department for Work and Pensions is the first public-sector department to use the system. Zanzibar works in a similar way to other exchanges, with the OGC saying that Zanzibar would only be open to businesses that were either currently allowed to bid for public-sector contracts or were invited to do so.

Mini case study 7.4 is an example of another e-government initiative for sourcing.

Mini Case Study 7.4   Source UK

Source UK (www.sourceuk.org.uk) is an example of a successful e-government initiative which has been responsible for the delivery and the management of the busiest electronic communication and e-procurement channels to UK government and wider public-sector departments in line with the 'Modernising Government Agenda' legislation. Approximately 250,000 senior managers, budget holders and decision makers have direct access to the channels for their on-the-minute must-have news and information needs and for the sourcing of their goods and services.

Source UK is proven to be one of the most accredited, respected, well-known and busiest portals of its sort available to this marketplace. The portal is currently receiving on average 500,000 visits each month.

Source: Source UK e-mail alert.

Debate 7.2

The future for independent B2B marketplaces

'There is no future for independent B2B marketplaces, exchanges or hubs; instead those sponsored by buyers in the industry (for example, Covisint in the car industry) will be dominant.'

Improved methods for facilitating purchasing using these types of sites will undoubtedly increase the adoption of the Internet for e-commerce since consumers will become aware of the lower prices available by these buying methods. For the business-to-business case this needs to be linked in with methods of making payment easier such as the Open Buying Initiative (www.obi.org).

Types of marketplace

Kaplan and Sawhney (2000) have developed a taxonomy of B2B marketplaces by applying existing classifications of corporate purchasing, namely *how* businesses buy (systematic purchasing or spot purchasing) and *what* businesses buy (manufacturing inputs or operating resource inputs). They identify the types of marketplace shown in Table 7.7. Note that manufacturing-input marketplaces tend to be vertical marketplaces set up for a particular industry such as steel, construction or chemicals, while operating resources tend to be horizontal marketplaces offering a range of products to differing industries.

Kaplan and Sawhney introduce another variation in the way marketplaces differ. This is according to whether the marketplace is direct between buyer and seller or whether some degree of aggregation occurs. In the same way that, for consumer products, volume discounts can be achieved through combining the purchasing power of individuals, this can also occur for small and medium businesses. Kaplan and Sawhney refer to this type of aggregation as 'reverse aggregation' since aggregation is back through the supply chain from customers to suppliers. They also identify 'forward aggregation' in which the supply chain operates through distributors in a traditional way. A distributor of PCs from different manufacturers aggregates supply from the different manufacturers. Marketplaces can also act as value chain integrators when they combine supply chain functions referred to in Chapter 6.

Table 7.7	Types of B2B marketplaces identified by Kaplan and Sawhney (2000) with examples

How businesses buy	What businesses buy	
	Operating resources	**Manufacturing resources**
Systematic sourcing	MRO hubs www.barclaysb2b.com	Catalogue hubs www.sciquest.com
Spot sourcing	Yield managers www.elance.com	Exchanges www.e-steel.com www.plasticsnet.com

Source: Adapted and reprinted by permission of *Harvard Business Review* from table on p. 99 from 'E-hubs: the new B2B marketplaces,' by Kaplan, S. and Sawhney, M., in *Harvard Business Review*, May–June 2000. Copyright © 2000 by the Harvard Business School Publishing Corporation, all rights reserved.

According to Sawhney (1999) companies looking to create exchanges typically specialize in one of the four sectors of Table 7.7, although some B2B marketplaces do offer both catalogue hubs and exchanges.

Metamediaries

Third parties that provide a single point of contact and deliver a range of services between customers and suppliers.

Some marketplaces also differ in the range of services they offer – some may go beyond procurement to offer a range of services that integrate the supply chain. Sawhney (1999) refers to these marketplaces as ' **metamediaries**'. An example of a metamediary is Plastics Net (www.plasticsnet.com). This provides services of supplier evaluation, procurement, tracking, marketplace information, certification monitoring, auctions and catalogues.

The future of e-procurement

Software (intelligent) agents

Software programs that assist humans by automatically gathering information from the Internet or exchanging data with other agents based on parameters supplied by the user.

In the future, some suggest that the task of searching for suppliers and products may be taken over by **software agents** which have defined rules or some degree of intelligence that replicates intelligence in humans. On the Internet, agents can already be used for marketing research by performing searches using many search engines and in the future they may also be used to search for products or even purchase products. Agents work using predetermined rules or may learn rules using neural network techniques. Such rules will govern whether purchases should be made or not.

Some of the implications of agent technology on marketing are explored by Gatarski and Lundkvist (1998). They suggest that agent technology may create artificial consumers who will undertake supplier search, product evaluation and product selection functions. The authors suggest that such actors in a supplier-to-consumer dialogue will behave in a more rational way than their human equivalents and existing marketing theories may not apply.

Tucker and Jones (2000) also review the use of intelligent agents for sourcing. They foresee agents undertaking evaluation of a wide range of possible alternative suppliers based on predefined quantitative selection criteria including price, availability and delivery. They believe the technology is already available – indeed, similar intelligent software is used for making investments in financial markets. What is not clear is how the software will assess trustworthiness of a supplier or their competence as a business partner or associate.

Summary

1   Procurement activities involved with purchasing items from a supplier include purchasing, but also transportation, goods-in and warehousing before the item is used.

2   E-procurement involves the electronic integration of all procurement activities.

3   The numbers of staff and stages involved in procurement are reduced through e-procurement by empowering the originator of orders and changing the role of buying staff.

4   E-procurement is intended to achieve reduced purchasing cycle time and cost savings, principally through reduced staff time spent in procurement and lower inventory.

5   Options for introducing e-procurement include:
   • Sell-side e-procurement – purchase direct from a seller's website that is typically not integrated with the buyer's procurement system.
   • Buy-side e-procurement – integration of sellers' catalogues with the buyer's procurement system.
   • Marketplace procurement – trading through an intermediary with many suppliers (may or may not be integrated with buyer's procurement system).

6   The main types of electronic marketplace in the terminology of Kaplan and Sawhney (2000) are combinations of:
   • Systematic sourcing of operating resources (MRO hubs)
   • Systematic sourcing of manufacturing resources (catalogue hubs)
   • Spot sourcing of operating resources (yield managers)
   • Spot sourcing of manufacturing resources (exchanges).

7   Organizational hurdles involved with the introduction of e-procurement include redeployment or redundancy of staff and overcoming fears of trust in suppliers.

8   The main technical challenges are the integration or replacement of a range of existing purchasing systems with a variety of supplier or marketplace systems.

Exercises

Self-assessment questions

1   Outline the two main methods by which companies purchase supplies and the two broad divisions of supplies needed.

2   Taking your answer from 1, give examples of B2B exchanges that have been created to meet these purchasing needs.

3   Draw a sketch that shows the main stages and people involved in traditional and e-procurement.

4   Outline the main reasons for e-procurement.

5   What is maverick purchasing? What safeguards need to be introduced into e-procurement to avoid this?

6   Explain the differences between the buy-side, sell-side and marketplace options for e-procurement.

7   Outline the benefits and disadvantages of each of the options in 6.

8   What are the organizational implications of introducing e-procurement?

Essay and discussion questions

1 Chris Miller of Shell Chemical has been quoted as saying:

   'E-procurement is not about screwing suppliers. It's about taking cost out for both suppliers and buyers and reducing institutionalized inefficiencies. Plus it supports smaller buyers and suppliers just as much as larger ones. It's not a big boys' club.'

   Discuss this statement through reviewing the benefits and disadvantages of e-procurement to both buyers and suppliers.

2 For an industry sector of your choice review the current alternative options for, and business adoption of B2B marketplaces available to, purchasing and IS professionals and attempt to forecast the situation in five years.

3 Critically assess the claims made for cost savings and increased profitability available from e-procurement.

4 Analyse the procurement process for an organization with which you are familiar. Explain the changes and possible problems involved with introducing e-procurement.

5 'Fully automated end-to-end procurement is not practical.' Discuss.

Examination questions

1 Draw a diagram explaining four types of B2B exchanges that are dependent on the type of purchasing and what is purchased. Give one example of a product that could be purchased at each, and the name of an exchange offering this service.

2 Describe the different elements of an e-procurement system.

3 Draw a diagram that summarizes the main differences in processes within an organization for traditional procurement and e-procurement.

4 Outline the main benefits of e-procurement.

5 Explain the differences between buy-side and sell-side e-procurement. Give an advantage for each type for the purchasing company.

6 Current adoption levels of e-procurement are low. Identify the main reasons for this.

7 Explain how cost savings may arise from e-procurement.

8 Why do some commentators suggest real cost savings from e-procurement may be nearer to 10% than higher figures suggested by e-procurement solutions providers?

References

Baily, P., Farmer, D., Jessop, D. and Jones, D. (1994) *Purchasing Principles and Management.* Pitman, London.

Caffrey, B. (1997) Dispelling e-commerce ROI myths. Published online only at **http://purchasing.about.com/industry/purchasing/library/weekly/aa032798.htm,** 18 July.

CIPS (2008) E-commerce / E-purchasing CIPS Knowledge Summary. **www1.cips.org/documents/e-commerce.pdf.** Accessed September 2008.

Computer World (2001a) B2B outlook still ominous. By Gary Kadet, 23 April. Available online at **www.computerworld.com.**

Computer World (2001b) Private exchanges drive B2B success. By Pimm Fox, 7 May. Available online at **www.computerworld.com**.

Conspectus (2006) Supply chain management and manufacturing systems. Prime Marketing Publications, June. PMP Research **www.conspectus.com**.

Covisint (2002) Press release, 4 February. Covisint.com.

FT.com (2006) SMEs miss out on online tendering. Article, published on FT.com site; 3 March.

Gatarski, R. and Lundkvist, A. (1998) Interactive media face artificial customers and marketing theory must rethink. *Journal of Marketing Communications*, 4, 45–59.

Hildebrand, C. (2002) How to: save money with e-procurement, *CIO.com News*. By Carl Hildebrand, 13 August.

IBF (2008) 12 ways to use your intranet to cut your costs. Member Briefing Paper, August. Published by the Intranet Benchmarking Forum (**www.ibforum.com**).

Johnson, M. (2010) Barriers to innovation adoption: a study of e-markets. *Industrial Management & Data Systems*, 110(2), 157–74.

Kalakota, R. and Robinson, M. (2000) *E-Business: Roadmap for Success*. Addison-Wesley, Reading, MA.

Kaplan, S. and Sawhney, M. (2000) E-hubs: the new B2B marketplaces. *Harvard Business Review*, May–June, 97–103.

Kluge, J. (1997) Reducing the cost of goods sold: role of complexity, design relationships. *McKinsey Quarterly*, 2, 212–15.

Knudsen, D. (2003) Aligning corporate strategy, procurement strategy and e-procurement tools. *International Journal of Physical Distribution and Logistics Management*, 33(8), 720–34.

Line56 (2004). Compuware buys last of Covisint. Article by Jim Ericson, *Line56* (**www.line56.com**), Friday, 6 February.

logistics.about (2003) EProcurement advances chat. Summary by Jeff Ashcroft of interview with Carrie Ericson of AT Kearney (**http://logistics.about.com**).

Ovans, A. (2000) E-procurement at Schlumberger. *Harvard Business Review*, May–June, 21–3.

Potter, C. (2000) Trust . . . not built at e-speed: trust issues in B2B e-procurement. PricewaterhouseCoopers Report, July, London.

Riggins, F. and Mitra, S. (2007) An e-valuation framework for developing net-enabled business metrics through functionality interaction. *Journal of Organizational Computing and Electronic Commerce*, 17(2), 175–203.

Sawhney, M. (1999) Making new markets. *Business 2.0*, May, 116–21.

Smart, A. (2010) Exploring the business case for e-procurement. *International Journal of Physical, Distribution and Logistics Management*, 40(3), 181–201.

Tranmit (1999) *Procurement Management Systems: A Corporate Black Hole. A survey of technology trends and attitudes in British industry*. Tranmit plc, UK. Survey conducted by Byline Research. Report available at **www.rswww.com/purchasing**.

Tucker, D. and Jones, L. (2000) Leveraging the power of the Internet for optimal supplier sourcing. *International Journal of Physical Distribution and Logistics Management*, 23 May, 30(3/4), 255–67.

Turban, E., Lee, J., King, D. and Chung, H. (2000) *Electronic Commerce: A Managerial Perspective*. Prentice-Hall, Upper Saddle River, NJ.

Further reading

Puschmann, T. and Alt., R. (2005) Successful use of e-procurement in supply chains. *Supply Chain Management: An International Journal,* 10/2, 122–33. A useful introduction to e-procurement with a review of alternative e-procurement strategies and catalogue management approaches.

Web links

Ariba.com (**www.ariba.com**) Guidelines on B2B e-commerce procurement from this 'spend management provider'.

Buy IT (**www.buyitnet.org**) UK-based.

The Chartered Institute of Purchasing and Supply (CIPS) (**www.cips.org**) Industry body in UK. Has research and best-practice advice on e-procurement including a 2006 survey on SME attitudes to e-commerce.

Conspectus (**www.conspectus.com**) Articles on different aspects of e-business including supply chain management.

Ebreviate (**www.ebreviate.com**) Articles on e-procurement best practice from solutions provider AT Kearney.

The Logistics web guide on About.com (http://logistics.about.com) Also has collection of links on the benefits and disadvantages of e-procurement.

Web support

The following additional case studies are available at
www.pearsoned.co.uk/chaffey

→ Personalized 'cybercycles' from DBS Oegland, Norway
→ Hamleys e-tail

The site also contains a range of study materials designed to help improve your results.

Learning outcomes

After completing this chapter the reader should be able to:

- Assess the need for separate e-business and e-marketing strategies
- Create an outline e-marketing plan intended to implement the e-marketing strategy
- Distinguish between marketing communication characteristics of traditional and new media

Management issues

The issues for managers raised in this chapter include:

- How do we integrate traditional marketing approaches with e-marketing?
- How can we use electronic communications to differentiate our products and services?
- How do we redefine our marketing and communications mixes to incorporate new media?

Links to other chapters

The main related chapters are:

- *Chapter 4* – e-environment provides underpinning on the macro-economic factors that support e-marketing planning
- *Chapter 5* – on e-business strategy acts as an introduction to Part 2 and the chapters that follow; in particular, the section on eight strategic decisions is relevant to this chapter
- *Chapter 9* – CRM details practical implementation of e-marketing plans through promotional techniques and customer relationship management
- *Chapter 10* – discusses the change management issues associated with introducing multi-channel marketing within an organization

Introduction

In Chapter 5 we explored approaches to developing e-business strategy. In this chapter we examine e-marketing strategy and planning separately since, in many organizations, a distinct e-marketing plan integrated with other marketing plans will often be developed by the marketing or e-commerce team. The e-marketing or Internet marketing plan will help define specific e-marketing objectives and develop strategies to ensure that resources are deployed to take advantage of the marketing opportunities provided by the Internet, and to counter its threats. E-marketing is focused on how a company and its brands use the web and other digital media such as e-mail and mobile media to interact with its audiences in order to meet its marketing goals. Figure 8.1 shows that there are three main operational processes involved in e-marketing. These are:

- **Customer acquisition**. Attracting visitors to a website or promoting a brand through reaching them via search engines or advertising on other sites.
- **Customer conversion**. Engaging site visitors to achieve the outcomes the site owner seeks such as leads, sales or browsing of other content.
- **Customer retention and growth**. Encouraging repeat usage of digital channels and, for transactional sites, repeat sales.

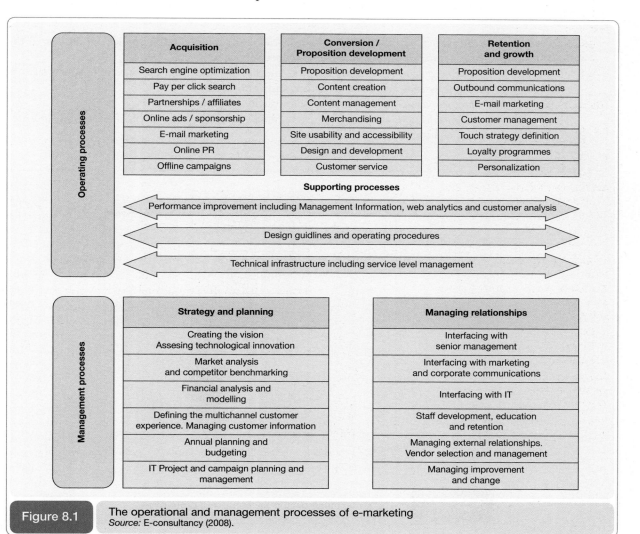

Figure 8.1   **The operational and management processes of e-marketing**
Source: E-consultancy (2008).

We discuss the tactics used to achieve these goals in more depth in Chapter 9. In this chapter we focus on the management issues involved in developing a strategy for e-marketing. The e-marketing strategy will naturally be informed by the wider business and marketing objectives and e-business strategy to ensure it supports the goals of the organization. Figure 8.2 shows that typically there is a hierarchy of plans in an organization with the corporate or business plan informing the marketing plan and this then informing specific market plans for different products or geographical markets. There is usually a separate communications plan which details the marketing campaigns that need to be executed to achieve the marketing objectives from the marketing plan.

Chapter structure

This chapter assumes limited previous knowledge of marketing, so we start with an introduction to the marketing and digital marketing concept and explain its relationship to e-business. A structured approach to developing an e-marketing plan is then described which is based on a similar strategy process model to that introduced in Chapter 5. The chapter also reviews how marketing concepts such as target marketing, the marketing mix and branding may require different treatment when we are using digital media.

Examples of typical ways in which organizations align their e-marketing strategy with business strategy are provided by Sultan and Rohm (2004) who, based on a study of three organizations, identify these strategic objectives:

- *Cost reduction and value chain efficiencies.* For example, B2B supplier AB Dick used the Internet to sell printer supplies to reduce service calls.
- *Revenue generation.* Reebok uses the Internet for direct licensed sales of products such as treadmills which do not have strong distribution deals.
- *Channel partnership.* Partnering with distributors using extranets.
- *Communications and branding.* Car company Saturn developed the MySaturn site to foster close relationships with customers.

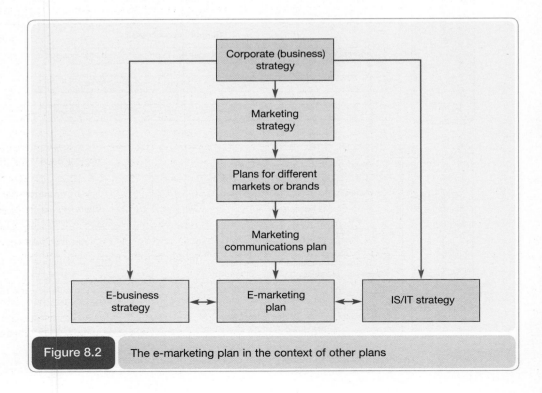

| **Figure 8.2** | The e-marketing plan in the context of other plans |

Real-world E-Business experiences   The E-consultancy interview

Steve Nicholas, Assistant Director of e-commerce at Guess

Overview and main concepts covered

Steve talks about the challenges of multi-channel retailing, especially for a well-known global brand in the fashion sector and one that has both wholesale and retail businesses to think about.

The interview

Q. Can you summarise where Guess is in terms of multi-channel retail?

Steve Nicholas, Guess: In terms of multi-channel, we're really in a good place from a merchandising and inventory perspective, because of the way we are set up. We're set up with virtual inventory that is tied to our e-commerce site and retail stores, so we get an initial allocation that's strictly for e-commerce and can pull from a reserve in our North American warehouse.

The warehouse ships out about 80% of its merchandise to the stores and holds back around 20% for replenishment. E-commerce can pull from that 20% for hot selling items and quickly push out to our stores any not so hot selling items that may have been included in the initial e-commerce-only allocation.

In our US stores, we also have a store portal or merchandise locator, which store personnel can use to order from the website in the store. If a store does not have a particular size or colour, we can accommodate that customer's order through the e-commerce site, from the store register. So in terms of inventory, we're in a solid position to accommodate the customer from a multi-channel perspective.

From a broader, assortment perspective, we have a debate going on about whether the e-commerce site should represent 'Guess – the brand' or 'Guess – the retail stores'.

If you go to Guess.com and want to buy shoes, do you expect to see all the shoes that Guess as a company markets through its wholesale, licensee and retail businesses or just the shoes we are currently selling in our retail stores? It's a question of strategy really.

Q. How does that affect how you market products online? Have you set up your site primarily as a place for consumers to research products, before buying instore?

Steve Nicholas, Guess: Sure. Our website is a shop window for the latest and greatest products that we have available in our North American retail stores.

We use a company called Foresee Results, which creates custom online visitor surveys and matches up the data with the American Consumer Satisfaction Index to compare our visitors' satisfaction with that of the satisfaction of visitors to other websites. We continually rank near the top in terms of multi-channel satisfaction scores.

From the surveys, we have visibility – we know that 69% of the people browsing on our site have made two or more purchases in our stores during the last year and 37% have made five or more. They view our site as an online catalogue to see what the new items are, and then go to the store to try it on and purchase.

Q. Have you found affiliate marketing and other performance-based online marketing techniques difficult to reconcile with your branding aims?

Steve Nicholas, Guess: We've just ventured into the affiliate world, launching an affiliate programme this summer. It's a bit too early to speak about the results from that, but it's a huge branding challenge for us.

Guess is such a well-known brand and we have to be very selective when picking our affiliate partners. We don't want the Guess name appearing just anywhere on the internet.

We are keeping it to affiliates that we feel are brand-appropriate and are covering the right demographic. We could be less selective, of course – picking affiliate partners and getting short term incremental sales, but only at the expense we feel of long term company success. We're using them for traffic more than anything – and making sure we protect the brand always.

We have a Guess Factory division and e-commerce site and we are being less selective with affiliate partners for that.

Q. You've yet to add transactional functionality to your UK and European sites. Is there any plan to?

Steve Nicholas, Guess: At some point, yes. As a company, we have moved in the last few years from a wholesaler to a global retailer with a wholesale operation as well. So it's all part and parcel of that.

The relationships and infrastructure are not yet ready for us to sell online in the UK or other countries. That's not to say it won't happen in the next few years – it's just getting the structure right. We are looking at the opportunities.

Source: www.econsultancy.com/news-blog/newsletter/3415/steve-nicholas-assistant-director-of-e-commerce-at-guess.html.

What is e-marketing?

Internet marketing has been described simply as '*achieving marketing objectives through applying digital technologies*' (Chaffey *et al.*, 2009). This succinct definition helps remind us that it is the results delivered by technology that should determine investment in Internet marketing, not the adoption of the technology!

Marketing defined

As with many terms with the 'e' prefix, we need to return to an original definition of the topic to more fully understand what e-marketing involves. The definition of marketing by the UK's Chartered Institute of Marketing is:

> *Marketing is the management process responsible for identifying, anticipating and satisfying customer requirements profitably.*

This definition emphasizes the focus of marketing on the customer, while at the same time implying a need to link to other business operations to achieve this profitability. In this chapter, and in Chapter 9, we will focus on how the Internet can be used to achieve the processes implied by this statement:

- *Identifying* – how can the Internet be used for marketing research to find out customers' needs and wants?
- *Anticipating* – we have seen in Chapter 5 that anticipating the demand for digital services (the online revenue contribution) is key to governing the resource allocation to e-business.
- *Satisfying* – a key issue for e-marketing is how to achieve customer satisfaction through the electronic channel; this raises issues such as: is the site easy to use, does it perform adequately, what is the standard of associated customer service and how are physical products dispatched?

Mini case study 8.1 gives a great example of how companies can use digital techniques to fulfil marketing aims. We introduced crowdsourcing in Chapter 4 where we defined it as '*Utilizing a network of customers or other partners to gain insights for new product or process innovations and to potentially help promote a brand*'.

Mini Case Study 8.1	Crowdsourcing – Penguin recruits teenagers to appeal to teenagers

Penguin used crowdsourcing to cover both the creation and management of Spinebreakers (Figure 8.3) , a new site proposition to enable them to interact with teenagers. In an interview with the *Marketer* (2009), Anna Rafferty, Managing Director of the Digital Division at Penguin Books, described the process. During the website development Penguin recruited hundreds of teenagers from every area and background for focus groups and usability testing. The teenagers made every decision, choosing the URL and the nature of the brand themselves. 'We decided not to make any assumptions,' says Rafferty.

The site is now run by three tiers of teenagers, or 'crews' as they elected to be called, who have varying levels of control over the site. The core crew of 12 teenagers write all of the website copy and come into the Penguin offices every month to discuss strategy; the second crew of 70 deputy editors are based all over the country and have back-end access to the site; while the third tier consists of the hundreds of teenage bloggers who participate on the site.

Figure 8.3	Spinebreakers *Source*: www.spinebreakers.co.uk.

According to Chaffey *et al.* (2009) the term 'marketing' tends to be used in two distinct respects in modern management practice. It can describe:

1 The range of specialist marketing functions carried out within many organizations. Such functions include market research, brand and product management, public relations and customer service.

2 An approach or concept (the marketing concept) that can be used as the guiding philosophy for all functions and activities of an organization. Business strategy is guided by an organization's market and competitor focus and everyone in the organization should be required to have a customer focus in their job.

The marketing concept
The management of the range of organizational activities that impact on the customer as part of marketing.

The modern **marketing concept** (Houston, 1986) unites these two meanings and stresses that marketing encompasses the range of organizational functions and processes that seek to determine the needs of target markets and deliver products and services to customers and other key stakeholders such as employees and financial institutions. Valentin (1996) argues that the marketing concept should lie at the heart of the organization, and the actions of directors, managers and employees should be guided by its philosophy.

Marketing orientation
Coordinating all organizational activities that impact on the customer to deliver customer requirements.

The modern concept of marketing is much broader than the lay person's view of marketing simply as advertising and sales. Modern marketing philosophy also requires that organizations be committed to a **marketing or customer orientation** (Jaworski and Kohli, 1993). This concept involves all parts of the organization coordinating activities to ensure that customer needs are met efficiently, effectively and profitably. The development of e-commerce services in response to changes in market needs is one example of market orientation, as Hughes (2001) has pointed out. In his study of new Internet start-ups and traditional banking operations which use e-commerce, he found that the Internet or e-business start-ups were more involved in conducting research to understand the customer experience and then adapting the service accordingly.

E-marketing defined

E-marketing
Achieving marketing objectives through use of electronic communications technology.

The term 'Internet marketing' tends to refer to an external perspective of how the Internet can be used in conjunction with traditional media to acquire and deliver services to customers. An alternative term is '**e-marketing**' (for example, McDonald and Wilson, 1999) which can be considered to have a broader scope since it refers to any use of technology to achieve marketing objectives and has an external and an internal perspective. This is more consistent with the concept of e-business which involves managing both internal and external communications.

Digital marketing is another similar term, explained in Chapter 1, which is used increasingly by online marketing agencies and trade publications.

E-marketing planning

E-marketing plan
A plan to achieve the marketing objectives of the e-business strategy.

An **e-marketing plan** is needed in addition to a broader e-business strategy to detail how the sell-side specific objectives of the e-business strategy will be achieved through marketing activities such as research and communications. Since the e-marketing plan is based on the objectives of the e-business or business strategy there is overlap between the elements of each approach, particularly for environment analysis, objective setting and strategic analysis. Figure 8.2 shows how e-marketing activities will inform the e-business strategy which, in turn, will inform the e-marketing plan.

We will use a similar strategy process model for e-marketing planning to that introduced in Chapter 5. In this chapter we use the SOSTAC™ framework developed by Paul Smith (1999), which summarizes the different stages that should be involved in a marketing strategy from strategy development to implementation (Figure 8.4):

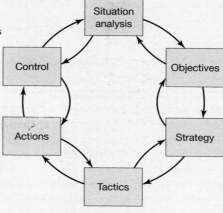

Where are we now?
- Goal performance (5Ss)
- Customer insight
- E-marketplace SWOT
- Brand perception
- Internal capabilities and resources

Where do we want to be?
5Ss objectives:
- Sell – customer acquisition and retention targets
- Serve – customer satisfaction targets
- Sizzle – site stickiness, visit duration
- Speak – trialogue; number of engaged customers
- Save – quantified efficiency gains

How do we monitor performance?
- 5Ss + web analytics – KPIs
- Usability testing/mystery shopper
- Customer satisfaction surveys
- Site visitor profiling
- Frequency of reporting
- Process of reporting and actions

The details of tactics, who does what and when
- Responsibilities and structures
- Internal resources and skills
- External agencies

How do we get there?
- Segmentation, targeting and positioning
- OVP (online value proposition)
- Sequence (credibility before visibility)
- Integration (consistent OVP) and database
- Tools (web functionality, e-mail, IPTV etc.)

How exactly do we get there?
(the details of strategy)
- E-marketing mix, including: the communications mix, social networking, what happens when?
- Details of contact strategy
- E-campaign initiative schedule

| Figure 8.4 | SOSTAC™ – a generic framework for e-marketing planning |

- Situation – where are we now?
- Objectives – where do we want to be?
- Strategy – how do we get there?
- Tactics – how exactly do we get there?
- Action – what is our plan?
- Control – did we get there?

Measurement of the effectiveness of e-marketing is an integral part of the strategy process in order to assess whether objectives have been achieved. The loop is closed by using the analysis of web analytics data (Chapter 12) metrics collected as part of the control stage to continuously improve e-marketing through making enhancements to the website and associated marketing communications.

We will now review the six elements of the SOSTAC™ approach to e-marketing planning. Overlap between this coverage and that in Chapter 5 is minimized by cross-referencing between these chapters.

Is a separate e-marketing plan required?

If there is a specific resource for e-marketing activities such as an e-marketing or e-commerce manager, then they will be responsible for the e-marketing plan. However, where there is no identified responsibility for e-marketing, which is still the case in many small and medium organizations, there is likely to be no e-marketing plan. This often occurs when marketing managers have limited resources or other priorities and a lack of recognition that a separate e-marketing plan is valuable.

These problems are typical and commonplace when there is no clear planning or control for e-marketing:

1 Customer demand for online services will be underestimated if this has not been researched and it is under-resourced and no or unrealistic objectives are set to achieve online marketing share.

2 Existing and start-up competitors will gain market share if insufficient resources are devoted to e-marketing and no clear strategies are defined.

3 Duplication of resources will occur, for example different parts of the marketing organization purchasing different tools or using different agencies for performing similar online marketing tasks.

4 Insufficient resource will be devoted to planning and executing e-marketing and there is likely to be a lack of specific specialist e-marketing skills which will make it difficult to respond to competitive threats effectively.

5 Insufficient customer data are collected online as part of relationship building and these data are not integrated well with existing systems.

6 Efficiencies available through online marketing will be missed, for example lower communications costs and enhanced conversion rates in customer acquisition and retention campaigns.

7 Opportunities for applying online marketing tools such as search marketing or e-mail marketing will be missed or the execution may be inefficient if the wrong resources are used or marketers don't have the right tools.

8 Changes required to internal IT systems by different groups will not be prioritized accordingly.

9 The results of online marketing are not tracked adequately on a detailed or high-level basis.

10 Senior management support of e-marketing is inadequate to drive what often needs to be a major strategic initiative.

However, managers responsible for a substantial investment in an Internet website and associated e-marketing communications will naturally want to ensure that the correct amount of money is invested and that it is used effectively. For these reasons and to avoid the 10 problems noted above, many leading adopters of e-commerce do have a distinct e-marketing plan, as an international e-consultancy survey of e-commerce managers shows (Figure 8.5).

For smaller organizations, the digital plan need not be exhaustive – a two-page summary defining objectives and outlining strategies may be sufficient. The important thing is to set clear objectives and strategies showing how the digital presence should contribute to the sales and marketing process. Specific initiatives that are required such as search marketing, e-mail marketing or features of a website redesign can be specified.

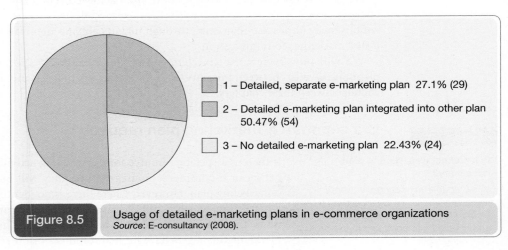

1 – Detailed, separate e-marketing plan 27.1% (29)

2 – Detailed e-marketing plan integrated into other plan 50.47% (54)

3 – No detailed e-marketing plan 22.43% (24)

Figure 8.5 Usage of detailed e-marketing plans in e-commerce organizations
Source: E-consultancy (2008).

In the longer term, once an organization has successfully defined its approaches to Internet marketing, it is likely that a separate Internet marketing strategy or e-marketing plan *will not* need to be developed each year since the Internet can be considered as any other communications medium and integrated into existing communications plans as suggested by Figure 8.5.

Situation analysis

Situation analysis
Environment analysis and review of internal processes and resources to inform strategy.

The aim of **situation analysis** is to understand the current and future environment in which the company operates in order that the strategic objectives are realistic in light of what is happening in the marketplace. Figure 8.6 shows the inputs from situation analysis that inform the e-marketing plan. These mainly refer to a company's external environment.

The study of an organization's online environment was introduced in Figure 2.1 and Figure 2.3 where it was noted that there was the immediate (micro-)environment of customers, competitors, suppliers and intermediaries and a broader (macro-)environment of social, legal, political, economic and technological characteristics. Situation analysis will

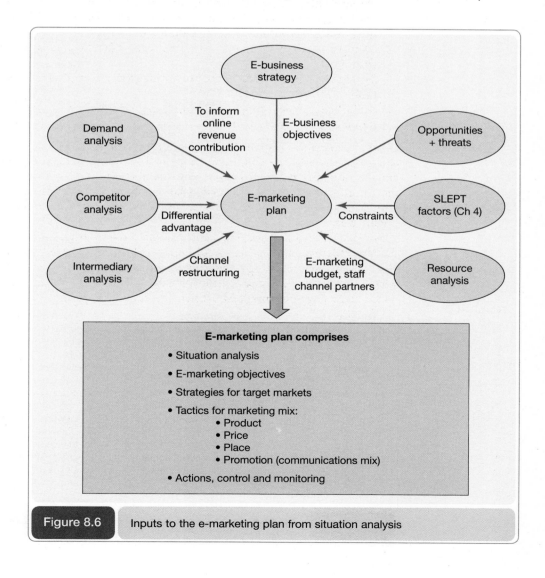

| **Figure 8.6** | Inputs to the e-marketing plan from situation analysis |

involve consideration of all of these factors and will form the basis for defining objectives, strategies and tactics. Consideration of the SLEPT or macro-environment factors is a major topic that is covered in Chapter 4. In this chapter we will concentrate on what needs to be analysed about the more immediate marketplace in terms of customers, competitors, intermediaries and market structure. An internal audit of the capability of the resources of the company such as its people, processes and technology also needs to take place.

In Chapter 5 we introduced the use of a SWOT analysis for an organization's digital channels. The SWOT can be used to summarize the range of analyses covered in this section. Figure 8.7 gives an example of a typical Internet SWOT.

Demand analysis

A key factor driving e-marketing and e-business strategy objectives is the current level and future projections of customer demand for e-commerce services in different market

The organization	Strengths – S 1 Existing brand 2 Existing customer base 3 Existing distribution	Weaknesses – W 1 Brand perception 2 Intermediary use 3 Technology/skills (poor web experience) 4 Cross-channel support 5 Churn rate
Opportunities – O 1 Cross-selling 2 New markets 3 New services 4 Alliances/co-branding	SO strategies Leverage strengths to maximize opportunities = attacking strategy **Examples:** 1 Migrate customers to web strategy 2 Refine customer contact strategy across customer life cycle or commitment segmentation (e-mail, web) 3 Partnership strategy (co-branding, linking) 4 Launch new web-based products or value-adding experiences, e.g. video streaming	WO strategies Counter weaknesses through exploiting opportunities = build strengths for attacking strategy **Examples:** 1 Countermediation strategy (create or acquire) 2 Search marketing acquisition strategy 3 Affiliate-based acquisition strategy 4 Refine customer contact strategy (e-mail, web)
Threats – T 1 Customer choice (price) 2 New entrants 3 New competitive products 4 Channel conflicts 5 Social network	ST strategies Leverage strengths to minimize threat = defensive strategy **Examples:** 1 Introduce new Internet-only products 2 Add value to web services – refine OVP 3 Partner with complementary brand 4 Create own social network/customer reviews	WT strategies Counter weaknesses and threats: = build strengths for defensive strategy **Examples:** 1 Differential online pricing strategy 2 Acquire/create pure-play company with lower cost-base 3 Customer engagement strategy to increase conversion, average order value and lifetime value 4 Online reputation management strategy/E-PR

Figure 8.7　Example SWOT analysis

segments (see Strategic analysis, Chapter 5, p. 250). This will influence the demand for products online and this, in turn, should govern the resources devoted to different online channels. **Demand analysis** examines current and projected customer use of each digital channel and different services within different target markets. It can be determined by asking for each market:

Demand analysis for e-business

Assessment of the demand for e-commerce services amongst existing and potential customer segments.

- What percentage of customer businesses have access to the Internet?
- What percentage of members of the buying unit in these businesses have access to the Internet?
- What percentage of customers are prepared to purchase your particular product online?
- What percentage of customers with access to the Internet are not prepared to purchase online, but are influenced by web-based information to buy products offline?
- What is the popularity of different online customer engagement devices such as Web 2.0 features such as blogs, online communities and RSS feeds?
- What are the barriers to adoption amongst customers of different channels and how can we encourage adoption?

Savvy e-marketers use tools provided by search engine services such as Google to evaluate the demand for their products or services based on the volume of different search terms typed in by search engine users. Table 8.1 shows the volume of searches for these generic, broad keywords. Most users also narrow their searches using phrases like 'free online banking', 'cuba holidays' and 'ski jackets'. This enables online suppliers to target their messages to consumers looking for these products through advertising services such as Google and Overture (Yahoo! Search Marketing).

Through evaluating the volume of phrases used to search for products in a given market it is possible to calculate the total potential opportunity and the current share of search terms for a company. 'Share of search' can be determined from web analytics reports from the company site which indicate the precise key phrases used by visitors to actually reach a site from different search engines.

Table 8.1	Volume of searches for single keywords in a single month

Keyword	Total global searches	Total estimated UK searches on Google
panasonic	45,500,000	7,480,000
playstation 2	13,600,000	823,000
kindle	7,480,000	301,000
dvd recorder	5,000,000	1,000,000
dvd players	5,000,000	1,220,000
digital camcorders	4,090,000	110,000
mens watches	4,090,000	1,220,000
online shopping	3,350,000	550,000
32 lcd tv	2,740,000	1,000,000
buy computer	1,830,000	49,500
dvd recorders	1,220,000	301,000
roller skates	1,220,000	301,000
tv lcd 42	1,220,000	301,000

Note: Estimates are based on the Google keyword tool in June 2010 based on products related to Amazon.

Thus the situation analysis as part of e-marketing planning must determine levels of access to the Internet in the marketplace and propensity to be influenced by the Internet to buy either offline or online. In a marketing context, the propensity to buy is an aspect of buyer behaviour (The online buying process, Chapter 9).

Figure 8.8 summarizes the type of picture the e-marketing planner needs to build up. For each geographic market the company intends to serve, research needs to establish:

1 Percentage of customers with Internet (or mobile) access.
2 Percentage of customers who access the website (and choose to use different types of services and channels such as mobile or social media options such as Facebook or Twitter).
3 Percentage of customers who will be favourably influenced.
4 Percentage of customers who buy online.

Now refer to Activity 8.1 where this analysis is performed for the car market. This picture will vary according to different target markets, so the analysis will need to be performed for each of these. For example, customers wishing to buy 'luxury cars' may have web access and a higher propensity to buy than those for small cars.

Activity 8.1	Customer activity in the car market in your country

Purpose

To illustrate the type of marketing research needed to inform demand analysis for e-marketing planning and approaches to finding this information.

Activity

For your country update Figure 8.8 to reflect current and future projections:

A For corporate buyers (known as the 'fleet market') where a specialist manager coordinates the purchase and management of company cars for efficiency purposes:

1 Percentage of customers with Internet access.
2 Percentage of customers who access the website.
3 Percentage of customers who will be favourably influenced (may be difficult to determine).
4 Percentage of customers who buy online.

If possible, try to gauge how these figures vary according to companies of different sizes and different members of the buying unit.

B For individual buyers (consumers):

1 Percentage of customers with Internet access.
2 Percentage of customers who access the website or social media services via web or mobile channels.
3 Percentage of customers who will be favourably influenced.
4 Percentage of customers who buy online or use other services such as brochure download, book a test drive or service.

If possible, try to gauge how these figures vary according to age, sex and social class.

Government sources and trade associations for car purchasing can be used to research the data.

No suggested answer supplied.

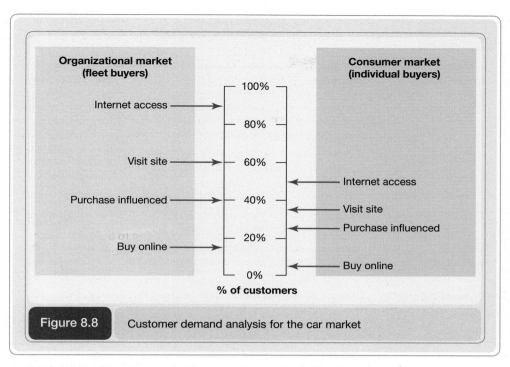

| Figure 8.8 | Customer demand analysis for the car market |

Qualitative customer research

It is important that customer analysis not be restricted to quantitative demand analysis. Variani and Vaturi (2000) point out that qualitative research provides insights that can be used to inform strategy. They suggest using graphic profiling, which is an attempt to capture the core characteristics of target customers, not only demographics, but also their needs and attitudes and how comfortable they are with the Internet. In Chapter 11 we will review how **customer personas** and **scenarios** are developed to help inform understanding of online buyer behaviour.

A summary of the categories of different sources of customer insight that an organization can tap into and their applications is shown in Table 8.2. The challenge within organizations seems to be selecting which paid-for and free services to select and then ensure sufficient time is spent reviewing and actioning the data to create value-adding insights. My experience shows that often data are only used by the digital team and not utilized more widely since in large organizations, staff are unaware of the existence of the data or service provider supplying it. There is also the significant issue of privacy; organizations need to be transparent about how they collect and use these data and give customers choice as discussed in Chapter 4.

As well as external sources, many online businesses are now harnessing customer viewpoints or innovation through their own programmes. Well-known examples from business and consumer fields include:

- Dell Ideastorm (www.ideastorm.com)
- MyStarbucks Idea (http://mystarbucksidea.com)
- BBC Backstage (http://backstage.bbc.co.uk)
- Lego MindStorm (http://mindstorms.lego.com/community/default.aspx)
- Oracle Mix (https://mix.oracle.com/listens)

You can see how web-savvy companies use the web for marketing research, as a listening channel. They use the web and e-mail channels as means of soliciting feedback and suggestions which contribute to shaping future services.

Customer scenario
Alternative tasks or outcomes required by a visitor to a website. Typically accomplished in a series of stages of different tasks involving different information needs or experiences.

Persona
A summary of the characteristics, needs, motivations and environment of typical website users.

| Table 8.2 | Categories of suppliers of digital customer insight and sample suppliers |

Insight type	Description	Sample suppliers
Voice of customer	Customer perceptions of online and multichannel experience including advocacy and Net Promoter Score. Online reputation (buzz) management tools	www.iperceptions.com www.opinionlab.com www.foreseeresults.com www.bazaarvoice.com www.davechaffey.com/online-reputation-management-tools
Customer profile data	Characteristics of customers in line with segments	Internal databases
Purchase behaviour	Transaction history including product category, recency, frequency and monetary value	Internal databases
Visitor behaviour from web analytics	Customer journeys on site and referral sources. Popularity of landing pages, content and products	www.google.com/analytics www.omniture.com www.clicktracks.com
Audience panel data	Audience volume/reach and profile on third-party sites	www.hitwise.com www.comscore.com www.netratings.com
Competitive benchmarking	Independent review of website functionality and features from independent review team or customers (mystery shoppers)	www.globalreviews.com www.psyma.com www.edigitalresearch.com
Campaign response	Combination of digital media touchpoints leading to website visits and conversion. Ad network behavioural targeting. Detailed keyphrase analysis	www.atlassolutions.com www.doubleclick.com www.lynchpin.com www.davechaffey.com/seo-keyword-tools
Experimentation	AB and multivariate testing. On-site behavioural targeting. On-site merchandising solutions	www.optimost.com www.offermatica.com www.maxymiser.com www.omniture.com www.atg.com

Competitor analysis

Competitor analysis for e-business
Review of e-business services offered by existing and new competitors and adoption by their customers.

Competitor analysis or the monitoring of competitor use of e-commerce to acquire and retain customers is especially important in the e-marketplace due to the dynamic nature of the Internet medium. This enables new services to be launched and promotions changed much more rapidly than through print communications. The implications of this dynamism are that competitor benchmarking is not a one-off activity while developing a strategy, but needs to be continuous.

Benchmarking of competitors' online services and strategy is a key part of planning activity and should also occur on an ongoing basis in order to respond to new marketing approaches such as price or promotions. According to Chaffey *et al.* (2009), competitor benchmarking has different perspectives which serve different purposes:

1 *Review of internal capabilities*: such as resourcing, structure and processes vs external customer facing features of the sites.
2 *From core proposition through branding to online value proposition (OVP)*. The core proposition will be based on the range of products offered, price and promotion. The OVP describes the type of web services offered which add to a brand's value.

3 *Different aspects of the customer life cycle*: customer acquisition, conversion to retention. Competitor capabilities should be benchmarked for all the digital marketing activities of each competitor, as shown in Figure 8.1. These should be assessed from the viewpoint of different customer segments or personas, possibly through usability sessions. Performance in search engines using the tools mentioned in Chapter 2 should be reviewed as a key aspect of customer acquisition and brand strength. In addition to usability, customer views should be sought on different aspects of the marketing mix such as pricing and promotions mentioned later in the chapter.

4 *Qualitative to quantitative*: from qualitative assessments by customers through surveys and focus groups through to quantitative analysis by independent auditors of data across customer acquisition (e.g. number of site visitors or reach within market, cost of acquisition, number of customers, sales volumes and revenues and market share); conversion (average conversion rates) and retention such as repeat conversion and number of active customers.

5 *In-sector and out-of-sector*: benchmarking against similar sites within sector and reviewing sectors which tend to be more advanced, e.g. online publishers, social networks and brand sites. Benchmarking services are available from analysts such as Bowen Craggs & Co (www.bowencraggs.com). An example of one of their benchmark reports is shown in Figure 8.9. You can see that this is based on the expert evaluation of the suitability of the site for different audiences as well as measures under the overall construction (which includes usability and accessibility), message (which covers key brand messages and suitability for international audiences) and contact (which shows integration between different audiences). The methodology states: 'it is not a "tick box": every metric is judged by its existence, its quality and its utility to the client, rather than "Is it there or is it not?"'

6 *Financial to non-financial measures*. Through reviewing competitive intelligence sources such as company reports or tax submissions additional information may be available on turnover and profit generated by digital channels. But other forward-looking aspects of the company's capability which are incorporated on the balanced scorecard measurement framework (see Chapter 4) should also be considered, including resourcing, innovation and learning.

7 *From user experience to expert evaluation*. Benchmarking research should take two alternative perspectives, from actual customer reviews of usability to independent expert evaluations.

Now complete Activity 8.2 to gain an appreciation of how benchmarking competitor e-business services can be approached.

Pos	Company	Construction	Message	Contact	Serving society	Serving investors	Serving the media	Serving job seekers	Serving customers	Total	URL	Country
	maximum score	60	48	12	32	32	32	32	32	280		
1	Siemens	47	40	10	27	21	28	24	24	221	www.siemens.com	Germany
2	Royal Dutch Shell	46	41	7	26	22	21	24	22	209	www.shell.com	Netherlands
3	BP	41	39	10	28	27	18	19	25	207	www.bp.com	UK
4	Nokia	44	36	8	26	24	24	16	25	203	www.nokia.com	Finland
5	AstraZeneca	48	33	9	20	20	27	16	27	200	www.astrazeneca.com	France
	Total	44	39	11	25	27	12	22	21	200	www.total.com	UK/Sweden
7	IBM	41	36	11	23	26	26	12	24	199	www.ibm.com	US
8	ING	43	40	8	22	25	21	16	22	197	www.ing.com	Netherlands
9	UBS	37	36	6	20	27	22	26	20	194	www.ubs.com	Switzerland
10	General Electric	42	37	10	25	17	19	17	24	191	www.ge.com	US

Figure 8.9 Benchmark comparison of corporate websites
Source: Bowen Craggs & Co (www.bowencraggs.com).

Activity 8.2	Competitor benchmarking

Purpose

To understand the services of a competitor website it is useful to benchmark and to assess the value of benchmarking.

Activity

You have been commissioned by a major company to evaluate the *marketing effectiveness* of their online services in comparison with their competitors'. You have to present your findings on their services and how they can be improved in a ten-minute PowerPoint presentation.

Choose a B2C industry sector such as airlines, book retailers, book publishers, CDs or clothing or for B2B a sector such as oil companies, chemical companies or construction industry companies.

Work individually or in groups to identify the type of information that should be available from the website (and which parts of the site you will access it from) which will be useful in terms of competitor benchmarking. Once your criteria have been developed, you should then benchmark companies and summarize which you feel is making best use of the Internet medium.

Table 5.10 may also prove useful.

Answers to activities can be found at www.pearsoned.co.uk/chaffey

Intermediary analysis

Chapter 2 highlighted the importance of web-based intermediaries such as portals in driving traffic to an organization's website or influencing visitors while they consume content. Situation analysis will also involve identifying relevant intermediaries for a particular marketplace. These will be different types of portal such as horizontal and vertical portals which will be assessed for suitability for advertising, PR or partnership. This activity can be used to identify strategic partners or will be performed by a media planner or buyer when executing an online advertising campaign.

For example, an online book retailer needs to assess which comparison or aggregator services such as Kelkoo (www.kelkoo.com) and Shopsmart (www.shopsmart.com) it and its competitors are represented on. Questions which are answered by analysis of intermediaries are do competitors have any special sponsorship arrangements and are micro-sites created with intermediaries? The other main aspect of situation analysis for intermediaries is to consider the way in which the marketplace is operating. To what extent are competitors using disintermediation or reintermediation? How are existing channel arrangements being changed?

Internal marketing audit

An internal audit will assess the capability of the resources of the company such as its people, processes and technology to deliver e-marketing compared with its competitors. In Chapter 10 we discuss how teams should be restructured and new resources used to deliver competitive online marketing and customer experience. The internal audit will also review the way in which a current website or e-commerce service performs. The audit is likely to review the following elements of an e-commerce site, which are described in more detail in '*Focus on* Web analytics: measuring and improving performance of e-business services' in Chapter 12:

1 *Business effectiveness.* This will include the contribution of the site to revenue, profitability and any indications of the corporate mission for the site. The costs of producing and updating the site will also be reviewed, i.e. cost–benefit analysis.

2 *Marketing effectiveness.* These measures may include:
   - leads;
   - sales;
   - cost of acquiring new customers;
   - retention;
   - market share;
   - brand engagement and loyalty;
   - customer service.

   These measures will be assessed for each of the different product lines delivered through the website. The way in which the elements of the marketing mix are utilized will also be reviewed.

3 *Internet effectiveness.* These are specific measures that are used to assess the way in which the website is used, and the characteristics of the audience. Such measures include specialist measures such as unique visitors and page impressions that are collected through web analytics, and also traditional research techniques such as focus groups and questionnaires to existing customers. From a marketing point of view, the effectiveness of the value proposition of the site for the customer should also be assessed.

Objective setting

Effective e-marketing plans are based on clearly defined objectives since these will inform the strategies and tactics and help in communicating the strategic aims to the workforce and investors.

Strategies are agreed to be most effective when they support specific business objectives. A useful technique to help align strategies and objectives is to present them together in a table together with the insight developed from situation analysis which may have informed the strategy. Table 8.3 gives an example which also shows the links between strategies of customer acquisition, conversion and retention and the tactics used to fulfil them such as e-mail marketing and search engine marketing which we discuss in Chapter 9.

Table 8.3	The relationship objectives, strategies and performance indicators for a B2B company (in order of priority)

Objectives	Substantiation (informed by situation analysis or insight, example)	Strategies to achieve goals	Key performance indicators (critical success factors)
1 *Acquisition objective.* Acquire 50,000 new online customers this financial year at an average cost per acquisition (CPA) of £30 with an average profitability of 5%	Based on growth forecast based on current sales of 40,000 sales per year, but with incremental sales arising from new affiliate programme and SEO development	Start affiliate marketing programme and improve SEO. Existing media mix based on pay-per-click and display advertising supported by offline media	Overall CPA for online sales. Incremental number and % of sales from affiliate marketing programme Number of strategic keywords ranked in top positions in natural search results page

Table 8.3	Continued		

Objectives	Substantiation (informed by situation analysis or insight, example)	Strategies to achieve goals	Key performance indicators (critical success factors)
2 *Acquisition (or conversion) objective.* Migrate 40% of existing customers to using online 'paperless' bill payment services and e-mail communications within 3 years	Extrapolation of current natural migration coupled with increased adoption from offline direct marketing campaign	Direct marketing campaign using direct mail, phone prompts and online persuasion to encourage adoption. Use of incentive to encourage change	Number and percentage of existing customers registering to use online services. Number and percentage of customers actively using online services at different points after initially registering
3 *Conversion objective.* Increase the average order value of online sales to £42 per customer	Growth estimated based on current AOV of £35 plus model suggesting 20% increase in AOV	Use of new merchandising system to show users related 'next best product' for different product categories	% of site visitors responding to merchandising / cross-selling messages
4 *Conversion objective.* Increase site conversion rate to 3.2%	Model showing separate increase in conversion for new and existing customers based on strategies shown on the right	Combination of strategies: • Incentivized e-mail follow-up on checkout abandonments for new customers • Introduction of more competitive pricing strategy on best sellers • AB and multivariate messaging improvement of landing pages • Refinement to quality of traffic purchased through pay-per-click programme	Variations in conversion rates for new and existing customers in different product categories
5 *Retention objective.* Increase annual repeat new customer conversion rate by 20%	Business case based on limited personalization of offers to encourage repeat purchases via e-mail.	• Delivery of personalized product offers by e-mail • 5% second purchase discount voucher	• Increased conversion rate of retention e-mail contact programme • Conversion to sale for second purchase discount campaigns
6 *Growth objective.* Increase new prospects recommended by friends (viral marketing or 'member get member') by 10,000 per annum	Model based on encouraging 2% of customers to recommend friends annually (based on trial scheme)	Supported by direct mail and e-mail recommendation programme	• Response rate to direct mail campaign

We also discussed the importance of SMART e-business objectives in Chapter 5. We also noted the value of using metrics which combined efficiency and effectiveness and could be applied in the context of the balanced scorecard. Table 8.4 presents detailed e-marketing metrics in this way.

Table 8.4	Example Internet marketing objectives within the balanced scorecard framework for a transactional e-commerce site

Balanced scorecard sector	Efficiency	Effectiveness
Financial results (business value)	• Channel costs • Channel profitability	• Online contribution (direct) • Online contribution (indirect) • Profit contributed
Customer value	• Online reach (unique visitors as % of potential visitors) • Cost of acquisition or cost per sale (CPA or CPS) • Customer satisfaction ratings	• Sales and sales per customer • New customers • Online market share • Customer propensity to defect • Customer loyalty index
Operational processes	• Conversion rates • Average order value • List size and quality • E-mail-active %	• Fulfilment times • Support response times
Innovation and learning (people and knowledge)	• Novel approaches tested • Internal e-marketing education • Internal satisfaction ratings	• Novel approaches deployed • Performance appraisal review

Online revenue contribution

An assessment of the direct contribution of the Internet or other digital media to sales, usually expressed as a percentage of overall sales revenue.

In Chapter 5, we also mentioned the importance of defining the **online revenue contribution** as a target to improve performance. Figure 8.10 gives an example combining the online revenue contribution and the online promotion contribution as a forecast based on marketing research of demand analysis and competitor analysis. Complete Case study 8.1 to review how easyJet increased their online revenue contribution.

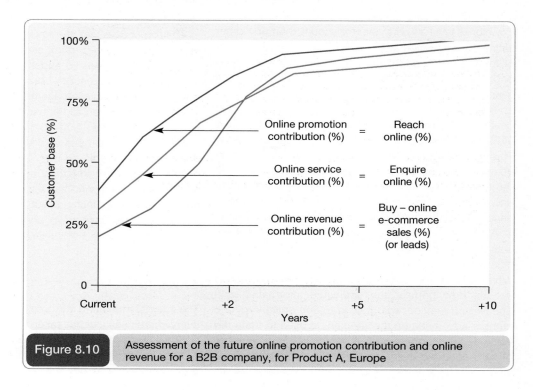

Figure 8.10	Assessment of the future online promotion contribution and online revenue for a B2B company, for Product A, Europe

This historical case shows how the easyJet website (Figure 8.11) became the main sales channel for easyJet from its launch in the 1990s. How the Internet was used for service delivery and marketing communications is also described. This case study has been retained since it is a popular case illustrating the benefits of management commitment to a planned, well-resourced strategy to help grow digital channels. By 2010, 98% of seats were sold online and easyJet still incentivizes people to book their cheap flights online through a £7.50 discount for each leg of a journey.

easyJet was founded by Stelios Haji-Ioannou, the son of a Greek shipping tycoon who reputedly used to 'hate the Internet'. In the mid-1990s Haji-Ioannou reportedly denounced the Internet as something 'for nerds', and swore that it wouldn't do anything for his business. This is no longer the case, since by August 1999 the site accounted for 38% of ticket sales or over 135,000 seats. This was past the company's original Internet contribution target at launch of 30% of sales by 2000. In the period from launch, the site had taken more than 800,000 bookings since it was set up in April 1998 after a shaky start of two sales in the first week and one thousand within the first month. In March 2000 easyJet increased its online discount to £2.50 for a single trip – a higher level of permanent discount than any other airline. By September 2000, Internet sales reached 85% of total sales. Since this time, the growth in proportion of online sales has decreased. By 2003, over 90% of all sales were online.

The company was originally set up in 1994. As a low-cost airline, looking to undercut traditional carriers such as British Airways, it needed to create a lean operation. To achieve this, Haji-Ioannou decided on a single sales channel in order to survive. He chose the phone. At the time this was ground-breaking, but the owner was encouraged by companies such as Direct Line insurance, and the savings which direct selling would bring.

Although Haji-Ioannou thought at the time that there was no time to worry about the Internet and that one risk was enough, he was adaptable enough to change. When a basic trial site was launched, he kept a close eye on how popular the dedicated information and booking phone line was (having a web-specific phone number advertised on the site can be used to trace the volume of users on the site). A steady rise in the number of calls occurred every week. This early success coincided with the company running out of space at its call centre due to easyJet's growth. Haji-Ioannou related,

'We either had to start selling over the Internet or build a new call centre. So our transactional site became a £10 million decision.'

Although the success of easyJet could be put down solely to the founder's adaptability and vision, the company was helped by the market it operated in and its chosen business model – it was already a 100% direct phone sales operation. This meant it was relatively easy to integrate the web into the central booking system. There were also no potential channel conflicts with intermediaries such as travel agents. The web also fitted in with the low-cost easyJet proposition of no tickets, no travel agents, no network tie-ups and no in-flight meals. Customers are given a PIN number for each order on the website which they give when they get to the airport.

Sales over the Internet began in April 1998, and although easyJet's new-media operations were then handled by Tableau, a few months later easyJet took them in-house.

The Internet is important to easyJet since it helps it to reduce running costs, important for a company where each passenger generates a profit of only £1.50. Savings to easyJet made through customers booking online enable it to offer at least £1 off to passengers who book online – this is part of the online proposition.

The owner says that 'the savings on the Internet might seem small compared to not serving a meal on a plane, which saves between £5 and £10, but when you think how much it would cost to build a new call centre, pay every easyJet reservation agent 80 pence for each seat sold – not to mention all the middlemen – you're talking much more than the £1 off we give online buyers'.

What about the risks of alienating customers who don't want to book online? This doesn't worry the owner. He says 'I'm sure there are people who live in the middle of nowhere who say they can't use the Internet and will fly Ryanair instead. But I'm more worried about keeping my cost base down, and finding enough people to fill my aeroplanes. I only need 6 million people a year, not all 56 million.'

Promotion

The Internet marketing gurus say 'put the company URL everywhere'; easyJet has taken this literally with its web address along the side of its Boeing 737s.

easyJet frequently varies the mix by running Internet-only promotions in newspapers. easyJet ran its first Internet-only promotion in a newspaper in *The Times* in

Figure 8.11   easyJet website
Source: www.easyjet.com.

February 1999, with impressive results. Some 50,000 seats were offered to readers and 20,000 of them were sold on the first day, rising to 40,000 within three days. And, according to the marketing director, Tony Anderson, most of these were seats that otherwise would have been flying along at 600 mph – empty. The scalability of the Internet helped deal with demand since everyone was directed to the website rather than the company needing to employ an extra 250 telephone operators. However, risk management did occur with a micro-site built for *Times* readers (www.times.easyjet. com) to avoid putting a strain on easyJet's main site.

Anderson says, 'The airline promotions are basically designed to get rid of empty seats.' He adds, 'If we have a flight going to Nice that's leaving in 20 minutes' time, it costs us very little to put some extra people on board, and we can get, say, £15 a head for it.' Flight promotions are intended to avoid attracting people who would fly with easyJet, so advanced booking schemes are intended to achieve that.

A later five-week promotion within *The Times* and *The Sunday Times* newspapers offered cheap flights to a choice of all easyJet destinations when 18 tokens were collected. In total, 100,000 seats were sold during the promotion, which was worth more than £2 million to the airline. Thirty per cent of the seats were sold online, with the rest of the transactions being completed by phone; 13,000 orders were taken over the Internet in the first day alone with over 15,000 people on the site at one point.

The website also acts as a PR tool. Haji-Ioannou uses its immediacy to keep newspapers informed about new promotions and offers.

The website is also used as an aggressive tool in what is a very competitive marketplace. Haji-Ioannou says, 'Once we had all these people coming to our site, I asked myself: Why pay a PR company to publicize what we think when we have a captive audience on the site?' For example, easyJet ran a competition in which people had to guess what BA's losses would be on

'Go', its budget rival to easyJet (the figure turned out to be £20 million). Within minutes of the BA results being announced on 7 September, the easyJet site had the 50 flight-ticket winners from an incredible 65,000 people who had entered. In a similar vein a section of the site was entitled 'Battle with Swissair', giving easyJet's view that Swissair's head had persuaded the Swiss government to stop easyJet being granted a commercial scheduled licence on the Geneva–Barcelona route. easyJet also called itself 'The web's favourite airline', in 1999, a direct counterpoint to British Airways' slogan of 'The world's favourite airline' for which it enjoyed a court battle.

easyEverything

Following the brand extension success of Virgin, easyJet has used the 'easy' prefix to offer additional services as part of the easyGroup:

- easyEverything, a chain of 400-seat-capacity Internet cafés originally offering access at £1 an hour. This is run as an independent company and will charge easyJet for banner ads, but clearly the synergy will help with clickthrough between 2 and 3%. The only concession easyEverything makes towards easyJet is that café customers can spend time on the easyJet site for free.
- easyRentacar, a low-cost car rental business offering car rental at £9 a day. These costs are possible through offering a single car type and being an Internet-only business.

Implementation

The articles report that Russell Sheffield, head of new-media agency Tableau, which initially worked with easyJet had an initial problem of colour! 'He says there was a battle to stop him putting his favourite colour all over the site.' The site was intended to be highly functional, simply designed and without any excess baggage. He says, 'The home page (orange) only had four options – buy online, news, info, and a topic of the moment such as BA "GO" losses – and the site's booking system is simpler to use than some of its competitors'. He adds: 'Great effort was put into making

the navigation intuitive – for example, users can move directly from the timetables to the booking area, without having to go via the home page.'

The site was designed to be well integrated into easyJet's existing business processes and systems. For example, press releases are fed through an electronic feed into the site, and new destinations appear automatically once they are fed into the company's information system.

Measurement of the effectiveness of the site occurred through the dedicated phone number on the site which showed exactly how many calls the site generated, and the six-month target was met within six weeks. Website log file analysis showed that people were spending an average of eight minutes a time on the site, and better still, almost everyone who called bought a ticket, whereas with the normal phone line, only about one in six callers buys. Instead of having to answer questions, phone operators were doing nothing but sell tickets.

Once the website generated two-fifths of easyJet business, it was taken in-house and Tableau now acts solely as a strategic adviser.

Source: Based on *Revolution* articles: EasyJet site a success in first month, 1 August 1998; EasyJet promotion sells 30,000 seats, 1 November 1998; Say hello to Mr e-Everything, 13 October 1999.

Questions

1 To what extent was the Internet revenue contribution of around 90% achieved 'more by luck than judgement'?

2 Explain the proposition of using the Internet for the customer and define the benefits for the company.

3 Explain how easyJet uses the website to vary the different elements of the marketing mix and as a marketing communications tool.

4 Use a news source such as www.ft.com or review its investors' relations site (www.easyjet.com/EN/ about/investorrelations.html) to find out how easyJet has extended its Internet applications.

Strategy

The strategy element of an e-marketing plan defines how e-marketing objectives will be achieved. Strategy definition has to be tightly integrated into the e-marketing planning process since e-marketing planning is an iterative process from situation analysis to objective setting to strategy definition (Figure 8.4). Key decisions in strategy definition for e-business were described in Chapter 5. To avoid significant overlap here, the reader is referred to that section. Another perspective on e-marketing strategy is provided by E-consultancy (2008) who explain that the output from the digital strategy will often be a series of strategic e-commerce initiatives in the key areas of customer acquisition, conversion or retention such as those shown in Table 8.5. These e-commerce initiatives will typically be prioritized and placed as part of a long-term e-commerce 'roadmap' defining required developments over a longer period of 18 months to three years.

Table 8.5	Summary of typical focus for main types of e-commerce-related strategic initiatives	
Type of digital marketing strategy initiative	**Commentary**	**Examples of strategy implementation**
1 **New customer proposition (Product, Place and Pricing)**	These are new site features or other online communications which are directly related to offering new products or services, potentially from new locations that will generate revenue.	• Bank – introduce new product requiring different quotes • Portal – introduce comparison service • Service company – introduce new functionality acquired through takeover of company • Magazine or music service offering new pricing options • See also channel integration initiatives
2 **Customer acquisition strategic initiatives**	These are strategic projects to enhance a site's capability to deliver new prospects on a continuous basis through different online marketing techniques. They may involve investment in the site itself (e.g. SEO) or the back-end, integrating with affiliates.	• SEO • PPC • Affiliate marketing • Aggregators • Enhance page type (to help increase conversion rate), e.g. category or product landing pages
3 **Customer conversion and customer experience strategic initiatives**	Investments in new customer features on the site. These will be based on a business case of increased conversion rate and average order value. May include major new functionality such as that for a new online store or more specific functionality integrated into existing site functionality. Many strategic initiatives are aimed at improving the customers' experience of a brand.	• Implement online shop / secure payment • Introduce customer reviews and ratings • Merchandising capability to offer tailored promotions • Interactive tools to help product selection • Refine on-site search engine • Buyers guides consisting of in-depth content about products or rich media (e.g. videos showcasing products)
4 **Customer development and growth strategic initiatives**	Investments to improve the experience and delivery of offers to existing customers.	• Personalized recommendations for existing customers • Development of e-mail welcome strategy for new online customers as part of development of an integrated contact or e-CRM strategy delivered through personalized web and e-mail messages and traditional direct communications • Introduce blogs or RSS feeds to encourage return visitors • Introduce more participation through customer communities

Table 8.5	Continued

Type of digital marketing strategy initiative	Commentary	Examples of strategy implementation
5 **Channel integration initiatives**	These may reference any of the strategies above.	• Offline retailer launches 'click and reserve' service • Digital facilities introduced in-store • Integration of mobile marketing into direct mail or e-mail campaigns
6 **Enhance marketing capabilities through site infrastructure improvements**	These typically involve 'back-end or back-office features' which won't be evident to users of the site, but will help in the management or administration of the site. Will often involve improving customer insight capabilities.	• CRM or personalization • Content management system • Performance improvement – improve management information, web analytics systems including systems for multivariate and AB testing • Improve customer feedback or other customer survey facilities • Update development approach for introducing new functionality

The amount invested on the Internet should be based on the anticipated contribution the Internet will make to a business, as explained in the sections on objectives. In Chapter 5 (p. 265) we saw how Kumar (1999) identified four different criteria for deciding whether the Internet would replace or complement other channels to market. In this chapter, we consider an alternative model, the Electronic Shopping Test (Box 8.1), for reviewing the likely strategic importance of the Internet to a company as developed by de Kare-Silver (2000).

Box 8.1	The Electronic Shopping or ES Test

This test was developed by Michael de Kare-Silver to assess the extent to which consumers are likely to purchase a retail product using the Internet. De Kare-Silver suggests factors that should be considered in the ES Test:

1 *Product characteristics*. Does the product need to be physically tried or touched before it is bought?
2 *Familiarity and confidence*. Considers the degree the consumer recognizes and trusts the product and brand.
3 *Consumer attributes*. These shape the buyer's behaviour – are they amenable to online purchases in terms of access to the technology skills available and do they no longer wish to shop for a product in a traditional retail environment?

In his book, de Kare-Silver describes a method for ranking products. Product characteristics, familiarity and confidence are each marked out of 10, and consumer attributes are marked out of 30. Using this method, he scores products as shown in Table 8.6.

De Kare-Silver states that any product scoring over 20 has good potential, since the score for consumer attributes is likely to increase through time. Given this, he suggests companies will regularly need to review the score for their products.

Table 8.6	Product scores in de Kare-Silver (2000), Electronic Shopping Potential Test			
Product	**1 Product characteristics (10)**	**2 Familiarity and confidence (10)**	**3 Consumer attributes (30)**	**Total**
Groceries	4	8	15	27
Mortgages	10	1	4	15
Travel	10	6	15	31
Books	8	7	23	38

Market and product positioning

The Internet offers new opportunities for selling new products into new markets. These present strategic alternatives that can be evaluated using the options first stated by Ansoff (1957). The risks involved with the four options of market penetration, market development, product development and both market and product development (diversification) vary, as shown in Figure 5.19 and explained in the commentary.

There may also be options for new digital products that could include information products that can be delivered over the web. Such products may not be charged for, but will add value to existing products. Ghosh (1998) suggested developing new products or adding 'digital value' to customers. He says companies should ask the following questions:

1 Can I offer additional information or transaction services to my existing customer base?
2 Can I address the needs of new customer segments by repackaging my current information assets or by creating new business propositions using the Internet?
3 Can I use my ability to attract customers to generate new sources of revenue such as advertising or sales of complementary products?
4 Will my current business be significantly harmed by other companies providing some of the value I currently offer?

In addition Ghosh (1998) suggests that companies should provide free digital value to help build an audience. He refers to this process as building a 'customer magnet'; today this would be known as a 'portal' or 'community'. There is good potential for customer magnets in specialized vertical markets served by business-to-business companies. For example, a customer magnet could be developed for the construction industry, agrochemicals, biotechnology or independent financial advisers.

In 2009, Chris Anderson of *Wired Magazine* gave the concept renewed impetus when he published the book *Free! Why $0.00 Is the Future of Business*. You can read his views on the issue of digital value here: www.wired.com/techbiz/it/magazine/16-03/ff_free.

Target market strategies

Target marketing strategy
Evaluation and selection of appropriate segments and the development of appropriate offers.

We have seen that we need to review the options for using the digital media to reach new markets or develop existing markets. Within both of these markets we need to analyse the target market in more detail to understand their needs and potential and then develop a strategy to satisfy these markets to maximize revenue. This is **target marketing strategy** and involves the four stages shown in Figure 8.12.

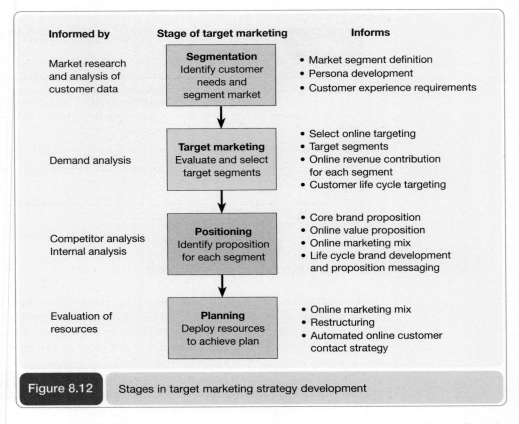

Informed by	Stage of target marketing	Informs
Market research and analysis of customer data	**Segmentation** Identify customer needs and segment market	• Market segment definition • Persona development • Customer experience requirements
Demand analysis	**Target marketing** Evaluate and select target segments	• Select online targeting • Target segments • Online revenue contribution for each segment • Customer life cycle targeting
Competitor analysis Internal analysis	**Positioning** Identify proposition for each segment	• Core brand proposition • Online value proposition • Online marketing mix • Life cycle brand development and proposition messaging
Evaluation of resources	**Planning** Deploy resources to achieve plan	• Online marketing mix • Restructuring • Automated online customer contact strategy

Figure 8.12   Stages in target marketing strategy development

Segmentation
Identification of different groups within a target market in order to develop different product offerings and communications for the groups.

The first stage in Figure 8.12 is **segmentation**. Segmentation involves understanding the groupings of customers in the target market to understand their needs and potential as a revenue source in order to develop a strategy to satisfy these segments while maximizing revenue. Dibb *et al.* (2000) say that:

> *Market segmentation is the key of robust marketing strategy development ... it involves more than simply grouping customers into segments ... identifying segments, targeting, positioning and developing a differential advantage over rivals is the foundation of marketing strategy.*

In an e-marketing planning context market segments will be analysed to assess:

1 Their current market size or value, future projections of size and the organization's current and future market share within the segment.
2 Competitor market shares within the segment.
3 Needs of each segment, in particular unmet needs.
4 Organization and competitor offers and proposition for each segment across all aspects of the buying process.

The targeting approaches used for online acquisition and retention campaigns will naturally depend on established segmentation. Table 8.7 summarizes options for targeting customers online. The power of digital technology is that it makes it easier and more cost-effective to deliver targeted messages on a web page or in an e-mail compared to traditional media.

Let's look at each targeting variable in a little more depth.

1 **Relationship with company.** Campaigns will often be intended to target new contacts *or* existing contacts. But remember, some communications will reach both. Marketers have to consider whether it will be cost-effective to have separate communications for new, existing and lapsed contacts – or to target each of these groups in the same communications but using different content aimed at each.

Table 8.7	A range of targeting and segmentation approaches for a digital campaign

Targeting variable	Examples of segments and potential online targeting attributes
1 Relationship with company	New contacts (prospects), existing customers, lapsed customers
2 Demographic segmentation	B2C: Age, sex, social group, geographic location B2B: Company size, industry served, individual members of decision-making unit
3 Psychographic or attitudinal segmentation	Attitudes to risk and value when buying, e.g. early adopter, brand loyal or price conscious
4 Value	Assessment of current or historical value and future value
5 Life cycle stage	Position in life cycle, related to value and behaviour, i.e. time since initial registration, number of products purchased, categories purchased in
6 Behaviour	• Search term entered into search engine • Responsiveness to different types of offers (promotion or product type) • Responsiveness to campaigns in different channels (channel preference) • Purchase history in product categories including recency, frequency and monetary value (Chapter 9)

When visitors click through to your website from online and offline campaigns, copy should be presented that recognizes the relationship or, again, provide a range of content to recognize each different relationship. Visit Microstrategy (www.microstrategy.com) to see how its registration page establishes the relationship.

2 **Demographic segmentation**. This is typically based on age, sex or social group. Online demographics are often used as the basis for which sites to purchase display advertising or for renting e-mail lists. Demographics can also be used to limit or focus who pay-per-click search ads are displayed to.

3 **Psychographic or attitudinal segmentation**. This includes attitudes to risk and value when buying. It is less straightforward to target on these attributes of a consumer since it is easier to buy media based on demographic breakdown. However, certain sites may be more suitable for reaching a particular psychographic audience. The psychographic characteristics of the audience are still an important part of the brief, to help develop particular messages.

It is possible to collect attitudinal information on a site and add it to the customer profile. For example, Wells Fargo asks investors to select:
● The type of investment preferred (individual stocks or mutual funds).
● What type of investor best describes you (aggressive growth to more cautious).

4 **Value**. The higher-value customers (indicated by higher average order value and higher modelled customer lifetime values) will often warrant separate communications with different offers. Sometimes digital channels are not the best approach for these customers – relationship managers will want direct contact with their most valuable customers, while digital channels are used to communicate more cost-effectively with lower-value customers. It is also worth considering reducing the frequency of e-mails to this audience.

5 **Life cycle stage**. This is very useful where customers follow a particular sequence in buying or using a service, such as online grocery shopping or online banking. As explained in

Chapter 9, automated event-triggered e-mail marketing can be developed for this audience. For example, bank First Direct uses a 6-month welcome strategy based on e-mail and direct mail communications. For other campaigns, the status of a customer can be used for targeting, for example not-purchased or used service, purchased once, purchased more than 5 times and active, purchased more than 5 times and inactive, etc.

6 **Behavioural.** Behavourial targeting is one of the big opportunities provided by digital marketing. It involves assessing customers' past actions in following links, reading content, using online services or buying products, and then follows up on these with a more relevant message based on the propensity to act based on the previous action.

Online options for behavioural targeting can be illustrated by a travel company such as lastminute.com:

- *Pay-per-click search engine marketing* such as Google AdWords makes targeting possible according to the type of keyphrase typed when a potential customer searches for information. A relevant ad specific to a holiday destination the prospect is looking for, e.g. 'Hotel New York' can then be shown.

- *Display advertising* makes behavioural targeting possible since cookies can be used to track visitors across a site or between sites and display relevant ads. If a site user visits the travel section of a newspaper site, then the ad about lastminute can be served as they visit other content on this site, or potentially on other sites.

- *E-mail marketing* can be targeted based on customer preferences indicated by links they have clicked on. For example, if a user has clicked a link about a holiday in North America, then a targeted e-mail can be delivered relevant to this product or promotion. More sophisticated analysis based on RFM analysis (Chapter 9) can also be used.

When reviewing the options for which variables to use to target, the campaign planner must keep in mind that the variables selected for targeting should be those which are most likely to influence the level of response for the campaign. Figure 8.13 indicates the general improvement in campaign response dependent on the type of targeting variables used. This approach is used by travel company Travelocity in their e-mail marketing. Speaking at the 2006 Internet Retailing Forum they described how they concentrate their efforts on behaviour suggesting purchase intent, i.e. when a visitor to their site clicks on a particular type of holiday, e-mails sent to the customer should be updated to reflect that.

Seybold (1999) identified five questions to help develop a customer-centric strategy for e-marketing (which are still relevant today; the questions apply equally to marketing). The questions are:

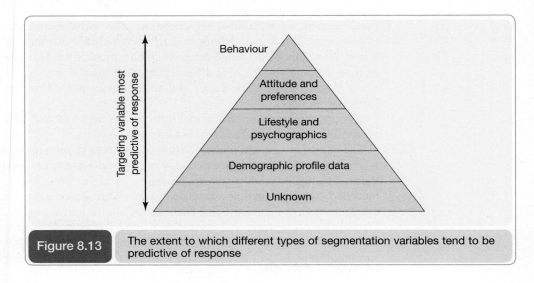

| Figure 8.13 | The extent to which different types of segmentation variables tend to be predictive of response |

1 Who are our customers?

This involves identifying target segments that share certain characteristics and needs. It was seen in Chapter 4 that different criteria for identifying segments include demographics and geographical location for the B2C market and organizational characteristics and members of the buying unit for the B2B market.

2 How are their needs changing?

Understanding the needs of different segments when they venture online is important to the next stages of delivering value to the customer. Some segments may have originally been motivated by price, but customer service may become more important. This is closely related to buyer behaviour (Chapter 9).

3 Which do we target?

This is an important strategic decision in e-marketing which we discussed in Chapter 5 under the strategic decision *Decision 2: Market and product development strategies*.

4 How can we add value?

We have seen in Chapters 5 and 6 that customer value is mainly dependent on the combination of product quality, customer service quality, fulfilment time and price. Companies need to decide for each segment which of these is most important and then seek to adjust these elements accordingly as part of the marketing mix described in the next section.

5 How do we become first choice?

To decide on this it is necessary to know how to position within the marketplace relative to competitor offerings. **Positioning** is related to how a consumer perceives a product in terms of the elements of value described above. It is stage 3 in Figure 8.12. A positioning statement is often developed to encapsulate this. Companies then need to decide how to highlight the benefits as a **differential advantage** over rivals' products.

Having a clear, powerful positioning is crucial online, since it is so easy for customers to compare service providers when initially selecting a product. It is also important to customer retention since the first experience of a brand will determine whether the customer naturally returns to the supplier as first choice or initiates another search to find alternatives.

As mentioned in Chapter 5, in an e-marketing context the differential advantage and positioning can be clarified and communicated by developing an **online value proposition (OVP)**. This is similar to a unique selling proposition, but is developed for e-commerce services. It *builds on the core proposition* for the company's services. In developing a proposition managers should identify:

- A clear differentiation of the proposition from competitors' based on product features or service quality.
- Target market segment(s) that the proposition will appeal to.
- How the proposition will be communicated to site visitors and in all marketing communications. Developing a tagline can help this.
- How the proposition is delivered across different parts of the buying process.
- How the proposition will be delivered and supported by resources.

Ideally, the e-commerce site should have an additional value proposition to further differentiate the company's products or services. The site design will also need to communicate the core proposition of the brand or products.

Having a clear online value proposition has several benefits:

- it helps distinguish an e-commerce site from its competitors' (this should be a website design objective);
- it helps provide a focus to marketing efforts and enables company staff to be clear about the purpose of the site;

Positioning

Influencing the customer's perception of a product within a marketplace.

Differential advantage

A desirable attribute of a product offering that is not currently matched by competitor offerings.

Online value proposition (OVP)

A statement of the benefits of e-commerce services that ideally should not be available in competitor offerings or offline offerings.

- if the proposition is clear it can be used for PR and word-of-mouth recommendations;
- it can be linked to the normal product propositions of a company or its product.

Variani and Vaturi (2000) have conducted a review of failures in B2C dot-com companies. They believe that many of the problems have resulted from a failure to apply established marketing orientation approaches. They summarize their guidelines as follows:

> *First identify customer needs and define a distinctive value proposition that will meet them, at a profit. The value proposition must then be delivered through the right product and service and the right channels and it must be communicated consistently. The ultimate aim is to build a strong, long-lasting brand that delivers value to the company marketing it.*

Conversely, Agrawal *et al.* (2001) suggest that the success of leading e-commerce companies is often due to matching value propositions to segments successfully.

Some of the best taglines have been developed by the start-up companies, for which the OVP is particularly important. For example:

> *'Compare. Buy. Save.'* Kelkoo (www.kelkoo.com)
> *'Earth's biggest selection.'* Amazon (www.amazon.com)

The Citibank site design (www.citibank.com) uses a range of techniques to illustrate its core proposition and OVP. The main messages are:

> *Welcome to Citibank: The one-stop solution for all your financial needs.*
> *Look for a product or service; Learn about a financial product; Find a location.*

Different OVPs can be developed for different products or different segments. For Citibank UK, the OVP for its Internet banking service is:

> *Bank whenever you want, from wherever you are. Citibank Internet Banking gives you the freedom and flexibility to manage your day-to-day finances. It's secure, convenient and very easy to use.*

Many strategic e-marketing planning decisions are based around the OVP and the quality of online customer experience delivered by a company. Interactive Web 2.0 features can be particularly important for transactional sites in that they may enhance the user's experience and so encourage conversion and repeat sales. Examples of how companies have developed their OVP through interactive features include customer reviews and ratings, podcast product reviews, a blog with customer comments enabled, buyers' guide and video reviews. Figure 8.14 gives one example of a company that has put Web 2.0 customer reviews at the heart of its OVP.

Content strategy

It is evident that a compelling OVP demands exceptional, compelling content and a compelling experience provided for customers through the website and other online presence on blogs, social networking sites and through mobile platforms. Today, by content we not only refer to the combination of static content forming web pages, but also dynamic rich media content which encourages interaction. Videos, podcasts, user-generated content and interactive product selectors should also be considered as content which should be refined to engage issues.

You can see the challenge **content strategy** presents since today there are so many different types of content delivered in different forms to different places on different access platforms, yet it is increasingly important to engage customers in social media.

The definition suggests these elements of content management that need to be planned and managed:

Content strategy
The management of text, rich media, audio and video content aimed at engaging customers and prospects to meet business goals published through print and digital media including web and mobile platforms which is repurposed and syndicated to different forms of web presence such as publisher sites, blogs, social media and comparison sites.

1 *Content engagement value.* Which types of content will engage the audience – is it simple product or services information, a guide to buying product, or a game to engage your audience?

| **Figure 8.14** | Firebox
Source: www.firebox.com. |

2 *Content media.* Plain text, rich media such as Flash or Rich Internet applications or mobile apps (see Chapter 3), audio (podcasts) and hosted and streamed video. Even plain text offers different format options from HTML text to e-book formats and PDFs.

3 *Content syndication.* Content can be syndicated to different types of site through feeds, APIs, microformats or direct submission by e-mail. Content can be embedded in sites through widgets displaying information delivered by a feed.

4 *Content participation.* Effective content today is not simply delivered for static consumption; it should enable commenting, ratings and reviews. These also need to be monitored and managed both in the original location and where they are discussed elsewhere.

5 *Content access platform.* The different digital access platforms such as desktops and laptops of different screen resolution and mobile devices. Paper is also a content access platform for print media.

It can be seen that managing the creation of quality content is part of a broader customer engagement strategy which looks at delivering effective content across the whole customer life cycle. As such it is an integral part of the CRM strategy development which we cover in more detail in the next chapter.

To help deliver a compelling OVP requires a change of mindset for many companies. They need to think more like a publisher and so invest in quality content that is superior to that of their competitors. This requires:

- Quality, compelling content – content is still king!
- Quality writers to create quality content who may be internal staff or external freelance writers.
- An editorial calendar and appropriate process to schedule and deliver the content.
- Investment in software tools to facilitate the process.
- Investment in customer research to determine the content their different audiences will engage with.
- Careful tracking of which content engages and which does not.

Pulizzi and Barrett (2010) recommend creating a content marketing roadmap which is underpinned by the BEST principles. BEST stands for:

- *Behavioural.* Does everything you communicate to customers have a purpose? What do you want them to do as a result of interacting with content?
- *Essential.* Deliver information that your best prospects need if they are to succeed at work or in life.
- *Strategic.* Your content marketing efforts must be an integral part of your overall business strategy.
- *Targeted.* You must target your content precisely so that it is truly relevant to your buyers. Different forms of content will need to be delivered through different social platforms.

It can be argued that companies already require many of the attributes of publishers to produce effective marketing campaigns. But a continuous process is needed to create compelling content for the web, mobile phones and traditional media. There are also many potential places consumers like to consume content – a blog, through news feeds, through Facebook, through Twitter or YouTube and other video options – so syndication to these other channels and management of interactions on them is also required.

Figure 8.15 shows a process using tools like RSS publication from a content management system, linked to Twitterfeed, a Twitter Facebook application and URL-shortening service Bit.ly to help with syndication.

Figure 8.15 suggests how these different content publishing and distribution options can be integrated to form a 'virtuous circle' which is more efficient for the company. Companies should also consider how differential value is offered through each channel – each needs an OVP to maximize engagement.

Once e-marketing strategies have been developed as part of the e-marketing plan, tactics need to be implemented to achieve these strategies. These tactics will be informed by the special marketing characteristics of electronic media. The *Focus on* section below summarizes some of the key differences before we review tactics.

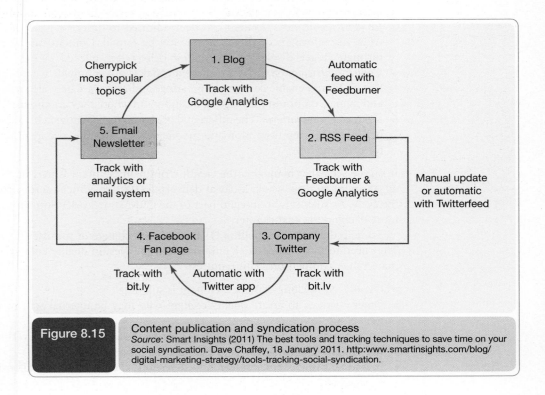

Figure 8.15

Content publication and syndication process
Source: Smart Insights (2011) The best tools and tracking techniques to save time on your social syndication. Dave Chaffey, 18 January 2011. http:www.smartinsights.com/blog/digital-marketing-strategy/tools-tracking-social-syndication.

Focus on	**Characteristics of digital media communications**

In this section, we explore the main differences between marketing communications in the traditional media such as TV, print and radio and new digital media such as websites, interactive TV and mobile commerce. This section is based on the summary presented in Chaffey (2000). Recognizing the differences between the Internet and other media is important to achieving success in channel promotion and channel satisfaction, and will lead in turn to positive channel outcomes and profitability.

A useful summary of the differences between the new media and traditional media has been developed by McDonald and Wilson (1999) as the '6 Is' of e-marketing. These highlight factors that apply to practical aspects of Internet marketing such as personalization, direct response and marketing research, but also strategic issues of industry restructuring and integrated channel communications. By considering each of these facets of the new media, marketing managers can develop marketing plans that accommodate the characteristics of the new media. This presentation of the '6 Is' is a new interpretation of these factors using new examples and diagrams to illustrate these concepts.

1 Interactivity

Deighton (1996) was one of the first authors to explain that interactivity is a key characteristic of the Internet which enables companies to communicate with customers in a new way. Figure 8.16(a) shows how traditional media are predominantly *push media* where the marketing message is broadcast from company *to* customer and other stakeholders. During this process, there is limited interaction with the customer. On the Internet, it is usually a customer who initiates contact and is *seeking* information on a website. In other words it is a **pull marketing communications** technique (but e-mail can be considered as a **push marketing communications** technique). Figure 8.16(b) shows how the Internet should be used to encourage two-way communication; these may be extensions of the direct-response approach. For example, FMCG (fast-moving consumer goods) suppliers such as Nestlé

Pull marketing communications

The consumer is proactive in interacting with companies through actively seeking information or entertainment on company websites or social media sites through search engines, comparison intermediaries or direct navigation

Push marketing communications

Communications are broadcast from an advertiser to consumers of the message who are passive recipients

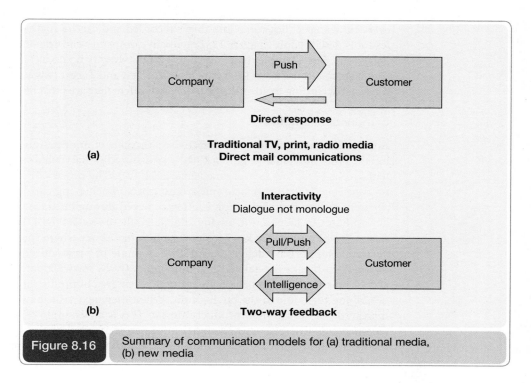

Figure 8.16	Summary of communication models for (a) traditional media, (b) new media

(www.nescafe.co.uk) use their website and social media presence as a method of generating interaction by providing incentives such as competitions and sales promotions to encourage the customer to respond with their names, addresses and profile information such as age and sex.

Hoffman and Novak (1997) realized early in the development of the web that interactivity was significant enough to represent a new model for marketing or a new marketing paradigm. They suggest that the facilities of the Internet represent a computer-mediated environment in which the interactions are not between the sender and receiver of information, but with the medium itself. They said:

> consumers can interact with the medium, firms can provide content to the medium, and in the most radical departure from traditional marketing environments, consumers can provide commercially-oriented content to the media.

The user-generated content customers can provide may be directly commercial such as auctioning of their possessions such as via eBay (www.ebay.com) or can include comments on products or suppliers on a neutral site (e.g. www.kelkoo.com) or a destination site (www.firebox.com). The *Focus on* Social media management section in Chapter 9 covers techniques for harnessing the interactivity of the web in more detail.

2 Intelligence

The Internet can be used as a relatively low-cost method of collecting marketing research, particularly about customer perceptions of products and services. In the competitions referred to above, Nestlé is able to profile its customers on the basis of the information received in questionnaires. The Internet can be used to create two-way feedback which does not usually occur in other media. Financial services provider Egg (www.egg.com) collects information about their online service levels through a questionnaire that is continuously available in the customer-service part of their site. What is significant is that the company responds via the website to the main concerns of the customer; if the length of time it takes to reply to customer-service e-mails is seen as a problem it will explain what the organization is trying to do to resolve this problem.

A wealth of marketing research information is also available from the website itself, since every time a user clicks on a link this is recorded and can be analysed with the web analytics tools described in Chapter 12. Potentially companies can respond in real time to buyer behaviour. For example, banks such as HSBC (www.hsbc.co.uk) and Lloyds TSB (www.lloydstsb.co.uk) use a service from Omniture Test and Target (www.omniture.com) to serve messages according to an evaluation of which offers they are most likely to respond to.

3 Individualization

Another important feature of interactive marketing communications is that they can be tailored to the individual (Figure 8.17(b)), unlike traditional media where the same message tends to be broadcast to everyone (Figure 8.17(a)). The process of tailoring is also referred to as *personalization* and is an important aspect of achieving customer relationship management online. Personalization is often achieved through extranets which are set up with key accounts to manage the buying and after-sales processes. Dell (www.dell.com/premier) set up 'Dell Premier' for key accounts such as the Abbey where special offers and bespoke customer support are delivered. Another example of personalization is that achieved by business-to-business e-tailer RS Components (www.rswww.com). Every customer who accesses their system is profiled according to their area of product interest and information describing their role in the buying unit. When they next visit the site information will be displayed relevant to their product interest. This is an example of what is known as *mass customization* where generic customer information is supplied for particular segments, i.e. the information is not unique to individuals, but to those with a common interest. Amazon

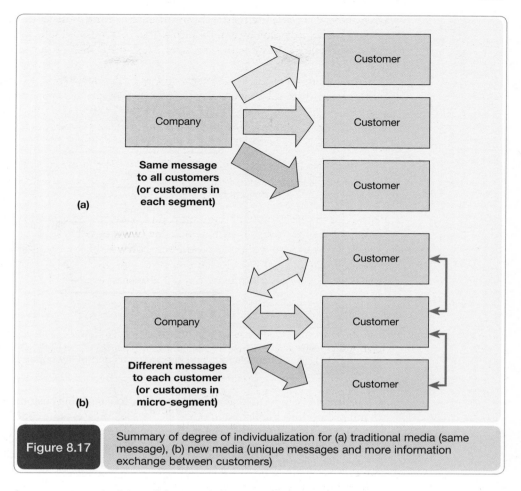

Figure 8.17	Summary of degree of individualization for (a) traditional media (same message), (b) new media (unique messages and more information exchange between customers)

(www.amazon.com) is well known for using a *collaborative filtering* approach or Amazon's 'Customers Who bought X ... also bought ... Y'. Amazon also has two other personalization features, 'Customers who shopped for X also SHOPPED for ...' and 'Customers who searched for X also BOUGHT ...' You can read about the approach that they use to achieve this in IEE (2003).

4 Integration

The Internet provides further scope for integrated marketing communications. Figure 8.18 shows how it is just one of many different media channels (these channels are also offered by intermediaries). When assessing the success of a website, the role of the Internet in communicating with customers and other partners can best be considered from two perspectives. First, organization-to-customer direction: how does the Internet complement other channels in communication of proposition for the company's products and services to new and existing customers with a view to generating new leads and retaining existing customers? Second, customer-to-organization: how can the Internet complement other channels to deliver customer service to these customers? Many companies are now considering how they integrate e-mail response and website callback into their existing call-centre or customer-service operation. This may require a substantial investment in training and new software.

Some practical examples of how the Internet can be used as an integrated communications tool are as shown by Figure 8.19 and Activity 8.3.

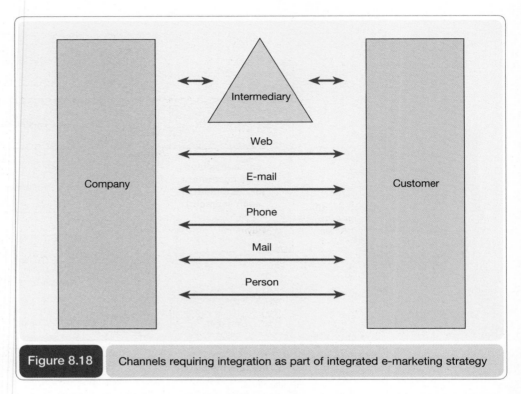

| Figure 8.18 | Channels requiring integration as part of integrated e-marketing strategy |

- The Internet can be used as a direct-response tool enabling customers to respond to offers and promotions publicized in other media. Dell uses 'e-value codes' which it publishes in magazines and offline material to direct people to specific pages (via a search) when they visit the website. CapitalOne uses a similar approach. These codes include a media code to assess which offline communications were most effective in driving sales on the website.
- The website can have a direct-response or callback facility built into it. The Automobile Association has a feature where a customer service representative will contact a customer by phone when the customer fills in their name, phone number and a suitable time to ring.
- The Internet can be used to support the buying decision even if the purchase does not occur via the website. For example, Dell has a prominent web-specific phone number on their website that encourages customers to ring a representative in the call centre to place their order. This has the benefits that Dell is less likely to lose the business of customers who are anxious about the security of online ordering and Dell can track sales that result partly from the website according to the number of callers on this line. This is alternative 3 in Figure 8.19. Changing from one channel to another during the buying process is referred to as **mixed-mode buying** or channel switching. It is a key aspect of devising online marketing communications since the customer should be supported in changing from one channel to another. Bazett *et al.* (2005) give the example of a high-street chain that estimated (through credit card tracking) that for every £1 of revenue it takes on the web, £3 are spent in-store after browsing online – so it has objectives for this and works equally hard to help these customers through facilities such as store locators and information on stock availability for that store.
- Customer information delivered on the website must be integrated with other databases of customer and order information such as those accessed via staff in the call centre to provide what Seybold (1999) calls a '360 degree view of the customer'.
- The Internet can be used to support customer service. For example, easyJet (www.easyjet. com), which receives over half its orders electronically, encourages users to check a list of frequently asked questions (FAQs) compiled from previous customer enquiries before contacting customer support via phone.

Mixed-mode buying
The process by which a customer changes between online and offline channels during the buying process.

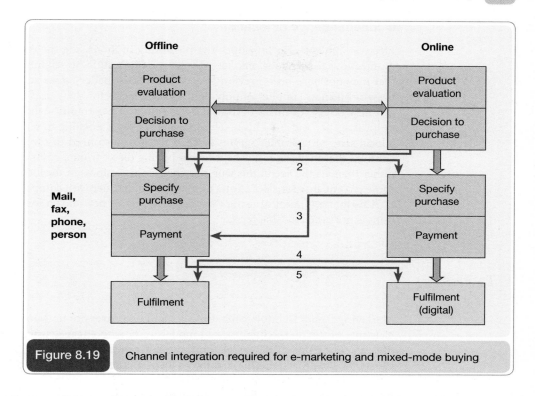

| Figure 8.19 | Channel integration required for e-marketing and mixed-mode buying |

Activity 8.3   Integrating online and offline communications

Purpose

To highlight differences in marketing communications introduced through the use of the Internet as a channel and the need to integrate these communications with existing channels.

Activity

List communications between a PC vendor and a home customer over the lifetime of a product such as a PC. Include communications using both the Internet and traditional media. Refer to channel swapping alternatives in the buying decision shown in Figure 8.19 to develop your answer.

Answers to activities can be found at www.pearsoned.co.uk/chaffey

---

5 Industry restructuring

Disintermediation, reintermediation and countermediation are key concepts of industry restructuring that should be considered by any company developing an e-marketing strategy (see Chapters 2 and 4). For the marketer defining their company's communications strategy it becomes very important to consider the company's representation on these intermediary sites by answering questions such as 'Which intermediaries should we be represented on?' and 'How do our offerings compare to those of competitors in terms of features, benefits and price?'

6 Independence of location

Electronic media also introduce the possibility of increasing the reach of company communications to the global market. This gives opportunities to sell into international markets that may not have been previously accessible. Scott Bader (www.scottbader.com), a business-to-business supplier of polymers and chemicals for the paints and coatings industry, can now target countries beyond the forty or so it has traditionally sold to via a network of local agents and franchises. The Internet makes it possible to sell to a country without a local sales or customer service force. Strategists also need to carefully consider channel conflicts that may arise. If a customer is buying direct from a company in another country rather than via the agent, this will marginalize the business of the local agent who may want some recompense for sales efforts or may look to partner with competitors.

A further appraisal of using the characteristics of new media for effective communications is presented in Chapter 9.

Tactics

Marketing tactics to implement strategies and objectives are traditionally based around the elements of the marketing mix and models of how to engage customers throughout their life cycle as part of customer relationship management. In Chapter 9, we will review the life cycle-based approach. In this chapter we focus on the marketing mix.

The marketing mix – the 4Ps of Product, Price, Place and Promotion originally proposed by Jerome McCarthy (1960) – is still used as an essential part of implementing marketing strategy by many practitioners. The 4Ps have been extended to the 7Ps by including three further elements that better reflect service delivery: People, Processes and Physical evidence (Booms and Bitner, 1981), although others argue that these are subsumed within the 4Ps. The marketing mix is applied frequently when developing marketing strategies since it provides a simple framework like that shown in Figure 8.20 for varying different elements of the offering to influence the demand for products within target markets. For example, to increase sales of a product the price can be decreased or the amount or type of promotion changed, or there can be some combination of these elements.

E-commerce provides new opportunities for the marketer to vary the marketing mix which have been summarized well by Allen and Fjermestad (2001).

Using the internet to vary the marketing mix

Product	Promotion	Price	Place	People	Process	Physical evidence
• Quality	• Marketing communications	• Positioning	• Trade channels	• Individuals on marketing activities	• Customer focus	• Sales/staff contact experience of brand
• Image	• Personal promotion	• List	• Sales support	• Individuals on customer contact	• Business-led	• Product packaging
• Branding	• Sales promotion	• Discounts	• Channel number	• Recruitment	• IT-supported	• Online experience
• Features	• PR	• Credit	• Segmented channels	• Culture/ image	• Design features	
• Variants	• Branding	• Payment methods		• Training and skills	• Research and development	
• Mix	• Direct marketing	• Free or value-added elements		• Remuneration		
• Support						
• Customer service						
• Use occasion						
• Availability						
• Warranties						

Figure 8.20   The elements of the marketing mix

There are some well-known criticisms of applying the marketing mix as a solitary tool for marketing strategy. First, the marketing mix is symptomatic of a push approach to marketing and does not explicitly acknowledge the needs of customers. As a consequence, the marketing mix tends to lead to a product rather than a customer orientation. To mitigate this effect, Lautenborn (1990) suggested the 4Cs framework which considers the 4Ps from a customer perspective. In an e-commerce context the 4Cs can be interpreted as follows:

- Customer needs and wants (from the product) – the website is a mechanism for explaining how the product proposition meets these needs and wants.
- Cost to the customer (price) – online the customer is likely to be comparing prices to other websites and traditional purchasing sources.
- Convenience (relative to place) – online this is the quality of customer experience in terms of the ordering process and fulfilment.
- Communication (promotion) – the website itself coupled with the methods of driving traffic to the site, such as search-engine marketing and e-mail marketing as described in Chapter 9.

The long tail concept

A frequency distribution suggesting the relative variation in popularity of items selected by consumers.

It follows that the selection of the marketing mix is based on detailed knowledge of buyer behaviour collected through market research. Furthermore, it should be remembered that the mix is often adjusted according to different target markets or segments. An increased focus on 'one-to-one marketing' which means tailoring of the offer for specific customers also sits uncomfortably within the 7Ps framework.

The **long tail concept** is useful for considering the role of Product, Place, Price and Promotion online as explained in Box 8.2.

Box 8.2	Applying the long tail concept

The phenomenon now referred to as the 'long tail', following an article by Anderson (2004), was arguably first applied to human behaviour by George Kingsley Zipf, professor of linguistics at Harvard, who observed the phenomenon in word usage (see http://en.wikipedia.org/wiki/Zipf%27s_law). He found that if the variation in popularity of different words in a language is considered, there is a systematic pattern in the frequency of usage or popularity. Zipf's 'law' suggests that if a collection of items is ordered or ranked by popularity, the second item will have around half the popularity of the first one and the third item will have about a third of the popularity of the first one and so on. In general:

The kth item is 1/k the popularity of the first.

Look at Figure 8.21 which shows how the 'relative popularity' of items is predicted to decline according to Zipf's law from a maximum count of 1,000 for the most popular item to 20 for the 50th item.

In an online context, application of this 'law' is now known as 'the long tail' thanks to Anderson (2004). It can be applied to the relative popularity of a group of websites or web pages or products on an individual site, since they tend to show a similar pattern of popularity. There are a small number of sites (or pages within sites) which are very popular (the head which may account for 80% of the volume) and a much larger number of sites or pages that are less popular individually, but still collectively important. Returning to the product context, Anderson (2004) argued that for a company such as Amazon, the long tail or Zipf's law can be applied to describe the variation in preferences for selecting or purchasing from a choice for products as varied as books, CDs, electronic items, travel or financial services. This pattern has also been identified by Brynjolfsson *et al.* (2003) who present a framework that quantifies the economic impact of increased product variety made available through electronic markets. They say:

> *One reason for increased product variety on the Internet is the ability of online retailers to catalog, recommend, and provide a large number of products for sale. For example, the number of book titles available at Amazon.com is more than 23 times larger than the number of books on the shelves of a typical Barnes & Noble superstore, and 57 times greater than the number of books stocked in a typical large independent bookstore.*

Looking at the issue from another perspective, they estimate that 40% of sales are from relatively obscure books with a sales rank of more than 100,000 (if you visit Amazon, you will see that every book has a sales rank from 1 for the most popular to over 1 million for the least popular). This indicates the importance of the long tail for online retailers like Amazon, since 40% of sales are from these less popular books which cannot be stocked in a conventional bookstore (a large real-world bookstore would typically hold 100,000 books). In a pricing context, another benefit for online retailers is that less popular products cannot be readily obtained in the real world, so Amazon can justify higher prices for these books. Brynjolfsson *et al.* (2003) estimated that average Amazon prices for an item in the top 100,000 is $29.26 and in less popular titles $41.60.

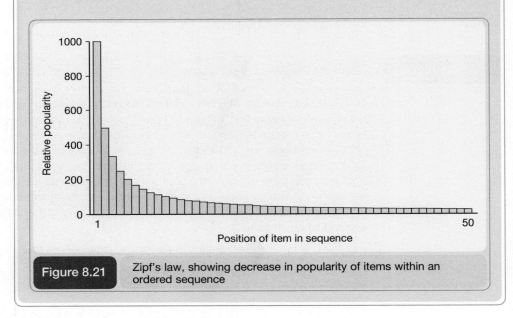

Figure 8.21   Zipf's law, showing decrease in popularity of items within an ordered sequence

Product variable
The element of the marketing mix that involves researching customers' needs and developing appropriate products.

Core product
The fundamental features of the product that meet the user's needs.

Extended product
Additional features and benefits beyond the core product.

Product

There are many alternatives for varying the **product** when a company is developing its online strategy. Internet-related product decisions can be usefully divided into decisions affecting the **core product** and the **extended product**. For some companies, there may be options for new digital products which will typically be information products that can be delivered over the web. In some cases, the core product offering has been replaced by information about the product. For example, a company providing oil-drilling equipment focusing instead on analysis and dissemination of information about drilling. In some cases, an online version of the product may be more valuable to customers in that it can be updated more regularly. The advertising directory BRAD (www.brad.co.uk) has been changed from a large paper-based document to an online version with searching facilities that were not available in the paper-based version. The Internet also introduces options for **mass customization** of products. Levi's provided a truly personal service that dates back to 1994, when Levi Strauss initiated its 'Personal Pair' programme. Women who were prepared to pay more than $15 more than the standard price and wait for delivery could go to Levi's stores and have themselves measured.

Companies can also consider how the Internet can be used to change the range or combination of products offered. Some companies only offer a subset of products online; others may have a fuller catalogue available online than is available through offline brochures. **Bundling** is a further alternative. For example, easyJet has developed a range of complementary travel-related services including flights, packages and car hire.

For many companies, using the Internet to vary the extended product is most practical. Chaffey and Smith (2008) suggest these examples of how the Internet can be used to vary the extended product:

- Endorsements
- Awards
- Testimonies
- Customer lists
- Customer comments
- Warranties
- Guarantees
- Money-back offers
- Customer service (see People, Process and Physical evidence)
- Incorporating tools to help users during their use of the product. Options for digital products.

Companies such as publishers, TV companies and other media owners who can offer digital products such as published content, music or videos now have great flexibility to offer a range of product purchase options at different price points including:

- **Subscription**. This is a traditional publisher revenue model, but subscription can potentially be offered for different periods at different price points, e.g. 3 months, 12 months or 2 years.
- **Pay-per-view**. A fee for a single download or viewing session at a higher relative price than the subscription service. Music service Napster offers vouchers for download in a similar way to a mobile company 'pay as you go' model. Travel publisher Lonely Planet enables visitors to a destination to download an introduction for a fraction of the price of a full printed guide.
- **Bundling**. Different channels or content can be offered as individual products or grouped at a reduced price compared to pay per view.
- **Ad-supported content**. The publisher's main revenue source is through adverts on the site (CPM display advertising using banners ads and skyscrapers, a fixed sponsorship arrangement or CPC, which stands for 'cost per click'). Other options include affiliate revenue from sales on third-party sites or offering access to subscriber lists. The UK's most popular newspaper site, *The Guardian* (www.guardian.co.uk), once trialled an ad-free subscription service, but it, like many online publishers, has reverted to ad-supported content.

Also related to the product element of the mix is how the Internet can be used to assist in new product development by assessing product needs from website logs (Chapter 12), testing new concepts, online surveys and focus groups.

Quelch and Klein (1996) also noted that the implication of the Internet and globalization is that to remain competitive, organizations will have to roll out new products more rapidly to international markets. More recently, Malcolm Gladwell in his book *The Tipping Point* (2000) has shown how word-of-mouth communication has a tremendous impact on the rate of adoption of new products and we can suggest this effect is often enhanced or facilitated through the Internet. The implications of the tipping point are discussed in Box 8.3.

Mass customization
Using economies of scale enabled by technology to offer tailored versions of products to individual customers or groups of customers.

Bundling
Offering complementary services.

Box 8.3	How does the tipping point apply to digital marketing?

Marsden (2004) provides a good summary of the implications of the **tipping point** for marketers. He says that 'using the science of social epidemics, *The Tipping Point* explains the three simple principles that underpin the rapid spread of ideas, products and behaviours through a population'. He advises how marketers should help create a 'tipping point' for a new product or service, the moment when a domino effect is triggered and an epidemic of demand sweeps through a population like a highly contagious virus.

There are three main laws that are relevant from *The Tipping Point*:

1 The law of the few

This suggests that the spread of any new product or service is dependent on the initial adoption by 'connectors' who are socially connected and who encourage adoption through word-of-mouth and copycat behaviour. In an online context, these connectors may use personal blogs, e-mail newsletters and podcasts to propagate their opinions.

2 The stickiness factor

Typically, this refers to how 'glued' we are to a medium such as a TV channel or a website, but in this context it refers to attachment to the characteristics and attributes of a product or a brand. Gladwell stresses the importance of testing and market research to make the product effective. Marsden suggests that there are key cross-category attributes which are key drivers for product success and he commends the work of Morris and Martin (2000) which summarizes these attributes as:

- *Excellence*: perceived as best of breed
- *Uniqueness*: clear one-of-a-kind differentiation
- *Aesthetics*: perceived aesthetic appeal
- *Association*: generates positive associations
- *Engagement*: fosters emotional involvement
- *Expressive value*: visible sign of user values
- *Functional value*: addresses functional needs
- *Nostalgic value*: evokes sentimental linkages
- *Personification*: has character, personality
- *Cost*: perceived value for money.

You can see that this list is also a useful prompt about the ideal characteristics of a website or online service.

3 The power of context

Gladwell suggests that like infectious diseases, products and behaviours spread far and wide only when they fit the physical, social and mental context into which they are launched. He gives the example of a wave of crime in the New York subway that came to an abrupt halt by simply removing the graffiti from trains and clamping down on fare-dodging. It can be suggested that products should be devised and tested to fit their context, situation or occasion of use.

Case study 8.2 shows how Dell has revised its marketing mix through deep customer understanding.

Case Study 8.2 | Dell gets closer to its customers online

Dell is a technology company, offering a broad range of product categories, including desktop computer systems, storage, servers and networking products, mobility products, software and peripherals and services to manage IT infrastructure for large organizations. Dell are the number one supplier of personal computer systems in the United States, and the number two supplier worldwide.

Dell proposition

The main Dell product offerings are:

1 *Desktop PCs*. Five lines of desktop computer systems are produced for different markets. For example, the OptiPlex line is designed to help business, government, and institutional customers manage their total cost of ownership by offering stability, security, and managed product transitions; the Dimension line is designed for small businesses and home users requiring the latest features for their productivity and entertainment needs. The XPS tm and Alienware lines are targeted at customers who require the highest-performance gaming or entertainment experience available. In July 2007, Dell introduced the Vostro™ line, which is designed to provide technology and services to suit the specific needs of small businesses.

2 *Servers and networking*. The PowerEdge™ line of servers is designed to offer customers affordable performance, reliability, and scalability. Again different options are available for different markets including high performance rack, blade, and tower servers for enterprise customers and lower priced tower servers for small organizations, networks, and remote offices.

3 *Storage*. For example, storage area networks, network-attached storage, direct-attached storage, disk and tape back-up systems, and removable disk back-up.

4 *Mobility*. Notebook computers are targeted at customers who require the highest performance gaming or entertainment experience available.

5 *Software and peripherals*. Office software and hardware including printers, televisions, notebook accessories, networking and wireless products, digital cameras, power adapters, scanners, and other products.

6 *Enhanced services*. Tailored solutions that help customers lower the cost of their services environment and maximize system performance, efficiency, and

return on investment. These include: Infrastructure Consulting Services; Deployment Services to install and integrate new systems; Asset Recovery and Recycling Services; Training Services; Enterprise Support Services and Managed Life Cycle Services (outsourced IT management).

7 *Financial services* for business and consumer customers in the US through a joint venture between Dell and CIT Group, Inc.

Dell business strategy

Dell's vision is to:

strive to provide the best possible customer experience by offering superior value; high-quality, relevant technology; customized systems; superior service and support; and differentiated products and services that are easy to buy and use.

The core elements of the strategy which are evident in Dell's marketing communications are:

- 'We simplify information technology for customers. Making quality personal computers, servers, storage, and services affordable is Dell's legacy. We are focused on making information technology affordable for millions of customers around the world. As a result of our direct relationships with customers, or "customer intimacy", we are best positioned to simplify how customers implement and maintain information technology and deliver hardware, services, and software solutions tailored for their businesses and homes.

- *We offer customers choice.* Customers can purchase systems and services from Dell via telephone, kiosks, and our website, www.dell.com, where they may review, configure, and price systems within our entire product line; order systems online; and track orders from manufacturing through shipping. We have recently launched a retail initiative and plan to expand that initiative by adding new distribution channels to reach additional consumers and small businesses through retail partners and value-added resellers globally.

- *Customers can purchase custom-built products and custom-tailored services.* Historically our flexible, build-to-order manufacturing process enabled us to turn over inventory every five days on average, thereby reducing inventory levels, and rapidly bring the latest technology to our customers. The market and our competition has evolved, and we are ▶

now exploring the utilization of original design manufacturers and new distribution strategies to better meet customer needs and reduce product cycle times. Our goal is to introduce the latest relevant technology more quickly and to rapidly pass on component cost savings to a broader set of our customers worldwide.

- *We are committed to being environmentally responsible in all areas of our business*. We have built environmental consideration into every stage of the Dell product life cycle – from developing and designing energy-efficient products, to reducing the footprint of our manufacturing and operations, to customer use and product recovery.'

Dell's sales and marketing

Dell sells products and services directly to customers through dedicated sales representatives, telephone-based sales, and online at www.dell.com.

Customer segments include large corporate, government, healthcare, and education accounts, as well as small-to-medium businesses and individual consumers.

Dell stresses the importance of its direct business model in providing direct and continuous feedback from customers, thereby allowing them to develop and refine their products and marketing programs for specific customer groups.

In its SEC filing Dell emphasizes how it listens to customers to develop relevant innovative technology and services they trust and value. Evidence for using the participative nature of Web 2.0 is that customers can offer suggestions for current and future Dell products, services, and operations on an interactive portion of the Dell website called Dell IdeaStorm. It says: '*This constant flow of communication, which is unique to our direct business model, also allows us to rapidly gauge customer satisfaction and target new or existing products*.'

For large business and institutional customers, Dell maintains a field sales force throughout the world. Dedicated account teams, which include field-based system engineers and consultants, form long-term relationships to provide their largest customers with a single source of assistance and develop specific tailored solutions for these customers. Dell also maintains specific sales and marketing programs targeted at federal, state, and local governmental agencies as well as specific healthcare and educational markets.

Dell Premier

For its large organizational customers, Dell offers Premier (http://premier.dell.com) which is a secure, customizable procurement and support site or extranet designed to save organizations time and money through all phases of IT product ownership. The main benefits of Dell Premier are described as:

- *Easy Ordering* – A custom online store ensures access to your products at your price.
- *Easy Tracking* – View real-time order status, online invoices and purchase history details.
- *Easy Control* – Custom access groups define what users can see and do within Premier.

Marketing communications

Dell markets its products and services to small-to-medium businesses and consumers primarily by advertising on television and the Internet, advertising in a variety of print media, and by mailing a broad range of direct marketing publications, such as promotional pieces, catalogs, and customer newsletters. In certain locations, they also operate Dell stores or kiosks, typically located within shopping centers, that allow customers to view their products in person and purchase online with the assistance of a Dell expert.

Dell online communications

The management of the consumer site was presented to E-consultancy (2008). Dell has a three-stage order funnel:

- Marketing communications execution measured by site visits
- Site merchandising measured by *consideration* % (site visits to e-store visits)
- Store merchandising measured by *conversion* % (e-store visits to e-receipts).

The presenter explained how Dell aims to understand and act on customer behaviour based on identification of a series of consideration drivers, for example, the quality of online advertising; path quality through site; merchandising/offers and conversion drivers, for example, configurator 'ease of use'; accessibility of decision support tools and consistency of message through entire path.

Dell will invest in strategic improvements to the site to improve these levers; examples mentioned included new merchandising approaches such as customer ratings and reviews, videos, major 'path' or customer journey changes created through decision support tools to 'help me choose'. There are also more tactical initiatives to help deliver the right message to each customer including customization/personalization, real estate optimization and message balancing.

More tactical persuasion of site visitors is based on price moves/optimized price position to market and the mix of product features. A wide range of different offers need to be managed. Tactical promotions are driven by promotional 'end dates' which are weekly or bi-weekly and include varying:

- Free shipping
- Money off discounts
- Free upgrades (e.g. memory)
- Free accessories
- Finance offers
- Service upgrades.

The presenter also noted how across Europe, the promotional mix has to vary to reflect the differences in buying psychology. He summarizes the main differences between customers as follows:

- UK – all about price
- CH – add value over price
- DE – all about high-end products in mix
- IT – design is important (!)
- DK – cheap is good
- NO – added value is key
- FR – tailored for France.

Dell's use of digital media channels

The main digital media channels used by Dell.com in Europe are:

- Paid search through programmes such as Google AdWords is used to promote value through time limited offers related to the phrase searched upon.
- Display advertising – for example advertising on technology websites is particularly important for the corporate market.

- Affiliate marketing – used to protect the Dell brand by enabling affiliates to bid on terms such as 'Dell laptops' and to target niche audiences such as owners of gaming machines.
- E-mail marketing – an e-newsletter is used to keep in touch with existing customers and deliver targeted offers when their hardware may be renewed.

Dell and indirect channels

Although the focus of Dell's business strategy has been selling directly to its customers, it also uses some indirect sales channels when there is a business need. In the US it sells products indirectly through third-party solution providers, system integrators, and third-party resellers. During financial year 2008, Dell began offering Dimension desktop computers and Inspiron notebook computers in retail stores in the Americas and announced partnerships with retailers in the UK, Japan, and China. Dell says: *'These actions represent the first steps in our retail strategy, which will allow us to extend our business model and reach customers that we have not been able to reach directly.'*

Source: Security Exchange Commission filing 10-K for Dell, 2007.

> ### Question
>
> Describe approaches used by Dell within their site design and promotion to deliver relevant offers for different types of online customers.

Price

Price variable

The element of the marketing mix that involves defining product prices and pricing models.

Pricing models

Describe the form of payment such as outright purchase, auction, rental, volume purchase and credit terms.

The **price** element of the marketing mix refers to an organization's pricing policies which are used to define **pricing models** and, of course, to set prices for products and services. The Internet has dramatic implications for pricing in many sectors and there is a lot of literature in this area. Baker *et al.* (2001) and more recently Xing *et al.* (2006) have noted two approaches that have been commonly adopted for pricing on the Internet. Start-up companies have tended to use low prices to gain a customer base, while many existing companies have transferred their existing prices to the web. However, Case study 8.1 showed how easyJet discounted online prices in an effort to meet its objectives of online revenue contribution. In this case, price reduction was possible because of the lower overhead of processing a customer transaction online in comparison with on the phone. Similarly, to acquire customers online booksellers may decide to offer a discount of 50% on the top 25 best-selling books in each category, for which no profit is made, but offer a relatively small discount on the less popular books of the long tail to give a profit margin.

The main implications of the Internet for the Price aspect of the mix are as follows.

1 Increased price transparency and its implications on differential pricing

Quelch and Klein (1996) describe two contradictory effects of the Internet on price that are related to price transparency. First, a supplier can use the technology for differential pricing, for example customers in different countries. However, if precautions are not taken about price, the customers may be able to quickly find out about the price discrimination and they will object to it. So, customer knowledge of pricing is enhanced through the Internet. This is particularly the case for standardized goods sold through online retailers. Not only can customers visit sites of rival suppliers, they can visit sites of price-comparison engines. It is difficult to retain price differentials if all customers are aware of these differences. Currently, this is probably not the case. However, research quoted by Baker *et al.* (2001) suggests that only around 8% of active online consumers are 'aggressive price shoppers'. Furthermore, they note that Internet price brands have remained quite broad. Online booksellers' prices varied by an average of 33% and CD sellers' by 25%.

There appear to be two main reasons for this: first, pricing is only one variable – consumers also decide on suppliers according to other aspects about the brand such as familiarity, trust and perceived service levels. Secondly, consumers often display **satisficing behaviour**. The term 'satisfice' was coined by Herbert Simon in 1957 when he said that people are only 'rational enough' and that they suspend or relax their rationality if they feel it is no longer required. This is called 'bounded rationality' by cognitive psychologists. In other words, although consumers may seek to minimize some variable (such as price) when making a product or supplier selection, most may not try too hard. Online, this is supported by research by Johnson *et al.* (2004) who showed that by analysing panel data from over 10,000 Internet households and three commodity-like products (books, CDs and air travel services) the amount of online search is actually quite limited. On average, households visit only 1.2 book sites, 1.3 CD sites and 1.8 travel sites during a typical active month in each category. Of course, these averages will reflect a range of behaviour.

A compromise approach used by many companies is to use differential pricing with lower prices or Internet offers for some of their products online. This has been the approach followed by online electrical retailers such as Comet (www.comet.co.uk), travel companies such as Thomson (www.thomson.co.uk) and companies with e-savings products.

Pricing online has to take into account the concept of **price elasticity of demand**. This is a measure of consumer behaviour based on economic theory that indicates the change in demand for a product or service in response to changes in price. Price elasticity of demand is determined by the price of the product, availability of alternative goods from alternative suppliers (which tends to increase online) and consumer income. A product is said to be 'elastic' (or responsive to price changes) if a small change in price increases or reduces the demand substantially. A product is 'inelastic' if a large change in price is accompanied by a small amount of change in demand. More details on price elasticity of demand are given in Box 8.4.

Satisficing behaviour
Consumers do not behave entirely rationally in product or supplier selection. They will compare alternatives, but then may make their choice given imperfect information.

Price elasticity of demand
Measure of consumer behaviour that indicates the change in demand for a product or service in response to changes in price.

Box 8.4	Price elasticity of demand

Price elasticity of demand assesses the extent to which a change in price will influence the demand for a product. It is calculated as the change in quantity demanded (expressed as a percentage divided by the change in price as a percentage). Different products will naturally have different coefficients of price elasticity of demand depending on where they lie on the continuum of consumer tastes from relatively undifferentiated commodities to luxury, highly differentiated products where the brand perception is important.

The formula for the price elasticity of demand is:

$$\text{Price Elasticity of Demand coefficient} = \frac{\%\ \text{Change in Quantity Demanded}}{\%\ \text{Change in Price}}$$

Price elasticity for products is generally described as:

- Elastic (*coefficient of price elasticity > 1*). Here, the percentage change in quantity demanded is greater than the percentage change in price. In elastic demand, the demand curve is relatively shallow and a small percentage increase in price leads to a reduction in revenue. On balance overall, when the price is raised, the total revenue of producers or retailers falls since the rise in revenue does not compensate for the fall in demand and when the price is decreased total revenue rises because the income from additional customers compensates in the decrease in revenue from reduced prices. Figure 8.22 shows the demand curve for a relatively elastic product (price elasticity = 1.67).

- Inelastic demand (*coefficient of price elasticity < 1*). Here, the percentage change in quantity demanded is smaller than the percentage change in price. In inelastic demand, the demand curve is relatively steep and a small percentage increase in price causes a small decrease in demand. On balance overall revenue increases as the price increases and falls as the price falls. Figure 8.23 shows the demand curve for a relatively inelastic product (price elasticity = 0.3125).

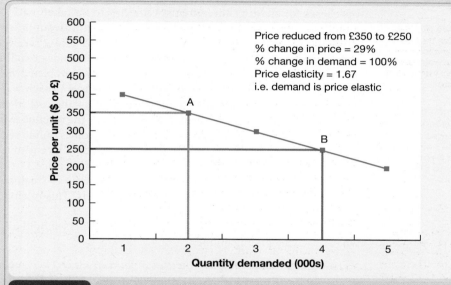

Price reduced from £350 to £250
% change in price = 29%
% change in demand = 100%
Price elasticity = 1.67
i.e. demand is price elastic

| Figure 8.22 | Price elasticity of demand for a relatively elastic product |

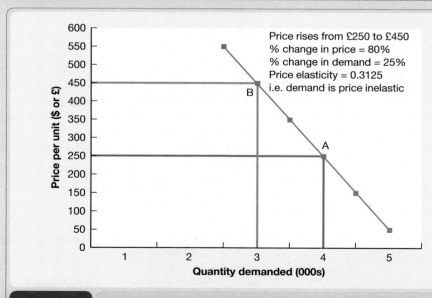

Price rises from £250 to £450
% change in price = 80%
% change in demand = 25%
Price elasticity = 0.3125
i.e. demand is price inelastic

| Figure 8.23 | Price elasticity of demand for a relatively inelastic product |

2 Downward pressure on price (including commoditization)

For business commodities, auctions on business-to-business exchanges (e.g. Emiliani, 2001) can also have a similar effect of driving down price. Many companies, such as GlaxoSmith-Kline (pharmaceuticals), Whitbread (entertainment and leisure) and DaimlerChrysler (automotive), have reported that price has been decreased by 10% or more using reverse auctions (see Case study 2.1). Purchase of some products that have not traditionally been thought of as commodities may become more price-sensitive. This process is known as '**commoditization**'. Goods that are becoming commoditized include electrical goods and cars.

Commoditization
The process whereby product selection becomes more dependent on price than on differentiating features, benefits and value-added services.

3 New pricing approaches (including dynamic pricing and auctions)

In addition to the auctions described above, the Internet introduces new opportunities for **dynamic pricing**, for example new customers could be automatically given discounted purchases for the first three items. Care has to be taken with differential pricing since established customers will be unhappy if significant discounts are given to new customers. Amazon trialled such a discounting scheme in 2000 and it received negative press and had to be withdrawn when people found out that their friends or colleagues had paid less. If the scheme had been a clear introductory promotion this problem might not have arisen.

Dynamic pricing
Prices can be updated in real time according to the type of customer or current market conditions.

A further approach is **aggregated buying**. This approach was promoted by LetsBuyit.com, but the business model did not prove viable – the cost of creating awareness for the brand and explaining the concept was not offset by the revenue from each transaction.

Aggregated buying
A form of customer union where buyers collectively purchase a number of items at the same price and receive a volume discount.

Baye *et al.* (2007) reported that European electronics online retailer Pixmania (www.pixmania.com) used price experimentation to learn about its customers' price sensitivity. They noted that for a PDA, Pixmania adjusted its product price 11 times in a 14-week period, from a low of £268 to a high of £283 as part of a series of small experiments that enabled it to learn about the price sensitivities of its customers. This pricing strategy also provides an additional strategic benefit – unpredictability.

Baye *et al.* (2007) recommend that online retailers should ask the following questions when reviewing pricing online:

1 *How many competitors are there at a point in time?* They suggest a product's mark-up should be increased when the number of rivals falls and decreased when the number of rivals increases. They also recommend that since the identity of competitors online will differ from traditional offline rivals it is important to include key online competitors.
2 *What is the position in the product life cycle?* A product's mark-up should be decreased over its life cycle or when new versions are introduced.
3 *What is the price sensitivity or elasticity of a product?* They suggest continuously experimenting to learn changes in the price sensitivity of a product.
4 *At what level is pricing set?* The optimal mark-up factor should be applied at the product rather than category or firm level based on price testing at the product level. They also note the variation of conversion rates and clickthrough fees from paid search engines and aggregators at the category or product level, which makes it important to have micromanagement of pricing.
5 *Are rivals monitoring my price?* Be unpredictable if rivals are watching. Exploit 'blind spots' if rivals are not watching.
6 *Are we stuck in the middle?* A middle pricing point is sub-optimal particularly if prices can be set to target the lowest point in the market.

4 Alternative pricing structure or policies

Different types of pricing may be possible on the Internet, particularly for digital, downloadable products. Software and music have traditionally been sold for a continuous right to use. The Internet offers new options such as payment per use, rental at a fixed cost per month or a lease arrangement. Bundling options may also be more possible. The use of software-as-a-service (SaaS) (Chapter 3) providers to deliver services such as website traffic monitoring also gives new methods of volume pricing. Web analytics companies such as Omniture (www.omniture.com) and Clicktracks (www.clicktracks.com) charge in price bands based on the number of visitors to the purchaser's site.

Further pricing options which could be varied online include:

- Basic price
- Discounts
- Add-ons and extra products and services
- Guarantees and warranties
- Refund policies
- Order cancellation terms.

Place

Place

The element of the marketing mix that involves distributing products to customers in line with demand and minimizing cost of inventory, transport and storage.

Allen and Fjermestad (2001) argue that the Internet has the greatest implications for **place** in the marketing mix since the Internet has a global reach. However, due to cost and time of international fulfilment together with issues of trust in the local country and the availability of phone support, most products are still sourced locally. The exception to this is digital products where there is no physical limitation on fulfilment, so for example Apple iTunes has proved successful in offering this service worldwide. The main implications of the Internet for the place aspect of the mix, which we will review in this section, are:

1 Place of purchase

In a B2B context, e-commerce is conducted on the manufacturer's own site, at an intermediary or is procured on a customer's site (Chapter 2, p. 64).

2 New channel structures

New channel structures such as changes introduced by disintermediation, reintermediation and countermediation referred to in Chapter 2 (pp. 62–3) and Chapter 5 (p. 286).

3 Channel conflicts

A significant threat arising from the introduction of an Internet channel is that while disintermediation gives a company the opportunity to sell direct and increase profitability on products, it can also threaten distribution arrangements with existing partners. Such channel conflicts are described by Frazier (1999), and need to be carefully managed. Frazier (1999) identifies some situations when the Internet should only be used as a communications channel. This is particularly the case where manufacturers offer an exclusive, or highly selective, distribution approach. To take an example, a company manufacturing expensive watches costing thousands of pounds will not in the past have sold direct, but will have used a wholesaler to distribute watches via retailers. If this wholesaler is a major player in watch distribution, then it is powerful, and will react against the watch manufacturer selling direct. The wholesaler may even refuse to act as distributor and may threaten to distribute only a competitor's watches, which are not available over the Internet.

Further channel conflicts involve other stakeholders including sales representatives and customers. Sales representatives may see the Internet as a direct threat to their livelihood. In some cases, such as Avon cosmetics and *Encyclopaedia Britannica*, this has proved to be the case with this sales model being partly or completely replaced by the Internet. For many B2B purchases, sales representatives remain an essential method of reaching the customer to support them in the purchase decision. Here, the Internet can be used as a sales support and customer education tool. Customers who do not use the online channels may also respond negatively if lower prices are available to their online counterparts. This is less serious than other types of channel conflict.

Internet channels can take these forms:

- a communication channel only;
- a distribution channel to intermediaries;

- a direct sales channel to customers;
- any combination of the above.

To avoid channel conflicts, the appropriate combination of channels must be arrived at.

Internet channel strategy will, of course, depend on the existing arrangements for the market. If a geographical market is new and there are no existing agents or distributors, there is unlikely to be channel conflict, in that there is a choice of distribution through the Internet only or appointments of new agents to support Internet sales, or a combination of the two. Often SMEs will attempt to use the Internet to sell products without appointing agents, but this strategy will only be possible for retail products that need limited pre-sales and after-sales support. For higher-value products such as engineering equipment, which will require skilled sales staff to support the sale and after-sales servicing, agents will have to be appointed.

For existing geographical markets in which a company already has a mechanism for distribution in the form of agents and distributors, the situation is more complex, and there is the threat of channel conflict.

4 Virtual organizations

The concept of virtual organizations was introduced in Chapter 6. From an e-marketing perspective, the Internet provides new options for forming partnerships to mutually benefit all parties.

Referring to small and medium businesses, Azumah *et al.* (2005) indicate three levels of development towards what they term an e-organization:

1 Half-fusion organizations (minimum use of the Internet and network technologies);
2 Fusion organization (committed and intensive use of the Internet and network technologies).
3 E-organization (uses technologies as the core of the business for managing the entire business processes).

Place tactics will have to review all the types of opportunities and threats described above and decide which are appropriate. Issues in distribution and fulfilment are described in Chapter 6.

Promotion

Promotion

The element of the marketing mix that involves communication with customers and other stakeholders to inform them about the product and the organization.

Specification of the **promotion** is usually part of a communications strategy. This will include selection of target markets, positioning and integration of different communications tools. The Internet offers a new marketing communications channel to inform customers of the benefits of a product and assist in the buying decision. The main elements of the promotional or communications mix and their online equivalents summarized by Chaffey and Smith (2008) are shown in Table 8.8:

One approach for developing promotion tactics is to specify the communications techniques required for different stages of the buying. Another approach is to look at how the Internet can supplement the range of promotional activities such as advertising, sales promotions, PR and direct marketing. These approaches are discussed in Chapter 9, where we also look at how customers can be persuaded to return to a site for future purchases.

The promotion element of the marketing plan also requires three important decisions about investment:

1 *Investment in promotion compared to site creation and maintenance.* Since there is often a fixed budget for site creation, maintenance and promotion, the e-marketing plan should specify the budget for each to ensure there is a sensible balance.
2 *Investment in online promotion techniques in comparison to offline promotion.* A balance must be struck between these techniques. Figure 8.24 summarizes the tactical options that companies have. Which do you think would be the best option for an established

Table 8.8	The main elements of the promotional mix

Communications tool	Online implementation
1 Advertising	Interactive display ads, pay per click search advertising
2 Selling	Virtual sales staff, site merchandising, chat and affiliate marketing
3 Sales promotion	Incentives such as coupons, rewards, online loyalty schemes
4 Public relations	Online editorial, blogs, feeds, e-newsletters, newsletters, social networks, links and viral campaigns
5 Sponsorship	Sponsoring an online event, site or service
6 Direct mail	Opt-in e-mail using e-newsletters and e-blasts (stand-alone e-mails)
7 Exhibitions	Virtual exhibitions and White Paper distribution
8 Merchandising	Promotional ad serving on retail sites, personalized recommendations and e-alerts
9 Packaging	Virtual tours, real packaging is displayed online
10 Word-of-mouth	Viral, affiliate marketing, e-mail a friend, links

company as compared to a dot-com company? It seems that in both cases, offline promotion investment often exceeds that for online promotion investment.

There will naturally be a variation in spend on online marketing tools depending upon level of adoption of e-commerce by a company and its customers. Factors that will affect the proportion of online media spend in any organization include:

- Proportion of customers in a segment that can be reached through traditional or digital media.
- Proportion of customers in target market in researching and purchasing products online.
- Propensity of customers to purchase products using traditional channels.
- The relative cost-effectiveness of different online media (see Chapter 9) in comparison with traditional media such as TV and print.

There is a delicate balance to be struck between driving visitors to a website where they may be less likely to convert, but the cost of sale will be lower. With any medium there is a point of diminishing returns where more spend on that medium will not result in improved results. It seems that many companies are following a strategy of gradually increasing their digital spend since they want to find this inflection point without overstepping it too far.

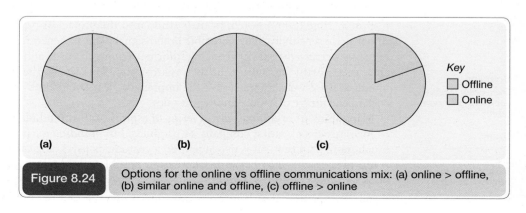

Figure 8.24	Options for the online vs offline communications mix: (a) online > offline, (b) similar online and offline, (c) offline > online

3 *Investment in different online promotion techniques.* For example, how much to pay for banner advertising as against online PR; how much to pay for search engine registration. These and other traffic building techniques are described in Chapter 9.

People, process and physical evidence

People variable
The element of the marketing mix that involves the delivery of service to customers during interactions with customers.

Process variable
The element of the marketing mix that involves the methods and procedures companies use to achieve all marketing functions.

Physical evidence variable
The element of the marketing mix that involves the tangible expression of a product and how it is purchased and used.

People, process and **physical evidence** are particularly important for service delivery. Since service delivery is an important aspect of e-commerce sites this is referred to in the '*Focus on* Excelling in e-commerce service quality' in Chapter 9; managing organizational change is the focus of Chapter 10; and user-centred design is in Chapter 11. Enhancing service is also an important element of online branding which is described in the next *Focus on* section. Physical evidence could be applied to site design or the accompanying packaging when products are delivered. Alternatively, these could be interpreted as part of the extended product.

Smith and Chaffey (2001) suggest that online, part of the consideration for the people element of the mix is the consideration of the tactics by which people can be replaced or their work automated. These are some of the options:

- *Autoresponders.* These automatically generate a response when a company e-mails an organization, or submits an online form.
- *E-mail notification.* Automatically generated by a company's systems to update customers on the status of their order, for example, order received, item now in stock, order dispatched.
- *Callback facility.* Customers fill in their phone number on a form and specify a convenient time to be contacted.
- *Frequently asked questions* (FAQs). For these, the art is in compiling and categorizing the questions so customers can easily find (a) the question and (b) a helpful answer.
- *On-site search engines.* These help customers find what they are looking for quickly and are popular when available. Site maps are a related feature.
- *Virtual assistants* come in varying degrees of sophistication and usually help to guide the customer through a maze of choices.

| Focus on | Online branding |

What comprises a successful online brand? Is it an e-commerce site with high levels of traffic? Is it a brand with good name recognition? Is it a profitable brand? Or is it a site with more modest sales levels, but one that customers perceive as providing good service? Although sites meeting only some of these criteria are often described as successful brands, we will see that a successful brand is dependent on a wide range of factors.

Erdem *et al.* (2002) noted, in their study into the impact of brand credibility on consumer price sensitivity, that a credible brand signal helps to generate customer value by: (i) reducing perceived risk, (ii) reducing information search costs, and (iii) creating a favourable, trustworthy perception of the organization. This shows the importance of online branding since websites must give the impression of trust and deliver a favourable experience to encourage first-time and repeat sales.

Branding
The process of creating and evolving successful brands.

Brand
The sum of the characteristics of a product or service perceived by a user.

Many think of **branding** only in terms of aspects of the brand identity such as the name or logo associated with a company or products, but branding gurus seem agreed that it is much more than that – it is dependent on a customer's psychological affinity for a product. A **brand** is described by Leslie de Chernatony and Malcolm McDonald in their classic 1992 book *Creating Powerful Brands as*:

an identifiable product or service augmented in such a way that the buyer or user perceives relevant unique added values which match their needs most closely. Furthermore, its success results from being able to sustain these added values in the face of competition.

This definition highlights three essential characteristics of a successful brand which we need to relate to the online environment:

- brand is dependent on customer perception;
- perception is influenced by the added-value characteristics of the product;
- the added-value characteristics need to be sustainable.

De Chernatony (2001) has evaluated the relevance of the brand concept on the Internet. He also believes that the main elements of brand values and brand strategy are the same in the Internet environment. However, he suggests that consumers on the Internet become active co-producers of value where they can contribute feedback through discussion groups to add value to a brand. De Chernatony argues for a looser form of brand control where the company facilitates rather than controls customer discussion.

A further method by which the Internet can change branding that was suggested by Jevons and Gabbot (2000) is that online, '*the first-hand experience of the brand is a more powerful token of trust than the perception of the brand*'. In the online environment, the customer can **experience** or interact with the brand more frequently and to a greater depth. As Dayal *et al.* (2000) say, '*on the world wide web, the brand is the experience and the experience is the brand*'. They suggest that to build successful online brands, organizations should consider how their proposition can build on these possible brand promises:

Brand experience
The frequency and depth of interactions with a brand can be enhanced through the Internet.

- *the promise of convenience* – making a purchase experience more convenient than the real-world one, or that with rivals;
- *the promise of achievement* – to assist consumers in achieving their goals, for example supporting online investors in their decision or supporting business people in their day-to-day work;
- *the promise of fun and adventure* – this is clearly more relevant for B2C services;
- *the promise of self-expression and recognition* – provided by personalization services such as Yahoo! Geocities where consumers can build their own website;
- *the promise of belonging* – provided by online communities.

De Chernatony (2001) suggests successful online branding requires delivering three aspects of a brand: rational values, emotional values and promised experience (based on rational and emotional values).

An alternative perspective on branding is provided by Aaker and Joachimsthaler (2000) who refer to '**brand equity**' which they define as:

Brand equity
The assets (or liabilities) linked to a brand's name and symbol that add to (or subtract from) a service.

a set of brand assets and liabilities linked to a brand, its name and symbol, that add to or subtract from the value provided by a product or service to a firm and/or to that firm's customers.

So, brand equity indicates the value provided to a company, or its customers, through a brand. Assessing brand equity on the web needs to address the unique characteristics of computer-mediated environments, as Christodoulides and de Chernatony (2004) have pointed out. These researchers set out to explore whether additional measures of brand equity were required online. Based on expert interviews they have identified the additional measures of brand equity which are important online, as summarized in Table 8.9. As we would expect, this includes attributes of the digital medium such as interactivity and customization which combine to form relevance and a great online brand experience. Content is not stressed separately, which is surprising, although they do mention its importance under site design and it is also a key aspect of other attributes such as customization, relevance and the overall experience. Their work on the need for rational, emotional appeal together with the promised experience of the website is presented in Figure 11.8.

Table 8.9	Traditional measures of brand equity and online measures of brand equity

Traditional measures of brand equity (Aaker and Joachimsthaler, 2000)	Online measures of brand equity (from Christodoulides and de Chernatony, 2004)
Price premium	Online brand experience
Satisfaction/loyalty	Interactivity
Perceived quality	Customization
Leadership popularity	Relevance
Perceived value	Site design
Brand personality	Customer service
Organizational associations	Order fulfilment
Brand awareness	Quality of brand relationships
Market share	Communities
Market price and distribution coverage	Website logs (see Chapter 9)

Brand identity

Brand identity

The totality of brand associations including name and symbols that must be communicated.

Aaker and Joachimsthaler (2000) also emphasize the importance of developing a plan to communicate the key features of the **brand identity** and increase brand awareness. Brand identity is again more than the name. These authors refer to it as a set of brand associations that imply a promise to customers from an organization. See 'Napster.com's brand identity', Mini case study 8.2, to see the different elements of brand identity which are effectively a checklist of what many e-tailers are looking to achieve.

Mini Case Study 8.2	Napster.com's brand identity

Aaker and Joachimsthaler (2000) suggest that the following characteristics of identity need to be defined at the start of a brand-building campaign. Marketing communications can then be developed that create and reinforce this identity. Here, we will apply them to Napster which forms the main case study at the end of this chapter.

- *Brand essence* (a summary of what the brand represents)
  This is not necessarily a tagline, but Napster has been described as an 'All you can eat music service which is fun and affordable'.
- Core identity (its key features)
  - choice – millions of tracks
  - value for money – under £10 per month subscription for as many tracks as you can listen to
  - easy to use – Napster runs as a separate application built for purpose
  - listen anywhere – on a PC or other computer, MP3 player or mobile phone
  - listen on anything – unlike iPod, Napster is compatible with most MP3 players rather than being tied in to a specific hardware manufacturer.
- *Extended identity*
  - personality – flouts what is standard for existing music providers thanks to its heritage as a peer-to-peer file-sharing service

- – personalization – Napster Radio based on particular genres or based on other songs you have downloaded
- – community – facility to share tracks with friends or other Napster members
- – symbols – Napster cat logo.
- ● *Value proposition*
  - – functional benefits – ease of use and personalization
  - – emotional benefits – community, non-conformist
  - – self-expressive benefit – build your own collection of your tastes.
- ● *Relationship*
  - – customers value and will be loyal to a company that isn't stuffy.

Ries and Ries (2000) suggest two rules for naming brands: (a) The Law of the Common Name – 'The kiss of death for an Internet brand is a common name.' This argues that common names such as Art.com or Advertising.com are poor since they are not sufficiently distinctive; (b) The Law of the Proper Name – 'Your name stands alone on the Internet, so you'd better have a good one.' This suggests that proper names are to be preferred to generic names, e.g. Handbag.com against Woman.com or Moreover.com against Business.com. The authors suggest that the best names will follow most of these eight principles: (1) short, (2) simple, (3) suggestive of the category, (4) unique, (5) alliterative, (6) speakable, (7) shocking and (8) personalized. Although these are cast as 'immutable laws' there will of course be exceptions!

The importance of brand online

The Internet presents a 'double-edged sword' to existing brands. A consumer who already has knowledge of a brand is more likely to trust it, but loyalty can be decreased because the Internet encourages consumers to trial other brands. This is suggested by Figure 8.25.

The BrandNewWorld (2004) survey showed that in some categories, a large proportion of buyers have purchased from different brands from those they initially considered, for example:

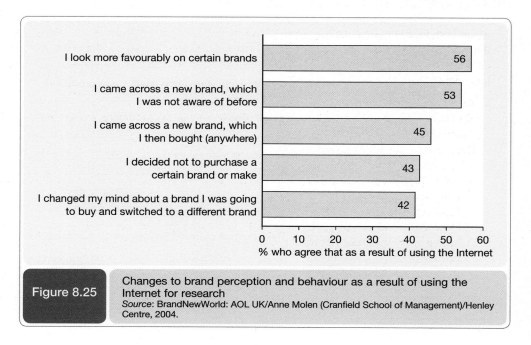

Figure 8.25	Changes to brand perception and behaviour as a result of using the Internet for research

Source: BrandNewWorld: AOL UK/Anne Molen (Cranfield School of Management)/Henley Centre, 2004.

- Large home appliances, 47%
- Financial products and services, 39%
- Holidays and travels, 31%
- Mobile phones, 28%
- Cars, 26%.

But, for other types of products, existing brand preferences appear to be more important:

- Clothing/accessories, 22%
- Computer hardware, 21%
- Garden/DIY products, 17%
- Home furnishings, 6%.

The survey also suggested that experienced Internet users were more likely to switch brands (52% agreed they were more likely to switch after researching online) compared to less-experienced users (33%).

Of course, the likelihood of a consumer purchasing from an established brand will depend upon the combination of their knowledge of the retailer brand or product brand. Figure 8.26 shows that many customers will still buy an unknown manufacturer brand if they are familiar with the retailer brand. This is less true if they don't know the retailer. Significantly, if they don't know the retailer or the brand, it is fairly unlikely they will buy.

The activity illustrates the importance of building brand awareness for an e-commerce service in a cost-effective manner at the same time as achieving good levels of service quality. Success factors for building a brand online are described further in Chapter 9. Key aspects of creating a positive customer experience are:

- Content quality (Can the customer easily find relevant, up-to-date content? Are there errors?).
- Adequate performance of website infrastructure in terms of availability and download speed.
- Ease of contacting a company for support.
- Quality of response to e-mail enquiries and fulfilment quality.
- Acknowledgement of customer privacy.
- Reflecting and supporting the characteristics of the offline brand.

Managing the technology and customer database necessary to deliver service is a key aspect of e-marketing and requires close interaction between marketers and the IS department or external consultants.

When buying online, I will buy a product if...

I am familiar with the retailer	Yes	Yes	No	No
I am familiar with the product brand	Yes	No	Yes	No
	90%	82%	54%	13%

Figure 8.26 The influence of brand knowledge on purchase. Matrix for question 'I will buy a product if …'
Source: BrandNewWorld: AOL UK/Anne Molen (Cranfield School of Management)/Henley Centre, 2004.

Actions

The actions component of e-marketing planning refers to activities conducted by managers to execute the plan. Questions that need to be resolved when specifying actions include:

- What level of investment in the Internet channel is sufficient to deliver these services? What will be the payback?
- What training of staff is required?
- What new responsibilities are required for effective Internet marketing?
- Are changes in organizational structure required to deliver Internet-based services?
- What activities are involved in creating and maintaining the website?

At this stage an e-marketing plan will be finalized to summarize actions that need to occur. An example of what appears in a typical e-marketing plan is presented in Box 8.5. This also acts as a summary for the chapter.

Box 8.5   A typical e-marketing plan framework

1   Situation analysis

Internal audits

- Current Internet marketing audit (business, marketing and Internet marketing effectiveness)
- Audience composition and characteristics
- Reach of website, contribution to sales and profitability
- Suitability of resources to deliver online services in face of competition.

External audits

- Macro-economic environment (Chapter 4)
- Micro-environment – new marketplace structures, predicted customer activity
- Competition – threats from existing rivals, new services, new companies and intermediaries.

Assess opportunities and threats (SWOT analysis)

- Market and product positioning
- Methods of creation of digital value and detailed statement of customer value proposition
- Marketplace positioning (buyer, seller and neutral marketplaces)
- Scope of marketing functions.

2   Objectives statement

- Corporate objectives of online marketing (mission statement)
- Detailed objectives: tangible and intangible benefits, specific critical success factors
- Contribution of online marketing to promotional and sales activities
- Online value proposition.

3   Strategy definition

- Investment and commitment to online channels (mixture of bricks and clicks)
- Market and product positioning – aims for increasing reach, new digital products and new business and revenue models
- Target market strategies – statement of prioritized segments, new segments, online value proposition and differential advantage. Significance of non-customer audiences?
- Change management strategy (Which new processes, structures and responsibilities will be required? Chapter 10).

4 **Tactics**
- *Product*. Creating new core and extended value for customers, options for migrating brand online
- *Promotion*. Specify balance of online and offline promotion methods. Role of CRM (see Chapter 9)
- *Price*. Discounting online sales, options for setting pricing, new pricing options, e.g. auctions
- *Place*. Disintermediation and reintermediation, seller, buyer or neutral sales
- *People, process and physical evidence*. Online service delivery through support and characteristics of website.

5 **Actions**

Specify:
- Tasks
- Resources
- Partnering and outsourcing
- Budget including costs for development, promotion and maintenance
- Timescale
- Staff.

Implementation
- Key development tasks (Chapters 11 and 12): analysis of business and audience needs, scenario-based design, development of content, integration of databases, migration of data, testing and changeover
- Project and change management (Chapter 10)
- Team organization and responsibilities
- Risk assessment (identify risks, measures to counter risks)
- Legal issues
- Development and maintenance process.

6 **Control**
- Identify a measurement process and metrics (Chapter 12) covering:
  - Business contribution (channel profitability – revenue, costs, return on investment)
  - Marketing effectiveness (channel outcomes – leads, sales, conversion rate, channel satisfaction)
  - Online marketing effectiveness (channel behaviour – page impressions, visitors, repeat visits, conversion rates).

Control

The control element of the e-marketing plan can be achieved through a combination of traditional techniques such as marketing research to obtain customer views and opinions and novel techniques such as analysis of web-server log files that use technology to monitor whether objectives are achieved. These techniques are reviewed in detail in Chapter 12 (p. 673). Intranets can be used to share information among marketers and consultants within an organization.

This case about the online music subscription service Napster illustrates how different elements of the mix can be varied online. It also highlights success factors for developing an online marketing strategy since Napster's proposition, objectives, competitors and risk factors are all reviewed.

The Napster brand has had a varied history. Its initial incarnation was as the first widely used service for 'free' peer-to-peer (P2P) music sharing. The record companies mounted a legal challenge to Napster due to lost revenues on music sales which eventually forced it to close. But the Napster brand was purchased and its second incarnation (Figure 8.27) offers a legal music download service in direct competition with Apple's iTunes. They also offer a music subscription service.

The original Napster

Napster was created between 1998 and 1999 by a 19-year-old called Shawn Fanning while he attended Boston's Northeastern University. He wrote the program initially as a way of solving a problem for a friend who wanted to find music downloads more easily online. The name 'Napster' came from Fanning's nickname.

The system was known as 'peer-to-peer' since it enabled music tracks stored on other Internet users' hard disks in MP3 format to be searched and shared with other Internet users. Strictly speaking, the service was not a pure P2P since central services indexed the tracks available and their locations in a similar way to how instant messaging (IM) works.

The capability to try a range of tracks proved irresistible and Napster use peaked with 26.4 million users worldwide in February 2001.

It was not long before several major recording companies backed by the RIAA (Recording Industry Association of America) launched a lawsuit. Of course, such an action also gave Napster tremendous PR and more users trialled the service. Some individual bands also responded with lawsuits. Rock band Metallica found that a demo of their song 'I disappear' began circulating on the Napster network and was eventually played on the radio. Other well-known artists who

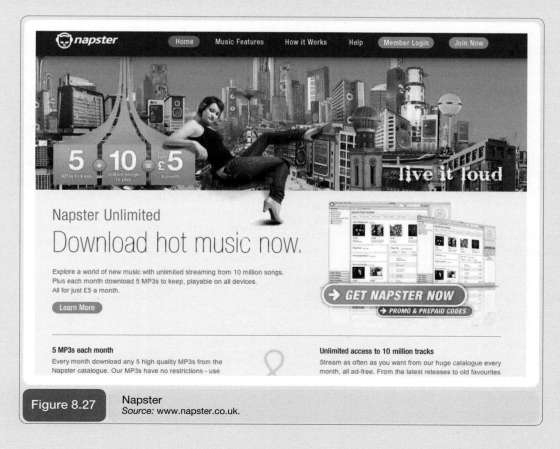

Figure 8.27	Napster
	Source: www.napster.co.uk.

vented their ire on Napster included Madonna and Eminem by posting false 'Cuckoo Egg' files instead of music; Madonna asked the downloader: 'What the fuck do you think you're doing?'! However, not all artists felt the service was negative for them. UK band Radiohead pre-released some tracks of their album *Kid A* on to Napster and subsequently became Number 1 in the US despite failing to achieve this previously.

Eventually, as a result of legal action an injunction was issued on 5 March 2001 ordering Napster to cease trading in copyrighted material. Napster complied with this injunction, but tried to do a deal with the record companies to pay past copyright fees and to turn the service into a legal subscription service.

In the following year, a deal was agreed with German media company Bertelsmann AG to purchase Napster's assets for $8 million as part of an agreement when Napster filed for Chapter 11 bankruptcy in the United States. This sale was blocked and the website closed. Eventually, the Napster brand was purchased by Roxio, Inc. which used the brand to rebrand their PressPlay service.

Since this time, other P2P services such as Gnutella, Grokster and Kazaa have prospered, which have been more difficult for the copyright owners to pursue in court; however, many individuals have now been sued in the US and Europe and the association of these services with spyware and adware has damaged them, which has reduced the popularity of these services.

New Napster in 2010

In September 2008, Napster was purchased by US electronics retailer Best Buy for $US121 million. It has continued to innovate and develop distribution deals, for example:

- Jan 2010: Named primary music partner for My Coke Rewards.
- Jan 2010: Release of an application programming interface (API). Consumer electronics and web developers of any size can easily integrate Napster content and services into their own products and web pages. Napster also used its own API to create a consistent look and feel to its services across all three screens – PC, mobile and TV.
- 2 October 2009: Dell consumer laptops and desktops in the US, UK and Germany to come with a year of Napster.
- 1 September 2009: Napster available on web-enabled phones via m.napster.com.

However, competitors such as Spotify, Last.fm and of course iTunes tend to gain the largest number of mentions in the media and the Napster brand seems often to be still associated with the free download service.

The online music download environment has also changed with legal music downloading propelled through increasing adoption of broadband, the success of Apple iTunes and its portable music player, the iPod.

Napster gains its main revenues from online subscriptions and permanent music downloads. The Napster service offers subscribers on-demand access to 15 million tracks that can be streamed or downloaded as well as the ability to purchase individual tracks or albums. Subscription fees are paid by end-user customers in advance. Napster also periodically licenses merchandising rights and resells hardware that its end-users use to store and replay their music.

The BBC (2005) reports Brad Duea, president of Napster, as saying:

The number one brand attribute at the time Napster was shut down was innovation. The second highest characteristic was actually 'free'. The difference now is that the number one attribute is still innovation. Free is now way down on the list. People are able to search for more music than was ever possible at retail, even in the largest megastore.

According to the Security Exchange Commission 2008 10-K filing for Napstar, Napster had fiscal 2008 revenue of $127.5 million, an increase of 15% over the prior fiscal year; a loss of $16.5 million, an improvement compared with a loss of $36.8 million the prior fiscal year; and positive cash flow for the fiscal year ended 31 March 2008.

The Napster proposition

Napster subscribers can listen to as many tracks as they wish which are contained within the catalogue of 15 million tracks. Napster users can listen to tracks on any mobile, MP3 player or computer compatible with Windows Digital Rights Management (DRM) and also through Napster apps on Android, Apple iOS and Blackberry phones. All these provide the option to save songs and playlists to play in an offline mode when not connected to the Internet.

Duea describes Napster as an 'experience' rather than a retailer. He says this because of features available such as:

- Napster recommendations
- Napster Radio based around songs by particular artists
- Napster Radio playlists based on the songs you have downloaded
- Swapping playlists and recommendations with other users.

iTunes and Napster are probably the two highest-profile services, but they have a quite different model of operating. There are no subscribers to iTunes, where users purchase songs either on a per-track basis or in the form of albums. By mid-2005, over half a billion tracks had been purchased on Napster. Some feel that iTunes locks people into purchasing Apple hardware; as one would expect, Duea of Napster says that Steve Jobs of Apple 'has tricked people into buying a hardware trap'.

But Napster's subscription model has also been criticized since it is a service where subscribers do not 'own' the music unless they purchase it at additional cost, for example to burn it to CD. The music is theirs to play either on a PC or on a portable player, but for only as long as they continue to subscribe to Napster. So it could be argued that Napster achieves lock-in in another form and requires a different approach to music ownership than some of its competitors.

Napster strategy

Napster (2005) describe their strategy as follows. The overall objective is to become the 'leading global provider of consumer digital music services'. They see these strategic initiatives as being important to achieving this:

- *Continue to build the Napster consumer brand* – as well as increasing awareness of the Napster brand identity, this also includes promoting the subscription service which encourages discovery of new music. Napster (2005) say, 'We market our Napster service directly to consumers through an integrated offline and online marketing program consistent with the existing strong awareness and perception of the Napster brand. The marketing message is focused on our subscription service, which differentiates our offering from those of many of our competitors. Offline marketing channels include television (including direct-response TV), radio and print advertising.'
- *Continue to innovate by investing in new services and technologies* – this initiative encourages support of a wide range of platforms: portable MP3 players, PCs, cars, mobile phones, etc. The large technical team in Napster shows the importance of this strategy. In the longer term, access to other forms of content such as video may be offered. Napster seem to view their ability to compete as depending substantially upon their intellectual property. They have a number of patents issued, but are also in dispute with other organizations over their patents.
- *Continue to pursue and execute strategic partnerships* – Napster has already entered strategic partnerships with technology companies (Microsoft and Intel), hardware companies (iRiver, Dell, Creative, Toshiba and IBM), retailers (Best Buy, Blockbuster, Radio Shack, Dixons Group, The Link,

PC World, Currys, Target), and others (Molson, Miller, Energizer, Nestlé).
- *Continue to pursue strategic acquisitions and complementary technologies* – this is another route to innovation and developing new services. Distribution partnerships with mobile providers are a key aspect of its strategy. In 2008, Napster launched mobile music services with Telecom Italia, which serves more than 35 million subscribers; Entel PCS, the leading Chilean mobile operator with more than 5.5 million subscribers; and in Japan Napster Mobile for NTT DoCoMo.

Customers

The Register (2005) reported that in the UK, by mid-2005, Napster UK's 750,000 users had downloaded or streamed 55 million tracks since the service launched in May 2004. The company said 80% of its subscribers are over the age of 25, and half of them have kids. Some three-quarters of them are male. Its subscribers buy more music online than folk who buy one-off downloads do and research shows that one in five of them no longer buy CDs, apparently.

Describing its marketing strategy Napster says in its SEC filing:

We primarily focus our marketing efforts on online advertising, where we can most cost effectively reach our target audience of 25–40-year-olds, as well as strategic partnerships where we can market our service with complementary products. In the United Kingdom and Germany, we also market our paid Napster service directly to consumers through a predominately online marketing program, consistent with the existing strong awareness and perception of the Napster brand. The marketing message is focused on our subscription service, which differentiates our offering from many of our competitors. Our online marketing program includes advertising placements on a number of websites (including affiliate partners) and search engines.

Distribution

Napster's online music services are sold directly to end-users through the website (www.napster.com). Affiliate networks and universities have procured site licences (in the US, a significant proportion of subscribers are university users). Prepaid cards are also available through retail partners such as Dixons in the UK, who also promote the service.

Napster also bundles its service with hardware manufacturers such as iRiver, Dell, Creative Labs, Gateway and Samsung.

Competition

Napster see their competitors for online music services in the US and Europe as Apple iTunes, Amazon MP3 downloads, Last.fm, Rhapsody and Spotify.

Napster (2005) believe that the main competitive factors affecting their market include programming and features, price and performance, quality of customer support, compatibility with popular hardware devices and brand.

Risk factors

In their annual report submission to the United States Securities and Exchange Commission, Napster is required to give its risk factors, which also give an indication of success factors for the business. Napster (2005) summarizes the main risk factors as follows:

1 The success of our Napster service depends upon our ability to add new subscribers and reduce churn.

2 Our online music distribution business has lower margins than our former consumer software products business. Costs of our online music distribution business as a percentage of the revenue generated by that business are higher than those of our former consumer software products business. The cost of third-party content, in particular, is a substantial portion of revenues we receive from subscribers and end-users and is unlikely to decrease significantly over time as a percentage of revenue.

3 We rely on the value of the Napster brand, and our revenues could suffer if we are not able to maintain its high level of recognition in the digital music sector.

4 We face significant competition from traditional retail music distributors, from emerging paid online music services delivered electronically such as ours, and from 'free' peer-to-peer services.

5 Online music distribution services in general are new and rapidly evolving and may not prove to be a profitable or even viable business model.

6 We rely on content provided by third parties, which may not be available to us on commercially reasonable terms or at all.

7 We must provide digital rights management solutions that are acceptable to both content providers and consumers.

8 Our business could be harmed by a lack of availability of popular content.

9 Our success depends on our music service's interoperability with our customer's music playback hardware.

10 We may not successfully develop new products and services.

11 We must maintain and add to our strategic marketing relationships in order to be successful.

12 The growth of our business depends on the increased use of the Internet for communications, electronic commerce and advertising.

13 If broadband technologies do not become widely available or widely adopted, our online music distribution services may not achieve broad market acceptance, and our business may be harmed.

14 Our network is subject to security and stability risks that could harm our business and reputation and expose us to litigation or liability.

15 If we fail to manage expansion effectively, we may not be able to successfully manage our business, which could cause us to fail to meet our customer demand or to attract new customers, which would adversely affect our revenue.

16 We may be subject to intellectual property infringement claims, such as those claimed by SightSound Technologies, which are costly to defend and could limit our ability to use certain technologies in the future.

Source: BBC (2005), Napster (2005), Wikipedia (2005), *The Register* (2005) and *Wired* (2005). Reprinted by kind permission of Napster, LLC. Napster disclaims any obligation to update or correct any information provided here.

Question

Assess how Napster competes with traditional and online music providers by reviewing the approaches it uses for different elements of the marketing mix.

Summary

1 E-marketing is the application of technology to achieve marketing objectives, defined by the Chartered Institute of Marketing as: '*the management process responsible for identifying, anticipating and satisfying customer requirements profitably.*'

2 E-marketing can be considered a subset of e-business and is equivalent to sell-side e-commerce.

3 An e-marketing plan is often developed separately from an e-business strategy. The SOSTAC™ framework is used to introduce the elements of an e-marketing plan.

4 Situation analysis – involves a consideration of the external environment with the emphasis on levels of customer access to the Internet, benchmarking of competitors and new entrants.

5 Objective setting – a key objective is setting the online revenue contribution or the percentage of sales that will be achieved online. For companies where direct sales are not practical because of the nature of the product companies may set objectives for how the web will affect marketing communications, customer service and cost reductions.

6 Strategies – through evaluating the suitability of product for direct sale a company may define a replacement (product suitable for direct sale, e.g. airline tickets) or complementary strategy (product unsuitable for direct sale, e.g. FMCG or consultancy services). Replacement strategies may involve changing distribution networks. Complementary strategies will involve using the Internet as an additional marketing communications channel.

7 Tactics – e-marketing tactics can be reviewed through varying the elements of the marketing mix: Price, Place, Product, Promotion, People, Processes and Physical evidence.

8 Actions – the planning of e-marketing strategy by identifying resources and timescales.

9 Control – control can be achieved through monitoring customer satisfaction and channel performance via the website and traditional channels.

Exercises

Self-assessment questions

1 Explain the link between e-marketing and e-business and why they may be considered separately.

2 Outline the stages in a strategic e-marketing planning process, for each stage noting two aspects that are of particular importance for e-marketing.

3 What is the Internet contribution and what is its relevance to e-marketing strategy?

4 What factors will govern the Internet contribution that is set for a given organization?

5 Why and how should a company approach benchmarking of online competitors?

6 Describe what is meant by a complementary and replacement Internet channel strategy and give examples of products for which companies follow a particular approach.

7 Summarize new opportunities to vary the marketing mix that arise through deploying the Internet.

8 How can online and offline techniques be used in the control stage of strategy?

Essay and discussion questions

1 Select a particular market sector and assess the past, current and future customer use of the Internet as a medium to select and buy products.

2 Develop an outline strategic e-marketing plan for an organization with which you are familiar.

3 'Traditional strategic planning has no relevance for the start-up company given the dynamism of the marketplace.' Discuss.

4 Assess the value and importance of the Internet contribution in setting e-marketing objectives in relation to other possible objectives.

5 Explain how the e-business can make use of technology to monitor and control its operations.

Examination questions

1 Outline the stages involved in developing a strategic e-marketing plan.

2 Explain what is meant by the Internet contribution and outline how companies will decide on a realistic objective.

3 What opportunities may there be to vary the Price and Place components of the marketing mix when delivering services through the Internet?

4 What is a complementary Internet channel strategy and for which companies will this be most appropriate?

5 What different aspects of e-marketing should be monitored as part of controlling e-marketing? Name three examples of how technology can be used to assist monitoring.

6 Explain the strategic options available for a company currently selling the majority of its products in a single country for product and marketplace positioning.

7 What do the concepts of reintermediation and disintermediation imply for the tactics a company employs for the Promotion and Place elements of the marketing mix?

8 Outline how the electronic medium requires different tactics for effective marketing communications.

References

Aaker, D. and Joachimsthaler, E. (2000) *Brand Leadership*. Free Press, New York.

Agrawal, V., Arjona, V. and Lemmens, R. (2001) E-performance: the path to rational exuberance. *McKinsey Quarterly*, no. 1, 31–43.

Allen, E. and Fjermestad, J. (2001) E-commerce marketing strategies: a framework and case analysis. *Logistics Information Management*, 14(1/2), 14–23.

Anderson, C. (2004) The Long Tail. *Wired*. 12(10), October. **www.wired.com/wired/archive/12.10/tail.html**.

Ansoff, H. (1957) Strategies for diversification. *Harvard Business Review*, September–October, 113–24.

Azumah, G., Loh, S. and McGuire, S. (2005) E-organisation and its future implication for SMEs. *Production Planning and Control*, 16(6), September, 555–62.

Baker, W., Marn, M. and Zawada, C. (2001) Price smarter on the Net. *Harvard Business Review*, February, 2–7.

Baye, M., Gatti, J., Kattuman, P. and Morgan, J, (2007) Dashboard for online pricing. *The California Management Review*, Fall, 50(1), 202–16.

Bazett, M., Bowden, I., Love, J., Street, R. and Wilson, H. (2005) Measuring multichannel effectiveness using the balanced scorecard. *Interactive Marketing*, 6(3), 224–31.

BBC (2005) Napster boss on life after piracy. By Derren Waters, 22 August. **http://news. bbc.co.uk/1/hi/entertainment/music/4165868.stm.**

Booms, B. and Bitner, M. (1981) Marketing strategies and organization structure for service firms. In *Marketing of Services*, eds J. Donelly and W. George, American Marketing Association, New York.

BrandNewWorld (2004) AOL Research published at **www.brandnewworld.co.uk.**

Brynjolfsson, E., Smith, D. and Hu, Y. (2003) Consumer surplus in the digital economy: Estimating the value of increased product variety at online booksellers, *Management Science*, 49(11), 1580–96: **http://ebusiness.mit.edu/research/papers/176_ErikB_ OnlineBooksellers2.pdf.**

Chaffey, D. (2000) Achieving success in Internet marketing. *Marketing Review*, 1, 1–23.

Chaffey, D. and Smith, P. (2008) *EMarketing Excellence. Planning and Optimising Your Digital Marketing*, 3rd edn. Butterworth-Heinemann, Oxford.

Chaffey, D., Mayer, R., Johnston, K. and Ellis-Chadwick, F. (2009) *Internet Marketing: Strategy, Implementation and Practice*, 4th edn. Financial Times Prentice Hall, Harlow.

Christodoulides, G. and de Chernatony, L. (2004) Dimensionalising on- and offline brands' composite equity. *Journal of Product and Brand Management*, 13(3), 168–79.

Dayal, S., Landesberg, H. and Zeissberg, M. (2000) Building digital brands. *McKinsey Quarterly*, no. 2.

de Chernatony, L. (2001) Succeeding with brands on the Internet. *Journal of Brand Management*, 8(3), 186–95.

de Chernatony, L. and McDonald, M. (1992) *Creating Powerful Brands*. Butterworth-Heinemann, Oxford.

Deighton, J. (1996) The future of interactive marketing. *Harvard Business Review*, November–December, 151–62.

Deise, M., Nowikow, C., King, P. and Wright, A. (2000) *Executive's Guide to E-Business. From Tactics to Strategy*. Wiley, New York.

de Kare-Silver, M. (2000) *EShock 2000. The Electronic Shopping Revolution: Strategies for Retailers and Manufacturers*. Macmillan, London.

Dibb, S., Simkin, L., Pride, W. and Ferrell, O. (2000) *Marketing. Concepts and Strategies*, 4th edn. Houghton Mifflin, Boston.

E-consultancy (2008) Managing Digital Teams. Integrating digital marketing into your organisation. 60-page report. Author: Dave Chaffey. Available from **www.econsultancy. com.**

Emiliani, V. (2001) Business-to-business online auctions: key issues for purchasing process improvement. *Supply Chain Management: An International Journal*, 5(4), 176–86.

Erdem, T., Swait, J. and Louviere, J. (2002) The impact of brand credibility on consumer price sensitivity, *International Journal of Research in Marketing*, 19(1), 1–19.

Evans, P. and Wurster, T. (1999) Getting real about virtual commerce. *Harvard Business Review*, November, 84–94.

Forrester (2007) The POST Method: A systematic approach to social strategy, Blog post by Josh Bernoff, 11 December 2007: **http://forrester.typepad.com/groundswell/2007/12/ the-post-method.html.**

Frazier, G. (1999) Organising and managing channels of distribution. *Journal of the Academy of Marketing Science*, 27(2), 222–40.

Ghosh, S. (1998) Making business sense of the Internet. *Harvard Business Review*, March–April, 126–35.

Gladwell, M. (2000) *The Tipping Point: How Little Things can Make a Big Difference*. Little, Brown, New York.

Hoffman, D.L. and Novak, T.P. (1997) A new marketing paradigm for electronic commerce. *The Information Society*, Special issue on electronic commerce, 13 (January–March), 43–54.

Houston, F. (1986) The marketing concept: what it is and what it is not. *Journal of Marketing*, 50 (April), 81–7.

Hughes, S. (2001) Market orientation and the response of UK financial services companies to changes in market conditions as a result of e-commerce. *International Journal of Bank Marketing*, 19(6), 222–31.

IEE (2003) Amazon.com recommendations: item-to-item collaborative filtering. *Internet Computing*, January–February, 76–80. Available online at: **http://agents.csie.ntu.edu.tw/ ~yjhsu/courses/u2010/papers/Amazon%20Recommendations.pdf.**

Jaworski, B. and Kohli, A. (1993) Market orientation: antecedents and consequences. *Journal of Marketing*, July, 53–70.

Jevons, C. and Gabbot, M. (2000) Trust, brand equity and brand reality in Internet business relationships: An interdisciplinary approach. *Journal of Marketing Management*, 16, 619–34.

Johnson, E., Moe, W., Fader, P., Bellman, S. and Lohse, G. (2004) On the depth and dynamics of online search behavior. *Management Science*, 50(3), 299–308.

Kumar, N. (1999) Internet distribution strategies: Dilemmas for the incumbent. *Financial Times*, Special Issue on Mastering Information Management, no. 7, Electronic Commerce.

Lautenborn, R. (1990) New marketing litany: 4Ps passes, 4Cs takeovers. *Advertising Age*, 1 October, 26.

McCarthy, J. (1960) *Basic Marketing: A Managerial Approach.* Irwin, Homewood, IL.

McDonald, M. and Wilson, H. (1999) *E-Marketing: Improving Marketing Effectiveness in a Digital World.* Financial Times Prentice Hall, Harlow.

Marsden, P. (2004) Tipping point marketing: a primer. *Brand strategy*, April. Available at **www.viralculture.com/pubs/tippingpoint2.htm.**

Morris, R.J. and Martin, C.L. (2000) Beanie Babies: A case study in the engineering of a high involvement/relationship-prone brand. *Journal of Product and Brand Management*, 9(2), 78–98.

Napster (2005) Annual Report, published at Investor relations site (**http://investor. napster. com**).

Pulizzi, J. and Barrett, T. (2010) *Get Content. Get Customers.* McGraw-Hill, Columbus, OH.

Quelch, J. and Klein, L. (1996) The Internet and international marketing. *Sloan Management Review*, Spring, 60–75.

Ries, A. and Ries, L. (2000) *The 11 Immutable Laws of Internet Branding.* HarperCollins Business, London.

Seybold, P. (1999) *Customers.com.* Century Business Books, Random House, London.

Simon, Herbert A. (1957) *Models of Man.* Wiley, New York.

Smith, P. (1999) *Marketing Communications: An Integrated Approach*, 2nd edn. Kogan Page, London.

Smith, P. and Chaffey, D. (2001) *E-Marketing Excellence at the Heart of E-Business.* Butterworth-Heinemann, Oxford.

Sultan, F. and Rohm, A. (2004) The evolving role of the Internet in marketing strategy. *Journal of Interactive marketing*, 19(2), Spring.

The Register (2005) Napster UK touts subscriber numbers. *The Register*, Tony Smith, 5 September. **www.theregister.co.uk/2005/09/05/napster_numbers.**

Valentin, E. (1996) The marketing concept and the conceptualization of marketing strategy. *Journal of Marketing Theory and Practice*, Fall, 16–27.

Variani, V. and Vaturi, D. (2000) Marketing lessons from e-failures. *McKinsey Quarterly*, no. 4, 86–97.

Weinberg, T. (2010) *The New Community Rules: Marketing on The Social Web.* Wiley, Hoboken, NJ.

Wikipedia (2005) Napster. Wikipedia. Wikipedia entry at **http://en.wikipedia.org/wiki/ Napster.**

Wired (2005) The day Napster died, **www.wired.com/news/mp3/0,1285,52540,00.html.**

Xing, X., Yang, S. and Tang, F. (2006) A comparison of time-varying online price and price dispersion between multichannel and dotcom DVD retailers. *Journal of Interactive Marketing* 20(2), 3–20.

Further reading

Bickerton, P., Bickerton, M. and Pardesi, U. (2000) *CyberMarketing*, 2nd edn. Butterworth-Heinemann, Oxford, Chartered Institute of Marketing series. Considers each element of the marketing mix in a separate chapter.

Chaffey, D., Mayer, R., Johnston, K. and Ellis-Chadwick, F. (2009) *Internet Marketing: Strategy, Implementation and Practice*, 4th edn. Financial Times Prentice Hall, Harlow. Chapters 2–5 cover e-marketing strategy.

Wilson, H., Hobbs, M., Dolder, C. and McDonald, M. (2004) Optimising multiple channels. *Interactive Marketing*, January–March, 252–68. A review of how companies have to select the best alternative channels.

Web links

Clickz (www.clickz.com) US site of statistics and advice about all aspects of digital marketing.

E-consultancy (www.econsultancy.com) Best-practice sections on different e-communications tools, newsletter features and interviews with e-commerce practitioners.

Marketing Sherpa (www.marketingsherpa.com) Articles and links on Internet marketing communications including e-mail and online advertising.

SmartInsights.com (www.smartinsights.com) A blog of links and articles about developments in e-marketing and digital communications managed by Dave Chaffey.

9

Customer relationship management

Web support

The following additional case studies are available at
www.pearsoned.co.uk/chaffey

The site also contains a range of study material designed to help improve your results.

Learning outcomes

After completing this chapter the reader should be able to:

- Outline different methods of acquiring customers via electronic media
- Evaluate different buyer behaviour amongst online customers
- Describe techniques for retaining customers and cross- and up-selling using new media

Management issues

Customer relationship management involves these management issues:

- What are the practical success factors digital media need to make customer acquisition more effective?
- What technologies can be used to build and maintain the online relationship?
- How do we deliver superior service quality to build and maintain relationships?

Links to other chapters

The main related chapters are:

- *Chapter 4* – CRM techniques are constrained by social, legal and ethical factors
- *Chapter 5* – CRM supports e-business strategy
- *Chapter 8* – CRM is one of the tactics aimed at fulfilling the objectives defined in the e-marketing plan

Introduction

Customer relationship management (CRM)
An approach to building and sustaining long-term business with customers.

The application of technology to achieve **customer relationship management (CRM)** is a key element of e-business. Building long-term relationships with customers is essential for any sustainable business. Failure to build relationships largely caused the failures of many dot-coms following huge expenditure on customer acquisition as explained in Chapters 2 and 5. The importance of customer retention to long-term profitability is well known from modelling of the type referred to in Chapter 4. But research summarized by Reichheld and Schefter (2000) shows that acquiring online customers is so expensive (20–30% higher than for traditional businesses) that start-up companies may remain unprofitable for at least two to three years. The research also shows that by retaining just 5% more customers, online companies can boost their profits by 25% to 95%. These authors say:

> but if you can keep customers loyal, their profitability accelerates much faster than in traditional businesses. It costs you less and less to service them.

Note that the relationship between customer loyalty and profitability has been questioned, notably by Reinartz and Kumar (2002), who discovered through analysis of four company databases that:

> there was little or no evidence to suggest that customers who purchase steadily from a company over time are necessarily cheaper to serve, less price sensitive, or particularly effective at bringing in new business.

They have suggested that companies that base their marketing focus on the simple assumption that loyal customers are the most profitable will miss opportunities in targeting other potentially profitable customers.

This chapter evaluates different techniques to both initiate and build relationships with customers by using a combination of online and offline techniques. The chapter is structured around the different stages of the classic **customer life cycle** of Select, Acquire, Retain, Extend, as is shown in Figure 9.1. The figure emphasizes the importance of integrating customer relationship management activities across the appropriate channels.

Customer life cycle
The stages each customer will pass through in a long-term relationship through acquisition, retention and extension.

An alternative view of how CRM can be achieved via a web or social media presence is the approach Yahoo! has used to build a profitable site. The managers of the site reported at industry conferences that an effective website should have three characteristics:

- *Magnetic*. Acquisition of visitors by promotion and by making the site attractive.
- *Sticky*. Retention – keeping customers on the site once they arrive and encouraging them to engage in revenue-generating activities.
- *Elastic*. Extension – persuading customers to return, particularly for revenue-generating activities.

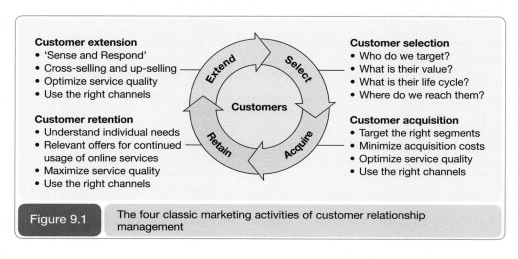

Customer extension
- 'Sense and Respond'
- Cross-selling and up-selling
- Optimize service quality
- Use the right channels

Customer retention
- Understand individual needs
- Relevant offers for continued usage of online services
- Maximize service quality
- Use the right channels

Customer selection
- Who do we target?
- What is their value?
- What is their life cycle?
- Where do we reach them?

Customer acquisition
- Target the right segments
- Minimize acquisition costs
- Optimize service quality
- Use the right channels

Extend · Select · Retain · Acquire · Customers

Figure 9.1 The four classic marketing activities of customer relationship management

The four marketing activities that comprise CRM involve the following.

1 **Customer selection** means defining the types of customers that a company will market to. It means identifying different groups of customers for which to develop offerings and to target during acquisition, retention and extension. Different ways of segmenting customers by value and by their detailed life cycle with the customer are reviewed. From an e-business perspective, as we see in Chapter 5, we may want to selectively target customer types who have adopted e-channels.

2 **Customer acquisition** refers to marketing activities intended to form relationships with new customers while minimizing acquisition costs and targeting high-value customers. Service quality and selecting the right channels for different customers are important.

3 **Customer retention** refers to the marketing activities taken by an organization to keep its existing customers. Identifying relevant offerings based on their individual needs and detailed position in the customer life cycle (e.g. number or value of purchases) is key.

4 **Customer extension** refers to increasing the depth or range of products that a customer purchases from a company. This is often referred to as 'customer development'.

There are a range of customer extension techniques for CRM that are particularly important to online retailers:

(a) **Re-sell**. Selling similar products to existing customers – particularly important in some B2B contexts as re-buys or modified re-buys.

(b) **Cross-sell**. Sell additional products which may be closely related to the original purchase.

(c) **Up-sell**. A subset of cross-selling, but in this case, selling more expensive products.

(d) **Reactivation**. Customers who have not purchased for some time, or have lapsed, can be encouraged to purchase again.

(e) **Referrals**. Generating sales from recommendations from existing customers.

Note that although the concept of CRM is prevalent in current marketing thinking and provides a valuable framework for tactics to increase loyalty and profitability, it may not accurately reflect the way the customer views their dealings with a company. Consumers may simply see their dealings with an organization as an exchange relationship and will not believe that they are tied to any company, i.e they may say 'I don't want a relationship'. O'Malley and Tynan (2001) note that the concept of a long-term relationship or partnership may be more readily applied to B2B marketing than consumer marketing. They say consumers:

> do not consider this false intimacy an interpersonal relationship. It is not driven primarily by trust, commitment, communication and shared values, but by convenience and self-interest.

It is useful to remember this consumer perspective on relationships when considering tactics to employ to help build and maintain relationships.

Marketing applications of CRM

A CRM system to support the four activities is made up of different marketing applications:

1 *Salesforce automation* (SFA). Sales representatives are supported in their account management and phone-based sales through tools to arrange and record customer enquiries and visits.

2 *Customer service management*. Representatives in contact centres respond to customer requests for information by using an intranet to access databases containing information on the customer, products and previous queries.

3 *Managing the sales process*. This can be achieved through e-commerce sites, or in a B2B context by supporting sales representatives by recording the sales process (SFA).

4 *Campaign management*. Managing ad, direct mail, e-mail and other campaigns.

5 *Analysis.* Through technologies such as data warehouses and approaches such as data mining, which are explained later in the chapter, customers' characteristics, their purchase behaviour and campaigns can be analysed in order to optimize the marketing mix.

Real-world E-Business experiences   **The E-consultancy interview**

Peter Cobb, co-founder of eBags, describes its approach to customer acquisition and retention

Overview and main concepts covered

Over the past 10 years, eBags has grown to be the largest seller of luggage and bags online. It offers bags from 500 brands with over 40,000 products available on its website. In the interview, eBags co-founder Peter Cobb talks about what eBags is doing to keep the growth continuing, why free shipping isn't so important online and the benefits of not having a warehouse. It combines discussion of how eBags varies elements of the marketing mix, as discussed in Chapter 8, and also approaches to customer acquisition and retention.

The interview

Q. Pure play online retail is performing well currently. Can multi-channel retailers catch up on the web?

Peter Cobb, eBags: Brick and mortar in our category is really struggling right now. Especially when you've got 200 products and you've got a competitor with 40,000. I think in a lot of categories, online is just such a better business model. We are so bullish on what's happening in the online retail world.

Our model is a drop ship model. We don't have a warehouse with 40,000 bags in it. We go to our brands and ask, what do you have on your website? We key in the information and feature it on our website. When brands sign up we tell them we don't ask much, but we need you to ship same day. This drop ship model is the reason we're alive. We don't have to spend tens of millions buying products and putting them in a warehouse.

Q: How much can e-commerce sales increases be attributed to a general online consumer shift?

Peter Cobb, eBags: I do think there's a general move toward online retail. This last holiday was one of the biggest shifts in people moving from brick and mortar to online. I heard that from multi-channel retailers. This was the year people realized online is a more efficient way to shop (depending on the product). Multi-channel retailers were hurt by a lack of inventory, and that pushed people online. Also, every year we're pushing how late into the season we can ship product. This year, it was all the way up to the 19th or 20th of December. In the past we just didn't want to risk it. That's all played into better efficiencies and more confidence from consumers. There are also more people that use the Internet for research.

Q. What have you changed at eBags in the past year?

Peter Cobb, eBags: From a marketing standpoint, we've gotten better. With our email platform, we've gone from a shotgun approach to 1 million email members to emails that have as many of 15 different segments in an email campaign. We have also instituted personalized emails. Based on what you've clicked on, you'll see products complementary to what you've purchased or clicked on at eBags.com. We've all gotten much smarter at using technology and making a better shopping experience.

Q. How do you organize your massive offering of products?

Peter Cobb, eBags: From a navigational standpoint it's challenging when you have 15,000 ladies' handbags. No one wants to wade through 15,000 handbags. Navigation taxonomy is really critical. It's also challenging on the marketing side. How do you create awareness for the products from a brand level? Some people shop from brand, some from product type, some at the price level.

Q. How important are special deals online, like free shipping?

Peter Cobb, eBags: I don't think free shipping is essential, or a requirement. I think it's one of the marketing tools that companies can use. I think there are some consumers that gravitate toward free shipping, but we've done tests where we've offered percent off and where we've done free shipping. We get more results from offering a percentage off. I think it boils down to value and a fair price.

Early on, we realized what was going on with luxury sale sites – Gilt, Groupon, etc. We realized you could sell upper end items, it just has to be a great value. We went to our upper end vendors and told them we'd want really great deals. It was a huge win for the customers. We specifically went to brands and said, give us 10 unbelievable products at fantastic prices. We featured those on our site, comparison shopping sites, etc. We used email, Twitter, Facebook and viral marketing to show that we had a great item on sale. All of those things add up.

Q. What has changed in online retail since last year?

Peter Cobb, eBags: A lot of us have gotten smarter on key words. We're monitoring those closely. We've also had fantastic partnerships. This holiday we launched with eBay. We realized they were committed to travel goods and handbags. We worked with ChannelAdviser to add an eBay store to eBags. Those customers want great value, and our products are on Buy It Now. That launched in November. We were amazed at how the eBay shoppers took to it. It ramped up during the holdays, but it's stayed high in the new year. Part of why it's been successful is because eBay has a bit of an issue with people buying products and not knowing whether they're legit or new. eBay has realized that there are some people who want the security of buying through a known entity but still want to use eBay and PayPal. Our feeling at eBags is that a lot of people go to eBags.com, but some people like using PayPal. Or shop via Amazon. eBags products are also featured on Amazon. Some want to use comparison shopping engines. We're agnostic on where we are.

Q. How important are comparison shopping engines?

Peter Cobb, eBags: We play in that arena for those customers who value price highest. We want to be price competitive. We see our eBags products in comparison shopping engines, but none of the things I've talked about are 20% or more of our marketing mix. It's really a nice balance. People don't just shop one specific way. Some people like using Nextag or Bing or Shopzilla. Others go straight to Google. Others start at eBay.

Q. How do you break out your marketing mix?

Peter Cobb, eBags: We break it up by marketing channel. We have people for every different channel. We divvy it all up. We have partners, like ChannelAdvisor that help us with the technology. Our 400,000 products are fed into ChannelAdvisor, they repackage that and feed it in to our marketing partners. Each of them has different flavors of how they like to receive information. It's been pretty cumbersome. But now it's not something where our IT people have to drop everything.

Q. What's coming next for eBags?

Peter Cobb, eBags: There are a couple of things we're doing site-wide. One of the things that's nice about technology today is that most people are on broadband. That gives us the opportunity to add bells and whistles that we couldn't do 5–10 years ago. We're ramping up video. We have interviews with designers and brand videos. That's something we're really excited about, that you couldn't even have done three years ago. We're also doing some things to make photographs larger. With broadband you can do that and it doesn't slow down the site.

A big area for us is behavioral targeting. If you came to the site and clicked on designer handbags, next time we're going to show you more of them. And show what others like you have purchased, rather than make you start from the very beginning.

We were just laughing about how we ever got a sale when there was dial up. It took 10 seconds to load each image. We don't have those issues now. You can whip through websites pretty easily.

Source: http://econsultancy.com/blog/5523-q-a-peter-cobb-of-ebags.

What is e-CRM?

The interactive nature of the web combined with e-mail communications provides an ideal environment in which to develop customer relationships, and databases provide a foundation for storing information about the relationship and providing information to strengthen it by improved, personalized services. This online approach to CRM is often known as '**e-CRM**', and it is on this we focus in this chapter. Although Figure 9.1 refers to the whole customer life cycle, typically it is used to refer to customer retention and extension activities.

It is difficult to state where CRM ends and e-CRM starts, since today they both make extensive use of digital technology and media. This is what Chaffey and Smith (2008) say:

> *What is e-CRM? Customer Relations Management with an 'e'? Ultimately, E-CRM cannot be separated from CRM, it needs to be integrated and seamlessly. However, many organisations do have specific E-CRM initiatives or staff responsible for E-CRM. Both CRM and E-CRM are not just about technology and databases, it's not just a process or a way of doing things, it requires, in fact, a complete customer culture.*

More specifically, we can say that important e-CRM challenges and activities which require management are:

- *Using the website for customer development* from generating leads through to conversion to an online or offline sale using e-mail and web-based information to encourage purchase.
- Managing e-mail list quality (coverage of e-mail addresses and integration of customer profile information from other databases to enable targeting).
- Applying *e-mail marketing* to support up-sell and cross-sell.
- *Data mining* to improve targeting.
- With a website with **personalization** or **mass customization** facilities to automatically recommend the 'next-best product'.

Electronic customer relationship management (e-CRM)
Using digital communications technologies to maximize sales to existing customers and encourage continued usage of online services.

Personalization
Delivering customized content for the individual through web pages, e-mail or push technology.

Mass customization
The creation of tailored marketing messages or products for individual customers or groups of customers typically using technology to retain the economies of scale and the capacity of mass marketing or production.

- Providing *online customer service facilities* (such as frequently asked questions, callback and chat support) that help achieve conversion to sale (these can be triggered automatically so that visitors to a site who show high intent or distress through multiple page visits can be prompted to enter a chat session or a callback).
- Managing *online service quality* to ensure that first-time buyers have a great customer experience that encourages them to buy again.
- Managing the *multi-channel customer experience* as customers use different media as part of the buying process and customer life cycle.

To help understand the scope of e-CRM, you may also find Figure 8.1 useful. This summarizes different marketing activities that need to be completed by an online retailer, structured according to customer acquisition, conversion and retention activities.

Sharma and Sheth (2004) have stressed the importance of a trend from mass marketing to what is now widely known as 'one-to-one' or '**customer-centric marketing**'. They note that e-channels can have advantages in terms of delivering relevant messages and offers to customers at relatively low cost. It can also be used to support customization of products. These authors give the example of the Dell model where each PC is manufactured and distributed 'on demand' according to the need of a specific customer. This is an example of what they refer to as 'reverse marketing' with the change on marketing execution from product supply to customer need. Another aspect of this transformation is that online, web marketers can track the past and current behaviours of customers in order to customize communications to encourage future purchases. This approach, which is another aspect of reverse marketing and also a key concept with e-CRM, can be characterized as '**sense and respond communications**'. The classic example of this is the personalization facilities provided by Amazon. Companies can also arrange triggered or follow-up e-mail activity after a customer event such as a quote (as used by insurer MORE TH>N, www.morethan.com) or an abandoned shopping basket (as used by Tesco.com) to encourage purchase.

Benefits of e-CRM

Using the Internet for relationship marketing involves integrating the customer database with websites to make the relationship targeted and personalized. Through doing this marketing can be improved as follows.

- *Targeting more cost-effectively.* Traditional targeting, for direct mail for instance, is often based on mailing lists compiled according to criteria that mean that not everyone contacted is in the target market. For example, a company wishing to acquire new affluent consumers may use postcodes to target areas with appropriate demographics, but within the postal district the population may be heterogeneous. The result of poor targeting will be low response rates, perhaps less than 1%. The Internet has the benefit that the list of contacts is *self-selecting* or pre-qualified. A company will only aim to build relationships with those who have visited a website and expressed an interest in its products by registering their name and address. The act of visiting the website and browsing indicates a target customer. Thus the approach to acquiring new customers with whom to build relationships is fundamentally different, as it involves attracting the customers to the website, where the company provides an offer to make them register.
- *Achieve mass customization of the marketing messages* (and possibly the product). This tailoring process is described in a subsequent section. Technology makes it possible to send tailored e-mails at much lower costs than is possible with direct mail and also to provide tailored web pages to smaller groups of customers (micro-segments).
- *Increase depth, breadth and nature of relationship.* The nature of the Internet medium enables more information to be supplied to customers as required. The nature of the relationship can be changed in that contact with a customer can be made more frequently. The frequency of contact with the customer can be determined by customers – whenever

Customer-centric marketing

This is based on customer behaviour within the target audience and then seeks to fulfil the needs and wants of each individual customer.

Sense and respond communications

Delivering timely, relevant communications to customers as part of a contact strategy based on assessment of their position in the customer life cycle and monitoring specific interactions with a company's website, e-mails and staff.

they have the need to visit their personalized pages – or they can be contacted by e-mail by the company according to their communications preferences.

- *A learning relationship can be achieved using different tools throughout the customer life cycle.* For example, tools summarize products purchased on-site and the searching behaviour that occurred before these products were bought; online feedback forms about the site or products are completed when a customer requests free information; questions asked through forms or e-mails to the online customer service facilities; online questionnaires asking about product category interests and opinions on competitors; new product development evaluation – commenting on prototypes of new products. Online facilitates learning about customer needs, as shown by Box 9.1.
- *Lower cost.* Contacting customers by e-mail or through their viewing web pages costs less than using physical mail, but perhaps more importantly, information only needs to be sent to those customers who have expressed a preference for it, resulting in fewer mail-outs. Once personalization technology has been purchased, much of the targeting and communications can be implemented automatically.

Customer engagement

Repeated interactions that strengthen the emotional, psychological or physical investment a customer has in a brand.

Customer engagement strategy

This difficulty in finding opportunities to achieve attention online on all types of sites has led to the emergence of the concept of **customer engagement** as a key challenge with

---

Box 9.1	Tapping into the wikinomics trend

'Wikinomics' is a term brought to prominence by Don Tapscott and Anthony Williams. It explains how businesses can generate business value through using the Internet to facilitate participation by individuals and collaboration by individuals.

These are my examples of business initiatives where companies have successfully taken advantage of wikinomics:

- *Dell Ideastorm* (www.ideastorm.com). Dell customers, or even non-customers, can suggest new products and features. In the separate 'Ideas in Action' section they update consumers on actions taken by the company. As well as improvements to customer service, they have explained how they have introduced systems with a non-Windows Linux operating system in response to suggestions on Ideastorm.
- *Procter and Gamble's Innocentive site* (www.innocentive.com) where freelance scientists, students and academics can work on problems posed by industry and sell solutions in return for cash rewards.
- Consumer-generated ads from Frito Lay, owners of the Doritos brand. Doritos used consumer-shot videos for its major ad slot at the Superbowl (major US baseball competition final). Doritos solicited ad executions through Yahoo! which hosted a contest for users to vote on their favourite submissions.
- *Ministry of Sound* (www.ministryofsound.com) encourages its web audience to vote on the best tracks and videos for its compilations and, although not a traditional media owner, now includes sponsored links and searches throughout its site to generate additional revenue.
- *Wikipedia* (www.wikipedia.com). Ironically, arguably the best-known example of wikinomics is an entirely altruistic initiative by its founder, Jimmy Wales; this is one of the few sites not to accept contextual advertising which could generate millions of dollars per month.

You can see that wikinomics can be used for a range of business applications, to create supplementary core revenue through contextual advertising, for market research or, as in the case of betting and lending exchanges, directly for generating income.

which digital marketers are increasingly concerned. cScape (2008) describe customer engagement as:

Repeated interactions that strengthen the emotional, psychological or physical invest-ment a customer has in a brand.

While for Haven (2007) customer engagement is:

the level of involvement, interaction, intimacy, and influence an individual has with a brand over time.

As we noted in Chapter 8, arguably the biggest difference in communications introduced by the growth of digital media and the web is the capability, or many would say necessity, to include customers' conversations as an integral part of communications. Today, proactively managing consumer participation through social media is seen as essential. The '*Focus on Social media*' section discusses this challenge.

Permission marketing

Permission marketing is an established approach which should form a practical founda-tion for CRM and online customer engagement. 'Permission marketing' is a term coined by Seth Godin. Godin (1999) notes that while research used to show we were bombarded by 500 marketing messages a day, with the advent of the web and digital TV this has now increased to over 3,000 a day! From an organization's viewpoint, this leads to a dilution in the effectiveness of the messages – how can the communications of any one company stand out? From the customer's viewpoint, time is seemingly in ever-shorter supply, cus-tomers are losing patience and expect reward for their attention, time and information. Godin refers to the traditional approach as '**interruption marketing**'. Permission market-ing is about seeking the customer's permission before engaging them in a relationship and providing something in exchange. The classic exchange is based on information or enter-tainment – a B2B site can offer a free report in exchange for a customer sharing their e-mail address, while a B2C site can offer a newsletter with valuable content and offers.

From an e-commerce perspective, a customer agrees to engage in a relationship when they check a box on a web form to indicate that they agree to receiving further communi-cations from a company. This is referred to as '**opt-in**'. This is preferable to **opt-out**, the situation where a customer has to consciously agree not to receive further information. You may recall from Chapter 4 that in many countries data protection laws requiring opt-in before customers receive communications and mandatory inclusion of opt-out have now been introduced in an attempt to stop spamming. Effectively, the law is mandating permis-sion marketing as best practice!

The importance of incentivization in permission marketing has been emphasized by Seth Godin who likens the process of acquisition and retention to dating someone. Godin (1999) suggests that dating the customer involves:

1 Offering the prospect an *incentive* to volunteer.
2 Using the attention offered by the prospect, offer a curriculum over time, teaching the consumer about your product or service.
3 Reinforce the *incentive* to guarantee that the prospect maintains the permission.
4 Offer additional *incentives* to get even more permission from the consumer.
5 Over time, use the permission to change consumer behaviour towards profits.

Notice the importance of incentives at each stage. The use of incentives at the start of the relationship and throughout it is key to successful rela-tionships. As we shall see in a later section, e-mail is very important in permission marketing to maintain the dialogue between company and customer.

Permission marketing
Customers agree (opt in) to be involved in an organization's marketing activities, usually as a result of an incentive.

Interruption marketing
Marketing communications that disrupt customers' activities.

Opt-in
A customer proactively agrees to receive further information.

Opt-out
A customer declines the offer to receive further information.

Debate 9.1

Is permission marketing the future?

'In the future, all marketing communications, regardless of medium, will be permission-based.'

Figure 9.2 summarizes the process of permission marketing in an online context. It shows how different methods are used to drive visitors to a website (1); incentives are then used to profile the customer (2). Subsequent e-mail or social network communications (3) and direct mail (4) are used to encourage repeat visits to the website for future purchase or to learn more about the customer and increase the information in the profile (5).

Customer profiling

Qualified lead

Contact information for a customer and an indication of his or her propensity to purchase different products.

Customer profile

Information that can be used to segment a customer.

To engage a customer in an online relationship, the minimum information that needs to be collected in an online form such as in Figure 9.2 is an e-mail address. This was an initial approach taken by the Peppers and Rogers site (www.1to1.com). What we really need, particularly for B2B sites, is a **qualified lead** that provides us with more information about the customer to help us decide whether that customer is a good prospect who should be targeted with further communications. For B2B this could mean a visit by field sales staff or a follow-up e-mail to arrange this. The Peppers and Rogers site has now been updated to reflect this approach.

To continue the relationship it is essential to build a **customer profile** that details each customer's product interest, demographics or role in the buying decision. This will affect the type of information and services delivered at the retention stage. For the customer to give this information a company will have to offer an incentive, establish trust and demonstrate credibility. Data protection and privacy law sets constraints on what can be collected from the customer, as described in Chapter 4 (p. 194).

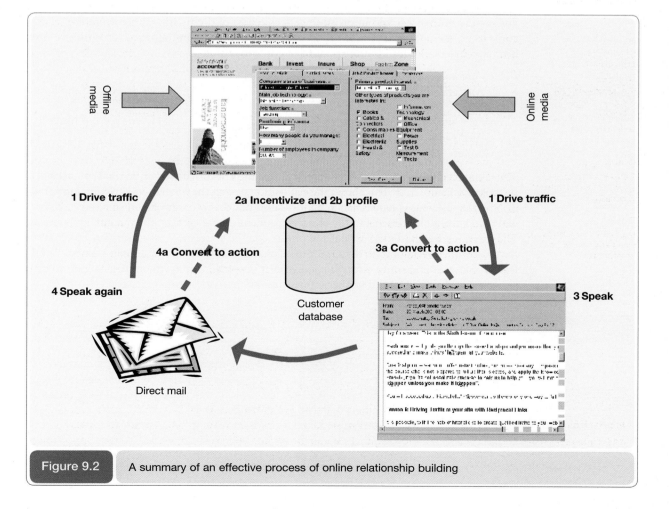

| Figure 9.2 | A summary of an effective process of online relationship building |

Peppers and Rogers (1999) have applied their work on building *one-to-one* relationships with the customer to the web. They suggest the IDIC approach as a framework for using the web effectively to form and build relationships:

1 *Customer identification.* This stresses the need to identify each customer on their first visit and subsequent visits. Common methods for identification are use of cookies or asking the customer to log on to a site.
2 *Customer differentiation.* This refers to building a profile to help segment customers. Characteristics for differentiating customers are described in Chapter 4 (p. 187).
3 *Customer interactions.* These are interactions provided on-site, such as customer service questions or creating a tailored product.
4 *Customization.* This refers to personalization or mass customization of content or e-mails according to the segmentation achieved at the acquisition stage. Approaches for personalization are explained in the section on *customer retention management.*

Note that although we are suggesting it is vital to capture the registration information, this should not be too 'up-front' since studies reported by Nielsen (2000) show that having to register acts as a barrier to entering sites. So the advice is to delay customer registration as late as possible.

Conversion marketing

Conversion marketing
Using marketing communications to maximize conversion of potential customers to actual customers and existing customers to repeat customers.

For managers to assess and improve the effectiveness of their CRM implementation, evaluation using the **conversion marketing** concept is useful. In an online context, this assesses how effective marketing communications are in converting:

- web browsers or offline audiences to site visitors;
- site visitors to engaged site visitors who stay on the site and progress beyond the home page;
- engaged site visitors to prospects (who are profiled for their characteristics and needs);
- prospects into customers;
- customers into repeat customers.

We referenced a high-level model based on this approach which can be used for planning purposes in Figure 5.14. This shows the acquisition part of the process and gives an indication of how the different channels can support each other. At each conversion step, some visitors will switch from one channel to the other, dependent on preferences and marketing messages. The dilemma for marketers is that the online channels are cheapest to service, but tend to have a lower conversion rate than traditional channels because of the human element. It follows that it is important to offer phone, live chat or e-mail contact in online channels to help convert customers who need further information or persuading to purchase.

Box 9.2 | Using the RACE marketing value framework to increase sales

RACE (Figure 9.3) is a practical framework designed to help marketers manage and improve the commercial value that their organizations gain from digital marketing. It is intended to help simplify their approach to reviewing the performance of their online marketing and taking actions to improve its effectiveness.

RACE consists of four steps designed to help engage prospects, customers and fans with brands throughout the customer life cycle:

REACH
Build awareness on other
sites and in offline media
and drive to web presences
KPIs:
• Unique visitors and fans
• Audience share
• Revenue or goal value
per visit

ACT
Engage audience with
brand on its website or
other online presence
KPIs:
• Bounce rate
• Pages per visit
• Product page conversion

ENGAGE
Build customer and fan
relationships through time
to achieve retention goals
KPIs:
• % active hurdle rates
• Fan engagement
• Repeat conversion

CONVERT
Achieve conversion to
marketing goals such as
fans, leads or sales on web
presences and offline
KPIs:
• Conversion rates
• Leads and sales
• Revenue and margin

Figure 9.3	Reach–Act–Convert–Engage model
	Source: Smart Insights (2010) Introducing RACE = A practical framework to improve your digital marketing. Dave Chaffey, 15 July 2010. http:wwwsmartinsights.com/blog/digital-marketing-strategy/race-a-practical-framework-to-improve-your-digital-marketing.

- *Step 1 Reach* – Build awareness of a brand, its products and services on other sites and in offline media and build traffic by driving visits to web presences.
- *Step 2 Act* – Engage audience with brand on its website or other online presence to encourage them to act or interact with a company or other customers.
- *Step 3 Convert* – Achieve conversion to marketing goals such as new fans, leads or sales on web presences and offline.
- *Step 4 Engage* – Build customer relationships through time to achieve retention goals.

Integrating RACE

Digital channels always work best when they are integrated with other channels, so where appropriate digital channels should be combined with the traditional offline media and channels. The most important aspects of integration are, first, using traditional media to raise awareness of the value of the online presences at the Reach and Act stages. Second, at the Convert and Engage steps, customers may prefer to interact with customer representatives.

Digital marketing – it's not just about the website

Today, the popularity of participation in social media means that how to reach, interact, convert and maintain ongoing engagement of customers through social networks is vital to the success of a brand. At each step in RACE you need to think how social media can help achieve your goals and how you can measure the effectiveness.

Note: RACE is an evolution of the REAN (Reach, Engage, Activate, Nurture) framework originally developed by Xavier Blanc and popularized by Steve Jackson in his book *Cult of Analytics* (Jackson, 2009).

Varianini and Vaturi (2000) suggest that many e-commerce failures have resulted from low conversion as a result of poorly targeted media spending. They suggest the communications mix should be optimized to minimize the cost of acquisition of customers. It can also be suggested that optimization of the conversion to action on-site is important to the success of marketing. Conversion to customer acquisition will be low if the site design, quality of service and marketing communications are not effective in converting visitors to prospects or buyers.

Agrawal *et al.* (2001) have developed a scorecard, assessed using a longitudinal study analysing hundreds of e-commerce sites in the USA and Europe. The scorecard is based on the **performance drivers** or critical success factors for e-commerce such as the costs for acquisition and retention, conversion rates of visitors to buyers to repeat buyers, together with churn rates. Note that to maximize retention and minimize churn, service-quality-based drivers need to be evaluated.

Performance drivers
Critical success factors that govern whether objectives are achieved.

There are three main parts to this scorecard:

1 *Attraction.* Size of visitor's base, visitor acquisition cost and visitor advertising revenue (e.g. media sites).
2 *Conversion.* Customer base, customer acquisition costs, customer conversion rate, number of transactions per customer, revenue per transaction, revenue per customer, customer gross income, customer maintenance cost, customer operating income, customer churn rate, customer operating income before marketing spending.
3 *Retention.* This uses similar measures to those for conversion customers.

The survey performed byAgrawal *et al.* (2001) shows that:

companies were successful at luring visitors to their sites, but not at getting these visitors to buy or at turning occasional buyers into frequent ones.

Agrawal *et al.* (2001) performed a further analysis where they modelled the theoretical change in net present value contributed by an e-commerce site in response to a 10% change in these performance drivers. This shows the relative importance of these drivers, or 'levers' as they refer to them:

Attraction
- Visitor acquisition cost: 0.74% change in net present value (NPV)
- Visitor growth: 3.09% change in NPV.

Conversion
- Customer conversion rate: 0.84% change in NPV
- Revenue per customer: 2.32% change in NPV.

Retention
- Cost of repeat customer: 0.69% change in NPV
- Revenue per repeat customer: 5.78% change in NPV
- Repeat customer churn rate: 6.65% change in NPV
- Repeat customer conversion rate: 9.49% change in NPV.

This modelling highlights the importance of on-site marketing communications and the quality of service delivery in converting browsers to buyers and buyers into repeat buyers. It also highlights the need to balance investment between customer acquisition and retention. Many start-up companies invest primarily in customer acquisition. For failed dot-com retailers such as LetsBuyit.com this was a strategic error since customer retention through repeat purchases is vital to the success of the online service.

The online buying process

Companies that understand how customers use the new media in their purchase decision-making can develop integrated communications strategies that support their customers at each stage of the buying process. Considering mixed-mode buying is a key aspect of devising online marketing communications since the customer should be supported in changing from one channel to another.

The simple model of the buying process shown in Figure 9.4 is valuable in developing the right online marketing tactics to support each stage of the process for each business.

Individual preferences for using the web will also differ. Lewis and Lewis (1997) identified five different types of web users who exhibit different **searching behaviour** according to the purpose of using the web:

Searching behaviours
Approaches to finding information vary from directed to undirected.

- *Directed information-seekers.* Will be looking for product, market or leisure information. This type of user tends to be experienced in using the web and is proficient in using search engines and directories.
- *Undirected information-seekers.* These are the users usually referred to as 'surfers', who like to browse and change sites by following hyperlinks. This group tends to be novice users (but not exclusively so) and they may be more likely to click on banner advertisements. The research in Figure 9.6 suggests that this behaviour is now less common.

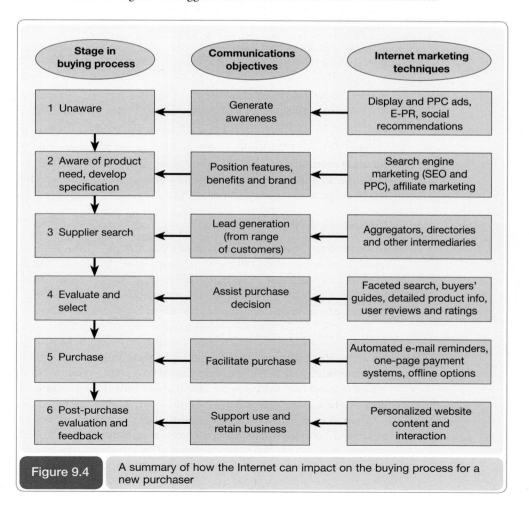

Figure 9.4 A summary of how the Internet can impact on the buying process for a new purchaser

- *Directed buyers.* These buyers are online to purchase specific products. For such users, brokers or intermediaries who compare product features and prices will be important locations to visit.
- *Bargain hunters.* These users want to use the offers available from sales promotions such as free samples or prizes.
- *Entertainment seekers.* Users looking to interact with the web for enjoyment through entering contests such as quizzes.

These different types of behaviour could be exhibited by the same person in different sessions online, or, less likely, in the same session.

Differences in buyer behaviour in target markets

As explained in Chapter 4, in the section *Understanding users' access requirements*, there is great variation in the proportion of user access in different countries. This gives rise to differences in buyer behaviour between different countries or between different segments according to how sophisticated customers are in their use of the Internet.

Differences between B2C and B2B buyer behaviour

Major differences in buyer behaviour exist between the B2B and B2C markets, and these must be accommodated in e-marketing communications. The main differences are:

1 Market structure
2 Nature of the buying unit
3 Type of purchase
4 Type of buying decision
5 Communication differences.

One of the main differences between business-to-business and business-to-consumer is the number of buyers. As Kotler (1997) points out, in B2B there tend to be *far fewer but larger buyers*. This means that the existence of suppliers tends to be well known, so efforts to promote the website using methods such as banner advertising or listing in search engines are less important than for consumer brands.

Influences on purchase

In the online environment, purchasers lack the physical reassurance we have when purchasing from a store or talking to someone over the phone. This is compounded because of stories of fraud and security problems. It follows that consumers are looking for cues of trust when they are on a site, which can include brand familiarity, site design, the type of content, accreditation and recommendations by other customers.

Bart *et al.* (2005) have developed a useful, widely referenced conceptual model that links website and consumer characteristics, online trust, and behaviour based on 6,831 consumers across 25 sites from 8 website categories including retail, travel, financial services, portals and community sites. We have summarized the eight main drivers of trust from the study in Figure 9.5 and have added some details about how these elements of trust can be substantiated or proved on the website.

The model of Bart *et al.* (2005) and similar models are centred on a site, but perceptions of trust are also built from external sources including the role of social media and friends, in particular, which can have a significant influence on purchase as research from Brand-NewWorld (2004) shows (Figure 9.6). A useful summary of influences on online purchase intention has been proposed by Dennis *et al.* (2009) where they do stress the importance of 'subjective norms' or 'social factors' in influencing purchase.

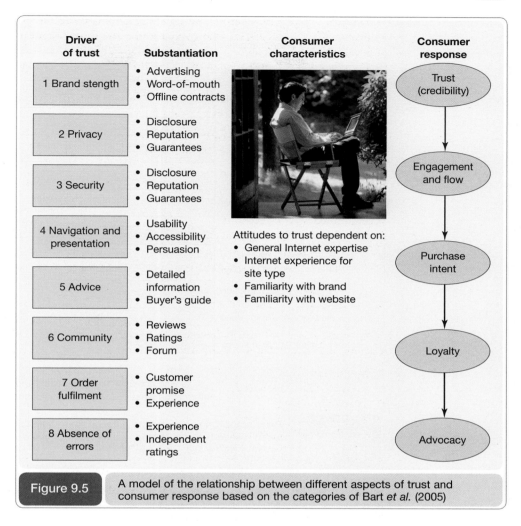

Driver of trust	Substantiation	Consumer characteristics	Consumer response

Figure 9.5 A model of the relationship between different aspects of trust and consumer response based on the categories of Bart *et al.* (2005)

The net promoter score

Net promoter score
A measure of the number of advocates a company (or website) has who would recommend it compared to the number of detractors.

Net promoter score (NPS) is a measure of customer advocacy originally popularized by Reichheld (2006) in his book *The Ultimate Question* which is essentially '*would you recommend us?*' It is highly relevant to CRM since recommendations are important to acquiring customers, but it is also the ultimate measure of customer satisfaction which is needed to drive retention.

Reichheld explains the main process for NPS as follows:

1 Systematically categorize customers into promoters, passives, or detractors. If you prefer, you can call them loyal advocates, fair-weather friends, and adversaries.
2 Creating closed-loop processes so that the right employees will directly investigate the root causes that drive customers into these categories.
3 Making the creation of more promoters and fewer detractors a top priority so employees up and down the organization take actions based on their findings from these root-cause investigations.

In practice, consumers are asked 'Would you recommend [Brand/Company X] to a friend or colleague', answered on a scale between 0 (not at all likely) and 10 (extremely likely). The actual score is calculated by subtracting the percentage of detractors (those giving 0–6 answers) from promoters (9–10s). The middle section, between 7 and 8, are the so-called passives.

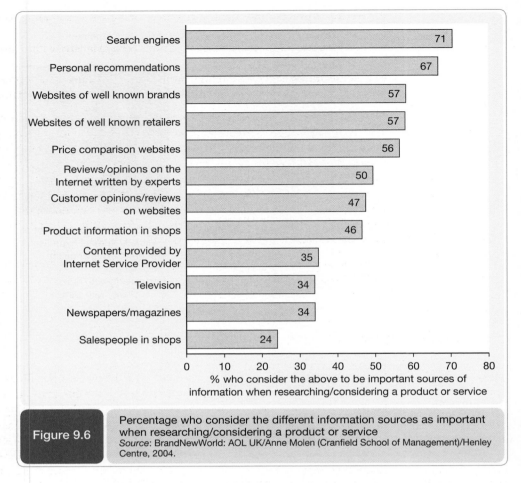

	Figure 9.6	Percentage who consider the different information sources as important when researching/considering a product or service

Source: BrandNewWorld: AOL UK/Anne Molen (Cranfield School of Management)/Henley Centre, 2004.

The concept of NPS is based on economic analysis of the customer base of a company. For Dell, Reichheld estimates that the average consumer is worth $210 (based on a lifetime-value calculation of future value over a five-year period calculated as Net Present Value), whereas a detractor costs the company $57 and a promoter generates $328. Online Dell uses software from Opinion Labs (www.opinionlabs.com) to both gather feedback and follow up on negative experiences and so reduce the number of detractors with major negative sentiment.

So, the idea is that after surveying as many customers as possible (to make it representative) and show you are listening, you then work backwards to determine which aspects of the experience of interacting with a brand creates 'promoters' or 'detractors'. Some specific approaches that can be used to help manage NPS in the online environment are:

Facilitating online advocacy:

- Page template contains 'forward/recommend to a friend' options.
- E-mail templates contain 'forward to a friend option'.
- Facilitate customer feedback through a structured programme of e-mailing customers for their opinions and NPS evaluations and by making it easy for site owners to comment.
- Showcase positive experiences, for example, e-retail sites often contain options for rating and commenting on products.
- Involve customers more in shaping your web services and core product offerings.

Managing online detractors

- Use online reputation management tools (www.davechaffey.com/online-reputation-management-tools) for notification of negative (and positive) comments.

- Develop a process and identify resource for rapidly responding to negative comments using a natural and open approach.
- Assess and manage the influence of negative comments within the natural listings of search engines.
- Practise fundamental marketing principles of listening to customer comments about products and services and aim to rectify them to win back the situation!

Kirby and Samson (2008) have critiqued the use of the NPS in practice. For example, they ask: 'Is an NPS of 40, consisting of 70% promoters and 30% detractors, the same as the same NPS consisting of 40% promoters and 0% detractors?' They also quote research by Kumar *et al.* (2007) which shows that while about three-quarters of US telecoms and financial service customers may intend to recommend when asked, only about one-third actually follow through and only about 13% of those referrals actually generate new customers. Keiningham *et al.* (2007) have assessed the value of recommendation metrics as determinants of customer lifetime value and also believe that the use of NPS could be misleading. They say the consequences of a simple focus on NPS are:

> *the potential misallocation of customer satisfaction and loyalty resources due to flawed strategies that are guided by a myopic focus on customers' recommend intentions.*

Customer acquisition management

Customer acquisition
Techniques used to gain new prospects and customers.

Offline marketing communications
Traditional techniques such as print and TV advertising used to generate website traffic.

Digital media channels
Online communications techniques used to achieve goals of brand awareness, familiarity, favourability and to influence purchase intent.

In an online context, '**customer acquisition**' can have two meanings. First, it may mean the use of the website to acquire new customers for a company as qualified leads that can hopefully be converted into sales. Second, it may mean encouraging existing customers to *migrate* to using online for purchase or service. Many organizations concentrate on the former, but where acquisition is well managed, campaigns will be used to achieve online conversion. For example, American Express developed a '*Go Paperless*' campaign to persuade customers to receive and review their statements online rather than by post. Phone bank First Direct used call centre representatives to persuade customers of the benefits of bypassing them by reviewing their statements online. They also encourage 'e-advocacy' amongst employees, i.e. encourage them to use the online services so they can better empathize with customer needs.

Before an organization can acquire customers through the content on its site, it must, of course, develop marketing communications strategies to attract visitors to the website.

Focus on	Marketing communications for customer acquisition including search engine marketing, online PR, online partnerships, interactive advertising, e-mail marketing and social media marketing

Online marketing communications
Internet-based techniques used to generate website traffic.

E-commerce managers constantly strive to deliver the most effective mix of communications to drive traffic to their e-commerce sites. The different techniques can be characterized as traditional **offline marketing communications** or rapidly evolving **online marketing communications** which are also referred to as **digital media channels**. The objective of employing these techniques is often to acquire new visitors or 'build traffic' using the diverse marketing communications techniques summarized in Figure 1.6. Some additional techniques to promote repeat visits are considered in the section on *Customer retention management*.

The characteristics of interactive marketing communications

To best exploit the characteristics of digital media, it is important to understand the different communications characteristics of traditional and new media. In this section, we look at eight key differences.

1 From push to pull

Push media

Communications are broadcast from an advertiser to consumers of the message who are passive recipients.

Pull media

The consumer is proactive in selection of the message through actively seeking out a website.

Traditional media such as print, TV and radio are **push media**, a one-way street where information is mainly unidirectional, from company to customer. In contrast, the web is an example of **pull media**. It means that as prospects and customers only visit a website when it enters their head to do so – when they have a defined need – they are proactive and self-selecting. But online pull means marketers have less control than in traditional communications where the message is pushed out to a defined audience. What are the e-marketing implications of the pull medium? First, we need to provide the physical stimuli to encourage visits to websites. This may mean traditional ads, direct mail or physical reminders. Second, we need to ensure our site is optimized for search engines. Third, e-mail is an online push medium, so it should be a priority objective of website design to capture customers' e-mail addresses in order that opt-in e-mail can be used to push relevant and timely messages to customers.

2 From monologue to dialogue

Interactivity

The medium enables a dialogue between company and customer.

Creating a dialogue through **interactivity** is important. Since the Internet is a digital medium and communications are mediated by software on the web server that hosts the web content, this provides the opportunity for two-way interaction with the customer. This is a distinguishing feature of the medium (Peters, 1998). For example, if a registered customer requests information, or orders a particular product, it will be possible for the supplier to contact them in future using e-mail with details of new offers related to their specific interest. Deighton (1996) proclaimed the interactive benefits of the Internet as a means of developing long-term relationships with customers.

A website, interactive digital TV and mobile phones all enable marketers to enter dialogue with customers. But digital dialogues have a less obvious benefit also – intelligence. Interactive tools for customer self-help can help collect intelligence – clickstream analysis recorded in web analytics can help us build up valuable pictures of customer preferences and help marketers 'sense and respond'.

3 From one-to-many to one-to-some and one-to-one

Traditional push communications such as TV and print are one-to-many: from one company to many customers, often the same message to different segments and often poorly targeted. With new media 'one-to-some' – reaching a niche or micro-segment becomes more practical – e-marketers can afford to tailor and target their message to different segments. We can even move to one-to-one communications where personalized messages can be delivered.

4 From one-to-many to many-to-many communications

New media also enable many-to-many communications. Hoffman and Novak (1996) noted that new media are many-to-many media. Here customers can interact with other customers via your website or in independent communities. The success of online auctions such as eBay also shows the power of many-to-many communications.

5 From 'lean-back' to 'lean-forward'

New media are also intense media – they are lean-forward media in which the website usually has the visitor's undivided attention. This intensity means that the customer wants to be in control and wants to experience flow and responsiveness to their needs. First impressions are important.

TV is more lean-back – the TV may be on, but its audience is not necessarily watching it. An article in the *Guardian* (2003) entitled 'TV ads "a waste of money"' summarizes research observing the reaction of consumers to ads. It supports those who argue that many consumers do not regularly watch TV ads. The study found people who watched television with family or friends were far more likely to talk to each other during the commercial breaks than to focus on the ads. Others spent the commercial break doing housework, reading or channel hopping.

6 The medium changes the nature of standard marketing communications tools such as advertising

In addition to offering the opportunity for one-to-one marketing, the Internet can be, and still is, widely used for one-to-many advertising. On the Internet the overall message from the advertiser becomes less important, and typically it is detailed information the user is seeking. The website itself can be considered as similar in function to an advertisement (since it can inform, persuade and remind customers about the offering, although it is not paid for in the same way as a traditional advertisement). Berthon *et al.* (1996) consider a website as a mix between advertising and direct selling since it can also be used to engage the visitor in a dialogue. Constraints on advertising in traditional mass media such as paying for time or space become less important.

Peters (1998) suggests that communication via the new media is differentiated from communication using traditional media in four different ways. First, *communication style* is changed, with *immediate* or synchronous transfer of information through online customer service being possible. Asynchronous communication, where there is a time delay between sending and receiving information as through e-mail, also occurs. Second, *social presence* or the feeling that a communications exchange is sociable, warm, personal and active may be lower if a standard web page is delivered, but can be enhanced, perhaps by personalization. Third, the consumer has more *control of contact*, and finally the user has control of *content*, through selection or through personalization facilities.

7 Increase in communications intermediaries

If we consider advertising and PR, with traditional media this occurs through a potentially large number of media owners for TV, radio and print publications. In the Internet era there is a vastly increased range of media owners or publishers through which marketers can promote their services and specifically gain links to their website. Traditional radio channels, newspapers and print titles have migrated online, but in addition there are a vast number of online-only publishers including horizontal portals (Chapter 2) such as search engines and vertical portals such as industry-specific sites. The online marketer needs to select the most appropriate of this plethora of sites to drive traffic to their website.

8 Integration remains important

Although new media have distinct characteristics compared to traditional media, this does not mean we should necessarily concentrate our communications solely on new media. Rather we should combine and integrate new and traditional media according to their strengths. We can then achieve synergy – the sum is greater than its parts. Most of us still spend most of our time in the real world rather than the virtual world, so offline promotion of the proposition of a website is important. It is also important to support mixed-mode buying.

Similarly, inbound communications to a company need to be managed. Consider what happens if the customer needs support for an error with their system. They may start by using the on-site diagnostics but these do not solve the problem. They then ring customer support. This process will be much more effective if support staff can access the details of the problem as previously typed in by the customer to the diagnostics package.

Assessing marketing communications effectiveness

A campaign will not be successful if it meets its objectives of acquiring site visitors and customers but the cost of achieving this is too high. This constraint is usually imposed simply by having a campaign budget. However, it is also essential to have specific objectives for the cost of getting the visitor to the site using different **referrers** combined with the cost of achieving the outcomes during their visit. This is stated as the **cost per acquisition (CPA)** (sometimes cost per action). Depending on context and market of a site, CPA may refer to different outcomes – the acquisition of a visitor, a lead or a sale.

To control costs, it is important for managers to define a target **allowable cost per acquisition** such as £30 for generating a business lead or £50 for achieving sign-up to a credit card.

Figure 9.7 shows the full range of measures used by digital marketers to control communications expenditure from least sophisticated to more sophisticated as follows:

0 *Volume or number of visitors*. This is usually measured as thousands of unique visitors. It is preferable to using page views or hits (see Chapter 12) as a measure of effectiveness, since it is opportunities to communicate with individuals. A more sophisticated measure is reach (%) or online audience share. This is only possible using panel data or audience data tools such as www.netratings.com or www.hitwise.com.

Example: An online bank has 1 million unique visitors per month.

1 *Quality or conversion rates to action*. This shows what proportion of visitors from different sources take specific marketing outcomes on the web such as lead, sale or subscription. **Bounce rates** can also be used to assess the relevance and appeal of the page that the visitor arrives on.

Example: Of these visitors 10% convert to an outcome such as logging in to their account or asking for a quote for a product.

2 *Cost (cost per click)*. The cost of visitor acquisition is usually measured specific to a particular online marketing tool such as paid search engine marketing since it is difficult to estimate for an entire site with many visitors referred from different sources.

Example: £2 CPC.

Referrer

The source of a website visit, e.g. paid search, affiliate marketing, online advertising or recorded as 'no referrer', i.e. when a URL is typed in directly.

Cost per acquisition (CPA)

The cost of acquiring a new customer. Typically limited to the communications cost and refers to cost per sale for new customers.

Allowable cost per acquisition

A target maximum cost for generating leads or new customers profitably.

Bounce rate

Percentage of visitors entering a site who leave immediately after viewing one page only (known as 'single-page visits').

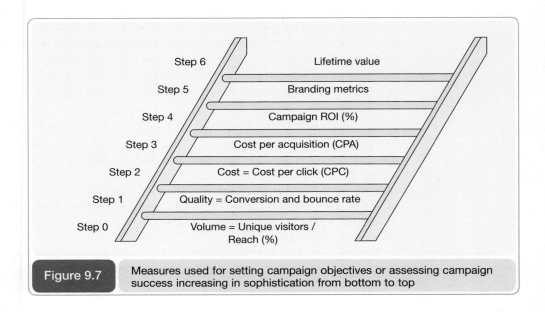

Step 6 — Lifetime value
Step 5 — Branding metrics
Step 4 — Campaign ROI (%)
Step 3 — Cost per acquisition (CPA)
Step 2 — Cost = Cost per click (CPC)
Step 1 — Quality = Conversion and bounce rate
Step 0 — Volume = Unique visitors / Reach (%)

Figure 9.7 Measures used for setting campaign objectives or assessing campaign success increasing in sophistication from bottom to top

3 *Cost (cost per action or acquisition).* When cost of visitor acquisition is combined with conversion to outcomes this is the cost of (customer) acquisition.

Example: £20 CPA (since only one in ten visitors take an action).

4 *Return on investment (ROI).* Return on investment is used to assess the profitability of any marketing activity or indeed any investment. There are different forms of ROI, depending on how profitability is calculated. Here we will assume it is just based on sales value or profitability based on the cost per click and conversion rate.

$$ROI = \frac{Profit\ generated\ from\ referrer}{Amount\ spent\ on\ advertising\ with\ referrer}$$

A related measure, which does not take profitability into account is return on advertising spend (ROAS) which is calculated as follows:

$$ROI = \frac{Total\ sales\ revenue\ generated\ from\ referrer}{Amount\ spent\ on\ advertising\ with\ referrer}$$

5 *Branding metrics.* These tend to be only relevant to interactive advertising or sponsorship. They are the equivalent of offline advertising metrics, i.e. brand awareness (aided and unaided), ad recall, brand favourability and purchase intent. Recorded using tools such as Dynamic Logic (www.dynamiclogic.com).

6 *Lifetime-value-based ROI.* Here the value of gaining the customer is not just based on the initial purchase, but the lifetime value (and costs) associated with the customer. This requires more sophisticated models which can be most readily developed for online retailers and online financial services providers.

Example: A bank uses a net present value model for insurance products which looks at the value over 10 years but the main focus is on a 5-year result and takes into account:
- acquisition cost
- retention rates
- claims
- expenses.

This is valuable since it helps give them a realistic 'allowable cost per sale' from different communications tools which is needed to get return over 5 years.

Figure 9.8 shows an example of effectiveness measures for an online ad campaign for an insurance product. Here an opportunity or lead is when a quote is requested. Note that the cost of acquisition is high, but this does not take into account the synergies of online advertising with offline campaigns, i.e. those who are influenced by the ad, but do not click through immediately.

Online marketing communications

In this section we will review approaches to online promotion using the different tools of Figure 1.6 from 1 to 6. These techniques are often combined in what is known as a '**traffic-building campaign**'; this is a method of increasing the audience of a site using different online (and offline) techniques.

A company's investment in the techniques in Figure 1.6 for customer acquisition should be based on the metrics discussed in the previous section. Most important is minimizing the cost of acquisition against volume required.

1 Search engine marketing (SEM)

As explained in Chapter 2, **search engines** and **directories** are the primary methods of finding information about a company and its products. It follows that if an organization is

---

Traffic-building campaign
The use of online and offline promotion techniques to increase the audience of a site (both new and existing customers).

Search engines
Provide an index of content on registered sites that can be searched by keyword.

Directories or catalogues
Provide a structured listing of registered websites and their function in different categories.

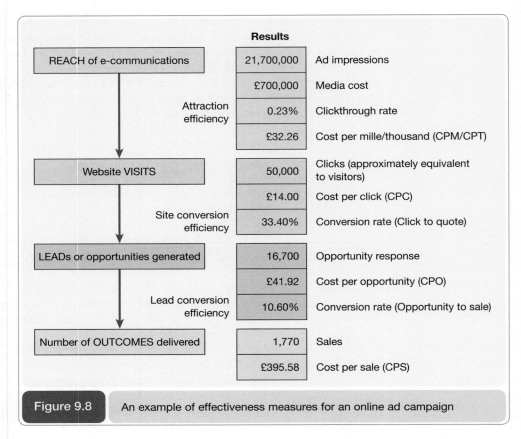

Figure 9.8 An example of effectiveness measures for an online ad campaign

not prominent in the search engines, then many potential sales could be lost since a company is dependent on the strength of its brand and offline communications to drive visitors to the website.

Consequently, Chaffey and Smith (2008) stress the importance of timing for traffic building. They say:

> Some e-marketers may consider traffic building to be a continuous process, but others may view it as a specific campaign, perhaps to launch a site or a major enhancement. Some methods tend to work best continuously; others are short term. Short-term campaigns will be for a site launch or an event such as an online trade show.

How does Google work?

It can help managers of search marketing campaigns to understand the technology behind Google which it discloses in many patents and in its Webmaster guidelines (www.google.com/ webmasters). Figure 9.9 shows that search technology involves these main processes:

Spiders or robots
Spiders are software processes, technically known as robots, employed by search engines to index web pages of registered sites on a regular basis.

1 *Crawling*. The purpose of the crawl is to identify relevant pages for indexing and assess whether they have changed. Crawling is performed by **robots** (bots), which are also known as **spiders**. These access web pages and retrieve a reference URL of the page for later analysis and indexing.

Although the terms 'bot' and 'spider' give the impression of something physical visiting a site, the bots are simply software processes running on a search engine's server which request pages, follow the links contained on that page and so create a series of page references with associated URLs. This is a recursive process, so each link followed will find additional links which then need to be crawled.

2 *Indexing*. An index is created to enable the search engine to rapidly find the most relevant pages containing the query typed by the searcher. Rather than searching each page for a

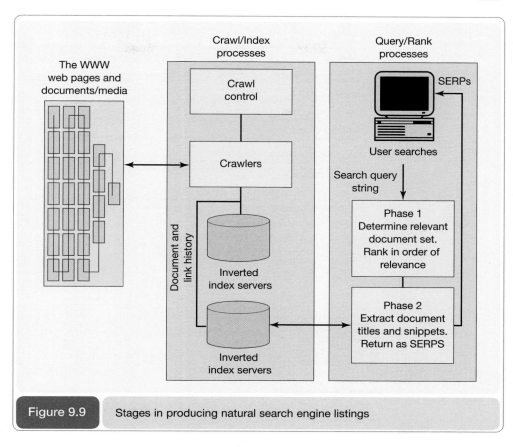

| Figure 9.9 | Stages in producing natural search engine listings |

query phrase, a search engine 'inverts' the index to produce a look-up table of documents containing particular words.

The index information consists of phases stored within a document and also other information characterizing a page such as the document's title, meta description, page rank, trust or authority, and spam rating. For the keywords in the document additional attributes will be stored such as semantic markup (<h1>, <h2> headings denoted within HTML), occurrence in **link anchor text**, proximity, frequency or density and position in document.

Link anchor text
The text used to form the blue underlined hyperlink viewed in a web browser defined in the HTML source.

3 *Ranking or scoring.* The indexing process has produced a lookup of all the pages that contain particular words in a query, but they are not sorted in terms of relevance. Ranking of the document to assess the most relevant set of documents to return in the SERPs (search engine results pages, Figure 9.10) occurs in real time for the search query entered. First, relevant documents will be retrieved from a run-time version of the index at a particular data centre, then a rank in the SERPs for each document will be computed based on many ranking factors of which we highlight the main ones in later sections.

4 *Query request and results serving.* The familiar search engine interface accepts the searcher's query. The user's location is assessed through their IP address and the query is then passed to a relevant data centre for processing. Ranking then occurs in real time for a particular query to return a sorted list of relevant documents and these are then displayed on the search results page.

Google has stated that it uses more than 200 factors or signals within its search ranking algorithms. These include positive ranking factors which help boost position and negative factors or filters which are used to remove search engine spam from the index. Further details (on ranking factors) can be found in Box 12.2, p. 657.

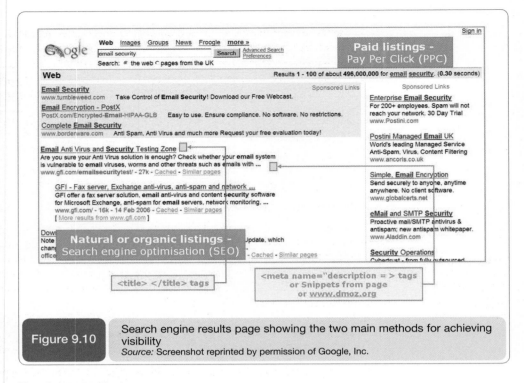

Figure 9.10

Search engine results page showing the two main methods for achieving visibility
Source: Screenshot reprinted by permission of Google, Inc.

Keyphrase analysis

Keyphrase (keyword phrase)
The combination of words users of search engines type into a search box which form a search query.

The starting point to successful search engine marketing is target the right keyphrases. Notice that I say '**keyphrase**' (short for 'keyword phrase') rather than 'keyword' since search engines such as Google attribute more relevance when there is a phrase match between the keywords that the user types and a phrase on a page. Companies should complete a 'gap analysis' which will identify keyphrases to target by showing, for each phrase, the number of visitors they could potentially attract compared to the actual positions or number of visitors they are receiving.

Key sources for identifying the keyphrases customers are likely to type when searching for products include your market knowledge, competitors' sites, keyphrases from visitors who arrive at the site (from web analytics), the internal site search tool and the keyphrase analysis tools listed at www.davechaffey.com/seo-keyword-tools. It is also useful to understand customer searching behaviour (Box 9.3).

Box 9.3   How do we search?

Search marketing firm iProspect conducted research on how we search by commissioning Jupiter research to survey 2,400 US searchers about their behaviour. Some of the key findings digital marketers need to be aware of:

- Searchers value brand credibility. 36% of search engine users believe that the companies whose websites are returned at the top of the search results are the top brands in their field.
- Many searchers don't look beyond the first page. Of search engine users who continue their search when not finding what they seek, 41% will change engines or change their search term if they don't find what they seek on the first page of search results. This figure was 28% in 2002.

- Search term refinement. Of search engine users 82% relaunch an unsuccessful search using the same search engine as they used for their initial search, but add more keywords to refine the subsequent search. This figure was just 68% in 2002.
- Searchers prefer natural listings. Between 60% and 80% of searches are on the natural rather than paid listings depending on the term. Note that separate audience panel research by comScore (2008) has shown that the paid click rate in Google is around 25% for search results pages with around 50% of searches containing paid ads.

Source: iProspect research, Spring 2006 (www.iprospect.com).

Search-engine optimization (SEO)

Search-engine optimization (SEO)

A structured approach used to improve the position of a company or its products in search engine natural or organic results listings for selected keyphrases.

Search-engine optimization (SEO) involves a structured approach used to increase the position of a company or its products in search-engine natural or organic results listings (shown in Figure 9.10) for selected keyphrases. It also involves controlling index inclusion or ensuring that as many pages of a site as possible are included within the search engine. There may be technical difficulties with this with some content management or e-commerce systems which need to be corrected.

Although each search engine has its own evolving algorithm with hundreds of weighting factors only known to the search engineers they employ, fortunately there are common factors that influence search engine rankings. These are, in approximate order of importance:

1 *Frequency of occurrence in body copy.* The number of times the keyphrase is repeated in the text of the web page is a key factor in determining the position for a keyphrase. Copy can be written to increase the number of times a word or phrase is used (technically, its 'keyphrase density') and ultimately boost position in the search engine. Note, though, that search engines make checks that a phrase is not repeated too many times such as 'cheap flights ... cheap flights ... cheap flights ... cheap flights ... cheap flights ... cheap flights ... cheap flights ... cheap flights ...' or the keyword is hidden using the same colour text and background and will not list the page if this keyphrase density is too high or it believes the page creator has tried to mislead the search engine ('search engine spamming'). Relevance is also increased by a gamut of legitimate 'tricks' such as including the keyphrase in headings (<H1>, <H2>), linking anchor text in hyperlinks and using a higher density towards the start of the document.

2 *Number of inbound links (page rank).* The more links you have from good-quality sites, the better your ranking will be. Evaluation of inbound links or backlinks to determine ranking is one of the key reasons Google became popular. Google uses an assessment called '**page rank**' to deliver relevant results since it counts each link from another site as a vote. However, not all votes are equal – Google gives greater weight to links from pages which themselves have high page rank and which have the same context or topical content as the page they link to. Weighting is also given where hyperlink anchor text or adjacent text contains text relevant to the keyphrase, i.e. the linking page must have context.

Page rank

A scale of 0 to 10 used by Google to assess the importance of websites according to the number of inbound links (link popularity).

Inclusion in directories such as Yahoo! or Business.com (for which a fee is payable) or the Open Directory (www.dmoz.org, which is currently free) is important since it can assist in boosting page rank. Another key aspect of linking is the architecture of internal links within the site. Keyphrases that occur within the hypertext of different forms of navigation are important to Google in indicating the context of a page.

3 *Title HTML tag.* The keywords in the title tag of a web page that appears at the top of a browser window are indicated in the HTML code by the <TITLE> keyword. For example, for my site (<title>E-business and Internet marketing articles – DaveChaffey.com</title>). This is significant in search engine listings since if a keyphrase appears in a title it is more likely to be listed high than if it is only in the body text of a page. It follows that each

page on a site should have a specific title giving the name of a company and the product, service or offer featured on a page. Greater weighting is given to keyphrases at the left of the title tag and those with a higher keyphrase density. The Title HTML tag is also vital in search marketing since this is typically the text underlined within the search results page which forms a hyperlink through to your website. If the Title tag appearing on the search results page is a relevant call-to-action that demonstrates relevance, you will receive more clicks, which equals more visits (incidentally, Google will monitor clickthroughs to a site and will determine that your content is relevant too and boost position accordingly).

Meta-tags

Keywords that are part of an HTML page that result in a higher search listing if they match the typed keyword.

4 *Meta-tags.* **Meta-tags** are part of the HTML source file, typed in by web page creators, which is read by the search engine spider or robot. They are effectively hidden from users, but are used by some search engines when robots or spiders compile their index. In the past, search engines assigned more relevance to a site containing keyphrases in its meta-tags than one that didn't. Search engine spamming of meta-tags resulted in this being an inaccurate method of assessing relevance and Google has reported that it assigns no relevance to meta-tags. However, other search engines such as 'Yahoo! Search' do assign some relevance to meta-tags, so it is best practice to incorporate these and to change them for each page with distinct content. There are two important meta-tags which are specified at the top of an HTML page using the `<meta name="'">` HTML keyword:

(i) The 'keywords' meta-tag highlights the key topics covered on a web page. Example:
`<meta name="keywords" content="E-business, E-commerce, E-marketing">`

(ii) The 'description' meta-tag denotes the information which will be displayed in the search results page so is very important to describe what the website offers to encourage searchers to click through to the site.

Example: `<meta name="description" content="Your guide to E-business and Internet marketing – DaveChaffey.com">`.

5 *Alternative graphic text.* A site that uses a lot of graphical material and/or plug-ins is less likely to be listed highly. The only text on which the page will be indexed will be the `<TITLE>` keyword. To improve on this, graphical images can have hidden text associated with them that is not seen by the user (unless graphical images are turned off), but will be seen and indexed by the search engine. For example, text about a company name and products can be assigned to a company logo using the 'ALT' tag as follows: `<IMG NAME="Logo" SRC="logo.gif" ALT="Internet marketing links and articles – DaveChaffey.com">`.

Again, due to search engine spamming this factor is assigned less relevance than previously (unless the image is also a link), but it is best practice to use this since it is also required by accessibility law (screen-readers used by the blind and visually impaired read out the text assigned through ALT tags).

Paid search marketing

Paid search marketing or paid listings are similar to conventional advertising; here a relevant text ad with a link to a company page is displayed when the user of a search engine types in a specific phrase. A series of text ads usually labelled as 'sponsored links' are displayed on the right and/or above and below the natural search engine listings. Unlike conventional advertising, the advertiser doesn't pay when the ad is displayed, but only when the ad is clicked on which then leads to a visit to the advertiser's website – hence this is often known as 'pay-per-click marketing'! The relative ranking of these 'paid performance placements' is typically based on the highest bid cost-per-click value for each keyphrase. The variation in bid amounts for clients of one search bid management tool are shown in Table 9.1.

Quality score

An assessment in paid search by Google AdWords (and now other search engines) of an individual ad triggered by a keyword which, in combination with the bid amount, determines the ranking of the ad relative to competitors.

But it is not a simple case that the company which is prepared to pay the most per click gets top spot as many think. The search engines also take the relative clickthrough rates of the ads dependent on their position (lower positions naturally have lower clickthrough rates) into account when ranking the sponsored links, so ads which do not appear relevant, because fewer people are clicking on them, will drop down or may even disappear off the listing. The analysis of CTR to determine position is part of the **quality score**, a concept originally developed by Google, but now integrated as part of the Microsoft Live and Yahoo! search networks.

Table 9.1	Variation in cost per click in campaigns, January 2008 different categories for US paid search

Category	CPC ($)
All finance	2.70
Credit	2.95
Mortgage	2.61
Auto finance	1.68
Travel	0.65
Automotive	0.57
Retail	0.36
Dating	0.40

Source: Efficient Frontier.

Contextual display network

Contextual ads are automatically displayed according to the type of content on partner publisher sites by the search engine.

Cost per thousand (CPM)

Cost per 1,000 ad impressions for a banner advert.

As well as paid search ads within the search engines, text ads are also displayed on third-party sites (for example, the ads on www.davechaffey.com) which form a **contextual 'display network'** such as Google Adsense (http://adsense.google.com) or Content Match on Yahoo! Search where 'contextual ads' are displayed automatically according to the type of content. These are typically paid for on a cost-per-click (CPC) basis but ads can also be paid for on a **CPM** basis. The search networks and publishers share the fees. They account for around 30% of Google's revenue. They enable marketers to reach a wider audience on selectable third-party sites, but they need to decide how to use these to deliver different messages.

Facebook pay-per-click advertising

Facebook has adopted the successful pay-per-click model from Google in an effort to monetise its audience. Mini case study 9.1, below, summarizes the benefits. The case study shows how you can target effectively in Facebook and increase awareness of a service beyond Google, while limiting your exposure through a CPC investment. But it also shows a much lower response rate than Google Adwords. This is to be expected since customers aren't in research or buy mode – they're socializing! So it's worth remembering that although not disclosed in this case study, conversion rates are likely to be lower too.

Mini Case Study 9.1	Saxo Bank uses Facebook to reach its audience

Saxo Bank is a global investment bank with headquarters in Denmark specializing in online trading and investment across international financial markets.

Saxo Bank uses Facebook's standard advertising units to advertise three products: Forex Trading, CFD Trading and Saxo Premium Account. It uses targeting by finance-related, sporting and luxury keywords which may be used in people's profiles when they express their interest and passion. It also targets by their demographics. Using both of these targeting characteristics enables them to reach around 600,000 people on Facebook.

Head of marketing at Saxo Bank UK, Stuart Rice, describes the advantages:

Facebook ads have a tremendous advantage over Google (which we also use) because we can target people who perhaps use words like 'Rolex', 'yachting' or 'shooting' in their profiles. It enables me to target to a better degree than Google.

Ads are bought on a cost-per-click (CPC) basis because it makes them easier to monitor; according to Rice:

I just know with CPC what it has cost me when someone clicks there. If I bought 100,000 impressions I'd have to spend a lot of time going through the data to see what I got for my money.

Campaign results

Average CPC paid is £1.31 and the CTR is 0.05%. The total clicks for the period 1 June to 1 September for the three Saxo Bank campaigns on Facebook was 4,344, giving a cost of c£6,000, with 7,439,276 impressions.

Source: New Media Age article Facebook Bidding, by Nicola Smith, 7 October 2010: http://www.nma.co.uk/features/facebook-bidding/3019000.article.

Beware of the fake clicks!

Whenever the principle of PPC marketing is described to marketers, very soon a light bulb comes on and they ask, 'So we can click on competitors and bankrupt them?' Well, actually no. The PPC ad networks detect multiple clicks from the same computer (IP address) and say they filter them out. However, there are techniques to mimic multiple clicks from different locations such as software tools to fake clicks and even services where you can pay a team of people across the world to click on these links. It is estimated that in competitive markets one in five of the clicks may be fake. While fake clicks can be monitored for and refunds obtained if proved, ultimately this could destroy PPC advertising.

In Mini case study 5.2 we saw how Arena Flowers defines KPIs to control its marketing spend. In Mini case study 9.2 Arena provides insights into its communications strategy and in particular the role of search engine and social marketing.

Mini Case Study 9.2	Arena Flowers online communications

Although we are florists in the traditional sense, at the heart of our business model is a website which makes shopping an enjoyable experience for our customers. Arena Flowers (www.arenaflowers.co.uk) has always prided itself in offering unique customer focused experiences and believes that technology plays a significant role in achieving this. Since its inception we have envisaged customer needs and requirements and tailored our website accordingly. We have continually sought customer feedback and worked extensively to make improvements to make ordering flowers and gifts an incredible experience for the customer. Everything from the website interface to product display, shopping cart and the checkout is an intuitive process.

We have leveraged the features of Web 2.0 to make Arena Flowers website an enjoyable experience while ensuring the highest security standards to protect our customers from Internet fraud.

However, that represents one dimension of our website. Like all other online businesses, it is vital for Arena Flowers to be found by customers and we rely extensively on Internet marketing to achieve this. The Internet has changed the way we interact with our stakeholders. It is a vibrant and rich advertising medium full of opportunities despite being multi-faceted. It requires a variety of strategies to be woven together to succeed. The significant aspect of Internet marketing is the ability to deliver relevant content to consumers at the right time. On the web, marketing and communications has shifted from the one size fits all approach of traditional advertising to delivering the right information at the right time to help consumers in making a decision.

The crux of our Internet marketing strategy is marketing for search engines. Search is an intrinsically buyer-led medium, which is flexible and responsive to consumer tastes. Research indicates that Internet users rarely type website addresses into the browser bars – they locate them through search engines such as Google, Yahoo, Ask or Live.

Therefore it is necessary for Arena Flowers to promote search rankings by improving our website's structure and content. It is important for us to appear as near as possible to the top of search engine results for a set of keywords. We achieve this by investing in considerable time and resources to research and identify a number of measures including keywords, onsite content, external link partners etc while ensuring that the structure of our website is search engine friendly to warrant a listing.

Apart from search engines, we focus on other broader Internet marketing strategies to insulate our reliance on search. Online mediums such as **blogs, podcasts, streaming video,** etc. are changing the way consumers research and buy products and services, necessitating Arena's presence on such mediums.

Furthermore, we also have a number of additional systems in place including Affiliate Marketing, Social Networking such as Facebook, Twitter, Squidoo etc., Comparison shopping, newsletters etc. We constantly evolve with the Web 2.0 medium to strengthen our web presence. These initiatives help in getting prospective customers to Arena Flowers.

From the beginning, we have strived to strike the right balance between technology and design to benefit from the important and powerful marketing channel – the Internet. Through the Internet, we are committed to engage in a personal relationship with our customers to provide them value added service. We regularly measure our Internet marketing efforts internally and we feel happy to see an increase in the number of visitors to our website, conversions, sales, customer feedback etc. But we certainly feel privileged when we get appreciated by an unexpected quarter – to be cited by an academic text on Internet marketing. It highlights the success of our Internet marketing efforts and motivates us further to take it to the next level.

Source: Blog posting, 9 September 2008, www.arenaflowers.com/blog/2008/09/09/wiser-about-web-from-a-flowers-website-to-academic-text/#comment-4361.

2 Online PR

The UK Institute of PR (IPR) defines PR as:

> *the management of reputation – the planned and sustained effort to establish and maintain goodwill and mutual understanding between an organisation and its publics.*

Online PR

Maximizing favourable mentions of your company, brands, products or websites on third-party websites which are likely to be visited by your target audience.

Online PR or e-PR leverages the network effect of the Internet. Remember, Internet is a contraction of 'interconnected networks'! Mentions of a brand or site on other sites are powerful in shaping opinions and driving visitors to your site. The main element of online PR is maximizing favourable mentions of an organization, its brands, products or websites on third-party websites which are likely to be visited by its target audience. Furthermore, as we noted in the topic on search engine optimization, the more links there are from other sites to your site, the higher your site will be ranked in the natural or organic listings of the search engines. Minimizing unfavourable mentions through online reputation management is also an aspect of online PR.

Activities which can be considered to be online PR include the following.

(a) Communicating with media (journalists) online

This uses the Internet as a new conduit to disseminate press releases (SEO-optimized) through e-mail and on-site and on third-party sites. Options include: setting up a press-release area on the website; creating e-mail alerts about news that journalists and other third parties can sign up to; submitting your news stories or releases to online news feeds.

(b) Link building

Link building

A structured activity to include good-quality hyperlinks to your site from relevant sites with a good page rank.

Reciprocal links

Links which are agreed between your and another's organization.

Link building is a key activity for search engine optimization. It can be considered to be an element of online PR since it is about getting your brand visible on third-party sites. Link building needs to be a structured effort to achieve as many links into a website as possible from referring websites (these commonly include **reciprocal links**), which will also improve your position in the search engine results pages.

McGaffin (2004) provides a great introduction to implementing a structured link-building programme. He says: '*Create great content, link to great content and great content will link to you*'. He describes how you should review existing links to your site and links to competitors, set targets and then proactively enquire to suitable site owners for links.

You can use the syntax 'link:site' in Google to see the number of quality links into a page on your site as judged by Google. e.g. 'link:www.davechaffey.com'.

Note that this also includes internal links. To exclude internal links and include pages with lower page rank or that do not have a true hyperlink, but contain the URL, Google this: 'www.url.com -site:www.url.com'.

For example, 'www.davechaffey.com -site:www.davechaffey.com'

(c) Blogs, podcasting and RSS

Blog
An online diary or news source prepared by an individual or a group of people.

Podcasts
Individuals and organizations post online media (audio and video) which can be accessed in the appropriate players including the iPod which first sparked the growth of this technique.

Introduced in Chapter 2, '**blogs**' give an easy method of regularly publishing web pages which are best described as online journals, diaries or news or events listings. They may include feedback (traceback) comments from other sites or contributors to the site. Frequency can be hourly, daily, weekly or less frequently, but daily updates are typical.

Podcasts are related to blogs since they can potentially be generated by individuals or organizations to voice an opinion either as audio (typically MP3) or video. They have been successfully used by media organizations such as the BBC which has used them for popular programmes such as film reviews or discussions and for live recording such as the Beethoven symphonies that received over 600,000 downloads in June 2005 alone. A big challenge for achieving visibility for podcasts is that contents can only currently be recognized by tags and it is difficult to assess quality without listening to the start of a podcast. All the main search engines are working on techniques to make searching of voice and video content practical. In the meantime, some start-ups such as Odeo (www.odeo.com) and Blinkx (www.blinkx.com) are developing solutions.

(d) Online communities and social networks

We explained in Chapter 8 that the power of the Internet to facilitate peer-to-peer interactions was evident from the mid-1990s. However, it is only relatively recently that this power to transform the way companies and customers interact has been apparent. The human need to socialize and share experiences is the real reason behind the popularity of online communities and social networks. In most countries, social networks are amongst the most popular sites due to this need. It follows that marketers will want to 'swim with the fishes' or try to communicate with customers in this environment. Certainly there are oppportunities to advertise on social networks, as shown in the Saxo Bank Mini case study, above. But if marketers perceive social media simply as an opportunity to push messages from a brand to passive recipients, then the opportunity to engage with customers to develop a deeper relationship is missing. Facebook aims to facilitate this through its ads which typically lead through to a brand page or company page within Facebook where brands can collect feedback.

So it is important for organizations to determine how their audiences use social networks and assess the opportunities to reach and interact with them. Dee *et al.* (2007) also note the importance of social networks in influencing perceptions about brands, products and suppliers. Their research shows large differences in gender and age on the types of products discussed, but recommendations on restaurants, computers, movies and vehicles being popular in all categories.

While many Facebook applications have been developed (www.facebook.com/apps/), the majority of well-known apps were not created by brands. Companies can also set up brand pages within Facebook, but these tend not to reach large numbers. Box 9.4 (see later) describes further advice on the use of social networks for marketing.

Focus on	Social media and social CRM strategy

We've seen throughout this book that the opportunities of communicating with customers through social network sites, online communities and interactions on company sites are so great today that a social media strategy has become a core element of e-business strategy. Yet creating a social media or customer engagement strategy is challenging since it requires a change in mindset for the company since they may have to give up some control on their messaging to enable them to communicate with customers effectively. The change in approach required is clear from a movement that originated in the USA in 1999, known as the Cluetrain manifesto (www.cluetrain.com). The authors, Levine *et al.* (2000), say:

> *Conversations among human beings sound human. They are conducted in a human voice. Most corporations, on the other hand, only know how to talk in the soothing, humorless monotone of the mission statement, marketing brochure, and your-call-is-important-to-us busy signal. Same old tone, same old lies. No wonder networked markets have no respect for companies unable or unwilling to speak as they do. Corporate firewalls have kept smart employees in and smart markets out. It's going to cause real pain to tear those walls down. But the result will be a new kind of conversation. And it will be the most exciting conversation business has ever engaged in.*

Of course, more than a change in mindset is required – to achieve change on this scale requires senior management sponsorship, investment and changes to processes and tools, as described in the next chapter on change management.

You can see that the Cluetrain manifesto is a call to action, encouraging managers to change their culture and provide processes and tools to enable employees of an organization to interact with and listen to customer needs in a responsible way.

Developing a social media strategy

When developing a social media strategy there seems to be a tendency for managers to turn straight to the tools they'll be using – should we start with Twitter or Facebook, or should we create a blog? This is the worst possible way to develop strategy; indeed, it's not strategy,

Mini Case Study 9.3	Best Buy offers, listens and responds in multiple channels

Best Buy is a multinational retailer of technology and entertainment products operating in the United States, Canada, Europe, China and Mexico. The Best Buy family of brands and partnerships collectively generates more than $45 billion in annual revenue and includes brands such as Best Buy; Audiovisions; The Carphone Warehouse; Future Shop; Geek Squad, Jiangsu Five Star; Magnolia Audio Video; Napster; Pacific Sales; The Phone House; and Speakeasy. Providing quality customer service is a large part of the customer experience. Best Buy explains:

Approximately 155,000 employees apply their talents to help bring the benefits of these brands to life for customers through retail locations, multiple call centers and websites, in-home solutions, product delivery and activities in our communities.

Figure 9.11 shows the customer support page for Bestbuy.com. You can see that there are a wide range of choices of customer service including:

- The Twelpforce (http://twitter.com/twelpforce). Immediate Twitter response followed by around 30,000 customers.
- Geek Squad Online Support. 'A live agent can fix your PC now! Prices starting at $49.99'.
- Discussion in communities.
- Standard e-mail and Click To Call options.

Video explanation: http://www.bby.com/about/.

Figure 9.11   Best Buy customer service

it's tactics! Strategy development for social media should be informed by demand analysis of customer channel adoption and the commercial potential of the approach.

Customer adoption of social media tools will vary according to customer segments and markets. So it's important to start by completing a marketplace analysis, as described in Chapter 2, to see which social tools and engagement techniques are most effective for the target audience.

Next, the commercial benefits of social media need to be reviewed and goals defined. Some marketers will see social media primarily as a way of gaining new customers through the viral effect of social media as existing customers or contacts discuss or recommend your content or products. For others, the benefits may be centred more on how recommendations, reviews and ratings can increase conversion rate. Public relations specialists will want to listen to the conversations for positive and negative sentiment about brand and then seek to manage this by increasing the positives and managing the negatives. Finally, social media can be viewed as a customer engagement and retention tool. Here social media are used to deliver customer service or are used as alternative channels to e-mail marketing to inform customers about new product launches or promotions.

POST is a useful framework for businesses to apply to help them develop a social media strategy, as summarized by Forrester (2007). POST is a simplified version of the SOSTAC framework introduced at the start of this chapter:

- *People.* Understanding the adoption of social media within an audience is an essential starting-point. The Forrester social media profiling tool shows how usage varies for different demographic groups: www.forrester.com/Groundswell/profile_tool.html.
- *Objectives.* Set different goals for different options to engage customers across different aspects of the customer life cycle from customer acquisition to conversion to retention. Josh Bernoff of Forrester recommends: '*decide on your objective before you decide on a technology. Then figure out how you will measure it.*'
- *Strategy.* How to achieve your goals. Bernoff suggests that because social media are a disruptive approach you should imagine how social media will support change. He says: '*Imagine you succeed. How will things be different afterwards? Imagine the endpoint and you'll know where to begin.*'
- *Technology.* Finally, decide on the best social media platforms to achieve your goals; we'll review these in a moment.

Social CRM strategy

We have seen that there are a diverse range of goals of applying social media within an organization, which is a significant challenge, particularly in larger organizations since success will require collaboration across different roles and functions. **Social CRM** is a relatively new term which helps define the broad scope of social media across the customer life cycle and value chain.

Conversations can occur across a range of site types, including 'social networks' such as Facebook and Twitter, but also in a company's own blog, third-party blogs, reviews-and-ratings sites or in neutral web self-service forums like Get Satisfaction. Many organizations have developed a social media governance policy to ensure that conversations are listened to and responded to accordingly. You can read examples at http://socialmediagovernance.com/policies.php.

The scope of social CRM is well illustrated as grouped within the six business application areas in Figure 9.12, which is presented by Altimeter (2010). The scope of each area is:

1 *Marketing.* Monitoring, analysis and response of customer conversations through social listening tools. I think the report misses a discussion on integration of social marketing into other campaign tactics such as e-mail marketing.
2 *Sales.* Understanding where prospects are discussing selection of products and services offered by you and competitors and determining the best way to get involved in the conversation to influence sales and generate leads. Within B2B, Linked In is an obvious location that should be monitored.
3 *Service and support.* Customer self-help through forums provided by you and neutral sites.
4 *Innovation.* Using conversations to foster new product development or enhance online offerings is one of the most exciting forms of social CRM.
5 *Collaboration.* This is e-business collaboration within an organization through an intranet and other software tools to encourage all forms of collaboration which support business processes.
6 *Customer experience.* This references the use of social CRM to enhance the customer experience and add value to a brand which is implied by many of the other aspects above. It gives the examples of using VIP programmes, offering collaboration between customers with shared characteristics to add value and create advocacy.

A social CRM strategy can be developed by reviewing and prioritizing options in each of the six business applications above.

The 5Ms provide another useful framework within the Altimeter (2010) report which can be used for reviewing strategy implementation. The 5Ms are:

Social CRM

The process of managing customer-to-customer conversations to engage existing customers, prospects and other stakeholders with a brand and so enhance customer relationship management.

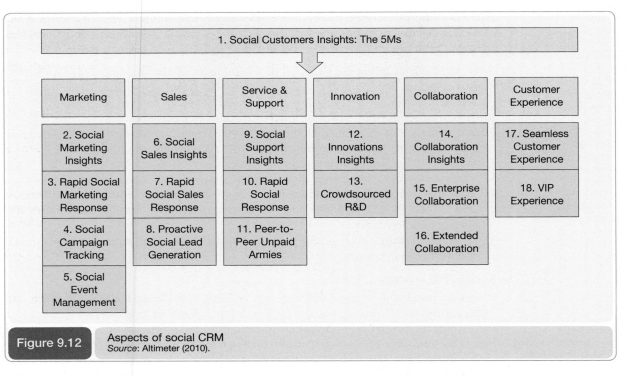

Figure 9.12 Aspects of social CRM
Source: Altimeter (2010).

1 *Monitoring.* Reviewing the method of social listening and deriving insights from these.
2 *Mapping.* Finding relationships between individual customers or grouped segments using different social platforms, e.g. Facebook and Twitter or e-mail marketing.
3 *Management.* Processes for implementing and reviewing strategy. More report detail on campaign management would be helpful here.
4 *Middleware.* The software tools and APIs used to monitor and gather insight.
5 *Measurement.* The measures used to assess social marketing effectiveness and ROI.

Categories of social media

There are many, many sites and tools which provide an environment for social media; to gain an idea of just how many, complete Activity 9.1 which lists hundreds of tools in 25 categories.

A social media site is much more than simply a website. From a technology viewpoint most of these sites can be considered as software applications or web services which give access to users at different levels of permission and then enable management and storage of

Activity 9.1 Understanding the range of social media marketing platforms

Purpose

To explore the range of social media sites and tools, to categorize them and assess their business applications.

Activity

Visit the Conversation Prism (www.conversationprism.com) or the Smart Insights Digital Marketing Radar (http://bit.ly/smartradar) and identify the types of social media sites you and your colleagues use. How do you think the popularity of tools would differ for different types of B2B and B2C sites? Discuss how businesses should decide on the most important to invest in to achieve their goals.

different forms of user-generated content. Messaging is also an important feature of many of these sites, particularly the main social networks which will alert users when new content related to their content or connections is published. APIs for exchanging data with other web services interfaces are also a key feature of social networks which enable them and their members to extend their reach and influence by being incorporated into other sites.

Since there are so many types of social presence, it is helpful to simplify the options to manage. For this we recommend these six categories based on chapters in Weinberg (2010). You can see there's more to social media than social networks:

1 *Social networking.* The emphasis here is on listening to customers and sharing engaging content. Facebook tends to be most important for consumer audiences and Linked In for business audiences.

2 *Social knowledge.* These are informational social networks like Yahoo! Answers, where you can help an audience by solving their problems and subtly showing how your products have helped others. Wikipedia is another site in this category, although it has relatively little application for marketing.

3 *Social sharing.* These are social bookmarking sites like Delicious (www.delicious.com) which can be useful for understanding the most engaging content within a category.

4 *Social news.* Twitter is the best-known example.

5 *Social streaming.* Rich and streaming media social sites for sharing photos, video and podcasting.

6 *Company user generated content and community.* Distinct from the other types of social presence which are independent of companies, these are the company's own social space which may be integrated into product content (reviews and ratings), a customer support community or a blog.

Community

A customer-to-customer interaction delivered via e-mail groups, web-based discussion forums or chat.

So, the popularity of **communities** implemented on company sites or within social networks means that it is important for companies to manage these effectively. But why is community important and how can companies best manage it? Hagel and Armstrong (1997) say:

> *The rise of virtual communities in online networks has set in motion an unprecedented shift from vendors of goods and services to the customers who buy them. Vendors who understand this transfer of power and choose to capitalize on it by organizing virtual communities will be richly rewarded with both peerless customer loyalty and impressive economic returns.*

Depending on market sector, an organization has a choice of developing different types of community for B2C, and communities of purpose, position, interest and profession for B2B.

1 *Purpose* – people who are going through the same process or trying to achieve a particular objective. Examples include those researching cars, such as Autotrader (www.autotrader.co.uk), or stocks online, such as the Motley Fool (www.motleyfool.co.uk). Price or product comparison services such as MySimon, Shopsmart and Kelkoo serve this community. At sites such as Bizrate (www.bizrate.com), the Egg Free Zone (www.eggfreezone.com) or Alexa (www.alexa.com), companies can share their comments on companies and their products.

2 *Position.* Communities set up specifically for people who are in a certain circumstance, such as having a health disorder or being at a certain stage of life. Examples are teenage chat site Dobedo (www.dobedo.co.uk), Cennet (www.cennet.co.uk) offering 'New horizons for the over 50s', www.babycenter.com and www.parentcentre.com for parents, and the Pet Channel (www.thepetchannel.com).

3 *Interest.* This community is for people who share an interest or passion such as sport (www.football365.com), music (www.pepsi.com), leisure (www.walkingworld.com) or any other interest (www.deja.com).

4 *Profession.* These are important for companies promoting B2B services.

These B2B vertical portals can be thought of as 'trade papers on steroids'. In fact, in many cases they have been created by publishers of trade papers, for example Emap Business Communications has created Construction Plus for the construction industry. Each has industry and company news and jobs, as expected, but they also offer online storefronts and auctions for buyers and sellers and community features such as discussion topics. Of course, the trade papers such as Emap's *Construction Weekly* are responding by creating their own portals.

Today social networks provide a low-cost method for companies to create a community. You will notice that most of these examples of community are intermediary sites that are independent of a particular manufacturer or retailer. A key question to ask before embarking on a community-building programme is: '*Can customer interests be best served through a company-independent community?*'

If the answer to this question is 'yes', then it may be best to form a community that is a brand variant, differentiated from its parent. For example, Boots the Chemist created Handbag.com as a community for its female customers. Another and less costly alternative is to promote your products through sponsorship or co-branding on an independent community site or portal or to get involved in the community discussions.

Alternatively, companies can create their own forums although successful examples are relatively rare since there is a fear that a brand may be damaged if customers criticize products, so some moderation is required. Honda UK (www.honda.co.uk/car) provide a good example of a community created by their brand on their site. Rather than having a separate community section, the community is integrated within the context of each car as 'second opinions' menu options. Interestingly, some negative comments are permitted to make the discussion more meaningful.

A potential problem with a company-hosted forum is that it may be unable to get sufficient people to contribute to a company-hosted community. But initial recruitment of contributors and moderation has been used to grow the forum by software services company SAP, which has successfully created several niche communities to support its business with over 1 million software engineers, partners and business people (www.sap.com/community). Contributions are rewarded through donations to international aid charities.

What tactics can organizations use to foster community? Parker (2000) suggests eight questions organizations should ask when considering how to create a customer community:

1 What interests, needs or passions do many of your customers have in common?
2 What topics or concerns might your customers like to share with each other?
3 What information is likely to appeal to your customers' friends or colleagues?
4 What other types of business in your area appeal to buyers of your products and services?
5 How can you create packages or offers based on combining offers from two or more affinity partners?
6 What price, delivery, financing or incentives can you afford to offer to friends (or colleagues) which your current customers recommend?
7 What types of incentives or rewards can you afford to provide customers who recommend friends (or colleagues) who make a purchase?
8 How can you best track purchases resulting from word-of-mouth recommendations from friends?

A good approach to avoiding problems is to think about the difficulties you may have with your community-building efforts. Typical problems are:

1 *Empty communities.* A community without any people is not a community. The traffic-building techniques mentioned earlier need to be used to communicate the proposition of the community.
2 *Silent communities.* A community may have many registered members, but a community is not a community if the conversation flags. How do you get people to participate? Here are some ideas:

- *Seed the community.* Use a moderator to ask questions or have a weekly or monthly question written by the moderator or sourced from customers. Have a resident independent expert to answer questions.
- *Make it select.* Limit it to key account customers or set it up as an extranet service that is only offered to valued customers as a value-add. Members may be more likely to get involved.

3 *Critical communities.* Many communities on manufacturer or retailer sites can be critical of the brand, for example an early community from the bank Egg (www.egg.com) was closed due to negative comments.

Finally, remember the *lurkers* – those who read the messages but do not actively contribute. There may be ten lurkers for every active participant. The community can also positively influence these people and build brand.

| Box 9.4 | Social networks – success factors for social network marketing |

Research by Microsoft (2007) based on interviews and surveys with social networkers found these human motivations for using social networks:

- 59% To keep in touch with friends and family
- 57% I like looking at other people's spaces
- 47% I want to meet people with similar interests
- 46% To express my opinions and views on topics
- 20% It is a good way to date
- 17% Using it for a specific reason, e.g. wedding, job networking.

In the same report, Microsoft, which part-owns Facebook, has developed these approaches for taking advantage of social networking either through buying ad space, or creating a brand space or brand channels that enable consumers to interact with or promote a brand:

1 *Understand consumers' motivations for using social networks*. Ads will be most effective if they are consistent with the typical lifestage of networkers or the topics that are being discussed.
2 *Express yourself as a brand*. Use the web to show the unique essence of your brand, but think about how to express a side of the brand that it is not normally seen.
3 *Create and maintain good conversations*. Advertisers who engage in discussions are more likely to resonate with the audience, but once conversations are started they must be followed through.
4 *Empower participants*. Social network users use their space and blogs to express themselves. Providing content or widgets to associate themselves with a brand may be appealing.
5 *Identify online brand advocates*. Use reputation management tools to identify influential social network members who are already brand advocates. Approach the most significant ones directly. Consider using contextual advertising such as Microsoft content ads or Google Adsense to display brand messages within their spaces when brands are discussed.
6 *The golden rule: behave like a social networker*. This means:

- Being creative
- Being honest and courteous (ask permission)
- Being individual
- Being conscious of the audience
- Updating regularly.

Members of a community or social network will differ in the extent to which they are connected with others. The most influential network members will be highly connected and will discuss issues of interests with a wider range of contacts than those who are less connected

It is generally believed by PR professionals seeking to influence marketplace perceptions that it is important to target the highly connected individuals since they are typically trusted individuals who other members of the community may turn to for advice. But there is much discussion about the influence of the influencers online. Researchers of community interactions believe that it is the collective interactions between typical network members (known as the '*moderately connected majority*') that are equally important. For example, Watts and Dodds (2007) argue that the 'influential hypothesis' is based on untested assumptions and in most cases does not match how diffusion operates in the real world. They comment that '*most social change is driven not by influentials, but by easily influenced individuals influencing other easily influenced individuals*'.

Although there is a clear wish to socialize online, site owners need to remember that it is not straightforward to engage an online audience as they move between different sites. Only a relatively small proportion will engage. Mini case study 9.4 shows that only a relatively small number of site visitors will actively participate.

(e) Managing how your brand is presented on third-party sites

As part of online PR it is useful to set up monitoring services. It is also necessary to have the resources to deal with negative PR as part of online reputation management. Microsoft's PR agency reputedly has a 'rapid response unit' that can respond to online PR. Examples of alerting services include Googlealert (www.googlealert.com) and the other tools listed at www.davechaffey.com/online-reputation-management-tools.

(f) Creating a buzz – online viral marketing

From a functional point of view, online viral marketing often involves generating word-of-mouth and links through to a website, as outlined in Chapter 4, so it can be considered part of online PR.

To summarize the section on online PR, see Figure 9.13. This highlights the importance of activities involving participation and how all online PR activities feed back into SEO through the links generated.

3 Online partnerships

Partnerships are an important part of today's marketing mix. Smith and Chaffey (2005) say that they are the eighth 'P' (Chapter 8). The same is true online. There are three key types of online partnerships: link building (covered in the previous section, this can also be considered to be part of online PR), affiliate marketing and online sponsorship. All should involve a structured approach to managing links through to a site. The important types of partner arrangement are as follows.

Mini Case Study 9.4	Nielsen's 90-9-1 rule of participation inequality: encouraging more users to contribute

To encourage online community participation is a challenge since the majority of visitors to a community lurk or don't participate. Usability expert Jakob Nielsen gives examples of participation on Wikipedia (just 0.2% of visitors are active) and Amazon (fewer than 1% post reviews). He explains:

- *90% of users are lurkers (i.e., read or observe, but don't contribute).*
- *9% of users contribute from time to time, but other priorities dominate their time.*
- *1% of users participate a lot and account for most contributions: it can seem as if they don't have lives because they often post just minutes after whatever event they're commenting on occurs.*

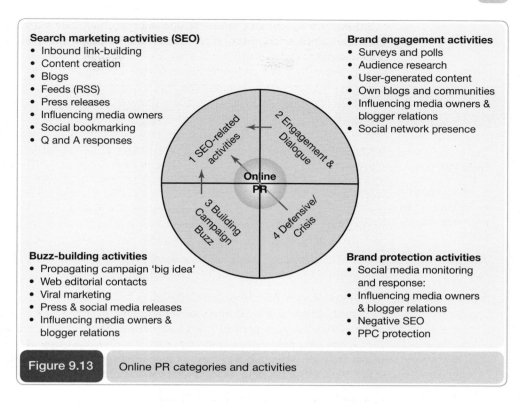

Search marketing activities (SEO)
- Inbound link-building
- Content creation
- Blogs
- Feeds (RSS)
- Press releases
- Influencing media owners
- Social bookmarking
- Q and A responses

Brand engagement activities
- Surveys and polls
- Audience research
- User-generated content
- Own blogs and communities
- Influencing media owners & blogger relations
- Social network presence

Buzz-building activities
- Propagating campaign 'big idea'
- Web editorial contacts
- Viral marketing
- Press & social media releases
- Influencing media owners & blogger relations

Brand protection activities
- Social media monitoring and response:
- Influencing media owners & blogger relations
- Negative SEO
- PPC protection

(circle diagram labels) Online PR; 1 SEO-related activities; 2 Engagement & Dialogue; 3 Building Campaign Buzz; 4 Defensive/Crisis

Figure 9.13   Online PR categories and activities

(a) Affiliate marketing

Affiliate marketing

A commission-based arrangement where an e-retailer pays sites that link to it for sales, leads (CPA-based) or, less commonly, visitors (CPC-based).

Affiliate marketing has become very popular with e-retailers since many achieve over 20% of their online sales through affiliates (also known as 'aggregators' since they aggregate offers from different providers). The great thing about affiliate marketing for the e-retailer is that they, the advertiser, do not pay until the product has been purchased or a lead generated. It is sometimes referred to as 'zero-risk advertising' (Figure 9.14).

Amazon was one of the earliest adopters of affiliate marketing and it now has hundreds of thousands of affiliates that drive visitors to Amazon through links in return for commission on products sold. Internet legend records that Jeff Bezos, the creator of Amazon, was chatting at a cocktail party to someone who wanted to sell books about divorce via her website. Subsequently, Amazon.com launched its Associates Program in July 1996 and it is still going strong. To manage the process of finding affiliates, updating product information, tracking clicks and making payments, many companies use an affiliate network or affiliate manager such as Commission Junction (www.cj.com) or Trade Doubler (www.tradedoubler.com).

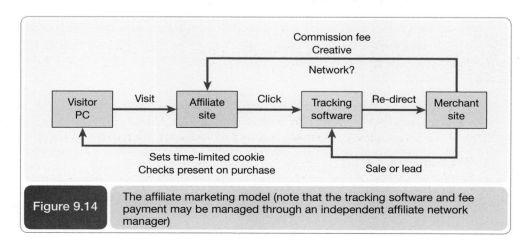

Commission fee
Creative
Network?

Visitor PC — Visit → Affiliate site — Click → Tracking software — Re-direct → Merchant site

Sets time-limited cookie
Checks present on purchase

Sale or lead

Figure 9.14   The affiliate marketing model (note that the tracking software and fee payment may be managed through an independent affiliate network manager)

Some of the issues with balancing spend between affiliate marketing and other online communications techniques and offline communications techniques are illustrated by Mini case study 9.5.

Mini Case Study 9.5	Electronic retailers cut back on their e-communications spend

Technology e-retailer dabs.com (featured in Case study 11.1) has traditionally used these as their main communications tools:

- Search engine marketing (the main investment)
- Referrals from affiliates (this has been reduced)
- Online display advertising on third-party sites (limited)
- PR.

Jonathan Wall, Dabs marketing director, explains (New Media Age, 2005a) how dabs.com reappraised their use of e-communications tools. He said:

We stopped all our affiliate and price-comparison marketing in February because we wanted to see what effect it had on our business and if we were getting value for money. It was proving a very expensive channel for us and we've found [stopping] it has had virtually no effect, because we're seeing that people will still go to Kelkoo to check prices and then come to our site anyway. It's like they're having a look around first and then coming to a brand they know they can trust. We're continuing with paid-for search on Google, but that's all we're doing with online marketing at the moment.

New Media Age (2005a) also reported that Empire Direct had adopted a similar approach to its communication mix, reporting that its co-founder and sales and marketing director, Manohar Showan, had revealed that the company has significantly moved from online to offline advertising. He said:

We've moved a lot more into national papers and specialist magazines. Two years ago, if you'd asked me where we marketed and advertised ourselves, I would have said the majority was online. But now it's turned right round and online's the minority.

New Media Age (2005a) believes that the reason for this is not a mistrust of the very medium it's using to take sales but, instead, the result of a growing realization that its acquisition costs were swelling online. Showan says:

We were very keen advocates of affiliate marketing and pay-per-click search. The trouble was we had to pay for every click and we were finding that the cost of acquiring each new customer was getting more and more. One big issue was that we were finding people would come to us through affiliates just to check information on a product they'd already bought, so we were basically paying for customers to find out how to hook up their new VCR. We still have affiliates – our main one is Kelkoo – and we still bid for clicks on Google, but not as much as we used to. One of the things we were finding with the search engines is that, with our own search optimisation and because so many people were coming to our site, we were normally very high up the list just through normal searching. In our experience, particularly with Google, if people can see what they want in the main list, they don't look to the right-hand side of the page.

(b) Online sponsorship

Online sponsorship is not straightforward. It's not just a case of mirroring existing 'real-world' sponsorship arrangements in the 'virtual world' although this is a valid option. There are many additional opportunities for sponsorship online which can be sought out, even if you don't have a big budget at your disposal.

Ryan and Whiteman (2000) define online sponsorship as:

the linking of a brand with related content or context for the purpose of creating brand awareness and strengthening brand appeal in a form that is clearly distinguishable from a banner, button, or other standardized ad unit.

For the advertiser, online sponsorship has the benefit that their name is associated with an online brand that the site visitor is already familiar with. Sponsorship builds on this existing relationship and trust. Closely related is online 'co-branding' where there is an association between two brands.

4 Interactive advertising

How positively do you view interactive advertising as a communications tool? Even today, there are relatively few advertisers who have used interactive advertising. The first 468 by 68 pixels banner ad was placed on Hotwired in 1995 and the call-to-action 'Click here!' generated a clickthough of 25%. Since then, the clickthrough rate (CTR) has fallen dramatically as many consumers suffer from 'banner blindness' – they ignore anything on a website that looks like an ad. The Doubleclick compilation of ad response (www.doubleclick.com) shows that today the average CTR is typically less than 0.1%, although video ads can receive a higher response rate. This low response rate, combined with relatively high costs of over £20 per thousands of ads served, has seemingly made some marketers prejudiced against interactive advertising. But we will see that there are many innovative approaches to interactive advertising which are proved to increase brand awareness and purchase intent. Given these limitations to banner ads, most media owners, digital marketing agencies and industry bodies now refer to 'interactive or display advertising', which is more suggestive of the range of options.

Media multiplier or halo effect

The role of one media channel on influencing sale or uplift in brand metrics. Commonly applied to online display advertising, where exposure to display ads may increase clickthrough rates when the consumer is later exposed to a brand through other media.

Online ads also seem to provide a **media multiplier or halo effect** which can help increase the response rates from other online media. For example, if a web user has been exposed to banner ads, this may increase their response to paid search ads and may also increase their likelihood of converting on a site since brand awareness and trust may be higher.

This effect is suggested by research reported by MAD (2007) in the travel market which involved asking respondents what their response to an online ad that appealed to them would be. Surely it would be a click? In fact, the results broke down as follows:

- Search for a general term relating to the advertisement (31%)
- Go straight to advertiser's site (29%)
- Search for the advertiser's name (26%)
- Click on banner to respond (26%)
- Visit a retail store (4%).

Of course, this methodology shows us reported behaviour rather than actual behaviour, but it is still significant that more than twice as many people are being driven to a search engine by banner advertising than by clicking directly on the banner! The research concludes that paid-search marketing needs to be optimized to work with banner advertising, by anticipating searches that are likely to be prompted by the banner and ensure a higher rank for search results. For example, a brand featuring a Cyprus holiday offer will generate generic search terms like 'package holiday Cyprus' rather than brand searches.

Abraham (2008) has also shown that online ads can stimulate offline sales. For one retailer with a turnover of $15 billion, their research showed that over a three-month period sales increased (compared to a control group) by 40% online and by 50% offline among people exposed to an online search marketing and display-ad campaign promoting the entire company. Because its baseline sales volumes are greater in physical stores than on the Internet, this retailer derived a great deal more revenue benefit offline than the percentages suggest.

Fundamentals of online advertising

Ad serving

The term for displaying an advertisement on a website. Often the advertisement will be served from a web server different from the site on which it is placed.

Advertising on the web takes place when an advertiser pays to place advertising content on another website. The process usually involves **ad serving** from a different server from that on which the page is hosted (ads can be served on destination sites in a similar way).

Destination site
The site reached on clickthrough.

Micro-site
A small-scale destination site reached on clickthrough which is part of the media owner's site

Advertising is possible on a range of sites in order to drive traffic to an organization's **destination site** or alternatively a **micro-site** or nested ad-content on the media owner's site or on the destination site.

The purpose of interactive advertising

Robinson *et al.* (2007) have noted that the two primary goals of online display advertising are, first, using display adverts as a form of marketing communication used to raise brand awareness and, second, as a direct response medium focused on generating a response. Cartellieri *et al.* (1997) identify the following objectives:

- *Delivering content.* This is the typical case where a clickthrough on a banner advertisement leads through to a destination site giving more detailed information on an offer. This is where a direct response is sought.
- *Enabling transaction.* If a clickthrough leads through to a merchant such as a travel site or an online bookstore this may lead directly to a sale. A direct response is also sought here.
- *Shaping attitudes.* An advertisement that is consistent with a company brand can help build brand awareness. Building awareness is a key aspect of online advertising.
- *Soliciting response.* An advertisement may be intended to identify new leads or as a start for two-way communication. In these cases an interactive advertisement may encourage a user to type in an e-mail address or other information.
- *Encouraging retention.* The advertisement may be placed as a reminder about the company and its service and may link through to on-site sales promotions such as a prize draw.

Interactive ad targeting options

Online ads can be targeted through placing ads:

1 *On a particular type of site (or part of site)* which has a specific visitor profile or type of content. So a car manufacturer can place ads on the home page of Handbag.com to appeal to a young female audience. A financial services provider can place an ad in the money section of the site to target those interested in these products. To reach large mass-market audiences, place an ad on a large portal home page such as MSN which has millions of visitors each day (sometimes known as a 'road-block' or 'takeover' if they take all ad inventory).
2 *To target a registered user's profile.* A business software provider could advertise on FT.com to target finance directors or IT managers.
3 At a particular time of day or week.

Behavioural ad targeting
Enables an advertiser to target ads at a visitor as they move elsewhere on the site or return to the site, thus increasing the frequency or number of impressions served to an individual in the target market.

4 *Online behaviour.* **Behavioural ad targeting** is all about relevance – dynamically serving relevant content, messaging or an ad which matches the interests of a site visitor according to inferences about their characteristics. These inferences are made by anonymously tracking the different types of pages visited by a site user during a single visit to a site or across multiple sessions. Other aspects of the environment used by the visitor can also be determined, such as their location, browser and operating system.

Interactive ad formats

As well as the classic 468 by 60 pixel rotating GIF banner ad which is decreasing in popularity, media owners now provide a choice of larger, richer formats which web users are more likely to notice. Research has shown that message association and awareness building are much higher for flash-based ads, rich-media ads and larger-format rectangles (multipurpose units, MPUs) and skyscrapers. View the rich-media ads at www.eyeblaster.com or www.tangozebra.com and you will agree that they definitely can't be ignored. Specific ad formats are available within the social networks, for example Facebook Engagement Ads, Twitter Promoted Tweets and YouTube Promoted videos.

Interstitial ads
Ads that appear between one page and the next.

Overlay
Typically an animated ad that moves around the page and is superimposed on the website content.

Other online ad terms you will hear include 'interstitials' (intermediate adverts before another page appears); the more common 'overlays' which appear above content; and of course pop-up windows that are now less widely used because of their intrusion. Online advertisers face a constant battle with users who deploy pop-up blockers or less commonly ad-blocking software, but they will persist in using rich-media formats where they generate the largest response.

Robinson *et al.* (2007) conducted research on the factors which increased clickthrough response to banner ads. The main variables they (and previous studies they reference) include are:

- Banner size
- Message length
- Promotional incentive
- Animation
- Action phrase (commonly referred to as a call to action)
- Company brand/logo.

Media planning – deciding on the online/offline mix for advertising

This decision is typically taken by the media planner. The mix between online and offline spend should reflect consumers' media consumption and the cost-response effectiveness of each medium. But, depending on the agency used, they may play it safe by putting the ad spend into what they are familiar with and what may be most rewarding in terms of commission – offline media. Many **cross-media optimization studies (XMOS)** have shown that the optimal online spend for low-involvement products is surprisingly high at 10–15% of total spend. Although this is not a large amount, it compares to previous spend levels below 1% for many organizations.

XMOS research is designed to help marketers and their agencies answer the (rather involved) question, 'What is the optimal mix of advertising vehicles across different media, in terms of frequency, reach and budget allocation, for a given campaign to achieve its marketing goals?'

The mix between online and offline spend is varied to maximize campaign metrics such as reach, brand awareness and purchase intent. Table 9.2 summarizes the optimal mix identified for four famous brands. For example, Dove found that increasing the level of interactive advertising to 15% would have resulted in an increase in overall branding metrics of 8%. The proportion of online is small, but remember that many companies are spending less than 1% of their ad budgets online, meaning that offline frequency is too high and they may not be reaching many consumers.

The reasons for using and increasing the significance of online in the media mix are similar to those for using any media mix as described by Sissors and Baron (2002):

- Extend reach (adding prospects not exposed by a single medium or other media).
- Flatten frequency distribution (if audience viewing TV ads is exposed too many times, there is a law of diminishing returns and it may be better to reallocate that budget to other media).

Cross-media optimization studies (XMOS)
Studies to determine the optimum spend across different media to produce the best results.

Table 9.2	Optimum media mix suggested by XMOS® studies		
Brand	**TV**	**Magazine**	**Online**
Colgate	75%	14%	11%
Kleenex	70%	20%	10%
Dove	72%	13%	15%
McDonald's	71%	16% (radio)	13%

Source: Interactive Advertising Bureau (www.iab.net/xmos). XMOS is a registered trademark of the IAB.

- To reach different kinds of audiences.
- To provide unique advantages in stressing different benefits based on the different characteristics of each medium.
- To allow different creative executions to be implemented.
- To add gross impressions if the other media are cost-efficient.
- Reinforce message by using different creative stimuli.

All of these factors, and the first three in particular, provide the explanation of why XMOS shows it is worthwhile to put double-digit percentages into online media.

5 E-mail marketing

When devising plans for e-mail marketing communications, marketers need to plan for:

Outbound e-mail marketing
E-mails are sent to customers and prospects from an organization.

Inbound e-mail marketing
Management of e-mails from customers by an organization.

- **outbound e-mail marketing**, where e-mail campaigns are used as a form of direct marketing to encourage trial and purchases and as part of a CRM dialogue;
- **inbound e-mail marketing**, where e-mails from customers such as support enquiries are managed. These are often managed today in conjunction with chat and co-browsing sessions.

Despite the increase in spam such that the vast majority of e-mails are spam or viruses (most estimates exceed 80%), e-mail can still drive good response levels; this is particularly the case with in-house lists, so e-mail communications to customers through e-newsletters or periodic e-mail blasts are today a vital communications technique for companies.

The main measures for evaluating e-mail marketing are:

- *Delivery rate* – this excludes e-mail 'bounces' – e-mails will bounce if the e-mail address is no longer valid or a spam filter blocks the e-mail. So, online marketers check their 'deliverability' to make sure their messages are not identified as 'false positives' by spam prevention software. Web-based e-mail providers such as Hotmail and Yahoo! Mail have introduced standard authentication techniques known as Sender ID and Domain Keys which make sure the e-mail broadcaster is who they say they are and doesn't spoof their address as many spammers do.
- *Open rate* – this is measured for HTML messages through downloaded images. It is an indication of how many customers open an e-mail, but is not accurate since some users have preview panes in their e-mail readers which load the message even if it is deleted without reading and some e-mail readers such as Outlook Express now block images by default (this has resulted in a decline in open rates through time).
- *Clickthrough rate* – this is the number of people who click through on the e-mail of those delivered (strictly unique clicks rather than total clicks). You can see that response rates are quite high at around 10%.

Mini case study 9.6 shows how an online intermediary has been able to launch a revolutionary service which now operates in several countries in Europe. It shows the importance of using strategic e-mail communications effectively to engage customers as part of its retention strategy by targeting them more closely through a defined contact strategy and then integrating with the website booking system.

Opt-in e-mail options for customer acquisition

For acquiring new visitors and customers to a site, there are three main options for e-mail marketing. From the point of view of the recipient, these are:

1 *Cold e-mail campaign.* In this case, the recipient receives an opt-in e-mail from an organization that has rented an e-mail list from a consumer or a business e-mail list provider. Although they have agreed to receive offers by e-mail, the e-mail is effectively cold.

| Mini Case Study 9.6 | Toptable uses CRM and e-mail to engage customers online |

Launched in February 2000, Toptable (toptable.co.uk, Figure 9.15) is now Europe's largest online restaurant booking and advisory service – a free service for customers to research, plan and book anything from a romantic dinner for two to a large corporate event. Toptable receives a fee for every booking and is on course to seat 3 million diners in 2008.

Challenges and objectives of e-mail usage

While Toptable was already utilizing an established industry solution for delivering and tracking its e-mail campaigns, expert input was required to help achieve its aggressive CRM sales targets.

The existing CRM programme consisted of two weekly e-mail sends that contained minimal segmentation and tailoring of content. As a result, in some cases open rates had fallen to as low as 10% and all the signs pointed to list fatigue as users lost interest in the communications.

Toptable chose to partner with Emailcenter in August 2007 to help them develop an industry-leading CRM programme and to move the communications strategy away from a mass broadcast model.

Key objectives included:

- Increase the frequency of bookings from regular customers
- Reactivate defected customers
- Encourage those users who had yet to make a booking to do so.

Emailcenter put a plan in place around their ROAD methodology to achieve these goals and continues to work closely with Toptable to project manage their entire CRM programme. ROAD is a model developed by Emailcenter that covers the four key areas that need to be addressed for a successful e-mail marketing programme:

| Figure 9.15 | Toptable
Source: www.toptable.co.uk. |

Applying ROAD to the Toptable CRM programme

Relevance

Prior to working with Emailcenter Toptable e-mails contained minimal personalization. Each recipient received the same restaurant offers and reviews no matter where they lived or worked in the UK.

Using existing RSS feeds from the Toptable site Emailcenter automated the production of content containing offers, reviews and news items for each of their 300 locations. All Toptable have to do now for each e-mail is change global elements such as subject lines, intro messages and advertising.

Not only did this see increases in performance (tailored e-mails have generated conversion rates over twice that of the generic versions), it enabled Toptable to offer a highly relevant e-mail to all of their customers no matter where they are based in the UK.

Increasing the relevance of the content always improves the performance of an e-mail programme. However, an additional tactic is to be relevant with the timing of the e-mail.

An effective tactic was put in place that sent targeted triggered messages that replaced the newsletter to a number of segments including:

- Defectors – customers that made their last booking 6 weeks ago
- Lookers – customers that registered a month ago but have yet to make a booking.

Each segment had a series of e-mails that were delivered a week apart, each with ever improving offers. If a customer makes a booking from one of these e-mails they do not get any further e-mails in future weeks and resume receipt of the newsletter.

These e-mails were over 17 times more effective at reactivating customers and changing their booking behaviour than the newsletter. These triggered e-mails also helped increase the number of paid bookings from e-mail activity by 26% per week, despite being less than 5% of the e-mails sent each week.

Optimization

Continually reviewing the e-mail campaigns and testing variables such as subject lines, from names, styles, content or timing enables Toptable to learn what works best for them and helps them maximize e-mail performance.

Two main areas of testing are run:

- **Subject line tests** – 3 to 4 variants on subject lines are sent to a test file the night before, enabling them to identify the best-performing subject line for the next day's send.
- **Ad-hoc tests** – testing any variant that may have an impact on performance from changing the type of content, the number of offers, position of content, automated content vs manual content, frequency of send and timing.

The subject line tests alone show a deviation of around 2% points between the best and worst subject lines open rates.

Analysis

In order to identify whether progress towards the sales targets is being met and to isolate areas within the e-mail programme which either require improvement or are succeeding, a range of custom reporting is carried out. These reports include:

- How does frequency of send impact on long-term booking rates?
- Analysis of generic newsletters versus tailored content and the impact on defection and reactivation rates

Other standard reports Toptable utilize from within Maxemail include the Heatmap report that shows visually where clients are clicking and comparison reports that make it easy to identify trends over time.

Deliverability

While deliverability was not considered a major issue previously it was discovered upon analysis that only around 65% of the e-mails were being delivered into the inbox due to their incumbent suppliers' sending reputation. More worrying, it was found that the bounce list contained a large number of addresses that were falsely classified as invalid due to a black listing bouncing them. Upon analysis of this bounce list and subsequent test sends the overall list size was increased by 25% by reactivating the e-mails.

For future sends through Maxemail Emailcenter took full ownership of deliverability issues. This involved:

- Set-up of SPF/Sender ID records
- Dedicated IP range for corporate domains and use of a shared IP for Hotmail for the ultimate IP configuration
- Using spam-checking tools and running test sends to major ISPs such as Hotmail and AOL using 'Inbox Seeding'
- White-listing and feedback loops set up with major ISPs.

Within one month of the first delivery an inbox placement rate of 99.87% was achieved which has remained in place since.

Results

Since partnering with Emailcenter on their CRM activity Toptable have seen the following year-on-year performance increases across the board.

Bookings	Open rates	Click-thru rates	Delivery rates
+60%	+28.3%	+49.4%	+53.6%

Source: Adapted from Emailcenter (2008).

2 *Co-branded e-mail.* Here, the recipient receives an e-mail with an offer from a company they have a reasonably strong affinity with. For example, the same credit card company could partner with a mobile service provider such as Vodafone and send out the offer to their customer (who has opted in to receive e-mails from third parties). Although this can be considered a form of cold e-mail, it is warmer since there is a stronger relationship with one of the brands and the subject line and creative will refer to both brands.

3 *Third-party e-newsletter.* In this visitor acquisition option, a company publicizes itself in a third-party e-newsletter. This could be in the form of an ad, sponsorship or PR (editorial) which links through to a destination site. These placements may be set up as part of an interactive advertising ad buy since many e-newsletters also have permanent versions on the website. Since e-newsletter recipients tend to engage with them by scanning the headlines or reading them if they have time, e-newsletter placements can be relatively cost-effective.

House list

A list of prospect and customer names, e-mail addresses and profile information owned by an organization.

Viral marketing, which is discussed in the next section, also uses e-mail as the mechanism for transferring messages. E-mail is most widely used as a prospect conversion and customer retention tool using an opt-in or **house list** of prospects and customers who have given permission to an organization to contact them. For example, Lastminute.com has built a house list of over 10 million prospects and customers across Europe. Successful e-mail marketers adopt a strategic approach to e-mail and develop a contact or touch strategy which plans the frequency and content of e-mail communications, as explained in Chapters 4 and 6. For customer retention, a house list is built where e-mail is used to communicate to existing customers.

6 Social media marketing

Social media marketing

Monitoring and facilitating customer–customer interaction and participation throughout the web to encourage positive engagement with a company and its brands. Interactions may occur on a company site, social networks and other third-party sites.

Viral marketing

E-mail is used to transmit a promotional message to another potential customer.

Social media marketing, covered in the 'Focus on' section earlier in this chapter, can often be assisted through **viral marketing** approaches which harness the network effect of the Internet and can be effective in reaching a large number of people rapidly in the same way as a natural virus or a computer virus. It is effectively an online form of word-of-mouth communications. Smith and Chaffey (2005) say ideally viral marketing is a clever idea, a game, a shocking idea, or a highly informative idea which makes compulsive viewing. It can be a video clip, TV ad, cartoon, funny picture, poem, song, political message, or news item. It is so amazing, it makes people want to pass it on. This is a challenge for commercial companies since, to be successful, it will need to challenge convention and this may not fit well with the brand.

To make a viral campaign effective, Justin Kirby of viral marketing specialists DMC (www.dmc.co.uk) suggests that three things are needed (Kirby, 2003):

1 *Creative material – the 'viral agent'.* This includes the creative message or offer and how it is spread (text, image, video).
2 *Seeding.* Identifying websites, blogs or people to send e-mail to start the virus spreading.
3 *Tracking.* To monitor the effect, to assess the return from the cost of developing the viral agent and seeding.

With the widespread adoption of high-speed broadband in many countries, rich media experiences are increasingly used to engage customers with the hope they will have a 'viral effect', i.e. they will be discussed online or offline and more people will become aware of or interact with the brand campaign. Mini case study 1.1 on WillItBlend.com gives one successful example which fulfils Kirby's criteria of an effective viral and it translated to increased product sales.

Offline marketing communications

Offline communications will never disappear – they are effective at reaching an audience to encourage them to visit a site, but are also useful as a way of having an impact or explaining a complex proposition, as Mini case study 9.7 shows.

Table 9.3 gives a summary of the strengths and weaknesses of the digital media channels discussed in this chapter (numbers reference the different boxes in Figure 1.6).

Mini Case Study 9.7	Offline communications vital for finding the perfect partner at Match.com

UK-based online dating company Match.com has over 1.5 million members and in 2004 was responsible for 200,000 marriages around the world. Match.com and partner company uDate.com compete against Yahoo! Personals, Dating Direct, traditional players and a host of smaller players. Given the intense competition, Samantha Bedford, UK MD believes it is essential to invest in offline communications for continued growth. In Autumn 2005, Match.com spent over £3 million on a TV advertising campaign since they wanted to generate brand awareness, given that they estimated that by 2008 the value of the online dating market would double. In addition to achieving reach and brand awareness, offline advertising is important because it enables Match.com to communicate a fairly complex message to potential customers. Focus groups showed that many singles felt they didn't need an online dating service and didn't realize how Match.com could help as part of the overall dating experience.

Source: New Media Age (2005b).

Table 9.3	Summary of the strengths and weaknesses of different communications channels for promoting an online presence	

Promotion technique	Main strengths	Main weaknesses
1a Search engine optimization (SEO)	Highly targeted, relatively low cost of PPC. High traffic volumes if effective. Considered credible by searchers	Intense competition, may compromise look of site. Complexity of changes to ranking algorithm
1b Pay-per-click (PPC) marketing	Highly targeted with controlled cost of acquisition. Extend reach through content network	Relatively costly in competitive sectors and low volume compared with SEO
1c Trusted feed	Update readily to reflect changes in product lines and prices	Relatively costly, mainly relevant for e-retailers
2 Online PR	Relatively low cost and good targeting. Can assist with SEO through creation of backlinks	Identifying online influencers and setting up partnerships can be time-consuming. Need to monitor comments on third-party sites
3a Affiliate marketing	Payment is by results (e.g. 10% of sale or leads goes to referring site)	Costs of payments to affiliate networks for set-up and management fees. Changes to ranking algorithm may affect volume from affiliates
3b Online sponsorship	Most effective if low-cost, long-term co-branding arrangement with synergistic site	May increase awareness, but does not necessarily lead directly to sales
4 Interactive advertising	Main intention to achieve visit, i.e. direct response model. But also role in branding through media multiplier effect	Response rates have declined historically because of banner blindness
5 E-mail marketing	Push medium – can't be ignored in user's inbox. Can be used for direct response link to website. Integrates as a response mechanism with direct mail	Requires opt-in for effectiveness. Better for customer retention than for acquisition? Inbox cut-through – message diluted amongst other e-mails. Limits on deliverability
6 Social media and viral marketing	With effective viral agent possible to reach a large number at relatively low cost. Influencers in social networks significant	Difficult to create powerful viral concepts and control targeting. Risks damaging brand since unsolicited messages may be received
Traditional offline advertising (TV, print, etc.)	Larger reach than most online techniques. Greater creativity possible, leading to greater impact	Targeting arguably less easy than online. Typically high cost of acquisition

Customer retention management

For an e-commerce site, customer retention has two distinct goals:

1 To retain customers of the organization (repeat customers).
2 To keep customers using the online channel (repeat visits).

These are similar to the two aims of customer acquisition as described in a previous section. Ideally marketing communications should address both aims.

Maintaining online customer relationships is difficult. Laurie Windham (2001) says:

> *That's what's so scary about customer retention in the online space. We've created this empowered, impatient customer who has a short attention span, a lot of choices, and a low barrier to switching.*

To create long-term online customer relationships that build on acquisition, to retain and extend, we need to analyse the drivers of satisfaction amongst these e-customers, since satisfaction drives loyalty and loyalty drives profitability. The relationship is shown in Figure 9.16. The objective of marketers is to drive customers up the curve towards the zone of affection. However, it is worth remembering that the majority are not in that zone and to achieve retention marketers must understand why customers defect or are indifferent.

It follows from Figure 9.16 that we need to understand different factors that affect loyalty. The type of approach that can be taken is highlighted by Reichheld and Schefter (2000). They reported that Dell Computer has created a customer experience council that has researched key loyalty drivers, identified measures to track these and put in place an action plan to improve loyalty (Table 9.4).

Since quality of service is so crucial in determining satisfaction and loyalty, see the '*Focus on* Excelling in e-commerce service quality' section later in this chapter.

Now let us consider key e-marketing tools that help retain customers. Repeat visits can be generated by a variety of means and brainstorming sessions can help generate these. Often it may simply be the expedient of regularly updated market and product or technical information that helps customers perform their day-to-day work. Such information can be delivered through extranets such as Dell Premier or through personalization services such as that described for RS Components. Information to help people perform their work is the proposition of the vertical portals such as industry-specific sites. Online communities are popular for both consumer and business markets since users can discuss topical issues or ask for answers to their queries. For example, the UK Net Marketing Group at

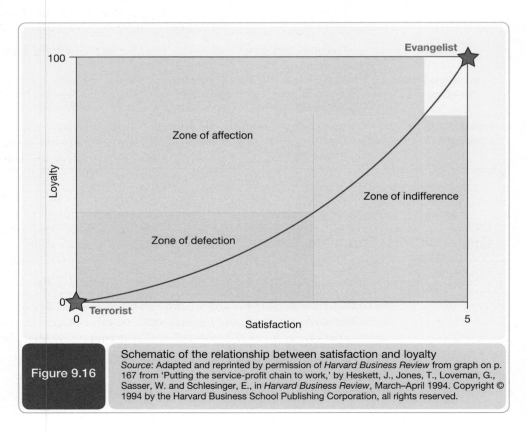

Figure 9.16	Schematic of the relationship between satisfaction and loyalty *Source*: Adapted and reprinted by permission of *Harvard Business Review* from graph on p. 167 from 'Putting the service-profit chain to work,' by Heskett, J., Jones, T., Loveman, G., Sasser, W. and Schlesinger, E., in *Harvard Business Review*, March–April 1994. Copyright © 1994 by the Harvard Business School Publishing Corporation, all rights reserved.

Table 9.4	Relationship between loyalty drivers and measures to assess their success at Dell Computer

Loyalty drivers	Summary metric
1 Order fulfilment	Ship to target. Percentage that ship on time exactly as the customer specified.
2 Product performance	Initial field incident rate – the frequency of problems experienced by customers.
3 Post-sale service and support	On-time, first-time fix – the percentage of problems fixed on the first visit by a service rep who arrives at the time promised.

Source: Adapted and reprinted by permission of *Harvard Business Review* from information on pp. 105–13 from 'Your secret weapon on the web', by Reichheld, F. and Schefter, P., in *Harvard Business Review*, July–August 2000. Copyright © 2000 by the Harvard Business School Publishing Corporation, all rights reserved.

www.chinwag.com discusses the benefits of new technologies such as mobile commerce and recommends suppliers of Internet services. Many such communities work because they are independent of suppliers, so it may be difficult to introduce these types of facilities on to a corporate site. Finally, traditional sales promotion techniques translate well to the Internet. RS Components use Product of the Week or Month to discount some items and offer competitions and prize draws to encourage repeat visits. These are often publicized in offline mail-outs to encourage repeat visits.

Personalization and mass customization

The potential power of personalization is suggested by these quotes from Evans *et al.* (2000) that show the negative effects of lack of targeting of traditional direct mail:

Don't like unsolicited mail ... haven't asked for it and I'm not interested.

(Female, 25–34)

Most isn't wanted, it's not relevant and just clutters up the table ... you have to sort through it to get to the 'real mail'.

(Male, 45–54)

It's annoying to be sent things that you are not interested in. Even more annoying when they phone you up ... If you wanted something you would go and find out about it.

(Female, 45–54)

Personalization
Delivering individualized content through web pages or e-mail.

Mass customization
Delivering customized content to groups of users through web pages or e-mail.

Collaborative filtering
Profiling of customer interest coupled with delivery of specific information and offers, often based on the interests of similar customers.

Personalization and **mass customization** can be used to tailor information and opt-in e-mail can be used to deliver it to add value and at the same time remind the customer about a product. 'Personalization' and 'mass customization' are terms that are often used interchangeably. In the strict sense, personalization refers to customization of information requested by a site customer at an *individual* level. Mass customization involves providing tailored content to a *group* with similar interests. This approach is sometimes also referred to as '**collaborative filtering**'.

All these personalization techniques take advantage of the dynamic possibilities of web content. Users' preferences are stored in databases and content is taken from a database. Personalization can be achieved through several dynamic variables including:

- the customers' preferences
- the date or time
- particular events
- the location.

Personalization can also be used to offer innovative services. Online bookseller BOL (www. bol.com) allows customers to choose their favourite parts from different types of travel guides, perhaps history from the Rough Guides and maps from Lonely Planet, but excluding night clubs and restaurants. The personalized book can then be printed on demand on the customer's printer.

A more typical personalization service is that provided by the portals such as Google, Yahoo! and NetVibes. These enable users to configure their home page so that it delivers the information they are most interested in: perhaps their regional weather, the results from their soccer team and the prices of shares they have purchased.

Turning to negative aspects of personalization, there are two chief difficulties. First, cost, for the reasons explained in the next section and, second, it may act as a barrier to users. For example, some personalization requires the user to log in. This may be a problem if a customer has mislaid a password. Equally, for a new visitor to the site the need to apply for a password can be offputting and a customer may disappear, never to return. Effective personalization will still enable a new visitor to view a good deal of content even if they do not have a password. Use of *cookies* can avoid the need for the customer to actively log in, with this occurring automatically.

Creating personalization

Personalization of web content is much more expensive than developing static content, since it requires database integration and specialized software tools such as Omniture Test and Target, which recognizes visitors when they return and then accesses and displays the relevant information from a database.

Mini case study 9.8 shows how implementation of personalization can result in more relevant messages and improved response rates.

Extranets

Extranets were introduced in Chapter 3. Since they require a user to log in they signify differential services through premium content and services. Many options are possible. A dynamic example of using an extranet is the use of the web to host online events that mirror traditional events such as seminars, trade shows and user group conferences, virtual seminars with a guest speaker by webcast, virtual trade shows where exhibitors, seminar speakers

---

Mini Case Study 9.8	HSBC uses personalization to deliver tailored propositions

When HSBC Bank International (HBIB) refined its website it wanted to use personalization with the goal of delivering specific offers and servicing to different customer segments and encourage customers to move into more valuable segments. This would enable it to capitalize on sales opportunities that would otherwise be missed. New Media Age (2007) reported that this was a challenge since '*60% of total weekly visitors to offshore.hsbc.com log on to the internet banking service, HSBC wanted to market to them effectively while they were engaged in this task, disrupting their banking experience without infuriating them*'. Business rules were created to serve promotions dependent on the type of content accessed and the level of balance in the customer's account.

HSBC was successful in meeting its goals and the results show the benefit of personalized, targeted banners. On average, New Media Age (2007) reported that the new banners had an 87.5% higher click-through rate than non-personalized banners (6.88% versus 3.67%). The number of savings accounts opened via Internet banking increased by 30% (based on six months pre- and post-launch). And the number of non-Premier customers upgrading to Premier accounts (requiring a balance of £60,000 or more) increased by 86% (based on four weeks pre- and post-launch of the targeted banners).

and delegates are linked by the web. Dell Computer has a special brand variant known as Dell Premier that can be used to provide value-added services for key accounts. Other traditional retention methods such as loyalty schemes and sales promotions translate well to the online environment.

The use of extranets presents a barrier to entry, particularly if users lose their passwords. To limit this effect RS Components sends out password reminders to help retention. A Dutch insurer combined online and offline techniques to use an extranet to deliver mass customization. Existing customers were divided into six segments and then contacted through a direct mail campaign. Members of each segment were given one of six passwords, so that when they accessed the extranet there were six different versions of content for the website giving product suggestions and offers consistent with the segment. Extranets provide good traceability of marketing outcomes and tagging of visitors. In this case the effectiveness of the campaign in terms of response rate from the e-mail and conversion to sales could also be monitored for different segments.

Opt-in e-mail

Opt-in e-mail is vital in communicating the retention offers either through regular e-mail communications such as a newsletter or higher-impact irregular e-mail communications such as details of a product launch. Remember that e-mail has the power of traditional push communication. It enables a targeted message to be pushed out to a customer to inform and remind and they are certain to view it within their e-mail inbox; even if it is only deleted, it cannot be ignored.

Spam
Unsolicited e-mail (usually bulk-mailed and untargeted).

Despite its potential, use of e-mail for marketing has negative connotations due to **spam** and privacy concerns as discussed in Chapter 3, so it's essential that e-mail marketing is permission-based.

Once an e-mail address has been collected, managers must plan the frequency of e-mail communications. Options include:

- *Regular newsletter type.* For example, once a day, once a week, once a month. It is best if customers are given choice about the frequency.
- *Event-related.* These tend to be less regular and are sent out perhaps every three or six months when there is news of a new product launch or an exceptional offer.
- *E-mail sequence.* Software can be purchased to send out a series of e-mails. For example, after subscription to a trial version of an online magazine, e-mails will be sent out at 3, 10, 25 and 28 days to encourage a subscription before the trial lapses.

Techniques for managing customer activity and value

Within the online customer base of an organization, there will be customers who have different levels of activity in usage of online services or in sales. A good example is a bank – some customers may use the online account once a week, others much less frequently and some not at all. Figure 9.17 illustrates the different levels of activity.

To improve the adoption of 'web self-service' which helps reduce costs it is important to define measures which indicate activity levels and then develop tactics to increase activity levels through more frequent use. Objectives and corresponding tactics can be set for:

- Increasing number of *new users per* month and annually (separate objectives will be set for existing bank customers and new bank customers) through promoting online services to drive visitors to the website.
- Increasing % of *active users* (an appropriate threshold can be used – for some other organizations it could be set at 7, 30 or 90 days). Using direct communications such as e-mail, personalized website messages, direct mail and phone communications to new, dormant and inactive users increases the percentage of active users.

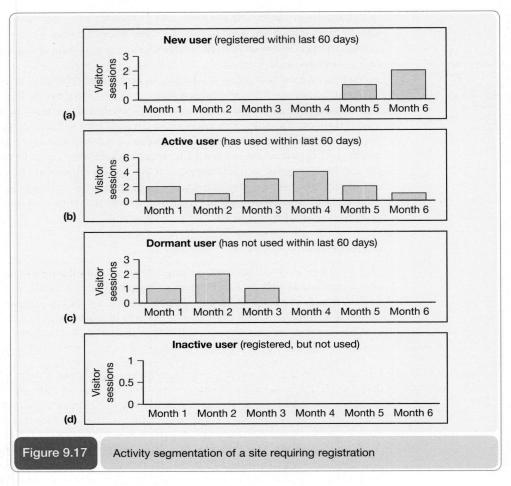

| Figure 9.17 | Activity segmentation of a site requiring registration |

- Decreasing % of *dormant users* (were once new or active, could be sub-categories), but have not used within a time period to be classified as active.
- Decreasing % of *inactive users* (or non-activated) users. These are those who signed up for a service such as online banking and username was issued, but they have not used the service.

You can see that corresponding strategies can be developed for each of these strategies.

Another key metric, in fact the key retention metric for e-commerce sites, refers to repeat business. The importance of retention rate metrics was highlighted by Agrawal *et al.* (2001). The main retention metrics they mention and show the impact on profitability are:

- *Repeat-customer conversion rate* – how many first-time customers purchase a second product?
- *Repeat-customer base* – the proportion of the customer base who have made repeat purchases.
- *Number of transactions per repeat customer* – this indicates the stage of development of the customer in the relationship (another similar measure is number of product categories purchased).
- *Revenue per transaction of repeat customer* – this is a proxy for lifetime value since it gives average order value.

Lifetime value modelling

Lifetime value (LTV)
Lifetime value is the total net benefit that a customer or group of customers will provide a company over their total relationship with the company.

An appreciation of **lifetime value (LTV)** is also key to the theory and practice of customer relationship management. However, while the term is often used, calculation of LTV is not straightforward, so many organizations do not calculate it. Lifetime value is defined as the total net benefit that a customer or group of customers will provide a company over their total relationship with a company. Modelling is based on estimating the income and costs associated with each customer over a period of time and then calculating the net present value in current monetary terms using a discount rate value applied over the period.

There are different degrees of sophistication in calculating LTV. These are indicated in Figure 9.18. Option 1 is a practical way or approximate proxy for future LTV, but the true LTV is the future value of the customer at an individual level. Lifetime value modelling at a segment level (4) is vital within marketing since it answers the question:

How much can I afford to invest in acquiring a new customer?

Lifetime value analysis enables marketers to:

- Plan and measure investment in customer acquisition programmes
- Identify and compare critical target segments
- Measure the effectiveness of alternative customer retention strategies
- Establish the true value of a company's customer base
- Make decisions about products and offers
- Make decisions about the value of introducing new e-CRM technologies.

Figure 9.19 gives an example of how LTV can be used to develop a CRM strategy for different customer groups. Four main types of customers are indicated by their current and future value as bronze, silver, gold and platinum. Distinct customer groupings (circles) are identified according to their current value (as indicated by current profitability) and future value as indicated by lifetime value calculations. Each of these groups will have a customer profile signature based on their demographics, so this can be used for customer selection. Different strategies are developed for different customer groups within the four main value groupings. Some bronze customers such as Groups A and B realistically do not have development potential and are typically unprofitable, so the aim is to reduce costs in communications and if they do not remain as customers, this is acceptable. Some bronze customers such as Group C may have potential for growth, so for these the strategy is to extend their purchases. Silver customers are targeted with customer extension offers and gold customers are extended where possible although these have relatively little growth

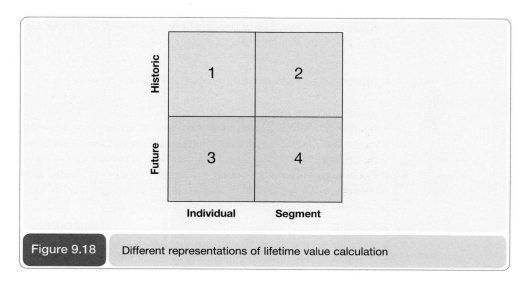

Figure 9.18 Different representations of lifetime value calculation

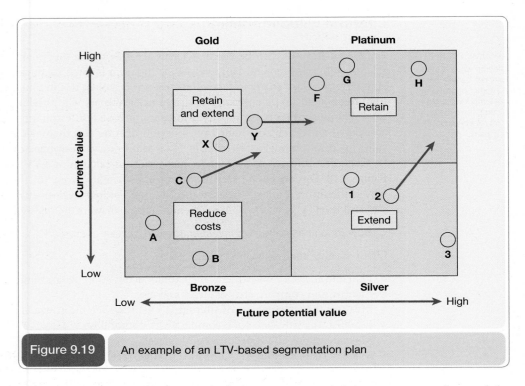

| Figure 9.19 | An example of an LTV-based segmentation plan |

potential. Platinum customers are the best customers, so it is important to understand the communication preferences of these customers and not to over-communicate unless there is evidence that they may defect.

Excelling in e-commerce service quality

In the virtual world customer service is a key difference between brands. Jevons and Gabbot (2000) explain: '*the first-hand experience of the brand is a more powerful token of trust than the perception of the brand*'.

Research across industry sectors suggests that the quality of service is a key determinant of loyalty. Feinberg *et al.* (2000) report that if reasons why customers leave a company are considered, over 68% leave because of 'poor service experience', with other factors such as price (10%) and product issues (17%) less significant.

Improving online service quality

Delivering service quality in e-commerce can be assessed through reviewing existing frameworks for determining levels of service quality. Those most frequently used are based on the concept of a 'service-quality gap' that exists between the customers' *expected* level of service (from previous experience and word-of-mouth communication) and their perception of the *actual* level of service delivery.

Parasuraman *et al.* (1985) suggested that these dimensions of service quality on which consumers judge expected and delivered service-quality levels are:

- tangibles – the physical appearance and visual appeal of facilities;
- reliability – the ability to perform the service consistently and accurately;
- responsiveness – a willingness to help customers and provide prompt service;

- assurance – the knowledge and courtesy of employees and their ability to convey trust and confidence;
- empathy – providing caring, individualized attention.

Note that there has been heated dispute about the validity of this SERVQUAL instrument framework (Parasuraman *et al.*, 1985) in determining service quality, see for example Cronin and Taylor (1992). Despite this it is still instructive to apply these dimensions of service quality to customer service on the web. We will now review each dimension of SERVQUAL.

Tangibles

It can be suggested that the tangibles dimension is influenced by ease of use and visual appeal based on the structural and graphic design of the site. The importance of these factors to consumers is indicated by a 1999 study by Forrester Research of 8,600 US consumers that found that the main reason for returning to a site were high-quality content (75%), ease of use (66%), speed to download (58%) and frequency of update (54%); these were the most important aspects of website quality mentioned.

Reliability

The reliability dimension is dependent on the availability of the website, or in other words, how easy it is to connect to the website as a user.

Reliability of e-mail response is also a key issue; Chaffey and Edgar (2000) report on a survey of 361 UK websites across different sectors. Of those in the sample, 331 (or 92%) were accessible at the time of the survey and, of these, 299 provided an e-mail contact point. E-mail enquiries were sent to all of these 299 websites; of these, 9 undeliverable mail messages were received. It can be seen that at the time of the survey, service availability is certainly not universal.

Responsiveness

The same survey showed that responsiveness was poor overall: of the 290 successfully delivered e-mails, a 62% response rate occurred within a 28-day period. For over a third of companies there was zero response!

Of the companies that did respond, there was a difference in responsiveness (excluding immediately delivered automated responses) from 8 minutes to over 19 working days! While the mean overall was 2 working days, 5 hours and 11 minutes, the median across all sectors (on the basis of the fastest 50% of responses received) was 1 working day and 34 minutes. The median result suggests that response within one working day represents best practice and could form the basis for consumer expectations.

Responsiveness is also indicated by the performance of the website – the time it takes for a page request to be delivered to the user's browser as a page impression. Since there is a wide variability in the delivery of information and hence service quality from web servers hosted at ISPs, companies should be careful to monitor this and specify levels of quality with suppliers in service-level agreements (SLAs). Zona Research (1999) conducted an analysis that suggests that $4.35 billion may be lost in e-commerce revenues due to customer 'bailout' when customers are unwilling to wait for information to download. The report notes that many customers may not be prepared to wait longer than eight seconds!

As explained in Chapter 7, effective fulfilment is also an essential part of responsiveness.

Assurance

In an e-mail context, assurance can best be considered as the quality of response. In the survey reported by Chaffey and Edgar (2000), of 180 responses received, 91% delivered a personalized human response with 9% delivering an automated response which did not address the individual enquiry; 40% of responses answered or referred to all three questions with 10% answering two questions, and 22% one. Overall, 38% did not answer any of the specific questions posed!

A further assurance concern of e-commerce websites is the privacy and security of customer information. A company that subscribes to the Internet Shopping is Safe – ISIS (www.imrg.org/is) – merchant accreditation or TRUSTe principles (www.truste.org) will provide better assurance than one that does not. The following actions can be suggested to achieve assurance in an e-commerce site:

1 Provide clear and effective privacy statements
2 Follow privacy and consumer protection guidelines in all local markets
3 Make security of customer data a priority
4 Use independent certification bodies
5 Emphasize the excellence of service quality in all communications.

Empathy

Although it might be considered that empathy requires personal human contact, it can still be achieved, to an extent, through e-mail. Chaffey and Edgar (2000) report that of the responses received, 91% delivered a personalized human response, with 29% passing on the enquiry within their organization. Of these 53, 23 further responses were received within the 28-day period and 30 (or 57%) of passed-on queries were not responded to further.

Provision of personalization facilities is also an indication of the empathy provided by the website, but more research is needed as to customers' perception of the value of web pages that are dynamically created to meet a customer's information needs.

An alternative approach for considering how service quality can be delivered through e-commerce is to consider how the site provides customer service at the different stages of the buying decision shown in Figure 9.3. Thus quality service is not only dependent on how well the purchase itself is facilitated, but also on how easy it is for customers to select products and on after-sales service, including fulfilment quality. The Epson UK site (www.epson.co.uk) illustrates how the site can be used to help in all stages of the buying process. Interactive tools are available to help users select a particular printer, diagnose and solve faults, and technical brochures can be downloaded. Feedback is solicited on how well these services meet customers' needs.

These SERVQUAL elements have been applied to online banking by Jun and Cai (2001) in a detailed study. This supports the importance of the original SERVQUAL elements in an online setting. For example, it highlights the importance of a timely, accurate response to customer queries. It also uncovers a particular feature of online service – that customers expect to see a continuous improvement to site services, and suggests their satisfaction will be reduced if positive changes are not made.

In summary, it can be suggested that for managers wishing to apply a framework such as SERVQUAL in an e-commerce context there are three stages appropriate to managing the process.

1 *Understanding expectations.* The SERVQUAL framework can be used with market research and benchmarking of other sites, as described in Chapter 12, to understand customer requirements such as responsiveness and empathy. Scenarios can also be used to identify the customer expectations of using services on a site.
2 *Setting and communicating the service promise.* Once expectations are understood, marketing communications can be used to inform the customers of the level of service. This can be achieved through customer service guarantees or promises. It is better to under-promise than over-promise. A book retailer that delivers the book in two days when three days were promised will earn the customer's loyalty better than the retailer that promises one day, but delivers in two! The enlightened company may also explain what it will do if it does not meet its promises – will the customer be recompensed? The

service promise must also be communicated internally and combined with training to ensure that the service is delivered.

3   *Delivering the service promise*. Finally, commitments must be delivered through on-site service, support from employees and physical fulfilment. If not, online credibility is destroyed and a customer may never return.

As a conclusion to this section review Mini case study 9.9 which shows how one company delivers service quality on line.

Mini Case Study 9.9   Online customer service at Barclays

In 2005, Barclays deployed web self-service to answer customers' question online and reduce the 100,000 monthly calls to its helpdesk. Accessible on every page, via 'Ask a question', the Barclays solution allows customers to ask questions and receive meaningful, accurate answers on any subject from credit card offers to information about how the company credit scores.

In the first 12 months, 'Ask a question' was used by 350,000 customers and answered more than half a million questions. Only 8% of customers escalated through to the call centre, pointing to high levels of customer satisfaction and resulting in improvements to call centre efficiency and quality of service. In 2007, more than 2 million customers used 'Ask a question' to find answers to their questions.

'Ask a question' is providing invaluable insight at the critical decision making process about what concerns customers have and what products are of interest. For example, it identified a higher demand from personal banking customers for making foreign currency payments than was previously known to Barclays. This information is being used to inform the bank about customer trends and requirements, and for creating customer-driven website content.

It was apparent that website visitors who ask questions through web self-service were more than casual browsers but customers with genuine buying requirements. There was potential to increase sales conversion by putting the right information and product offer in front of these customers based on what they were asking about. 'Ask a question' was enhanced to incorporate ad-serving, which serves up targeted advertising and sales promotions in response to questions asked by customers via the bank's website. The adverts change automatically depending on their relevance to customer questions, or to products and services Barclays wants to promote. For example, when customers ask questions about foreign currency accounts, 'Ask a question' will provide a specific answer and display adverts for travel insurance, the use of debit cards abroad and foreign mortgages. As well as promoting products directly relevant to the customers' search, ad serving is used to cross-promote related products and services. These ads provide customers with an appealing call to action that speeds sales completion and increases response rates.

Advertising products alongside search results is producing high conversion rates with 12% of customers responding to a product advertisement. 'Ask a question' is also improving usability, allowing customers to access all of the content relevant to them from a single click or question. By integrating ad serving with 'Ask a question', Barclays have been able to achieve high levels of behavioural targeting that have previously only been available through expensive and complicated website analytic tools. Because advertisements and promotions are served in response to customer enquiries, there is no need for the system to log or track vast amounts of historical customer data to analyse and predict customer behaviour in order to deliver targeted information. This cuts the complexity of delivering targeted information and increases sales.

Source: Transversal (2008) UK companies fail the multi-channel customer service test. Research report, March.

Customer extension

Customer extension
Deepening the
relationship with the
customer through
increased interaction and
product transactions.

Lifetime value (LTV)
The combined revenue
attributable to a customer
during their relationship
with a company.

**Share of wallet or
share of customer**
The proportion of
customer expenditure
in a particular category
that belongs to a single
customer.

Customer extension has the aim of increasing the **lifetime value** of the customer to the company by encouraging cross-sales, for example an Egg credit card customer may be offered the option of a loan or a deposit account. When a customer returns to a website this is an opportunity for cross-selling and such offers can be communicated. Direct e-mail is also an excellent way for informing a customer about other company products and it is also useful in encouraging repeat visits by publicizing new content or promotions. E-mail is vitally important to achieving online CRM as it is a push medium where the customer can be reminded why they should visit the website.

Many companies are now only proactively marketing to favoured customers. Seth Godin (1999) says, '*Focus on share of customer, not market share – fire 70 per cent of your customers and watch your profits go up!*' One UK financial services provider has analysed characteristics of high-churn-rate customers, and when a new prospect fitting this profile contacts the call centre they are actively discouraged. Using these techniques it is possible to increase **share of customer**.

Advanced online segmentation and targeting techniques

The most sophisticated segmentation and targeting (see Chapter 8 for an introduction) schemes for extension are often used by e-retailers, who have detailed customer profiling information and purchase history data as they seek to increase customer lifetime value through encouraging increased use of online services over time. However, the general principles of this approach can also be used by other types of companies online. The segmentation and targeting approach used by e-retailers is based on five main elements which in effect are layered on top of each other. The number of options used, and so the sophistication of the approach, will depend on resources available, technology capabilities and opportunities afforded by the list:

1 *Identify customer life cycle groups.* Figure 9.20 illustrates this approach. As visitors use online services they can potentially pass through seven or more stages. Once companies have defined these groups and set up the customer relationship management infrastructure to categorize customers in this way, they can then deliver targeted messages, either by personalized on-site messaging or through e-mails that are triggered automatically due to different rules.

2 *Identify customer profile characteristics.* This is a traditional segmentation based on the type of customer. For B2C e-retailers it will include age, sex and geography. For B2B companies, it will include size of company and the industry sector or application they operate in.

3 *Identify behaviour in response and purchase.* As customers progress through the life cycle shown in Figure 9.20, though analysis of the database, they will be able to build up a detailed response and purchase history which considers the details of recency, frequency, monetary value and category of products purchased. This approach, which is known as 'RFM or FRAC analysis', is reviewed below. See Case study 9.1 for how Tesco target their online customers.

4 *Identify multi-channel behaviour (channel preference).* Regardless of the enthusiasm of the company for online channels, some customers will prefer using online channels and others will prefer traditional channels. This will, to an extent, be indicated by RFM and response analysis since customers with a preference for online channels will be more responsive and will make more purchases online. Customers that prefer online channels can be targeted mainly by online communications such as e-mail, while customers who prefer traditional channels can be targeted by traditional communications such as direct mail or phone. This is 'right-channelling', which was introduced in Chapter 5.

5 *Tone and style preference.* In a similar manner to channel preference, customers will respond differently to different types of message. Some may like a more rational appeal, in which case a detailed e-mail explaining the benefits of the offer may work best. Others will prefer an emotional appeal based on images and with warmer, less formal copy. Sophisticated companies will test for this in customers or infer it using profile characteristics and response behaviour and then develop different creative treatments accordingly. Companies that use polls can potentially use this to infer style preferences.

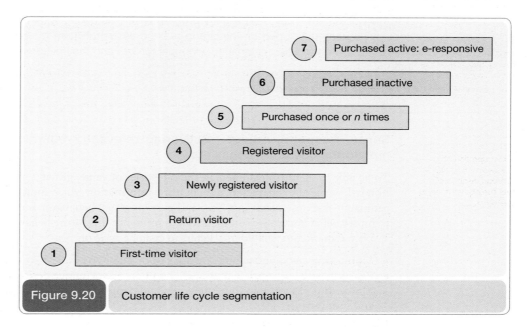

Figure 9.20   Customer life cycle segmentation

To summarize this section, read Mini case study 9.10 which illustrates the combination of these different forms of communication.

Mini Case Study 9.10   **Euroffice segment office supplies purchasers using 'touch marketing funnel' approach**

Euroffice (www.euroffice.co.uk) targets small and mid-sized companies. According to George Karibian, CEO, '*getting the message across effectively required segmentation*' to engage different people in different ways. The office sector is fiercely competitive, with relatively little loyalty since company purchasers will often simply buy on price. However, targeted incentives can be used to reward or encourage buyers' loyalty. Rather than manually developing campaigns for each segment, which is time-consuming, Euroffice mainly uses an automated event-based targeting approach based on the system identifying the stage at which a consumer is in the life cycle, i.e. how many products they have purchased and the types of product within their purchase history. Karibian calls this a '*touch marketing funnel approach*' i.e. the touch strategy is determined by customer segmentation and response. Three main groups of customers are identified in the life cycle and these are broken down further according to purchase category. Also layered on this segmentation is breakdown into buyer type – are they a small home-user, an operations manager at a mid-size company or a purchasing manager at a larger company? Each will respond to different promotions.

The first group, at the top of the funnel and the largest are 'Group 1: Trial customers' who have made one or two purchases. For the first group, Euroffice believes that creating impulse-buying through price promotions is most important. These will be based on categories purchased in the past. The second group, 'Group 2: The nursery', have made three to eight purchases. A particular issue, as with many e-retailers, is encouraging customers from the third to fourth purchase; there is a more significant drop-out at this point which the company uses marketing to control. Karibian says: '*When they get to group two, it's about creating frequency of purchase to ensure they don't forget you*'. Euroffice sends a printed catalogue to Group 2 separately from their merchandise as a reminder about the company. The final group, 'Group 3: Key accounts or Crown Jewels', have made nine or more orders. They also tend to have a higher basket value. These people are the Crown Jewels and will spend an average of £135 per order compared to an average of £55 for trial customers. They have a 90% probability of re-ordering within a six-month period. For this group, tools have been developed on the site to make it easier for them to shop. The intention is that these customers find these tools help them in making their orders and they become reliant on them, so achieving 'soft lock-in'.

Source: Adapted from the company website press releases and Revolution (2005).

Sense, Respond, Adjust – delivering relevant e-communications through monitoring customer behaviour

To be able to identify customers in the categories of value, growth, responsiveness or defection risk we need to characterize them using information which indicates their purchase and campaign-response *behaviour*. Past and current actual behaviour is often the best predictor of future behaviour so we can then seek to influence this future behaviour.

Digital marketing enables marketers to create a cycle of:

- Monitoring customer actions or behaviours and then ...
- Reacting with appropriate messages and offers to encourage desired behaviours
- Monitoring response to these messages and continuing with additional communications and monitoring.

Or, if you prefer, simply:

$$Sense \rightarrow Respond \rightarrow Adjust$$

The sensing is done through using technology to monitor visits to particular content on a website or clicking on particular links in an e-mail. Purchase history can also be monitored, but since purchase information is often stored in a legacy sales system it is important to integrate this with systems used for communicating with customers. The response can be done through messages on-site, or in e-mail, and then adjustment occurs through further sensing and responding.

This 'Sense and Respond' technique has traditionally been completed by catalogue retailers such as Argos or Littlewoods Index using a technique known as 'RFM analysis'. This technique tends to be little known outside retail circles, but e-CRM gives great potential to applying it in a range of techniques since we can use it not only to analyse purchase history, but also visit or log-in frequency to a site or online service and response rates to e-mail communications.

Recency, Frequency, Monetary value (RFM) analysis

RFM is sometimes known as 'FRAC', which stands for: Frequency, Recency, Amount (obviously equivalent to monetary value), Category (types of product purchased – not included within RFM). We will now give an overview of how RFM approaches can be applied, with special reference to online marketing. We will also look at the related concepts of latency and hurdle rates.

Recency

This is the recency of customer action, e.g. purchase, site visit, account access, e-mail response, e.g. 3 months ago. Novo (2004) stresses the importance of recency when he says:

Recency, or the number of days that have gone by since a customer completed an action (purchase, log-in, download, etc.) is the most powerful predictor of the customer repeating an action ... Recency is why you receive another catalogue from the company shortly after you make your first purchase from them.

Online applications of analysis of recency include: monitoring through time to identify vulnerable customers and scoring customers to preferentially target more responsive customers for cost savings.

Frequency

Frequency is the number of times an action is completed in the period of a customer action, e.g. purchase, visit, e-mail response, e.g. five purchases per year, five visits per month, five log-ins per week, five e-mail opens per month, five e-mail clicks per year. Online applications of this analysis include combining with recency for RF targeting.

Monetary value

The monetary value of purchase(s) can be measured in different ways, e.g. average order value of £50, total annual purchase value of £5,000. Generally, customers with higher monetary values tend to have a higher loyalty and potential future value since they have purchased more items historically. One example application would be to exclude these customers from special promotions if their RF scores suggested they were actively purchasing. Frequency is often a proxy for monetary value per year since the more products purchased, the higher the overall monetary value. It is possible then to simplify analysis by just using recency and frequency. Monetary value can also skew the analysis for high-value initial purchases.

Latency

Latency is related to frequency, being the average time between customer events in the customer life cycle. Examples include the average time between website visits, second and third purchase and e-mail clickthroughs. Online applications of latency include putting in place triggers that alert companies to customer behaviour outside the norm, for example increased interest or disinterest, then managing this behaviour using e-communications or traditional communications. For example, a B2B or B2C organization with a long interval between purchases would find that if the average latency decreased for a particular customer, then they may be investigating an additional purchase (their recency and frequency would likely increase also). E-mails, phone calls or direct mail could then be used to target this person with relevant offers according to what they were searching for.

Hurdle rate

According to Novo (2004), hurdle rate refers to the percentage of customers in a group (such as in a segment or on a list) who have completed an action. It is a useful concept, although the terminology doesn't really describe its application. Its value is that it can be used to compare the engagement of different groups or to set targets to increase engagement with online channels as the examples below show:

- 20% of customers have visited in the past 6 months
- 5% of customers have made three or more purchases in the year
- 60% of registrants have logged on to the system in the year
- 30% have clicked through on e-mail in the year.

Grouping customers into different RFM categories

In the examples above, each division for recency, frequency and monetary value is placed in an arbitrary position to place a roughly equal number of customers in each group. This approach is also useful since the marketer can set thresholds of value relevant to their understanding of their customers.

RFM analysis involves two techniques for grouping customers:

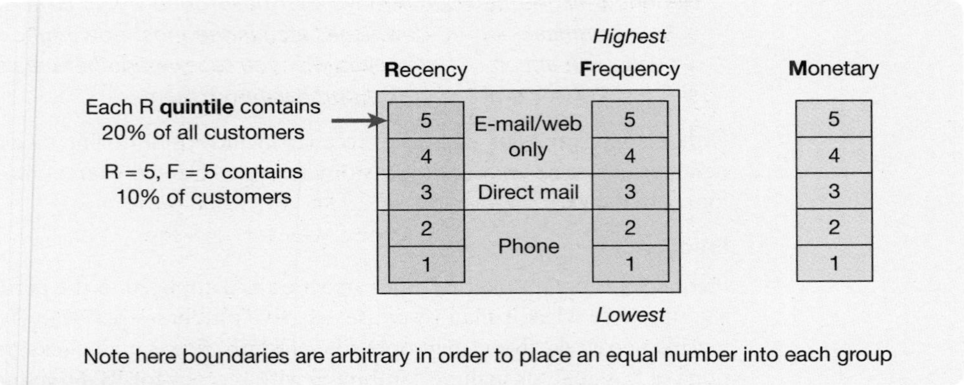

	Recency		**Highest** Frequency		Monetary	

Each R **quintile** contains 20% of all customers

R = 5, F = 5 contains 10% of customers

Recency: 5, 4, 3, 2, 1

E-mail/web only — 5, 4
Direct mail — 3
Phone — 2, 1

Frequency: 5, 4, 3, 2, 1

Monetary: 5, 4, 3, 2, 1

Lowest

Note here boundaries are arbitrary in order to place an equal number into each group

Figure 9.21   RFM analysis

1 *Statistical RFM analysis.* This involves placing an equal number of customers in each RFM category using quintiles of 20% (10 deciles can also be used for larger databases), as shown in Figure 9.21. The figure also shows one application of RFM with a view to using communications channels more effectively. Lower-cost e-communications can be used to communicate with customers who use online services more frequently since they prefer these channels and more expensive communications can be used for customers who seem to prefer traditional channels. This process is sometimes known as 'right-channelling' or 'right-touching'.

2 *Arbitrary divisions of customer database.* This approach is also useful since the marketer can set thresholds of value relevant to their understanding of their customers.

For example, RFM analysis can be applied for targeting using e-mail according to how a customer interacts with an e-commerce site. Values could be assigned to each customer as follows:

Recency:
    1 – Over 12 months
    2 – Within last 12 months
    3 – Within last 6 months
    4 – Within last 3 months
    5 – Within last 1 month

Frequency:
    1 – More than once every 6 months
    2 – Every 6 months
    3 – Every 3 months
    4 – Every 2 months
    5 – Monthly

Monetary value:
    1 – Less than £10
    2 – £10–£50
    3 – £50–£100
    4 – £100–£200
    5 – More than £200

Simplified versions of this analysis can be created to make it more manageable, for example a theatre group uses these nine categories for its direct marketing:

Oncers (attended theatre once)
- Recent oncers   attended <12 months
- Rusty oncers   attended >12, <36 months
- Very rusty oncers   attended 36+ months

Twicers:
- Recent twicer   attended <12 months
- Rusty twicer   attended >12, <36 months
- Very rusty twicer   attended in 36+ months

2+ subscribers:
- Current subscribers   booked 2+ events in current season
- Recent   booked 2+ last season
- Very rusty   booked 2+ more than a season ago

Product recommendations and propensity modelling

Propensity modelling

A name given to the approach of evaluating customer characteristics and behaviour and then making recommendations for future products.

Propensity modelling is one name given to the approach of evaluating customer characteristics and behaviour, in particular previous products or services purchased, and then making recommendations for the next suitable product. However, it is best known as 'recommending the "next best product" to existing customers'.

A related acquisition approach is to target potential customers with similar characteristics through renting direct mail or e-mail lists or advertising online in similar locations.

The following recommendations are based on those in van Duyne *et al.* (2002).

1 *Create automatic product relationships* (i.e. next best product). A low-tech approach to this is, for each product, to group together products previously purchased together. Then for each product, rank product by number of times purchased together to find relationships.
2 *Cordon off and minimize the 'real estate' devoted to related products.* An area of screen should be reserved for 'next-best product prompts' for up-selling and cross-selling. However, if these can be made part of the current product they may be more effective.
3 *Use familiar 'trigger words'.* This is familiar from using other sites such as Amazon. Such phrases include:

'Related products', 'Your recommendations', 'Similar', 'Customers who bought...'
'Top 3 related products'.

4 Editorialize about related products, i.e. within copy about a product.
5 Allow quick purchase of related products.
6 Sell related products during checkout. And also on post-transaction pages, i.e. after one item has been added to basket or purchased.

Note that techniques do not necessarily require an expensive recommendations engine except for very large sites.

Technology solutions for CRM

Database technology is at the heart of delivering CRM applications. Often the database is accessible through an intranet website accessed by employees, or an extranet accessed by customers or partners provides an interface with the entire customer relationship management system. Today, on-demand web services such as Siebel CRM On Demand (www.crmondemand.com) and Salesforce.com (www.salesforce.com) are becoming increasingly popular.

E-mail is used to manage many of the inbound, outbound and internal communications managed by the e-CRM system. Using e-mail for communications is a service provided by e-CRM systems such as Salesforce (www.salesforce.com) or Siebel (www.siebel.com), or smaller businesses can use an e-mail marketing ASP service such as EmailReaction (www.emailreaction).

A workflow system is often used for automating CRM processes. For example, a workflow system can remind sales representatives about customer contacts or can be used to manage service delivery such as the many stages of arranging a mortgage. The three main types of customer data held as tables in customer databases for CRM are typically:

1 *Personal and profile data.* These include contact details and characteristics for profiling customers such as age and sex (B2C) and business size, industry sector and individual's role in the buying decision (B2B).
2 *Transaction data.* A record of each purchase transaction including specific product purchased, quantities, category, location, date and time, and channel where purchased.
3 *Communications data.* A record of which customers have been targeted by campaigns, and their response to them (outbound communications). Also includes a record of inbound enquiries and sales representative visits and reports (B2B).

The behavioural data available through 2 and 3 are very important for targeting customers to more closely meet their needs.

Research completed by Stone *et al.* (2001) illustrates how customer data collected through CRM applications can be used for marketing. The types of data that are held, together with the frequency of their usage, are:

Basic customer information	75%
Campaign history	62.5%
Purchase patterns (sales histories)	50%
Market information	42.5%
Competitor information	42.5%
Forecasts	25%

The data within CRM systems that were reported to be used for marketing applications were as follows:

Targeted marketing	80%
Segmentation	65%
Keeping the right customers	47.5%
Trend analysis	45%
Increased loyalty	42.5%
Customized offers	32.5%
Increase share of customer	27.5%

The Hewson Consulting Group (www.hewson.co.uk) identifies the following benefits of CRM systems to customers:

- Improved response times to customer requests for information.
- Delivered product meets customer requirements.
- Reduced costs of buying and using a product or service.
- Immediate access to order status and more responsive technical support.

Customer self-service

Customers perform information requests and transactions through a web interface rather than contact with customer support staff.

It is apparent that while many of these benefits could be achieved by phoning customer support staff who then access a CRM system, it may increase customer convenience, and reduce costs to the company, if they can access this information through a web interface. This approach is referred to as '**customer self-service**'.

Despite the benefits of CRM described in this chapter, it must be stressed that failure rates are high. Research conducted independently in 2000 by analysts Gartner and the Butler Group suggested that around 60 to 70% of CRM projects fail (Mello, 2001). This is not necessarily indicative of weaknesses in the CRM concept, rather it indicates the difficulty of implementing a complex information system that requires substantial changes to organizations' processes and has major impacts on the staff. Such failure rates occur in many other information systems projects. In addition to the change management issues, discussed in Chapter 10, key technical issues for managers selecting e-CRM systems are:

1 Type of applications.
2 Integration with back-office systems.
3 The choice of single-vendor solutions or a more fragmented choice.
4 Data quality.

Types of CRM applications

Figure 9.22 is intended to convey the complexity of providing CRM solutions. The aim of CRM technology is to provide an interface between the customer and the employee that replaces or facilitates direct interaction. From both customer and employee perspectives, the ultimate aim of CRM systems is to enable contact regardless of the communications channel that the customer wants to use, whether this is traditional methods such as phone or fax or newer digital technologies. Thus the ideal CRM system will support multi-channel communication or the customer-preferred channel. Regardless of channel, the customer will have different needs depending on their stage in the buying process (see section on 'Differences in buyer behaviour in target markets'). In the figure, we identify three core needs for the customer – to find out more information about a product, to place an order and to

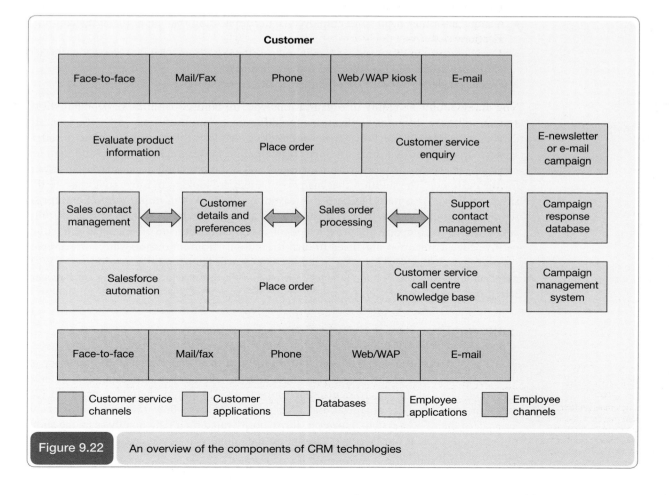

| **Figure 9.22** | An overview of the components of CRM technologies |

receive post-sales support. Applications must be provided to support each of these needs. Likewise, the employee will have applications requirements to support the customer and the sales and marketing objectives of the organization; in the figure these are sales force automation, to place an order received by phone, by fax or in person and to answer customers' questions via a support system and knowledge base. At the heart of the system is the database storage needed to support these applications. The IT infrastructure described in Chapter 3 such as servers, middleware and networking is not shown in the figure.

Integration with back-office systems

When introducing a CRM system to an organization, a company will have previously invested in systems for other key business functions such as sales order processing or customer support. These existing, legacy systems appear at both the applications and database levels in Figure 9.22. It will not be financially viable to discard these applications, but integration with them is vital to give visibility of the customer information to everyone in the organization and provide excellent customer support. Thus integration of legacy systems is a vital part of deciding on and implementing CRM systems.

The choice of single-vendor solutions or a more fragmented choice

Figure 9.22 highlights the key issues in deciding on and designing a system to support CRM. Think about the ideal situation; it would be:

- A single customer-facing and employee-facing application that supports all the communications channels.
- A single integrated database such that any employee has total visibility about a customer – they can access all visit, sales and support histories.
- From a single vendor for ease of implementation and support.

Now think about the reality in organizations you are familiar with: in all probability the system will have different applications for different communications channels, separate databases in different functional areas and multiple vendors. E-commerce systems are often separate from traditional systems. Such fragmentation makes implementation and maintenance of such systems a headache for managers and will often result in poor levels of service for the customer. The solution that many companies are looking to move to is close to the situation above. This need has been the reason for the growth in importance of enterprise resource planning systems from companies such as SAP and Oracle. However, the difficulty is that no single company can provide best-of-breed applications in all areas. To gain competitive edge, companies may need to turn to solutions from innovators who, for example, support new channels such as WAP, and provide knowledge management solutions or sales management solutions. Thus managers are faced with a precarious balancing act between selecting standardized products or integrating more leading systems for each CRM capability.

Data quality

All CRM systems are critically dependent on the currency, completeness and accuracy of their databases. One of the biggest challenges after installation is maintaining data quality. The importance of this was recognized in a survey of CRM and marketing managers in 120 medium–large UK B2C organizations (QAS, 2002). Of these, 86% rated accurate data as 'crucial' to their CRM system. However, the majority rated their data quality as falling short of their objectives. It can be suggested that for data quality to be managed successfully, the following are important:

1 *Establish a business owner.* This issue is too important to be managed solely by technologists and it requires management at customer contact points, which are part of the responsibility of marketing. All staff involved with managing customer data should be made clear about their responsibilities.

2 *Optimize quality on capture.* Validation checks can be built in at data entry to check that fields such as postcode are complete and accurate.

3 *Continuously improve quality.* Customer contact details constantly change. Changes of e-mail address are even more difficult to manage than changes of physical address. As a consequence, all contact points should be used to help maintain data quality.

4 *Work towards a single view of customer.* Many errors result because different data are stored in different databases so unifying the data in a single database is the aim for many organizations.

5 *Adopt a data quality policy.* Of the sample in the QAS (2002) survey 40% had no data quality policy, but this is essential to help achieve the four steps above.

As a conclusion to this chapter, read Case study 9.1 as an example of how Tesco has used CRM technology to improve their customers' 'share of wallet'. It is estimated that for every £8 spent on groceries in the UK £1 is spent at Tesco, which is now seeking its share of all retail category sales.

Case Study 9.1 — Tesco.com increases product range and uses triggered communications to support CRM

Context

Tesco, well known as Britain's leading food retail group with a presence in Europe and Asia, has also been a pioneer online.

Product ranges

The Tesco.com site acts as a portal to most of Tesco's products, including various non-food ranges, Tesco Personal Finance and the telecoms businesses, as well as services offered in partnership with specialist companies, such as clothing, dieting clubs, flights and holidays, music downloads, gas, electricity and DVD rentals.

Competitors

Tesco currently leads the UK's other grocery retailers in terms of market share. This pattern is repeated online. The compilation below is from Hitwise (2005) and the figures in brackets show market share for traditional offline retail formats from the Taylor Nelson Softres Super Panel (see http://superpanel.tns-global.com).

1 Tesco Superstore, 27.28% (29% of retail trade)
2 ASDA, 13.36%
3 ASDA@t Home, 10.13% (17.1%)
4 Sainsburys, 8.42%
5 Tesco Wine Warehouse, 8.19%
6 Sainsburys to You, 5.86% (15.9%)
7 Waitrose.com, 3.42% (3.6%)

8 Ocado, 3.32% (owned by Waitrose, 3.6%)
9 Lidl, 2.49% (1.8%)
10 ALDI-UK, 2.10% (2.3%).

Some companies are repeated since their main site and the online shopping site are reported on separately. Asda.com now seems to be performing in a consistent manner online to its offline presence. However, Sainsburys' online performance seems to be significantly lower compared to its offline performance. Some providers such as Ocado which originally just operated within the London area have a strong local performance.

Notably, some of Tesco.com's competitors are absent from the Hitwise listing since their strategy has been to focus on retail formats. These are Morrisons (12.5% retail share), Somerfield (5.5%) and Co-op (5.0%).

Promotion of service

As with other online retailers, Tesco.com relies on in-store advertising and marketing to the supermarket's Clubcard loyalty scheme's customer base to persuade customers to shop online. New Media Age (2005c) quotes Nigel Dodd, marketing director at Tesco.com, as saying: '*These are invaluable sources as we have such a strong customer base.*' However, for non-food goods the supermarket does advertise online using keyword targeted ads.

For existing customers, e-mail marketing and direct mail marketing to provide special offers and promotions to customers are important.

According to Humby and Hunt (2003), e-retailer Tesco.com uses what they describe as a 'commitment-based segmentation' or 'loyalty ladder' which is based on recency of purchase, frequency of purchase and value which is used to identify six life cycle categories which are then further divided to target communications:

- 'Logged-on'
- 'Cautionary'
- 'Developing'
- 'Established'
- 'Dedicated'
- 'Logged-off' (the aim here is to win back).

Tesco then uses automated event-triggered messaging to encourage continued purchase. For example, Tesco.com has a touch strategy which includes a sequence of follow-up communications triggered after different events in the customer life cycle. In the example given below, communications after event 1 are intended to achieve the objective of converting a website visitor to action; communications after event 2 are intended to move the customer from a first-time purchaser to a regular purchaser and for event 3 to reactivate lapsed purchasers.

- *Trigger event 1: Customer first registers on site (but does not buy)*
  Auto-response (AR) 1: 2 days after registration e-mail sent offering phone assistance and £5 discount off first purchase to encourage trial.
- *Trigger event 2: Customer first purchases online*
  AR1: Immediate order confirmation.
  AR2: Five days after purchase e-mail sent with link to online customer satisfaction survey asking about quality of service from driver and picker (e.g. item quality and substitutions).
  AR3: Two weeks after first purchase – direct mail offering tips on how to use service and £5 discount on next purchases intended to encourage re-use of online services.
  AR4: Generic monthly e-newsletter with online exclusive offers encouraging cross-selling.
  AR5: Bi-weekly alert with personalised offers for customer.
  AR6: After two months – £5 discount for next shop.
  AR7: Quarterly mailing of coupons encouraging repeat sales and cross-sales.
- *Trigger event 3: Customer does not purchase for an extended period*
  AR1: Dormancy detected – reactivation e-mail with survey of how the customer is finding the service (to identify any problems) and a £5 incentive.
  AR2: A further discount incentive is used in order to encourage continued usage to shop after the first shop after a break.

Tesco's online product strategy

New Media Age (2005c) ran a profile of Laura Wade-Gery, CEO of Tesco.com since January 2004, which provides an interesting insight into how the business has run. In her first year, total sales were increased 24% to £719 million. Laura is 40 years old, a keen athlete and has followed a varied career developing through an MA in History at Magdalen College, Oxford, and an MBA from Insead; Manager and partner in Kleinwort Benson; Manager and senior consultant, Gemini Consulting; Targeted marketing director (Tesco Clubcard), and Group strategy director, Tesco Stores.

The growth overseen by Wade-Gery has been achieved through a combination of initiatives. Product range development is one key area. In early 2005, Tesco.com fulfilled 150,000 grocery orders a week but now also offers more intangible offerings, such as e-diets and music downloads.

Wade-Gery has also focused on improving the customer experience online – the time it takes for a new customer to complete their first order has been decreased from over an hour to 35 minutes through usability work culminating in a major site revision.

To support the business as it diversifies into new areas, Wade-Gery's strategy was 'to make home delivery part of the DNA of Tesco', according to New Media Age (2005c). She continues: *'What we offer is delivery to your home of a Tesco service – it's an obvious extension of the home-delivered groceries concept.'* By May 2005, Tesco.com had 30,000 customers signed up for DVD rental, through partner Video Island (which runs the rival Screenselect service). Over the next year, Wade-Gery's target is to treble this total, while also extending home-delivery services to the likes of bulk wine and white goods.

Wade-Gery looks to achieve synergy between the range of services offered. For example, its partnership with eDiets can be promoted through the Tesco Clubcard loyalty scheme, with mailings to 10 million customers a year. In July 2004, Tesco.com Limited paid £2 million for the exclusive licence to eDiets.com in the UK and Ireland under the URLs www.eDietsUK.com and www.eDiets.ie. Through promoting the services through the URLs, Tesco can use the dieting business to grow use of the Tesco.com service and in-store sales.

To help keep focus on home retail delivery, Wade-Gery sold women's portal iVillage (www.ivillage.co.uk) back to its US owners for an undisclosed sum in March 2004. She explained to New Media Age:

> *It's a very different sort of product to the other services that we're embarking on. In my mind, we stand for providing services and products that you buy, which is slightly different to the world of providing information.*

The implication is that there was insufficient revenue from ad sales on iVillage and insufficient opportunities to promote Tesco.com sales. However, iVillage was a useful learning experience in that there are some parallels with iVillage, such as message boards and community advisers.

Wade-Gery is also director of Tesco Mobile, the joint 'pay-as-you-go' venture with O$_2$ which is mainly serviced online, although promoted in-store and via direct mail. Tesco also offers broadband and dial-up ISP services, but believes the market for Internet telephony (provided through Skype and Vonage, for example) is not sufficiently developed. Tesco.com have concentrated on more traditional services which have the demand, for example Tesco Telecom fixed-line services attracted over a million customers in their first year.

However, this is not to say that Tesco.com will not invest in relatively new services. In November 2004, Tesco introduced a music download service, and just six months later Wade-Gery estimates they have around 10% market share – one of the benefits of launching relatively early. Again, there is synergy, this time with hardware sales. New Media Age (2005c) reported that as MP3 players were unwrapped, sales went up – even on Christmas Day! She says:

The exciting thing about digital is where can you take it in the future. As the technology grows, we'll be able to turn Tesco.com into a digital download store of all sorts, rather than just music. Clearly, film [through video on demand] would be next.

But it has to be based firmly on analysis of customer demand. Wade-Gery says: 'The number one thing for us is whether the product is something that customers are saying they want; has it reached a point where mass-market customers are interested?' There also has to be scope for simplification. New Media Age (2005c) notes that Tesco is built on a core premise of convenience and value and Wade-Gery believes what it's already done with mobile tariffs, broadband packages and music downloads are good examples of the retailer's knack for streamlining propositions. She says: 'We've actually managed to get people joining broadband who have never even had a dial-up service.'

Source: Humby and Hunt (2003), New Media Age (2005c), Hitwise (2005), Wikipedia (2005).

Question

Based on the case study and your own research on competitors, summarize the strategic approaches which have helped Tesco.com achieve success online.

Summary

1 The objective of customer relationship management (CRM) is to increase customer loyalty in order to increase profitability. CRM is aimed at improving all aspects of the level of customer service.

2 CRM tactics can be based around the acquisition–retention–extension model of the ideal relationship between company and customer.

3 In an e-commerce context, acquisition refers to gaining new customers to a company and converting existing customers to online services. To enable an online relationship it is important to profile customers to find out their needs and expectations and obtain an opt-in e-mail agreement to continue the dialogue.

4 Marketing communications techniques to achieve acquisition, retention and extension include traditional online mass-media techniques and specialized online techniques such as search engine registration, link-building, e-mail marketing and banner advertising.

5 Techniques for customer retention include the use of extranets, online communities, online sales promotions and e-mail marketing.

6 Customer extension involves better understanding of the customer through feedback on new product development and encouraging customers to increase the depth of their relationship by offering complementary products for purchase or increasing purchase frequency.

7 Knowledge of online buyer behaviour, and in particular, the differing needs of the customer through the different stages of the buying decision can be used to improve CRM management.

8 Customer service quality is important in achieving loyalty and the SERVQUAL framework can be used to consider how to use the Internet to achieve this.

9 Technology solutions for CRM are aimed at providing interaction between employees and customers across multiple communications channels with all customer information stored in a single database to provide complete visibility of the customer by employees. Managers look to minimize the number of solutions partners they work with to achieve these goals.

10 Specific technology application requirements for CRM are salesforce automation (contact management) and call centre applications which integrate workflow to manage queries and a knowledge base from which queries can be reviewed.

Exercises

Self-assessment questions

1 What are the goals of acquisition and retention in an online context?

2 Outline the differences between permission marketing and interruption marketing including reference to the terms 'opt-in' and 'opt-out'.

3 Summarize the main types of online marketing communications for traffic building.

4 Explain why mixed-mode buying needs to be understood by those managing an e-commerce site.

5 Explain a range of techniques for attracting repeat visits to a website.

6 What is the difference between personalization and mass customization?

7 How can an e-commerce site be used to achieve extension in CRM?

8 What are the management issues in managing data and applications integration in CRM?

Essay and discussion questions

1 On what basis should marketing managers decide on the communications mix for an e-commerce site?

2 Evaluate the current communications mix for an online e-tailer and make recommendations for future communications to achieve customer acquisition and retention.

3 Show how an understanding of the online buying process can be used to revise marketing communications.

4 Explain, using examples, typical differences between a traffic-building campaign for a B2B and a B2C company.

5 Examine the relationship between customer satisfaction, loyalty and sales in relation to a pureplay e-commerce site.

6 Examine the benefits and disadvantages of personalization, community building and direct e-mail. For an organization of your choice recommend a suitable balance between these e-marketing tools.

7 Assess whether a multi-vendor or single (limited number) vendor strategy is best for the implementation of e-CRM systems.

8 Recommend a social CRM data and application architecture for a B2C company that provides integration with related legacy systems.

Examination questions

1 Explain the concept of mixed-mode buying with reference to a pureplay e-commerce bookseller.

2 You are the e-commerce manager for a B2C site. Write an explanation to be included in a report to the managing director of why a permission marketing approach is required.

3 What different types of searching behaviour are exhibited by online users and what are the implications for someone responsible for traffic building on a site?

4 With reference to customer acquisition and retention, explain two goals for each required by an e-commerce site manager.

5 Outline four different methods of building website traffic.

6 Explain three factors that will influence the balance of online and offline website promotion for an organization.

7 How can an e-commerce site be used to inform new product development?

8 What is a legacy system and what is its relevance to CRM?

References

Abraham, M. (2008) The off-line impact of online ads. *Harvard Business Review*, 86(4), 28.

Agrawal, V., Arjona, V. and Lemmens, R. (2001) E-performance: the path to rational exuberance. *McKinsey Quarterly*, no. 1, 31–43.

Altimeter (2010) Social CRM: The New Rules of Relationship Management. White Paper published April 2010, Editor Charlene Li. Published online at **http:www.altimetergroup. com/2010/03/altimeter-report-the-18-use-cases-of-social-crm-the-new-rules-of-relationship-management.html**.

Bart, Y., Shankar, V., Sultan, E. and Urban, G. (2005) Are the drivers and role of online trust the same for all web sites and consumers? A large-scale exploratory empirical study. *Journal of Marketing*, October, 133–52.

Berthon, B., Pitt, L. and Watson, R. (1996) Resurfing W3: research perspectives on marketing communication and buyer behaviour on the World Wide Web. *International Journal of Advertising*, 15, 287–301.

BrandNewWorld (2004) AOL Research originally published at **www.brandnewworld.co.uk**.

Cartellieri, C., Parsons, A., Rao, V. and Zeisser, M. (1997) The real impact of Internet advertising. *McKinsey Quarterly*, no. 3, 44–63.

Chaffey, D. and Edgar, M. (2000) Measuring online service quality. *Journal of Targeting, Analysis and Measurement for Marketing*, 8(4), 363–78.

Chaffey, D. and Smith, P. (2008) *EMarketing Excellence Planning and Optimising Your Digital Marketing*, 3rd edn. Butterworth-Heinemann, Oxford.

comScore (2008) *Why Google's surprising paid click data are less surprising*, by Magid Abraham, 28 February. Published at **www.comscore.com/blog/2008/02/whygoogle's surprisingpaidclickdataarelesssurprising.html**.

Cronin, J. and Taylor, S. (1992) Measuring service quality: a re-examination and extension. *Journal of Marketing*, 56, 55–63.

cScape (2008) Second Annual Online Customer Engagement Report (2008). Produced by E-consultancy in association with cScape. Published online at **www.cscape.com**.

Dee, A., Bassett, B. and Hoskins, J. (2007) Word-of-mouth research: principles and applications. *Journal of Advertising Research*, 47(4), 387–97.

Deighton, J. (1996) The future of interactive marketing. *Harvard Business Review*, November–December, 151–62.

Dennis, C., Merrilees, B., Jayawardhena, C. and Wright, L.T. (2009) E-consumer behaviour. *European Journal of Marketing*, 43(9/10), 1121–39.

Emailcenter (2008) Toptable. Utilising Maxemail ROAD to increase bookings by 60%. Case study published at: **www.emailcenteruk.com/case%20studies/toptable.php**, accessed 9 September.

Evans, M., Patterson, M. and O'Malley, L. (2000) Bridging the direct marketing-direct consumer gap: some solutions from qualitative research. *Proceedings of the Academy of Marketing Annual Conference*, Derby.

Feinberg, R., Trotter, M. and Anton, J. (2000) At any time – from anywhere – in any form. In D. Renner (ed.) *Defying the Limits, Reaching New Heights in Customer Relationship Management*. Report from Montgomery Research Inc, San Francisco, CA: **http://feinberg.crmproject.com**.

Forrester Research (1999) Strong content means a loyal audience. Forrester Research report. 27 January.

Guardian (2003) TV ads 'a waste of money', Claire Cozens. Tuesday 4 February.

Godin, S. (1999) *Permission Marketing*. Simon & Schuster, New York.

Graham, J. and Havlena, W. (2007) Finding the 'missing link': advertising's impact on word of mouth, web searches, and site visits. *Journal of Advertising Research*, 47(4), 427–35.

Hagel, J. and Armstrong, A. (1997) *Net Gain: Expanding Markets through Virtual Communities*. Harvard Business School Press, Cambridge, MA.

Haven, B. (2007) Marketing's New Key Metric: Engagement, 8 August, Forrester.

Heskett, J., Jones, T., Loveman, G., Sasser, W. and Schlesinger, E. (1994) Putting the service-profit chain to work. *Harvard Business Review*, March–April, 164–74.

Hitwise (2005) Press release: The top UK Grocery and Alcohol websites, week ending 1 October, ranked by market share of website visits, from Hitwise.co.uk. Press release available at **www.hitwise.co.uk**.

Hoffman, D.L. and Novak, T.P. (1996) Marketing in Hypermedia computer-mediated environments: conceptual foundations. *Journal of Marketing*, 60 (July), 50–68.

Humby, C. and Hunt, T. (2003) *Scoring Points. How Tesco is Winning Customer Loyalty*. Kogan Page, London.

iProspect (2006) iProspect Search Engine User Behavior Study (April 2006). Available at **www.iprospect.com**.

Jevons, C. and Gabbot, M. (2000) Trust, brand equity and brand reality in Internet business relationships: an interdisciplinary approach. *Journal of Marketing Management*, 16(6), 619–34.

Jun, M. and Cai, S. (2001) The key determinants of banking service quality: a content analysis. *International Journal of Bank Marketing*, 19(7), 276–91.

Justgiving (2007) Justgiving Widget version 2.0. Blog posting, 24 July. **http://justigiving. typepad. com/charities/2007/07/justgiving-widg.html**.

Keiningham, T., Cooil, B., Aksoy, L., Andreassen, T. and Weiner, J. (2007) The value of different customer satisfaction and loyalty metrics in predicting customer retention, recommendation and share-of-wallet. *Managing Service Quality*, 17(4), 172–81.

Kirby, J. (2003) Online viral marketing: next big thing or yesterday's fling? *New Media Knowledge*. Published online at **www.newmediaknowledge.co.uk**.

Kirby, K. and Samson, A. (2008) Customer advocacy metrics: the NPS theory in practice, *AdMap*, February, 17–19.

Kotler, P. (1997) *Marketing Management – Analysis, Planning, Implementation and Control*. Prentice-Hall, Englewood Cliffs, NJ.

Kumar, V., Peterson, J. and Leone, R. (2007) How valuable is word of mouth? *Harvard Business Review*, 85(10), 139–46.

Levine, R., Locke, C., Searls, D. and Weinberger, D. (2000) *The Cluetrain Manifesto.* Perseus Books, Cambridge, MA.

Lewis, H. and Lewis, R. (1997) Give your customers what they want. *Selling on the Net. Executive book summaries*, 19(3).

McGaffin, K. (2004) Linking matters: how to create an effective linking strategy to promote your website. Published at **www.linkingmatters.com.**

MAD (2007) How online display advertising influences search volumes. Published 4 June 2007. MAD Network (*Marketing Week*), Centaur Communications. **http:// technologyweekly.mad.co.uk/Main/InDepth/SearchEngineMarketing/Articles/ f66d813eeab74e93ad8f252ae9c7f02a/How-online-display-advertising-influences-search-volumes.html.**

Mello, A. (2001) Watch out for CRM's hidden costs. ZdNet online, 15 October. Available online at: **http://techupdate.zdnet.com/techupdate/stovies/main/0,14179,2818163, 00.html.**

Microsoft (2007) Word of the web guidelines for advertisers: Understanding trends and monetising social networks. Research report.

New Media Age (2005a) Product placement. By Sean Hargrave. *New Media Age*, 12 May, **www.nma.co.uk.**

New Media Age (2005b) Perfect match. By Greg Brooks. *New Media Age*, 29 September, **www.nma.co.uk.**

New Media Age (2005c) Delivering the goods. By Nic Howell. *New Media Age*, 5 May.

New Media Age (2006) Banking on Search. *New Media Age* 16 March.

New Media Age (2007) Impulse Buying. By Emma Rubach. *New Media Age*, 30 August, **www.nma.co.uk.**

Nielsen, J. (2000) Web research: believe the data. *Jakob Nielsen's Alertbox*, 11 July 1999: **www.useit.com/alertbox/990711 .html.**

Novo, J. (2004) Drilling Down: Turning customer data into profits with a spreadsheet. Available from **www.jimnovo.com.**

O'Malley, L. and Tynan, C. (2001) Reframing relationship marketing for consumer markets. *Interactive Marketing*, 2(3), 240–46.

Parasuraman, A., Zeithaml, V. and Berry, L. (1985) A conceptual model of service quality and its implications for future research. *Journal of Marketing*, 49, Fall, 41–50.

Parker, R (2000) *Relationship Marketing on the Web.* Adams Streetwise, Avon, MA.

Peppers, B. and Rogers, P. (1999) *One-to-One Field Book.* Currency/Doubleday, New York.

Peters, L. (1998) The new interactive media: one-to-one but to whom? *Marketing Intelligence and Planning*, 16(1), 22–30.

QAS (2002) Data Quality – the Reality Gap. Executive summary of a report commissioned by QAS. Available online at **www.qas.com/uk.**

Reichheld, F. (2006) *The Ultimate Question: Driving Good Profits and True Growth.* Harvard Business School Press, Boston.

Reichheld, F. and Schefter, P. (2000) E-loyalty, your secret weapon on the web. *Harvard Business Review*, July–August, 105–13.

Reinartz, W. and Kumar. V. (2002) The mismanagement of customer loyalty. *Harvard Business Review*, July, 4–12.

Revolution (2005) E-mail Marketing Report by Justin Pugsley. *Revolution.* September, 58–60.

Robinson, H., Wysocka, A. and Hand, C. (2007) Internet advertising effectiveness: The effect of design on click-through rates for banner ads. *International Journal of Advertising*, 26(4), 527–41.

Ryan, J. and Whiteman, N. (2000) Online Advertising Glossary: Sponsorships. ClickZ Media Selling Channel, 15 May.

Seybold, P. (1999) *Customers.com.* Century Business Books, Random House, London.

Sharma, A. and Sheth, J. (2004) Web-based marketing: the coming revolution in marketing thought and strategy. *Journal of Business Research*, 57(7), 696–702.

Sissors, J. and Baron, R. (2002) *Advertising Media Planning*, 6th edn. McGraw-Hill, Chicago.

Smith, P.R. and Chaffey, D. (2005) *EMarketing Excellence – at the Heart of EBusiness*, 2nd edn. Butterworth-Heinemann, Oxford.

Stone, M., Abbott, J. and Buttle, E (2001) Integrating customer data into CRM strategy. In B. Foss and M. Stone (eds) *Successful Customer Relationship Marketing*. Wiley, Chichester.

Transversal (2008) UK companies failt the multi-channel customer service test. Research report, March.

van Duyne, D., Landay, J. and Hong, J. (2002) *The Design of Sites: Patterns, Principles, and Processes for Crafting a Customer-centered Web Experience*. Addison-Wesley, Reading, MA.

Varianini, V. and Vaturi, D. (2000) Marketing lessons from e-failures. *McKinsey Quarterly*, no. 4, 86–97.

Watts, D. and Dodds, S. (2007) Influentials, networks, and public opinion formation. *Journal of Consumer Research*, 34(4), 441–58.

Webster, R and Wind, Y. (1972) *Organizational Buying Behavior*. Prentice-Hall, Englewood Cliffs, NJ.

Weinberg, T. (2010) *The New Community Rules: Marketing on The Social Web*. Wiley, Hoboken, NJ.

Wikipedia (2005) Tesco. *Wikipedia*, the free encyclopedia: **http://en.wikipedia.org/wiki/Tesco**.

Windham, L. (2001) *The Soul of the New Consumer: The Attitudes, Behaviors and Preferences of E-Customers*. Allworth Press, New York.

Zona Research (1999) The economic impacts of unacceptable website download speeds. White Paper, April (**www.zonaresearch.com**).

Further reading

Chaffey, D., Mayer, R., Johnston, K. and Ellis-Chadwick, F. (2009) *Internet Marketing: Strategy, Implementation and Practice*, 4th edn. Financial Times Prentice Hall, Harlow. Chapter 6 covers online relationship building and Chapters 8 and 9 interactive communications.

Chatterjee, P. (2010) Multiple-channel and cross-channel shopping behavior: Role of consumer shopping orientations. *Marketing Intelligence & Planning*, 28(1), 9–24. This paper explores buyer behaviour implications for multi-channel transactions.

Dennis, C., Merrilees, B., Jayawardhena, T. and Wright, L.T. (2009) E-consumer behaviour. *European Journal of Marketing*, 43(9/10) 1121–39. A good overview of consumer behaviour.

Jackson, S. (2009) *Cult of Analytics: Driving online marketing strategies using web analytics*. Elsevier, Oxford, UK.

Møller, K. and Halinen, A. (2000) Relationship marketing theory: its roots and direction. *Journal of Marketing Management*, 16, 29–54.

Sargeant, A. and West, D. (2001) *Direct and Interactive Marketing*. Oxford University Press, Oxford. An excellent coverage of traditional direct marketing, although the specific chapter on e-marketing is brief.

Winer, R. (2001) A framework for customer relationship management. *California Management Review*, 43(4). A good overview of CRM and e-CRM.

Web links

Direct Marketing Association (**www.dma.org.uk**) Best-practice guidelines and benchmarks of response rates.

DoubleClick (www.doubleclick.net) An e-mail broadcaster and advertising network worldwide, with offices in many countries. Its site provides research of ad and e-mail marketing response rates across its clients.

Internet-advertising-related links

Atlas (www.atlasdmt.com) Ad-serving and tracking provider with research about ad effectiveness.

ClickZ (www.clickz.com/experts/) An excellent collection of articles on online marketing communications. US-focused. Relevant sections for this chapter include: affiliate marketing, advertising technology, e-mail marketing, media buying.

EyeBlaster (www.eyeblaster.com) One of the main providers of rich media ad serving technologies. Its galleries have good examples.

eMarketer (www.emarketer.com) Includes reports on media spend based on compilations of other analysts.

iMediaConnection (www.imediaconnection.com) Media site reporting on best practice in online advertising.

Internet Advertising Bureau (www.iab.net) The widest range of studies about Internet advertising effectiveness. In UK: **www.iabuk.net**. Internet Advertising Bureau XMOS micro-site (**www.iab.net/xmos**).

Tangozebra (www.tangozebra.co.uk) UK-based provider of ad-serving technology which showcases many of the most recent ad campaigns by industry category.

Search-engine-related links

ClickZ (www.clickz.com/) An excellent collection of articles on online marketing communications. US-focused. Relevant sections for this chapter include: affiliate marketing, advertising technology, e-mail marketing, media buying.

Searchenginewatch (www.searchenginewatch.com) A complete resource on SEO and PPC marketing.

Webmasterworld (www.webmasterworld.com) A forum where search practitioners discuss best practice.

CRM and database marketing

CRM Today (www.crm2day.com) A portal with articles about the practical aspects of deploying CRM technology.

Database Marketing Institute (www.dbmarketing.com/articles) Good source of articles, some of which refer to e-CRM.

Direct Marketing Association UK (www.dma.org.uk) Source of up-to-date data protection advice and how-to guides about online direct marketing.

Jim Novo (www.jimnovo.com) A site by a US consultant that has a lot of detail on techniques to profile customers online.

Peppers and Rogers One-to-one marketing website (**www.1to1.com**) A site containing a lot of information on the techniques and tools of relationship marketing.

Permission marketing (www.permission.com) Site supporting book by Seth Godin of Yahoo! on permission marketing. No content, but four sample chapters.

REAN framework Definition of REAN framework at **http://en.wikipedia.org/wiki/ REAN** and discussion of the REAN framework is available at: **www.blackbeak. com/2008/01/29/measuring-online-engagement-re-visited-and-introducing-the-rean-model/**.

Part 3 Implementation

Management of e-business implementation is described in Part 3 of the book in which we examine practical management issues involved with creating and maintaining e-business solutions.

10

Change management p. 530

- The challenges of e-business transformation
- Different types of change in business
- Planning change
- Human resource requirements
- Revising organizational structures
- Approaches to managing change
- Risk management

Focus on . . .
- Knowledge management

11

Analysis and design p. 577

- Analysis for e-business
- Process modelling
- Data modelling
- Design for e-business

Focus on . . .
- User-centred site design
- Security design for e-business

12

E-business service implementation and optimization p. 649

- Alternatives for acquiring e-business systems
- Development of web-based content and services
- Testing
- Changeover
- Content management and maintenance

Focus on . . .
- Web analytics: measuring and improving performance of e-business services

10

Change management

Web support

The following additional case studies are available at
www.pearsoned.co.uk/chaffey

→ Orange evolves customer services to achieve 12,000 visitors to site each week
→ Staff acquisition and retention at Netdecisions
→ Managing global change at Guinnesss

The site also contains a range of study material designed to help improve your results.

Learning outcomes

After completing this chapter the reader should be able to:

- Identify the different types of change that need to be managed for e-commerce
- Develop an outline plan for implementing e-commerce change
- Describe alternative approaches to organizational structure resulting from organizational change

Management issues

The issues for managers raised in this chapter include:

- What are the success factors in managing change?
- Should we change organizational structure in response to e-business? If so, what are the options?
- How do we manage the human aspects of the implementation of organizational change?
- How do we share knowledge between staff in the light of high staff turnover and rapid changes in market conditions?

Links to other chapters

The main related chapters are:

- Chapters in *Part 2* on strategy development should be read before this chapter since they explain the reasons for change. *Chapter 5* describes structural change for e-business
- *Chapters 11* and *12* on strategy implementation that follow this chapter describe how the change management approach is implemented through analysis, design and implementation

Introduction

What we anticipate seldom occurs: what we least expect generally happens.

(Benjamin Disraeli)

Disraeli's quote, referring to changes that need to be responded to in government, could equally be applied to the responses that are necessary from an organization venturing into e-business. Perhaps the greatest challenge faced by both B2B and B2C companies as they adopt e-business practices is how to manage the change that is necessitated by e-business.

However, for managing e-business within a particular organization it is possible to anticipate many of the changes that will be required by learning lessons from the pioneers of e-business. Through applying best practice and adopting risk management, it is possible to be proactive and manage change successfully. However, achieving this is not straightforward, as suggested by Mini case study 10.1.

Approaches to managing changes to organizational processes and structures and their impact on organization staff and culture are known as **change management**. Approaches to managing change associated with e-business are the subject of this chapter.

The introduction of e-business often requires its users to learn how to use new internal information systems, but more significantly it will require new methods of working. The changes experienced by staff tend to be greatest for large-scale projects which are intended to achieve **business transformation**. For example, the introduction of an e-business system to support online sales or online procurement may introduce major changes for staff working in these areas. Both types of systems represent a potential threat to existing staff. Some staff may have been working face-to-face with customers or suppliers for many years and they are now asked to use technology which decreases the human element of contact. They

Change management
Managing process, structural, technical, staff and culture change within an organization.

Business transformation
Significant changes to organizational processes implemented to improve organizational performance.

Mini Case Study 10.1 — The reasons behind a failed e-project

McLaughlin (2010) has reviewed a case study of a project where, after significant financial investment (approximately US$300m), and three years of development, the project was deemed a failure. The initiative was designed to link the sales, marketing, fulfilment, manufacturing and distribution systems together in order to reduce supply chain stock levels, increase responsiveness to customer demands and increase profit margins by providing a direct link to customers (circumventing business partners for some product lines).

The project was managed centrally from the North American headquarters, with input sought from the other geographies (Europe/Middle East/Africa, Asia Pacific, and Latin America). The geographies had responsibility to respond to the central team on local aspects of the e-CRM project. The central team had responsibility for the overall scope of the project and the back office, or the e-CRM 'engine', whilst the geographies had responsibility to ensure the system, once deployed, considered local and cultural aspects of how the organization interacted with customers and business partners.

In this study, McLaughlin surveyed the level of employee awareness of the e-CRM system; employee buy-in; employee confidence in an e-CRM system; and employee awareness of barriers to successful implementation. Although most employees had heard of the e-CRM project, the depth of awareness was not consistent across the organization. From the surveyed population, 24% had heard of e-CRM but were unaware of what the project would deliver; 28% understood the deliverables and received regular communications on the project's progress. But 48% of the surveyed workforce, whilst understanding what e-CRM was about and what it was trying to achieve, did not receive any communications on a regular basis updating them on the project's progress. In effect, 72% of the workforce was not aware of how e-CRM was progressing, and how the objectives and deliverables were changing.

may consider this reduces the efficiency of the work, they may feel their jobs are less interesting or even that their jobs are under threat.

We start this chapter by reviewing some of the challenges of implementing and managing e-commerce. We then go on to consider different aspects of change management and the chapter is structured around the different aspects of change we need to plan for; these include:

- *Scheduling* – what are the suitable stages for introducing change?
- *Budgeting* – how do we cost e-business?
- *Resources needed* – what type of resources do we need, what are their responsibilities and where do we obtain them?
- *Organizational structures* – do we need to revise organizational structure?
- *Managing the human impact of change* – what is the best way to introduce large-scale e-business change to employees?
- *Technologies to support e-business change* – the roles of knowledge management, groupware and intranets are explored.

Finally, we summarize different aspects of change management through looking at risk management approaches to e-business-led change.

Real-world E-Business experiences   The E-consultancy interview

Confused.com integrates digital marketing with marketing

Overview and main concepts covered

Tom Beverley is Customer Marketing Director for Confused.com, the insurance aggregator which launched originally in 2002. He leads the customer insight, below the line marketing, customer service and content teams.

One of the challenges for Confused.com, as for many e-businesses, is how digital marketing approaches are integrated with traditional media. In this interview Tom explains how traditional and digital marketing can work together and how Confused.com is joining up its marketing efforts.

Confused.com does a lot of TV advertising, how do you measure the impact of these ads online?

Tom Beverley, Confused.com: Confused.com uses a variety of methods to understand the impact of TV advertising, a couple of which should be familiar to any offline TV advertiser:

- Econometric analysis: using thousands of variables to isolate the impact of TV spend and ROI based on visits, quotes and sales. This has some unique challenges in a market as young, competitive and volatile as price comparison.
- Customer attribution: we ask customers who came direct to site to indicate which media channel influenced their decision to visit. This method provides long-term trends.
- Regional hold-back control groups: provide some insight for TV copy changes but with multi-channel TV's rise this method is becoming less and less reliable.
- Brand search versus competition and market: using insights for search we can get a rough and ready indication of how our TV is performing.

None of these methods provides us with 'the answer' to the impact of TV advertising but together they give us a feel – a flare in the dark. We can't wait for IPTV.

How can traditional marketing and digital work well together? What has worked for you?

Tom Beverley, Confused.com: We are always looking for ways to make traditional and digital marketing work well together. We've seen particular success in combining PR, social media and digital together.

For example, our recent Confused Nation campaign combined traditionally commissioned PR research to find out what consumers were confused about, the Twitter and Googlemaps APIs to produce content mash ups on a campaign site and our PR network to push the story (and site) out to journalists and the wider public. This campaign has generated significant coverage both in national and regional press, and online, leading to some great equivalent advertising values.

Conversely, we've experienced times when traditional marketing and digital haven't worked well together. Our recent ATL executions led with the line 'you could save £150 in 5 minutes', a claim that tested well in traditional research groups. However, when using this claim in the competitive car insurance paid search arena, it significantly reduced the effectiveness of our adword copy. This particular message looked weak when directly alongside competitor claims that promised significantly higher savings.

Insurance is a very competitive area in terms of SEO and paid search – can you use offline advertising to reduce PPC spend and reduce the reliance on search to acquire customers?

Tom Beverley, Confused.com: Absolutely. Indeed, we have seen a steady decrease in the number of consumers searching for generic car insurance terms as price comparison sites have dominated ATL spend in the insurance sector.

Conversely, we've seen an increase in branded search for comparison sites which is heavily correlated to brand awareness and salience driven by TV spend. This has made getting the right strategy on brand defence increasingly important to our search marketing team.

Presumably you can use online data to feed into your offline marketing – can you give me some examples of this?

Tom Beverley, Confused.com: Presently, we use some online data to help target and understand our best consumers (demographics, attitudes, behaviour). We also develop our savings claims from online data which invariably end up in our advertising. However, this is an area we're looking at exploiting further in the future. Watch this space.

Insurance quotes can be a lengthy and potentially frustrating process for customers – how do you approach form design to maximize conversions?

Tom Beverley, Confused.com: Simplicity is the guiding principle for our form design. We need to go through the process as seamlessly as possible. We made big strides in 2009 to remove as many unnecessary questions as possible, as well as moving non-standard questions into overlays (e.g. additional drivers, claims or convictions).

This reduced the length of our forms for a significant proportion of our customers. In addition, we pre-populate fields where possible and provide contextual help throughout the form. However, it's a never-ending process and our product teams are continually working to identify problem areas and find innovative IA and UX solutions.

What have been the major points of friction in the process for customers? How have you solved these issues?

Tom Beverley, Confused.com: Log-in was and is our major area of friction for returning customers for various reasons. We've implemented a number of changes to improve the log-in process as well as improve the password retrieval process.

One of these is to allow returning customers to go through the quote process without logging in immediately but moving that to the end of the process. On password retrieval we've improved the copy on the log-in page to direct consumers to our customer support team as a last resort and increased the priority of these requests to ensure a timely response.

For new customers our main area of friction is on the sign-up pages. Surrendering the level of data required for an accurate car insurance quote does put some visitors off. For example, for historical reasons we capture mother's maiden name.

We know consumers don't like this and are working with our partners on alternatives. These issues have been identified through a combination of web analytics analysis, session replaying and speaking to customers.

Do you have any 'quick wins' in terms of website usability that you can share with us?

Tom Beverley, Confused.com: Don't overload pages with too many competing messages. Use traditional customer insight methods to understand your two or three most important messages for consumers, prioritize them and then implement a simple information architecture and design that highlights them.

For example, if you find that free is an important message then your call-to-action button could contain the word 'Free, sign up now' rather just 'Sign up now'.

I know it's boring but keeping it simple and clean is the best trick. Cut copy relentlessly. Confused.com is as guilty as any website for not following this rule.

Source: E-consultancy: http://econsultancy.com/uk/ blog/6624-q-a-confused-com-s-tom-beverley-on-multichannel-marketing.

The challenges of e-business transformation

Figure 10.1 shows key aspects or levers of change that need to be assessed in order to maximize the benefits of e-business. The main change levers required are:

1 Market and business model (described in Chapter 2).
2 Business process (described in Chapter 4).
3 Organizational structure, culture and staff responsibilities (described in this chapter).
4 Technology infrastructure changes (described in Chapters 3, 9 and 11).

These are all major changes that are required in order for an organization to be agile enough to respond to marketplace changes and deliver competitive customer service. To help achieve these different aspects of change, a series of success factors seem to be required. These include:

- management buy-in and ownership;
- effective project management;
- action to attract and keep the right staff to achieve change;
- employee ownership of change.

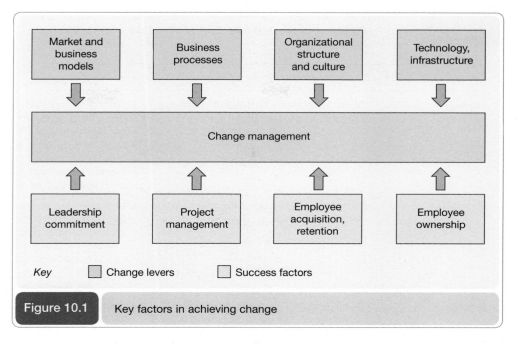

Figure 10.1 Key factors in achieving change

This chapter focuses on how to best achieve these success factors. Activity 10.1 introduces some of the changes required by e-business.

| Activity 10.1 | Managing change at a B2C company |

Purpose

To investigate the impacts of change on employees associated with e-business.

Activity

Speculate how the introduction of changes by a CEO or managing director such as those illustrated by the top four boxes of Figure 10.1 would affect different employees at a B2C company. Imagine you are each of the following people. What would your reaction be on a professional and a personal level? What would be your role in affecting change?

- Marketing manager
- Warehouse manager
- HR manager
- IS manager
- Employee in call centre.

Answers to activities can be found at www.pearsoned.co.uk/chaffey

The challenges of sell-side e-commerce implementation

A useful framework for reviewing an organization's capabilities to manage e-business-related change is shown in Table 10.1. This 7S framework was developed by McKinsey consultants in the 1970s and summarized by Waterman *et al.* (1980).

Table 10.1	The 7S strategic framework and its application to e-business management

Element of 7S mode	Relevance to e-business management	Key issues
Strategy	The contribution of e-business in influencing and supporting organizations' strategy	• Gaining appropriate budgets and demonstrating/delivering value and ROI from budgets. Annual planning approach • Techniques for using e-business to impact organization strategy • Techniques for aligning e-business strategy with organizational and marketing strategy
Structure	The modification of organizational structure to support e-businesss	• Integration of e-commerce team with other management, marketing (corporate communications, brand marketing, direct marketing) and IT staff • Use of cross-functional teams and steering groups • Insourcing *vs* outsourcing
Systems	The development of specific processes, procedures or information systems to support Internet marketing	• Campaign planning approach-integration • Managing/sharing customer information • Managing content quality • Unified reporting of digital marketing effectiveness • In-house *vs* external best-of-breed *vs* external integrated technology solutions
Staff	The breakdown of staff in terms of their background, age and sex and characteristics such as IT *vs* marketing, use of contractors/consultants	• Insourcing *vs* outsourcing • Achieving senior management buy-in/involvement with digital marketing • Staff recruitment and retention. Virtual working • Staff development and training
Style	Includes both the way in which key managers behave in achieving the organization's goals and the cultural style of the organization as a whole	• Relates to role of the e-commerce team in influencing strategy – is it dynamic and influential or conservative and looking for a voice?
Skills	Distinctive capabilities of key staff, but can be interpreted as specific skill-sets of team members	• Staff skills in specific areas: supplier selection, project management, content management, specific e-marketing approaches (search engine marketing, affiliate marketing, e-mail marketing, online advertising)
Superordinate	The guiding concepts of the e-commerce organization which are also part of shared values and culture. The internal and external perception of these goals may vary	• Improving the perception of the importance and effectiveness of the e-commerce team amongst senior managers and staff it works with (marketing generalists and IT)

Table 10.1 summarizes some of the main issues which need management, but what are the main challenges in implementing strategy? E-consultancy (2005) surveyed UK e-commerce managers to assess their views on the main challenges of managing e-commerce within an organization. In the context of the 7Ss, we can summarize the main challenges as follows:

• *Strategy* – Limited capabilities to integrate Internet strategy into core marketing and business strategy as discussed in Chapter 5 is indicated by frustration on gaining appropriate budgets.

- *Structure* – Structural and process issues are indicated by the challenges of gaining resource and buy-in from traditional marketing and IT functions.
- *Skills and staff* – These issues were indicated by difficulties in finding specialist staff or agencies.

E-consultancy research I completed in 2005 and updated in 2008 highlighted some of the main challenges of implementing e-commerce. My initial sample for interviews was e-commerce managers for transactional sites – for example, mobile phones (Orange, The Carphone Warehouse), travel (Tui and MyTravel), financial services (Lloyds TSB and Bradford and Bingley) and direct marketers such as BCA.

One of the aims of the research was to gain a picture of the organizational processes and activities that need to be managed as part of sell-side e-commerce and the organizational structures that had been created to manage this. Figure 10.2 gives an indication of the number of operational e-CRM processes that need to be managed across the three core e-CRM areas (acquisition, conversion, retention) which we reviewed in Chapter 9. It also shows the management activities needed to support these. Some large organizations in the study had between 10 and 50 specialist staff managing these activities. For smaller companies, there is also the challenge that only 1 or 2 people are responsible for these activities, so they will need to work smart and outsource many of the activities!

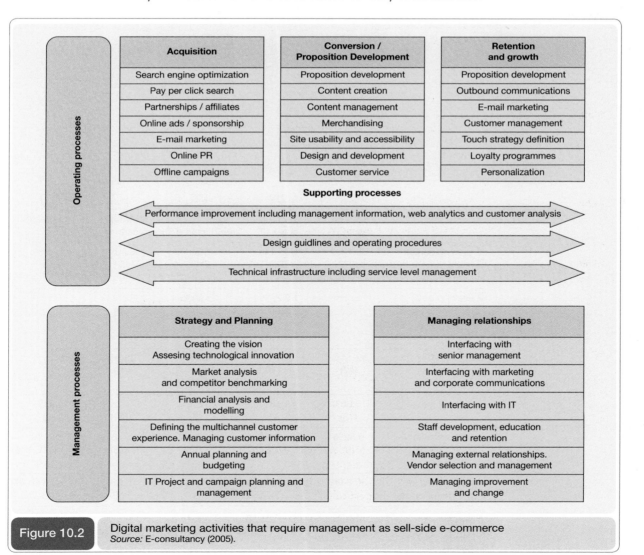

Figure 10.2 Digital marketing activities that require management as sell-side e-commerce
Source: E-consultancy (2005).

As part of the research, respondents were asked what their main challenges were and these highlighted the issues of gaining sufficient resources for Internet marketing. Their key challenges included:

- *Gaining buy-in and budget* consistent with audience media consumption and value generated.
- *Conflicts of ownership and tensions* between a digital marketing team, traditional marketing, IT, and finance and senior management.
- *Coordination with different channels* in conjunction with teams managing marketing programmes elsewhere in the business.
- *Managing and integrating customer information* about characteristics and behaviours collected online.
- *Achieving a unified reporting* and performance improvement process throughout the business including reporting, analysis and actioning suggested changes.
- *Structuring the specialist digital team* and integrating into the organization by changing responsibilities elsewhere in the organization.
- *Insourcing vs outsourcing online marketing tactics*, i.e. search, affiliate, e-mail marketing, PR.
- *Staff recruitment and retention* since there is a shortage of e-marketing skills given the rapid growth in demand for these skills, which gives great opportunities for everyone reading this book!

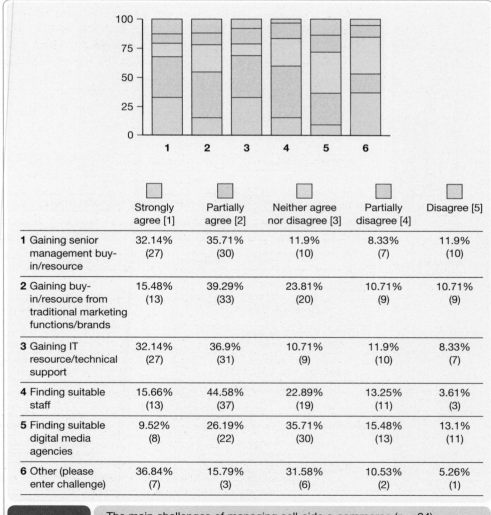

	Strongly agree [1]	Partially agree [2]	Neither agree nor disagree [3]	Partially disagree [4]	Disagree [5]
1 Gaining senior management buy-in/resource	32.14% (27)	35.71% (30)	11.9% (10)	8.33% (7)	11.9% (10)
2 Gaining buy-in/resource from traditional marketing functions/brands	15.48% (13)	39.29% (33)	23.81% (20)	10.71% (9)	10.71% (9)
3 Gaining IT resource/technical support	32.14% (27)	36.9% (31)	10.71% (9)	11.9% (10)	8.33% (7)
4 Finding suitable staff	15.66% (13)	44.58% (37)	22.89% (19)	13.25% (11)	3.61% (3)
5 Finding suitable digital media agencies	9.52% (8)	26.19% (22)	35.71% (30)	15.48% (13)	13.1% (11)
6 Other (please enter challenge)	36.84% (7)	15.79% (3)	31.58% (6)	10.53% (2)	5.26% (1)

Figure 10.3 The main challenges of managing sell-side e-commerce (*n* = 84)
Source: E-consultancy (2005).

After initial qualitative interviews, identifying the type of challenges faced by an e-commerce manager, a wider survey identified how common these problems were. The responses of e-commerce managers are summarized in Figure 10.3.

The research showed that managing the interfaces between the e-commerce team and other parts of the organization was a major challenge for many organizations. Managing these interfaces is a key role of the head of e-commerce and managers within their team. Every respondent articulated the need for education of colleagues in the organization about the benefits of e-commerce and the changes in processes required to achieve these benefits. This need for education was mentioned with respect to three main parts of the organization:

1 *Senior management.* Managing the senior management team interface was mainly an issue for less-evolved adopters of e-commerce. Leading adopters mentioned it had been a problem, but they now felt they had achieved understanding of the strategic importance of online channels and this was matched by financial resources and sufficient input into planning to achieve alignment between business objectives and e-commerce initiatives.

2 *Marketing, different brands, businesses or countries.* Similarly, this was more of an issue for the less-evolved organizations. Others had created processes for collaboration between e-commerce and marketing teams and defined responsibilities for e-commerce within these marketing teams.

3 *Information technology.* This interface was mentioned as a challenge by nearly every respondent – there was a belief that insufficient resource for applications development was limiting the potential of e-commerce to deliver value to customers and the organization. Where this was less of an issue, companies had either incorporated some development function within the e-commerce function, or had outsourced parts of development.

Different types of change in business

Incremental change
Relatively small adjustments required by an organization in response to its business environment.

Discontinuous change
Change involving a major transformation in an industry.

Organizational change
Includes both incremental and discontinuous change to organizations.

Anticipatory change
An organization initiates change without an immediate need to respond.

Reactive change
A direct response by an organization to a change in its environment.

Viewed at a large scale across an entire industry, change takes two forms. **Incremental change** involves relatively small adjustments required by changes in the business environment (Chapter 4). Organizations scan their environment and make adjustments according to the introduction of new products from competitors, new laws or long-term changes in customer behaviour. Organizations also make changes to improve the efficiency of their processes. More significant **discontinuous change** or transformational change involves a major change in the business environment which changes the basis for competition. The opportunities and threats presented by widespread availability of low-cost Internet connectivity is a discontinuous change.

Organizational change mirrors that at industry level. It can occur on a continuous or incremental basis or on a discontinuous basis. The introduction of e-business requires organizations to manage both types of change.

Nadler *et al.* (1995) developed a useful way of classifying types of organizational change. This uses the concepts of incremental and discontinuous change together with anticipatory or reactive change. **Anticipatory change** occurs when an organization makes proactive changes in order to improve its efficiency or to create an advantage within the competitive environment. **Reactive change** is a direct response to a change in the external environment. The four different forms of organizational change identified by Nadler *et al.* (1995) are:

1 *Tuning.* This is an incremental form of change when there is no immediate need for change. It can be categorized as 'doing things better'. New procedures or policies may be used to improve process efficiency, e.g. to reduce time to market or reduce costs of doing business. E-business involves 'tuning' as Internet technologies are applied to improve efficiency.

2 *Adaptation.* Also an incremental form of change, but in this case it is in response to an external threat or opportunity. It can also be categorized as 'doing things better'. For example, a competitor may introduce a new product or there may be a merger between two rivals. A response is required, but it does not involve a significant change in the basis for competition. Managing e-business-related change also requires adaptation.

3 *Re-orientation.* A significant change or transformation to the organization is identified as a priority in the short-to-medium term. There is not an immediate need for change, but a significant change is anticipation of change. When IBM was one of the first organizations to introduce the concept of 'e-business' in the mid-1990s, this was a re-orientation in the way it delivered its service (with an increased focus on consultancy services rather than hardware and software) which helped to spark a wider change in the way businesses worked. Successful adoption of e-business also requires re-orientation for many organizations.

4 *Re-creation.* In re-creation, the senior management team of an organization decides that a fundamental change to the way it operates is required to compete effectively. In the airline industry, established airlines have had to establish change programmes to respond to the low-cost carriers, for example by emphasizing service quality or introducing rival low-cost services. Both re-orientation and re-creation can be categorized as 'doing things differently'. E-business has also caused 're-creation' in the airline industry, with the low-cost airlines now gaining more than 90% of bookings online. However, as we saw in Chapter 4, such dramatic change has not been caused in every industry.

Business process management

So, some forms of e-business initiative related to internal processes such as the introduction of a human resources management system are simply about improving efficiency – they involve incremental change. The practice of improving the efficiency of business processes with the assistance of information systems is an important activity in many organizations as is shown by Case study 10.1. It can be seen that the label in vogue at the time of writing is '**business process management**' (BPM). This encompasses different scales of improving business process that are introduced above.

Business process management (BPM)
An approach supported by software tools intended to increase process efficiency by improving information flows between people as they perform business tasks.

The BPM concept has been defined by Gartner (2003) as follows:

> BPM is a methodology, as well a collection of tools that enables enterprises to specify step-by-step business processes. Proper analysis and design of BPM flows require a strong understanding of the atomic business steps that must be performed to complete a business process. As BPM executes a business process, these atomic steps will often correspond to well-known business activities, such as checking credit ratings, updating customer accounts and checking inventory status. In effect, the BPM process flow is often just a sequence of well-known services, executed in a coordinated fashion.
>
> Classic document workflow, which was BPM's predecessor, focused on humans performing the services. Fueled by the power of application integration, BPM focuses on human and automated agents doing the work to deliver the services.

Discontinuous process change

Although BPM often refers to continuous, incremental change, other forms of information-management-related applications such as e-ticketing for an airline will be associated with discontinuous change – with low-cost airlines such as easyJet and Ryanair now selling over 90% of their tickets online this has had a fairly significant impact on the airline industry. The introduction of e-business applications or enterprise resource planning systems described in Chapter 2 are also often related to transformational change programmes. Three degrees of business-process change are shown in Table 10.2.

Table 10.2	Alternative terms for using IS to enhance company performance		
Term	**Involves**	**Intention**	**Risk of failure**
Business process re-engineering	Fundamental redesign of all main company processes through organization-wide initiatives	Large gains in performance (>100%?)	Highest
Business process improvement	Targets key processes in sequence for redesign	(<50%)	Medium
Business process automation	Automating existing process. Often uses workflow software (Chapter 2)	(<20%)	Lowest

Business process re-engineering (BPR)

Identifying radical, new ways of carrying out business operations, often enabled by new IT capabilities.

In the early-to-mid 1990s organization-wide transformational change was advocated under the label of '**business process re-engineering**' (**BPR**). It was popularized through the pronouncements of Hammer and Champy (1993) and Davenport (1993). The essence of BPR is the assertion that business processes, organizational structures, team structures and employee responsibilities can be fundamentally altered to improve business performance. Hammer and Champy (1993) defined BPR as:

> *the fundamental rethinking and radical redesign of business processes to achieve dramatic improvements in critical, contemporary measures of performance, such as cost, quality, service, and speed.*

The key terms from this definition that encapsulate the BPR concept are:

- *Fundamental rethinking* – re-engineering usually refers to changing of significant business processes such as customer service, sales order processing or manufacturing.
- *Radical redesign* – re-engineering involves a complete rethinking about the way business processes operate.
- *Dramatic improvements* – the aim of BPR is to achieve improvements measured in tens or hundreds of percent. With automation of existing processes only single-figure improvements may be possible.
- *Critical contemporary measures of performance* – this point refers to the importance of measuring how well the processes operate in terms of the four important measures of cost, quality, service and speed.

Willcocks and Smith (1995) characterize the typical changes that arise in an organization with process innovation as:

- work units changing from functional departments to process teams;
- jobs changing from simple tasks to multi-dimensional work;
- people's roles changing from controlled to empowered;
- focus of performance changing from activities to results;
- values changing from protective to productive.

In *Re-engineering the Corporation* (1993) Hammer and Champy have a chapter giving examples of how IS can act as a catalyst for change (disruptive technologies). These technologies are familiar from applications of e-business such as those described in Chapter 2 and include tracking technology, decision support tools, telecommunications networks, teleconferencing and shared databases. Hammer and Champy label these as 'disruptive technologies' which can force companies to reconsider their processes and find new ways of operating. It is arguable though whether technology is commonly disruptive in the sense of achieving major changes such as those in the re-orientation and re-creation categories.

Many re-engineering projects were launched in the 1990s and failed due to their ambitious scale and the problems of managing large information systems projects. Furthermore, BPR was also often linked to downsizing in many organizations, leading to an outflow of staff and knowledge from businesses. As a result BPR as a concept has fallen out of favour and more caution in achieving change is advocated.

Business process improvement (BPI)

Optimizing existing processes, typically coupled with enhancements in information technology.

Less radical approaches to organizational transformation are referred to as '**business process improvement**' **(BPI)** or by Davenport (1993) as 'business process innovation'. Taking the example of a major e-business initiative for supply chain management, an organization would have to decide on the scope of change. For instance, do all supply chain activities need to be revised simultaneously or can certain activities such as procurement or outbound logistics be targeted initially? Modern thinking would suggest that the latter approach is preferable.

Business process automation (BPA)

Automating existing ways of working manually through information technology.

If a less radical approach is adopted, care should be taken not to fall into the trap of simply using technology to automate existing processes which are sub-optimal – in plain words, using information technology 'to do bad things faster'. This approach of using technology to support existing procedures and practices is known as '**business process automation**' **(BPA)**. Although benefits can be achieved through this approach, the improvements may not be sufficient to generate a return on investment.

A staged approach to the introduction of BPR has been suggested by Davenport (1993). This can also be applied to e-business change. He suggests the following stages that can be applied to e-business:

- *Identify the process for innovation* – these are the major business processes from the organization's value chain which add most to the value for the customer or achieve the largest efficiency benefits for the company. Examples include customer relationship management, logistics and procurement.
- *Identify the change levers* – these can encourage and help achieve change. The main change levers are innovative technology and, as we have seen, the organization's culture and structure.
- *Develop the process vision* – this involves communication of the reasons for changes and what can be achieved in order to help achieve buy-in throughout the organization.
- *Understand the existing processes* – current business processes are documented. This allows the performance of existing business processes to be benchmarked and so provides a means for measuring the extent to which a re-engineered process has improved business performance.
- *Design and prototype the new process* – the vision is translated into practical new processes which the organization is able to operate. Prototyping the new process operates on two levels. First, simulation and modelling tools can be used to check the logical operation of the process. Second, assuming that the simulation model shows no significant problems, the new process can be given a full operational trial. Needless to say, the implementation must be handled sensitively if it is to be accepted by all parties.

Cope and Waddell (2001) have assessed approaches managers in manufacturing industry in Australia use to introduce e-commerce services. They tested for different stages of transformation from fine-tuning through incremental adjustment, modular transformation and corporate transformation. They found that in this particular industry at the time of the survey, a relatively conservative approach of 'fine-tuning' was predominant.

Process management: making complex business simpler **FT**

This case gives a modern perspective on approaches to improve business processes using information systems. It summarizes the tools, benefits and some of the problems associated with business process management.

Steven S. Smith, chief technology officer for the US bank Wells Fargo Financial, introduced his company to business process management last year.

Note how he did it: 'I didn't go to our divisional chief executive and say: "We are going to invest in this tool." Instead, we brought the technology in and worked together with the business on a specific issue. It was the business manager who presented to the divisional CEO. He said: "Look at the benefits of this new technology."

'All the IT people were sitting in the room with big smiles on their faces. They didn't have to say a word. It was the business bragging about how wonderful it is,' he says.

When the business side of an organization has good things to say, unprompted, about a new technology, something unusual is happening and, for many companies, that something is business process management.

It is a methodology underpinned by a technology and it is a hot ticket.

Accenture, the world's largest consultancy, already has a global director for BPM, Jim Adamczyk.

He describes it as a mindset: 'It is something that has mostly been going on for a long time. What has changed is the convergence of the business need for process engineering with the evolution of technology that lets people build systems flexible enough to supply the need.'

In a new book, Kiran Garimella, Michael Lees and Bruce Williams (2008) of Software AG, the European consultancy, say that BPM represents a culmination of all the collective experience, thinking and professional development in business management over the past several decades.

'It's customer first. It's business focused, it empowers people in all corners of a business to be more successful. It brings people and systems together. BPM is where all the lofty goals and best strategies are coming home to roost,' they say.

It sounds too good to be true and it has already attracted the attention of a string of software houses and consultancies from the 'pure play' vendors such as Pegasystems, Savvion and Lombardi at one end to the big 'stack' vendors including Oracle and IBM at the other.

It is easy to see why Mr Adamczyk worries: 'I fear that this is being hyped as one of our endless series of silver bullets, but at core we are trying to align the domain of the business – what the business needs – with what IT can understand and build.'

What is driving the adoption of BPM? Ram Menon, head of worldwide marketing for the pure play vendor Tibco, argues that increasing business complexity is the chief cause: 'At the core, it's about agility, efficiency and productivity. Businesses are continually under pressure to get more work done with fewer resources.

'Regulatory compliance is another driver. Rules such as the European Union's Markets in Financial Instruments directive (MiFID) and Sarbanes-Oxley in the US have a significant process dimension. In healthcare, it's HIPAA. Almost every industry has its list of compliance requirements.

'Used appropriately, BPM helps companies streamline processes, reduce cycle times and get things done faster. This frees employees to focus on areas where they can add real value.'

BPM provides the tools to enable organizations to examine, analyse and improve their processes, with a process being anything that transforms resources and materials into products or services.

'This transformation is how a business works; it's the magic elixir of the enterprise,' say the Software AG authors. 'The more effective this transformation, the more successfully you create value.'

BPM software provides the technological underpinning that facilitates communication and mobility of data across applications. Only in the past few years has the software become mature enough to be used reliably for this purpose.

There are four main phases: process analysis, process design, process automation and business activity monitoring – which provides the feedback for further improvements.

Here are two examples of BPM in action.

University College London Hospitals comprises seven large hospitals in central London treating hundreds of thousands of in and out-patients each year through a bewilderingly large number of specialisms.

Government targets demand that no more than 18 weeks elapse between first referral and the start of treatment. James Thomas, UCLH IT director, knew the existing manual methods of tracking patients through what are known as 'care pathways' could not cope.

He wanted to introduce technology that would enable tracking by exception. Only if a staging post on the care pathway failed – a missing laboratory report, for example – would a warning flag be raised. The UCLH system sends an e-mail to the individual responsible to alert them to the deficiency.

In conjunction with Logica CMG, the consultancy, Mr Thomas used BPM software from Lombardi to map the care pathway for a single specialism, discovering in the process that the first and last thirds of the process are identical. The middle third depends on the particular specialism involved.

Business activity monitoring (BAM) software was used to monitor the progress of the patient along the pathway. 'It's your conscience. It's an incredibly good policeman,' Mr Thomas says.

The system will be live across one hospital in the group by the end of this month; the whole of UCLH by the end of the year. But it has not been easy: 'Getting people to acknowledge that they work to processes and to document those processes and then work through harmonising those processes is not easy. You're talking about administrative and clinical staff in different hospital buildings.

'Potentially, people might see this as a form of electronic Big Brother that sends them e-mails when they haven't done something. We have to turn that on its head and say the task facing us is too big for our current way of working – this is something to help us break up and digest the problem.'

At Wells Fargo Financial, Mr Smith was concerned that it was taking too long to complete certain business processes. The test bed for the BPM software that he brought in was the process that tracked the answers the bank gave customers who asked for a loan.

'The specific issue was: how to track the salesperson's response to the customer after a decision had been made on a loan. If the customer failed to take up the loan even if it was approved, what was the reason,' Mr Smith says.

Tracking the process manually would have required hiring another 20 staff across the US; four were already in place.

The BPM software took four months to install – Mr Smith blames the delay on his team's reluctance to use 'agile' development methods rather than the tried and tested 'waterfall' technique – but it resulted in automating the process for the whole of North America using three rather than the four existing staff.

The bank has implemented a number of BPM systems after that first deployment. In one, the process

for adding a new merchant to the bank's private label credit card product, which used to take weeks now takes only a day or so.

Mr Smith says that, with so many BPM vendors, it is important to choose the most appropriate by bringing them into the facility and asking them to interface with the existing systems.

These two examples demonstrate important principles of BPM deployment.

First, the need to start in a small way – a single process such as Mr Thomas's patient care pathway or Mr Smith's loan agreement is enough for proof of concept.

Second, the need to capture the hearts and the minds of the people who have to use the system. Mr Thomas insisted, for example, that hospital staff would not have to use new techniques or undergo extra training to make full use of the system.

Rod Favaron, chief executive of Lombardi, says companies will see three kinds of benefits from BPM, properly deployed: effficiency, effectiveness and agility.

'In the era of Service Oriented Architecture and on-demand market messages, agility is a well understood concept. In the world of process management, the ability to change quickly is essential,' he says.

'Customers on average change their key processes between four and seven times a year. New opportunities can arise. New partners or customers need you to support a different way of doing business.

'Government regulations can require companies to change their processes. BPM provides the platform they need to be able to change processes faster and in a more controlled fashion than any other option.'

Source: Alan Cane, Process Management: Making complex business a lot simpler? *The Financial Times*, 14 May 2008. Reprinted with permission.

Questions

1 How does the article suggest that business thinking and practice has evolved since the exhortations for business process re-engineering in the 1990s?

2 Summarize the benefits for BPM discussed in the article.

3 Discuss the need for a concept such as BPM when all new information systems and e-business initiatives are ultimately driven by process improvement.

Planning change

Our starting point for managing change is when the objectives, strategy and tactics for introducing e-business change have already been specified as outlined in Part 2. Here, we are concerned with how to implement the strategy to achieve the objectives through the activities performed by the project management team as part of project planning.

The imperative for project governance?

A recent survey of the challenges of managing e-business implementation projects is indicated by a survey of over 600 European and US businesses involved in management of web-related projects (E-consultancy, 2007). The research found that:

- Only 58% of respondents say that their projects always achieve their goals, and yet only 21% of them say they always achieve deadlines.
- Only 39% always achieve budget and a positive ROI.
- Over 8% of respondents never meet their project deadlines and nearly 6% never deliver their projects within budget.
- Nearly half of all respondents (45.5%) do *not* have a structured approach to managing their web projects.

Respondents to the E-consultancy (2007) research believed that web-related projects are different from other projects because of their need to be responsive to:

- changing customer requirements and market conditions;
- the breadth of people and skills involved;
- the raft of stakeholders;
- frequently tight or fixed deadlines;
- a degree of uncertainty;
- and the need for interaction with real customers.

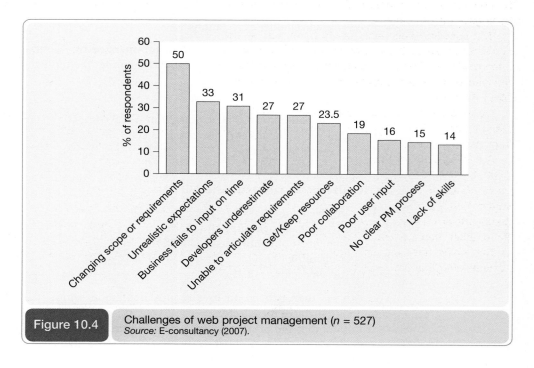

| Figure 10.4 | Challenges of web project management (*n* = 527)
Source: E-consultancy (2007). |

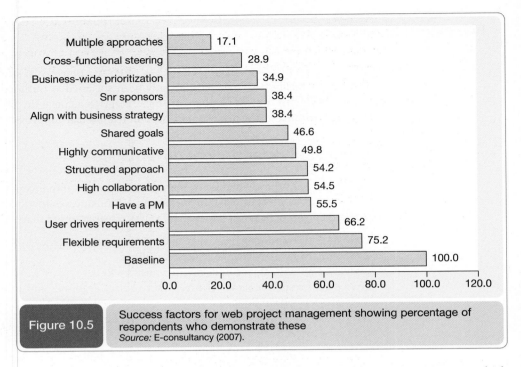

| Figure 10.5 | Success factors for web project management showing percentage of respondents who demonstrate these
Source: E-consultancy (2007). |

E-consultancy (2007) also looked at the main challenges of web project management which are shown in Figure 10.4 and corresponding approaches to overcome these challenges in Figure 10.5.

The research concluded that web projects require a project management approach that helps with:

- evolving requirements;
- putting focus on the end-customer;
- collaboration between different skill sets;
- managing stakeholder expectations.

Further research by the Standish Group summarized by Clarety (2009) reveals further insights into the reasons for project failure. It identifes the top five reasons for 'challenged projects' mentioned by respondents:

1 Lack of user input (12.8%)
2 Incomplete requirements and specifications (12.3%)
3 Changing requirements and specifications (11.8%)
4 Lack of executive support (7.5%)
5 Technology incompetence (7%)

The top five success factors were identified as:

1 User involvement (15.9%)
2 Executive management support (13.9%)
3 Clear statement of requirements (13.0%)
4 Proper planning (9.6%)
5 Realistic expectations (8.2%)

You can see that a focus on user requirements and senior management support are common to many of these factors.

It follows that the project governance of e-business projects, like that of other major information systems, is essential to success. The COBIT framework provides a good summary of the requirements from a governance approach. COBIT is the widely adopted IT governance model for Control Objectives for Information and related Technology. This definition is also helpful since it highlights some of the success factors in project management which we will cover later in this chapter. Project management is one of the key processes COBIT identifies for the effective governance of IT. It defines its control objective PO10 (COBIT, 2001) as follows.

Managing projects should satisfy the business requirement:

to set priorities and to deliver on time and within budget

and be enabled by

the organisation identifying and prioritising projects in line with the operational plan and the adoption and application of sound project management techniques for each project undertaken and takes into consideration:

- *business management sponsorship for projects*
- *program management*
- *project management capabilities*
- *user involvement*
- *task breakdown, milestone definition and phase approvals*
- *allocation of responsibilities*
- *rigorous tracking of milestones and deliverables*
- *cost and manpower budgets, balancing internal and external resources*
- *quality assurance plans and methods*
- *program and project risk assessments*
- *transition from development to operations.*

For effective project management the following elements need to be incorporated as part of the project management process as described, for example, by Chaffey and Wood (2005):

- *Estimation* – identifying the activities involved in the project, sometimes referred to as a 'work breakdown structure' (WBS). The sequence of activities for implementation of a typical e-business system is shown in Figure 10.6.
- *Resource allocation* – after the initial WBS, appropriate resources can be allocated to the tasks.
- *Schedule/plan* – after resource allocation, the amount of time for each task can be determined according to the availability and skills of the people assigned to the tasks. Effort time is the total amount of work that needs to occur to complete a task. Elapsed time indicates how long in time (such as calendar days) the task will take, and is dependent on the number of people working on the task, and their skills.
- *Monitoring and control* – monitoring involves ensuring the project is working to plan once it has started. Control is taking corrective action if the project deviates from the plan. In particular the project manager will want to hit **milestones** – events that need to happen on a particular date are defined for which performance against objectives can be measured.

Milestone
Key deadline to be achieved during project, usually with defined deliverable.

The project plan and schedule for an e-business system

The project plan for an e-business system will involve all of the stages shown in Figure 10.6. This diagram also shows how the final part of the book is structured.

Initiation
The start-up phase of the project.

- In Chapter 10 we review the activities needed during the **initiation** phase of a project that involves the creation of a change management programme including project planning, managing organizational change and risk management. In this chapter we do not consider feasibility analysis since assessment of the costs and benefits of the e-business system have already been considered as an aspect of strategy as described in Part 2.

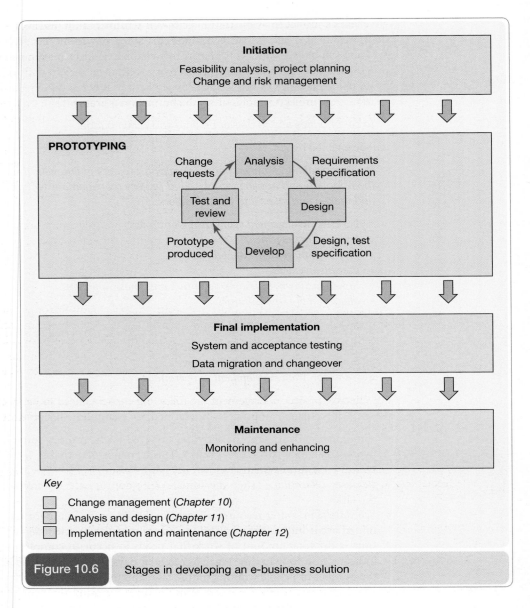

Figure 10.6   Stages in developing an e-business solution

- In Chapter 11 the analysis and design phases are described. In these the requirements of the organization and users of the system are defined and translated into a design from which the system can be built. Analysis and design occur in an iterative fashion through prototyping as described in the section that follows.
- In Chapter 12 the final stages of developing the e-business system are described. These include writing the program code, building the databases, migrating data, testing the system and managing the changeover to the live system. Chapter 12 also describes the maintenance of the system once it is live. This is monitoring the system and enhancing it as bugs and opportunities arise.

Systems development life cycle

The sequence in which a system is created from initiation, analysis, design, implementation, build and maintenance.

These stages in developing an e-business system use well-established approaches to building IS based on the **systems development life cycle**. But significant differences project managers need to take into account are:

- The timescales for delivery of the system are compressed compared to traditional applications – the system needs to be developed in 'Internet time'. Prototyping and making activities such as analysis, design and testing which occur in parallel are used to achieve tight deadlines, as is the use of off-the-shelf systems perhaps hosted with an ASP (Chapter 3).

- The e-commerce system may be hosted outside of an organization so we need to consider the constraints imposed by hosting the site externally with an ISP and integrating external components of the system with data stored and processes occurring inside the organization.
- The focus of the project is on content and services rather than on application; this means that delivery of information is the key. Linking different information sources and different applications through APIs is also becoming more important.
- Because the system is customer-facing and on the public Internet, speed and availability are crucial, as is securing the system from malicious hackers and spammers.
- Analysis and design are arguably more closely related in an e-commerce implementation since the usability of the site is critically dependent on the needs of the user and the proto-typing approach is used to achieve users' needs.
- Once launched the site or service should be more dynamic than a traditional applica-tion: an effective site will be updated continuously in response to customer demands and testing. The solution is never complete. Mini case study 10.2 illustrates how continuous improvements to a site can improve permformance.

With increasing use of the SaaS services introduced in Chapter 3, the analysis, design and build stages tend to be different from bespoke IS implementation. The analysis stage is equally important, but will focus on mapping the facilities of the off-the-shelf software with the existing business practices. A vital decision is the extent to which the company will change or adapt its practices and processes to match the software or web services or the extent it will be possible to tailor the system to match the processes. The degree of customi-zation to a company's needs also becomes a key issue.

The design phase will require much less input than for a bespoke system. It will focus on issues of how to tailor the user interface, database structures and security of the off-the-shelf

Mini Case Study 10.2	Conversion optimization leads to increased sales for one of Europe's leading hip hop stores

Def-Shop.com provides Europe's largest selection of hip hop clothing. Most of its sales are to the German market.

In April 2009, Def-Shop began working with Conversion Rate Experts to help increase its profits. Early tests on key pages have resulted in increases in conversion rate of 20%, 63% and 115%.
Here are some of the activities that Def-Shop and Conversion Rate Experts have collaborated on:

- E-commerce sites have several core functions, one of which is 'matchmaking' – the site needs to show products that the visitor is most likely to be interested in. There are several ways of doing this, such as product recommendation engines, search boxes, information architecture and navigation. An analysis of Def-Shop's site revealed great opportunities for improving the information architecture and navigation.
- It's important to give visitors reasons to buy from your site rather than from your competitors. Conversations with Def-Shop's staff revealed ten compelling advantages to ordering from Def-Shop; for example, Def-Shop has the largest selection, it has a great returns policy, and it has great credibility, in the form of associations with MTV and hip hop celebrities. This information was made prominent at key points in the conversion funnel.

Many successful businesses are based around a community of customers that share the same passions, values and interests. Def-Shop's CEO, Alexander Buchler, is passionate about hip hop culture, and feels that hip hop lacks a cultural focus in Europe. Conversion Rate Experts have encouraged Alex to invest in creating a whole community around Def-Shop, so the company becomes a focus for hip hop culture, rather than being just a web store.

package to the needs of the e-business solution. The build and implementation phases will still be involved and, as for any implementation, the project manager will have to schedule software and database configuration, data migration, testing and training.

An illustration of a typical project schedule for a sell-side e-commerce system is illustrated in Box 10.1.

Box 10.1	Example task breakdown and schedule

This case illustrates the different tasks that need to be performed as part of a sell-side e-commerce implementation for a company that does not have a website presence.

The schedule can be structured as followed:

1 *Pre-development tasks*. These include domain name registration and deciding on the company to host the website. It is important to register the domain name for the site as early as possible. It also includes preparing a brief of the aims and objectives of the site, then, if intending to outsource, presenting this to rival companies to bid.
2 *Content planning*. This is the detailed analysis and design of the site, including prototyping.
3 *Content development and testing*. Writing the HTML pages, producing the graphics and testing.
4 *Publishing the site*. This is a relatively short stage.
5 *Pre-launch promotion*. This is the marketing communications techniques described in Chapter 9.
6 *Ongoing promotion*. The schedule should also allow for periodic promotion which might involve discount promotions or competitions. These are often reused.

Figure 10.7 gives an indication of the relationship between these tasks, and how long they may take for a typical initial e-commerce site.

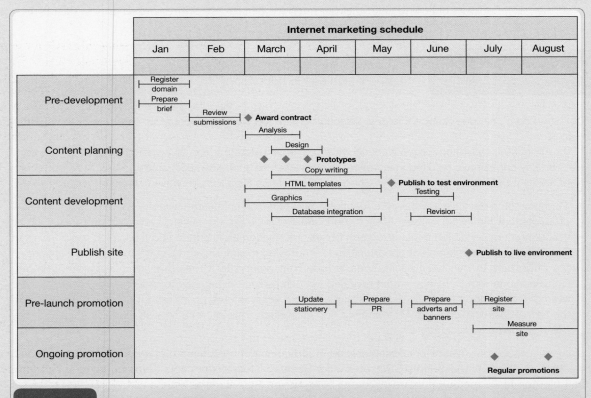

Figure 10.7	An example website development schedule

Prototyping

Prototyping is a common approach to the development of e-business systems; its essence is that it is:

- *Rapid* – Prototyping is part of a systems development approach known as '**RAD – Rapid Application Development**' since the time from inception to completion is reduced to months rather than years. More rapid development is achieved through reducing the length of time of the analysis, design and build stages by combining them in conjunction with the use of graphical software tools with which applications can be built quickly from pre-assembled components.
- *Simple* – Skeleton applications are produced as **prototypes** that do not contain all the functions of a system but are a framework which gives a good indication to users of the information available and the look and feel of an application. They can then comment on it and say, for example, 'this information is missing' or 'we like that feature, but it would be nice to do that also' or 'that feature isn't necessary, it's not what we meant'.
- *Iterative* – Prototypes are produced often at a frequency of one every few days or weeks so that the comments from the last review can be fed into the evolving system.
- *Incremental* – Each prototype incorporates the feedback from the previous review, so each version of the application has a limited number of new features.
- *User-centred* – Users are involved at all stages of development, in describing the existing system, reviewing the prototypes and testing the system.

The prototyping approach is now ubiquitous since it reduces the risk of major design, functional or informational errors during the construction of the application that may be costly and time-consuming to fix at a later stage in development.

Agile software development

Today, the concept of prototyping has been extended across the whole life cycle for developing website functionality or software applications where it is known as **agile software development**. The goal of agile development is to be able to create stable releases more frequently than traditional development methodologies, i.e. new functionality will be introduced through several releases each month rather than a more significant release every few weeks, months or even years. The approach is sometimes known as 'permanent beta'. Another difference from agile development is the emphasis on face-to-face communication to define requirements rather than detailed requirements specifications.

Scrum is a methodology that supports agile software development. Scrum involves the *scrum master* who is effectively a project manager, the *product owner* who represents the stakeholders such as the business owners and customers, and the *scrum team* which includes the developers.

Scrum is based on focused sprints of a 15–30-day period where the team creates an increment of potentially releasable software. Potential functionality for each sprint is agreed at a *sprint planning meeting* from the *product backlog*, a prioritized set of high-level requirements. The sprint planning meeting is itself iterative with the product owner stating their requirements from the product backlog and the technical team then determining how much of this they can commit to complete during the forthcoming sprint. The term 'scrum' refers to a daily project status meeting during the sprint. See www.softhouse.se/Uploades/Scrum_eng_webb.pdf for an overview of the process.

The principles of agile development are encapsulated in the *Agile Manifesto* (http://agile-manifesto.org/) which was agreed in 2001 by proponents of previous rapid development methodologies including the Dynamic Systems Development Methodology and Extreme Programming. The Agile Manifesto is useful in illustrating the principles of agile programming which it contrasts with traditional approaches. The text of the manifesto is:

We are uncovering better ways of developing software by doing it and helping others do it. Through this work we have come to value:

- *Individuals and interactions over processes and tools*
- *Working software over comprehensive documentation*
- *Customer collaboration over contract negotiation*
- *Responding to change over following a plan*

That is, while there is value in the items on the right, we value the items on the left more.

Human resource requirements

E-business implementation requires specialist skills that may not be present within an organization. The range of specialist skill requirements is indicated in Figure 10.8. The E-consultancy (2005) research showed that over half of respondents felt it was a challenge, although there were more pressing challenges.

E-business project managers have a choice of building a new skills set within their organization or outsourcing and partnering with other organizations.

Even more problematic than selecting the right type of staff is attracting and retaining e-business staff. If we want effective, experienced staff then these will demand high salaries. We will be competing for these staff with dot-com companies that are trying to recruit and also other established medium-to-large companies that are looking to build an e-business capability. Smaller companies will have an even trickier problem of needing to find all of these skills rolled into one person!

Staff retention

The difficulties in staff resourcing for e-business do not end with the recruitment of staff. As Crush (2000) says, 'Getting good staff is difficult, keeping them is a nightmare!' Since there is a highly competitive marketplace for e-business staff, many staff will want to move on to further their career. This will often be after the company has spent some time training them. The job characteristics model developed by Hackman and Oldham (1980) provides a useful framework for designing jobs that provide a good experience to improve staff motivation and so help retention. The five intrinsic characteristics of a job are:

1 Skill variety.
2 Task identity, how well the work is defined relative to other tasks and whether an employee sees a job through 'from start to finish'.
3 Task significance or the importance of the work.
4 Autonomy or freedom in completing work.
5 Feedback from employer.

To enhance these psychological characteristics Hackman and Oldham (1980) suggest the following approaches can be used:

- *Task combination* – by combining tasks employees see more of the whole task.
- *Natural workgroups* – this also helps in task combination through creating a team to complete tasks.
- *Establish customer relations* – this helps in task significance.
- *Vertical loading* – employees take responsibility for tasks completed by supervisors.
- *Opening feedback channel* – from internal or external customers, via managers where necessary.

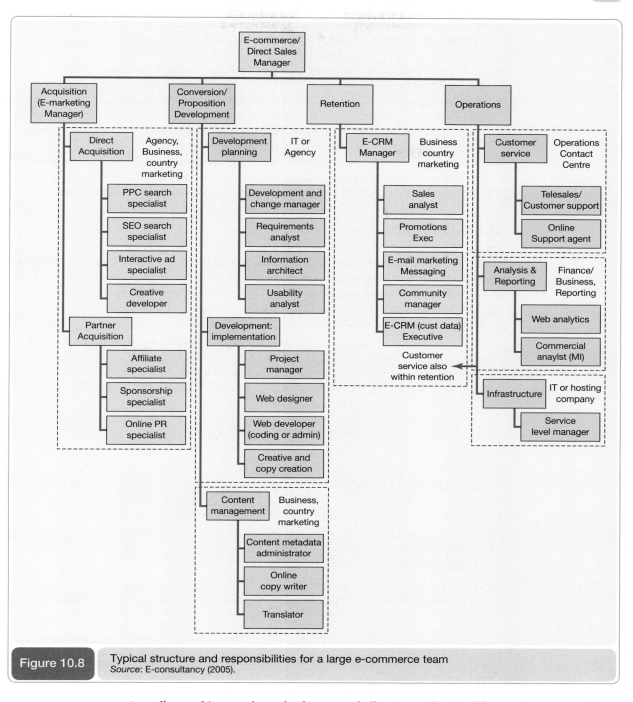

Figure 10.8 Typical structure and responsibilities for a large e-commerce team
Source: E-consultancy (2005).

As well as making employees' roles more challenging and enjoyable, another approach is to share the skills between staff, so that if key staff leave, then not all their knowledge will leave with them. Certain types of collaboration referred to in the E-consultancy (2005) report can assist with staff sharing knowledge and experience:

- *Co-locating staff* – including marketing staff in the digital team or e-commerce staff in the marketing team was mentioned.
- *Job-swapping* – a slightly different approach, which also involves co-location, was noted as effective.

- *Interim collaborative teams ('SWAT' teams)* – a temporary multi-disciplinary team (for example, teams from e-commerce, marketing and technology) is formed to drive a particular initiative or performance improvement, e.g. home page improvement, web analytics or supporting customer journeys between channels. This approach is reported to be used by Amazon.
- *Creation of a central 'Centre of Excellence for Digital Marketing'* can provide a clear resource which marketing staff can turn to for advice and best-practice documentation. Members of this team can also be involved in proactively 'spreading the word' through involvement in training or operational campaign planning.
- *Combined planning sessions* – rather than the digital team developing a plan and then discussing with the marketing team who may then incorporate it into their plan, a more collaborative approach is used with both working on creating an integrated plan.

Outsourcing

Given the difficulties of recruiting new business staff referred to above, many companies turn to third parties to assist with their e-business implementation. However, there is a bewildering series of supplier choices. Complete Activity 10.2 to help understand the choices required.

Activity 10.2	Options for outsourcing different e-business activities

Purpose

To highlight the outsourcing available for e-business implementation and to gain an appreciation of how to choose suppliers.

Activity

A B2C company is trying to decide which of its sell-side e-business activities it should outsource. Select a single supplier (single tick for each function) that you think can best deliver each of these services indicated in Table 10.3. Justify your decision.

Table 10.3	Options for outsourcing different e-business activities

E-marketing function	Traditional marketing agency	New media agency	ISP or traditional IT supplier	Management consultant
1 Strategy				
2 Design				
3 Content and service development				
4 Online promotion				
5 Offline promotion				
6 Infrastructure				

Answers to activities can be found at www.pearsoned.co.uk/chaffey

We are seeing a gradual blurring between the types of supplier shown in Table 10.3 as they recruit expertise so as to deliver a 'one-stop shop' service, though they still tend to be strongest in particular areas. Companies need to decide whether to partner with the best of breed in each, or to compromise and choose the one-stop shop that gives the best balance; this would arguably be the new media agency or perhaps a traditional marketing agency that has an established new media division. Which approach do you think is best?

The increased use of outsourcing marks a move towards the virtual organization. With the introduction of electronic networks such as the Internet it becomes easier to outsource aspects of the production and distribution of goods to third parties. Hallowell (2001) notes that the degree to which businesses can automate or outsource their human resources is strongly dependent on the type and level of service expected for a particular type of product. This can be significant in governing their **scalability** or capacity for growth without taking on additional staff. He says that customer services in e-commerce are:

Scalability
The ability of an organization or system to adapt to increasing demands being placed on it.

> described as 'virtual' (either pure information or automated) and 'physical' (requiring some degree of human intervention) ... because the nature and quantity of physical service necessary to deliver value to customers influences the quantity of human intervention required, it also influences a firm's ratio of variable to fixed costs, which alters its 'scalability'. The paradox comes in that while reduced scalability is viewed negatively by many venture capitalists and proponents of ecommerce, the cause of that reduction in scalability, human intervention, may help a firm to differentiate its offering to customers, thus providing a source of competitive advantage.

He concludes:

> For firms that are very high on the scalability continuum, the need for physical service does not present a 'scalability' problem. At these firms, information is the core service offering. Physical service is relatively insignificant, both from customers' perspectives (use of physical service is infrequent, if at all) and from the firm's perspective (it represents a very small portion of total costs). Thus, these firms do not rely on physical service (and the employees it requires) to differentiate their offering; their differentiation tends to come from the quality of their content and the ease with which users can access it.
>
> In contrast, firms that sell non-information services such as travel, or goods such as books, toys, or antiques require significantly more complex physical service operations. The degree to which they need more physical service is inversely proportional to the degree to which they are 'scalable'.

Case study 10.1 explores the extent to which outsourcing of core business processes is possible.

Revising organizational structures

When a company first embarks on e-business, perhaps through creating a new website to promote its products, it will normally operate within the existing company structure, perhaps using outsourcing to make good a resource deficit. However, as the contribution of the website to the company increases, the work involved increases and more staff from different parts of the organization are involved in e-business, it may be necessary to adopt new organizational structures and working practices. This issue has been considered by Parsons *et al.* (1996) from a sell-side e-commerce perspective. They recognize four stages in the growth of what they refer to as 'the digital marketing organization':

1 *Ad hoc activity.* At this stage there is no formal organization related to e-commerce and the skills are dispersed around the organization. It is likely that there is poor integration between online and offline marketing communications. The website may not reflect the offline brand, and the website services may not be featured in the offline marketing

communications. Maintenance of the website will be informal and errors may occur as information becomes out of date.

2 *Focusing the effort.* At this stage, efforts are made to introduce a controlling mechanism for Internet marketing. Parsons *et al.* (1996) suggest that this is often achieved through a senior executive setting up a steering group which may include interested parties from marketing and IT and legal experts. At this stage the efforts to control the site will be experimental with different approaches being tried to build, promote and manage the site.

3 *Formalization.* At this stage the authors suggest that Internet marketing will have reached a critical mass and there will be a defined group or separate business unit within the company which manages all digital marketing.

4 *Institutionalizing capability.* This stage also involves a formal grouping within the organization, with formal links created between digital marketing and a company's core activities. Baker (1998) argues that a separate e-commerce department may be needed as the company may need to be restructured in order to provide the necessary levels of customer service over the Internet.

Although this is presented as a stage model with evolution implying all companies will move from one stage to the next, many companies will find that true formalization with the creation of a separate e-commerce or e-business department is unnecessary. For small and medium companies with a marketing department numbering a few people and an IT department perhaps consisting of two people, it will not be practical to have a separate group. Even large companies may find it is sufficient to have a single person or small team responsible for e-commerce with their role being to coordinate the different activities within the company using a matrix management approach.

Activity 10.3 reviews different types of organizational structures for e-commerce. Table 10.4 reviews some of the advantages and disadvantages of each.

> **Debate 10.1**
>
> **Organizing for e-business**
> *'The introduction of a separate e-business function is necessary in large organizations to implement e-business effectively.'*

| **Activity 10.3** | **Which is the best organization structure for e-commerce?** |

Purpose

To review alternative organizational structures for e-commerce.

1 Match the four types of companies and situations to the structures (a) to (d) in Figure 10.9.

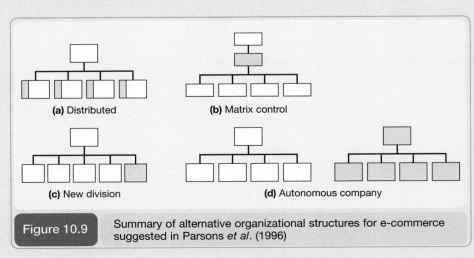

(a) Distributed   (b) Matrix control

(c) New division   (d) Autonomous company

| Figure 10.9 | Summary of alternative organizational structures for e-commerce suggested in Parsons *et al.* (1996) |

(a) A separate operating company. Examples: Prudential and Egg (www.egg.com).

(b) A separate business unit with independent budgets. Examples: RS Components Internet Trading Company (www.rswww.com).

(c) A separate committee or department manages and coordinates e-commerce. Example: Derbyshire Building Society (www.derbyshire.co.uk).

(d) No formal structure for e-commerce. Examples: many small businesses.

2 Under which circumstances would each structure be appropriate?

3 Summarize the advantages and disadvantages of each approach.

Answers to activities can be found at www.pearsoned.co.uk/chaffey

Table 10.4	Advantages and disadvantages of the organizational structures shown in Figure 10.9		
Organizational structure	**Circumstances**	**Advantages**	**Disadvantages**
(a) No formal structure for e-commerce	Initial response to e-commerce or poor leadership with no identification of need for change	Can achieve rapid response to e-commerce service responses (e-mail, phone). Priorities not decided logically. Insufficient resources	Poor-quality site in terms of content quality and customer
(b) A separate committee or department manages and coordinates e-commerce	Identification of problem and response in (a)	Coordination and budgeting and resource allocation possible	May be difficult to get different departments to deliver their input due to other commitments
(c) A separate business unit with independent budgets	Internet contribution (Chapter 6) is sizeable (>20%)	As for (b), but can set own targets and not be constrained by resources. Lower-risk option than (d)	Has to respond to corporate strategy. Conflict of interests between department and traditional business
(d) A separate operating company	Major revenue potential or flotation. Need to differentiate from parent	As for (c), but can set strategy independently. Can maximize market potential	High risk if market potential is overestimated due to start-up costs

Where the main e-commerce function is internal, the E-consultancy (2005) research suggested that it was typically located in one of four areas (see Figure 10.10) in approximate decreasing order of frequency:

(a) Main e-commerce function in separate team.

(b) Main e-commerce function part of operations or direct channel.

(c) Main e-commerce function part of marketing, corporate communications or other central marketing function.

(d) Main e-commerce function part of information technology (IT).

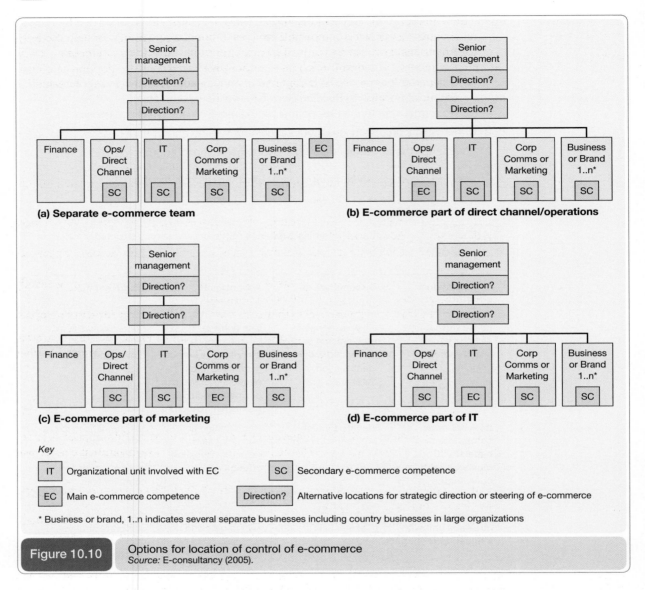

Key

IT — Organizational unit involved with EC

EC — Main e-commerce competence

SC — Secondary e-commerce competence

Direction? — Alternative locations for strategic direction or steering of e-commerce

* Business or brand, 1..n indicates several separate businesses including country businesses in large organizations

Figure 10.10	Options for location of control of e-commerce
	Source: E-consultancy (2005).

There is also often one or several secondary areas of e-commerce competence and resource. For example, IT may have a role in applications development and site build and each business, brand or country may have one or more e-commerce specialists responsible for managing e-commerce in their unit. Consider which of the options would be preferable for organizations you are familiar with. The research suggested that the approach which was appropriate depended strongly on the market(s) the company operated in and their existing channel structures.

Approaches to managing change

Hayes (2002) notes that for external forces of change, it may be difficult for those in an organization to manage and control the impact of change – the deterministic view. However, the voluntarist view is that managers can make an important difference to managing the impact of change. In the case of information systems management, it is clear that much can be done to reduce the impact of change. Change management is conducted by **change agents** who are the managers responsible for controlling change. In the context of e-business, the change agent could be the project manager responsible for implementing a new information system, an e-business manager responsible for increasing adoption of e-business by an organization, or specialist digital marketing or supply chain managers seeking to increase adoption of e-channels.

Senior management involvement

Cope and Waddell (2001) have assessed the role of leadership style in e-commerce implementations. They assessed the most common approaches to e-commerce implementation, distinguishing between these approaches:

- *Collaborative* – widespread participation of employees occurs to define the changes required and techniques to achieve them.
- *Consultative* – management takes the final decision, after calling on some employees for input.
- *Directive* – the management team takes the decisions, with the employees generally trusting them to do so and being generally informed.
- *Coercive* – the management team takes the decision with very limited recourse to employees.

Of these approaches, the consultative approach was, as might be expected, most common, but other statements used in the research suggested that there were elements of other approaches.

Models for achieving change

There are many process models for achieving change which can be usefully applied to managing e-business-related change. A classic model for achieving organizational change was suggested by Lewin and Schein. It involves three stages:

1 Unfreeze the present position by creating a climate of change by education, training and motivation of future participants.
2 Quickly move from the present position by developing and implementing the new system.
3 Refreeze by making the system an accepted part of the way the organization works.

Note that Lewin and Schein did not collaborate on developing this model of personal and organizational change. Kurt Lewin developed the model in unpublished work and this was then extended by Edgar Schein (1956) who undertook research into psychology based on Lewin's ideas. More recently, Lewin (1972) summarized some of his ideas. Later, Schein (1992) concluded that three variables are critical to the success of any organizational change:

1 The degree to which the leaders can break from previous ways of working.
2 The significance and comprehensiveness of the change.
3 The extent to which the head of the organization is actively involved in the change process.

To achieve the unfreeze stages different staff can be identified for different roles by the project manager:

- *System sponsors* are senior managers or board members who have bought into the e-business initiative, are committed to major change and want to achieve success. The sponsors will try to fire up staff with their enthusiasm and stress why introducing the system is important to the business and its workers.
- *System owners* are managers in the organization of key processes such as a procurement manager or marketing manager who will use the e-business system to achieve benefits in their area.

- *System users*. These are staff in the different areas of the business who are actively involved in making the process happen. They could be a buyer in procurement or a brand manager within the marketing department.

Special types of system users can be identified, and it is important for the change manager to try to influence these staff to help achieve commitment among other staff. The three main types of system users that should be influenced are as follows:

- *Stakeholders* should be identified for each of the process areas where change will be introduced. These will be staff who are respected by their co-workers and will again act as a source of enthusiasm for the system. The user representatives used in specification, testing and sign-off are key stakeholders.
- *The legitimizer* protects the norms and values of the system; they are experienced in their job and regarded as the experts by fellow workers; they may initially be resistant to change and therefore need to be involved early.
- *Opinion leaders* are people whom others watch to see whether they accept new ideas and changes. They usually have little formal power, but are regarded as good ideas people who are receptive to change and again need to be involved early in the project.

For e-business implementation these roles will need to be identified for each implementation project as well as the overall change.

A more detailed change model proposed by Jay and Smith (1996) identifies four phases:

1 *Initial orientation*. In the orientation phase, it is necessary that there be a clear understanding of the reasons for bringing about change. This should be identified as part of the e-business, e-marketing or SCM strategies. A change strategy must be developed that includes an indication of how results will be measured, the project milestones, and how objectives would be measured and the change project organized. A skilled change team should be established and committed change sponsors identified.

2 *Preparation*. The preparation phase will involve an analysis of the environment within which the change is to take place. This includes an identification of the critical success factors for change along with a threat analysis. A work-plan for the change process must also be developed that includes detailed tasks and timings. The change direction must be announced to those affected and there should be an emphasis on maximizing communication effectiveness. The final step in this phase is to provide direction, particularly through strong communication of the goals and how they will be achieved.

3 *Change implementation*. In the third phase, Jay and Smith suggest that the changes are implemented by piloting the change, introducing the new procedures, conducting training and finally rolling out the change. Choosing a pilot department or site may be difficult. However, the organizational aspects as they relate to reporting relationships, job definitions, training schedules, working procedures and reward systems must be still be defined and communicated.

4 *A supportive phase*. In the final phase, the change must be stabilized. This means that management must openly commit itself to the change and fine-tune or adjust procedures where necessary. Measuring acceptance and new behaviour and producing a formal report can be used to evaluate the effectiveness of the change. There must be prevention of a relapse, such as an attempt to revert to old systems and practices or even bypassing the new system altogether. Conducting regular review meetings along with continual training and procedure reviews can help this.

Hayes (2002) has summarized how change managers can facilitate progress through the overall change process and progress through the transitions an individual makes during change. He notes the following general implications of the transition model for change managers:

- The overall form of the transition curve will take different forms – individual stages may be longer or shorter and the degree of mood change at each stage can vary considerably.
- There will often be a time lag between the announcement of a change and a reaction to it. It is possible to mistake initial shock and denial for acceptance of the change.
- Different people and different parts of the organization will pass through the change cycle at different rates and in different ways.
- Change managers will typically be out of step with other staff since they are involved earlier and deeper.
- The cycle cannot be avoided, but there is much that change managers can do to facilitate people's progress through it.

Hayes (2002) gives specific advice about how change managers can facilitate change through different change transitions. This advice is summarized in Table 10.5 together with typical implications for e-business initiatives and applications.

Table 10.5	Facilitating organizational change through a transition model	
Transition phase	**Typical actions by change managers**	**Implications for e-business implementation**
1 **Shock/ awareness**	Create a climate of receptivity to change. Announcement sufficiently in advance in involving senior managers.	Pre-announcement and involvement are readily practicable for e-business. Announcement and ownership by a senior manager is important.
2 **Denial**	Diagnosis of the reason for denial is important. Gently support the staff through denial. Repeat message of reason for change and justify. Find ways to get staff involved in change early.	Involvement is typically a requirement of e-business projects, so this is usually practical for some staff; for others communication of the benefits and progress of the project and the implications for them should be considered.
3 **Depression**	Providing support and listening are required at this stage rather than ignoring complaints.	This stage can be accommodated through prototyping and recording feedback in the live system.
4 **Letting go**	Continued explanation of the benefits of the new system without denigrating the past approach. Setting targets associated with the new system.	Around this stage prototypes of the new system will be available which will help with the process of letting go since tangible evidence of the new system and, hopefully, its benefits will be available.
5 **Testing**	Testing is encouraged by encouraging experimentation without blame where problems occur.	Testing corresponds to the testing phase of the system or adoption of the new system dependent on involvement. Positive or negative feedback on the new system should be encouraged, discussed and acted upon where appropriate.
6 **Consolidation**	This is facilitated by reviewing performance and learning and recognizing, rewarding and communicating benefits.	Improvements achieved through the system should be assessed and communicated.
7 **Reflection and learning**	This is achieved through structured learning about the change through reviews and encouraging unstructured learning such as feedback about the system.	Post-implementation reviews should occur at this stage, since this acknowledges that no system can be perfect first time and future improvements are planned for. The use of a structured system to log problems with the system or process can also help.

Source: The middle column is based on a summary of the commentary in Hayes (2002).

Organizational culture

Bocij *et al.* (2005) suggest that social relationships in an organization that are part of its **culture** are important. They say '*the efficiency of any organization is dependent on the complex formal and informal relationships that exist within it*'. Formal relationships include the hierarchical work relationships within and between functional business areas. Informal relationships are created through people working and socializing with each other on a regular basis and will cut across functional boundaries. E-business-led change has the capacity to alter both types of relationships as it brings about change within and between functional business areas.

Boddy *et al.* (2001) summarize four different types of cultural orientation that may be identified in different companies:

1 *Survival (outward-looking, flexible)* – the external environment plays a significant role (an open system) in governing company strategy. The company is likely to be driven by customer demands and will be an innovator. It may have a relatively flat structure.
2 *Productivity (outward-looking, ordered)* – interfaces with the external environment are well structured and the company is typically sales-driven and is likely to have a hierarchical structure.
3 *Human relations (inward-looking, flexible)* – this is the organization as family, with interpersonal relations more important than reporting channels, a flatter structure and staff development, and empowerment is thought of as important by managers.
4 *Stability (inward-looking, ordered)* – the environment is essentially ignored, with managers concentrating on internal efficiency and again management is through a hierarchical structure.

Now complete Activity 10.4 to investigate how companies may need to realign their culture to succeed in e-business.

Activity 10.4	Changing the culture for e-business

Purpose

To identify appropriate cultural changes that may be necessary for e-business success.

Activity

Review the four general categories of organizational cultural orientation summarized by Boddy *et al.* (2001) and take each as characterizing four different companies and then suggest which is most appropriate for e-business. State whether you think they are most likely to occur in a small or a larger organization.

Answers to activities can be found at www.pearsoned.co.uk/chaffey

---

Focus on	Knowledge management

Knowledge management has an important role within e-business since business success is critically dependent on staff knowledge about all aspects of the micro-environment such as customers, suppliers, intermediaries, competitors and how to shape internal processes to best deliver customer service.

Knowledge management is only introduced here. A more detailed coverage of how knowledge management can support business processes is available in Chaffey and White (2011).

With the move towards globalization and responding more rapidly to changing market conditions knowledge transfer is a key to competitiveness. Knowledge management is also a change management response to the problems of staff retention referred to earlier. As Saunders (2000) puts it:

Every day, knowledge essential to your business walks out of your door, and much of it never comes back. Employees leave, customers come and go and their knowledge leaves with them. This information drain costs you time, money and customers.

What is knowledge?

Knowledge
Applying experience to problem solving.

Knowledge management (KM)
Techniques and tools disseminating knowledge within an organization.

The concept of **knowledge** is more difficult to state than that of data or information. However, knowledge can be regarded as the next level of sophistication or business value in the cycle from data through information to knowledge. **Knowledge management (KM)** seeks to share this experience within a company. Useful summaries have been produced by Mekhilef *et al.* (2004):

Knowledge is the combination of data and information, to which is added expert opinion, skills and experience, to result in a valuable asset which can be used to aid decision making. Knowledge may be explicit and/or tacit, individual and/or collective.

Knowledge Management is the management of activities and processes for leveraging knowledge to enhance competitiveness through better use and creation of individual and collective knowledge resources.

Theorists have identified two different types of knowledge, and different approaches can be used to disseminate each type of knowledge within an organization:

Explicit knowledge
Knowledge that can be readily expressed and recorded within information systems.

Tacit knowledge
Mainly intangible knowledge that is typically intuitive and not recorded since it is part of the human mind.

1 **Explicit** – details of processes and procedures. Explicit knowledge can be readily detailed in procedural manuals and databases.
2 **Tacit** – less tangible than explicit knowledge, this is experience on how to react to a situation when many different variables are involved. It is more difficult to encapsulate this knowledge, which often resides in the heads of employees. Techniques for sharing this knowledge include learning stories and histories. To acquire tacit knowledge may rely on sharing knowledge with partners outside the company or others in different sectors. So knowledge management should not be considered solely as confining corporate knowledge within the firewalls.

It follows that one goal of knowledge management is to turn tacit knowledge into explicit knowledge which can then be shared between employees and used to train new employees.

A framework for the different activities that comprise knowledge management is given in Figure 10.11. The main activities are:

1 *Identify knowledge.* This is an analysis of the availability of existing knowledge to support the activities forming existing processes and a gap analysis showing what is missing.
2 *Create new knowledge.* This reviews methods to create new knowledge. At the personal and team levels, recommended techniques are through training, process problem improvement sessions or brainstorming. At the departmental or organizational levels, knowledge creation can occur through benchmarking against other organizations and through establishing expert groups known as 'communities of practice' or use of consultants or other companies to acquire new knowledge.
3 *Store knowledge.* Mekhilef *et al.* point out that much knowledge is typically 'stored' in people's brains and so will often remain there as 'tacit knowledge'. Knowledge can also

be embedded or become part of the 'organizational memory' through revising processes that form team routines. Storing explicit knowledge requires a structured approach to selecting, updating, organizing or categorizing knowledge within information systems.

4 *Share knowledge.* This increases knowledge availability to ensure it is available in the right context – i.e. for the right person, at the right time to support their current activity. Mekhilef *et al.* (2004) identify the *stock* method of distribution where knowledge is made available through databases and the *flow* method where knowledge is transferred directly from person to person through collaboration, workshops or mentoring.

These authors also say that approaches to support knowledge sharing include: intranets or portals, databases, collaboration, communities of practice, job rotation, coaching, seminars and training. Technology can be used to assist this through making information available through an intranet which enables browsing and searching of document databases or more collaborative approaches such as 'wikis' (web-based discussions which can be authored by several people) or 'webinars' (staff learn through dialling into a presentation or discussion hosted by an expert member of staff).

5 *Use knowledge.* Since a lot of knowledge remains under-utilized, the authors suggest that the purpose of this stage is to ensure that all effort that is spent in the previous activities pays off! It also involves managing further additions to the knowledge base.

Sveiby (1997–2000) suggests that one of the best ways to understand knowledge management is by looking at how people use the term 'knowledge management'. This includes academic researchers, consultants and industry practitioners. The two different views of knowledge management are:

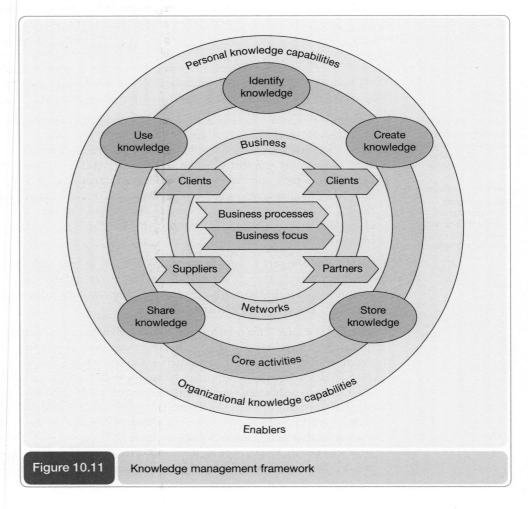

| Figure 10.11 | Knowledge management framework |

- IT-based view – knowledge can be stored as objects within databases and information systems.
- People-track view – knowledge management is about trying to improve individual skills and behaviour.

Objectives of knowledge management

The reasons for moving to knowledge management are highlighted by a 1999 IDC survey. The main reasons, which you can see are still relevant today, given by 355 US IS manager respondents were:

- Improving profit/growing revenue (67%)
- Retaining key talent/expertise (54%)
- Increasing customer retention and/or satisfaction (52%)
- Defending market share against new entrants (44%)
- Gaining faster time to market with products (39%)
- Penetrating new market segments (39%)
- Reducing costs (38%)
- Developing new products/services (35%).

It is evident that although employee retention is important, knowledge management is also seen as a competitive force for acquiring and retaining customers. Unlike other e-business initiatives cost reduction is relatively unimportant.

Sveiby (1997–2000) identifies an evolution of knowledge management objectives through time starting with a realization around 1992 that many companies were reinventing the wheel by not applying the experience acquired through previous, similar projects. Sharing knowledge was achieved by using best-practice databases using groupware such as Lotus Notes. Later the database was again the focus as companies aimed to learn more about their customers through data warehousing and data mining. The third phase is, he says, associated with sell-side e-commerce and learning more about *interactions* with customers through web-based forms and online purchases.

Implementing knowledge management

The reasons for difficulties in moving to knowledge management (KM) are also highlighted by the 1999 IDC survey. The main problems, which are again still relevant, are:

- Lack of understanding of KM and its benefits (55%)
- Lack of employee time for KM (45%)
- Lack of skill in KM techniques (40%)
- Lack of encouragement in the current culture for sharing (35%)
- Lack of incentives/rewards to share (30%)
- Lack of funding for KM initiatives (24%)
- Lack of appropriate technology (18%)
- Lack of commitment from senior management (15%).

Note that lack of the appropriate technology is not a major issue, although selecting the right technology may be important. All the main barriers relate to organizational structure and culture. A key finding seems to be the need to explain the benefits of knowledge management, develop skills and encourage sharing. Marianne Hedin, Research Manager at IDC Research (IDC, 2000) says:

> It is impossible to achieve full benefits from knowledge management unless individuals are willing and motivated to share their knowledge or unless organizations lose their structural rigidity to permit information and knowledge flow.

David Snowden (2002) puts it more simply when he says:

> *Knowledge can only be volunteered – it cannot be conscripted.*

Hansen *et al.* (1999) suggest that incentives are required to encourage staff to share knowledge such as making knowledge sharing a factor in the employees' performance review.

For example, with ShareNet, a knowledge management system at Siemens, contributors could collect points called ShareNet shares, similar to frequent-flier miles. Users earned shares for entering knowledge objects into the library (20 shares for a success story), answering urgent requests (3 shares), reusing knowledge and rating one another's contributions (single shares). In May 2000, the top 50 point collectors were invited to New York for a conference on ShareNet. Redemption of shares was possible against prizes such as textbooks, mobile phones, computers, PDAs and business trips. One share was roughly equivalent to one euro at the time. Different countries and business units were then compared on their success in generating shares.

Technologies for implementing knowledge management

The implementation of e-business applications can support knowledge management through providing different applications which support the five different steps of knowledge management described above. Binney (2001) identifies six different classes of KM applications as follows:

1 *Transactional.* Helpdesk and customer service applications.
2 *Analytical.* Data warehousing and data mining for CRM applications.
3 *Asset management.* Document and content management.
4 *Process support.* Total quality management, benchmarking, BPR, Six Sigma (see www.isixsigma.com for further information).
5 *Developmental.* Enhancing staff skills and competencies – training and e-learning.
6 *Innovation and creation.* Communities, collaboration and virtual teamwork.

Today, there is much discussion about the opportunities for using collaborative tools like Yammer, which we introduced in Chapter 2, to enable sharing of information using social networking approaches. Collectively this approach and these tools is often referred to as Enterprise 2.0. You can see that these are potentially applicable across all six stages identified above and can help share tacit and explicit knowledge.

Vendors now offer many tools for knowledge management, but it must be recognized that these tools only facilitate knowledge management. Major changes to knowledge creation and dissemination processes within the organization are likely to be required to reap the benefits of this technology.

Alternative tools for managing knowledge include:

- Knowledge capture tools such as software for devising knowledge maps and mind maps.
- Knowledge sharing techniques such as chat, discussion groups, wikis, webinars and video-conferencing.
- Knowledge delivery tools such as intranets and e-mail.
- Knowledge storage in document databases or knowledge bases such as Lotus Notes/Domino and content management systems.
- Electronic document management systems such as Interleaf publisher.
- Expert systems used to capture specific task-based knowledge and deliver a solution.

Chaffey and Wood (2005) point out that intranets tend to have three stages of sophistication for knowledge management:

1 *Static.* Basic web pages stored on a web server. Information publishing is centrally controlled. Employees browse and search for information but do not interact. Content is refreshed on an irregular basis. The danger is that the intranet will become a silo of underused and untrustworthy information.

2 *Interaction.* The intranet evolves into a dynamic environment developing around the knowledge needs of employees. Publishing becomes a regular process that many employees are involved with. Discussion boards and bulletin boards are introduced. Employees start to develop trust in using the intranet to share and locate knowledge.

3 *Collaborative electronic workspace.* The intranet becomes a 'self-service' environment where all employees are empowered to share knowledge via publishing mechanisms and collaborative tools. It becomes the starting point for discovering explicit knowledge. All core business processes will take place across the intranet platform.

Hansen *et al.* (1999) identify two contrasting approaches for implementing knowledge management which they illustrate through case studies of management consultancies. They refer to these approaches as 'codification' and 'personalization'. They found that companies tend to focus on one approach or the other, although there was some overlap. In the codification approach, used by Andersen Consulting and Ernst & Young, knowledge is codified or translated into a form suitable for searching using a database. Hansen *et al.* (1999) give the example of a partner in the Los Angeles office of Ernst & Young who needed assistance in creating a bid for implementation of an ERP system. Since he did not have this type of implementation he tapped into the knowledge management repository to find similar bids completed by others in the past. The reuse of a previous bid made it possible to complete the bid in half the normal period of four to six weeks, even though the partner was relatively inexperienced in this area. The codification process has been a major initiative at Ernst & Young with over 250 employed at the Center for Business Knowledge to codify information and help others perform searches. In addition, each of Ernst & Young's forty practice areas has a specialist in codifying documents.

The personalization approach has been adopted more by strategy consulting firms such as Bain and McKinsey. Hansen *et al.* (1999) relate the case of a partner in the London office of Bain who had to advise a UK financial institution how to solve a particular strategy dilemma. This assignment required knowledge of different market and geographical sectors and creative input. She used the Bain people-finder system to find those with suitable information, then convened a meeting in Europe that involved video-conferencing with others in Singapore and Sydney. Over the next four months, the partner then consulted regularly through e-mail, video-conferencing and phone. As well as using these technological approaches, McKinsey also fosters knowledge transfer by moving staff between offices, by having directories of experts and by having a culture that encourages prompt return of calls.

Knowledge management has been beset by difficulties of project implementation. Storey and Barnett (2000) review the literature on project failure and report on a detailed case study. They highlight six key learnings:

(1) Listen very carefully to the expectations, agendas and wants of all parties involved. They may appear to be using the same language and to be supporting the programme but in fact their understandings and plans may be very different.

(2) Check continuously that top management support is continuing and is delivered in a practical and public way.

(3) Be alert to the potential differences between a paradigm based on knowledge management which is IT-led and infused with priorities relating to knowledge capture, archiving and mining, and one based on the learning organization concept which may be inspired by wider developmental values. If handled with extraordinary skill the two approaches may reinforce each other but this cannot be expected simply to occur by happenchance.

(4) It will be found useful to ensure that the purpose and reason for expending effort on knowledge sharing is clarified and understood by everyone involved. It needs to be seen to be useful to those who are, in effect, being asked to behave differently.

(5) The interrelationship between knowledge sharing, knowledge creation and organizational change needs to be understood and realized. Reversal to traditional ways of operating based on low trust and direct command are too easily adopted when problems arise as our case demonstrates.

(6) *If knowledge is to be more widely shared and more readily created and used, there is an implication that innovation in process and probably service or products will also ensue and indeed should be sought. There are different types or levels of organizational KM systems: at the lower level, expert practitioners simply make available their operating routines and information. At the second level, the new knowledge is used as a basis for the shift in the kind of products and services offered to customers.*

Using Enterprise 2.0 approaches for knowledge management

Throughout this book we have discussed the power of Web 2.0 approaches for web communications. But these approaches are increasingly used within business. Web 2.0 concepts such as social networks, blogs and microblogging (Chapter 3) are increasingly being used for knowledge management within companies. Here are some approaches:

- Use of content management systems such as Microsoft Sharepoint Server for managing intranet content.
- Use of internal blogs where staff can blog about project work in different categories.
- Use of microblogging using tools like Yammer which has been dubbed Twitter for business (see *Mini case study 3.4* on Twitter).
- Use of social networks within a business. Services such as Ning (www.ning.com) can potentially be used for this. The open-source knowledge management solution CY.in (www.cyn.in) allows users to 'create organized workspaces to collaborate with colleagues'. Permissions can be selectively allocated to view, edit and review the space content. Applications include wikis, file repositories, discussion boards, event calendars, blogs and galleries.
- Use of wikis, as shown by Case study 10.2.

| Case Study 10.2 | Using Enterprise 2.0 tools to support knowledge management at Janssen-Cilag Australia |

About Janssen-Cilag

Janssen-Cilag is one of the fastest growing, research based pharmaceutical companies in Australia. It has more than 300 employees, split across Australia and New Zealand with around half based in the field. It is one of 250 Johnson & Johnson operating companies, which total about 121,000 employees across 57 countries.

Intranet history

In 2006, Janssen-Cilag completely replaced our simple, static HTML intranet with a Wiki solution. Over the 16 months since its launch, it has dramatically transformed internal communication and continues to increase in both visits and content contributions each month.

Intranet requirements gathering

The culture at Janssen-Cilag is highly consultative and relationship based. As such, gathering information and buy-in is often achieved through a series of conversations and discussions, building a coalition of support.

Requirements for a new Intranet site were collected through 27 interviews with a variety of people from all levels of the business. Three themes emerged:

1 We need a trusted source of information
2 Whatever we do has to be simple
3 Just do something!

Each conversation varied widely in focus, but the format usually went as follows:

1 The floodgates open with a dump of information the user considers vital for the Intranet, which lasts about 15 minutes. (What can I get?)
2 They highlight search as a key requirement.
3 I would steer the conversation to questions about how content should be maintained. (What can you give?)

Pitching a Wiki to the business

With many years of experience building one of the first large scale completely open collaboration platforms for the web and then building heavyweight enterprise CMS systems for large organisations, I've personally come full-circle to the idea that the best collaboration systems are incredibly simple and open. Wikis are a powerful starting point for any organisation, but latent demand at Janssen-Cilag created the perfect environment.

As such, I used the requirements gathering session as a chance to pitch the idea of a Wiki as the solution to our Intranet problem. After bringing the conversation to understand our content maintenance requirements, I'd talk through the Wiki approach and how it may work for Janssen-Cilag. My sales pitch went as follows:

1 We need a system where editing is immediate and very simple.
2 Getting people to contribute at all is hard, so we need to concentrate on letting people do things rather than worrying about what they shouldn't do.
3 The risk of letting anyone change anything is low, since we'll keep a complete history of changes so we can quickly undo mistakes and we can hold irresponsible individuals accountable for anything improper. (Reactive moderation rather than Proactive moderation.)

In general, the response was incredibly positive. Predictably, the main argument against this system was fear of improper changes to content, particularly for information subject to regulatory control. I would counter this argument in two ways:

1 There are two ways to control people's behaviour: social forces and technical forces. Currently, we successfully rely on social forces to control a wide range of things like who calls or emails the CEO with their latest crazy idea. Technical forces are powerful, but with each technical feature we increase training and raise the bar against collaboration. Surely, we can see if social forces will be enough for all but the most critical of content?
2 Anyone can choose to monitor any content that they are concerned about (e.g. automatic email alert with changes). So, they can quickly jump in and correct any mistakes.
3 For exceptional cases, we may choose to lock down critical content and define clear ownership and responsibility for its maintenance.

At the end, showing people around Wikipedia was an incredibly powerful way to seal the deal, particularly since they have often used it to find information in the past.

There were no major objections to trying a Wiki-style concept.

Implementing a Wiki for your Enterprise Intranet

We purchased, customised and launched a pilot Wiki Intranet within two weeks and with a budget of $11,000 AUD. This included all graphic design and single sign on integration.

After evaluating a wide range of alternatives including MediaWiki, Twiki and FlexWiki, we selected Confluence by Atlassian. Our main concerns were support for a hierarchy of pages, strong attachment capabilities,

news features, LDAP integration, high quality search and a decent rich text editor.

Our customisation focused almost completely on usability. People shouldn't know or care that they are using a Wiki. All that matters is that they can easily browse, search and contribute content. (In fact, after 16 months, only a small set of Janssen-Cilag staff would think of our Intranet as a Wiki. To them, it just seems natural that Intranet software would have evolved to something this simple to use.)

Here were our implementation decisions:

Integration with LDAP and use of NTLM for automatic single sign on is essential. We even hacked someone's starting point and open sourced our improved version.

Rich text editing must be available and as Word-like as possible.

Users like hierarchy and structure, the Wiki should not feel disorganised or completely free-form. (Confluence supports this with an exact page hierarchy capability.)

Sacrifice power and flexibility for simplicity. For example, our page design is fixed into a title, alphabetical list of subpages, page content, alphabetical list of attachments. While it would be nice to be able to change this at times, or order the attachments, or change the look and feel, it's far more important that everyone can contribute and clearly understands how things work.

Remove as many unnecessary features as possible. For example, labels are a great idea, but we already have hierarchy and most users don't really know what labels are.

Launch & user training

We started the new site as a pilot, launching as the source of information for a relocation of our head office. (Nothing drives traffic like the seating plan for a new office!) Information around the relocation was fast moving and changing daily for the two weeks between announcement of the move and our actual relocation.

Building on that success, we obtained executive approval to replace the existing Intranet. Over the next two weeks we worked with key content owners (most particularly HR) to show them how to create pages and migrate appropriate information. We made the decision to not automatically migrate any content, mostly because it was so old and trust in the existing intranet information was so low.

Our launch was timed with an informal head office monthly meeting, where around 100 people stand and listen to an update from senior management. We switched the site to live during the meeting, and had 5 minutes to present:

1 1 min: Highlight the desire for a trusted source of information that was simple to use.
2 3 mins: Full training that showed how easy it was to view, search, edit & maintain.
3 1 min: Point out that responsibility for building that trusted source is now in your hands!

That launch presentation remains the only formal training we've ever provided on how to use the system.

Continuing training has been provided through short one-on-one demonstrations (we only show, we never do) and a detailed help section (I'm happy to show you now, but for future reference here is the help page).

Adoption, statistics & business impact

The adoption of JCintra has been remarkable. After only 3 months, 111 people had contributed more than 5,000 changes. After 12 months, we had 18,000 contributions from 184 people within the business.

Most significantly, our contributions per month has continued to grow since launch. People are engaging and collaborating more with time, they are not losing steam as you might expect.

To drive adoption, we've primarily focused on owning the flow of new information. Early on, we established a policy that all announcements must be on JCintra. When necessary, they may be sent via email in addition to posting as news on the Intranet. Today, announcements ranging from major restructures to new babies for employees flow through the news page without clogging up email inboxes.

Owning the flow of news has established JCintra as a trusted source for the latest information. This translates into an expectation that the stocks of information (e.g. policies) will be available and up to date. Own the flow and the stock will come.

Business information that was previously scattered in email (e.g. Business Planning presentations) is now collected into a permanent, secure online space. We have a growing reference and history of information to build on and make available to newcomers. Knowledge management, previously a big concern, has moved off the agenda for the time being.

Content ownership model

For many Intranet owners, the model for content ownership is a key point of focus. With JCintra, our philosophy (successfully so far) has been:

1 If someone isn't willing to maintain a piece of content, it can't be that important to the business.

2 We happily show people how to do things with the site, but we don't do it for them.
3 Occasionally we highlight sections of the site on the home page, which is a great way to drive the defacto owners to clean it up a little.
4 We encourage people to have high expectations for content on the Intranet. If something is missing, please report it to the appropriate area of the business, or better still, add it for them.
5 The answer to verbal queries for many departments has become, 'it's on JCintra'. This reminds people to search first and ask later.
6 In the end, the quality of content in an area is a reflection on the defacto department owner, not the Intranet itself.

As a result, we've seen some departments embrace the Intranet in a big way, while others don't update content as much as we'd like. As expected, service areas of the business have been strong adopters, which means the main areas of Intranet content have been well maintained.

We've not yet adopted a formal content review process, but believe this will become more important in the next year of the site's life.

Keeping momentum & next steps

The primary barrier to continued success of JCintra remains the same as our initial barrier: encouraging a culture of collaboration and transparency. Some areas of JCintra have been highly successful in this regard, while other sections have never gained clear ownership or momentum.

JCintra works best when it is established as the source of truth for information and becomes the place where the work is done on a day-to-day basis. While the Intranet is a place that has to hold a published copy, it will remain as 'extra work' and struggle in the competition for people's time.

Source: (Janssen Cilag): e-gineer.com blog by Nathan Wallace, Associate Director – Information Technology (i.e. CIO) for Janssen-Cilag Australia, a pharmaceutical subsidiary of Johnson & Johnson. www.e-gineer.com/v2/blog/2007/08/our-intranet-wiki-case-study-of-wiki.htm.

Questions

1 What does this case study suggest are the main challenges for different stages of introducing a wiki or other Enterprise 2.0 approaches in a large organization?
2 Which solutions does Nathan Wallace describe as being effective for overcoming these problems?

Risk management

Risk management
Evaluating potential risks, developing strategies to reduce risks and learning about future risks.

To conclude this chapter and act as a bridge to the final two chapters we review the problems associated with change when managing an e-business implementation. **Risk management** is intended to identify potential risks in a range of situations and then take actions to minimize the risks. We all unconsciously perform risk management throughout our lives. For example, when crossing a country road we will assess the likely risk of a car approaching, or a silent cyclist approaching around the blind bend, and perhaps increase our pace accordingly. Activity 10.5 is intended to illustrate these risks. Risk management involves these stages:

1 Identify risks, including their probabilities and impacts.
2 Identify possible solutions to these risks.
3 Implement the solutions, targeting the highest-impact, most-likely risks.
4 Monitor the risks to learn for future risk assessment.

Activity 10.5	E-business risk management

Purpose

To highlight risks that are part of an e-business implementation and suggest solutions. This activity acts as a summary of many of the change management concepts reviewed in this chapter.

Activity

Review this chapter with reference to Chapters 4 and 5 and produce a grid with four columns describing the risk for a company with which you are familiar, or for a typical B2C company, assessing its probability on a scale of 0 (no risk) to 10 (very high risk), its impact from a scale of 0 (no impact) to 10 (catastrophic), and possible solutions.

Answers to activities can be found at www.pearsoned.co.uk/chaffey

Table 10.6	Organizational risk exposure factors (from Simon, 1999)

Growth risks	Culture risks	Information management risks
Pressures for performance (over-ambitious targets due to external demands)	Rewards for entrepreneurial risk-taking	Transaction complexity and velocity (a particularly high risk for companies having to purchase or sell raw materials in bulk)
Rate of expansion (expansion difficult to control and recruit new employees)	Executive resistance to bad news (and lack of action)	Gaps in diagnostic performance measures (poor reporting capabilities)
Inexperience of key employees	Levels of internal competition (Is the culture cooperative or too competitive?)	Degree of decentralized decision making (lack of central control and management of other risks)

Source: Adapted and reprinted by permission of *Harvard Business Review* from table on p. 87 from 'How risky is your company?' by Simon, R., in *Harvard Business Review*, May–June 1999. Copyright © 1999 by the Harvard Business School Publishing Corporation, all rights reserved.

As an alternative view of risks with a wider organization context, Simon (1999) presents a simple risk calculator based on different types of risks faced at a company level (Table 10.6). This calculator can be usefully applied to e-business change or a high-growth dot-com company since significant change may accentuate these risks.

Summary

1 Change as a result of e-business needs to be managed on two levels. First, the change that needs to be managed as part of projects to introduce e-business. Second, organization-wide change is required for e-business. We focus on this change in this chapter.

2 Sound project management is required to achieve change. Traditional project management activities such as estimation, resource allocation, scheduling, planning and monitoring are all important here. A project manager also needs to facilitate change by communicating the need for change.

3 Traditional life cycle stages – analysis, design and build – can be used to estimate the tasks required for an e-business implementation. Since most e-business solutions will be based on tailoring off-the-shelf packages, there will be a change in balance between the analysis, design, build and implementation phases in comparison with a bespoke solution. Prototyping is essential to achieve the fast timescales required by e-business.

4 Building a team for e-business will require technical, marketing and project management skills. This will be difficult in the face of a competitive marketplace for these skills and high staff turnover. Tactics should be developed to help retain staff in this environment.

5 To implement e-business, a company will need to partner with a variety of companies. The e-business manager will need to decide whether to outsource activities such as strategy, content development and site promotion at the outset of an e-business project and whether it may be necessary to bring these activities back in-house at a later stage.

6 Changes to organizational structures are likely to be required to build the e-business. Coordination of e-business-related activities can be achieved through a working party, e-business manager or separate department. Companies may also spin off sell-side e-commerce to a completely separate business.

7 Managing staff responses to change is an important aspect of change. Managers will need to consider how to achieve commitment and action from senior managers and also how to gain staff acceptance of the new system and new working practices. Techniques that may be used are user education, user involvement and achieving support from respected staff. Companies with an outward-looking cultural orientation will be predisposed to e-business-led change while others that have an inward-facing, inflexible cultural orientation may have to consider changes in culture.

Exercises

Self-assessment questions

1 Summarize the main types of change that need to be managed during introduction of e-business.

2 What approaches must managers take to achieve change management successfully?

3 Outline the main stages of a sell-side e-commerce implementation.

4 Explain the role of prototyping in developing a sell-side e-commerce solution.

5 Describe four different approaches to retaining staff.

6 What alternative approaches are there to structuring e-commerce within an organization?

7 Which type of organizational culture is most amenable to e-business-related change?

8 What are some of the risks of e-business change, and how can they be managed?

Essay and discussion questions

1 Write an essay on approaches to managing e-business change.

2 'Total outsourcing of e-business operations is the best method to overcome the skills shortage.' Discuss.

3 Contrast the project management stages involved with sell-side and buy-side e-commerce implementations (referring to Chapters 11 and 12 will help with this question).

4 'High turnover of technical staff is a fact of life in a buoyant job market and there is little that can be done to reduce turnover.' Discuss.

5 Develop a change management plan for a company you are familiar with.

6 You are the HR manager at a new-media design agency and are evaluating the use of overseas contract workers to help on projects. Write a report summarizing the feasibility of this approach.

7 Write a report on how the knowledge within a company can be better managed. Refer to particular technologies and procedures for managing explicit and tacit knowledge.

8 Assess the merits of virtualization in an organization of your choice.

Examination questions

1 Explain what prototyping is and why it may be used on an e-commerce implementation.

2 Summarize the main human-resource requirements for an e-commerce implementation.

3 A company has implemented a brochureware site without any changes to managerial or organizational structure. They are now seeking to achieve one-third of their revenues via the website. What changes to managerial and organizational structure would you suggest?

4 Explain how knowledge management differs from information management.

5 Explain the concept of the virtual organization. What are the advantages over a traditional organization?

6 Name four approaches a company can take to increase retention of technical staff.

7 Prioritize, with justification, your recommendations for outsourcing these functions: e-commerce strategy, e-commerce hosting, e-commerce content updating.

8 You are project manager of an e-procurement implementation. How would you maximize acceptance of the new system among staff?

References

Alvesson, M. and Karreman, D. (2002) Odd couple – making sense of the curious concept of knowledge management. *Journal of Management Studies*, 38(7), 995–1018.

Baker, P. (1998) *Electronic Commerce. Research Report 1998*. KPMG Management Consulting.

Binney, D. (2001) The KM spectrum – understanding the KM landscape. *Journal of Knowledge Management*, 5(1), 33–42.

Bocij, P., Chaffey, D., Greasley, A. and Hickie, S. (2005) *Business Information Systems. Technology, Development and Management*, 3rd edn. Financial Times Prentice Hall, Harlow.

Boddy, D., Boonstra, A. and Kennedy, G. (2001) *Managing the Information Revolution*. Financial Times Prentice Hall, Harlow.

Chaffey, D. and White, S. (2011) *Business Information Management: Improving Performance Using Information Systems*, 2nd edn. Financial Times Prentice Hall, Harlow.

Clarety (2009) Project and programme failure rates, posted by Kevin Brady on Sat 27 June 2009, **http://www.claretyconsulting.com/it/comments/ project-and-programme-failure-rates/2009-06-27/**.

COBIT (2001) Control Objectives. COBIT (3rd edn). Released by the COBIT Steering Committee and the IT Governance Institute. Available online at: **www.isacf.org/cobit**.

Cope, O. and Waddell, D. (2001) An audit of leadership styles in e-commerce. *Managerial Auditing Journal*, 16(9), 523–9.

Crush, P. (2000) What's my motivation? *Revolution*, 2 August, 34–6.

Davenport, T.H. (1993) *Process Innovation: Re-engineering Work through Information Technology*. Harvard Business School Press, Boston.

E-consultancy (2005) Managing an E-commerce team. Integrating digital marketing into your organisation. 60-page report by Dave Chaffey. Available from **www.econsultancy. com**.

E-consultancy (2007) Web Project Management. The practices behind successful web projects. Research report by Sonia Kay available from E-consultancy (**www.econsul-tancy.com**).

Garimella, K., Lees, M. and Williams, B. (2008) *BPM Basics for Dummies*. Wiley, New York.

Gartner (2003) Gartner Application Integration and Middleware Strategies Research Note T-19-4751, J. Sinur, D. McCoy and J. Thompson, 14 April. The Gartner Group (**www.gartner.com**).

Hackman, J. and Oldham, G. (1980) *Work Redesign*. Addison-Wesley, Reading, MA.

Hallowell, R. (2001) 'Scalability': the paradox of human resources in e-commerce. *International Journal of Service Industry Management*, 12(1), 34–43.

Hammer, M. and Champy, J. (1993) *Re-engineering the Corporation: A Manifesto for Business Revolution*. HarperCollins, New York.

Hansen, M., Nohria, N. and Tierney, T. (1999) What's your strategy for measuring knowledge? *Harvard Business Review*, May–June, 106–16.

Hayes, J. (2002) *The Theory and Practice of Change Management*. Palgrave, Basingstoke.

IDC (1999) Knowledge Management Survey. IDC Research (**www.idcresearch.com**).

IDC (2000) Capitalizing on Knowledge Management. IDC Research Report (**www. idcresearch. com#W18864**).

Jay, K.E. and Smith, D.C. (1996) A generic change model for the effective implementation of information systems. *South African Journal of Business Management*, 27(3).

Lewin, K. (1972) Quasi-stationary social equilibrium and the problems of permanent change. In *Organizational Development: Values, Process, and Technology*, N. Margulies and A. Raia (eds). McGraw-Hill, New York, pp. 65–72.

McLaughlin, S. (2010) Dangerous solutions: case study of a failed e-project. *Journal of Business Strategy*, 31(2).

Mekhilef, M., Kelleher, D. and Oleson, A. (2004) *European Guide to Good Practice in Knowledge Management* – Chapter 5, Terminology. Published by European Committee for Standardization at **www.cenorm.be**.

Nadler, D., Shaw, R. and Walton, E. (1995) *Discontinuous Change*. Jossey-Bass, San Francisco.

Parsons, A., Zeisser, M. and Waitman, R. (1996) Organizing for digital marketing. *McKinsey Quarterly*, no. 4, 183–92.

Saunders, R. (2000) Managing knowledge. *Harvard Management Communication Letter*, June, 3–5.

Schein, E. (1956) The Chinese indoctrination program for prisoners of war. *Psychiatry*, 19, 149–72.

Schein, E. (1992) *Organizational Culture and Leadership*. Jossey-Bass, San Francisco.

Simon, R. (1999) How risky is your company? *Harvard Business Review*, May–June, 85–94.

Snowden, D. (2002) Complex acts of knowing – paradox and descriptive self awareness. IBM Global Services, July: **www-1.ibm.com/services/files/complex.pdf**.

Storey, J. and Barnett, E. (2000) Knowledge management initiatives: learning from failure. *Journal of Knowledge Management*, 4(2), 145–56.

Sveiby, K.E. (1997–2000) *The New Organizational Wealth: Managing and Measuring Knowledge-Based Assets*. Berrett-Koehler, San Francisco. Updated on author's website (**www.sveiby.com.au/KnowledgeManagement.html**).

Waterman, R.H., Peters, T.J. and Phillips, J.R. (1980) Structure is not organization. *McKinsey Quarterly*, in-house journal. McKinsey & Co., New York.

Willcocks, L. and Smith, G. (1995) IT enabled business process reengineering: organisational and human resource dimension. *Strategic Information Systems*, 4(3), 279–301.

Further reading

Alavi, M. and Leidner, D. (2001) Knowledge Management and Knowledge Management Systems: Conceptual foundations and research issues. *MIS Quarterly*, 25(1), 107–153. An informative grounding in knowledge management concepts and challenges of implementation within businesses.

Boddy, D., Boonstra, A. and Kennedy, G. (2001) *Managing the Information Revolution*. Financial Times Prentice Hall, Harlow. Chapter 5, Information and people, and Chapter 6, Information and structure, are relevant to this chapter and contain good examples.

Chaffey, D. and Wood, S. (2005) *Business Information Management*. Financial Times Prentice Hall, Harlow. Chapter 5 focuses on knowledge management and Chapter 8 on change management.

Rubenstein-Montano, B., Liebowitz, J., Buchwalter, J., McCaw, D., Newman, B. and Rebeck, K. (2001) SMARTVision: a knowledge-management methodology. *Journal of Knowledge Management*, 5(4), 300–10. Reviews different methodologies for implementing knowledge management and suggests a detailed methodology.

Web links

David Snowden's Cognitive Edge (**www.cognitive-edge.com**) Blog by ex-IBM knowledge management expert.

E20Portal (**www.e20portal.com**) A site focusing on developments in Enterpise 2.0 applications includes case studies: **http://e20portal.com/index.php/case-studies**.

Information Research – an International Journal (**http://informationr.net**) An online journal focusing on information and knowledge management moderated by staff at the Department of Information Studies, University of Sheffield.

Knowledge Board (**www.knowledgeboard.com**) Forum focusing on knowledge management with database of articles on the topic.

Knowledge Management Central (**www.icasit.org/km/**) KM Central provides practical advice and support for business professionals working on knowledge management issues and projects.

Knowledge Management – Ark Group (**www.kmmagazine.com**) European monthly trade magazine – 'Inside Knowledge'.

Office of Government Commerce (**www.ogc.gov.uk**) Offers good guidelines in the IT Community section on successful IT including project and risk management (**www.ogc.gov.uk/index.asp?id=36**).

11

Analysis and design

Web support

The following additional case studies are available at
www.pearsoned.co.uk/chaffey

→ Legacy data integration
→ User interface enhancements at Waterstones
→ Additional activity – creating a database for a B2C company

The site also contains a range of study material designed to help improve your results.

Learning outcomes

After completing this chapter the reader should be able to:

• Summarize approaches for analysing requirements for e-business systems
• Identify key elements of approaches to improve the interface design and security design of e-commerce systems

Management issues

Analysis and design of e-business systems raises these issues for management:

• What are the critical success factors for analysis and design of e-business systems?
• What is the balance between requirements for usable and secure systems and the costs of designing them in this manner?

Links to other chapters

The main related chapters are:

• *Chapter 10* places analysis and design into the context of change management for e-business as shown in Figure 10.6
• *Chapter 12* – the sections on measurement and marketing research show how the effectiveness of analysis and design are evaluated

Introduction

Analysis and design
Analysis of system requirements and design for creation of a system.

In the context of strategy implementation, **analysis and design** activities are required to specify the business and user needs for a system and to develop a plan for building it (Figure 10.6).

This chapter reviews new approaches to analysis and design required for e-business systems. It does not aim to explain how to follow well-established techniques for analysis and design such as data flow diagramming, information flow diagrams and entity relationship diagramming. These have been described many times before, for example in Bocij *et al.* (2008).

The chapter is intended to provide managers with an appreciation of some analysis and design techniques for e-business, to provide familiarity with techniques such as process analysis, data modelling and use-case design. This familiarity should aid collaboration when the managers are involved in discussing the requirements of the system with technical staff.

It is in two main parts. In the first part we review analysis techniques and in particular process analysis for re-engineering which is important in many e-business implementations. We also touch on data modelling.

The second part looks at the design of e-business systems. The techniques described are aimed at improving the information quality of end-users of e-business systems – ensuring information is timely and secure, has the correct content in terms of accuracy, relevance and completeness, and is in a form that is easy to interpret. The section on architectural design looks at how systems are integrated to improve flow of information and also to achieve timely delivery of information. '*Focus on* User-centred site design' demonstrates how using use-case analysis and interface design guidelines can be applied to produce usable sell-side or buy-side e-commerce systems with good information quality. '*Focus on* Security design' reviews security requirements for the e-business, reviews generic approaches to security and finally looks at the current usage of e-commerce security techniques.

The importance of analysis and design is such that even if an effective strategy has been developed, its execution can be destroyed by ineffectual analysis and design. Complete Activity 11.1 to review some of the consequences of poor analysis and design.

Activity 11.1	The consequences of poor analysis and design

Purpose

To highlight the impact of poor analysis and design on customer satisfaction and business performance.

Activity

Form a focus group and discuss your own experiences of online purchasing. What have been your problems and frustrations? Refer to a particular example such as purchasing a book – what are your expectations? Alternatively, visit GetSatisfaction.com to see the types of complaints about different brands.

Answers to activities can be found at www.pearsoned.co.uk/chaffey

Arena Flowers's Sam Barton on web design and development

Overview and main concepts covered

Online florist Arena Flowers has had quite a lucrative time since its launch in late 2006. The site generated GBP 2m in revenues in its first year, helped by a strong focus on SEO, a bespoke e-commerce platform and a Facebook app that provides 15% of its traffic (albeit at lower conversion rates). We also featured Arena Flowers as mini case studies in *Chapters 5* and *8*. Here, head of design and development Sam Barton talks about the Arena Flowers web strategy and plans for the future.

The interview

Q. Can you give us a quick introduction to the business?

Sam Barton, Arena Flowers: We're an online florist based in Park Royal. We're based there as London is a big marketplace for us. Fifty per cent of our orders go to Greater London, but Park Royal is also a big logistics hub so it is good for distribution to the rest of our markets.

The business was incorporated in July 2006 and we went live with the transactional website in September 2006. The process of getting the company going was quite the reverse of some businesses. From February of 2006, we built the website in our free time as we were all employed full time elsewhere. We used that period to test the market. Not a lot of people were doing long tail flowers so we wanted to see how it would go.

The reason we were able to prove the test case and get angel funding was we were able to get Pagerank 5 by August 2006, before we went transactional. In most live e-commerce sites, bread and butter traffic comes from PPC (lining Google's pockets!) but it's expensive. We felt that if we could get alternative sources of traffic, we would have a more viable proposition. The early SEO work helped secure the funding and also allowed us to jump straight into the marketplace with a good foothold, so when we turned on PPC we were already on a par with incumbents.

But visibility is nothing without a good product offering. We cut out all middlemen and buy direct from growers, so we get great prices and our flowers are exceedingly fresh. There are no 'relay' fees with us and, because of our high stock turnover, we get fresh flowers in daily and they go straight to the customer, rather than sitting in a hot shop window.

In terms of usability, we are fairly obsessive about all elements of our site and its features, to try to maximise the user experience. For example, you can upload a video to go with your flowers. And we send a text message to tell you exactly when your flowers were delivered.

We also put a lot of emphasis on customer retention; we have a very good customer services team and different ways of handling customers to encourage them to come back to us. We have different tactics. Customers that make a certain number of orders will be rewarded with an upgrade or a bottle of champagne, for example. Our emails also have a very high return rate and we don't bombard our users.

Q. Where are you in terms of sales and profitability?

Sam Barton, Arena Flowers: We did GBP 2m net sales in year one and broke even within the first 12 months of trading. We should do GBP 4m+ in year two and make a healthy profit. We see opportunities to keep growing both sales and profitability at a similar rate going forward through various initiatives.

Q. How have your average order values developed since the launch of the site?

Sam Barton, Arena Flowers: We started off with low-30s [GBP] and that has grown month on month. We're now at [GBP] 42, even though the volume of orders has grown substantially as we have grown as a business and widened our offering.

The business has really grown fast in a relatively short period of time. We sell Prestat's chocolates on our website, and they were so surprised at the volumes we were selling that they have asked us to develop their e-commerce platform.

Q. Is there any one thing you could point to as being responsible for that rise in order value?

Sam Barton, Arena Flowers: When we went live, the site looked very similar to how it looks now in terms of its framework. But the offerings were much simpler. For example, we didn't have an 'add vase' option for our dozen red roses, or a 'make deluxe' option.

Adding cross-sell options and expanding our offering has been a big thing. Not many florists have an alcohol licence, for example, but ours really helps us to add volume. Nor can any other UK florist offer the opportunity to include a photo, a video or a sound file with your order.

Q. How was your experience with Ruby on Rails while developing the site?

Sam Barton, Arena Flowers: The Rails framework made development very easy and allowed us to grow the site very quickly in the run up to its launch.

By using it, we were able to further our long tail strategy by replicating thousands of pages very quickly. By May, we were able to have 60,000 pages up and were seeing traffic to each one of them. That exercise alone was very important and was a bit of a milestone for us.

The reason I was keen to use Ruby on Rails was that I wanted a content management system that generated dynamic URLs but had keywords in. That's now regarded as pretty much common sense, but in 2005, when we started talking about it, it was fairly novel. That was something I was adamant about from the outset.

We're fortunate to have an in-house development team. We are very attentive to the latest SEO chatter and making sure the site is optimised is a very high priority. We went into this with the knowledge that we had to be the best in order to compete.

Q. What are the main downsides? Did you have any support or staff issues?

Sam Barton, Arena Flowers: Finding people to support Ruby is the main issue. You are limited by the people who can support it. There are a handful of people I would trust to look at our code.

It's not complicated to sit people down and train them if they're a developer. We've done that – I have brought someone in who was fluent in PHP but not in Ruby, and is now part of the working team. It took six weeks and it could have been quicker, but we have a very complicated set of tools.

Q. What are you doing in terms of content optimisation?

Sam Barton, Arena Flowers: We've got quite a unique facility for managing our content, which is all done through Ajax. Products can be dragged around a category page to suit a high ranking position, so we can move them up if they are selling well or if we have stock we would like to shift. Likewise, we can move them down if they are not converting.

Our homepage is key for us and it's quite extraordinary how a day's sales can fluctuate as you move products around on it.

We have people monitoring both sales and stock throughout the day and moving products up and down. We're also talking with a company that wants to test some code on our site that will do the job I just described automatically. It puts in some dynamic scripts that monitors clicks and success rates.

I won't go into too much depth because it is a new company but we're planning to implement it in the next few weeks to see how it works.

There are lots of tools like this that we have already set up.

Q. What prompted you to launch your Facebook app and how has that benefited the business?

Sam Barton, Arena Flowers: Facebook was an obvious thing to do. It's amazing how many people use it. A blog and Facebook app were things we wanted to do quickly before they became commonplace. We're not Sainsbury's and don't have a shop to present our offering from, so creating awareness through Facebook is an obvious thing to do.

We get something like 15% of our traffic through Facebook. It might not be the best converting traffic but it's important for spreading our brand. It was also easy for us to put together – it took us a week to get the functionality going and perhaps another five days of tweaking.

Q. Going forward, would you consider developing a multi-channel presence?

Sam Barton, Arena Flowers: We know from our competitors' experience that offline for this product doesn't work as well in terms of margins.

You can, of course, sell flowers offline because there are high street florists. But it is much more profitable for us to refine our proposition rather than expand into offline. Direct marketing for offline alone is very expensive and the conversion rate is terrible. It just doesn't warrant it.

Q. Have you thought about developing your e-commerce platform into a side-business?

Sam Barton, Arena Flowers: It has occurred to us. The Prestat partnership has been very successful and we know we could do another one of those. We have built both a great technology solution and a highly efficient operational platform, meaning we can offer a full blown solution to third parties if we wish to.

The question is where is our time best spent – creating value in the Arena brand or white labelling what we've done to date? Or both?

Q. What about launching other sites?

Sam Barton, Arena Flowers: There is a lot to be gained by improving our core offering – we know a lot about flowers and we are very good at them. But we may expand the Arena brand.

We own various other Arena domains but we are in no rush to push them until we feel that we have really delivered the best possible service for UK flower lovers.

Things like expanding our offering for business customers, where we've already developed Arena For Business, a unique set of tools to save business time and increase accountability. Pushing that side of the business will be important for us, as well as other areas like weddings, which is a huge market in the UK and often not that well served.

Source: www.econsultancy.com/news-blog/newsletter/3722/arena-flowers-8217-sam-barton-on-web-design-and-development.html.

Analysis for e-business

Analysis for e-business
Using analytical techniques to capture and summarize business and user requirements.

Analysis for e-business is concerned with understanding the business and user requirements for a new system. Typical analysis activity can be broken down into: understanding the current process and then reviewing possible alternatives for implementing the e-business solution. In the following sections we will review different techniques. In this section we focus on using diagrams to demonstrate the business processes. User requirements capture techniques that help determine the function required by a system are described in the '*Focus on* User-centred site design' section.

Analysts recognize that delivering quality information to employees and partners, or exchanging it between processes, is the key to building information systems that improve efficiency and customer service. Pant and Ravichandran (2001) say:

> *Information is an agent of coordination and control and serves as a glue that holds together organisations, franchises, supply chains and distribution channels. Along with material and other resource flows, information flows must also be handled effectively in any organisation.*

This shows that in the era of e-business analysis should be used as a tool to optimize the flow of information both inside and outside organizations. In this chapter we start by looking at how workflow management is a key to managing time-based information flows. We then review how process modelling is used to analyse information flows to optimize business processes and then look at information storage analysis through a brief review of data modelling.

Process modelling

Traditional approaches to process analysis use established systems analysis and design methods that are part of methodologies such as Structured Systems Analysis and Design Methodology (SSADM), like the data flow diagram technique outlined in Bocij *et al.* (2008). Such approaches often use a hierarchical method of establishing

- the processes and their constituent sub-processes
- the dependencies between processes
- the inputs (resources) needed by the processes and the outputs.

Activity-based process definition methods
Analysis tools used to identify the relationship between tasks within a business process.

Process
Part of a system that has a clearly defined purpose or objective and clearly defined inputs and outputs.

The processes and sub-processes are essentially the activities or tasks that need to be performed by the business information system, so these are sometime referred to as '**Activity-based process definition methods**'. A **process** can be defined at the business level in terms of the main activities of a business. Each process can be broken down further as explained in the section on 'Task analysis and task decomposition'. Significant business processes are elements of the value chain; they include inbound logistics (including procurement), manufacture, outbound logistics or distribution, and customer relationship management or sales and marketing activity. Davenport (1993) notes that even for large multinational organizations the number of main processes will rarely exceed ten.

Note that in addition to the approaches shown here, use-case analysis to assist in defining interface requirements is described in the '*Focus on* User-centred site design section'.

Process mapping

Existing business processes often overlap different functional areas of a business. So, before detailed activities are identified the analyst needs to identify where in the organization proc-

Process mapping
Identification of location and responsibilities for processes within an organization.

esses occur and who is responsible for them. This procedure is often known as '**process mapping**'. Such process mapping is clearly important for identifying potential users of an e-business system. Table 11.1 shows an outline process map that might be used for a B2B company to prepare a proposal for a new major account.

Table 11.1	Process map for activities with process 'prepare proposal'

Process activity	Marketing	Engineering	Finance	Senior management
1 Cost estimation		M		
2 Assess financial risk		m	M	
3 Publicity presentation	M	m		
4 Review	M	M	M	m
5 Authorization			M	M

M = major role in function, m = minor role in function

Task analysis and task decomposition

Task analysis
Identification of different tasks, their sequence and how they are broken down.

Before a process such as 'prepare proposal' can be designed and implemented, a more detailed breakdown is required. This is usually referred to as '**task analysis**'.

Noyes and Baber (1999) point out that a difficulty with this type of process or task decomposition is that there are no set rules for what to call the different levels of decomposition or how far to decompose the process. The number of levels and the terminology used for the different levels will vary according to the application you are using and the consultant you may be working with. Georgakoupoulos *et al.* (1995) talk about 'task nesting' of tasks broken down into sub-tasks as part of the activity-based method for describing workflows. They give the example of a workflow process for procurement where the task 'procure materials' is broken down further into the sub-tasks of 'verify status', 'get bids' and 'place order'. Curtis *et al.* (1992) provide a useful framework, referring to *process units* or *elements* at each process level as follows:

Level 1 *business processes* are decomposed into:
Level 2 *activities* which are further divided to:
Level 3 *tasks* and finally:
Level 4 *sub-tasks.*

An example of a four-level task decomposition is presented in Figure 11.1.

Attempts to standardize the meanings of these terms have been produced by the Workflow Management Coalition, an industry standards body (WfMC, 1996), which describes the different process elements as follows:

1 *Business process.* A set of one or more linked procedures or activities which collectively realize a business objective or policy goal, normally within the context of an organizational structure defining functional roles and relationships.
2 *Activity.* A description of a piece of work that forms one logical step within a process. An activity may be a manual activity, which does not support computer automation, or a workflow (automated) activity. A workflow activity requires human and/or machine resource(s) to support process execution; where human resource is required an activity is allocated to a workflow participant.

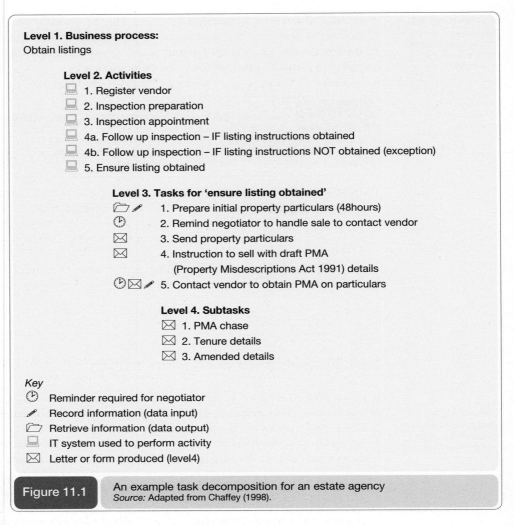

Level 1. Business process:
Obtain listings

    Level 2. Activities
    1. Register vendor
    2. Inspection preparation
    3. Inspection appointment
    4a. Follow up inspection – IF listing instructions obtained
    4b. Follow up inspection – IF listing instructions NOT obtained (exception)
    5. Ensure listing obtained

        Level 3. Tasks for 'ensure listing obtained'
        1. Prepare initial property particulars (48hours)
        2. Remind negotiator to handle sale to contact vendor
        3. Send property particulars
        4. Instruction to sell with draft PMA
            (Property Misdescriptions Act 1991) details
        5. Contact vendor to obtain PMA on particulars

            Level 4. Subtasks
            1. PMA chase
            2. Tenure details
            3. Amended details

Key
  Reminder required for negotiator
  Record information (data input)
  Retrieve information (data output)
  IT system used to perform activity
  Letter or form produced (level4)

Figure 11.1	An example task decomposition for an estate agency
	Source: Adapted from Chaffey (1998).

3 *Work item.* The representation of the work to be processed (by a workflow participant) in the context of an activity within a process instance. An activity typically generates one or more work items which together constitute the task to be undertaken by the user (a workflow participant) within this activity.

Process dependencies

Process dependencies summarize the order in which activities occur according to the business rules that govern the processes. Normally, activities occur in a sequence and are *serial;* sometimes activities can occur simultaneously, when they are known as *parallel*. Data flow diagrams and flow charts are widely used as diagramming techniques to show process dependencies. In this section we will review three techniques for showing dependencies that are more commonly applied in e-business analysis. These are flow process charts and network diagrams including the EPC (event-driven process chain) standard used by the SAP product.

Workflow management

Workflow management (WFM)
The automation of information flows; provides tools for processing the information according to a set of procedural rules.

Process dependencies are a core part of analysing and revising an organization's workflow as part of **workflow management (WFM)**, a concept that is integral to many e-business applications, so before we look at process analysis techniques, let us look at why workflow is integral to e-business.

WFM was defined by the Workflow Management Coalition (WfMC, 1996) as

the automation of a business process, in whole or part during which documents, information or tasks are passed from one participant to another for action, according to a set of procedural rules.

Workflow systems automate e-business processes by providing a *structured* framework to support a process. Applications of workflow in e-business include actioning queries from external customers or handling internal support queries. E-mail enquiries can be analysed and routed to the right person depending on their subject. Letters may need to be scanned before being added to the workflow queue.

Workflow helps manage business processes by ensuring that tasks are prioritized to be performed:

→ as soon as possible
   → by the right people
      → in the right order.

The workflow approach gives a consistent, uniform approach for improved efficiency and better customer service. Workflow software provides functions to:

- assign tasks to people
- remind people about their tasks which are part of a workflow queue
- allow collaboration between people sharing tasks
- retrieve information needed to complete the task such as a customer's personal details
- provide an overview for managers of the status of each task and the team's performance.

What type of workflow applications will exist in a company? For a B2B company, e-business applications of workflow might include:

1 *Administrative workflow.* Internal administrative tasks such as managing purchase orders for procurement and booking holidays and training.
2 *Production workflows.* Customer-facing or supplier-facing workflows such as an intranet- or extranet-based customer support database and stock management system integrated with a supplier's system.

Flow process charts

A simple flow chart is a good starting point for describing the sequence of activities of a workflow. Despite their simplicity, flow charts are effective in that they are easy to understand by non-technical staff and also they highlight bottlenecks and inefficiencies. Flow process charts are used commonly when solving e-business problems, whether in the front office or the back office. Each symbol in the chart refers to a particular operation within the overall process. An explanation of the symbols used in flow process chart analysis is shown in Figure 11.2. Box 11.1 and Figure 11.3 show one way of laying out flow process charts. Another example of how flow process charts are applied in practice using a tabular arrangement is presented in Activity 11.2. An example of how tabular flow process charts can be applied to e-procurement analysis is given in Chapter 7 (p. 358).

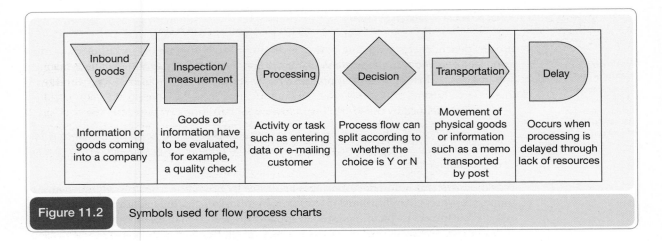

Symbols used for flow process charts

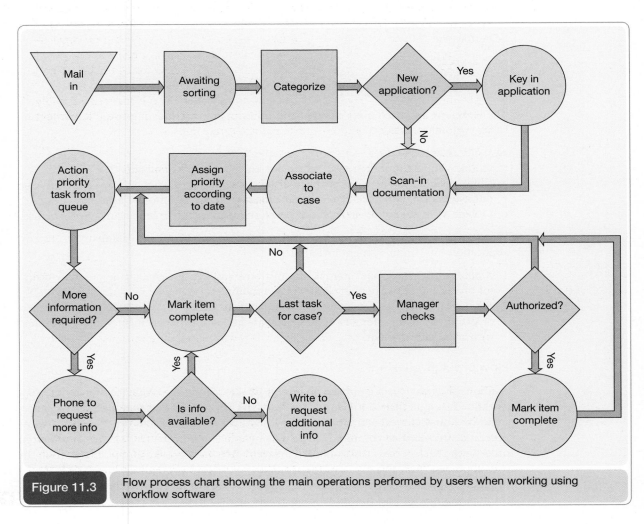

Flow process chart showing the main operations performed by users when working using workflow software

| Box 11.1 | Use of flow process charts for design of workflow systems |

In this example mortgage (loan) applications are received by post. It is then necessary to identify *new applications* and supporting documentation for applications already received. (This is a decision point indicated by a diamond-shaped decision box.) New applications are keyed into the workflow system as a new case and the original form is scanned in for reference (these are processes shown as circles on the chart). Supporting material such as ID (driving licences) and letters from employers are also scanned in. A team member will then assign or associate all scanned images of material which has been scanned in to a particular case. Assigning new documents (*assignment tasks*) is always the most important task, so these need to be automatically placed by the software at the head of the workflow queue. Once assigned the documents will need to be actioned (*action tasks*) by the operator, so according to the type of document and when it needs to be chased the workflow system will assign a priority to the task and place it in the workflow queue. Team members will then have to action tasks from the workflow queue which are prioritized according to date. Processing an action task will usually involve phoning the customer for clarification or writing a letter to request additional information. After this has been achieved the operator will mark the item as complete and a new workflow task will be created if necessary: for example, to follow up if a letter is not received within ten days.

This diagram is also useful for summarizing system design since it can identify different modules of a system and the hardware and software necessary to support these modules. In this case some of the modules are:

- Scan document (scanner and scanning software)
- Associate document to customer case (link to customer database)
- Prioritize document (specialized workflow module)
- Review document (link to customer database)
- Contact customer (link to phone system and letter printer).

| Activity 11.2 | Transforming invoice processing at a B2B company |

Purpose

To illustrate how the flow process chart can be used to simplify a business process.

Background

Table 11.2 has been drawn up following observation of tasks performed during a systems analysis project at a B2B company. The main problem is the delay currently occurring when the MD has to authorize an invoice of £10,000. The company can obtain a discount of 10% if payment is made in 10 days. This is not achievable currently and the MD wants to use IT to make this possible. As part of this re-engineering, restructuring may be required also – the MD believes that fewer staff are needed for invoice payment.

No.	Task description	Chart symbols	Distance (m)	Average time (hours)
				Flow process chart for invoice processing – original situation

Table 11.2 Flow process chart for invoice processing – original situation

No.	Task description	Chart symbols	Distance (m)	Average time (hours)
1	Receive invoice, stamp date	O⇨□D▼	–	0.1
2	To first payable clerk	O➔□D▽	50	5
3	On first payable clerk's desk	O⇨□▶▽	–	1
4	Write and attach purchase order	●⇨□D▽	–	0.1
5	To cost accountant	O➔□D▽	20	5
6	On cost accountant's desk	O⇨□▶▽	–	5
7	Code to appropriate job number	●⇨□D▽	–	0.1
8	Return to first payable clerk	O➔□D▽	20	5
9	On first payable clerk's desk	O⇨□▶▽	–	1
10	Make copies	●⇨□D▽	–	0.1
11	To Managing Director	O➔□D▽	200	5
12	On Managing Director's desk	O⇨□▶▽	–	48
13	Reviewed and approved by MD	●⇨□D▽	–	0.1
14	To second payable clerk	O➔□D▽	200	5
15	On second payable clerk's desk	O⇨□▶▽	–	1
16	Add vendor number and due date	●⇨□D▽	–	0.1
17	Write to accounts payable ledger in accounting systems	●⇨□D▽	–	0.5
18	Pay invoice – write cheque	●⇨□D▽	–	0.1
19	To file clerk	O➔□D▽	20	5
20	On file clerk's desk	O⇨□▶▽	–	1
21	File invoice	●⇨□D▽	–	0.1

Activity

As a business analyst you have to produce a more efficient way of working. You should restructure the workflow by filling in a blank table. You should also write down assumptions about changed roles and give details of new software needed to support the new workflow. You can assume each member of staff has access to a networked PC and the MD has access to a notebook with fax/modem that they use twice daily.

See Table 11.3 opposite.

Answers to activities can be found at www.pearsoned.co.uk/chaffey

Effort duration analysis

Effort duration analysis is an analytical tool that can be used to calculate the overall efficiency of a process when we have performed a detailed analysis such as that in Activity 11.2. To do this, we sum the average time it takes workers to complete every activity making up the overall process, then divide this by the total length of time the whole process takes to

No.	Task description	Chart symbols	Distance (m)	Average time (hours)
1	Receive invoice, stamp and scan	●⇨□D▼	–	0.1
2	E-mail to first payable clerk	○➜□D▽	–	0.1
3	In worklist of first payable clerk	○⇨□◗▽	–	5
4	Fill in purchase order, code job number	●⇨□D▽	–	0.5
5	E-mail to MD	○➜□D▽	–	0.1
6	In MD's worklist	○⇨□◗▽	–	12
7	Review and approval by MD	●⇨□D▽	–	0.1
8	E-mail to second payable clerk	○➜□D▽	–	0.1
9	In worklist of second payable clerk	○⇨□◗▽	–	5
10	Add vendor number and due date	●⇨□D▽	–	0.1
11	Key into accounting system	●⇨□D▽	–	0.1
12	Pay invoice and mark task as complete	●⇨□D▽	–	0.1

Table 11.3 Flow process chart for invoice processing – re-engineered process

occur. The total process time is often much longer since this includes time when the task is not being worked on. Here this is during transport of the forms, and when they are waiting in out-trays and in-trays. The efficiency relationship can be given as:

$$Efficiency = \frac{\sum(T(\textit{effort on tasks}))}{T(\textit{total process time})}$$

If we apply effort duration analysis to the first scenario in Activity 11.2, with delays and transport not contributing to the overall process, we can see that the efficiency is barely 2%! This measure can be extended by noting the activities that add value to the customer rather than simply being administrative.

Network diagrams

While data flow diagrams and flow process charts may give a good indication of the sequence in which activities and tasks occur, they often do not give a sufficiently tight, formal definition of the process sequence necessary for input into an e-business, workflow or ERP system. To do this we can use a network diagram known as a GAN (generalized activity network). Here, nodes are added between the boxes representing the tasks, to define precisely the alternatives that exist following completion of a task. The most common situation is that one activity must follow another, for example a check on customer identity must be followed by a credit check. Where alternatives exist, the logic is defined at the node as follows: where a single pathway is taken from two or more alternatives, the node is defined as an OR node, and when several pathways may be followed this is an AND node. Join nodes combine previous activities, and splits determine which activities occur next. Where there are alternatives, business rules are defined as pre-conditions or post-conditions. A summary of the alternative dependencies is given in Table 11.4.

Event-driven process chain (EPC) model

One of the most widely used methods for describing business events and processes is the event-driven process chain method (EPC). This has been popularized by its application to re-engineering of enterprises performed using the SAP R/3 ERP product which accounts for worldwide sales of several billion dollars. Over 800 standard business EPCs are defined to support the SAP R/3 system; they are intended to illustrate business rules clearly for interpretation by business users before enactment in the software. The different elements of the EPC model are shown in Table 11.5; these include the different types of dependencies previously reviewed in Table 11.4. Figure 11.4 is an EPC meta-model illustrating how the different elements relate to one another. This figure shows how business functions are triggered through transactions on *business objects* which also lead to a *business event*. *Control flows* link the activities, events and logical operators. Entities or information objects are items such as sales orders or invoices.

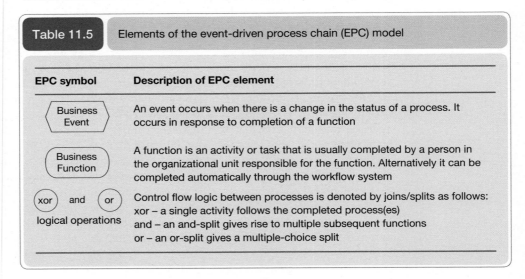

Table 11.4	Workflow dependencies at a node on a network diagram	
Node type	**Description**	**Summary**
AND-SPLIT	Workflow splits into two or more parallel activities which all execute	
OR-SPLIT	Workflow splits into multiple branches of which only one is followed	
AND-JOIN	Multiple executing activities join into a single thread of control	
OR-JOIN	An exclusive alternative activity joins into a single thread of execution	
Iteration	Repetition of one or more workflow activities until a condition is met	
Must follow	No alternative paths exist	

Table 11.5	Elements of the event-driven process chain (EPC) model
EPC symbol	**Description of EPC element**
Business Event	An event occurs when there is a change in the status of a process. It occurs in response to completion of a function
Business Function	A function is an activity or task that is usually completed by a person in the organizational unit responsible for the function. Alternatively it can be completed automatically through the workflow system
xor and or logical operations	Control flow logic between processes is denoted by joins/splits as follows: xor – a single activity follows the completed process(es) and – an and-split gives rise to multiple subsequent functions or – an or-split gives a multiple-choice split

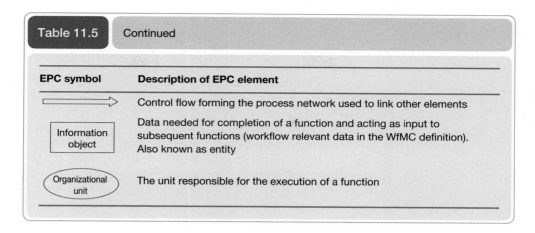

Table 11.5	Continued

EPC symbol	Description of EPC element
⇒	Control flow forming the process network used to link other elements
Information object	Data needed for completion of a function and acting as input to subsequent functions (workflow relevant data in the WfMC definition). Also known as entity
Organizational unit	The unit responsible for the execution of a function

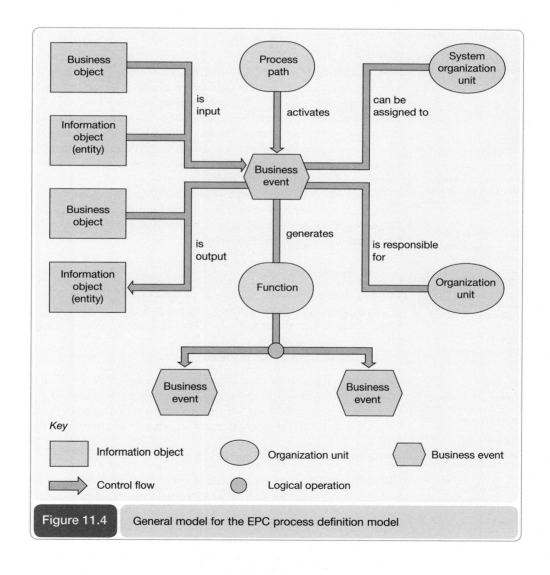

Figure 11.4	General model for the EPC process definition model

Validating a new process model

Whichever method has been used to arrive at the process definition, we need to check that the process definition is realistic. When developing a wish list of process capabilities and corresponding business rules the stages described by David Taylor in his book on concurrent engineering (Taylor, 1995) may be useful. He suggests that once new processes have been established they are sanity checked by performing a 'talk-through, walk-through and run-through'. Here, the design team will describe the proposed business process as a model in which different business objects interact. Once the model has been adjusted, the walk-through stage involves more detail in the scenario and the design team will role-play the services the objects provide. The final run-through stage is a quality check in which no on-the-spot debugging occurs – just the interactions between the objects are described. Increasing use is made of simulation software to model alternative scenarios.

Data modelling

Data modelling of e-business and e-commerce systems uses well-established techniques such as normalization that are used for relational database analysis and design. As a consequence, this section is brief in comparison with that on process modelling which introduces some novel techniques. See Bocij *et al.* (2008, Chapter 11) for an introduction to normalization and relational database design. Some basic definitions are given in this section as a reminder of key terms. Before we start it is worth mentioning that the advent of data mining and object-oriented approaches has meant increasing use of non-relational database design. These are outlined further in Chapters 6 and 11 of Bocij *et al.* (2008).

The approach we use to explore data modelling for e-commerce is to use examples that identify typical elements of data modelling for a sell-side e-commerce system. We will use ER (entity relationship) modelling to review typical structures for these databases. In simple ER modelling there are three main stages.

1 Identify entities

Entities define the broad groupings of information such as information about different people, transactions or products. Examples include customer, employee, sales orders, purchase orders. When the design is implemented each design will form a **database table**.

2 Identify attributes for entities

'**Attributes**' describe the characteristics of any single instance of an entity. For example, the customer entity has attributes such as name, phone number and e-mail address. When the design is implemented each attribute will form a **field**, and the collection of fields for one instance of the entity such as a particular customer will form a **record**.

3 Identify relationships between entities

The **relationships** between entities require identification of which fields are used to link the tables. For example, for each order a customer places we need to know which customer has placed the order and which product they have ordered. As is evident from Figure 11.5, the fields 'customer ID' and 'product ID' are used to relate the order information between the three tables. The fields that are used to relate tables are referred to as 'key fields'. A **primary key** is used to uniquely identify each instance of an entity and a **secondary key** is used to link to a primary key in another table. In Figure 11.5 the primary key of the customer table is customer ID, but the field customer ID in the order table is here a secondary key that

Entity
A grouping of related data, such as customer entity, implemented as a table.

Database table
Each database comprises several tables.

Attribute
A property or characteristic of an entity, implemented as a field.

Field
Attributes of products, such as date of birth.

Record
A collection of fields for one instance of an entity, such as Customer Smith.

Relationship
Describes how different tables are linked.

Primary key
The field that uniquely identifies each record in a table.

Secondary key
A field that is used to link tables, by linking to a primary key in another table.

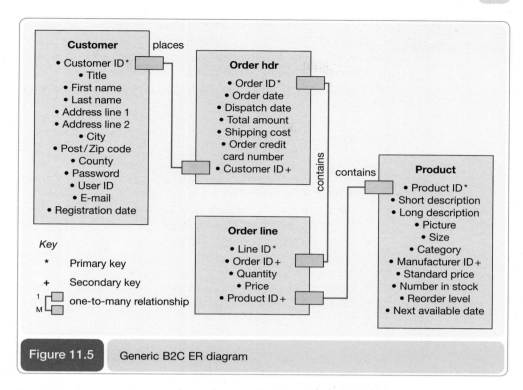

Key

*	Primary key
+	Secondary key
1 M	one-to-many relationship

Figure 11.5　Generic B2C ER diagram

links back to the customer table. This relationship is an example of a one-to-many relationship since each customer may place many orders over the lifetime of the relationship.

Normalization is an additional stage, not covered here, used to optimize the database to minimize redundancy or duplication of information.

If you have previous experience in analysis and design for databases, complete Activity 11.3 to develop an ER diagram for a typical B2C company. If you do not have this experience then refer to the generic answers to gain an appreciation of how databases are structured.

Applying the star schema for data warehousing

E-business systems manage a vast number of transactions with data recorded for each. A key design issue is how the information about these transactions can usefully be applied to improve the effectiveness and business contribution of these systems. In Chapter 12 we describe how web analytics systems are used to analyse and improve the effectiveness of sell-side e-commerce systems.

While independent analytics systems are available, larger companies are increasingly finding that to apply the insights available they have to integrate web analytics information with internal sales and ordering systems to form **data warehouses**. Managers involved with planning and using these systems need to be aware of the **star schema data model** which is a specific form of ER model which is then implemented as a design most suitable for storage and rapid analysis of time-based data (which are not updated with live transactions).

Data warehouses
Large database systems used for storing a history of integrated company data on customer interactions, sales and supply chain transactions.

Star schema data model
A form of data model based on a central fact table referencing a transaction linked through database indexes to several dimensions (arranged to form a star) which give alternative methods of breaking down these transactions.

Activity 11.3	ER modelling for a B2C company

Purpose

To gain an understanding of the generic structure for transactional e-commerce databases.

Activity

Create a normalized ER diagram for the B2C company, or a B2C consumer transactional site.

For answers see Figure 11.5.

Comments

- Customer. May also have a separate delivery address.
- Order. Many items may be required on each order, so each order header can have many line items.
- Product. Includes catalogue information, such as description and a picture.
- Product. Informs the customer the number in stock and when they will be available.
- There will be a separate manufacturer table not shown here.

Design for e-business

System design

Defines how an information system will operate.

The **design** element of creating an e-business system involves specifying how the system should be structured.

In the two *Focus on* sections that follow we look at two aspects of design that are of great importance to how e-business systems are perceived by customers – security and interface design. Before that, we consider the overall architectural design of e-business systems.

Architectural design of e-business systems

The starting point for design of e-business systems is to ensure that a common architecture exists across the company in terms of hardware and software technology, applications and business processes. This goal is summarized in Figure 3.17(b).

Client–server model

A system architecture in which end-user machines such as PCs, known as 'clients', run applications while accessing data and possibly programs from a server.

E-business systems follow the same **client–server model** architecture of many business information systems created in the 1990s. For the e-business, the clients are typically employees, suppliers or customers' desktop PCs which give the 'front-end' access point to e-business applications. The clients are connected to a 'back-end' server computer via an intranet, extranet or Internet.

In Chapters 3 and 6 we have discussed the management issues involved with selecting 'software as a service' (SaaS) e-business systems which are client–server systems where the client is a web browser on a computer or mobile device and the server is located outside the organization and the application process is commonly shared with many other companies in a 'multi-tenancy' model.

Debate 11.1

E-business vs ERP architectures

'Designing an appropriate architecture for e-business is effectively the same as the architecture for enterprise resource planning systems.'

A key design decision in client–server systems is how different tasks involved in delivering a working application to the users are distributed between client and server. The typical situation for these tasks in an e-business system is:

- *Data storage.* Predominantly on server. Client storage is ideally limited to cookies, which are then related to the data for the user which are stored on a database server.
- *Query processing.* Predominantly on the server, although some validation can be performed on the client.
- *Display.* This is largely a client function.
- *Application logic.* Traditionally, in early PC applications this has been a client function, but for e-business systems the design aim is to maximize the application logic processing including the business rules on the server.

Three-tier client–server

The first tier is the client that handles display, second is application logic and business rules, third is database storage.

Thin client

An end-user access device (terminal) where computing requirements such as processing and storage (and so cost) are minimized.

A typical e-business architecture uses a **three-tier client–server** model where the client is mainly used for display with application logic and the business rules partitioned on a server, which is the second tier, and the database server is the third tier. Since most of the processing is executed on the servers rather than the client, this architecture is sometimes referred to as a '**thin client**', because the size of the executable program is smaller. The application server provider (ASP) described in Chapter 3 is typically based upon the three-tier model. This is shown in Figure 11.6.

Although the three-tier model of an e-business system suggests a relatively simple architectural design, the reality is more complex. Different servers are needed which combine applications logic and database storage for different requirements. These may be physically separate servers or may be combined. Figure 11.7 shows a typical e-business architecture. The purpose of each of the servers is as follows:

- *Web server.* Manages http requests from client and acts as a passive broker to other servers. Returns or serves web pages.
- *Merchant server.* This is the main location of the application logic and integrates the entire application by making requests to the other server components.
- *Personalization server.* Provides tailored content – may be part of commerce server functionality.
- *Payment commerce server.* Manages payment systems and secure transactions.
- *Catalogue server.* A document management server used to display detailed product information and technical specifications.
- *CRM server.* Stores information on all customer contacts.
- *ERP server.* Required for information on stock availability and pricing from the customer. Will need to be accessed for sales order processing and histories, and logistics for distribution.

It is evident that designing the method of integration between different components is not straightforward – creating a fully integrated e-business is not straightforward! As was discussed in Chapter 9, the best approach to simplifying the design is to reduce the number of suppliers of components to improve the ease of data and applications integration.

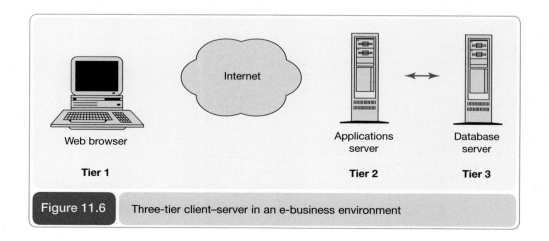

| Web browser | Internet | Applications server | Database server |
| Tier 1 | | Tier 2 | Tier 3 |

Figure 11.6   Three-tier client–server in an e-business environment

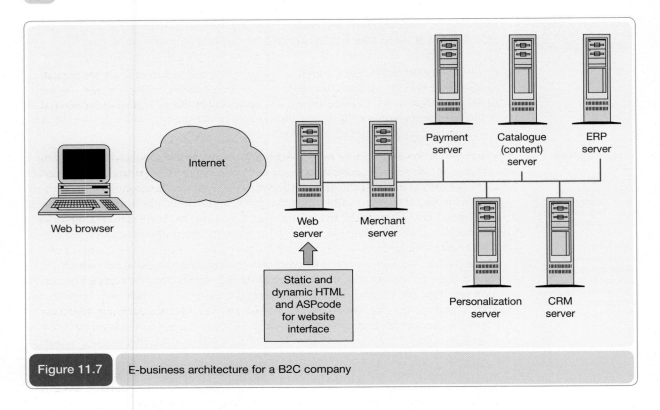

| Figure 11.7 | E-business architecture for a B2C company |

User-centred site design

Since e-business systems are often customer- or employee-facing systems, the importance of human–computer interaction in the design of web applications is high. Referring to website design, Nigel Bevan says:

> *Unless a web site meets the needs of the intended users it will not meet the needs of the organization providing the web site. Web site development should be user-centred, evaluating the evolving design against user requirements.* (Bevan, 1999a)

User-centred design
Design based on optimizing the user experience according to all factors, including the user interface, which affect this.

Noyes and Baber (1999) explain that **user-centred design** involves more than user interface design. It can be conceived of as centring on the human, but surrounded concentrically by factors that affect usability such as user interface, computers, workplace and the environment. Here we will be specifically looking at the user interface.

User-centred design starts with understanding the nature and variation within the user groups. According to Bevan (1999a), issues to consider include:

- Who are the important users?
- What is their purpose in accessing the site?
- How frequently will they visit the site?
- What experience and expertise do they have?
- What nationality are they? Can they read English?
- What type of information are they looking for?
- How will they want to use the information: read it on the screen, print it or download it?
- What type of browsers will they use? How fast will their communication links be?
- How large a screen/window will they use, with how many colours?

Box 11.2 gives a modern perspective on mistakes companies continue to make with their websites and suggests how companies can be persuaded to invest in usability initiatives.

Box 11.2	Why do websites torture their visitors?

Bruce Tognazzini was Apple's 66th employee, developing the company's first usability guidelines and founding its Human Interface team. Almost thirty years later, he's a principal at Nielsen Norman Group and still making his feelings known when companies commit design errors.

The main web usability/user experience mistakes
The level of open hostility that websites display is breathtaking. For every Bed, Bath & Beyond, with its smooth, comfortable user experience, there are a thousand amateurish websites that appear to feel that torturing their customers is a really good idea.

In the main, this has resulted from striving to achieve mediocrity, rather than excellence, but it is as devastating to the user experience as if they had set out to achieve hostility.

The worst single fault is throwing away the user's work. You see this in travel sites, where the user spends an hour selecting airline tickets for dates five months hence, then tries searching for a hotel for that same period, only to find the site has thrown away the dates and is assuming the user wants a hotel for tomorrow night.

The customer playing 'what if' with different airlines and different hotels may have to enter the same group of dates as many as a dozen times during these transactions – often resulting in their making a mistake the last, fateful time, and ending up with worthless airline tickets for the wrong dates.

Then there's the worst single bit of information that can be discarded: the user's decision to uncheck the box saying, 'Yes! I want you to spam me fourteen times a day for the rest of my life!' that appears embedded in the order page.

Go back to change anything on that page, and they'll turn the checkbox back on. How do these people imagine customers feel later when the spam they specifically rejected starts rolling in?

Recommendations on a faster web experience
Bruce Tognazzini recommends:

1 Rid your site of time-dependent media. Specifically, eliminate all Flash and video that is not specifically directed at the product or service being sold or discussed and that is not under the direct and voluntary control of the user.
2 8Support tabbed browsing.
3 Limit the number of pages and interactions necessary for a user to accomplish his or her task.
4 Do 'boredom testing', where you observe new and experienced users and see where they fidget, their mind and eyes wander, or they sit back with arms crossed.
5 Work out solutions so that when you must do some work 'behind the scenes', the user is engaged in decision-making and doesn't miss your presence. Use Firefox's ability to pre-fetch pages, for example, so when the user is ready to go, you are ready to go, too.

Will all companies have grasped the importance of user experience in another 12 years?
If you look back at my 1980 guidelines, above, and compare them with what is out there in 2007, you will see that the vast majority of companies don't yet grasp even the rudiments of human–computer interaction (HCI).

We still see, for example, most websites demanding that users enter difficult-to-check data, such as phone and credit card numbers, without spaces, all to save the programmer five minutes and a single line of code.

Such ignorance and laziness ensures full employment for HCI designers for the foreseeable future, and also ensures that the original promise of the web, with its sweeping aside of 'bricks and mortar stores', will continue unfulfilled.

Persuade senior management to buy in to usability/user experience?
Pore over your log files [web analytics] and be prepared to point out the places where users are 'bailing out', along with cogent arguments as to why, mentioning things like your lovely, design-award-winning Flash animated-splash screen that takes a minute to load and does nothing toward selling the product.

Then, convert those bail-outs into dollars:

We are losing 20% of our customers before they ever even enter the site because of our splash screen. Last year, our sales were $140,000,000. If we hadn't lost all these people, we could have realised an additional $11,420,000. Total lost profit: Around $750,000. A single HCI designer could have prevented that, at a savings of around $700,000 dollars. We also will no longer have to put out release x.01, x.1, and x.2 every time we come out with a new design, because the design will be right. That would save us millions more in engineering resources.

Companies not only save millions by having HCI talent available to them; they often move back from the brink of extinction.

HCI can be a no-brainer to senior management if the case is made clearly and expressed in terms they understand – money.

Failing buy-in, do it anyway. All that's needed is a broom closet and a couple of tables.

Forget about video. Just see if people can use your site. A single test with a single user in a broom closet can be such an eye-opener, it can change the course of a whole project. (Of course, even with qualitative testing, 20 or 30 users, over time, are better.)

Even a really bad designer, with sufficient user-testing, will eventually be able to cobble together a decent design – the infinite number of monkeys theory – the worst crime is to not test at all.

Also consider becoming an HCI designer yourself. If you're concerned enough to petition management, you have the most important prerequisite – you care.

Source: E-consultancy (2007).

Before we study best practice in user-centred design, it should be noted that usability and accessibility are only one part of the overall experience which determines a visitor's experience. In Chapter 5, in the section on competitor analysis, we explained how it is important to provide a promise of what the online representation of the brand will deliver to customers. The concept of online brand promise is closely related to that of delivering **online customer experience**. In this chapter, we will explore different practical actions that companies can take to create and maintain satisfactory online experiences. An indication of the effort required to produce a customer-centric online presence is given by Alison Lancaster, at the time the head of marketing and catalogues at John Lewis Direct and currently Marketing Director at Charles Tyrrwhit (www.ctshirts.co.uk), who says:

A good site should always begin with the user. Understand who the customer is, how they use the channel to shop, and understand how the marketplace works in that category. This includes understanding who your competitors are and how they operate online. You need continuous research, feedback and usability testing to continue to monitor and evolve the customer experience online. Customers want convenience and ease of ordering. They want a site that is quick to download, well-structured and easy to navigate.

Online customer experience
The combination of rational and emotional factors of using a company's online services that influences customers' perceptions of a brand online.

You can see that creating effective online experiences is a challenge since there are many practical issues to consider which we present in Figure 11.8. This is based on a diagram by de Chernatony (2001) who suggested that delivering the online experience promised by a brand requires delivering rational values, emotional values and promised experience (based on rational and emotional values). The factors that influence the online customer experience can be presented in a pyramid form of success factors as is shown in Figure 11.8 (the different success factors reflect current best-practice and differ from those of de Chernatony). The diagram also highlights the importance of delivering service quality online, as has been indicated by Trocchia and Janda (2003).

Research by Christodoulides *et al.* (2006) has tested the importance of a range of indicators of online brand equity for online retail and service companies. This analysis was performed across these five dimensions of brand equity assessed by asking the questions which are listed below:

1 Emotional connection

Q1: I feel related to the type of people who are [X]'s customers
Q2: I feel like [X] actually cares about me
Q3: I feel as though [X] really understands me

2 Online experience

Q4: [X]'s website provides easy-to-follow search paths
Q5: I never feel lost when navigating through [X]'s website
Q6: I was able to obtain the information I wanted without any delay

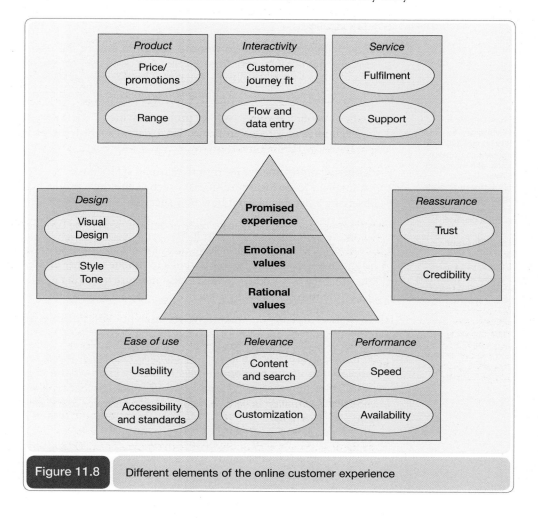

Figure 11.8   Different elements of the online customer experience

3 Responsive service nature

Q7: [X] is willing and ready to respond to customer needs

Q8: [X]'s website gives visitors the opportunity to 'talk back' to [X]

4 Trust

Q9: I trust [X] to keep my personal information safe

Q10: I feel safe in my transactions with [X]

5 Fulfilment

Q11: I got what I ordered from [X]'s website

Q12: The product was delivered by the time promised by [X]

Usability

Usability
An approach to website design intended to enable the completion of user tasks.

Usability is a key concept within user-centred design that is applied to the analysis and design for a range of products which defines how easy they are to use. The British Standards Institute ISO Standard: Human-centred Design Processes for Interactive Systems (1999) defines usability as the:

> *extent to which a product can be used by specified users to achieve specified goals with effectiveness, efficiency and satisfaction in a specified context of use.*

You can see how the concept can be readily applied to website design – web visitors often have defined *goals* such as finding particular information or completing a particular action.

In Jakob Nielsen's classic book, *Designing Web Usability* (Nielsen, 2000b), he describes usability as follows:

> *An engineering approach to website design to ensure the user interface of the site is learnable, memorable, error free, efficient and gives user satisfaction. It incorporates testing and evaluation to ensure the best use of navigation and links to access information in the shortest possible time. A companion process to information architecture.*

Expert review
An analysis of an existing site or prototype, by an experienced usability expert who will identify deficiencies and improvements to a site based on their knowledge of web design principles and best practice.

In practice, usability involves two key project activities. **Expert reviews** are often performed at the beginning of a redesign project as a way of identifying problems with a previous design. **Usability testing** involves:

1 Identifying representative users of the site and typical tasks.
2 Asking them to perform specific tasks such as finding a product or completing an order.
3 Observing what they do and how they succeed.

For a site to be successful, the user tasks or actions need to be completed:

Usability/user testing
Representative users are observed performing representative tasks using a system.

- Effectively – web usability specialists measure task completion, for example, only 3 out of 10 visitors to a website may be able to find a telephone number or other piece of information.
- Efficiently – web usability specialists also measure how long it takes to complete a task on site, or the number of clicks it takes.

Jakob Nielsen explains the imperative for usability best in his 'Usability 101' (www.useit. com/ alertbox/20030825.html). He says:

> *On the Web, usability is a necessary condition for survival. If a website is difficult to use, people leave. If the **homepage** fails to clearly state what a company offers and what users can do on the site, people leave. If users get lost on a website, they **leave**. If a website's information is hard to read or doesn't answer users' key questions, they **leave**. Note a pattern here?*

For these reasons, Nielsen suggests that around 10% of a design project budget should be spent on usability, but often actual spend is significantly less.

Evaluating designs

A test of effective design for usability is, according to Bevan (1999b), dependent on three areas:

1 *Effectiveness* – can users complete their tasks correctly and completely?
2 *Productivity (efficiency)* – are tasks completed in an acceptable length of time?
3 *Satisfaction* – are users satisfied with the interaction?

User involvement is vital to assess the effectiveness of design and focus groups have traditionally been used as part of a website prototyping approach described in Chapter 10.

E-consultancy (2009) describes how insurance company Hiscox (www.hiscox.co.uk) approached a site redesign using 3 different models of user interaction which were prototyped:

- A distribution model in which visitors pick the type of customer they are, then choose their product.
- A retail model, where customers pick the product they want, then choose how to buy it.
- A needs-based model to help customers choose products.

Eyetracking

A usability testing technique that provides a visual overlay of where visitors most commonly look at on the screen (heatmaps) and individual or common paths (gaze trails).

Eyetracking is an effective technique for assessing design effectiveness. Eyetracking of prospects is offered by many usability agencies as part of a focus group (see for example, the Video Explanation at : http://www.etre.com/blog/ and Eyetracking examples at http://www.youtube.com/user/SimpleUsability) or through remote testing through services such as WhatUsersDo.com.

Traditionally usability tests have been completed during analysis and design, but many businesses now gain feedback continuously via tools. Smart Insights (2010) identifies five types of tools.

1 **Website feedback tools.** Sometimes described as 'Voice of Customer', these provide a permanent facility for customers to feed back by prompts on every page.
2 **Crowdsourcing product opinion software.** Feedback on new features or service delivery.
3 **Simple page or concept feedback tools.** These give basic feedback from other site users.
4 **Site exit survey tools.** These tools rate intent (reason to visit site) against satisfaction. Some companies use for redesign, others for permanent tracking of site effectiveness.
5 **General online survey tools.** Many companies use generic low-cost or free survey tools to research audience opinions.

Use-case analysis

Use-case modelling

A user-centred approach to modelling system requirements.

Unified Modelling Language (UML)

A language used to specify, visualize and document the artefacts of an object-oriented system.

Web design personas

A summary of the characteristics, needs, motivations and environment of typical website users.

The **use-case method** of process analysis and modelling was developed in the early 1990s as part of the development of object-oriented techniques. It is part of a methodology known as **'Unified Modelling Language' (UML)** that attempts to unify the approaches that preceded it such as the Booch, OMT and Objectory notations. Jacobsen *et al.* (1994) give an accessible introduction and describe how object modelling can be applied to workflow analysis.

Persona and scenario analysis

Website designers and marketers use a similar model, but using different terminology. Marketers create **web design personas** for typical site visitors; this is a powerful technique for influencing the planning of online campaigns and the usability and customer-centricity of a website. Forrester (2005) researched the use of personas and found that ethnographic researchers averaged 21 interviews with typical users per project to create with an average of between four and eight personas and this cost between $47,000 and $500,000! Ford uses three buyer personas at Ford.com, Staples.com has seven personas for shoppers and Microsoft had seven for Windows XP.

Personas are essentially a 'thumbnail' description of a type of person. They have been used for a long time in research for segmentation and advertising, but in recent years have also proved effective for improving website design by companies that have applied this technique.

Customer scenarios are developed for different personas. Patricia Seybold in the book *The Customer Revolution* (Seybold and Marshak, 2001) explains them as follows:

> *A customer scenario is a set of tasks that a particular customer wants or needs to do in order to accomplish his or her desired outcome.*

You will see that scenarios can be developed for each persona. Each scenario is split up into a series of steps or tasks, which can be best thought of as a series of questions a visitor asks. By identifying questions website designers identify the information needs of different customer types at different stages in the buying process.

The use of scenarios is a simple, but very powerful web design technique that is still relatively rare in website design. They can also be used when benchmarking competitor sites as part of situation analysis.

The following are some guidelines and ideas on what can be included when developing a persona. The start or end point is to give each persona a name. The detailed stages are:

1 *Build personal attributes into personas:*
   - Demographic: age, sex, education, occupation and for B2B, company size, position in buying unit
   - Psychographic: goals, tasks, motivation
   - Webographics: web experience (months), usage location (home or work), usage platform (dial-up, broadband), usage frequency, favourite sites.
2 *Remember that personas are only models of characteristics and environment:*
   - Design targets
   - Stereotypes
   - Three or four usually suffice to improve general usability, but more are needed for specific behaviours
   - Choose one primary persona which, if satisfied, means others are likely to be satisfied.
3 *Different scenarios can be developed for each persona as explained further below.* Write three or four, for example:
   - Information-seeking scenario (leads to site registration)
   - Purchase scenario – new customer (leads to sale)
   - Purchase scenario – existing customer (leads to sale).

Once different personas have been developed that are representative of key site-visitor types or customer types, a **primary persona** is sometimes identified. Wodtke (2002) says:

> *Your primary persona needs to be a common user type who is both important to the business success of the product and needy from a design point of view – in other words, a beginner user or a technologically challenged one.*

She also says that secondary personas can also be developed such as super-users or complete novices. Complementary personas are those that don't fit into the main categories which display unusual behaviour. Such complementary personas help 'out-of-box thinking' and offer choices or content that may appeal to all users.

For another example of the application of personas, see the mini case study about paint manufacturer Dulux.

Stages in use-case analysis

The following stages are identified by Schneider and Winters (1998) for analysis using the use-case method.

Customer scenarios (user journeys)
Alternative tasks or outcomes required by a visitor to a website. Typically accomplished in a series of stages of different tasks.

Primary persona
A representation of the typical site user, who is strategically important to the effectiveness of the site, but one whose needs are challenging to fulfil.

Mini Case Study 11.1	Dulux paints a picture of consumers with personas

Campaign aims

The aims behind this brand initiative were to reposition Dulux from a paint brand to a colour help brand by meeting customer needs in a way competitors don't to help differentiate the Dulux brand. The aim was to position Dulux.co.uk (Figure 11.9) as '*the online destination for colour scheming and visualisation to help you achieve your individual style from the comfort of your home*'. Specific outcomes on the site are to browse colours, add colours to a personal scrapbook, use the paint calculator and find a stockist. Further aims were to 'win the war before the store', i.e. to provide colour help tools that can help develop a preference for Dulux before consumers are in-store and to prompt other ideas to sell more than one colour at a time.

Specific SMART objectives were to increase the number of unique visitors from 1m p.a. in 2003 to 3.5m p.a. in 2006 and to drive 12% of visitors to a desired outcome (e.g. ordering swatches).

Target audience

Based on research, it was found that the main audience for the site was female with these typical demographics and psychographics:

- Would-be adventurous 25–44 women, online
- Lack of confidence with previous site:
  - Gap between inspiration (TV, magazines, advertising) and lived experience (large DIY retail premises, nervous discomfort)
  - No guidance or reassurance previously available currently on their journey

Figure 11.9	Dulux.co.uk website

- Colours and colour combining are key
- Online is a well-used channel for help and guidance on other topics
- 12-month decorating cycle
- Propensity to socialize
- Quality, technical innovation and scientific proficiency of Dulux are given.

Specific personas were developed as follows:

- *First-time buyer*. Penny Edwards, Age: 27, Partner: Ben, Location: North London, Occupation: Sales Assistant
- *Part-time mum*. Jane Lawrence, Age: 37, Husband: Joe, Location: Manchester, Occupation: Part time PR consultant
- *Single mum*. Rachel Wilson, Age: 40, Location: Reading, Occupation: Business Analyst

Each has a different approach to interacting with the brand. For Penny it is summarized by the statement:

I've got loads of ideas and enthusiasm, I just don't know where to start.

Each persona was also characterized by their media consumption and preferences such as types of website, TV, magazines and radio channels and their favourite hobbies and socializing activities.

A storyboard was developed to illustrate the typical 'customer journey' for each persona, and these informed the final site design.

Brand campaign

To support the relaunch of the site, digital channels such as online banner advertising and interactive TV, with traditional channels such as press, in-store and PR. The main theme of the ads was 'colour chemistry' which was developed through featuring personas in the ads such as Candy Love, Forest Lake and Treacle Tart. The ads had a clear call-to-action to visit the website to find the right match for the consumer's personality and style.

Source: Case study developed by Agency.com available through the IAB (www.iabuk.net) and presented at the Engage 2007 Online Marketing conference.

1 Identify actors

Actors

People, software or other devices that interface with a system.

Actors are those objects which are involved in using or interacting with a system. They are not part of the system. The obvious actors are the users of a system. In a customer service application the actors may be a customer and the customer service person at the company. When performing process analysis to define use-cases we ask questions such as 'Who are the actors for this process?' 'What services do these actors provide?' 'What are the actors' tasks?' and 'What changes do they make to the status of the overall process?' Actors may add information to the system or receive it through reporting facilities. Note that an employee who has several roles would be represented by two different actors.

Schneider and Winters (1998) point out that other actors include software and hardware control devices that change the state of the process and external systems that interface with the system under consideration. These are effectively human actors who have been automated. Actors are denoted using the straightforward approach shown in Figure 11.10.

2 Identify use-cases

Use-case

The sequence of transactions between an actor and a system that supports the activities of the actor.

Use-cases are the different things users of a system want it to perform. These can be described as activities or tasks that are part of a dialogue between an actor and the system. They summarize the requirements of a system from each actor since they describe the functionality that will be provided by the system. Common use-cases are:

- Starting up, shutting down or amending a system.
- Adding or amending information on a system. Examples include placing an e-commerce order or recording a complaint via e-mail.
- Using a system for reporting or decision support.

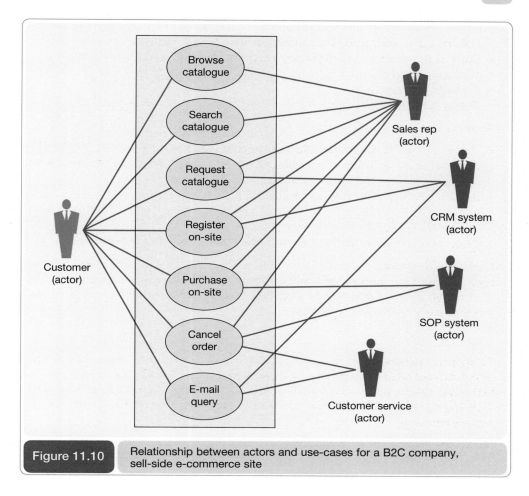

| Figure 11.10 | Relationship between actors and use-cases for a B2C company, sell-side e-commerce site |

Some use-cases for a B2C company are shown in Figure 11.10.

Bevan (1999b) also notes the importance of defining key scenarios of use. This stage, often known as 'knowledge elicitation', involves interviewing users and asking them to talk through their current or preferred way of working. Once the scenarios have been established, card sorting techniques, as described by Noyes and Baber (1999), can be used. They describe how after interviewing users, typical tasks or actions were written down on cards. These were then used to identify the sequence of actions users required from a menu system. They explain that the menu system devised was quite different from that envisaged by the software engineers. Card sorting techniques can also be used to check that no stages have been missed during the **talk-through** – a **walk-through** of the cards is performed.

3 Relate actors to use-cases

Figure 11.10 also shows how actors relate to use-cases. It can be used to identify responsibilities and check for missing activities. For example, 'Check order status' is a use-case that is missing and the company would have to discuss whether it was acceptable for a customer service rep to place an order for a customer who was complaining about a particular product.

4 Develop use-case scenarios

A detailed **scenario** is then developed to detail the different paths of events and activities for each use-case. The primary scenario describes the typical case where nothing goes wrong. The use-case includes detail of activities or functions, what happens when there is an alternative or decision, or if there is an error. Pre-conditions for entering and post-conditions for exiting the use-case are also specified.

Talk-through
A user verbally describes their required actions.

Walk-through
A user executes their actions through using a system or mock-up.

Scenario
A particular path or flow of events or activities within a use-case.

Figure 11.11 shows a primary scenario for the complete e-commerce purchase cycle. A more detailed primary scenario for the particular use-case 'Register' written from the point of view of the customer actor from Figure 11.12 is as follows:

Pre-condition: A user is active on the website.
Scenario: Register.
Basic path:

1 Use-case starts when customer presses 'register'.
2 Customer enters name, postal address and e-mail.
3 The post/zip code and e-mail address (@ symbol) will be checked for validity after entry and the user prompted if there is an error.
4 The customer will select 'submit'.
5 The system will check all fields are present and the customer information will be passed to the CRM system.
6 A redirect page will be displayed to thank the customer for registering and provide an option to return to the home page, and the use-case ends.

Post-condition: The customer details have been saved.
Alternative paths: The customer can cancel at stages 2 to 4 before pressing 'submit' and the use-case ends.

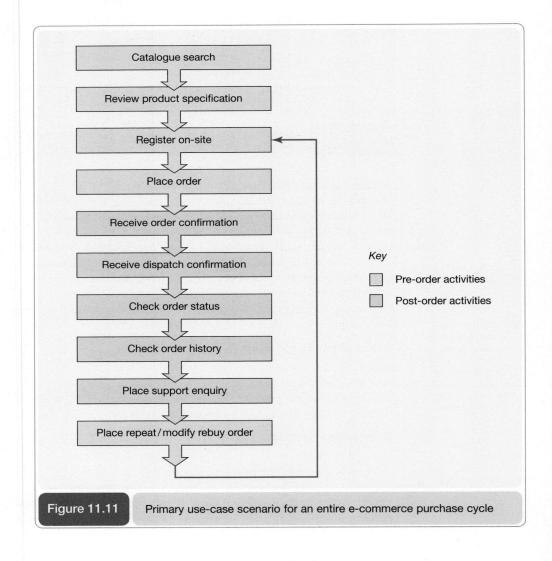

| **Figure 11.11** | Primary use-case scenario for an entire e-commerce purchase cycle |

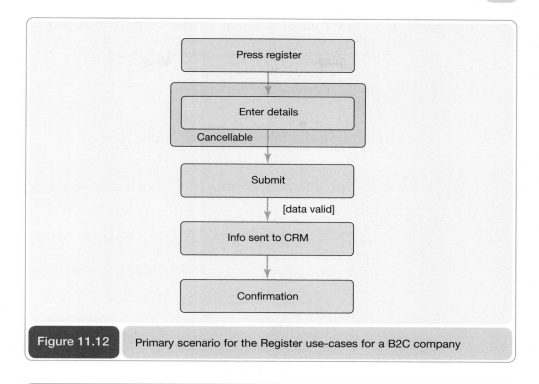

| Figure 11.12 | Primary scenario for the Register use-cases for a B2C company |

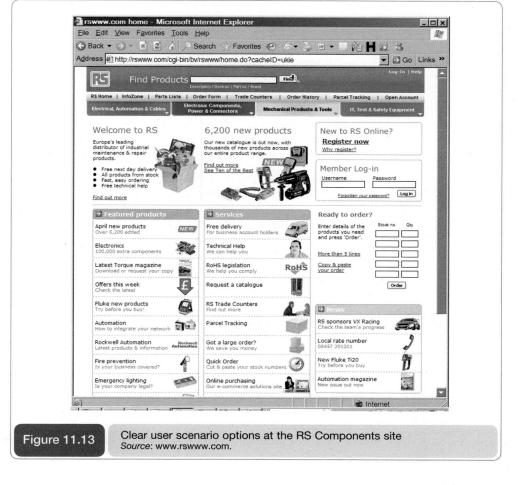

| Figure 11.13 | Clear user scenario options at the RS Components site
Source: www.rswww.com. |

It can be seen that by stating the use-case in this way different issues can be clarified. After the primary scenario is complete, second or alternative scenarios can be developed and added to the primary scenarios as alternatives. For the register scenario, cancel is a secondary scenario; others could include error conditions such as whether the postcode is invalid.

Figure 11.13 illustrates an e-commerce site with clear menu options which is consistent with use-case analysis.

Designing the information architecture

Information architecture

The combination of organization, labelling and navigation schemes composing an information system.

Rosenfeld and Morville (2002) emphasize the importance of **information architecture** to an effective website design. In their book, they give alternative definitions of an information architecture.

They say it is:

1 *The combination of organization, labelling, and navigation schemes within an information system.*
2 *The structural design of an information space to facilitate task completion and intuitive access to content.*
3 *The art and science of structuring and classifying web sites and intranets to help people find and manage information.*
4 *An emerging discipline and community of practice focused on bringing principles of design and architecture to the digital landscape.*

Essentially, in practice, creation of an information architecture involves creating a plan to group information logically – it involves creating a site structure which is often represented as a **site map**. Note, though, that whole books have been written on information architecture, so this is necessarily a simplification! A well-developed information architecture is very important to usability since it determines navigation options. It is also important to search engine optimization (Chapter 9), since it determines how different types of content that users may search for are labelled and grouped.

Site map

A graphical or text depiction of the relationship between different groups of content on a website.

A planned information architecture is essential to large-scale websites that include a large volume of product or support documentation. Information architectures are less important to small-scale websites and brand sites, but even here, the principles can be readily applied and can help make the site more visible to search engines and usable.

The benefits of creating an information architecture include:

- A defined structure and categorization of information will support user and organization goals, i.e. it is a vital aspect of usability.
- It helps increase 'flow' on the site – a user's mental model of where to find content should mirror that of the content on the website.
- Search engine optimization – a higher listing in the search rankings can often be used through structuring and labelling information in a structured way.
- Applicable for integrating offline communications – ads or direct mail can link to a product or campaign landing page to help achieve direct response. A sound URL strategy as explained in Chapter 8 can help this.
- Related content can be grouped to measure the effectiveness of a website as part of design for analysis which is also explained below.

Card sorting

Card sorting or web classification

The process of arranging a way of organizing objects on the website in a consistent manner.

Websites are frequently designed from the perspective of the designer rather than the information user, leading to labels, subject grouping and categories that are not intuitive to the user. **Card sorting or web classification** should categorize web objects (e.g. documents) in order to facilitate information task completion or information goals the user has set.

Robertson (2003) identifies the following questions when using card sorting to aid the process of modelling web classification systems:

- Do the users want to see the information grouped by: subject, task, business or customer groupings, or type of information?
- What are the most important items to put on the main menu?
- How many menu items should there be, and how deep should it go?
- How similar or different are the needs of the users throughout the organization?

Selected groups of users or representatives will be given index cards with the following written on them depending on the aim of the card sorting process:

- Types of document
- Organizational key words and concepts
- Document titles
- Descriptions of documents
- Navigation labels.

The user groups may then be asked to:

- group together cards that they feel relate to each other;
- select cards that accurately reflect a given topic or area;
- organize cards in terms of hierarchy – high-level terms (broad) to low-level terms.

At the end of session the analyst must take the cards away and map the results into a spreadsheet to find out the most popular terms, descriptions and relationships. If two or more different groups are used the results should be compared and reasons for differences should be analysed.

Blueprints

Blueprints
Show the relationships between pages and other content components.

According to Rosenfeld and Morville (2002), **blueprints:**

Show the relationships between pages and other content components, and can be used to portray organization, navigation and labelling systems.

They are often thought of, and referred to, as site maps or site structure diagrams and have much in common with these, except that they are used as a design device clearly showing grouping of information and linkages between pages, rather than a page on the website to assist navigation.

Refer to Figure 11.14 for an example of a site structure diagram for a toy manufacturer website which shows the groupings of content and an indication of the process of task completion also.

Wireframes

Wireframes
Also known as 'schematics', a way of illustrating the layout of an individual web page.

A related technique to blueprints is **wireframes**, which are used by web designers to indicate the eventual layout of a web page. Figure 11.15 shows that the wireframe is so called because it just consists of an outline of the page with the 'wires' of content separating different areas of content or navigation shown by white space.

Wodtke (2002) describes a wireframe (sometimes known as a 'schematic') as:

a basic outline of an individual page, drawn to indicate the elements of a page, their relationships, and their relative importance.

A wireframe will be created for all types of similar page groups, identified at the blueprint (site map) stage of creating the information architecture.

A wireframe focuses on individual pages; the navigation focus becomes where it will be placed on the page.

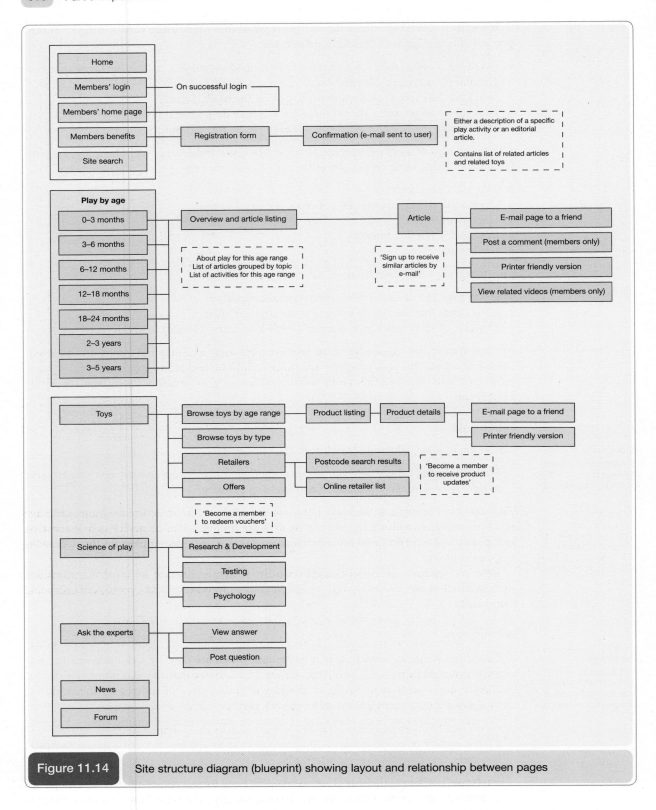

Figure 11.14   Site structure diagram (blueprint) showing layout and relationship between pages

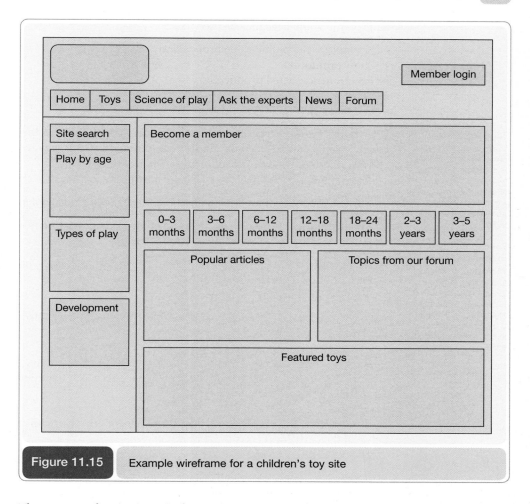

Figure 11.15   Example wireframe for a children's toy site

Storyboarding

The use of static drawings or screenshots of the different parts of a website to review the design concept with user groups.

The process of reviewing wireframes is sometimes referred to as '**storyboarding**', although the term is often applied to reviewing creative ideas rather than formal design alternative. Early designs are drawn on large pieces of paper, or mock-ups are produced using a drawing or paint program.

At the wireframe stage, emphasis is not placed on use of colour or graphics, which will be developed in conjunction with branding or marketing teams and graphic designers and integrated into the site towards the end of the wireframe process.

According to Chaffey and Wood (2005), the aim of a wireframe will be to:

- Integrate consistently available components on the web page (e.g. navigation, search boxes).
- Order and group key types of components together.
- Develop a design that will focus the user on to core messages and content.
- Make correct use of white space to structure the page.
- Develop a page structure that can be easily reused by other web designers.

Common wireframe or template features you may come across are:

- Navigation in columns on left or right and at top or bottom.
- Header areas and footer areas.
- 'Slots' or 'portlets' – these are areas of content such as an article or list of articles placed in boxes on the screen. Often slots will be dynamically populated from a content management system.

Slots on the home page may be used to:

- Summarize the online value proposition
- Show promotions
- Recommend related products
- Feature news, etc.
- Contain ads.

Page template

A standard page layout format which is applied to each page of a website. Typically defined for different page categories (e.g. category page, product page, search page).

Cascading style sheets (CSS)

A simple mechanism for adding style (e.g. fonts, colours, spacing) to web documents. CSS enables different style elements to be controlled across an entire site or section of site.

Wireframes are then transformed into physical site design **page templates** which are now created using standardized **cascading style sheets (CSS)** which enable a standard look and feel to be enforced across different sections of the site.

The standards body W3C (www.w3.org) defines cascading style sheets (CSS) as

a simple mechanism for adding style (e.g. fonts, colors, spacing) to Web documents.

CSS enables different style elements to be controlled across an entire site or section of site. Style elements that are commonly controlled include:

- Typography
- Background colour and images
- Borders and margins.

A style sheet consists of a series of rules that controls the way selected elements should be displayed. For example:

```
body { font-family: Verdana, Arial, Helvetica, Sans Serif, Sans; font-
size: 0.7em; text-align:center; margin: 0; background-color: white;
color: black; }
```

In this example, the HTML 'body' tag is the *selector* and the required style for text defined between the curly brackets is the *declaration*.

The benefits of CSS are:

- *Bandwidth* – pages download faster after initial page load since style definitions only need to be downloaded once as a separate file, not for each page.
- *More efficient development* – through agreeing site style and implementing in CSS as part of page templates, it is more efficient to design a site.
- *Reduces updating and maintenance time* – presentational mark-up is stored in one place separate from the content, making it quicker to update the site globally.
- *Increased interoperability* – adhering to W3C recommendations helps with support of multiple browsers.
- *Increases accessibility* – users can more readily configure the way a site looks or sounds using browsers and other accessibility support tools. Site is more likely to render on a range of access platforms like PDAs and Smartphones and appear well formatted on printers.

Customer orientation

Customer orientation

Developing site content and services to appeal to different customer segments or other members of the audience.

A well-designed site will have been developed to achieve **customer orientation** or customer-centricity. This involves the difficult task of trying to provide content and services to appeal to a wide range of audiences. For a B2B company the three main types of audience are customers, other companies and organizations, and staff. The detailed breakdown of these audiences is illustrated in Figure 11.16. Visit the Dell website (www.dell.com) to see how Dell segments its customer base on the home page into:

- Small office and home users
- Small businesses

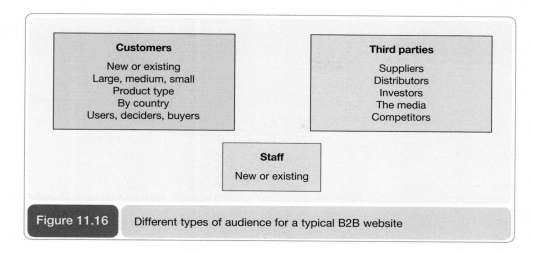

Customers	**Third parties**
New or existing Large, medium, small Product type By country Users, deciders, buyers	Suppliers Distributors Investors The media Competitors

Staff

New or existing

Figure 11.16 — Different types of audience for a typical B2B website

- Medium businesses
- Large businesses
- Corporates
- Government organizations.

Think about how well this approach works. What would be your reaction to being classified as a mere small business or home owner? Do you think this is a valid approach? A similar approach, by Microsoft, is to offer specialized content for IS managers to help them in their investment decisions. Is a more straightforward product-centric structure to the website appropriate?

As well as customer segments, designers also need to take into account variations in the backgrounds of visitors to the site. These can be thought of as four different types of familiarity:

1 *Familiarity with the Internet* – are short cuts provided for those familiar with the Internet? And for novices is there help to lead them through your site?
2 *Familiarity with organization* – for customers who do not know the organization, content is needed to explain who the company is and demonstrate credibility through 'About Us' options and customer testimonials.
3 *Familiarity with organization's products* – even existing customers may not know the full range of your product offering.
4 *Familiarity with your site* – site maps, search and help options are essential, because you may lose potential customers if they cannot be helped when they are lost.

Jakob Nielsen (2000a) says this about novice users:

> *Web users are notoriously fickle: they take one look at a home page and leave after a few seconds if they can't figure it out. The abundance of choice and the ease of going elsewhere puts a huge premium on making it extremely easy to enter a site.*

But he notes that we also need to take account of experts. He says we may eventually move to interfaces where the average site visitor gets a simplified design that is easy to learn and loyal users get an advanced design that is more powerful. But, for now, '*in-depth content and advanced information should be added to sites to provide the depth expected by experts*'.

The principles of customer orientation can be extended from the design of the site to the tactics that are used to deliver services via a website, as explained through Activity 11.4.

Activity 11.4	Applying Patricia Seybold's Customers.com approach to customer orientation

Purpose

To highlight how the principles of customer orientation of services offered can be applied to site design.

Activity

Read the extract of the eight success factors outlined by US industry analyst Patricia Seybold in her book, *Customers.com* (Seybold, 1999). Explain how each of these could be applied to customer-oriented site design for a B2B company.

The eight critical success factors she suggests are:

1 *Target the right customers.* This first and most important principle suggests concentrating on either the most profitable customers, which is one of the tenets of CRM (Chapter 9), or those that cannot be reached so well by other media.

2 *Own the customer's total experience.* By managing the customer's entire experience it should be possible to increase the quality of service and hence promote loyalty. Note that since many services such as delivery are now outsourced, this requires careful selection of partners to deliver this quality service.

3 *Streamline business processes that impact on the customer.* Seybold (1999) gives the example of Federal Express as a company that has used the Internet to re-engineer the service it delivers to customers – ordering, tracking and payment are now all available from the Fedex website.

4 *Provide a 360-degree view of the customer relationship.* This means that different parts of the company must have similar information about the customer to provide a consistent service. It implies integration of the personalization facilities of a website with other databases holding information about the customer. If these databases are not integrated then customer trust may be lost. Integration of call centres with a website is also an implication of this guideline.

5 *Let customers help themselves.* This has the benefit of reducing costs, while at the same time providing faster, more efficient customer service.

6 *Help customers do their jobs.* This guideline is similar to the previous one, but focuses more on providing them with the information needed to do their jobs.

7 *Deliver personalized service.* The importance of delivering personalized service to build a one-to-one relationship with the customer formed the basis for Chapter 9.

8 *Foster community.* Business websites afford good opportunities to create communities of interest since information can be generated which helps customers in their work and again encourages returns to the website. Independent business community sites are also important places for companies to have representation.

No suggested answers supplied.

Elements of site design

Once the requirements of the user are established we can turn our attention to the design of the human–computer interface. Nielsen (2000b) structures his book on web usability according to three main areas, which can be interpreted as follows:

1 *Site design and structure.*
2 *Page design.*
3 *Content design.*

Site design and structure

The structures created by designers for websites will vary greatly according to their audience and the site's purpose, but we can make some general observations about design and structure. We will review the factors designers consider in designing the style, organization and navigation schemes for the site.

Site style

An effective website design will have a style that is communicated through use of colour, images, typography and layout. This should support the way a product is positioned or its brand.

Site personality

The style elements can be combined to develop a personality for a site. We could describe site personalities in the same way we can describe people, such as 'formal' or 'fun'. This personality has to be consistent with the needs of the target audience. A business audience often requires detailed information and prefers an information-intensive style such as that of the Cisco site (www.cisco.com). A consumer site is usually more graphically intensive. Designers need to consider the constraints on the user experience, such as screen resolution and colour depth, the browser used and download speed. The list of constraints which must be tested is illustrated in Chapter 12.

Rosen and Purinton (2004) have assessed the relative importance of design factors which influence a consumer (based on questionnaires of a group of students). They believe there are some basic factors that determine the effectiveness of an e-commerce site:

(i) *Coherence* – simplicity of design, easy to read, use of categories (for browsing products or topics), absence of information overload, adequate font size, uncrowded presentation.
(ii) *Complexity* – different categories of text.
(iii) *Legibility* – use of 'mini home page' on every subsequent page, same menu on every page, site map.

You can see that these authors suggest that simplicity in design is important. Another example of research into website design factors supports the importance of design. Fogg *et al.* (2003) asked students to review sites to assess the credibility of different suppliers based on the website design. They considered these factors most important:

Design look	46.1%
Information design/structure	28.5%
Information focus	25.1%
Company motive	15.5%
Usefulness of information	14.8%
Accuracy of information	14.3%
Name recognition and reputation	14.1%
Advertising	13.8%
Bias of information	11.6%
Tone of the writing	9.0%
Identity of site sponsor	8.8%
Functionality of site	8.6%
Customer service	6.4%
Past experience with site	4.6%
Information clarity	3.7%
Performance on a test	3.6%
Readability	3.6%
Affiliations	3.4%

However, it should be borne in mind that such generalizations can be misleading based on the methodology used. Reported behaviour may be quite different from actual observed behaviour.

Site organization

In their book on information architectures for the web, Rosenfeld and Morville (2002) identify several different **information organization schemes**. These can be applied for different aspects of e-commerce sites, from the whole site through to different parts of the site.

Rosenfeld and Morville (2002) identify the following information organization schemes:

1 *Exact*. Here information can be naturally indexed. If we take the example of books, these can be alphabetical – by author or title; chronological – by date; or for travel books, for example, geographical – by place. Information on an e-commerce site may be presented alphabetically, but this is not suitable for browsing.

2 *Ambiguous*. Here the information requires classification; again taking the examples of books, the Dewey decimal system is an ambiguous classification scheme since the librarians classify books into arbitrary categories. Such an approach is common on an e-commerce site since products and services can be classified in different ways. Content can also be broken down by topic, by task or by audience. The use of metaphors is also common, where the website corresponds to a familiar real-world situation. The Microsoft Windows Explorer, where information is grouped according to Folders, Files and Trash, is an example of a real-world metaphor. The use of the shopping basket metaphor is widespread within e-commerce sites. It should be noted, though, that Nielsen (2000b) believes that metaphors can be confusing if the metaphor is not understood immediately or is misinterpreted.

3 *Hybrid*. Here there will be a mixture of organization schemes, both exact and ambiguous. Rosenfeld and Morville (2002) point out that using different approaches is common on websites but this can lead to confusion, because the user is not clear what mental model is being followed. It is probably best to minimize the number of information organization schemes.

Site navigation schemes

Devising a site that is easy to use is critically dependent on the design of the **site navigation scheme**. Hoffman and Novak (1997) stress the importance of the concept of '**flow**', which essentially describes how easy it is for the users to find the information they need as they move from one page of the site to the next, but also includes other interactions such as filling in on-screen forms. Rettie (2001) summarizes the meaning of flow and gives guidelines on how this concept can be used to enhance the visitor experience. These statements describing flow were used originally by Csikszentmihalyi and more recently by Rettie's research to test for a flow experience on a website:

> (1) *My mind isn't wandering. I am not thinking of something else. I am totally involved in what I am doing. My body feels good. I don't seem to hear anything. The world seems to be cut off from me. I am less aware of myself and my problems.*
>
> (2) *My concentration is like breathing. I never think of it. I am really oblivious to my surroundings after I really get going. I think that the phone could ring, and the doorbell could ring, or the house burn down or something like that. When I start, I really do shut out the whole world. Once I stop, I can let it back in again.*
>
> (3) *I am so involved in what I am doing, I don't see myself as separate from what I am doing.*

Rettie (2001) suggests that the following factors limit flow: long download times, delays to download plug-ins, long registration forms, limited stimulation, boring sites, slow responses, sites which are not intuitive, navigation links that fail, challenge greater than skill, irrelevant advertising. Conversely, reversing these factors can improve flow: quick download times, alternative versions (e.g. text and graphics), automatic completion of forms,

Information organization schemes
The structure chosen to group and categorize information.

Site navigation scheme
Tools provided to the user to move between different information on a website.

Flow
Flow describes how easy it is for users of a site to move between the different pages of content of the site.

opportunities for interaction, rapid responses, navigation which creates choices, predictable navigation for control, segmentation by Internet experience.

Most navigation systems are based upon a hierarchical site structure. When creating the structure, designers have to compromise between the two approaches shown in Figure 11.17. The **narrow and deep** approach has the benefit of fewer choices on each page, making it easier for the user to make their selection, but more clicks are required to reach a particular piece of information (see Figure 11.17(a)). The **broad and shallow** approach requires fewer clicks to reach the same piece of information, but the design of the screen potentially becomes cluttered (Figure 11.17(b)). These approaches are appropriate for the non-technical and technical audiences respectively. A rule of thumb is that site designers should ensure it only takes three clicks to reach any piece of information on a site. This implies the use of a broad and shallow approach on most large sites. This may also be beneficial for SEO purposes. Lynch and Horton (1999) recommend a broad and shallow approach and note that designers should not conceive of a single home page where customers arrive on the site, but of different home pages according to different audience types. Each of the pages in the second row of Figure 11.15(b) could be thought of as an example of a home page which the visitors can bookmark. Nielsen (2000b) points out that many users will not arrive on the home page, but may be referred from another site or advert to a particular page. He calls this process 'deep linking' and site designers should ensure that navigation and context are appropriate for users arriving on these pages.

As well as compromises on depth of links within a site it is also necessary to compromise on the amount of space devoted to menus. Nielsen (2000c) points out that some sites devote so much space to navigation bars that the space available for content is limited. Nielsen (2000c) suggests that the designer of navigation systems should consider the following information that a site user wants to know:

Narrow and deep navigation

Fewer choices, more clicks to reach required content.

Broad and shallow navigation

More choices, fewer clicks to reach required content.

Deep linking

Jakob Nielsen's term for a user arriving at a site deep within its structure.

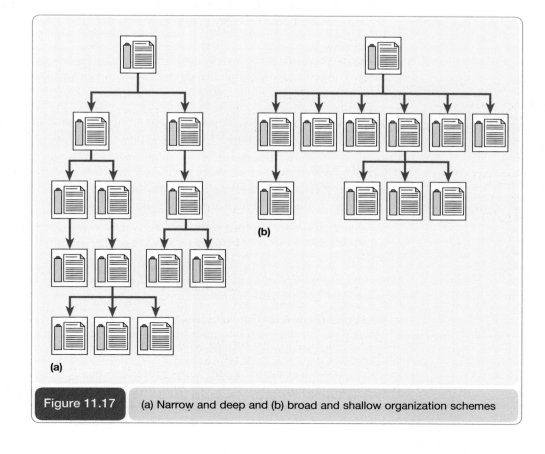

| Figure 11.17 | (a) Narrow and deep and (b) broad and shallow organization schemes |

- *Where am I?* The user needs to know where they are on the site and this can be indicated by highlighting the current location and clear titling of pages. Chaffey *et al.* (2009) refer to this as *context*. *Consistency* of menu locations on different pages is also required to aid cognition. Users also need to know where they are on the web. This can be indicated by a logo, which by convention is at the top or top left of a site.
- *Where have I been?* This is difficult to indicate on a site, but for task-oriented activities such as purchasing a product, the display can show the user that they are at the *n*th stage of an operation, such as making a purchase.
- *Where do I want to go?* This is the main navigation system which gives options for future operations.

To answer these questions, clear succinct labelling is required. Widely used standards such as Home, Main page, Search, Find, Browse, FAQ, Help and About Us are preferable. But for other particular labels it is useful to have what Rosenfeld and Morville (2002) call 'scope notes' – an additional explanation. These authors also argue against the use of iconic labels or pictures without corresponding text since they are open to misinterpretation and take longer to process.

Since using the navigation system may not enable the user to find the information they want rapidly, alternatives have to be provided by the site designers. These alternatives include search, advanced search, browse and site map facilities.

Page design

The page design involves creating an appropriate layout for each page. The main elements of a particular page layout are the title, navigation and content. Standard content such as copyright may be added to every page as a footer. Issues in page design include:

- *Page elements.* The proportion of page devoted to content compared to all other content such as headers, footers and navigation elements. The location of these elements also needs to be considered. It is conventional for the main menu to be at the top or on the left. The use of a menu system at the top of the browser window enables more space for content below.
- *The use of frames.* This is generally discouraged for the reasons given in Chapter 12.
- *Resizing.* A good page layout design should allow for the user to change the size of text or work with different monitor resolutions.
- *Consistency.* Page layout should be similar for all areas of the site unless more space is required, for example for a discussion forum or product demonstration.
- *Printing.* Layout should allow for printing or provide an alternative printing format.

Content design

Copywriting for the web is an evolving art form, but many of the rules for good copywriting are as for any medium. Common errors we see on websites are:

- too much knowledge assumed of the visitor about the company, its products and services;
- using internal jargon about products, services or departments – using undecipherable acronyms.

Web copywriters also need to take account of the user reading the content on-screen. Approaches to deal with the limitations imposed by the customer using a monitor include:

- writing more concisely than in brochures;
- chunking or breaking text into units of 5–6 lines at most; this allows users to scan rather than read information on web pages;
- using lists with headline text in larger font;
- never including too much on a single page, except when presenting lengthy information such as a report which may be easier to read on a single page;
- using hyperlinks to decrease page sizes or help achieve flow within copy, either by linking to sections further down a page or linking to another page.

Hofacker (2001) describes five stages of human information processing when a website is being used. These can be applied to both page design and content design to improve usability. Each of the five stages summarized in Table 11.6 acts as a hurdle, since if the site design or content is too difficult to process, the customer cannot progress to the next stage.

Table 11.6	A summary of information web stages described by Hofacker (2001)

Stage	Description	Applications
1 **Exposure**	Content must be present for long enough to be processed.	Content on banner ads may not be on screen long enough for processing and cognition.
2 **Attention**	User's eyes will be drawn towards headings and content, not graphics and moving items on a web page (Nielsen, 2000b).	Emphasis and accurate labelling of headings is vital to gain a user's attention. Evidence suggests that users do not notice banner adverts, suffering from 'banner blindness'.
3 **Comprehension and perception**	The user's interpretation of content.	Designs that use common standards and metaphors and are kept simple will be more readily comprehended.
4 **Yielding and acceptance**	Is the information (copy) presented accepted by customers?	Copy should reference credible sources and present counter-arguments as necessary.
5 **Retention**	As for traditional advertising, this describes the extent to which the information is remembered.	An unusual style or high degree of interaction leading to flow and user satisfaction is more likely to be recalled.

Source: Adapted from Hofacker (2001).

Using these layers we can map content across different access levels to produce a site which is integrated across the needs of its audiences. This also relates to the section on security since different access levels may be given for different information.

Web accessibility

Accessibility
An approach to site design intended to accommodate site usage using different browsers and settings particularly required by the visually impaired.

Web accessibility is another core requirement for websites. It is about allowing all users of a website to interact with it regardless of disabilities they may have or the web browser or platform they are using to access the site. The visually impaired are the main audience that designing an accessible website can help. However, increased usage of mobile or wireless access devices make consideration of accessibility important.

The quote below shows the importance of the accessibility to a visually impaired user of a website who uses a screen-reader which reads out the navigation options and content.

For me being online is everything. It's my hi-fi, it's my source of income, it's my super-market, it's my telephone. It's my way in.

(Lynn Holdsworth, screen-reader user, web developer and programmer, RNIB, www.rnib.org.uk)

Accessibility legislation
Legislation intended to protect users of websites with disabilities, including those with visual disability.

Remember that many countries now have specific **accessibility legislation** to which website owners are subject. This is often contained within disability and discrimination acts. In the UK, the relevant act is the Disability and Discrimination Act (DDA) 1995. Recent amendments to the DDA makes it unlawful to discriminate against disabled people in the way in which a company recruits and employs people, provides services or provides education. Providing accessible websites is a requirement of Part II of the Disability and

Discrimination Act published in 1999 and required by law from 2002. This is most important for sites which provide a service; the 2002 code of practice gives this example:

An airline company provides a flight reservation and booking service to the public on its website. This is a provision of a service and is subject to the Act.

Although there is a moral imperative for accessibility, there is also a business imperative. The main arguments in favour of accessibility are:

1 *Number of visually impaired people* – in many countries there are millions of visually impaired people varying from 'colour blind' to partially sighted to blind.
2 *Number of users of less popular browsers or variation in screen display resolution.* Microsoft Internet Explorer is now the dominant browser, but other browsers have a loyal following amongst the visually impaired (for example screen-readers and Lynx, a text-only browser) and early adopters (for example Mozilla Firefox, Safari and Opera). If a website does not display well in these browsers, then you may lose these audiences. Complete Activity 11.5 to review variation in access rate.
3 *More visitors from natural listings of search engines.* Many of the techniques used to make sites more usable also assist in search engine optimization. Clearer navigation, text alternatives for images and site maps can all help improve a site's position in the search engine rankings.
4 *Legal requirements.* In many countries it is a legal requirement to make websites accessible.

Guidelines for creating accessible websites are produced by the governments of different countries and non-government organizations such as charities. Internet standards organizations such as the World Wide Web Consortium have been active in promoting guidelines for web accessibility through its Website Accessibility Initiative (WAI), see www.w3.org/WAI.

Activity 11.5 — Allowing for the range in access devices

One of the benefits of accessibility requirements is that it helps website owners and web agencies consider the variation in platforms used to access websites.

Questions

1 Update the compilation in Table 11.7 to the latest values using Onestat.com or other data from web analytics providers.

2 Explain the variations. Which browsers and screen resolutions do you think should be supported?

Table 11.7 Summary of the range in browsers and screen resolutions used at the time of writing

	Web browser popularity			Screen resolution popularity	
1	Firefox	39.7%	1	1200 × 800	20%
2	Internet Explorer	27.9%	2	1280 × 1024	16%
3	Chrome	19%	3	1440 × 900	12.3%
4	Safari	10.3%	4	1024 × 768	10%
5	Opera	0.8%	5	1680 × 1050	9%

Source: Visitors to DaveChaffey.com, September 2008, used by students and professionals worldwide. Note that the formerly standard resolution of 800 by 600 is now less than 3%.

There are three different priority levels which it describes as follows:

- *Priority 1 (Level A).* A Web content developer must satisfy this checkpoint. Otherwise, one or more groups will find it impossible to access information in the document. Satisfying this checkpoint is a basic requirement for some groups to be able to use Web documents.
- *Priority 2 (Level AA).* A Web content developer should satisfy this checkpoint. Otherwise, one or more groups will find it difficult to access information in the document. Satisfying this checkpoint will remove significant barriers to accessing Web documents.
- *Priority 3 (Level AAA).* A Web content developer may address this checkpoint. Otherwise, one or more groups will find it somewhat difficult to access information in the document. Satisfying this checkpoint will improve access to Web documents.

So, for many companies the standard is to meet Priority 1 and Priority 2 or 3 where practical.

Some of the most important Priority 1 elements are indicated by these 'Quick Tips' from the WAI:

Alt tags

Alt tags (alternative tags) appear after an image tag and contain a phrase associated with that image.

- Images and animations. Use **alt tags** to describe the function of each visual.
- Image maps. Use the client-side map and text for hotspots.
- Multimedia. Provide captioning and transcripts of audio, and descriptions of video.
- Hypertext links. Use text that makes sense when read out of context. Avoid 'click here'.
- Page organization. Use headings, lists and consistent structure. Use CSS for layout and style where possible.

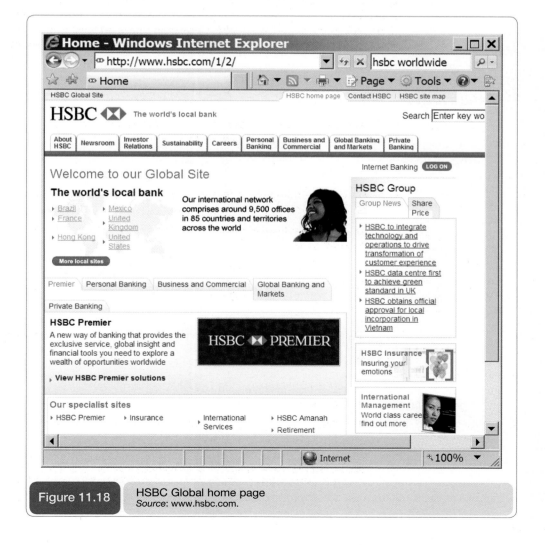

Figure 11.18	HSBC Global home page

Source: www.hsbc.com.

- Graphs and charts. Summarize or use the longdesc attribute.
- Scripts, applet and plug-ins. Provide alternative content in case active features are inaccessible or unsupported.
- Frames. Use the noframes element and meaningful titles.
- Tables. Make line-by-line reading sensible. Summarize.
- Check your work. Validate. Use the tools, checklist and guidelines at www.w3.org/TR/WCAG.

Figure 11.18 is an example of a site which meets brand and business objectives while supporting accessibility through resizing of screen resolution, text resizing and alternative image text.

Case Study 11.1   Dabs.com refines its web store

This case study highlights the importance placed on website design as part of the customer experience by dabs.com. It shows the need to upgrade the infrastructure regularly to deliver a satisfactory experience which is competitive with other e-retailers. dabs.com is one of the UK's leading Internet retailers of IT and technology products from manufacturers such as Sony, Hewlett-Packard, Toshiba and Microsoft. The case also highlights some of the strategic issues with operating an e-business as it describes the growth of the company.

Company background and history

Dabs.com was originally created by entrepreneur David Atherton in partnership with writer Bruce Smith (the name 'Dabs' comes from the combined initials of their two names). Dabs.com is a wholly owned subsidiary of BT, but the Dabs branding remains on its site. But BT has used the Dabs website design and catalogue system for its own BT Shop (www.shop.bt.com). Turnover for the 2006 financial year was £160 million (£15 million from elsewhere in Europe) with a gross profit of £24 million.

Dabs Direct was launched in 1990, as a mail order firm which mainly promoted itself through ads in home technology magazines such as *Personal Computer World* and *Computer Shopper*.

Dabs.com was launched in 1999 at the height of the dot-com boom, but unlike many dot-com start-up businesses, it was based on an existing offline business.

In its first year, dabs.com was loss-making with £1.2 million lost in 2000–1, which was partly due to including free delivery as part of the proposition to acquire new customers.

In 2003, the company opened its first 'bricks and mortar' store at Liverpool John Lennon Airport and it has also opened an operation in France (www.dabs.fr). The French site remains, but the retail strategy has now ended

since margins were too low, despite a positive effect in building awareness of the brand in retail locations.

Strategy

The importance that dabs.com owners place on customer experience and usability is suggested by their mission statement, which places customer experience at its core together with choice and price. dabs.com's mission is:

> *to provide customers with a quick and easy way of buying the products they want, at the most competitive prices around, delivered directly to their door.*

Growth has been conservatively managed, since as a privately held company dabs.com has to grow profitably rather than take on debts. Dabs.com has reviewed the potential of other European countries for distribution and may select a country where broadband access is high, such as Sweden or the Netherlands. A country such as Italy, where consumers traditionally prefer face-to-face sales, would not be an early candidate to target for an opening. Dabs.com targets the B2B market as well as the consumer market, offering a different version of the site for business users and 60% of sales are from this source. In terms of products, dabs.com has focused on computers and related products, but is considering expanding into new categories or even ranges. Initially these will be related to what computer users need while they are working.

Dabs.com in 2005

In 2005, dabs.com is a £200 million company with 235 staff, holding 15,000 lines for a customer base of almost 1.5 million and processing around 5,000 customer orders every day. Dabs.com has 8 million visits a month from around 750,000 unique users. Its catalogue contains 20,000 products with laptops, LCD monitors and external hard drives among the main sales lines.

NCC (2005) reports that dabs.com believes that what its customers require is a dynamic site that provides comprehensive information on its product ranges, delivery charges, returns policy, financing services and rewards scheme. It also provides dabs.tv, a video service that allows customers to see more complex products in greater detail.

Jonathan Wall, dabs.com's marketing director, sees security as important as part of the customer experience, and to protect the business. He says:

> We were one of the first e-businesses to adopt Visa's 'Verified by Visa' 3D secure payment authentication system and we've also implemented MasterCard's SecureCode variant. We've always worked closely with both credit card companies and it's a concern that dates back to our mail order side. The threat of being attacked and defrauded is always in the forefront of our thoughts.

Delivery

To ensure delivery as promised, Jonathan Wall explains the importance dabs.com attach to IT. 'We invest as much in our highly automated warehouse as we do in our marketing,' says Wall. 'Our systems use a sophisticated combination of dynamic bins and unique product numbering. A lot of the management team come from technical backgrounds. Our back office system was written in OpenVMS by our IT director. Our sales processing system was written in-house.'

Talking to *IT Week* (2003), Wall explained how the initial growth occurred, and how future growth will be sustained: 'We dominate the PC hobbyist/IT professional sector, but our business must evolve. We want to cast our net further so that we are appealing to people who are interested in technology as a whole. New customers need a new approach. We have built a new environment and a new website for this target audience.'

In mid-2003 dabs.com launched a site to help it achieve sales to the new audience. Research was used to help develop the new site. The usability of the existing website was tested and the new concept was also shown to a focus group. After analysing the responses dabs.com created a pilot site, which the same focus group then approved. In total, the new site took 10 months to develop and was an investment of £750,000.

The 2005 site update

NCC (2005) says Wall makes the business case for the new site as follows:

> Our new site will take us right up there to the top of the field. You have to try and stay ahead. We'll have

guided navigation, still quite rare on a UK site, which will help customers to find what they're looking for more intuitively. Early e-commerce customers knew that they specifically wanted a Sony Vaio laptop, for example. New customers just know that they want a laptop that's small and fast and costs less than £1,000. Guided navigation means they can search according to a product's attributes rather than specific brands and models.

Since the average selling price of laptops is going down, slim margins are decreased further. Wall says: 'Selling electronic equipment on the web has traditionally been passive but by redesigning our site we'll be able to show customers what another extra £50 spent on a laptop will buy them.'

Although the previous site was updated only 2 years before, he describes the need to keep ahead of competitors as 'a cat and mouse thing'.

But new site advances must be combined with competitive prices, Wall says:

> Online customers are price-loyal, not retailer-loyal. The customer is only as loyal as the cheapest price they can pay for a product. It means your competitors are only ever one click away. We have to do everything to keep our customers on our site. Getting them to pay that price to you, rather than your competitor, means that you'll need to exploit the constantly-evolving benefits of digital technology to make their buying experience on your site as fluent and satisfactory as possible.

On-site search capabilities

Part of the new site is improved on-site search capabilities from Endeca, which powers the search of Wal-Mart and Circuit City sites in the US. Search is important to increasing conversion rates, and so increasing sales, since if a user is not presented with a relevant product when they search, they are likely to try another retailer. The search capability should strike a balance between delivering too many results and too few. *Channel Register* (2005) reports that dabs.com hopes to increase conversion rate by up to 50% by updating the site's search and navigation features. Current conversion rate is 3.5% and it is hoped this will be increased to nearer 5%.

Endeca's new search allows users to select products by attributes including price, brand and even size and weight. This method of narrowing down the search should result in the customer being left to choose from a list of 10 or 20 products rather than hundreds.

Another aspect of the business case for the new site is to ensure the customer makes the right decision since product returns are costly for dabs.com and annoying for the customer.

Jonathan Wall explained: 'When we launched the website in 1999 people knew what they wanted. Now we find a large tranche of customers might know the type of product they want to buy but not which model they want. The new site is about guiding them through the process.'

Accessibility

Since dabs.com has tech-savvy customers, it has to support them as they adopt new ways of browsing. Dabs.com found that by 1995 nearly a fifth of its users were using the Mozilla Firefox browser, so a further requirement for the new site was to make it accessible to users browsing with a range of browsers such as Firefox, Opera and Apple's Safari.

Marketing communications

Marketing communications approaches used by dabs.com are summarized in Mini case study 9.3 'Electronic retailers cut back on their e-communications spend'. For customer acquisition, the main communications tools that are used are:

- Search engine marketing (the main investment)
- Referrals from affiliates (this has been reduced)
- Online display advertising on third-party sites (limited)
- PR
- Sponsorship (shirt sponsorship for Premiership team Fulham).

Source: Channel Register (2005); IT Week (2003); NCC (2005).

Questions

1 The management of dabs.com has invested in several major upgrades to its online presence in order to improve the online customer experience. Assess the reasons for the need to invest in site upgrades by referring to the dabs.com example. To what extent do you think major, regular site upgrades are inevitable?

2 Compare the quality of the online customer experience of dabs.com by visiting the site and those of its competitors such as www.ebuyer.com and www.euroffice.com. Explain the categories of criteria you have used to make your assessment.

Focus on   Security design for e-business

Security is a prime concern of e-business managers. The principal concern is the security of information: both about customers and internal company data about finance, logistics, marketing and employees. Indeed, we saw in Chapter 4 that securing customer information is a legal requirement under data protection laws in many countries. These risks apply to all companies, but larger companies tend to be more at risk from targeted attacks. Information used within e-business systems must be safeguarded from a range of hazards. The range of risks faced by organizations is summarized in Box 11.3.

Box 11.3   Common security threats and solutions for the e-business

The BERR (2008) Information Security Breaches Survey highlights the extent of the security problem for e-businesses. Companies that had a security incident are shown in Table 11.8.

Figure 11.19 shows the most common security incidents. You can see that internal security problems are an increasing issue.

The main website security risks

There are also more specific threats to website owners. Specialist website security consultants Watson Hall (www.watsonhall.com) consider the top 10 Internet security risks and solutions to be:

Table 11.8	Security incidents		
	Small < 50 staff	**Large > 250 staff**	**Very large > 500 staff**
Companies that had security incident last year	45%	72%	96%
Average number incidents (median of average in brackets)	6 (100)	15 (200)	> 400 (> 1300)
Average cost of worst incident	£10 to £20K	£90k to £170K	£1 million to £2 million

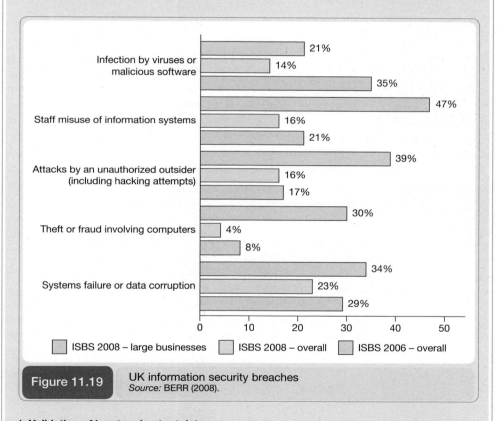

Figure 11.19   UK information security breaches
Source: BERR (2008).

1 Validation of input and output data

All data used by the website (from users, other servers, other websites and internal systems) must be validated for type (e.g. numeric, date, string), length (e.g. 200 characters maximum, or a positive integer), syntax (e.g. product codes begin with 2 letters and are followed by 5 digits) and business rules (e.g. televisions can only cost between £100 and £2,000, daily credit limit must not be exceeded). All data written as output (displayed) need to be safe to view in a browser, e-mail client or other software and the integrity of any data that are returned must be checked. Utilizing Asynchronous JavaScript and XML (AJAX) or Adobe Flex increases complexity and the possible attack vectors.

SEO spamming is a common problem to site owners where disreputable companies use scripts to automate adding links to their sites for search engine optimization purposes through comment forms, in blogs, forums and social networks. To combat this a **CAPTCHA** system such as reCAPTCHA (www.recaptcha.net) is required.

2 Direct data access (and theft)

If data exist, they can potentially be viewed or extracted. Avoid storing data that you do not need on the website and its database(s) – for example, some data relating to payment cards should never be stored. Poorly developed systems may allow access to data through SQL injection compromises, insufficient input and output data validation (see No 1 above) or poor system security.

3 Data poisoning

If users can amend or delete data inappropriately and these are then used to update your internal systems, business information is being lost. This can be hard to detect and it is important that the business rules are examined and enforced to validate data changes to ensure poisoning is not occurring.

4 Malicious file execution

Uploaded files or other data feeds may not be what they seem. Never allow user-supplied input to be used in any file name or path (e.g. URLs or file system references). Uploaded files may also contain a malicious payload so should not be stored in web-accessible locations. Note that Google will automatically identify some sites that contain malware within the search results listings. **Malware** such as key loggers are also a significant problem for infection of end-user computers. They are often delivered as Trojan e-mail attachments.

5 Authentication and session management

Websites rely on identifying users to provide access permissions to data and functions. If authentication, authorization and session management can be circumvented or altered, a user could access resources they are not allowed to. Beware especially of how password reminders, remember-me, change password, log-out and updating account details are handled and how session tokens are used, and always have log-in forms on dedicated and encrypted (SSL) pages.

6 System architecture and configuration

The information system architecture model should address the sensitivity of data identified during the requirements and specification phase of a website project. This may entail having separate web, application and database servers or involve clustering, load balancing or virtualization. Sufficient and safe logging, monitoring and alerting facilities need to be built in to allow audit.

7 Phishing

Phishing, where users are misled into believing some other entity is or belongs to their own organization, is best tackled through user education, but the way the website is designed, its architecture and how it communicates with users can reduce the risk.

Phishing (pronounced 'fishing') is a specialized form of online identity theft. The most common form is where a spam e-mail is sent out purporting to be from an organization such as a bank or payment service. Recipients are then invited to visit a website to update their details after entering their username and password.

Phishing involves 'spoofing' or where one party masquerades as someone else. Spoofing can be of two sorts:

- IP spoofing is used to gain access to confidential information by creating false identification data such as the originating network (IP) address. The objective of

CAPTCHA
CAPTCHA stands for 'Completely Automated Public Turing test to tell Computers and Humans Apart'. It requires a person submitting a web form to enter letters or numbers from an image to validate that they are a genuine user.

Malware
Malicious software or toolbars, typically downloaded via the Internet, which acts as a 'Trojan horse' by executing unwanted activities such as key-logging of user passwords or viruses which may collect e-mail addresses

Phishing
Obtaining personal details online through sites and e-mails masquerading as legitimate businesses.

Firewall

A specialized software application mounted on a server at the point where the company is connected to the Internet to prevent unauthorized access.

this access can be espionage, theft or simply to cause mischief, generate confusion and damage corporate public image or political campaigns. **Firewalls** can be used to reduce this threat.

- Site spoofing, i.e. fooling the organization's customers using a similar URL such as www.amazno.com, can divert customers to a site which is not the bona fide retailer.

Firewalls can be used to minimize the risk of security breaches by hackers and viruses. Firewalls are usually created as software mounted on a separate server at the point the company is connected to the Internet. Firewall software can then be configured to accept only links from trusted domains representing other offices in the company or key account customers.

8 Denial of service

Whilst malicious users might try to swamp the web server with a vast number of requests or actions that degrade its performance (filling up logs, uploading large files, undertaking tasks that require a lot of memory repeatedly), **denial-of-service** attacks include locking out valid user accounts or may be caused by coding problems (e.g. memory leaks, resources not being released).

Denial-of-service attack

Also known as a distributed denial-of-service (DDOS) attack, these involve a hacker group taking control of many 'zombie' computers attached to the Internet whose security has been comprised. This 'botnet' is then used to make many requests to a target server, so overloading it and preventing access to other visitors.

9 System information leakage

Web servers, errors, staff, partner organizations, search engines and rubbish can all be the source of important information about your website – its technologies, business logic and security methods. An attacker can use such information to their advantage so it is important to avoid system information leakage as far as possible.

10 Error handling

Exceptions such as user data validation messages, missing pages and server errors should be handled by the code so that a custom page is displayed that does not provide any system information to the user (see No. 9 above). Logging and alerting of unusual conditions should be enabled and these should allow subsequent audit.

Given the level of threats, it seems that many companies still do not have solutions in place, judging by these figures from BERR (2008):

- 10% of websites that accept payment details do not encrypt them.
- 21% spend less than 1% of their IT budget on information security.
- 35% have no controls over staff use of Instant Messaging.
- 48% of disaster recovery plans have not been tested in the last year.
- 52% do not carry out any formal security risk assessment.
- 67% do nothing to prevent confidential data leaving on USB sticks, etc.
- 78% of companies that had computers stolen did not encrypt hard disks.
- 79% are not aware of the contents of BS 7799/ISO 27001.
- 84% of companies do not scan outgoing e-mail for confidential data.

Information security management system

An organizational process to protect information assets.

Information security policy

A definition of the organizational approaches to information security and the responsibilities of employees in protecting information.

Given the extent of the security risks described in Figure 11.19, many organizations now implement a formal **information security management system**.

The information management strategy will mandate that there is an **information security policy**. This may be a policy developed in-house, or adoption of a security standard such as British Standard BS 7799 which has now been upgraded and ratified as international standard ISO/IEC 17799.

ISO 17799 has comprehensive coverage of different risks and approaches to management of security. It recommends the following processes:

1 *Plan* – perform business risk analysis
2 *Do* – internal controls to manage the applicable risks

3 *Check* – a management review to verify effectiveness

4 *Act* – action changes required as part of the review as necessary.

ISO 17799/BS 7799 helps give a framework by which to manage the risks to the information evident from Figure 11.19. It requires the following areas of information security management to be defined:

- *Section 1: Security policy.* Describes the organization's requirements and scope of security for different business areas and sites. It also should demonstrate the support of senior management in controlling and owning security.
- *Section 2: Organizational security.* Describes how the company manages security including different staff responsibilities for security, how security incidents are reported, actioned and reviewed as a standard business activity to improve security.

> **Information asset register (IAR)**
> A repository for the types, value and ownership of all information within an organization.

- *Section 3: Asset classification and control.* BS 7799 recommends that an **information asset register (IAR)** be created, detailing every information asset within the organization such as databases, personnel records, contracts, software licences, publicity material. For each asset, responsibility is defined. The value of each asset can then be determined to ensure appropriate security is in place.
- *Section 4: Personnel security.* This ensures there is clarity within job definitions and employment contracts, to reduce the risk of human error leading to information loss and to ensure that staff understand what their rights and responsibilities are concerning information security. Staff training is also important to achieve this.
- *Section 5: Physical and environmental security.* This defines physical access to buildings. It also considers how information can be protected from threats such as fire and flood.
- *Section 6: Communications and operations management.* Guidelines on the day-to-day operation of information systems is the largest section of BS 7799. It covers acceptance criteria for new or updated systems, virus defence software, e-mail and website usage, network access and back-up and restore systems.
- *Section 7: Access control.* This defines how to protect access to information systems through access control mechanisms (username and password procedures with different security clearance for different applications and types of information).
- *Section 8: System development and maintenance.* This specifies how new systems must be designed and procured with security in mind.

> **Business continuity management or disaster recovery**
> Measures taken to ensure that information can be restored and accessed if the original information and access method are destroyed.

- *Section 9: Business continuity management.* **Business continuity management or disaster recovery** specifies how the organization will be able to continue to function in the event of a major event such as a fire or flood or other damage to information systems. Use of off-site back-ups and alternative systems is key to this.
- *Section 10: Compliance.* This specifies how an organization will comply with the relevant UK and EU law related to information security management. Implementing BS 7799 is a good way of helping ensure that a business does comply with these requirements. Regular audit and review needs to occur to ensure the organization remains compliant.

We will now cover some of the main threats to security in the e-business which need to be managed.

Managing computer viruses

> **Computer virus**
> A program capable of self-replication allowing it to spread from one machine to another. It may be malicious and delete data, or benign.

Computer viruses are a significant threat to company and personal information since it is estimated that there are now over 100,000 of them.

Types of virus

There are many different mechanisms by which computer viruses reproduce or 'self-replicate' and spread from one machine to another. The main different types are:

Boot-sector virus
Occupies boot record of hard and floppy disks and is activated during computer start-up.

Worm
A small program that self-replicates and transfers across a network from machine to machine. A form of virus.

Trojan
A virus that masquerades as a bona fide application.

1 *Boot-sector virus.* **Boot-sector viruses** were most important when floppy disks were widely used.

2 *Worms.* A **worm** is a small computer program that replicates itself and then transfers itself from one machine to the next. Since no human interaction is required, worms can spread very rapidly. For example, the 'Code Red' worm replicated itself over 250,000 times in just nine hours on 19 July 2001. In 2003, the 'Slammer' worm exploited a security loophole in the Microsoft SQL server database product and rapidly infected 75,000 machines. Each infected machine sent out so much traffic that many other servers failed also. This was one of the fastest spreading viruses of all time, as Figure 11.20 shows. In future it seems such worms will bring the Internet to a complete standstill.

3 *Macro-viruses.* Macro-viruses are piggybacked on documents created by office applications such as Microsoft Word and Excel. Office software such as this has a macro-facility to help users record common actions. One of the best-known macro-viruses is 'Melissa'. This struck in March 1999 and it marked a new trend as it combined a macro-virus with one that accessed the address book of Microsoft Outlook to e-mail itself to new victims. This was one of the fastest spreading viruses in history and it is estimated that it affected over a million PCs. In 2002, the author of the 'Melissa' virus, David L. Smith, was sentenced to 20 months in prison in the US.

4 *E-mail attachment viruses.* These viruses are activated when a user of an e-mail program opens an attachment. 'Melissa' is an example of such a virus. The 'Love Bug' virus contains the subject line 'I love you', while the message contains the text 'kindly check the attached LOVELETTER from me' which is an attached file called LOVE-LETTER-FOR-YOU. TXT.VBS. The virus deleted image and audio files and accessed Internet servers to send out different versions of itself. According to ClickZ (2003) it was estimated that nearly $9 billion damage was done through this virus. Much of the cost is not the loss of data, but the cost of hiring specialists to rectify the problem or staff time lost.

5 *Trojan viruses.* A **Trojan** is a virus that masquerades as a bona fide application. They are named after the Greek myth of the giant wooden horse used by attackers to gain access to Troy. Examples include utilities such as a file-sharing program, a screen saver, upgrades to some system components and even imitation anti-virus programs. The advantage for

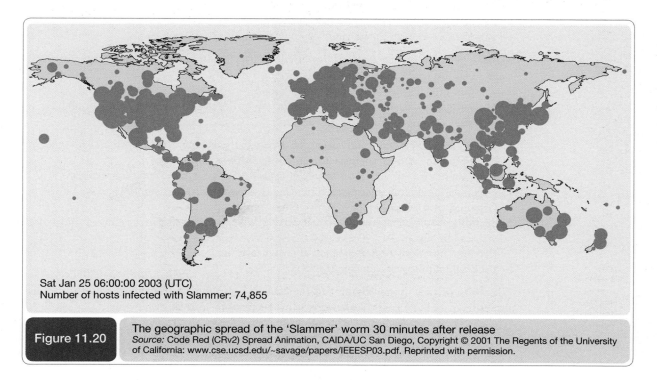

Sat Jan 25 06:00:00 2003 (UTC)
Number of hosts infected with Slammer: 74,855

Figure 11.20

The geographic spread of the 'Slammer' worm 30 minutes after release
Source: Code Red (CRv2) Spread Animation, CAIDA/UC San Diego, Copyright © 2001 The Regents of the University of California: www.cse.ucsd.edu/~savage/papers/IEEESP03.pdf. Reprinted with permission.

virus writers is that the programs can be much larger. One of the most famous Trojans is 'Back Orifice', reputedly developed by a hacking group known as 'Cult of the Dead Cow'. This could be attached to other larger files and gave complete access to a machine for a hacker.

6 *Hoax e-mail viruses.* These are warnings about non-existent viruses which ask the recipient to send the warning on to their friends. They are usually malicious, but can contain instructions on how to remove the virus by deleting files which could cause damage. They cause disruption through time lost.

Protecting computer systems against viruses

All organizations and individuals require a policy to combat the potential impact of viruses given the frequency with which new, damaging viruses are released. Even individual computer users at home should think through the steps they can take to counter viruses. There are two approaches that can be combined to counter viruses. These are using the right tools and educating staff to change practices.

Anti-virus software
Software to detect and eliminate viruses.

Anti-virus software is well known as a tool to protect systems from viruses. Many businesses and homes now use products such as McAfee Virus Scan and Symantec Norton Anti-Virus to protect themselves against the threat of viruses. Unfortunately, a lot more action is required than initial purchase for the anti-virus software to be effective. New viruses are continually released so it is essential that regular updates be obtained.

Companies also need to decide on the frequency of scanning memory and computer files, since a full scan on start-up can take a long time. Most anti-virus software now seeks to identify viruses when they first arrive (real-time scanning). A further issue is how good the anti-virus tool is at identifying e-mail and macro-viruses, since it is less straightforward for these types of virus to be identified.

Managed e-mail service
Receipt and transmission of e-mails is managed by a third party.

Another approach is to use an external **managed e-mail service** which scans e-mails before they arrive in the organization and then scans e-mails for viruses when they are sent. For example, Messagelabs (www.messagelabs.com) scans 2.7 billion e-mails a day for 7,500 companies worldwide. In August 2008 it reported that:

- 78% of messages were spam
- 1 in 88 contained a virus
- 1 in 522 was a phishing attempt.

Managed e-mail services are likely to be more effective than using internal anti-virus software since the service providers are experts in this field. They will also be able to identify and respond to e-mail worm attacks more rapidly.

To summarize, organizations need a policy to be developed for use of anti-virus software. This should specify:

1 The preferred anti-virus software to be used on all machines.
2 The frequency and mechanism for updating anti-virus software.
3 The frequency with which the whole end-user PC is system-scanned for viruses.
4 Organizational blocking of attachments with uncommon extensions.
5 Organizational disabling of macros in office applications.
6 Scanning to be performed on mail servers when e-mails are first received and before viruses are sent.
7 Recommendations on use of spam-filtering software.
8 Back-up and recovery mechanisms.

Education of staff in identifying and then acting upon the different types of virus can also limit the impact of viruses. Some general instructions include the following:

1 Do not open attachments to e-mails from people you don't know (reduce transmission of e-mail attachment viruses). Only open attachments which look legitimate, for example Word documents with relevant names. Some viruses use file extensions that are not

commonly used such as .pif, .scr or .vbs. Viewing documents rather than opening them for editing can also reduce the risk of transmission.

2 Download software only from the official source, and always check for viruses before installing the software (reduces risk of Trojan horse viruses).

3 Disable or turn off macros in Word or Excel unless you use them regularly (reduces risk of macro-viruses).

4 Back up important files daily if this function is not performed by a system administrator.

Controlling information service usage

Issues in controlling information service typically involve one of two problems from the employer's perspective. First, hardware and software resources provided for work purposes are used for personal purposes, thus reducing productivity. Secondly, monitoring the use of information introduces legal issues of surveillance. Monitoring of information service usage includes checking for:

- Use of e-mail for personal purposes.
- Inappropriate use of e-mail, possibly leading to legal action against the company.
- Use of Internet or websites for personal use.

The problems in e-mail usage are covered in the later section on e-mail management. The extent of these issues, particularly in larger organizations, is apparent from Figure 11.21.

Monitoring of electronic communications

Employee communications monitoring
Companies monitor staff e-mails and web sites they access.

Employee communications monitoring or surveillance is used by organizations to reduce productivity losses through time wasting.

Simple calculations highlight the wastage when staff time is spent on non-productive work. If an employee earning £25,000 per year spends 30 minutes each day of a 5-day week

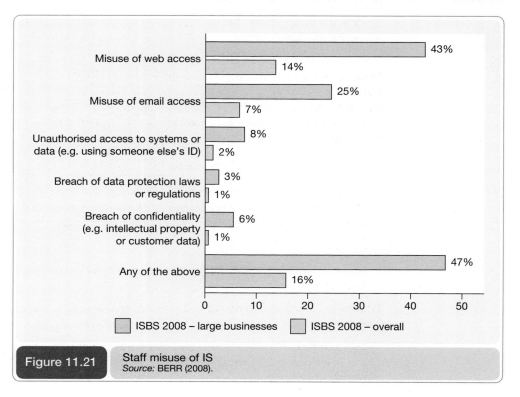

Figure 11.21	Staff misuse of IS
	Source: BERR (2008).

answering personal e-mails or visiting non-work-related websites, this will cost the company over £1,500 per year. Activities such as using streaming media to view the news or download audio clips can also place strain on the company networks.

A typical example of alleged time wasting where the company dismissed the employee involved Lois Franxhi, a 28-year-old IT manager who was sacked in July 1998 for making nearly 150 searches over four days in office hours for a holiday. She claimed unfair dismissal – she was pregnant at the time of the dismissal. As with many unfair dismissals, the case was not clear-cut, with Mrs Franxhi claiming the company sacked her because of sex discrimination. The tribunal dismissed these claims, finding that the employee had lied about the use of the Internet, saying she had only used it for one lunchtime when in fact records showed she had used it over four days.

More recently DTI (2006) reported on a member of staff at a small services company who accessed adult websites at work. He used someone else's computer to conceal his activity. Communications monitoring of employees may also be warranted if it is felt they are sending or receiving e-mails or accessing websites which contain content the organization deems unacceptable. Typical examples of such content are pornography or racist material. However, some organizations even block access to news, sports or web-based e-mail sites because of the amount of time staff spend in accessing them. To define permissible content, many organizations now have an '**acceptable-use policy**'. This will describe the types of material it is not acceptable to access and is also a means of explaining monitoring procedures.

Scanning and filtering are the two most common forms of monitoring. **Scanning software** identifies the content of e-mails sent or received and web pages accessed. Tools such as WebSense or MailMarshal SMTP from Marshal or Web Marshal will look for the occurrence of particular words or images – pornography is indicated by skin colour tones for example. Rules will also be set up, for example to ban e-mail attachments over a particular size or containing swearing, as indicated by Figure 11.22. Such tools can also give a picture of the most popular types of site or content. This might show, for example, how much time is being wasted accessing news and sports sites.

Such software usually also has blocking or filtering capabilities. **Filtering software** such as Websense (www.websense.com) can detect and block other activities such as:

Acceptable-use policy
Statement of employee activities involving use of networked computers that are not considered acceptable by management.

Scanning software
Identifies e-mail or web-page access that breaches company guidelines or acceptable-use policies.

Filtering software
Software that blocks specified content or activities.

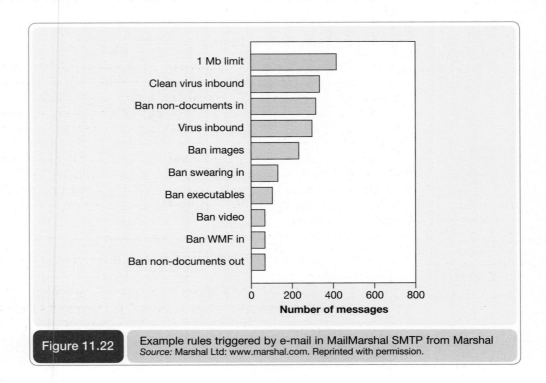

| Figure 11.22 | Example rules triggered by e-mail in MailMarshal SMTP from Marshal
Source: Marshal Ltd: www.marshal.com. Reprinted with permission. |

- Peer-to-peer (P2P) file sharing, for example of MP3 audio files.
- Instant messaging using Yahoo! Messenger or Microsoft Instant Messenger.
- The use of streaming media (e.g. audio and video) and other high-bandwidth applications.
- Accessing specified sites, e.g. social networks, news sites or personal e-mail programs since analysis has shown that staff spend so much time using them.
- Spyware which seeks to send out information collected from computers.
- Adware programs which place adverts or pop-ups.
- Employee hacking.

Websense and similar products can block sites in different categories, for different types of staff, according to the acceptable-use policy of the organization using a database (www.websense.com/products/about/database/categories.cfm) that contains over 1.5 million websites in many categories of which we list just some to illustrate the degree of control available to the employer. Examples of the categories include:

- Abortion or Pro-Choice or Pro-Life
- Adult Material
- Parent category that contains the categories: Adult Content, Lingerie and Swimsuit, Nudity, Sex, Sex Education
- Adult Content
- Advocacy Groups
- Business and Economy
- Financial Data and Services
- Drugs

Consider how many of those listed above you may visit when studying, at business or at home. It will be apparent that if an employer wishes, they can block virtually every site. When search engines are blocked, management-grade employees are likely to be restricted in their understanding of the business environment and are restricted from self-development! Employees are likely to view negatively an employer who does not trust them to use their time judiciously.

The popularity of different methods of monitoring and blocking is shown in Figure 11.23.

Employee monitoring legislation

In June 2003, the Office of the Information Commissioner published *Monitoring at Work*, to provide practical guidance for employers on how they should approach monitoring of employees in the workplace. These guidelines seek to achieve a balance between employees' wishes for privacy and the need for employers to run their businesses efficiently. The code does not prevent monitoring, but is based on the concept of proportionality. Proportionality means that any adverse impacts from monitoring must be justified by the benefits to the employer and others. This addresses an apparent anomaly in that data protection law refers to individual consent for processing of personal data being 'freely given' and it is not normal for employees to give this consent. The code makes it clear that individual consent is not required provided that an organization has undertaken an '**impact assessment**' of monitoring activities.

According to the code, an impact assessment involves:

Impact assessment
An assessment of the employee monitoring process in the workplace to identify improvements to minimize infringement of employee privacy.

- *identifying clearly the **purpose(s)** behind the monitoring arrangement and the benefits it is likely to deliver*
- *identifying any likely **adverse impact** of the monitoring arrangement*
- *considering **alternatives** to monitoring or different ways in which it might be carried out*
- *taking into account the **obligations** that arise from monitoring*
- *judging whether monitoring is **justified**.*

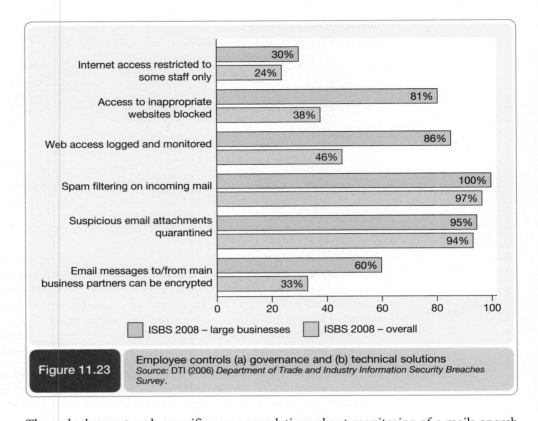

Figure 11.23	**Employee controls (a) governance and (b) technical solutions**
	Source: DTI (2006) *Department of Trade and Industry Information Security Breaches Survey.*

The code does not make specific recommendations about monitoring of e-mails or web traffic, but it does refer to them as typical monitoring activities which it suggests may be acceptable if staff are informed of them and an impact assessment has been conducted. The code does ask employers to consider whether alternatives may be better than systematic monitoring. Alternatives may include training or clear communication from managers and analysis of stored e-mails where it is thought an infringement has taken place rather than continuous monitoring. For example, automated monitoring is preferred to IT staff viewing personal e-mails of staff. The code also makes clear that the company should not undertake any **covert monitoring**. An 'acceptable-use policy' will describe the types of material it is not acceptable to access and is also a means of explaining monitoring procedures. It does appear that if an employee was disciplined or dismissed for sending too many personal e-mails for instance, they would have legitimate grounds to appeal if they had not been informed that monitoring was occurring and their managers had not made it clear that this was acceptable practice.

Covert monitoring
Monitoring which the employer undertakes without notification of staff.

Other European countries have different laws on monitoring. Some, such as Germany, are much more restrictive than the UK in terms of the level of monitoring that organizations are able to perform. Organizations opening offices abroad clearly need to be aware of local variations in legal constraints on employee monitoring and data protection.

E-mail management

E-mail is now an essential business communication tool and is also widely used for personal use. Billions of messages are sent each day. Four main controls need to be considered to reduce the amount of time effectively wasted by staff reading e-mail by minimizing the volume of:

1 Spam (unsolicited e-mail).
2 Internal business e-mail.

3 External business e-mail.

4 Personal e-mail (friends and family).

Despite the potential time loss through e-mail misuse an AMA (2003) survey suggested that only 34% of employers had a written e-mail retention and deletion policy in place. Furthermore, there are issues of legal liability about what employees say in their e-mail which also need to be considered. We will look at the risk and controls of each e-mail risk in turn.

1 Minimizing spam (unsolicited e-mail)

Spam is now a potential problem for every company and individual using the Internet. At the time of writing over 75% of e-mails were spam or virus-related in some countries and individuals whose inboxes are unprotected can receive hundreds of spam e-mails each day. The spammers rely on sending out millions of e-mails often from **botnets** of infected PCs in the hope that even if there is only a 0.01% response they may make some money, if not necessarily get rich.

Legal measures to combat spam have had limited success. So, many information services managers are now using a range of methods to control spam. Figure 11.24 summarizes alternative techniques to combat spam. Figure 11.24(a) is the original situation where all mail is allowed into an inbox. Figure 11.24(b) uses different techniques to reduce the volume of e-mail through identification and blocking of spam. Figure 11.24(c) is a closed inbox where only known, trusted e-mails are allowed into an organization.

The full range of techniques that can be used in combination to combat spam include:

1 *Avoid harvesting of addresses.* Spammers harvest e-mails from e-mail addresses published on web pages and even the program code used to convert online form content to an e-mail to a company. By reducing the number of e-mail addresses published, or changing their format, the number of e-mail addresses can be reduced.

2 *Educate staff not to reply to spam.* The worst thing an individual can do on receiving spam is to reply to it to complain or to attempt to unsubscribe. This merely confirms to the

Spam
Unsolicited e-mail (usually bulk-mailed and untargeted).

Botnet
Independent computers, connected to the Internet, are used together, typically for malicious purposes through controlling software. For example, they may be used to send out spam or for a denial-of-service attack.

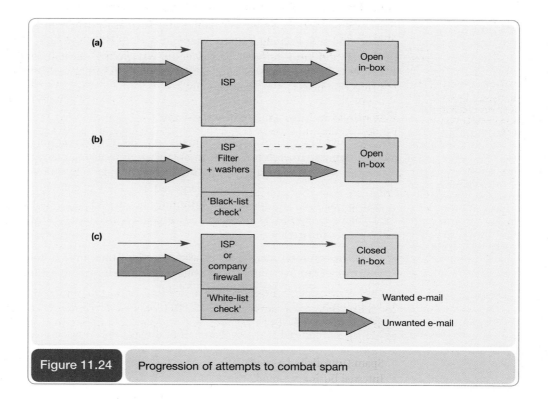

| Figure 11.24 | Progression of attempts to combat spam |

spammer that the address is valid and they are likely to send more junk e-mail and sell your address on to other spammers.

3 *Use filters.* Filtering software can identify spam from key words and phrases such as 'For Free', 'Sex' or 'Viagra'. **E-mail filters** are provided for users of web-based e-mail. Microsoft Outlook Express has its own filter. Filtering software such as Mailwasher (www.mailwasher.net) or Mcaffee Spamkiller (www.mcaffee.com) can also be installed. Unfortunately, many spammers know how to avoid the keywords in the filters. The problem with filters and other services is that there can be 'false positives' or valid e-mails that are classified as junk. Additionally, spammers find ways to work around filters by putting 'gobbeldy gook' in the footer of their messages that is not recognized by the filters or using variants of words such as V1agra, or Via-gra. Review of these may still be necessary. This technique is represented by Figure 11.24(b).

4 *Use 'peer-to-peer' blocking services.* These take advantage of humans being good at identifying spam and then notifying a central server which keeps an index of all spam. CloudMark (www.cloudmark.com), a peer-to-peer solution, requires users to identify spam by pressing a 'Block' button in Outlook Express which then updates a central server, so when others download the same message at a later time, it is automatically identified as spam. This technique is represented by Figure 11.24(b).

5 *Use blacklist services.* **Blacklists** are lists of known spammers such as those reported to Spamhaus Project (www.spamhaus.com) or SpamCop (www.spamcop.net). They are often used in conjunction with filters to block e-mails. Brightmail (www.brightmail.com) uses a global network of e-mail addresses set up to trap and identify spam. Brightmail is increasingly used by ISPs such as BT OpenWorld to block spam, but it is not a cheap service, costing $5 to $15 per year. This price could easily be justified by the time staff save over the year. This technique is also represented by Figure 11.24(b).

6 *Use whitelist services.* The **whitelist** approach has not been adopted widely since it is difficult to set up, but it probably offers the best opportunity for the future. A whitelist gives a list of bona fide e-mail addresses that are likely to want to contact people within an organization. It will include all employees, partners, customers and suppliers who have obtained opt-in from employees to receive e-mail. E-mail from anyone not on the list will be blocked. However, maintaining such as list will require new software and new procedures for keeping it up to date.

7 *Ensure anti-virus software and blocking is effective.* E-mail viruses are increasingly perpetrated by spammers since they are a method of harvesting e-mail addresses. Virus protection needs to be updated daily.

2 Minimizing internal business e-mail

The ease and low cost of sending e-mails to a distribution list or copying people in on a message can lead to each person in an organization receiving many messages each day from colleagues within the organization. This problem tends to be worse in large organizations, simply because each individual has a larger address book of colleagues.

A press release from the British Computer Society summarizing research conducted by the Henley Management College in 2002 suggested that a lot of time is wasted by managers when processing irrelevant e-mails:

- Of seven common management tasks, meetings took up 2.8 hours on average, dealing with e-mail came second with an average of 1.7 hours and accessing information from the Internet accounted for a further 0.75 hour.
- Respondents reported receiving on average 52 e-mails per day while 7% received 100 e-mails per day or more.
- Managers reported that less than half of e-mails (42%) warranted a response, 35% were read for information only and nearly a quarter were deleted immediately. On average only 30% of e-mails were classified as essential, 37% as important and 33% as irrelevant or unnecessary.

E-mail filter

Software used to identify spam according to its characteristics such as keywords.

Blacklist

A compilation of known sources of spam that are used to block e-mail.

Whitelist

A compilation of trusted sources of e-mail that is permitted to enter an inbox.

- Despite the reservations about the quality and volume of e-mails received, the majority of respondents (81%) regarded e-mail as the communications technology which has had the most positive impact on the way they carried out their job, alongside the Internet and the mobile phone.

To overcome this type of business e-mail overuse, companies are starting to develop e-mail policies which explain best practice. For example, Chaffey and Wood (2005) devised these guidelines:

- Only send the e-mail to employees who must be informed or who must act upon it.
- Banning certain types of e-mail, such as the classic 'e-mail to the person who sits next to you' or individuals in the same office.
- Avoid 'flaming' – these are aggressive e-mails which often put voice to feelings that wouldn't be said face-to-face. If you receive an annoying e-mail it is best to wait 10 minutes to cool down rather than 'flaming' the sender.
- Avoid 'trolls' – these are a species of e-mail closely related to flame-mails. They are postings to a newsgroup deliberately posted to 'wind up' the recipient.
- Combine items from separate e-mails during the day or week into a single e-mail for the day/week.
- Write clear subject lines.
- Structure e-mails so that they can be scanned quickly using sub-heads and numbered and bulleted lists.
- Make follow-up actions clear.
- When reading e-mail, use folders to categorize e-mails according to content and priority.
- Perform e-mail reading and checking in batches, e.g. once per morning or afternoon rather than being alerted to and opening every e-mail that arrives.
- Delete e-mails which are not required for future reference (large volumes are taken up on servers through staff not deleting e-mails and their attachments).
- And so on – all common-sense guidelines, but often common sense isn't common!

3 Minimizing external business e-mail

People within an organization can receive many e-mails from legitimate suppliers. For example, an IT manager might receive e-mails from hardware and software manufacturers, service providers, event or conference organizers and e-newsletters from magazines. It is usually left to the judgement of the individual employee to select appropriate e-newsletters. Spam filters will not usually block such messages, but primitive filters may. The challenge/respond system will still enable such e-mails to be received. If certain websites are blocked, e-newsletters will be less effective since images are not downloaded from blocked sites. Many individuals use a separate e-mail address from the main inbox when opting in. This means the e-newsletter can be read at the office or at home and is also available when the individual changes jobs.

4 Minimizing personal e-mail (friends and family)

Although there are many surveys about the volume of spam and amount of time spent processing e-mail at work, there is relatively little data published on the amount of time spent writing personal e-mails.

To minimize this problem and some of the problems of over-using e-mail for business use, the following steps can be taken:

1 Create written guidelines defining the policy on acceptable e-mail use and disciplinary procedures for when guidelines are breached.
2 Use increasing levels of control or sanctions for breaches including performance reviews, verbal warnings, removal of e-mail privileges, termination and legal action.
3 Providing training for staff on acceptable and efficient e-mail use.
4 Monitor e-mails for signatures of personal use and any breaches of the policy, e.g. swearing, and take action accordingly.

Hacking

'**Hacking**' refers to the process of gaining unauthorized access to computer systems, typically across a network. Hacking can take different forms. Hacking for monetary gain is usually aimed at identity theft where personal details and credit card details are accessed for the purpose of fraud. Hacking could also occur with malicious intent. For example, a former employee might gain access to a network with a view to deleting files or passing information on to a competitor. Notorious hackers who have been prosecuted, but often seem to have ultimately gained from their misdemeanours, include:

- *Robert Morris* – The son of the chief scientist at the US National Computer Security Center, this graduate student created a destructive Internet worm in 1988 which took advantage of a security flaw in the Unix operating system. When unleashed it caused thousands of computers to crash. The disruption was partly accidental and he released instructions to system administrators on how to resolve the problem. He was sentenced to three years of probation, 400 hours of community service and a fine of $10,050. He is now an assistant professor at MIT, where he originally released his worm to disguise its creation at Cornell University.
- *Kevin Poulsen* – In 1990 Poulsen took over all telephone lines into the Los Angeles radio station KIIS-FM, assuring that he would be the 102nd caller. Poulsen won a Porsche 944 S2. This was one of many hacks conducted while he worked for hi-tech company SRI International by day and hacked at night. He was eventually traced and, in June 1994, he pleaded guilty to seven counts of mail, wire and computer fraud, money laundering and obstruction of justice, and was sentenced to 51 months in prison and ordered to pay $56,000 in restitution. It was the longest sentence ever given for hacking. He is now a computer security journalist.
- *Kevin Mitnick* – The first hacker to be featured on an FBI 'Most wanted' poster, Mitnick was arrested in 1995. He later pleaded guilty to four counts of wire fraud, two counts of computer fraud and one count of illegally intercepting a wire communication. He admitted that he broke into computer systems and stole proprietary software belonging to Motorola, Novell, Fujitsu, Sun Microsystems and other companies. He was sentenced to 46 months. Following his sentence he became a security consultant and is now a leading commentator on security and has made many TV appearances and written books and articles.

Gaining access to a system may be perceived by the hacker as simply a technical challenge. The term 'hacking' traditionally refers to the process of creating program code, another form of technical challenge. This can almost be considered as a pastime, albeit an unethical one. The BBC (2003) reported that TruSecure, a US hacking monitoring organization, currently tracks more than 11,000 individuals in about 900 different hacking groups and gangs.

Three main forms of gaining unauthorized access to computer systems can be identified. First, the normal entry points to systems through usernames and passwords can be used. Tools are available to try different alternative log-ins, although most modern systems will refuse access after several attempts. Hacking can be combined with identity theft to gain an idea of the passwords used.

The second form of hacking exploits known vulnerabilities in systems. Although these vulnerabilities are publicly known and will be posted on the vendor's website and specialist security websites, there will be many system administrators who have not updated their systems with the latest security update or 'patch'. This is partly because there are so many security vulnerabilities, with new ones being announced every week.

Thirdly, Kevin Mitnick refers to '**social engineering**' which typically involves impersonating employees of an organization to access security details. One example of this, given in Mitnick and Simon (2002), is when the attacker contacts a new employee and advises them of the need to comply with security policies. The attacker then asks the user for their password to check it is in line with the policy of choosing a difficult-to-guess password. Once the user reveals their password, the caller makes recommendations to construct future passwords in such a way that the attacker will be able to guess them.

Protecting computer systems against hackers

Protecting computer systems against hackers involves creating counter-measures to the three main types of hacking outlined above. For gaining access to systems via passwords, policies can be developed to reduce the risk of access. One simple approach is to mandate that new passwords are required every month and that they contain at least one number and a mix of upper and lower case. This prevents users using simple passwords which are easily guessed. Education is required to reduce the risk of passwords falsely obtained through 'social engineering', but this will never completely remove the threat.

Computer systems can also be protected by limiting access at the point the external network enters the company. **Firewalls** are essential to prevent outside access to confidential company information, particularly where an extranet has been set up. Firewall software can then be configured to only accept links from trusted domains representing other offices in the company.

Measures must also be put in place to stop access to systems through published security vulnerabilities. The BBC (2003) reported that in 2003 there were 5,500 security vulnerabilities that could be used. A policy on updating operating systems and other software with the latest versions is also required. It is not practical to make all updates, but new vulnerabilities must be monitored and patches applied to the highest-risk categories. This is a specialist task and is often outsourced. TruSecure (www.trusecure.com) is an example of a specialist company that monitors security vulnerabilities and advises organizations on prevention. They also employ a team of people who attempt to infiltrate hacker groups to determine the latest techniques. TruSecure gave the FBI over 200 documents about the 'Melissa' virus author. Although they did not know his real name, they knew his three aliases and had built a detailed profile of him.

'**Ethical hackers**' are former hackers who now apply their skills to test the vulnerabilities of existing systems.

Sometimes 'low-tech' techniques can be used too. The *Guardian* (2003) reported cases where criminals had impersonated call-centre staff in order to gain access to customer accounts!

Firewall
A specialized software application typically mounted on a server at the point where the company is connected to the Internet. Its purpose is to prevent unauthorized access into the company.

Ethical hacker
Hacker employed legitimately to test the quality of system security.

Secure e-commerce transactions

For e-businesses offering online sales there are also additional security risks from the customer or merchant perspective:

(a) Transaction or credit card details stolen in transit.
(b) Customer's credit card details stolen from merchant's server.
(c) Merchant or customer is not who they claim to be.

In this section we assess the measures that can be taken to reduce the risk of these breaches of e-commerce security. We start by reviewing some of the theory of online security and then review the techniques used.

Principles of secure systems

Before we look at the principle of secure systems, it is worth reviewing the standard terminology for the different parties involved in the transaction:

- *Purchasers*. These are the consumers buying the goods.
- *Merchants*. These are the retailers.
- *Certification authority (CA)*. This is a body that issues digital certificates that confirm the identity of purchasers and merchants.

- *Banks.* These are traditional banks.
- *Electronic token issuer.* A virtual bank that issues digital currency.

The basic requirements for security systems from these different parties to the transaction are as follows:

1 *Authentication* – are parties to the transaction who they claim to be (risk (c) above)?
2 *Privacy and confidentiality* – are transaction data protected? The consumer may want to make an anonymous purchase. Are all non-essential traces of a transaction removed from the public network and all intermediary records eliminated (risks (b) and (c) above)?
3 *Integrity* – checks that the message sent is complete, i.e. that it is not corrupted.
4 *Non-repudiability* – ensures sender cannot deny sending message.
5 *Availability* – how can threats to the continuity and performance of the system be eliminated?

Kesh *et al.* (2002) explore the security requirements for e-commerce in more detail.

Approaches to developing secure systems

Digital certificates

Digital certificates (keys)
Consist of keys made up of large numbers that are used to uniquely identify individuals.

There are two main methods of encryption using **digital certificates**.

1 Secret-key (symmetric) encryption

Symmetric encryption
Both parties to a transaction use the same key to encode and decode messages.

Symmetric encryption involves both parties having an identical (shared) key that is known only to them. Only this key can be used to encrypt and decrypt messages. The secret key has to be passed from one party to the other before use in much the same way as a copy of a secure attaché case key would have to be sent to a receiver of information. This approach has traditionally been used to achieve security between two separate parties, such as major companies conducting EDI. Here the private key is sent out electronically or by courier to ensure it is not copied.

This method is not practical for general e-commerce, as it would not be safe for a purchaser to give a secret key to a merchant since control of it would be lost and it could not then be used for other purposes. A merchant would also have to manage many customer keys.

2 Public-key (asymmetric) encryption

Asymmetric encryption
Both parties use a related but different key to encode and decode messages.

Asymmetric encryption is so called since the keys used by the sender and receiver of information are different. The two keys are related by a numerical code, so only the pair of keys can be used in combination to encrypt and decrypt information. Figure 11.25 shows how public-key encryption works in an e-commerce context. A customer can place an order

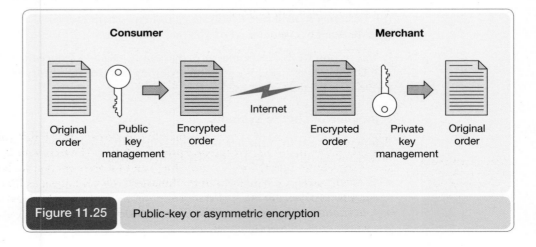

| Figure 11.25 | Public-key or asymmetric encryption |

with a merchant by automatically looking up the public key of the merchant and then using this key to encrypt the message containing their order. The scrambled message is then sent across the Internet and on receipt by the merchant is read using the merchant's private key. In this way only the merchant who has the only copy of the private key can read the order. In the reverse case the merchant could confirm the customer's identity by reading identity information such as a digital signature encrypted with the private key of the customer using their public key.

Pretty Good Privacy (PGP) is a public-key encryption system used to encrypt e-mail messages.

Digital signatures

Digital signatures
A method of identifying individuals or companies using public-key encryption.

Digital signatures can be used to create commercial systems by using public key encryption to achieve authentication: the merchant and purchaser can prove they are genuine. The purchaser's digital signature is encrypted before sending a message using their private key and, on receipt, the public key of the purchaser is used to decrypt the digital signature. This proves the customer is genuine. Digital signatures are not widely used currently due to the difficulty of setting up transactions, but they will become more widespread as the public-key infrastructure (PKI) stabilizes and use of certificate authorities increases.

The public-key infrastructure (PKI) and certificate authorities (CAs)

Certificate and certificate authorities (CAs)
A certificate is a valid copy of a public key of an individual or organization together with identification information. It is issued by a trusted third party (TTP) or certificate authority (CA).

In order for digital signatures and public-key encryption to be effective it is necessary to be sure that the public key intended for decryption of a document actually belongs to the person you believe is sending you the document. The developing solution to this problem is the issuance by a trusted third party (TTP) of a message containing owner identification information and a copy of the public key of that person. The TTPs are usually referred to as '**certificate authorities**' **(CAs)**, and various bodies such as banks and the Post Office are likely to fulfil this role. That message is called a '**certificate**'. In reality, as asymmetric encryption is rather slow, it is often only a sample of the message that is encrypted and used as the representative digital signature.

Example certificate information could include:

- user identification data;
- issuing authority identification and digital signature;
- user's public key;
- expiry date of this certificate;
- class of certificate;
- digital identification code of this certificate.

It is proposed that different classes of certificates would exist according to the type of information contained. For example:

- name, e-mail address
- driver's licence, national insurance number, date of birth
- credit check
- organization-specific security clearance data.

Virtual private networks

Virtual private network
Private network created using the public network infrastructure of the Internet.

A **virtual private network (VPN)** is a private wide-area network that runs over the public network, rather than a more expensive private network. The technique by which VPN operates is sometimes referred to as 'tunnelling', and involves encrypting both packet headers and content using a secure form of the Internet Protocol known as IPSec. As explained in Chapter 3, VPNs enable the global organization to conduct its business securely, but using the public Internet rather than more expensive proprietary systems.

Current approaches to e-commerce security

In this section we review the approaches used by e-commerce sites to achieve security using the techniques described above.

Secure Sockets Layer Protocol (SSL)

Secure Sockets Layer (SSL)
A commonly used encryption technique for scrambling data as it is passed across the Internet from a customer's web browser to a merchant's web server.

SSL is a security protocol used in the majority of B2C e-commerce transactions since it is easy for the customer to use without the need to download additional software or a certificate.

When a customer enters a secure checkout area of an e-commerce site SSL is used and the customer is prompted that 'you are about to view information over a secure connection' and a key symbol is used to denote this security. When encryption is occurring they will see that the web address prefix in the browser changes from 'http://' to 'https://' and a padlock appears at the bottom of the browser window.

The main facilities it provides are security and confidentiality. SSL enables a private link to be set up between customer and merchant. Encryption is used to scramble the details of an e-commerce transaction as it is passed between sender and receiver and also when the details are held on the computers at each end. It would require a determined attempt to intercept such a message and decrypt it. SSL is more widely used than the rival S-HTTP method.

Secure Electronic Transaction (SET)
A standard for public-key encryption intended to enable secure e-commerce transactions; lead-development by MasterCard and Visa.

Since, with enough computing power, time and motivation, it is possible to decrypt messages encrypted using SSL, much effort is being put into finding more secure methods of encryption such as **SET**. From a merchant's point of view there is also the problem that authentication of the customer is not possible without resorting to other methods such as credit checks.

Certificate authorities (CAs)

For secure e-commerce, there is a requirement for the management of the vast number of public keys. This management involves procedures and protocols necesssary throughout the lifetime of a key – generation, dissemination, revocation and change – together with the administrative functions of time/date stamping and archiving. The successful establishment of a CA is an immense challenge of trust building and complex management. There are two opposing views on how that challenge should be met:

- *Decentralized*: market-driven, creating brand-name-based 'islands of trust' such as the Consumers Association. There is a practical need for a local physical office to present certificates of attestable value, e.g. passports, drivers' licences. Banks and the Post Office have a huge advantage.
- *Centralized*: in the UK, the Department of Trade and Industry (DTI) has proposed a hierarchical tree leading ultimately to the government.

The best-known commercial CA is Verisign (www.verisign.com) and this is commonly used for merchant verification. Post Offices and telecommunications suppliers are also acting as CAs. Examples in the UK include BT (Trust Wise) and the Post Office (ViaCode).

Reassuring the customer

Once the security measures are in place, content on the merchant's site can be used to reassure the customer, for example Amazon (www.amazon.com) takes customer fears about security seriously, judging by the prominence and amount of content it devotes to this issue. Some of the approaches used indicate good practice in allaying customers' fears. These include:

- use of customer guarantee to safeguard purchase;
- clear explanation of SSL security measures used;

- highlighting the rarity of fraud ('ten million customers have shopped safely without credit card fraud');
- the use of alternative ordering mechanisms such as phone or fax;
- the prominence of information to allay fears – the guarantee is one of the main menu options.

Companies can also use independent third parties that set guidelines for online privacy and security. The best-known international bodies are TRUSTe (www.truste.org) and Verisign for payment authentication (www.verisign.com). Within particular countries there may be other bodies such as, in the UK, the ISIS or Internet Shopping is Safe scheme (http://isis.imrg.org)

Case Study 11.2 Building an e-business fortress

FT

In the lead-up to the industrial revolution, many European cities stopped relying on walls that for centuries kept them safe from marauding armies. Cities weighed up the risks and decided trade and collaboration were more important to survival than defence, so expanded beyond the city perimeter.

Businesses today face a similar predicament when it comes to securing computer networks, says Paul Dorey, chief information security officer (CISO) at energy giant BP.

With the growth of outsourcing, managed services, remote working and joint-ventures changing the business landscape, companies can no longer adopt a siege mentality when protecting corporate IT networks, he says.

'Outsourcers, contractors and third parties need to access corporate information. At the same time new technologies, such as wireless and instant messaging, are providing a security headache for those guarding the network perimeter.' Instead of repelling hackers and viruses using firewalls at the network edge, Mr Dorey, and other CISOs from companies including HSBC, ICI, Rolls-Royce and Royal Mail, advocate businesses re-think their security.

They have formed the Jericho Forum, an international pressure group aimed at making vendors listen to user requirements. It plans to lobby for product design changes so companies can trade securely over the internet. By doing so, it hopes businesses will not see electronic assets pillaged or destroyed to the biblical proportions its namesake did.

'The easiest model is something akin to internet banking where you access corporate systems through a highly secure web-portal, using authentication,' says Mr Dorey. 'Sensitive data is encrypted and there is a demilitarised zone, so even if one person accessing the system is compromised, the whole system is not,' he says.

Pharmaceutical company AstraZeneca is looking at this. In 2004 it spent $3.8bn (£2.15bn) on drugs research and development through collaboration with research organizations, universities and biotechnology partners. With dozens of organizations and 11,900 employees communicating in the R&D process over multiple networks, protection of intellectual property (IP) was not feasible through a 'walled castle' approach to security. So last year it replaced an in-house collaboration system with electronic vaulting technology from IT security company Cyber-Ark, says Patrick Meehan, lead technical architect at AstraZeneca. The original system had high costs and hindered collaboration, because the virtual private network on which it relied needed software installed on every user's system. By transporting data in an 'electronic safe' AstraZeneca is guarding intellectual property using inbuilt authentication, encryption and firewalls.

Enterprise rights management (ERM) software to restrict who can access, print and e-mail sensitive documents is also used. Paul Stamp, security analyst at Forrester Research believes protecting data assets is an improvement on the 'fortress approach', but current proprietary technologies and differences in global legislation could hamper progress. 'It's not going to happen overnight,' he says. 'The Jericho Forum is pushing for open-standards and that's going to be tough for the likes of Microsoft and Cisco to achieve from the very beginning.'

And with countries such as China, Israel, Russia and Saudi Arabia restricting the use of strong data encryption products, ERM is not immediately workable globally, he says.

Steve Wylie, EMEA managing partner at Accenture's security practice, adds that investment in encryption and ERM software could be costly in time spent managing user privileges. 'The negative impact of leaked R&D into drugs will justify the investment, but if employees spend time setting up access rights every time they produce documents like a company newsletter then it could hamper productivity,' he says. But while Mr Dorey admits re-defining a company's electronic boundaries has problems, advances in networking and business practices may force the IT industry's hand.

Source: Daniel Thomas, A different approach to protection. *The Financial Times*, 9 November 2005. Reprinted with permission.

Question

Summarize the change in security model needed to protect corporate assets.

Summary

1 Analysis of business and user requirements for e-business systems is important in delivering usable and relevant systems.

2 Process modelling is used to assess existing business processes and suggest revised processes. Techniques such as task analysis and flow process charts from workflow design are useful in understanding tasks that must be supported by the system and weaknesses in the current process.

3 Data modelling for e-business systems mainly involves traditional entity relationship approaches.

4 Architectural designs involve assessing appropriate integration between legacy systems and new e-commerce systems. Such designs are based on the client–server approach.

5 User interface design can be improved through using structured approaches such as use-case and following evolving standards for site structure, page structure and content.

6 Security design is important to maintain trust amongst the customer base. Security solutions target protecting servers from attack and prevent interception of messages when they are in transit.

Exercises

Self-assessment questions

1 What are the risks if analysis and design are not completed adequately?

2 Distinguish between process analysis and data analysis.

3 What are workflow analysis and workflow management systems?

4 What are legacy data and what are the options for their incorporation into an e-commerce system?

5 What are the four requirements of a secure e-commerce site?

6 Explain the concepts of digital keys and digital signatures and how they relate.

7 Explain the notation used for use-case analysis.

8 Summarize the characteristics of a usable website according to Jakob Nielsen (www.useit.com).

Essay and discussion questions

1 Write a plan for the analysis and design of an e-commerce site, recommending which aspects of process and data analysis should be conducted and explaining how they should be integrated.

2 Write an essay on the significance of workflow systems to e-business, illustrating your answer with examples of organizations of your choice.

3 Write a report summarizing the characteristics of a website with good usability.

4 How can the concept of customer orientation be translated into e-commerce site design?

5 Assess the success of e-tailers in designing secure e-commerce systems.

Examination questions

1 Summarize the purpose of process analysis.

2 What is meant by 'user-centred design'?

3 Explain the concept of task analysis with reference to a customer placing an order online.

4 Explain the stages involved in use-case analysis with reference to a customer placing an order online.

5 Describe the stages of data modelling with reference to a database for an e-procurement system.

6 Outline the different types of services that need to be provided by different servers on an e-commerce site based on the three-tier client–server system.

7 How do the attributes of a secure e-commerce site differ from customer and company viewpoints?

8 Explain the relationship between analysis, design and implementation for an e-commerce site.

References

AMA (2003) American Managment Association 2003 E-Mail Rules, Policies and Practices Survey: **www.amanet.org/research/pdfs/Email_Policies_Practices.pdf.**

BBC (2003) Cracking the hacker underground. BBC News Online: **http://news.bbc.co.uk/ 1/hi/technology/3246375.htm.**

BERR (2008) Information Security Breaches Survey 2008, managed by Pricewaterhouse-Cooper for UK Department of Business, Enterprise and Regulatory Reform (BERR), published at **www.pwc.co.uk/eng/publications/berr_information_security_breaches_ survey_2008.html.**

Bevan, N. (1999a) Usability issues in web site design. *Proceedings of the 6th Interactive Publishing Conference*, November. Available online at **www.usability.serco.com.**

Bevan, N. (1999b) Common industry format usability tests. *Proceedings of UPA 98*, Usability Professionals Association, Scottsdale, AZ, 29 June–2 July. Available online at **www. usability. serco.com.**

Bocij, P., Greasley, A. and Hickie, S. (2008) *Business Information Systems. Technology, Development and Management*, 4th edn. Financial Times Prentice Hall, Harlow.

British Standards Institute (1999) BS 13407 Human-centred Design Processes for Interactive Systems.

Chaffey, D. (1998) *Groupware, Workflow and Intranets – Re-engineering the Enterprise with Collaborative Software*. Digital Press, Woburn, MA.

Chaffey, D. and Wood, S. (2005) *Business Information Management: Improving Performance using Information Systems*. Financial Times Prentice Hall, Harlow.

Chaffey, D., Mayer, R., Johnston, K. and Ellis-Chadwick, F. (2009) *Internet Marketing: Strategy, Implementation and Practice,* 3rd edn. Financial Times Prentice Hall, Harlow.

Channel Register (2005) Dabs.com in £500k makeover. By John Leyden. *Channel Register,* 2 September: **www.channelregister.co.uk.**

Christodoulides, G., de Chernatony, L., Furrer, O., Shiu, E and Temi, A. (2006) Conceptualising and measuring the equity of online brands. *Journal of Marketing Management,* 22(7/8), 799–825.

ClickZ (2003) Virus damage worst on record for August 2003. By Sharon Gaudin. News alert published online at ClickZ Stats, 2 September: **www.clickz.com/stats.**

Curtis, B., Kellner, M. and Over, J. (1992) Process modeling. *Communications of the ACM,* 35(9), 75–90.

Davenport, T.H. (1993) *Process Innovation: Re-engineering Work through Information Technology.* Harvard Business School Press, Boston.

de Chernatony, L. (2001) Succeeding with brands on the Internet. *Journal of Brand Management,* 8(3), 186–95.

DTI (2006) Identity access and E-mail and Web Usage factsheets. A survey of UK business practice, managed by PricewaterhouseCoopers on behalf of the Department of Trade and Industry (DTI). Published at DTI Information Security Breaches Survey, E-consultancy.

E-consultancy (2007) E-business briefing interview. Bruce Tognazzini on human–computer interaction. Interview published November: **www.econsultancy.com/news-blog/ newsletter/link_track.asp?id=3515&link_id=#1.**

E-consultancy (2009) Q&A: Hiscox's Mike Beddington on selling financial services online, Posted 16 July 2009: **http://econsultancy.com/blog/4227-q-a-hiscox-on -selling-financial-services-online.**

Fogg, B., Soohoo, C., Danielson, D., Marable, L., Stanford, J. and Tauber, E. (2003) How do people evaluate a web site's credibility? A Consumer WebWatch research report, prepared by Stanford Persuasive Technology Lab.

Forrester (2005) Site Design Personas: How Many, How Much. By Harley Manning, 3 June. Forrester Research publication.

Georgakoupoulos, D., Hornick, M. and Sheth, A. (1995) An overview of workflow management: from process modeling to workflow automation infrastructure. *Distributed and Parallel Databases,* 3, 119–53.

Guardian (2003) Hijacked your bank balance, your identity, your life. *The Guardian,* 25 October: **www.guardian.co.uk/weekend/story/0,3605,1069646,00.html.**

Hofacker, C. (2001) *Internet Marketing.* Wiley, New York.

Hoffman, D.L. and Novak, T.P. (1997) A new marketing paradigm for electronic commerce. *The Information Society,* Special issue on electronic commerce, 13 (Jan.–Mar.), 43–54.

IT Week (2003) E-shop adds to attractions. By David Neal. *IT Week,* 12 September, 24: **www.itweek.co.uk.**

Jacobsen, I., Ericsson, M. and Jacobsen, A. (1994) *The Object Advantage. Business Process Re-engineering with Object Technology.* Addison-Wesley, Wokingham.

Kesh, S., Ramanujan, S. and Nerur, S. (2002) A framework for analyzing e-commerce security. *Information Management and Computer Security,* 10(4), 149–58.

Lynch, P. and Horton, S. (1999) *Web Style Guide. Basic Design Principles for Creating Web Sites.* Yale University Press, New Haven, CT. Available online at: **http://info.med.yale. edu/ caim/manual/contents.html.**

Messagelabs (2008) Threat Statistics, published monthly at **www.messagelabs.com.**

Mitnick, K. and Simon, W. (2002) *The Art of Deception: Controlling the Human Element of Security.* Wiley, New York.

NCC(2005) Dabs.com benefits from innovative approach. *Principra,* NCC Members Magazine, no. 37, May/June.

Nielsen, J. (2000a) *Novice vs. Expert Users.* Jakob Nielsen's Alertbox, 6 February. **www.useit. com/alertbox/20000206.html.**

Nielsen, J. (2000b) *Designing Web Usability.* New Riders, San Francisco.

Nielsen, J. (2000c) *Details in Study Methodology Can Give Misleading Results.* Jakob Nielsen's Alertbox, 21 February: **www.useit.com/alertbox/990221.html**

Noyes, J. and Baber, C. (1999) *User-Centred Design of Systems.* Springer-Verlag, Berlin.

Pant, S. and Ravichandran, T. (2001) A framework for information systems planning for e-business. *Logistics Information Management,* 14(1), 85–98.

Rettie, R. (2001) An exploration of flow during Internet use. *Internet Research: Electronic Networking Applications and Policy,* 11(2), 103–13.

Robertson, J. (2003) Information design using card sorting. Step Two. Available online at **www.steptwo.com.au/papers/cardsorting/index.html.**

Rosen, D. and Purinton, E. (2004) Website design: viewing the web as a cognitive landscape, *Journal of Business Research,* 57(7), 787–94.

Rosenfeld, L. and Morville, P. (2002) *Information Architecture for the World Wide Web,* 2nd edn. O'Reilly, Sebastopol, CA.

Schneider, G. and Winters, J. (1998) *Applying Use Cases. A Practical Guide.* Addison-Wesley, Reading, MA.

Seybold, P. (1999) *Customers.com.* Century Business Books, Random House, London.

Seybold, P. and Marshak, R. (2001) *The Customer Revolution.* Crown Business, London.

Smart Insights (2010) Website Feedback Tools review, published 7 April 2010: **http://www.smartinsights.com/digital-marketing-software/website-feedback-tools-review/.**

Taylor, D. (1995) *Business Engineering with Object Technology.* Wiley, New York.

Trocchia, P. and Janda, S. (2003) How do consumers evaluate Internet retail service quality? *Journal of Services Marketing,* 17(3), 243–53.

Wodtke, C. (2002) *Information Architecture: Blueprints for the Web.* New Riders, Indianapolis, IN.

Workflow Management Coalition (WfMC) (1996) Reference model. Version 1. In *The Workflow Management Coalition Specification. Terminology and Glossary.* Workflow Management Coalition, Brussels.

Further reading

Bevan, N. (1999a) Usability issues in web site design. *Proceedings of the 6th Interactive Publishing Conference,* November 1999. Available online at **www.usability.serco.com.** Accessible, lists of web-design pointers.

Jakob Nielsen's UseIt (**www.useit.com**). Detailed guidelines (alertboxes) and summaries of research into usability of web media.

Noyes, J. and Baber, C. (1999) *User-Centred Design of Systems.* Springer-Verlag, Berlin. Details the user-centred design approach.

Web links

British web site trade associations BIMA (**www.bima.co.uk**) and BWDMA (**www.bwdma. co.uk**) Have good resources for the specialist in this area.

DTI Information Security (**www.dti.gov.uk/industries/information_security**) Guidelines on information security.

DTI Information Security Breaches Survey (**www.security-survey.gov.uk**) A survey of security in UK businesses.

Jakob Nielsen's UseIt (**www.useit.com**) Detailed guidelines (alertboxes) and summaries of research into usability of web media.

Royal National Institute for the Blind (**www.rnib.org.uk/accessibility**) Web accessibility guidelines.

Usability News (**www.usabilitynews.com**).

User Interface Engineering (**www.uie.com**) Articles on usability which often provide a counterpoint to those of Nielsen.

UI Access (**www.uiaccess.com/access_links.html**) Resources on website accessibility.

Web Design References (**www.d.umn.edu/itss/support/Training/Online/webdesign**) A collection from the University of Minnesota, Duluth, including articles and references on accessibility, information architecture and usability.

Web Style Guide (**www.webstyleguide.com**) Supporting site for the style guide book of P. Lynch and S. Horton of Yale Medical School. Complete text online.

Worldwide Web Consortium Web accessibility guidelines (see **www.w3.org/WAI**).

12

E-business service implementation and optimization

Web support

The following additional case studies are available at
www.pearsoned.co.uk/chaffey

→ Change management at the Woolwich Group
→ Guide to smarter searching

The site also contains a range of study materials designed to help improve your results.

Learning outcomes

After completing this chapter the reader should be able to:

- Produce a plan to minimize the risks involved with the launch phase of an e-business application
- Define a process for the effective optimization of an e-business system
- Create a plan to measure and improve the effectiveness of sell-side e-business applications using web analytics tools

Management issues

Implementation and optimization of e-business systems raises these issues for management:

- What actions can we take to minimize the risks of implementation?
- How do we select the most appropriate systems?
- How do we achieve transition from previous systems to a new e-business system?
- What techniques are available to measure and optimize our services?

Links to other chapters

- This chapter follows naturally from *Chapters 10* and *11*. The context is given in Figure 10.6. The change management plan defined in *Chapter 10* will be enacted in the implementation phase. The coding, testing and changeover aspects of implementation will be based on the analysis and design documentation produced using the techniques described in *Chapter 11*

Introduction

In the traditional software development life cycle the **implementation** and **maintenance** phases are well-defined steps involved with the transition of new software application or system from the production to live environment. The increasing usage of web-based e-business services has rendered the concept of maintenance less useful since this suggests changes are limited to improving performance and bug fixing. Instead, a **dynamic e-business application** requires that content and services will be continuously updated in response to marketplace forces. As competitors introduce new services and offers, and as marketing research reveals problems or opportunities with the site from a customer perspective, ongoing **maintenance activities** will be required for the e-business to remain competitive. Consider the services of Google (Case study 3.1) which are continually updated to improve the user experience, performance and monetization of the service. For example, Google has stated that it makes over 300 changes a year to its search algorithm to combat search spam and deliver more relevant results.

We saw in Chapter 10 how agile development methodologies such as scrum promote continuous development in what is sometimes referred to as a 'permanent beta'. So today there is generally less distinction between development and live phases, and many pureplay e-businesses seek a model of '*continuous release project*' to enable more regular, incremental releases to web functionality. This approach is shown in Figure 12.1.

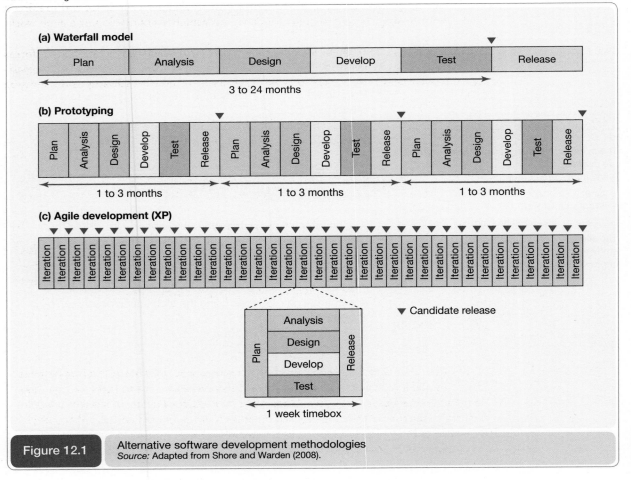

(a) Waterfall model

| Plan | Analysis | Design | Develop | Test | Release |

3 to 24 months

(b) Prototyping

| Plan | Analysis | Design | Develop | Test | Release | Plan | Analysis | Design | Develop | Test | Release | Plan | Analysis | Design | Develop | Test | Release |

1 to 3 months   1 to 3 months   1 to 3 months

(c) Agile development (XP)

Iteration (repeated)

Analysis / Design / Develop / Test — Plan — Release

1 week timebox

▼ Candidate release

| **Figure 12.1** | **Alternative software development methodologies**
Source: Adapted from Shore and Warden (2008). |

While analysis of requirements is occurring, design and implementation will be occurring simultaneously in order to produce storyboards and prototypes. This prototyping may occur in timeboxes of a certain duration, perhaps 30 days or 60 days, with a prototype produced at the end of each timebox. It is evident that implementation activities such as testing and review follow analysis and design and occur for each increment.

Optimization of e-business services

Optimization suggests a rigorous, ongoing approach to improving the effectiveness and efficiency of e-business services. When we reviewed goals for effectiveness and efficiency in Chapter 5, we explained the importance of defining both type of goals. Managers of e-business services need to continually revisit these questions:

- *Service effectiveness.* Is the service meeting business goals? Is the experience and service delivered satisfactory for users? Are new technology approaches or information available that could improve the experience?
- *Service efficiency.* Is the operation of the system measured through speed of response, usability and cost appropriate to lead to an effective service? Are new technology approaches available that could improve the system efficiency?

Web analytics is the discipline which helps answer the questions about experience and service levels for sell-side e-commerce. We see that through techniques like AB and multivariate testing many companies are optimizing through continuous reviews of their sites and services. Producing quality content is also important to an effective experience and requires a sound process to keep content up to date and we cover methods of developing a good workflow for this.

In this chapter we also explore criteria for selecting key e-business technology platforms such as content management systems and web analytics. The 'Real-world e-business experiences' interview below introduces some of the issues involved with selecting and managing a CMS.

Real-world E-Business experiences   The E-consultancy interview

Dane Atkinson, CEO of Squarespace, on selecting a content management system (CMS)

Context

Squarespace is an example of a paid hosted service CMS that is distinct from the free solutions used by many bloggers and small businesses and the large content management systems such as Interwoven. The interview highlights many of the important factors in selecting a CMS and addresses the selection issue of free or fee service.

The interview

Q. What is Squarespace?

Dane Atkinson, Squarespace: Squarespace is an online, fully hosted web publishing platform offering a slick, easy-to-use CMS. Customers are able to build, design, and create fully customized websites, blogs and portfolios in a fraction of the time it would normally take them if they were relying on other services or hard coding it themselves. Because of the flexibility of the Squarespace platform, it appeals to both less experienced, less tech-savvy people (who are able to easily accomplish full site buildouts without knowing a line of code) as well as experienced designers and developers (who are able to access and easily manipulate their site's CSS in order to quickly and more easily create incredibly feature-rich, well designed websites).

Q. On your website, you describe why Squarespace isn't free. With all of the talk about 'free' over the past several years, what led you to avoid the free business model?

Dane Atkinson, Squarespace: We do not aspire to the 'free' business model for a variety of reasons. The most important being that we believe that free is almost never actually free. There are, obviously, costs associated with operating a business: providing server space, hiring employees, maintaining an office space, purchasing equipment, providing customer support, etc.

Though many free services may not require direct payments from their customers to cover these expenses, they are often 'paying' for them in other ways: perhaps they need to contend with advertising, or deal with minimal or unsatisfactory customer support. Or perhaps their free service requires hours upon hours of their own valuable time to maintain, update and customize. Maybe their site is down often, or their site gets hacked and they have no recourse to deal with it. These are the things that people often forget about when they embark upon these 'free' relationships with companies.

We have a very 'clean' and transparent relationship with our customers. They pay us a fee every month and we provide them with an excellent product, round the clock customer support and reliability you often don't find with other hosting providers. When you consider all of the factors mentioned above, our fees often end up being lower than what others are shelling out in hosting, extra bandwidth, professional designers, troubleshooting assistance, and certainly, opportunity costs. None of this is necessary with Squarespace and our customers are happy to pay a monthly fee for their own peace of mind.

Q. Thanks to the economy, more and more companies have started looking to charge their users over the past year. What are some of the key things that companies need to do when building a paid business model?

Dane Atkinson, Squarespace: While there are certainly a wide variety of differences in companies, industries and services, there are a few things that will always remain key factors in building a successful paid business model:

1 Provide an excellent service
2 Fulfil a need that is not currently being met (or do it better than everyone else out there)
3 Focus on customer service
4 Focus on innovation

Our company has grown organically over the past 6 years with very little marketing or advertising. Though we have expanded our efforts in this area over the past year, we continue to get an astonishing number of 'word of mouth' customers or referrals from existing customers. This is in spite of the fact that there are a number of free, direct competitors in our marketplace – which is both inspiring and incredibly humbling.

Q. One interesting thing I noticed is that you offer a 14-day free trial. For an entrepreneur grappling with the best way to offer a free taste of his or her product, what advantages has the free trial model offered you over, say, a freemium model?

Dane Atkinson, Squarespace: We allow customers to try our service, build a site, and then decide whether or not it's for them. That is in stark contrast to a business that offers a free (sometimes degraded version) of their service to a large swath of their customer base in the hopes that they will one day upgrade to a higher paying account level.

Squarespace customers are not of the mindset that any of our services are free or will remain free. We provide a short window of time in which customers can 'test drive' our product, and at the end of that trial period, their choices are very clear cut: remain a valued customer of the company and purchase an account, or not. Happily, our conversion rates speak to the fact that a good chunk of our customers choose to stay.

Q. The market you're competing in is quite competitive. WordPress and Movable Type are both very popular, both free and can be self-hosted. How have you approached defining your target market and differentiating yourself?

Dane Atkinson, Squarespace: While our competitors offer customers products that offer the possibility of achieving similar final results as Squarespace, the process of getting there is very different. We tend to appeal more to a creative, design-savvy customer base that is willing to pay for our services. And as a website building and CMS tool, we believe there simply is nothing else out there that provides the ease, flexibility, and time savings of Squarespace. While we are, admittedly, behind the competition in visibility right now, this is changing very quickly as more and more people turn to us as a solution.

Q. A lot of people found out about Squarespace through your recent Twitter campaign, which went viral. What metrics, if any, did you employ to track ROI?

Dane Atkinson, Squarespace: We paid close attention to our daily traffic, number of Twitter followers, trial account sign-ups, conversions as well as the number of uses (and popularity of) the Squarespace hashtag on Twitter. Though it was more difficult to measure, we also tried to look at our public awareness perception levels throughout the course of the month.

Q. Overall, did you find that the campaign created more buzz and more business, or primarily buzz?

Dane Atkinson, Squarespace: The campaign created much of both. For a company that is not as well known as some of the other major players, the buzz factor was definitely a nice result of the campaign. We learned some lessons as well, and definitely enjoyed watching the trajectory of the campaign play out over the course of 30 days. We saw significant increases in traffic to our site that month, as well as in trial account sign-ups. Our conversions netted out at about 10% higher than average.

Q. Squarespace is an interesting company. Your founder, Anthony Casalena, was 20 years old when he started building the product, you're based in New York, you haven't raised any venture capital and according to your Inc. 500 profile, you generated over $2m in revenue in 2008. Given the economy, do you think more start-ups will resemble Squarespace going forward?

Dane Atkinson, Squarespace: I think it's hard to say how things will shake out. This recession is certainly putting an unexpected spin on many people's business models and forcing many to take stock of how they can ensure their business remains viable in this sort of economy. We are grateful that we've taken the time to thoughtfully put in place a model for Squarespace that seems to be working well both for our customers, and for the growth of our company.

Source: http://econsultancy.com/blog/4647-q-a-dane-atkinson-ceo-of-squarespace.

Alternatives for acquiring e-business systems

Acquisition method
Defines whether the system is purchased outright or developed from scratch.

Bespoke development
Information system development specifically for purpose.

Packaged implementation
Standard software is installed with limited configuration required.

Hosted solution
Standard software which is managed externally on the supplier's server.

Tailored development
The standard solution requires major configuration or integration of different modules.

The basic alternative **acquisition methods** for e-business systems are similar to those for traditional business information systems:

1 *Bespoke development.* With a **bespoke development**, the application is developed from 'scratch' through programming of a solution by an in-house or external development team or systems integrator.
2 *Off-the-shelf.* In a **packaged implementation** a standard existing system is purchased from a solution vendor and installed on servers and clients located within the organization. Alternatively, free or low-cost open-source software may be used. A web design tool such as Dreamweaver is a simple example of an off-the-shelf packaged implementation.
3 *Hosted Software as a Service (SaaS) solution.* With a **hosted solution**, a standard system is used, but it is managed using a third-party applications service provider variously known as 'on-demand', 'web services' or a 'managed solution'. The merits and examples of the SaaS approach have been discussed in Chapters 3 and 6.
4 *Tailored development.* In a **tailored development**, an off-the-shelf system or SaaS solution is tailored according to the organization's needs. This form of project is often based on integrating components from one or several vendors.

Chaffey and Wood (2005) demonstrated that the prevalent approach is the tailored off-the-shelf or hosted approach, which is often the best compromise between meeting an organization's specific needs and reliability while minimizing cost and development time. Decisions also have to be taken as to whether bespoke development or tailoring occurs in-house or using a consultant who is familiar with the latest e-commerce development tools.

Regardless of the source of the system, the main criteria used to select the solution are common. They are:

1 *Functionality.* The features of the application. Describes how well the e-business application meets the business need.
2 *Ease of use.* Systems should be intuitive to minimize the time needed to learn how to use them. A well-constructed piece of software will make it fast to conduct common tasks.
3 *Performance.* The speed of the application to perform different functions. This is measured by how long the user has to wait for individual functions to be completed such as data retrieval, calculation and screen display.
4 *Scalability.* Scalability is related to performance; it describes how well a system can adapt to higher workloads which arise as a company grows. For example, an ERP system will require more customer details, suppliers and products to be held on it as the company grows. The workload will also be higher as the number of internal and external users of the system increases.
5 *Compatibility or interoperability.* This refers to how easy it is to integrate the application with other applications. For example, does it have import and export facilities, does it support transfer of data using XML?
6 *Extensibility.* This describes how easy it is to add new functions or features to a package by adding new modules from the original vendor or other vendors.
7 *Stability or reliability.* All applications have errors or bugs and applications vary in the number of times they fail depending on how well they have been tested since they were first introduced.
8 *Security.* Capabilities for restricting access to applications should be assessed. This is particularly important for hosted solutions.
9 *Support.* Levels of support and the cost of support from the software vendor will vary. There is a risk that small companies may cease trading and the product may no longer be supported.

Now complete Activity 12.1 to consider how these different factors are balanced.

Activity 12.1   Selecting applications software for a small business

Purpose

To aid understanding of the different factors to assess when selecting applications software and the relative importance of them.

Activity

A start-up office supplies business which specializes in supply of printers is reviewing its alternatives for different types of e-business system. Form groups with each group selecting one type of e-business service from the list below and then discussing the importance of the nine criteria for selecting software described above. A ranked list of the criteria in order of importance should be produced. These can be put on a whiteboard, with one type of software in each column to assess the commonality in requirements.

E-business service types:

1 Customer relationship management application.

2 Supply chain management application.

3 Employee management system.

4 Web analytics software (see later in chapter).

Development of web-based content and services

Static web content

A web page view that is identical every time it is loaded.

The delivery of e-business services via a web interface may initially appear straightforward. Everyone has heard apocryphal tales such as a 12-year-old creating a website to sell used cars. Indeed, the creation of **static web content** is straightforward as we will see. In this example, simple HTML code is used for layout and formatting of information to create a simple catalogue of perhaps ten cars, with a web page for each that is accessed from a home page or simple menu. But imagine the situation for a real car dealership where a customer will want to select from a range of hundreds or thousands of cars with different specifications from different manufacturers. Here, it is impractical for the user to select from a menu of hundreds of cars. At the very least, they will expect the cars to be grouped into categories by manufacturer and perhaps sorted by age. But finding the right car through browsing these categories could take a long time and most users will demand a basic search facility by which they type in, or select, the make of car or an advanced search facility by which they choose the make, plus the specification such as engine size and year of registration. In this case the page delivered to the user will depend on their preferences and will be

Dynamic web content

A web page view that varies according to user preferences or environment constraints.

dynamic web content. Here, it is apparent that more than simple formatting and presentation is required – the site is interactive, that is to say it must accept text input from the user and respond to the request with the appropriate information. The development process will involve coding to accept the user's preferences, passing the request to a database, performing a query, returning the results and formatting them for the user.

In this section we briefly introduce how simple static web pages can be developed using HTML and how scripts and databases can be used in conjunction with HTML to produce dynamic content.

Creating static web content

HTML (Hypertext Markup Language)

A standard format used to define the text and layout of web pages. HTML files usually have the extension .HTML or .HTM.

HTML or hypertext markup language, which was introduced in Chapter 3, is the standard that is most commonly used for producing static web content. HTML files can be written with an ordinary text editor or the specialist tools described in a later section.

The operation of HTML is based on a web browser interpreting HTML tags or codes on a web page when it is loaded into the browser, as explained in Chapter 3 (see the example in Figure 3.14). Managers need to be aware of some aspects of HTML development:

1 *Standards compliance.* The World Wide Web Consortium (www.w3.org) has been prominent in defining web standards. Promoting standards has been taken up by other advocacy groups such as the WaSP, the Web Standards Project (www.webstandards. org/about/mission/) and many web design agencies. The use of web standards affects the quality of service and accessibility levels of sites.

   In his seminal reference on web standards, Jeffrey Zeldman says that the best way to view web standards is as '*a continuum, not a set of inflexible rules*'. In practice a combination of the standards shown in Box 12.1 will be required. In particular the use of plug-ins and Ajax should be carefully discussed prior to implementation since this may exclude some site users or force them to use another plug-in.

2 *Cross-browser support.* Dependent on the standards used and how they are implemented, the site may appear different in different browsers since they may have interpreted some of the W3.org standards differently. This can result in a site rendering (appearing) differently in different browsers. Prior to implementation a list of browsers and versions should be targeted and then subsequently tested using tools such as BrowserShots (Figure 3.9).

   Increases accessibility – users can more readily configure the way a site looks or sounds using browsers and other accessibility support tools. Site is more likely to render on a range of access platforms like PDAs and smartphones.

Cascading Style Sheets (CSS)

A simple mechanism for adding style (e.g. fonts, colours, spacing) to web documents. CSS enables different style elements to be controlled across an entire site or section of site.

3 *Use of stylesheets for different platforms.* We introduced **Cascading Style Sheets (CSS)** in Chapter 11 as a mechanism for enabling different style elements such as typography and layout to be controlled across an entire site or section of site.

   Managers need to check with designers that the CSS will be designed to be flexible for making minor changes to presentation (for example in the case of a re-branding) and that it supports different platforms such as mobile access or print output.

4 *Accessibility support.* We saw in the section on user-centred design in Chapter 11 that **web accessibility** is about allowing all users of a website to interact with it regardless of disabilities they may have or the web browser or platform they are using to access the site. The level of accessibility support provided (Level A, AA and AAA) should be defined before implementation and then validated as part of implementation.

Web accessibility

An approach to website design that enables sites and web applications to be used by people with visual impairment or other disabilities such as motor impairment. Accessibility also demands that web users should be able to use websites and applications effectively regardless of the browser or access platform they use and its settings.

5 *SEO support.* We saw in Chapter 9 that different on-page optimization techniques are important to indicate to search engine algorithms the context of the page. Box 12.2 highlights some of the main standards. Unless SEO support is strictly defined as part of a site redesign it may be difficult to change these attributes of a page through a content management system. The on-page factors should be uniquely defined for each page within the site to avoid a 'duplicate content penalty' meaning that the search engine does not index a page since it is considered similar to another page.

   It is also important that staff creating and reviewing content are aware of these factors and can then modify the way their site is described through the content management system. So SEO mark-up needs to be part of a page creation and review process.

6 *Form validation.* Forms are vital pages in a site since they create value from a visit through leads (via a contact us form for example), forum postings or the shopping trolley and checkout. It is vital that they use cross-browser web standards and that they use an appropriate approach to check user inputs are valid.

Box 12.1	Which web standards should the site support?

The main standards typically followed with current versions are:

1 *Structural and semantic standards:*
   HTML (www.w3.org/TR/html401)
   XHTML (www.w3.org/TR/xhtml1)
   XML (www.w3.org/TR/2000/REC-xml-20001006)
2 *Presentation languages:*
   Cascading Style Sheets (CSS) (www.w3.org/TR/css21)
3 *Object models:*
   The Document Object Model (DOM), which describes the structural relationship between objects within an HTML or XML document enabling them to be accessed and updated, for example for form validation www.w3.org/DOM/DOMTR#dom2.
4 *Scripting languages:*
   ECMA Script (the standard to which Javascript has evolved) which is used for form validation, for example www.ecma-international.org/publications/standards/Ecma-262.htm.
5 *Plug-in technology for rich Internet applications:*
   - Adobe Flash and Shockwave (a proprietary standard) for building interactive applications and displaying video http://en.wikipedia.org/wiki/Macromedia_Flash.
   - Adobe Acrobat (www.adobe.com/acrobat), the de facto document display standard.
   - Adobe Flex (www.adobe.com/products/flex) and Microsoft Silverlight (www.microsoft.com/silverlight) for building rich Internet applications (RIA).
   - Streaming media (proprietary standards for audio and video such as Real Networks .rm and Microsoft .wma).
   - Java for rich Internet applications (www.java.com).
6 *Ajax:*
   Ajax is based on other standards, notably JavaScript and XML supported by the DOM and CSS. A key feature of Ajax is that the XMLHttpRequest object is used to exchange data asynchronously with the web server without requiring new browser page loads. http://en.wikipedia.org/wiki/AJAX.

Box 12.2	Key search engine optimization (SEO) requirements

This compilation of the main factors that affect the position of a site within the search engines is taken from SEOMoz (www.seomoz.org), a resource created for webmasters and online marketers to help them achieve better rankings in the search engines.

This compilation shows an assessment of the most important ranking success factors by 30 experts in SEO where they rate each factor out of 5 and then the average is presented. Terms such as <title> and meta description are described in more detail in Chapter 9.

1 *Key on-page optimization factors:*
   These are attributes of the page which are defined through HTML tags with the exception of keyword frequency and density (the number of times a word is repeated on the page in relation to its length) and document name.

- `<title>` tag = 4.9/5
- Keyword frequency and density = 3.7/5
- Keyword in headings = `<h1>` = 3.1, `<h2>` = 2.8
- Keyword in document name = 2.8
- Alt tags and image titles = 2.6 (particularly when linked to destination page)
- Meta name description = 2/5
- Meta name keywords = 1/5

2 *Key off-page optimization factors:*
Off-page optimization describes the characteristics of links to a page from within the site and most importantly from external sites:
- More backlinks (higher page rank) = 4/5
- Link anchor text contains keyword = 4.4/5
- Page assessed as a hub = 3.5/5
- Page assessed as an authority = 3.5/5
- Link velocity (rate at which changes) = 3.5/5

The importance of keyword text in anchor links means that sites which have a linking system based on text rather than image links will perform better for SEO. Another issue to consider when obtaining links from other sites is the use of the nofollow tag on a link, e.g. `<a href= www.domain.com rel="nofollow">Link anchor text</a>`. This indicates to search engines that the link should not be counted in the index and the destination page not indexed (unless it is linked to from another source). This means that many links in social networks and forums are effectively worthless for SEO since their owners have implemented the 'nofollow' to reduce 'SEO spamming'.

Source: SEOMoz (2007).

Software and services for developing e-business applications

Tools are available with different levels of complexity and managers must decide which are most suitable to invest in. The types of tools to choose between are listed below.

Specialized HTML editors

These tools provide facilities for adding HTML and CSS tags automatically. For example, adding the bold text tag `<B> </B>` to the HTML document will happen when the user clicks the bold tag.

Examples

There are many freeware and shareware editors in this category, but most business users will now have WYSIWYG editing integrated into their CMS, so the quality of editor and support for managing workflow of reviewing and publishing posts is a key criteria for these CMSS.

Basic tools

- Dreamweaver (www.macromedia.com/products/dreamweaver).
- Modern versions of word processors such as Microsoft Word or OpenOffice now have these facilities through using the Save As Web Page option but they may add to 'page weight' through additional XML markup code, so cannot typically be used for commercial sites.

Advanced graphics tools

- Adobe Photoshop (extensively used by graphic designers, www.adobe.com).
- Macromedia Flash and Director-Shockwave (used for graphical animations, www.macromedia.com).

Web application frameworks and application servers

Web application frameworks

A standard programming framework based on reusable library functions for creating dynamic websites through a programming language.

Web application frameworks provide a foundation for building dynamic interactive websites and web services. They use standard programming conventions or Application Programming Interface (APIs) in combination with data storage to achieve different tasks such as simply adding a user to a system or rendering the different page elements of a site. They provide standard functions in libraries to make it quicker to develop functionality than starting from lower-level coding. Functions in the web application framework are executed by **web application servers** which are software processes running on the server which accept and action requests via the principal web server software (e.g. Apache or Microsoft Information Server). The Common Gateway Interface (CGI) was a forerunner of this concept since it enabled standard functions to be accessed on a server, for example to perform form validation.

Web application server

Software processes which are accessed by a standard programming interface (API) of a web application framework to serve dynamic website functionality in response to requests received from browsers.

Examples

- *Adobe ColdFusion* (www.adobe.com/products/coldfusion/). An established commercial framework.
- *Microsoft ASP.Net* (www.asp.net) is an evolution of the former Micosoft ASP script-based approach to an entirely different approach based on running compiled code on a server.
- *PHP* (www.php.net) An open-source script-based alternative for development of web applications which can be used to create web applications. Open-source CMS such as Drupal (www.drupal.org) are based on this.
- *JavaBeans Enterprise and Java Server Pages.* Widely used enterprise open-source system promoted by Sun Microsystems which are implemented using the Java language (www.java.com). The ERP system SAP makes extensive use of this framework within its web application versions.
- *Zope* (www.zope.org) An object-based open-source application server using the Python language on which the widely used Plone (www.plone.org) CMS is based.
- *Ruby on Rails* (www.rubyonrails.org) Another relatively new open-source application framework feted for its rapid production of systems and reusability of modules as part of agile development.

A technical discussion of the issues involved with selection of application frameworks and servers is outside the scope of this text. Essentially all of the solutions above have been successfully used to develop enterprise web services and what is most important to successful project delivery is finding the right level of skills for implementation and a project methodology or development process which is effective. The open-source alternatives have lower costs associated, but there may be difficulty in obtaining the right in-house or third-party resources to create applications of some of the less widely used frameworks and servers. This is indicated by Figure 12.2 which shows a survey of the application frameworks used by Fortune 1000 companies in 2007.

Content management systems

Content management system (CMS)

A software tool for creating, editing and updating documents accessed by intranet, extranet or Internet.

A **content management system (CMS)** provides a method for non-specialists to update website pages. This is an efficient method of publishing content since the facility can be made available to people throughout the company. Today there are two main forms of CMS, both of which are delivered as web services which can be accessed through a web browser. Enterprise CMSs can be used for large, complex sites (and other corporate documents) and as well as the standard page creation and editing facilities offer version control and review of documents through workflow systems which notify reviewers when new documents are ready for editing. CMS for smaller companies traditionally lack workflow or multi-author facilities, but offer many of the other features to create content. But blogging platforms such as Wordpress and Moveable Type are increasingly used by smaller businesses for managing their entire site since they have enterprise features.

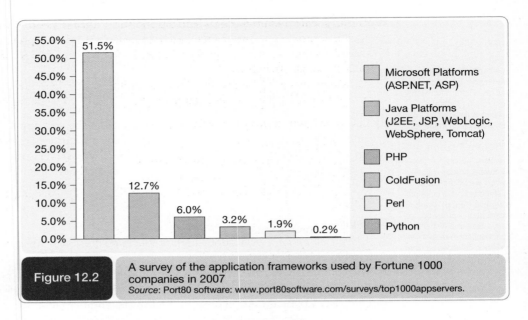

Figure 12.2	A survey of the application frameworks used by Fortune 1000 companies in 2007 *Source*: Port80 software: www.port80software.com/surveys/top1000appservers.

Criteria for selecting a content management system

A professional content management systems should provide these facilities:

- *Easy authoring system.* Editing of new and existing documents should be possible through a WYSIWYG (what you see is what you get) facility similar to a word processor which makes it easy to embed images and supports a range of markup necessary for SEO.
- *Search engine robot crawling.* The content must be stored and linked such that it can be indexed by search engine crawlers to add it to their index. Sometimes URL rewriting to a search-engine-friendly format without many parameters is required. The Google Webmaster pages describe the requirements: www.google.com/webmasters.
- *Search-engine-optimization-friendly markup.* Some bespoke content management systems created by design agencies do not enable easy editing of the key fields shown in Box 12.2, such as <title>, <h1> and <meta name= "description" content="page description">.
- *Different page templates.* The design and maintenance of content structure (sub-compo-nents, templates, etc.), web-page structure and website structure. It should be possible to create different layouts and designs for different site sections or categories of pages.
- *Link management.* The maintenance of internal and external links through content change and the elimination of dead links.
- *Input and syndication.* The loading (spidering) of externally originating content and the aggregation and dissemination of content from a variety of sources.
- *Versioning.* The crucial task of controlling which edition of a page, page element or the whole site is published. Typically this will be the most recent, but previous editions should be archived and it should be possible to roll back to a previous version.
- *Security and access control.* Different permissions can be assigned to different roles of users and some content may only be available through log-in details. In these cases, the CMS maintains a list of users.
- *Use of plug-ins and widgets.* Mashups are possible through embedding widgets such as links to social networks or third-party applications. But a content management system may not readily support embedding within the main content or sidebars.
- *Publication workflow.* Content destined for a website needs to pass through a publication process to move it from the management environment to the live delivery environment. The process may involve tasks such as format conversion (e.g. to PDF, or to WAP), rendering to HTML, editorial authorization and the construction of composite docu-ments in real time (personalization and selective dissemination).

- *Tracking and monitoring.* Providing logs and statistical analysis of use to provide performance measures, tune the content according to demand and protect against misuse. It should also be possible to rapidly add tags to the page templates for web analytics tools such as Google Analytics.
- *Navigation and visualization.* Providing an intuitive, clear and attractive representation of the nature and location of content using colour, texture, 3D rendering or even virtual reality.

The main open source CMSs are:

- Plone (www.plone.org)
- Drupal (www.drupal.org), a PHP version
- Mambo/Joomla (www.mamboserver.com)
- Magento (www.magentocommerce.com), a CMS for managing e-commerce content and sales

Examples of commercial CMSs:

- Interwoven (www.interwoven.com)
- RedDot (www.reddot.com)
- Microsoft Office Sharepoint Server (MOSS, www.microsoft.com)

Blogging systems (personal CMSs):

- Blogger (www.blogger.com)
- Movable Type/TypePad (www.movabletype.com)
- WordPress (www.wordpress.org)

Many of these are open source CMSs, meaning that the cost of ownership is low.

Selecting e-commerce servers

E-commerce servers provide many of the capabilities of a CMS, but they focus on the needs of promoting product information and supporting the purchase process. The basic facilities of display of product content in different categories will be similar, so many of the most important requirements will relate to integration with other internal and external systems. Specific requirements of e-commerce servers include integration with:

- *Product catalogue systems* to import the latest products.
- *Feeds* to support shopping comparison engines such as Google Product Search or Shopzilla.
- *Advanced shopping search* or faceted browsing systems such as Endeca (www.endeca.com), Mercado and Google Mini Search appliance (www.google.com/enterprise).
- *Merchandising systems* which recommend appropriate products and promotions to visitors, for example ATG (www.atg.com).
- *Customer service solutions* including click-to-call or click-to-chat systems (e.g. www.atg.com).
- *Customer reviews and ratings systems*, for example BazaarVoice (www.bazaarvoice.com) and Feefoo (www.feefo.com).
- *Payment systems*, for example Netbanx (www.netbanx.com), Verisign (www.verisign.com), Worldbank (www.worldbank.com) and consumer systems Google Checkout (www.google. com/checkout) and Paypal (www.paypal.com).
- *Enterprise resource management systems* for supply chain management and order fulfilment, for example SAP (www.sap.com).
- *Testing and web analytics systems* since retailers will want to optimize their pages by trialling different versions to increase conversion rates.

Some providers such as ATG seek to include many of these facilities, but many online retailers will want to incorporate 'best-of-breed' technologies for these different applications.

Examples:

- *Actinic* (www.actinic.com) and *Intershop* (www.intershop.com), generally smaller business solutions
- *ATG Commerce Suite* (www.atg.com), generally an enterprise system
- *NetSuite Ecommerce module* (www.netsuite.com), for a range of company sizes integrating with other systems such as accounting and fulfilment.

Testing

Testing

Aims to identify non-conformance in the requirements specification and errors.

Testing has two main objectives: first, to check for non-conformance with the business and user requirements, and, second, to identify bugs or errors. In other words, it checks that the site does what users need and is reliable. Testing is an iterative process that occurs throughout development. As non-conformances are fixed by the development team, there is a risk that the problem may not have been fixed and that new problems have been created. Further testing is required to check that solutions to problems are effective.

The testing process

Test specification

A description of the testing process and tests to be performed.

A structured testing process is necessary in order to identify and solve as many problems as possible before the system is released to users. This testing is conducted in a structured way by using a **test specification** which is a comprehensive specification of testing in all modules of the system. If the use-case method of analysis described in Chapter 11 is used then it will specify the different use-cases or scenarios to be tested in detailed test scripts. The comprehensive testing specification will also cover all the different types of test outlined in Table 12.1.

Table 12.1	Types of testing required for an e-commerce site

Type of testing	Description
Developer tests	Code-level tests performed by developers of modules
Feasibility testing	Tests a new approach, often near the start of a project to make sure it is acceptable in terms of user experience
Module (component) tests	Checks individual modules have the correct functionality, i.e. correct outputs are produced for specified inputs (black-box testing)
Integration testing	Checks interactions between groups of modules
System testing	Checks interactions between all modules in the system
Database transaction taken	Can the user connect to the database and are transactions executed correctly?
Performance/capacity testing	Tests the speed of the system under high load
Usability and accessibility testing	Check that the system is easy to use, follows the conventions of user-centred design and meets accessibility requirements described in Chapter 11
Acceptance tests	Checks the system is acceptable for the party that commissioned it
Content or copy testing	Tests the acceptability of copy from a marketing view

Testing in the web environment requires new constraints. Unfortunately the list of constraints is long and sometimes neglected, to disastrous effect. Retailer Boo.com used a complex graphic to display clothes that was too time-consuming to use for visitors to the site. If there are a thousand potential users of an e-commerce site, all of the following constraints on design may exclude a proportion:

- *Speed of access* – everyone has used sites with huge graphics that take minutes to download. Good designers will optimize graphics for speed and then test using a slow modem across phone lines. Yahoo! downloads in just one second, so this is the performance that users expect from other sites.
- *Screen resolutions* – designing for different screen resolutions is necessary since some users with laptops may be operating at low resolution such as 640 by 480 pixels, the majority at 800 by 600 pixels, a few at higher resolutions of 1064 by 768 pixels or greater. If the designers have designed the site using PCs with high resolutions, they may be difficult to read for the majority.
- *Number of colours* – some users may have monitors capable of displaying 16 million colours giving photo-realism while others may only have the PC set up to display 256 colours.
- *Changing font size* – choosing large fonts on some sites causes unsightly overlap between the different design elements – depends on the type of web browser used.
- *Different browsers* and different versions of browsers may display graphics or text slightly differently or process JavaScript differently, so it is essential to test on a range of browser platforms.
- *Plug-ins such as Macromedia Flash and Shockwave* – if a site requires plug-ins, then a business will be cutting down its audience by the number of people who are unable or unprepared to download these plug-ins.

Development environment
Software and hardware used to create a system.

Testing environments

Test environment
Separate software and hardware used to test a system.

Production or live environment
Software and hardware used to host operational system.

Testing occurs in different environments during the project. Prototypes are tested in a **development environment** which involves programmers' testing data across a network on a shared server. In the implementation phase a special **test environment** may be set up which simulates the final operating environment for the system. This test environment will be used for early user training and testing and for system testing. Finally, the **production or live environment** is that in which the system will be used operationally. This will be used for user acceptance testing and when the system becomes live.

Changeover

Changeover
The term used to describe moving from the old to the new information system.

Soft launch
A preliminary site launch with limited promotion to provide initial feedback and testing of an e-commerce site.

Migration or changeover from a previous information system to a new system is particularly important for mission-critical e-business systems where errors in management of **changeover** will result in a negative customer experience or disruption to the supply chain.

When introducing a new sell-side e-commerce system there are two basic choices. First, the company can fully test the system in a controlled environment before it goes live and thus minimize the risk of adverse publicity due to problems with the site. Second, the company can perform what is known as a '**soft launch**'. Here, after initial testing, the site will be tested in a live environment where customers can use it.

The alternatives for migrating from different versions of a system are reviewed in Bocij *et al.* (2005) and summarized in Table 12.2. Complete Activity 12.2 to review the relative merits of these approaches.

Table 12.2	Advantages and disadvantages of the different methods of implementation	

Method	Main advantages	Main disadvantages
1 **Immediate cutover.** Straight from old system to new system on a single date	Rapid, lowest cost	High risk. Major disruption if serious errors with system
2 **Parallel running.** Old system and new system run side-by-side for a period	Lower risk than immediate cutover	Slower and higher cost than immediate cutover
3 **Phased implementation.** Different modules of the system are introduced sequentially	Good compromise between methods 1 and 2	Difficult to achieve technically due to interdependencies between modules
4 **Pilot system.** Trial implementation occurs before widespread deployment	Essential for multinational or national rollouts	Has to be used in combination with the other methods
5 **'Perpetual beta'**	Used by on-demand service providers such as the search engines to introduce new functionality in modules	Errors not identified in testing may impact large numbers of users, but can be updated to users rapidly

Activity 12.2	Understanding e-commerce and e-business

Purpose

Highlight the most suitable techniques for changeover.

Activity

1 Identify the variables which will determine the choice of changeover method.

2 Which changeover alternative would you recommend for a B2B company if it introduces a new intranet-based virtual helpdesk?

3 Justify your answer by analysing in a table the degree of risk, from high to low for each factor across each approach.

Answers to activities can be found at www.pearsoned.co.uk/chaffey

Database creation and data migration

Data migration
Transfer of data from old systems to new systems.

A final aspect of changeover that should be mentioned, and is often underestimated, is **data migration**. For an e-commerce system for a bank, for example, this would involve transferring or exporting data on existing customers and importing them to the new system. This is sometimes also referred to as 'populating the database'. Alternatively, a middleware layer may be set up such that the new system accesses customers from the original legacy database. Before migration occurs it is also necessary for a member of the development team known as 'the database administrator' to create the e-commerce databases. This can be time-consuming since it involves:

- Creating the different tables by entering the field definitions arising from the data modelling described in Chapter 11.
- Creating the different roles of users such as their security rights or access privileges. These need to be created for internal and external users.

- Creating stored procedures and triggers, which is effectively server-side coding to implement business rules.
- Optimizing the database for performance.

Supporting search engines is significant where companies migrate their content to a new domain name or use a different CMS or commerce server which uses different document names. There is a risk that the search engine will lose the history of previous ranking based on backlinks to the site and its pages. To manage this a mapping can be provided to redirect from the old to the new pages known as a '301 redirect' on Apache servers.

Deployment planning

Deployment plan
A schedule which defines all the tasks that need to occur in order for changeover to occur successfully. This includes putting in place all the infrastructure such as cabling and hardware.

Systems integrator
A company that organizes the procurement and installation of hardware and software needed for implementation.

A **deployment plan** is needed to put in place the hardware and software infrastructure in time for user acceptance testing. This is not a trivial task since often a range of equipment will be required from a variety of manufacturers. Although the project manager is ultimately responsible for deployment planning, many companies employ **systems integrators** to coordinate these activities, particularly where there is a national rollout.

Content management and maintenance

Sell-side e-commerce sites are continuously under development, even when they become live. The sites need to be dynamic to deal with errors reported by customers and in response to innovations by competitors. Additionally the content, such as information about different events or new product launches and price promotions, will need to be updated if the site is to generate repeat visits from customers.

Buy-side e-commerce sites are less dynamic and are more akin to traditional business information systems, so in this section we will focus on maintenance of e-commerce sites, although this description will also apply to e-business implementations of intranets and extranets.

What are the management issues involved with maintenance? These are some of the challenges:

- Deciding on the frequency and scope of content updating.
- Processes for managing maintenance of the site and responsibilities for updating.
- Selection of content management system (covered in the previous section).
- Testing and communicating changes made.
- Integration with monitoring and measurement systems.
- Managing content in the global organization.

As realization of content as a strategic asset grows, more senior roles are being created to manage content quality. See Box 12.3.

| Box 12.3 | Logitech appoint a content strategist |

Computer peripheral provider Logitech advertised for a content strategist. This job description for a content strategist in a large company helps show us the key aspects of content strategy. These requirements summarize the essence of a sound content strategy:

- Senior management must understand the importance of content strategy to invest in good quality resources with high-profile roles.

- Content must be of exceptional quality to be most effective – the job description says: '*useful, compelling and meaningful*'.
- Involves a strategy for syndication – not limited to company's own site.
- Blends improving customer experience, customer engagement and SEO.
- Requires an editorial calendar to manage creation of content.
- Content quality improved through a continuous process applying analytics and customer satisfaction.
- Integrates copywriting, web platform design and implementation, marketing communications, PR and SEO resources or teams.
- Supports goals and essence of company brand.

Content strategist responsibilities

- Drive the development and organization of content that is useful, compelling and meaningful – directly on logitech.com and indirectly through distributed content.
- Create user flows, information hierarchies, wireframes and content strategy for Logitech.com in support of campaigns, product launches and ongoing improvement.
- Determine content requirements for logitech.com, inventory existing content, identify gaps, evaluate possible sources for additional material, and manage the process of getting that content into production.
- Creatively look for opportunities to improve content, consumer experience and SEO performance.
- Manage the Logitech.com editorial calendar to proactively keep content useful and up to date.
- Use analytics, consumer and usability testing and business requirements to help improve the experience and the content of Logitech.com in the long and short term.
- Work with the web, writing, PR and marcomm teams to determine the most effective ways to support campaigns and product launches on the web.
- Lead projects that make our web and component communication more intuitive and useful to consumers and internal partners.
- Work with brand architecture and terminology to guide the effective organization of products and activities on Logitech.com.
- Drive the architecture of and improvements to the internal product content management system (worldwide product database) to fit the needs of the organization.
- Occasionally write or edit content – particularly metadata, titles, alt text and edit general content to optimize for natural search.

Content strategist requirements

- 4-year college degree in a relevant field required, Masters degree preferred.
- 5–7 years of experience in an information architecture role, with 2–3 years working on complex websites.
- 2–3 years of experience being directly responsible for content strategy on a dynamic, complex or ever-evolving website.
- Experience with web content management systems, component content management systems (DITA or otherwise) and authoring systems (XML or other).
- Strong strategic, analytical skills with a solid ability to articulate information requirements clearly.
- A creative and collaborative approach that elevates the creative and communication opportunities – rather than straight analysis.
- Expertise in content strategy – including strong experience in SEO and keyword analysis as well as planning flexible approaches to keep content accurate and fresh.
- Accomplishments in the effective use of syndication (in and out) and user-generated content as well as working collaboratively with writers and designers.

- The ability to be measured by hard metrics – views, time on site, consumer feedback – as well as soft metrics – support of the brand vision and architecture, consumer perception.
- Demonstrated ability to visualize and communicate complex information using Microsoft Visio or similar software.
- Deep experience with all levels of UX strategy and testing – but the ability to act quickly on consumer insights and best practices.
- Solid work ethic, ability to perform under pressure, meet deadlines, prioritize and deliver multiple tasks on time.
- Willing to learn and contribute to a strong team environment.
- Enthusiastic about the products and the possibilities of Logitech.

Other Information

Logitech knows the value of strategic communication and content and now we're expanding our team to make the most of it. The global marketing team needs an expert who is ready to add his or her brain, talent and creativity to the cause of making our content work smarter, harder and around the globe. This is an opportunity for an IA/content strategy professional to put both strategy and executional excellence into practice every day and make an immediate and visible impact on the efficacy of a global organization.

This role reports directly into the Global Director of Writing and Brand Architecture, with a direct and ongoing relationship with the Director of Global Web Marketing.

Source: Job description, Information Architect/ Content Strategist for Logitech, posted 29 September 2010: http://jobs.mashable.com/a/jbb/job-details/379895.

Frequency and scope of content updating

The moment an e-commerce system is live it will require updates to the content and services. Different types of content updating can be identified, and a different approach will be required for each. We can apply the fault taxonomy of Jorgensen (1995) to an e-commerce site to decide on the timing of the action required according to the type of problem. We can see that the approach is quite different from that for a traditional information system or packaged software that is distributed to thousands of customers. For example, with a mild problem such as a spelling mistake within software, it would be too costly to update and redistribute the software. With the e-commerce site, a spelling mistake, although trivial, can be updated immediately by correcting it on the web page or in the database or content management system where it is stored. Indeed, minor problems need to be corrected because they reduce the credibility of the site.

For more major errors, it is essential to fix the problems as soon as possible since revenue will be lost, both from customers who are unable to complete their current purchases and from users who will be unprepared to use the site in future because of their bad experience. Data from transactional e-commerce sites show that very few have continuous availability. If the site revenue for a 24-hours, 7-days-a-week site is £10 million per week then if availability falls to 95% this is the equivalent of losing £500,000 before the loss of future revenues from disgruntled customers is taken into account. A modular or component-based approach to e-commerce systems should enable the location of the problem module or cartridge to be identified rapidly and the problem in the module to be fixed, or possibly to revert to the previous version.

As well as fixing the problems shown in Table 12.3 companies will also wish to update the functionality of the e-commerce system in response to customer demands, sales promotions or competitor innovations. Again, a component-based approach can enable self-contained, discrete, new modules or cartridges to be plugged into the system which are

Table 12.3	Fault taxonomy described in Jorgensen (1995) applied to an e-commerce site

Category	Example	Action – traditional BIS or packaged software	Action – e-commerce site
1 Mild	Misspelt word	Ignore or fix when next major release occurs	Fix immediately
2 Moderate	Misleading or redundant information. Problem with font readability	Ignore or defer to next major release	Fix immediately
3 Annoying	Truncated text, failed JavaScript, but site still usable	Defer to next major release	Fix immediately
4 Disturbing	Some transactions not processed correctly, intermittent crashes in one module	Defer to next maintenance release	Urgent patch required for module
5 Serious	Lost transactions	Defer to next maintenance release. May need immediate fix and release	Urgent patch required for module
6 Very serious	Crash occurs regularly in one module	Immediate solution needed	Urgent patch required for module, revert to previous version
7 Extreme	Frequent very serious errors	Immediate solution needed	Urgent patch required for module, revert to previous version
8 Intolerable	Database corruption	Immediate solution needed	Urgent patch required for module, revert to previous version
9 Catastrophic	System crashes, cannot be restarted – system unusable	Immediate solution needed	Urgent patch required for module, revert to previous version
10 Infectious	Catastrophic problem also causes failure of other systems	Immediate solution needed	Revert to previous version

Source: Copyright © 1995 from *Software Testing: A Craftsman's Approach* by Paul C. Jorgensen. Reproduced by permission of Routledge/Taylor & Francis Group, LLC.

designed to provide new functionality with only minimal changes to existing modules. For each such update, a small-scale prototyping process involving analysis, design and testing will need to occur.

Maintenance process and responsibilities

For efficient updating of an e-commerce system, it is vital to have a clearly defined process for content and service changes. Different processes will apply depending on the scope of the change, as described in the previous section. We can identify two different types of changes – routine content changes such as updates to documents on the site or new documents and major changes where we make changes to the structure, navigation or services on the site.

Process for routine content changes

The process for routine content changes should be communicated to all staff providing content to the site, with responsibilities clearly identified in their job descriptions. The main stages involved in producing an updated web page are to design it, write it, test it and publish it. A more detailed process is indicated here which distinguishes between review of the content and technical testing of the completed web page.

According to Chaffey *et al.* (2009), the different tasks involved in the maintenance process for new copy are as follows:

1 *Write.* This stage involves writing copy and, if necessary, designing the layout of copy and associated images.
2 *Review.* An independent review of the copy is necessary to check for errors before a document is published. Depending on the size of organization, review may be necessary by one person or several people covering different aspects of site quality such as corporate image, marketing copy, branding and legality.
3 *Correct.* This stage is straightforward and involves updates necessary as a result of stage 2.
4 *Publish (to test environment).* The publication stage involves putting the corrected copy on a web page which can be checked further. This will be in a test environment that can only be viewed from inside the company.
5 *Test.* Before the completed web page is made available over the World Wide Web a final test will be required for technical issues such as whether the page loads successfully on different browsers.
6 *Publish (to live environment).* Once the material has been reviewed and tested and is signed off as satisfactory it will be published to the main website and will be accessible by customers.

The difficulty is that all these stages are required for quality control, but if different people are involved, then rapid, responsive publication is not possible. Activity 12.3 illustrates a typical problem of content maintenance, involving the six stages described above, and assesses changes that could be made to improve the situation.

Activity 12.3	Optimizing the content review process at a B2C company

Purpose

Assess how quality control and efficiency can be balanced for revisions to web content.

Activity

The extract below and Figure 12.3 illustrate a problem of updating encountered by a B2C company. How can they solve this problem?

Problem description

From when the brand manager identifies a need to update copy for their product, the update might happen as follows: brand manager writes copy (1–2 days), one day later the web manager reviews copy, three days later the marketing manager checks the copy, seven days later the legal department checks the copy, two days later the revised copy is implemented on the test site, two days later the brand manager reviews the test site, the next day the web manager reviews the website followed by updating and final review before the copy is added to the live site two days later and over a fortnight from when a relatively minor change to the site was identified!

Answers to activities can be found at www.pearsoned.co.uk/chaffey

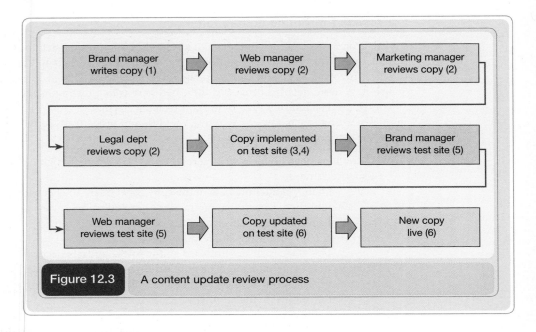

Brand manager writes copy (1)	Web manager reviews copy (2)	Marketing manager reviews copy (2)
Legal dept reviews copy (2)	Copy implemented on test site (3,4)	Brand manager reviews test site (5)
Web manager reviews test site (5)	Copy updated on test site (6)	New copy live (6)

Figure 12.3   A content update review process

Frequency of content updates

Since the web is perceived as a dynamic medium, customers expect new information to be posted to a site straightaway. If material is inaccurate or 'stale' then the customer may not return to the site.

As information on a web page becomes outdated and will need to be updated, it is important to have a mechanism defining what triggers this update process. Trigger procedures should be developed such that when price changes, PR release or product specifications are updated in promotional leaflets or catalogues, these changes are also reflected on the website. Without procedures of this type, it is easy for there to be mismatches between online and offline content.

As part of defining a website update process and standards, a company may want to issue guidelines which suggest how often content is updated. This may specify that content is updated as follows:

- within two days of a factual error being identified;
- a new 'news' item is added at least once a month;
- when product information has been static for two months.

Process for major changes

For major changes to a website, such as changing the menu structure, adding a new section of content or changing the services for users, a different process is required. Such changes will involve a larger investment and there will be limited funds, so priorities must be agreed. The approach that is usually used is to set up a steering committee to ratify proposed changes. Such a decision usually needs an independent chair such as the e-commerce manager or marketing manager to make the final decision. The typical structure of such a committee is shown in Figure 12.4(a). It is made up of both technical and business staff and is useful for encouraging integration between these roles. Typical roles of some members of the committee who may also be involved in update of the site are shown in Figure 12.4(b). Figure 12.4(a), which could apply to Internet, extranet or intranet content, shows how a pyramid arrangement is used to ensure content quality on the site.

The committee will typically have a range of responsibilities such as:

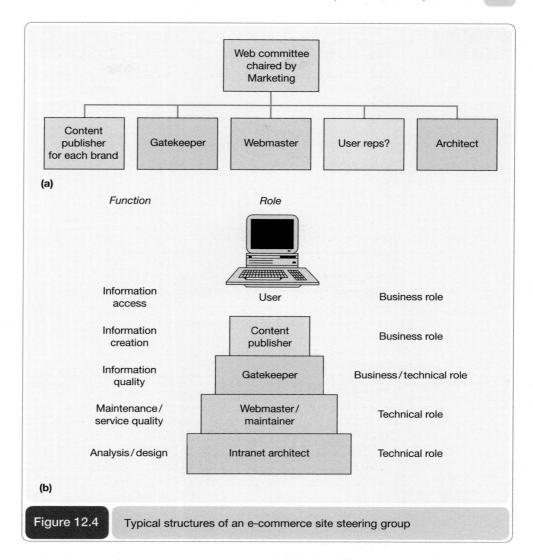

| Figure 12.4 | Typical structures of an e-commerce site steering group |

- Defining agreed update process and responsibilities for different types of changes.
- Specifying site standards for structure, navigation and look and feel (Table 12.4).
- Specifying the tools that are used to update and manage content.
- Assessing proposals for major changes to site standards, content and services.
- Reviewing quality of service in terms of customer service and security.
- Specifying online promotion methods for the site (e.g. search engine registration) and evaluating the business contribution delivered via the site.
- Managing the budget for the site.

Initiatives to keep content fresh

It is often said that up-to-date content is crucial to site 'stickiness', but fresh content will not happen by accident, so companies have to consider approaches that can be used to control the quality of documents and in particular to keep them up to date and relevant. Generic approaches that can work well are:

- Assign responsibility for particular content types or site sections to individuals.
- Make the quality of web content produced part of employees' performance appraisal.
- Produce a target schedule for publication of content.

Table 12.4	Website standards	
Standard	**Details**	**Applies to**
Site structure	Will specify the main areas of the site, e.g. products, customer service, press releases, how to place content and who is responsible for each area.	Content developers
Navigation	May specify, for instance, that the main menu must always be on the left of the screen with nested (sub) menus at the foot of the screen. The home button should be accessible from every screen at the top-left corner of the screen.	Website designer/webmaster usually achieves these through site templates
Copy style	General guidelines, for example, reminding those writing copy that copy for the web needs to be briefer than its paper equivalent. Where detail is required, perhaps with product specifications, it should be broken up into chunks that are digestible on screen.	Individual content developers
Testing standards	Check site functions for: • different browser types and versions • plug-ins and invalid links • speed of download of graphics • spellchecking each page.	Website designer/webmaster
Corporate branding and graphic design	Specifies the appearance of company logos and the colours and typefaces used to convey the brand message.	Website designer/webmaster
Process	The sequence of events for publishing a new web page or updating an existing page. Who is responsible for reviewing and updating?	All
Performance	Availability and download speed figures.	Webmaster and designers

- Identify events which trigger the publication of new content, e.g. a new product launch, price change or press release.
- Identify stages and responsibilities in updating – who specifies, who creates, who reviews, who checks, who publishes.
- Measure the usage of content through web analytics or get feedback from site users.
- Publish a league table of content to highlight when content is out of date.
- Audit and publish content to show which is up to date.

Managing content for a global site

The issues in developing content management policies that are described above are complicated for a large organization with many lines of business and particularly for a multinational company. Centralization can give economies of scale and can achieve consistency in the way brand values are communicated nationally and internationally. However, content will need to be developed locally for regional audiences and this may require variations from central guidelines. Some regional autonomy needs to be allowed to enable buy-in from the different regions. It can be suggested that the following are required at an international level:

1 *Technology platform.* A common software system (CMS) will reduce costs of purchase, update and training. Integration with common software for customer relationship management (Chapter 9) and evaluation and measurement systems (see later in this chapter) will also be most efficient.

2 *System architecture.* A consistent architecture will avoid 'reinventing the wheel' in each country and will enable staff, partners and customers who need to access the CMS in different countries to be immediately familiar with it. Standards include:
- Common page layout and navigation through templates.
- Common directory structures and consistent URL structure.
- Programming standard and languages and version control systems.

3 *Process/standards.* Update procedures for review of content for marketing, data protection and legal reasons as described in previous sections. Back-up and archiving policies will also be required.

Focus on	Web analytics: measuring and improving performance of e-business services

We review measuring and improving the effectiveness of e-commerce system in detail since it is a key part of optimizing e-commerce. We focus on measurement of sell-side e-commerce, since the approach is most advanced for this sector, but the principles and practice can be readily applied to other types of e-business system such as intranets and extranets.

Companies that have a successful approach to e-commerce often seem to share a common characteristic. They attach great importance and devote resources to monitoring the success of their online marketing and putting in place the processes to continuously improve the performance of their digital channels. This culture of measurement is visible in the UK bank Alliance and Leicester (Santander). Stephen Leonard, head of e-commerce, described their process as 'Test, Learn, Refine' (*Revolution*, 2004). Graeme Findlay, senior manager, customer acquisition of e-commerce at A&L, explains further: '*Our online approach is integrated with our offline brand and creative strategy, with a focus on direct, straightforward presentation of strong, value-led messages. Everything we do online, including creative, is driven by an extensive and dynamic testing process.*'

Seth Romanow, Director of Customer Knowledge at Hewlett-Packard, speaking at the 2004 E-metrics summit, described their process as 'Measure, Report, Analyse, Optimize'. Amazon refers to its approach as 'The Culture of Metrics' (see Case study 12.1). Jim Sterne, who convenes an annual event devoted to improving online performance (www.emetrics. org), has summarized his view on the required approach in his book *Web Metrics* (Sterne, 2002) as 'TIMITI' which stands for 'Try It! Measure It! Tweak It!' i.e. online content should be reviewed and improved continuously rather than as a periodic or ad hoc process. The importance of defining an appropriate approach to measurement and improvement is such that the term '**web analytics**' has developed to describe this key Internet marketing activity. A web analytics association (www.webanalyticsassociation.org) has been developed by vendors, consultants and researchers in this area. Eric Petersen (2004), an analyst specializing in web analytics, defines it as follows:

> *Web analytics is the assessment of a variety of data, including web traffic, web-based transactions, web server performance, usability studies, user submitted information [i.e. surveys], and related sources to help create a generalised understanding of the visitor experience online.*

Web analytics
Techniques used to assess and improve the contribution of e-marketing to a business.

You can see that in addition to what are commonly referred to as 'site statistics' about web traffic, sales transactions, usability and researching customers' views through surveys are also included. However, this suggests analysis for the sake of it – whereas the business purpose of analytics should be emphasized. The definition could also refer to comparison of site visitor volumes and demographics relative to competitors using panels and ISP collected data. Our definition is:

Web analytics is the customer-centred evaluation of the effectiveness of Internet-based marketing in order to improve the business contribution of online channels to an organization.

A more recent definition from the Web Analytics Association (WAA, www. webanalyticsassociation.org) in 2005 is:

Web Analytics is the objective tracking, collection, measurement, reporting and analysis of quantitative Internet data to optimize websites and web marketing initiatives.

Principles of performance management and improvement

To improve results for any aspect of any business, performance management is vital. As Bob Napier, Chief Information Officer, Hewlett-Packard, was reported to have said back in the 1960s:

You can't manage what you can't measure.

The processes and systems intended to monitor and improve the performance of an organization and specific management activities such as Internet marketing are widely known as '**performance management systems**' and are based on the study of **performance measurement systems**.

Measurement is often neglected when a website is first created. Measurement is often highlighted as an issue once early versions of a site have been 'up and running' for a few months or even years, and employees start to ask questions such as '*How many customers are visiting our site, how many sales are we achieving as a result of our site and how can we improve the site to achieve a return on investment?*' The consequence of this is that performance measurement is often built into an online presence retrospectively. If measurement is built into site management, a more accurate approach can be developed and it is more readily possible to apply a technique known as '**design for analysis**' (**DFA**). Here, the site is designed so companies can better understand the types of audience and their decision points. For example, for Dell (www.dell.com), the primary navigation on the home page is by business type. This is a simple example of DFA since it enables Dell to estimate the proportion of different audiences to their site and at the same time connect them with relevant content. Other examples of DFA include:

- Breaking up a long page or form into different parts, so you can see which parts people are interested in.
- A URL policy used to recommend entry pages for printed material.
- Group content by audience type or buying decision and setting up content groups of related content within web analytics systems.
- Measure attrition at different points in a customer journey, e.g. exit points on a five-page buying cycle.

In this section, we will review approaches to performance management by examining three key elements of an e-commerce performance improvement system. These are, first, the *process* for improvement, secondly, the measurement framework which specifies groups of relevant **Internet marketing metrics** and, finally, an assessment of the suitability of tools and techniques for collecting, analysing, disseminating and actioning results.

Stage 1: Creating a performance management system

The essence of performance *management* is suggested by the definition for performance *measurement* used by Andy Neely of Cranfield School of Management's Centre for Business Performance. He defines (Neely *et al.*, 2002) performance measurement as:

the process of quantifying the efficiency and effectiveness of past actions through acquisition, collation, sorting, analysis, interpretation and dissemination of appropriate data.

Performance management system

A process used to evaluate and improve the efficiency and effectiveness of an organization and its processes.

Performance measurement system

The process by which metrics are defined, collected, disseminated and actioned.

Design for analysis (DFA)

The required measures from a site are considered during design to better understand the audience of a site and their decision points.

Internet marketing metrics

Measures that indicate the effectiveness of Internet marketing activities in meeting customer, business and marketing objectives.

Performance management extends this definition to the process of analysis and actioning change in order to drive business performance and returns. Online marketers can apply many of the approaches of business performance management to Internet marketing. As you can see from the definition, performance is measured primarily through information on process **effectiveness** and **efficiency** as introduced in Chapter 5 in the section on objective setting where we noted that it is important to include both effectiveness and efficiency measures.

The need for a structured performance management process is clear if we examine the repercussions if an organization does not have one. These include: poor linkage of measures with strategic objectives or even absence of objectives; key data not collected; data inaccuracies; data not disseminated or analysed; or no corrective action. Many of the barriers to improvement of measurement systems reported by respondents in Adams *et al.* (2000) also indicate the lack of an effective process. The barriers can be grouped as follows:

- *senior management myopia* – performance measurement not seen as a priority, not understood or targeted at the wrong targets – reducing costs rather than improving performance;
- *unclear responsibilities for delivering and improving the measurement system;*
- *resourcing issues* – lack of time (perhaps suggesting lack of staff motivation), the necessary technology and integrated systems;
- *data problems* – data overload or of poor quality, limited data for benchmarking.

To avoid these pitfalls, a coordinated, structured measurement process such as that shown in Figure 12.5 is required. Figure 12.5 indicates four key stages in a measurement process. These were defined as key aspects of annual plan control by Kotler (1997). Stage 1 is a goal-setting stage where the aims of the measurement system are defined – this will usually take the strategic Internet marketing objectives as an input to the measurement system. The aim of the measurement system will be to assess whether these goals are achieved and specify corrective marketing actions to reduce variance between target and actual key performance indicators. Stage 2, performance measurement, involves collecting data to determine the different metrics that are part of a measurement framework as discussed in the next section. Stage 3, performance diagnosis, is the analysis of results to understand the reasons for variance from objectives (the 'performance gap' of Friedman and Furey, 1999) and selection of marketing solutions to reduce variance. The purpose of Stage 4, corrective action, according to Wisner and Fawcett (1991), is:

> to identify competitive position, locate problem areas, assist the firm in updating strategic objectives and making tactical decisions to achieve these objectives and supply feedback after the decisions are implemented.

Effectiveness

Meeting process objectives, delivering the required outputs and outcomes. 'Doing the right thing.'

Efficiency

Minimizing resources or time needed to complete a process. 'Doing the thing right.'

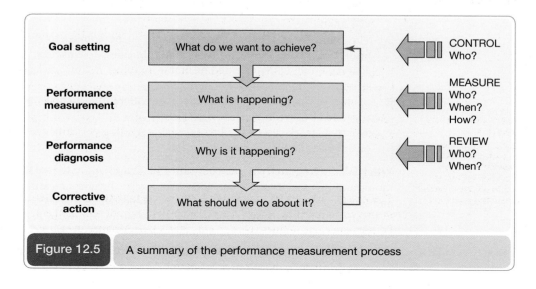

Goal setting	What do we want to achieve?	CONTROL Who?
Performance measurement	What is happening?	MEASURE Who? When? How?
Performance diagnosis	Why is it happening?	REVIEW Who? When?
Corrective action	What should we do about it?	

Figure 12.5 A summary of the performance measurement process

In an Internet marketing context, corrective action is the implementation of these solutions as updates to website content, design and associated marketing communications. At this stage the continuous cycle repeats, possibly with modified goals. Bourne *et al.* (2000) and Plant (2000) suggest that in addition to reviewing objectives, the suitability of the metrics should also be reviewed and revised.

Measurement is not something that can occur on an ad hoc basis because if it is left to the individual they may forget to collect the data needed. A 'measurement culture' is one in which each employee is aware of the need to collect data on how well the company is performing and on how well it is meeting its customers' needs.

Stage 2: Defining the performance metrics framework

Measurement for assessing the effectiveness of Internet marketing can be thought of as answering these questions:

1 Are corporate objectives identified in the Internet marketing strategy being met?
2 Are marketing objectives defined in the Internet marketing strategy and plan achieved?
3 Are marketing communications objectives identified in the Internet marketing plan achieved?
4 How efficient are the different promotional techniques used to attract visitors to a site?

Efficiency measures are more concerned with minimizing the costs of online marketing while maximizing the returns for different areas of focus such as acquiring visitors to a website, converting visitors to outcome or achieving repeat business.

Chaffey (2000) suggests that organizations define a measurement framework which defines groupings of specific metrics used to assess Internet marketing performance. He suggests that suitable measurement frameworks will fulfil these criteria:

A Include both macro-level effectiveness metrics which assess whether strategic goals are achieved and indicate to what extent e-marketing contributes to the business (revenue contribution and return on investment).

B Include micro-level metrics which assess the efficiency of e-marketing tactics and implementation. Wisner and Fawcett (1991) note that typically organizations use a hierarchy of measures and they should check that the lower-level measures support the macro-level strategic objectives. Such measures are often referred to as *performance drivers*, since achieving targets for these measures will assist in achieving strategic objectives. E-marketing performance drivers help optimize e-marketing by attracting more site visitors and increasing conversion to desired marketing outcomes.

C Assess the impact of the e-marketing on the satisfaction, loyalty and contribution of key stakeholders (customers, investors, employees and partners) as suggested by Adams *et al.* (2000).

D The framework must be flexible enough to be applied to different forms of online presence whether business-to-consumer, business-to-business, not-for-profit or transactional e-tail, CRM-oriented or brand-building. Adams *et al.* (2000) note that a 'one-size-fits-all' framework is not desirable.

E Enable comparison of performance of different e-channels with other channels as suggested by Friedman and Furey (1999).

F The framework can be used to assess e-marketing performance against competitors' or out-of-sector best-practice.

When identifying metrics it is common practice to apply the widely used SMART mnemonic and it is also useful to consider three levels – business measures, marketing measures and specific Internet marketing measures (see objective setting section in Chapter 5).

Chaffey (2000) presents a framework of measures, shown in Figure 12.6, which can be applied to a range of different companies. Metrics for the categories are generated as objectives from Internet marketing planning which then need to be monitored to assess the

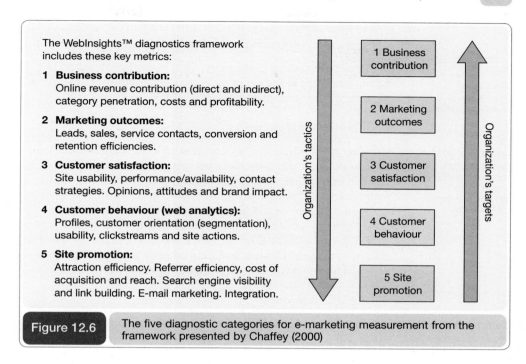

The WebInsights™ diagnostics framework includes these key metrics:

1 **Business contribution:**
   Online revenue contribution (direct and indirect), category penetration, costs and profitability.

2 **Marketing outcomes:**
   Leads, sales, service contacts, conversion and retention efficiencies.

3 **Customer satisfaction:**
   Site usability, performance/availability, contact strategies. Opinions, attitudes and brand impact.

4 **Customer behaviour (web analytics):**
   Profiles, customer orientation (segmentation), usability, clickstreams and site actions.

5 **Site promotion:**
   Attraction efficiency. Referrer efficiency, cost of acquisition and reach. Search engine visibility and link building. E-mail marketing. Integration.

Figure 12.6	The five diagnostic categories for e-marketing measurement from the framework presented by Chaffey (2000)

success of strategy and its implementation. Objectives can be devised in a top-down fashion, starting with strategic objectives for business contribution and marketing outcomes leading to tactical objectives for customer satisfaction, behaviour and site promotion. An alternative perspective is bottom-up – success in achieving objectives for site promotion, on-site customer behaviour and customer satisfaction lead sequentially to achieving objectives for marketing outcomes and business contribution.

1 Channel promotion

Channel promotion

Measures that assess why customers visit a site – which adverts they have seen, which sites they have been referred from.

Referrer

The site that a visitor previously visited before following a link.

Channel-promotion measures consider where the website users originate – online or offline, and what are the sites or offline media that have prompted their visit. Log file analysis can be used to assess which intermediary sites customers are **referred** from and even which keywords they typed into search engines when trying to locate product information. Promotion is successful if traffic is generated that meets objectives of volume and quality. Quality will be determined by whether visitors are in the target market and have a propensity for the service offered (conversion rates for different referrers). Overall hits or page views are not enough – inspection of log files for companies shows that a high proportion of visitors get no further than the home page! Differences in costs of acquiring customers via different channels also need to be assessed.

Key measure: referral mix. For each referral source such as offline or banner ads online it should be possible to calculate:

- % of all referrals (or visitors);
- cost of acquisition (CPA) or cost per sale (CPS);
- contribution to sales or other outcomes.

2 Channel buyer behaviour

Channel buyer behaviour

Describes which content is visited, time and duration.

Once customers have been attracted to the site we can monitor content accessed, when they visit and how long they stay, and whether this interaction with content leads to satisfactory marketing outcomes such as new leads or sales. If visitors are incentivized to register on-site it is possible to build up profiles of behaviour for different segments. It is also important to recognize return visitors for whom cookies or log-in are used.

Key measures are:

Bounce rates for different pages, i.e. proportion of single page visits:

Home page views/all page views, e.g.	20% = (2,358/11,612)
Stickiness: Page views/visitor sessions, e.g.	6 = 11,612/2,048
Repeats: Visitor sessions/visitors, e.g.	2 = 2,048/970.

Stickiness

An indication of how long a visitor stays on-site.

3 Channel satisfaction

Channel satisfaction

Evaluation of the customer's opinion of the service quality on the site and supporting services such as e-mail.

Channel satisfaction with the online experience is vital in achieving the desired channel outcomes, although it is difficult to set specific objectives. However, it is not directly reported through web analytics, so is often not reported. Online methods such as online questionnaires, focus groups and interviews can be used to assess customers' opinions of the website content and customer service and how it has affected overall perception of brand. We reviewed five classes of website feedback tools in Chapter 11 in the section on user-centred design.

Key measure: channel satisfaction indices. These are discussed in Chapter 8 and include ease of use, site availability and performance, and e-mail response. To compare customer satisfaction with other sites, benchmarking services can be used.

4 Channel outcomes

Conversion rate

Percentage of site visitors who perform a particular action such as making a purchase.

Traditional marketing objectives such as number of sales, number of leads, **conversion rates** and targets for customer acquisition and retention should be set and then compared to other channels. Dell Computer (www.dell.com) records on-site sales and also orders generated as a result of site visits, but placed by phone to a specific number unique to the site.

Key measure: channel contribution (direct and indirect).

Channel outcomes

Record customer actions taken as a consequence of a site visit.

A widely used method of assessing **channel outcomes** is to review the conversion rate, which gives an indication of the percentage of site visitors who take a particular outcome. For example:

Conversion rate, visitors to purchase = 2% (10,000 visitors, of which 200 make purchases).
Conversion rate, visitors to registration = 5% (10,000 visitors, of which 500 register).

Attrition rate

Percentage of site visitors who are lost at each stage in making a purchase.

A related concept is the **attrition rate** which describes how many visitors are lost at each stage of visiting a site. Figure 12.7 shows that for a set time period, only a proportion of site visitors will make their way to product information, a small proportion will add an item to a basket and a smaller proportion still will actually make the purchase. A key feature of e-commerce sites is that there is a high attrition rate between a customer's adding an item to a basket and subsequently making a purchase. Online marketers work to decrease this 'shopping basket abandonment rate' through improving usability and modifying messaging to persuade visitors to continue the 'user journey'.

5 Channel profitability

Channel profitability

The profitability of the website, taking into account revenue and cost and discounted cash flow.

A contribution to business **profitability** is always the ultimate aim of e-commerce. To assess this, leading companies set an Internet contribution target of achieving a certain proportion of sales via the channel. When easyJet (www.easyjet.com) launched its e-commerce facility in 1998, it set an Internet contribution target of 30% by 2000. They put the resources and communications plan in place to achieve this and their target was reached in 1999. Assessing contribution is more difficult for a company that cannot sell products online, but the role of the Internet in influencing purchase should be assessed. Discounted cash flow techniques are used to assess the rate of return over time. Service contribution from e-channels should also be assessed.

Multi-channel evaluation

The frameworks we have presented in this chapter are explained in the context of an individual channel. But, as Wilson (2008) has pointed out, there is a need to evaluate how different channels support each other.

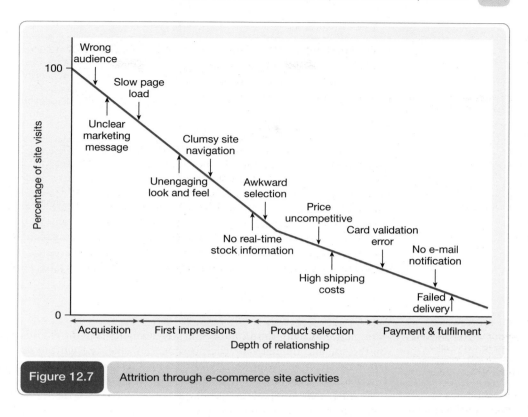

| Figure 12.7 | Attrition through e-commerce site activities |

He suggests the most important aspect of multi-channel measurement is to measure 'channel cross-over effects'. This involves asking, for example: 'How can the impact of a paid search campaign be measured if it is as likely to generate traffic to a store, salesforce or call centre as to a website? How can the impact of a direct mail campaign be tracked if it generates website traffic as well as direct responses?'

1to1Media (2008) summarize recommendations by Forrester, which are:

1 *Total number of hybrid customers.* These include the number and proportion who research online and purchase offline.
2 *Distribution and spend levels of those hybrid customers.* Proportion, average order value and type of category spend for these customers.
3 *Cross-channel conversion.* For example, online researchers who buy offline and potentially vice versa.
4 *Customer spend with competitors by channel.* This would have to be established by primary research for each brand. Audience measurement services such as Hitwise will give information on share of search, share of visitors and upstream/downstream patterns of visitors.

An example of a balanced scorecard-style dashboard developed to assess and compare channel performance for a retailer is presented in Figure 12.8.

Stage 3: Tools and techniques for collecting metrics and summarizing results

Techniques to collect metrics include the collection of site-visitor activity data such as that collected from site log-files, the collection of metrics about outcomes such as online sales or e-mail enquiries and traditional marketing research techniques such as questionnaires and focus groups which collect information on the customer's experience on the website.

Results (6)	Customers & stakeholders (5)
• Revenue • Multi-channel contribution • Degree multi-channel sells up • Costs per channel • Degree of sweating assets • Multi-channel infrastructure costs	• Overall customer satisfaction • Customer propensity to defect • Customer propensity to purchase • Customer perception of added value • Integration of customer experience
Core processes (3)	**People and knowledge (4)**
• Productive multichannel usage • Price (relative to competitors/other channels) • Quality of integrated customer view	• Staff satisfaction • Appropriate behaviours 'Living the brand' • Willingness to diversify/extend the brand • Knowledge of target customer

Figure 12.8 Multi-channel performance scorecard for a retailer

Collecting site-visitor activity data

Site-visitor activity data
Information on content and services accessed by e-commerce site visitors.

Site-visitor activity data captured in web analytics systems records the number of visitors on the site and the paths or clickstreams they take through the site as they visit different content. There is a wide variety of technical terms to describe these activity data which Internet marketers need to be conversant with.

Traditionally this information has been collected using a log-file analysis web analytics tool. The server-based log file is added to every time a user downloads a piece of information (a **hit**) and is analysed using a **log-file analyser**, as illustrated by Figure 3.7. Examples of transactions within a log file are:

Hit
Recorded for each graphic or text file requested from a web server. It is not a reliable measure for the number of people viewing a page.

> *www.davechaffey.com – [05/Oct/2012:00:00:49 -000] "GET/index.html HTTP/1.0" 200 33362*
> *www.davechaffey.com – [05/Oct/2012:00:00:49 -000] "GET/logo.gif HTTP/1.0" 200 54342*

Despite their wide use in the media, hits are not a useful measure of website effectiveness since if a page consists of 10 graphics, plus text, this is recorded as 11 hits. **Page impressions** or page views and **unique visitors** are better measures of site activity.

Log-file analyser
A separate program such as WebTrends that is used to summarize the information on customer activity in a log file.

An example of visitor volume to a website using different measures based on real, representative data for one month is presented in Figure 12.9. You can see how hits are much higher than page views and unique visitors and are quite misleading in terms of the 'opportunities to see' a message. We can also learn from the ratio between some of these measures – the figure indicates:

Page impression
A more reliable measure than a hit, denoting one person viewing one page.

- *Pages per visit (PPV)* – the average number of pages viewed per visitor to a site (this is indicative of engagement with a site since the longer a visitor stays on a 'sticky site', the higher this value will be). Duration on a site in minutes is inaccurate since this figure is skewed upwards by visitors who arrive on a site and are inactive before their session times out at 30 minutes.

Unique visitors
Individual visitors to a site measured through cookies or IP addresses on an individual computer.

- *Visits per (unique) visitor (VPV)* – this suggests the frequency of site visits. These data are reported for a month, during which time one would not expect many returning visitors. So it is often more relevant to present these data across a quarter or a year.

Other information giving detailed knowledge of customer behaviour that can be reported by any web analytics package include:

- Top pages.
- Entry and exit pages.
- Path or clickstream analysis showing the sequence of pages viewed.
- Country of visitor's origin (actually dependent on the location of their ISP).

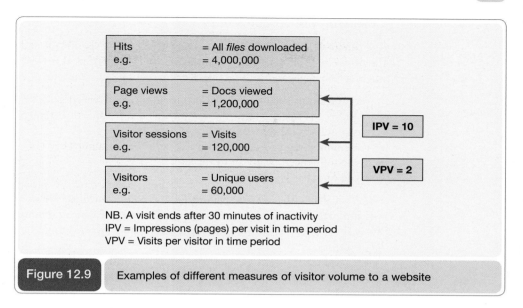

Figure 12.9 Examples of different measures of visitor volume to a website

- Browser and operating system used.
- Referring URL and domain (where the visitor came from).

Comparing apples to oranges?

With many different web analytics tools being used on different sites, it is important that there be standards for measuring visitor volumes. In particular, there are different techniques for measuring unique visitors which can be measured through IP addresses, but this is more accurate if it is combined with cookies and browser types. International standards bodies such as the IFABC (www.ifabc.org) and Web Analytics Association (www.webanalyticsassociation.org) and UK organizations such as ABC electronic (www.abce.org.uk) and JICWEBS (www.jicwebs.org) have worked to standardize the meaning of and data collection methods for different measures. See Table 12.5 or visit these sites for the latest precise definition of the terms in this section. Media buyers are particularly interested in accurate audited figures of media sites and organizations such as ABC electronic are important for this.

Table 12.5 Terminology for key website volume measures

Measure	Measure	Definition
1 How many? (Audience reach)	Unique users	A unique and valid identifier [for a site visitor]. Sites may use (i) IP + user-agent, (ii) cookie and/or (iii) registration ID
2 How often? (Frequency metric)	Visit	A series of one or more PAGE IMPRESSIONS, served to one USER, which ends when there is a gap of 30 minutes or more between successive PAGE IMPRESSIONS for that USER
3 How busy? (Volume metric)	Page impression	A file, or combination of files, sent to a valid USER as a result of that USER's request being received by the server
4 What see?	Ad impressions	A file or a combination of files sent to a valid USER as an individual advertisement as a result of that USER's request being received by the server
5 What do?	Ad clicks	An AD IMPRESSION clicked on by a valid USER

Source: ABC electronic (www.abce.org.uk).

Collecting site outcome data

Site outcome data refer to a customer performing a significant action which is of value to the marketer. This is usually a transaction that is recorded. It involves more than downloading of a web page, and is proactive. Key marketing outcomes include:

- registration to site or subscriptions to an e-mail newsletter;
- requests for further information such as a brochure or a request for a callback from a customer service representative;
- responding to a promotion such as an online competition;
- a sale influenced by a visit to the site;
- a sale on-site.

When reviewing the efficiency of different e-communications tools referred to in Chapter 9, it is important to assess the outcomes generated. Measuring quantity of clickthroughs to a site is simplistic, it is conversion to these outcomes which should be used to assess the quality of traffic.

An important aspect of measures collected offline is that the marketing outcomes may be recorded in different media according to how the customer has performed mixed-mode buying. What we are really interested in is whether the website influenced the enquiry or sale. For all contact points with customers staff need to be instructed to ask how they found out about the company, or made their decision to buy. Although this is valuable information it is often intrusive, and a customer placing an order may be annoyed to be asked such a question. To avoid alienating the customer, these questions about the role of the website can be asked later, perhaps when the customer is filling in a registration or warranty card. Another device that can be used to identify use of the website is to use a specific phone number for customers coming from the website.

It will be apparent that to collect some of these measures we may need to integrate different information systems. Where customers provide details such as an e-mail address and name in response to an offer, these are known as 'leads' and they may need to be passed on to a direct-sales team or recorded in a customer relationship management system. For full visibility of customer behaviour, the outcomes from these systems need to be integrated with the site-visitor activity data.

Selecting a web analytics tool

There is a bewildering range of hundreds of web analytics tools varying from shareware packages with often primitive reporting through to complex systems which may cost hundreds of thousands of dollars a year for a popular site. You can gain an idea of the range of tools by visiting the Web Analytics Demystified 'Vendor Discovery Tool' (www.webanalytics demystified.com/vendor_discovery_tool.asp) to find the tools used to monitor your sites or competitors' sites.

Given this, it is difficult for the Internet marketer to select the best tool or tools to meet their needs. One of the first issues to consider is the different types of measures that need to be integrated within the performance management system. Figure 12.10 gives an indication of the types of data that need to be integrated which include:

1 *Operational data.* Data would be ideally collected and reported within a single tool at this level, but unfortunately to obtain the best reporting it is often necessary to resort to four different types of tools or data source:
   - Referrer data from acquisition campaigns such as search marketing or online advertising. Separate tools are often also required for retention e-mail marketing.
   - Site-centric data about visitor volume and clickstream behaviour.
   - Customer response and profile data.
   - Transactional data about leads and sales which are often obtained from separate legacy systems.

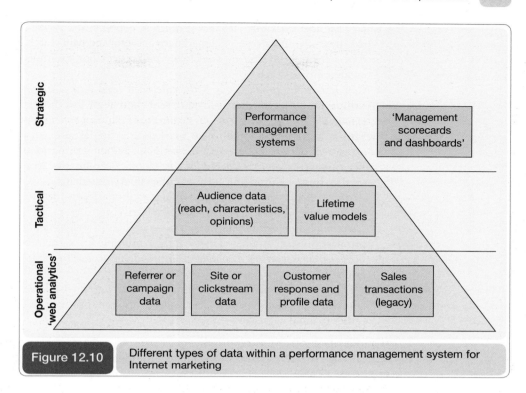

Figure 12.10	Different types of data within a performance management system for Internet marketing

2 *Tactical data*. These data are typically models of required response such as:
   - Reach models with online audience share data for different demographic groupings from sources such as Hitwise and Netratings.
   - Lifetime value models which are created to assess profitability of visitors to the site from different sources and so need to integrate with operational data.
3 *Strategic data*. Performance management systems for senior managers will give the big picture presented as scorecards or dashboards showing the contribution of digital channels to the organization in terms of sales, revenue and profitability for different products. These data indicate trends and relative performance within the company and to competitors such that the Internet marketing strategy can be reviewed for effectiveness.

So an important requirement of a web analytics tool is that it should seek to integrate all these different data sources. The other main requirements of a web analytics tool to consider include:

- Reporting of marketing performance (many are technical tools which do not clearly report on results from a marketing perspective).
- Accuracy of technique.
- Analysis tools.
- Integration with other marketing information systems (export).
- Ease of use and configuration.
- Cost, which often varies according to site visitor volumes and number of system users.
- Suitability for reporting on e-marketing campaigns.

Many online tracking tools were originally developed to report on the performance of the site and the pages accessed rather than specifically to report on e-marketing campaigns. It is therefore important that companies have an excellent campaign reporting capability, such as:

1 *Can the tool track through to point entry on site through to outcome such as site registration or sale?* Integration with data to reflect actual leads or sales in a legacy system should also be reported.

2 *Can the tool track and compare a range of online media types?* For example, interactive (banner) ads, affiliates, e-mail marketing, natural and paid search, explained in Chapter 8.

3 *Can return-on-investment models be constructed?* For example, by entering costs and profitability for each product?

4 *Can reports be produced at both a detailed level and a summary level?* This enables comparison of performance for different campaigns and different parts of the business.

5 *Capability to track clickthroughs at an individual respondent level for e-mail campaigns.* This is important for follow-up marketing activities after an e-mail list member has expressed interest in a product through clicking on a promotion link.

6 *Are post-view responses tracked for ads?* Cookies can be used to assess visitors who arrive on the site at a later point in time, rather than immediately.

7 *Are post-click responses tracked for affiliates?* Similarly, visitors from affiliates may buy the product not on their first visit, but on a later visit.

8 *Do e-mail campaign summaries give unique clicks as well as total clicks?* If an e-mail communication such as a newsletter contains multiple links, then total clicks will be higher.

9 *Is real-time reporting available?* Is immediate access to campaign performance data available?

10 *Is cross-campaign and cross-product or content reporting available?* Is it readily possible to compare campaigns and sales levels across different products or different parts of the site rather than an aggregate?

Accuracy is another an important aspect of web analytics tool. Perhaps the worst problems of log-file analysis are the problems of under-counting and over-counting. These are reviewed in Table 12.6.

A relatively new approach is to use the alternative *browser-based* or *tag-based* measurement system that records access to web pages every time a page is loaded into a user's web browser through running a short script, program or tag inserted into the web page. Potentially it is more accurate than server-based approaches for the reasons explained in Table 12.7. This approach usually runs as a hosted solution with the metrics recorded on a remote server. An example of the output reporting from a web analytics service is shown in Figure 12.11 and the data available from a web analytics tool designed for improving the performance of online retailers (and other site types) are shown in Box 12.4.

Table 12.6	Inaccuracies caused by server-based log-file analysis

Sources of under-counting	Sources of over-counting
Caching in user's web browsers (when a user accesses a previously accessed file, it is loaded from the memory of the user's computer on a server-based cache on their PC)	Frames (a user viewing a framed page with three frames will be recorded as three page impressions or page views)
Caching on proxy servers (proxy servers are used within organizations or ISPs to reduce Internet traffic by storing copies of frequently used pages)	Spiders and robots (traversing of a site by spiders from different search engines is recorded as page impressions. These spiders can be excluded, but this is time-consuming)
Firewalls (these do not usually exclude page impressions, but they usually assign a single IP address for the user of the page, rather than referring to an individual's PC)	Executable files (these can also be recorded as hits or page impressions unless excluded)
Dynamically generated pages, generated 'on-the-fly', are difficult to assess with server-based log files	

Box 12.4	Measuring online retailer performance

It is important for retailers to benchmark their performance through time in comparison to both their own and competitor performance. This highlights changes in performance according to updates to the site, marketing campaigns and competitor activity. Aggregated web analytics data from Coremetrics retail customers provide these data, as shown in Table 12.7.

Table 12.7	Typical retailer performance measures

Session Traffic Summary	**Nov-08**
One Page Session[1]	22.28%
Multi-Page Session[2]	77.72%
Browser Session[3]	55.55%
Shopping Cart Sessions[4]	9.40%
Order Sessions[5]	4.63%
Visitor Experience Summary	**Nov-08**
Page Views Per Session[6]	11.59
Product Page Views Per Session[7]	2.14
Average Time on Site (in seconds)[8]	462.55
Transaction Summary	**Nov-08**
Average Items/Order[9]	2.53
Average Order Value[10]	£55.75
Shopping Cart Conversion Rate[11]	49.90%
Shopping Cart Abandonment[12]	50.10%
New Visitor Conversion Rate[13]	2.98%
On-Site Search Summary	**Nov-08**
On-Site Search Session[14]	34.27%
On-Site Search Conversion Rate[15]	8.28%
On-Site Search Average Order Value[16]	£45.84
Marketing Summary Direct Load	**Nov-08**
Traffic%[17]	50.34%
Sales%[18]	60.23%
Conversion Rate[19]	5.88%
Natural Search	**Nov-08**
Traffic%[20]	21.67%
Sales%[21]	13.28%
Conversion Rate[22]	2.83%

Table 12.7	Continued

Referrals	Nov-08
Traffic%[23]	6.18%
Sales%[24]	3.78%
Referral Conversion Rate[25]	3.32%

Explanation of metrics

1	One Page Session%	Out of all sessions, the percentage in which visitors immediately departed the site (i.e. only one page was viewed by the visitor during the session).
2	Multi-Page Session%	Out of all sessions, the percentage in which visitors did not immediately depart the site (i.e. more than one page viewed by the visitor during the session).
3	Browser Session%	Out of all sessions, the percentage in which visitors viewed at least one product page.
4	Shopping Cart Session%	Out of all sessions, the percentage in which visitors placed at least one item in their shopping cart.
5	Order Session%	Out of all sessions, the percentage in which visitors completed an order.

Visitor Experience Summary Metrics

6	Page Views/Session	The average number of pages viewed by visitors per session.
7	Product Views/Session	The average number of products viewed by visitors per session.
8	Average Session Length	The average length of time for a visitor session.

Transactions Summary Metrics

9	Average Items per Order	The average number of items purchased per order.
10	Average Order Value	The average value of each order.
11	Shopping Cart Conversion%	Out of all visitors who placed items in their shopping carts, this is the percentage that went on to place an order.
12	Shopping Cart Abandonment%	Out of visitors who placed items in their shopping carts, this is the percentage that did not go on to place an order.
13	New Visitor Conversion%	Out of all new visitor sessions, this is the percentage that completed an order.

On-Site Search Summary Metrics

14	On-Site Search Session	Out of all sessions, the percentage in which visitors used on-site search capabilities.
15	On-Site Search Conversion	Out of all sessions where visitors used your on-site search capabilities, this is the percentage that also completed an order.
16	On-Site Search Average Order Value	The average value of orders that were placed during sessions involving one or more on-site search.

Marketing Summary Metrics

17	Direct Load – % of Site Traffic	Out of all tracked visitor sessions for the specified time period, the percentage attributable to a direct load of the site.
18	Direct Load – % of Sales	Out of all sales for tracked visitor sessions for the specified time period, the percentage attributable to a direct load of the site.
19	Direct Load – Session Conversion Rate	Out of all sessions tracked for the specified time period attributable to a direct load of the site, the percentage including an order.
20	Natural Search – % of Site Traffic	Out of all tracked visitor sessions for the specified time period, the percentage attributable to a natural search link from a search engine.
21	Natural Search – % of Sales	Out of all sales for tracked visitor sessions for the specified time period, the percentage attributable to a natural search link from a search engine.
22	Natural Search – Session Conversion Rate	Out of all sessions, the percentage that included visitors viewing at least one product page.
23	Referrals – % of Site Traffic	Out of all tracked visitor sessions for the specified time period, the percentage attributable to a referring site.
24	Referrals – % of Sales	Out of all sales for tracked visitor sessions for the specified time period, the percentage attributable to a referring site.
25	Referrals – Session Conversion Rate	Out of all sessions tracked for the specified time period that was attributable to a referring site, the percentage that included an order.

Source: Coremetrics monthly metrics benchmark produced for UK retailers, July 2008 www.coremetrics. co.uk/ solutions/benchmarking.php.
Permissions: Sylvia Jensen, Senior Director of Marketing EMEA, Coremetrics. She can be reached via e-mail at sjensen@coremetrics.com.

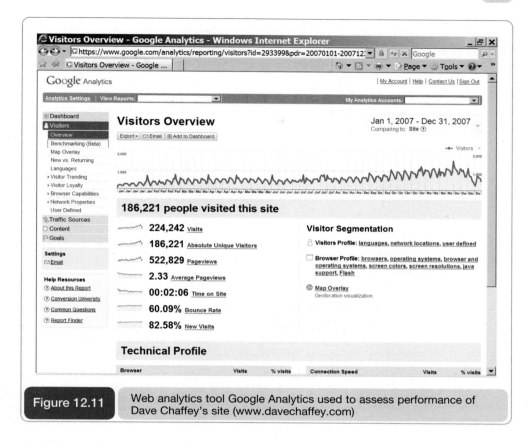

| Figure 12.11 | Web analytics tool Google Analytics used to assess performance of Dave Chaffey's site (www.davechaffey.com) |

In addition to the quantitative web analytics measurement approaches discussed, traditional **marketing research** can be used to help determine the influence of the website and related communications on customer perception of the company and its products and services. The options for conducting survey research include interviews, questionnaires, focus groups and mystery shoppers. Each of these techniques can be conducted offline or online. The advantages and disadvantages of the different approaches are shown in Table 12.8.

Internet-based market research
The use of online questionnaires and focus groups to assess customer perceptions of a website or broader marketing issues.

AB and multivariate testing

Often site owners and marketers reviewing the effectiveness of a site will disagree and the only method to be certain of the best performing design or creative alternatives is through designing and running experiments to evaluate the best to use. Matt Round, then director of personalization at Amazon, speaking at the E-metrics summit in 2004, said the Amazon philosophy, described further in Case study 12.1, is:

Data trumps intuition.

AB testing and multivariate testing are two measurement techniques that can be used to review design effectiveness to improve results.

AB testing

A/B or AB testing
Refers to testing two different versions of a page or a page element such as a heading, image or button for effectiveness.

In its simplest form, **A/B or AB testing** refers to testing two different versions of a page or a page element such as a heading, image or button. Some members of the site are served alternately with the visitors to the page randomly split between the two pages. Hence it is sometimes called 'live split testing'. The goal is to increase page or site effectiveness against key performance indicators including clickthrough rate, conversion rates and revenue per visit.

Table 12.8	A comparison of different online metrics collection methods

Technique	Strengths	Weaknesses
1 **Server-based log-file analysis of site activity**	Directly records customer behaviour on site plus where they were referred from Low cost	Not based around marketing outcomes such as leads, sales Size, even summaries may be over 50 pages long Doesn't directly record channel satisfaction Under-counting and over-counting Misleading unless interpreted carefully
2 **Browser-based site activity data**	Greater accuracy than server-based analysis Count all users, cf. panel approach	Relatively expensive method Similar weaknesses to server-based technique apart from accuracy Limited demographic information
3 **Panel activity and demographic data**	Provide competitor comparisons Give demographic profiling Avoid under-counting and over-counting	Depend on extrapolation from limited sample that may not be representative
4 **Outcome data,** e.g. enquiries, customer service e-mails	Record marketing outcomes	Difficulty of integrating data with other methods of data collection when collected manually or in other information systems
5 **Online questionnaires** Customers are prompted randomly – every *n*th customer or after customer activity or by e-mail	Can record customer satisfaction and profiles Relatively cheap to create and analyse	Difficulty of recruiting respondents who complete accurately Sample bias – tend to be advocates or disgruntled customers who complete
6 **Online focus groups** Synchronous recording	Relatively cheap to create	Difficult to moderate and coordinate No visual cues, as from offline focus groups
7 **Mystery shoppers** Customers are recruited to evaluate the site, e.g. www. emysteryshopper.com	Structured tests give detailed feedback Also tests integration with other channels such as e-mail and phone	Relatively expensive Sample must be representative

Control page

The page against which subsequent optimization will be assessed. Typically a current landing page.

When completing AB testing it is important to identify a realistic baseline or **control page** (or audience sample) to compare against. This will typically be an existing landing page. Two new alternatives can be compared to previous control, which is known as an ABC test. Different variables are then applied as in Table 12.9.

Table 12.9	AB test example

Test	A (Control)	B (Test page)
Test 1	Original page	New headline, existing button, existing body copy
Test 2	Original page	Existing headline, new button, existing body copy
Test 3	Original page	Existing headline, existing button, new body copy

An example of the power of AB testing is an experiment Skype performed on their main topbar navigation, where they found that changing the main menu options 'Call Phones', to 'Skype Credit' and 'Shop' to 'Accessories' gave an increase of 18.75% revenue per visit (Skype were speaking at the 2007 E-metrics summit). That's significant when you have hundreds of millions of visitors! It also shows the importance of being direct with navigation and simply describing the offer available rather than the activity.

Multivariate testing

Multivariate testing is a more sophisticated form of AB testing which enables simultaneous testing of pages for different combinations of page elements that are being tested. This enables selection of the most effective combination of design elements to achieve the desired goal.

An example of a multivariate test is shown in Mini case study 12.1.

Mini Case Study 12.1   Multivariate testing at National Express Group increases conversion rate

The National Express Group is the leading provider of travel solutions in the UK. Around 1 billion journeys a year are made worldwide on National Express Group's bus, train, light rail and express coach and airport operations. A significant proportion of ticket bookings are made online through the company's website at www.nationalexpress.com.

The company used multivariate testing provider Maxymiser to run an experiment to improve conversion rate of a fare selection page which was the penultimate step in booking (Figure 12.12). The analysis team identified a number of subtle alterations to content (labelled A to E) and calls to action on the page with the

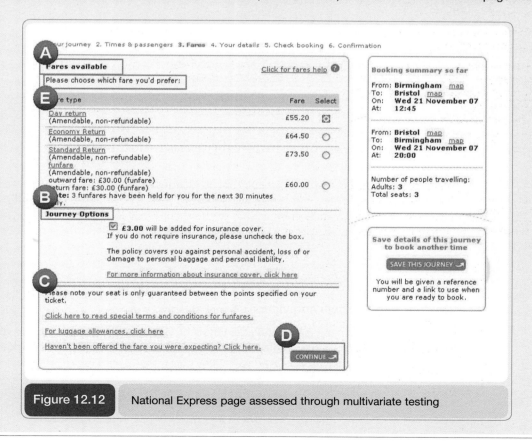

Figure 12.12   National Express page assessed through multivariate testing

aim of stimulating visitor engagement and driving a higher percentage of visitors through to successful conversion without changing the structure of the page or National Express brand identity. In order to aid more effective up-sell to insurance add-ons, changes to this call to action were also proposed.

It was decided that a multivariate test would be the most effective approach to determine the best-performing combination of content. The variants jointly developed by Maxymiser and the client were tested with all live site visitors and the conversion rate of each combination monitored. They tried 3,500 possible page combinations and during the live test the underperforming combinations were taken out to maximize conversion rates at every stage.

At the end of the testing period, after reaching statistical validity, results showed that the best combination of elements showed a 14.11% increase in conversion rates for the page, i.e. 14.11% more visitors were sent through to the fourth and final step in the registration process, immediately hitting bottom line revenue for National Express (Figure 12.13).

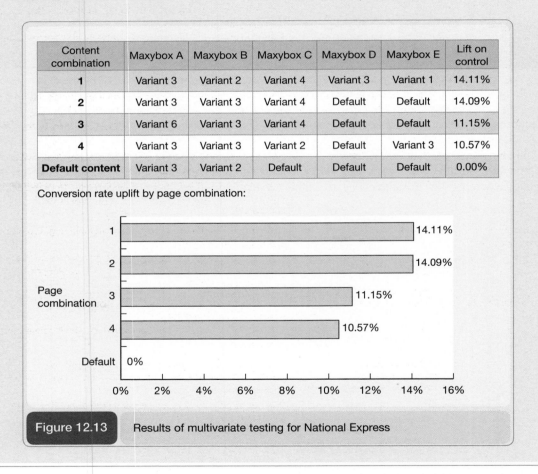

Content combination	Maxybox A	Maxybox B	Maxybox C	Maxybox D	Maxybox E	Lift on control
1	Variant 3	Variant 2	Variant 4	Variant 3	Variant 1	14.11%
2	Variant 3	Variant 3	Variant 4	Default	Default	14.09%
3	Variant 6	Variant 3	Variant 4	Default	Default	11.15%
4	Variant 3	Variant 3	Variant 2	Default	Variant 3	10.57%
Default content	Variant 3	Variant 2	Default	Default	Default	0.00%

Conversion rate uplift by page combination:

Figure 12.13 Results of multivariate testing for National Express

Clickstream analysis and visitor segmentation

Clickstream analysis refers to detailed analysis of visitor behaviour in order to diagnose problems and opportunities. Table 12.10 gives an indication of the type of questions asked by web analyst Dave Chaffey (www.davechaffey.com) when reviewing clients' sites.

Table 12.10	A summary of how an analyst will interpret web analytics data. GA is terminology for Google Analytics (www.google.com/analytics), one of the most widely used tools

Analyst question	Typical web analytics report terminology	Diagnosis of analyst used to improve performance
How successful is the site at achieving engagement and outcomes?	Conversion goals (GA) Bounce rates (GA) Pages/visit (GA)	• Is engagement and conversion consistent with other sites in sector? • What are maximum engagement and conversion rates from different referrers?
Where are visitors entering the site?	Top entry pages Top landing pages (GA)	• How important is home page compared to other page categories and landing pages? Does page popularity reflect product popularity? • Check that messaging and calls to action are effective on these pages • Assess source of traffic, in particular keywords from search engines and apply elsewhere
What are sources of visitors (referrers)?	Referrers Traffic sources Filters set up to segment visitors	• Are the full range of digital media channels relevant for a company represented? • Is the level of search engine traffic consistent with the brand reputation? • What are the main link partners driving free traffic (potential for more)?
What is the most popular content?	Top content (GA)	• Is page popularity as expected? Are there problems with findability caused by navigation labelling? • Which content is most likely to influence visitors to outcome? • Which content is most popular with returning visitors segment?
Which are the most popular findability methods?	Site search (GA)	• How popular are different forms of navigation, e.g. top menu, sidebar menus? • What are the most popular searches? Where do searches tend to start? Are they successfully finding content or converting to sale?
Where do visitors leave the site?	Top exit pages (GA)	• Are these as expected (home page, About Us page, transaction completion)? • Are there error pages (e.g. 404 not found) which cause visitors to leave?
Which clickstreams are taken?	Path analysis Top paths (GA)	• How can attrition in conversion funnels be improved? • What does forward path analysis show are the most effective calls-to-action? • What does reverse path analysis indicate about the pages which influence sale?

Path analysis

Aggregate clickstreams are usually known within web analytics software as 'forward' or 'reverse' paths. This is a fairly advanced form of analysis, but the principle is straightforward – you seek to learn from the most popular paths.

Viewed at an aggregate level across the site through 'top paths' type reports, this doesn't appear particularly useful as the top paths are often:

• Home page : Exit
• Home page : Contact Us : Exit
• News page : Exit

Clickstream analysis becomes more actionable when the analyst reviews clickstreams in the context of a single page – this is **forward path analysis** or **reverse path analysis**.

On-site search effectiveness

On-site search is another crucial part of clickstream analysis since it is a key way of finding content, so a detailed search analysis will pay dividends. Key search metrics to consider are:

- Number of searches.
- Average number of searches per visitor or searcher.
- % of searches returning zero results.
- % of site exits from search results.
- % of returned searches clicked.
- % of returned searches resulting in conversion to sale or other outcome.
- Most popular search terms – individual keyword and keyphrases.

Visitor segmentation

Segmentation is a fundamental marketing approach, but it is often difficult within web analytics to relate customer segments to web behaviour because the web analytics data aren't integrated with customer or purchase data, although this is possible in the most advanced systems such as Omniture, Visual Sciences and WebTrends.

However, all analytics systems have a capability for segmentation and it is possible to create specific filters or profiles to help understand one type of site visitor behaviour. Examples include:

- First-time visitors or returning visitors
- Visitors from different referrer types including:
  - Google natural
  - Google paid
  - Strategic search keyphrases, brand keyphrases, etc.
  - Display advertising
- Converters against non-converters
- Geographic segmentation by country or region (based on IP addresses)
- Type of content accessed, e.g. are some segments more likely to convert? For example, speaking at Ad Tech London '06, MyTravel reported that they segment visitors into:
  - Site flirt (2 pages or less)
  - Site browse (2 pages or more)
  - Saw search results
  - Saw quote
  - Saw payment details
  - Saw booking confirmation details.

Budgeting

To estimate profitability and return on investment of e-channels as part of budgeting, companies need to consider both tangible and intangible costs and benefits. A suggested checklist of these is shown in Box 12.5.

A similar approach can be used to calculating the ROI of enhancements to an e-commerce site. Hanson (2000) suggests an approach to this which requires identification of revenue from the site, costs from site and costs from supporting it via a call centre. These are related to profit as follows:

Operating profit = Net income from sales – E-commerce site costs – Call centre costs
Net income from sales = (Product price – Unit cost) × Sales – Fixed product costs

E-commerce site costs = Site fixed costs + ((% site support contacts) ×
Cost site support contact × Sales)

Call centre (CC) costs = CC fixed costs + ((% CC support contacts) ×
Cost CC support contact × Sales)

Forward path analysis

Reviews the combinations of clicks that occur from a page. This form of analysis is most beneficial from important pages such as the home page, product and directory pages. Use this technique to identify: messaging / navigation combinations which work best to yield the most clicks from a page.

Reverse path analysis

Indicates the most popular combination of pages and/or calls-to-action which lead to a page. This is particularly useful for transactional pages such as the first checkout page on a consumer site; a lead generation or contact us page on a business-to-business site; an e-mail subscription page or a call-me back option.

Box 12.5	Suggested worksheet for calculating return on investment for an e-commerce site

Tangible business benefits

1 *Reduced costs*
   (a) Promotional materials, including catalogues – creative, printing, paper, distribution
   (b) Product support materials – creation, printing, paper, distribution
   (c) Lower infrastructure or communication costs – fewer outbound calls required
   (d) Support staff savings
   (e) Sales staff savings
   (f) Order inaccuracies
   (g) Lower cost of supporting channel
2 *Increased revenue*
   (a) New sales to new geo-demographic segments
   (b) Penetration/retention/repeat orders
   (c) Cross-sales to existing purchasers
   (d) Penetration/cross-sales to new purchasers in an organization

Intangible business benefits

3 *Faster time to market*
   ● Reduce product introduction by *n* weeks
4 *Improved customer satisfaction/brand equity*
   ● How does this affect retention?

Tangible costs

1 *Physical costs*
   (a) Hardware, software
   (b) Network costs
2 *Planning costs*
3 *Implementation costs*
   (a) Project management
   (b) Software development, testing
   (c) Data migration
   (d) Training
   (e) Promotion (online and offline)
4 *Operational costs*
   (a) Hardware and software maintenance
   (b) Network maintenance
   (c) Technical staff costs
   (d) Content maintenance staff costs
   (e) Support staff costs
   (f) Management staff costs
   (g) Ongoing promotional costs (online and offline)

Source: This worksheet was originally based on White Paper 'A Return on Investment Guide for Business-to-Business Internet Commerce' provided by e-commerce solution provider Openmarket (www.openmarket.com).

Different approaches for estimating costs are recommended by Bayne (1997):

● *Last year's Internet marketing budget.* This is assuming the site has been up and running for some time.
● *Percentage of company sales.* It is again difficult to establish this for the first iteration of a site.

- *Percentage of total marketing budget.* This is a common approach. Typically the percentage will start small (less than 5%, or even 1%), but will rise as the impact of the Internet increases.
- *Reallocation of marketing dollars.* The money for e-marketing will often be taken by cutting back other marketing activities.
- *What other companies in your industry are spending.* This is definitely necessary in order to assess and meet competitive threats, but competitors may be over-investing.
- *Creating an effective online presence.* In this model of 'paying whatever it takes', a company spends sufficient money to create a website which is intended to achieve their objectives. This may be a costly option, but for industries in which the Internet is having a significant impact, it may be the wise option. A larger than normal marketing budget will be necessary to achieve this.
- *A graduated plan tied into measurable results.* This implies an ongoing programme in which investment each year is tied into achieving the results established in a measurement programme.
- *A combination of approaches.* Since the first budget will be based on many intangibles it is best to use several methods and present high, medium and low expenditure options for executives with expected results related to costs.

As a summary to this section, complete Activity 12.4.

Activity 12.4	Creating a measurement plan for a B2C company

Purpose

To develop skills in selecting appropriate techniques for measuring e-business effectiveness.

Activity

This activity acts as a summary to this section on e-business measurement. Review Table 12.11 and assess the frequency with which metrics in each of the following categories should be reported for a sell-side e-commerce site and acted upon. For each column, place an R in the column for the frequency with which you think the data should be recorded.

Table 12.11	Alternative timescales for reporting e-commerce site performance

	Promotion	Behaviour	Satisfaction	Outcomes	Profitability
Hour					
Day					
Week					
Month					
Quarter					
Relaunch					

Answers to activities can be found at www.pearsoned.co.uk/chaffey

In Chapter 1, we started this book with a case study of the world's largest e-business retailer. We conclude with a case of the world's second largest e-retailer, showing how the culture of test, learn, refine is key to their success.

Case Study 12.1	Learning from Amazon's culture of metrics

Context

Why a case study on Amazon? Surely everyone knows about who Amazon are and what they do? Yes, well, that may be true, but this case goes beyond the surface to review some of the 'insider secrets' of Amazon's success.

Like eBay, Amazon.com was born in 1995. The name reflected the vision of Jeff Bezos to produce a large-scale phenomenon like the River Amazon. This ambition has proved justified since, just 8 years later, Amazon passed the $5 billion sales mark – it took Wal-Mart 20 years to achieve this.

Vision and strategy

In their 2008 SEC filing, Amazon describes the vision of their business as to:

Relentlessly focus on customer experience by offering our customers low prices, convenience, and a wide selection of merchandise.

The vision is to offer Earth's biggest selection and to be Earth's most customer-centric company. Consider how these core marketing messages summarizing the Amazon online value proposition are communicated both on-site and through offline communications.

Of course, achieving customer loyalty and repeat purchases has been key to Amazon's success. Many dot-coms failed because they succeeded in achieving awareness, but not loyalty. Amazon achieved both. In their SEC filing they stress how they seek to achieve this. They say:

We work to earn repeat purchases by providing easy-to-use functionality, fast and reliable fulfillment, timely customer service, feature-rich content, and a trusted transaction environment. Key features of our websites include editorial and customer reviews; manufacturer product information; Web pages tailored to individual preferences, such as recommendations and notifica-tions; 1-Click® technology; secure payment systems; image uploads; searching on our websites as well as the Internet; browsing; and the ability to view selected interior pages and citations, and search the entire contents of many of the books we offer with our 'Look Inside the Book' and 'Search Inside the Book' features. Our community of online customers also creates feature-rich content, including product reviews, online recommendation lists, wish lists, buying guides, and wedding and baby registries.

In practice, as is the case for many online retailers, the lowest prices are for the most popular products, with less popular products commanding higher prices and a greater margin for Amazon. Free shipping offers are used to encourage increase in basket size since customers have to spend over a certain amount to receive free ship-ping. The level at which free shipping is set is critical to profitability and Amazon has changed it as competition has changed and for promotional reasons.

Amazon communicates the fulfilment promise in several ways including presentation of latest inventory availability information, delivery date estimates, and options for expedited delivery, as well as delivery ship-ment notifications and update facilities.

This focus on the customer has translated to excellence in service with the 2004 American Customer Satisfaction Index giving Amazon.com a score of 88, which was at the time the highest customer satisfaction score ever recorded in any service industry, online or offline.

Round (2004) notes that Amazon focuses on customer satisfaction metrics. Each site is closely monitored with standard service availability monitoring (for example, using Keynote or Mercury Interactive) site availability and download speed. Interestingly, it also monitors per-minute site revenue upper/lower bounds – Round describes an alarm system rather like a power plant where if revenue on a site falls below $10,000 per minute, alarms go off! There are also internal performance service-level agreements for web services where T% of the time, different pages must return in X seconds.

Competition

In its SEC (2005) filing Amazon describes the envi-ronment for its products and services as 'intensely competitive'. It views its main current and potential competitors as: (1) physical-world retailers, catalogue retailers, publishers, vendors, distributors and manufac-turers of products, many of which possess significant brand awareness, sales volume and customer bases, and some of which currently sell, or may sell, products or services through the Internet, mail-order or direct marketing; (2) other online e-commerce sites; (3) a number of indirect competitors, including media companies, web portals, comparison shopping websites, and web search engines, either directly or in collaboration with other retailers; and (4) companies that provide e-commerce services, including website development, third-party fulfilment and customer service.

It believes the main competitive factors in its market segments include 'selection, price, availability, convenience, information, discovery, brand recognition, personalized services, accessibility, customer service, reliability, speed of fulfillment, ease of use, and ability to adapt to changing conditions, as well as our customers' overall experience and trust in transactions with us and facilitated by us on behalf of third-party sellers'.

For services offered to business and individual sellers, additional competitive factors include the quality of their services and tools, their ability to generate sales for third parties they serve, and the speed of performance for their services.

From auctions to marketplaces

Amazon auctions (known as zShops) were launched in March 1999, in large part as a response to the success of eBay. They were promoted heavily from the home page, category pages and individual product pages. Despite this, a year after launch they had only achieved a 3.2% share of the online auction compared to 58% for eBay and it only declined from this point.

Today, competitive prices of products are available through third-party sellers in the 'Amazon Marketplace' which are integrated within the standard product listings. The strategy to offer such an auction facility was initially driven by the need to compete with eBay, but now the strategy has been adjusted such that Amazon describes it as part of the approach of low pricing.

Although it might be thought that Amazon would lose out on enabling its merchants to sell products at lower prices, in fact Amazon makes greater margin on these sales since merchants are charged a commission on each sale and it is the merchant who bears the cost of storing inventory and fulfilling the product to customers. As with eBay, Amazon is just facilitating the exchange of bits and bytes between buyers and sellers without the need to distribute physical products.

How 'the culture of metrics' started

A common theme in Amazon's development is the drive to use a measured approach to all aspects of the business, beyond the finance. Marcus (2004) describes an occasion at a corporate 'boot-camp' in January 1997 when Amazon CEO Jeff Bezos 'saw the light':

'At Amazon, we will have a Culture of Metrics,' he said while addressing his senior staff. He went on to explain how web-based business gave Amazon an *'amazing window into human behavior.'* Marcus says: *'Gone were the fuzzy approximations of focus groups, the anecdotal fudging and smoke blowing from the marketing department. A company like Amazon could (and did) record every move a visitor made, every last click and twitch of the mouse. As the data piled up into virtual heaps, hummocks and mountain ranges, you could draw all sorts of conclusions about their chimerical nature, the consumer. In this sense, Amazon was not merely a store, but an immense repository of facts. All we needed were the right equations to plug into them.'*

James Marcus then goes on to give a fascinating insight into a breakout group discussion of how Amazon could better use measures to improve its performance. Marcus was in the Bezos group, brainstorming customer-centric metrics. Marcus (2004) summarizes the dialogue, led by Bezos:

'First, we figure out which things we'd like to measure on the site,' he said. *'For example, let's say we want a metric for customer enjoyment. How could we calculate that?'*

There was silence. Then somebody ventured: 'How much time each customer spends on the site?'

'Not specific enough,' Jeff said.

'How about the average number of minutes each customer spends on the site per session,' someone else suggested. *'If that goes up, they're having a blast.'*

'But how do we factor in purchase?' I [Marcus] said feeling proud of myself. *'Is that a measure of enjoyment?'*

'I think we need to consider frequency of visits, too,' said a dark-haired woman I didn't recognize. *'Lot of folks are still accessing the web with those creepy-crawly modems. Four short visits from them might be just as good as one visit from a guy with a T-1. Maybe better.'*

'Good point,' Jeff said. *'And anyway, enjoyment is just the start. In the end, we should be measuring customer ecstasy.'*

It is interesting that Amazon was having this debate about the elements of RFM analysis (described in Chapter 6) in 1997, after already having achieved $16 million of revenue in the previous year. Of course, this is a miniscule amount compared with today's billions of dollar turnover. The important point was that this was the start of a focus on metrics which can be seen through the description of Matt Round's work later in this case study.

From human to software-based recommendations

Amazon has developed internal tools to support this 'culture of metrics'. Marcus (2004) describes how the 'Creator Metrics' tool shows content creators how well their product listings and product copy are working. For each content editor such as Marcus, it retrieves all recently posted documents including articles, interviews, booklists and features. For each one it then gives a conversion rate to sale plus the number of page views, adds (added to basket) and repels (content requested, but the back button then used). In time, the work of editorial reviewers such as Marcus was marginalized since Amazon found that the majority of visitors used the search tools rather than read editorials and they responded to the personalized recommendations as the matching technology improved (Marcus likens early recommendation techniques to 'going shopping with the village idiot').

Experimentation and testing at Amazon

The 'culture of metrics' also led to a test-driven approach to improving results at Amazon. Matt Round, speaking at E-metrics 2004 when he was director of personalization at Amazon, describes the philosophy as '*data trumps intuitions*'. He explained how Amazon used to have a lot of arguments about which content and promotion should go on the all-important home page or category pages. He described how every category VP wanted top-centre and how the Friday meetings about placements for next week were getting 'too long, too loud, and lacked performance data'.

But today 'automation replaces intuitions' and real-time experimentation tests are always run to answer these questions since actual consumer behaviour is the best way to decide upon tactics.

Marcus (2004) also notes that Amazon has a culture of experiments, of which A/B tests are key components. Examples where A/B tests are used include new home page design, moving features around the page, different algorithms for recommendations, changing search relevance rankings. These involve testing a new treatment against a previous control for a limited time of a few days or a week. The system will randomly show one or more treatments to visitors and measure a range of parameters such as units sold and revenue by category

(and total), session time, session length, etc. The new features will usually be launched if the desired metrics are statistically significantly better. Statistical tests are a challenge though, as distributions are not normal (they have a large mass at zero, for example, of no purchase). There are other challenges since multiple A/B tests are running every day and A/B tests may overlap and so conflict. There are also longer-term effects where some features are 'cool' for the first two weeks and the opposite effect where changing navigation may degrade performance temporarily. Amazon also finds that as its users evolve in their online experience the way they act online has changed. This means that Amazon has to constantly test and evolve its features.

Technology

It follows that the Amazon technology infrastructure must readily support this culture of experimentation and this can be difficult to achieve with standardized content management. Amazon has achieved its competitive advantage through developing its technology internally and with a significant investment in this which may not be available to other organizations without the right focus on the online channels. As Amazon explains in SEC (2005):

> using primarily our own proprietary technologies, as well as technology licensed from third parties, we have implemented numerous features and functionality that simplify and improve the customer shopping experience, enable third parties to sell on our platform, and facilitate our fulfillment and customer service operations. Our current strategy is to focus our development efforts on continuous innovation by creating and enhancing the specialized, proprietary software that is unique to our business, and to license or acquire commercially-developed technology for other applications where available and appropriate. We continually invest in several areas of technology, including our seller platform; A9.com, our wholly-owned subsidiary focused on search technology on www.A9.com and other Amazon sites; web services; and digital initiatives.

Round (2004) describes the technology approach as 'distributed development and deployment'. Pages such as the home page have a number of content 'pods' or 'slots' which call web services for features. This makes it relatively easy to change the content in these pods and even change the location of the pods on-screen. Amazon uses a flowable or fluid page design, unlike many sites, which enables it to make the most of real estate on-screen.

Technology also supports more standard e-retail facilities. SEC (2005) states:

We use a set of applications for accepting and validating customer orders, placing and tracking orders with suppliers, managing and assigning inventory to customer orders, and ensuring proper shipment of products to customers. Our transaction-processing systems handle millions of items, a number of different status inquiries, multiple shipping addresses, giftwrapping requests, and multiple shipment methods. These systems allow the customer to choose whether to receive single or several shipments based on availability and to track the progress of each order. These applications also manage the process of accepting, authorizing, and charging customer credit cards.

Data-driven automation

Round (2004) said that 'data is king at Amazon'. He gave many examples of data-driven automation including customer channel preferences, managing the way content is displayed to different user types such as new releases and top-sellers, merchandising and recommendation (showing related products and promotions) and also advertising through paid search (automatic ad generation and bidding).

The automated search advertising and bidding system for paid search has had a big impact at Amazon. Sponsored links were initially done by humans, but this was unsustainable due to the range of products at Amazon. The automated programme generates keywords, writes ad creative, determines best landing page, manages bids, and measures conversion rates, profit per converted visitor and updates bids. Again the problem of volume is there: Matt Round described how the book *How to Make Love Like a Porn Star* by Jenna Jameson received tens of thousands of clicks from pornography-related searches, but few actually purchased the book. So the update cycle must be quick to avoid large losses.

There is also an automated e-mail measurement and optimization system. The campaign calendar used to be manually managed with relatively weak measurement and it was costly to schedule and use. A new system:

- automatically optimizes content to improve customer experience;
- avoids sending an e-mail campaign that has low clickthrough or high unsubscribe rate;
- includes inbox management (avoid sending multiple e-mails/per week);

- has a growing library of automated e-mail programmes covering new releases and recommendations;
- but there are challenges if promotions are too successful and inventory isn't available.

Your recommendations

'Customers Who Bought X … also bought Y' is Amazon's signature feature. Round (2004) describes how Amazon relies on acquiring and then crunching a massive amount of data. Every purchase, every page viewed and every search is recorded. So there are now two new versions: 'Customers who shopped for X also shopped for Y' and 'Customers who searched for X also bought Y'. They also have a system codenamed 'Goldbox' which is a cross-sell and awareness-raising tool. Items are discounted to encourage purchases in new categories!

He also describes the challenge of techniques for sifting patterns from noise (sensitivity filtering) and clothing and toy catalogues change frequently so recommendations become out of date. The main challenges though are the massive data size arising from millions of customers, millions of items and recommendations made in real time.

Partnership strategy

As Amazon grew, its share price growth enabled partnership or acquisition with a range of companies in different sectors. Marcus (2004) describes how Amazon partnered with Drugstore.com (pharmacy), Living.com (furniture), Pets.com (pet supplies), Wineshopper.com (wines), HomeGrocer.com (groceries), Sothebys.com (auctions) and Kozmo.com (urban home delivery). In most cases, Amazon purchased an equity stake in these partners, so that it would share in their prosperity. It also charged them fees for placements on the Amazon site to promote and drive traffic to their sites. Similarly, Amazon charged publishers for prime position to promote books on its site which caused an initial hue and cry, but this abated when it was realized that paying for prominent placements was widespread in traditional booksellers and supermarkets. Many of these new online companies failed in 1999 and 2000, but Amazon had covered the potential for growth and was not pulled down by these partners, even though for some, such as Pets.com, it had an investment of 50%.

Analysts sometimes refer to 'Amazoning a sector', meaning that one company becomes dominant in an online sector such as book retail such that it becomes very difficult for others to achieve market share. In addition to developing, communicating and delivering a very strong proposition, Amazon has been able to consolidate its strength in different sectors through its partnership arrangements and through using technology to facilitate product promotion and distribution via these partnerships. The Amazon retail platform enables other retailers to sell products online using the Amazon user interface and infrastructure through their 'Syndicated Stores' programme. Similarly, in the US, Borders, a large book retailer, uses the Amazon merchant platform for distributing its products. Toy retailer Toys 'Я' Us has a similar arrangement. Such partnerships help Amazon extend its reach into the customer base of other suppliers, and of course, customers who buy in one category such as books can be encouraged to purchase from other areas such as clothing or electronics.

Another form of partnership referred to above is the Amazon Marketplace which enables Amazon customers and other retailers to sell their new and used books and other goods alongside the regular retail listings. A similar partnership approach is the Amazon 'Merchants@' programme which enables third-party merchants (typically larger than those who sell via the Amazon Marketplace) to sell their products via Amazon. Amazon earns fees either as fixed fees or as sales commissions per unit. This arrangement can help customers who get a wider choice of products from a range of suppliers with the convenience of purchasing them through a single checkout process.

Finally, Amazon has also facilitated formation of partnerships with smaller companies through its affiliates programme. Internet legend records that Jeff Bezos, the creator of Amazon, was chatting at a cocktail party to someone who wanted to sell books about divorce via her website. Subsequently, Amazon.com launched its Associates Program in July 1996 and it is still going strong. Googling www.google.com/search?q=www.amazon.com+-site%3Awww.amazon.com for sites that link to the US site shows over 4 million pages, many of which will be affiliates. Amazon does not use an affiliate network, which would take commissions from sale, but, thanks to the strength of its brand, has developed its own affiliate programme. Amazon has created tiered performance-based incentives to encourage affiliates to sell more Amazon products.

Marketing communications

In their SEC filings Amazon state that the aims of their communications strategy are (unsurprisingly) to:

1 Increase customer traffic to their websites.
2 Create awareness of their products and services.
3 Promote repeat purchases.
4 Develop incremental product and service revenue opportunities.
5 Strengthen and broaden the Amazon.com brand name.

Amazon also believes that their most effective marketing communications are a consequence of their focus on continuously improving the customer experience. This then creates word-of-mouth promotion which is effective in acquiring new customers and may also encourage repeat customer visits.

As well as this, Marcus (2004) describes how Amazon used the personalization enabled through technology to reach out to a difficult-to-reach market which Bezos originally called 'the hard middle'. Bezos's view was that it was easy to reach 10 people (you called them on the phone) or the 10 million people who bought the most popular products (you placed a superbowl ad), but more difficult to reach those in between. The search facilities in the search engine and on the Amazon site, together with its product recommendation features, meant that Amazon could connect its products with the interests of these people.

Online advertising techniques include paid search marketing, interactive ads on portals, e-mail campaigns and search engine optimization. These are automated as far as possible as described earlier in the case study. As previously mentioned, the affiliate programme is also important in driving visitors to Amazon and Amazon offers a wide range of methods of linking to its site to help improve conversion. For example, affiliates can use straight text links leading direct to a product page and they also offer a range of dynamic banners which feature different content such as books about Internet marketing or a search box.

Amazon also uses cooperative advertising arrangements, better known as 'contra-deals', with some vendors and other third parties. For example, a print advertisement in 2005 for a particular product such as a wireless router with a free wireless laptop card promotion was to feature a specific Amazon URL in the ad. In product fulfilment packs, Amazon may include a leaflet for a non-competing online company such as Figleaves.com (lingerie) or Expedia (travel). In return, Amazon leaflets may be included in customer communications from the partner brands.

Amazon's associates programme directs customers to its websites by enabling independent websites to make millions of products available to its audiences with fulfilment performed by Amazon or third parties. It pays commissions to hundreds of thousands of participants in its associates programme when its customer referrals result in product sales.

In addition, it offers everyday free shipping options worldwide and recently announced Amazon.com Prime in the US, its first membership programme in which members receive free two-day shipping and discounted overnight shipping. Although marketing expenses do not include the costs of free shipping or promotional offers, it views such offers as effective marketing tools.

Source: *Internet Retailer* (2004); Marcus (2004); Round (2004); SEC (2005).

Questions

1 By referring to the case study, Amazon's website for your country and your experience of Amazon offline communications, evaluate how well Amazon communicates its core proposition and promotional offers.
2 Using the case study, characterize Amazon's approach to marketing communications.
3 Explain what distinguishes Amazon in its uses of technology for competitive advantage.
4 How does the Amazon 'culture of metrics' differ from that in other organizations from your experience?

All figures in millions:

	2007	2006	2005
Net sales	$14,835	$10,711	$8,490
Cost of sales	11,482	8,255	6,451
Gross profit	3,353	2,456	2,039
Operating expenses (1):			
Fulfillment	1,292	937	745
Marketing	344	263	198
Technology and content	818	662	451
General and administrative	235	195	166
Other operating expense, net	9	10	47
Total operating expenses	2,698	2,067	1,607
Income from operations	655	389	432
Interest income	90	59	44
Interest expense	(77)	(78)	(92)
Other income (expense), net	(1)	(4)	2
Remeasurements and other	(7)	11	42
Total non-operating income (expense)	5	(12)	(4)
Income before income taxes	660	377	428
Provision for income taxes	184	187	95
Income before cumulative effect of change in accounting principle	476	190	333
Cumulative effect of change in accounting principle	–	–	26
Net income	$ 476	$ 190	$ 359

Summary

1. Implementation is an iterative process of managing changes involving analysis, design, testing and review as part of an evolutionary prototyping process.

2. Maintenance is a continuous process of monitoring, assessing required changes and then implanting them using evolutionary prototyping.

3. Simple web pages are developed in static HTML. Most e-business systems require dynamic pages that are implemented using client- and server-side scripting, of which the most popular are JavaScript and ASP.

4. Testing has two main objectives: first, to check for non-conformance with the business and user requirements and, second, to identify bugs or errors. There are many specialized techniques to test either part of the system (component testing) or all of the system (system testing).

5. Changeover has to be managed to include elements of piloting, phased implementation, immediate cutover and parallel running.

6. Content management requires a clearly defined update process and responsibilities according to different types of changes required.

7. Measurement also requires process and responsibilities and also a measurement framework. A suggested framework for sell-side e-commerce assesses channel promotion, channel behaviour, channel satisfaction, channel outcomes and channel profitability. Selection of appropriate web analytics tools is important to assess the effectiveness of e-commerce.

Exercises

Self-assessment questions

1. Summarize how the activities involved with implementation and maintenance relate to analysis and design activities in previous chapters.

2. What are the risks of launching a new e-commerce site if implementation is not conducted effectively?

3. Distinguish between static and dynamic content and methods of achieving them.

4. What are the objectives of testing? How do these relate to an e-commerce site?

5. Summarize the advantages and disadvantages of the different changeover methods.

6. What are the issues for managers of content management?

7. What are the main elements of an e-commerce site measurement plan?

8. What are the elements of a budget for an e-commerce site enhancement?

Essay and discussion questions

1. Write a report to a manager recommending particular techniques that should or should not be implemented on an e-commerce site. Examples may include frames, Flash or Shockwave plug-ins, JavaScript, Java and active server pages.

2. Develop a plan for measuring the marketing effectiveness of an e-commerce site.

3. Discuss the balance of using a website and traditional methods for marketing research.

4. Choose an example of a simple brochureware website. Develop an implementation plan for this site, recommending development techniques that will be used to enhance the site.

Examination questions

1   You are developing a testing plan for an e-commerce site. Outline five key aspects of the site you would test.

2   Data migration is often overlooked in implementation planning. Explain what data migration is and explain when it may need to occur for creation of an e-commerce site for an existing business.

3   Analyse the advantages and disadvantages of a soft versus hard website launch.

4   Explain the following terms and suggest which is the most useful in measuring the effectiveness of a website.

    (a) hit

    (b) page impression

    (c) site visit.

5   Why are conversion and attrition rates important in evaluating the performance of an e-commerce site?

6   Suggest three key measures that indicate the contribution of an e-commerce site to overall business performance for a company with online and offline presence.

References

1to1media (2008) The Time for Cross-Channel Measurement Is Now, Article by Kevin Zimmerman, 22 September.

Adams, C., Kapashi, N., Neely, A. and Marr, B. (2000) Managing with measures. Measuring ebusiness performance. *Accenture White Paper*. Survey conducted in conjunction with Cranfield School of Management.

Agrawal, V., Arjana, V. and Lemmens, R. (2001) E-performance: the path to rational exuberance. *McKinsey Quarterly*, no. 1, 31–43.

Bayne, K. (1997) *The Internet Marketing Plan*. Wiley, New York.

Bocij, P., Chaffey, D., Greasley, A. and Hickie, S. (2005) *Business Information Systems: Technology, Development and Management*, 3rd edn. Financial Times Prentice Hall, Harlow.

Bourne, M., Mills, J., Willcox, M., Neely, A. and Platts, K. (2000) Designing, implementing and updating performance measurement systems. *International Journal of Operations and Production Management*, 20(7), 754–71.

Chaffey, D. (2000) Achieving Internet marketing success. *Marketing Review*, 1(1), 35–60.

Chaffey, D. and Wood, S. (2005) *Business Information Management: Improving Performance Using Information Systems*. Financial Times Prentice Hall, Harlow.

Chaffey, D., Mayer, R., Johnston, K. and Ellis-Chadwick, F. (2009) *Internet Marketing: Strategy, Implementation and Practice*, 4th edn. Financial Times Prentice Hall, Harlow.

Friedman, L. and Furey, T. (1999) *The Channel Advantage*. Butterworth-Heinemenn, Oxford.

Hanson, W. (2000) *Principles of Internet Marketing*. South Western College Publishing, Cincinnati, OH.

Internet Retailer (2004) The New Wal-Mart? By Paul Demery. *Internet Retailer*, 1 May. **www.internetretailer.com**.

Jorgensen, P. (1995) *Software Testing: A Craftsman's Approach*. CRC Press, Boca Raton, FL.

Kotler, P. (1997) *Marketing Management – Analysis, Planning, Implementation and Control*. Prentice-Hall, Englewood Cliffs, NJ.

Marcus, J. (2004) *Amazonia: Five Years at the Epicentre of the Dot-com Juggernaut*. The New Press, New York.

Neely, A., Adams, C. and Kennerley, M. (2002) *The Performance Prism: The Scorecard for Measuring and Managing Business Success*. Financial Times Prentice Hall, Harlow.

Petersen, E. (2004) *Web Analytics Demystified*. Self-published. Available from **www. webanlyticsdemystified.com**.

Plant, R. (2000) *ECommerce: Formulation of Strategy*. Prentice-Hall, Upper Saddle River, NJ.

Revolution (2004) Alliance and Leicester Banks on E-commerce. *Revolution*. Article by Philip Buxton. **www.revolutionmagazine.com**, 28 July.

Round, M. (2004) Presentation to E-metrics, London, May. **www.emetrics.org**.

SEC (2005) United States Securities and Exchange Commission submission Form 10-K from Amazon. For the fiscal year ended 31 December 2004.

SEOMoz (2007) Search engine ranking factors v2, 2 April, **www.seomoz.org/article/ search-ranking-factors**.

Shore, J. and Warden, S. (2008) *The Art of Agile Development*. O'Reilly, Sebastopol, CA.

Sterne, J. (2002) *Web Metrics: Proven Methods for Measuring Web Site Success*. Wiley, New York.

Wilson, H. (2008) *The Multichannel Challenge*. Butterworth-Heinemann, Oxford.

Wisner, J. and Fawcett, S. (1991) Link firm strategy to operating decisions through performance measurement. *Production and Inventory Management Journal*, Third Quarter, 5–11.

Further reading

Barron, D. (2000) *The World of Scripting Languages*. Wiley, Chichester. An accessible introduction to scripting languages such as Perl and JavaScript.

Deitel, H., Deitel, P. and Nieto, T. (2001) *E-Business and E-Commerce: How to Program*. Prentice-Hall, Upper Saddle River, NJ. An excellent guide to creating static and dynamic pages and many other issues of e-business technology.

Friedlein, A. (2002) *Maintaining and Evolving Successful Commercial Web Sites*. Morgan Kaufmann, San Francisco. An excellent book for professionals covering managing change, content, customer relationships and site measurement.

Inan, H. (2002) *Measuring the Success of Your Website: A Customer-centric Approach to Website Management*. Pearson Education/Prentice Hall, Frenchs Forest, NSW. A detailed guide to online measurement options.

Sterne, J. (2002) *Web Metrics: Proven Methods for Measuring Web Site Success*. Wiley, New York. A guide to measurement online, with many case studies and examples of tools.

Wilson, H. (2008) *The Multichannel Challenge*. Butterworth-Heinemann, Oxford.

Zeldman, J. (2007) *Designing with Web Standards*, 2nd edn. New Riders, Berkeley, CA. **www.zeldman.com**.

Web links

Web analytics expertise

ABC electronic (**www.abce.org.uk**) Audited Bureau of Circulation is standard for magazines in the UK. This is the electronic auditing part. Useful for definitions and examples of traffic for UK organizations.

Avinash Kaushik's blog (**www.kaushik.net**) Avinash is an expert in web analytics and his popular blog shows how web analytics should be used to control and improve return on e-marketing investments.

E-consultancy (**www.econsultancy.com**) Has a section on web analytics including buyers' guides to the tools available.

Emetrics (**www.emetrics.org**) Jim Sterne's site has many resources for online marketing metrics.

Epikone (**www.epikone.com/resources**) A specialist web analytics blog and e-book giving guidance on how to tailor Google Analytics.

Neil Mason of Applied Insights (**www.applied-insights.co.uk**) Blog featuring Neil's insights related to measurement and control of e-marketing.

Jim Sterne of Target Marketing (**www.targeting.com**) Leading commentator on the topic.

Web Analytics Demystified (**www.webanalyticsdemystified.com**) Analyst Eric Peterson on web analytics.

Web Analytics Association (**www.webanalyticsassociation.org**) The trade association site has definitions and advice.

Content management

Gerry McGovern New Thinking (**www.gerrymcgovern.com**) Resources about user-centric content management.

ReadWriteWeb (**www.readwriteweb.com**) Site focusing on trends and developments in content management, web applications and social media.

Glossary

A

AB testing A/B or AB testing refers to testing two different versions of a page or a page element such as a heading, image or button for effectiveness. The alternatives are served alternately with the visitors to the page randomly split between the two pages. Changes in visitor behaviour can then be compared using different metrics such as clickthrough rate on page elements like buttons or images or macro-conversion rates, such as conversion to sale or sign-up.

Acceptable-use policy Statement of employee activities involving use of networked computers that are not considered acceptable by management.

Accessibility An approach to website design that enables sites and web applications to be used by people with visual impairment or other disabilities such as motor impairment. Accessibility also demands that web users should be able to use websites and applications effectively regardless of the browser and access platform they use and its settings.

Accessibility legislation Legislation intended to protect users of websites with disabilities, including those with visual disability.

Acquisition method Defines whether the system is purchased outright or developed from scratch.

Activity-based process definition methods Analysis tools used to identify the relationship between tasks within a business process.

Actors People, software or other devices that interface with a system. See **use-case**.

Ad serving The term for displaying an advertisement on a website. Often the advertisement will be served from a web server different from the site on which it is placed.

Affiliate A company promoting a merchant typically through a commission-based arrangement either direct or through an affiliate network.

Affiliate marketing A commission-based arrangement where an e-tailer pays sites that link to it for sales, leads (CPA-based) or less commonly visitors (CPC-based).

Affiliate networks An e-tailer pays commission on sales referred from other sites.

Agents Software programs that assist humans by automatically gathering information from the Internet or exchanging data with other agents based on parameters supplied by the user.

Aggregated buying A form of customer union where buyers collectively purchase a number of items at the same price and receive a volume discount.

Aggregators An alternative term for price comparison sites. Aggregators include product, price and service information, comparing competitors within a sector such as financial services, retail or travel. Their revenue models commonly include affiliate revenues (CPA), pay-per-click advertising (CPC) and display advertising (CPM).

Agile development An iterative approach to developing software and website functionality with the emphasis on face-to-face communications to elicit, define and test requirements. Each iteration is effectively a mini-software project including stages of planning, requirements analysis, design, coding, testing and documentation.

Allowable cost per acquisition A target maximum cost for generating leads or new customers profitably.

Alt tags Alt tags appear after an image tag and contain a phrase associated with that image. For example: `<img src="logo.gif" alt="Company name, company products"/>`.

Analysis and design Analysis of system requirements and design for creation of a system.

Analysis for e-business Using analytical techniques to capture and summarize business and user requirements.

Anticipatory change An organization initiates change without an immediate need to respond.

Anti-virus software Software to detect and eliminate viruses.

Application server An application server provides a business application on a server remote from the user.

Applications service provider (ASP) A provider of business applications such as e-mail, workflow or groupware or any business application on a server remote from the user. A service often offered by ISPs.

Asymmetric encryption Both parties use a related but different key to encode and decode messages.

Atomization In a Web 2.0 context refers to a concept where the content on a site is broken down into smaller fundamental units which can then be distributed via the web through links to other sites. Examples of atomization include the stories and pages in individual feeds being syndicated to third-party sites and widgets.

Attribute A property or characteristic of an entity, implemented as a field; see **Database**.

Attrition rate Percentage of site visitors that are lost at each stage in making a purchase.

Auction A buying model where traders make **offers** and **bids** to sell or buy under certain conditions.

Augmented reality Blends real-world digital data capture typically with a digital camera in a webcam or mobile phone to create a browser-based digital representation or experience mimicking that of the real world.

B

B2B electronic marketplace Virtual locations with facilities to enable trading between buyers and sellers.

Backbones High-speed communications links used to enable Internet communications across a country and internationally.

Balanced scorecard A framework for setting and monitoring business performance. Metrics are structured according to customer issues, internal efficiency measures, financial measures and innovation.

Bandwidth Indicates the speed at which data are transferred using a particular network media. It is measured in bits per second (bps).

Behavioural ad targeting Enables an advertiser to target ads at a visitor as they move within or between sites dependent on their viewing particular sites or types of content that indicate their preference. This approach increases ad relevance and the frequency or number of impressions served to an individual in the target market, so increasing response.

Bespoke development Information system development specifically for a purpose.

Bid A commitment by a trader to *purchase* under certain conditions. See **Auction**.

Blacklist A compilation of known sources of **spam** that is used to block e-mail.

Blog An online diary or news source prepared by an individual or a group of people.

Bluecasting Bluecasting involves messages being automatically pushed to a consumer's Bluetooth-enabled phone or they can pull or request audio, video or text content to be downloaded from a live advert. In the future ads will be able to respond to those who view them.

Bluejacking Sending a message from a mobile phone or transmitter to another mobile phone which is in close range via Bluetooth technology.

Blueprints Show the relationships between pages and other content components, and can be used to portray organization, labelling and navigation systems.

Bluetooth A wireless standard for transmission of data between devices over short ranges (less than 100 m).

Boot-sector virus Occupies boot record of hard and floppy disks and is activated during computer start-up.

Botnet Independent computers, connected to the Internet, are used together, typically for malicious purposes through controlling software. For example, they may be used to send out spam or for a denial-of-service

attack where they repeatedly access a server to degrade its service. Computers are often initially infected through a virus when effective anti-virus measures are not in place.

Bounce rate Percentage of visitors entering a site who leave immediately after viewing one page only (known as 'single-page visits').

Brand The sum of the characteristics of a product or service perceived by a user.

Brand equity A brand's assets (or liabilities) linked to the brand's name and symbol that add to (or subtract from) a service.

Brand experience The frequency and depth of interactions with a brand can be enhanced through the Internet.

Brand identity The totality of brand associations including name and symbols that must be communicated.

Branding The process of creating and developing successful brands.

Bricks and mortar A traditional organization with limited online presence.

Broad and shallow navigation More choices, fewer clicks to reach required content.

Broadband connection Access to the Internet via phone lines using a digital data transfer mechanism.

Brochureware Brochureware describes a website in which a company has migrated its existing paper-based promotional literature on to the Internet without recognizing the differences required by this medium.

Browsers See **Web browsers**.

Browser compatibility Cross-browser compatibility is the capability of a site to render and deliver interactivity correctly in different versions of web browsers, in particular the most popular browsers: Microsoft Internet Explorer, Mozilla Firefox, Apple Safari and Google Chrome.

Browser extensions The capability of a browser to add new services through new add-ons or plug-ins or customizing through different visual themes, particularly used in Mozilla Firefox browser.

Browser plug-in An add-on program to a web browser, providing extra functionality such as animation.

Bundling Offering complementary services.

Burn rate The speed at which dot-coms spend investors' money.

Business-alignment IS strategy The IS strategy is generated from the business strategy through techniques such as Critical Success Factor analysis.

Business continuity management Measures taken to ensure that information can be restored and accessed if the original information and access method are destroyed.

Business-impacting IS strategy IS strategy analyses opportunities for new technologies and processes to favourably impact the business strategy.

Business model A summary of how a company will generate revenue identifying its product offering, value-added services, revenue sources and target customers.

Business process automation (BPA) Automating existing ways of working manually through information technology.

Business process improvement (BPI) Optimizing existing processes typically coupled with enhancements in information technology.

Business process management (BPM) An approach supported by software tools intended to increase process efficiency by improving information flows between people as they perform business tasks.

Business process re-engineering (BPR) Identifying radical, new ways of carrying out business operations, often enabled by new IT capabilities.

Business-to-business (B2B) Commercial transactions between an organization and other organizations.

Business-to-consumer (B2C) Commercial transactions between an organization and consumers.

Business transformation Significant changes to organizational processes implemented to improve organizational performance.

Buy-side e-commerce E-commerce transactions between a purchasing organization, its suppliers and partners.

C

CAPTCHA Stands for 'Completely Automated Public Turing test to tell Computers and Humans Apart'. It requires a person submitting a web form such as a comment to enter letters or numbers from an image to validate that they are a genuine user.

Card sorting The process of arranging a way of organizing objects on a website in a consistent manner.

Cascading style sheets (CSS) Enable web designers to define standard styles (e.g. fonts, spacing and colours) to hypertext mark-up language documents. By separating the presentation style of documents from the content of documents, CSS simplifies web authoring and site maintenance since style can be defined across a whole site (or sections of sites).

Certificate and certificate authorities (CAs) A certificate is a valid copy of a public key of an individual or organization together with identification information. It is issued by a trusted third party (TTP) or certificate authority (CA). CAs make public keys available and also issue private keys.

Change agents Managers involved in controlling change transitions.

Change management Managing process, structural, technical, staff and culture change within an organization.

Changeover The term used to describe moving from the old information system to the new information system.

Channel buyer behaviour Describes which content is visited, time and duration.

Channel outcomes Record customer actions taken as a consequence of a site visit.

Channel profitability The profitability of the website, taking into account revenue and cost and discounted cash flow.

Channel promotion Measures that assess why customers visit a site – which adverts they have seen, which sites they have been referred from.

Channel satisfaction Evaluation of the customer's opinion of the service quality on the site and supporting services such as e-mail.

Churn rate The proportion of customers (typically subscribers) that no longer purchase a company's products in a time period.

Clicks and mortar A business combining an online and offline presence.

Clicks-only or Internet pureplay An organization with principally an online presence.

Client–server The client–server architecture consists of client computers such as PCs sharing resources such as a database stored on more powerful **server** computers.

Client–server model A system architecture in which end-user machines such as PCs known as clients run applications while accessing data and possibly programs from a server.

Cloud computing The use of distributed storage and processing on servers connected by the Internet, typically provided as software or data storage as a subscription service provided by other companies.

Cold list Data about individuals that are rented or sold by a third party.

Collaborative filtering Profiling of customer interests coupled with delivery of specific information and offers, often based on the interests of similar customers.

Commoditization The process whereby product selection becomes more dependent on price than on differentiating features, benefits and value-added services.

Community A customer-to-customer interaction delivered via e-mail groups, web-based discussion forums or chat.

Competitor analysis for e-business Review of e-business services offered by existing and new competitors and adoption by their customers.

Computer virus A program capable of self-replication allowing it to spread from one machine to another. It may be malicious and delete data, or benign.

Consumer-to-business (C2B) Customer is proactive in making an offer to a business, e.g. the price they are prepared to pay for an airline ticket.

Consumer-to-consumer (C2C) Interactions between customers on a website, e.g. posting and reading of topics on an electronic bulletin board.

Content Content is the design, text and graphical information which forms a web page. Good content is the key to attracting customers to a website and retaining their interest or achieving repeat visits.

Content management system (CMS) Software used to manage creation, editing and review of web-based content.

Content strategy The management of text, rich media, audio and video content aimed at engaging customers and prospects to meet business goals published through print and digital media including web and mobile platforms which is repurposed and syndicated to different forms of web presence such as publisher sites, blogs, social media and comparison sites.

Contextual display network Contextual ads are automatically displayed according to the type of content on partner publisher sites by the search engine.

Control page The page against which subsequent optimization will be assessed. Typically a current landing page. When a new page performs better than the existing control page, it becomes your control page in subsequent testing. Also known as 'champion-challenger'.

Conversion marketing Using marketing communications to maximize conversion of potential customers to actual customers and existing customers to repeat customers.

Conversion rate Percentage of site visitors that perform a particular action such as making a purchase.

Cookies Cookies are small text files stored on an end-user's computer to enable websites to identity them.

Co-opetition Interactions between competitors and marketplace intermediaries which can mutually improve the attractiveness of a marketplace.

Core competencies Resources, including skills or technologies, that provide a particular benefit to customers.

Core product The fundamental features of the product that meet the user's needs.

Cost per acquisition (CPA) The cost of acquiring a new customer. Typically limited to the communications cost and refers to cost per sale for new customers. May also refer to other outcomes such as cost per quote or enquiry.

Cost per click (CPC) The cost to the advertiser (or the revenue received by the publisher) of each click of a link to a third-party site.

Cost per thousand (CPM) Cost per 1,000 ad impressions for a banner advert.

Countermediation Creation of a new intermediary by an established company.

Covert monitoring Monitoring which the employer undertakes without notification of staff.

Cross-media optimization studies (XMOS) Studies to determine the optimum spend across different media to produce the best results.

Crowdsourcing Utilizing a network of customers or other partners to gain insights for new product or process innovations.

Culture This concept includes shared values, i.e. cultures are created when a group of employees interact over time and are relatively successful in what they undertake.

Customer acquisition Techniques used to gain new prospects and customers.

Customer-centric marketing An approach to marketing based on detailed knowledge of customer behaviour within the target audience which seeks to fulfil the individual needs and wants of customers.

Customer engagement Repeated interactions that strengthen the emotional, psychological or physical investment a customer has in a brand.

Customer extension Techniques to encourage customers to increase their involvement with an organization.

Customer insight Knowledge about customers' needs, characteristics, preferences and behaviours based on analysis of qualitative and quantitative data. Specific insights can be used to inform marketing tactics directed at groups of customers with shared characteristics.

Customer journey A description of modern multi-channel behaviour as consumers use different media to select suppliers, make purchases and gain customer support.

Customer life cycle The stages each customer will pass through in a long-term relationship through acquisition, retention and extension. There are more detailed stages within this.

Customer orientation Developing site content and services to appeal to different customer segments or other members of the audience.

Customer profile Information that can be used to segment a customer.

Customer relationship management (CRM) An approach to building and sustaining long-term business with customers.

Customer scenario Alternative tasks or outcomes required by a visitor to a website. Typically accomplished in a series of stages of different tasks involving different information needs or experiences.

Customer self-service Customers perform information requests and transactions through a web interface rather than contact with customer support staff.

Customer value Dependent on product quality, service quality, price and fulfilment time.

D

Data controller Each company must have a defined person responsible for data protection.

Data migration Transfer of data from old to new systems.

Data subject The individual whose privacy is protected through data protection legislation.

Data warehouses Large database systems (often measured in gigabytes or terabytes) containing detailed company data on sales transactions which are analysed to assist in improving the marketing and financial performance of companies.

Database A database can be defined as a collection of related information. The information held in the database is stored in an organized way so that specific items can be selected and retrieved quickly. See **Database management system**.

Database management system (DBMS) The information held in an electronic database is accessed via a database management system. A DBMS can be defined as one or more computer programs that allow users to enter, store, organize, manipulate and retrieve data from a database. For many users, the terms *database* and *database management system* are interchangeable. A *relational database management system (RDBMS)* is an extension of a DBMS and allows data to be combined from a variety of sources.

Database table Each database comprises several tables.

Dedicated server Server only contains content and applications for a single company.

Deep linking Jakob Nielsen's term for a user arriving at a site deep within its structure.

Demand analysis Assessment of the demand for e-commerce services amongst existing and potential customer segments.

Denial-of-service attacks Websites are disabled through bombardment with many requests for information originating from computers around the world that have been hijacked.

Deployment plan A deployment plan is a schedule which defines all the tasks that need to occur in order for changeover to occur successfully. This includes putting in place all the infrastructure such as cabling and hardware.

Design for analysis (DFA) The required measures from a site are considered during design to better understand the audience of a site and their decision points.

Destination site Typically a retailer or manufacturer site with sales and service information. Intermediaries such as media sites may be destination sites for some.

Development environment Software and hardware used to create a system.

Dial-up connection Access to the Internet via phone lines using analogue modems.

Differential advantage A desirable attribute of a product offering that is not currently matched by competitor offerings.

Digital certificates (keys) Consist of keys made up of large numbers that are used to uniquely identify individuals.

Digital marketing This has a similar meaning to 'electronic marketing' – both describe the management and execution of marketing using electronic media such as the web, e-mail, interactive TV and wireless media in conjunction with digital data about customers' characterstics and behaviour.

Digital media channels Online communications techniques used to achieve goals of brand awareness, familiarity and favourability and to influence purchase intent by encouraging users of digital media to visit a website to engage with the brand or product and ultimately to purchase online or offline through traditional media channels such as by phone or in-store.

Digital rights management (DRM) The use of different technologies to protect the distribution of digital services or content such as software, music, movies or other digital data.

Digital signatures A method of identifying individuals or companies using public-key encryption.

Directories or catalogues Structured listings of registered sites in different categories such as Yahoo! categories.

Disaster recovery See **Business continuity management**.

Discontinuous change Change involving a major transformation in an industry.

Disintermediation The removal of intermediaries such as distributors or brokers that formerly linked a company to its customers.

Disruptive Internet technologies New Internet-based communications approaches which change the way in which information about products is exchanged, which impact the basis for competition in a marketplace.

Domain name The domain name refers to the name of the web server and it is usually selected to be the same as the name of the company, e.g. www.<company-name>. com, and the extension will indicate its type.

Domain name registration The process of reserving a unique web address that can be used to refer to the company website.

Dot-coms Businesses whose main trading presence is on the Internet.

Downstream supply chain Transactions between an organization and its customers and intermediaries, equivalent to sell-side e-commerce.

Dynamic e-business application The application is continuously updated in response to competitive forces.

Dynamic pricing Prices can be updated in real time according to the type of customer or current market conditions.

Dynamic web content See **Dynamic web page**.

Dynamically created web page A page that is created in real time, often with reference to a database query, in response to a user request.

E

Early adopter Company or department that invests in new technologies and techniques.

Early (first) mover An early entrant into the marketplace.

Effectiveness Meeting process objectives, delivering the required outputs and outcomes: 'doing the right thing'.

Efficiency Minimizing resources or time needed to complete a process: 'doing the thing right'.

Efficient consumer response (ECR) ECR is focused on demand management aimed at creating and satisfying customer demand by optimizing product assortment strategies, promotions, and new product introductions. It creates operational efficiencies and costs savings in the supply chain through reducing inventories and deliveries.

Electronic business (e-business) All electronically mediated information exchanges, both within an organization and with external stakeholders supporting the range of business processes.

Electronic business applications infrastructure Applications that provide access to services and information inside and beyond an organization.

Electronic business infrastructure The architecture of hardware, software, content and data used to deliver e-business services to employees, customers and partners.

Electronic business strategy Definition of the approach by which applications of internal and external electronic communications can support and influence corporate strategy.

Electronic channel service contribution The proportion of service-type processes that are completed using electronic channels.

Electronic channel strategies Define how a company should set specific objectives and develop specific differential strategies for communicating with its customers and partners through electronic media such as the Internet, e-mails and wireless media.

Electronic commerce (e-commerce) All electronically mediated information exchanges between an organization and its external stakeholders. See **Sell-side** and **Buy-side e-commerce**.

Electronic customer relationship management (e-CRM) Using digital communications technologies to maximize sales to existing customers and encourage continued usage of online services.

Electronic data interchange (EDI) The exchange, using digital media, of structured business information, particularly for sales transactions, such as purchase orders and invoices between buyers and sellers.

Electronic economy (e-economy) The dynamic system of interactions between a nation's citizens, businesses and government that capitalize upon online technology to achieve a social or economic good.

Electronic funds transfer (EFT) Automated digital transmissions of money between organizations and banks.

Electronic government (e-government) The use of Internet technologies to provide government services to citizens.

Electronic mail (e-mail) filter Software used to identify **spam** according to its characteristics such as keywords.

Electronic marketing (e-marketing) Achieving marketing objectives through use of electronic communications technology.

Electronic marketing (e-marketing) plan A plan to achieve the marketing objectives of the e-business strategy.

Electronic marketplace A virtual marketplace such as the Internet in which no direct contact occurs between buyers and sellers.

Electronic procurement (e-procurement) The electronic integration and management of all procurement activities including purchase request, authorization, ordering, delivery and payment between a purchaser and a supplier.

Electronic procurement system (EPS) An electronic system used to automate all or part of the procurement function by enabling the scanning, storage and retrieval of invoices and other documents; management of approvals; routeing of authorization requests; interfaces to other finance systems; and matching of documents to validate transactions.

Emergent strategy Strategic analysis, strategic development and strategy implementation are interrelated and are developed together.

Employee communications monitoring Companies monitor staff e-mails and websites they access.

Encryption See **Asymmetric encryption** and **Symmetric encryption**.

Enterprise application integration (EAI) Software used to facilitate communications between business applications including data transfer and control.

Enterprise resource planning (ERP) applications Enterprise applications used to manage information about organizational resources such as raw materials, products, staff and customers as part of delivery of a product or service.

Enterprise social media software Systems used inside organizations to enable real-time collaboration between employees and other stakeholders such as customers and suppliers to support business processes such as customer service, supply chain management and new product development. Collectively these tools are sometimes referenced as Enterprise 2.0.

Entity A grouping of related data, such as a customer entity. Implemented as a table.

Environmental scanning and analysis The process of continuously monitoring the environment and events and responding accordingly.

Ethical hacker Hacker employed legitimately to test the quality of system security.

Ethical standards Practice or behaviour which is morally acceptable to society.

Exchange See **B2B electronic marketplace**.

Expert review An analysis of an existing site or prototype by an experienced usability expert who will identify deficiencies and improvements to a site based on their knowledge of web design principles and best practice.

Explicit knowledge Knowledge that can be readily expressed and recorded within information systems.

Extended product Additional features and benefits beyond the core product.

External value chain or value network The links between an organization and its strategic and non-strategic partners that form its external value chain.

Extranet A service provided through Internet and web technology delivered by extending an intranet beyond a company to customers, suppliers and collaborators.

Eyetracking A usability testing technique that provides a visual overlay of where visitors most commonly look on the screen (heatmaps) and individual or common paths (gaze trails).

F

Feed Information is regularly exchanged between a server and another server or a client using a standardized XML format enabling the latest version of the information to be exchanged.

Field Attributes of products, such as date of birth. See **Database**.

Filtering software Software that blocks specified content or activities.

Financial EDI Aspect of electronic payment mechanism involving transfer of funds from the bank of a buyer to a seller. See **Electronic data interchange**.

Firewall A specialized software application mounted on a server at the point where the company is connected to the Internet. Its purpose is to prevent unauthorized access into the company from outsiders.

First-party cookies Served by the site you are currently using – typical for e-commerce sites.

Flow Flow describes how easy it is for users of a site to move between the different pages of content of the site.

Folksonomy A contraction of 'folk taxonomy', a method of classifying content based on tagging that has no hierarchy, i.e. without parent–child relationships.

Forward path analysis Reviews the combinations of clicks that occur from a page. This form of analysis is most beneficial from important pages such as the home page, product and directory pages. Use this technique to identify: messaging / navigation combinations which work best to yield the most clicks from a page.

G

GIF (Graphics Interchange Format) A graphics format and compression algorithm best used for simple graphics.

Globalization The increase of international trading and shared social and cultural values.

H

Hacking The process of gaining unauthorized access to computer systems, typically across a network.

Hit Recorded for each graphic or text file requested from a web server. It is not a reliable measure for the number of people viewing a page.

Hosted solution Standard software which is managed externally on the supplier's server.

Hosting provider A service provider that manages the server used to host an organization's website and its connection to the Internet backbones.

House list Data about existing customers used to market products to encourage future purchase.

HTML (Hypertext Markup Language) HTML is a standard format used to define the text and layout of web pages. HTML files usually have the extension .HTML or .HTM.

HTML parameters These occur within the tags to specify particular characteristics of the HTML statement.

HTML meta-tags Markup codes denoted by <start code> and </end code> that instruct the browser to format information or perform a particular operation.

HTTP (Hypertext Transfer Protocol) HTTP or Hypertext Transfer Protocol is a standard which defines the way information is transmitted across the Internet between web browsers and web servers.

Hub See **B2B electronic marketplace**.

Hype cycle A graphic representation of the maturity, adoption and business application of specific technologies.

Hyperlink A method of moving between one website page and another, indicated to the user by an image or text highlighted by underlining and/or a different colour.

I

Infrastructure as a Service (IaaS) Hardware used to provide support for end-user applications is outsourced and paid for according to level of usage. The hardware infrastructure used includes servers and networks.

Identity theft The misappropriation of the identity of another person, without their knowledge or consent.

i-Mode A mobile access platform that enables display of colour graphics and content subscription services.

Impact assessment An assessment of the **employee communications monitoring** process in the workplace to identify improvements to minimize infringement of employee privacy.

Implementation The creation of a system based on analysis and design documentation.

Inbound e-mail E-mail received from outside the organization such as customer and supplier enquiries.

Inbound e-mail marketing Management of e-mails from customers by an organization.

Inbound logistics The management of material resources entering an organization from its suppliers and other partners.

Incremental change Relatively small adjustments required by an organization in response to its business environment.

Infomediary A business whose main source of revenue derives from capturing consumer information and developing detailed profiles of individual customers for use by third parties.

Information and communication technology (ICT or IT) The software applications, computer hardware and networks used to create e-business systems.

Information architecture The combination of organization, labelling and navigation schemes making up an information system.

Information asset register A repository for the types, value and ownership of all information within an organization.

Information asymmetry Imperfect information sharing between members of a supply chain which increases uncertainty about demand and pricing.

Information organization schemes The structure chosen to group and categorize information.

Information security management system An organizational process to protect information assets.

Information security policy A definition of the organizational approaches to information security and the responsibilities of employees in protecting information.

Information society A society with widespread access and transfer of digital information within business and the community.

Information supply chain An information-centric view of the supply chain which addresses the organizational and technological challenges of achieving technology-enabled supply chain management efficiency and effectiveness.

Initiation The start-up phase of the project.

Intellectual property rights (IPR) Protect the intangible property created by corporations or individuals that is protected under copyright, trade secret and patent laws.

Interactivity The medium enables a dialogue between company and customer.

Intermediary An organization or e-commerce site that typically brings buyers and sellers together.

Internet The Internet refers to the physical network that links computers across the globe. It consists of the infrastructure of network servers and communication links between them that are used to hold and transport information between the client PCs and web servers.

Internet-based market research The use of online questionnaires and focus groups to assess customer perceptions of a website or broader marketing issues.

Internet EDI Use of **electronic data interchange** data standards delivered across non-proprietary IP networks.

Internet governance Control of the operation and use of the Internet.

Internet marketing metrics Measures that indicate the effectiveness of Internet marketing activities in meeting customer, business and marketing objectives.

Internet pureplay An organization with principally an online presence.

Internet service provider (ISP) A provider enabling home or business users a connection to access the Internet. They can also host web-based applications.

Interruption marketing Marketing communications that disrupt customers' activities.

Interstitial ads Ads that appear between one page and the next.

Intranet A private network within a single company using Internet standards to enable employees to access and share information using web publishing technology.

IP address The unique numerical address of a computer.

IPTV (Internet Protocol Television) Digital television service is delivered using Internet Protocol, typically by a broadband connection. IPTV can be streamed for real-time viewing or downloaded before playback.

J

JPEG (Joint Photographics Experts Group) A graphics format and compression algorithm best used for photographs.

K

Keyphrase (keyword phrase) The combination of words users of search engines type into a search box which form a search query.

Knowledge Applying experience to problem solving.

Knowledge management Techniques and tools for disseminating knowledge within an organization.

L

Lead See **Qualified lead**.

Lifetime value (LTV) Lifetime value is the total net benefit that a customer or group of customers will provide a company over their total relationship with the company.

Link anchor text The text used to form the blue underlined hyperlink viewed in a web browser defined in the HTML source.

Link building A structured activity to include good-quality hyperlinks to your site from relevant sites with a good **page rank**.

Localization Tailoring of web-site information for individual countries or regions.

Log-file analyser A log-file analyser is a separate program such as Webtrends that is used to summarize the information on customer activity contained in a log file.

Logistics See **Inbound logistics** and **Outbound logistics**.

Long tail concept A frequency distribution suggesting the relative variation in popularity of items selected by consumers.

M

Maintenance activities Involve measurement of an information system's effectiveness and updating to correct errors or introduce new features necessary to improve its value to the organization.

Maintenance phase Commences after the system is live.

Malicious virus A virus that causes damage through destruction of data or software.

Malware Malicious software or toolbars, typically downloaded via the Internet, which acts as a 'Trojan horse' by executing other unwanted activites such as keylogging of user passwords or viruses which may collect e-mail addresses.

Managed e-mail service Receipt and transmission of e-mails is managed by a third party.

Marketing concept The management of the range of organizational activities that impact on the customer as part of marketing.

Marketing orientation Meeting customer requirements through the coordination of all organizational activities that impact the customer.

Marketplace See **B2B electronic marketplace**.

Mashups Websites, pages or widgets that combine the content or functionality of one website or data source with another to create something offering a different type of value to web users from the separate types of content or functionality.

Mass customization Delivering customized content to groups of users through web pages or e-mail.

Mbps One megabit per second or 1,000,000 bps (company networks operate at 10 or more Mbps).

Media multiplier or halo effect The role of one media channel on influencing sale or uplift in brand metrics. Commonly applied to online display advertising, where exposure to display ads may increase clickthrough rates when the consumer is later exposed to a brand through other media, for example sponsored links or affiliate ads. It may also refer to conversion rates on a destination site through higher confidence in the brand or familiarity with the offer.

Meta-data A definition of the structure and content of a collection of data or documents. 'Data about data'.

Metamediaries Intermediaries providing information to assist with selection and discussion about different product and services.

Meta-tags Text within an HTML file summarizing the characteristics of the document. The most relevant to search engines are the meta-keywords tag used to list keywords relevant to the page and the content meta-tag, the description of which forms part of the listings snippet in the search results page. They are not used for ranking purposes in Google.

Microblogging Publishing of short posts through services such as Twitter.com and Tumblr.com.

Middleware Software used to facilitate communication between business applications including data transfer control.

Milestone Key deadline to be achieved during project, usually with defined deliverable criteria.

Micro-formats A simple set of formats based on XHTML for describing and exchanging information about objects including product and travel reviews, recipes and event information.

Micro-site A small-scale destination site reached on clickthrough which is part of the media owner's site.

Mission statement See **Vision or mission statement.**

Mixed-mode buying The process by which a customer changes between online and offline channels during the buying process.

Mobile apps A software application that is designed for use on a mobile phone, typically downloaded from an App store. iPhone Apps are best known, but all Smartphones support the use of apps which can provide users with information, entertainment or location-based services such as mapping.

Mobile commerce (m-commerce) Electronic transactions and communications conducted using mobile devices such as laptops, PDAs and mobile phones, and typically with a wireless connection.

MRO Maintenance, repairs and operations of manufacturing facilities.

Multi-channel e-business strategy Defines how different marketing and supply chain channels should integrate and support each other to drive business efficiency and effectiveness.

Multi-channel marketing Customer communications and product distribution are supported by a combination of digital and traditional channels at different points in the buying cycle.

Multi-channel marketing strategy Defines how different marketing channels should integrate and support each other in terms of their proposition development and communications based on their relative merits for the customer and the company.

Multi-tenancy SaaS A single instance of a web service is used by different customers (tenants) run on a single server or load-balanced across multiple servers. Customers are effectively sharing processor, disk usage and bandwidth with other customers.

N

Narrow and deep navigation Fewer choices, more clicks to reach required content.

Net neutrality The principle of provision of equal access to different Internet services by telecommunications service providers.

Net promoter score A measure of the number of advocates a company (or website) has who would recommend it compared to the number of detractors.

Notification The process whereby companies register with the data protection registrar to inform about their data holdings.

O

Offer A commitment by a trader to sell under certain conditions. See **Auction**.

Offline marketing communications Traditional techniques such as print and TV advertising used to generate website traffic.

Online business model A summary of how a company will generate a profit identifying its core product or service value proposition, target customers in different markets, position in the competitive online marketplace or value chain and its projections for revenue and costs.

Online buyer behaviour An assessment of how consumers and business people use the Internet in combination with other communications channels when selecting and buying products and services.

Online customer experience The combination of rational and emotional factors of using a company's online services that influences customers' perceptions of a brand online.

Online intermediaries Websites which help connect web users with content they are seeking on **destination sites**. Include new online intermediaries such as search engines and shopping comparison sites and traditional brokers, directories and newspaper and magazine publishers that now have an online presence.

Online marketplace Exchanges of information and commercial transactions between consumers, businesses and governments completed through different forms of online presence such as search engines, social networks, comparison sites and destination sites.

Online marketing communications Internet-based techniques used to generate website traffic.

Online PR Maximizing favourable mentions of your company, brands, products or websites on third-party websites which are likely to be visited by your target audience.

Online revenue contribution (ORC) An assessment of the direct contribution of the Internet or other digital media to sales, usually expressed as a percentage of overall sales revenue.

Online value proposition (OVP) A statement of the benefits of e-commerce services that ideally should not be available in competitor offerings or offline offerings.

Open-source software Software that is developed collaboratively, independent of a vendor, by a community of software developers and users.

Opt-in A customer proactively agrees to receive further information.

Opt-out A customer declines the offer to receive further information.

Organizational change Includes both **incremental** and **discontinuous change** to an organization.

Outbound e-mail E-mail sent from the company to other organizations.

Outbound e-mail marketing E-mails are sent to customers and prospects from an organization.

Outbound logistics The management of resources supplied from an organization to its customers and intermediaries such as retailers and distributors.

Overlay Typically an animated ad that moves around the page and is superimposed on the website content.

P

PaaS (Platform as a Service) Provision of software services for application design, development, data storage, testing and hosting together with messaging tools for collaboration on the development project.

Packaged implementation Standard software is installed with limited configuration required.

Packet Each Internet message such as an e-mail or http request is broken down into smaller parts for ease of transmission.

Page impression (view) A more reliable measure than a hit denoting one person viewing one page.

Page rank A scale of 0 to 10 used by Google to assess the importance of websites according to the number of inbound links (link popularity).

Page template A standard page layout format which is applied to each page of a website. Typically defined for different page categories (e.g. category page, product page, search page).

Pay-per-click (PPC) search marketing A company pays for text adverts to be displayed on the search engine results pages when a specific keyphrase is entered by the search users. It is so called since the marketer pays for each time the hypertext link in the ad is clicked on.

People variable The element of the marketing mix that involves the delivery of service to customers during interactions with customers.

Performance drivers Critical success factors that govern whether objectives are achieved.

Performance management system A process used to evaluate and improve the **efficiency** and **effectiveness** of an organization and its processes.

Performance measurement system The process by which metrics are defined, collected, disseminated and actioned.

Permission marketing Customers agree (opt in) to be involved in an organization's marketing activities, usually as a result of an incentive.

Persistent cookies Cookies that remain on the computer after a visitor session has ended. Used to recognize returning visitors.

Persona A summary of the characteristics, needs, motivations and environment of typical website users.

Personal data Any information about an individual stored by companies concerning their customers or employees.

Personalization Delivering individualized content through web pages or e-mail.

Phishing Obtaining personal details online through sites and e-mails masquerading as legitimate businesses.

Physical evidence variable The element of the marketing mix that involves the tangible expression of a product and how it is purchased and used.

Place variable The element of the marketing mix that involves distributing products to customers in line with demand and minimizing cost of inventory, transport and storage.

Plug-in An add-on program to a web browser providing extra functionality such as animation.

PNG (Portable Network Graphics) A graphics format defined to supersede the GIF format. Its features include compression, transparency and progressive loading.

Podcasts Individuals and organizations post online media (audio and video) which can be accessed in the appropriate players including the iPod, which first sparked the growth of this technique.

Portal An **intermediary site** focused on providing a gateway to other information on other sites, but often also providing its own content and services. Examples include search engines, ISPs and online newspapers and magazines.

Positioning Influencing the customer's perception of a product within a marketplace.

Prescriptive strategy The three core areas of strategic analysis, strategic development and strategy implementation are linked together sequentially.

Price elasticity of demand Measure of consumer behaviour that indicates the change in demand for a product or service in response to changes in price. Price elasticity of demand is used to assess the extent to which a change in price will influence demand for a product.

Price variable The element of the marketing mix that involves defining product prices and pricing models.

Pricing models Describe the form of payment such as outright purchase, auction, rental, volume purchase and credit terms.

Primary key The field that uniquely identifies each record in a table. See **Database**.

Primary persona A representation of the typical website user, who is strategically important to the effectiveness of the site, but one whose needs are challenging to fulfil.

Privacy The right of an individual to control the information held about them by third parties.

Privacy and Electronic Communications Regulations (PECR) Act A law intended to control the distribution of e-mail and other online communications including **cookies.**

Privacy statement A web page explaining how personal data will be collected, stored, disseminated and updated.

Private B2B exchanges A manufacturer or major supplier to different manufacturers creates a **portal** which is used for managing all aspects of procurement.

Private key See **Encryption.**

Process Part of a system that has a clearly defined purpose or objective and clearly defined inputs and outputs.

Process mapping Identification of location and responsibilities for processes within an organization.

Process variable The element of the marketing mix that involves the methods and procedures companies use to achieve all marketing functions.

Product variable The element of the marketing mix that involves researching customers' needs and developing appropriate products.

Production or live environment Software and hardware used to host an operational system.

Productivity paradox Research results indicating a poor correlation between organizational investment in information systems and organizational performance measured by return on equity.

Promotion variable The element of the marketing mix that involves communication with customers and other stakeholders to inform them about the product and the organization.

Propensity modelling A name given to the approach of evaluating customer characteristics and behaviour and then making recommendations for future products.

Prototype A preliminary version of part or all of an information system reviewed by its users and business sponsors.

Prototyping Prototyping is an iterative process whereby website users suggest modifications before further prototypes and the live version of the site are developed.

Proximity marketing Marketing messages are delivered in real time according to customers' presence based on the technology they are carrying, wearing or have embedded. Bluecasting is the best-known example.

Psychographic segmentation A breakdown of customers according to different characteristics.

Public key See **Encryption**.

Pull media The consumer is proactive in selection of the message through actively seeking out a website.

Pull supply chain An emphasis on using the supply chain to deliver value to customers who are actively involved in product and service specification.

Punchout catalogue A purchasing company accesses through its firewall a dynamic real-time catalogue hosted by a supplier or intermediary containing detailed product information, pricing and product images. These can be potentially integrated with their own purchasing systems.

Pull marketing communications The consumer is proactive in interacting with companies through actively seeking information or entertainment on company websites or social media sites through search engines, comparison intermediaries or direct navigation.

Push marketing communications Communications are broadcast from an advertiser to consumers of the message who are passive recipients or may respond by visiting a website through direct navigation or clickthrough.

Push media Communications are broadcast from an advertiser to consumers of the message who are passive recipients.

Push supply chain A supply chain that emphasizes distribution of a product to passive customers.

Q

Qualified lead Contact information for a customer and an indication of their propensity to purchase different products.

Quality score An assessment in paid search by Google AdWords (and now other search engines) of an individual ad triggered by a keyword which, in combination with the bid amount, determines the ranking of the ad relative to competitors. The primary factor is the clickthrough rate for each ad, but Quality Score also considers the match between the keyword and the occurrence of the keyword in the text, historical clickthrough rates, the engagement of the searcher when they click through to the site and the speed at which the page loads.

Quick Response (QR) Code AQR code is a two-dimensional matrix bar code. QR codes were invented in Japan where they are a popular type of two-dimensional code used for direct response.

R

RAD – Rapid Application Development An approach to information systems development that includes incremental development using **prototypes**.

Radio-frequency identification (RFID) Microchip-based electronic tags are used for monitoring anything they are attached to, whether inanimate (products) or animate (people).

Reactive change A direct response by an organization to a change in its environment

Really Simple Syndication (RSS) feeds Blog, news or other content is published by an XML standard and syndicated for other sites or read by users in RSS reader software services. Now typically shortened to 'feed', e.g. news feed or sports feed.

Reciprocal links An exchange of links between two site owners.

Record A collection of fields for one instance of an entity, such as Customer Smith. See **Database**.

Referrer The source of a website visit, e.g. paid search, affiliate marketing, online advertising or recorded as 'no referrer', i.e. when a URL is typed in directly.

Reintermediation The creation of new intermediaries between customers and suppliers providing services such as supplier search and product evaluation.

Relationship Describes how different tables are linked. See **Database**.

Repurposing Developing content for a new access platform which was previously used for a different platform such as the web.

Resource analysis Review of the technological, financial and human resources of an organization and how they are utilized in business processes.

Revenue models Describe methods of generating income for an organization.

Reverse path analysis Indicates the most popular combination of pages and/or calls-to-action which lead to a page. This is particularly useful for transactional pages such as the first checkout page on a consumer site; a lead generation or contact us page on a business-to-business site; an e-mail subscription page or a call-me back option.

Rich media Digital assets such as ads are not static images, but provide animation, audio or interactivity as a game or form to be completed.

Right-channelling This is selective adoption of e-channels by business for some products or markets in order to best generate value for the organization according to stakeholder preferences.

Risk management Evaluating potential risks, developing strategies to reduce risks and learning about future risks.

Robots Automated tools known as 'spiders' or 'robots' index registered sites. Users search by typing keywords into a search engine and are presented with a list of pages.

S

Satisficing behaviour Consumers do not behave entirely rationally in product or supplier selection. They will compare alternatives, but then may make their choice given imperfect information.

Scalability The ability of an organization or system to adapt to increasing demands being placed on it.

Scanning software Identifies e-mail or website access that breaches company guidelines or **acceptable-use policies**.

Scenario A particular path or flow of events or activities within a use-case.

Scenario-based analysis Models of the future environment are developed from different starting points.

Schematics See **wireframes**.

Scrum Scrum is a methodology that supports agile software development based on 15–30-day sprints to implement features from a product backlog. 'Scrum' refers to a daily project status meeting during the sprint.

Search engines Automated tools known as 'spiders' or 'robots' index registered sites. Users use search engines by typing keywords and are presented with a list of ranked pages from the index.

Search-engine optimization (SEO) A structured approach used to increase the position of a company or its products in search-engine results according to selected keywords.

Searching behaviours Approaches to finding information vary from directed to undirected.

Secondary key A field that is used to link tables, by linking to a primary key in another table. See **Database**.

Secure Electronic Transaction (SET) A standard for public-key encryption intended to enable secure e-commerce transactions, lead-developed by Mastercard and Visa.

Secure Sockets Layer (SSL) A commonly used encryption technique for scrambling data as they are passed across the Internet from a customer's web browser to a merchant's web server.

Segmentation Identification of different groups within a target market in order to develop different offerings for the groups.

Sell-side e-commerce E-commerce transactions between a supplier organization and its customers.

Semantic web Interrelated content including data with defined meaning, enabling better exchange of information between computers and between people and computers.

Sense and respond communications Delivering timely, relevant communications to customers as part of a contact strategy based on assessment of their position in the customer life cycle and monitoring specific interactions with a company's website, e-mails and staff.

Servers See **Web servers**.

Service-level agreement A contractual specification of service standards a contractor must meet.

Service-oriented architecture (SOA) A service-oriented architecture is a collection of services that communicate with each other as part of a distributed systems architecture comprising different services.

Session cookies Cookies used to manage a single visitor session.

Share of search The audience share of Internet searches achieved by a particular audience in a particular market.

Share of wallet or share of customer The proportion of customer expenditure in a particular category that belongs to a single customer.

Short code 5-digit numbers combined with text that can be used by advertisers or broadcasters to encourage consumers to register their interest. They are typically followed up by an automated text message from the advertiser with the option to opt-in to further information by e-mail or to link through to a WAP site.

Single-tenancy SaaS A single instance of an application (and/or database) is maintained for all customers (tenants) who have dedicated resources of processor, disk usage and bandwidth. The single instance may be load-balanced over multiple servers for improved performance.

Site map A graphical or text depiction of the relationship between different groups of content on a website.

Site navigation scheme Tools provided to the user to move between different information on a website.

Site-visitor activity data Information on content and services accessed by e-commerce site visitors.

Situation analysis Environment analysis and review of internal processes and resources to inform strategy.

SMS (Short Message Services) The formal name for text messaging.

Social commerce Social commerce is a subset of e-commerce which encourages participation and interaction of customers in rating, selecting and buying products through group buying. This participation can occur on an e-commerce site or on third-party sites.

Social CRM The process of managing customer-to-customer conversations to engage existing customers, prospects and other stakeholders with a brand and so enhance customer-relationship management.

Social location-based marketing Where social media tools give users the option of sharing their location, and hence give businesses the opportunity to use proximity or location-based marketing to deliver targeted offers and messages to consumers and collect data about their preferences and behaviour.

Social media A category of media focusing on participation and peer-to-peer communication between individuals with sites providing the capability to develop user-generated content (UGC) and to exchange messages and comments between different users.

Social media marketing Monitoring and facilitating customer–customer interaction and participation throughout the web to encourage positive engagement with a company or its brands. Interactions may occur on a company site, social networks and other third-party sites.

Social engineering Exploiting human behaviour to gain access to computer security information from employees or individuals.

Social network A site-facilitating exchange of text, audio or video content.

Soft launch A preliminary site launch with limited promotion to provide initial feedback and testing of an e-commerce site.

Soft lock-in Customers or suppliers continue to use online services because of the switching costs.

Software A series of detailed instructions that control the operation of a computer system. Software exists as programs which are developed by computer programmers.

Software (intelligent) agents Software programs that assist humans by automatically gathering information from the Internet or exchanging data with other agents based on parameters supplied by the user.

Spam Unsolicited e-mail (usually bulk mailed and untargeted).

Spiders Automated tools known as 'spiders' or 'robots' index registered sites. Users search by typing keywords and are presented with a list of pages.

Stage models Used to review how advanced a company is in its use of information and communications technology (ICT) to support different processes.

Star schema data model A form of data model based on a central fact table referencing a transaction linked through database indexes to several dimensions (arranged to form a star) which give alternative methods of breaking down these transactions. A data warehouse will typically integrate several fact tables for different forms of transaction.

Static web content See **Static web page**.

Static web page A page on the web server that is invariant.

Stickiness An indication of how long a visitor stays on a site.

Storyboarding The use of static drawings or screenshots of the different parts of a website to review the design concept with user groups. It can be used to develop the

structure – an overall 'map' with individual pages shown separately.

Strategic agility The capability to innovate and so gain competitive advantage within a marketplace by monitoring changes within an organization's marketplace and then to efficiently evaluate alternative strategies and select, review and implement appropriate candidate strategies.

Strategic analysis Collection and review of information about an organization's internal processes and resources and external marketplace factors in order to inform strategy definition.

Strategic objectives Statement and communication of an organization's mission, vision and objectives.

Strategy Definition of the future direction and actions of a company defined as approaches to achieve specific objectives. See **Prescriptive** and **Emergent strategy**.

Strategy definition Formulation, review and selection of strategies to achieve strategic objectives.

Strategy implementation Planning, actions and controls needed to achieve strategic goals.

Strategy process model A framework for approaching strategy development.

Streaming media Sound and video that can be experienced within a web browser before the whole clip is downloaded.

Subject access request A request by a **data subject** to view **personal data** from an organization.

Supply chain management (SCM) The coordination of all supply activities of an organization from its suppliers and partners to its customers. See **Upstream** and **Downstream supply chain**.

Supply chain network The links between an organization and all partners involved with multiple supply chains.

Supply chain visibility Access to up-to-date, accurate, relevant information about a supply chain's process to different stakeholders.

SWOT analysis Strengths, weaknesses, opportunities and threats.

Symmetric encryption Both parties to a transaction use the same key to encode and decode messages.

System A system can be defined as a collection of interrelated components that work together towards a collective goal.

System design Defines how an information system will operate.

Systems development life cycle The sequence in which a system is created through initiation, analysis, design, implementation, build and maintenance.

Systems integrator A company that organizes the procurement and installation of hardware and software needed for implementation.

Systems software This form of software manages and controls the operation of the computer system as it performs tasks on behalf of the user.

T

Tacit knowledge Mainly intangible knowledge that is typically intuitive and not recorded since it is part of the human mind.

Tagging (Web 2.0) Users or web page creators categorize content on a site through adding descriptive terms. A common approach in blog posts.

Tailored development The standard solution requires major configuration or integration of different modules.

Talk-through A user verbally describes his or her required actions.

Target marketing strategy Evaluation and selection of appropriate segments and the development of appropriate offers.

Task analysis Identification of different tasks, their sequence and how they are broken down.

TCP/IP The Transmission Control Protocol is a transport-layer protocol that moves data between applications. The Internet Protocol is a network-layer protocol that moves data (**packets**) across networks.

Technology convergence A trend in which different hardware devices such as TVs, computers and phones merge and have similar functions.

Technology scouting A structured approach to reviewing technology innovations akin to football scouting.

Test environment Separate software and hardware used to test a system.

Test specification A description of the testing process and tests to be performed.

Testing Aims to identify non-conformance in the requirements specification and errors.

Thin client An end-user device (terminal) where computing requirements such as processing and storage (and so cost) are minimized.

Third-party cookies Served by another site to the one you are visiting – typical for **portals** where an ad network will track remotely or where the web analytics software places a **cookie**.

Three-tier client–server The first tier is the client that handles display, second is application logic and business rules, third is database storage.

Tipping point Using the science of social epidemics explains principles that underpin the rapid spread of ideas, products and behaviours through a population.

Total cost of ownership (TCO) The sum of all cost elements of managing information systems for end-users including purchase, support *and* maintenance.

Trademark A trademark is a unique word or phrase that distinguishes your company. The mark can be registered as plain or designed text, artwork or a combination. In theory, colours, smells and sounds can also be trademarks.

Trading hub See **B2B electronic marketplace**.

Traffic-building campaign The use of online and offline promotion techniques such as banner advertising, search engine promotion and reciprocal linking to increase the audience of a site (both new and existing customers).

Transaction log files A web server file that records all page requests.

Trojan A virus that masquerades as a bona fide application.

U

Unified Modelling Language (UML) A language used to specify, visualize and document the artefacts of an object-oriented system.

Uniform (universal) resource locators (URL) A web address used to locate a web page on a web server.

Unique visitors Individual visitors to a site measured through cookies or IP addresses on an individual computer.

Upstream supply chain Transactions between an organization and its suppliers and intermediaries, equivalent to buy-side e-commerce.

URL (uniform or universal resource locator) A web address used to locate a web page on a web server.

URL strategy A defined approach to forming URLs including the use of capitalization, hyphenation and sub-domains for different brands and different locations. This has implications for promoting a website offline through promotional or vanity URLs, search engine optimization and findability. A clean URL which fits many of these aims is http://www.domain.com/folder-name/document-name. Care must be taken with capitalization since Linux servers parse capitals differently from lower-case letters.

Usability An approach to website design intended to enable the completion of user tasks.

Usability/user testing Representative users are observed performing representative tasks using a system.

Use-case The sequence of transactions between an actor and a system that supports the activities of the actor.

Use-case modelling A user-centred approach to modelling system requirements.

User-centred design Design based on optimizing the user experience according to all factors, including the user interface, which affect this.

Utility computing IT resources and in particular software and hardware are utilized on a pay-per-use basis and are managed externally as 'managed services'.

V

Value-added network (VAN) A secure wide-area network that uses proprietary rather than Internet technology.

Value chain A model for analysis of how supply chain activities can add value to products and services delivered to the customer.

Value network The links between an organization and its strategic and non-strategic partners that form its external value chain.

Value stream The combination of actions required to deliver value to the customer as products and services.

Vendor-managed inventory (VMI) Supply chain partners manage the replenishment of parts or items for sale through sharing of information on variations in demand and stocking level for goods used for manufacture or sale.

Vertical integration The extent to which supply chain activities are undertaken and controlled within the organization.

Viral marketing In an online context, 'Forward to a Friend' e-mail is used to transmit a promotional message from one person to another. 'Online word of mouth'.

Virtual integration The majority of supply chain activities are undertaken and controlled outside the organization by third parties.

Virtual organization An organization which uses information and communications technology to allow it to operate without clearly defined physical boundaries between different functions. It provides customized services by outsourcing production and other functions to third parties.

Virtual private network (VPN) A secure, encrypted (tunnelled) connection between two points using the Internet, typically created by ISPs for organizations wanting to conduct secure Internet trading.

Virtual world An electronic environment which simulates interactions between online characters known as avatars. Also known as Massively Multiplayer Online Roleplaying Games (MMORPG).

Virtualization (company) The process of a company developing more of the characteristics of the virtual organization.

Virtualization (technology) The indirect provision of technology services through another resource (abstraction). Essentially one computer is using its processing and storage capacity to do the work of another.

Vision or mission statement A concise summary defining the scope and broad aims of an organization's digital channel in the future, explaining how they will contribute to the organization and support customers and interactions with partners.

Voice over IP (VOIP) Voice data are transferred across the Internet – it enables phone calls to be made over the Internet.

W

Walk-through A user executes their actions through using a system or mock-up.

Web 2.0 concept Web 2.0 refers to a collection of web services which facilitate certain behaviours online such as community participation and user-generated content, rating and tagging.

Web 3.0 concept Next-generation web incorporating high-speed connectivity, complex cross-community interactions, full range of digital media (text, voice, video) and an intelligent or semantic web where automated applications can access data from different online services to assist searchers perform complex tasks of supplier selection.

Web accessibility An approach to website design that enables sites and web applications to be used by people with visual impairment or other disabilities such as motor impairment. Accessibility also demands that web users should be able to use websites and applications effectively regardless of the browser or access platform they use and its settings.

Web address See **URL**.

Web analytics Techniques used to assess and improve the contribution of e-marketing to a business including reviewing traffic volume, referrals, clickstreams, online reach data, customer satisfaction surveys, leads and sales.

Web analytics system Information on visitor volumes, sources and pages visited are analysed through web analytics systems.

Web application frameworks A standard programming framework based on reusable library functions for creating dynamic websites through a programming language.

Web application server Software processes which is accessed by a standard programming interface (API) of a web application framework to serve dynamic website functionality in response to requests received from browsers. They are designed to manage multiple requests from multiple users and will provide load-balancing to support high volumes of usage.

Web browsers Browsers such as Microsoft Internet Explorer provide an easy method of accessing and viewing information stored as web documents on different servers.

Web classification See **Card sorting**.

Web design personas A summary of the characteristics, needs, motivations and environment of typical website users.

Web logs Web logs or blogs are a method of publishing web pages, particularly those with news listings.

Web page See **Static web page, Dynamically created web page** and **Web servers**.

Web servers Store and present the web pages accessed by web browsers.

Web services Business applications and software services are provided through Internet and web protocols with the application managed on a separate server from where it is accessed.

Whitelist A compilation of trusted sources of e-mail that is permitted to enter an inbox.

Widgets A badge or button incorporated into a site or social network space by its owner, with content or services typically served from another site making widgets effectively a mini-software application or web service. Content can be updated in real time since the widget interacts with the server each time it loads.

Wi-Fi ('wireless-fidelity') A high-speed wireless local-area network enabling wireless access to the Internet for mobile, office and home users.

Wiki A collaborative interactive web service which enables users to modify content contributed by others.

Wireframes Also known as 'schematics' – a way of illustrating the layout of an individual web page.

Wireless Application Protocol (WAP) WAP is a technical standard for transferring information to wireless devices, such as mobile phones.

Wireless communications Electronic transactions and communications conducted using mobile devices such as laptops and mobile phones (and fixed access platforms) with different forms of wireless connection.

Workflow management (WFM) Workflow management is the automation of information flows; it provides tools for processing the information according to a set of procedural rules.

World Wide Web (WWW) The most common technique for publishing information on the Internet. It is accessed through web browsers which display web pages of embedded graphics and HTML- or XML-encoded text.

Worm A small program that self-replicates and transfers across a network from machine to machine. A form of virus.

X

XML or eXtensible Markup Language A standard for transferring structured data, unlike HTML which is purely presentational.

Index

Note: Terms which feature in the Glossary have **emboldened** page numbers.